Mobil
Travel Guide

Northern Great Lakes 2004

Michigan

Minnesota

Wisconsin

ExxonMobil
Travel Publications

Maps by

RAND M^{c}NALLY

Acknowledgements

We gratefully acknowledge the help of our representatives for their efficient and perceptive inspections of the lodging and dining establishments listed; the establishments' proprietors for their cooperation in showing their facilities and providing information about them; the many users of previous editions who have taken the time to share their experiences; and for their time and information, the thousands of chambers of commerce, convention and visitors bureaus, city, state, and provincial tourism offices, and government agencies who assisted in our research.

Mobil Travel Guide is also grateful to all the highly talented writers who contributed entries to this book.

Maps Copyright © 2004 Rand McNally & Company

Printing Acknowledgement: North American Corporation of Illinois

www.mobiltravelguide.com

The information contained herein is derived from a variety of third-party sources. Although every effort has been made to verify the information obtained from such sources, the publisher assumes no responsibility for inconsistencies or inaccuracies in the data or liability for any damages of any type arising from errors or omissions.

Neither the editors nor the publisher assumes responsibility for the services provided by any business listed in this guide or for any loss, damage, or disruption in your travel for any reason.

ISBN: 0-7627-2892-2

Manufactured in the United States of America.

10 9 8 7 6 5 4 3 2 1

Contents

MAP SYMBOLS

━━━━ Free limited-access highway	⊙⊙⊙ Interstate highway	Urbanized area in state maps; in city maps
▬▬▬ New — under construction	⊙⊙⊙ U.S. highway	Separate cities within metro area
━━━━ Toll limited-access highway	⊙⊙⊙ State or provincial highway	⊛ ⊛ National capital; state capital; cities; towns
▬▬▬ New — under construction		(size of type indicates relative population)
━━━ Other multilane highway	⊡⊡⊡ Other highway	● ● ○
━━━ Principal highway		U.S. or Canadian National Park
━━━ Other through highway	Miles between arrows	State/Provincial Park or Recreation Area
━━━ Other road	One mile or less not shown	National Forest or Grassland, city park
┈┈┈ Unpaved road	Interchanges and interchange	▪ Point of interest
┅┅┅ Ferry	numbers	Hospital, medical center
	┄┄┄┄ Time zone boundary	┄┄┄┄ Continental divide

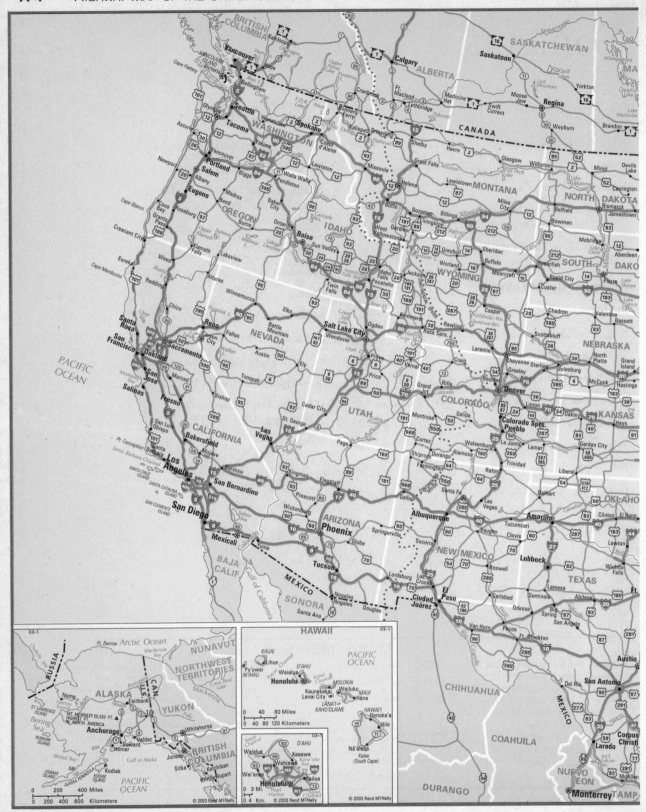

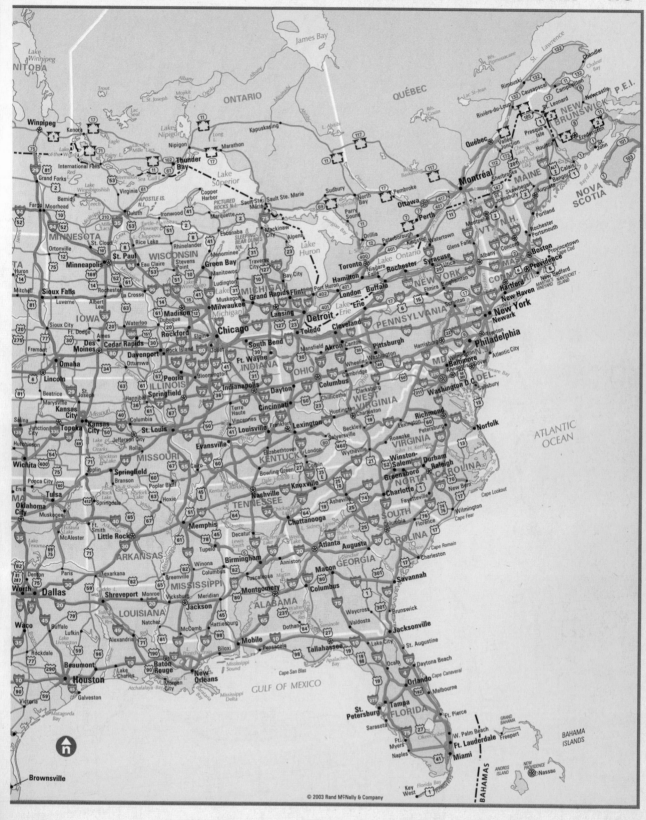

© 2003 Rand McNally & Company

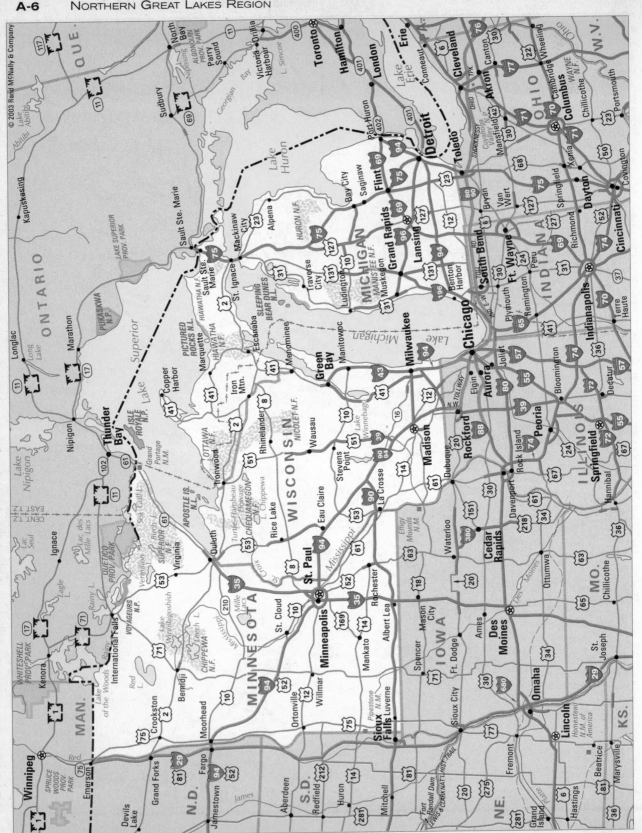

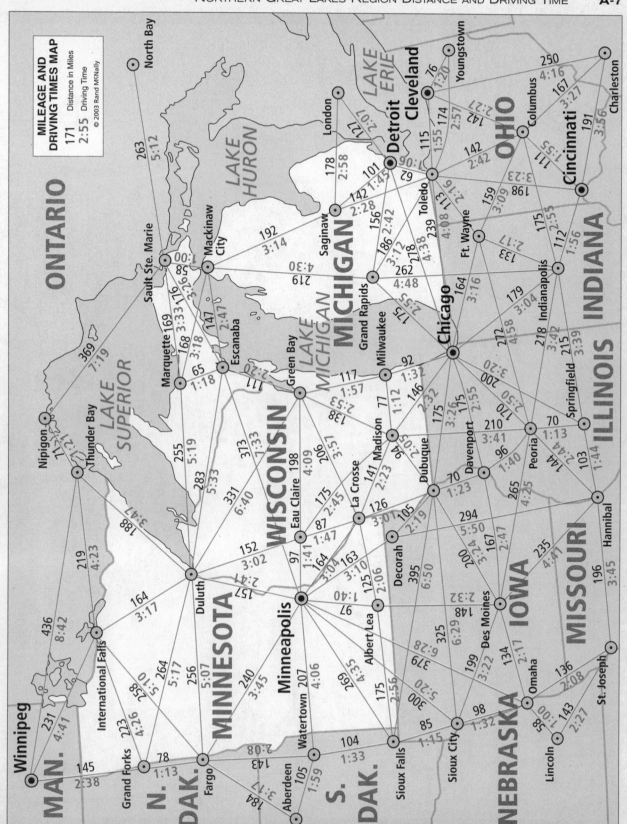

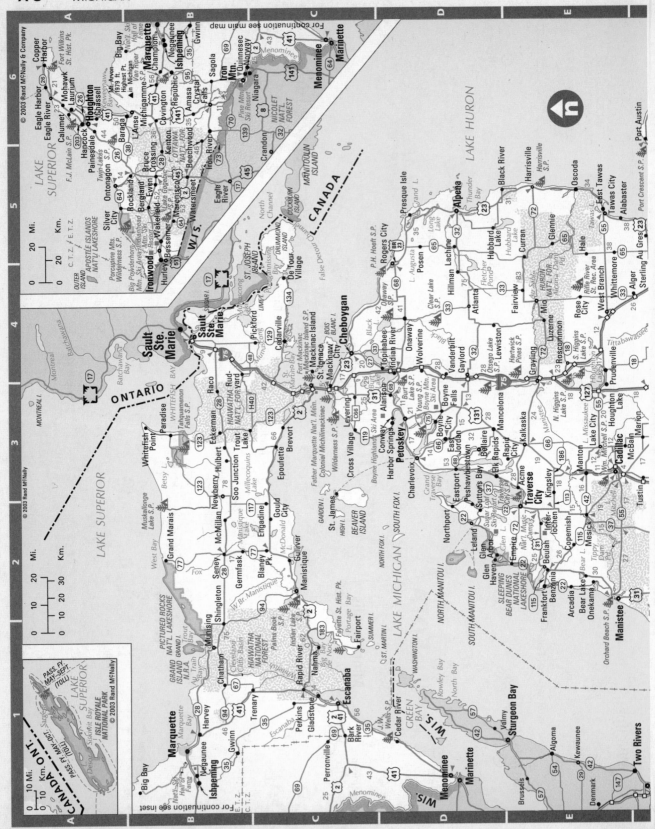

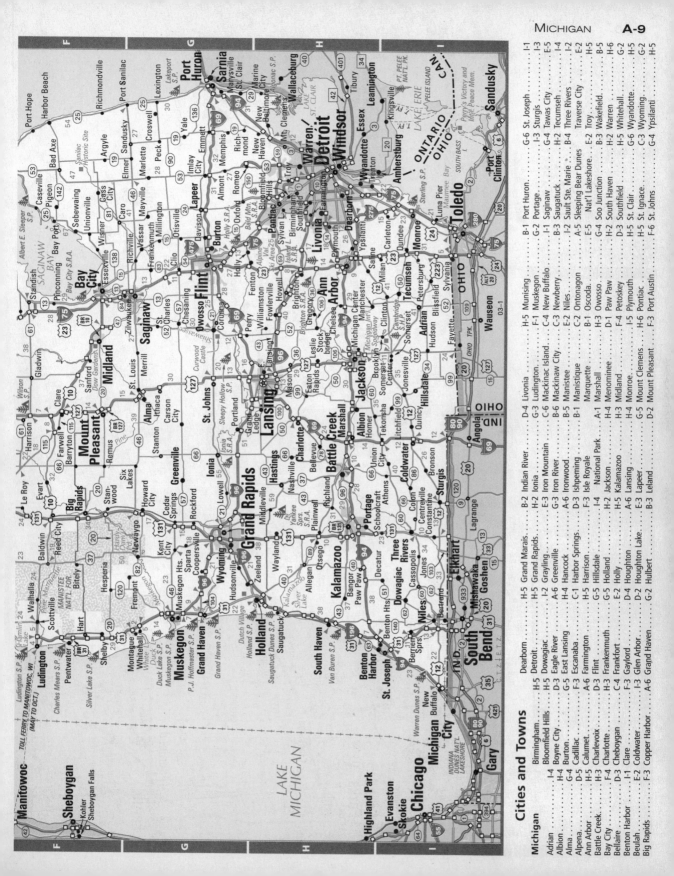

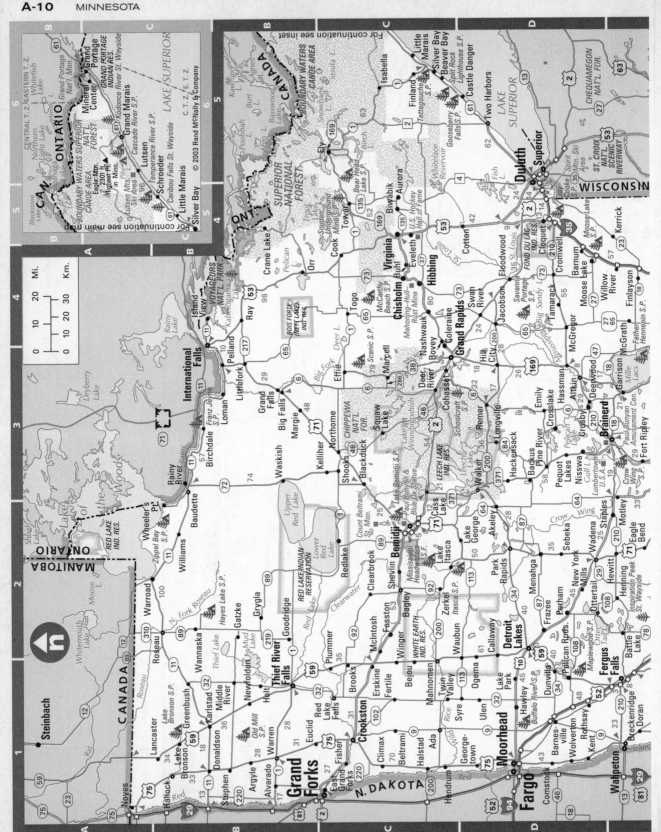

© 2003 Rand McNally & Company

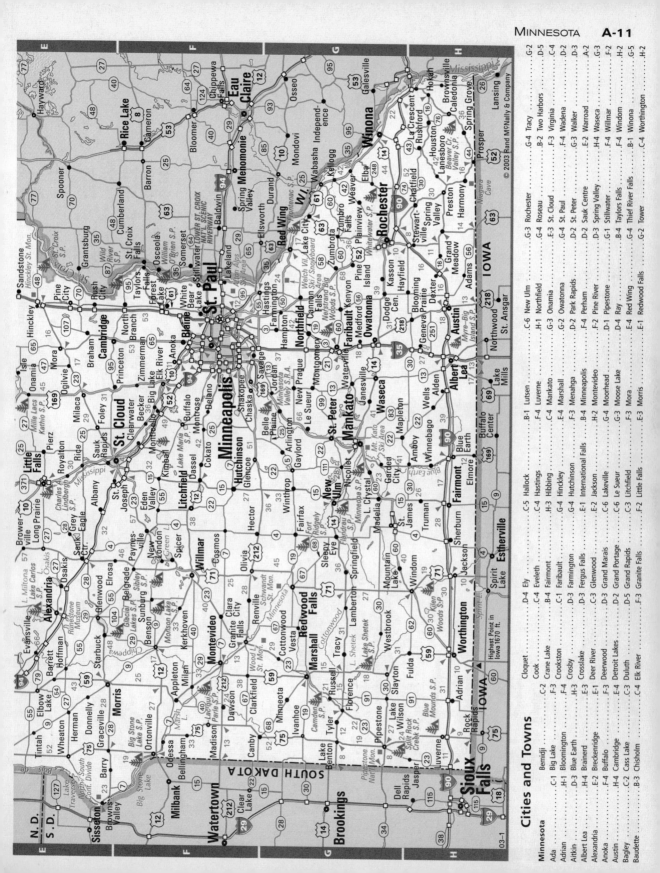

© 2003 Rand McNally & Company

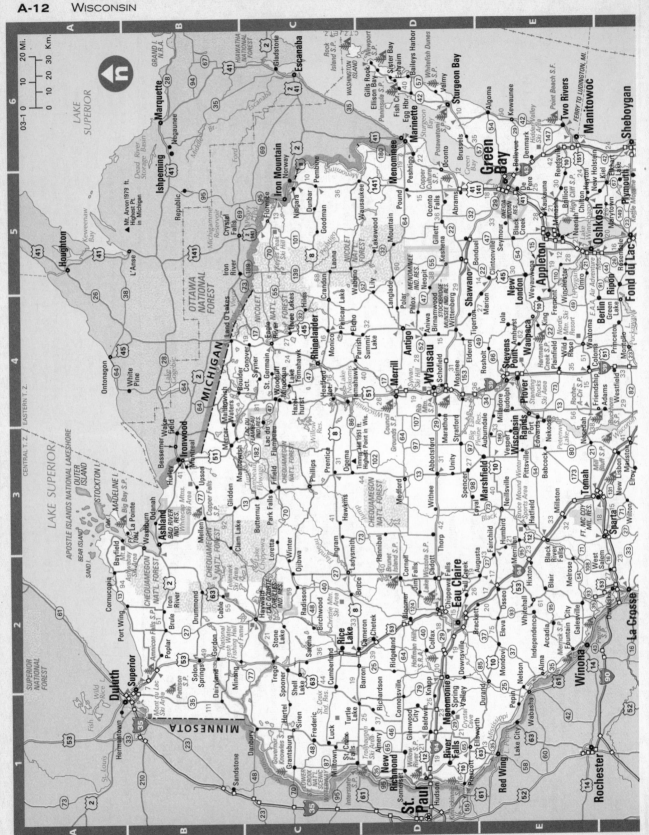

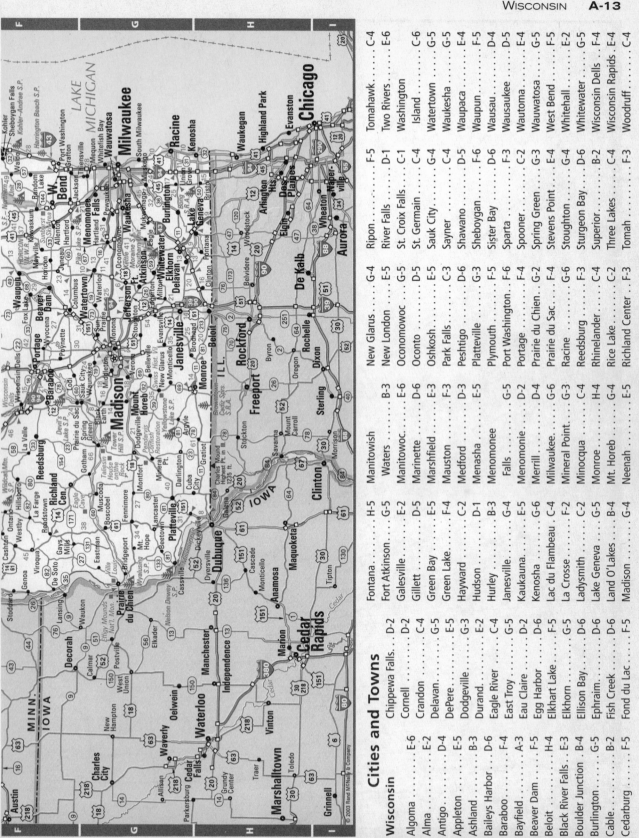

Cities and Towns

Wisconsin

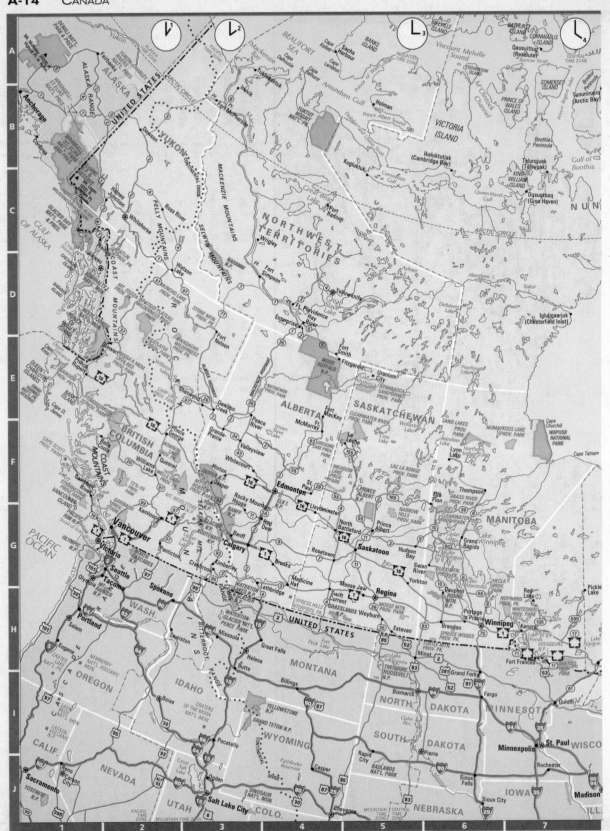

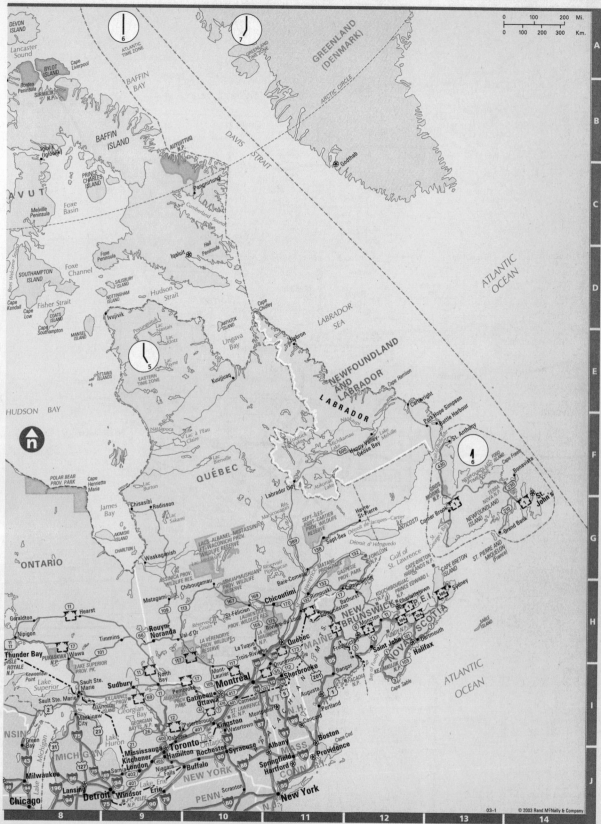

Detroit, MI & Vicinity

© 2003 Rand McNally

Pine Knob Ski Resort · Voorheis Lake · Bald Mt. St. Rec. Area · Ray Center · New Haven · W.C. Wetzel S.P. (Undev.) · Meade · New Haven · Davis

Maceday Lake · Oronville Rd. · Judah Lake · Palace of Auburn Hills · Washington · Macomb · Chesterfield

Waterford · Pontiac · Rochester Hills · Shelby · Waldenburg · New Baltimore

Union Lake · Sylvan Lake · Keego Harbor · Auburn Hills · Rochester · Disco · Utica · Sterling Hts. · Clinton · Mt. Clemens · Harrison

W. Bloomfield · Bloomfield · Bloomfield Hills · Troy · Birmingham · Clawson · Madison Hts. · Warren · Fraser · Roseville · St. Clair Shores

Farmington Hills · Franklin · Beverly Hills · Royal Oak · Berkley · Lathrup Village · Huntington Woods · Pleasant Ridge · Center Line · Eastpointe · Grosse Pointe Woods · Harper Woods

Livonia · Farmington · Southfield · Oak Park · Ferndale · Hazel Park · Grosse Pointe Farms · Grosse Pointe

Redford · Highland Park · Hamtramck · Grosse Pointe Park

Westland · Detroit · Grosse Pte. · Belle Isle · Peche Island

Garden City · Dearborn Hts. · Dearborn · Melvindale · River Rouge · Ecorse · Windsor · Tecumseh · Elmstead · Puce

Inkster · Wayne · Allen Park · Lincoln Park · Fighting Island

Romulus · Taylor · Southgate · Wyandotte · Riverview

New Boston · Brownstown · Trenton · Grosse Ile · Amherstburg

Willow · Woodhaven · Flat Rock · Gibraltar

Lake St. Clair · U.S. / CANADA · ONTARIO · MICHIGAN · Monroe Co. · Wayne Co.

Central Detroit, MI

© 2003 Rand McNally

Scale: 0 1 2 3 4 5 MI. / 0 1 2 3 4 5 6 7 8 Km.

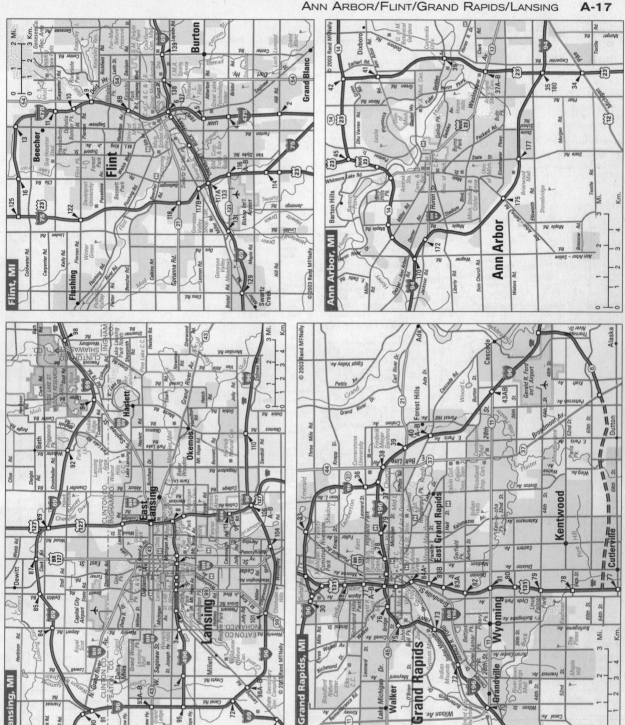

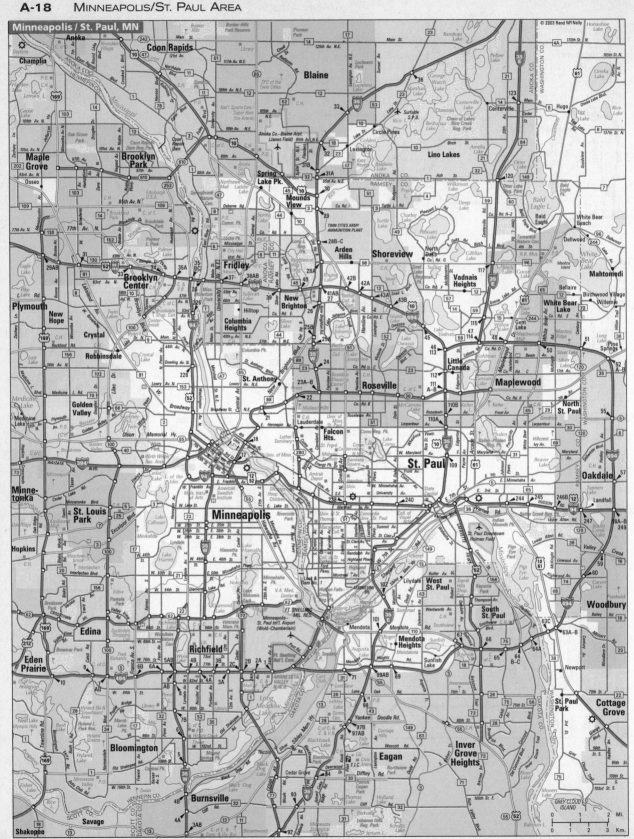

Minneapolis / St. Paul, MN

© 2003 Rand McNally

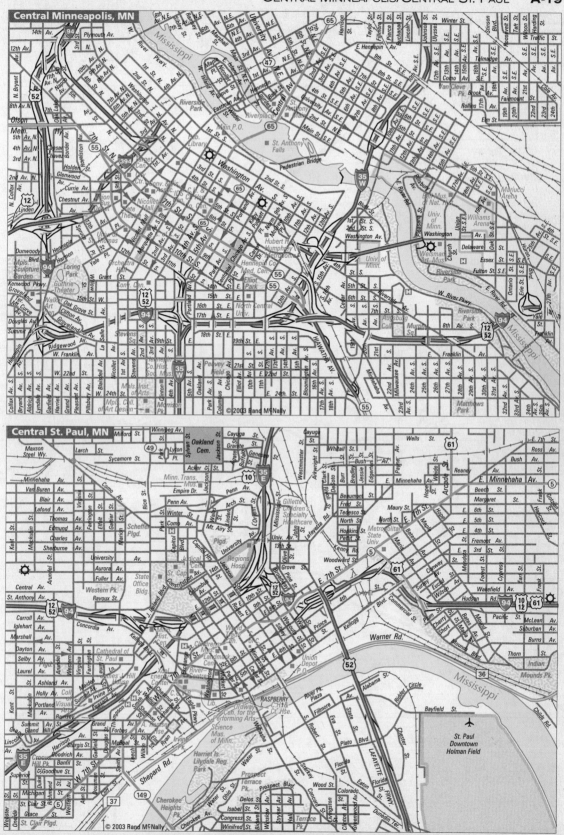

Central Minneapolis, MN

Central St. Paul, MN

© 2003 Rand McNally

Milwaukee, WI & Vicinity

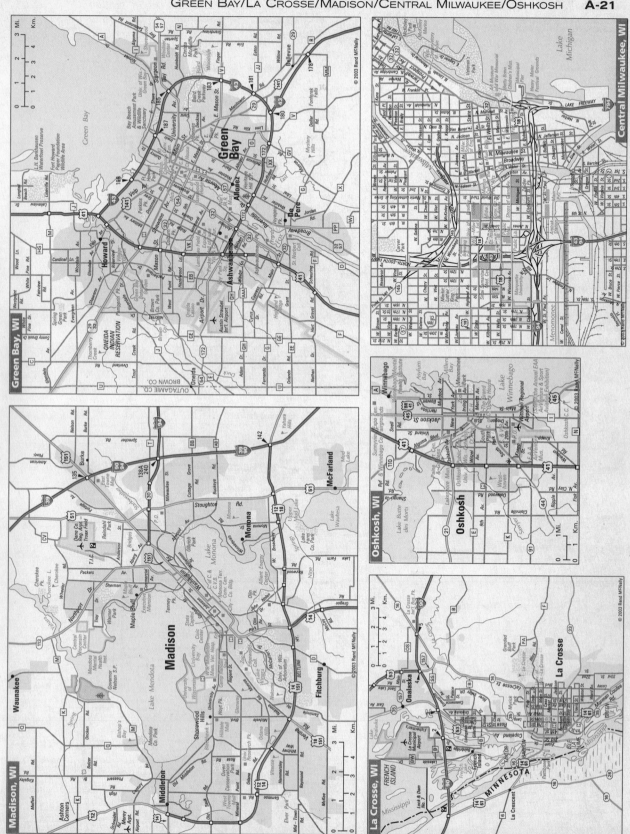

Green Bay, WI

Central Milwaukee, WI

Madison, WI

Oshkosh, WI

La Crosse, WI

© 2003 Rand McNally

Chicago, IL & Vicinity

© 2003 Rand McNally

LAKE MICHIGAN
El. 579 ft. above sea level

Toronto, ON

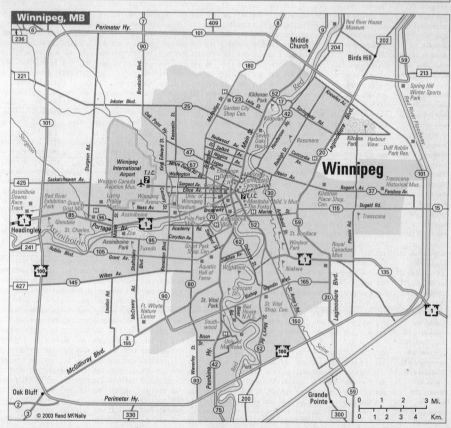

Winnipeg, MB

	Atlanta, GA	Billings, MT	Boston, MA	Charlotte, NC	Chicago, IL	Cincinnati, OH	Cleveland, OH	Dallas, TX	Denver, CO	Detroit, MI	Houston, TX	Indianapolis, IN	Kansas City, MO	Los Angeles, CA	Memphis, TN	Miami, FL	Milwaukee, WI	Minneapolis, MN	New Orleans, LA	New York, NY	Omaha, NE	Philadelphia, PA	Phoenix, AZ	Pittsburgh, PA	Portland, OR	St. Louis, MO	Salt Lake City, UT	San Francisco, CA	Seattle, WA	Tulsa, OK	Washington, D.C.	Wichita, KS
Albany, NY	1014	2076	166	777	820	727	478	1682	1814	648	1770	791	1287	2833	1230	1407	921	1236	1441	153	1274	238	2544	472	2927	1040	2206	2953	2899	1433	365	1477
Albuquerque, NM	1406	994	2247	1629	1341	1397	1606	644	439	1591	890	1290	783	799	1014	1960	1424	1222	1170	2019	979	1939	463	1649	1385	1041	626	1097	1456	650	1886	593
Amarillo, TX	1121	971	1962	1344	1056	1112	1321	359	424	1306	605	1005	604	1084	729	1675	1139	1043	885	1734	716	1654	748	1364	1666	756	911	1382	1737	365	1601	417
Atlanta, GA		1890	1100	243	712	463	715	791	1415	723	797	529	810	2205	393	661	811	1132	468	896	1000	816	1862	686	2604	556	1883	2503	2675	798	635	972
Baltimore, MD	673	1960	407	436	704	523	379	1366	1693	532	1454	592	1088	2681	914	1080	805	1120	1125	203	1158	102	2345	251	2811	841	2090	2837	2783	1234	38	1278
Billings, MT	1890		2242	2055	1247	1547	1598	1429	555	1534	1676	1433	1078	1239	1606	2551	1176	843	1954	2067	896	2017	1206	1716	891	1333	549	1179	821	1238	1961	1064
Birmingham, AL	148	1839	1185	391	661	467	719	647	1364	727	671	478	759	2058	246	783	760	1081	342	981	949	901	1722	753	2553	505	1832	2356	2624	651	743	825
Bismarck, ND	1558	417	1828	1610	833	1133	1184	1274	709	1120	1521	1019	790	1595	1318	2219	762	429	1709	1653	608	1603	1515	1302	1310	1045	927	1598	1240	1037	1547	802
Boise, ID	2184	621	2673	2349	1702	1959	2029	1704	830	1965	1951	1852	1372	846	1900	2845	1741	1466	2229	2498	1233	2448	995	2147	425	1627	338	648	496	1513	2392	1339
Boston, MA	1100	2242		863	986	893	644	1768	1980	814	1856	957	1453	2999	1316	1483	1087	1402	1527	211	1440	313	2710	586	3093	1206	2372	3119	3065	1599	441	1643
Buffalo, NY	896	1787	461	659	531	438	189	1376	1525	359	1495	502	998	2544	924	1381	632	947	1243	417	985	412	2255	216	2638	751	1917	2664	2610	1144	388	1188
Charleston, SC	321	2196	966	207	911	619	721	1112	1721	850	1113	730	1116	2526	714	580	1010	1325	784	762	1306	661	2183	654	2910	862	2189	2824	2981	1119	525	1306
Charlotte, NC	243	2055	863		770	478	516	1034	1580	645	1040	589	975	2428	617	724	869	1184	711	659	1165	534	2092	449	2769	721	2048	2726	2840	1021	398	1165
Cheyenne, WY	1450	455	1939	1615	968	1225	1295	974	100	1231	1221	1118	638	1102	1166	2111	1007	878	1499	1764	499	1714	906	1413	1155	893	434	1181	1226	783	1658	609
Chicago, IL	712	1247	986	770		293	342	933	1009	278	1089	179	529	2028	536	1373	92	407	927	811	469	761	1804	460	2122	300	1401	2148	2070	693	705	719
Cincinnati, OH	463	1547	893	478	293		252	938	1208	260	1057	112	603	2196	486	1124	392	707	805	660	726	580	1860	290	2379	356	1658	2405	2370	749	524	793
Cleveland, OH	715	1598	644	516	342	252		1190	1336	170	1309	316	812	2355	738	1238	443	758	1057	486	796	436	2069	135	2449	565	1728	2475	2421	958	380	1002
Columbus, OH	574	1606	783	433	352	111	142	1049	1276	204	1168	175	671	2264	597	1155	451	766	916	553	794	473	1928	183	2447	424	1726	2473	2429	817	417	861
Dallas, TX	791	1429	1768	1034	933	938	1190		882	1198	247	882	552	1440	454	1316	1016	991	526	1564	664	1484	1069	1228	2124	633	1403	1741	2195	262	1326	365
Davenport, IA	792	1166	1135	898	175	421	491	915	843	427	1095	314	363	1862	550	1453	214	359	941	960	303	910	1609	609	1956	266	1235	1982	1989	612	854	553
Denver, CO	1415	555	1980	1580	1009	1208	1336	882		1272	1129	1101	605	1022	1097	2076	1048	919	1407	1805	540	1750	809	1460	1250	858	529	1276	1321	691	1694	517
Des Moines, IA	961	997	1304	1067	333	590	660	746	674	596	926	483	194	1693	623	1622	372	243	1014	1129	134	1079	1440	778	1787	350	1066	1813	1820	443	1023	384
Detroit, MI	723	1534	814	645	278	260	170	1198	1272		1317	310	792	2291	746	1367	379	694	1065	639	732	589	2054	288	2385	550	1664	2411	2357	943	533	955
Duluth, MN	1189	861	1459	1241	464	764	815	1145	1073	751	1325	650	593	2092	965	1850	393	157	1356	1284	533	1234	1839	933	1754	681	1465	2042	1684	842	1178	783
El Paso, TX	1426	1178	2394	1669	1488	1544	1753	633	623	1738	753	1437	930	807	1087	1939	1571	1369	1100	2197	1016	2117	436	1796	1627	1188	868	1188	1698	797	1959	740
Fargo, ND	1369	607	1639	1421	644	944	995	1087	901	931	1334	830	603	1785	1131	2030	573	240	1522	1464	421	1414	1707	1113	1500	858	1117	1788	1430	850	1358	725
Flagstaff, AZ	1733	1070	2574	1956	1668	1724	1933	971	673	1918	1217	1617	1110	472	1341	2287	1751	1549	1497	2346	1210	2266	136	1976	1279	1368	520	770	1350	977	2213	920
Houston, TX	797	1676	1856	1040	1089	1057	1309	247	1129	1317		1025	732	1560	573	1190	1179	1171	351	1652	911	1572	1189	1347	2371	837	1650	1941	2442	505	1414	612
Indianapolis, IN	529	1433	957	589	179	112	316	882	1101	310	1025		496	2089	472	1190	278	593	816	729	619	649	1753	359	2272	249	1551	2298	2256	642	593	686
Jackson, MS	383	1817	1424	626	747	692	944	408	1225	952	442	683	737	1850	212	908	837	1119	180	1220	927	1140	1479	982	2467	495	1746	2149	2538	534	982	708
Jacksonville, FL	346	2236	1142	383	1058	795	897	1001	1761	1026	875	875	1156	2431	712	341	1157	1478	546	938	1346	837	2060	830	2950	902	2229	2742	3021	1117	701	1291
Kansas City, MO	810	1078	1453	975	529	603	812	552	605	792	732	496		1626	526	1471	568	439	917	1225	188	1145	1246	855	1792	253	1071	1818	1863	249	1089	190
Knoxville, TN	215	1826	928	229	542	250	502	840	1351	510	928	361	746	2199	388	876	641	956	599	724	936	644	1863	496	2540	492	1819	2497	2611	792	486	936
Las Vegas, NV	1982	966	2726	2205	1755	1956	2082	1220	749	2018	1466	1849	1353	275	1590	2536	1794	1665	1746	2551	1286	2498	292	2208	1021	1606	416	569	1122	1226	2462	1265
Lexington, KY	386	1669	935	401	375	83	335	874	1194	343	993	188	589	2175	422	1047	474	789	741	731	779	645	1839	373	2383	335	1662	2409	2454	728	543	779
Little Rock, AR	531	1513	1453	754	655	623	875	315	966	883	434	591	389	1682	139	1165	745	826	441	1249	577	1169	1346	913	2208	403	1487	1980	2279	275	1011	449
Los Angeles, CA	2205	1239	2999	2428	2028	2196	2355	1440	1022	2291	1560	2089	1626		1813	2746	2067	1938	1907	2824	1559	2738	371	2448	967	1840	689	381	1141	1449	2685	1392
Louisville, KY	415	1595	996	475	297	103	355	835	1120	363	954	114	515	2101	383	1076	396	711	702	763	705	683	1765	393	2309	261	1588	2335	2380	654	617	705
Memphis, TN	393	1606	1316	617	536	486	738	454	1097	746	573	472	526	1813		1027	626	908	392	1112	716	1032	1477	776	2320	284	1599	2111	2391	406	874	580
Miami, FL	661	2551	1483	724	1373	1124	1238	1316	2076	1367	1190	1190	1471	2746	1027		1472	1793	861	1279	1661	1178	2375	1171	3265	1217	2544	3057	3336	1432	1042	1606
Milwaukee, WI	811	1176	1087	869	92	392	443	1016	1048	379	1179	278	568	2067	626	1472		336	1017	912	508	862	1887	561	2069	383	1440	2187	1999	776	806	758
Minneapolis, MN	1132	843	1402	1184	407	707	758	991	919	694	1171	593	439	1938	908	1793	336		1299	1227	379	1177	1685	876	1736	624	1311	2058	1666	688	1121	629
Mobile, AL	329	2003	1429	572	920	726	978	598	1415	986	472	737	923	2028	398	718	1019	1305	143	1225	1113	1145	1657	1009	2657	681	1936	2339	2728	724	964	898
Montréal, QC	1227	1909	324	990	848	829	590	1767	1842	575	1886	879	1362	2861	1315	1632	949	1264	1654	384	1302	463	2632	617	2955	1128	2234	2981	2732	1521	590	1525
Nashville, TN	242	1650	1106	407	472	278	530	663	1175	538	782	289	570	2022	211	903	571	892	527	902	760	822	1686	568	2364	316	1643	2320	2435	615	664	760
New Orleans, LA	468	1954	1527	711	927	805	1057	526	1407	1065	351	816	917	1907	392	861	1017	1299		1323	1107	1243	1536	1095	2649	675	1928	2267	2720	679	1085	890
New York, NY	896	2067	211	659	811	660	486	1564	1805	639	1652	729	1225	2824	1112	1279	912	1227	1323		1265	109	2482	388	2918	978	2197	2944	2890	1371	237	1415
Norfolk, VA	557	2147	577	320	891	601	566	1348	1781	719	1384	713	1176	2729	918	948	992	1307	1055	373	1366	276	2393	438	2970	922	2249	2996	3041	1315	196	1366
Odessa, TX	1147	1204	2122	1390	1244	1292	1509	354	649	1494	546	1193	792	1088	808	1672	1327	1231	882	1918	904	1838	717	1552	1784	944	1025	1469	1855	553	1680	605
Oklahoma City, OK	862	1221	1702	1085	796	852	1061	208	674	1046	455	745	344	1343	470	1496	879	783	733	1474	456	1394	1007	1104	1916	496	1195	1641	1987	105	1342	157
Omaha, NE	1000	896	1440	1165	469	726	796	664	540	732	911	619	188	1559	716	1661	508	379	1107	1265		1215	1346	914	1653	443	932	1679	1724	435	1159	302
Orlando, FL	440	2330	1284	525	1152	903	1039	1095	1855	1163	969	969	1250	2525	806	229	1251	1572	640	1080	1440	979	2154	972	3044	996	2323	2836	3115	1211	843	1385
Philadelphia, PA	816	2017	313	534	761	580	436	1484	1750	589	1572	649	1145	2738	1032	1178	862	1177	1243	109	1215		2402	308	2868	898	2147	2894	2840	1291	136	1335
Phoenix, AZ	1862	1206	2710	2092	1804	1860	2069	1069	809	2054	1189	1753	1246	371	1477	2375	1887	1685	1536	2482	1346	2402		2112	1338	1504	656	752	1486	1113	2349	1056
Pittsburgh, PA	686	1716	586	449	460	290	135	1228	1460	288	1347	359	855	2448	776	1171	561	876	1095	388	914	308	2112		2567	608	1846	2593	2539	1001	252	1045
Portland, ME	1229	2343	117	964	1087	994	745	1897	2081	915	1985	1058	1554	3100	1445	1584	1188	1503	1656	312	1541	414	2811	687	3194	1307	2473	3220	3166	1700	542	1744
Portland, OR	2604	891	3093	2769	2122	2379	2449	2124	1250	2385	2371	2272	1792	967	2320	3265	2069	1736	2649	2918	1653	2868	1338	2567		2047	758	636	174	1933	2812	1759
Rapid City, SD	1521	373	1904	1686	909	1209	1260	1069	400	1196	1316	1095	709	1312	1237	2182	838	609	1628	1729	527	1679	1206	1378	1266	964	644	1391	1196	878	1623	704
Reno, NV	2406	955	2895	2571	1924	2181	2251	1665	1052	2187	1911	2074	1594	473	2122	3067	1963	1834	2193	2720	1455	2670	735	2369	578	1849	522	224	752	1735	2614	1561
Roanoke, VA	430	1917	678	193	663	370	429	1098	1550	558	1186	482	945	2457	646	915	762	1077	857	474	1135	394	2121	365	2739	691	2018	2765	2810	1050	236	1135
St. Louis, MO	556	1333	1206	721	300	356	565	633	858	550	837	249	253	1840	284	1217	383	624	675	978	443	898	1504	608	2047		1326	2073	2118	393	878	443
Salt Lake City, UT	1883	549	2372	2048	1401	1658	1728	1403	529	1664	1650	1551	1071	689	1599	2544	1440	1311	1928	2197	932	2147	656	1846	758	1326		746	829	1212	2091	1038
San Antonio, TX	992	1483	2051	1235	1210	1215	1467	277	936	1475	199	1159	817	1365	731	1385	1293	1256	546	1847	929	1767	994	1505	2100	910	1341	1746	2171	539	1609	630
San Diego, CA	2154	1299	3064	2397	2088	2214	2423	1361	1082	2351	1481	2107	1600	124	1831	2667	2127	1998	1828	2836	1619	2756	354	2466	1091	1858	749	505	1265	1467	2703	1410
San Francisco, CA	2503	1179	3119	2726	2148	2405	2475	1741	1276	2411	1941	2298	1818	381	2111	3057	2187	2058	2267	2944	1679	2894	752	2593	636	2073	746		810	1747	2838	1785
Sault Ste Marie, ON	1047	1282	943	960	452	584	506	1357	1446	350	1510	537	966	2465	957	1708	404	549	1347	939	906	925	2228	624	2175	724	1838	2585	2105	1117	869	1129
Seattle, WA	2675	821	3065	2840	2070	2370	2421	2195	1321	2357	2442	2256	1863	1141	2391	3336	1999	1666	2720	2890	1724	2840	1486	2539	174	2118	829	810		2004	2784	1830
Shreveport, LA	605	1614	1646	848	851	819	1071	186	1067	1079	239	787	566	1628	335	1130	941	1005	347	1442	752	1362	1257	1109	2309	599	1588	1927	2380	339	1204	550
Sioux Falls, SD	1177	717	1564	1342	569	876	920	849	654	856	1096	769	365	1673	893	1838	498	269	1284	1389	183	1339	1460	1038	1610	620	989	1736	1540	612	1283	487
Spokane, WA	2431	539	2783	2596	1788	2088	2139	1970	1096	2075	2217	1974	1619	1215	2147	3092	1717	1384	2495	2608	1437	2558	1377	2257	352	1874	720	885	282	1779	2502	1605
Springfield, MO	684	1247	1418	849	512	568	777	423	761	762	666	461	169	1630	283	1345	595	606	674	1190	357	1110	1294	820	1961	212	1240	1928	2032	183	1090	263
Tallahassee, FL	270	2143	1301	470	965	733	985	839	1668	993	713	782	1063	2269	550	478	1064	1385	384	1097	1253	996	1898	917	2857	809	2136	2580	2928	955	860	1129
Tampa, FL	458	2348	1340	581	1170	921	1095	1113	1873	1181	987	987	1268	2543	824	273	1269	1590	658	1136	1458	1035	2172	1028	3062	1014	2341	2854	3133	1229	899	1403
Toronto, ON	961	1773	566	766	517	498	296	1436	1511	244	1555	548	1031	2530	984	1488	618	933	1303	528	971	517	2301	323	2624	797	1903	2650	2596	1190	495	1194
Tulsa, OK	798	1238	1599	1021	693	749	958	262	691	943	505	642	249	1449	406	1432	776	688	679	1371	435	1291	1113	1001	1933	393	1212	1747	2004		1271	174
Washington, D.C.	635	1961	441	398	705	524	380	1326	1694	533	1414	593	1089	2685	874	1042	806	1121	1085	237	1159	136	2349	252	2812	878	2091	2838	2784	1271		1279
Wichita, KS	972	1064	1643	1165	719	793	1002	365	517	955	612	686	190	1392	580	1606	758	629	890	1415	302	1335	1056	1045	1759	443	1038	1785	1830	174	1279	

Making road trips easy is our driving ambition.

Come and see how easy and convenient our Exxon and Mobil locations are. Before you head off for your next road trip, stop into your local Exxon or Mobil retailer and fill up on the essentials: film, batteries, cold soda for your thirst, salty snacks and candy for your hunger and, of course, automotive services and quality fuels. With over 16,000 locations nationwide, we make it effortless.

And don't forget to use your *Speedpass*™ to get back on the road even faster. After all, getting there is half the fun. How do we know? We're drivers too.

We're drivers too.

Meet The Stars

Mobil Travel Guide 2004 *Five-Star* Award Winners

LODGINGS

California
The Beverly Hills Hotel, *Beverly Hills*
Chateau du Sureau, *Oakhurst*
Four Seasons, San Francisco, *San Francisco*
Hotel Bel-Air, *Los Angeles*
The Peninsula Beverly Hills, *Beverly Hills*
Raffles L'Ermitage Beverly Hills, *Beverly Hills*
The Ritz-Carlton San Francisco, *San Francisco*

Colorado
The Broadmoor, *Colorado Springs*
The Little Nell, *Aspen*

Connecticut
The Mayflower Inn, *Washington*

Florida
Four Seasons Resort Palm Beach, *Palm Beach*
The Ritz-Carlton, Naples, *Naples*
The Ritz-Carlton, Palm Beach, *Palm Beach*

Georgia
Four Seasons Hotel Atlanta, *Atlanta*
The Lodge at Sea Island Golf Club, *Sea Island*

Illinois
Four Seasons Hotel Chicago, *Chicago*
Peninsula Chicago, *Chicago*
The Ritz-Carlton, A Four Seasons Hotel, *Chicago*

Massachusetts
Four Seasons Hotel Boston, *Boston*
Blantyre, *Lenox*

New York
Four Seasons Hotel New York, *Manhattan*
The Point, *Saranac Lake*
The Ritz-Carlton New York Central Park, *Manhattan*
The St. Regis, *Manhattan*

North Carolina
Fearrington House, *Pittsboro*

South Carolina
Woodlands Resort and Inn, *Summerville*

Texas
The Mansion on Turtle Creek, *Dallas*

Vermont
Twin Farms, *Woodstock*

Virginia
The Inn at Little Washington, *Washington*
The Jefferson Hotel, *Richmond*

RESTAURANTS

California
The Dining Room at The Ritz-Carlton San Francisco, *San Francisco*
The French Laundry, *Yountville*
Gary Danko, *San Francisco*

Georgia
The Dining Room, *Atlanta*
Seeger's, *Atlanta*

Illinois
Charlie Trotter's, *Chicago*
Trio, *Evanston*

New York
Alain Ducasse, *Manhattan*
Jean Georges, *Manhattan*

Ohio
Maisonette, *Cincinnati*

Pennsylvania
Le Bec-Fin, *Philadelphia*

South Carolina
The Dining Room at Woodlands, *Summerville*

Virginia
The Inn at Little Washington, *Washington*

The Mobil Travel Guide has been rating establishments with a One- to Five-Star system since 1958. Each establishment awarded the Mobil Five-Star rating is "one of the best in the country." Detailed information on each award winner can be found in the corresponding regional edition listed on the back cover.

Welcome

Dear Traveler,

Since its inception in 1958, Mobil Travel Guide has served as a trusted advisor to auto travelers in search of value in lodging, dining, and destinations. Now in its 46th year, the Mobil Travel Guide is the hallmark of our ExxonMobil family of travel publications, and we're proud to offer an array of products and services from our Mobil, Exxon, and Esso brands in North America to facilitate life on the road.

Whether you're looking for business or pleasure venues, our nationwide network of independent, professional evaluators offers their expertise on thousands of travel options, allowing you to plan a quick family getaway, a full-service business meeting, or an unforgettable Five-Star celebration.

Your feedback is important to us as we strive to improve our product offerings and better meet today's travel needs. Whether you travel once a week or once a year, please take the time to contact us at www.mobiltravelguide.com. We hope to hear from you soon.

Best wishes for safe and enjoyable travels.

Lee R Raymond

Lee R. Raymond
Chairman and CEO
Exxon Mobil Corporation

A Word to Our Readers

Travelers are on the roads in great numbers these days. They're exploring the country on day trips, weekend getaways, business trips, and extended family vacations, visiting major cities and small towns along the way. Because time is precious and the travel industry is ever-changing, having accurate, reliable travel information at your fingertips is critical. Mobil Travel Guide has been providing invaluable insight to travelers for more than 45 years, and we are committed to continuing this service well into the future.

The Mobil Corporation (known as Exxon Mobil Corporation since a 1999 merger) began producing the Mobil Travel Guide books in 1958, following the introduction of the US highway system in 1956. The first edition covered only five southwestern states. Since then, our books have become the premier travel guides in North America, covering the 48 contiguous states and Canada. Now, ExxonMobil presents the latest editions of our annual travel guides, with a fresh new look. We also recently introduced road atlases and specialty publications, a robust new Web site, as well as the first fully integrated, auto-centric travel support program called MobilCompanion, the driving force in travel. (See the inside back cover for more information).

Since its founding, Mobil Travel Guide has served as an advocate for travelers seeking knowledge about hotels, restaurants, and places to visit. Based on an objective process, we make recommendations to our customers that we believe will enhance the quality and value of their travel experiences. Our trusted One- to Five-Star rating system is the oldest and most respected lodging and restaurant inspection and rating program in North America. Most hoteliers, restaurateurs, and industry observers favorably regard the rigor of our inspection program and understand the prestige and benefits that come with receiving a Mobil Travel Guide star rating.

The Mobil Travel Guide process of rating each establishment includes:

☼ Unannounced facility inspections
☼ Incognito service evaluations for Mobil Four- and Five-Star properties
☼ A review of unsolicited comments from the general public
☼ Senior management oversight

For each property, more than 450 attributes, including cleanliness, physical facilities, employee attitude, and courtesy, are measured and evaluated to produce a mathematically derived score, which is then blended with the other elements to form an overall score. These quantifiable scores allow comparative analysis among properties and form the basis that Mobil Travel Guide uses to assign its Mobil One- to Five-Star ratings.

This process focuses largely on guest expectations, guest experience, and consistency of service, not just physical facilities and amenities. It is fundamentally a relative rating system that rewards those properties that continually strive for and achieve excellence each year. Indeed, the very best properties are consistently raising the bar for those that wish to compete with them. These properties proactively respond to consumers' needs even in today's uncertain times.

Only facilities that meet Mobil Travel Guide's standards earn the privilege of being listed in the guide. Deteriorating, poorly managed establishments are deleted. A Mobil Travel Guide listing constitutes a positive quality recommendation; every listing is an accolade, a recognition of achievement. Our One- to Five-Star rating system highlights its level of service. Extensive in-house research is constantly underway to determine new additions to our lists.

☼ The Mobil Five-Star Award indicates that a property is one of the very best in the country and consistently provides gracious and courteous service, superlative quality in its facility, and a unique ambience. The lodgings and restaurants at the Five-Star level consistently and proactively respond to consumers' needs and continue their commitment to excellence, doing so with grace and perseverance.

☼ Also highly regarded is the Mobil Four-Star Award, which honors properties for outstanding achievement in overall facility and for providing very strong service levels in all areas. These award-winners provide a distinctive experience for the ever-demanding and sophisticated consumer.

☼ The Mobil Three-Star Award recognizes an excellent property that provides full services and amenities. This category ranges from exceptional hotels with limited services to elegant restaurants with a less-formal atmosphere.

- A Mobil Two-Star property is a clean and comfortable establishment that has expanded amenities or a distinctive environment. A Two-Star property is an excellent place to stay or dine.
- A Mobil One-Star property is limited in its amenities and services but focuses on providing a value experience while meeting travelers' expectations. The property can be expected to be clean, comfortable, and convenient.

Allow us to emphasize that we do not charge establishments for inclusion in our guides. We have no relationship with any of the businesses and attractions we list and act only as a consumer advocate. In essence, we do the investigative legwork so that you won't have to.

Keep in mind, too, that the hospitality business is ever-changing. Restaurants and lodgings—particularly small chains and standalone establishments—change management or even go out of business with surprising quickness. Although we make every effort to double-check information during our annual updates, we nevertheless recommend that you call ahead to make sure the place you've selected is still open and offers all the amenities you're looking for. We've provided phone numbers; when available, we also list fax numbers and Web site addresses.

We hope that your travels are enjoyable and relaxing and that our books help you get the most out of every trip you take. If any aspect of your accommodation, dining, or sightseeing experience motivates you to comment, please drop us a line. We depend a great deal on our readers' remarks, so you can be assured that we will read your comments and assimilate them into our research. General comments about our books are also welcome. You can write to us at Mobil Travel Guide, 1460 Renaissance Drive, Suite 401, Park Ridge, IL 60068, or send an e-mail to info@mobiltravelguide.com.

Take your Mobil Travel Guide books along on every trip you take. We're confident that you'll be pleased with their convenience, ease of use, and breadth of dependable coverage.

Happy travels!

How to Use This Book

The Mobil Travel Guide travel planners are designed for ease of use. The book begins with a general introduction that provides a geographical and historical orientation to the state and gives basic statewide tourist information, from climate to popular highways to seatbelt laws. The remainder is devoted to travel destinations within the state—mainly cities and towns, but also national and state parks and tourist areas—which are arranged alphabetically.

The following sections explain the wealth of information you'll find about those travel destinations: information about the area, things to see and do there, and where to stay and eat.

Maps and Map Coordinates

At the front of this book in the full-color section, we have provided state maps as well as maps of selected larger cities to help you find your way around once you leave the highway. You'll find a key to the map symbols on the Contents page at the beginning of the map section.

Next to most cities and towns throughout the book, you'll find a set of map coordinates, such as C-2. These coordinates reference the maps at the front of this book and help you find the location you're looking for quickly and easily.

Destination Information

Because many travel destinations are close to other cities and towns where travelers might find additional attractions, accommodations, and restaurants, we've included cross-references to those cities and towns when it makes sense to do so. We also list addresses and phone numbers for travel information resources—usually the local chamber of commerce or office of tourism—as well as pertinent statistics and, in many cases, a brief introduction to the area.

Information about airports, ground transportation, and suburbs is included for large cities.

Driving and Walking Tours

The driving tours that we include for many states are usually day trips that make for interesting side excursions, although they can be longer. They offer you a way to get off the beaten path and visit an area that travelers often overlook. These trips frequently cover areas of natural beauty or historical significance.

Each walking tour focuses on a particularly interesting area of a city or town. Again, these tours can provide a break from everyday tourist attractions. The tours often include places to stop for meals or snacks.

What to See and Do

The Mobil Travel Guide offers information about nearly 20,000 museums, art galleries, amusement parks, historic sites, national and state parks, ski areas, and many other types of attractions. A white star on a black background ★ signals that the attraction is a must-see—one of the best in the state. Because municipal parks, public tennis courts, swimming pools, and small educational institutions are common to most towns, they generally are not mentioned.

In an attraction's description, you'll find the months, days, and, in some cases, hours of operation; the address/directions, telephone number, and Web site (if there is one); and the admission price category. The following are the ranges we use for admission fees:
- ✪ **FREE**
- ✪ **$** = Up to $5
- ✪ **$$** = $5.01-$10
- ✪ **$$$** = $10.01-$15
- ✪ **$$$$** = Over $15

Special Events

Special events are either annual events that last only a short time, such as festivals and fairs, or longer, seasonal events such as horseracing, summer theater and concerts, and professional sports. The Mobil Travel Guide Special Events listings also include infrequently occurring occasions that mark certain dates or events, such as a centennial or other commemorative celebration.

Side Trips

We recognize that your travels don't always end where state lines fall, so we've included some side trips that technically fall outside the scope of this book but that travelers frequently visit when they're in this region. Nearby national park, major cities, and other major draws fall into this category. You'll find side trips for a particular area at the end of that state's city listings.

Lodging and Restaurant Listings

Lodgings and restaurants are usually listed under the city or town in which they are located. Make sure to check the related cities and towns that appear right beneath the city heading for additional options, especially if you're traveling to a major metropolitan area that includes many suburbs. In large cities, lodgings located within 5 miles of major commercial airports are listed under a separate "Airport Area" heading that follows the city section.

LODGINGS

Travelers have different wants and needs when it comes to accommodations. To help you pinpoint properties that meet your particular needs, each lodging property is classified by type according to the following characteristics:

- **Motels/Motor Lodges.** These accommodations are in low-rise structures with rooms that are easily accessible to parking, which is usually free. Properties have small, functional lobbies, and guests enter their rooms from the outdoors. Service is often limited, and dining may not be offered in lower-rated motels. Shops and businesses are generally found only in higher-rated properties, as are bell staff, room service, and restaurants serving three meals daily.

- **Hotels.** A hotel is an establishment that provides lodging in a clean, comfortable environment. Guests can expect private bathrooms as well as some measure of guest services, such as luggage assistance, room service, and daily maid service.

- **Resorts.** A resort is an establishment that provides lodging in a facility that is typically located on a larger piece of land. Recreational activities are emphasized and often include golf, spa, and tennis. Guests can expect more than one food and beverage establishment on the property, which aims to provide a variety of food choices at a variety of price points.

- **All Suites.** In an all suites property, guest accommodations consist of two rooms: a bedroom and a living room. Higher-rated properties offer facilities and services comparable to regular hotels.

- **B&Bs/Small Inns.** The hotel alternative for those who prefer the comforts of home and a personal touch. It may be a structure of historic significance and often is located in an interesting setting. Breakfast is usually included and often is treated as a special occasion. Cocktails and refreshments may be served in the late afternoon or evening. Rooms are often individually decorated, but telephones, televisions, and private bathrooms may not be available in every room.

- **Boutique Hotels.** Frequently a small hotel of fewer than 150 guest rooms, a boutique hotel is more about décor than about functionality and service. In many cases, the unique décor is trendsetting and hip, but don't let it fool you…there are, more often than not, inherent weaknesses in the facility with regard to size of the guest rooms, bathrooms, and so on. Services offered usually match those of a larger hotel but are done on a more personal and, often, more interesting manner.

- **Guest Ranches.** Like resorts, guest ranches specialize in stays of three days or more. These lodgings also offer meal plans and extensive outdoor activities. Horseback riding is usually a feature; stables and trails are found on the ranch property, and trail rides and daily instruction are part of the program. Many guest ranches are working ranches, ranging from casual to rustic, and guests are encouraged to participate in ranch life. Eating is often family style and may include cookouts. Western saddles are assumed; phone ahead to inquire about English saddle availability.

- **Extended Stay.** These hotels specialize in stays of three days or more and usually offer weekly room rates. Service is often limited, and dining may not be offered at lower-rated properties.

- **Casino Hotels.** Casino hotels incorporate areas that offer games of chance such as blackjack, poker, and slot machines and are found only in states where gambling is legal. These hotels offer a wide range of services and amenities comparable to regular hotels.

Because most lodgings offer the following features and services, information about them does not appear in the listings unless exceptions exist:

- Year-round operation with a single rate structure
- Major credit cards accepted (note that Exxon or Mobil Corporation credit cards cannot be used to pay for room or other charges)
- Air-conditioning and heat, often with individual room controls
- Bathroom with tub and/or shower in each room
- Cable television
- Cots and cribs available
- Daily maid service
- Elevators
- In-room telephones

Each lodging listing gives the name, address/location (when no street address is available), neighborhood and/or directions from downtown (in major cities), phone number(s), fax number, total number of guest rooms, and seasons open (if not year-round). Also included are details on business, luxury, recreational, and dining facilities on the property or nearby. A key to the symbols at the end of each listing can be found on the inside front cover of this book.

For every property, we also provide pricing information. Because lodging rates change frequently, we often opt to list a pricing category rather than specific prices; however, we provide specific room rates wherever possible. The pricing categories break down as follows:

- ✪ **$** = Up to $150
- ✪ **$$** = $151-$250
- ✪ **$$$** = $251-$350
- ✪ **$$$$** = $351 and up

All prices quoted by the Mobil Travel Guide are in effect at the time of publication; however, prices cannot be guaranteed. In some locations, short-term price variations may exist because of special events or holidays. Whenever possible, these price variations are noted. Certain resorts have complicated rate structures that vary with the time of year; always confirm rates when making your plans.

RESTAURANTS

All dining establishments listed in our books have a full kitchen and offer table service and a complete menu. Parking on or near the premises, in a lot or garage, is assumed. If parking is not available, we note that fact in the listing.

Each listing also gives the cuisine type, address (or directions if no street address is available), neighborhood and/or directions from downtown (in major cities), phone and fax numbers, Web site (if available), meals served, days of operation (if not open daily year-round), reservation policy, and pricing category or, whenever possible, specific à la carte entrée prices. We also indicate if a child's menu is offered. The price categories are defined as follows per diner and assume that you order an appetizer, entrée, and one drink:

- ✪ **$** = $15 and under
- ✪ **$$** = $16-$35
- ✪ **$$$** = $36-$85
- ✪ **$$$$** = $86 and up

QUALITY RATINGS

The Mobil Travel Guide has been rating lodgings and restaurants in the United States since the first edition was published in 1958. For years, the guide was the only source of such ratings, and it remains among the few guidebooks to rate restaurants across the country and in Canada.

All listed establishments have been inspected by experienced field representatives and/or evaluated by a senior staff member. Our ratings are based on detailed inspection reports of the individual properties, on written evaluations of staff members who stay and dine anonymously, and on an extensive review of reader comments. Rating categories reflect both the features a property offers and its quality in relation to similar establishments.

Here are the definitions for the star ratings for lodgings:

- ✪ ★ : A Mobil One-Star lodging is a limited-service hotel, motel, or inn that is considered a clean, comfortable, and reliable establishment.
- ✪ ★★ : A Mobil Two-Star lodging is considered a clean, comfortable, and reliable establishment that has expanded amenities, such as a full-service restaurant on the premises.
- ✪ ★★★ : A Mobil Three-Star lodging is well appointed, with a full-service restaurant and expanded amenities, such as a fitness center, golf course, tennis courts, 24-hour room service, and optional turndown service.
- ✪ ★★★★ : A Mobil Four-Star lodging provides a luxury experience with expanded amenities in a distinctive environment. Services may include, but are not limited to, automatic turndown service, 24-hour room service, and valet parking.
- ✪ ★★★★★ : A Mobil Five-Star lodging provides consistently superlative service in an exceptionally distinctive luxury environment, with expanded services. Attention to detail is evident throughout the hotel, resort, or inn, from bed linens to staff uniforms.

The Mobil Travel Guide star ratings for restaurants are defined as follows:

- ✪ ★ : A Mobil One-Star restaurant provides a distinctive experience through culinary specialty, local flair, or individual atmosphere.
- ✪ ★★ : A Mobil Two-Star restaurant serves fresh food in a clean setting with efficient service. Value is considered in this category, as is family friendliness.
- ✪ ★★★ : A Mobil Three-Star restaurant has good food, warm and skillful service, and enjoyable décor.
- ✪ ★★★★ : A Mobil Four-Star restaurant provides professional service, distinctive presentations, and wonderful food.
- ✪ ★★★★★ : A Mobil Five-Star restaurant offers one of few flawless dining experiences in the country. These establishments consistently provide their guests with exceptional food, superlative service, elegant décor, and exquisite presentations of each detail surrounding a meal.

TERMS AND ABBREVIATIONS IN LISTINGS

The following terms and abbreviations are used throughout the Mobil Travel Guide lodging and restaurant listings to indicate which amenities and services are available at each establishment. We've done our best to provide accurate and up-to-date information, but things do change, so if a particular feature is essential to you, please contact the establishment directly to make sure that it is available.

Complete meal Soup and/or salad, entrée, and dessert, plus a nonalcoholic beverage.

Continental breakfast Usually coffee and a roll or doughnut.

D Followed by a price, indicates the room rate for a double room—two people in one room in one or two beds (the charge may be higher for two double beds).

Each additional The extra charge for each additional person beyond the stated number of persons.

In-room modem link Every guest room has a connection for a modem that's separate from the main phone line.

Kitchen(s) A kitchen or kitchenette that contains a stove or microwave, sink, and refrigerator and is either part of the room or a separate, adjoining room. If the kitchen is not fully equipped, the listing will indicate "no equipt" or "some equipt."

Laundry service Either coin-operated laundry facilities or overnight valet service is available.

Luxury level A special section of a lodging, spanning at least an entire floor, that offers increased luxury accommodations. Management must provide no less than three of these four services: separate check-in and check-out, concierge, private lounge, and private elevator service (with key access). Complimentary breakfast and snacks are commonly offered.

Movies Prerecorded videos are available for rental or check-out.

Prix fixe A full, multicourse meal for a stated price; usually available at finer restaurants.

Valet parking An attendant is available to park and retrieve your car.

VCR VCRs are present in all guest rooms.

VCR available VCRs are available for hookup in guest rooms.

SPECIAL INFORMATION FOR TRAVELERS WITH DISABILITIES

The Mobil Travel Guide **D** symbol indicates establishments that are at least partially accessible to people with mobility problems. Our criteria for accessibility are unique to our publications. Please do not confuse them with the universal symbol for wheelchair accessibility.

When the **D** symbol follows a listing, the establishment is equipped with facilities to accommodate people using wheelchairs or crutches or otherwise needing easy access to doorways and rest rooms. Travelers with severe mobility problems or with hearing or visual impairments may or may not find the facilities they need. Always phone ahead to make sure that an establishment can meet your needs.

All lodgings bearing our **D** symbol have the following facilities:

- ISA-designated parking near access ramps
- Level or ramped entryways to buildings
- Swinging building entryway doors a minimum of 39 inches wide
- Public rest rooms on the main level with space to operate a wheelchair and handrails at commode areas
- Elevator(s) equipped with grab bars and lowered control buttons
- Restaurant(s) with accessible doorway(s), rest rooms with space to operate a wheelchair, and handrails at commode areas
- Guest room entryways that are at least 39 inches wide
- Low-pile carpet in rooms
- Telephones at bedside and in the bathroom
- Beds placed at wheelchair height
- Bathrooms with a minimum doorway width of 3 feet
- Bath with an open sink (no cabinet) and room to operate a wheelchair
- Handrails at commode areas and in the tub
- Wheelchair-accessible peepholes in room entry door
- Wheelchair-accessible closet rods and shelves

All restaurants bearing our **D** symbol offer the following facilities:

- ISA-designated parking beside access ramps
- Level or ramped front entryways to the building
- Tables that accommodate wheelchairs
- Main-floor rest rooms with an entryway that's at least 3 feet wide
- Rest rooms with space to operate a wheelchair and handrails at commode areas

Making the Most of Your Trip

A few hardy souls might look back with fondness on a trip during which the car broke down, leaving them stranded for three days, or a vacation that cost twice what it was supposed to. For most travelers, though, the best trips are those that are safe, smooth, and within budget. To help you make your trip the best it can be, we've assembled a few tips and resources.

Saving Money

ON LODGING

Many hotels and motels offer discounts—for senior citizens, business travelers, families, you name it. It never hurts to ask—politely, that is. Sometimes, especially in the late afternoon, desk clerks are instructed to fill beds, and you might be offered a lower rate or a nicer room to entice you to stay. Simply ask the reservation agent for the best rate available. Also, make sure to try both the toll-free number and the local number. You may be able to get a lower rate from one than the other.

Becoming a member of MobilCompanion will entitle you to discounted rates at many well-known hotels around the country. For more information, call 877/785-6788 or visit www.mobilcompanion.com.

Timing your trip right can cut your lodging costs as well. Look for bargains on stays over multiple nights, in the off-season, and on weekdays or weekends, depending on the location. Many hotels in major metropolitan areas, for example, have special weekend packages that offer considerable savings on rooms; they may include breakfast, cocktails, and dinner discounts.

Another way to save money is to choose accommodations that give you more than just a standard room. Rooms with kitchen facilities enable you to cook some meals yourself, reducing your restaurant costs. A suite might save money for two couples traveling together. Even hotel luxury levels can provide good value, as many include breakfast or cocktails in the price of a room.

State and city taxes, as well as special room taxes, can increase your room rate by as much as 25 percent per day. We are unable to include information about taxes in our listings, but we strongly urge you to ask about taxes when making reservations so that you understand the total cost of your lodgings before you book.

Watch out for telephone-usage charges that hotels frequently impose on long-distance, credit-card, and other calls. Before phoning from your room, read the information given to you at check-in, and then be sure to review your bill carefully when checking out. You won't be expected to pay for charges that the hotel didn't spell out. Consider using your cell phone if you have one; or, if public telephones are available in the hotel lobby, your cost savings may outweigh the inconvenience of using them.

Here are some additional ways to save on lodgings:
- Stay in B&B accommodations; they're generally less expensive than standard hotel rooms, and the complimentary breakfasts cut down on food costs.
- If you're traveling with children, find lodgings at which kids stay free.
- When visiting major cities, stay just outside the city limits; these rooms are usually less expensive than those in downtown locations.
- Consider visiting national parks during the low season, when prices of lodgings near the parks drop 25 percent or more.
- When calling a hotel, ask whether it is running any special promotions or if any discounts are available; many times reservationists are told not to volunteer deals unless specifically asked about them.
- Check for hotel packages; some offer nightly rates that include a rental car or discounts on major attractions.

ON DINING

There are several ways to get a less expensive meal at a more expensive restaurant. Early-bird dinners are popular in many parts of the country and offer considerable savings. If you're interested in sampling a Mobil Four- or Five-Star establishment, consider going at lunchtime. Although the prices are probably still relatively high at midday, they may be half of those at dinner, and you'll experience the same ambience, service, and cuisine.

As a member of MobilCompanion, you can enroll in iDine. This program earns you up to 20 percent cash back at more than 1,900 restaurants on meals purchased with the credit card you register; the rebate appears on your credit card bill. For more information about MobilCompanion and iDine, call 877/785-6788 or go to www.mobilcompanion.com.

ON ENTERTAINMENT

Although many national parks, monuments, seashores, historic sites, and recreation areas may be used free of charge, others charge an entrance fee (ranging from $1 to $6 per person or $5 to $20 per carload) and/or a usage fee for special services and facilities. If you plan to make several visits to national recreation areas, consider one of the following money-saving programs offered by the National Park Service:

- National Parks Pass. This annual pass is good for entrance to any national park that charges an entrance fee. If the park charges a per-vehicle fee, the pass holder and any accompanying passengers in a private noncommercial vehicle may enter. If the park charges a per-person fee, the pass applies to the holder's spouse, children, and parents as well as the holder. It is valid for entrance fees only; it does not cover parking, camping, or other fees. You can purchase a National Parks Pass in person at any national park where an entrance fee is charged; by mail from the National Park Foundation, PO Box 34108, Washington, DC 20043-4108; by calling 888/GO-PARKS; or at www.nationalparks.org. The cost is $50.

- Golden Eagle. When affixed to a National Parks Pass, this sticker, available to people who are between 17 and 61 years of age, extends coverage to sites managed by the US Fish and Wildlife Service, the US Forest Service, and the Bureau of Land Management. It is good until the National Parks Pass to which it is affixed expires and does not cover usage fees. You can purchase one at National Park Service, Fish and Wildlife Service, and Bureau of Land Management fee stations. The cost is $15.

- Golden Age Passport. Available to citizens and permanent US residents 62 and older, this passport is a lifetime entrance permit to fee-charging national recreation areas. The fee exemption extends to those accompanying the permit holder in a private noncommercial vehicle or, in the case of walk-in facilities, to the holder's spouse and children. The passport also entitles the holder to a 50 percent discount on federal usage fees charged in park areas, but not on concessions. Golden Age Passports must be obtained in person and are available at most National Park Service units that charge an entrance fee. The applicant must show proof of age, such as a driver's license or birth certificate (Medicare cards are not acceptable proof). The cost is $10.

- Golden Access Passport. Issued to citizens and permanent US residents who are physically disabled or visually impaired, this passport is a free lifetime entrance permit to fee-charging national recreation areas. The fee exemption extends to those accompanying the permit holder in a private noncommercial vehicle or, in the case of walk-in facilities, to the holder's spouse and children. The passport also entitles the holder to a 50 percent discount on usage fees charged in park areas, but not on concessions. Golden Access Passports must be obtained in person and are available at most National Park Service units that charge an entrance fee. Proof of eligibility to receive federal benefits (under programs such as Disability Retirement, Compensation for Military Service-Connected Disability, and the Coal Mine Safety and Health Act) is required, or an affidavit must be signed attesting to eligibility.

A money-saving move in several large cities is to purchase a CityPass. If you plan to visit several museums and other major attractions, CityPass is a terrific option because it gets you into several sites for one substantially reduced price. Currently, CityPass is available in Boston, Chicago, Hollywood, New York, Philadelphia, San Francisco, Seattle, and southern California (which includes Disneyland, Sea World, and the San Diego Zoo). For more information or to buy one, call 888/330-5008 or visit www.citypass.net. You can also buy a CityPass from any participating CityPass attraction.

Here are some additional ways to save on entertainment and shopping:

- Check with your hotel's concierge for various coupons and special offers; they often have two-for-one tickets for area attractions and coupons for discounts at area stores and restaurants.

- Purchase same-day concert or theater tickets for half-price through the local cheap-tickets outlet, such as TKTS in New York City or Hot Tix in Chicago.

- Visit museums on their free or "by donation" days, when you can pay what you wish rather than a specific admission fee.

- Save receipts from purchases in Canada; visitors to Canada can get a rebate on federal taxes and some provincial sales taxes.

ON TRANSPORTATION

Transportation is a big part of any vacation budget. Here are some ways to reduce your costs:

- If you're renting a car, shop early over the Internet; you can book a car during the low season for less, even if you'll be using it in the high season.

- Rental car discounts are often available if you rent for one week or longer and reserve in advance.

- Get the best gas mileage out of your vehicle by making sure that it's properly tuned up and keeping your tires properly inflated. If your tires need to be replaced, you can save money on a new set of Michelins by becoming a member of MobilCompanion.

⊘ Travel at moderate speeds on the open road; higher speeds require more gasoline.

⊘ Fill the tank before you return your rental car; rental companies charge to refill the tank and do so at prices of up to 50 percent more than at local gas stations.

⊘ Make a checklist of travel essentials and purchase them before you leave; don't get stuck buying expensive sunscreen at your hotel or overpriced film at the aiport.

FOR SENIOR CITIZENS

Look for the senior-citizen discount symbol SC in this book's lodging and restaurant listings. Always call ahead to confirm that a discount is being offered, and be sure to carry proof of age. At places not listed in this book, it never hurts to ask if a senior-citizen discount is offered. Additional information for mature travelers is available from the American Association of Retired Persons (AARP), 601 E St NW, Washington, DC 20049; phone 202/434-2277; www.aarp.org.

Tipping

Tips are expressions of appreciation for good service. However, you are never obligated to tip if you receive poor service.

IN HOTELS

⊘ Door attendants usually get $1 for hailing a cab.

⊘ Bell staff expect $2 per bag.

⊘ Concierges are tipped according to the service they perform. Tipping is not mandatory when you've asked for suggestions on sightseeing or restaurants or for help in making dining reservations. However, a tip of $5 is appropriate when a concierge books you a table at a restaurant known to be difficult to get into. For obtaining theater or sporting event tickets, $5 to $10 is expected.

⊘ Maids should be tipped $1 to $2 per day. Hand your tip directly to the maid, or leave it with a note saying that the money has been left expressly for the maid.

IN RESTAURANTS

Before tipping, carefully review your check for any gratuity or service charge that is already included in your bill. If you're in doubt, ask your server.

⊘ Coffee shop and counter service waitstaff usually receive 15 percent of the bill, before sales tax.

⊘ In full-service restaurants, tip 18 percent of the bill, before sales tax.

⊘ In fine restaurants, where gratuities are shared among a larger staff, 18 to 20 percent is appropriate.

⊘ In most cases, the maitre d' is tipped only if the service has been extraordinary, and only on the way out. At upscale properties in major metropolitan areas, $20 is the minimum.

⊘ If there is a wine steward, tip $20 for exemplary service and beyond, or more if the wine was decanted or the bottle was very expensive.

⊘ Tip $1 to $2 per coat at the coat check.

AT AIRPORTS

Curbside luggage handlers expect $1 per bag. Car-rental shuttle drivers who help with your luggage appreciate a $1 or $2 tip.

Staying Safe

The best way to deal with emergencies is to avoid them in the first place. However, unforeseen situations do happen, so you should be prepared for them.

IN YOUR CAR

Before you head out on a road trip, make sure that your car has been serviced and is in good working order. Change the oil, check the battery and belts, make sure that your windshield washer fluid is full and your tires are properly inflated (which can also improve your gas mileage). Other inspections recommended by the vehicle's manufacturer should also be made.

Next, be sure you have the tools and equipment needed to deal with a routine breakdown:

⊘ Jack

⊘ Spare tire

⊘ Lug wrench

⊘ Repair kit

⊘ Emergency tools

⊘ Jumper cables

⊘ Spare fan belt

⊘ Fuses

⊘ Flares and/or reflectors

⊘ Flashlight

⊘ First-aid kit

⊘ In winter, a windshield scraper and snow shovel

Many emergency supplies are sold in special packages that include the essentials you need to stay safe in the event of a breakdown.

Also bring all appropriate and up-to-date documentation—licenses, registration, and insurance cards—and know what your insurance covers. Bring an extra set of keys, too, just in case.

En route, always buckle up! In most states, wearing a seatbelt is required by law.

If your car does break down, do the following:

- ✪ Get out of traffic as soon as possible—pull well off the road.
- ✪ Raise the hood and turn on your emergency flashers or tie a white cloth to the roadside door handle or antenna.
- ✪ Stay in your car.
- ✪ Use flares or reflectors to keep your vehicle from being hit.

If you are a member of MobilCompanion, remember that En Route Support is always ready to help when you need it. Just give us a call and we'll locate and dispatch an emergency roadside service to assist you, as well as provide you with significant savings on the service.

IN YOUR HOTEL OR MOTEL

Chances are slim that you will encounter a hotel or motel fire, but you can protect yourself by doing the following:

- ✪ Once you've checked in, make sure that the smoke detector in your room is working properly.
- ✪ Find the property's fire safety instructions, usually posted on the inside of the room door.
- ✪ Locate the fire extinguishers and at least two fire exits.
- ✪ Never use an elevator in a fire.

For personal security, use the peephole in your room door and make sure that anyone claiming to be a hotel employee can show proper identification. Call the front desk if you feel threatened at any time.

PROTECTING AGAINST THEFT

To guard against theft wherever you go:

- ✪ Don't bring anything of more value than you need.
- ✪ If you do bring valuables, leave them at your hotel rather than in your car.
- ✪ If you bring something very expensive, lock it in a safe. Many hotels put one in each room; others will store your valuables in the hotel's safe.
- ✪ Don't carry more money than you need. Use traveler's checks and credit cards or visit cash machines to withdraw more cash when you run out.

For Travelers with Disabilities

To get the kind of service you need and have a right to expect, don't hesitate when making a reservation to question the management about the availability of accessible rooms, parking, entrances, restaurants, lounges, or any other facilities that are important to you, and confirm what is meant by "accessible."

The Mobil Travel Guide D symbol indicates establishments that are at least partially accessible to people with special mobility needs (people using wheelchairs or crutches or otherwise needing easy access to buildings and rooms). Keep in mind that our criteria for accessibility are unique to our publication and should not be confused with the universal symbol for wheelchair accessibility. Further information about these criteria can be found in the earlier section "How to Use This Book."

A thorough listing of published material for travelers with disabilities is available from the Disability Bookshop, Twin Peaks Press, Box 129, Vancouver, WA 98666; phone 360/694-2462; disabilitybookshop. virtualave.net. Another reliable organization is the Society for Accessible Travel & Hospitality (SATH), 347 Fifth Ave, Suite 610, New York, NY 10016; phone 212/447-7284; www.sath.org.

Traveling to Canada

Citizens of the United States should be aware of these conditions when entering Canada:

- ✪ Visas are not required.
- ✪ Visitors may tour the provinces for up to three months without paying a fee.
- ✪ Proof of citizenship, such as a passport, birth certificate, or voter registration card, is required. A driver's license is not acceptable proof of citizenship.
- ✪ Naturalized citizens will need their naturalization certificates or their US passports to reenter the United States.
- ✪ Children under 18 traveling on their own should carry a letter from a parent or guardian giving them permission to travel in Canada.
- ✪ Drivers are advised to carry their motor vehicle registration cards.
- ✪ If the car is not registered in the driver's name, a letter from the registered owner authorizing use of the vehicle should be available.
- ✪ If the car is a rental, carry a copy of the rental contract stipulating permission for use in Canada.

- Ask your car insurer for a Canadian Non-Resident Inter-Province Motor Vehicle Liability Insurance Card. This card ensures that your insurance company will meet the minimum insurance requirements in Canada.
- The use of seatbelts by drivers and passengers is compulsory in all provinces.
- Rabies vaccination certificates are required for dogs or cats.
- A permit is required for the use of citizens band (CB) radios.

The Canadian dollar's rate of exchange with the US dollar varies; contact your local bank for the latest figures.

For the most current and detailed listing of Customs regulations and sources, ask for the annually revised brochure *Canada: Travel Information,* available upon request from the Canadian consulate or embassy in your area.

Important Toll-Free Numbers and Online Information

Hotels and Motels

Adams Mark 800/444-2326
www.adamsmark.com

AmericInn 800/634-3444
www.americinn.com

AmeriHost Inn Hotels 800/434-5800
www.amerihostinn.com

Amerisuites 800/833-1516
www.amerisuites.com

Baymont Inns 877/BAYMONT
www.baymontinns.com

Best Inns & Suites 800/237-8466
www.bestinn.com

Best Value Inns 888/315-BEST
www.bestvalueinn.com

Best Western International 800/WESTERN
www.bestwestern.com

Budget Host Inn 800/BUDHOST
www.budgethost.com

Candlewood Suites 888/CANDLEWOOD
www.candlewoodsuites.com

Clarion Hotels 800/252-7466
www.choicehotels.com

Comfort Inns and Suites 800/252-7466
www.choicehotels.com

Country Hearth Inns 800/848-5767
www.countryhearth.com

Country Inns & Suites 800/456-4000
www.countryinns.com

Courtyard by Marriott 888/236-2427
www.courtyard.com

Cross Country Inn 800/621-1429
www.crosscountryinns.com

Crowne Plaza Hotels and Resorts 800/227-6963
www.crowneplaza.com

Days Inn 800/544-8313
www.daysinn.com

Delta Hotels 800/268-1133
www.deltahotels.com

Destination Hotels & Resorts 800/434-7347
www.destinationhotels.com

Doubletree Hotels 800/222-8733
www.doubletree.com

Drury Inns 800/378-7946
www.druryinn.com

Econolodge 800/553-2666
www.econolodge.com

Economy Inns of America 800/826-0778
www.innsofamerica.com

Embassy Suites 800/362-2779
www.embassysuites.com

ExelInns of America 800/FOREXEL
www.exelinns.com

Extended StayAmerica 800/EXTSTAY
www.extstay.com

Fairfield Inn by Marriott 888/236-2427
www.fairfieldinn.com

Fairmont Hotels 800/441-1414
www.fairmont.com

Four Points by Sheraton 888/625-5144
www.starwood.com

Four Seasons 800/545-4000
www.fourseasons.com

Hampton Inn/Hampton Inn and Suites 800/426-7866
www.hamptoninn.com

Hard Rock Hotels, Resorts and Casinos 800/HRDROCK
www.hardrock.com

Harrah's Entertainment 800/HARRAHS
www.harrahs.com

Harvey Hotels 800/922-9222
www.bristolhotels.com

Hawthorn Suites 800/527-1133
www.hawthorn.com

Hilton Hotels and Resorts (US) 800/774-1500
www.hilton.com

Holiday Inn Express 800/HOLIDAY
www.sixcontinentshotel.com

Holiday Inn Hotels and Resorts 800/HOLIDAY
www.holiday-inn.com

Homestead Studio Suites 888/782-9473
www.stayhsd.com

Homewood Suites 800/225-5466
www.homewoodsuites.com

Howard Johnson 800/406-1411
www.hojo.com

Hyatt 800/633-7313
www.hyatt.com

Ian Schrager . . . . Contact individual hotel
www.ianschragerhotels.com

Inter-Continental 888/567-8725
www.intercontinental.com

Joie de Vivre 800/738-7477
www.jdvhospitality.com

Kimpton Hotels 888/546-7866
www.kimptongroup.com

Knights Inn 800/843-5644
www.knightsinn.com

La Quinta 800/531-5900
www.laquinta.com

Le Meridien 800/543-4300
www.lemeridien.com

Leading Hotels of the World 800/223-6800
www.lhw.com

Loews Hotels 800/235-6397
www.loewshotels.com

MainStay Suites 800/660-6246
www.choicehotels.com

Mandarin Oriental 800/526-6566
www.mandarin-oriental.com

Marriott Conference Centers 888/236-2427
www.conferencecenters.com

Marriott Hotels, Resorts, and Suites 888/236-2427
www.marriott.com

Marriott Vacation Club International 800/845-5279
www.marriott.com/vacationclub

Microtel Inns & Suites 800/771-7171
www.microtelinn.com

Millennium & Copthorne Hotels 866/866-8086
www.mill-cop.com

Motel 6 . . . . 800/4MOTEL6
www.motel6.com

Omni Hotels 800/843-6664
www.omnihotels.com

Pan Pacific Hotels and Resorts 800/327-8585
www.panpac.com

Park Inn & Park Plaza 888/201-1801
www.parkhtls.com

The Peninsula Group . . . . Contact individual hotel
www.peninsula.com

Preferred Hotels & Resorts Worldwide 800/323-7500
www.preferredhotels.com

Quality Inn 800/228-5151
www.qualityinn.com

Radisson Hotels 800/333-3333
www.radisson.com

Raffles International Hotels and Resorts 800/637-9477
www.raffles.com

Ramada International 888/298-2054
www.ramada.com

Ramada Plazas, Limiteds, and Inns 800/2RAMADA
www.ramadahotels.com

Red Lion Inns 800/733-5466
www.redlion.com

Red Roof Inns 800/733-7663
www.redroof.com

Regal Hotels 800/222-8888
www.regal-hotels.com

Regent International 800/545-4000
www.regenthotels.com

Relais & Chateaux 800/735-2478
www.relaischateaux.com

Renaissance Hotels 888/236-2427
www.renaissancehotels.com

Residence Inns 888/236-2427
www.residenceinn.com

Ritz-Carlton 800/241-3333
www.ritzcarlton.com

Rockresorts 888/FORROCKS
www.rockresorts.com

Rodeway Inns 800/228-2000
www.rodeway.com

Rosewood Hotels & Resorts 888/767-3966
www.rosewood-hotels.com

Scottish Inn 800/251-1962
www.bookroomsnow.com

Select Inn 800/641-1000
www.selectinn.com

Sheraton 888/625-5144
www.sheraton.com

Shilo Inns 800/222-2244
www.shiloinns.com

Shoney's Inns 800/552-4667
www.shoneysinn.com

Signature/Jameson Inns 800/822-5252
www.jamesoninns.com

Sleep Inns 800/453-3746
www.sleepinn.com

Small Luxury Hotels of the World 800/525-4800
www.slh.com

Sofitel 800/763-4835
www.sofitel.com

SpringHill Suites 888/236-2427
www.springhillsuites.com

SRS Worldhotels 800/223-5652
www.srs-worldhotels.com

St. Regis Luxury Collection 888/625-5144
www.stregis.com

Staybridge Suites by Holiday Inn 800/238-8000
www.staybridge.com

Summerfield Suites by Wyndham 800/833-4353
www.summerfieldsuites.com

Summit International 800/457-4000
www.summithotels.com

Super 8 Motels 800/800-8000
www.super8.com

The Sutton Place Hotels 866/378-8866
www.suttonplace.com

Swissotel 800/637-9477
www.swissotel.com

TownePlace Suites 888/236-2427
www.towneplace.com

Travelodge 800/578-7878
www.travelodge.com

Universal 800/23LOEWS
www.loewshotel.com

Vagabond Inns 800/522-1555
www.vagabondinns.com
W Hotels 888/625-5144
www.whotels.com
Wellesley Inn and Suites 800/444-8888
www.wellesleyinnandsuites.com
WestCoast Hotels 800/325-4000
www.westcoasthotels.com
Westin Hotels & Resorts 800/937-8461
www.westin.com
Wingate Inns 800/228-1000
www.wingateinns.com
Woodfin Suite Hotels 800/966-3346
www.woodfinsuitehotels.com
Wyndham Hotels & Resorts 800/996-3426
www.wyndham.com

Airlines

Air Canada 888/247-2262
www.aircanada.ca
Alaska 800/252-7522
www.alaskaair.com
American 800/433-7300
www.aa.com
America West 800/235-9292
www.americawest.com
ATA 800/435-9282
www.ata.com
British Airways 800/247-9297
www.british-airways.com
Continental 800/523-3273
www.flycontinental.com
Delta 800/221-1212
www.delta-air.com
Island Air 800/323-3345
www.islandair.com
Mesa 800/637-2247
www.mesa-air.com
Northwest 800/225-2525
www.nwa.com
Southwest 800/435-9792
www.southwest.com
United 800/241-6522
www.ual.com
US Airways 800/428-4322
www.usairways.com

Car Rentals

Advantage 800/777-5500
www.arac.com
Alamo 800/327-9633
www.goalamo.com
Allstate 800/634-6186
www.bnm.com/as.htm

Avis 800/831-2847
www.avis.com
Budget 800/527-0700
www.budgetrentacar.com
Dollar 800/800-4000
www.dollarcar.com
Enterprise 800/325-8007
www.pickenterprise.com
Hertz 800/654-3131
www.hertz.com
National 800/227-7368
www.nationalcar.com
Payless 800/729-5377
www.800-payless.com
Rent-A-Wreck.com 800/535-1391
www.rent-a-wreck.com
Sears 800/527-0770
www.budget.com
Thrifty 800/847-4389
www.thrifty.com

Four-Star Establishments in the Northern Great Lakes

Michigan

★★★★ Lodgings
The Townsend Hotel, *Birmingham*

★★★★ Restaurants
The Lark, *Bloomfield Hills*
Tapawingo, *Charlevoix*

Wisconsin

★★★★ Lodgings
The American Club, *Kohler*
Canoe Bay, *Rice Lake*

Michigan

Michigan has a mighty industrial heritage and is well-known as the birthplace of the automobile industry, but rivaling the machines, mines, and mills is the more than $9 billion-a-year tourist industry. The two great Michigan peninsulas, surrounded by four of the five Great Lakes, unfold a tapestry of lakeshore beaches, trout-filled streams, more than 11,000 inland lakes, nearly 7 million acres of public hunting grounds—and the cultural attractions of Dearborn, Detroit, Ann Arbor, Grand Rapids, and other cities.

Michigan has a geographically split personality linked by a single—but magnificent—five-mile-long bridge. The Upper Peninsula faces Lake Superior on one side and Lake Michigan on the other. It revels in its north-country beauty and ruggedness. The Lower Peninsula has shores on Lakes Michigan, Huron, and Erie. Its highly productive Midwestern-style farmland is dotted with diversified cities.

Michigan is a four-season vacationland, with the tempering winds off the Great Lakes taming what might otherwise be a climate of extremes. In a land of cherry blossoms, tulips, ski slopes, and sugar-sand beaches, you can fish through the ice, hunt deer with a bow and arrow, follow the trail of a bobcat, rough it on an uncluttered island, trace Native American paths, or hunt for copper, iron ore, and Lake Superior agates or Petoskey stones. One of the country's finest art museums is in Detroit, and Dearborn's Henry Ford Museum and historic Greenfield Village attract visitors from all over the world. Michigan has an increasing array of challenging resort golf courses as well as more than 750 public courses. Ann Arbor, Detroit, and East Lansing offer outstanding universities.

A world center for automobile manufacture, Michigan leads in the production of automobiles and light trucks. More than two-thirds of the nation's tart red cherries are harvested here; so are more than 90 percent of the dry edible beans. This state is also one of the nation's leading producers of blueberries. Wheat, hay, corn, oats, turkeys, cattle, and hogs are produced in vast quantities. The Soo Locks at Sault Ste. Marie boast the two longest locks in the world, which can accommodate superfreighters 1,000 feet long.

French explorers were the first known Europeans to penetrate the lakes, rivers, and streams of Michigan. In their wake came armies of trappers eager to barter with the natives and platoons of soldiers to guard the newly acquired territory. Frenchmen and Native Americans teamed to unsuccessfully fight the British, who in turn were forced to retreat into Canada after the American colonies successfully revolted. The British briefly forged into Michigan again during the War of 1812, retreating finally to become Michigan's good neighbors in Canada.

Population: 9,295,297
Area: 56,954 square miles
Elevation: 570-1,980 feet
Peak: Mount Arvon (Baraga County)
Entered Union: January 26, 1837 (26th state)
Capital: Lansing
Motto: If you seek a pleasant peninsula, look around you
Nickname: Wolverine State
Flower: Apple Blossom
Bird: Robin
Tree: White Pine
Fair: Late August-early September in Detroit
Time Zone: Eastern and Central (Menominee, Dickinson, Iron, and Gogebic counties)
Website: www.michigan.org
Fun Facts:

1. Forty of the state's 83 counties adjoin at least one of the Great Lakes. Michigan is the only state that touches four of the five Great Lakes.
2. Michigan was the first state to guarantee every child the right to tax-paid high school education.

Calendar Highlights

JANUARY

Ice Sculpture Spectacular (*Plymouth*). *Phone 734/453-1540*. Hundreds of ice sculptures line the streets and fill Kellogg Park, as professional and student chefs compete with each other carving huge blocks of ice. Sculptures are lighted at night.

MAY

Tulip Time Festival (*Holland*). *Phone 616/396-4221 or 800/822-2770*. A celebration of Dutch heritage: 1,800 klompen dancers, 3 parades, street scrubbing, Dutch markets, entertainment, and millions of tulips.

JUNE

Bavarian Festival (*Frankenmuth*). *Heritage Park. Phone 800/BAVARIA*. Celebration of German heritage. Music, dancing, parades, and other entertainment; food; art demonstrations and agricultural displays.

Cereal City Festival (*Battle Creek*). *On Michigan Ave. Phone 616/962-2240*. Children's Parade, Queen's Pageant, arts and crafts exhibits; also the world's longest breakfast table.

International Freedom Festival (*Detroit and Windsor, ON*). *Phone 313/923-7400*. Joint celebration with Detroit and Windsor; nearly 100 events, including fireworks.

JULY

Sailing Races (*Mackinac Island*). *Phone 810/985-7101 for Port Huron race; 312/861-7777 for Chicago race*. Port Huron-to-Mackinac and Chicago-to-Mackinac.

Street Art Fairs (*Ann Arbor*). *Contact Convention and Visitors Bureau, 800/888-9487*. Nearly 1,000 artists and craftspeople display and sell works.

AUGUST

Michigan State Fair (*Detroit*). *Michigan Exposition and Fairgrounds. Phone 313/369-8428*.

SEPTEMBER

Historic Home Tour (*Marshall*). *Phone 616/781-5163 or 800/877-5163*. Informal tours of nine 19th-century homes, including Honolulu House, Governor's Mansion, and Capitol Hill School.

Mackinac Bridge Walk (*Mackinaw City and St. Ignace*). *Phone 231/436-5574 or 800/666-0160*. 70,000 participants take a recreational walk across Mackinac Bridge (some lanes open to motor vehicles).

DECEMBER

Dickens Christmas (*Holly*). Re-creates the Dickensian period with carolers, town crier, strolling characters, skits, bell choirs, street hawkers, carriage rides. Thanksgiving weekend-weekend before Dec 25.

There has been a wavelike pattern to Michigan's economic development. First there were the trees that created a great lumber industry. These were rapidly depleted. The copper and iron-ore mines followed. They also are now mostly inactive, although the discovery of new copper deposits is leading to renewed activity. Finally, the automobile industry, diversified industries, and tourism have become successful. Today, the St. Lawrence Seaway makes the cities of Michigan international ports and the state's future a prosperous one.

When to Go/Climate

Long, hard winters and hot, humid summers are common on Michigan's Upper Peninsula. The Lower Peninsula benefits from the moderating influence of the Great Lakes. Summers are warm; and brilliant fall foliage spreads southward from the Upper Peninsula beginning in September.

AVERAGE HIGH/LOW TEMPERATURES (°F)

Detroit

Jan 30/16	May 70/47	Sept 74/63
Feb 33/18	June 79/56	Oct 62/41
Mar 44/27	July 83/61	Nov 48/32
Apr 58/37	Aug 81/60	Dec 35/21

Grand Rapids

Jan 29/15	May 79/55	Sept 72/50
Feb 43/25	June 83/60	Oct 60/39
Mar 57/35	July 81/58	Nov 46/30
Apr 69/46	Aug 81/58	Dec 34/21

Parks and Recreation

Water-related activities; hiking, riding, various other sports, picnicking and visitor centers, as well as camping, are available in many of these areas. Motor vehicle permits are required to enter parks: $4/day (excluding Warren Dunes, $5/day for nonresidents); annual sticker: $20. From May through Sep, about 80 percent of the campsites in each park are available by reservations for stays of 1-15 nights. The fee is $9-$23/night. Pets on leash only. For reservations phone 800/44-PARKS. For reservations applications and further info about state parks, contact Dept of Natural Resources, Parks and Recreation Division, PO Box 30257, Lansing 48909-7757; 517/373-9900. For info on state forests, contact Dept of Natural Resources, Forest Management Division, PO Box 30452, Lansing 48909. Phone 517/373-1275.

FISHING AND HUNTING

In the 1960s coho and chinook salmon were transplanted from the Pacific Northwest into the streams feeding into Lake Michigan and subsequently into Lakes Huron and Superior. The success of the program was immediate and today salmon fishing, especially for chinook, is a major sport. Chinook fishing is good throughout the summer in the Great Lakes and through the early fall during the spawning season in the rivers; the fish may weigh as much as 45 pounds. Information on charter boat fishing can be obtained from Travel Michigan, Michigan Jobs Commission, PO Box 3393, Livonia 48151. Phone 888/78-GREAT.

Nonresident restricted fishing licenses: annual $26; all-species fishing incl spike, salmon, and brook, brown, rainbow, and lake trout: $41. A fishing license for all waters is required for everyone 17 years of age and older. Resident and nonresident 24-hr fishing license $7.

Nonresident hunting licenses: small game $65; deer $129; bear $150; archery (deer only) $129. For further information on hunting and fishing, write Dept of Natural Resources, Retail Sales Section, PO Box 30181, Lansing 48909. Phone 517/373-1204.

Driving Information

Safety belts are mandatory for all persons in front seat of vehicle. Children ages 4-16 must be in an approved passenger restraint anywhere in vehicle. Children ages 1-4 may use a regulation safety belt in back seat, but must use an approved safety seat in front seat of vehicle. Children under age 1 must use an approved safety seat anywhere in vehicle. Phone Office of Highway Safety Planning, 517/336-6477.

INTERSTATE HIGHWAY SYSTEM

The following alphabetical listing of Michigan towns in this book show that these cities are within 10 miles of the indicated interstate highways. Check a highway map for the nearest exit.

Highway Number	Cities/Towns within ten miles
Interstate 69	Coldwater, Flint, Lansing, Marshall, Owosso, Port Huron.
Interstate 75	Bay City, Birmingham, Bloomfield Hills, Cheboygan, Dearborn, Detroit, Flint, Frankenmuth, Gaylord, Grayling, Holly, Mackinaw City, Monroe, Pontiac, Saginaw, St. Ignace, Sault Ste. Marie, Warren.
Interstate 94	Ann Arbor, Battle Creek, Dearborn, Detroit, Jackson, Kalamazoo, Marshall, Mount Clemens, Port Huron, St. Clair, St. Joseph, Warren, Ypsilanti.
Interstate 96	Detroit, Grand Haven, Grand Rapids, Lansing, Muskegon.

Additional Visitor Information

Travel Michigan, Michigan Jobs Commission, PO Box 30226, Lansing 48909; phone 888/78-GREAT, distributes publications including an annual travel planner, seasonal travel guides and calendars of events, and directories of lodgings, campgrounds, golf courses, and charter boat and canoe companies. Travel counselors are available (daily) to assist in planning a Michigan getaway.

There are 13 Welcome Centers in Michigan, open daily; visitors who stop will find information, brochures and an extensive database of lodging facilities and attractions most helpful in planning stops at points of interest. Their locations are as follows: Clare, off US 27; Coldwater, off I-69; Dundee, off US 23; Iron Mountain, off US 2; Ironwood, off US 2; Mackinaw City, off I-75; Marquette, off US 41; Menominee, off US 41/MI 35; Monroe, off I-75; New Buffalo, off I-94; Port Huron, off I-94; St Ignace, off I-75; and Sault Ste. Marie, off I-75.

THE KEWEENAW PENINSULA

The drive up the Keweenaw Peninsula is Michigan's most popular road trip—and with good reason. This route offers everything you could ever want in a driving tour: awe-inspiring waterfalls, amazing coastal scenery, colorful history, sunny beaches, and picturesque towns. Surrounded on three sides by spectacular Lake Superior, the Keweenaw Peninsula also offers visitors the rare treat of watching the sun rise and set over the same body of water.

No visit to the Keweenaw, often referred to as "Copper Country," would be complete without exploring the history of its days as a copper mining boom town. Quincy Mine, located in the town of Hancock, offers guided copper mine tours, as well as a passenger cog rail tram. The nearby town of Houghton was runner-up in the Chicago Tribune's "Best Little Town in the Midwest" contest and is well worth a visit. Houghton also offers seasonal ferry service to Isle Royale National Park, the United States' most isolated national park and an amazing wilderness experience that outdoor enthusiasts won't want to miss. Advance reservations are required. Isle Royale can also be accessed by seaplane. 11 miles north of Hancock/Houghton is Calumet, an almost perfectly preserved mining town, replete with flagstone streets and entire districts of restored dwellings. Keweenaw National Historic Park, located here, features a self-guided walking tour commemorating the history of copper mining in the area. From Calumet, head north on Route 26 to Eagle River, pausing at Eagle River Falls for a look at the beautiful scenery and a photograph or two. Route 26 between Eagle Harbor and Copper Harbor is Brockway Mountain Drive, believed by some to be the most beautiful road in the state. This 9 mile drive is the highest above-sea-level road between the Rockies and Alleghenies—the views are superlative from this commanding height! Fall paints this route with an amazing palate of colors; spring brings the migration of hawks and eagles. Whatever the season, Brockway Mountain is an ideal place to watch the sunset over Lake Superior—the perfect end to a perfect day in the Keweenaw Peninsula.

If you have more than one day—and we hope you do because there is so much yet to see—spend tomorrow exploring attractions in and around Copper Harbor. Take the 20-minute boat ride out to Copper Harbor Lighthouse for a guided tour of one of the oldest lighthouses on Lake Superior. Visit Delaware Mine for a copper mine tour that will take you 110 feet down a mine shaft. Stop at Estivant Pines, located a few miles south of Copper Harbor, to see some of the oldest trees in Michigan. Take the ferry out to Isle Royale for a wilderness experience you won't soon forget. Scuba dive at the Keweenaw Preserve to explore the eighteen shipwrecks submerged there (note: it is illegal to remove anything from the wrecks). Whatever you choose to see and do, you are sure to enjoy your time in the Keweenaw Peninsula! **(Approximately 45 miles)**

Allen Park

See also Dearborn

Restaurant

★ ★ ★ **MORO'S.** *6535 Allen Rd (48101). Phone 313/382-7152.* Veal is king here, straight from the on-site butcher. Many dishes are prepared tableside. Service and atmosphere are Old World and professional. Italian menu. Specializes in veal, steak. Hours: 11 am-10 pm; Sat 4-10 pm; Sun 2-8 pm. Closed most major holidays; also Sun June-Aug. Lunch $5-$15 , dinner $10-$25. Casual, Italian décor. Cr cds: A, MC, V.

Ⓓ

Alma (G-4)

See also Mount Pleasant

Pop 9,034 **Elev** 736 ft **Area code** 989 **Zip** 48801

Information Gratiot Area Chamber of Commerce, 110 W Superior St, PO Box 516; 989/463-5525

Web www.gratoit.org

What to See and Do

Alma College. *614 W Superior St. 614 W Superior St. Phone 989/463-7111.* (1886) 1,400 students. On 87-acre campus. Campus tours. 190,000-volume library. Frank Knox Memorial Room in Reid-Knox building has mementos of former secretary of the Navy (by appt).

Special Event

Highland Festival & Games. *614 W Superior St # 1. Bahlke Field at Alma College. Phone 989/463-8979.* Piping, drumming, fiddling, Ceilidh, dancing; caber toss, sheaf toss, hammer throw competitions; art fair, parade. Memorial Day weekend.

Motels/Motor Lodges

★ **COMFORT INN.** *3110 W Monroe Rd (48801). Phone 989/463-4400; fax 989/463-2970. www.comfortinn.com.* 87 rooms, 2 story. S, D $53-$89; each additional $5; under 18 free. Crib free. TV; cable (premium), VCR available (movies). Indoor pool; whirlpool. Complimentary continental breakfast. Restaurant 4:30-10 pm; closed Sun, Mon. Room service. Bar. Check-out 11 am. Meeting rooms. Business services available. Valet service. Some bathroom phones. Cr cds: A, C, D, DS, JCB, MC, V.

Ⓓ ⌦ ⋈ ⚐

★ **PETTICOAT INN.** *2454 W Monroe Rd (48801). Phone 989/681-5728.* 11 rooms. S $36-$40; D $45-$52; each additional $3; higher rates special events. Pet accepted. TV; cable (premium). Restaurant adjacent open 24 hours. Check-out 11 am. Country setting. Cr cds: A, DS, MC, V.

⌦ ⋈ **SC**

Alpena (D-5)

Pop 11,354 **Elev** 593 ft **Area code** 989 **Zip** 49707

Information Convention and Visitors Bureau, 235 W Chisholm St, PO Box 65; 989/354-4181 or 800/4-ALPENA

Web www.oweb.com/upnorth/cvb/

Located at the head of Thunder Bay, Alpena is a center for industry as well as recreation. Approximately 80 shipwrecks have occurred in this area, making it an excellent diving location.

What to See and Do

Dinosaur Gardens Prehistorical Zoo. *11168 US23, 10 miles south in Ossineke. Phone 989/471-5477.* Authentic reproductions of prehistoric birds and animals. (Mid-May-mid-Oct, daily). **$**

Island Park and Alpena Wildfowl Sanctuary. *US 23 N and Long Rapids Rd.* Intown wildfowl sanctuary and self-guided nature trails, fishing platforms, and picnic area.

Jesse Besser Museum. *491 Johnson St, 2 blocks E off US 23. Phone 989/356-2202.* Historical exhibits feature agricultural, lumber, and early industrial era; reconstructed avenue of 1890 shops and businesses; restored cabins, Maltz Exchange Bank (1872), Green School (1895). Jesse Besser exhibit. Science exhibits include geology, natural history, and archaeological displays. Also planetarium, shows (Sun; fee). Museum (daily; closed holidays). **$**

Old Presque Isle Lighthouse and Museum. *5295 Grand Lake Rd. 23 miles N via US 23 on Presque Isle. Phone 989/595-2787.* Nautical instruments, marine artifacts, and other antiques housed in lighthouse and keeper's cottage (1840). Antiques from mid-1800s. (May-mid-Oct, daily) **$**

Special Events

Alpena County Fair. *603 S Eleventh St. Alpena County Fairgrounds. Phone 517/356-1174.* First week Aug.

Art on the Bay–Thunder Bay Art Show. *313 N 2nd Ave. Bay View Park. Phone 989/356-6678.* Third weekend July.

Brown Trout Festival. *235 W Chisholm St. Phone 989/354-4181.* Third full week July.

Motels/Motor Lodges

★ **BEST WESTERN OF ALPENA.** *1286 MI 32 W (49707). Phone 989/356-9087; fax 989/354-0543. www.bestwestern.com.* 36 rooms, 1-2 story. $59-$70; each additional $6; under 12 free. Complimentary continental breakfast. Check-out 11 am. TV; cable (premium). Bar. Game room. Indoor pool, whirlpool. Cr cds: A, C, D, DS, MC, V.

⊡ ☒ ☒ SC

★ **FLETCHER.** *1001 US 23 N (49707). Phone 989/354-4191; toll-free 800/334-5920; fax 989/354-4056.* 96 rooms, 2 story. June-Oct: S $58; D $64; each additional $6; suites $115; kitchen units $85; under 16 free; weekly rates; lower rates rest of year. Crib $6. Pet accepted. TV; cable. Indoor pool; whirlpool, sauna. Restaurant 7 am-9 pm. Room service. Bar 11-2 am; Sun from noon. Check-out 11 am. Meeting rooms. Bellhops. Free airport, bus depot transportation. Tennis. Nature trail. Refrigerators; some in-room whirlpools. Some balconies. Grills. Overlooks wooded acres. Cr cds: A, DS, MC, V.

⊡ ☒ ☒ ☒ ☒ ☒ ☒

★ ★ **HOLIDAY INN.** *1000 US 23 N (49707). Phone 989/356-2151; toll-free 800/465-4329; fax 989/356-2151. www.holiday-inn.com.* 148 rooms, 2 story. S $69-$99; D $79-$109; each additional $10; studio rooms $99; under 19 free. Crib free. Pet accepted. TV; cable. Indoor pool; whirlpool, poolside service. Restaurant 6:30 am-2 pm, 5-10 pm. Room service. Bar 4 pm-2 am; entertainment. Check-out noon. Coin laundry. Meeting rooms. Business services available. Bellhops. Valet service. Sundries. Gift shop. Free airport, bus depot transportation. Putting green. Cross-country ski 8 miles. Exercise equipment; sauna. Game room. Cr cds: A, D, DS, JCB, MC, V.

⊡ ☒ ☒ ☒ ☒ ☒ ☒ ☒ ☒ ☒ ☒

Ann Arbor (H-5)

See also Dearborn, Detroit, Jackson, Ypsilanti

Settled 1823 **Pop** 109,592 **Elev** 840 ft **Area code** 734

Information Convention & Visitors Bureau, 120 W Huron, 48104; 734/995-7281 or 800/888-9487

Web www.annarbor.org

Most famous as the home of the University of Michigan, Ann Arbor has a college-town atmosphere enjoyed by both students and residents. The community's economy is diversified, with more than 100 research and high-technology firms.

There are two interesting theories about the origin of the town's unusual name. One explanation is that two of the pioneer settlers had wives named Ann who liked to sit together under a wild grape arbor—hence, "Ann Arbor." The other theory, recognized by many historians, claims that the latter part of the name came from the many openings, or, in those days, "arbors," which appeared in the thick forests covering the nearby hills. The "arbors" were said to have resulted from agricultural methods of the Native Americans.

What to See and Do

Huron-Clinton Metroparks. *17845 Savage Rd. Phone 800/477-3191.* A regional park system with 13 recreation areas located along the Huron and Clinton rivers in southeast Michigan. A motor vehicle entry permit, which is good at all metroparks, is required (free on Tues). (Also see FARMINGTON, MOUNT CLEMENS, TROY)

> **Delhi.** *8801 N Territorial Rd. 5 1/2 miles NW on Delhi Rd, near Huron River Dr. Phone 734/426-8211.* On this 50-acre site are the Delhi Rapids. Fishing, canoeing, rentals (May-Sept); hiking trails, cross-country skiing, picnicking, playground.

> **Dexter-Huron.** *8801 N Territorial Rd. 7 1/2 miles NW along Huron River Dr. Phone 734/426-8211.* Fishing, canoeing; hiking trails, cross-country skiing, picnicking, playground.

> **Hudson Mills.** *8801 N Territorial Rd. 12 miles NW on N Territorial Rd. Phone 734/426-8211.* More than 1,600-acre recreation area; fishing, boating, canoe rentals; hiking, bicycle trail (rentals), 18-hole golf, cross-country skiing (winter), picnicking, playground, camping, activity center.

Kempf House Center for Local History. *312 S Division. Phone 734/994-4898.* (1853) Unusual example of Greek Revival architecture, restored structure owned and maintained by the city of Ann Arbor. Antique Victorian furnishings; displays of local historical artifacts. Tours (Sun afternoons; closed Jan and Aug). **$**

⊡ **University of Michigan.** *530 S State St. Phone 734/764-INFO.* (1817) 36,000 students. Established here in 1837, after having moved from Detroit where it was founded. One of the largest universities in the country, it makes significant contributions in teaching and research. Points of particular interest are

> **Exhibit Museum of Natural History.** *1109 Geddes Ave. Phone 734/764-0478.* Anthropology, Michigan wildlife, geology, and prehistoric life exhibits. (Daily; closed holidays Planetarium shows (Sat and Sun; fee). **DONATION**

> **Gerald R. Ford Presidential Library.** *1000 Beal Ave. Phone 734/741-2218.* Research library that houses Ford's presidential, vice-presidential, and congressional documents. (Mon-Fri; closed holidays) **FREE**

> **Kelsey Museum of Ancient and Medieval Archaeology.** *434 S State St. Phone 734/764-9304.* (Tues-Sun) **FREE**

Law Quadrangle. *S State St and S University Ave. Phone 734/764-9322.* Quadrangle includes four beautiful Gothic-style buildings. The law library, with an underground addition, has one of the nation's most extensive collections.

Matthaei Botanical Gardens. *1800 N Dixboro Rd, 3 miles NE of campus. Phone 734/998-7060 or 734/998-7061.* Approximately 250 acres including greenhouses (daily; closed holidays). Seasonal exhibits. Grounds (daily). **$$**

Museum of Art. *530 S State St. Phone 734/764-0395.* (Tues-Sun) **DONATION**

Nichols Arboretum. *Geddes Ave. Phone 734/998-9540.* Approximately 125 acres. (Daily) **FREE**

North Campus. *2 miles NE of central campus.* Contains research areas; School of Music designed by Eero Saarinen; School of Art and Architecture with public art gallery (Mon-Sat); School of Engineering.

Power Center for the Performing Arts. *121 S Fletcher. Phone 734/763-3333.* A 1,414-seat theater houses performances of drama, opera, music, and dance.

Special Events

Ann Arbor Summer Festival. *120 W Huron St. Phone 734/647-2278.* A performing arts festival of mime, dance, theater, and music; also lectures, films, and exhibits. June-early July.

Street Art Fair. *450 S Main St Phone 734/994-5260.* Nearly 1,000 artists and craftspeople display and sell works. Four days mid-July.

Motels/Motor Lodges

★★ **COURTYARD BY MARRIOTT.** *3205 Boardwalk (48108). Phone 734/995-5900; fax 734/995-2937. www.marriott.com.* 160 rooms, 4 story, 40 suites. S $89-$159; D $89-$169; each additional $10; suites $99-$179; under 18 free. Crib free. Check-out noon. TV; cable (premium). Many refrigerators. Valet service. Restaurant 6:30 am-1 pm. Bar 4:30 pm-midnight. Exercise equipment. Indoor pool, whirlpool. Cross-country ski 3 miles. Meeting rooms. Cr cds: A, C, D, DS, MC, V.

★ **FAIRFIELD INN.** *3285 Boardwalk Dr (48108). Phone 734/995-5200; toll-free 800/228-2800; fax 734/995-5394. www.fairfieldinn.com.* 110 rooms, 4 story. S, D $59-$129; each additional $6; under 18 free; higher rates: football weekends, some university events. Crib free. Complimentary continental breakfast. Check-out noon. TV; cable (premium). Refrigerators. Valet service. Restaurant adjacent 6:30 am-1 pm. Indoor pool, whirlpool. Cross-country ski 3 miles. Cr cds: A, C, D, DS, JCB, MC, V.

★ **HAMPTON INN.** *2300 Green Rd (48105). Phone 734/996-4444; toll-free 800/426-7866; fax 734/996-0196. www.hamptoninn.com.* 130 rooms, 4 story. S $59-$85; D $66-$95; under 18 free. Crib free. Pet accepted, some restrictions. Complimentary continental breakfast. Check-out noon. TV; cable (premium). Valet service. Restaurant nearby. Exercise equipment. Indoor pool, whirlpool. Cross-country ski 3 miles. Meeting rooms, business services. Cr cds: A, C, D, DS, MC, V.

★ **HAMPTON INN.** *925 Victors Way (48108). Phone 734/665-5000; fax 734/665-8452. www.hamptoninn.com.* 150 rooms, 4 story. June-Nov: S $65-$75; D $80-$95; under 18 free; higher rates special events (2-day min); lower rates rest of year. Crib free. TV; cable (premium). Indoor pool; whirlpool. Complimnetary continental breakfast. Complimentary coffee in lobby. Restaurant nearby. Check-out noon. Coin laundry. Meeting rooms. Business services available. Valet service Mon-Fri. Exercise equipment. Refrigerators. Cr cds: A, C, D, DS, MC, V.

★★ **HOLIDAY INN.** *3600 Plymouth Rd (48105). Phone 734/769-9800; toll-free 800/800-5560; fax 734/761-1290. www.holiday-inn.com.* 223 rooms, 2-5 story. S $77-$99; D $109-$139; under 18 free; weekend rates. Crib free. Pet accepted, some restrictions; $50 refundable. TV; cable. Indoor/outdoor pool, whirlpool. Restaurant 6:30 am-10 pm; Fri, Sat to 11 pm; Sun 7:30 am-9 pm. Room service. Bar. Check-out 11 am. Meeting rooms. Business services available. Valet service. Tennis. Cross-country ski 2 1/2 miles. Exercise equipt, sauna. Game room. Picnic tables. Cr cds: A, C, D, DS, JCB, MC, V.

★ **LAMP POST INN.** *2424 E Stadium Blvd (48104). Phone 734/971-8000; fax 734/971-7483. www.lamppostinn.com.* 54 rooms, 16 kitchen units, 27 with shower only, 2 story. S, D $44.95-$89.95; family, weekly rates; higher rates special events. Crib free. Pet accepted, some restrictions. TV; cable, VCR available. Pool. Complimentary continental breakfast. Check-out 11 am. Downhill ski 20 miles; cross-country ski 1 1/2 miles. Health club privileges. Microwaves, refrigerators. Cr cds: A, D, DS, MC, V.

★ **RED ROOF INN - NORTH.** *3621 Plymouth Rd (48105). Phone 734/996-5800; fax 734/996-5707. www.redroof.com.* 108 rooms, 2 story. S $39.99-$61.99; D $48.99-$71.99; 3 or more persons $51.99-$64.99; under 18 free; higher rates special events. Crib free. Pet accepted. TV; cable (premium). Restaurant adjacent 6 am-midnight. Check-out noon. Cr cds: A, C, D, DS, MC, V.

🅳 🌊 🕸

★★★ **WEBER'S INN.** *3050 Jackson Ave (48103). Phone 734/769-2500; toll-free 800/443-3050; fax 734/769-4743. www.webersinn.com.* This is a full service, deluxe hotel, restaurant and conference facility. It offers 48 poolside guestrooms and suites, located near the University of Michigan and only 30 minutes outside of downtown Detroit. 160 rooms, 4 story. S, D $95-$135; each additional $10; suites $199-$275; under 18 free. Crib free. TV; cable (premium), VCR available (movies). Indoor pool; whirlpool, poolside service. Complimentary continental breakfast. Restaurant 6:30 am-10:30 pm; Mon to 9:30 pm; Fri to midnight; Sat 8 am-midnight; Sun 8 am-9:30 pm. Room service. Bar 11-1:30 am; entertainment. Check-out noon. Meeting rooms. Business center. In-room modem link. Valet service. Sundries. Tennis privileges. Cross-country ski 5 miles. Exercise equipment; sauna. Some refrigerators. Some rooms with spiral staircase to pool. Cr cds: A, C, D, DS, JCB, MC, V.

🅳 🏊 🎿 🌊 🕸 🚶

Hotels

★★ **BELL TOWER HOTEL.** *300 S Thayer St (48104). Phone 734/769-3010; toll-free 800/562-3559; fax 734/769-4339. www.belltowerhotel.com.* 66 rooms, 3-4 story, 10 suites. S $125; D $140; each additional $15; suites $154-$238; under 3 free. Crib free. TV; cable, VCR available. Complimentary continental breakfast. Restaurant 6-10 pm; closed Sun. Check-out noon. Meeting rooms. Business services available. In-room modem link. Free valet parking. Cross-country ski 2 miles. Health club privileges. Refrigerator, minibar in suites. European-style décor, ambience. Cr cds: A, C, D, ER, MC, V.

🅳 🏊 🌊 🆂🅲

★★★ **CROWNE PLAZA HOTEL.** *610 Hilton Blvd (48108). Phone 734/761-7800; toll-free 800/465-4329; fax 734/995-1085. www.crowneplazaaa.com.* This hotel is conveniently located two miles from the University of Michigan and situated next to a regional shopping center. Guests will enjoy the spacious and handsomely appointed guestrooms, as well as the exceptional service. 200 rooms, 3 story. S, D $125-$164; suites $200-$300; family, weekend rates. Crib free. TV; cable (premium). Indoor pool; whirlpool. Complimentary coffee. Restaurant 6 am-11 pm; Sun from 7 am. Room service. Bar 5 pm-midnight. Check-out

11 am. Meeting rooms. Concierge. Bellhops. Valet service. Sundries. Gift shop. Cross-country ski 10 miles. Exercise equipment; sauna. Cr cds: A, D, DS, JCB, MC, V.

🅳 🏊 🕴 🌊 🕸 🚶

★★★ **THE DAHLMANN CAMPUS INN - ANN ARBOR.** *615 E Huron St (48104). Phone 734/769-2200; toll-free 800/666-8693; fax 734/769-6222. www.campusinn.com.* This inn is located near the University of Michigan's campus and offers a restaurant, pool, sauna and small exercise room for its guests. The property is also near many local shops, galleries and restaurants. 208 rooms, 15 story. S $138-$150; D $153-$200, each additional $15; suites $175-$350. Cross-country ski 3 miles. Cr cds: A, C, D, DS, MC, V.

🅳 🏊 🌊 🕸 🚶

★★ **SHERATON INN ANN ARBOR.** *3200 Boardwalk (48108). Phone 734/996-0600; toll-free 800/848-2770; fax 734/996-8136. www.sheraton.com.* 197 rooms, 6 story. S, D, studio rooms $79-$135; each additional $10; suites $109-$175; under 18 free; weekend rates. Crib free. TV; cable (premium). Indoor/outdoor pool; whirlpool, poolside service. Restaurant 6:30 am-10:30 pm; Fri, Sat to 11:30 pm. Room service. Bar noon-1 am. Check-out noon. Meeting rooms. Business center. In-room modem link. Bellhops. Sundries. Cross-country ski 10 miles. Exercise equipment; sauna. Health club privileges. Some refrigerators, microwaves. Cr cds: A, C, D, DS, JCB, MC, V.

🅳 🏊 🌊 🕸 🆂🅲 🚶

Extended Stay

★★ **RESIDENCE INN BY MARRIOTT.** *800 Victors Way (48108). Phone 734/996-5666; fax 734/996-1919. www.residenceinn.com.* 114 kitchen suites, 2-3 story. S $109-$139; D $169. Crib free. Pet accepted; fee. Complimentary continental breakfast. Check-out noon. TV; cable (premium). Balconies. Valet services, coin laundry. Restaurant opposite 6 am-11 pm. Heated pool, whirlpool. Picnic tables. Meeting room. Cr cds: A, C, D, DS, ER, JCB, MC, V.

🅳 🌊 🌊 🕸 🚶

Restaurants

★ **BELLA CIAO.** *118 W Liberty St (48104). Phone 734/995-2107. www.bellaciao.com.* Hours: 5:30-10 pm. Closed Sun; major holidays. Reservations accepted. Italian menu. Service bar. A la carte entrees: dinner $16-$24. Specializes in veal, pasta, seafood. Outdoor dining. Cr cds: A, D, DS, MC, V.

★★ **DANIELS ON LIBERTY AND THE MOVEABLE FEAST.** *326 W Liberty (48103). Phone 734/663-3278; fax 734/663-9154. www.danielsonliberty.com.* Specializes in duck, seafood, veal. Hours: 5:30-9-pm. Closed Sun; major holidays. A la carte entrees: dinner $19-$29.

Complete meals: dinner $30-$50. Service bar. Historic Victorian house (1870). Reservations accepted. Outdoor dining. Cr cds: A, C, D, DS, MC, V.

D

★ ★ **EARLE.** *121 W Washington (48104). Phone 734/994-0211; fax 734/994-3466. www.theearle.com.* French menu, Italian menu. Hours: 5:30-10 pm; Fri to midnight; Sat 6 pm-11:30 pm; Sun 5-9 pm. Closed holidays; Sun June-Aug. Dinner $10-$30. Bar. In historic brick building (1885). Reservations accepted. Outdoor dining. Own sorbet. Cr cds: A, D, DS, MC, V.

D

★ ★ ★ **ESCOFFIER.** *300 S Thayer St (48104). Phone 734/995-3800; fax 734/769-4339.* This Continental restaurant resides in the historic Bell Tower Hotel near the University of Michigan's central campus. Enjoy the upscale menu, extensive wine list, and classy bar in a refined environment of warm gold walls, white tablecloths, and polished wood. Hours: 5:30-9:30 pm. Closed Sun; major holidays. Reservations accepted. French menu. Bar. Wine list. A la carte entrees: dinner $20-$35. Complete meals: dinner $30. Own pastries. Pianist. Valet parking. Cr cds: A, D, MC, V.

D

★ ★ **GANDY DANCER.** *401 Depot St (48104). Phone 734/769-0592; fax 734/769-0415. www.muer.com.* Hours: 11:30 am-4 pm, 5-10 pm; Sat from 5 pm; Sun 3:30-9 pm; early-bird dinner Mon-Sat 4:30-5:30 pm; Sun brunch 10 am-2 pm. Closed Jan 1, Dec 25. Reservations accepted. Bar. Lunch $5.50-$14, dinner $16-$35. Sun brunch $18.95. Child's meals. Specializes in fresh seafood, rack of lamb, pasta. Own pasta. Valet parking. Historic converted railroad station. Cr cds: A, D, DS, MC, V.

D

★ **PAESANO'S.** *3411 Washtenaw Ave (48104). Phone 734/971-0484; fax 734/971-0419.* Italian menu. Specializes in pasta, fresh seafood. Hours: 11 am-11 pm; Fri to midnight; Sat noon-midnight; Sun noon-10 pm. Closed Jan 1, Thanksgiving, Dec 25. Lunch $5.50-$9, dinner $10.95-$21.95. Bar. Child's meals. Reservations accepted. Outdoor dining. Strolling mandolinists Fri. Cr cds: A, D, DS, MC, V.

D

★ **ZINGERMAN'S DELICATESSEN.** *422 Detroit St (48104). Phone 734/663-3354; fax 734/769-1235. www.zingermans.com.* Hours: 7 am-10 pm. Closed major holidays. Dinner $7.50-$12.99. Children's menu. Cr cds: A, MC, V.

D

Battle Creek (H-3)

See also Kalamazoo, Marshall

Settled 1831 **Pop** 53,540 **Elev** 830 ft **Area code** 616

Information Greater Battle Creek/Calhoun County Visitor and Convention Bureau, 77 E Michigan, Suite 100, 49017; 616/962-2240 or 800/397-2240

Web www.battlecreek.org

Battle Creek's fame was built by two cereal tycoons, W.K. Kellogg and C.W. Post. The Kellogg and Post cereal plants are the largest of their type anywhere. The city has a variety of other food-packing industries plus many heavy industries. Post and Kellogg have influenced more than the economy; signs, streets, parks, and many public institutions also bear their names. The city takes its name from a "battle" that took place on the banks of the creek in 1825 between a native and a land surveyor.

What to See and Do

Binder Park Zoo. *7400 Division Dr. Phone 616/979-1351.* Exotic, endangered, and domestic animals in natural exhibits. Fifty-acre Wild Africa exhibit including giraffes, zebras, antelope, African wild dogs; trading village, ranger station, research camp, and working diamond mine alongside a panoramic African savanna. Ride the Wilderness Tram and the Z.O. & O. Railroad (fee). Miller Children's Zoo. (Mid-Apr-Mid-Oct, daily) Special events during Halloween and Christmas. **$$$**

Fort Custer State Recreation Area. *5163 W Fort Custer Dr. 8 miles W via MI 96, in Augusta. Phone 616/731-4200.* Swimming beach, fishing, boating (launch); nature, bridle, and bicycle trails, picnic areas, hunting. Improved campgrounds (res required). Cross-country skiing, snowmobiling. (Daily) Standard fees. **$$**

Kimball House Museum. *196 Capital Ave NE. Phone 616/966-2496.* (1886). Restored and refurnished Victorian home; displays trace development of use of appliances, tools, medical instruments; herb garden; country store. (Fri afternoons; closed Jan-Mar) **$**

Leila Arboretum. *W Michigan Ave at 20th St. Phone 616/969-0270.* A 72-acre park containing native trees and shrubs. On ground is

Kingman Museum of Natural History. *175 Limit St (49017). Phone 616/965-5117.* Exhibits include Journey Through the Crust of the Earth, Walk in the Footsteps of the Dinosaurs, Mammals of the Ice Age, Window to the Universe, Planetarium, Wonder of Life, Discovery Room, and others. (Wed-Sun afternoons; closed holidays) **$**

Sojourner Truth Grave. *Oak Hill Cemetery, South Ave and Oak Hill Dr.* On the cemetery's Fifth St is the plain square monument marking the resting place of this remarkable fighter for freedom. Born a slave in the 1790s, Truth gained her freedom in the 1820s and crusaded against slavery until her death in 1883. Although uneducated, she had a brilliant mind as well as unquenchable devotion to her cause.

W. K. Kellogg Bird Sanctuary of Michigan State University. *13 miles NW off MI 89, 12685 E C Ave. Phone 616/671-2510.* Experimental farm and forest nearby. Seven kinds of swans and more than 20 species of ducks and geese inhabit the ponds and Wintergreen Lake. One of the finest bird of prey collections in the Midwest, along with free-roaming upland game birds. Colorful viewing all seasons of the year. Observation deck and educational displays. Grounds and reception center (daily).

Willard Beach. *2 miles S, on shores of Goguac Lake.* Lavishly landscaped; has a wide bathing beach. Supervised swimming; picnicking, pavilion. (Memorial Day-Labor Day, daily) **$**

Special Event

Cereal City Festival. *171 W Michigan Ave. Phone 616/962-2240.* Children's Parade, Queen's Pageant, arts and crafts exhibits; also the world's longest breakfast table. Second Sat June.

Motels/Motor Lodges

★ ★ **BATTLE CREEK INN.** *5050 Beckley Rd (49015). Phone 616/979-1100; toll-free 800/232-3405; fax 616/979-1899. www.battlecreekinn.com.* 211 rooms, 2 story. S $60-$70; D $73-$77; each additional $8; family rates; golf plans. Crib free. Pet accepted. TV; cable (premium). Indoor heated pool; poolside service. Coffee in rooms. Complimentary continental breakfast. Restaurant 6:30 am-2 pm, 5-10 pm. Room service. Bar 4 pm-midnight. Check-out noon. Coin laundry. Meeting rooms. Business services available. Valet service. Putting green. Exercise equipment. Health club privileges. Game room. Refrigerators available. Cr cds: A, D, DS, MC, V.

🄳 🐾 ⛱ 🏌 🛬 SC

★ **DAYS INN.** *4786 Beckley Rd (49017). Phone 616/979-3561; fax 616/979-1400. www.daysinn.com.* 88 rooms, 9 kitchen units. S $40.75-$44.75; D $42.75-$62.75; each additional $4; kitchen units $51.25-$63.75; under 18 free; weekly rates; golf plans; higher rates Balloon Festival. Crib free. Pet accepted. TV; cable (premium). Coffee in rooms. Complimentary continental breakfast. Restaurant opposite open 24 hours. Check-out noon, check-in 4 pm. Meeting room. Business services available. Tennis privileges. Cross-country ski 4 miles. Health club privileges. Some in-room whirlpools. Cr cds: A, C, D, DS, MC, V.

🄳 🐾 ⚓ 🏌 🛬 🏊 SC

★ **SUPER 8 MOTEL.** *5395 Beckley Rd (49015). Phone 616/979-1828; toll-free 800/800-8000; fax 616/979-1828. www.super8.com.* 62 rooms, 3 story. No elevator. S,D $37-$72; each additional $5; suites $51-$100; under 12 free; higher rates special events. Crib free. Complimentary coffee. Check-out 11 am, check-in 2 pm. TV; cable (premium). Restaurant adjacent 6 am-midnight. Cross-country ski 4 miles. Business services available. Cr cds: A, C, D, DS, MC, V.

🄳 ⛱ 🛬 SC

Hotel

★ ★ ★ **MCCAMLY PLAZA.** *50 SW Capital Ave (49017). Phone 616/963-7050; toll-free 888/622-2659; fax 616/963-3880. www.mccamlyplazahotel.com.* This hotel offers 242 well-appointed guestrooms and suites along with a large indoor pool and whirlpool, a new exercise room and more. Golf packages are available for visitors and the location of the property places it near many attractions. 242 rooms, 16 story. S $149; D $159; each additional $20; suites $200-$300; under 17 free; weekly, weekend rates. Crib free. Check-out 1 pm. TV; cable, VCR available (movies). Refrigerators, minibars. Coffee in rooms. Restaurant 6:30 am-1:30 pm, 5:30-10 pm. Bar 4 pm-1 am; entertainment Mon-Sat. Cross-country ski 3 miles. Meeting rooms, business services. Cr cds: A, C, D, DS, JCB, MC, V.

🄳 ⛱ 🍴 🏌 ⚓ 🏋 🛬 SC 🚶

B&B/Small Inns

★ ★ **GREENCREST MANOR.** *6174 Halbert Rd (49017). Phone 269/962-8633; fax 269/962-7254. www.greencrestmanor.com.* 8 rooms, 3 story. Complimentary continental breakfast. Check-out 11 am, check-in 4:30 pm. TV; cable (premium). Marble fireplaces. Totally nonsmoking. Cr cds: A, D, MC, V.

🅱 🛬

Bay City (F-4)

See also Midland, Saginaw

Settled 1831 **Pop** 38,936 **Elev** 595 ft **Area code** 989

Information Bay Area Convention & Visitors Bureau, 901 Saginaw St, 48708; 989/893-1222 or 888/BAY-TOWN

Web www.tourbaycitymi.org

Bay City is a historic port community located on Saginaw Bay, which services Great Lakes freighters as well as seagoing vessels in the handling of millions of tons of products annually. The city, which is the county seat, is noted for tree-shaded streets and residential areas with new homes and Victorian and Georgian mansions built by the 19th-century lumber barons. Industries include shipbuilding, automobile parts, petrochemicals, and electronics. Sugar beet production and potato and melon crops are important to its economy.

Retail, service, specialty dining, and entertainment businesses can be found in the Historic Midland Street area on the west side of Bay City.

What to See and Do

Bay City State Recreation Area. *3582 State Park Dr. 5 miles N on MI 247, along Saginaw Bay. Phone 989/684-3020.* Approximately 200 acres. Swimming, bathhouse, fishing, boating; hiking, picnicking, concession, camping. Standard fees.

Jennison Nature Center. *3582 State Park Dr (48706). Phone 989/667-0717.* Displays on the history, geology, wildlife, and general ecology of the area. Hiking trails. (Tues-Sun; closed holidays) **FREE**

Tobico Marsh. *3582 State Park Dr (48706). Phone 989/684-3020.* 1,700 acres of wetland, the largest remaining wildlife refuge on Saginaw Bay's western shore. Two 32-foot towers allow panoramic viewing of deer, beaver, mink, and hundreds of species of waterfowl and song, shore, and marsh birds. Visitor Center (Tues-Sun). Killarney Beach Rd. **FREE**

Bay County Historical Museum. *321 Washington Ave. Phone 989/893-5733.* Preserving and displaying the heritage of Bay County. Exhibits interpret life of Native Americans; depict fur trading, lumbering, shipbuilding, industrial development; life of pioneering women; changing exhibits. (Mon-Sat; closed holidays) **DONATION**

City Hall and Bell Tower. *301 Washington Ave. Phone 989/893-1222.* (Circa 1895) Meticulously restored Romanesque structure; council chamber has 31-foot-long woven tapestry depicting history of Bay City. View of city and its waterway from bell tower. (Mon-Fri; closed holidays) **FREE**

Deer Acres. *2346 MI 13 in Pinconning. Phone 989/879-2849.* Storybook theme park with petting zoo. Train rides (fee), antique cars, more. (Mid-May-Labor Day, daily; after Labor Day-mid-Oct, Sat and Sun) **$$$**

Scottish Rite Cathedral. *614 Center Ave. Phone 989/893-3700.* The only Scottish Rite Cathedral in the state; contains Lord Cornwallis's surrender chair. (Mon-Fri) **FREE**

Special Events

Munger Potato Festival. *1920 S Finn Rd (48747). SE on MI 15, then E on MI 138 in Munger. Phone 989/659-3270.* Four days late July.

St. Stanislaus Polish Festival. *Lincoln Ave, S end of Bay City. Phone 989/893-1749.* Late June.

Motels/Motor Lodges

★★ **BEST VALUE INN & SUITES.** *6285 Westside Saginaw Rd (48706). Phone 989/686-0840; toll-free 888/315-BEST; fax 989/686-0840. www.bestvalueinn.com.* 70 rooms, 2 story. S $55-$60; D $55-$65; each additional $5; under 12 free. Crib free. TV; cable (premium). Heated pool; whirlpool, sauna. Restaurant adjacent 6 am-9 pm. Check-out 11 am. Meeting rooms. Business services available. Game room. Some refrigerators. Private patios, balconies. Cr cds: A, C, D, DS, MC, V.

★ **EUCLID.** *809 N Euclid Ave (48706). Phone 989/684-9455; fax 989/686-6440.* 36 rooms. S $36; D $46; each additional $4. Crib $5. Check-out 11 am. TV; cable (premium). Some refrigerators. Restaurant nearby. Playground. Heated pool. Picnic tables. Cr cds: A, C, D, DS, MC, V.

★★ **HOLIDAY INN.** *501 Saginaw St (48708). Phone 989/892-3501; fax 989/892-9342. www.holiday-inn.com.* 100 rooms, 4 story. S, D $84; each additional $7; under 18 free. Crib free. Pet accepted. TV; cable. Indoor pool; whirlpool, sauna. Restaurant 6:30 am-10 pm; Sat, Sun from 7 am. Room service. Bar from noon. Check-out noon. Coin laundry. Meeting rooms. Business services available. Valet service. Sundries. Cr cds: A, C, D, DS, JCB, MC, V.

Resort

★★ **BAY VALLEY HOTEL & RESORT.** *2470 Old Bridge Rd (48706). Phone 989/686-3500; toll-free 800/241-4653; fax 989/686-6950. www.bayvalley.com.* Located on 470 acres of beautiful landscape, this resort offers its guests tons of recreational activities including biking, tennis, water sports, and great golf. The hotel is full service and has 150 rooms and suites along with a fine dining restaurant. Mid-Apr-Oct: S, D $55-$95; each additional $10; suites $150; under 12 free; package plans; lower rates rest of year. Crib free. Pet accepted. Check-out noon. TV; cable (premium), VCR available. In-room modem link. Private patios, balconies. Valet service. Restaurant 7 am-10 pm; Fri, Sat to 11 pm. Bar 11-1:30 am; Sun from noon; entertainment. Room service. Playground. Exercise room, sauna. Game room. Heated indoor/outdoor pool, whirlpool, poolside service. 18-hole golf, greens fee $39-$54, pro, putting green, driving range, golf carts. Cross-country ski on site, instruction. Picnic tables. Lawn games. Free airport transportation. Meeting rooms, business services. Concierge. Sundries. Gift shop. Cr cds: A, C, D, DS, MC, V.

Restaurants

★ ★ **LINDEN HOF.** *201 N Euclid Ave (48706). Phone 517/686-2209. www.lindenhoff.com.* American menu. Salad bar. Hours: 11 am-11 pm; Sun 11:30 am-10 pm. Closed Dec 25. Dinner $7.95-$15.95. Bar to 1 am. Child's menu. Casual attire. Cr cds: DS, MC, V.

[D] [SC]

★ ★ **O SOLE MIO.** *1005 Saginaw St (48708). Phone 989/893-3496; fax 989/893-8393.* Italian menu. Hours: 5-10 pm; Fri, Sat to 10:30 pm. Closed Sun, Mon; most major holidays. Dinner $14-$37.50. Bar. Children's meals. Casual attire. Cr cds: A, D, MC, V.

[D]

Bellaire (D-3)

Pop 1,104 **Elev** 616 ft **Area code** 231 **Zip** 49615

Information Bellaire Chamber of Commerce, PO Box 205; 231/533-6023

Web www.bellairemichigan.com/chamber

What to See and Do

Shanty Creek Resort. *1 Shanty Creek Rd. 2 miles SE off MI 88. Phone 231/533-8621 or 800/678-4111.* Two separate mountains: five quad, two double chairlifts, four surface lifts; patrol, school, rentals; snowmaking; nursery; night skiing; lodge (see RESORT), restaurant, snack bar, entertainment; indoor/outdoor pool, two whirlpools; health club. Thirty trails on two mountains; longest run approximately one mile; vertical drop 450 feet. Cross-country trails (25 miles). (Thanksgiving-Mar, daily) $$$$

Resort

★ ★ ★ **SHANTY CREEK RESORT.** *1 Shanty Creek Rd (49615). Phone 231/533-8621; toll-free 800/678-4111; fax 231/533-7001. www.shantycreek.com.* This resort offers three distinct lodges. The Schuss Village offers European style, the Summit Village gives visitors a great view of the snow covered lakes and forests, while the Cedar River Village overlooks the Tom Weiskopf golf course. 600 rooms, 1-3 story, 259 kitchen units (some equipment). June-Aug, winter weekends (2-day minimum), Christmas week (4-day minimum): S, D $86-$148; each additional $10; kitchen units, chalets $145-$325; under 18 free; package plans; lower rates rest of year. Crib $10. Check-out noon, check-in 6 pm. TV; cable (premium), VCR available. Private patios, balconies. Refrigerators in suites. Some fireplaces. Dining room 7 am-9 pm. Bar 11-2 am; Sun from noon. Entertainment, movies. Room service. Supervised children's activities (seasonal). Playground. Massage. Exercise room, sauna, steam room. Sports director. Game room. Recreation room. 5 pools, 2 indoor; whirlpool, poolside service. Four 18-hole golf courses, pro, putting green, pro shop, driving range, carts available. Tennis $20/hr, pro. Downhill/cross-country ski on site. Picnic tables. Lawn games. Mountain bike trails (rentals). Exercise course, hiking trails. Ice skating. Sleighing. Airport transportation. Meeting rooms, business center. Concierge. Gift shop. Extensive grounds. Coffee in lobby. Private sand beach nearby. Cr cds: A, C, D, DS, MC, V.

[D] [symbols] [SC]

Beulah (E-2)

See also Frankfort, Traverse City

Pop 421 **Elev** 595 ft **Area code** 231 **Zip** 49617

Information Benzie County Chamber of Commerce, PO Box 204, Benzonia 49616; 231/882-5801 or 800/882-5801

Web www.benzie.org

This resort town is at the east end of Crystal Lake, which offers excellent fishing for salmon, trout, perch, bass, and smelt. Skiing, ice fishing, golf, and boating are also popular in the area.

What to See and Do

Benzie Area Historical Museum. *6941 Traverse Ave. 3 miles S on US 31 in Benzonia. Phone 231/882-5539.* Exhibits and artifacts depict area's lumbering, shipping, farming, transportation, homelife; display on Civil War author Bruce Catton. (June-Sept, Tues-Sat; Apr-May and Oct-Nov, Fri and Sat only; special tours by appt) $

Crystal Mountain Resort. *12500 Crystal Mountain Dr. Phone 231/378-2000.* High-speed lift, five chairlifts, two rope tows; night skiing; patrol, school, rentals; snowmaking; nursery; lodge, condominiums, restaurant, cafeteria, bar. 34 trails; longest run 1/2 mile; vertical drop 375 feet. (Thanksgiving-early Apr, daily) Groomed, track-set cross-country trails (14 miles), lighted night trail; rentals, instruction (Dec-Mar, daily). Snowboard half-pipe. Also 2 golf courses; indoor pool, fitness center; hiking, mountain bike trails; tennis courts. $$$$

Gwen Frostic Prints. *5140 River Rd, 3 miles S on US 31, 2 miles W in Benzonia.* Original block prints designed by artist and poet Gwen Frostic are featured at this wildlife sanctuary and printing shop. Display room lets visitors observe the printing presses in operation. (Early May-Oct, daily; rest of year Mon-Sat; closed holidays).

Platte River State Anadromous Fish Hatchery. *15120 US 31, 10 miles E via US 31. Phone 231/325-4611.* Michigan's largest hatchery annually produces about nine million anadromous salmon (salmon that live in oceans or lakes and return to the rivers to spawn). This is the birthplace of the coho salmon in the Great Lakes; also produces chinook salmon. Self-guided tours (daily). **FREE**

Restaurants

★ ★ **BROOKSIDE INN.** *115 US 31 (49617). Phone 231/882-9688; fax 231/882-4600. www.brooksideinn.com.* American, German, Italian menu. Hours: 8 am-9:30 pm; Fri, Sat to 11 pm; summer to midnight. Dinner $6.75-$25.95. Tableside stone cooking. Bar. Service bar. Child's menu. Casual attire. Outdoor dining. Guest rooms available. Cr cds: A, D, DS, MC, V.

[D]

★ **CHERRY HUT.** *211 N Michigan Ave (US 31) (49617). Phone 231/882-4431; fax 231/882-9203. www.cherryhut products.com.* American menu. Hours: 11 am-9 pm; mid-June-Labor Day 10 am-10 pm. Closed late Oct-Memorial Day. Dinner $11.95-$13.50. Child's menu. Casual attire. Outdoor dining. Cr cds: DS, MC, V.

[D]

★ **SAIL INN.** *US 31 (49616). Phone 231/882-4971; fax 231/882-7111.* American, Eclectic menu. Salad bar. Hours: 9 am-10 pm; Fri, Sat to 11 pm; Sun brunch 11 am-2 pm. Closed Thanksgiving, Dec 25. Dinner $11.95-$19.95. Bar. Child's menu. Totally nonsmoking. Cr cds: A, DS, MC, V.

[D] [icon]

Big Rapids (F-3)

Settled 1854 **Pop** 12,603 **Elev** 920 ft **Area code** 231 **Zip** 49307

Information Mecosta County Convention & Visitors Bureau, 246 N State St; 231/796-7640 or 800/833-6697

Web www.bigrapids.org

What to See and Do

Mecosta County Parks. *Phone 616/832-3246.* Parks open May-Oct. No pets permitted in Brower and School Section Lake parks. **$$$$**

Brower. *6 miles S on US 131 to Stanwood, then 1 mile W to Old State Rd, then 3 miles S on Polk Rd. Phone 231/823-2561.* Swimming, fishing, boating (launch); playgrounds, tennis courts, softball diamond, camping.

Merrill Lake. *3275 Evergreen Rd (49678). E on MI 20 to MI 66, then N, 3 miles N of Barryton. Phone 517/382-7158.* Swimming (two beaches), fishing, boating (launch, ramps); picnicking (shelters), playgrounds, camping.

Paris. *6 miles N on MI 131, in Paris. Phone 231/796-3420.* Fishing, canoeing (ramp); wildlife area, picnicking (shelter), camping.

School Section Lake. *9003 90th Ave (49332). Approximately 23 miles E via MI 20. Phone 231/972-7450.* Swimming beach, boating (launch); picnicking (shelters), concessions, playgrounds, camping. **$$$$**

Special Event

Labor Day Arts Fair. *Warren Ave and Hemlock Dr (49307). Phone 231/796-7649.* Hemlock Park on Muskegon River. More than 150 exhibitors of various arts and crafts; concessions. Labor Day.

Motel/Motor Lodge

★ ★ **HOLIDAY INN.** *1005 Perry Ave (49307). Phone 616/796-4400; toll-free 800/465-4329; fax 616/796-0220. www.holiday-inn.com.* 118 rooms, 4 story. S $68-$77; D $78-$87; each additional $10; suites $150; under 18 free; golf plans. Crib free. TV; cable (premium). Indoor pool; whirlpool, sauna. Restaurant 6:30 am-10 pm; Fri, Sat 7 am-11 pm; Sun 7 am-8 pm. Room service. Bar 11 am-11 pm; Fri, Sat to midnight; Sun noon-9 pm. Check-out noon. Meeting rooms. Business services available. In-room modem link. Valet service. Gift shop. Tennis privileges, pro. 18-hole golf, greens fee, pro, putting green, driving range. Cr cds: A, C, D, DS, ER, JCB, MC, V.

[D] [icons]

Birmingham (H-5)

See also Bloomfield Hills, Detroit, Southfield

Pop 19,997 **Elev** 781 ft **Area code** 248

Information Birmingham-Bloomfield Chamber of Commerce, 124 W Maple, 48009; 248/644-1700

Web www.bbcc.com

Motel/Motor Lodge

★ **HOLIDAY INN EXPRESS.** *34952 Woodward Ave (48009). Phone 248/646-7300; fax 248/646-4501. www.hiexpressbirmingham.com.* 126 rooms, 2-5 story. S, D $109-$169; suites $125-$250; under 18 free; weekend rates. Crib free. TV; cable (premium). Complimentary continental breakfast. Coffee in rooms. Restaurant nearby. Business services available. In-room modem link. Check-out noon. Valet service. Health club privileges. Refrigerators. Cr cds: A, C, D, DS, ER, JCB, MC, V.

[D] [icons]

Hotel

★ ★ ★ ★ **THE TOWNSEND HOTEL.** *100 Townsend St (48009). Phone 248/642-7900; toll-free 800/548-4172; fax 248/645-9061. www.townsendhotel.com.* The Townsend Hotel brings the refinement of Europe to the heart of Michigan. Tucked away in the quiet community of Birmingham, where tree-lined streets brim with unique stores and bustling cafés, the hotel is conveniently located less than an hour from Detroit. The guest rooms are handsomely furnished with regal décor. Jewel tones add panache, four-poster beds add charm, and full kitchens in the suites and penthouses ensure that guests never need to leave the comforts of home behind. The cherry-wood paneling and the warm glow of the fireplace make for a particularly inviting space at the Rugby Grille, and its airy gallery filled with the fragrance of fresh flowers is a sunny alternative. The sleek city chic of the Townsend Corner Bar has made it one of the hotspots on the local scene. Its appealing interiors are a perfect match for its Asian-inspired appetizers and creative cocktails. 150 rooms, 4 story, 51 suites. suites, 150 rooms, 4 story, 51 suites. story. S, D $275-$290; each additional $20; suites $229-$700; under 12 free. Check-out noon. TV; cable (premium), VCR (movies). In-room modem link. Restaurant. Bar to 2 am. Room service 24 hours. Health club privileges. Exercise bicycle brought to room on request. Tennis privileges. Downhill ski 20 miles; cross-country ski 5 miles. Covered parking. Valet parking $17. Business center. Concierge. Afternoon tea Tues-Sat by reservation; pianist. Located opposite park. Cr cds: A, D, DS, MC, V.

D 🏊 🛏 🏃 🎿

Restaurants

★ ★ ★ **FORTE'.** *201 S Old Woodward Ave (48009). Phone 248/594-7300; fax 734/594-7353. www.forterestaurant.com.* Hours: 11:30 am-2 pm 5-10 pm; Thurs-Sat to 11 pm, closed Sun; holidays. Lunch $7-$14, dinner $15-$38. Entertainment, Thurs. Reservations accepted. Cr cds: A, D, DS, MC, V.

D 🛏

★ ★ ★ **RUGBY GRILLE.** *100 Townsend St (48009). Phone 248/642-5999; fax 248/645-9061. www.townsendhotel.com.* Located in the European-style Townsend Hotel, this internationally inspired, Continental restaurant's dinner menu features fine steak and chops, fresh seafood and homemade pastas. Breakfast and lunch, with slightly more standard menu options, are also available in the polished-wood, burgundy-toned space. Hours: 6:30 am-midnight; Fri, Sat 7-1 am. Reservations accepted. Bar. Wine cellar. Prix fixe: breakfast $7.95-$19.95. A la carte entrees: lunch $9.95-$18.95, dinner $20-$40. Specialties: steak tartare, Caesar salad, Black Angus beef, Dover sole. Own baking. Valet parking. Intimate dining room with cherry woodwork, marble-top tables, French doors. Cr cds: A, D, DS, MC, V.

D

Bloomfield Hills (H-5)

See also Birmingham, Detroit, Pontiac, Southfield, Troy, Warren

Settled 1819 **Pop** 4,288 **Elev** 830 ft **Area code** 248

Information Birmingham-Bloomfield Chamber of Commerce, 124 W Maple, Birmingham 48009; 248/644-1700

Web www.bbcc.com

Amasa Bagley followed a Native American trail and cleared land on what is today the business section of this small residential city. It was known as Bagley's Corners, later as Bloomfield Center, and then as Bloomfield Hills. In 1904, Ellen Scripps Booth and George G. Booth, president of the *Detroit News*, bought 300 acres of farmland here, naming it Cranbrook after the English village in which Mr. Booth's father was born. Since then, they have turned the estate into a vast cultural and educational complex.

What to See and Do

Cranbrook Educational Community. *1221 N Woodward Ave. Phone 248/645-3000.* This famous campus is the site of the renowned center for the arts, education, science, and culture. Located on more than 300 acres, Cranbrook is noted for its exceptional architecture, gardens, and sculpture. Cranbrook is composed of

Cranbrook Academy of Art and Museum. *39221 Woodward Ave. Phone 248/645-3312.* 150 students. Graduate school for design, architecture, and the fine arts. Museum has international arts exhibits and collections. (Wed-Sun afternoons; closed holidays) **$$**

Cranbrook Gardens. *1221 N Woodward Ave. Phone 248/645-3149.* 40 acres of formal and informal gardens; trails, fountains, outdoor Greek theater. (May-Aug, daily; Sept, afternoons only; Oct, Sat and Sun afternoons) **$$**

Cranbrook House. *380 Lone Pine Rd. Phone 248/645-3149.* (1908) Tudor-style structure designed by Albert Kahn. Contains exceptional examples of decorative and fine art from the late 19th and early 20th centuries. **$$**

Cranbrook Institute of Science. *39221 Woodward Ave. Phone 248/645-3200.* Natural history and science museum with exhibits, observatory, nature center; planetarium and laser demonstrations. (Mon-Sat, also Sun afternoons; closed holidays) **$$**

Motel/Motor Lodge

★ ★ ★ **KINGSLEY HOTEL AND SUITES.** *39475 Woodward Ave (48304). Phone 248/644-1400; toll-free*

800/544-6835; fax 248/644-5449. This quiet hotel offers the friendly service expected from a small inn along with the amenities and facilities of a large hotel. Located near shopping, this hotel offers, a pool and Jacuzzi, a seafood restaurant, deli and much more. Room service 7 am-11 pm; Sun to 10 pm. Exercise equipment. Downhill ski 20 miles. Barber, beauty shop. Meeting rooms, business services. Cr cds: A, C, D, DS, ER, JCB, MC, V.

Restaurant

★ ★ ★ ★ **THE LARK.** 6430 Farmington Rd. Phone 248/661-4466; fax 248/661-8891. www.thelark.com. A pleasant destination during any season, this European country-style restaurant offers chef Marcus Haight's classic French and internationally flavored dishes. In winter, two fireplaces warm the cozy interior of terracotta and Portuguese-tiled walls. In summer, outdoor dining rests beside a walled garden, a grape trellis, and a quiet fountain. The name refers to the obvious as well as to owners Jim and Mary Lark. French menu. Hours: 6-10:30 pm (last sitting 9 pm); Fri, Sat to 9 pm (last sitting). Closed Sun, Mon; Dec 25, Thanksgiving, Easter, also 1st week Jan and 1st week Aug. Dinner $60-$70. Bar. Reservations required. Totally nonsmoking. Cr cds: A, D, MC, V.

Boyne City (D-3)

See also Charlevoix, Petoskey

Pop 3,400 **Elev** 600 ft **Area code** 231 **Zip** 49712

Information Chamber of Commerce, 28 S Lake St; 231/582-6222

Web www.boynecity.com

What to See and Do

Boyne Mountain. *1 Boyne Mountain Rd. SE via MI 75 to Boyne Falls, off US 131. Phone 231/549-6000 or 800/462-6963.* Triple, sicross-passenger, three quad, three double chairlifts; rope tow; patrol, school, rentals; snowmaking; lodge (see RESORT), cafeteria, restaurant, bar, nursery. Longest run one mile; vertical drop 500 feet. Cross-country trails (35 miles), rentals. (Trail ticket; fee) (Late Nov-mid-Apr, daily) **$$$$**

Motel/Motor Lodge

★ **WATER STREET INN.** 240 Front St (49712). Phone 231/582-3000; fax 616/582-3001. 27 rooms, 3 story. S, D $145-$165; each additional $10; under 13 free. Check-out 11 am. TV; cable (premium). Private swimming beach.

Downhill ski 6 miles, cross-country ski 1 1/2 miles. Cr cds: A, D, MC, V.

Resort

★ ★ **BOYNE MOUNTAIN LODGE.** 1 Boyne Mountain Rd (49713). Phone 231/549-6000; fax 616/549-6094. www.boynemountain.com. 265 units in lodges, villas, condos, 1-3 story, 109 kitchens Dec-mid-Mar, mid-June-Aug: S, D $72-$105; 1-3 bedroom kitchen apartments $135-$325; AP; package plans; lower rates rest of year. Crib free. TV; cable, VCR available (movies). 2 pools, heated; whirlpool. Dining room 7 am-10 pm. Box lunches. Bar noon-2 am. Check-out 1 pm, check-in 5 pm. Meeting rooms. Business services available. Tennis, pro. 9-hole and two 18-hole golf courses, greens fee $70-$80, pro. Private beach. Paddleboats. Downhill/cross-country ski on site. Ice rink; rentals. Lawn games. Bicycles. Entertainment. Exercise equipment; sauna. 5,000-ft paved, lighted airstrip. Many minibars. Some balconies. Alpine-style décor; fireplace in lobby. Cr cds: A, C, D, DS, MC, V.

Restaurant

★ **PIPPINS.** 5 W Main St (49712). Phone 231/582-3311; fax 231/582-3201. www.pippinsrestaurant.com. American menu. Hours: 8 am-9 pm; Sun to 2 pm. Closed Mid-Mar-May, Oct-Dec 25. Dinner $6-$15. Bar. Child's menu. Casual attire. Cr cds: DS, MC, V.

Cadillac (F-3)

Settled 1871 **Pop** 10,104 **Elev** 1,328 ft **Area code** 231 **Zip** 49601

Information Cadillac Area Visitor Bureau, 222 Lake St; 231/775-0657 or 800/22-LAKES

Web www.cadillacmichigan.com

On the shores of lakes Cadillac and Mitchell, Cadillac was founded as a lumber camp and was once the major lumber center of the area. The city today prospers on diversified industry and tourism. Named for Antoine de la Mothe Cadillac, founder of Detroit, it is also headquarters for the Huron-Manistee National Forest (see MANISTEE and OSCODA). A Ranger District office of the forests is also located here.

What to See and Do

Adventure Island. 6083 E MI 1155 (49601). Phone 231/775-2527. Park includes mountain miniature golf, go-karts, batting cages, bumper boats, waterslides, concessions, arcade, hydro-tube waterslide. (Daily May-Oct) **$$$$**

Caberfae Peaks Ski Resort. *12 miles W on MI 55. Phone 231/862-3300.* Quad, triple, three double chairlifts, two T-bars, two rope tows; patrol, school, rentals; snowmaking; bar, cafeteria, lodge, motel, nursery, restaurant; snowboard, cross-country, and snowmobile trails. (Late Nov-Mar, daily) **$$$$**

Johnny's Game and Fish Park. *504 Haynes St (49601). 5 miles SW on MI 115, follow signs. Phone 231/775-3700.* Wild and tame animals; 75-ft-long elevated goat walk; fishing for rainbow trout (no license, no limit; fee). (Mid-May-Labor Day, daily) **$$$**

William Mitchell State Park. *6093 E MI 115. 2 1/2 miles W via MI 55 and 115. Phone 231/775-7911.* Approximately 260 acres between Cadillac and Mitchell lakes. Swimming beach, bathhouse, fishing, boating (launching, rentals); interpretive hiking trail, picnicking, playground, camping (tent and trailer facilities). Visitor center. Nature study area. Standard fees.

Motels/Motor Lodges

★ ★ **BEST VALUE INN.** *5676 MI 55 E (49601). Phone 231/775-2458; toll-free 800/654-8375; fax 231/775-8383. www.bestwestern.com.* 66 rooms. May-mid-Oct, Dec 26-mid-Mar: D $72-$87; each additional $5; lower rates rest of year. Crib $3. TV; cable (premium). Indoor pool; whirlpool, sauna. Playground. Restaurant 7 am-10 pm. Room service. Check-out 11 am. Business services available. Tennis. Golf privileges. Downhill ski 12 miles; cross-country ski 1/2 mile. Bowling. Game room. Lawn games. Cr cds: A, C, D, DS, MC, V.

[D] [symbols]

★ ★ **CADILLAC SANDS RESORT.** *6319 E MI 115 (49601). Phone 231/775-2407; toll-free 800/647-2637; fax 231/775-6422. www.cadillacsands.com.* 55 rooms, 2 story. June-Sept: S, D $69.95-$125; each additional $5; under 12 free. Crib $2. Pet accepted. Complimentary continental breakfast. Check-out 11 am. TV; cable (premium). Some private patios, balconies. Restaurant 5-10:30 pm; also Sat, Sun 8-11 am (in season). Bar 4 pm-2:30 am; entertainment. Indoor pool. Golf privileges, putting green. Downhill ski 13 miles; cross-country ski 3 1/2 miles. Lawn games. Boat rentals, paddleboats. Free airport transportation. Meeting room, business services. Private beach; dockage. Cr cds: A, D, DS, MC, V.

[D] [symbols]

★ **DAYS INN.** *6001 E MI 115 (49601). Phone 231/775-4414; toll-free 800/329-7466; fax 231/779-0370. www.daysinn.com.* 60 rooms, 2 story. June-Sept, Dec-Feb: S, D $68-$121; family, mid-wk rates; lower rates rest of year. Crib free. TV; cable (premium), VCR available (movies). Indoor pool; whirlpool. Complimentary con-

tinental breakfast. Restaurant nearby. Check-out 11 am. Meeting room. Business services available. Valet service. Downhill ski 12 miles; cross-country ski 2 miles. Volleyball. Some refrigerators. Lake 1/4 mile; swimming beach. Cr cds: A, C, D, DS, JCB, MC, V.

[D] [symbols] [SC]

★ **HAMPTON INN.** *1650 S Mitchell (49601). Phone 231/779-2900; fax 231/779-0846. www.hamptoninn.com.* 120 rooms, 4 story. Memorial Day-Labor Day: S $79; D $99; family rates; under 18 free; lower rates rest of year. Crib free. TV; cable (premium). Indoor pool; whirlpool. Complimentary continental breakfast. Coffee in rooms. Restaurant nearby. Check-out 11 am. Meeting rooms. Business services available. Valet service. Downhill ski 20 miles; cross-country ski 1 mile. Cr cds: A, C, D, DS, ER, JCB, MC, V.

[D] [symbols]

★ ★ ★ **MCGUIRE'S RESORT.** *7880 Mackinaw Tr (49601). Phone 231/775-9947; toll-free 800/632-7302; fax 231/775-9621. www.mcguiresresort.com.* This resort is the perfect spot for visitors to relax and enjoy their vacation, with walking and biking trails, two golf courses, a pool, tennis facilities, volleyball and basketball courts, and more. It is near shopping, the movie theater and the lake. 122 rooms, 1-3 story. May-Sept: S, D $69-$124; each additional $10; suites $109-$189; under 18 free; ski, golf plans; higher rates Dec 26-Jan 1. Cribs $15. Pet accepted; $15. TV; cable. Whirlpool, sauna. Restaurant 7 am-10 pm; off-season to 9 pm. Room service. Bar 11:30-1:30 am; entertainment. Coffee in rooms. Check-out 11 am. Meeting room. Business services available. In-room modem link. Valet service. Gift shop. Free airport, bus depot transportation. 27-hole golf, greens fee $45-$62, putting green, driving range. Downhill ski 15 miles; cross-country ski on site. Health club privileges. Game room. Lawn games. Refrigerators. Some, Fireplaces, private patios. Panoramic view of countryside. Cr cds: A, C, D, DS, MC, V.

[D] [symbols]

★ **SUN-N-SNOW MOTEL.** *301 S Lake Mitchell Dr (49601). Phone 231/775-9961. www.cadillacmichigan.com.* 29 rooms. June-Labor Day, winter weekends, Christmas wk: S $39-$59; D $49-$69; suites $90-$115; lower rates rest of year. Crib free. Pet accepted. TV; cable. Restaurant nearby. Check-out 11 am. Business services available. Downhill ski 15 miles; cross-country ski 1/4 mile. Golf privileges. Lawn games. Private beach. On Lake Mitchell. Park opposite. Cr cds: A, DS, MC, V.

[symbols] [SC] [symbols]

★ **SUPER 8 MOTEL.** *211 W MI 55 (49601). Phone 231/775-8561; fax 231/775-9392. www.super8.com.* 27 rooms, 2 story. Jan-Feb, June-Aug: S $46; D $65; each additional $5; under 12 free; lower rates rest of year. Crib free. TV. Indoor pool; whirlpool. Complimentary continental breakfast. Restaurant opposite 8 am-3 pm. Check-out 11 am. Downhill ski 15 miles; cross-country ski 1/4 mile. Health club privileges. Some refrigerators. Cr cds: A, C, D, DS, MC, V.

Restaurants

★ ★ **HERMANN'S EUROPEAN CAFE.** *214 N Mitchell (49601). Phone 231/775-9563. www.chefhermann. com.* Continental menu. Hours: 11 am-9:30 pm; Fri, Sat to 10 pm. Closed Sun; major holidays. Dinner $9.50-$25.95. Bar. Child's menu. Casual attire. Reservations required over 10 persons. Outdoor dining. Guest rooms available. Cr cds: A, D, DS, MC, V.

D

★ ★ **LAKESIDE CHARLIE'S.** *301 S Lake Mitchell (49601). Phone 231/775-5332; fax 231/775-8100.* American menu. Hours: 11:30 am-10 pm; Fri, Sat to 11 pm; Sun 11 am-8 pm; early-bird dinner 4-6 pm. Closed Mon. Dinner $7.45-$18.25. Bar to midnight; Fri, Sat to 1:30 am. Entertainment Fri, Sat. Child's menu. Casual attire. Outdoor dining. Cr cds: A, DS, MC, V.

D SC

Calumet (A-6)

See also Copper Harbor, Hancock, Houghton

Pop 818 **Elev** 1,208 ft **Area code** 906 **Zip** 49913

Information Keweenaw Peninsula Chamber of Commerce, 326 Shelden, Houghton 49931; 906/482-5240 or 800/338-7982

Web www.keweenaw.org

What to See and Do

Calumet Theatre. *340 6th St. Phone 906/337-2610.* (1899) Built with boom town wealth and continually being restored, this ornate theater was host to such great stars as Lillian Russell, Sarah Bernhardt, Lon Chaney, Otis Skinner, James O'Neil, Douglas Fairbanks, and John Philip Sousa. Guided tours (mid-June-Sept, daily). Live performances throughout the year. **$$**

Keweenaw National Historical Park. *100 Red Jacket Rd (49913). Phone 906/337-3168.* Established in Oct, 1992, to commemorate the heritage of copper mining on the Keweenaw Peninsula—its mines, machinery, and people. Self-guided walking tour brochures of the historic business and residential districts are available. Fees for cooperating sites include mine tours, museums. Calumet Unit and Quincy Unit. **FREE**

Upper Peninsula Firefighters Memorial Museum. *327 6th St. Phone 906/296-2561.* Housed in the historic Red Jacket Fire Station, this museum features memorabilia and exhibits spanning almost a century of firefighting history. (Mon-Sat) **$**

Charlevoix (D-3)

Pop 3,116 **Elev** 599 ft **Area code** 231 **Zip** 49720

Information Charlevoix Area Chamber of Commerce, 408 Bridge St; 231/547-2101

Web www.charlevoix.org

What to See and Do

Beaver Island Boat Company. *103 Bridge Park Dr, City Dock, Phone 231/547-2311.* A 2 1/4 hour trip to Beaver Island, the largest island of the Beaver Archipelago. (June-Sept, daily; mid-Apr-May and Oct-mid-Dec, limited schedule) Advance car reservations necessary. **$$$$**

Lake Michigan and Lake Charlevoix Beaches. Swimming, picnicking. Depot and Ferry Ave beaches; charter fishing, boat rentals (power and sail), launching ramp; tennis courts; municipal nine-hole golf course (June-Labor Day).

Special Events

Apple Festival. *408 Bridge St (49720). Phone 231/547-2101.* Second weekend Oct.

Venetian Festival. *408 Bridge St (49720). Phone 231/547-2101.* Midway, street, and boat parades, fireworks. Fourth full weekend July.

Waterfront Art Fair. *East Park. Phone 231/547-2675.* Second Sat Aug.

Motels/Motor Lodges

★ **ARCHWAY MOTEL.** *1440 Bridge St (49720). Phone 231/547-2096.* 14 rooms. Mid-June-mid-Aug: S, D $48-$99; higher rates: holidays, special events; lower rates rest of year. TV; cable (premium). Heated pool. Playground. Restaurant adjacent 5:30 am-3 pm. Check-out 10 am. Free airport, ferry transportation. Downhill/cross-country ski 2 miles. Picnic tables. Cr cds: DS, MC, V.

★ **LODGE.** *120 Michigan Ave (49720). Phone 231/547-6565; fax 231/547-0741.* 40 rooms, 2 story. July-mid-Aug, holiday weekends, Christmas holidays: S, D $80-$115; each additional $5; suites $155-$165; under 12 free; lower rates rest of year. Crib free. Pet accepted. TV; cable (premium). Pool. Complimentary coffee. Restaurant nearby. Check-out 11 am. Business services available. Downhill/cross-country ski 1 mile. Some private patios, balconies. Overlooks harbor. Cr cds: A, MC, V.

★ **WEATHERVANE TERRACE HOTEL.** *111 Pine River Ln (49720). Phone 231/547-9955; toll-free 800/552-0025; fax 231/547-0070.* 68 rooms, 2-3 story. S, D $90-$115; under 12 free; ski plans. Complimentary continental breakfast. Check-out 11 am. TV; cable (premium), VCR available (movies). Some fireplaces. Pool, whirlpool. Downhill/cross-country ski 1 mile. Cr cds: A, D, DS, MC, V.

All Suites

★★★**EDGEWATER INN.** *100 Michigan Ave (49720). Phone 231/547-6044; toll-free 800/748-0424; fax 231/547-0038. www.edgewater-charlevoix.com.* This inn offers one and two bedroom condominium suites that overlook Round Lake. It has both an indoor and an outdoor pool, a Jacuzzi, sauna and much more. It is also located downtown, close to many local restaurants and attractions. 60 kitchen suites, 3 story. June-late Aug: 1 bedroom (up to 4) $178-$242; 2 bedroom (up to 6) $235-$325; each additional (after 4) $5; under 17 free; weekly rates; higher rates: Christmas holidays, special events (2-day min); lower rates rest of year. Crib free. TV; cable; VCR, DVD. Restaurant 7 am-10 pm. Service bar. Coffee in rooms. Check-out 11 am. Coin laundry. Meeting room. Massage (by appt). Beauty shop. Downhill/cross-country ski 1 mile. Exercise equipment; sauna. Some in-room whirlpools. Refrigerators, fireplaces, private patios, balconies. Picnic tables. On lake; boat slips. Cr cds: A, MC, V.

Restaurants

★★★ **MAHOGANY'S.** *9600 Clubhouse Dr (49720). Phone 231/547-3555.* Located at the Charlevoix Country Club, the fieldstone fireplace and handcrafted mahogany bar set the scene for an elegant experience. Serving casual lunches on the porch and international cuisine in the dining room, this restaurant is the perfect post-game stopping place. Hours: noon-2:30 pm, 6-10 pm. Closed Dec 24, 25. Reservations accepted. Continental menu. Bar to midnight. Wine list. Lunch $5.50-$9, dinner $15-$26. Child's meals. Specializes in veal, seafood. Entertainment Fri, Sat. Victorian country cottage. Cr cds: A, MC, V.

★★ **STAFFORD'S WEATHERVANE.** *106 Pine River Ln (49720). Phone 231/547-4311; fax 231/547-0079. www.staffords.com.* American, Continental menu. Hours: 11:30 am-11 pm; Sun to 10 pm; early-bird dinner 5-6 pm. Closed Jan 25. Dinner $16.95-$28.50. Bar. Entertainment Fri, Sat. Child's menu. Casual attire. Reservations required. Outdoor dining. Cr cds: A, DS, MC, V.

★★★ **TAPAWINGO.** *9502 Lake St (49729). Phone 231/588-7971. www.tapawingo.net.* Lake view. Hours: 6-9:30 pm; days vary Sept-mid-Nov, mid-Dec-June. Closed mid-Nov-mid-Dec. Reservations required. Bar. Wine cellar. Prix fixe: dinner $47-$55. Specializes in regional dishes. Own baking. Country atmosphere. Landscaped setting on small lake. Fieldstone fireplace. Totally nonsmoking. Cr cds: A, D, MC, V.

Cheboygan (C-4)

See also Indian River, Mackinaw City

Settled 1871 **Pop** 4,999 **Elev** 600 ft **Area code** 231 **Zip** 49721

Information Cheboygan Area Chamber of Commerce, 124 N Main St, PO Box 69; 231/627-7183 or 800/968-3302

Web www.cheboygan.com

Surrounded by two Great Lakes and large inland lakes, the city has long been famous as a premier boating area. Cheboygan was once a busy lumber port, but now has a wide variety of industry.

What to See and Do

Aloha. *4347 3rd St (49721). 9 miles S on MI 33, then W on MI 212, on Mullett Lake. Phone 231/625-2522.* Approximately 95 acres with swimming, sand beach, fishing, boating (launch); picnicking, camping (dump station). Standard fees. (Daily) **$$**

Cheboygan. *4490 Beach Rd (49721). 3 miles NE off US 23, on Lake Huron. Phone 231/627-2811.* More than 1,200 acres with swimming, fishing, boating; hunting, hiking, cross-country skiing, picnicking, camping. Nature study. Standard fees. (Daily) **$$**

Cheboygan Opera House. *403 N Huron St. Phone 231/627-5432; fax 231/627-2643.* (1877) Renovated 580-seat auditorium featuring events ranging from bluegrass to ballet. Contact Chamber of Commerce for show schedule.

Fishing. Locks here lift boats to Cheboygan River leading to inland waterway which includes Mullett and Burt lakes, famous for muskie, walleye, salmon, and bass. Cheboygan County is the only place in the state where sturgeon spearing is legal each winter (Feb). Along the route, marinas supply cruise needs; swimming, boating. Contact the Chamber of Commerce.

The US Coast Guard Cutter *Mackinaw.* One of the world's largest icebreakers, with a complement of 80 officers and crew. When in port, the *Mackinaw* is moored at the turning basin on the east side of the Cheboygan River.

Special Event

Cheboygan County Fair. *Fairgrounds. Phone 231/627-7183.* Early Aug.

Motels/Motor Lodges

★**BEST WESTERN RIVER TERRACE.** *847 S Main St (49721). Phone 231/627-5688; toll-free 877/627-9552; fax 616/627-2472. www.bestwestern.com.* 53 rooms, 2 story. D $67-$127; each additional $10. Check-out 11 am. TV; cable (premium). Exercise equipment. Indoor pool, whirlpool. Cross-country ski 5 miles. Spacious grounds; excellent view of river. Cr cds: A, C, D, DS, MC, V.

🄳 ⬚ ⬚ ⬚ ⬚ ⬚

★ **DAYS INN.** *889 S Main St (49721). Phone 231/627-3126; fax 616/627-2889. www.daysinn.com.* 42 rooms, 2 story. Mid-June-mid-Sept: S $58-$110; D $68-$125; suites $85-$175; under 16 free; higher rates Labor Day wkend; lower rates rest of year. Crib free. TV; cable (premium). Complimentary continental breakfast. Restaurant adjacent 6 am-11 pm. Check-out 11 am. Free airport, bus depot transportation. Cross-country ski 3 miles. Refrigerators. Balconies. On river; dockage. Cr cds: A, C, D, DS, JCB, MC, V.

🄳 ⬚ ⬚ ⬚ ⬚ ⬚ ⬚

Restaurant

★ ★ **HACK-MA-TACK INN.** *8131 Beebe Rd (49721). Phone 231/625-2919. www.hack-ma-tack.com.* Hours: 5 pm-closing; May-Oct from noon. Closed mid-Oct-mid-Apr. No A/C. Bar. Dinner $18.95-$29.95. Specializes in whitefish, prime rib. Early American décor; fireplace. Set in wooded area. Overlooks Cheboygan River, 400-foot dock. Guest rooms available. Cr cds: A, D, DS, MC, V.

Chesaning

Restaurant

★ ★ ★ **CHESANING HERITAGE HOUSE.** *605 Broad St (48616). Phone 989/845-7700; fax 989/845-4249. www.bonnymillinn.com.* This 1908, Georgian Revival mansion is located across the street from the Bonnymill Inn. Hours: 11 am-8 pm; Fri, Sat to 9 pm; Sun 9:30 am-8 pm. Closed Dec 24, 25. Reservations accepted. Bar to 10 pm; Fri, Sat to midnight. Lunch $5-$15, dinner $12-$22. Child's meals. Specializes in stuffed pork tenderloin, prime rib, seafood. Outdoor dining. Victorian décor; crystal chandelier, fireplace. Georgian Revival mansion (1908) converted into nine dining areas. Cr cds: A, DS, MC, V.

🄳

Clare (F-3)

See also Harrison, Midland, Mount Pleasant

Pop 3,021 **Elev** 841 ft **Area code** 989 **Zip** 48617

Information Chamber of Commerce, 429 McEwan St; 989/386-2442 or 888/282-5273

Web www.claremichigan.com

What to See and Do

Chalet Cross-Country. *5931 Clare Ave. 6 miles N via Old US 27. Phone 989/386-9697.* Groomed cross-country trails (approximately 8 1/2 miles) graded to skier's experience; patrol, school, rentals; store. (Dec-Mar, daily; closed Dec 25) **$$**

Special Event

Irish Festival. *McEwan St (48617). Phone 989/386-2442.* Mid-Mar.

Motel/Motor Lodge

★ **DOHERTY HOTEL.** *604 N McEwan St (48617). Phone 517/386-3441; toll-free 800/525-4115; fax 517/386-4231. www.dohertyhotel.com.* 92 rooms, 3 story. S $39-$65; D $49-$90; each additional $5; suites $102-$115; weekly rates; golf plans. Crib $5. Pet accepted. Indoor pool; whirlpool, poolside service. Complimentary full breakfast. Restaurant (see DOHERTY). Bar 11-2 am; entertainment Wed-Sat. Check-out noon. Meeting rooms. Business services available. Bellhops. Valet service. Free airport transportation. Golf privileges. Downhill ski 5 miles; cross-country ski 7 miles. Game room. Balconies. Cr cds: A, D, DS, MC, V.

🄳 ⬚ ⬚ ⬚ ⬚

Restaurant

★ **DOHERTY.** *604 McEwan St (48617). Phone 989/386-3441; fax 989/386-4231. www.dohertyhotel.com.* Hours: 6 am-2 pm, 5-10 pm; Fri, Sat to 11 pm; Sun to 9 pm. Breakfast $4.75-$9.25, lunch $4.95-$10.25 , dinner $10-$27. Bar 11-2 am. Salad bar. Entertainment Fri, Sat. Child's meals. Established 1924. Reservations accepted. Cr cds: A, D, DS, MC, V.

🄳

Coldwater (I-3)

See also Marshall

Pop 9,607 **Elev** 969 ft **Area code** 517 **Zip** 49036

Information Coldwater/Branch County Chamber of Commerce, 20 Division St; 517/278-5985 or 800/968-9333

Web www.branch-county.com

What to See and Do

Tibbits Opera House. *14 S Hanchett St. Phone 517/278-6029.* (1882) Renovated 19th-century Victorian opera house. Presently home to professional summer theater series, art exhibits, a winter concert series, children's programs, and community events. Originally owned and operated by businessman Barton S. Tibbits, the house attracted such performers as John Phillip Sousa, Ethel Barrymore, P. T. Barnum, John Sullivan, and William Gillette. Tours (Mon-Fri). **FREE**

Wing House Museum. *27 S Jefferson St. Phone 517/278-2871.* (1875) Historical house museum exhibiting Second Empire architectural style. Includes original kitchen and dining room in basement, collection of Oriental rugs, oil paintings, three generations of glassware, Regina music box; furniture from Empire to Eastlake styles. (Wed-Sun, afternoons; also by appointment) **$**

Special Events

Branch County 4-H Fair. *31 Division St. Phone 517/279-4313.* Exhibits, animal showing, carnival booths, rides, tractor pulling. Second week Aug.

Bronson Polish Festival Days. *SW on US 12 in Bronson. Phone 800/968-9333.* Heritage fest; games, vendors, concessions, dancing. Third week July.

Car Show Swap Meet. *4-H Fairgrounds. Phone 800/968-9333.* Antique and class car show, arts and crafts, vendors; trophies. Early May.

Quincy Chain of Lakes Tip-Up Festival. *5 miles E via US 12 on Tip-Up Island in Quincy. Phone 800/968-9333.* Parade, fishing and woodcutting contests; torchlight snowmobile ride; dancing, polar bear splash, pancake breakfast, fish fry. Second weekend Feb.

Tibbits Professional Summer Theatre Series. *14 S Hanchett St. Phone 517/278-6029.* Resident professional company produces comedies, musicals. Phone 517/278-6029. Late June-Aug.

Motel/Motor Lodge

★★RAMADA INN & SUITES CONVENTION CENTER. *1000 Orleans Blvd (49036). Phone 517/278-2017; toll-free 800/806-8226; fax 517/279-7214. www.ramada.com.* 128 rooms, 2 story, 24 kitchens May-Oct: S $60-$65; D $67-$72; each additional $7; suites, kitchen units $72-$77; under 18 free; higher rates race weekends; lower rates rest of year. Crib free. Pet accepted. TV; cable (premium). Indoor pool; whirlpool. Complimentary continental breakfast. Restaurant 11 am-2 pm, 5-8 pm; weekend hours vary. Room service. Bar 5 pm-midnight; Fri, Sat to 2 am; closed Sun; entertainment Thurs-Sat. Check-out 11 am. Meeting rooms. Business services available. Valet service. Cross-country ski 2 miles. Game room. Cr cds: A, D, DS, MC, V.

B&B/Small Inns

★★CHICAGO PIKE. *215 E Chicago St (49036). Phone 517/279-8744; toll-free 800/471-0501; fax 517/278-8597. www.chicagopikeinn.com.* 8 rooms, 2 story. 2 A/C. S $100; D $165; each additional $20; suite $155. Closed Thanksgiving, Dec 24, 25. Children over 12 years only. TV; cable (premium), VCR available (free movies). Complimentary full breakfast; afternoon refreshments. Restaurant nearby. Check-out noon, check-in 3 pm. Free airport transportation. Golf privileges. Cross-country ski 20 miles. Bicycles. Horse and carriage rental. Picnic tables, grills. Victorian residence (1903); antiques; period furnishings; fireplace in sitting room. Cr cds: A, DS, MC, V.

Copper Harbor (A-6)

Pop 55 **Elev** 621 ft **Area code** 906 **Zip** 49918

Information Keweenaw Peninsula Chamber of Commerce, 325 Shelden, Houghton 49931 49913; 906/482-5240 or 800/338-7982

Web www.copperharbor.org

Lumps of pure copper studded the lakeshore and attracted the first explorers to this area, but deposits proved thin and unfruitful. A later lumbering boom also ended. Today this northernmost village in the state is a small but beautiful resort. Streams and inland lakes provide excellent trout, walleye, bass, and northern pike fishing. Lake Superior yields trout, salmon, and other species.

What to See and Do

Astor House Antique Doll & Indian Artifact Museum. *560 Gratiot St (US 41). Phone 906/289-4449 or 800/833-2470.* Early mining boom-days items and hundreds of antique dolls. (June-Oct, daily) **$**

Brockway Mountain Drive. *10 miles begins 1/4 mile W of junction US 41 and MI 26.* Lookouts; views of Lake Superior and forests.

Delaware Mine Tour. *11 miles W on US 41. Phone 906/289-4688.* Underground guided tour of copper mine dating back to 1850s. (Mid-May-mid-Oct, daily) **$$$**

Ferry service to Isle Royale National Park. *60 5th St. Phone 906/482-0984.* (see) Four ferries and a float plane provide transportation (June-Sept, daily; some trips in May). For fees and schedule contact Park Superintendent.

Fort Wilkins State Park. *1 mile E on US 41. Phone 906/289-4215.* Approximately 200 acres. A historic army post (1844) on Lake Fanny Hooe. The stockade has been restored and the buildings have been preserved to maintain the frontier post atmosphere. Costumed guides demonstrate old army lifestyle. Fishing, boating (launch); cross-country ski trails, picnicking, playground, concession, camping. Museum with relics of early mining days and various exhibits depicting army life in the 1870s. Standard fees. (Daily)

Isle Royale Queen III Evening Cruises. *Phone 906/289-4437.* Narrated 1 1/2-hour cruise on Lake Superior. Reservations advised. (July 4-Labor Day, eves)

Special Events

Art in the Park. *Main St. Phone 906/337-4579.* Community Center grounds. Juried art show featuring local and regional artists; food; live entertainment. Mid-Aug.

Brockway Mountain Challenge. *Phone 906/337-4579.* 15-kilometer cross-country ski race. Feb.

Motels/Motor Lodges

★ **ASTOR HOUSE-MINNETONKA RESORT.** *560 Gratiot (49918). Phone 906/289-4449; toll-free 800/433-2770; fax 906/289-4326. www.exploringthenorth. com.* 13 motel rooms, 12 cottages, 8 kitchens. No A/C. Early May-late Oct: S $48-$50; D $50-$53; cottages for 2-10, $46-$95; $300-$525/wk. Closed rest of year. Crib $5. Pet accepted; $5. TV; cable (premium). Restaurant opposite 8 am-10 pm. Check-out 10:30 am. Gift shop. Saunas. Picnic tables, grill. Pine-paneled cottages, many overlooking harbor, lake. Astor House Museum on premises. 8 rooms across street. Cr cds: DS, MC, V.

D ◆ ✕ ⊠

★ **BELLA VISTA MOTEL.** *160 6th St (49918). Phone 906/289-4213. www.bellavistamotel.com.* 22 rooms, 1-2 story, 8 kitchen cottages. No A/C. Late June-mid-Oct: S, D $45-$55; each additional $4; cottages for 2-5, $39-$60; lower rates May-mid-June. Crib available. Closed rest of year. TV; cable (premium). Restaurant nearby. Check-out 10 am. Some balconies. Picnic tables. Most rooms overlook harbor. On Lake Superior; dock. Cr cds: DS, MC, V.

🖛 ✕ ⊠

Restaurant

★ **TAMARACK INN.** *512 Gratiot St (49918). Phone 906/289-4522.* Hours: 8 am-9 pm. Breakfast $2-$6,

lunch $3.75-$6 , dinner $4-$20. Salad bar. Reservations accepted. Cr cds: DS, MC, V.

Dearborn (H-5)

See also Detroit, Ypsilanti

Settled 1763 **Pop** 89,286 **Elev** 605 ft **Area code** 313

Information Chamber of Commerce, 15544 Michigan Ave, 48126; 313/584-6100

Web www.dearborn.org

Dearborn is the home of the Ford Motor Company Rouge Assembly Plant, Ford World Headquarters, the Henry Ford Museum, and Greenfield Village. Although Dearborn has a long and colorful history, its modern eminence is due to Henry Ford, who was born here in 1863.

What to See and Do

✪ **Henry Ford Estate-Fair Lane.** *4901 Evergreen Rd (follow signs), on the University of Michigan-Dearborn Campus. Phone 313/593-5590.* (1913-1915) Built by automotive pioneer Henry Ford in 1915, the mansion cost in excess of $2 million and stands on 72 acres of property. The mansion, designed by William Van Tine, reflects Ford's penchant for simplicity and functionalism; its systems for heating, water, electricity, and refrigeration were entirely self-sufficient at that time. The powerhouse, boathouse, and gardens have been restored, and some original furniture and children's playhouse have been returned to the premises. (Apr-Dec, daily; rest of year, Sun; closed Jan 1, Dec 25) **$$$**

✪ **Henry Ford Museum and Greenfield Village.** *20900 Oakwood Blvd, 1/2 mile S of US 12, 1 1/2 miles W of Southfield Rd. Phone 313/271-1620 or 313/982-6150.* On a 254-acre setting, this is an indoor-outdoor complex that preserves a panorama of American life of the past—an unequaled collection of American historical artifacts. Built by Henry Ford as a tribute to the culture, resourcefulness, and technology of the United States, the museum and village stand as monuments to America's achievements. Dedicated in 1929 to Thomas Edison, they attract visitors each year from around the world. (Daily; closed Thanksgiving, Dec 25)

Greenfield Village. *20900 Oakwood Blvd. Phone 313/271-1620.* Comprised of more than eighty 18th- and 19th-century buildings moved here from all over the country. Historic homes, shops, schools, mills, stores, and laboratories that figured in the lives of such historic figures as Lincoln, Webster, Burbank, McGuffey, Carver, the Wright brothers, Firestone, Edison, and Ford. Among the most interesting are the courthouse where Abraham Lincoln practiced law, the Wright brothers' cycle shop, Henry Ford's birthplace,

Edison's Menlo Park laboratory, homes of Noah Webster and Luther Burbank, 19th-century farmstead of Harvey Firestone; steam-operated industries, crafts workers, demonstrations, home activites. (Daily; closed Thanksgiving, Dec 25; interiors also closed Jan-mid-Mar) Also winter sleigh tours. **$$$$**

Henry Ford Museum. *Phone 313/271-1620.* Occupies 12 acres, includes major collections in transportation, power and machinery, agriculture, lighting, communications, household furnishings and appliances, ceramics, glass, silver, and pewter. Special exhibits, demonstrations, and hands-on activities. (Daily; closed Thanksgiving, Dec 25)

Suwanee Park. Turn-of-the-century amusement center with antique merry-go-round, steamboat, train ride; restaurant, soda fountain. (Mid-May-Sept) Some fees. In addition, visitors can take narrated rides in a horse-drawn carriage (fee), on a steam train (fee), or on a riverboat; 1931 Ford bus rides are also available (mid-May-Sept). Varied activities are scheduled throughout the year (see SPECIAL EVENTS). Meals and refreshments are available. Combination ticket for Henry Ford Museum and Greenfield Village. **$$$$**

Special Events

Fall Harvest Days. *20900 Oakwood Blvd. Greenfield Village. Phone 313/271-1620.* Celebrates turn-of-the-century farm chores, rural home life, and entertainment. Three days early Oct.

Old Car Festival. *20900 Oakwood Blvd. Greenfield Village. Phone 313/271-1620.* Two days Sept.

Motels/Motor Lodges

★ ★ **BEST WESTERN GREENFIELD INN.** *3000 Enterprise Dr (48101). Phone 313/271-1600; toll-free 800/528-1234; fax 313/271-1600. www.bestwestern.com.* 210 rooms, 3 story. S $75-$95; D $85-$105; each additional $10; suites $99-$129; under 20 free. Crib $10. TV; cable (premium), VCR (movies). Indoor pool; whirlpool, poolside service. Restaurant 6 am-10 pm. Room service. Bar 11 am-midnight. Check-out noon. Coin laundry. Meeting rooms. Business services available. In-room modem link. Bellhops. Valet service. Sundries. Free airport, train station, bus depot, transportation. Downhill ski 14 miles; cross-country ski 4 miles. Exercise equipment; sauna. Bathroom phones, refrigerators; some in-room whirlpools. Cr cds: A, C, D, DS, ER, JCB, MC, V.

D ⚓ ☕ ⨉ ⊠ SC

★ ★ **COURTYARD BY MARRIOTT.** *5200 Mercury Dr (48126). Phone 313/271-1400; toll-free 800/321-2211; fax 313/271-1184. www.marriott.com.* 147 rooms, 14 suites, 2-3 story. S, D $89-$105; suites $105-$114; under 12 free; weekend rates. Crib free. TV; cable (premium). Indoor pool; whirlpool. Coffee in rooms. Breakfast available. Bar Sun-Thurs 5:30-9:30 pm. Check-out

noon. Coin laundry. Meeting rooms. Business services available. In-room modem link. Valet service (Mon-Fri). Exercise equipment. Some refrigerators. Private patios, balconies. Cr cds: A, C, D, DS, MC, V.

D ⚓ ⨉ ⊠ SC

★**HAMPTON INN.** *20061 Michigan Ave (48124). Phone 313/436-9600; fax 313/436-8345. www.hamptoninn.com.* 119 rooms, 4 story. S, D $83-$93; suites $122-$132; under 18 free. Crib free. TV; cable (premium). Indoor pool. Complimentary continental breakfast. Complimentary coffee in rooms. Restaurant nearby. Check-out noon. Coin laundry. Meeting room. Business services available. In-room modem link. Valet service. Exercise equipment. Refrigerator, wet bar in suites. Overlooks Henry Ford Museum and Greenfield Village. Cr cds: A, C, D, DS, MC, V.

D ⚓ ⨉ ⊠ SC

★**QUALITY INN.** *21430 Michigan Ave (48124). Phone 313/565-0800; toll-free 800/221-2222; fax 313/565-2813. www.qualityinn.com.* 100 rooms, 2 story. S, D $89-$119; each additional $5; under 18 free. Complimentary continental breakfast. Check-out noon. TV; cable (premium). In-room modem link. Pool. Near Henry Ford Museum and Greenfield Village. Cr cds: A, C, D, DS, ER, JCB, MC, V.

D ⚓ ⊠ SC

★ **RED ROOF INN.** *24130 Michigan Ave (48124). Phone 313/278-9732; fax 313/278-9741. www.redroof.com.* 112 rooms, 2 story. June-Aug: S $39.99-$59.99; D $49.99-$69.99; 1-2 additional $59.99-$69.99; under 18 free; lower rates rest of year. Crib free. Pet accepted, some restrictions. TV; cable (premium). Complimentary coffee in lobby. Restaurant adjacent 6:30 am-5:30 pm; cafe opposite to 11 pm. Check-out noon. Business services available. Cr cds: A, C, D, DS, MC, V.

D ☕ ⨉ ⊠

Hotels

★ ★ ★**HYATT REGENCY DEARBORN.** *Fairlane Town Center (48126). Phone 313/593-1234; fax 313/593-3366. www.hyatt.com.* Located near museums and historical sites and within walking distance of many shops and restaurants, this hotel is great for those guests visiting the area along with business travelers. It also offers a pool, hot tub, and fitness room. 772 rooms, 16 story. S, D $160-$185; each additional $25; suites $350-$720; under 18 free; weekend rates. Crib free. Valet parking $10. TV; cable (premium). Restaurants 6:30 am-midnight. Bars, 1 revolving. Check-out noon. Convention facilities. Business center. In-room modem link. Exercise equipment; sauna. Health club privileges. 16-story atrium, glass elevators. Near Henry Ford Museum and Greenfield Village. Cr cds: A, C, DS, JCB, MC, V.

D ⚓ ⨉ ☂ ⊠ SC ⚷

★ ★ ★ **MARRIOTT HOTEL, THE DEARBORN INN.** *20301 Oakwood Blvd (48124). Phone 313/271-2700; fax 313/271-7464. www.marriotthotels.com/dtwdi.* Built in 1931, this 222-room historic hotel is located on 23 beautifully landscaped acres with gardens. 2-4 story, 22 suites. S $149-$179; D $159-$189; suites $200-$275; under 18 free; weekend rates; package plans. Crib free. Pet accepted, some restrictions. Check-out noon. TV; cable (premium), VCR available. In-room modem link. Some refrigerators. Coffee in rooms. Restaurant 6:30 am-11 pm. Bar 11-1 am; entertainment. Health club privileges. Exercise equipment. Heated pool, wading pool, poolside service. Tennis. Lawn games. Meeting rooms. Concierge. Luxury level. Consists of Georgian-style inn built by Henry Ford (1931), two Colonial-style lodges and five Colonial-style houses; early American décor and furnishings. Cr cds: A, C, D, DS, ER, JCB, MC, V.

★ ★ ★ **THE RITZ-CARLTON, DEARBORN.** *300 Town Center Dr (48126). Phone 313/441-2000; fax 313/253-2051. www.ritzcarlton.com.* Located 15 minutes from both downtown Detroit and the airport. Massachusetts designer Frank Nicholidayson is behind the exquisite interiors, filled with 18th- and 19th-century antiques, marble, and chandeliers. 308 rooms, 11 story. S, D $195-$225; suites $375-$1,500; under 18 free; weekend rates. Crib free. Check-out noon. TV; cable (premium). In-room modem link. Bathroom phones, minibars. Restaurant (see THE GRILLE ROOM). Bar 11-1 am; entertainment. Room service 24 hours. Health club privileges. Exercise equipment, sauna. Massage. Indoor pool, whirlpool, poolside service. Golf privileges. Tennis privileges. Valet/garage parking $15. Business center, convention facilities. Concierge. Gift shop. Luxury level. Ballroom. Cr cds: A, C, D, DS, ER, JCB, MC, V.

Restaurants

★ ★ ★ **THE GRILLE ROOM.** *300 Town Center Dr (48126). Phone 313/441-2000; fax 313/441-2051. www.ritzcarlton.com.* Any time of day, this Ritz-Carlton, mahogany-clad dining room is a civilized retreat for Chef de cuisine Christian Schmidt's American-continental cuisine featuring steaks, chops and seafood. Hours: 6:30 am-2:30 pm, 6-9:30 pm; Fri, Sat 6-11 pm; Sun brunch 11 am-2 pm. Buffet lunch $25.50. Breakfast A la carte entrees: $6.50-$14.50, lunch A la carte entrees: $12-$26, dinner A la carte entrees: $18-$50. Sun brunch $39. Bar 11-1 am; Sun to midnight. Club-like setting; brass chandeliers, 18th- and 19th-century oil paintings. Reservations accepted. Valet parking. Cr cds: A, DS, MC, V.

★ ★ **KIERNAN'S STEAK HOUSE.** *21931 Michigan Ave (US 12) (48124). Phone 313/565-4260; fax 313/565-3712.* Hours: 11 am-11 pm; Sat from 5 pm; Sun 4-9 pm. Closed most major holidays. Reservations accepted. Bar to midnight. Lunch $7-$35, dinner $9.95-$35. Specializes in steak, seafood, veal. Valet parking. Intimate atmosphere. Cr cds: A, DS, MC, V.

Detroit (H-5)

Founded 1701 **Pop** 1,027,974 **Elev** 600 ft **Area code** 313

Information Metropolitan Detroit Convention and Visitors Bureau, 211 W Fort St, Suite 1000, 48226; 800/DETROIT

Web www.visitdetroit.com

Suburbs Ann Arbor, Birmingham, Bloomfield Hills, Dearborn, Farmington, Mount Clemens, Plymouth, Pontiac, St. Clair, Southfield, Troy, Warren, Ypsilanti.

Detroit, a high-speed city geared to the tempo of the production line, is the symbol throughout the world of America's productive might. Its name is almost synonymous with the word "automobile." The city that put the world on wheels, Detroit is the birthplace of mass production and the producer of nearly 25 percent of the nation's automobiles, trucks, and tractors. Every year a new generation of vehicles is hammered out in its factories. This is the city of Ford, Chrysler, Dodge, the Fishers, and the UAW. Detroit is a major producer of space propulsion units, automation equipment, plane parts, hardware, rubber tires, office equipment, machine tools, fabricated metal, iron and steel forging, and auto stampings and accessories. Being a port and border city, Detroit puts the Michigan Customs District among the nation's top five customs districts.

Founded by Antoine de la Mothe Cadillac in the name of Louis XIV of France at *le place du détroit*—"the place of the strait"—this strategic frontier trading post was 75 years old when the Revolution began. During the War of Independence, Detroit was ruled by Henry Hamilton, the British governor hated throughout the colonies as "the hair buyer of Detroit." He encouraged Native Americans to take rebel scalps rather than prisoners. At the end of the war, the British ignored treaty obligations and refused to abandon Detroit. As long as Detroit remained in British hands, it was both a strategic threat and a barrier to westward expansion; however, the settlement was finally wrested away by Major General Anthony Wayne at the Battle of Fallen Timbers. On July 11, 1796, the Stars and Stripes flew over Detroit for the first time.

During the War of 1812, the fortress at Detroit fell mysteriously into British hands again, without a shot fired. It was recaptured by the Americans the following year. In 1815, when the city was incorporated, Detroit was still just a trading post; by 1837, it was a city of 10,000 people. Then, the development of more efficient transportation opened the floodgates of immigration, and the city was on its way as an industrial and shipping hub. Between 1830-1860, population doubled with every decade. At the turn of the century, the auto industry took hold. Today, Detroit is a leader in the fields of automation and space exploration equipment. Yet it is a city that acknowledges its traditions as a French fort and frontier trading post. It looks to the future as well as the past.

Detroit was a quiet city before the automobile—brewing beer and hammering together carriages and stoves. Most people owned their own homes—they called it "the most beautiful city in America." All this swiftly changed when the automobile age burst upon it. Growth became the important concern; production stood as the summit of achievement. The automobile lines produced a new civic personality—there was little time for culture at the end of a day on the line. The city rocketed out beyond its river-hugging confines, developing nearly 100 suburbs. Today growing pains have eased, the automobile worker has more leisure time, and a new Detroit personality is emerging. Civic planning is remodeling the face of the community, particularly downtown and along the riverfront. Five minutes from downtown, twenty separate institutions form Detroit's Cultural Center—all within easy walking distance of one another.

Detroit is one of the few cities in the United States where you can look due south into Canada. The city stretches out along the Detroit River between lakes Erie and St. Clair, opposite the Canadian city of Windsor, Ontario. Detroit is 143 square miles in size and almost completely flat. The buildings of the Renaissance Center and Civic Center are grouped about the shoreline, and a network of major highways and expressways radiate from this point like the spokes of a wheel. The original city was laid out on the lines of the L'Enfant plan for Washington, D.C., with a few major streets radiating from a series of circles. As the city grew, a gridiron pattern was superimposed to handle the maze of subdivisions that had developed into Detroit's 200 neighborhoods.

These main thoroughfares all originate near the Civic Center: Fort Street (MI 3); Michigan Avenue (US 12); Grand River Avenue (I-96); John Lodge Freeway (US 10); Woodward Ave (MI 1); Gratiot Avenue (MI 3); and Fisher and Chrysler freeways (I-75). Intersecting these and almost parallel with the shoreline are the Edsel Ford Freeway (I-94) and Jefferson Avenue (US 25).

What to See and Do

Belle Isle. *E Jefferson Ave and E Grand Blvd. An island park in middle of Detroit River, reached by MacArthur Bridge.* Between US and Canada, in sight of downtown Detroit, this 1,000-acre island park offers 9-hole golf, a nature center, guided nature walks, swimming, fishing (piers, docks). Picnicking, ball fields, tennis and lighted handball courts. **FREE** Also here are

Aquarium. *E Jefferson and E Grand Blvd. Phone 313/852-4141.* One of the largest and oldest freshwater collections in the country. (Daily) **$**

Belle Isle Zoo. *E Jefferson Ave and E Grand Blvd. Phone 313/852-4083.* Animals in natural habitat. (May-Oct, daily) **$$**

Dossin Great Lakes Museum. *100 Strand Dr. Phone 313/852-4051.* Scale models of Great Lakes ships; restored "Gothic salon" from Great Lakes liner; marine paintings, reconstructed ship's bridge, and full-scale racing boat, *Miss Pepsi.* (Wed-Sun) **DONATION**

Whitcomb Conservatory. *E Jefferson Ave and E Grand Blvd. Phone 313/852-4064.* Exhibits of ferns, cacti, palms, orchids; special exhibits. (Wed-Sun) **$**

Canada. Windsor, Ontario is only a five-minute drive through the Detroit-Windsor tunnel or via the Ambassador Bridge. Tunnel and bridge tolls. Buses run every 12 minutes (fee). For Border Crossing Regulations, see MAKING THE MOST OF YOUR TRIP.

Children's Museum. *67 E Kirby Ave. Phone 313/873-8100.* Exhibits include "America Discovered," Inuit culture, children's art, folk crafts, birds and mammals of Michigan, holiday themes. Participatory activities relate to exhibits. Special workshops and programs and planetarium demonstrations on Sat and during vacations. (Mon-Sat; closed holidays) **FREE**

Civic Center. *Woodward and Jefferson aves.* Dramatic group of buildings in a 95-acre downtown riverfront setting. Included in this group are

Cobo Hall-Cobo Arena. *W Jefferson Ave and Washington Blvd. Phone 313/877-8111; fax 313/877-8577.* Designed to be the world's finest convention-exposition-recreation building; features an 11,561-seat arena and 720,000 square feet of exhibit area and related facilities. (Daily)

Coleman A. Young Municipal Center. *2 Woodward Ave. Phone 313/224-5585.* A $27-million, 13-story white marble office building and 19-story tower housing more than 36 government departments and courtrooms. At front entrance is massive bronze sculpture *Spirit of Detroit.* Building (Mon-Fri; closed holidays). **FREE**

Hart Plaza and Dodge Fountain. *Jefferson Ave. Phone 313/877-8077.* A $2-million water display designed by sculptor Isamu Noguchi.

Mariners' Church. *170 E Jefferson Ave. Phone 313/259-2206.* Oldest stone church in the city, completed in 1849, was moved 800 feet to its present site as part of Civic Center plan. Since that time it has been extensively restored and a belltower with carillon has been added. Tours (by appointment). **FREE**

Michigan Consolidated Gas Company Building. *1 Woodward Ave.* Glass-walled skyscraper designed by Minoru Yamasaki.

Veterans' Memorial Building. *151 W Jefferson Ave.* Rises on site where Cadillac and first French settlers landed in 1701. This $5.75-million monument to the Detroit area war dead was the first unit of the $180-million Civic Center to be completed. The massive sculptured-marble eagle on the front of the building is by Marshall Fredericks, who also sculpted *Spirit of Detroit* at City-County Building.

Detroit Historical Museum. *5401 Woodward Ave. Phone 313/833-1805.* Presents a walk through history along reconstructed streets of Old Detroit, period alcoves, costumes; changing exhibits portray city life. The museum now showcases a new automotive exhibition, celebrating the 100th anniversary of the automotive industry. (Tues-Sun; closed holidays) **$$**

Detroit Institute of Arts. *5200 Woodward Ave, between Farnsworth Ave and Kirby St. Phone 313/833-7900.* (1885) One of the great art museums of the world, tells history of humankind through artistic creations. Every significant art-producing culture is represented. Exhibits include *The Detroit Industry* murals by Diego Rivera, Van Eyck's *St. Jerome*, Bruegel's *Wedding Dance*, and Van Gogh's *Self-Portrait*; African, American, Indian, Dutch, French, Flemish, and Italian collections; medieval arms and armor; an 18th-century American country house reconstructed with period furnishings. Frequent special exhibitions (fee); lectures, films. (Wed-Sun; closed holidays) **$$**

Detroit Lions (NFL). *Ford Field. Phone 248/335-4131.*

Detroit Public Library. *5201 Woodward Ave. Phone 313/833-1000.* Murals by Coppin, Sheets, Melchers, and Blashfield; special collections include National Automotive History, Burton Historical (Old Northwest Territory), Hackley (African Americans in performing arts), Labor, Maps, Rare Books, US Patents Collection from 1790 to present. (Tues-Sat; closed holidays) **FREE**

Detroit Red Wings (NHL). *600 Civic Center Dr. Joe Louis Arena. Phone 810/654-6666.*

Detroit Shock (WNBA). *2 Championship Dr (48326). Phone 248/377-0100.* Team plays at the Palace of Auburn Hills.

Detroit Symphony Orchestra Hall. *3711 Woodward Ave. Phone 313/576-5100; fax 313/576-5101.* (1919) Restored public concert hall features classical programs. The Detroit Symphony Orchestra performs here.

Detroit Tigers (MLB). *2100 Woodward Ave and I-75. Phone 313/962-4000.* Team plays at Comerica Park.

Detroit Zoo. *10 miles N via Woodward Ave, at I-696 in Royal Oak. Phone 248/398-0900.* One of the world's outstanding zoos, with 40 exhibits of more than 1,200 animals in natural habitats. Outstanding chimpanzee, reptile, bear, penguin, and bird exhibits. (Daily; closed Jan 1, Thanksgiving, Dec 25) **$$$**

Eastern Market. *2934 Russell, via I-75 at Gratiot. Phone 313/833-1560.* (1892) Built originally on the site of an early hay and wood market, this and the Chene-Ferry Market are the two remaining produce/wholesale markets. Today the Eastern Market encompasses produce and meat-packing houses, fish markets, and storefronts offering items ranging from spices to paper. It is also recognized as the world's largest bedding flower market. (Mon-Sat; closed holidays) **FREE**

Fisher Building. *3011 W Grand Blvd. Phone 313/874-4444.* (1928) Designed by architect Albert Kahn, this building was recognized in 1928 as the most beautiful commercial building erected and given a silver medal by the Architectural League of New York. The building consists of a 28-story central tower and two 11-story wings. Housed here are the Fisher Theater, shops, restaurants, art galleries, and offices. Underground pedestrian walkways and skywalk bridges connect to parking deck and 11 separate structures, includes General Motors World Headquarters and New Center One.

Gray Line bus tours. *1301 E Warren Ave (48207). Phone 313/870-5012.*

Historic Trinity Lutheran Church. *1345 Gratiot Ave. Phone 313/567-3100.* (1931) Third church of congregation founded in 1850; 16th-century-style pier-and-clerestory, neo-Gothic small cathedral. Luther tower is a copy of the tower at a monastery in Erfurt, Germany. Much statuary and stained glass. Bell tower. (Tours by appt) **DONATION**

Huron-Clinton Metroparks. *Phone 810/463-4581.* A system of 13 recreation areas in the surrounding suburbs of Detroit (see ANN ARBOR, FARMINGTON, MOUNT CLEMENS, and TROY).

International Institute of Metropolitan Detroit. *111 E Kirby Ave. Phone 313/871-8600.* Hall of Nations has cultural exhibits from five continents (Mon-Fri; closed holidays). Cultural programs and ethnic festivals throughout the year. **FREE**

Motown Museum. *2648 W Grand Blvd. Phone 313/875-2264.* "Hitsville USA," the house where legends like Diana Ross and the Supremes, Stevie Wonder, Marvin

Gaye, the Jackson Five, and the Temptations recorded their first hits. Motown's original recording Studio A; artifacts, photographs, gold and platinum records, memorabilia. Guided tours. (Daily) **$$$**

Museum of African-American History. *315 E Warren Ave. In the University Cultural Center. Phone 313/494-5800.* Exhibits trace the history and achievements of black people in the Americas. (Tues-Sun; closed holidays) **$$$**

Renaissance Center. *100-400 E Jefferson Ave. Phone 313/568-5600; fax 313/568-5606.* 7-tower complex on the riverfront; includes 73-story hotel (see HOTELS), offices, restaurants, bars, movie theaters, retail shops, and business services.

★ **Washington Boulevard Trolley Car.** *Phone 313/933-1300.* Antique electric trolley cars provide a unique transit service to downtown hotels, the Civic Center, and the Renaissance Center. From late May-Labor Day Detroit operates the only open-top double-decker trolley car in the world. (Daily).

Wayne State University. *656 W Kirby. Phone 313/577-2972; 313/577-2424 for University Information.* (1868) 34,950 students. Has 13 professional schools and colleges. The campus has almost 100 buildings, some of the most notable being the award-winning McGregor Memorial Conference Center designed by Minoru Yamasaki and its sculpture court; the Walter P. Reuther Library of Labor and Urban Affairs; and the Yamasaki-designed College of Education. Wayne has a medical campus of 16 acres adjacent in the Detroit Medical Center. Three theaters present performances.

Special Events

Detroit Grand Prix. *1249 Washington Blvd. Phone 800/489-RACE. Belle Isle.* Indy car race. Fri is Free Prix Day. June.

Ford International Detroit Jazz Festival. *1 Hart Plaza. Phone 313/963-7622.* Five days of free jazz concerts. Late Aug.

Hazel Park. *1650 E Ten Mile Rd. Phone 248/398-1000.* Harness racing. Mon, Tues, Thurs-Sat. Apr-mid-Oct.

International Auto Show. *1 Washington Blvd. Cobo Hall. Phone 248/643-0250.* Jan.

Meadow Brook Music Festival. *Oakland University Campus 207 Wilson Hall. Phone 248/377-0100.* (see PONTIAC).

Meadow Brook Theatre. *Oakland University Campus 207 Wilson Hall. Phone 248/377-3300.* (see PONTIAC).

Michigan State Fair. *1120 W State Fair Ave. Phone 313/366-3300.* Late Aug-early Sept.

Northville Downs. *301 Center St (48167). Phone 248/349-1000.* Harness racing. Over 12 years only. Mon, Tues, Thurs, Sat. Jan, Oct-Mar.

Riverfront Festivals. *1 Hart Plaza. Phone 313/877-8077.* Weekend festivals featuring entertainment, costumes, history, artifacts, and handicrafts of Detroit's diverse ethnic populations. Different country featured most weekends. May-Sept.

The Theatre Company-University of Detroit Mercy. *8200 W Outer Dr. Phone 313/993-1130.* Dramas, comedies in university theater. Sept-May.

Motels/Motor Lodges

★**BEST WESTERN.** *16999 S Laurel Park Dr (48154). Phone 734/464-0050; fax 734/464-5869. www.bestwestern.com.* 123 rooms, 2 story. D $74-$120; under 18 free. Complimentary continental breakfast. Check-out noon. TV; cable (premium). In-room modem link. Exercise equipment. Pool. Cross-country ski 5 miles. Cr cds: A, C, D, DS, MC, V.

⬛⬛⬛⬛⬛

★★**COURTYARD BY MARRIOTT DETROIT DOWNTOWN.** *333 E Jefferson St (48226). Phone 313/222-7700; fax 313/222-8517. www.courtyard.com.* 255 rooms, 21 story. S $180-$250; D $190-$250; each additional $20; suites $250-$1,000; under 18 free; weekend rates. Valet parking $9. Crib free. TV; cable. Indoor pool; whirlpool, poolside service. Coffee in rooms. Restaurant 6:30 am-10 pm; Fri, Sat to 11 pm. Bar 11-2 am. Meeting rooms. Business center. In-room modem link. Shopping arcade. Barber, beauty shop. Tennis. Racquetball. Exercise room; sauna. Bathroom phone and TV, refrigerator in suites. Opposite river. Cr cds: A, C, D, DS, MC, V.

⬛⬛⬛⬛⬛⬛

★★**COURTYARD BY MARRIOTT DETROIT LIVONIA.** *17200 N Laurel Park Dr (48152). Phone 734/462-2000; fax 734/462-5907. www.marriott.com.* 149 rooms, 3 story. S, D $96-$106; suites $125-$135; weekend rates. Crib free. TV; cable (premium). Indoor pool; whirlpool. Restaurant 6:30-10 am; Sat 7-11 am; Sun 7 am-1 pm. Bar 4-11 pm; closed Sat, Sun. Check-out noon. Coin laundry. Meeting rooms. Business services available. In-room modem link. Valet service. Downhill/cross-country ski 20 miles. Exercise equipment. Refrigerator in suites. Private patios, balconies. Cr cds: A, C, D, DS, JCB, MC, V.

⬛⬛⬛⬛

★ ★ **HOLIDAY INN.** *5801 Southfield Service Dr (48228). Phone 313/336-3340; fax 313/336-7037. www.holiday-inn.com.* 347 rooms, 6 story. S, D $99; suites $250; under 18 free; weekend rates. Crib free. TV; cable (premium). 2 pools, 1 indoor; whirlpool. Coffee in rooms. Restaurant 6 am-2 pm, 5-10 pm; Sat, Sun from 7 am. Room service. Bar 11 am-midnight. Check-out noon. Convention facilities. Business center. Bellhops. Gift shop. Exercise equipment; sauna. Game room. Cr cds: A, D, DS, JCB, MC, V.

★ ★ **PARKCREST INN.** *20000 Harper Ave (48225). Phone 313/884-8800; fax 313/884-7087.* 49 rooms, 2 story. S $59; D $67-$72; kitchen units $84; family rates. Crib free. Pet accepted. TV; cable (premium). Heated pool. Restaurant 6:30-2:30 am; Sun 7:30 am-10 pm. Room service. Bar to 2 am. Check-out 11 am. Valet service. Cross-country ski 15 miles. Cr cds: A, C, D, DS, MC, V.

★ **THE SHORECREST MOTOR INN.** *1316 E Jefferson Ave (48207). Phone 313/568-3000; toll-free 800/992-9616; fax 313/568-3002. www.shorecrestmi.com.* 54 rooms, 2 story. S $69-$89; D $89-$99; family, weekly, weekend rates. Crib free. TV; cable (premium). Restaurant from 6 am; weekends from 7 am. Room service. Check-out noon. Business services available. Valet service. Health club privileges. Refrigerators. Cr cds: A, C, D, DS, MC, V.

Hotels

★ ★ ★ **MARRIOTT DETROIT LIVONIA.** *17100 Laurel Park Dr N (48152). Phone 734/462-3100; toll-free 800/321-2211; fax 734/462-2815. www.marriott.com.* 224 rooms, 6 story. S, D $129-$149; suites $225; family, weekend rates. Crib free. TV; cable (premium), VCR available. Indoor pool; whirlpool, poolside service. Restaurant 6:30 am-10 pm. Bar noon-midnight. Check-out noon. Meeting rooms. Business center. In-room modem link. Gift shop. Free garage parking. Downhill/cross-country ski 20 miles. Exercise equipment; sauna. Health club privileges. Connected to Laurel Park Mall. Luxury level. Cr cds: A, C, D, DS, ER, JCB, MC, V.

★ ★ ★ **MARRIOTT DETROIT METROPOLITAN AIRPORT TERMINAL.** *Detroit Metropolitan Airport (48242). Phone 734/941-9400. www.marriott.com.* 160 rooms, 5 story. S, D $145-$225; each additional $20; under 17 free. Crib available. Pet accepted. TV; cable (premium), VCR available. Complimentary continental breakfast. Check-out noon. Meeting rooms. Business center. Gift shop. Some refrigerators, minibars. Cr cds: A, C, D, DS, ER, JCB, MC, V.

★ ★ **MARRIOTT RENAISSANCE CENTER.** *Renaissance Center (48243). Phone 313/568-8000; toll-free 800/352-0831; fax 313/568-8146. www.marriott.com.* 1,306 rooms, 50 story. S $175-$195; D $190-$210; each additional $15; suites $330-$1,200; under 18 free; weekend rates. Crib free. Pet accepted. TV; cable, VCR available (movies). Indoor pool. Restaurants 6 am-11 pm. Room service 24 hours. Bar 11:30-1:30 am. Check-out 1 pm. Convention facilities. Business center. In-room modem link. Shopping arcade. Barber, beauty shop. Exercise room; sauna. Many minibars. Luxury level. Cr cds: A, C, D, DS, ER, JCB, MC, V.

★ ★ ★ **OMNI DETROIT RIVER PLACE.** *1000 River Place Dr (48207). Phone 313/259-9500; fax 313/259-3744. www.omnihotels.com.* This elegant hotel is located in downtown Detroit on the historic waterfron. Guestrooms boast views of the river and the Canadian border. The hotel has a championship croquet court which is the only U.S.C.A. sanctioned croquet court in Michigan. 108 rooms, 18 suites, 5 story. S $115-$185; D $135-$205; each additional $20; suites $165-$500; under 12 free; holiday rates; higher rates some special events. Crib free. Pet accepted. Check-out noon. TV; cable (premium), VCR available. In-room modem link. Restaurant (see BARON'S STEAKHOUSE). Bar 11 am-11 pm; Fri, Sat to 1 am. Exercise room, sauna. Massage. Indoor pool, whirlpool. Tennis privileges. Valet parking $6. Meeting rooms, business services. Croquet court. Cr cds: A, C, D, DS, MC, V.

All Suite

★ ★ ★ **ATHENEUM SUITE HOTEL.** *1000 Brush St (48226). Phone 313/962-2323; toll-free 800/772-2323; fax 313/962-2424. www.atheneumsuites.com.* This property is located downtown in Greek town, near many restaurants, shops, and other area attractions. 174 suites, 10 story. Suites $195; each additional $20; family, weekly rates. Crib free. Check-out noon. TV; cable (premium), VCR available. In-room modem link. Minibars; some bathroom phones. Coffee in rooms. Restaurant adjacent 8 am-midnight. Bar, room service 24 hours. Health club privileges. Exercise equipment. Valet parking $12. Meeting rooms, business services. Concierge. Neoclassical structure adjacent International Center. Cr cds: A, C, D, DS, ER, JCB, MC, V.

★ ★ ★ **EMBASSY SUITES HOTEL.** *19525 Victor Pkwy (48512). Phone 734/462-6000; fax 734/462-6003. www.embassysuites.com.* The property is located near the Detroit Zoo, Tiger Stadium, the Twelve Oaks Mall, many restaurants, and other attractions. 239 suites, 5 story. S $129-$149; D $139-$159; each additional $10; under 18 free (max 2); weekend rates; higher rates special events. Crib free. TV; cable (premium). Indoor pool; whirlpool. Complimentary full breakfast. Complimentary coffee in rooms. Restaurant 6-9 am, 11 am-4 pm, 5-10 pm; hours vary Fri-Sun. Bar 5 pm-midnight; closed Sun. Check-out noon. Coin laundry. Meeting rooms. Business services available. In-room modem link. Gift shop. Exercise equipment; sauna. Refrigerators, microwaves. Balconies. Five-story atrium. Cr cds: A, C, D, DS, JCB, MC, V.

D X ~ X ~ SC ↗

B&B/Small Inns

★ **BOTSFORD INN.** *28000 Grand River Ave (48336). Phone 248/474-4800.* 65 rooms. S $65-$75; D $70-$85; each additional $5; suites $75-$95; under 12 free; monthly rates. Crib $5. TV; cable (premium). Complimentary full breakfast. Coffee in rooms. Dining room 7 am-10 pm. Bar 11 am-midnight. Check-out 1 pm, check-in 3 pm. Guest laundry. Meeting rooms. Tennis. Early American, Victorian furnishings; many antiques. Built in 1836; restored by Henry Ford. Cr cds: A, C, D, DS, MC, V.

D ~ ~ SC

Restaurants

★ ★ ★ **BARON'S STEAKHOUSE.** *1000 River Place Dr (48207). Phone 313/259-4855; fax 313/259-3744. www.omnihotels.com.* The snug dining room and patio in the River Palace Hotel overlook the Detroit River. Specializes in beef, chicken, seafood. Hours: 7 am-10 pm; Fri, Sat to 11 pm; Sun 7 am-10 pm, open for holidays. Breakfast $4.95-$11.95, lunch $4.95-$16.95, dinner $13.95-$28.95. Bar to 11 pm. Child's meals. Reservations accepted. Outdoor dining. Cr cds: A, D, DS, MC, V.

D

★ ★ ★ **CAUCUS CLUB.** *150 W Congress St (48226). Phone 313/965-4970.* One of the city's culinary legends, this English-style dining room serves American-Continental cuisine with European accents. The jumbo Dover sole in lemon butter is a signature dish and the cozy, dimly lit bar a popular, after-work hangout. Continental menu. Specialties: fresh fish, steak, ribs. Hours: 11:30 am-8:30 pm; Fri to 10 pm; Sat 5 pm-10 pm; summer hours vary. Closed Sun; major holidays. Lunch $7.75-$17.25, dinner $15-$24. Entertainment Fri-Sat. Reservations accepted. Cr cds: A, D, DS, MC, V.

D

★ **EL ZOCALO.** *3400 Bagley (48216). Phone 313/841-3700.* Mexican menu. Hours: 11-1 am; Fri, Sat to 2:30 am. Closed some major holidays. Lunch $4.50-$4.65, dinner $6.65-$10.95. Bar. Reservations accepted Sun-Thurs. Cr cds: A, D, DS, MC, V.

D

★ ★ **FISHBONE'S RHYTHM KITCHEN CAFE.** *400 Monroe St (48226). Phone 313/965-4600; fax 313/965-1449.* Southern Louisiana, Creole, Cajun menu. Hours: 6:30 am-midnight; Fri, Sat to 1:45 am; Sun brunch 10:30 am-2 pm, closed Dec 25. Lunch $5.95-$12.95, dinner $5.95-$19.95. Sun brunch $17.95. Bar. Valet parking. Cr cds: A, D, DS, MC, V.

D

★ ★ ★ **INTERMEZZO.** *1435 Randolph St (48226). Phone 313/961-0707; fax 313/961-5387. www.intermezzo detroit.com.* Located in the heart of the Harmonie Park theater district, this contemporary restaurant serves Italian cuisine in a lively atmosphere. Hours: 11 am-10 pm; Fri, Sat to 11 pm. Closed Sun, Mon; major holidays. Lunch $6-$22, dinner $18-$42. Bar. Entertainment Fri, Sat. Reservations accepted. Outdoor dining. Cr cds: A, D, DS, MC, V.

D

★ ★ ★ **OPUS ONE.** *565 E Larned (48226). Phone 313/961-7766; fax 313/961-9243. www.opus-one.com.* Partners Jim Kokas and Ed Mandziara have overseen this dressy dining room for over 10 years. Executive chef Tim Giznsky creates inventive, American-Continental cuisine that can be enjoyed for dinner, weekday power lunches or pared with local theater tickets. American menu. Continental menu. Specializes in seafood, aged beef. Hours: 1:30 am-10 pm; Fri to 11 pm; Sat 5-11 pm. Closed Sun; major holidays. Lunch $8.95-$24.95, dinner $24.95-$38.95. Dinner Pianist Tues-Sat . Bar. Reservations accepted. Valet parking. Cr cds: A, D, DS, MC, V.

D

★ ★ **PEGASUS TAVERNA.** *558 Monroe St (48226). Phone 313/964-6800.* American menu. Greek menu. Specializes in lamb chops, seafood, spinach cheese pie. Hours: 11-1 am; Fri, Sat to 2 am; Sun to midnight. Lunch A la carte entrees: $4.95-$7.95, , dinner A la carte entrees: $7-$27, Bar. Child's meals. Lattice-worked ceiling; hanging grape vines. Cr cds: A, D, DS, MC, V.

D

★ ★ ★ **RATTLESNAKE CLUB.** *300 Stroh River Pl (48207). Phone 313/567-4400; fax 313/567-2063. www.rattlesnakeclub.com.* This Rivertown destination is where well-known chef Jimmy Schmidt offers seasonal, worldly American cuisine, a beautiful riverside dining room, and a superior, well-priced wine list. The flagship restaurant has been open for over 10 years, a testament to its popularity. Specializes in seasonal dishes. Hours:

11:30 am-10 pm; Fri to midnight; Sat 5:30-midnight. Closed Sun; most major holidays. Lunch $11.95-$32.95, dinner $12.95-$34.95. Bar. Reservations accepted. Valet parking. Outdoor dining. Cr cds: A, C, D, DS, MC, V.

D

★ **TRAFFIC JAM & SNUG.** *511 W Canfield St (48201). Phone 313/831-9470; fax 313/831-4022. www. traffic-jam.com.* Hours: 11 am-10:30 pm; Fri to midnight; Sat noon-midnight. Closed Sun; most major holidays. Dinner $9-$15. Microbrewery and dairy on premises. Children's menu. Cr cds: A, DS, MC, V.

D

★★★**THE WHITNEY.** *4421 Woodward Ave (48201). Phone 313/832-5700; fax 313/832-2159. www.thewhitney.com.* Set in the Whitney family home, this mansion with Tiffany windows and crystal chandeliers serves updated versions of traditional favorites. Guests can dine in their choice of rooms including the Music Room, Library, or Oriental Room. American cuisine. Specializes in veal, beef, seafood. Menu changes monthly. Hours: 11 am-2 pm, 6-9:00 pm; Wed, Thurs 5-9 pm; Fri, Sat 5-10 pm; Sun 5-8 pm; closed major holidays. Lunch A la carte entrees: $6.95-$16.95, dinner A la carte entrees: $18-$35. Dinner Prix fixe: $40-$60. Sun brunch 11 am-2 pm. Sun brunch $27.95. Bar 5 pm-2 am; closed Sun and Mon. Entertainment. Reservations accepted. Complimentary valet parking. Cr cds: A, D, DS, MC, V.

D

Detroit Wayne County Airport Area (H-5)

See also Dearborn, Detroit, Ypsilanti

Information 313/942-3550.

Motels/Motor Lodges

★★ **COURTYARD BY MARRIOTT.** *30653 Flynn Dr (48174). Phone 734/721-3200; fax 734/721-1304. www.marriott.com.* 146 rooms, 3 story. S, D $93; each additional $10; suites $110; under 16 free; weekend rates. Crib free. TV; cable (premium). Indoor pool; whirlpool. Complimentary coffee in rooms. Restaurant 6:30 am-2 pm, 5-10 pm; Sat 7 am-1 pm, 5-10 pm; Sun 7 am-1 pm. Bar. Check-out noon. Coin laundry. Meeting rooms. Business services available. In-room modem link. Valet service. Free airport transportation. Exercise equipment. Refrigerator in suites. Balconies. Cr cds: A, C, D, DS, MC, V.

D ⊱ 🕇 ✕ 🖳

★ **HAMPTON INN.** *30847 Flynn Dr (48174). Phone 734/721-1100; fax 734/721-9915. www.hamptoninn.com.* 136 rooms, 3 story. S, D $69.95-$89.95; under 17 free. Crib $5. TV; cable (premium). Pool. Complimentary continental breakfast. Restaurant adjacent 6 am-10 pm; Fri, Sat to 11:30 pm. Check-out noon. Meeting rooms. Business center. In-room modem link. Valet service. Free airport transportation. Cr cds: A, C, D, DS, MC, V.

D ⊱ ✈ 🖳 SC 🕇

★★ **PARK INN.** *8270 Wickham (48174). Phone 734/729-6300; fax 734/722-8740.* 243 rooms, 4 story. S, D $79-$89; each additional $10; suites from $150; family, weekend rates; package plans. Crib free. Check-out noon. TV; cable (premium). Valet service. Restaurant 6 am-10 pm. Bar 11-2 am; Sun from noon; entertainment. Room service. Playground. Exercise equipment, sauna. Indoor pool. Cross-country ski 4 miles. Free airport transportation. Meeting rooms, business services. Sundries. Cr cds: A, C, D, DS, ER, JCB, MC, V.

D ⋗ ⊱ 🕇 ✕ 🖳

★ **QUALITY INN.** *7600 Merriman Rd (48174). Phone 734/728-2430; toll-free 800/937-0005; fax 734/728-3756. www.choicehotels.com.* 140 rooms. D $74-$79; each additional $5; under 12 free. Complimentary continental breakfast. Check-out noon. TV; cable (premium). In-room modem link. Laundry services. Bar. Free airport transportation. Cr cds: A, C, D, DS, JCB, MC, V.

D ✕ 🖳

Hotels

★★★ **CROWNE PLAZA DETROIT METRO.** *8000 Merriman Rd (48174). Phone 734/729-2600; toll-free 800/227-6963; fax 734/729-9414. www.crowneplaza.com.* Situated at the entrance to the Detroit Metro Airport and offering guests courtesy van service, this luxury hotel welcomes the weary traveler with its spacious guestrooms, some offering walk out balconies, and a well-maintained fitness center with pool and whirlpool guaranteed to relax the tendons and ease the mind. Nearby attractions include the Greenfield Village, Henry Ford Museum, and Ford Headquarters. 365 rooms, 11 story. S, D $149; each additional $10; suites $179-$229; family, weekend rates. Crib free. Pet accepted, some restrictions. TV; cable (premium), VCR available. Indoor pool; whirlpool. Coffee in rooms. Restaurant 6 am-10 pm. Bar noon-1 am. Check-out noon. Convention facilities. Business center. In-room modem link. Gift shop. Free airport transportation. Exercise equipment. Game room. Some balconies. Luxury level. Cr cds: A, C, D, DS, JCB, MC, V.

D 🕽 ⊱ 🕇 ✕ 🖳 🕇

★★★ **MARRIOTT ROMULUS DETROIT.** *30559 Flynn Dr (48174). Phone 734/729-7555; toll-free 800/228-9290; fax 734/729-8634.* Whether guests are traveling for business, pleasure, or attending a meeting, this hotel's focus is on the facilities and services that will make even the most discerning guest relax and appreciate all the luxury being offered. 245 rooms, 4 story. S $134-$144; D $144-$154; suites $350; family, weekend rates. Crib free. TV; cable (premium). Indoor pool; whirlpool. Restaurant 6:30 am-10 pm. Bar from 11 am. Check-out noon. Meeting rooms. Business services available. In-room modem link. Gift shop. Free airport transportation. Downhill ski 15 miles. Exercise equipment. Some bathroom phones. Refrigerator, minibar in suites. Luxury level. Cr cds: A, C, D, DS, ER, JCB, MC, V.

D ⊠ ⇌ ✕ ✈ ⊠ ✕

All Suites

★★★ **HILTON SUITES DETROIT METRO AIRPORT.** *8600 Wickham Rd. Phone 734/728-9200; fax 734/728-9278. www.detroitmetroairport.hilton.com.* Offering an oasis of comfort and relaxation, and situated just 1 mile from the Detroit Metro Airport, this hotel is guaranteed to provide the perfect home-away-from-home. 151 suites, 3 story. S $89-$169; D $99-$179; each additional $10; family, weekend rates. Crib free. Complimentary full bkfst, coffee in rooms. Check-out noon. TV; cable (premium), VCR (movies $6). In-room modem link. Some balconies. Refrigerators. Valet services, coin laundry. Restaurant 6 am-11 pm. Bar. Exercise equipment. Game room. Indoor/outdoor pool, whirlpool, poolside service. Downhill ski 10 miles. Free airport transportation. Meeting rooms, business center. Sundries. Cr cds: A, C, D, DS, ER, JCB, MC, V.

D ⇌ ✕ ✉ ⇌ ✕ ✈ ⊠ SC ✕

East Tawas

Restaurant

★ **GENII'S FINE FOODS.** *601 W Bay St (48730). Phone 989/362-5913.* Specializes in Chinese food, steak, spaghetti, and fish. Hours: 7 am-9 pm; weekends to 10 pm in season. Closed Dec 25. Breakfast $1.35-$8, lunch $3.75-$7, dinner $4.95-$15. Child's meals. Reservations accepted. Cr cds: A, DS, MC, V.

SC

Ellsworth

Restaurant

★★★ **ROWE INN.** *6303 County 48 (49729). Phone 231/588-7351; toll-free 800/432-5823; fax 231/588-2365. www.roweinn.com.* This elegant fine dining restaurant is located on the lake in Ellsworth. They focus on cuisine native to Michigan and boast an extensive wine list. American, French menu. Hours: 6-10 pm. Closed Thanksgiving, Dec 25. Dinner $19.50-$36.50. Service bar. Children's meals. Casual attire. Reservations required. Outdoor dining, totally nonsmoking. Cr cds: A, DS, MC, V.

D ⊠

Escanaba (C-1)

See also Gladstone

Settled 1830 **Pop** 13,659 **Elev** 598 ft **Area code** 906 **Zip** 49829

Information Delta County Area Chamber of Commerce, 230 Ludington St; 906/786-2192 or 888/335-8264

Web www.deltami.org

The first European settlers in this area were lured by the pine timber, which they were quick to log; however, a second growth provides solid forest cover once again. Escanaba is the only ore-shipping port on Lake Michigan. Manufacture of paper is another important industry. Sports enthusiasts are attracted by the open water and huge tracts of undeveloped countryside. Fishing is excellent. Escanaba is the headquarters for the Hiawatha National Forest.

What to See and Do

Hiawatha National Forest. *2727 N Lincoln Rd. Phone 906/786-4062.* This 893,000-acre forest offers scenic drives, hunting, camping, picnicking, hiking, horseback riding, cross-country skiing, snowmobiling, winter sports; lake and stream fishing, swimming, sailing, motorboating, and canoeing. It has shoreline on three Great Lakes—Huron, Michigan, and Superior. The eastern section of the forest is close to Sault Ste. Marie, St. Ignace, and the northern foot of the Mackinac Bridge. Fees charged at developed campground sites. (Daily) For further information contact the Supervisor. **FREE**

Ludington Park. *On MI 35, overlooks Little Bay de Noc. Phone 906/786-4141.* Fishing, boating (launch, marina; fee), swimming, bath house; tennis courts, playground, volleyball court, ball fields, picnic area, tables, stoves, scenic bike path, pavilion, bandshell. (Apr-Nov, daily) **FREE** In the park is

Delta County Historical Museum and Sand Point Lighthouse. *12 Water Plant Rd. Phone 906/786-3763.* Local historical artifacts; lumber, railroad, and maritime industry exhibits; 1867 restored lighthouse (fee). (June-Labor Day, daily) **$**

Pioneer Trail Park and Campground. *3 miles N on US 2/41, MI 35. Phone 906/786-1020.* A 74-acre park on the Escanaba River. Shoreline fishing; picnicking, nature trails, playground, camping (fee). (May-Sept, daily) **$**

Special Event

Upper Peninsula State Fair. *2401 12th Ave N. Phone 906/786-4011.* Agricultural and 4-H exhibits, midway, entertainment. Six days mid-Aug.

Motels/Motor Lodges

★ **BAYVIEW.** *7110 US 2/41 (MI 35) (49837). Phone 906/786-2843; toll-free 800/547-1201; fax 906/786-6218. www.baydenoc.com/bayview.* 22 rooms, 1-2 story. June-mid-Sept: S $35-$45; D $45-$60; family rates; some lower rates rest of year. Crib free. Pet accepted; $8. TV; cable (premium). Indoor pool. Playground. Complimentary coffee in rooms. Restaurant adjacent 7 am-8 pm. Check-out 11 am. Business services available. Sauna. Some refrigerators. Picnic tables, barbecue area. Cr cds: A, MC, V.

D ⬛🍴🎿🏌🏊🎣⛷ 🚶

★★ **BEST WESTERN PIONEER INN.** *2635 Ludington St (49829). Phone 906/786-0602; toll-free 800/528-1234; fax 906/786-3938. www.bestwestern.com.* 72 rooms, 2 story. S $45-$91; D $55-$101; each additional $5. Crib $5. TV; cable (premium). Indoor pool. Restaurant 7 am-2 pm, 5-10 pm. Bar 5 pm-2 am. Check-out 11 am. Meeting rooms. Business services available. Sundries. Downhill/cross-country ski 7 miles. Many balconies. Cr cds: A, C, D, DS, MC, V.

D ✈ 🏊 ⛷ SC

★ **DAYS INN.** *2603 N Lincoln Rd (49829). Phone 906/789-1200; toll-free 800/548-2822; fax 906/789-0128. www.daysinn.com.* 123 rooms, 4 story. Mid-Jun-mid Sept: S, D $65-$83; each additional $6; under 12 free; lower rates rest of year. Crib free. Check-out noon. TV; cable. Restaurant adjacent 6 am-10 pm. Bar 11:30 am-midnight; Fri, Sat to 2 am. Indoor pool, whirlpool. Downhill/cross-country ski 7 miles. Free airport transportation. Meeting rooms. Cr cds: A, C, D, DS, JCB, MC, V.

D ⬛🍴🏊🎿🏌⛷

★ **ECONO LODGE ESCANABA.** *921 N Lincoln Rd (49829). Phone 906/789-1066; toll-free 800/929-5997; fax 906/789-9202.* 50 rooms, 2 story. June-Sept: S $44.99; D $50.99; each additional $6; under 12 free; higher rates Upper Peninsula State Fair; lower rates rest of year. TV; cable (premium). Whirlpool. Complimentary continen-

tal breakfast. Restaurant nearby. Check-out 11 am. Meeting room. Downhill/cross-country ski 7 miles. Exercise equipment; sauna. Cr cds: A, C, D, DS, JCB, MC, V.

D ✈ 🏌 ⛷ SC

★★ **TERRACE BLUFF BAY INN.** *7146 P Rd (49829). Phone 906/786-7554; toll-free 800/283-4678; fax 906/786-7597.* 71 rooms, 1-2 story. Mid-June-Aug: S $52; D $72-$79 each additional $5; under 16 free; package plans; lower rates rest of year. Crib $2. TV; cable, VCR available. Indoor pool; whirlpool. Restaurant 5-9 pm; June-Aug 7-11 am, 5-10 pm. Bar 5-11 pm. Check-out 11 am. Meeting rooms. Business services available. Sundries. Tennis. Golf, driving range. Downhill ski 5 miles; cross-country ski 7 miles. Exercise equipment; sauna. Game room. Fish cleaning, storage. Boat launch. Private patios, balconies. Overlooks Little Bay de Noc. Cr cds: A, DS, MC, V.

D ⬛ ✈ 🎿 🏌 🍴 🏊 ⛷

Restaurant

★★ **STONEHOUSE.** *2223 Ludington St (49829). Phone 906/786-5003; fax 906/786-5189.* Specializes in prime rib, seafood, veal. Hours: 11 am-2 pm, 5-9:30 pm; Sat from 5 pm. Closed Sun; also some major holidays. Lunch $4-$10, , dinner $4-$30. Bar to midnight. Child's meals. Reservations accepted. Cr cds: A, D, DS, MC, V.

Farmington (H-5)

See also Birmingham, Detroit, Milford, Northville, Novi, Southfield

Pop 10,132 **Elev** 750 ft **Area code** 248

Information Chamber of Commerce, 30903-B Ten Mile Rd, 48336; 248/474-3440

Web www.ffhchamber.com

What to See and Do

Kensington Metropark. *2240 W Buno Rd (48380). 14 miles NW on I-96, Kent Lake Rd or Kensington Rd exits. Phone 248/685-1561 or 248/227-2757.* More than 4,000 acres on Kent Lake. Two swimming beaches (Memorial Day-Labor Day, daily), boating (rentals), ice fishing; biking/hiking trail, tobogganing, skating, picnicking, concessions, 18-hole golf (fee). 45-minute boat cruises on the Island Queen (summer, daily; fee). Nature trails; farm center, nature center. Park (daily). Free admission Tues.

Special Event

Farmington Founders Festival. *Grand River & Farmington Rd. Phone 248/474-3440.* Ethnic food, arts and crafts, sidewalk sales, carnival, rides, concert, fireworks. Mid-July.

Motels/Motor Lodges

★ **COMFORT INN.** *30715 W Twelve Mile Rd (48334). Phone 248/471-9220; toll-free 800/228-5150; fax 248/471-2053. www.comfortinn.com.* 135 rooms, 4 story. S, D $69-$84, each additional $6; suites $109; under 18 free; weekend rates. Crib free. TV; cable (premium). Complimentary continental breakfast. Restaurant nearby. Check-out noon. Meeting rooms. Valet service. Health club privileges. Refrigerator in suites. Balconies. Cr cds: A, C, D, DS, JCB, MC, V.

D X S SC X

★ ★ **EXECUTIVE HOTEL & SUITES.** *Phone 248/553-0000; fax 248/553-7630.* 204 rooms, 3 story, 44 suites. S $129-$149; D $139-$149; suites $99-$129; under 19 free; weekend rates. Crib free. TV; cable. Indoor pool. Restaurant 6:30 am-11 pm. Room service. Bar 11 am-midnight. Check-out noon. Meeting rooms. Business center. In-room modem link. Bellhops. Valet service. Downhill ski 20 miles. Exercise equipment; sauna. Some in-room whirlpools; bathroom phone in suites. Cr cds: A, C, D, DS, MC, V.

S X X S X S SC

★ **HAMPTON INN.** *20600 Haggerty Rd (48167). Phone 734/462-1119; toll-free 800/426-7866; fax 734/462-6270. www.hamptoninn.com.* 125 rooms, 4 story. S, D $75-$89; under 18 free; weekend rates. Crib free. TV; cable (premium). Heated pool. Complimentary continental breakfast. Check-out noon. Meeting rooms. Business services available. In-room modem link. Valet service. Downhill ski 20 miles. Exercise equipment; sauna. Cr cds: A, C, D, DS, MC, V.

D S S X S SC

★ ★ **HOTEL BARONETTE.** *27790 Novi Rd (48377). Phone 248/349-7800; fax 248/349-7467.* Perched amidst rolling hills and beautifully lush and well maintained landscape, this hotel offers all the comforts of home, as well as the convenience of being adjoined to Michigan's largest shopping center, Twelve Oaks Mall. 150 rooms, 3 story. S $116; D $126; each additional $10; under 6 free. Complimentary full breakfast. Check-out noon. TV; cable; VCR (movies). Restaurant, bar. Exercise equipment, sauna. Indoor pool, whirlpool. Cr cds: A, C, D, DS, ER, JCB, MC, V.

D S X S

★ **RAMADA LIMITED OF NOVI.** *21100 Haggerty Rd (48167). Phone 248/349-7400; fax 248/349-7454. www.ramada.com.* 125 rooms, 2 story. D $48-$55; each additional $6; under 18 free. Complimentary continental breakfast. Check-out noon. TV; cable (premium). Cr cds: A, C, D, DS, MC, V.

D S

★ **RED ROOF INN.** *24300 Sinacola Ct NE (48335). Phone 248/478-8640; toll-free 800/843-7663; fax 248/478-4842. www.redroof.com.* 108 rooms. S $31.99-$33.99; D $37.99-$39.99; 3 or more $47.99; under 18 free. Crib free. Pet accepted. TV; cable. Restaurant adjacent open 24 hours. Check-out noon. Cr cds: A, C, D, DS, MC, V.

D X S

★ ★ **WYNDHAM NOVI GARDEN.** *42100 Crescent Blvd (48375). Phone 248/344-8800; toll-free 800/822-4200; fax 248/344-8535. www.wyndham.com.* 148 rooms, 2 story, 22 suites. S $118; D $128; each additional $10; suites $94-$104; under 18 free; weekend rates. Crib free. TV; cable. Indoor pool; whirlpool, sauna. Complimentary coffee in rooms. Restaurant 6:30 am-2 pm, 5-10 pm; Sat, Sun from 7 am. Room service (dinner). Bar. Check-out noon. Meeting rooms. Valet service. Health club privileges. Refrigerators available. Cr cds: A, C, D, DS, JCB, MC, V.

D S X S X

Hotels

★ ★ ★ **DOUBLETREE.** *2700 Sheraton Dr (48377). Phone 248/348-5000; toll-free 800/222tree; fax 248/348-2315. www.doubletree.com.* 217 rooms, 3 story. S $88-$140; D $93-$150; each additional $10; suites $175-$275; under 18 free; weekend rates. Crib free. TV; cable (premium). 2 pools, 1 indoor; whirlpool. Restaurant 6:30 am-10:30 pm. Room service. Bar 11-1 am; entertainment. Check-out noon. Meeting rooms. Business services available. Bellhops. Valet service. Exercise equipment; sauna. Health club privileges. Cr cds: A, MC, V.

D S X X S SC

★ ★ ★ **HILTON NOVI.** *21111 Haggerty Rd (48375). Phone 248/349-4000; fax 248/349-4066. www.hilton.com.* Conveniently situated near the intersection to all the major highways, this hotel offers a comfortable stay while being minutes from some of Novi's fun quaint attractions. 239 rooms, 7 story. S $115-$175; D $130-$190; each additional $15; suites $275-$525; family, weekend rates. Crib free. TV; cable (premium). Pool; whirlpool. Restaurant 6:30 am-11 pm. Room service 24 hours. Bar 11-2 am. Check-out noon. Meeting rooms. Business services available. In-room modem link. Downhill ski 10 miles; cross-country ski 2 miles. Exercise equipment; sauna. Refrigerator in suites. Cr cds: A, C, D, DS, ER, JCB, MC, V.

D S X X S SC

★ ★ ★ **RADISSON HOTEL.** *37529 Grand River Ave (48335). Phone 248/477-7800; toll-free 0/333-3333; fax 248/477-6512. www.radisson.com.* This hotel offers guests a comfortable stay along with warm and friendly service. 137 suites, 4 story. S, D $114; weekend rates. Crib free. TV; cable (premium), VCR available. Indoor pool; whirlpool.

Complimentary continental breakfast. Coffee in rooms. Restaurant 6:30 am-2 pm, 5-10 pm. Room service. Bar 5 pm-midnight. Check-out noon. Meeting rooms. Business services available. Valet service. Downhill ski 20 miles. Exercise equipment; sauna. Health club privileges. Refrigerators. Cr cds: A, C, D, DS, ER, JCB, MC, V.

D ⊠ ≊ 🏃 ⬛ SC

Farmington Hills

Restaurant

★ ★ ★ **TRIBUTE.** *31425 W Twelve Mile Rd (48334). Phone 248/848-9393; fax 248/848-1919. www.tribute-restaurant.com.* Chef Takashi Yagihashi spent 17 years in some of the most renowned kitchens in Europe and America before settling down to serve his Asian-inspired, contemporary French creations. The industrial building and luxuriously whimsical dining room are the property of Lawrence Wisne, a Detroit automotive-industry millionaire whose lavish investment has put this restaurant on the nation's culinary map. Contemporary French cuisine with Asian accents. Hours: 5:30-9:30 pm. Closed Sun, Mon; also holidays. Reservations accepted. Valet parking only. Degustation menu $90. Vegetable vegustation menu $70. Cr cds: A, D, DS, MC, V.

D

Flint (G-5)

See also Holly, Owosso, Saginaw

Settled 1819 **Pop** 140,761 **Elev** 750 ft **Area code** 810

Information Flint Area Convention and Visitors Bureau, 519 S Saginaw St, 48502; 810/232-8900 or 800/25-FLINT

Web www.visitflint.org

Once a small, wagon-producing town, Flint is now an important automobile manufacturer. The fur trade brought Flint its first prestige; lumbering opened the way to carriage manufacturing, which prepared the city for the advent of the automobile. General Motors, the city's major employer, has Buick plants here. One of the largest cities in the state, it also has many other industrial firms.

What to See and Do

County recreation areas. *5045 E Stanley Rd.*

Genesee-C. S. Mott Lake. Approximately 650 acres. Swimming, fishing, boating (launches, fee); snowmobiling. Picnicking with view of Stepping Stone Falls. Riverboat cruises (fee).

Holloway Reservoir. *7240 N Henderson Rd. 12 miles E on MI 21, then 8 miles NE via MI 15. Phone 810/653-4062.* Approximately 2,000 acres. Swimming, water sports, fishing, boating (launches, fee); snowmobiling, picnicking, camping (fee). (Daily) **FREE**

⭐ **Crossroads Village/Huckleberry Railroad.** *G-6140 Bray Rd, 6 miles NE via I-475, at exit 13. Phone 810/736-7100.* Restored living community of the 1860-1880 period; 28 buildings and sites including a railroad depot, carousel, Ferris wheel, general store, schoolhouse, and several homes; working sawmill, gristmill, cidermill, blacksmith shop; 8-mile steam train ride; entertainment. Paddlewheel riverboat cruises (fee). Special events most weekends. (Memorial Day-Labor Day, daily; Sept, weekends; also special Halloween programs, Dec holiday lighting spectacular). **$$$**

Flint College and Cultural Corporation. *817 E Kearsley St. Phone 810/237-7330 (Cultural Center).* A complex that includes the University of Michigan-Flint (5,700 students), Mott Community College, Whiting Auditorium, Flint Institute of Music, Bower Theater. Also here are

Flint Institute of Arts. *In the Cultural Center, 1120 E Kearsley St. Phone 810/234-1695.* Permanent collections include Renaissance decorative arts, Oriental Gallery, 19th- and 20th-century paintings and sculpture, paperweights; changing exhibits. (Tues-Sun; closed holidays) **FREE**

Robert T. Longway Planetarium. *1310 E Kearsly St. Phone 810/760-1181.* Ultraviolet, fluorescent murals; Spitz projector. Exhibits. Programs. (Phone for schedule) **$$**

Sloan Museum. *1221 E Kearsley St. Phone 810/237-3450.* Collection of antique autos and carriages, most manufactured in Flint; exhibitions of Michigan history; health and science exhibits. (Daily; closed holidays) **$$**

For-Mar Nature Preserve and Arboretum. *22142 N Genesee Rd. Phone 810/789-8567.* Approximately 380 acres. Nature trails, indoor and outdoor exhibits, two interpretive buildings. Guided hikes available for groups of ten or more (fee). **$**

Motels/Motor Lodges

★ **HOLIDAY INN EXPRESS.** *1150 Longway Blvd (48503). Phone 810/238-7744; toll-free 800/278-1810; fax 810/233-7444. www.holiday-inn.com.* 124 rooms, 5 story. S, D $79-$89; under 18 free. Crib free. Complimentary continental breakfast. Check-out noon. TV; cable (premium). In-room modem link. Some in-room whirlpools. Valet service. Health club privileges. Downhill ski 20 miles. Free airport transportation. Meeting room, business center. Cr cds: A, D, DS, JCB, MC, V.

D 🐾 ⬛ 🏃 🐾 ✕ ⬛ SC

★★HOLIDAY INN. *5353 Gateway Centre (48507). Phone 810/232-5300; toll-free 888/570-1770; fax 810/232-9806. www.holiday-inn.com.* 171 rooms, 4 story. S $99-$129; D $99-$149; each additional $10; suites $114-$229; family, weekly rates. Crib free. TV; cable. Indoor pool; whirlpool. Restaurant 6:30 am-10 pm; Fri, Sat 7 am-11 pm. Room service. Bar 11:30 am-midnight; Fri, Sat to 2 am. Check-out noon. Coin laundry. Meeting rooms. Business services available. In-room modem link. Bellhops. Valet service. Concierge. Free airport, train station, bus depot transportation. Game room. Exercise equipment; sauna. Health club privileges. Some refrigerators, wet bars. Picnic tables. Cr cds: A, D, DS, JCB, MC, V.

$\boxed{D}$ ⌦ 🏃 ⌘ ✈ ⌦ SC

★RED ROOF INN. *G3219 Miller Rd (48507). Phone 810/733-1660; toll-free 800/843-7663; fax 810/733-6310. www.redroof.com.* 107 rooms, 2 story. June-mid-Sept: S $34.99-$42; D $42-$49; 3 or more $52-$56; under 18 free; lower rates rest of year. Crib free. TV; cable (premium). Restaurant adjacent 6:30 am-11 pm. Business services available. Check-out noon. Cr cds: A, C, D, DS, MC, V.

$\boxed{D}$ 🐾 ⌦

★ SUPER 8 MOTEL. *3033 Claude Ave (48507). Phone 810/230-7888; toll-free 800/800-8000; fax 810/230-7888. www.super8.com.* 61 rooms, 3 story. No elevator. S $38.98; D $44.98; each additional $6; under 12 free; higher rates Buick Open: Pet accepted. TV; cable. Complimentary coffee in lobby. Restaurant nearby. Check-out 11 am. Cr cds: A, C, D, DS, JCB, MC, V.

$\boxed{D}$ 🐾 ⌦ SC

Hotel

★★CHARACTER INN. *1 W Riverfront Center (48502). Phone 810/239-1234; fax 810/239-5843.* 369 rooms, 16 story. S, D $89; suites $99-$295; under 18 free. Crib free. Check-out noon. TV; cable. Some refrigerators. Restaurant 6:30 am-11 pm; Fri, Sat to 1 am. Bar. Exercise equipment. Game room. Indoor pool, whirlpool. Free garage parking. Free airport transportation. Meeting rooms, business center. Concierge. On river. Cr cds: A, DS, MC, V.

$\boxed{D}$ ⌦ 🏃 ⌦ 🏃 ✈

Restaurant

★★★MAKUCH'S RED ROOSTER. *3302 Davison Rd (48506). Phone 810/742-9310.* This family-owned restaurant specializes in Caesar salad, fresh seafood, and steak. They do their own baking, and several of the menu items are prepared table side. Hours: 11 am-9 pm; Fri to 9:30 pm; Sat 5-9:30 pm. Closed Sun; major holidays. Lunch $4.50-$12.95, dinner $18.95-$32.95. Bar. Child's meals. Reservations accepted. Cr cds: MC, V.

Frankenmuth (G-5)

See also Bay City, Flint, Saginaw

Settled 1845 **Pop** 4,408 **Elev** 645 ft **Area code** 989 **Zip** 48734

Information Convention & Visitors Bureau, 635 S Main St; 989/652-6106, 800/386-8696 or 800/386-3378

Web www.frankenmuth.org

This city was settled by 15 immigrants from Franconia, Germany, who came here as Lutheran missionaries to spread the faith to the Chippewas. Today, Frankenmuth boasts authentic Bavarian architecture, flower beds, and warm German hospitality.

What to See and Do

⭐ **Bronner's Christmas Wonderland.** *25 Christmas Ln. Phone 989/652-9931; toll-free 800/ALL-YEAR (recording).* Thought to be the world's largest Christmas store: more than 50,000 trims and gifts from around the world. Multi-image presentation "World of Bronner's" (18 min); outdoor Christmas lighting display along Christmas Lane (dusk-midnight). (Daily; closed holidays).

Factory Outlet Stores. *12240 S Beyer Rd. Approximately 5 miles S on I-75, exit 136. Phone 989/624-7467.* More than 175 outlet stores can be found at The Outlets at Birch Run. (Daily)

Frankenmuth Historical Museum. *613 S Main St. Phone 989/652-9701.* Local historical exhibits, hands-on displays, audio recordings, and cast-form life figures. Gift shop features folk art. (Mon-Sat, also Sun afternoons; closed holidays) **$**

Frankenmuth Riverboat Tours. *445 S Main St. Board at dock behind Riverview Cafe. Phone 989/652-8844.* Narrated tours (45 minutes) along Cass River. (May-Oct, daily, weather permitting) **$$**

Glockenspiel. *713 S Main St. Phone 989/652-9941.* Tops the Bavarian Inn (see RESTAURANTS); 35-bell carillon with carved wooden figures moving on a track acting out the story of the Pied Piper of Hamelin.

Michigan's Own Military & Space Museum. *1250 S Weiss St. Phone 989/652-8005.* Features uniforms, decorations, and photos of men and women from Michigan who served the nation in war and peace; also displays on Medal of Honor recipients, astronauts, former governors. (Mar-Dec, daily; closed Easter, Dec 25) **$$**

Special Events

Bavarian Festival. *335 S Main St. Phone 989/652-8155. Heritage Park.* Celebration of German heritage. Music, dancing, parades and other entertainment; food; art demonstrations and agricultural displays. Four days early-June.

Frankenmuth Oktoberfest. *635 S Main St. Phone 989/652-6106.* Serving authentic Munich Oktoberfest and American beer. German food, music, and entertainment. Third weekend Sept.

Motels/Motor Lodges

★ ★ ★ **FRANKENMUTH BAVARIAN INN LODGE.** *1 Covered Bridge Ln (48734). Phone 989/652-7200; toll-free 888/775-6343; fax 989/652-6711. www.bavarianinn.com.* Perched on the banks of the Cass River, this three generation family owned lodge continues to delight guests year after year. Offering a totally unique visit, this impressive lodge sets itself apart from the rest with its 5 indoor pools, 3 whirlpools, a Children's Village guranteed to delight the kid in all of us, plus an 18-hole indoor minature golf center, 2 lounges and restaurants, and to top off this exciting assortment of amenities, there are 4 outdoor tennis courts. Guests may come for the relaxation of it all but are guranteed to leave with the fairy tale of this truly delightful lodge. 354 units, 4 story. June-Oct: S, D $89-$135; suites $145-$210; lower rates rest of year. Crib $5. Check-out 11 am. TV; cable, VCR available. Balconies. Restaurant 7 am-9 pm. Bar to 12:30 am; entertainment. Room service. Exercise equipment. 5 indoor pools; 3 whirlpools. Tennis. Lawn games. Airport transportation. Business services, convention facilities. Gift shops. Game rooms. Cr cds: A, DS, MC, V.

[icons]

★★★**ZENDER'S BAVARIAN HAUS.** *730 S Main St (48734). Phone 989/652-0400; toll-free 800/863-7999; fax 989/652-9777.* Resembling a cozy chalet in the early European tradition, this inn offers a comfortable stay amidst delightful old world charm. From the spacious and well appointed guestrooms, to the beautiful and lush gardens and brick walkway that surrounds a pond and floating fountain, guests are guaranteed to be enchanted by it all. 137 rooms, 2 story. Early June-late Oct: D $85-$125; suites $165-$200; lower rates rest of year. Crib free. TV; cable (premium). Indoor/outdoor pool; whirlpool. Restaurant 7:30-10:30 am. Check-out 11 am. Business services available. 18-hole golf privileges. Exercise equipment; sauna. Game room. Private balconies. Cr cds: DS, MC, V.

[icons]

Restaurants

★★**FRANKENMUTH BAVARIAN INN.** *713 S Main St (MI 83) (48734). Phone 989/652-9941; fax 989/652-3481. www.bavarianinn.com.* American, German menu. Hours: 11 am-9:30 pm. Closed Dec 24 evening; also 1st week Jan. Lunch $7.50-$12.95, dinner $12.95-$26. Bar. Child's meals. Established 1888. Reservations accepted. Specializes in Bavarian dinner, family-style chicken dinner. Cr cds: A, DS, MC, V.

[icons]

★★**ZEHNDER'S.** *730 S Main St (MI 83) (48734). Phone 989/652-0400; fax 989/652-3544. www.zehnders.com.* American menu. Specializes in all-you-can-eat family-style chicken dinner, steak, seafood. Hours: 8 am-9:30 pm. Closed Dec 24. Lunch $5.95-$12.95 , dinner $14.50-$19. Bar. Child's meals. Family style dining. Cr cds: DS, MC, V.

[icon]

Frankfort (E-2)

Pop 1,546 **Elev** 585 ft **Area code** 231 **Zip** 49635

Information Benzie County Chamber of Commerce, PO Box 204, Benzonia 49616; 231/882-5801 or 800/882-5801

Web www.benzie.org

An important harbor on Lake Michigan, Frankfort is a popular resort area. Fishing for coho and chinook salmon is excellent here. Frankfort is the burial site of Father Marquette. Nearby is Sleeping Bear Dunes National Lakeshore. Development of the lakeshore is complete with 40-slip marina, gas, sewage pumpout, electricity, and bathing facilities.

Motels/Motor Lodges

★ **BAY VALLEY INN.** *1561 Scenic Hwy (49635). Phone 616/352-7113; fax 616/352-7114.* 20 rooms. Memorial Day-Labor Day: S $45-$55; D $65-$75; suite $90; family, weekly rates; lower rates rest of year. Crib free. Pet accepted. TV; cable, VCR available (free movies). Playground. Complimentary continental breakfast. Check-out 11 am. Free laundry. Meeting rooms. Business services available. Downhill/cross-country ski 18 miles. Recreation room. Refrigerators. Picnic tables, grills. Cr cds: A, DS, MC, V.

[icons] **SC**

★**HARBOR LIGHTS MOTEL & CONDOS.** *15 2nd St (49635). Phone 231/352-9614; fax 231/352-6580.* 57 rooms, 2 story. D $85-$95; ski, golf plans. Check-out 11 am. TV; cable (premium). Park, beach opposite. Indoor pool, whirlpool. Downhill ski 18 miles, cross-country ski 3 miles. Lawn games. Cr cds: C, DS, MC, V.

[icons]

Resort

★ ★ **CHIMNEY CORNERS RESORT.** *1602 Crystal Dr (49635). Phone 231/352-7522; fax 616/352-7252. www.benzie.com.* 8 rooms in lodge, 2 share bath, 1-2 story, 7 kitchen apartments (1-2 bedroom), 13 kitchen cottages for 1-20. No A/C. Closed rest of year. Crib free. Pet accepted, some restrictions. May-Nov: lodge rooms for 2, $60-$55 (maid service available); kitchen apartments for 2-6 $825-$875/week; kitchen cottages $1,175-$1,500/week.

Check-out 10 am, check-in 3 pm. TV in lobby; cable. Many private patios. Fireplaces. Grocery, coin lndry, package store 7 miles. Dining room in season 8-10:30 am, noon-2 pm. Playground. Tennis. Picnic tables. Private beach; rowboats, hoists; paddleboats. Sailboats. 1,000-foot beach on Crystal Lake, 300 acres of wooded hills. Cr cds: A, MC, V.

Restaurants

★ **HOTEL FRANKFORT.** *231 Main St (49635). Phone 231/352-4303; fax 231/352-6383. www.hotelfrankfort.com.* Hours: 8 am-9 pm; Fri, Sat to 10 pm; June-Aug to 10 pm. Breakfast $2.05-$6.95, lunch $2.95-$7, dinner $7.95-$19.95. Bar. Child's meals. Victorian décor; gingerbread woodwork on exterior. Reservations accepted. Guest rooms available. Cr cds: A, D, DS, MC, V.

D SC

★ **MANITOU.** *4349 Scenic Hwy (MI 22) (49635). Phone 231/882-4761.* Hours: 4:30-10 pm; early-bird dinner to 6 pm; closed Jan-Apr. Dinner $15-$35. Reservations accepted. Outdoor dining. Cr cds: MC, V.

D

★★**RHONDA'S WHARFSIDE.** *300 Main St (49635). Phone 231/352-5300; fax 231/352-7271.* Specializes in California cuisine. Continental. Hours: vary seasonally. Closed Dec 25. Lunch $4.50-$10.95, dinner $14.25-$20.25. Service bar. Child's meals. Totally nonsmoking. Cr cds: A, DS, MC, V.

D

Gaylord (D-4)

See also Boyne City, Grayling

Settled 1873 **Pop** 3,256 **Elev** 1,349 ft **Area code** 989 **Zip** 49735

Information Gaylord Area Convention & Tourism Bureau, 101 W Main, PO Box 3069; 989/732-4000 or 800/345-8621

Web www.gaylordmichigan.net

What to See and Do

Otsego Lake State Park. *7 miles S off I-75 on Old US 27. Phone 517/732-5485.* Approximately 60 acres. Swimming beach, bathhouse, waterskiing, boating (rentals, launch); fishing for pike, bass, and perch; picnicking, playground, concession, camping. (Mid-Apr-mid-Oct) Standard fees. **$$**

Treetops Sylvan Resort. *3962 Wilkinson Rd. 5 miles E via MI 32 to Wilkinson Rd. Phone 989/732-6711; toll-free 888/TREETOPS.* Double, two triple chairlifts, four rope tows; patrol, school, rentals; cafeteria, bar. Nineteen runs; longest run 1/2 mile; vertical drop 225 feet. (Dec-mid-Mar, daily) 10 miles of cross-country trails; 3 1/2 miles of lighted trails. **$$$$**

Special Events

Alpenfest. *1535 Opal Lake Rd. Phone 989/732-6333.* Participants dressed in costumes of Switzerland; carnival, pageant, grand parade; "world's largest coffee break." Third weekend July.

Otsego County Fair. *Phone 989/732-4119.* Mid-Aug.

Winterfest. *M South Ct (49735). Phone 800/345-8621.* Ski racing and slalom, cross-country events, snowmobile events, activities for children, snow sculpting, downhill tubing. Early Feb.

Motels/Motor Lodges

★ **BEST VALUE INN OF GAYLORD.** *803 S Otsego Ave (49735). Phone 989/732-6451; toll-free 800/876-9252; fax 989/732-7634.* 44 rooms, 1-2 story. D $69-$99; each additional $6; under 16 free. Pet accepted. Complimentary continental breakfast. Check-out 11 am. TV; cable. Exercise equipment, sauna. Downhill/cross-country ski 3 miles. Cr cds: A, C, D, DS, MC, V.

D SC

★★ **BEST WESTERN ALPINE LODGE.** *833 W Main St (49735). Phone 989/732-2431; toll-free 800/684-2233; fax 989/732-9640. www.bestwestern.com.* 137 rooms, 2 story. Mid-June-Sept, ski weekends, Christmas week: S, D $85-$91; each additional $6; under 19 free; golf plans; lower rates rest of year. Crib free. Pet accepted. TV; cable, VCR available (movies). Indoor pool; whirlpool. Restaurant 6 am-10 pm. Room service. Bar 3 pm-midnight. Check-out 11 am. Coin laundry. Meeting rooms. Business services available. Valet service. Sundries. Downhill/cross-country ski 4 miles. Exercise equipment; sauna. Game room. Cr cds: A, C, D, DS, MC, V.

D

★ **DAYS INN.** *1201 W Main St (49735). Phone 989/732-2200; toll-free 800/952-9584; fax 989/732-0300. www.daysinn.com.* 95 rooms, 2 story. Mid-June-early Sept: S $57-$84; D $67-$94; each additional $5; family rates; ski, golf plans; higher rates late Dec-Jan 1; lower rates rest of year. Crib free. TV; cable (premium). Indoor pool; whirlpool. Complimentary continental breakfast. Restaurant adjacent 6 am-10 pm. Check-out 11 am. Coin laundry. Meeting room. Business services available. Downhill ski 4 miles; cross-country ski 1 1/2 miles.

Exercise equipment; sauna. Game room. Refrigerators. Cr cds: A, C, D, DS, MC, V.

★★ **QUALITY INN.** *137 W Main St (49735). Phone 989/732-7541; toll-free 800/228-5151; fax 989/732-0930. www.qualityinn.com.* olf plans; lower rates rest of year. Crib free. TV; cable (premium). Indoor pool; whirlpool. Restaurant 7 am-10 pm; Sun to 9 pm. Check-out 11 am. Business services available. Downhill/cross-country ski 1/2 mile. Exercise equipment. Cr cds: A, C, D, DS, JCB, MC, V.

Resorts

★ **EL RANCHO STEVENS.** *2332 E Dixon Lake Rd (49735). Phone 989/732-5090; fax 989/732-5059. www.elranchostevens.com.* 32 rooms in 2 lodges, 2-3 story. No A/C. Memorial Day-Sept (2-day min), MAP: S $110-$150; D $83-$115/person. Closed rest of year. Crib free. Heated pool. Free supervised children's activities. Teen club. Dining room 6-9 pm. Snacks; barbecues. Bar noon-midnight. Check-out 11 am, check-in 3 pm. Grocery, coin lndry, package store 3 miles. Meeting rooms. Free airport transportation. Sports director; instructors. Tennis. Sand beach; water sports, paddleboats, boats. Waterskiing available. Hayrides. Nature hike. Lawn games. Social director; entertainment. Game room. Recreation room. Picnic tables. 1,000 acres on Lake Dixon. Cr cds: DS, MC, V.

★★★ **GARLAND RESORT & GOLF COURSE.** *4700 N Red Oak (49756). Phone 989/786-2211; fax 989/786-2254. www.garlandusa.com.* Located on 3,500 lush acres and offering spectacular views, this property will make guests feel right at home. Serving savory concoctions amidst elegant surroundings, the restaurant here is guaranteed to delight the senses and tickle the tastebuds with its gourmet cuisine. 58 rooms in main building, 60 cottages. May-Oct, MAP: S, D $79-$179; cottages $159; family, weekly, weekend, holiday rates; golf, ski plans; lower rates rest of year. Closed week of Thanksgiving, mid-Mar-Apr. Crib free. Check-out 11 am, check-in 4 pm. TV; cable, VCR available. Balconies. Refrigerators. Valet service. Coin laundry 5 miles. Restaurant 6 am-11 pm; winter hours vary. Bar 6-2 am; entertainment. Room service. Massage. Exercise equipment, sauna, steam room. Social director. Sports director. 2 pools, 1 indoor; whirlpool, poolside service. 72-hole golf course, pro, greens fee $75, putting green, driving range. Lighted tennis. Downhill ski 12 miles, cross-country ski on site. Picnic tables. Lawn games. Bicycles. Hiking. Sleighing. Airport transportation. Meeting rooms, business services. Concierge. Cr cds: A, DS, MC, V.

★★ **MARSH RIDGE RESORT.** *4815 Old 27 S (49735). Phone 989/705-3900; toll-free 800/743-7529; fax 989/732-2134. www.marshridge.com.* 50 rooms, 1-2 story, 4 kitchen units. Mid-May-late Oct, late Dec-late Mar: S, D $135-$139; each additional $10; kitchen units up to 4 $129-$165; under 16 free; ski, golf plans; weekend rates; lower rates rest of year. Crib free. TV; cable (premium); VCR available (fee). Heated pool; whirlpool, sauna. Restaurant 7 am-10 pm; 5-9 pm off season. Coffee in lobby. Complimentary continental breakfast. Check-out 11 am. Meeting rooms. Valet service. 18-hole golf, greens fee (incl cart) $55, putting green, lighted driving range. Downhill ski 5 miles; lighted cross-country ski on site. Recreation room. Lawn games. Some fireplaces. Refrigerators, private patios, balconies. Picnic tables. Cr cds: A, MC, V.

★★★ **TREETOPS RESORT.** *3962 Wilkinson Rd (49735). Phone 989/732-6711; fax 989/732-6595. www.treetops.com.* This modern Alpine getaway offers guestrooms, suites, condominiums and resort homes, all overlooking the Pigeon River Valley. 260 rooms in main buildings, 2-3 story, 30 rooms in chalets, 2 story, 8 kitchens May-Sept, Dec 25-Feb: S, D $115-$358; each additional $6; chalet rooms, kitchen units $300-$380; under 18 free; MAP available; ski, golf plans; Christmas week (4-day minimum); winter weekends (2-day minimum); lower rates rest of year. Crib $5. Check-out noon, check-in 4 pm. TV; cable (premium), VCR available. Private patios, balconies. Many refrigerators. Coffee in rooms. Dining room (public by res) 8 am-10 pm; Fri, Sat to 10:30 pm. Bar to 2 am. Room service 4 pm-midnight. Supervised children's activities, ages 1-12 years. Playground. Exercise equipment, sauna. Massage. Social director. Game room. 4 pools, 2 heated indoor; children's pool, whirlpools, poolside service. 18-hole golf, greens fee $36-$99, pro, putting green, 2 driving ranges, golf cart. Lighted tennis. Downhill/cross-country ski on site; rentals. Snack bar; picnics. Picnic tables. Lawn games. Hiking trails. Ice skating. Volleyball. Barber, beauty shop. Free airport transportation. Meeting rooms, business services. Concierge. Arcade shops. 4,000-acre hilltop complex on the crest of Pigeon River Valley. Cr cds: A, D, MC, V.

Restaurants

★ **SCHLANG'S BAVARIAN INN.** *Old US 27 S (49735). Phone 989/732-9288.* German, American menu. Hours: 5-10 pm. Closed Sun; most major holidays. Dinner $12.95-$18.95. Bar. Children's meals. Casual attire. Outdoor dining, Authentic Bavarian atmosphere; fireplace. Cr cds: MC, V.

★★**SUGAR BOWL.** *216 W Main St (MI 32) (49734). Phone 989/732-5524; fax 989/732-3448.* Greek, American menu, Greek gourmet table. Salad bar. Hours: 7 am-11 pm; Sun to 10 pm. Closed Easter, Thanksgiving, Dec 25; also last week Mar and 1st week Apr. Dinner $6.95-$19.95. Bar. Child's menu. Fireplace. Cr cds: A, DS, MC, V.
D

Gladstone (C-1)

See also Escabana

Restaurant

★★**LOG CABIN SUPPER CLUB.** *7531 US 2 (49837). Phone 906/786-5621; fax 906/786-6594. www.logcabinbythebay.com.* Hours: 11 am-10 pm; Sun from 4 pm. Closed most major holidays. Bar to midnight. Lunch $4-$6, dinner $10.95-$22.95. Complete meals: dinner $10.95-$22.95. Child's meals. Specializes in steak, fresh fish. Salad bar. Rustic décor. Overlooks Little Bay de Noc. Cr cds: MC, V.
D

Glen Arbor (D-2)

See also Leland, Traverse City

Settled 1848 **Pop** 250 **Elev** 591 ft **Area code** 231 **Zip** 49636

Information Sleeping Bear Area Chamber of Commerce, PO Box 217; 231/334-3238

Web www.sleepingbeararea.com

This community, situated on Lake Michigan, lies just north of Sleeping Bear Dunes National Lakeshore.

Resort

★★★**THE HOMESTEAD.** *Wood Ridge Rd (49636). Phone 231/334-5000; fax 616/334-5246. www.thehomestead resort.com.* Visitors can choose to stay in a small hotel, an inn, a lodge, or privately owned guest homes when they stay at this resort. Guests will find beaches, four pools, a small craft harbour, golf, and tennis facilities along with restauants and shops. 130 condos condos, 2-3 story, 94 lodge rooms. No A/C in condos. July-Labor Day: condos (2-day min) $140-$740; lodge rooms $76-$311; suite $165-$445; MAP available; lower rates May-June, early Sept-Oct. Closed mid-March-Apr, Nov-late-Dec. Check-out 11 am, check-in 5 pm. TV; cable, VCR available. In-room modem link. Patios, balconies. Many fireplaces. Coffee in rooms. Restaurant 8 am-10 pm. Entertainment. Supervised children's activities (July-Sept, to age 10; $32-$75). Playground. Exercise equipment, sauna. Massage (by appt). Sports director. 4 heated pools, children's pool, lifeguard, whirlpool, poolside service in season. 9-hole par-3 golf, greens fee $34-$76, pro, putting green, driving range, carts available. Tennis, pro (July-Sept). Downhill/cross-country ski on site. Bicycles. Sailboats, canoes. Charter fishing. Skating. Meeting rooms, business services. On Lake Michigan shoreline. Private beach. Cr cds: DS, MC, V.
D 🚲 🍴 🎿 ⚓ 🎿 🏊 SC

Restaurants

★★**LA BECASSE.** *Phone 231/334-3944; fax 231/334-7503.* French menu. Hours: 5:45-9:15 pm. Closed Mon; most major holidays; Tues May-mid-June; also mid-Oct-late Dec, mid-Feb-early May. Dinner $19-$32. Service bar. Reservations required. Outdoor dining. Cr cds: A, DS, MC, V.
D

★**WESTERN AVENUE GRILL.** *6410 Western Ave (49636). Phone 231/334-3362; fax 231/334-6378.* American menu. Hours: 11 am-9 pm. Closed Mon-Wed; Thanksgiving, Dec 25. Dinner $8.95-$22.95. Bar. Children's meals. Casual attire. Cr cds: MC, V.
D

Grand Haven (G-2)

See also Grand Rapids, Holland, Muskegon

Settled 1834 **Pop** 11,951 **Elev** 590 ft **Area code** 616 **Zip** 49417

Information Grand Haven/Spring Lake Area Visitors Bureau, One S Harbor Dr; 616/842-4910 or 800/303-4092

Web www.grandhavenchamber.org

Through this port city at the mouth of the Grand River flows a stream of produce for all the Midwest. The port has the largest charter fishing fleet on Lake Michigan and is also used for sportfishing, recreational boating, and as a Coast Guard base. Connecting the pier to downtown shops is a boardwalk and park.

What to See and Do

Grand Haven State Park. *1001 Harbor Ave. 1 mile SW. Phone 616/798-3711.* Almost 50 acres on Lake Michigan beach. Swimming, bathhouse, fishing; picnicking (shelter), playground, concession, camping. Standard fees. (Daily) **$$**

Harbor Trolleys. *Phone 616/842-3200.* Two different routes: Grand Haven trolley operates between downtown and state park; second trolley goes to Spring Lake. Transfer point at Chinook Pier. (Memorial Day-Labor Day, daily). **$**

Municipal Marina. *101 N Harbor Dr (49147). At foot of Washington St, downtown.* Phone 616/847-3478. Contains 57 transient slips; fish cleaning station; stores and restaurants; trolley stop.

Harbor Steamer. *301 N Harbor.* Phone 616/842-8950. Stern-wheel paddleboat cruises to Spring Lake; scenic views, narrated by captain. (Mid-May-Sept, daily)

Musical Fountain. *1 N Harbor St. Dewey Hill.* Phone 616/842-2550. Said to be the world's largest electronically controlled musical fountain; water, lights, and music are synchronized. Programs (Memorial Day-Labor Day, eves; May and rest of Sept, Fri and Sat only). Special Christmas nativity scene in Dec covering all of Dewey Hill.

Special Events

Coast Guard Festival. *310 S Harbor Dr.* Phone 888/207-2434. Includes a parade, carnival, craft exhibit, ship tours, pageant, and variety shows, fireworks. Late July-early Aug.

Great Lakes Kite Festival. *106 Washington Ave. Grand Haven State Park.* Phone 616/846-7501. May.

On the Waterfront Big Band Concert Series. *Phone 616/842-2550.* Wed evenings. July-Aug.

Polar Ice Cap Golf Tournament. *1 S Harbor Dr. Spring Lake.* Phone 800/303-4097. 18-hole, par-three golf game on ice. Late Jan.

Winterfest. *120 Washington Ave.* Phone 616/842-4499. Music, dance, parade, children's activities. Late Jan.

Motels/Motor Lodges

★ **BEST WESTERN.** *1525 S Beacon Blvd (49417).* Phone 616/842-4720; toll-free 800/780-7234; fax 616/847-7821. www.bestwestern.com. 101 rooms. D $62-$130; each additional $4; under 12 free. Check-out 11 am. TV; cable (premium). Pool. Cross-country ski 8 miles. Free airport transportation. Cr cds: A, C, D, DS, MC, V.

★ **DAYS INN.** *1500 S Beacon Blvd (49417).* Phone 616/842-1999; toll-free 800/547-1855; fax 616/842-3892. www.daysinn.com. 100 rooms, 2 story. May-early Sept: S, D $69-$110; each additional $6; lower rates rest of year. Crib free. TV; cable. Indoor pool; whirlpool. Restaurant 8 am-10 pm; Sun 10:30 am-2 pm. Room service. Bar noon-midnight. Check-out noon. Coin laundry. Meeting rooms. Business services available. Downhill ski 2 miles; cross-country ski 6 miles. Health club privileges. Game room. Cr cds: A, C, D, DS, JCB, MC, V.

★ **FOUNTAIN INN.** *1010 S Beacon Blvd (49417).* Phone 616/846-1800; toll-free 800/745-8660; fax 616/846-9287. 47 rooms, 2 story. Mid-May-Labor Day: S, D $49.95-$89.95;

each additional $5; higher rates special events; lower rates rest of year. TV; cable. Complimentary continental breakfast. Restaurant nearby. Check-out 11 am. Meeting rooms. Cross-country ski 3 miles. Cr cds: A, DS, MC, V.

B&B/Small Inns

★ ★ **HARBOR HOUSE INN.** *114 S Harbor Dr (49417).* Phone 616/846-0610; fax 616/846-0530. 17 rooms, 3 story. Closed Dec 24, 25. Complimentary continental breakfast. Check-out 11 am, check-in 2 pm. TV in sitting room; cable. Health club privileges. Game room. Early American décor. Totally nonsmoking. Cr cds: A, MC, V.

★ ★ **THE ROYAL PONTALUNA BED & BREAKFAST.** *1870 Pontaluna Rd (49456).* Phone 231/798-7271; toll-free 800/856-3545; fax 616/798-3352. www.bbonline.com/mi/pontaluna. 5 rooms, 2 story. No room phones. May-Sept: S, D $119-$169; each additional $25; lower rates rest of year. TV; cable (premium), VCR (movies). Indoor pool; whirlpool, sauna. Complimentary continental breakfast. Restaurant nearby. Check-out 11 am, check-in 4 pm. Lighted tennis. Cross-country ski on site. Recreation room. Totally nonsmoking. Cr cds: A, MC, V.

Grand Marais (B-2)

Pop 350 **Elev** 640 ft **Area code** 906 **Zip** 49839

Information Chamber of Commerce, PO Box 139; 906/494-2447

Web www.grandmaraismichigan.com

On the shore of Lake Superior, Grand Marais has a harbor with marina and is surrounded by cool, clear lakes, trout streams, and agate beaches. In the winter, there is snowmobiling and cross-country skiing.

What to See and Do

Pictured Rocks National Lakeshore. *Phone 906/387-3700.* This scenic stretch of shoreline begins at the western edge of Grand Marais and continues west to Munising (See also). Recreational opportunities include swimming, fishing, hiking, hunting, rock climbing, cross-country skiing, and snowmobiling.

Special Events

500-Miler Snowmobile Run. *Downtown Grand Marais.* Phone 906/494-2447. Mid-Jan.

Music and Arts Festival. *Downtown Grand Marais. Phone 906/494-2447.* Second weekend Aug.

Motel/Motor Lodge

★ ★ **WELKER'S LODGE.** *Canal St (49839). Phone 906/494-2361; fax 906/494-2371.* 41 rooms, 1-2 story, 9 kitchen cottages. Some A/C. Some room phones. S $35-$47; D $48-$57; each additional $5; kitchen cottages $235-$325/wk. Crib $5. Pet accepted. Check-out 11 am, cottages 10 am. TV; cable (premium), VCR available (movies $5). Coin laundry. Restaurant 7:30 am-8:30 pm. Bar. Playground. Sauna. Indoor pool, whirlpool. Tennis. Lawn games. Meeting room, business services. On Lake Superior; private beach. Cr cds: A, DS, MC, V.

Grand Rapids (H-2)

See also Holland, Muskegon

Settled 1826 **Pop** 189,126 **Elev** 657 ft **Area code** 616

Information Grand Rapids/Kent County Convention & Visitors Bureau, 140 Monroe Center NW, Suite 300, 49503; 616/459-8287 or 800/678-9859

Web www.grcvb.org

Grand Rapids, a widely known furniture center and convention city, is located on the site where Louis Campau established a Native American trading post in 1826. The city derives its name from the rapids in the Grand River, which flows through the heart of the city. There are 50 parks here, totalling 1,270 acres. Calvin College and Calvin Seminary (1876) are located here; several other colleges are in the area.

Thirty-eighth president Gerald R. Ford was raised in Grand Rapids and represented the Fifth Congressional District in Michigan from 1948-1973, when he became the nation's vice president.

What to See and Do

Berlin Raceway. *3411 Leonard St NW (49504). Phone 616/677-1140.* Late-model stock car, sportsman stock car, and super stock car racing. (May-Sept, Fri-Sun)

Blandford Nature Center. *1715 Hillburn Ave NW. Phone 616/453-6192.* More than 140 acres of woods, fields, and ponds with self-guiding trails; guided tours (fee); interpretive center has exhibits, live animals; furnished pioneer garden; one-room schoolhouse. (Mon-Fri, also Sat and Sun afternoons; closed holidays) **FREE**

Cannonsburg. *6800 Cannonsburg Rd, 10 miles NE via US 131, W River Dr. Phone 616/874-6711 or 800/253-8748 (IL, IN, OH) for snow conditions.* Quad, triple, double chairlift, two T-bars, 8 rope tows. Longest run approximately 1/3 mile; vertical drop 250 ft. Patrol, school, rentals, snowmaking; nursery, cafeteria, bar. (Thanksgiving-mid-Mar, daily) **$$$$$**

Fish Ladder. *Sixth St Dam.* A unique fish ladder for watching salmon leap the rapids of the Grand River during spawning season.

⭐ **Frederik Meijer Gardens and Sculpture Park.** *3411 Bradford NE. Phone 616/957-1580.* Botanic garden and sculpture park includes 15,000-square-foot glass conservatory, desert garden, exotic indoor and outdoor gardens, more than 60 bronze works in sculpture park. Also outdoor nature trails and tram tour. Gift shop, restaurant. (Daily; closed Jan 1, Dec 25) **$$$**

⭐ **Gerald R. Ford Museum.** *303 Pearl St NW. Phone 616/451-9263.* A 28-minute introductory film on Ford; reproduction of the White House Oval Office; educational exhibits on the US House of Representatives and the presidency; original burglar tools used in the Watergate break-in. (Daily; closed Jan 1, Thanksgiving, Dec 25) **$$**

Grand Rapids Art Museum. *155 Division St N. Phone 616/831-1000.* Collections include Renaissance, German Expressionist, French, and American paintings; graphics and a children's gallery augmented by special traveling exhibitions. (Tues-Sun; closed holidays) **$$**

John Ball Zoo. *1300 W Fulton St. Phone 616/336-4300.* Located in 100-acre park, zoo features more than 700 animals, Living Shores Aquarium, African Forest exhibit, and children's zoo. (Daily; closed Dec 25) **$$**

La Grande Vitesse. *County Building, downtown.* This 42-ton stabile was created by Alexander Calder.

Meyer May House. *450 Madison St SE. Phone 616/246-4821.* (1908) Frank Lloyd Wright house from the late prairie period. Authentically restored with all architect-designed furniture, leaded-glass windows, lighting fixtures, rugs, and textiles. Tours begin at visitor center, 442 Madison St SE. (Tues, Thurs, Sun; schedule varies) **FREE**

Pando. *8076 Belding Rd NE, 12 miles NE on MI 44, in Rockford. Phone 616/874-8343.* Six rope tows, seven lighted runs; patrol, school, rentals, grooming equipment, snowmaking; cafeteria. Vertical drop 125 feet. (Dec-Mar, daily) Seven miles of cross-country trails; three miles of lighted trails, track-setting equipment; rentals. Night skiing. **$$$$**

The Public Museum of Grand Rapids. *272 Pearl St NW. Phone 616/456-3997 or 616/456-3663 (planetarium).* Located in the Van Andel Museum Center; exhibits of interactive history and natural science, include mammals, birds, furniture, Native American artifacts, re-creation of 1890s Grand Rapids street scene and 1928 carousel. Chaffee Planetarium offers sky shows and laser light shows (fee). (Daily; closed Jan 1, Easter, Dec 25) **$$**

Special Events

Community Circle Theater. *1300 W Fulton St. Phone 616/456-6656.* John Ball Park Pavilion; mid-May-Sept.

Festival. *Calder Plaza. Phone 616/459-2787.* Arts and crafts shows, entertainment, international foods. First full weekend June.

Motels/Motor Lodges

★ **AMERIHOST INN.** *2171 Holton Court (49544). Phone 616/791-8500; fax 616/791-8630.* 60 rooms, 2 story. D $63-$78; each additional $8; under 17 free. Complimentary continental breakfast. Check-out noon. TV; cable (premium). Exercise equipment, sauna. Indoor pool, whirlpool. Downhill, cross-country ski 15 miles. Cr cds: A, C, D, DS, MC, V.

[icons]

★ **BEST WESTERN GRANDVILLE INN.** *3425 Fairlane Ave (49418). Phone 616/532-3222; toll-free 800/237-8737; fax 616/532-4959. www.bestwestern.com.* 82 rooms, 2 story. D $69-$120; each additional $5; under 12 free. Complimentary continental breakfast. Check-out 11 am. TV; cable (premium). Laundry services. Game room. Indoor pool. Indoor pool. Downhill ski 20 miles, cross-country ski 10 miles. Adjacent to Grand Village Mall. Cr cds: A, C, D, DS, MC, V.

[icons]

★ ★ **BEST WESTERN MIDWAY HOTEL.** *4101 SE 28th St (49512). Phone 616/942-2550; toll-free 888/280-0081; fax 616/942-2446. www.bestwestern.com.* 146 rooms, 3 story. S $85; D $95; each additional $10; under 18 free; wkend, holiday rates. Crib free. TV; cable (premium). Indoor pool; whirlpool, poolside service. Complimentary full breakfast. Complimentary coffee in rooms. Restaurant 7 am-2 pm, 5-10 pm; Sun 6:30 am-2 pm, 5-9 pm. Room service. Bar noon-midnight; Fri, Sat to 2 am. Check-out noon. Meeting rooms. Business services available. Bellhops. Valet service. Free airport transportation. Downhill ski 14 miles; cross-country ski 4 miles. Exercise equipment; sauna. Health club privileges. Game room. Recreation room. Some refrigerators. Picnic tables. Cr cds: A, C, D, DS, MC, V.

[icons]

★ **COMFORT INN.** *4155 SE 28th St (49512). Phone 616/957-2080; toll-free 800/638-7949; fax 616/957-9712. www.comfortinn.com.* 109 rooms, 3 story. S, D $89; suites $73; under 18 free; weekend rates. Crib free. TV; cable (premium). Complimentary continental breakfast. Restaurant adjacent 6 am-10 pm. Check-out noon. Meeting room. Business services available. Valet service. Downhill ski 15 miles; cross-country ski 4 miles. Some balconies. Cr cds: A, C, D, DS, JCB, MC, V.

[icons]

★★ **COUNTRY HEARTH INN.** *2985 SE Kraft Ave (49512). Phone 616/940-1777; fax 616/940-9809.* 40 suites, 2 story. S, D $85. Crib free. Pet accepted. Complimentary bkfst, coffee in rooms. Check-out noon. TV; cable (premium), VCR (free movies). Refrigerators. Valet service. Restaurant nearby. Business services available. Cr cds: A, C, D, DS, MC, V.

[icons]

★ **DAYS INN.** *310 NW Pearl St (49504). Phone 616/235-7611; toll-free 800/329-7466; fax 616/235-1995. www.daysinn.com.* 175 units, 8 story. S, D $49-$96; each additional $7; suites $74-$96; under 16 free; ski plans; higher rates special events. Crib free. TV; cable (premium), VCR available. Indoor pool; whirlpool. Restaurant 6 am-10 pm; weekend hours vary. Room service. Bar 11-1 am; Sun to 10 pm. Check-out 11 am. Meeting rooms. Business services available. Bellhops. Valet service. Downhill/cross-country ski 12 miles. Exercise equipment. Refrigerator in suites. Cr cds: A, C, D, DS, ER, JCB, MC, V.

[icons]

★ **EXEL INN GRAND RAPIDS.** *4855 28th St SE (49512). Phone 616/957-3000; toll-free 800/367-3935; fax 616/957-0194. www.exelinns.com.* 110 rooms, 2 story. S $36.99-$38.99; D $41.99-$47.99; each additional $4; under 18 free. Crib free. Pet accepted. TV. Complimentary continental breakfast. Check-out noon. Downhill ski 15 miles; cross-country ski 4 miles. Cr cds: A, C, D, DS, MC, V.

[icons]

★ **HAMPTON INN.** *4981 S 28th St (49512). Phone 616/956-9304; toll-free 800/426-7866; fax 616/956-6617. www.hamptoninn.com.* 120 rooms, 2 story. S $72; D $79; each additional $7; under 18 free. Crib free. Pet accepted. TV; cable (premium). Heated pool. Complimentary continental breakfast. Coffee in rooms. Restaurant adjacent 11 am-10 pm. Check-out noon. Meeting room. Business services available. Valet service. Downhill ski 15 miles; cross-country ski 4 miles. Exercise equipment. Cr cds: A, C, D, DS, MC, V.

[icons]

★ **HOLIDAY INN.** *255 SW 28th St (49548). Phone 616/241-6444; toll-free 800/465-4329; fax 616/241-1807. www.holiday-inn.com.* 156 rooms, 5 story. D $75; under 19 free. Check-out noon. TV; cable (premium), VCR available. In-room modem link. Restaurant, bar, room service. Health club privileges. Exercise equipment, sauna. Game room. 2 pools, 1 indoor, whirlpool, poolside service. Downhill ski 12 miles, cross-country ski 3 miles. Cr cds: A, C, D, DS, JCB, MC, V.

[icons]

★ **LEXINGTON HOTEL SUITES.** *5401 SE 28th Ct (49546). Phone 616/940-8100; toll-free 800/441-9628; fax 616/940-0914. www.lexingtonsuites.com.* 121 suites, 3 story. D $87-$107; each additional $8; under 18 free. Complimentary continental breakfast. Check-out noon. TV; cable (premium). Laundry services. Exercise equipment. Indoor pool, whirlpool. Downhill ski 15 miles, cross-country ski 5 miles. Free airport transportation. Cr cds: A, MC, V.

★ **QUALITY INN TERRACE CLUB.** *4495 SE 28th St (49512). Phone 616/956-8080; fax 616/956-0619. www.qualityinn.com.* 126 rooms, 3 story. D $79-$109; each additional $10; under 18 free; ski, golf plans. Complimentary full breakfast. Check-out noon. TV; cable (premium). In-room modem link. Laundry services. Health club privileges. Exercise equipment. Indoor pool, whirlpool. Downhill ski 15 miles, cross-country ski 3 miles. Free airport transportation. Cr cds: A, C, D, DS, ER, JCB, MC, V.

★★ **RADISSON HOTEL.** *3333 SE 28th St (49512). Phone 616/949-9222; fax 616/949-3841. www.radisson.com.* 200 rooms, 5 story. S, D $85; family, weekend rates. Crib free. TV; cable (premium). Indoor pool; whirlpool, sauna, poolside service. Restaurant 6:30 am-10 pm; Fri to 11 pm; Sat 7 am-11 pm; Sun 7 am-10 pm. Room service. Bar 4 pm-midnight. Check-out noon. Meeting rooms. Business services available. Bellhops. Valet service. Free airport transportation. Downhill ski 15 miles; cross-country ski 3 miles. Recreation room. Putting green. Cr cds: A, C, D, DS, ER, JCB, MC, V.

★ **RED ROOF INN.** *5131 SE 28th St (49512). Phone 616/942-0800; toll-free 800/843-7663; fax 616/942-8341. www.redroof.com.* 107 rooms, 2 story. S $40.99-$47.99; D $46.99-$54.99; 1st additional $6; under 18 free. Crib free. Pet accepted. TV; cable (premium). Complimentary coffee in lobby. Restaurant adjacent 6 am-11 pm; Fri, Sat open 24 hrs; Sun to 10 pm. Check-out noon. Business services available. Downhill ski 15 miles; cross-country ski 5 miles. Cr cds: A, C, D, DS, MC, V.

★ **SWAN INN.** *5182 NW Alpine Ave (49321). Phone 616/784-1224; toll-free 800/875-7926; fax 616/784-6565.* 38 rooms, 1-2 story, 4 kitchens S $40-$50; D, kitchen units $48-$65; each additional $2; under 12 free; weekly rates. Crib free. TV; cable (premium). Heated pool. Restaurant 6 am-10 pm; Sun to 4 pm. Room service. Check-out 11:30 am. Coin laundry. Meeting rooms. Business services available. Downhill/cross-country ski 12 miles. Cr cds: A, MC, V.

★ **TRAVELODGE HOTEL & CONFERENCE CENTER.** *4041 Cascade Rd SE (49546). Phone 616/949-8800; toll-free 800/578-7878; fax 616/949-4303. www.travelodge.com.* 149 rooms, 2 story. S, D $70; each additional $10; suites $180; family, weekend rates. Crib free. TV; cable (premium). Indoor/outdoor pool; sauna. Restaurant 6:30 am-10 pm; Fri, Sat to 11 pm. Room service. Bar 4 pm-midnight; Fri, Sat to 1 am; entertainment Fri, Sat. Check-out 11 am. Meeting rooms. Business services available. Bellhops. Valet service. Sundries. Free airport transportation. Lighted tennis. Downhill/cross-country ski 4 miles. Lawn games. Private patios, balconies. Cr cds: A, C, D, DS, ER, JCB, MC, V.

Hotels

★★★ **AMWAY GRAND PLAZA.** *187 Monroe Ave NW (49503). Phone 616/774-2000; toll-free 800/253-3590; fax 616/776-6489. www.amwaygrand.com.* Opened in 1913, the Amway Grand Plaza Hotel is a cherished Michigan landmark. Fronting the Grand River, the hotel is conveniently located in the heart of Grand Rapids' business and entertainment district. Exuding the elegance of the early 1900s, the hotel's lobby is topped by a magnificent golf-leaf ceiling. The guest rooms are beautifully appointed in traditional or contemporary décor, the Tower Rooms featuring sweeping views of the river and city. Fitness and business centers are provided for guests' convenience. From dinner and dancing atop the tower at Cygnus and informal dining at the Garden Court Lounge to family dining with a river view at Bentham's and casual fare at GP Sports, this hotel has it all. The nine restaurants and lounges satisfy demanding appetites, but the 1913 Room, with its fine continental cuisine, is the jewel in the crown. 682 rooms, 29 story. S, D $115-$215 ; each additional $15; suites $315-$465; under 12 free; weekend rates. Check-out noon. TV; cable (premium), VCR available. Restaurant. Bars 11:30-2 am; Sun from noon; entertainment Mon-Sat. Room service 24 hours. Exercise room; sauna. Massage. Indoor pool; whirlpool, poolside service. Tennis. Downhill ski 15 miles; cross-country ski 10 miles. Garage parking $9, valet $13. Airport transportation $10. Concierge. Luxury level. Cr cds: A, C, D, DS, MC, V.

★★★ **CROWNE PLAZA HOTEL.** *5700 28th St SE (49546). Phone 616/957-1770; toll-free 800/957-9575; fax 616/957-0629. www.crowneplaza.com/grr-airport.* Located only 3 miles from the Kent County International Airport and minutes from the largest shopping center in West Michigan, this hotel is very convenient. It offers guests free passes to the nearby country and athletic clubs. 320 rooms, 5 story. S, D $87-$163; suites $250; under 18 free; weekend packages. Crib free. Check-out noon.

TV; cable (premium), VCR available (movies). In-room modem link. Some private patios, balconies. Refrigerators in suites. Coffee in rooms. Valet service. Coin laundry. Restaurant 6:30 am-10 pm. Bar 11-2 am; Sun noon-midnight. Room service. Exercise equipment, sauna. 2 pools, 1 heated indoor, whirlpool, poolside service. 18-hole golf privileges, greens fee $33, pro, putting green. Tennis privileges. Downhill ski 14 miles, cross-country ski 5 miles. Free self and valet parking. Free airport transportation. Meeting rooms, business center. Concierge. Gift shop. Cr cds: A, C, D, DS, ER, JCB, MC, V.

★ ★ ★ **HILTON GRAND RAPIDS AIRPORT.** *4747 SE 28th St SE (49512). Phone 616/957-0100; toll-free 877/ 944-5866; fax 616/957-2977. www.hilton.com/GRRHIHF/ index.html.* Located five minutes from the Kent County International Airport, this hotel offers guests large rooms with oversized beds, full room service, an indoor heated pool and health club, a complimentary airport shuttle service and more. 224 rooms, 4 story. S, D $72-$152; each additional $10; suites $165-$375; family, ski, weekend rates. Crib free. TV; cable (premium). Heated indoor pool; whirlpool; poolside service. Restaurant 6:30 am-11 pm; Sat, Sun from 7 am. Room service. Bar 11-2 am; entertainment Tues-Sat. Coffee in rooms. Check-out noon. Meeting rooms. Business services available. In-room modem link. Bellhops. Valet service. Free 24-hour airport transportation. Downhill ski 14 miles; cross-country ski 4 miles. Exercise equipment; sauna. Health club privileges. Game room. Some refrigerators. Cr cds: A, C, D, DS, ER, JCB, MC, V.

Extended Stay

★ ★ **RESIDENCE INN BY MARRIOTT.** *2701 E Beltline Ave SE (49546). Phone 616/957-8111; fax 616/957-3699. www.residenceinn.com.* 96 kitchen suites, 2 story. Suites $102-$135; under 12 free. Crib free. Pet accepted, some restrictions; $60 and $6/day. TV; cable (premium), VCR available. Heated pool; whirlpool. Complimentary continental breakfast. Restaurant adjacent 11-2 am. Check-out noon. Coin laundry. Meeting room. Business services available. Valet service. Free airport transportation. Downhill ski 15 miles; cross-country ski 5 miles. Exercise equipment. Health club privileges. Private patios; some balconies. Picnic tables, grills. Cr cds: A, C, D, DS, ER, JCB, MC, V.

Restaurants

★ ★ **ARNIE'S.** *3561 SE 28th St (49512). Phone 616/ 956-7901; fax 616/956-2138.* American menu. Hours: 7 am-10:30 pm; Sat from 8 am; Sun 9 am-3 pm. Closed some major holidays. Dinner $7.99-$9.99. Piano bar. Child's menu. Cr cds: A, MC, V.

★ ★ **DUBA'S.** *420 E Beltline NE (49506). Phone 616/ 949-1011; fax 616/949-4462.* American menu. Hours: 11 am-10 pm; Fri, Sat to 11 pm. Closed Sun; holidays. Dinner $22-$26. Bar. Child's menu. Casual attire. Cr cds: A, MC, V.

★ ★ ★ **GIBSON'S.** *1033 Lake Dr (49506). Phone 616/ 774-8535; fax 616/774-9102.* Housed in an old monastery, this romantic destination sits majestically on a wooded, parklike property. Visitors are attracted with fine food and many, uniquely decorated dining spaces. Continental menu. Hours: 11:30 am-11 pm; Sat from 5 pm. Closed July 4, Thanksgiving, Dec 25; also Sun from June-Aug. Dinner $18.75-$29.95. Bar 11:30-1 am. Piano/piano bar. Children's meals. In former Franciscan friary (1860s). Casual attire. Patio dining. Cr cds: A, D, DS, MC, V.

★ **JOHN BRANN'S STEAKHOUSE.** *5510 SE 28th St (49512). Phone 616/285-7800; fax 616/285-5966.* Hours: 11 am-10 pm; Fri, Sat to 11 pm; Sun 10 am-9 pm; early-bird dinner Sun-Thurs 4-8 pm; Sun brunch to 2:30 pm. Closed Thanksgiving, Dec 25. Reservations accepted. Bar to 2 am. Lunch $5.99-$8.99, dinner $7.99-$15.99. Sun brunch $8.99. Child's meals. Specializes in steak, prime rib. Salad bar. Family-owned. Cr cds: A, D, DS, MC, V.

★ ★ **PIETRO'S BACK DOOR PIZZERIA.** *2780 SE Birchcrest St (49506). Phone 616/452-3228; fax 616/452-0172. www.rcfc.com.* Northern Italian, American menu. Hours: 11:30 am-10 pm; Fri to 11 pm; Sat 3-11 pm; Sun noon-10 pm. Closed Thanksgiving, Dec 25. Dinner $7-$15. Bar. Child's menu. Casual attire. Outdoor dining. Cr cds: A, D, DS, MC, V.

★ ★ **SAYFEE'S.** *3555 SE Lake Eastbrook Blvd (49546). Phone 616/949-5750; fax 616/949-1446.* Continental menu. Hours: 11 am-11 pm. Closed Sun except Mother's Day, Easter; some major holidays. Dinner $9.95-$24.95. Bar. Band Tues-Sat. Child's menu. Casual attire. Valet parking. Outdoor dining. Cr cds: A, D, DS, MC, V.

★ ★ **SCHNITZELBANK.** *342 SE Jefferson Ave (49503). Phone 616/459-9527; fax 616/459-9272. www.schnitzel.kvi.net.* German, American menu. Hours: 11 am-8 pm; Fri to 9 pm; Sat 4:30-9 pm. Closed Sun; holidays. Dinner $9.95-$19.95. Bar. Children's meals. Casual attire. Totally nonsmoking. Cr cds: A, DS, MC, V.

Grayling (E-3)

See also Houghton Lake

Pop 1,944 **Elev** 1,137 ft **Area code** 517 **Zip** 49738

Information Grayling Area Visitors Council, PO Box 406; 800/937-8837

Web www.grayling-mi.com

What to See and Do

Canoe trips. There are many canoe liveries in the area, with trip itineraries for the Manistee and Au Sable rivers. Contact Grayling Area Visitors Council for details.

Hartwick Pines State Park. *4216 Ranger Rd. 7 miles NE on MI 93. Phone 517/348-7068.* Approximately 9,700 acres. Fishing for trout, perch, and largemouth bass; hunting, marked cross-country ski trails, picnicking, playground, concession, camping. Three-dimensional exhibits in interpretive center tell the story of the white pine. Log memorial building, lumberman's museum near virgin pine forest; "Chapel in the Pines." Naturalist. Standard fees. (Daily) **$$**

Skyline Ski Area. *4020 Skyline Rd. 2 miles S off I-75, exit 251. Phone 517/275-5445.* Double chairlift, five rope tows; patrol, school, rentals; cafeteria, ski shop. Longest run approximately 1/2 mile; vertical drop 210 feet. (Mid-Dec-Mar, daily) **$$$$$**

Special Events

Au Sable River Festival. *213 N James St (49738). Phone 800/937-8837.* Arts and crafts, parade, car show. Last full weekend July.

Winter Wolf Festival. *213 N James St (49738). Phone 800/937-8837.* Early Feb.

Motels/Motor Lodges

★★**HOLIDAY INN.** *2650 I-75 Business Loop (49738). Phone 517/348-7611; toll-free 800/292-9095; fax 517/348-7984. www.holiday-inn.com.* 151 rooms, 2 story. July-Aug: S, D $69-$119; each additional $6; suites $150-$175; under 19 free; lower rates rest of year. Pet accepted. TV; cable (premium), VCR available. Indoor pool; wading pool, whirlpool, poolside service. Playground. Restaurant 6 am-2 pm, 5-10 pm; Sun 6 am-9 pm. Room service. Bar 11-2 am; entertainment. Check-out 11 am. Meeting rooms. Business services available. Bellhops. Valet service. Sundries. Airport, bus depot transportation. Downhill ski 5 miles; cross-country ski on site. Game room. Lawn games. Exercise equipment; sauna. Picnic tables. On wooded property. Some refrigerators. Cr cds: A, C, D, DS, JCB, MC, V.

★**HOSPITALITY HOUSE.** *1232 I-75 Business Loop (49738). Phone 517/348-8900; toll-free 800/722-4151; fax 517/348-6509.* 80 rooms, 1-2 story. Memorial Day-Labor Day, weekends: S, D $65-$92; each additional $5; suites $125-$175; under 16 free; lower rates rest of year. Crib free. TV; cable (premium), VCR available (movies $4). Indoor pool; whirlpool. Restaurant 6:30 am-2 pm, 5-9 pm. Room service. Check-out 11 am. Business services available. Valet service. Free airport, bus depot transportation. Downhill/cross-country ski 3 miles. Game room. Refrigerators, microwaves. Cr cds: A, C, D, DS, MC, V.

★**NORTH COUNTRY LODGE.** *615 I-75 Business Loop (49738). Phone 517/348-8471; toll-free 800/475-6300; fax 517/348-6114. www.grayling-mi.com/northcountrylodge.* 24 rooms, 8 kitchens Mid-June-Labor Day, winter weekends, Christmas week: S $40-$50; D $45-$60; each additional $5; kitchen units $55-$70; suite $140-$160; family, weekly rates; lower rates rest of year. Crib free. Pet accepted. TV; cable. Restaurant nearby. Check-out 11 am. Free airport, bus depot transportation. Downhill/cross-country ski 3 miles. Cr cds: A, C, D, DS, MC, V.

★**POINTE NORTH OF GRAYLING MOTEL.** *1024 S I-75 Business Loop N (49738). Phone 517/348-5950.* 21 rooms. Mid-June-Labor Day, Christmas week, winter weekends: S $40-$50; D $45-$65; each additional $5; kitchen unit $65-$85; lower rates rest of year. TV; cable (premium). Check-out 10 am. Downhill ski 3 miles; cross-country ski 2 miles. Refrigerators, microwaves. Picnic table, grill. Cr cds: A, C, D, DS, MC, V.

★**SUPER 8 MOTEL.** *5828 Nelson A Miles Pkwy (49738). Phone 517/348-8888; fax 517/348-2030. www.super8.com.* 61 rooms, 2 story. Apr-Sept: S $46.69; D $55.88-$67.88; each additional $4; under 12 free; lower rates rest of year. TV; cable (premuim). Pet accepted. Complimentary continental breakfast. Restaurant adjacent open 24 hours. Check-out 11 am. Meeting room. Coin laundry. Downhill ski 1 mile; cross-country ski 6 miles. Lawn games. Cr cds: A, C, D, DS, MC, V.

Hancock (A-6)

See also Copper Harbor, Houghton

Pop 4,547 **Elev** 686 ft **Area code** 906 **Zip** 49930

Information Keweenaw Peninsula Chamber of Commerce, 326 Shelden Ave, PO Box 336, Houghton 49931; 906/482-5240 or 800/338-7982

Web www.portup.com/snow

Named for John Hancock, the town is the home of Suomi College (1896), the only Finnish college in the United States.

What to See and Do

Finnish-American Heritage Center. *601 Quincy St. Phone 906/487-7367.* Center houses the Finnish-American Historical Archives, a museum, theater, art gallery, and the Finnish-American Family History Center. (Mon-Fri; closed holidays) Special events evenings and weekends. Located on the campus of Suomi College, **FREE**

Special Event

Houghton County Fair. *North Lincoln Rd & 12th Ave N. Fairgrounds. Phone 906/482-6200.* Late Aug.

Motel/Motor Lodge

★ **BEST WESTERN COPPER CROWN MOTEL.** *235 Hancock Ave (49930). Phone 906/482-6111; toll-free 800/528-1234; fax 906/482-0185. www.bestwestern.com.* 47 rooms, 2 story. D $50-$60; each additional $3; under 12 free. Check-out 11 am. TV; cable (premium). Saunas. Indoor pool, whirlpool. Downhill, cross-country ski 1 miles. Cr cds: A, C, D, DS, MC, V.

Harbor Springs (D-3)

See also Petoskey

Settled 1827 **Pop** 1,540 **Elev** 600 ft **Area code** 231 **Zip** 49740

Information Chamber of Commerce, 205 State St; 231/526-7999

Web www.harborsprings-mi.com

Known as a year-round vacation spot, Harbor Springs is a picturesque town on Little Traverse Bay.

What to See and Do

Andrew J. Blackbird Museum. *368 E Main St. Phone 231/526-7731.* Museum of the Ottawa; artifacts. (Memorial Day-Labor Day, daily; Sept-Oct, weekends) Special exhibits (fee). **$**

Boyne Highlands. *600 Highlands Dr. 4 1/2 miles NE off MI 119. Phone 231/526-2171 or 800/462-6963.* Four triple, four quad chairlifts, rope tow; patrol, school, rentals, snowmaking; cafeteria, restaurant, bar, nursery, lodge (see RESORT). (Thanksgiving weekend-mid-Apr, daily) Weekend plan. Cross-country trails (4 miles); rentals. **$$$$**

Nub's Nob. *500 Nub's Nob Rd, 5 miles. Phone 231/526-2131 or 800/SKI-NUBS.* Two double, three quad, three triple chairlifts; patrol, school, rentals, snowmaking; cafeteria, bar. Longest run one mile; vertical drop 427 feet. (Thanksgiving-Easter, daily) Half-day rates. Cross-country trails (same seasons, hours as downhill skiing); night skiing (5 nights/week). **$$$$**

Shore Drive. *Along MI 119.* One of the most scenic drives in the state. Passes through Devil's Elbow and Springs area, said to be haunted by an evil spirit.

Motels/Motor Lodges

★ **BIRCHWOOD INN.** *7077 S Lake Shore Dr (49740). Phone 231/526-2151; toll-free 800/530-9955; fax 231/526-2108.* 48 rooms, 1-2 story, 2 suites in lodge. Mid-June-mid-Oct: S, D, suites $55-$99; each additional $10; kitchen units $105-$215; lower rates rest of year. Crib $10. TV; cable. Heated pool. Playground. Complimentary continental breakfast. Restaurant adjacent 5:30-10 pm. Check-out 11 am. Meeting rooms. Business services available. Tennis. Downhill ski 8 miles; cross-country ski 1 mile. Refrigerators available. Private patios, balconies. Cr cds: MC, V.

★ **COLONIAL INN.** *210 Artesian Ave (49740). Phone 231/526-2111; fax 231/526-5458. www.harborsprings.com.* 45 rooms, 2 story. D $108-$158. Complimentary continental breakfast (July-Aug). Check-out 11 am. TV; cable. Some fireplaces. Bar. Pool, whirlpool. Built 1894; landscaped grounds. Cr cds: MC, V.

★ **HARBOR SPRINGS COTTAGE INN.** *Phone 231/526-5431; fax 231/526-8094.* 21 rooms, 2 A/C, 4 kitchens Mid-June-Labor Day: S $58-$90; D $68-$100; kitchen units $100; under 14 free; lower rates rest of year. Crib $5. Pet accepted. TV; cable. Complimentary continental breakfast. Check-out 11 am. Downhill/cross-country ski 5 miles. Guest bicycles, sailboats. Little Traverse Bay opposite. Cr cds: A, D, DS, MC, V.

Resort

★★ **BOYNE HIGHLANDS RESORT.** *600 Highlands Dr (49740). Phone 231/526-3000; toll-free 800/462-6963; fax 231/526-3100. www.boyne.com.* 228 rooms, 3 story, 195 condo units. June-Sept, Dec-Mar: D $119-$187; condo units $187; ski, golf plans; lower rates rest of year. Crib free. TV; cable. 4 heated pools; wading pool, whirlpool, poolside service. Children's activities, 4-10 yrs, summer. Dining room 7:30 am-10:30 pm. Room service. Bar 4 pm-2 am. Check-out 1 pm, check-in 5 pm. Coin laundry. Meeting rooms. Business center. Grocery 2 miles; package store 1 mile. Tennis. May-late-Oct: 18-hole golf, greens fee $39-$129, 2 driving ranges, 2 putting greens, 2 pro shops. Downhill/cross-country ski on site. Ice skating. Lawn games. Hiking. Game room. Gift shop. Entertainment. Exercise equipment; sauna, steam room. Massage (by appointment). Refrigerators. Some private patios, balconies. European atmosphere. On 6,000 acres. Cr cds: A, C, D, DS, MC, V.

B&B/Small Inn

★ ★ ★ **KIMBERLY COUNTRY ESTATE.** *2287 Bester Rd (49740). Phone 231/526-7646; fax 231/526-8054. www.kimberlycountryestate.com.* Just four minutes outside town, this Colonial plantation home is wrapped in pillared balconies overlooking the swimming pool and Wequetonsing Golf Course. Rooms have English country decor and four-poster beds and include evening wine reception and bedtime sherry and truffles. 6 rooms, 2 story. Children over 12 years only. Complimentary full breakfast. Check-out 11 am, check-in 2-6 pm. TV, VCR in library. Downhill/cross-country ski 5 miles. Some fireplaces, whirlpools. Heated pool. Totally nonsmoking. Cr cds: A, MC, V.

Restaurants

★ ★ **LEGS INN.** *Phone 231/526-2281; fax 231/526-2615. www.legsinn.com.* Polish, American menu. Hours: noon-9 pm; July-Labor Day noon-10 pm. Closed late-Oct-late-May. Dinner $11-$18. Bar. Entertainment Fri-Sun. No A/C. Child's menu. Outdoor dining. Totally nonsmoking. Cr cds: DS, MC, V.

★ **THE NEW YORK.** *101 State St (49740). Phone 231/526-1904; fax 231/526-6286. www.thenewyork.com.* Continental menu. Hours: 5-10 pm; Fri, Sat to 11 pm; Sun brunch Mothers Day-Labor Day. Closed Thanksgiving, Dec 25; also Apr and early Nov. Dinner $14.50-$24. Bar. Children's meals. Victorian-style former hotel building. Casual attire. Cr cds: A, MC, V.

★ ★ **STAFFORD'S PIER.** *102 Bay St (49740). Phone 231/526-6201; fax 231/526-2370. www.staffords.com.* American menu. Hours: 11:30 am-11 pm; Sun to 10 pm. Closed Dec 25. Dinner $9.95-$27.95. Bar. Entertainment Fri, Sat. Child's menu. Casual attire. Outdoor dining. Cr cds: A, DS, MC, V.

Harrison (F-3)

See also Houghton Lake

Pop 1,835 **Elev** 1,186 ft **Area code** 989 **Zip** 48625

Information Chamber of Commerce, 809 N 1st St, PO Box 682; 989/539-6011

Web www.harrisonchamber.com

What to See and Do

Snowsnake Mountain. *3407 Mannsiding Rd. 5 miles S on US 27. Phone 517/539-6583.* Triple chairlift, five rope tows; patrol, school, rentals, snowmaking; snack bar. Longest run is 1/2 mile; vertical drop 210 feet. Night skiing. (Mid-Dec-mid-Mar, daily) Cross-country trails. **$$$$**

Wilson State Park. *910 First St. 1 mile N on Old US 27. Phone 517/539-3021.* Approximately 35 acres on the shore of Budd Lake. Swimming; fishing for largemouth bass, bluegill, perch; picnicking, playground, camping. Standard fees. **$$**

Special Events

Clare County Fair. *418 Fairlane St. Clare County Fairgrounds. Phone 989/539-9011.* Late July-early Aug.

Frostbite Open. *809 N 1st St. Phone 989/539-6011.* Winter golf tournament. Feb.

Holland (H-2)

See also Saugatuck

Settled 1847 **Pop** 30,745 **Elev** 610 ft **Area code** 616

Information Holland Area Chamber of Commerce, 272 E 8th St, PO Box 1888, 49422-1888; 616/392-2389 or Holland Convention and Visitors Bureau, 76 E 8th St; 616/394-0000 or 800/506-1299

Web www.holland.org

In 1847, a group of Dutch seeking religious freedom left the Netherlands and settled in this area because its sand dunes and fertile land reminded them of their homeland. Today much of the population is of Dutch descent. The town prides itself on being the center of Dutch culture in the United States. The city is located at the mouth of the Black River, on the shores of Lake Macatawa, and has developed a resort colony along the shores of lakes Macatawa and Michigan.

What to See and Do

Cappon House. *228 W 9th St. Phone 616/392-6740 or 616/392-9084.* (1874) Italianate house of first mayor of

Holland. Original furnishings, millwork. (May-Sept, Fri and Sat afternoons or by appt) **$$**

Dutch Village. *1 mile NE on US 31. Phone 616/396-1475.* Buildings of Dutch architecture; canals, windmills, tulips, street organs, Dutch dancing; animals, movies, rides; wooden shoe carving and other crafts; museum, tours; restaurant. (Mid-Apr-late Oct, daily).

Holland Museum. *31 W 10th St. Phone 616/392-9084 or 616/392-1362.* Features decorative arts from the Netherlands Collection, the Volendam Room. Permanent and changing exhibits pertaining to local history. Gift shop. (Mon, Wed-Sun; closed holidays) **$$**

Holland State Park. *2215 Ottawa Beach Rd. 7 miles W off US 31. Phone 616/399-9390.* This 143-acre park includes a 1/4 mile beach on Lake Michigan. Swimming, bathhouse, boating (launch), fishing; picnicking, playground, concessions, camping. Standard fees. **$$**

Hope College. *141 E 12th St. Between College and Columbia aves. Phone 616/392-5111.* (1866) 2,550 students. Liberal arts. Tours of campus. Theater series (July-Aug, fee; phone 616/395-7000).

Veldheer's Tulip Gardens and Deklomp Wooden Shoe & Delftware Factory. *12755 Quincy St. Phone 616/399-1900.* The only Delftware factory in the US; factory tours (free). Visitors can try on wooden shoes and talk to the artisans who made them. (Daily)

⭐ **Windmill Island.** *7th St and Lincoln. Phone 616/836-1490.* The 225-year-old windmill, "De Zwaan" (the swan), is the only operating imported Dutch windmill in the US. It was relocated here by special permission of the Dutch government, as the remaining windmills in the Netherlands are considered historic monuments. It is still used today to grind flour. The imported carousel, "Draaimolen," offers free rides. (May-Aug, daily; Labor Day-Oct, limited hrs) **$$** Included

> **Little Netherlands.** *7th & Lincoln. Phone 616/355-1030.* A miniature reproduction of old Holland; 20-minute film on Dutch windmills in the posthouse; klompen dancing in summer; exhibits, tulips. **$$**

Wooden Shoe Factory. *12755 Quincy. 447 Phone 616/396-6513.* Factory operations can be viewed by public (Mon-Sat). Also gift shop (daily; hours may be limited off-season). **$**

Special Event

Tulip Time Festival. *171 Lincoln Ave. Phone 800/822-2770.* A celebration of Dutch heritage: 1,800 klompen dancers, three parades, street scrubbing, Dutch markets, musical and professional entertainment, and millions of tulips. Eight days mid-May.

Motels/Motor Lodges

⭐ **COUNTRY INN BY CARLSON.** *12260 James St (49424). Phone 616/396-6677; fax 616/396-1197.* 116 rooms, 2 story. D $89-$99; each additional $5; under 18 free. Complimentary continental breakfast. Check-out noon. TV; cable; VCR available. Cross-country ski 5 miles. Country-style decor. Cr cds: A, D, DS, MC, V.

D ⊠ ⊠

⭐⭐ **HOLIDAY INN.** *650 E 24th St (49423). Phone 616/394-0111; toll-free 800/279-5286; fax 616/394-4832. www.holiday-inn.com.* 168 units, 4 story. May-Nov: S, D $109-$129; under 17 free; lower rates rest of year. Check-out noon. TV; cable (premium). In-room modem link. Patios, balconies. Refrigerator in suites. Coffee in rooms. Restaurant 6 am-10 pm. Bar 4 pm-2 am; entertainment Mon-Sat. Room service. Exercise equipment, sauna. Game room. Recreation room. Indoor pool. Cross-country ski 3 miles. Free airport transportation. Meeting rooms, business services. Cr cds: A, D, DS, JCB, MC, V.

D ⊠ ⊠ ⊠ ⊠ ⊠ ⊠ ⊠ SC

⭐ **SUPER 8 MOTEL.** *680 E 24th St (49423). Phone 616/396-8822; toll-free 800/800-8000; fax 616/396-2050. www.super8.com.* 68 rooms, 3 story, 6 suites. May-Labor Day: S $52.88; D $57.88; each additional $6; suites $85; under 12 free; weekend rates; lower rates rest of year. Crib free. TV; cable (premium). Complimentary coffee in lobby. Restaurant nearby. Check-out 11 am. Coin laundry. Business services available. In-room modem link. Valet service. Cross-country ski 3 miles. Cr cds: A, C, D, DS, MC, V.

D ⊠ ⊠ SC

B&B/Small Inns

⭐⭐ **DUTCH COLONIAL INN.** *560 Central Ave. Phone 616/396-3664; fax 616/396-0461. www.dutchcolonialinn.com.* 4 rooms, 1-3 story. Complimentary full breakfast. Check-out 11 am, check-in 3 pm. TV. Cross-country ski 3 miles. Some fireplaces. Built in 1928. Totally nonsmoking. Cr cds: A, DS, MC, V.

⊠

Restaurants

⭐ **84 EAST PASTA ETC.** *84 E 8th St (49423). Phone 616/396-8484; fax 616/393-8848.* American menu, Italian menu. Hours: 11 am-11 pm. Closed Sun; major holidays. Lunch A la carte entrees: $5-$7, dinner A la carte entrees: $6-$9. Bar. Child's meals. Casual décor. Cr cds: A, DS, MC, V.

D

★ ★ ★ **ALPENROSE.** *4 E 8th St (49423). Phone 616/393-2111; fax 616/393-0027. www.alpenroserestaurant.com.* Hours: 7:30 am-9 pm; Sun brunch 10 am-2 pm; summer hours vary. Closed Dec 25. Reservations accepted. Austrian, continental menu. Service bar. Extensive wine list. Lunch $5.95-$9.95, dinner $8.95-$18.95. Sun brunch $16.95. Child's meals. Specialties: chicken shortcake, Wiener schnitzel. Outdoor dining. Authentic Austrian-style dining. Totally nonsmoking. Cr cds: A, D, DS, MC, V.

D

★ **PEREDDIE'S.** *447 Washington Sq (49423). Phone 616/394-3061; fax 616/394-9810. www.pereddies.net.* Italian menu. European-style café with deli and Italian galleria. Hours: 10 am-9 pm; Fri, Sat to 10 pm. Closed Sun; major holidays. Lunch $5-$10, dinner $12-$25. Service bar. Reservations accepted required Fri, Sat. Cr cds: A, DS, MC, V.

D

★ ★ **PIPER.** *Phone 616/335-5866; fax 616/335-6797. www.piperrestaurant.com.* With its light and airy interior overlooking Lake Macatawa, this casually elegant restaurant serves cuisine with professional, friendly service. Closed most major holidays; also Sun, Mon in winter. Dinner. Bar. Children's menu. Cr cds: A, DS, MC, V.

D

★ ★ **TILL MIDNIGHT.** *208 College Ave (49423). Phone 616/392-6883; fax 616/392-9638. www.tillmidnight.com.* Eclectic menu. Hours: 11 am-2:30 pm, Mon-Thurs 5-10 pm, Fri-Sat 5 pm-midnight, closed Sun; most major holidays. Lunch A la carte entrees: $6-$8 , dinner A la carte entrees: $18-$25. Bar. Child's meals. Reservations accepted. Totally nonsmoking. Cr cds: A, DS, MC, V.

D

Holly (H-5)

See also Detroit, Flint, Pontiac

Pop 5,595 **Elev** 937 ft **Area code** 248 **Zip** 48442

Information Chamber of Commerce, 120 S Saginaw St, PO Box 214; 248/634-1900

Web www.hollymi.com

What to See and Do

Davisburg Candle Factory. *6634 Broadway; 2 miles S, then 3 miles E on Davisburg Rd. Phone 248/634-4214.* Located in 125-year-old building; produces unique and beautiful handcrafted candles. Unusual taper production line. Showroom and gift shop. Demonstrations by appointment (weekdays). (Daily) **FREE**

★ **Historic Battle Alley.** *110 Battle Alley. Phone 810/634-5208.* Once known for its taverns and brawls, Battle Alley is now a restored 19th-century street featuring antiques, boutiques, specialty shops, crafters; dining at the Historic Holly Hotel (see RESTAURANT). On the Alley is a mosaic of the bicentennial logo made from 1,000 red, white, and blue bricks. (Daily; closed holidays) **FREE**

Mount Holly Ski Area. *13536 S Dixie Hwy, 7 miles NE off I-75. Phone 248/634-8260.* Three quad, three triple, double chairlift, six rope tows; patrol, school, rentals, snowmaking; two cafeterias, two bars. Vertical drop 350 feet. Night skiing. (Dec-Mar, daily; closed Dec 24 eve)

Special Events

Carry Nation Festival. *103 N Saginaw (48442). Phone 248/634-1055.* Re-creation of Carry Nation's 1908 visit to Holly. The "temperance crusader" charged down Battle Alley with her famed umbrella, smashing bottles and a few heads along the way. Pageant, parade, antique car show, race, games, arts and crafts show, model railroad. Weekend after Labor Day.

Dickens Festival. *Phone 248/634-1900.* Re-creates the Dickensian period with carolers, town crier, strolling characters, skits, bell choirs, street hawkers, carriage rides. Thanksgiving-weekend before Dec 25.

Michigan Renaissance Festival. *12500 Dixie Hwy. Phone 248/634-5552.* Festivities include jousting tournaments, entertainment, food, and crafts in Renaissance-style village. Eight weekends Aug-Sept.

Restaurant

★ ★ **HISTORIC HOLLY HOTEL.** *110 Battle Alley (48442). Phone 248/634-5208; fax 248/634-7977. www.hollyhotel.com.* Hours: 11 am-3 pm, 5-10 pm; Fri, Sat to 11 pm; Sun noon-8 pm; Sun brunch 11 am-3 pm. Closed Dec 25, Jan 1, Labor & Memorial Day, July 4. Dinner $23-$40. Sun brunch $19. Bar. In restored hotel (1891); Victorian décor. Reservations accepted. Cr cds: A, MC, V.

Houghton (A-6)

Settled 1843 **Pop** 7,498 **Elev** 607 ft **Area code** 906 **Zip** 49931

Information Keweenaw Peninsula Chamber of Commerce, 326 Shelden Ave, PO Box 336; 906/482-5240 or 800/338-7982

Web www.cityofhoughton.com

Houghton and its sister city, Hancock (see), face each other across the narrowest part of Portage Lake. This is the area of America's first mining capital, the scene of the first great mineral strike in the Western Hemisphere. The copper-bearing geological formations are believed to be the oldest rock formations in the world. The great mining rush of 1843 and the years following brought people from all over Europe. Two main ethnic groups are identifiable today: Cornishmen, who came from England; and Finns, who have made this their cultural center in the United States.

What to See and Do

Ferry service to Isle Royale National Park. *800 E Lakeshore Dr (49931). Phone 906/482-0984.* Four ferries and a float plane provide transportation (June-Sept, daily; some trips in May). For fees and schedule contact Park Superintendent.

Michigan Technological University. *1400 Townsend Dr. Phone 906/487-1885.* (1885) 6,200 students. Campus tours leave from University Career Center in Administration Building. (See SPECIAL EVENTS) On campus is

    A. E. Seaman Mineralogical Museum. *In Electrical Energy Resources Center. Phone 906/487-2572.* Exhibits one of the nation's best mineral collections. (May-Oct, Mon-Sat; rest of year, Mon-Fri; closed holidays)

Mont Ripley Ski Area. *1400 Townsend Dr (49931). 1/2 mile E on MI 26. Phone 906/487-2340.* Double chairlift, T-bar; patrol, school, rentals, snowmaking; cafeteria. (Early Dec-late Mar, daily; closed Dec 25) **$$$$**

Special Events

Bridgefest. *326 Shelden Ave. On the Houghton and Hancock waterfronts. Phone 906/482-2388.* Parade, arts and crafts show, entertainment, powerboat races, fireworks. Phone 906/482-2388. Father's Day weekend. Mid-June.

Winter Carnival. *1400 Townsend Dr (49931). 2818.* Late Jan-early Feb.

Motels/Motor Lodges

★ ★ **BEST WESTERN INN FRANKLIN SQUARE.** *820 Shelden Ave (49931). Phone 906/487-1700; toll-free 888/487-1700; fax 906/487-9432. www.bestwestern.com.* 105 rooms, 7 story. June-Oct: S $65-$75; D $72-$82; each additional $6; suites $95-$110; under 12 free; higher rates special events; lower rates rest of year. Crib $4. TV; cable (premium). Indoor pool; whirlpool, sauna. Restaurant 6:30 am-10 pm. Room service. Bar 2 pm-2 am. Check-out 11 am. Meeting rooms. Business services available. Downhill ski 3 miles; cross-country ski 5 miles. Refrigerator available. Cr cds: A, C, D, DS, JCB, MC, V.

★ **BEST WESTERN KING'S INN.** *215 Shelden Ave (49931). Phone 906/482-5000; toll-free 800/780-7234; fax 906/482-9795. www.bestwestern.com.* 68 rooms, 4 story. D

$63-$79; each additional $6; under 17 free. Pet accepted. Complimentary continental breakfast. Check-out 11 am. TV; cable (premium), VCR available (movies). Sauna. Indoor pool, whirlpool. Downhill ski 2 miles, cross-country ski 3 miles. Cr cds: A, C, D, DS, MC, V.

★**CHIPPEWA MOTEL.** *217 Willson Memorial Dr. Phone 906/523-4611.* 15 rooms, 7 kitchen units. June-mid-Oct: S $36; D $44-$46; kitchen units for 2-6, $50-$70; lower rates rest of year. Crib $2. TV; cable. Coffee in rooms. Restaurant adjacent 7 am-8 pm; Sun 8 am-7 pm. Check-out 10 am. Meeting rooms. Downhill ski 9 miles; cross-country ski 1 block. Picnic tables. Some rooms overlook bay of Portage Lake. City park with beach, playground, picnic area and boat launch adjacent. Cr cds: C, D, DS, MC, V.

★ **L'ANSE MOTEL AND SUITES.** *Rte 2 & US 41 Box 606 (49946). Phone 906/524-7820; toll-free 800/800-6198; fax 906/524-7247.* 21 rooms, 2 with shower only. S $31; D $40; each additional $2. Crib $5. TV; cable (premium). Complimentary coffee in lobby. Check-out 11 am. Cross-country ski 2 miles. Cr cds: A, C, D, DS, MC, V.

★ **SUPER 8.** *790 Michigan Ave (49908). Phone 906/353-6680; fax 906/353-7246. www.super8.com.* 40 rooms, 2 story. S $41.88; D $49.88; each additional $4; under 12 free. Crib $2. Pet accepted. TV; cable. Complimentary continental breakfast. Restaurant opposite. Check-out 11 am. Meeting room. Business services available. Cross-country ski 8 miles. Cr cds: A, C, D, DS, MC, V.

★ **SUPER 8 MOTEL.** *1200 E Lakeshore Dr (49931). Phone 906/482-2240; fax 906/482-0686. www.super8.com.* 86 rooms, 2 story. S $48-$53; D $53-$58; each additional $3; suites $75; under 12 free. Crib $3. TV; cable (premium). Indoor pool; whirlpool, sauna. Complimentary continental breakfast. Restaurant nearby. Check-out 11 am. Meeting room. Downhill ski 1 mile; cross-country ski 1/2 mile. Cr cds: A, C, D, DS, MC, V.

★ **VACATIONLAND MOTEL.** *US 41 Box 93 (49931). Phone 906/482-5351; toll-free 800/822-3279.* 24 rooms, 1-2 story. July-Labor Day: S $34-$58; D $44-$58; family rates; lower rates rest of year. Crib $2. TV; cable (premium). Heated pool. Complimentary continental breakfast. Restaurant nearby. Check-out 11 am. Sundries. Downhill ski 5 miles; cross-country ski 3 miles. Picnic tables. 18-hole golf adjacent. Cr cds: A, C, D, DS, MC, V.

Houghton Lake (E-3)

Pop 3,353 **Elev** 1,162 ft **Area code** 517 **Zip** 48629

Information Chamber of Commerce, 1625 W Houghton Lake Dr; 989/366-5644 or 800/248-5253

Web www.houghtonlakechamber.org

The Houghton Lake area is the gateway to a popular north country resort area including three of the largest inland lakes in the state and 200,000 acres of state forests.

What to See and Do

Higgins Lake. *Between US 27 and I-75.* One of the most beautiful in America, Higgins Lake covers 10,317 acres and has 25 miles of sandy shoreline.

Houghton Lake. *Between US 27 and I-75.* Largest inland lake in Michigan and the source of the Muskegon River. This lake has a 32-mile shoreline and 22,000 acres of water, as well as 200 miles of groomed and marked snowmobile trails. A variety of resorts are in the area.

St. Helen Lake. *E on MI 55, then N on MI 76.* This pine-bordered lake has 12 miles of shoreline.

Special Event

Tip-Up-Town USA Ice Festival. *1625 W Houghton Lake Dr. Phone 989/366-5644.* Ice-fishing contests, games, food, parade, carnival. Third and fourth weekend Jan.

Motels/Motor Lodges

★ **VAL HALLA MOTEL.** *9869 W Houghton Lake Dr (48629). Phone 517/422-5137.* 21 rooms. D $45-$62; each additional $5. Pet accepted. Check-out 11 am. TV. Pool. Downhill ski 17 miles, cross-country ski 2 miles. Lawn games. Free airport transportation. Cr cds: A, DS, JCB, MC, V.

★ **VENTURE INN MOTEL.** *8939 W Houghton Lake Dr (48629). Phone 517/422-5591.* 12 rooms. Mid-June-Labor Day: S $40-$45; D $50; each additional $5; higher rates holidays; lower rates rest of year. Crib $2. TV. Heated pool. Complimentary coffee in rooms. Restaurant opposite open 24 hours. Check-out 11 am. Downhill ski 20 miles; cross-country ski 10 miles. Cr cds: MC, V.

Hulbert (B-3)

See also Newberry, Soo Junction

Pop 250 **Elev** 750 ft **Area code** 906 **Zip** 49748

North of Hulbert is a particularly wild portion of the Upper Peninsula with much wildlife. Popular activities are fishing for northern pike, bass, perch, and trout on Hulbert Lake; canoeing; and other outdoor sports.

What to See and Do

Tahquamenon Falls State Park. *41382 W MI 123. E on MI 28, then approximately 15 miles N on MI 123. Phone 906/492-3415.* (see NEWBERRY)

Indian River (D-4)

See also Petoskey

Pop 2,500 **Elev** 616 ft **Area code** 231 **Zip** 49749

Information Chamber of Commerce, 3435 S Straits Hwy, PO Box 57; 231/238-9325 or 800/394-8310

Web www.irmi.org

What to See and Do

Burt Lake State Park. *6635 State Park Dr (49749). 1/2 mile S off I-75, exit 310. Phone 231/238-9392.* Approximately 400 acres. Beach, beachhouse, waterskiing, fishing for walleyed pike and perch, boating (ramp, rentals); picnicking, playground, concession, camping. Standard fees. (May-Oct, daily) **$$**

Canoeing. *4752 Onaway Rd. Phone 231/238-9092.* Trips on Sturgeon and/or Pigeon rivers; difficulty varies with streams. Various trips offered. Reservations advised.

  Sturgeon & Pigeon River Outfitters. *4271 S Straits Hwy. Phone 231/238-8181.* Canoeing, tubing, kayaking. (May-mid-Sept) Contact 4271 S Straits Hwy.

  Tomahawk Trails Canoe Livery. *6225 State Route 68 (49749). Phone 231/238-8703.* (May-Oct, daily) Contact PO Box 814.

Cross in the Woods. *7078 MI 68. 1 mile W of I-75 exit 310, on MI 68. Phone 231/238-8973.* Wooden crucifix 55 ft tall. Outdoor shrines. (Mar-Nov, daily) **FREE**

Motel/Motor Lodge

★ **NOR-GATE.** *4846 Straits Hwy (49749). Phone 231/238-7788.* 12 rooms, 3 kitchens S $34; D $44; each additional $3; kitchen units $40-$69; weekly rates. Crib $5. TV; cable (premium). Complimentary coffee in lobby.

Restaurant nearby. Check-out 11 am. Picnic tables. State park 1/2 mile. Cr cds: A, DS, MC, V.

⊠ ⫚ ⊠

Iron Mountain (C-6)

See also Iron River, Ishpeming

Settled 1878 **Pop** 8,525 **Elev** 1,138 ft **Area code** 906 **Zip** 49801

Information Tourism Association of the Dickinson County Area, 600 S Stephenson Ave, PO Box 672; 906/774-2002 or 800/236-2447

Web www.dickinsonchamber.com

After more than a half-century of production, the underground shaft mines of high-grade ore deposits here have closed. Logging, tourism, and wood products are the main economic factors now, and Iron Mountain is the distribution point for the entire Menominee Range area. A nearby bluff heavily striped with iron ore gave the city its name. Abandoned mines, cave-ins, and a huge Cornish mine pump, preserved as tourist attractions, are reminders of mining days.

What to See and Do

Iron Mountain Iron Mine. *8 miles E on US 2 in Vulcan. Phone 906/563-8077.* Mine train tours 2,600 feet of underground drifts and tunnels 400 feet below surface. Working machinery, museum. Tours (June-mid-Oct, daily). **$$$**

Lake Antoine Park. *N33393 Quinnesec. 2 miles NE. Phone 906/774-8875.* Swimming, boating, waterskiing; nature trail, picnicking, concession, improved county campgrounds (fee); band concerts. (Memorial Day-Labor Day, daily) **$$$**

Menominee Range Historical Museum. *300 E Ludington St. In the Carnegie Public Library. Phone 906/774-4276.* More than 100 exhibits depict life on the Menominee Iron Range in the 1880s and early 1900s; 1-room school, Victorian parlor, trapper's cabin, country store. (Mid-May-Sept, daily; rest of year, by appointment) **$$$** Combination ticket includes

Cornish Pumping Engine & Mining Museum. *300 Kent St (49801). Kent St. Phone 906/774-1086.* Features largest steam-driven pumping engine built in US, with 40-foot-diameter flywheel in engine and weighing 160 tons; also display of underground mining equipment used in Michigan; WWII glider display. (Mid-May-Sept, daily; rest of year, by appointment) **$$**

Pine Mountain Lodge. *N3332 Pine Mountain Rd, 2 1/2 miles N off US 2/141. Phone 906/774-2747 or 800/553-PINE (Nov-Apr).* Triple, two double chairlifts, rope tow; snowmaking, patrol, school, rentals; nine-hole golf; two tennis courts; indoor/outdoor pools; restaurant, cafeteria, bar; lodge, condos. Longest run 3/4 mile; vertical drop 500 feet. (Late Nov-early Apr, daily) Cross-country trails.

Special Events

Festival of the Arts. *Phone 906/774-2945.* Crafts demonstrations, antique car show, concerts, square and folk dancing, community theater, international foods. Mid-June-mid-Aug.

Pine Mountain Ski Jumping Tournament. *Pine Mountain Lodge. Phone 906/774-2747.* Jan.

Wood-Bee Carvers Show. *Premiere Center. Phone 906/774-2945.* Wood carvers competition and show. Oct.

Motels/Motor Lodges

★ **BEST WESTERN EXECUTIVE INN.** *1518 S Stephenson Ave (US 2) (49801). Phone 906/774-2040; toll-free 800/528-1234; fax 906/774-0238. www.bestwestern.com.* 57 rooms, 2 story. D $63; each additional $6. Pet accepted. Complimentary continental breakfast. Check-out 11 am. TV; cable (premium), VCR available (movies $2.50). Indoor pool. Downhill/cross-country ski 3 miles. Cr cds: A, C, D, DS, MC, V.

D ⫚ ⊠ ⊠ ⊠ SC

★ **COMFORT INN.** *1555 N Stephenson Ave (49801). Phone 906/774-5505; toll-free 800/638-7949; fax 906/774-2631. www.comfortinn.com.* 48 rooms, 2 story. S $52; D $59; each additional $6; under 18 free. Crib free. TV; cable (premium), VCR available. Complimentary continental breakfast. Restaurant nearby. Check-out 11 am. Meeting room. Business services available. Valet service. Coin laundry. Downhill/cross-country ski 2 miles. Exercise equipment. Some refrigerators. Cr cds: A, C, D, DS, ER, JCB, MC, V.

⫚ ⊠ ⊠

★ **SUPER 8 MOTEL.** *2702 N Stephenson Ave (49801). Phone 906/774-3400; toll-free 888/711-8090; fax 906/774-9903. www.super8.com.* 90 rooms, 2 story. S $44.88; D $56.88; each additional $6; suites from $64.88; under 12 free. Crib free. TV; cable (premium), VCR available. Pool; whirlpool, sauna. Complimentary continental breakfast. Restaurant nearby. Check-out 11 am. Coin laundry. Meeting room. Business services available. Downhill/cross-country ski 4 miles. Some refrigerators. Picnic tables. Cr cds: A, D, DS, MC, V.

D ⊠ ⊠ ⊠ SC

★ **TIMBERS MOTOR LODGE.** *200 S Stephenson Ave (49801). Phone 906/774-7600; toll-free 800/433-8533; fax 906/774-6222. www.thetimbers.com.* 53 rooms, 2 story. S $40; D $50; each additional $5; suites $54. Crib $4. Check-out noon. TV; cable (premium). In-room modem link. Restaurant nearby. Exercise equipment, sauna. Indoor pool, whirlpool. Downhill/cross-country ski 1 1/2 miles. Meeting rooms, business services. Cr cds: A, C, D, DS, MC, V.

🄳 ⛷ 🎿 ⛴ 🛖 🏊 🏃

Iron River (B-6)

See also Iron Mountain

Pop 2,095 **Elev** 1,510 ft **Area code** 906 **Zip** 49935

Information Iron County Chamber of Commerce, 50 E Genesee St; 906/265-3822 or 888/879-IRON

Web www.iron.org

Just north of the Wisconsin-Michigan state line, Iron River was one of the last of the large mining towns to spring up on the Menominee Range. Lumbering has also played a prominent part in the town's past. Ottawa National Forest (see IRONWOOD) lies a few miles to the west, and a Ranger District office is located here.

What to See and Do

Iron County Museum. *Museum Rd (49915). 2 miles S on County 424 in Caspian. Phone 906/265-2617.* Indoor/outdoor museum of 22 buildings. Miniature logging exhibit with more than 2,000 pieces; iron mining dioramas; more than 100 major exhibits; log homestead; 1896 1-room schoolhouse; logging camp, home of composer Carrie Jacobs-Bond; Lee LeBlanc Wildlife Art Gallery. Annual ethnic festivals (Scandinavian, Polish, Italian, Yugoslavian; inquire for schedule). (Mid-May-Oct, daily; rest of year, by appt) **$$**

Ski Brule. *119 Big Bear Rd, 3 miles SW off MI 189. Phone 906/265-4957 or 800/362-7853.* Four chairlifts, two T-bars, pony lift, rope tow; patrol, school, rentals, snowmaking; chalet and condo lodging, restaurant, cafeteria, bar, nursery. Seventeen runs, longest run 1 mile; vertical drop 500 feet. (Nov-Apr, daily) Cross-country trails. **$$$$**

Special Events

Bass Festival. *Phone 906/265-3822.* Canoe races on the Paint River, softball game, barbecue, music, and events at Runkle Park and Runkle Lake. First weekend July.

Ferrous Frolics. *100 Museum Dr. Phone 906/265-2617.* Iron County Museum. Arts, crafts, demonstrations, band concert, flea market. Third weekend July.

Iron County Fair. *N 7th Ave and W Franklin St. Fairgrounds. Phone 888/879-4766.* Four days late Aug.

Upper Peninsula Championship Rodeo. *50 E Genesee St. Fairgrounds. Phone 906/265-3822.* Late July.

Ironwood (B-5)

See also Wakefield, Hurley

Settled 1885 **Pop** 6,849 **Elev** 1,503 ft **Area code** 906 **Zip** 49938

Information Ironwood Area Chamber of Commerce, 150 N Lowell; 906/932-1122

Web www.ironwoodmi.org

Ironwood is a center for summer and winter recreation. The first part of Gogebic County to be settled, the town was linked at first with fur trading. It quickly blossomed into a mining town when a deposit of iron was found in what is now the eastern section of the city. John R. Wood, one of the first mining captains, was known as "Iron" because of his interest in ore—thus, the name Ironwood.

What to See and Do

Big Powderhorn Mountain. *N11375 Powderhorn Rd. Phone 906/932-4838 or 906/932-3100 (reservations only).* Nine double chairlifts; patrol, school, rentals; three restaurants, cafeteria, three bars, nursery. Twenty-five runs; longest run 1 mile; vertical drop 600 feet. (Thanksgiving-early Apr, daily)

Blackjack. *N11251 Baker Blackjack Rd. 12 miles E of MI 51 via US 2, Blackjack exit. Phone 906/229-5115 or 906/229-5157 (reservations only).* Four double chairlifts, two rope tows; patrol, school, rentals; cafeteria, restaurant, bar, nursery, lodging. Longest run one mile; vertical drop 465 feet. (Nov-Mar, daily) **$$$$**

Black River Harbor. *N15725 Black River Rd. 4 miles E, then 15 miles N on County 513. Phone 906/932-7250.* Deep-sea fishing boats for rent, boat rides, Lake Superior cruises; picnicking, playground, camping.

Copper Peak Ski Flying. *N13870 Copper Peak Rd. 12 miles N on County 513. Phone 906/932-3500.* The only ski flying facility in North America, and one of six in the world, where athletes test their skills in an event that requires more athletic ability than ski jumping. Skiers reach speeds of more than 60 miles per hour and fly farther than 500 feet. International tournament is held every winter. In summer, chairlift and elevator rides take visitors 240 feet above the crest of Copper Peak for a view of three states, Lake Superior, and Canada. (Mid-June-Labor Day, daily; Sept-Oct, weekends) **$$**

Hiawatha—World's Tallest Indian. *Houk St.* Statue of famous Iroquois stands 52 feet high and looks north to the legendary "shining big-sea-water"—Gitchee Gumee, also known as Lake Superior.

Little Girl's Point Park. *104 S Lowell St (49938). County 505 N, 18 miles N, off US 2; on Lake Superior. Phone 906/*

932-1420. Notable for the agate pebbles on the beaches. Picnic tables (fee), campsites (fee); Native American burial grounds. (May-Sept)

Mount Zion. *3/4 mile N of US 2 at E4946 Jackson Rd. Phone 906/932-3718.* One of the highest points on the Gogebic Range, with 1,750-foot altitude, 1,150 feet above Lake Superior. Double chairlift, two rope tows; patrol, school, rentals; snack bar. Longest run is 3/4 mile; vertical drop 300 feet. (Mid-Dec-Mar, Tues-Sun; closed Dec 25) Two miles of cross-country ski trails, equipment rentals.

Ottawa National Forest. *2100 E Cloverland Dr (49938). E via US 2, MI 28. Contact Supervisor, phone 906/932-1330.* Wooded hills, picturesque lakes and streams, waterfalls, J. W. Toumey Nursery, Black River Harbor, North Country National Scenic Trail, Watersmeet Visitor Center and Sylvania, Sturgeon River Gorge, and McCormick Wildernesses are all part of this 953,600-acre forest. Fishing for trout, muskie, northern pike, walleye, bass, and panfish; swimming, canoeing, boat landing; hunting for big and small game, hiking, cross-country and downhill skiing, picnicking, camping. Some fees. (Daily) **FREE**

Special Event

Gogebic County Fair. *104 S Lowell St. Fairgrounds. Phone 906/932-1420.* Second weekend Aug.

Motels/Motor Lodges

★**BLACK RIVER LODGE.** *N12390 Black River Rd (49938). Phone 906/932-3857; fax 906/932-6601.* 25 rooms, 12 A/C, 2 story, 4 townhouses (no A/C), some kitchens Dec-Mar: S $30-$45; D $35-$65; Suites $35-$98; kitchen units $45-$100; townhouses $80-$180; weekly rates; ski plans; AP, MAP available; lower rates rest of year. Crib free. TV; cable (premium), VCR available. Indoor pool; whirlpool. Playground. Restaurant (hrs vary). Bar 6 pm-2 am. Check-out 11 am. Meeting rooms. Downhill ski 1 1/2 miles; cross-country ski on site. Lawn games. Game room. Hiking. Fishing/hunting guides. Some refrigerators. Picnic tables, grill. Cr cds: DS, MC, V.

D ⊠ ⟲ 🛌 ⤢ ⛽ ➤ ✈ ⊠ 🏃

★**COMFORT INN.** *210 E Cloverland Dr (49938). Phone 906/932-2224; toll-free 800/572-9412; fax 906/932-9929. www.comfortinn.com.* 63 rooms, 2 story. S $52-$100; D $59-$125; each additional $6; under 18 free. Crib free. TV; cable (premium), VCR available (movies). Indoor pool; whirlpool. Complimentary continental breakfast. Restaurant opposite open 24 hours. Check-out 11 am. Meeting room. Business services available. Downhill/cross-country ski 6 miles. Some refrigerators, wet bars. Cr cds: A, C, D, DS, JCB, MC, V.

D ⊠ 🏃 🛌 ⤢ 🏃 ⊠ ⊠

Ishpeming (B-1)

See also Marquette

Settled 1844 **Pop** 7,200 **Area code** 906 **Zip** 49849

Information Ishpeming-Negaunee Area Chamber of Commerce, 661 Palms Ave; 906/486-4841

Web www.marquette.org

Iron mines gave birth to this city and still sustain it. Skiing is the basis of its recreation and tourism business. In 1887, three Norwegians formed a ski club in Ishpeming, which is a Native American word for "high grounds." That ski club eventually became a national ski association.

What to See and Do

⭐ **National Ski Hall of Fame and Ski Museum.** *Between 2nd and 3rd sts, on US 41. Phone 906/485-6323 or 906/485-6324.* Affiliated with the US Ski Association. Houses national trophies and displays of old skis and ski equipment, includes a replica of the oldest-known ski and ski pole in the world. Roland Palmedo National Ski Library, collection of ski publications for researchers in-house only. (Daily; closed holidays) **$$**

Suicide Bowl. *On Cliffs Dr at E end of city. Phone 906/485-4242.* Includes five ski-jumping hills from mini-hill to 70-meter hill. There are also four cross-country trails; one is lighted for evening use. **$$**

Van Riper State Park. *17 miles W on US 41. Phone 906/339-4461.* Approximately 1,000 acres on Lake Michigamme. Swimming, waterskiing, bathhouse, fishing, boating (ramp, rentals); hunting, hiking, picnic grounds, concession, playground, camping. Standard fees. (Daily) **$$**

Special Event

Annual Ski Jumping Championships. *US National Ski Hall of Fame. US Hwy 41 W (49849). Phone 906/485-6323.* Paul Bietila Memorial. Also cross-country ski race. Feb.

Motel/Motor Lodge

★ ★ **BEST WESTERN COUNTRY INN.** *850 US 41 W (49849). Phone 906/485-6345; toll-free 800/780-7234; fax 906/485-6348. www.bestwestern.com.* 60 rooms, 2 story. Mid-June-Oct: S $70; D $75; each additional $5; family rates; ski plans; lower rates rest of year. Crib free. Pet accepted. TV; cable (premium). Indoor pool; whirlpool. Complimentary continental breakfast. Complimentary coffee in lobby. Restaurant adjacent 6 am-10 pm; Fri, Sat to 11 pm. Check-out noon. Business services available. Downhill ski 15 miles; cross-country ski 2 miles. Health club privileges. Game room. Cr cds: A, C, D, DS, MC, V.

D ⊠ ⟲ ⤢ ⊠ SC

Isle Royale National Park (A-1)

(N of Upper Peninsula, on island in Lake Superior.)

This unique wilderness area, covering 571,790 acres, is the largest island in Lake Superior, 15 miles from Canada (the nearest mainland), 18 miles from Minnesota, and 45 miles from Michigan. There are no roads and no automobiles are allowed. The main island, 45 miles long and 8 1/2 miles across at its widest point, is surrounded by more than 400 smaller islands. Isle Royale may be reached by boat from Houghton or Copper Harbor in Michigan, from Grand Portage in Minnesota, or by seaplane from Houghton. Schedules vary; inquire each year around January 1. Contact Superintendent, Isle Royale National Park, 800 E Lakeshore Dr, Houghton, MI 49931; phone 906/482-0984.

The only wildlife here are those animals able to fly, swim, drift across the water, or travel on ice. Moose, wolf, fox, and beaver are the dominant mammals; however, before 1900 no moose existed on the island. The current population of 700 evolved from a few moose that swam to the island around 1912. In the winter of 1949 wolves came across the ice and stayed. More than 200 species of birds have been observed, including loons, bald eagles, and ospreys.

Prehistoric peoples discovered copper on the island 4,000 years ago. Later, white men tried to mine in a number of places. The remains of these mining operations may still be seen; some of the ancient mining pits date back 3,800 years.

There are more than 165 miles of foot trails leading to beautiful inland lakes, more than 20 of which have game fish, including pike, perch, walleye, and in a few, whitefish cisco. There are trout in many streams and lakes. Fishing is under National Park Service and Michigan regulations (see FISHING AND HUNTING in state text). Boat rental and charter fishing are available at Rock Harbor Lodge. Basic supplies are available on the island in limited quantities. Nights are usually cold; bring warm clothing and be prepared to rough it. Group camping is available for parties of seven to ten people; inquire for group information; group campsites must be reserved. The park is open from approximately May to October.

Rock Harbor Lodge is at the east end of the island, about 3 1/2 miles east of Mott Island, which is the Park Service headquarters during the summer. The lodge offers rooms, cabins, restaurant, and a camp store. Room reservations should be made at least three months in advance. The lodge is open June through Labor Day. For lodge information write National Park Concessions, Inc., PO Box 605, Houghton, MI 49931, phone 906/337-4993 (summer); or National Park Concessions, Inc., PO Box 27, Mammoth Cave, KY 42259, phone 270/773-2191 (winter).

Jackson (H-4)

See also Battle Creek, Lansing

Settled 1829 **Pop** 37,446 **Elev** 960 ft **Area code** 517

Information Convention & Tourist Bureau, 6007 Ann Arbor Rd, 49201; 517/764-4440 or 800/245-5282

Web www.jackson-mich.org

Four major highways and heavy rail traffic make this a transportation center. Industries are the foundation of the city's economy. In Jackson on July 6, 1854, the Republican Party was officially born at a convention held "under the green spreading oaks," as there was no hall large enough to accommodate the delegates. Each year, the city attracts thousands of tourists, who use it as a base to explore more than 200 natural lakes in Jackson County.

What to See and Do

Cascades Falls Park. *1992 Warren Ave (49203). Brown St via I-94 to exit 138. Phone 517/788-4320.* Approximately 465 acres. Fishing ponds and pier, paddle-boating (rentals); picnicking, playground; 18-hole miniature golf, driving range; fitness and jogging trail; basketball, tennis, and horseshoe courts; restaurant. Some fees. Also here are

Cascades-Sparks Museum. *Brown St & Denton Rd. Phone 517/788-4320.* Depicts early history of falls and its builder, Captain William Sparks; original drawings, models, audiovisual displays. (Memorial Day-Labor Day, nightly)

Sparks Illuminated Cascades Waterfalls. *1992 Warren Ave. Phone 517/788-4320 or 517/788-4277.* Approximately 500 feet of water cascading over 16 waterfalls and six fountains in continually changing patterns of light, color, and music. (Memorial Day-Labor Day, nightly) **$$**

Dahlem Environmental Education Center. *7117 S Jackson Rd. Phone 517/782-3453.* Nature center with 5 miles of trails through forests, fields, marshes; 1/2 mile "special needs" trail for the disabled; visitor center with exhibits, gift shop. (Tues-Sun). **FREE**

Ella Sharp Park. *3225 4th St. Phone 517/788-4040.* Approximately 530 acres with 18-hole golf course, tennis courts, ballfields, swimming pool, miniature golf, picnic facilities, formal gardens. (Daily) In park is

Ella Sharp Museum. *3225 4th St (49203). Phone 517/787-2320.* Complex includes Victorian farmhouse, historic farm lane, one-room schoolhouse, log cabin, galleries with rotating art and historic exhibits;

studios; planetarium; visitor center. (Tues-Sun; closed holidays) **$$**

⭐ **Michigan Space Center.** *2111 Emmons Rd (49201). Phone 517/787-4425.* US space artifacts and memorabilia displayed in geodesic dome, incl Gemini trainer, Apollo 9 Command Module, replica of space shuttle, Challenger memorial, space food, space suits, lunar rover, moon rock, satellites, orbiters, landers, giant rocket engines; films and special presentations. Picnicking and children's play areas. Gift shop. (May-Labor Day, daily; Jan-Apr, Tues-Sun) **$$**

Republican Party founding site. *W Franklin and 2nd sts.* Marked with a tablet dedicated by President William Howard Taft.

Waterloo Farm Museum. *9998 Waterloo-Munith Rd. Phone 517/596-2254.* Tours of furnished pioneer farmhouse (1855-1885), bakehouse, windmill, farm workshop, barn, milk cellar, log house, granary. (June-Aug, Tues-Sun afternoons; Sept, Sat and Sun; Pioneer Festival second Sun Oct) **$$**

Waterloo State Recreation Area. *16345 McClure Rd. 15 miles E on I-94, then N on unnumbered road.* This is the state's largest recreation area, with 20,072 acres. Swimming, beach, bathhouse, waterskiing, fishing, boating (ramp, rentals) on numerous lakes; horseback riding, nature trails, hunting, picnicking, concession, cabins, tent and trailer sites; geology center. Standard fees.

Special Events

Civil War Muster & Battle Reenactment. *1992 Warren Ave. Phone 517/788-4320.* Cascade Falls Park. Thousands of participants re-create a different Civil War battle each year; living history demonstrations, parades, food, entertainment. Third weekend Aug.

Harness racing. *200 W Ganson St. Phone 517/788-4500.* Jackson Harness Raceway, Jackson County Fairgrounds. Pari-mutuel betting. Spring and fall races.

Hot-Air Balloon Jubilee. *3606 Wildwood Ave. Phone 517/782-1515.* Jackson County Airport. Competitive balloon events; skydivers; arts and crafts. Phone 517/782-1515. Mid-July.

Jackson County Fair. *200 W Ganson St. Phone 517/788-4405.* Stage shows; displays of produce, handicrafts, farm animals; midway shows; rides. Second week Aug.

Michigan Speedway. *12626 US 12. Phone 800/354-1010.* NASCAR, ARCA, IROC and Indy Car races on a 2-mile oval track. Contact 12626 US 12, Brooklyn 49230; 800/354-1010. Mid-June-mid-Aug.

Rose Festival. *212 W Michigan Ave. Phone 517/787-2065.* Ella Sharp Park. Parade, pageant, garden tours, entertainment. Mid-May-mid-June.

Motels/Motor Lodges

⭐ **BAYMONT INN.** *2035 N Service Dr (49202). Phone 517/789-6000; toll-free 800/428-3438; fax 517/782-6836. www.baymontinns.com.* 67 rooms, 2 story. D $46.95-$59.95. Pet accepted. Complimentary continental breakfast. Check-out noon. TV; cable (premium). Cr cds: A, C, D, DS, MC, V.

D ⏴ ⌧ SC

⭐ **COUNTRY HEARTH INN.** *1111 Boardman Rd (49202). Phone 517/783-6404; toll-free 800/267-5023; fax 517/783-6529.* 73 rooms, 2 story. D $59-$73; each additional $6; under 18 free. Complimentary continental breakfast. Check-out noon. TV; cable. Health club privileges. Cr cds: A, C, D, DS, MC, V.

D ⌧ SC

⭐ **HOLIDAY INN.** *2000 Holiday Inn Dr (49202). Phone 517/783-2681; fax 517/783-5744. www.holiday-inn.com.* 184 rooms, 2 story. D $79-$89; under 19 free. Pet accepted; fee. Check-out 11 am. TV; cable; VCR available. Laundry services. Restaurant, bar, room service. Sauna. Game room. Miniature golf. Pool, whirlpool. Cross-country ski 10 miles. Cr cds: A, D, DS, JCB, MC, V.

D ⏴ ⌧ ⌧ ⌧ SC

Restaurants

⭐⭐ **GILBERT'S STEAK HOUSE.** *2323 Shirley Dr (49202). Phone 517/782-7135. www.gilbertsteakhouse.com.* Specializes in steak, prime rib, seafood. Hours: 11 am-10 pm; Fri, Sat to 11 pm; Sun Noon-7 pm. Closed some major holidays. Buffet on Sun $13.95, lunch $4.95-$8.50, dinner $9.95-$19.95. Bar. Child's meals. Victorian atmosphere. Reservations accepted. Cr cds: A, D, DS, MC, V.

D

⭐⭐ **KNIGHT'S STEAKHOUSE & GRILL.** *2125 Horton Rd (49203). Phone 517/783-2777.* Specializes in steak. Hours: 11 am-10 pm; Fri, Sat to 11 pm, closed Sun; most major holidays. Dinner $5-$25. Bar. Child's meals. Reservations accepted. Cr cds: A, MC, V.

D

Kalamazoo (H-3)

See also Battle Creek, Paw Paw, Three Rivers

Settled 1829 **Pop** 80,277 **Elev** 780 ft **Area code** 616

Information Kalamazoo County Convention and Visitors Bureau, 346 W Michigan Ave, 49007; 616/381-4003 or 800/222-6363

Web www.kazoofun.com

Yes, there really is a Kalamazoo—a unique name, immortalized in song and verse. The name is derived from the Native American name for the Kalamazoo River, which means "where the water boils in the pot." The concept is noted not only in the community's name but also in its cultural, industrial, and recreational makeup. Diversified industry from bedding plants to pharmaceuticals thrive here. Many recreational activities complete the picture.

What to See and Do

Bittersweet Ski Area. *600 River Rd. 18 miles N via US 131, MI 89 W to Jefferson Rd exit. Phone 616/694-2820.* Quad, four triple chairlifts, double chairlift, five rope tows; school, rentals; lodge, cafeteria, bar. Sixteen trails; longest run 2,300 feet; vertical drop 300 feet. Night skiing. (Dec-Mar, daily) **$$$$**

Bronson Park. *200 W South St.* A bronze tablet marks the spot where Abraham Lincoln made an antislavery speech in 1856.

Crane Park. *Park St, at the crest of Westnedge Hill overlooking city.* Formal floral gardens, tennis courts.

Echo Valley. *8495 E H Ave. Phone 616/349-3291 or 616/345-5892.* 60-mph tobogganing (toboggans furnished), ice-skating (rentals). (Dec-Mar, Fri-Sun; closed Dec 25) **$$$**

Gilmore-CCCA Museum. *6865 Hickory Rd, 15 miles NE via MI 43 in Hickory Corners. Phone 616/671-5089.* More than 120 antique autos tracing the significant technical developments in automotive transportation; on 90 acres of landscaped grounds. (Mid-May-mid-Oct, daily) **$$$**

⭐ **Kalamazoo Air Zoo.** *3101 E Milham Rd, on the grounds of Kalamazoo/Battle Creek Airport. Phone 616/382-6555.* It is home to over 70 beautiful historic and restored aircraft of the WWII period, many in flying condition; exhibits, video theater, flight simulator, observation deck. Tours of Restoration Center (May-Sept). Flight of the Day (May-Sept, afternoons). (Daily; closed major holidays) **$$$**

Kalamazoo College. *1200 Academy St. Phone 616/337-7000.* (1833) 1,300 students. Private, liberal arts college. Red-brick streets and Georgian architecture characterize this school, one of the 100 oldest colleges in the nation. A 3,023-pipe organ is in Stetson Chapel; Bach Festival (Mar); Festival Playhouse (June-July).

Kalamazoo Institute of Arts. *314 S Park St. Phone 616/349-7775 or 616/349-3959.* Galleries, school, shop, library, and auditorium. Collection of 20th-century American art; circulating exhibits. (Tues-Sun; closed holidays; also Aug) **DONATION**

Kalamazoo Nature Center. *7000 N Westnedge Ave. Phone 616/381-1574.* Interpretive Center; restored 1860s pioneer homestead; nature trails (tours by appt); barnyard (May-Labor Day); Public Orientation Room programs, slides, movies, live animals. (Daily; closed holidays) **$$**

Kalamazoo Valley Museum. *230 N Rose St. Phone 616/373-7990.* Includes Mary Jane Stryker Interactive Learning Hall with an interactive theater, science gallery, Challenger Learning Center, Egyptian artifacts, and Universe Theater and Planetarium. (Mon-Sat, Sun afternoons) **$**

Timber Ridge Ski Area. *5 miles N on US 131, then W at D Ave exit. Phone 616/694-9449 or 800/253-2928.* Four chairlifts, Pomalift, three rope tows; patrol, school, snowmaking; snack bar, cafeteria, two bars. Store, repairs, rentals. Fifteen trails; longest run 2/3 mile; vertical drop 250 feet. (Late Nov-mid-Mar, daily) **$$$$**

Western Michigan University. *1903 W Michigan Ave. Phone 616/387-1000.* (1903) 28,000 students. Contemporary plays, musical comedies, operas, and melodramas offered in Shaw and York theaters. Touring professional shows, dance programs, and entertainers in Miller Auditorium; dance and music performances are featured in the Irving S. Gilmore University Theatre Complex. Art exhibits in Sangren Hall and East Hall. Inquire for schedules.

Special Events

Kalamazoo County Fair. *2900 Lake St (49001). Phone 616/381-4003.* Aug.

Kalamazoo County Flowerfest. *350 S Burdick St (49007). Phone 616/381-3597.* July.

Wine and Harvest Festival. *Bronson Park. Phone 800/222-6363.* Kalamazoo-Paw Paw. First weekend Sept.

Motels/Motor Lodges

★ **BEST WESTERN HOSPITALITY INN.** *3640 E Cork St (49001). Phone 616/381-1900; fax 616/373-6136. www.bestwestern.com.* 124 rooms, 3 story. D $69-$89; each additional $8; under 14 free. Complimentary continental breakfast. Check-out noon. TV; cable. Exercise equipment, sauna. Indoor pool, whirlpool. Downhill, cross-country ski 15 miles. Cr cds: A, C, D, DS, ER, MC, V.

[D] 🛏 🖾 🏋 ✕ 🖾 SC

★ **DAYS INN.** *3522 Sprinkle Rd (49001). Phone 616/381-7070; fax 616/381-4341. www.daysinn.com.* 146 rooms, 2 story. S, studio rooms $75; D $83; under 18 free. Crib free. Pet accepted. TV; cable (premium), VCR available. 2 pools, 1 indoor; whirlpool, sauna, poolside service. Restaurant 6:30 am-10 pm; Fri, Sat to 11 pm. Room service. Bar 11:30 am-midnight; closed Sun. Check-out noon. Coin laundry. Meeting rooms. Business services available. Bellhops. Valet service. Sundries. Free airport transportation. Downhill/cross-country ski 15 miles. Adjacent to stadium. Cr cds: A, D, DS, MC, V.

[D] 🏊 🖾 ✕ 🖾 ✈

★ **FAIRFIELD INN.** *3800 E Cork St (49001). Phone 616/ 344-8300; fax 616/344-8300. www.fairfieldinn.com.* 133 rooms, 3 story. Late May-mid-Sept: S $39.95; D $55.95; each additional $3; under 18 free; lower rates rest of year. Crib free. TV; cable. Heated pool. Complimentary continental breakfast. Restaurant adjacent 6 am-midnight. Check-out noon. Meeting room. Business services available. Valet service. Downhill/cross-country ski 15 miles. Cr cds: A, C, D, DS, MC, V.

[icons]

★ ★ **HOLIDAY INN KALAMAZOO.** *2747 S 11th St (49009). Phone 616/375-6000; fax 616/375-1220. www.holiday-inn.com.* 186 rooms, 4 story. S, D $79-$89; studio rooms $79; under 19 free. Crib free. Pet accepted. TV. Indoor pool; whirlpool, poolside service. Restaurant 6:30 am-10:30 pm; Fri, Sat to 11 pm. Room service. Bar 11:30 am-midnight; Fri, Sat to 1 am. Check-out 11 am. Coin laundry. Meeting room. Business services available. Bellhops. Valet service. Putting green. Downhill ski 8 miles; cross-country ski 3 miles. Exercise room; sauna. Game room. Cr cds: A, D, DS, JCB, MC, V.

[icons]

★ ★ **QUALITY INN & SUITES.** *3750 Easy St (49001). Phone 616/388-3551; toll-free 800/687-6667; fax 616/342-9132. www.qualityinn.com.* 116 rooms, 2 story. S $61; D $67; each additional $6; under 18 free. Crib free. Pet accepted. TV; cable (premium). Heated pool. Complimentary continental breakfast. Restaurant adjacent 6 am-11 pm. Check-out noon. Meeting rooms. Business services available. Valet service. Free airport, train station, bus depot transportation. Downhill/cross-country ski 15 miles. Cr cds: A, C, D, DS, JCB, MC, V.

[icons]

★ **RED ROOF INN.** *5425 W Michigan Ave (49009). Phone 616/375-7400; fax 616/375-7533. www.redroof.com.* 108 rooms, 2 story. S $36-$45; D $40-$52; 3 or more $50; under 18 free; higher rates special events. Crib free. Pet accepted. TV. Complimentary coffee. Restaurant nearby. Check-out noon. Business services available. Downhill ski 8 miles; cross-country ski 3 miles. Picnic tables, grill. Cr cds: A, C, D, DS, MC, V.

[icons]

★ **SUPER 8 MOTEL.** *618 Maple Hill Dr (49009). Phone 616/345-0146; fax 616/345-0146. www.super8.com.* 62 rooms, 3 story. No elevator. Apr-Oct: S $43.99; D $48.99-$52.99; under 12 free; higher rates wkends; lower rates rest of year. Crib free. Pet accepted. TV; cable (premium). Restaurant adjacent 7 am-10 pm. Check-out 11 am. Downhill ski 11 miles. Some refrigerators, microwaves. Cr cds: A, C, D, DS, MC, V.

[icons]

Hotel

★ ★ **RADISSON PLAZA.** *100 W Michigan Ave (49007). Phone 616/343-3333; toll-free 800/333-3333; fax 616/381-1560. www.radisson.com.* This hotel is located in the heart of Kalamazoo, near the campus of Western Michigan University and the local international airport. 281 rooms, 9 story. D $149; each additional $10. Check-out noon. TV. In-room modem link. Restaurant, bar. Exercise room, sauna. Indoor pool, whirlpool. Valet parking. Free airport transportation. Concierge. Cr cds: A, C, D, DS, ER, JCB, MC, V.

[icons]

B&B/Small Inns

★ ★ **HALL HOUSE BED & BREAKFAST.** *106 Thompson St (49006). Phone 269/343-2500; toll-free 888/ 761-2525; fax 269/343-1374. www.hallhouse.com.* 6 rooms, 3 story. Complimentary breakfast. TV; cable, VCR. Georgian Colonial Revival building (1923). Original artwork. Cr cds: A, MC, V.

[icons]

★ ★ **STUART AVENUE INN BED & BREAKFAST.** *229 Stuart Ave (49007). Phone 269/342-0230; toll-free 800/461-0621; fax 269/385-3442. www.stuartaveinn.com.* 10 rooms, 4 suites, 12 kitchen units, 2-3 story. S $85, D $95-$105; each additional $10; suites $120-$150; kitchen units $150-$250/week (4-week min); weekly rates. Complimentary continental breakfast; afternoon refreshments. Check-out 11am, check-in 3pm. TV; cable. Some fireplaces. Restaurant nearby. Downhill/cross-country ski 15 miles. Totally nonsmoking. Cr cds: A, C, D, DS, MC, V.

[icons]

Extended Stay

★ ★ **RESIDENCE INN BY MARRIOTT.** *1500 E Kilgore Rd (49001). Phone 616/349-0855; toll-free 800/331-3131; fax 616/373-5971. www.marriott.com.* 83 kitchen suites, 2 story. S, D $105-$130; weekly rates. Crib free. Pet accepted, some restrictions; fee. TV; cable, VCR available (movies). Heated pool; whirlpool. Complimentary continental breakfast. Complimentary coffee in rooms. Restaurant nearby. Check-out noon. Coin laundry. Meeting room. Business services available. In-room modem link. Valet service. Free airport transportation. 9-hole golf privileges. Downhill/cross-country ski 20 miles. Health club privileges. Some fireplaces. Picnic tables, grills. Cr cds: A, C, D, DS, ER, JCB, MC, V.

[icons]

Restaurants

★ ★ ★ **BLACK SWAN.** *3501 Greenleaf Blvd (49008). Phone 616/375-2105; fax 616/375-5516. www.millennium restaurants.com.* Classic continental cuisine is served in the quiet dining room overlooking beautiful Willow Lake. Hours: 11:30 am-2 pm, 5-10 pm; Sun 4-8 pm. Closed major holidays. Reservations accepted. Continental menu. Bar to midnight. Lunch $5.95-$15.95, dinner $14.95-$23.95. Sun brunch $11.95. Child's meals. Specializes in seafood, steak. Valet parking. Cr cds: A, D, DS, MC, V.

D

★ ★ **BRAVO.** *5402 Portage Rd (49002). Phone 269/344-7700. www.bravokalamazoo.com.* American, Italian menu. Contemporary Italian décor. Hours: 11:30 am-10 pm; Fri to 11 pm; Sat 5-11 pm; Sun 4-9 pm; closed for holidays, except for Thanksgiving Day. Lunch $5-$12, dinner $10.95-$21.95. Sun brunch 10:30 am-2 pm. Sun brunch $14.95. Bar. Child's meals. Reservations accepted. Cr cds: A, DS, MC, V.

D

★ ★ ★ **WEBSTER'S.** *100 W Michigan Ave (49007). Phone 269/343-4444; fax 269/381-1560.* The elegant copper and brass display kitchen turns out fresh seafood and grilled steaks as well as tableside Caesar salads and freshly prepared desserts. Contemporary American menu. Closed Sun; some major holidays. Dinner. Bar. Entertainment Fri-Sat. Cr cds: A, D, DS, MC, V.

D

Lansing (H-4)

Settled 1847 **Pop** 127,321 **Elev** 860 ft **Area code** 517

Information Greater Lansing Convention & Visitors Bureau, 1223 Turner St, Suite 200, 48906; 517/487-6800 or 888/252-6746

Web www.lansing.org

When the capital of Michigan moved here in 1847 for lack of agreement on a better place, the "city" consisted of one log house and a sawmill. Today, in addition to state government, Lansing is the headquarters for many trade and professional associations and has much heavy industry. R. E. Olds, who built and marketed one of America's earliest automobiles, started the city's industrial growth. Lansing is the home of the Lansing Automotive Division of General Motors and many allied industries. East Lansing, a neighboring community, is the home of the Michigan State University Spartans and is part of the capital city in all respects except government.

What to See and Do

BoarsHead Theater. *Center for the Arts, 425 S Grand Ave. Phone 517/484-7800.* A regional center with a professional resident theater company.

Brenke River Sculpture and Fish Ladder. *2 miles N via Washington Ave.* Located at North Lansing Dam on the Riverfront Park scenic walk, sculpture encompasses the ladder designed by artist/sculptor Joseph E. Kinnebrew and landscape architect Robert O'Boyle.

Fenner Nature Center. *2020 E Mt Hope Ave, at Aurelius Rd. Phone 517/483-4224.* Park features a bald eagle, two waterfowl ponds, replica of a pioneer cabin and garden, 5 miles of nature trails through a variety of habitats; picnicking. Nature center with small animal exhibits (Tues-Sun). Trails (daily). **FREE**

Impression 5 Science Center. *200 Museum Dr. Phone 517/485-8116.* Center has more than 200 interactive, hands-on exhibits, incl computer lab, chemistry experiments; restaurant. (Mon-Sat; closed holidays) **$$**

The Ledges. *10 miles W via MI 43 in Grand Ledge. Phone 517/627-7351.* Edging the Grand River, the Ledges are quartz sandstone 300 million years old. They are considered a good rock climbing area for the experienced. (Daily) **$**

Michigan Historical Museum. *717 W Allegan St. Phone 517/373-3559.* (Michigan Library & Historical Center) Exhibits include a copper mine, sawmill, and 54-foot-high relief map of Michigan; audiovisual programs, hands-on exhibits. (Daily; closed holidays) **FREE**

Michigan State University. *Phone 517/353-1855.* (1855) 42,000 students. Founded as the country's first agricultural college and forerunner of the nationwide land-grant university system, MSU, located on a 5,300-acre landscaped campus with 7,800 different species and varieties of trees, shrubs, and vines, is known for its research, Honors College, and many innovations in education. Among the interesting features of the campus are Abrams Planetarium (shows: Fri-Sun, fee; phone 517/355-4672); Horticultural Gardens; W. J. Beal Botanical Garden; Breslin Student Events Center (box office, phone 517/432-5000); Wharton Center for Performing Arts (box office, phone 517/432-2000); Michigan State University Museum (Mon-Sat, also Sun afternoons, closed holidays); and Kresge Art Museum (Daily; closed holidays).

Potter Park Zoo. *1301 S Pennsylvania Ave. Phone 517/483-4222.* Zoo on the Red Cedar River; has more than 400 animals. Educational programs, camel and pony rides, playground, concession, and picnic facilities. (Daily) **$$**

★ **R. E. Olds Transportation Museum.** *240 Museum Dr. Phone 517/372-0422.* Named after Ransom Eli Olds, the museum houses Lansing-built vehicles include Oldsmobile, REO, Star, and Durant autos; REO and

Duplex trucks, bicycles, airplanes; period clothing, photographic display of Olds' Victorian home, and a "Wall of Wheels" from the Motor Wheel Corp. (Tues-Sat; closed Jan 1, Dec 25)

State Capitol Building. *Capitol and Michigan aves. Phone 517/373-2353.* Dedicated in 1879, this was one of the first state capitol buildings to emulate the dome and wings of the US Capitol in Washington, D.C. Interior walls and ceilings reflect the work of many skilled artisans, muralists, and portrait painters. Tours (daily). **FREE**

Woldumar Nature Center. *5539 Lansing Rd. Phone 517/322-0030.* A 188-acre wildlife preserve; nature walks, interpretive center (Mon-Sat; closed holidays). Trails open for hiking and skiing (daily, dawn-dusk). **DONATION**

Special Events

East Lansing Art Festival. *Phone 517/337-1731.* Artists' work for sale, continuous performances, ethnic foods, children's activities. Third weekend May.

Mint Festival. *18 miles N via US 27 in St. Johns. Phone 517/224-7248.* Queen contest, parade, mint farm tours, antiques, arts and crafts, flea market, entertainment. Second weekend Aug.

Motels/Motor Lodges

★ ★ **BEST WESTERN MIDWAY HOTEL.** *7111 W Saginaw Hwy (48917). Phone 517/627-8471; toll-free 877/772-6100; fax 517/627-8597. www.bestwestern.com.* 149 rooms, 2-3 story. Sept-May: S $78; D $88; each additional $5; under 12 free; lower rates rest of year. Crib free. Pet accepted. TV; cable (premium). Indoor pool; whirlpool. Coffee in rooms. Restaurant 6:30 am-10 pm; weekend hours vary. Room service. Bar 11-2 am. Check-out noon. Meeting rooms. Business services available. Bellhops. Valet service. Sundries. Free airport transportation. Exercise equipment; sauna. Game room. Refrigerators available. Cr cds: A, C, D, DS, MC, V.

★ ★ **CLARION HOTEL & CONFERENCE CENTER.** *3600 Dunckel Dr (48910). Phone 517/351-7600; fax 517/351-4640.* Located 10 minutes from Michigan State University. A restaurant and lounge are on site for guests dining pleasure. 150 rooms, 2 story. S $71-$110; D $81-$112; each additional $10; suites $175; under 18 free; weekly rates. Crib free. Check-out 11 am. TV; cable (premium). Private patios, balconies. Valet service. Restaurant 6:30 am-11 pm; Sat, Sun from 7 am. Bar 11-1 am; entertainment Mon-Sat. Room service. Exercise equipment, sauna. Game room. 2 pools, 1 indoor, whirlpool. Putting green. Lighted tennis. Cross-country ski 7 miles. Lawn games. Free airport transportation. Meeting room, business services. Sundries. Cr cds: A, C, D, DS, JCB, MC, V.

★ **COMFORT INN & EXECUTIVE SUITES.** *2209 University Park Dr (48864). Phone 517/349-8700; toll-free 800/228-5150; fax 517/349-5638. www.comfortinn.com.* 160 rooms, 2 story. S, D $59-$95; each additional $6; suites $85-$115; under 18 free; higher rates special events. Crib free. TV; cable. Indoor pool; whirlpool. Complimentary continental breakfast. Restaurant adjacent 6 am-midnight. Check-out 11 am. Meeting room. Business services available. Cross-country ski 5 miles. Exercise equipment; sauna, steam room. Whirlpool in suites. Cr cds: A, C, D, DS, JCB, MC, V.

★ ★ **COURTYARD BY MARRIOTT.** *2710 Lake Lansing Rd (48912). Phone 517/482-0500; fax 517/482-0557. www.marriott.com.* 129 rooms, 2 story, 17 suites. S $56; D $64; suites $70-$105; under 16 free. Crib free. Complimentary full breakfast. Check-out noon. TV; cable (premium), VCR available. Private patios, balconies. Valet services, coin laundry. Indoor pool, whirlpool. Cross-country ski 5 miles. Picnic tables. Meeting rooms, business center. Cr cds: A, C, D, DS, MC, V.

★ **FAIRFIELD INN.** *2335 Woodlake Dr (48864). Phone 517/347-1000; toll-free 800/568-4421; fax 517/347-5092. www.fairfieldinn.com.* 79 rooms, 2 story. S $59; D $64; each additional $5; suites $125; under 18 free. Crib free. TV; cable (premium). Indoor pool; whirlpool. Complimentary continental breakfast. Restaurant nearby. Check-out noon. Valet service. Some refrigerators. Cr cds: A, C, D, DS, ER, JCB, MC, V.

★ **HAMPTON INN.** *525 N Canal Rd (48917). Phone 517/627-8381; fax 517/627-5502. www.hamptoninn.com.* 109 rooms, 3 story. S $71; D $79; suites $84; under 18 free. Crib free. TV; cable (premium). Complimentary continental breakfast. Restaurant adjacent 6 am-10 pm. Check-out noon. Meeting rooms. Business services available. Valet service. Refrigerator in suites. Some balconies. Cr cds: A, C, D, DS, MC, V.

★ ★ **HOLIDAY INN.** *6820 S Cedar St (48911). Phone 517/694-8123; toll-free 800/465-4329; fax 517/699-3753. www.holiday-inn.com.* 300 rooms, 5 story. S $120; D $130; each additional $10; suites $200-$390; under 18 free; weekend rates. Crib free. TV; cable. Indoor pool; whirlpool. Coffee in rooms. Restaurant 6:30 am-10 pm. Bar 4 pm-1 am. Check-out noon. Convention facilities. Business services available. Airport, train station, bus depot transportation. Cross-country ski 3 miles. Exercise equipment; sauna. Sun deck. Game room. Refrigerators. Cr cds: A, C, D, DS, JCB, MC, V.

★ **QUALITY SUITES.** *901 Delta Commerce Dr (48917). Phone 517/886-0600; fax 517/886-0103. www.qualityinn.com.* 117 suites, 4 story. D $99; each additional $10; under 18 free. Complimentary full breakfast. Check-out 11 am. TV; cable (premium), VCR available (movies). Exercise equipment, sauna. Free airport transportation. Cr cds: A, C, D, DS, JCB, MC, V.

⬚ 🛉 ✈ 🛇

★**RED ROOF INN LANSING EAST.** *3615 Dunckel Rd (48910). Phone 517/332-2575; toll-free 800/843-7663; fax 517/332-1459. www.redroof.com.* 80 rooms, 2 story. S $41-$51; D $42-$54; each additional $6; under 18 free. Crib free. Pet accepted. TV. Restaurant opposite 7 am-11 pm. Check-out noon. Business services available. Cr cds: A, C, D, DS, MC, V.

⬚ 🐾 🛇 SC

Hotels

★ ★ ★ **MARRIOTT AT UNIVERSITY PLACE EAST LANSING.** *300 M.A.C. Ave (48823). Phone 517/337-4440; fax 517/337-5001. www.marriott.com.* 180 rooms, 7 story. S, D $119; weekend rates; higher rates: university football wkends, graduation. Crib free. TV; cable (premium). Indoor pool; whirlpool. Complimentary coffee in lobby. Restaurant 6:30 am-midnight; Sat from 7 am; Sun 7 am-10 pm. Room service. Bar 11 am-midnight; Sun to 10 pm. Check-out noon. Coin laundry. Meeting rooms. Business services available. Bellhops. Valet service. Sundries. Free garage parking. Free airport transportation. Exercise equipment; sauna. Balconies. Cr cds: A, C, D, DS, ER, JCB, MC, V.

⬚ 🛏 🛉 🛇 🚶

★ ★ ★ **RADISSON.** *111 N Grand Ave (48933). Phone 517/482-0188; toll-free 800/333-3333; fax 517/487-6646. www.radisson.com.* This is the only hotel located in downtown Lansing and is near many attractions including Oldsmobile Park and the Lansing Convention Center. 260 rooms, 11 story. S, D $79-$139; suites $185-$199; under 19 free. Crib free. TV; cable (premium). Indoor pool; whirlpool. Coffee in rooms. Restaurant 6 am-11 pm. Bar 11-1 am. Check-out noon. Convention facilities. Business services available. Concierge. Gift shop. Free valet parking. Free airport, train station, bus depot transportation. Cross-country ski 6 miles. Exercise equipment; sauna. Bathroom phone, refrigerator in suites. Cr cds: A, C, D, DS, ER, JCB, MC, V.

⬚ 🛉 🛏 🛉 ✈ 🛇 SC 🚶

★ ★ ★ **SHERATON HOTEL.** *925 S Creyts Rd (48917). Phone 517/323-7100; toll-free 800/325-3535; fax 517/323-2180. www.sheratonlansing.com.* 219 rooms, 5 story. S $89-$119; D $99-$129; each additional $12; suites $225; under 18 free; weekend rates. Crib free. TV; cable

(premium). Indoor pool. Coffee in rooms. Restaurant 6:30 am-midnight. Room service. Bar 11-2 am. Check-out noon. Meeting rooms. Business services available. Bellhops. Gift shop. Free airport transportation. Cross-country ski 5 miles. Exercise equipment; sauna. Some refrigerators. Cr cds: A, C, D, DS, ER, MC, V.

⬚ 🛉 🛉 🛏 🛉 ✈ 🛇 🚶

B&B/Small Inns

★ ★ **THE ENGLISH INN.** *677 S Michigan Rd (48827). Phone 517/663-2500; toll-free 800/858-0598; fax 517/663-2643. www.englishinn.com.* 10 rooms, 3 story. Children over 12 years only. Complimentary continental breakfast. Check-out 11 am, check-in 3 pm. TV; cable (premium), VCR available. Restaurant. Pool. Cross-country ski on site. Built in 1927; antiques. Totally nonsmoking. Cr cds: A, DS, MC, V.

🛉 🛉 🛏 🛇

Extended Stay

★ ★ **RESIDENCE INN BY MARRIOTT EAST LANSING.** *1600 Grand River (48823). Phone 517/332-7711; fax 517/332-7711. www.marriott.com.* 60 kitchen suites, 2 story. S $115; D $165; each additional $10; family rates. Crib free. TV; cable (premium), VCR available (movies). Heated pool; whirlpool. Complimentary continental breakfast. Complimentary coffee in rooms. Restaurants nearby. Check-out noon. Coin laundry. Business services available. Valet service. Health club privileges. Balconies. Picnic table, grill. Cr cds: A, C, D, DS, ER, JCB, MC, V.

⬚ 🛏 🛇

Leland (D-2)

Pop 400 **Elev** 602 ft **Area code** 231 **Zip** 49654

What to See and Do

⭐ **Boat trips to Manitou Islands.** *207 W River St. Leland Harbor. Phone 231/256-9061.* The Mishe-mokwa makes daily trips in summer, incl overnight camping excursions, to North and South Manitou islands; also evening cocktail cruise. (June-Aug, daily; May, Sept-Oct, Mon, Wed, Fri-Sun) $$$$

Motel/Motor Lodge

★ ★ **LELAND LODGE.** *565 E Pearl St (49654). Phone 616/256-9848; fax 616/256-8812.* 18 rooms, 2 story, 4 kitchens Mid-June-Labor Day: S, D $89-$149; each additional $10; kitchen units $805-$995/wk; lower rates rest of year. Crib free. TV; cable. Complimentary continental breakfast weekends (in season). Restaurant 11 am-10 pm; off-season to 9 pm. Room service. Bar 11 am-11 pm.

Check-out 11 am. Business services available. 18-hole golf privileges. Cr cds: A, DS, MC, V.

D 🛅

B&B/Small Inns

★★ **MANITOU MANOR BED & BREAKFAST.** *Phone 231/256-7712; fax 231/256-7941.* Day-mid-Oct: S, D $140; each additional $15; family, weekly rates; lower rates rest of year. Complimentary full breakfast. Check-out 11am, check-in Noon. TV in sitting room; VCR. Downhill ski 5 miles; cross-country ski on site. Historic (1873) farmhouse with 6 acres of cherry trees. Totally nonsmoking. Cr cds: DS, MC, V.

🔧 ⚞ ⚟ SC

Restaurants

★★ **BLUE BIRD.** *102 River St (49654). Phone 231/256-9081; fax 231/256-7052. www.leelanav.com/bluebird.* Hours: 11:30 am-3 pm, 5-9 pm; Sun 5-9 pm; Late-Nov-Mar: Sun brunch 10 am-2 pm; Fri, Sat 5-9 pm. Closed first 3 weeks Nov; also Mon Apr-mid-June, after Labor Day-Oct. Reservations accepted. Bar 11:30 am-midnight. Lunch $4-$8.50, dinner $8.95-$16.95. Child's meals. Specializes in prime rib, seafood, Great Lakes fish. Salad bar. Overlooks channel. Family-owned. Cr cds: DS, MC, V.

D

★★ **COVE.** *111 River St (49654). Phone 231/256-9834; fax 231/256-2704.* Specializes in seafood. Hours: 11 am-10 pm. Closed Mid-Oct-mid-May. Lunch $3.95-$8.95, dinner $12.95-$25. Bar. Child's meals. Reservations accepted. Outdoor dining. Cr cds: A, MC, V.

D

★★ **LEELANAU COUNTRY INN.** *149 E Harbor Hwy (49664). Phone 231/228-5060. www.leelanaucountryinn.com.* Specializes in fresh seafood, prime rib, pasta. Hours: 5-9 pm; early-bird dinner 5-6 pm; hours vary Nov-May. Closed Dec 24, 25, 26. Dinner $10.95-$22.95. Child's meals. Converted house (1891); guest rooms available. Reservations accepted. Cr cds: MC, V.

D SC

Ludington (F-1)

See also Manistee

Settled 1880 **Pop** 8,507 **Elev** 610 ft **Area code** 231 **Zip** 49431

Information Ludington Area Convention & Visitor Bureau, 5300 W US 10; 231/845-0324 or 877/420-6618

Web www.ludingtoncvb.com

A large passenger car ferry and freighters keep this important Lake Michigan port busy. First named Père Marquette, in honor of the missionary explorer who died here in 1675, the community later adopted the name of its more recent founder, James Ludington, a lumber baron. Ludington draws vacationers because of its long stretch of beach on Lake Michigan and miles of forests, lakes, streams, and dunes surrounding the town. The Père Marquette River has been stocked with chinook salmon; fishing boats may be chartered.

What to See and Do

Auto Ferry/SS Badger. *701 Maritime Dr. At the end of US 10. Phone 231/845-5555; toll-free 800/841-4243.* Instead of driving all the way around Lake Michigan, you can drive right onto the SS Badger and ride across. This car ferry takes passengers and vehicles on a 4-hour trip to Manitowoc, WI, and back (if you wish). Amenities include a nautical history display, game room, movie screenings, staterooms, and food service. (May-Oct, daily) **$$$$**

Ludington Pumped Storage Hydroelectric Plant. *3225 S Lakeshore Dr (49431). Phone 800/477-5050.* Scenic overlooks beside Lake Michigan and the plant's 840-acre reservoir. One of the world's largest facilities of this type. (Apr-Nov, daily) **FREE** Footpaths connect to

> **Mason County Campground and Picnic Area.** *5906 W Chauvez Rd (49431). S Old US 31 to Chauvez Rd, then 1 1/2 miles S. Phone 231/845-7609.* Picnicking, playground, camping (hookups). (Memorial Day-Labor Day, daily) **$$$**

Ludington State Park. *MI 116 N (49431). 8 1/2 miles N on MI 116. Phone 231/843-8671.* Approximately 4,500 acres on lakes Michigan and Hamlin and the Sable River. Swimming, bathhouse, waterskiing, fishing, boating (ramp, rentals); hunting, cross-country skiing, picnicking, playground, concession, camping. Visitor center (May-Sept). Standard fees. **$$**

Pere Marquette Memorial Cross. Towers high into the skyline, overlooks the harbor and Lake Michigan.

Stearns Park. Half-mile swimming beach (lifeguard, June-Labor Day), fishing, boating, ramps, launch, 150-slip marina; picnicking, playground, miniature golf, shuffleboard. Fee for some activities.

White Pine Village. *1687 S Lakeshore Dr (49431). 3 miles S via US 31 to Iris Rd, follow signs. Phone 231/843-4808.* Historical buildings re-create small-town Michigan life in the late 1800s; general store, trapper's cabin, courthouse/jail, town hall, one-room school, and others. (June-early Sept, Tues-Sun) **$$**

Motels/Motor Lodges

★ **FOUR SEASONS MOTEL.** *717 E Ludington Ave (49431). Phone 616/843-3448; toll-free 800/968-0180;*

fax 616/843-2635. www.fourseasonsmotel.com. 33 rooms. Mid-June-mid-Oct: S, D $45-$99; higher rates: holidays, festivals; lower rates rest of year. Crib free. TV; cable (premium), VCR available. Complimentary continental breakfast. Coffee in rooms. Restaurant nearby. Check-out 11 am. Free airport transportation. Golf privileges. Cross-country ski 6 miles. Cr cds: DS, MC, V.

⬛ 🏊 ⬛ SC

★ **MARINA BAY MOTOR LODGE.** 604 W Ludington Ave (49431). Phone 616/845-5124; toll-free 800/968-1440; fax 616/843-7929. 24 rooms, 1-2 story. Late June-early Sept: S, D $60-$135; each additional $5; higher rates special events; lower rates rest of year. Crib free. TV; cable (premium), VCR available (movies $2). Complimentary coffee in lobby. Restaurant nearby. Check-out 11 am. Business services available. Free airport transportation. Cross-country ski 4 miles. Some in-room whirlpools. Cr cds: DS, MC, V.

🏊

★ **MILLERS LAKESIDE MOTEL.** 808 W Ludington Ave (49431). Phone 616/843-3458; toll-free 800/843-2177; fax 616/843-3450. 52 rooms. Mid-May-mid-Sept: S, D $65-$80; each additional $5; suites $95; higher rates: holidays, special events; weekly rates off-season; lower rates rest of year. Crib free. TV; cable (premium), VCR available. Heated pool. Restaurant nearby. Check-out 11 am. Business services available. Free airport transportation. Cross-country ski 5 miles. Public beach, launching ramp, park, miniature golf opposite. Cr cds: A, DS, MC, V.

⬛ 🏊 ⬛ ⬛ SC

★ **RAMADA INN & CONVENTION CENTER.** 4079 W US 10 & Brye Rd (49431). Phone 616/845-7311; toll-free 800/707-7475; fax 616/843-8551. 116 rooms, 4 story. Mid-May-early Sept: S $89; D $99; each additional $10; suites $125; under 16 free; weekly rates; golf plans; lower rates rest of year. Crib free. TV; cable (premium). Indoor pool; whirlpool. Restaurant 6:30 am-10 pm. Room service. Bar 5 pm-midnight; entertainment Thurs-Sat. Check-out 11 am. Coin laundry. Meeting rooms. Business services available. Exercise equipment; sauna. Game room. Cr cds: A, C, D, DS, MC, V.

⬛ ⬛ 🏋 ⬛ SC

★ **SNYDER'S SHORELINE INN.** 903 W Ludington Ave (49431). Phone 231/845-1261; fax 616/843-4441. 44 rooms, 2 story. D $89-$249; each additional $20. Complimentary continental breakfast. Check-out 11 am. TV; cable (premium), VCR available (free movies). On lake; swimming beach. Pool, whirlpool. Free airport transportation. Cr cds: A, MC, V.

⬛ ⬛ ⬛ ⬛ ⬛

★ **VIKING ARMS INN.** 930 E Ludington Ave (49431). Phone 231/843-3441; toll-free 800/748-0173; fax 231/845-7703. www.vikingarmsinn.com. 45 rooms. D $50-$150; each additional $5. Complimentary continental breakfast. Check-out 11 am. TV; cable; VCR (movies $3). Some fireplaces. Pool, whirlpool. Cross-country ski 7 miles. Free airport transportation. Cr cds: MC, V.

⬛ 🏊 ⬛ ✈ ⬛

B&B/Small Inns

★ ★ **NICKERSON INN.** 262 W Lowell (48858). Phone 231/869-6731; fax 616/869-6151. 13 rooms, 3 suites, 3 story. No room phones. Children over 12 years only. Complimentary full breakfast. Check-out 11 am, check-in 2 pm. Restaurant. Built in 1914; antiques. Cr cds: DS, MC, V.

⬛ ⬛ ⬛ ⬛

Restaurant

★ ★ **SCOTTY'S.** 5910 E Ludington Ave (US 10) (49431). Phone 231/843-4033. American menu. Hours: 11:30 am-2 pm, 5-10 pm; Sat from 5 pm; Sun 9 am-1 pm; early bird winter only. Closed Thanksgiving, Dec 25. Dinner $9.95-$25.95. Bar. Child's menu. Casual attire. Parking. Cr cds: A, MC, V.

⬛

Mackinac Island (C-4)

See also Mackinaw City, Saint Ignace

Pop 469 **Elev** 600-925 ft **Area code** 906 **Zip** 49757

Information Chamber of Commerce, PO Box 451; 906/847-3783 or 800/454-5227

Web www.mackinac.com

Labeled the "Bermuda of the North," Mackinac (MAK-i-naw) Island retains the atmosphere of the 19th century and the imprint of history. In view of the Mackinac Bridge, it has been a famous resort for the last century. The island was called "great turtle" by Native Americans who believed that its towering heights and rock formations were shaped by supernatural forces. Later, because of its strategic position, the island became the key to the struggle between England and France for control of the rich fur trade of the great Northwest. Held by the French until 1760, it became English after Wolfe's victory at Québec, was turned over to the United States at the close of the American Revolution, reverted to the British during the War of 1812, and finally was restored to the United States.

With the decline of the fur trade in the 1830s, Mackinac Island began to develop its potential as a resort area.

Exploring Mackinac Island

Mackinac is truly an island that time forgot: the clippety-clop of horse-drawn wagons echoes in the streets, period-garbed docents stroll among historical reconstructions, and quaint candy shops roll out fudge by the ton. And yet, many tourists manage to go there and only see the two or three square-blocks off the tour-boat docks and miss all the rest. Mackinac Island is the perfect approximation of living history, tacky tourism, sublime aesthetics, and lovely natural scenery-all contained on an island that can be circumnavigated in one but rewarding day hike.

The best option is to take the early-morning ferry. Spend some time lolling around the anachronistic downtown, the make a quick visit to historic Fort Mackinac. Then head a few miles to Arch Rock for stunning views of the sun rising steadily over the Great Lake. From there, head inland to the modest but occasionally daunting central rise of the island, bypassing an old fort and two cemeteries where original settlers and soldiers are buried. Next head south via British Landing Road for a look at the Governor"s Residence before returning to the downtown. Or, if you are in marathon shape, you may want to hike from the cemeteries all the way to the northwest shoreline, where historic markers indicate the site of the British invasion that occurred over a century ago. If you stay along the main road to the south, you may be lucky enough to witness a most resplendent sunset as you waltz back into downtown.

German Village

German Village is a neighborhood to its roots. Uneven brick streets hand-laid in a herringbone pattern are lined with trees and the plain, simple brick cottages of German brewery workers. Boxlike brick houses feature carved limestone lintels and steps, slate roofs, and miniscule well-kept yards. The village offers weekend zither concerts, a huge Oktoberfest, a clutch of German restaurants, and genuine old-world charm. There is a noticeable absence of neon. In fact, the entire historic district is listed on the National Register of Historic Places. Start at the German Village Meeting Haus (588 S Third St), where an 11-minute video tells the story of the settlement. An exhibit includes a timeline of German Village and items from the Wagner Brewery collection. Head south to the Golden Hobby Shop (630 S Third St). This 125-year-old former schoolhouse is chock-full of items crafted by local seniors. Included are handmade quilts, Afghans, ceramics, jewelry, stained glass, woodcrafts, and holiday decorations-all

at great prices. The Boot Loft (631 S Third St) is a city-block long with 32 rooms of bargain paperbacks and hardcovers, many 50-90 percent off original prices. One of the nation's largest independents, this rambling bookstore stocks more than one million items. It is contained (barely) in pre-Civil War era buildings that once housed general stores, a saloon, and nickelodeon cinema. The courtyard provides a great space to sit, relax, and people-watch. Next door is Cup O" Joe (627 S Third St), where comfy couches and chairs make it a favorite hangout for locals and visitors. Grab a cup of house blend or a latte and indulge from an irresistible assortment of pastries, cheesecake, scones, and muffins. Hausfrau Haven (769 S Third St) is a whimsical general store with an eclectic stock of wine, beer, outrageous greeting cards, political put-down T-shirts, and a scrumptious local confection known as buckeyes: rich peanut-butter-filled chocolates resembling the horse chestnuts that give Ohio its nickname. Turn left to Kossuth and Helen Winnemore's Contemporary Craft Gallery (150 E Kossuth St), one of the nation's oldest, continuously operating fine crafts shops, with jewelry and works of clay, metal, and wood. Housed in a charming brick cottage, it is the ultimate customer-friendly shop. Visitors are greeted with coffee or tea and invited not only to browse items on display, but also to check out drawers of jewelry and other items.

Mohawk dead-ends into Schiller Park, a beautiful, 23-acre urban park named after German poet-philosopher Frederich Schiller. Actors Summer Theatre stages Shakespeare productions and musicals in the amphitheater. The park, containing a large statue of the eponymous Schiller, is ringed by large homes built by German brewery owners in the early and mid-19th century. Stroll north down City Park Ave, arguably the prettiest street in the village. It"s a great place to enjoy beautiful landscaping, peek into backyard gardens, and greet a few neighborhood dogs. Quilts & Stuff (911 City Park) has been selling quilted items at this location for many years. Continue north, make a left on Beck, a right on Third, and end your tour at Katzinger's Delicatessen (475 S Third St). Sandwich #59—a hot corned beef and Swiss on pumpernickel—was renamed ""Bill's Day at the Deli"" after former President Clinton enjoyed one. Other eateries include Schmidt's Sausage Haus (240 E Kossuth St), an historic landmark specializing in German/American foods. At Juergen's German Village Backerei & Konditorei (525 S Fourth St), proprietor Rosemarie Keidel serves up German pastries and foods in a former boarding house where waitresses wear traditional dirndls.

Southern planters and their families summered here prior to the Civil War; wealthy Chicagoans took their place in the years following. No automobiles are allowed on the island; transportation is by horse and carriage or bicycle. Horse and carriages and bicycles can be rented. Passenger ferries make regularly scheduled trips to the island from Mackinaw City and St. Ignace, or visitors can reach the island by air from St. Ignace, Pellston, or Detroit.

What to See and Do

Mackinac Island Carriage Tours, Inc. *Main St. Phone 906/847-3307.* Narrated, historic, and scenic horse-drawn carriage tour (1-3/4 hrs) covering 20 sights. (Mid-May-mid-Oct, daily; some tours available rest of year) **$$$$**

⭐ **Mackinac Island State Park.** *300 S Washington Sq. Phone 906/847-3328.* Comprises approximately 80 percent of the island. Michigan's first state park has views of the Straits of Mackinac, prehistoric geological formations such as Arch Rock, and shoreline and inland trails. Visitor center at Huron St has informative exhibits, a slide presentation, and guidebooks (mid-May-mid-Oct, daily). British Landing Nature Center (May-Labor Day). Included in the admission price are Mission Church (1830), Biddle House (1780), and McGulpin House. **FREE** Here is

Beaumont Memorial. Monument to Dr. William Beaumont, who charted observations of the human digestive system by viewing this action through an opening in the abdomen of a wounded French-Canadian. (Mid-June-Labor Day, daily)

Benjamin Blacksmith Shop. *Market St.* A working forge in replica of blacksmith shop dating from 1880s. (Mid-June-Labor Day, daily)

Fort Mackinac. *Fort St. Phone 906/847-3328.* (1780-1895) High on a bluff overlooking the Straits of Mackinac, this 18th-19th-century British and American military outpost is complete with massive limestone ramparts, cannon, guardhouse, blockhouses, barracks; costumed interpreters, reenactments, children's discovery room, crafts demonstrations; rifle and cannon firings; audiovisual presentation. (Mid-May-mid-Oct, daily) **$$$**

Indian Dormitory. *(1838)* Built as a place for Native Americans to live during annual visits to the Mackinac Island office of the US Indian Agency; interpretive displays, craft demonstrations; murals depicting scenes from Longfellow's "Hiawatha." (Mid-June-Labor Day, daily)

Marquette Park. *401 E Fair Ave. Main St. Phone 906/228-0460.* Statue of Father Marquette, historic marker, and 66 varieties of lilacs dominate this park.

Shepler's Mackinac Island Ferry. *556 E Central Ave. Phone 616/436-5023.* Departs 556 E Central Ave, Macki-naw City or from downtown St. Ignace. (Early May-early Nov) **$$$$**

Star Line Ferry. *587 N State St. Phone Toll 800 638-9892.* "Hydro Jet" service from Mackinaw City and St. Ignace. (May-Oct) **$$$$**

Special Events

Lilac Festival. *Main St (49757). Phone 800/4-LILACS.* Second week June.

Sailing races. *Main St (49757). Phone 906/847-3783.* Port Huron to Mackinac and Chicago to Mackinac. Mid-late July.

Hotels

⭐⭐⭐ **IROQUOIS MOTEL.** *Phone 906/847-3321; fax 906/847-6274. www.iroquoishotel.com.* This Victorian hotel offers guestrooms and suites at a lakefront location. Guests can enjoy fine dining at the Carriage House or a drink at the Piano Bar. Visitors can rent bicycles from the property to take a tour of the local area. 47 rooms, 3 story. No A/C. Mid-June-mid-Sept: S, D $115-$280; each additional $15; suites $360; spring, fall packages; lower rates mid-May-mid-June, mid-Sept-late Oct. Closed rest of year. TV in some rooms, sitting room. Restaurant (see CARRIAGE HOUSE). Room service. Check-out noon, check-in 3 pm. Business services available. Luggage handling. Valet service. 18-hole golf privileges. Overlooks water, private beach. Cr cds: A, MC, V.
✈

⭐⭐ **ISLAND HOUSE.** *100 Main St (49757). Phone 906/847-3347; toll-free 800/626-6304; fax 906/847-3819. www.theislandhouse.com.* This hotel, built in 1852, offers a great getaway where visitors can relax and enjoy their time. The property has beautifully decorated guestrooms that overlook the marina and Mackinac Harbor. A short ferry will bring guests to the island. 97 rooms, 50 A/C, 4 story. Mid-June-Labor Day: S, D $145-$165; each additional $20; suites $400; under 13 free; MAP available; lower rates mid-May-mid-June, after Labor Day-mid-Oct. Closed rest of year. Crib free. Check-out 11 am. Restaurant (see GOVNOR'S LOUNGE). Bar noon-2 am; entertainment Tues-Sun. No room service. Indoor pool, whirlpool. Steam room. Golf privileges. Tennis privileges. Airport transportation. Meeting rooms, business services. One of first summer hotels on island (1852); Victorian architecture. Lake opposite. Cr cds: A, DS, MC.
🄳 🗱 🛠 🕌 🛍 🛥 🕴 🛏 🎿

⭐⭐⭐ **LAKE VIEW.** *1 Huron St (49757). Phone 906/847-3384; fax 906/847-6283. www.mackinac.com.* With furnishings reflecting the early Victorian influence on Mackinac Island, this small and unique hotel has cozy guest suites, on-site shops, a restaurant, and pub. Guests, though, will find no automobiles on the island. 85 rooms, some A/C, 4 story. May-Oct: S $99-$179; D $139-$275; each additional $20; under 16 free. Closed rest of year. Crib free. Indoor pool; whirlpool, sauna. Restaurant 7:30 am-10 pm, off season to 8 pm. Check-out 11 am. Meeting rooms. Business services available. Lake opposite. Cr cds: DS, MC, V.

★ ★ **LILAC TREE HOTEL.** *Main St (49757). Phone 906/847-6575; fax 906/847-3501.* 39 suites, 3 story. July-Aug: S, D $175-$250; family, holiday rates; lower rates May-June, Sept-Oct. Closed rest of year. Crib free. TV; cable (premium). Complimentary coffee in rooms. Restaurant 11 am-2 pm. No room service. Check-out 11 am. In-room modem link. Shopping arcade. Refrigerators. Balconies. Each suite uniquely decorated; antique and reproduction furnishings. Cr cds: A, MC, V.

Resorts

★ ★ ★ **GRAND HOTEL.** *1 Grand Ave (49757). Phone 906/847-3331; toll-free 800/334-7263; fax 906/847-3259. www.grandhotel.com.* From the moment one arrives on the island and is delivered to the hotel in a horse-drawn carriage, they are transported back to the 19th-century. The hotel rides regally on a bluff overlooking the straits of Mackinac. Sit in one of the giant rocking chairs on the longest front porch in America and watch the Great Lake freighters glide by while sipping a favorite beverage. Long a popular retreat for the romantic at heart, the hotel offers a variety of accommodations, shops, afternoon tea, and carriage rentals. 387 rooms, 6 story. Mid-May-Nov, MAP and FAP: S $275-$315; D $340-$360; each additional $99. Closed rest of year. Crib available. Service charge 18%. Check-out noon, check-in 3 pm. TV; cable. Some balconies. Restaurant 8 am-8:45 pm. Bar to 2 am. Entertainment, room service. Exercise equipment. Sauna. Recreation room. Heated pool, whirlpool, lifeguard. 18-hole golf, greens fee $75, putting green. Tennis, pro. Lawn games. Bicycles. Convention facilities. Afternoon tea. Large veranda overlooks Straits of Mackinac, formal gardens. On 500 acres; 2,000-acre state park adjacent. Cr cds: A, DS, MC, V.

★ ★ ★ **MISSION POINT RESORT.** *1 Lakeshore Dr (49757). Phone 906/847-3312; fax 906/847-3408. www.missionpoint.com.* 236 air-cooled rooms, 90 suites, 2-3 story. Late June-early Sept: S, D $189-$269; each additional $20; suites $210-$695; under 18 free; MAP available; higher rates: July 4, yacht races (3-day min); lower rates mid-May-late June, early Sept-mid-Oct. Closed rest of year. Crib free. Check-out 11 am, check-in 3 pm. TV; cable (premium), VCR available. Grocery, coin laundry, package store 1/2 mile. Dining room 7 am-11 pm. Snack bar. Bar 11-2 am. Room service. Supervised

children's activities; ages 4-12. Exercise equipment, sauna. Soc director. Game room. Heated pool, whirlpool, poolside service. Golf privileges. Tennis. Picnics. Lawn games. Bicycle rentals. Sailing nearby. Meeting rooms, business center. Concierge. Gift shop. Sunset cruises Sat evenings (in season). Movies nightly. 18 acres on lakefront. Cr cds: A, D, DS, MC, V.

B&B/Small Inns

★ ★ **BAY VIEW AT MACKINAC.** *100 Huron St (49757). Phone 906/847-3295; fax 906/847-6219. www.mackinacbayview.com.* 20 rooms, 3 story. Closed Nov-Apr. Adults only. Complimentary full breakfast. Check-out 11 am, check-in 3 pm. TV; VCR in suites. Built 1891 in Grand Victorian style; on bay. Totally nonsmoking. Cr cds: A, DS, MC, V.

Restaurants

★ ★ **CARRIAGE HOUSE.** *298 Main St (49757). Phone 906/847-3321; fax 906/847-6274. www.iroquoishotel.com.* Closed mid-Oct-Memorial Day. Breakfast, lunch, dinner. Bar. Children's menu. Outdoor dining. Cr cds: DS, MC, V.

★ ★ **OUNGE.** *Main St (49757). Phone 269/847-3347. www.theislandhouse.com.* Specialties: prime rib, pasta. Hours: 7:30-10:30 am, 5:30-10 pm. Closed mid-Oct-mid-May. A la carte entrees: dinner $12.95-$26.95. Buffet: Breakfast $13.95. Bar noon-2 am. Entertainment Tues-Sun. In Mackinac Island's oldest hotel (1852). Cr cds: A, DS, MC, V.

Mackinaw City (C-3)

See also St. Ignace

Settled 1681 **Pop** 875 **Elev** 590 ft **Area code** 231 **Zip** 49701

Information Greater Mackinaw Area Chamber of Commerce, 706 S Huron, PO Box 856, phone 231/436-5574; or the Mackinaw Area Tourist Bureau, 708 S Huron, PO Box 160, phone 800/666-0160

Web www.mackinawcity.com

The only place in America where one can see the sun rise on one Great Lake (Huron) and set on another (Michigan), Mackinaw City sits in the shadow of the Mackinac Bridge. The French trading post built here became Fort Michilimackinac about 1715. It was taken over by the British in 1761 and two years later was captured by Native

Americans. The British reoccupied the fort in 1764. The fort was rebuilt on Mackinac Island between 1780-1781.

What to See and Do

⭐ **Colonial Michilimackinac.** *207 W Sinclair. At south end of Mackinac Bridge. Phone 231/436-5563.* Reconstructed French and British outpost and fur-trading village of 1715-1781; costumed interpreters provide music and military demonstrations, pioneer cooking and crafts, children's program, and reenactments of French colonial wedding and arrival of the Voyageurs. Working artisans, musket and cannon firing (mid-June-Labor Day, daily). Murals, dioramas in restored barracks (mid-May-mid-Oct, daily). Re-created Native American encampment (mid-June-Labor Day). Archaeoligical tunnel "Treasures from the Sand"; visitors can view the longest ongoing archaeological dig in US (mid-June-Labor Day, daily). Visitor Center, audiovisual presentation. **$$$**

> **Mill Creek.** *9001 S US 23. 3 miles SE via US 23. Phone 231/436-7301.* Scenic 625-acre park features working water-powered sawmill (1790); nature trails, forest demonstration areas, maple sugar shack, active beaver colony, picnicking. Sawmill demonstrations; archaeological excavations (mid-June-Labor Day, Mon-Fri). Visitor center, audiovisual presentation. (Mid-May-mid-Oct, daily) **$$**

Mackinac Bridge. This imposing structure has reduced crossing time to the Upper Peninsula over the Straits of Mackinac to 10 minutes. Connecting Michigan's upper and lower peninsulas between St. Ignace and Mackinaw City, the 8,344-foot distance between cable anchorages makes it one of the world's longest suspension bridges. (Total length of steel superstructure: 19,243 feet; height above water at midspan: 199 feet; clearance for ships: 155 feet) Fine view from the bridge. Auto toll **$**

Mackinac Bridge Museum. *231 E Central Ave. Phone 231/436-5534.* Displays on the construction and maintenance of the bridge. Features original pieces of equipment. (Daily)

Shepler's Mackinac Island Ferry. *556 E Central. Phone 231/436-5023.* (Early May-early Nov) **$$$$**

Star Line Ferry. *711 S Huron. Phone 231/436-5045.* "Hydro-Jet" (May-Oct). **$$$$**

Wilderness State Park. *898 Wilderness Park Dr. 11 miles W of I-75, on Lake Michigan and Straits of Mackinac. Phone 231/436-5381.* Approximately 8,200 acres. Beaches, waterskiing, fishing, boating (launch); hunting in season, snowmobiling, cross-country skiing, picnic areas, playgrounds. Trailside cabins, camping. Standard fees. **$$**

Special Events

Colonial Michilimackinac Pageant. *Phone 231/436-5574.* Pageant and reenactment of Chief Pontiac's capture of the frontier fort in 1763; parade, muzzle-loading contests. Three days Memorial Day weekend.

Mackinac Bridge Walk. *Phone 231/436-5574.* Recreational walk for all across Mackinac Bridge (some lanes open to motor vehicles). Labor Day morning.

Mackinaw Mush Sled Dog Race. *Phone 231/436-5574.* The biggest dog sled race in the contiguous US. First week Feb.

Spring/Fall Bike Tours. *Phone 231/436-5574.* Biannual bicycle rides, ranging from 25-100 miles. Mid-June-mid-Sept.

Vesper Cruises. *Arnold's Line Dock. Phone 231/436-5902.* Sun evening. July-Sept.

Winterfest. *Phone 231/436-5574.* Late Jan.

Motels/Motor Lodges

⭐ **BEACHCOMBER MOTEL ON THE WATER.** *1011 S Huron St (49701). Phone 231/436-8451; toll-free 800/968-1383.* 22 rooms. July-early Aug: S $30-$125; D $35-$125; each additional $3; cottage $550/week; higher rates: July 4, antique car show, Labor Day weekend (2-day minimum); lower rates mid-Apr-June, early Sept-Oct. Closed rest of year. Crib free. Pet accepted, some restrictions. TV; cable (premium). Restaurant nearby. Check-out 10 am. Refrigerators available. Picnic tables. On lake; private beach. Cr cds: A, DS, MC, V.

⬛🏊🐾🍴🏖️ SC

⭐ **BEST WESTERN INN.** *112 Old US 31 (49701). Phone 616/436-5544; toll-free 800/528-1234; fax 616/436-7180. www.bestwestern.com.* 73 rooms, 2 story. D $52-$95; each additional $5. Nov-mid-Apr. Complimentary contintental breakfast. Check-out 11 am. TV; cable (premium), VCR available. In-room modem link. Laundry services. Indoor pool, whirlpool. Cr cds: A, C, D, DS, MC, V.

🏖️🏊 SC

⭐ **CHIPPEWA MOTOR LODGE.** *929 S Huron Ave (49701). Phone 616/436-8661; toll-free 800/748-0124; fax 616/436-8661. www.largestbeach.com.* 39 rooms, 1-3 story. D $49-$85; each additional $3-$5; under 12 free. Closed Nov-Apr. Check-out 10:30 am. TV; cable (premium). Game room. Private beach on Lake Huron. Indoor pool, whirlpool. Lawn games. Landscaped grounds. Cr cds: DS, MC, V.

⬛🐾🏖️🏊

⭐ **COMFORT INN.** *611 S Huron St (49701). Phone 616/436-5057; toll-free 800/221-2222; fax 616/436-7385. www.comfortinn.com.* 60 rooms, 3 story. No elevator. Late June-early Sept: S, D $88-$130; each additional $6; under 18 free; higher rates: Labor Day weekend, antique auto show (3-day minimum); lower rates May-late June, early Sept-Oct. Closed rest of year. Crib $6. TV; cable (premium). Indoor pool; whirlpool. Restaurant nearby. Check-out 10 am. Refrigerators. Balconies. On lake, beach. Cr cds: A, C, D, DS, ER, JCB, MC, V.

D ≈ ⊠ SC

★ **DAYS INN.** *825 S Huron St (49701). Phone 231/436-5557; toll-free 800/329-7466; fax 231/436-5703. www.daysinn.com.* 84 rooms, 2 story. Late June-early Sept: S $64-$144; D $68-$148; each additional $6; under 18 free; higher rates: summer holidays, antique car show, special events; Labor Day, antique car show (2-day minimum); lower rates Apr-late June, early Sept-Oct. Closed rest of year. Crib available. TV; cable, VCR available. Indoor pool; whirlpool, sauna. Playground. Complimentary coffee. Restaurant 7 am-9 pm. Room service. Check-out 11 am. Coin laundry. Meeting room. Putting green. Game room. Lawn games. Refrigerators available. Balconies. Picnic table. On lake; ferry terminal adjacent. Cr cds: A, C, D, DS, MC, V.

D ≈ ⊠ SC

★ **GRAND MACKINAW INN AND SUITES.** *907 S Huron (49701). Phone 231/436-8831; toll-free 800/822-8314. www.grandmackinaw.com.* 40 rooms, 1-2 story. D $65-$95; each additional $5. Closed Nov-Apr. Pet accepted, some restrictions; fee. Check-out 11 am. TV; cable (premium). Private sand beach; overlooks Lake Huron. Indoor pool, whirlpool. Lawn games. Cr cds: A, MC, V.

D ⊸ ≈ ⊠ SC

★ **HOLIDAY INN EXPRESS.** *364 Lowingney (49701). Phone 616/436-7100; toll-free 800/465-4329; fax 616/436-7070. www.holiday-inn.com.* 71 rooms, 3 story. Mid-June-early Sept: S $75-$145; D $81-$145; each additional $6; family rates; higher rates special events; lower rates rest of year. Crib free. TV; cable (premium), VCR (movies). Indoor pool; whirlpool. Complimentary continental breakfast. Restaurant opposite 8 am-10 pm. Check-out 11 am. Coin laundry. Business services available. Cross-country ski 7 miles. Exercise equipment; sauna. Game room. Some refrigerators. Balconies. Lake, swimming beach 3 blocks. Cr cds: A, C, D, DS, JCB, MC, V.

D ⊠ ≈ ⌖ ⊠ SC

★ **HOWARD JOHNSON.** *150 Old US 31 (49701). Phone 231/436-5733; toll-free 800/446-4656; fax 616/436-5733. www.hojo.com.* 46 rooms, 1-2 story. Late June-Aug: S $75; D $98; each additional $5; family rates; higher rates July 4; higher rates (2-day minimum): Labor Day, Antique Car Show; lower rates May-late June, Sept-Oct. Closed rest of year. Crib free. TV; cable (premium). 2 pools, 1 indoor; whirlpool. Playground. Complimentary coffee in lobby. Restaurant nearby. Check-out 11 am. Cr cds: A, C, D, DS, JCB, MC, V.

D ≈ ⊠ SC

★ **KEWADIN.** *619 S Nicolet St (MI 108) (49701). Phone 616/436-5332; toll-free 800/503-9699; fax 616/436-7726.* 76 rooms, 2 story. Mid-June-early Sept: S $64.50-$84.50; D $69.50-$84.50; each additional $5; family rates; higher rates special events; lower rates May-mid-June, early Sept-mid-Oct. Closed rest of year. Crib free. Pet accepted. TV; cable. Heated pool. Playground. Restaurant nearby. Check-out 11 am. Refrigerators. Cr cds: A, C, D, DS, MC, V.

⊸ ≈ ⊠ SC

★ **LIGHTHOUSE VIEW.** *699 N Huron St (49701). Phone 231/436-5304; fax 616/436-5304.* 25 rooms, 2 story. D $45-$95; each additional $5. Closed Nov-Apr. Pet accepted, some restrictions. Check-out 11 am. TV; cable. Beach opposite. Indoor pool, whirlpool. Cr cds: A, C, D, DS, MC, V.

D ⊸ ⌂ ⌖ ≈ ⊠

★ **MOTEL 6.** *206 N Nicolet St (49701). Phone 616/436-8961; toll-free 800/466-8356; fax 616/436-7317. www.motel6.com.* 53 rooms, 2 story. Mid-June-Labor Day: S, D $38.95-$88.95; each additional $6; higher rates: holiday weekends, special events; Labor Day weekend (2-day minimum); lower rates rest of year. Crib free. Pet accepted; $3. TV; cable (premium). Indoor pool; whirlpool. Restaurant adjacent 7 am-10 pm. Check-out 11 am. Cross-country ski on site. Some refrigerators. Cr cds: A, C, D, DS, MC, V.

D ⊸ ≈ ⊠

★ **PARKSIDE.** *711 N Heron (49701). Phone 231/436-8301; fax 616/436-8301.* 44 rooms, 1-2 story. D $48-$88. Closed Nov-Apr. Pet accepted, some restrictions. Check-out 10 am. TV; cable (premium). Game room. Indoor pool, whirlpool. Colonel Michilimackinac State Park opposite. Cr cds: A, DS, MC, V.

D ⊸ ⌂ ⌖ ≈ ⊠

★ **QUALITY INN & SUITES BEACHFRONT.** *917 S Huron Ave (49701). Phone 231/436-5051; toll-free 877/436-5051; fax 231/436-7221.* 60 rooms, 1-2 story. D $35-$149; each additional $5. Closed Nov-mid-Apr. Pet accepted, some restrictions. Check-out 10 am. TV; cable (premium), VCR available. Sauna. Private beach on Lake Huron. Indoor pool, whirlpool. Lawn games. Near ferry dock. Cr cds: A, C, D, DS, ER, JCB, MC, V.

D ⊸ ⌂ ≈ ⊠ SC

★ ★ **RAMADA INN.** *450 S Nicolet St (49701). Phone 231/436-5535; fax 616/436-5849. www.ramada.com.* 162 rooms, 3 story. Mid-June-early Sept: S $60.50-$115; D $66.50-$115; each additional $8; under 18 free; lower rates rest of year. Crib free. TV; cable (premium), VCR available. Indoor pool; whirlpool, sauna. Complimentary coffee. Restaurant 6:30 am-11 pm; off season to 9 pm. Room service. Bar 3 pm-2 am. Check-out 11 am. Coin laundry. Meeting rooms. Cross-country ski 5 miles. Game room. Refrigerators; some in-room whirlpools. Cr cds: A, C, D, DS, JCB, MC, V.

⊡ 🐾 🛏 🖼 🚶

★ **RAMADA LIMITED WATERFRONT.** *723 S Huron Ave (49721). Phone 231/436-5055; toll-free 888/852-4165; fax 616/436-5921. www.ramada.com.* 42 rooms, 3 story. D $79-$159; each additional $5. Closed Nov-mid-Apr. Complimentary continental breakfast. Check-out 11 am. TV; cable (premium), VCR available. On beach. Indoor pool, whirlpool. Cr cds: A, C, D, DS, JCB, MC, V.

⊡ ⚓ 🛏 🖼

★ **STARLITE BUDGET INN.** *116 Old US 31 (49701). Phone 231/436-5959; toll-free 800/288-8190; fax 616/436-5988. www.mackinawcity.com/lodging/starlite.* 33 rooms. Mid-June-late Aug: S $42-$89; D $42-$149; family, weekly rates; higher rates: July 4, Labor Day, auto show; lower rates May-mid-June, late Aug-Oct. Closed rest of year. Crib free. Pet accepted, some restrictions; $5. TV; cable (premium). Heated pool. Playground. Complimentary coffee in rooms. Restaurant nearby. Check-out 10 am. Refrigerators. Cr cds: A, MC, V.

⊡ 🐾 🏊 🍴 🏊 🛏

★ **SUPER 8 MOTEL.** *601 N Huron Ave (49701). Phone 616/436-5252; toll-free 800/800-8000; fax 616/436-7004. www.super8.com.* 50 rooms, 2 story. July-mid-Oct: S $74-$135; D $79-$145; each additional $6; higher rates special events (2-day minimum); lower rates rest of year. Crib $6. Pet accepted, some restrictions. TV; cable, VCR available. Indoor pool; whirlpool, sauna. Complimentary coffee in lobby. Restaurant nearby. Check-out 11 am. Coin laundry. Game room. Refrigerators available. Some balconies. Cr cds: A, C, D, DS, MC, V.

⊡ 🐾 🛏 🖼 SC

★ **WATERFRONT INN.** *1009 S Huron St (US 23) (49701). Phone 231/436-5527; fax 616/436-8661. www.largestbeach.com.* 69 rooms. D $49-$96.95; each additional $5. Check-out 11 am. TV; cable (premium). Private beach on Lake Huron. Pool, whirlpool. Cr cds: A, DS, MC, V.

⊡ ⚓ 🛏 🖼

Restaurants

★ **EMBERS.** *810 S Huron Ave (US 23) (49701). Phone 231/436-5773; fax 231/436-7763.* Hours: 7am-9pm. Closed Nov-early Apr. Buffet breakfast $5.99, lunch $6.49, dinner $10.95. Breakfast $1.95-$8, lunch $3.95-$8.95, dinner $6.95-$16.99. Bar 8 pm-midnight. Cr cds: DS, MC, V.

⊡ SC

★ ★ **'NEATH THE BIRCHES.** *14277 Mackinaw Hwy (49701). Phone 231/436-5401; fax 231/436-7178.* Closed late Oct-mid-May. Dinner. Bar. Children's menu. Cr cds: A, D, DS, MC, V.

★ **PANCAKE CHEF.** *327 Central (49701). Phone 231/436-5578; fax 231/436-5579. www.pancakechef.com.* American menu. Breakfast, lunch, dinner. Cr cds: A, D, DS, MC, V.

⊡

Manistee (E-2)

Pop 6,734 **Elev** 600 ft **Area code** 231 **Zip** 49660

Information Manistee Area Chamber of Commerce, 11 Cypress St; 231/723-2575 or 800/288-2286

Web www.manistee.com

With Lake Michigan on the west and the Manistee National Forest on the east, this site was once the home of 1,000 Native Americans who called it Manistee—"spirit of the woods." In the mid-1800s this was a thriving lumber town, serving as headquarters for more than 100 companies. When the timber supply was exhausted, the early settlers found other sources of revenue. Manistee is rich in natural resources including salt, oil, and natural gas. A Ranger District office of the Huron-Manistee National Forest is located in Manistee.

What to See and Do

Huron-Manistee National Forest. *E and S of town, via US 31 and MI 55. Phone 800/821-6263.* This 520,968-acre forest is the Manistee section of the Huron-Manistee National Forest (for Huron section see OSCODA). The forest includes the Lake Michigan Recreation Area, which contains trails and panoramic views of the sand dunes and offers beaches; fishing in lakes and in the Pine, Manistee, Little Manistee, White, Little Muskegon, and Pere Marquette rivers; boating, hiking, bicycle, and vehicle trails; hunting for deer and small game, camping, and picnicking. Winter sports include downhill and cross-country skiing, snowmobiling, ice fishing, and ice sailing. Fees charged at recreation sites. (Daily) **FREE**

Manistee County Historical Museum. *425 River St. Russell Memorial Building, 425 River St. Phone 231/723-5531.* Fixtures and fittings of 1880 drugstore and early general store; Victorian period rooms, historical photographs; Civil War, marine collections; antique dolls, costumes, housewares. (June-Sept, Mon-Sat; rest of year, Tues-Sat; closed holidays) **$**

Old Waterworks Building. *W 1st St. Phone 231/723-5531.* Logging wheels, early lumbering, shipping, and railroad exhibits; Victorian parlor, barbershop, shoe shop, kitchen. (Late June-Aug, Tues-Sat) **DONATION**

Orchard Beach State Park. *2064 Lakeshore Rd. 2 miles N on MI 110. Phone 231/723-7422.* High on a bluff overlooking Lake Michigan; 201 acres. Swimming beach; hiking, picnicking, playground, stone pavilion, camping. **$$**

Ramsdell Theatre and Hall. *101 Maple St. Phone 231/723-9948 or 231/723-7188.; fax 231/723-6982. (1903)* Constructed by T. J. Ramsdell, pioneer attorney, this opulent building is home to the Manistee Civic Players, who present professional and community productions throughout the year; also art and museum exhibits. Tours (June-Aug, Wed and Sat; rest of year, by appointment). **DONATION**

Special Events

National Forest Festival. *50 Filer St. Phone 231/723-2575.* Boat show; car show; US Forestry Service forest tours; parades, athletic events, raft and canoe races, Venetian boat parade, fireworks. Sponsored by the Chamber of Commerce. Phone 231/723-2575. July 4 week.

Shoot Time in Manistee. *Old Fort Rendezvous. Phone 231/723-9006.* Traditional shooting events, costumed participants. Late June.

Victorian Port City Festival. *Phone 231/723-2575.* Musical entertainment, street art fair, antique auto exhibit, food, schooner rides. Early Sept.

Motels/Motor Lodges

★ ★ **BEST WESTERN INN.** *200 Arthur St (US 31 N) (49660). Phone 231/723-9949; toll-free 800/296-6835; fax 616/723-9949. www.bestwestern.com.* 72 rooms, 2 story. Late May-Oct: S $48-$90; D $54-$130; each additional $6; lower rates rest of year. Crib $6. TV; cable (premium). Indoor pool. Restaurant 6 am-10 pm. Bar 2 pm-2 am. Check-out 11 am. Meeting rooms. Business services available. Sundries. Free airport transportation. Cross-country ski 3 miles. Exercise equipment. Game room. Sun deck. Manistee Lake opposite. Cr cds: A, D, DS, MC, V.

⊡ ⬙ 🛠 ⚲ 🏊 ⛷ 🧖 🏌 📷 ⊠

★ **DAYS INN MANISTEE.** *1462 US 31S (49660). Phone 231/723-8385; toll-free 888/626-4783; fax 616/723-2154. www.daysinn.com.* 90 rooms, 2 story. July-Sept: S, D $55-$120; each additional $6; under 12 free; lower rates rest of year. Crib free. TV; cable, VCR available (movies). Indoor pool; whirlpool. Continental breakfast. Restaurant opposite 5 am-midnight. Check-out 11 am. Coin laundry. Meeting rooms. Business services available. Sundries. Free airport transportation. Cross-country ski 3 miles. Game room. Cr cds: A, C, D, DS, JCB, MC, V.

⊡ 🍴 ⚲ ⊠

★ **MANISTEE INN & MARINA.** *378 River St (49660). Phone 231/723-4000; toll-free 800/968-6277; fax 231/723-0007. www.manisteeinn.com.* 25 rooms, 2 story.

Mid-May-mid-Sept: S $59-$73; D $64-$77; each additional $9; whirlpool rooms $91-$129; lower rates rest of year. Crib free. TV; cable, VCR (movies $2). Complimentary continental breakfast. Restaurant nearby. Check-out 11 am. Coin laundry. Meeting room. Business services available. Cross-country ski 10 miles. Cr cds: A, D, DS, MC, V.

⊡ ⬙ 🚣 🏌 ⊠ 🏊

Manistique (C-2)

Pop 3,456 **Elev** 600 ft **Area code** 906 **Zip** 49854

Information Schoolcraft County Chamber of Commerce, 1000 W Lakeshore Dr; 906/341-5010

Web www.manistique.com

Manistique, the county seat of Schoolcraft County, has a bridge in town named "The Siphon Bridge" that is partially supported by the water that flows underneath it. The roadway is approximately four feet below the water level. Fishing for salmon is good in the area. A Ranger District office of the Hiawatha National Forest (see ESCANABA) is located here.

What to See and Do

Fayette. *15 miles W on US 2, then 17 miles S on MI 183 to Fayette on Big Bay de Noc. Phone 906/644-2603.* Approximately 700 acres. Fayette, formerly an industrial town producing charcoal iron (1867-1891), is now a ghost town; self-guided tour of restored remains; interpretive center (May-Oct). Swimming, fishing; picnicking, playground, camping. **$$**

Indian Lake. *6 miles W on US 2, then 3 miles N on MI 149, 1/2 mile E on County Rd 442. Phone 906/341-2355.* Hiking. **$$**

Palms Book. *S on US 2 to Thompson, then 12 miles NW on MI 149. Phone 906/341-2355.* Approximately 300 acres. Here is Kitch-iti-ki-pi, the state's largest spring, 200 ft wide, 40 ft deep; 16,000 gallons of water per min form a stream to Indian Lake. Observation raft for viewing the spring. Picnicking, concession. No camping allowed. Standard fees. Closed in winter. **$$**

Thompson State Fish Hatchery. *7 miles SW via US 2, MI 149. Phone 906/341-5587.* **FREE**

Special Events

Folkfest. *Phone 906/341-5010.* Mid-July.

Schoolcraft County Snowmobile Poker Run. *Phone 906/341-5010.* Late Jan.

Motels/Motor Lodges

★ **BEST WESTERN BREAKERS.** *1199 E Lakeshore Dr (49854). Phone 906/341-2410; toll-free 888/335-3674; fax 906/341-2207. www.bestwestern.com.* 40 rooms. D $54-$74; each additional $5. Check-out 11 am. TV; cable (premium). Overlooks Lake Michigan. Private beach opposite. Indoor pool, outdoor pool, whirlpool. Cr cds: A, C, D, DS, MC, V.

⌖ ⚡ 🏊 ✈ 🐾 SC

★ **BUDGET HOST/MANISTIQUE MOTOR INN.** *RR 1, Box 1505 (49854). Phone 906/341-2552; toll-free 800/283-4678; fax 906/341-2552. www.budgethost.com.* 26 rooms, 13 A/C. Mid-June-Labor Day: S $44-$55; D $46-$58; each additional $5; suites $65-$100; lower rates rest of year. Crib $3. TV; cable (premium). Heated pool. Restaurant adjacent 5 am-11 pm; bar. Check-out 11 am. Business services available. Free airport, bus depot transportation. Cross-country ski 5 miles. Lawn games. Cr cds: A, C, D, DS, ER, MC, V.

🐾 🍴 🏊 ✈ 🐾

★ **ECONO LODGE.** *US 2 E (49854). Phone 906/341-6014; fax 906/341-2979. www.econolodge.com.* 31 rooms. July-Labor Day: S $49-$59; D $59-$66; each additional $5; under 18 free; lower rates rest of year. TV; cable (premium). Complimentary continental breakfast. Restaurant nearby. Check-out 11 am. Cross-country ski 10 miles. Lake Michigan boardwalk opposite. Cr cds: A, C, D, DS, JCB, MC, V.

🍴 🏊 🐾

★ **HOLIDAY MOTEL.** *E US Hwy 2 (49854). Phone 906/341-2710.* 20 rooms. No A/C. June-Labor Day: D $48; lower rates rest of year. Crib $5. Pet accepted. TV; cable (premium). Heated pool. Playground. Complimentary continental breakfast. Restaurant nearby. Check-out 10 am. Lawn games. Picnic tables. Cr cds: A, DS, MC, V.

🐾 🏊 🐾 SC

★ **NORTHSHORE MOTOR INN.** *Rte 1 Box 1967, US 2 E (49854). Phone 906/341-2420; toll-free 800/297-7107.* 12 rooms. July-Aug: S $28-$36; D $38-$52; each additional $4; under 12 free; lower rates rest of year. Crib free. TV; cable (premium). Restaurant nearby. Check-out 11 am. Cross-country ski 6 miles. Picnic tables. Opposite lake. Cr cds: A, C, D, DS, MC, V.

🏂 ✈ 🐾

B&B/Small Inns

★ **CELIBETH HOUSE.** *Phone 906/283-3409. www.celibeth house.com.* 7 air-cooled rooms, 3 story. No room phones. Closed Dec-Apr. Complimentary continental breakfast. Check-out 11 am, check-in 3 pm. Renovated house (1895) used as logging company's headquarters and then as part of resort. Totally nonsmoking. Cr cds: DS, MC, V.

⌖ ⚡ 🐾

Marquette (B-1)

See also Ishpeming

Settled 1849 **Pop** 21,977 **Elev** 628 ft **Area code** 906 **Zip** 49855

Information Marquette Area Chamber of Commerce, 501 S Front St; 906/226-6591

Web www.marquette.org

The largest city in the Upper Peninsula, Marquette is the regional center for retailing, government, medicine, and iron ore shipping. Miles of public beaches and picnic areas flank the dock areas on Lake Superior. Rocks rise by the water and bedrock runs just a few feet below the surface. The city is named for the missionary explorer Father Jacques Marquette, who made canoe trips along the shore here between 1669 and 1671. At the rear flank of the city is sand-plain blueberry country, as well as forests and mountains of granite and iron.

What to See and Do

Marquette County Historical Museum. *213 N Front St. Phone 906/226-3571.* Exhibits of regional historical interest; J. M. Longyear Research Library. (Mon-Fri; closed holidays) **$**

Marquette Mountain Ski Area. *3 miles SW on County 553. Phone 906/225-1155 or 800/944-SNOW.* Three double chairlifts, rope tow; patrol, school, rentals, snowmaking, night skiing, weekly NASTAR; cafeteria, bar, nursery. Longest run 1 1/4 miles vertical drop 600 feet. (Late Nov-Apr, daily) Cross-country trails (three miles) nearby.

Mount Marquette Scenic Outlook Area. *1 mile S via US 41.* Provides lovely view. (May-mid-Oct, daily)

Northern Michigan University. *140 Presque Isle Ave. Phone 906/227-1700.* The school has been designated an Olympic Education Center. For information on Olympic Education Center, phone 906/227-2888. Tours available.

Presque Isle Park. *401 E Fair. On the lake in NE part of city. Phone 906/228-0460.* Picnic facilities (four picnic sites for the disabled), swimming, water slide (fees), boating (launch, fee); nature trails, cross-country skiing, tennis courts, playground. Bog walk features 4,000-foot trail with plank walkways and observation decks; self-guided with interpretive sign boards at ten conservation points. (May-Oct, daily; rest of year, open only for winter sports) **FREE** Near the park is

  Upper Harbor ore dock. Several million tons of ore are shipped annually from this site; the loading of ore freighters is a fascinating sight to watch. Adjacent parking lot for viewing and photography.

Statue of Father Marquette. *401 E Fair Ave. Marquette Park. Phone 906/228-0460.* On top of a bluff overlooking the site of the first settlement.

Sugar Loaf Mountain. *7 miles N on County 550.* A 3,200-foot trail leads to the summit for a panoramic view of the Lake Superior coastline and forestland.

Tourist Park. *401 E Fair Ave. Phone 906/225-1555 (summer); 906/228-0460 (winter).* Swimming, fishing; playground, tent and trailer sites (mid-May-mid-Oct, daily; fee). Entrance fee charged during Hiawatha Music Festival (see SPECIAL EVENTS). **FREE**

Upper Peninsula Children's Museum. *123 W Baraga Ave. Phone 906/226-3911.* All exhibits are products of kids' imaginations; regional youth planned their conceptual development. (Tues-Sun; closed holidays) **$$**

Special Events

Art on the Rocks. *Phone 609/228-4137.* Presque Isle Park. Nationwide art display and sale. Last full weekend July.

Hiawatha Music Festival. *Phone 906/226-8575.* Tourist Park. Bluegrass, traditional music festival. Third weekend July.

International Food Festival. *Phone 906/249-1595.* Ellwood Mattson Lower Harbor Park. Ethnic foods, crafts, music. July 4 weekend.

Seafood Festival. *Phone 906/226-6591.* Ellwood Mattson Lower Harbor Park. Weekend before Labor Day.

UP 200 Dog Sled Race. *Phone 800/544-4321.* Dog sled race; features food, games, entertainment, dog-sledding exhibitions. Mid-late Feb.

Motels/Motor Lodges

★**CEDAR MOTOR INN.** *2523 US Hwy 41 W (49855). Phone 906/228-2280; fax 906/228-2280.* 44 rooms, 1-2 story. Mid-June-mid-Oct: S, D $44-$58; each additional $3; lower rates rest of year. Crib $5. TV; cable (premium). Indoor pool; whirlpool, sauna. Coffee in rooms. Restaurant nearby. Check-out 11 am. Meeting room. Business services available. In-room modem link. Downhill ski 5 miles; cross-country ski 3 miles. Sun deck. Cr cds: A, D, DS, MC, V.

D ⊠ ⤢ ≋ ⊠

★**DAYS INN.** *2403 US 41 W (49855). Phone 906/225-1393; fax 906/225-9845. www.daysinn.com.* 65 rooms. July-Sept: S $55-$60, D $60-$65; each additional $6; family rates; lower rates rest of year. Crib free. TV; cable (premium). Indoor pool; whirlpool, sauna. Complimentary continental breakfast. Restaurant nearby. Check-out 11 am. Downhill ski 5 miles; cross-country ski 3 miles. Some refrigerators. Cr cds: A, C, D, DS, JCB, MC, V.

D ⊠ 🏃 ≋ ⊠ 🚶 ✈ ⊠ SC 🚶

★★**HOLIDAY INN.** *1951 US 41 W (49855). Phone 906/225-1351; toll-free 800/465-4329; fax 906/228-4329. www.holiday-inn.com.* 203 rooms, 5 story. S, D $69-$104; each additional $4; family rates; ski plans. Crib free. Pet accepted. TV; cable (premium). Indoor pool; whirlpool. Restaurant 6 am-2 pm, 5-10 pm. Room service. Bar 3 pm-2 am; Sun to midnight. Check-out noon. Meeting room. Business services available. Bellhops. Valet service. Sundries. Free airport transportation. Downhill ski 7 miles; cross-country ski 3 miles. Sauna. Health club privileges. Nature trails. Picnic tables. Cr cds: A, C, D, DS, JCB, MC, V.

D 🐾 ⊠ 🏃 ⊱ ≋ 🚶 ✈ ✕ ⊠

★**IMPERIAL MOTEL.** *2493 US 41(49855). Phone 906/228-7430; toll-free 800/424-9514; fax 906/228-3883. www.imperialmotel.com.* 43 rooms, 2 story. June-Oct: S $38-$45; D $48-$57; each additional $4; lower rates rest of year. Crib $7. TV; cable (premium). Indoor pool; sauna. Coffee in lobby. Restaurants nearby. Check-out 11 am. Business services available. Downhill ski 5 miles; cross-country ski 3 miles. Game room. Cr cds: A, C, D, DS, MC, V.

D ⊠ 🏃 ≋ ⊠ SC 🚶

★★**RAMADA INN.** *412 W Washington St (49855). Phone 906/228-6000; toll-free 800/272-6232; fax 906/228-2963. www.ramada.com.* 113 rooms, 2-7 story. S $84-$89; D $89-$94; each additional $5; under 18 free. Crib free. Pet accepted. TV; cable (premium). Indoor pool; whirlpool, sauna. Restaurant 6 am-10 pm; Fri, Sat to 11 pm. Room service. Bar 11-2 am. Check-out noon. Coin laundry. Meeting rooms. Business services available. Airport transportation. Downhill ski 3 miles; cross-country ski 1/2 mile. Many poolside rooms. Health club privileges. Cr cds: A, C, D, DS, JCB, MC, V.

D 🐾 ⤢ ⊠ 🏃 ⊱ ≋ 🚶 ✈ 🚶 ⊠ 🚶

★★**TIROLER HOF INN.** *1880 US 41 S (49855). Phone 906/226-7516; toll-free 800/892-9376; fax 906/226-0699.* 44 rooms, 36 A/C, 2 story. Mid-May-mid-Oct: S $42; D $50-$52; each additional $5; suites $68; studio rooms $50-$52; lower rates rest of year. Crib available. TV; cable (premium). Playground. Restaurant (in season) 7:30-10 am, 5:30-9 pm. Check-out 11 am. Coin laundry. Meeting room. Downhill/cross-country ski 1 1/2 miles. Recreation room. Sauna. Private patios, balconies. Picnic tables, grills. On 13 acres; pond. Overlooks Lake Superior. Cr cds: A, DS, MC, V.

⊠ ⊠

★**VALUE HOST MOTOR INN.** *1101 US 41 W (49801). Phone 906/225-5000; toll-free 800/929-5996; fax 906/225-5096.* 52 rooms, 2 story. May-Oct: S $34.45-$37.45; D $38.45-$48.50; each additional $5; family rates; lower rates rest of year. Crib free. TV; cable (premium). Complimentary continental breakfast. Restaurant nearby. Check-out 11 am. Meeting room. Business services available.

Downhill/cross-country ski 4 miles. Sauna. Whirlpool. Some refrigerators. Picnic tables. Cr cds: A, MC, V.

D ⌧ ⌧

Restaurant

★ ★ **NORTHWOODS SUPPER CLUB.** *260 Northwoods Rd (49855). Phone 906/228-4343; fax 906/228-5718.* Closed Dec 24-26. Lunch, dinner, Sun brunch. Bar. Entertainment Fri, Sat. Children's menu. Cr cds: A, DS, MC, V. **$**

D SC

Marshall (H-3)

Settled 1830 **Pop** 6,891 **Elev** 916 ft **Area code** 616 **Zip** 49068

Information Chamber of Commerce, 424 E Michigan; 616/781-5163 or 800/877-5163

Web www.marshallmi.org

Marshall was, at one time, slated to be Michigan's capital—a grand governor's mansion was built, land was set aside for the capitol, and wealthy and influential people swarmed into the town. In 1847, Marshall lost its capital bid to Lansing. Today, many of the elaborate houses and buildings of the period remain, and more than 30 historical markers dot the city's streets.

What to See and Do

American Museum of Magic. *107 E Michigan Ave. Phone 616/781-7674.* Display of vintage magical equipment, rare posters, photographs, and personal effects of some of the well-known magicians of history. (By appt) **$$**

Honolulu House Museum. *107 N Kalamazoo Ave. Phone 616/781-8544 or 800/877-5163.* (1860) This exotic structure, blending traditional Italianate architecture with tropical motifs of island plantation houses, was built by first US Consul to the Sandwich Islands (now Hawaii); period furnishings, artifacts. Also headquarters of Marshall Historical Society, which provides free self-guided walking tour brochures listing town's many interesting 19th-century buildings and more than 30 historical markers. (May-Oct, daily; rest of year, wkends) **$$**

Special Events

Historic Home Tour. *Phone 800/877-5163.* Informal tours of nine 19th-century homes, including Honolulu House, Governor's Mansion, and Capitol Hill School. First weekend after Labor Day.

Welcome to My Garden Tour. *Phone 616/781-5434.* Tour of Marshall's most distinctive gardens. Second weekend July.

B&B/Small Inns

★ ★ **MCCARTHY'S BEAR CREEK INN.** *15230 C Drive N (49068). Phone 616/781-8255.* 14 rooms, 2-3 story. No room phones. S, D $65-$98; each additional $10. Complimentary continental breakfast. Check-out Noon, check-in 3 pm. Cross-country ski 12 miles. Rooms in renovated house and dairy barn (1948); country décor, antiques. On wooded knoll overlooking Bear Creek; handbuilt fieldstone fencing. Cr cds: A, MC, V.

⌧ ⌧ ⌧

★ ★ **NATIONAL HOUSE INN.** *102 S Parkview St (49068). Phone 616/781-7374; fax 616/781-4510. www.nationalhouseinn.com.* 16 rooms, 2 story. S, D $69-$130; each additional $10; under 6 free. Closed Dec 24-25. Crib free. TV; cable (premium), VCR available. Complimentary breakfast. Restaurant nearby. Check-out noon, check-in after 3 pm. Business services available. Airport transportation. Cross-country ski 10 miles. Oldest operating inn in state; authentically restored, antique furnishings. Established in 1835. Cr cds: A, MC, V.

D ⌧ ⌧ ⌧ ⌧

Restaurants

★ **CORNWELL'S TURKEYVILLE.** *18935 15 1/2 Mile Rd (49068). Phone 616/781-4293. www.turkeyville.com.* Hours: 11 am-8 pm. Closed late Dec-mid-Jan. Children's menu. Outdoor seating. Cr cds: DS, MC, V. **$**

D

★ ★ **SCHULER'S OF MARSHALL.** *115 S Eagle St (49068). Phone 269/781-0600; fax 269/781-4361. www.schulersrestaurant.com.* Closed Dec 25. Lunch, dinner, Sun brunch. Bar. Children's menu. Patio dining. Cr cds: A, D, DS, MC, V. **$**

D

Menominee (D-1)

See also Marinette, WI

Settled 1796 **Pop** 9,398 **Elev** 600 ft **Area code** 906 **Zip** 49858

Information Menominee Area Chamber of Commerce, 1005 10th Ave, PO Box 427; 906/863-2679

Because of water transportation and water power, many manufacturing industries have located in Menominee. Green Bay and the Menominee river form two sides of the triangle-shaped city. Across the river is the sister city of Marinette, Wisconsin. Established as a fur-trading post, later a lumbering center, Menominee County is the largest dairy producer in the state of Michigan. Menominee is a Native American word for "wild rice," which once grew profusely on the riverbanks.

What to See and Do

First Street Historic District. *From 10th Ave to 4th Ave.* Variety of specialty shops located in a setting of restored 19th-century buildings. Marina, parks, restaurants, galleries.

Henes Park. *Henes Park Dr and 3rd St. Phone 906/863-2656.* Small zoo with deer yards, nature trails, bathing beach, and picnic area. (Memorial Day-mid Oct, daily) **FREE**

J. W. Wells State Park. *23 miles NE on MI 35, Cedar River. Phone 906/863-9747.* Approximately 700 acres, including 2 miles along Green Bay and 1,400 feet along Big Cedar River. Swimming, bathhouse, waterskiing, fishing, boating (ramp); hunting, snowmobiling, cross-country skiing, picnicking, playground, camping, cabins and shelters. Standard fees.

Menominee Marina. *1st St between 8th and 10th aves. Phone 906/863-8498 or 906/863-5101.* One of the best small-craft anchorages on the Great Lakes. Swimming beach, lifeguard. (May-Oct, daily)

Stephenson Island. *In middle of Menominee River.* Reached by bridge that also carries traffic between the sister cities on US 41. On island are picnic areas and a historical museum.

Special Event

Waterfront Festival. *Phone 906/863-2679.* Entertainment, music, dancing, footraces, fireworks, food, parade. Four days, first weekend Aug.

Midland (F-4)

See also Bay City, Mount Pleasant, Saginaw

Pop 38,053 **Elev** 629 ft **Area code** 989

Information Midland County Convention & Visitors Bureau, 300 Rodd St, Suite 101, 48640; 989/839-9522 or 888/4-MIDLAND

Web www.midlandcvb.org

Midland owed its prosperity to the lumber industry until Herbert Henry Dow founded The Dow Chemical Company in 1897.

What to See and Do

Architectural Tour. Self-guided driving tour of buildings designed by Alden B. Dow, son of Herbert H. Dow. The younger Dow studied under Frank Lloyd Wright at Taliesin. He designed more than 45 buildings in Midland,

including the architect's house and studio, churches, Stein House (his Taliesin apprentice project), and the Whitman House, for which he won the 1937 Grand Prix for residential architecture. Many buildings are privately owned and not open to the public. Maps and audio cassettes are available at the Midland Center for the Arts. Audio cassettes **$$**

Chippewa Nature Center. *400 S Badour Rd. Phone 517/631-0830.* On more than 1,000 acres; 14 miles of marked and mowed trails; wildflower walkway and pond boardwalk; Homestead Farm; reconstructed 1870s log cabin, barn, sugarhouse, one-room schoolhouse; visitor center; museum depicting evolutionary natural history of the Saginaw Valley; auditorium, library; seasonal programs. (Daily; closed Thanksgiving, Dec 25) **FREE**

★ **Dow Gardens.** *1018 W Main St. Entrance at Eastman Rd and W St. Andrews. Phone 517/631-2677 or 800/362-4872.* Gardens, originally grounds of the residence of Herbert H. Dow, founder of The Dow Chemical Company, include more than 100 acres of trees, flowers, streams, waterfalls; greenhouse, conservatory. (Daily; closed holidays) Tours by appointment. **$$**

Herbert H. Dow Historical Museum. *3200 Cook Rd, 2 miles NW via W Main St. Phone 517/832-5319.* Composed of replicated Evans Flour Mill and adjacent buildings that housed Dow's Midland Chemical Company, predecessor to The Dow Chemical Company. Interpretive galleries include Joseph Dow's workshop, Herbert Dow's office, drillhouse with steam-powered brine pump, laboratory; audiovisual theater. (Wed-Sat, also Sun afternoons; closed holidays) **$**

Midland Center for the Arts. *1801 W St. Andrews. Phone 517/631-5930.* Designed by Alden B. Dow. Houses Hall of Ideas, a museum of science, technology, health, history, and art exhibits. Also concerts, plays. Architectural tour begins here. (Daily; closed holidays) **$$**

Special Events

Fall Festival. *400 S Badour Rd (48640). Phone 989/631-0830.* Chippewa Nature Center. Second weekend Oct.

Maple Syrup Festival. *400 S Badour Rd. Phone 989/631-0830.* Chippewa Nature Center. Third Sat Mar.

Matrix: Midland Festival. *1801 W St. Andrews Rd. County Fairgrounds.* Celebration of the arts, sciences, humanities; classical and popular music, theater, dance; lectures by noted professionals. *Phone 989/631-7980.* Late June-Sept.

Michigan Antique Festivals. *2156 N Rudy Ct. Phone 989/687-9001.* Midland Center for the Arts. 1,000 vendors inside and outside. Mid-May-mid-June.

Motels/Motor Lodges

★ ★ BEST WESTERN VALLEY PLAZA RESORT.
5221 Bay City Rd (48642). Phone 517/496-2700; toll-free 800/825-2700; fax 517/496-9233. www.valleyplazaresort. com. 162 rooms, 2 story. S $67; D $77; suites $125-$175; under 18 free; higher rates weekends. Crib free. Pet accepted, some restrictions. TV; cable. Indoor pool; wading pool. Playground. Complimentary continental breakfast. Restaurant 6 am-9 pm; Sat from 7 am; Sun to noon. Room service. Bar noon-1 am. Check-out noon. Meeting rooms. In-room modem link. Bellhops. Valet service. Gift shop. Free airport transportation. Exercise room. Game room. Lawn games. Bowling. Movie theater. Small lake with beach. Cr cds: A, C, D, DS, JCB, MC, V.

🄳 ⬛⬛⬛⬛⬛⬛⬛⬛⬛⬛

★ ★ HOLIDAY INN.
1500 W Wackerly St (48640). Phone 517/631-4220; toll-free 800/622-4220; fax 517/631-3776. www.holiday-inn.com. 235 rooms, 2 story. S, D $85; under 18 free; weekend rates. Crib free. Pet accepted, some restrictions. TV; cable (premium). Indoor pool; whirlpool, poolside service. Playground. Restaurant 6 am-3 pm, 5:30-10 pm. Room service. Bar 11:30 am-11 pm; entertainment. Check-out 11 am. Meeting rooms. Business center. In-room modem link. Bellhops. Valet service. Sundries. Free airport transportation. Tennis privileges. Cross-country ski 2 miles. Exercise equipment; sauna. Game room. Cr cds: A, C, D, DS, JCB, MC, V.

🄳 ⬛⬛⬛⬛⬛⬛⬛⬛⬛⬛

★ SUPER 8 MOTEL.
4955 Garfield Rd (68467). Phone 517/662-7888; toll-free 800/866-4322; fax 517/662-7607. www.super8.com. 60 rooms, 3 story. S $44; D $52-$58; each additional $3; suites $66-$77; under 12 free; weekly rates. Crib free. TV; cable (premium). Complimentary continental breakfast. Complimentary coffee in lobby. Check-out 11 am. Coin laundry. Airport transportation. Downhill ski 15 miles. Game room. Some refrigerators. Cr cds: A, DS, MC, V.

🄳 ⬛⬛⬛⬛⬛

Milford

See also Farmington

Restaurant

★ ★ FIVE LAKES GRILL.
424 N Main St (48381). Phone 248/684-7455; fax 248/684-5935. Hours: 4-10 pm; Fri, Sat to 11 pm. Closed Sun; most major holidays. Reservations accepted. Bar. Dinner $11.50-$30. Child's meals. Specializes in contemporary American cooking. Modern bistro decor. Cr cds: A, MC, V.

🄳

Monroe (I-5)

See also Detroit, Toledo

Settled 1780 **Pop** 22,902 **Elev** 599 ft **Area code** 734 **Zip** 48161

Information Monroe County Chamber of Commerce, 106 W Front St, PO Box 1094; 734/457-1030

Web www.monroeinfo.com

Originally called Frenchtown because of the many French families that settled here, this city on Lake Erie was renamed in 1817 in honor of President James Monroe. The river that flows through the center of the city was named the River Aux Raisin because of the many grapes growing in the area. At one time, Monroe was briefly the home of General George Armstrong Custer of "Little Big Horn" fame.

What to See and Do

Monroe County Historical Museum. *126 S Monroe St. Phone 734/243-7137.* Exhibits of General George Custer, Woodland Native Americans, pioneers, War of 1812; trading post, country store museum. (Summer, daily; rest of year, Wed-Sun; closed holidays) **$**

River Raisin Battlefield Visitor Center. *1402 Elm Ave, just off I-75 at Elm Ave exit. Phone 734/243-7136 or 734/243-7137.* Interprets fierce War of 1812 battle of River Raisin (Jan 1813). Nearly 1,000 US soldiers from Kentucky clashed with British, Native American, and Canadian forces on this site; only 33 Americans escaped death or capture. Exhibits of weapons and uniforms, dioramas; fiber optic audiovisual map program. (Memorial Day-Labor Day, daily; rest of year, wkends; closed holidays) **FREE**

Sterling State Park. *2800 State Park Rd (48162). N of city, off I-75. Phone 734/289-2715.* On 1,001 acres. Swimming, waterskiing, fishing, boating (ramp); hiking, picnicking, playground, concession, camping. Standard fees. **$$**

Special Event

Monroe County Fair. *3775 S Custer Rd. Phone 734/241-5775.* Monroe County Fairgrounds. Rides, concessions, merchant buildings. Late July-early Aug.

Motels/Motor Lodges

★ DAYS INN.
1440 N Dixie Hwy (48162). Phone 734/289-4000; fax 734/289-4262. www.daysinn.com. 115 rooms, 2 story. S $50-$70; D $50-$85; each additional $10; under 12 free. Crib free. TV; cable (premium). Indoor pool; whirlpool, sauna. Restaurant 5 am-10 pm. Room service. Bar 11-2 am. Check-out noon. Meeting rooms.

Business services available. In-room modem link. Game room. Private patios, balconies. Cr cds: A, DS, MC, V.

[D] [symbols]

★ **HOLIDAY INN EXPRESS HOTEL & SUITES MONROE.** *1225 N Dixie Hwy (48162). Phone 734/ 242-6000; toll-free 800/242-6008; fax 734/242-0555. www.holiday-inn.com.* 161 rooms, 4 story, 34 suites. S $60; D $68; each additional $8; under 18 free; weekend rates off-season; golf plans. Crib free. Pet accepted. Check-out noon. TV; cable (premium), VCR available. In-room modem link. Valet service. Restaurant 6 am-10 pm. Bar 11-2 am; Sun noon-midnight; entertainment Mon-Sat. Room service. Sauna. Game room. Indoor pool, whirlpool, poolside service. Golf privileges. Meeting rooms. Sundries. Cr cds: A, D, DS, JCB, MC, V.

[symbols]

Mount Clemens (H-6)

Pop 18,405 **Elev** 614 ft **Area code** 586

Information Central Macomb County Chamber of Commerce, 58 S Gratiot, 48043; 586/493-7600

What to See and Do

Art Center. *125 Macomb Pl. Phone 810/469-8666.* Exhibits and classes, sponsors tours. Sales gallery, gift shop. Holiday Fair (Dec). (Mon-Fri, limited hours Sat; closed July and Aug) **FREE**

Crocker House. *15 Union St. Phone 810/465-2488. (1869)* This Italianate building, home of the Macomb County Historical Society, was originally owned by the first two mayors of Mount Clemens; period rooms, changing exhibits. (Mar-Dec, Tues-Thurs; also first Sun month) **$**

Metro Beach Metropark. *4 miles SE off I-94 on Lake St. Clair, exit 236. Phone 810/463-4581.* Park features 3/4-mi beach (late May-Sept, daily), pool (Memorial Day-Labor Day, daily; fee), bathhouse, boating, marinas, ramps, launch, dock (fee); 18-hole par-three golf course, miniature golf, shuffleboard, tennis, group rental activity center, playgrounds. Picnicking, concessions. Nature center. (Daily, hours vary) No pets. Free admission Tues. **$**

Special Event

Farm City Festival. *Phone 810/463-1528.* Late Aug.

Motel/Motor Lodge

★ **COMFORT INN UTICA, MI.** *11401 Hall Rd (48317). Phone 810/739-7111; fax 810/739-1041. www.comfortinn.com.* 104 rooms, 3 story. S $69-$84; D $69-$94; each additional $5; under 16 free. Crib free. TV; cable (premium), VCR available (movies). Complimentary

continental breakfast. Restaurant nearby. Check-out noon. Coin laundry. Business services available. In-room modem link. Valet service. Airport transportation. Cr cds: A, C, D, DS, JCB, MC, V.

[D] [symbols] [SC]

Mount Pleasant (F-3)

See also Alama, Clare, Midland

Pop 23,285 **Elev** 770 ft **Area code** 989 **Zip** 48858

Information Convention & Visitors Bureau, 114 E Broadway; 800/772-4433

Web www.mt-pleasant.net

What to See and Do

Center for Cultural & Natural History. *Rowe Hall.* Includes 45 exhibits and dioramas on anthropology, history, and natural science. (Daily; closed holidays) **FREE**

Central Michigan University. *204 W Hall. Phone 989/774-4000. (1892)* 16,300 students. Here is

Clarke Historical Library. *409 Park Library. Phone 989/774-3352.* Rare books, manuscripts; historical documents of Northwest Territory; children's library; changing exhibits. (School year, Mon-Fri) **FREE**

Soaring Eagle Casino. *2395 S Leaton Rd. Phone 888/732-4537.* Includes 2,500-seat Bingo Hall, slot machines, blackjack, craps, and roulette. Saginaw Chippewa Campground is nearby. (Daily) **FREE**

Special Events

Apple Fest. *Phone 989/773-3028.* First weekend Oct.

Maple Syrup Festival. *Approximately 5 miles S via US 27, in Shepherd. Phone 989/828-6486.* Last weekend Apr.

Motels/Motor Lodges

★ **COMFORT INN.** *2424 S Mission St (48858). Phone 989/772-4000; fax 989/773-6052. www.comfortinn.com.* 138 rooms, 2 story, 12 suites. S, D $48.50-$119.50; each additional $5; suites $135; under 18 free; weekly, weekday rates; golf plans; higher rates: CMU football weekends, festivals. Crib free. Pet accepted. TV; cable (premium), VCR (movies). Indoor pool. Complimentary continental breakfast. Restaurant nearby. Check-out noon. Coin laundry. Meeting rooms. Business services available. In-room modem link. Game room. Cr cds: A, C, D, DS, JCB, MC, V.

[D] [symbols]

★ ★ **HOLIDAY INN.** *5665 E Pickard St (48858). Phone 989/772-2905; toll-free 800/299-8891; fax 989/772-4952. www.holiday-inn.com.* 184 rooms, 2-3 story. S, D $58-$145; each additional $10; under 12 free; golf plan.

Crib free. Pet accepted. Check-out 11 am. TV; cable (premium). In-room modem link. Balconies. In-room whirlpools, refrigerators; some minibars. Coffee in rooms. Valet services, coin laundry. Restaurant 6:30 am-10 pm; Sun to 8 pm. Bar noon-2 am; Sun to 8 pm; entertainment Mon-Sat. Room service. Playground. Exercise room, sauna. Recreation room. 2 pools, 1 indoor; whirlpool. 36-hole golf, greens fee $35-$65, putting green, driving range. Lighted tennis. Lawn games. Free airport transportation. Meeting rooms, business services. Sundries. Cr cds: A, D, DS, JCB, MC, V.

★ **SUPER 8 MOTEL.** *2323 S Mission St (48858).* *Phone 989/773-8888; toll-free 800/868-5252; fax 989/772-5371. www.super8.com.* 143 rooms, 3 story. Apr-Sept: S $59.88-$84; D $59.88-$89; each additional $5; under 16 free; lower rates rest of year. Crib free. Pet accepted. Complimentary continental breakfast. Check-out noon. TV; cable (premium), VCR available (movies). Some in-room whirlpools, refrigerators. Valet service. Restaurant nearby. Tennis privileges. Cross-country ski 3 miles. Meeting room, business services. Cr cds: A, C, D, DS, JCB, MC, V.

Resort

★ ★ ★ **SOARING EAGLE CASINO & RESORT.** *6800 Soaring Eagle Blvd (48858). Phone 989/775-7777; toll-free 888/732-4537; fax 989/775-5383. www.soaringeaglecasino.com.* 512 rooms, 7 story, 20 suites. S, D $119-$179; suites $199-$350; children $10; under 17 free; lower rates rest of year. Crib Free. Complimentary coffee in rooms, newspaper, toll-free calls. Check-out 11 am, check-in 4 pm. TV; cable (premium). Refrigerators available. Some fireplaces, balconies. Valet services. Restaurant 7 am-11 pm. Bar, room service 24-hour. Supervised children's activities. Video games. Exercise room, sauna, steam room. Heated indoor pool, children's pool, lifeguard, lap pool, whirlpool, poolside service. Golf. Salon/barber. Free valet parking available. Meeting rooms, business services. Conference center. Concierge. Gift shop. Casino. Bingo. Native Americam theme. Cr cds: A, D, DS, MC, V.

Restaurants

★ ★ ★ **EMBERS.** *1217 S Mission St (US 27 Business) (48858). Phone 989/773-5007; fax 989/773-9436.* The signature "one pound pork chop" is the main attraction at this elegant restaurant in Mount Pleasant. Tease, a more casual dining option, is also available within the building. American menu. Hours: 5 pm-9 pm; Fri, Sat to 10 pm; Sun 10 am-7 pm; Sun brunch to 2 pm. Closed most major holidays. Dinner $16.95-$36.95. Bar. Child's menu. Casual attire. Smorgasbord 1st and 3rd Thurs. Cr cds: A, D, DS, MC, V.

★ ★ ★ **WATER LILY.** *6800 Soaring Eagle Blvd (48858). Phone 517/775-5496.* American menu. Hours: 6:30 am-9:30 pm; Fri, Sat to 10 pm; Sun 10:30 am-2 pm, 5:30-9:30 pm; Sun brunch buffett. Dinner $13-$32. Bar. Entertainment. Casual attire. Valet parking. Cr cds: A, D, DS, MC, V.

Munising (B-1)

Pop 2,783 **Elev** 620 ft **Area code** 906 **Zip** 49862

Information Alger Chamber of Commerce, 422 E Munising Ave, PO Box 405; 906/387-2138

Web www.algercounty.org

Colorful sandstone formations, waterfalls, sand dunes, agate beaches, hiking trails, and outdoor recreational facilities are part of the Hiawatha National Forest and the Pictured Rocks National Lakeshore, which stretches eastward from Munising along 42 miles of the south shore of Lake Superior. Camping areas are plentiful in the Lakeshore, Hiawatha National Forest, and on Lake Superior. A Ranger District office of the Hiawatha National Forest (see ESCANABA) is located in Munising.

What to See and Do

Pictured Rocks Boat Cruise. *355 Elm Ave. City Pier, Elm Ave. Phone 906/387-2379.* A 37-mi cruise on the Miners Castle, Pictured Rocks, Grand Island, or Miss Superior. (June-early Oct, daily) **$$$$**

★ **Pictured Rocks National Lakeshore.** *Phone 906/387-2379.* Museum (summer) and Munising Falls Interpretive Center (summer, daily). There are three drive-in campgrounds (fee) and numerous hike-in backcountry campsites (permit required, free, obtain from any visitor station). Pets are not permitted in the backcountry; must be on leash in other areas. Visitors can obtain information at Pictured Rocks National Lakeshore-Hiawatha National Forest Visitor Information Station (daily); Munising Headquarters (Mon-Fri); or Grand Sable Visitor Center (summer). Contact the Superintendent, PO Box 40.

Special Event

Pictured Rocks Road Race. *Phone 906/387-2379.* Course runs over wooded, hilly trails, roads passing waterfalls, streams, and Lake Superior. Late June.

Motels/Motor Lodges

★ **ALGER FALLS MOTEL.** *MI 28 E (49862). Phone 906/387-3536; fax 906/387-5228.* 17 rooms. July-Labor

Day: S $39-$45; D $45-$50; kitchen cottages $55-$65; lower rates rest of year. Crib $4. Pet accepted. TV; cable. Restaurant nearby. Check-out 11 am. Cross-country ski 3 miles. Recreation room. Picnic tables. Wooded area with trails. Cr cds: A, DS, MC, V.

★ ★ **BEST WESTERN.** *MI 28 E (49895). Phone 906/387-4864; toll-free 800/528-1234; fax 906/387-2038. www.bestwestern.com.* 80 rooms, 2 story. Late June-Aug: S, D $59-$64; each additional $5; suites $80-$95; lower rates rest of year. Crib $5. Pet accepted. TV. Indoor pool; whirlpool, sauna. Restaurant 7 am-10 pm. Bar 11-1 am; Sun from noon. Check-out 11 am. Meeting room. Business services available. Picnic tables. Some refrigerators. Cr cds: A, D, DS, MC, V.

★ **COMFORT INN.** *MI 28 E (49862). Phone 906/387-5292; fax 906/387-3753. www.comfortinn.com.* 61 rooms, 2 story. S $69-$98, D $74-$103. Crib free. Pet accepted. TV; cable (premium), VCR (movies). Indoor pool; whirlpool. Complimentary continental breakfast. Check-out 11 am. Coin laundry. Meeting rooms. Business services available. Cross-country ski 6 miles. Exercise equipment. Game room. Cr cds: A, C, D, DS, JCB, MC, V.

★ **DAYS INN.** *MI 28 E (49862). Phone 906/387-2493; toll-free 800/329-7466; fax 906/387-5214. www.daysinn.com.* 66 rooms. July-Sept, late Dec: S, D $65-$85; kitchen units $125; lower rates rest of year. Crib free. Check-out 11 am. TV; cable (premium), VCR (movies). Restaurant adjacent 6 am-11 pm. Sauna. Indoor pool; whirlpool. Cross-country ski 1 mile. Business services available. Cr cds: A, MC, V.

★ **SUNSET RESORT MOTEL.** *1315 Bay St (49862). Phone 906/387-4574. www.exploringthenorth.com.* Kitchen units $56-$60; lower rates rest of year. Closed 3rd week Oct-Apr. Crib $1. Pet accepted. TV; cable. Playground. Complimentary coffee. Restaurant nearby. Check-out 11 am. Lawn games. Picnic tables, grills. On Lake Superior; dockage. Cr cds: DS, MC, V.

★ **SUPER 8.** *M 28 and US 13 (49862). Phone 906/387-2466; fax 906/387-2355. www.super8.com.* 43 rooms, 2 story. Mid-June-Labor Day, Dec-Mar: S $45.88; D $55.88-$65.88; each additional $5; suite $73.88; under 12 free; lower rates rest of year. Crib free. TV; cable (premium). Complimentary continental breakfast. Restaurant nearby. Check-out 11 am. Cross-country ski 3 miles. Whirlpool, sauna. Some refrigerators. Cr cds: A, DS, MC, V.

Restaurant

★ **SYDNEY'S.** *MI 28 E (49862). Phone 906/387-4067.* Breakfast, lunch, dinner, Sun brunch. Bar. Cr cds: A, MC, V. **$**

Muskegon (G-2)

See also Grand Haven, Whitehall

Settled 1810 **Pop** 40,283 **Elev** 625 ft **Area code** 231

Information Muskegon County Convention & Visitors Bureau, 610 W Western Ave, 49440; 800/235-3866 or 800/250-WAVE

Web www.visitmuskegon.org

Muskegon County is located in the western part of the lower peninsula, along 26 miles of Lake Michigan shoreline. Muskegon Channel, which runs from Lake Michigan through the sand dunes to Muskegon Lake, opens the harbor to world trade. It has 80 miles of waterfront, including ten miles of public waterfront, and 3,000 acres of public parks—an acre for every 50 persons in the county. The downtown has been enclosed as a climate-controlled shopping and business mall.

Muskegon Lake, largest of 40 lakes in Muskegon County, is the focal point of the area comprised of Muskegon, Muskegon Heights, North Muskegon, Norton Shores, Roosevelt Park, and surrounding townships. Fishing for coho, chinook salmon, lake trout, perch, walleye, and other fish is good here; ice fishing is popular in the winter months. The first freshwater reef in North America, a natural fish attractant, is located in Lake Michigan, off Pére Marquette Park.

What to See and Do

Hackley and Hume Historic Site. *472 and 484 W Webster. Phone 231/722-7578.* Restored Queen Anne/Victorian mansions (1888-1889) built by two wealthy lumbermen; elaborately carved woodwork, stenciled walls, 15 Renaissance-style stained-glass windows, tiled fireplaces with carved mantels, period furniture. Tours (mid-May-Sept, Wed, Sat, Sun; also some weekends in Dec).

Michigan's Adventure Amusement Park. *4750 Whitehall Rd, 8 miles N on US 31 via Russell Rd exit. Phone 231/766-3377; fax 231/766-3295.* More than 24 amusement rides, includes Wolverine Wildcat, largest wooden roller coaster in the state; Corkscrew roller coaster, Mammoth River water slide, log flume; games, arcade. Also water park with wave pool, lazy river, body flumes, tube slides. Family play areas. (Mid-May-early Sept, daily) **$$$$**

Muskegon Museum of Art. *296 W Webster Ave. Phone 231/722-2600.* Permanent collection includes American and European paintings, an extensive print collection, Tiffany and contemporary glass, paintings by Hopper, Inness, Whistler, Homer, Wyeth, and others. (Tues-Sun; closed holidays) **DONATION**

Muskegon State Park. *3560 Memorial Dr. Phone 231/744-3480 or 800/447-2757 (camping).* Per vehicle. A 1,165-acre area with replica of frontier blockhouse on one of the park's highest sand dunes, observation point. Swimming, beaches, bathhouse, waterskiing, fishing, boating (ramp, launch); 12 miles of hiking trails, cross-country skiing, skating rink, luge run, picnicking, concession, playground, camping (electrical hookups). Standard fees. **$$**

Muskegon Trolley Company. *923 Witham Rd. Phone 231/724-6420.* Two routes cover north side, south side, and downtown; each trolley stops at 11 locations, including Hackley and Hume Historic Site, *USS Silversides,* Muskegon State Park. (Memorial Day-Labor Day, daily; no trips during special events) **$**

P. J. Hoffmaster State Park. *S on Henry St to Pontaluna Rd, then W on Lake Harbor Rd. Phone 231/798-3711 or 800/447-2757.* More than 1,000 acres include forest-covered dunes along 2 1/2 miles of Lake Michigan shoreline. Swimming, sandy beach. Ten miles of trails, Dune Climb Stairway to top of one of highest dunes, observation deck. Cross-country ski trails (three miles), picnicking, concession, camping (electric hookups, dump station). Visitor center has displays, exhibits on dune formation (daily). Standard fees. Also here is

> **Gillette Visitor Center.** *6585 Lake Harbor Rd. Phone 231/798-3573.* Sand dune interpretive center. Multi-image slide presentations on the Great Lakes and dune habitats; dune ecology exhibit, hands-on classrm; seasonal animal exhibits. (Daily)

***USS Silversides* and Maritime Museum.** *Bluff St at Muskegon Channel. Phone 231/755-1230.* Famous WWII submarine that served with Pacific Fleet along Japan's coasts. The Silverside's outstanding aggressive war record includes sinking 23 enemy ships, embarking on special minelaying and reconnaisance missions, and rescuing two American aviators downed in air strikes over Japan. Guided tours. (June-Aug, daily; Apr-May and Sept-Oct, Sat and Sun) No high heels, skirts.

Special Events

Blueberry Festival. *4545 Nestrom Rd. Fruitland Township Park. Phone 231/766-3208.* Late July.

Luge Run. *462 Scenic Dr. Phone 231/744-9629.* Muskegon Winter Sports Complex in Muskegon State Park. Jan-Mar.

Muskegon Air Fair. *101 Sinclair Dr. Phone 231/798-4596.* More than 100 military and civilian aircraft; displays. Phone 231/798-4596. Mid-July.

Muskegon Shoreline Spectacular. *Phone 231/737-5791.* Père Marquette Park. Concerts, sporting events, arts and crafts, hot-air balloon rides. Labor Day weekend.

Muskegon Summer Celebration. *587 W Western Ave. Phone 231/722-6520.* Family music and entertainment parade, midway, food and beer tents, Venetian boat parade. June-July.

Motels/Motor Lodges

★ **BEL-AIRE MOTEL.** *4240 Airline Rd (49444). Phone 321/733-2196; fax 321/733-2196.* 16 rooms. June-Aug: S $48; D $58; each additional $5; higher rates special events; lower rates rest of year. Crib $3. TV; cable (premium). Restaurant nearby. Check-out 11 am. Cross-country ski 5 miles. Cr cds: A, DS, MC, V.

🐾 ⛷ SC

★ **BEST WESTERN PARK PLAZA HOTEL.** *2967 Henry St (49441). Phone 231/733-2651; fax 616/733-5202. www.bestwestern.com.* 111 rooms, 4 story. D $64-$80; each additional $6; under 18 free. Check-out noon. TV; cable. Bar, entertainment. Sauna. Game room. Indoor pool. Free airport transportation. Cr cds: A, C, D, DS, JCB, MC, V.

D 🏊 ⛷ ✈

★ **DAYS INN.** *3450 Hoyt St (49444). Phone 231/733-2601; fax 616/733-2601. www.daysinn.com.* 106 rooms, 2 story. S $50-$80; D $60-$85; each additional $5. Crib free. TV; cable (premium). Heated pool; whirlpool. Complimentary continental breakfast. Restaurant nearby. Check-out 11 am. Coin laundry. Meeting rooms. Business services available. Health club privileges. Cross-country ski 5 miles. Cr cds: A, C, D, DS, JCB, MC, V.

D 🐾 🎿 🏊 🍽 ⛷

★★ **HOLIDAY INN.** *939 3rd St (49440). Phone 231/720-7100; toll-free 800/846-5253; fax 231/722-5118. www.holiday-inn.com.* 200 rooms, 8 story. S, D $99-$125; each additional $10; suites $220-$325; under 18 free. Crib free. TV; cable. Indoor pool; whirlpool. Restaurant 6:30 am-10 pm; weekends 7 am-11 pm. Room service. Bar 2 pm-midnight; Fri, Sat to 1 am. Check-out 11 am. Meeting rooms. Business services available. Bellhops. Valet service. Gift shop. Free airport, bus depot transportation. Exercise equipment; steam rm, sauna. Cr cds: A, C, D, DS, MC, V.

D 🏊 🍽 ⛷

★ **SUPER 8.** *3380 Hoyt St (49444). Phone 231/733-0088; fax 616/733-0088. www.super8.com.* 62 rooms, 2 story. Apr-Sept: S, D $35-$70; each additional $5; under 12 free; lower rates rest of year. TV; cable (premium), VCR available (movies). Pet accepted. Restaurant nearby. Check-out 11 am. Business services available. Cr cds: A, D, DS, MC, V.

D 🐾 🎿 🏊 🍽 ⛷

Restaurants

★**HOUSE OF CHAN.** *375 Gin Chan Ave (49444). Phone 231/733-9624; fax 231/739-1809.* Chinese, American menu. Hours: 11:30 am-10 pm; Fri to 11 pm; Sat 4-11 pm; Sun 11 am-9 pm; Sun brunch. Closed Mon; Dec 25. Dinner $11-$25. Bar. Child's menu. Casual attire. Cr cds: A, MC, V.

D

★★**RAFFERTY'S DOCKSIDE.** *601 Terrace Point Blvd (49440). Phone 231/722-4461; fax 231/722-2422. www.shorelineinn.com.* American menu. Hours: 11:30 am-11 pm; Sun to 8 pm; Sun brunch. Closed some major holidays. Dinner $13.95-$33. Bar. Child's menu. Casual attire. Outdoor dining. Cr cds: A, DS, MC, V.

D

★★**TONY'S.** *785 W Broadway (49441). Phone 231/739-7196; fax 231/739-7056.* Closed Sun; most major holidays. Lunch, dinner. Bar. Children's menu. Cr cds: A, D, DS, MC, V. **$$**

D

Newberry (B-3)

See also Soo Junction

Pop 1,873 **Elev** 788 ft **Area code** 906 **Zip** 49868

Information Newberry Area Chamber of Commerce, PO Box 308; 906/293-5562 or 800/831-7292

Web www.exploringthenorth.com/newbchamb/main.html

What to See and Do

Luce County Historical Museum. *411 W Harrie St. Phone 906/293-5753 or 906/293-5946.* (1894) Restored Queen Anne structure; the stone on the lower portion is Marquette or Jacobsville sandstone, some of the oldest rock in the country. Originally a sheriff's residence and jail, it was saved from razing and is now a museum. The staterm fireplace is original; many of the rooms have been refurbished to hold records, books, and other artifacts; jail cells are still intact. (Tues-Thurs) **FREE**

Seney National Wildlife Refuge. *3 miles S on MI 123, then 23 miles W on MI 28 to Seney, then 5 miles S on MI 77. Phone 906/586-9851.* On 95,455 acres. Canada geese, bald eagles, sandhill cranes, loons, deer, beaver, otter; several species of ducks. Visitor center has exhibits, films and information on wildlife observation (mid-May-Sept, daily). Headquarters (Mon-Fri). Self-guided auto tour (mid-May-mid-Oct). 1/2 mile nature trail (daylight hours). Fishing; picnicking, limited hunting. Pets on leash only. **FREE**

Tahquamenon Falls State Park. *41382 W MI 123. 30 miles NE on MI 123. Phone 906/492-3415.* Approximately 35,000 acres of scenic wilderness; includes Upper (40 feet) and Lower Falls (a series of several scenic falls of lesser height). Swimming, fishing, boating (rentals, launch); snowmobiling, cross-country skiing, hunting in season, playground, picnicking, concession; camping near rapids and near shore of Whitefish Bay, Lake Superior. Standard fees. **$$**

Special Events

Lumberjack Days. *Phone 800/831-7292. 1 mile N on MI 123, at Tahquamenon Logging Museum.* Wood carvings, traditional music, logging contests, lumberjack breakfast. Weekend late Aug.

Michigan Fiddlers' Jamboree. *At American Legion. Phone 906/293-8711.* Weekend late Sept.

Motels/Motor Lodges

★ **BEST WESTERN.** *Rte 1 Box 680 (60611). Phone 906/293-4000; toll-free 800/329-7466; fax 906/293-4005. www.bestwestsern.com.* 66 rooms, 2 story. June-Aug, mid-Dec-Feb: S $60-$90; D $66-$105; each additional $6; under 12 free; lower rates rest of year. Crib free. TV; cable (premium). Indoor pool; whirlpool, sauna. Complimentary continental breakfast. Restaurant nearby. Check-out 11 am. Meeting room. Business services available. Coin laundry. Cross-country ski 2 miles. Game room. Some refrigerators. Cr cds: A, C, D, DS, ER, JCB, MC, V.

D ⛽ 🏊 🔌 SC

★ **COMFORT INN.** *Hwy MI 28 & MI 123 (49868). Phone 906/293-3218; toll-free 800/228-5150; fax 906/293-9375. www.comfortinn.com.* 54 rooms, 2 story. Early June-Oct, Dec-Mar: S, D $50-$84; each additional $10; under 18 free; lower rates rest of year. Crib free. TV; cable. Complimentary continental breakfast. Restaurant opposite 6 am-midnight. Check-out 10 am. Coin laundry. Meeting room. Business services available. Valet service. Cross-country ski 3/4 mile. Game room. Some in-room whirlpools. Cr cds: A, C, D, DS, ER, JCB, MC, V.

D ⛽ 🔌 SC

★ **GATEWAY MOTEL.** *MI 123 S (49868). Phone 906/293-5651; toll-free 800/791-9485.* 11 rooms, 1 story. No room phones. July-Sept, late Dec-Apr: S $32-$52; D $42-$62; each additional $4; suite $66-$78; lower rates rest of year. Crib free. TV; cable (premium). Restaurant nearby. Check-out 10 am. Cross-country ski 4 miles. Refrigerator, microwave in suite. Cr cds: DS, MC, V.

🐾 ⛽ 🧍 ⛷ ✈ 🔌

★ **MANOR MOTEL.** *MI 123 Newberry Ave (49868). Phone 906/293-5000.* 12 rooms. Mid-June-mid-Oct, Christmas wk: S $44-$54; D $52-$59; each additional $4; suites $54-$72; family rates; lower rates rest of year. Crib free. Pet accepted. TV; cable (premium). Restaurant nearby. Check-out 10 am. Game room. Lawn games. Cr cds: DS, MC, V.

★ **ZELLAR'S VILLAGE INN.** *MI 123 S (Newberry Ave) (49868). Phone 906/293-5114; fax 906/293-5116.* 20 rooms. S $40; D $50-$60; each additional $4. Crib $5. Pet accepted. TV; cable (premium). Restaurant 6 am-10 pm. Room service. Bar. Check-out 11 am. Meeting rooms. Business services available. In-room modem link. Sundries. Game room. Cr cds: A, D, DS, MC, V.

New Buffalo (I-1)

See also Niles, Saint Joseph

Pop 2,317 **Elev** 630 ft **Area code** 616 **Zip** 49117

Information Harbor County Chamber of Commerce, 530 S Whittaker, Suite F; 616/469-5409

Web www.harborcountry.com

Because of its proximity to large midwestern cities, Lake Michigan, and beaches, New Buffalo and the Harbor County area have become a popular resort community for year-round vacationers.

What to See and Do

Red Arrow Highway. *I-94 and Union Pier. I-94, exits 4B, 6, or 12.* Many antique stores, inns, galleries, shops, and restaurants can be found along this road that travels from Union Pier to Sawyer, between Lake Michigan and the Interstate.

Niles (I-2)

See also New Buffalo, St. Joseph

Pop 12,458 **Elev** 658 ft **Area code** 616 **Zip** 49120

Information Four Flags Area Council on Tourism, 321 E Main, PO Box 1300; 616/684-7444

Web www.ci.niles.mi.us

Niles calls itself the "city of four flags" because the banners of France, England, Spain, and the United States each have flown over the area. Montgomery Ward and the Dodge brothers are native sons of the town.

What to See and Do

Fernwood Botanic Gardens. *13988 Range Line Rd, 5 miles NW via US 31/33, Walton Rd exit. Phone 616/695-6491.* The scenic grounds comprise 100 acres of woodland trails, spring-fed ponds, a tall grass prairie and nearly 20 gardens, incl rock and fern gardens and Japanese garden. Nature center features hands-on educational exhibits and panoramic bird observation windows. (Tues-Sun; closed Thanksgiving, Dec 25) **$$**

Fort St. Joseph Museum. *508 E Main St. Phone 616/683-4702.* Contains one of the top five Sioux art collections in the nation. Includes autobiographical pictographs by Sitting Bull and Rain-In-The-Face. Other collections are Fort St. Joseph (1691-1781) and Potawatomi artifacts, local history memorabilia. (Wed-Sat; closed holidays)

Special Events

Four Flags Area Apple Festival. *1740 Lake St. Phone 616/683-8870.* Fourth week Sept.

Riverfest. *Riverfront Park. Phone 616/683-8888.* Crafts, games, food, entertainment, raft race. Early Aug.

Northville

See also Farmington

Restaurants

★ ★ **LITTLE ITALY.** *227 Hutton St (48167). Phone 248/348-0575; fax 248/347-6204. www.littleitalynorthville.com.* Italian menu. Specializes in veal, seafood. Hours: 5 pm-10 pm; Fri, Sat to 11 pm; Sun 4-9 pm; , closed some major holidays, open on New Year's Eve. Lunch $6.95-$18.95, dinner $10.95-$28.95. Bar. Converted residence; small, intimate dining areas; antiques, original art. Reservations accepted. Cr cds: A, D, DS, MC, V.

★ ★ **MACKINNON'S.** *126 E Main St (48167). Phone 248/348-1991; fax 248/348-9470. www.mackinnonrestaurant.com.* Continental menu. Hours: 11:30 am-10 pm; Fri, Sat to 11 pm. Closed Sun. Lunch $4.95-$10.95, dinner $13.95-$25.95. Bar to 2 am. Victorian atmosphere; stained-glass windows. Reservations accepted. Outdoor dining. Lobster tank. Cr cds: A, D, DS, MC, V.

★ **ROCKY'S OF NORTHVILLE.** *41122 W Seven Mile Rd (48167). Phone 248/349-4434; fax 248/349-8517.* Specializes in seafood, pasta, steak. Hours: 11:30 am-10 pm; Fri, Sat to 11 pm; Sun 1-9 pm. Closed Jan 1, Dec 25. Lunch $6-$9, dinner $13-$18. Bar. Child's meals. Cr cds: A, D, DS, MC, V.

Novi

See also Farmington

Restaurant

★ ★ **AH-WOK.** *41563 W Ten Mile Rd (48375). Phone 248/349-9260.* Chinese menu. Specialties: Peking duck, seafood casserole, double butterfly shrimp, hot and sour soup. Hours: 11 am-9:30 pm; Fri to 11:30 pm; Sat 4 pm-11:30 pm; Sun 2:30-9:30 pm. Lunch $5.25-$7.95, dinner $7.50-$35. Service bar. Reservations accepted everyday. Cr cds: A, D, DS, MC, V.

Ⓓ

Ontonagon (A-5)

Pop 2,040 **Elev** 620 ft **Area code** 906 **Zip** 49953

Information Ontonagon County Chamber of Commerce, PO Box 266; 906/884-4735

Web www.ontonagonmi.com

A Ranger District office of the Ottawa National Forest (see IRONWOOD) is located here.

What to See and Do

Adventure Copper Mine. *200 Adventure Rd, in Greenland. Phone 906/883-3371.* Guided tour 300 feet underground; walk through passages worked by miners 100 years ago. Also above ground walking tour encompasses the historical aspects of copper mining from the pre-historic period to the 1930s. (Memorial Day-mid-Oct, daily) **$$$**

Porcupine Mountains Wilderness State Park. *412 S Boundry Rd. 20 miles W on MI 107, on shore of Lake Superior. Phone 906/885-5275.* This 63,000-acre forested, mountainous semiwilderness area harbors otters, bears, coyotes, bald eagles, and many other species. There are many streams and lakes with fishing for bass, perch, and trout; boating (launch); hunting in season for grouse, deer, and bear; downhill and cross-country skiing, snowmobiling; hiking trails with overnight rustic cabins (reservations available) and shelters; scenic overlooks, waterfalls, abandoned mine sites. Visitor center. Picnicking, playground, camping. Standard fees. (Daily) **$$** In the park is

　Ski area. *412 S Boundary Rd. Phone 906/885-5275.* Triple, double chairlifts, T-bar, rope tow; patrol, school, rentals; snack bar. Longest run 1 mile; vertical drop 641 feet. 25 miles of cross-country trails. (Mid-Dec-Mar, daily; closed Dec 25) **$$$$**

Motels/Motor Lodges

★ ★ **AMERICINN.** *120 Lincoln (49953). Phone 906/885-5311; fax 906/885-5847. www.americinns.com.* 71 rooms, 3 story. June-mid-Oct, late Dec-late Mar: S, D $75-$100; each additional $5; family rates; ski plan; lower rates rest of year. Crib free. TV; cable (premium), VCR available. Indoor pool; whirlpool. Complimentary continental breakfast. Restaurant 7 am-9:30 pm; off season from 4:30 pm. Bar 1 pm-2 am. Check-out 11 am. Meeting rooms. Business services available. Gift shop. Airport transportation. Downhill/cross-country ski 3 miles. Sauna. Game room. Recreation room. Picnic tables. On lake; swimming beach. Cr cds: A, C, D, DS, MC, V.

Ⓓ 🐾 ⚓ 🏊 ➗ 🏃

★ **MOUNTAIN VIEW LODGES.** *237 MI 107 (49953). Phone 906/885-5256. www.mtnviewlodges.com.* 11 (2 bedroom) cabins. No A/C. D $89-$109; each additional $11. Check-out 11 am. TV; cable; VCR (movies). Fireplaces. Downhill/cross-country ski 1 mile. Cr cds: A, DS, MC, V.

Ⓓ ⚓ ➗ ✈ 🏊

★ **PETERSON'S CHALET COTTAGES.** *287 Lakeshore Rd (49953). Phone 906/884-4230; fax 906/884-2965. www.petersonschaletcottages.com.* 13 kitchen cottages for 2-8 (1-2-bedrm), 2 vacation homes for 2-12 (3-bedrm). No A/C. S $60-$90; D $72-$110; each additional $10; vacation homes $225; under 18, $5. Crib available. TV; cable (premium). Restaurant nearby. Check-out 11 am. Gift shop. Free airport transportation. Downhill/cross-country ski 15 miles. Many fireplaces. Picnic tables, grills. Private beach on Lake Superior. Cr cds: A, DS, MC, V.

⚓ ➗ 👫 ➗ ✈ 🏊

Oscoda (E-5)

See also Tawas City

Pop 1,061 **Elev** 590 ft **Area code** 517 **Zip** 48750

Information Oscoda-Au Sable Chamber of Commerce, 4440 N US 23; 517/739-7322 or 800/235-4625

Web www.oscoda.com

This is a resort community where the Au Sable River, a famous trout stream, empties into Lake Huron. In 1890, when it was a logging town, Oscoda reached a population of 23,600.

What to See and Do

Huron-Manistee National Forest. *W of town on River Rd. Phone 989/739-0728.* This 427,000-acre forest is the Huron section of the Huron-Manistee National Forest. A major attraction of the forest is the Lumberman's Monument overlooking the Au Sable River. A three-figure bronze memorial, depicting a timber cruiser, sawyer, and river driver, commemorates the loggers who cut the virgin timber in Michigan in the latter part of the 19th-century. The visitor center at the monum ent offers interpretations of this colorful era (Memorial Day-Labor Day). Scenic drives; beaches, swimming, streams, lakes, trout fishing, canoe trips down the Au Sable River; hunting for deer and small game, camping, picnicking, winter sports areas. (Daily) **FREE**

Paddle-wheeler boat trips. *1775 W River Rd. Au Sable River Queen, Foote Dam, 6 miles W on River Rd. Phone 517/739-7351.* Boat makes 19-miles (2-hour) round-trips on Au Sable River. (Memorial Day-mid-Oct, daily; schedule may vary, reservations advised) **$$$**

Special Events

Au Sable River International Canoe Marathon. *Phone 989/739-7322.* This 120-mile marathon begins in Grayling and ends in Oscoda. Last weekend July.

Paul Bunyan Days. *Phone 989/739-7322.* Lumberjack show, chainsaw carving competition, children's events. Third weekend Sept.

Motels/Motor Lodges

★ **LAKE TRAIL.** *5400 US 23 N (48750). Phone 517/739-2096; toll-free 800/843-6007; fax 517/739-2565.* 42 rooms, 1-2 story, 20 suites, 2 kitchen cottages. S $50-$55; D $50-$60; each additional $6; suites $72-$125; kitchen cottages $85 ($525/week in season); under 12 free. Crib free. Complimentary continental breakfast. Check-out 11 am. TV; cable, VCR available (movies $4). Balconies. Some refrigerators. Health club privileges. Paddleboats, waverunners available; swimming beach. Lighted tennis. Picnic tables. Lawn games. Airport transportation. On lake. Cr cds: A, DS, MC, V.

[D] [🛩] [⚓] [🍴] [⛱] [🏃] [⊠]

★ **REDWOOD MOTOR LODGE.** *3111 US 23 N (48750). Phone 517/739-2021; fax 517/739-1121. www.redwoodmotorlodge.com.* 37 rooms, 1-2 story, 9 cabins. D $70-$80; each additional $5; under 5 free. Complimentary continental breakfast. Check-out 11 am. TV; cable (premium). Bar. Sauna. Game room. Private beach on Lake Huron opposite. Indoor pool, whirlpool. Lawn games. Cr cds: A, C, D, DS, MC, V.

[D] [🏊] [⊠]

OWOSSO (G-4)

See also Flint, Lansing

Settled 1836 **Pop** 16,322 **Elev** 730 ft **Area code** 989 **Zip** 48867

Information Owosso-Corunna Area Chamber of Commerce, 215 N Water St; 989/723-5149

Web www.shianet.org

Owosso's most famous sons were James Oliver Curwood, author of many wildlife novels about the Canadian wilderness, and Thomas E. Dewey, governor of New York and twice Republican presidential nominee. The city, rising on the banks of the Shiawassee River, has five parks and many industries.

What to See and Do

Curwood Castle. *224 Curwood Castle Dr. Phone 517/723-8844, ext 554.* This replica of a Norman castle, thought to be architecturally unique in the state, was used as a studio by James Oliver Curwood, author and conservationist. It is maintained as a museum with Curwood memorabilia and local artifacts displayed. (Tues-Sun afternoons; closed holidays) **DONATION**

Special Events

Curwood Festival. *Phone 989/723-2161.* River raft, bed, and canoe races, juried art show, pioneer displays and demonstrations, fun run, parade, entertainment. First full weekend June.

Shiawassee County Fair. *2900 E Hibbard Rd. Phone 989/743-3611.* Agricultural and home economics exhibits, rides. First week Aug.

Paw Paw (H-2)

See also Kalamazoo

Pop 3,169 **Elev** 740 ft **Area code** 269 **Zip** 49079

Information Chamber of Commerce, 804 S Kalamazo St; PO Box 105; 616/657-5395

Web www.pawpaw.net

The center of an important grape-growing area, this town takes its name from the Paw Paw River, so designated by Native Americans for the papaw trees that grew along its banks.

What to See and Do

Maple Lake. Created in 1908 when river waters were dammed for electric power. Boating and swimming on Maple Island; picnicking.

St. Julian Wine Company. *716 S Kalamazoo St, 2 blocks N of I-94 exit 60. Phone 269/657-5568.* The oldest and largest winery in the state; wine tasting. Tours every 1/2 hour. (Mon-Sat, also Sun afternoons; closed holidays)

Warner Vineyards. *706 S Kalamazoo St, 3 blocks N of I-94. Phone 269/657-3165.* Produce wine, champagne, and juices. Tours and tasting. (Daily; closed holidays) **FREE**

Motel/Motor Lodge

★ **DEERFIELD INN.** *139 Ampey Rd (49079). Phone 269/657-2578.* 43 rooms, 2 story. S $45-$55; D $55-$65; 3-4 persons $44.95. Crib free. TV. Complimentary coffee in lobby. Restaurant nearby. Check-out 11 am. Downhill ski 20 miles. Cr cds: A, DS, MC, V.

Pellston

Restaurant

★ ★ **DAM SITE INN.** *6705 Woodland Rd (49769). Phone 231/539-8851; fax 231/539-7002. www.damsiteinn.com.* Hours: 5-9 pm; Sun 3-8 pm, Apr-Oct. Closed late Oct-late Apr; also Mon Sept-June. No A/C. Bar. Dinner $12.75-$37.00. Specializes in own noodles, buttermilk biscuits, whitefish. Family-style chicken dinner. Fireplace. Overlooks dam. Cr cds: MC, V.

Pentwater

Restaurant

★ **HISTORIC NICKERSON INN.** *262 W Lowell St (49449). Phone 231/869-6731. www.nickersoninn.com.* Eclectic menu. Hours: 6-9 pm; Sun 8 am-1 pm, 6-9 pm. Closed Sun-Thurs (Apr-May);Jan-Mar; Dec 25. Dinner $14-$28. Children's menu. Casual attire. Outdoor dining. Totally nonsmoking. Cr cds: DS, MC, V.

Petoskey (D-3)

See also Boyne City, Charlevoix, Harbor Springs

Settled 1852 **Pop** 6,056 **Elev** 786 ft **Area code** 231 **Zip** 49770

Information Petoskey Regional Chamber of Commerce, 401 E Mitchell St; 231/347-4150

Web www.petoskey.com

A popular resort stretching along Little Traverse Bay, Petoskey is known for its historic Gaslight Shopping District. A diverse industrial base provides a viable year-round economy.

What to See and Do

Little Traverse Historical Museum. *100 Depot Ct. Phone 231/347-2620.* Housed in a former railroad depot, visitors can see historical exhibits from the area's Native American, pioneer, and Victorian past. (May-Nov, daily).

Petoskey State Park. *2475 MI 119 . 4 miles NE, on MI 119. Phone 231/347-2311.* A 305-acre park with swimming beach, beach house, fishing; hiking, cross-country skiing, picnicking, playground, camping (electrical hookups, dump station). Standard fees.

St. Francis Solanus Indian Mission. *W Lake St.* (1859) Built of square hand-cut timbers, held together by dovetailed corners. Native American burial grounds (not open to public) adjacent the church.

Special Event

Art in the Park. *401 E Mitchell St. Phone 231/347-4150.* Third Sat July.

Motels/Motor Lodges

★ **BAYWINDS INN.** *909 Spring St (49770). Phone 231/347-4193; toll-free 800/204-1748; fax 231/347-5927.* 48 rooms, 2 story. D $89-$97; each additional $5. Complimentary continental breakfast. Check-out 11 am. TV; cable (premium). Exercise equipment. Game room. Indoor pool, whirlpool. Downhill/cross-country ski 10 miles. Cr cds: A, D, DS, MC, V.

★ **ECONO LODGE.** *1858 US 131 (49770). Phone 231/348-3324; toll-free 800/748-0417; fax 616/348-3521. www.econolodge.com.* 59 rooms, 2 story. Mid-June-early Sept: S $46-$95; D $56-$120; family rates; package plans; lower rates rest of year. Crib available. Pet accepted; fee. TV; cable. Indoor pool; whirlpool. Complimentary continental breakfast. Restaurant nearby. Check-out 11 am. Business services available. Downhill ski 15 miles;

cross-country ski 10 miles. Cr cds: A, C, D, DS, JCB, MC, V.

⊡ ⊠ ⚗ ⚘ ⊠ ⊠

★ ★ **HOLIDAY INN.** *1444 S US 131 (49770). Phone 231/347-6041; fax 616/347-6041. www.holiday-inn.com.* 144 rooms, 5 story. July-Aug: S, D $115; under 19 free; holiday rates; ski, golf plans; higher rates wkends, Dec 20-Jan 2; lower rates rest of year. Crib free. TV; cable (premium). Indoor pool; whirlpool. Playground. Complimentary coffee in rooms. Restaurant 7 am-2 pm, 5-10 pm. Room service. Bar 4 pm-midnight; Fri, Sat to 2 am; entertainment Fri, Sat. Check-out noon. Coin laundry. Meeting rooms. Business services available. Bellhops. Valet service. Gift shop. Downhill/cross-country ski 15 miles. Health club privileges. Game room. Balconies. Cr cds: A, C, D, DS, JCB, MC, V.

⊡ ⊠ ⚗ ⊠

Hotel

★ ★ **STAFFORD'S PERRY HOTEL.** *Bay and Lewis Sts (49770). Phone 231/347-4000; toll-free 800/737-1899; fax 231/347-0636. www.staffords.com.* 81 rooms, 3 story. Late June-early Sept, weekends Sept-Feb, Christmas wk: S $80-$125; D $95-$185; suites $185; ski packages; lower rates rest of year. Crib $5. TV; cable, VCR available. Restaurant 7-10:30 am, 11:30 am-2:30 pm, 5:30-10 pm. Bar noon-11 pm. Check-out 11 am. Meeting rooms. Business services available. Downhill/cross-country ski 8 miles. Exercise equipment. Whirlpool. Some private patios, balconies. Cr cds: A, DS, MC, V.

⊡ ⚗ ⊠ ⚘ ⚗ ⚗ ⊠

Resort

★ ★ ★ **THE INN AT BAY HARBOR.** *3600 Village Harbor Dr (49770). Phone 231/439-4000; toll-free 800/362-6963. www.innatbayharbor.com.* 85 suites, 5 story. S, D $99-$334; suite $481-$1,808. Crib available. Complimentary continental breakfast. Check-out noon. TV; cable (premium). Some fireplaces, balconies, kitchenettes. Refrigerators, minibars. Coffee in rooms. Valet services. Restaurant 6 am-10 pm. Room service. Supervised children's activities, ages 4-15 (summer). Exercise room. Heated pool, whirlpool, poolside service. 27-hole golf, greens fee, golf carts, pro, putting green, driving range, pro shop. Free valet parking. Meeting rooms, business center. Concierge. Gift shop. Outdoor chess board. Beach. On Lake Michigan. Cr cds: A, C, D, DS, JCB, MC, V.

⊡ ⚗ ⊠ ⊠ ⚘

B&B/Small Inns

★ ★ ★ **STAFFORD'S BAY VIEW INN.** *2011 Woodland Ave (49770). Phone 231/347-2771; toll-free 800/258-1886; fax 201/347-3413. www.staffords.com.* 31 rooms, 3 story, 10 suites. No room phones. July-Aug, late-Dec, wkends: S, D $135-$260; each additional $18; suites $260; under 3 free; ski plan; lower rates rest of year. Crib free. Pet accepted; $20. TV in library. Complimentary full breakfast. Coffee in library 24 hours. Restaurant (see STAFFORD'S BAY VIEW INN). Check-out 11 am, check-in after 3 pm. Business services available. Valet service. Gift shop. Tennis privileges. Downhill ski 6 miles; cross-country ski on site. Sleigh rides. Bicycles. Lawn games. Picnic tables. Some fireplaces, balconies. Airport/local transportation. Victorian-style inn with green, mansard roof (1886); antiques, reproductions. Overlooks Little Traverse Bay. Cr cds: A, DS, MC, V.

⊡ ⚗ ⚘ ⚗ ⊠ ⚗ ⊠

Restaurants

★ ★ **ANDANTE.** *321 Bay St (49770). Phone 231/348-3321.* Hours: 5:30-9 pm. Closed Sun, Mon Oct-May; most major holidays. Reservations accepted. Eclectic menu. Service bar. Dinner $26-$39. Overlooks Little Traverse Bay. Totally nonsmoking. Cr cds: A, MC, V.

⊡

★ ★ **STAFFORD'S BAY VIEW INN.** *2011 Woodland Ave (49770). Phone 231/347-2771. www.staffords.com.* American menu. Hours: 8-10:30 am, noon-2:30 pm, 5:30-9 pm; Fri, Sat to 10 pm; Sun brunch 10 am-2 pm. Lunch $7.95-$12.95, dinner $17.95-$25.95, Sun Brunch $17.95. Entertainment. Children's menu. Casual attire. Outdoor seating. Cr cds: A, DS, MC, V.

⊡ ⊠

Plymouth (H-5)

Pop 9,560 **Elev** 730 ft **Area code** 734 **Zip** 48170

Information Chamber of Commerce, 386 S Main St; 734/453-1540

Web www.plymouthchamber.org

Plymouth is a quaint town with historical attractions and unique shopping areas.

Special Events

Fall Festival. *Phone 734/453-1540.* Antique mart, music, ethnic food. First weekend after Labor Day.

Ice Sculpture Spectacular. Hundreds of ice sculptures line the streets and fill Kellogg Park, as professional and student chefs compete with each other carving huge blocks of ice; the sculptures are lighted at night. Jan.

Motels/Motor Lodges

★ **FAIRFIELD INN DETROIT.** *West. 5700 Haggerty (48187). Phone 734/981-2440; fax 734/981-2440. www.fairfieldinn.com.* 133 rooms, 3 story. D $55-$75; each additional $7; under 18 free. Complimentary continental breakfast. Check-out noon. TV; cable (premium). Pool. Cr cds: A, C, D, DS, MC, V.

D ⊠ ⊠ SC

★ **QUALITY INN.** *40455 E Ann Arbor Rd (48170). Phone 734/455-8100; fax 734/455-5711. www.qualityinn.com.* 123 rooms, 2 story. D $75.95-$139.95. Complimentary continental breakfast. Check-out noon. TV; cable (premium). In-room modem link. Health club privileges. Pool. Cr cds: A, C, D, DS, ER, JCB, MC, V.

D ⊠ ⊠

★ **RED ROOF INN.** *39700 Ann Arbor Rd (48170). Phone 734/459-3300; toll-free 800/843-7663; fax 734/459-3072. www.redroof.com.* 109 rooms, 2 story. S $33.99-$48.99; D $41.99-$50.99; under 18 free. Crib free. Pet accepted. TV; cable (premium). Restaurant opposite open 24 hours. Check-out noon. In-room modem link. Cr cds: A, C, D, DS, MC, V.

D ⊠ ⊠

Restaurants

★ ★ ★ **CAFE BON HOMME.** *844 Penniman (48170). Phone 734/453-6260; fax 734/453-4699.* The modern European cuisine in this very upscale, tranquil restaurant tucked away in the Plymouth boutique shopping district serves such dishes as Southern French lamb pie, and pan-seared breast of duck. Closed Sun; major holidays. Lunch, dinner. Cr cds: A, D, DS, MC, V. **$$$**

D

★ ★ **ERNESTO'S.** *41661 Plymouth Rd (48170). Phone 734/453-2002; fax 734/453-7490.* Italian menu. Hours: 11 am-3 pm, 5-10 pm; Fri, Sat 11 am-11 pm; Sun noon-9 pm. Closed Mon; Jan 1, Dec 25. Lunch $7.25-$12.95 , dinner $13.95-$24.95. Bar. Reservations accepted. Outdoor dining. Cr cds: A, D, DS, MC, V.

D

Pontiac (H-5)

See also Bloomfield Hills, Detroit, Southfield

Settled 1818 **Pop** 71,166 **Elev** 943 ft **Area code** 248

Information Chamber of Commerce, 30 N Saginaw, Suite 404, 48342; 248/335-9600

Web www.pontiacchamber.com

What was once the summer home of Chief Pontiac of the Ottawas is now the home of the Pontiac division of General Motors. A group of Detroit businessmen established a village here that became a way station on the wagon trail to the West. The Pontiac Spring Wagon Works, in production by the middle 1880s, is the lineal ancestor of the present industry. Pontiac is surrounded by 11 state parks, and 400 lakes are within a short distance.

What to See and Do

Alpine Valley Ski Resort. *6775 E Highland. 12 miles W of Telegraph Rd on MI 59 (Highland Rd), in White Lake. Phone 248/887-2180 or 248/887-4183 (snow conditions).* Ten chairlifts, ten rope tows; patrol, school, rentals, snowmaking; bar, cafeteria. Longest run 1/3 mile; vertical drop 320 feet. (Nov-Mar, daily; closed Dec 24 afternoon and Dec 25 morning) **$$$$**

Detroit Lions (NFL). *1200 Featherstone Rd. Phone 248/355-4131.* Pontiac Silverdome.

Highland. *3500 Wixon Rd. 17 miles W on MI 59. Phone 248/685-2433.* On 5,524 wooded acres. Swimming, bathhouse, fishing, boating (launch); hiking, horseback riding, hunting in season, cross-country skiing, picnicking, playground, concession, camping. Standard fees.

Oakland University. *2200 N Squirrel Rd (48309). 3 miles NE off I-75, in Rochester. Phone 248/370-2100.* (1959) 12,500 students. On the grounds of the former Meadow Brook Farms estate of Mr. and Mrs. Alfred G. Wilson. The Eye Research Institute is internationally recognized; Center for Robotics and Advanced Automation promotes education, research, and development in high technology and manufacturing methods. (See SPECIAL EVENT) Also on campus are

Meadow Brook Art Gallery. *2200 N Squirrel Rd. Phone 248/370-3005.* Series of contemporary, primitive, and Asian art exhibitions, including permanent collection of African art; outdoor sculpture garden adjacent to music festival grounds. (Oct-May, Tues-Sun) **FREE**

Meadow Brook Hall. *2200 N Squirrel Rd. Phone 248/370-3140.* (1926-1929) English Tudor mansion (100 rooms) with nearly all original furnishings and art objects; antique needlepoint draperies, 24 fireplaces; library has hand-carved paneling; dining room has sculptured ceiling; ballroom has elaborate stone and woodwork. Serves as cultural and conference center of the university. (July-Aug, afternoons; rest of year, Sun afternoons) **$$$**

Meadow Brook Theatre. *Oakland University Campus 207 Wilson Hall. Phone 248/377-3300; fax 248/370-3343.* Professional company. (Early Oct-mid-May, Tues-Sun; matinees Wed, Sat, Sun)

Pontiac Lake. *7 miles W on MI 59. Contact Park Manager, 7800 Gale Rd, Rte 2, 48327. Phone 248/666-1020.* Approximately 3,700 acres. Swimming, bathhouse, waterskiing, fishing, boating (launch); horseback riding, riding stable, hunting in season, archery and rifle ranges, winter sports, picnicking, playground, concession, camping. Standard fees. **$$**

Special Event

Meadow Brook Music Festival. *207 Wilson Hall. Oakland University. Phone 248/567-6000.* Concerts featuring popular and classical artists. Dining and picnicking facilities. Mid-June-Aug.

Motels/Motor Lodges

★★ **COURTYARD BY MARRIOTT.** *1296 N Opdyke Rd (48326). Phone 248/373-4100; fax 248/373-1885. www.marriott.com.* 148 rooms, 10 suites, 2-3 story. Apr-July: S $92; D $102; each additional $10; suites $110-$120; under 14 free; weekly, wkend, holiday rates; ski plans; higher rates sports wkends; lower rates rest of year. Crib free. Complimentary coffee in rooms. Check-out noon. TV; cable (premium), VCR available. In-room modem link. Balconies. Some refrigerators, minibars. Valet services, coin laundry. Bar 4-11 pm. Exercise equipment. Indoor pool, whirlpool. Downhill ski 10 miles; cross-country ski 2 miles. Meeting rooms, business center. Cr cds: A, C, D, DS, MC, V.

[icons]

★ **FAIRFIELD INN.** *1294 N Opdyke Rd (48326). Phone 248/373-2228; fax 248/373-2228. www.fairfieldinn.com.* 134 rooms, 3 story. S $36.95-$49.95; D $48.95-$59.95; under 18 free; higher rates: special events, weekends. Crib free. TV; cable (premium). Heated pool. Complimentary continental breakfast. Restaurant adjacent 6 am-11 pm. Check-out noon. Valet service (Mon-Fri). In-room modem link. Downhill/cross-country ski 10 miles. Near Palace, Silverdome, Pine Knob Music Theatre. Cr cds: A, C, D, DS, MC, V.

[icons]

★ **HAMPTON INN.** *1461 N Opdyke Rd (48326). Phone 248/370-0044; fax 248/370-9590. www.hamptoninn.com.* 124 rooms, 3 story. S $58-$65; D $65-$72; under 17 free. Crib free. TV; cable (premium), VCR available (movies). Pool. Complimentary continental breakfast. Check-out noon. Meeting rooms. In-room modem link. Valet service. Downhill/cross-country ski 10 miles. Exercise equipment. Cr cds: A, C, D, DS, MC, V.

[icons]

Hotel

★★★ **MARRIOTT PONTIAC.** *3600 Centerpoint Pkwy (48341). Phone 248/253-9800. www.marriott.com.* 290 rooms, 11 story. S, D $175-$255; each additional $25; under 17 free. Crib available. Indoor pool. TV; cable (premium), VCR available. Restaurant 6 am-10 pm. Check-out noon. Meeting rooms. Business center. Exercise room. Gift shop. Some refrigerators, minibars. Cr cds: A, C, D, DS, MC, V.

[icon]

All Suites

★★★ **HILTON SUITES.** *2300 Featherstone Rd (48326). Phone 248/334-2222; fax 248/322-2321. www.hilton.com.* Hotel guests can enjoy complimentary cookies and milk by the lobby fireplace each night. 224 suites, 5 story. S, D $89-$149; each additional $15; family, weekend rates; package plans. Crib free. Pet accepted, some restrictions. Complimentary full breakfast, coffee in rooms. Check-out noon. TV; cable (premium), VCR (movies $3). In-room modem link. Some balconies. Refrigerators. Valet services, coin laundry. Restaurant 6-9:30 am, 11:30 am-1:30 pm, 5:30-10 pm; weekend hours vary. Bar, room service. Exercise equipment, sauna. Game room. Indoor pool, whirlpool. Golf privileges. Downhill/cross-country ski 12 miles. Meeting rooms, business center. Sundries. Gift shop. Cr cds: A, C, D, DS, ER, MC, V.

[icons]

Port Austin (F-6)

Pop 815 **Elev** 600 ft **Area code** 989 **Zip** 48467

Information Port Austin Chamber of Commerce, 2 W Spring St, PO Box 274; 989/738-7600

Web www.port-austin.com

What to See and Do

Albert E. Sleeper State Park. *6573 State Park Rd. 13 miles S on MI 25, on Saginaw Bay, Lake Huron. Phone 517/856-4411.* On 723 acres. Sand beach, bathhouse, fishing; hunting, hiking, cross-country skiing, picnicking, playground, camping. Standard fees. (Daily) **$$**

Huron City Museum. *7930 Huron City Rd, 8 miles E on MI 25. Phone 517/428-4123.* Nine preserved buildings from the 1850-1890 Victorian era, incl the LaGasse Log Cabin, Phelps Memorial Church, Point Aux Barques US Life Saving Station, Hubbard's General Store, Community House/Inn, Brick Museum, Carriage Shed, and Barn House of Seven Gables, former residence of Langdon Hubbard and later Dr. William Lyon Phelps (additional fee). Buildings house period furnishing and memorabilia. Tours (July-Labor Day, Thurs-Mon) **$$$**

Port Huron (G-6)

See also St. Clair

Pop 33,694 **Elev** 600 ft **Area code** 810 **Zip** 48060

Information Greater Port Huron Area Chamber of Commerce, 920 Pine Grove Ave; 810/985-7101

Web www.porthuron-chamber.org

Fort Gratiot Lighthouse, oldest on the Great Lakes, marks the St. Clair Straits. The famous International Blue Water Bridge (toll), south of the lighthouse, crosses to Sarnia, Ontario (see). (For Border Crossing Regulations see MAKING THE MOST OF YOUR TRIP.)

What to See and Do

Lakeport State Park. *7605 Lakeshore Rd (48059). 10 miles N on MI 25. Phone 810/327-6765.* 565 acres on Lake Huron. Beach, bathhouse, waterskiing, fishing for perch, boating (ramp); hiking, picnicking, concession, playground, camping (fee). (Daily) **$$**

Museum of Arts and History. *1115 6th St. Phone 810/982-0891.* Historical and fine arts exhibits; pioneer log home, Native American collections, Thomas Edison's boyhood home archaeological exhibit, marine lore, natural history exhibits, period furniture; also lectures. (Wed-Sun; closed holidays (See SPECIAL EVENTS) **DONATION** Also here is

Huron **Lightship Museum.** Lightships were constructed as floating lighthouses, anchored in areas where lighthouse construction was not possible, using their powerful lights and fog horns to guide ships safely past points of danger. Built in 1920, the *Huron* was stationed at various shoals in Lake Michigan and Lake Huron until her retirement in 1971. (June-Sept, Wed-Sun afternoons or by appointment)

Special Events

Feast of the Ste. Claire. *Pine Grove Park. Phone 810/985-7101.* Reenactment of 18th-century crafts, lifestyles, battles; also foods, fife and drum corps. Memorial Day weekend.

Mackinac Race. *Phone 810/985-7101.* Mid-July.

Motels/Motor Lodges

★ **COMFORT INN.** *1700 Yeager St (48060). Phone 810/982-5500; fax 810/982-7199. www.comfortinn.com.* 80 rooms, 2 story, 16 suites. June-Aug: S, D $69-$109; each additional $5; suites $89-$99; under 18 free; higher rates special events; lower rates rest of year. Crib free. TV; cable (premium), VCR available. Indoor pool; whirlpool. Complimentary continental breakfast. Complimentary coffee in lobby. Restaurant opposite 6 am-10 pm. Check-out 11 am. Coin laundry. Meeting rooms. In-room modem link. Valet service. Exercise equipment. Game room. Refrigerator in suites. Cr cds: A, C, D, DS, JCB, MC, V.

⊡ ⧠ ⧠ ⧠ ⧠ ⧠

★ **KNIGHTS INN.** *2160 Water St (48060). Phone 810/982-1022; toll-free 800/843-5644; fax 810/982-0927. www.knightsinn.com.* 104 units. Apr-Oct: S $51.95-$62.95; D $57.99-$67.95; each additional $5; kitchen units $61.95-$77.95; under 18 free; lower rates rest of year. Crib free. Pet accepted. TV; cable (premium), VCR available. Pool. Coffee in rooms. Restaurant nearby. Check-out noon. Cr cds: A, C, D, DS, MC, V.

⊡ ⧠ ⧠ ⧠ **SC**

★ ★ ★ **THOMAS EDISON INN.** *500 Thomas Edison Pkwy (48060). Phone 810/984-8000; toll-free 800/451-7991; fax 810/984-3230. www.thomasedisoninn.com.* 149 rooms, 3 story, 12 suites. S, D $85-$120, each additional $10; suites $150-$345. Crib free. Check-out noon. TV; cable (premium), VCR available. Balconies. Bathroom phones. Restaurant 7 am-11 pm; Sun 8 am-9 pm. Bar 11-2 am; entertainment (days vary). Room service. Exercise room, sauna. Indoor pool, whirlpool. Golf privileges. Tennis privileges. Meeting rooms, business center. Sundries. Gift shop. Opposite river. Cr cds: A, D, DS, MC, V.

⧠ ⧠ ⧠ ⧠ ⧠ ⧠

Restaurant

★ ★ **FOGCUTTER.** *511 Fort St (48060). Phone 810/987-3300; fax 810/987-3306. www. fogcutterrestaurant.com.* Hours: 11 am-10 pm; Sat from noon; Sun noon-7 pm. Closed most major holidays. Lunch $6.35-$14.95, dinner $13.95-$25.95. Bar. Child's meals. Reservations accepted. Cr cds: A, D, DS, MC, V.

⊡

Saginaw (G-4)

See also Bay City, Midland

Settled 1816 **Pop** 69,512 **Elev** 595 ft **Area code** 517

Information Saginaw County Convention and Visitors Bureau, One Tuscola St, Suite 101, 48607; 517/752-7164 or 800/444-9979

Web www.saginawcvb.org

When this was the land of the Sauk, the trees grew so thick that it was always night in the swamps on both sides of the Saginaw River. When the loggers "brought daylight to the swamp," the city became the timber capital of the world. When the trees were depleted, Saginaw turned its attention to industry and agriculture. Today, it is the home of numerous General Motors plants and is a leading manufacturer of malleable castings, as well as marketer of sugar beets, beans, bran, and wheat.

What to See and Do

Castle Museum of Saginaw County History. *500 Federal Phone 517/752-2861.* Housed in a replica of a French chateau; collections pertaining to the history of the Saginaw Valley and central Michigan. (Daily; closed holidays) **$**

Children's Zoo. *S Washington Ave and Ezra Rust Dr, in Celebration Sq. Phone 517/759-1657.* Small animals, including llamas, macaws, swans, snakes, and porcupines. Contact yard featuring goats; train and pony rides (fees); lectures; educational programs. (Mid-May-Labor Day, daily) **$**

Japanese Cultural Center & Tea House. *527 Ezra Rust Dr. Phone 517/759-1648.* Unique showplace on Lake Linton, designed by Yataro Suzue; gift from sister city of Tokushima, Japan. Tea service (fee); garden. (Tues-Sun)

Kokomo's Family Fun Center. *5200 Kokomo Dr. Phone 517/797-5656; fax 989/797-2313.* Go-karts, bumper boats, laser tag, batting cages, miniature golf, indoor driving range. More than 50 arcade games. (Daily) Fee for individual activities.

Marshall M. Fredericks Sculpture Gallery. *2250 Pierce Rd, at Saginaw Valley State University. Phone 517/790-5667.* Houses an extraordinary collection of more than 200 works by the world-renowned sculptor. (Tues-Sun) **DONATION**

Saginaw Art Museum. *1126 N Michigan Ave. Phone 517/754-2491.* Permanent and changing exhibits of paintings, sculpture, fine art; children's gallery; historic formal garden. (Tues-Sun; closed holidays) **DONATION**

Special Events

Great Lakes Rendezvous. *Phone 989/754-2928.* Third weekend Aug.

Saginaw County Fair. *2701 E Genesee Ave. Phone 989/752-7164.* Late July.

Saginaw Harness Raceway. *2701 E Genesee Ave, N via I-75, Bridgeport exit. For schedule phone 989/755-3451.* Over 12 years only. Racing season May-late Aug.

Motels/Motor Lodges

★★ **FOUR POINTS BY SHERATON.** *4960 Towne Centre Rd (48604). Phone 517/790-5050; toll-free 800/428-1470; fax 517/790-1466. www.fourpoints.com.* 156 rooms, 6 story. S, D $69-$139; each additional $10; under 18 free; weekend plan. Crib free. Pet accepted, some restrictions; $20 refundable. TV; cable (premium), VCR available. Indoor/outdoor pool; whirlpool. Restaurant 6:30

am-10 pm. Room service. Bar 11-2 am; entertainment. Check-out noon. Meeting rooms. Business services available. Bellhops. Valet service. Free airport transportation. Exercise equipment; sauna. Health club privileges. Game room. Country French décor. Cr cds: A, C, D, DS, ER, JCB, MC, V.

★ **HAMPTON INN.** *2222 Tittabawassee Rd (48604). Phone 517/792-7666; fax 517/792-3213. www.hampton inn.com.* 120 rooms, 2 story. S $56-$60; D $63-$67; under 18 free. Crib free. TV; cable (premium), VCR available. Heated pool. Complimentary continental breakfast. Restaurant nearby. Check-out noon. Meeting rooms. Valet service. Downhill ski 10 miles. Game room. Cr cds: A, C, D, DS, MC, V.

★ **SUPER 8 MOTEL.** *4848 Towne Center Rd (48603). Phone 517/791-3003; fax 517/791-3003. www.super8.com.* 62 rooms, 3 story. Apr-Sept: S $37.88; D $43.88-$47.88; each additional $5; suite $53.88; under 12 free; lower rates rest of year. Crib free. Pet accepted, some restrictions. TV; cable (premium). Restaurant nearby. Check-out 11 am. Health club privileges. Cr cds: A, C, D, DS, MC, V.

Saint Clair (G-6)

See also Detroit, Mount Clemens, Warren

Pop 5,116 **Elev** 600 ft **Area code** 810 **Zip** 48079

Information St. Clair Chamber of Commerce, 505 N Riverside Ave; 810/329-2962

Web www.stclairchamber.com

Motels/Motor Lodges

★★ **BLUE WATER INN.** *1337 N River Rd (48079). Phone 810/329-2261; toll-free 800/468-3727; fax 810/329-6056. www.muer.com.* Beautiful sunsets, fishing, and water sports galore are why the Blue Water area is so popular. Located on the St. Clair River. Guests will enjoy the fresh seafood the restaurant has to offer. 21 rooms. D $92.50; each additional $5; under 16 free. Complimentary continental breakfast. Check-out 11 am. TV; cable (premium). Restaurant, bar. Pool. All rooms overlook river. Cr cds: A, D, DS, MC, V.

★★ **ST CLAIR INN.** *500 N Riverside (48079). Phone 810/329-2222; toll-free 800/482-8327; fax 810/329-2348. www.stclairinn.com.* 78 rooms, 3 story. S, D $80-$145; each additional $10; suites $100-$300; family rates. Crib free. TV; cable. Indoor pool; whirlpool. Restaurant. Room service. Bar 11-2 am; entertainment Wed-Sat. Check-out noon, check-in 3 pm. Business services available. Bellhops. Valet service. Tennis privileges. 18-hole golf privileges. Game room. Some bathroom phones. Private patios, balconies. Overlooks St. Clair River. Cr cds: A, C, D, DS, MC, V.

D ⬇ 📷 ➿ ⊠ SC

Restaurants

★ ★ **RIVER CRAB.** *1337 N River Rd (MI 29) (48079). Phone 810/329-2261; fax 810/329-6056. www.muer.com.* Hours: 11:30 am-9 pm; Sat-Sun to 10 pm; early-bird dinner Mon-Fri 4-6 pm. Closed Dec 25. Lunch $6-$15, dinner $9-$30. Sun brunch $17.95. Bar. Entertainment. Child's meals. Reservations accepted. Valet parking. Outdoor dining. Cr cds: A, D, DS, MC, V.

D

★ ★ **ST. CLAIR INN.** *500 N Riverside (48079). Phone 810/329-2222. www.stclairinn.com.* Hours: 7-10:30 am, 11:30 am-4 pm, 5-10 pm; Fri, Sat to midnight; Sun 8 am-noon, 1-9 pm. Reservations accepted. Bar. Breakfast $4-$11, lunch $8-$14, dinner $15-$40. Child's meals. Specializes in prime rib, seafood, steak. Entertainment Tues-Sat. Valet parking Fri, Sat. Outdoor dining. River view. Cr cds: A, D, DS, MC, V.

D

Saint Ignace (C-3)

Pop 2,568 **Elev** 600 ft **Area code** 906 **Zip** 49781

Information St. Ignace Area Chamber of Commerce, 560 N State St; 906/643-8717 or 800/338-6660

Web www.stignace.com

Located at the north end of the Mackinac Bridge, across the Straits of Mackinac from Mackinaw City (see), St. Ignace was founded more than 300 years ago by the famous missionary/explorer, Piére Marquette. St. Ignace is the gateway to Michigan's Upper Peninsula, which offers beautiful scenery and vast opportunities for outdoor recreation. A Ranger District office of the Hiawatha National Forest (see ESCANABA) is located in St. Ignace.

What to See and Do

Castle Rock. *Castle Rock Rd. Phone 906/643-8268.* Climb the 170 steps to the top of this 200-foot-high rock to see excellent views of Mackinac Island and Lake Huron. Also features statue of Paul Bunyan and Babe, the blue ox. (Daily).

Father Marquette National Memorial. *Adjacent to Mackinac Bridge Authority Plaza.* This 52-acre memorial pays tribute to the life and work of the famed Jesuit explorer who came to area in the 1600s.

Mackinac Island ferries. Fifteen-minute trips to the island.

Shepler's. *556 E Central Ave. Phone 616/436-5023.* (Early May-early Nov, daily) **$$$$**

Star Line Ferry. *587 N State St. Phone 906/643-7635.* "Hydro Jet" service (May-Oct). Contact 590 N State St.

Marquette Mission Park and Museum of Ojibwa Culture. *Phone 906/643-9161.* Gravesite of Father Marquette. Museum interprets 17th-century Native American life and the coming of the French. (Memorial Day-Labor Day, daily; after Labor Day-rest of Sept, Tues-Sat) **$**

Special Events

Arts and Crafts Dockside and St. Ignace Powwow. *Phone 906/643-8717.* Juried show held in conjunction with the Bridge Walk; traditional Native American powwow. Labor Day weekend.

Down Memory Lane Parade and Straits Area Antique Auto Show. *268 Hillcrest Blvd. Phone 906/643-9402.* Last Sat June.

Mackinac Bridge Walk. *Phone 906/643-8717.* The only day each year when walking across the bridge is permitted (some lanes open to motor vehicles). Labor Day.

Motels/Motor Lodges

★ **AURORA BOREALIS MOTOR INN.** *635 W US 2 (49781). Phone 906/643-7488; toll-free 800/462-6783.* 56 rooms, 2 story. D $50-$75; each additional $5. Closed Nov-Apr. Check-out 10 am. TV; cable (premium). Cr cds: DS, MC, V.

D ⊠ SC

★ **BAY VIEW BEACHFRONT MOTEL.** *1133 N State St (49781). Phone 906/643-9444.* 19 rooms. Late June-Labor Day: S, D $42-$72; each additional $4; lower rates mid-May-late June, after Labor Day-late Oct. Closed rest of year. Crib free. Pet accepted. TV; cable. Restaurant nearby. Check-out 10 am. Free airport transportation. Picnic tables, grill. On Lake Huron; private beach. Cr cds: DS, MC, V.

D 🐾 ⬇ ➿ ⊠

★ **BEST WESTERN GEORGIAN HOUSE LAKEFRONT.** *1131 N State St (49781). Phone 906/643-8411; toll-free 800/322-8411; fax 906/643-8924. www.bestwestern.com.* 85 rooms, 2-3 story. D $69-$129; each additional $5; under 12 free. Check-out 11 am. TV; cable (premium). Laundry services. Game room. Miniature golf. Indoor pool, whirlpool. Downhill ski 5 miles, cross-country ski 2 miles. Cr cds: A, D, DS, MC, V.

📷 ➿ ✈ ⊠

★**BUDGET HOST INN.** *700 N State St (49781). Phone 906/643-9666; toll-free 800/872-7057; fax 906/643-9126. www.stignacebudgethost.com.* 56 rooms, 2 story. Mid-June-Labor Day: S $64-$66; D $94-$98; each additional $4; higher rates special events, holidays, auto show (3-day minimum); Labor day (2-day minimum); lower rates rest of year. Crib free. Pet accepted; $20 refundable. TV; cable (premium). Indoor pool; whirlpool. Guest laundry. Playground. Check-out 11 am. Business services available. In-room modem link. Downhill/cross-country ski 5 miles. Some refrigerators, in-room whirlpools. Sun deck. Overlooks Moran Bay. Ferry 1 block. Cr cds: A, C, D, DS, MC, V.

★**COMFORT INN.** *927 N State St (49781). Phone 906/643-7733; toll-free 800/228-5150; fax 906/643-6420. www.comfortinn.com.* 100 rooms, 4 story. July-late Aug: S, D $68-$130; each additional $5; under 18 free; higher rates (2-day minimum) auto show, Labor Day; lower rates late Apr-June, Aug-Dec. Closed rest of year. Crib $5. TV; cable (premium). Indoor pool; whirlpool. Playground. Complimentary continental breakfast. Check-out 11 am. Meeting room. Business services available. Exercise equipment. Game room. Lawn games. Refrigerators. Balconies. On beach. Cr cds: A, C, D, DS, JCB, MC, V.

★**DAYS INN.** *1067 N State St (49781). Phone 906/643-8008; toll-free 800/732-9746; fax 906/643-9400. www.daysinn.com.* 119 rooms, 2-3 story. Late June-early Sept: S $59-$99; D $64-$104; each additional $6; suites $96-$156; under 13 free; higher rates (3-day minimum) Labor Day, auto show; lower rates rest of year. Crib free. TV; cable (premium). Indoor pool; whirlpools. Playground. Complimentary continental breakfast. Restaurant opposite 7 am-10 pm. Check-out 10 am. Coin laundry. Free airport, bus depot transportation. Game room. Sauna. Refrigerators available. Lakefront balconies. Cr cds: A, C, D, DS, JCB, MC, V.

★**ECONO LODGE.** *1030 N State St (49781). Phone 906/643-8060; toll-free 800/638-7949; fax 906/643-7251. www.econolodge.com.* 47 rooms, 2 story. Late June-late Aug: S, D $62-$92; each additional $6; under 18 free; higher rates (2-day minimum) Labor Day, auto show; lower rates May-late June, late Aug-mid-Oct. Closed rest of year. Crib free. TV; cable (premium). Indoor pool; whirlpool. Playground. Restaurant adjacent 7:30 am-9 pm. Check-out 10 am. In-room modem link. Some refrigerators. Cr cds: A, D, DS, MC, V.

★**HARBOUR POINTE MOTOR INN.** *797 N State St (49781). Phone 906/643-9882; toll-free 800/642-3318; fax 906/643-6946.* 123 rooms, 1-3 story. No elevator. D $69-$135. Closed Nov-Apr. Complimentary continental breakfast. Check-out 11 am. TV; cable (premium), VCR available. Laundry services. Game room. 2 pools, 1 indoor. Whirlpool. Lawn games. Free airport transportation. On lake. Cr cds: A, C, D, DS, MC, V.

★**KEWADIN INN.** *1140 N State St (49781). Phone 906/643-9141; toll-free 800/345-9457; fax 906/643-9405.* 71 rooms. D $59-$79; package plans. Complimentary continental breakfast. Check-out 11 am. TV; cable (premium). Pool. Lawn games. Nature trail. Free airport transportation. Cr cds: A, C, D, DS, MC, V.

★**K ROYALE MOTOR INN.** *1037 N State St (49781). Phone 906/643-7737; toll-free 800/882-7122; fax 906/643-8556. www.stignace.com.* 95 rooms, 3 story. D $38-$125; each additional $5. Closed Nov-Mar. Complimentary continental breakfast. Check-out 10 am. TV; cable (premium). Laundry services. Game room. Overlooks Lake Huron; private beach. Indoor pool, whirlpool. Free airport transportation. Cr cds: A, MC, V.

★ ★ **QUALITY INN.** *913 Boulevard Dr (49781). Phone 906/643-9700; toll-free 800/906-4656; fax 906/643-6762. www.qualityinn.com.* 57 rooms, 2 story. Mid-June-mid-Sept: S $68-$76; D $73-$87; each additional $6; under 18 free; higher rates Labor Day (2-day minimum), auto show (3-day min); lower rates rest of year. Crib free. Pet accepted; $6. Indoor pool; whirlpool. TV; cable, VCR available. Complimentary continental breakfast. Complimentary coffee in lobby. Restaurant nearby. Check-out noon. Coin laundry. Meeting rooms. Sundries. Cross-country ski 7 miles. Game room. Cr cds: A, C, D, DS, JCB, MC, V.

★**THUNDERBIRD MOTOR INN.** *10 South St (49781). Phone 906/643-8900; fax 906/643-8596.* 34 rooms, 2 story. Mid-June-Labor Day: S, D $70-$125; each additional $5; higher rates (3-day min) Labor Day, auto show; lower rates mid-May-mid-June, Labor Day-Oct. Closed rest of year. Crib $4. TV; cable (premium). Restaurant nearby. Check-out 11 am. Cr cds: A, MC, V.

★**TRADEWINDS.** *1190 N State St (49781). Phone 906/643-9388; fax 906/643-9388.* 25 rooms. No room phones. Late June-Labor Day: S, D $55; each additional $4; higher rates (3-day minimum) Labor Day, auto show; lower rates late May-late June, Labor Day-mid-Oct. Closed rest of year. TV; cable (premium). Pool. Playground. Complimentary coffee in rooms. Restaurant adjacent 7 am-11 pm. Check-out 11 am. Picnic tables. Overlooks Lake Huron. Cr cds: DS, MC, V.

Saint Joseph (I-1)

See also New Buffalo, Niles

Pop 9,214 **Elev** 630 ft **Area code** 616 **Zip** 49085

Information Cornerstone Chamber Services, 38 W Wall St, PO Box 428, Benton Harbor 49023-0428; 616/925-6100

Web www.cstonealliance.org

This town is opposite Benton Harbor on the St. Joseph River.

What to See and Do

Curious Kids' Museum. *415 Lake Blvd. Phone 616/983-2543.* Interactive museum for children; kids can interact with such exhibits as balloon flying and apple picking and can even run their own TV station. (Wed-Sat 10 am-5 pm, Sun noon-5 pm) **$**

Deer Forest. *6800 Marquette Ave. Approximately 12 miles NE via I-94, in Coloma. Phone 616/468-4961 or 800/752-DEER.* Approximately 30 acres; more than 500 animals and birds; Story Book Lane, "Santa's Summer Home," train, children's rides, stage events, picnicking. (Memorial Day-Labor Day, daily) **$$**

Krasl Art Center. *707 Lake Blvd. Phone 616/983-0271.* Three galleries house contemporary and traditional works, fine and folk arts, local and major museum collections; art reference library; lectures, tours, films; gift shop. (Daily; closed holidays) **FREE**

Warren Dunes State Park. *12032 Red Arrow Hwy. 14 miles S via MI 63 and I-94, in Sawyer. Phone 616/426-4013.* On 1,499 acres on Lake Michigan. Swimming, beach house; hiking, picnicking, playground, concession, camping, cabins. 200 acres of virgin forest in Warren Woods. Standard fees. (Daily) **$$**

Special Events

Blossomtime Festival. *151 E Napier Ave. Phone 616/926-7397.* A spring salute to agriculture, industry, and recreation in southwest Michigan; Blessing of the Blossoms; Blossomtime Ball, Grand Floral Parade. Early May.

Krasl Art Fair. *Lake Bluff Park. Phone 616/983-0271.* One of the major art shows in the state. Second weekend July.

Sailing Festival. *Phone 616/982-0032.* Labor Day weekend.

Venetian Festival. *305 Lake Blvd. Phone 616/983-7917.* Boat parades, fireworks, concerts, land and water contests, races, sand-castle sculptures, food booths, photography competition. Mid-July.

Motels/Motor Lodges

★★**BENTON HOTEL SUITES.** *2860 MI 139 S (54547). Phone 616/925-3234; fax 616/925-6131.* 150 rooms, 2 story. June-Sept: S $63-$75; D $68-$75; each additional $5; under 18 free; golf plan; lower rates rest of year. Crib free. TV; cable (premium). Indoor/outdoor pool; whirlpool. Restaurant 6:30 am-10 pm; Sat 7 am-11 pm; Sun 7 am-9 pm. Room service. Bar 4 pm-midnight. Check-out 11 am. Meeting rooms. Business services available. Bellhops. Gift shop. Free train station, bus depot transportation. Exercise equipment; sauna. Game room. Recreation room. Cr cds: A, MC, V.

★★**BEST WESTERN.** *1598 Mall Dr (49022). Phone 616/925-1880; toll-free 800/228-5150; fax 616/925-1880. www.bestwestern.com.* 52 rooms, 2 story. Mid-May-mid-Sept: S $59.95; D $64.95; under 18 free; family rates; lower rates rest of year. Crib free. Pet accepted. TV; cable (premium). Indoor pool; whirlpool. Complimentary continental breakfast. Restaurant nearby. Check-out 11 am. Business services available. Game room. Health club privileges. Some refrigerators. Cr cds: A, C, D, DS, MC, V.

★★**COMFORT INN.** *1592 Mall Dr (49022). Phone 616/925-3000; fax 616/925-8796. www.marriott.com.* 98 rooms, 2 story. May-Sept: S, D $77-$96; suites $129-$299; lower rates rest of year. Crib free. Complimentary coffee. Check-out noon. TV; cable. In-room modem link. Valet service. Restaurant nearby. Exercise equipment. Indoor/outdoor pool. Cross-country ski 5 miles. Picnic tables. Meeting rooms, business services. Cr cds: A, C, D, DS, MC, V.

★**DAYS INN.** *2699 US 31 (49022). Phone 616/925-7021; fax 616/925-7115. www.daysinn.com.* 120 rooms, 2 story. May-Labor Day: S $47-$58; D $59-$70; each additional $5; under 16 free; higher rates festivals; lower rates rest of year. Crib free. TV, VCR available (movies). Indoor pool; whirlpool. Complimentary continental breakfast. Restaurant open 24 hours. Room service 8 am-9 pm. Check-out noon. Coin laundry. Meeting room. Business services available. Sundries. Cross-country ski 20 miles. Exercise equipment; sauna. Health club privileges. Game room. Some refrigerators. Private patios, balconies. Cr cds: A, C, D, DS, JCB, MC, V.

★**ECONO LODGE.** *2723 Niles Ave (49085). Phone 616/983-6321; fax 616/983-7630. www.econolodge.com.* 36 rooms, 2 story, 2 kitchens May-Sept: S $31-$38; D $49-$55; each additional $4; suite $52-$55; kitchen units $38-$52; under 12 free; weekly rates off-season; lower rates rest of year. Crib $4. TV; cable (premium). Heated pool. Complimentary continental breakfast. Restaurant adjacent open 24 hours. Check-out noon. Cross-country ski 5 miles. Many refrigerators. Cr cds: A, C, D, DS, JCB, MC, V.

★ **SUPER 8 MOTEL.** *1950 E Napier Ave (49022). Phone 616/926-1371; toll-free 800/800-8000; fax 616/926-1371. www.super8.com.* 62 rooms, 3 story. S $35.88-$47.88; D $46.88-$60.88; under 12 free; higher rates: wkends, special events. Crib free. Pet accepted. TV; cable (premium). Complimentary coffee in lobby. Restaurant nearby. Check-out 11 am. Business services available. Cr cds: A, C, D, DS, MC, V.

Hotel

★★ **BOULEVARD INN.** *521 Lake Blvd (49085). Phone 616/983-6600; toll-free 800/875-6600; fax 616/983-0520.* 85 suites, 7 story. Suites $97-$128; each additional $10; under 12 free; golf plans; higher rates (2-day minimum): Memorial Day wkend, Venetian Festival; lower rates rest of year. Crib free. Complimentary continental breakfast. Coffee in rooms. Check-out noon. TV; cable (premium), VCR available. Refrigerators. Restaurant 7 am-2 pm, 5:30-10 pm. Bar from 5 pm. Health club privileges. Meeting rooms, business center. Cr cds: A, D, DS, MC, V.

Saugatuck (H-2)

See also Holland, South Haven

Pop 954 **Elev** 600 ft **Area code** 616 **Zip** 49453

Information Saugatuck-Douglas Visitors & Convention Bureau, PO Box 28; 269/857-1701

Web www.saugatuck.com

Long one of the major art colonies in the Midwest, Saugatuck/Douglas is growing as a year-round resort area. It offers beautiful beaches for swimming and surfing on Lake Michigan, hiking and cross-country skiing in the dunes, canoeing and boating on the Kalamazoo River, yachting from marinas, and a charming shopping area. The northern end of the village covers an ancient Native American burial ground. During the summer months, arts and crafts shows are abundant.

What to See and Do

City of Douglas. *Docked just S of the Douglas-Saugatuck Bridge. Phone 269/857-2107 or 269/857-2151, ext 415.* Scenic afternoon, buffet brunch luncheon, and dinner cruises to Lake Michigan via Kalamazoo River. (Memorial Day weekend-Labor Day, daily)

Fenn Valley Vineyards and Wine Cellar. *6130 122nd Ave. 5 miles SE via I-196 exit 34. Phone 269/561-2396.* Self-guided tour overlooking wine cellar; audiovisual program, wine tasting. (Daily; closed holidays) **FREE**

Keewatin Marine Museum. *219 Union. Harbour Village, just S of the Saugatuck-Douglas Bridge. Phone 269/857-2107 or 269/857-2151, ext 415.* Tours of restored, turn-of-the-century, passenger steamship of the Canadian Pacific Railroad; maintained as "in-service" ship; features original, elegant furnishings, carved paneling, brass fixtures. Quadruple-expansion engine room also open to tours. (Memorial Day-Labor Day, daily) **$$**

Saugatuck Dune Rides. *6495 Washington Rd. 1/2 mile W of I-196, exit 41. Phone 269/857-2253.* Buggy rides over the sand dunes near Lake Michigan. (May-Sept, daily; Oct, weekends only) **$$$**

Star of Saugatuck. *At the Fish Dock, 716 Water St. Phone 269/857-4261.* Stern-wheel paddleboat with narrated tours on the Kalamazoo River and Lake Michigan (weather permitting). (Early May-Sept, daily; Oct, weekends only)

Special Events

Halloween Harvest Festival. *Phone 269/857-1701.* Late Oct.

Harbor Days. *132 Mason St. Phone 269/857-1701.* Venetian boat parade, family activities. Last weekend July.

Taste of Saugatuck. *Phone 269/857-1701.* Late Aug.

Motels/Motor Lodges

★ **LAKE SHORE RESORT.** *2885 Lakeshore Dr (49453). Phone 269/857-7121. www.lakeshoreresort saugatuck.com.* 30 rooms. D $80-$150; each additional $30. Closed Nov-Apr. Complimentary continental breakfast. Check-out 11 am. TV; cable. Pool. Nature trails. Viewing decks overlook lake. Cr cds: MC, V.

★ **SHANGRA-LA MOTEL.** *6190 Blue Star Hwy (49453). Phone 269/857-1453; toll-free 800/877-1453; fax 269/857-5905.* 20 rooms. D $50-$140; each additional $5. Closed Jan. Check-out 11 am. TV; VCR (movies $3). Pool. Cross-country ski 4 miles. Lawn games. Cr cds: DS, MC, V.

★ **TIMBERLINE.** *3353 Blue Star Hwy (49453). Phone 269/857-2147; toll-free 800/257-2147; fax 269/857-2147. www.timberlinemotel.com.* 28 rooms. D $65-$150; each additional $5. Check-out 11 am. TV; cable (premium). Game room. Pool, whirlpool. Cross-country ski 2 1/2 miles. Lawn games. Free airport transportation. Cr cds: A, DS, MC, V.

B&B/Small Inns

★★KINGSLEY HOUSE BED & BREAKFAST. *626 W Main St (49408). Phone 269/561-6425; fax 269/561-2593. www.kingsleyhouse.com.* 8 rooms, 3 suites, 3 story. 4 with shower only. No room phones. Children over 12 years only. Complimentary full breakfast. Check-out 11 am, check-in 4 pm. TV in suites; VCR available. Bicycles. Cross-country ski 5 miles. Victorian house built 1886; antiques. Totally nonsmoking. Cr cds: A, DS, MC, V.

★ ★ MAPLEWOOD HOTEL. *428 Butler (49453). Phone 269/857-1771; toll-free 800/650-9790; fax 269/857-1773. www.maplewoodhotel.com.* 15 rooms, 11 with shower only, 2 story. May-Oct: S, D $115-$185; each additional $15; under 3 free; lower rates rest of year. Crib free. TV; cable. Heated pool. Complimentary full breakfast. Restaurant nearby. Check-out noon, check-in 3-6 pm. 18-hole golf privileges. Cross-country ski 3 miles. Built in 1860; antiques. Totally nonsmoking. Cr cds: A, DS, MC, V.

★ ★ PARK HOUSE BED & BREAKFAST. *888 Holland St (49453). Phone 269/857-4535; toll-free 800/321-4535; fax 269/857-1065. www.parkhouseinn.com.* 9 rooms, 3 suites, 2 story. S, D $115-$185; suites $165; cottage $125-$225; weekly rates; 2-day min weekends Sept-June, 3-day min weekends July-Aug. Complimentary full breakfast. Check-out 11 am, check-in 3 pm. TV; in parlor, suites, cottages; VCR available (movies). Many fireplaces. Restaurant adjacent (in season) 7 am-3 pm. Cross-country ski 2 miles. White, clapboard house built for lumberman (1857); oldest house in Saugatuck, once visited by Susan B.Anthony. Some room phones. Totally nonsmoking. Cr cds: A, DS, MC, V.

★ ★ ROSEMONT INN RESORT. *83 Lakeshore Dr (49453). Phone 269/857-2637; toll-free 800/721-2637. www.rosemontinn.com.* 14 rooms, 2 story. Mid-June-mid-Sept: S $95-$145; D $205-305; holidays (3-day min); lower rates rest of year. No pets allowed, Adults only. Complimentary full breakfast; afternoon refreshments. Check-out Noon, check-in 3 pm. TV; cable. In-room modem link. Restaurant nearby. Sauna. Heated pool; whirlpool. Golf privileges. Cross-country ski on site. Built 1901. Totally nonsmoking. Cr cds: A, MC, V.

★ ★ SHERWOOD FOREST BED & BREAKFAST. *938 Center St (49406). Phone 269/857-1246; toll-free 800/838-1246; fax 269/857-1996. www.sherwoodforestbandb.com.* 5 rooms, shower only rooms, 1 cottage. kitchen units, 2 story. No room phones. Memorial Day-Labor Day: S, D $85-$165; cottage $850/wk; higher rates

weekends (2-day minimum); lower rates rest of year. Complimentary full breakfast. Check-out Noon , check-in 3 pm. TV in sitting room; VCR (free movies). Heated pool; whirlpool. Bicycles. Victorian-style house built 1890s; many antiques. Totally nonsmoking. Cr cds: DS, MC, V.

★ TWIN GABLES INN. *900 Lake St (49453). Phone 269/857-4346; toll-free 800/231-2185; fax 269/857-3482. www.twingablesinn.com.* 14 rooms, 2 story, 3 cottages (1-2 bedroom). No room phones. May-Oct: S, D $75-$170; each additional $10-$15; cottages $495-$720/wk; under 3 free; weekly rates; lower rates rest of year. TV in sitting room. Heated pool; whirlpool. Complimentary breakfast buffet (inn). Check-out 11 am, check-in 3 pm. Free airport, train station, bus depot transportation. Cross-country ski 3 miles. Some fireplaces. Picnic tables, grills. Fireplace in sitting rm, embossed tin ceilings and walls; antiques. Near lake. Cr cds: A, D, DS, MC, V.

★ ★ ★ WICKWOOD INN. *510 Butler St (49453). Phone 269/857-1465; fax 269/857-1552. www.wickwoodinn.com.* This romantic inn, adorned with antiques and fireplaces, is located in a resort village near Lake Michigan. Guests will discover intimate and quiet moments here. With a best selling cookbook author as innkeeper, it's no wonder the food is superb. 11 rooms, 2 story. No room phones. D $175-$325. Closed Dec 24, 25. Complimentary full breakfast. Check-out noon, check-in 3 pm. Restaurant nearby. Cr cds: MC, V.

Restaurants

★CHEQUERS. *220 Culver St (49453). Phone 269/857-1868; fax 269/857-2298. www.chequersofsaugatuck.com.* Hours: 11:30 am-10 pm; Sat to 11 pm; Sun noon-10 pm; winter hours vary. Closed Jan 1, Dec 25. Lunch $6-$10, dinner $10-$19. Bar. English pub menu. English-style pub. Cr cds: A, D, MC, V.

★ ★ TOULOUSE. *248 Culver St (49453). Phone 269/857-1561; fax 269/857-2298. www.restauranttoulouse.com.* French menu. Specializes in French casual country cuisine. French country atmosphere. Hours: 5:30-10 pm; Wed,Thurs to 9 pm. Opens during Jan.1 and Dec.25: closed Mar. Dinner $20-$30. Bar. Reservations accepted. Patio dining. Cr cds: A, MC, V.

Sault Sainte Marie (B-4)

Settled 1668 **Pop** 14,689 **Elev** 613 ft **Area code** 906 **Zip** 49783

Information Sault Convention and Visitors Bureau, 2581 I-75 Business Spur; 906/632-3301 or 800/MI-SAULT

Web www.ssmcoc.com

Sault Ste. Marie (SOO-Saint-Marie) is the home of one of the nation's great engineering marvels—the locks of St. Mary's River. Along the river the locks lower or raise lake and ocean vessels 21 feet between Lake Superior and Lake Huron in 6 to 15 minutes. From April to December, about 100 vessels a day pass through with no toll charge. The cascades of the river, which made the locks necessary, give the city its name: the French word for a cascade is *sault* and the name of the patron saint was Mary; combined, the two made Sault de Sainte Marie or "Leap of the Saint Mary's."

The only entrance into Canada for almost 300 miles, the Sault Ste. Marie community began in 1668 when Father Jacques Marquette built the first mission church here. An international bridge spans the St. Mary's River to Sault Ste. Marie, Ontario (toll). (For Border Crossing Regulations see MAKING THE MOST OF YOUR TRIP.) A Ranger District office of the Hiawatha National Forest (see ESCANABA) is located in Sault Ste. Marie.

What to See and Do

Federal Building. *E Portage Ave.* Grounds occupy what was the site of Jesuit Fathers' mission and later the original site of Fort Brady (1822) before it was moved. Ground floor houses River of History Museum, an interpretive center depicting the history of the St. Mary's River.

Lake Superior State University. *6550 W Easter Day.* Phone 906/635-2315. (1946) 3,000 students. This hillside campus was the second site of historic Fort Brady after it was moved from its original location; many old buildings, incl some that were part of the fort, still stand. Library's Marine Collection on Great Lakes Shipping open on request. Carillon concerts (June-Sept, twice daily; free). Headquarters of the famous Unicorn Hunters, official keepers of the Queen's English. Tours.

Museum Ship Valley Camp and Great Lakes Maritime Museum. *501 E Water St.* Phone 906/632-3658. Great Lakes Marine Hall of Fame. Ship's store, picnic area, and park. (Mid-May-mid-Oct, daily) 5 blocks E of locks. **$$$**

⭐ **Soo Locks.** *119 Park Pl.* Phone 906/632-3311. The famous locks can be seen from both the upper and lower parks paralleling the locks. The upper park has three observation towers. There is a scale model of the locks at the east end of the MacArthur Lock and a working lock model, photos, and a movie in visitor building in upper park. (Mar-Feb, daily) **FREE**

Soo Locks Boat Tours. *Docks located at 515 and 1157 E Portage Ave.* Phone 906/632-6301 or 906/632-2512. Two-hour narrated excursions travel through the Soo Locks, focusing on their history. Sunset dinner cruises (approximately 2 3/4 hours; reservations suggested). (Mid-May-mid-Oct, daily) **$$$$**

Tower of History. *501 E Waterstreet.* Phone 906/632-3658. A 21-story observation tower with a 20-mile view of Canadian and American cities; show in lobby, displays. (Mid-May-mid-Oct, daily) **$$**

Twin Soo Tour. *315-317 W Portage Ave. 315-317 W Portage Ave.* Phone 906/635-5241. Guided tour (two to four hrs) of both Canadian and American cities of Sault Ste. Marie; provides view of Soo Locks; passengers may disembark in Canada. (June-Oct, daily) **$$** Also here is

> **The Haunted Depot.** *Phone 906/635-5912.* Guided tours through depot's many unusual chambers; visitors can "fall uphill" in the mystery bedroom, walk through a "storm" in the cemetery, "lose their heads" at the guillotine. (June-Oct, daily)

Motels/Motor Lodges

⭐ **BEST WESTERN SAULT STE. MARIE.** *4281 I-75 Business Spur (49783).* Phone 906/632-2170; toll-free 800/297-2858; fax 906/632-7877. www.bestwestern.com. 110 rooms, 2 story. D $49-$109; package plans. Complimentary continental breakfast. Check-out 11 am. TV; cable (premium), VCR available. In-room modem link. Laundry services. Sauna. Game room. Indoor pool. Cr cds: A, C, D, DS, ER, JCB, MC, V.

🅳 ⊠ ⊠

⭐ **BUDGET HOST CRESTVIEW INN.** *1200 Ashmun St (49783).* Phone 906/635-5213; toll-free 800/955-5213; fax 906/635-9672. www.crestviewinn.com. 44 rooms. July-mid-Oct: S $54; D $64-$74; package plans; under 18 free; lower rates rest of year. Crib free. Pet accepted. TV; cable (premium). Complimentary continental breakfast. Complimentary coffee in lobby. Restaurant nearby. Check-out 11 am. In-room modem link. Health club privileges. Some refrigerators. Locks 1 miles. Cr cds: A, MC, V.

🐾 ⊠ SC

⭐ **COMFORT INN.** *4404 I-75 Business Spur (49783).* Phone 906/635-1118; toll-free 800/228-5150; fax 906/635-1119. www.comfortinn.com. 86 rooms, 2 story. May-Oct: S, D $59-$79; each additional $8; under 18 free; lower rates rest of year. Crib free. TV; cable (premium). Heated pool; whirlpool. Complimentary continental breakfast. Restaurant adjacent. Check-out 11 am. Exercise equipment. Cr cds: A, C, D, DS, JCB, MC, V.

🅳 ⊠ 🖾 🖾 🖾 ⊠ SC 🖾

★ **DAYS INN.** 3651 I-75 Business Spur (49783). Phone 906/635-5200; toll-free 800/329-7466; fax 906/635-9750. www.daysinn.com. 85 rooms, 2 story. June-Oct: S, D $49-$89; each additional $6; under 12 free; higher rates special events, holidays; lower rates rest of year. Crib free. TV; cable (premium), VCR available (movies). Indoor pool; whirlpool. Complimentary coffee in lobby. Restaurant adjacent 7 am-10 pm. Check-out 11 am. Coin laundry. In-room modem link. Valet service. Cross-country ski 5 miles. Game room. Refrigerator available. Cr cds: A, C, D, DS, JCB, MC, V.

⬚🏊🛏🏂🌊⬚ SC

★ **DORAL MOTEL.** 518 E Portage Ave (49783). Phone 906/632-6621; toll-free 800/998-6720. 20 rooms, 2 story. Mid-June-Oct: S $56; D $66; each additional $6; under 12 free; lower rates mid-Apr-mid-June. Closed rest of year. Crib $2.50. TV; cable. Heated pool; whirlpool. Restaurant nearby. Check-out 10 am. Sauna. Game room. Lawn games. Picnic tables. Cr cds: DS, MC, V.

🏊🌊

★ **LAWSON MOTEL.** 2049 Ashmun St (49783). Phone 906/632-3322; fax 906/632-4234. 16 rooms, 3 story. July-Oct: S $48; D $62; each additional $4; lower rates rest of year. Crib available. TV; cable (premium), VCR available. Complimentary coffee in lobby. Restaurant nearby. Check-out 11 am. Airport transportation. Cross-country ski 1/4 mile. Some refrigerators. Cr cds: A, DS, MC, V.

🛠🏊🏂🐾🌊🏃

★ **QUALITY INN.** 3290 I-75 Business Spur (49783). Phone 906/635-1523; toll-free 877/923-7887; fax 906/635-2941. www.qualityinn.com. 130 rooms, 2 story. D $70-$95; each additional $10; under 18 free. Check-out noon. TV; cable. Restaurant, bar, entertainment, room service. Exercise equipment, sauna. Game room. Indoor pool, whirlpool. Cross-country ski on site. Cr cds: A, C, D, DS, JCB, MC, V.

⬚🏊🌊🐾🏃

★★ **RAMADA PLAZA HOTEL OJIBWAY.** 240 W Portage Ave (49783). Phone 906/632-4100; toll-free 800/654-2929; fax 906/632-6050. www.ramada.com. 71 rooms, 6 story. June-mid-Oct: S, D $119; each additional $15; suites $210; under 18 free; package plans; lower rates rest of year. Crib free. TV; cable (premium). Indoor pool; whirlpool. Coffee in rooms. Restaurant (see FREIGHTERS). No room service. Bar 11:30-1 am. Check-out 11 am. Meeting rooms. Business services available. In-room modem link. Sauna. Some in-room whirlpools. Soo Locks adjacent. Cr cds: A, DS, MC, V.

⬚🛠🌊🐾🌊🏃

★ **SEAWAY MOTEL.** 1800 Ashmun St (49783). Phone 906/632-8201; toll-free 800/782-0466; fax 906/632-8210. 18 rooms. May-mid-Oct: S $58; D $62. Closed rest of year. Crib free. Pet accepted, some restrictions. TV; cable. Complimentary coffee in lobby. Restaurant opposite 5 am-midnight. Check-out 10 am. Free airport transportation. Downhill ski 18 miles; cross-country ski 1/4 mile. Cr cds: D, DS, MC, V.

🐾🛠🏂🌊🐾✈🌊

★ **SUPER 8.** 3826 I-75 Business Spur (49783). Phone 906/632-8882; toll-free 800/800-8000; fax 906/632-3766. www.super8.com. 61 rooms, 2 story. July-Aug: S $54.88-$70.88; D $60.88-$75.88; under 12 free; lower rates rest of year. Crib free. Pet accepted, some restrictions; $50 deposit. TV; cable (premium). Complimentary continental breakfast. Restaurant nearby. Check-out 11 am. Coin laundry. Cr cds: A, C, D, DS, MC, V.

⬚🐾🛠🏂🐾🐾🌊

Restaurants

★ **ANTLER'S.** 804 E Portage Ave (49783). Phone 906/632-3571; fax 906/632-6463. www.antlersgiftshop.com. Specializes in steak, seafood and barbecue ribs. Hours: 11 am-closing. Closed only during Christmas, Easter and Thanksgiving Day; Lunch $4.95-$22.95. Dinner $4.95-$22.95. Bar. Child's meals. Historic building (1800s). Same owner since 1948. Cr cds: MC, V.

⬚

★★ **FREIGHTERS.** 240 W Portage St (49783). Phone 906/632-4211; fax 906/632-6050. Hours: 6 am-2 pm, 4 pm-9 pm; Sun brunch 10 am-2 pm. Closed Dec 25. Bar noon-2 am. Breakfast $5-$8, lunch $7-$12, dinner $14-$30. Sun brunch $12.95. Child's meals. Specializes in seafood, prime rib. Extensive beer selection. Bi-level dining on river, overlooking Soo Locks. Cr cds: A, D, DS, MC, V.

⬚

Sleeping Bear Dunes National Lakeshore (E-2)

See also Glen Arbor, Leland, Traverse City

(On Lake Michigan shoreline between Frankfort and Leland)

In 1970, Congress designated the Manitou Islands and 35 miles of mainland Lake Michigan shoreline, in the vicinity of Empire, as Sleeping Bear Dunes National Lakeshore. An Ojibway legend tells of a mother bear, who with her two cubs tried to swim across Lake Michigan from Wisconsin to escape from a forest fire. Nearing the Michigan shore, the exhausted cubs fell behind. Mother bear climbed to the top of a bluff to watch and wait for her offspring. They never reached her. Today she can still be seen as the

Sleeping Bear, a solitary dune higher than its surroundings. Her cubs are the Manitou Islands, which lie a few miles offshore.

The lakeshore's variety of landforms support a diversity of interrelated plant habitats. Sand dune deserts contrast sharply with hardwood forests. There are strands of pine, dense cedar swamps, and a few secluded bogs of sphagnum moss. Against this green background are stand of white birch. In addition, the park supports many kinds of animal life, including porcupine, deer, rabbit, squirrel, coyote, and raccoon. More than 200 species of birds may be seen. Fishing and hunting are state-regulated; a Michigan license is required. Bass, bluegill, perch, and pike are plentiful; salmon are numerous in the fall.

Dune Climb takes visitors up 150 feet on foot through the dunes for a panoramic view of Glen Lake and the surrounding countryside. Pierce Stocking Scenic Drive, a 7-mile loop, is a road with self-guiding brochure available that offers visitors an opportunity to view the high dunes and overlooks from their cars (May-Oct; park pass is required).

Sleeping Bear Point Maritime Museum, 1 mile west of Glen Haven on MI 209, located in the restored US Coast Guard Station, contains exhibits on the activities of the US Life-Saving Service and the US Coast Guard and the general maritime activities these organizations have aided on the Great Lakes. A restored boathouse contains original and replica surf boats and other related rescue equipment. (Memorial Day-Labor Day, daily).

South Manitou Island, an 8-square-mile, 5,260-acre island with 12 miles of shoreline, has a fascinating history. Formed from glacial moraines more than 10,000 years ago, the island slowly grew a covering of forest. European settlers and the US Lighthouse Service, attracted by the forest and natural harbor, established permanent sites here as early as the 1830s. On the southwest corner is the Valley of the Giants, a grove of white cedar trees more than 500 years old. There are three developed campgrounds on the island, and ranger-guide tours of the 1873 lighthouse.

North Manitou Island, nearby, is a 28-square-mile wilderness with 20 miles of shoreline. There are no facilities for visitors. All travel is done by foot and is dependent on weather. Camping is allowed under wilderness regulations; no ground fires are permitted. There is no safe harbor or anchorage on either of the Manitou islands; however, from May-Oct, the islands are accessible by commercial ferry service from Leland.

Camping is available at D.H. Day Campground (May-Nov; dump station; fee) and Platte River Campground (year-round); camping is limited to 14 days. Pets on leash only. Information may be obtained from Headquarters in Empire (daily; closed off-season holidays). The visitor center there has information on park passes, self-guided trails, hiking, cross-country skiing, evening campfire programs, maritime and natural history exhibits, and other park activities (daily; closed off-season holidays). For further information and fees contact Chief of Interpretation, 9922 Front St, Empire 49630; 231/326-5134,

Soo Junction (B-3)

See also Hulbert, Newberry

Pop 100 **Elev** 840 ft **Area code** 906 **Zip** 49868

What to See and Do

Toonerville Trolley and Riverboat Trip to Tahquamenon Falls. *Soo Jct. Phone 906/876-2311 or 888/77-TRAIN.* Narrated 6 1/2-hour, 53-mile round-trip through Tahquamenon region via narrow-gauge railroad and riverboat, with 1 1/4-hour stop at Upper Tahquamenon Falls. Trolley leaves Soo Junction (mid-June-early Oct, daily). Also 1 3/4-hour train tour (July-Aug, Tues-Sat). Contact Tahquamenon Boat Service, Inc, Rural Rte 2, Box 938, Newberry 49868. **$$$$**

Southfield (H-5)

See also Birmingham, Bloomfield Hills, Detroit, Farmington, Pontiac

Pop 75,728 **Elev** 684 ft **Area code** 248

Information Chamber of Commerce, 17515 W 9 Mile Rd, Suite 750; 248/557-6661

Web www.southfieldchamber.com

Southfield, a northwestern suburb of Detroit, is the largest office center in the Detroit metro area. It is also home to the Lawrence Institute of Technology and has branch campuses of Wayne State University, Central Michigan University, and the University of Phoenix.

Motels/Motor Lodges

★★**COURTYARD BY MARRIOTT.** *27027 Northwestern Hwy (MI 10) (48034). Phone 248/358-1222; fax 248/354-3820. www.marriott.com.* 147 rooms, 2-3 story. S $119; D $129; suites $129-$149; under 18 free; weekend rates; higher rates special events. Crib free. TV; cable (premium). Indoor pool; whirlpool. Restaurant 6:30-10 am. Service bar. Check-out noon. Coin laundry. Meeting rooms. Business services available. In-room modem link. Valet service. Exercise equipment. Health club privileges. Balconies. Cr cds: A, C, D, DS, MC, V.

★ **HAMPTON INN.** *27500 Northwestern Hwy (MI 10) (48034). Phone 248/356-5500; fax 248/356-2083. www.hamptoninn.com.* 153 rooms, 2 story. S $65-$75; D $75-$85; under 18 free; some weekly, weekend rates. Crib free. Complimentary continental breakfast. Check-out noon. TV; cable. In-room modem link. Valet services, coin laundry. Restaurant nearby. Exercise equipment. Indoor pool, whirlpool. Downhill/cross-country ski 20 miles. Picnic tables. Meeting rooms, business services. Cr cds: A, C, D, DS, MC, V.

⊡ ⊡ ⊡ ⊡ ⊡

★ ★ **HOLIDAY INN.** *26555 Telegraph Rd (48034). Phone 248/353-7700; toll-free 800/465-4329; fax 248/353-8377. www.holiday-inn.com.* 417 rooms, 2 story, 16 suites. S, D $109; each additional $8; suites $275-$350; under 19 free; weekend rates. Crib free. Pet accepted, some restrictions. Check-out noon. TV; cable (premium). Coin laundry. Restaurant 6:30 am-2 pm, 5-10 pm; Sat, Sun from 7 am. Bar 11-1 am. Room service. Exercise equipment. Game room. Recreation room. Indoor pool, whirlpool. Downhill/cross-country ski 20 miles. Barber, beauty shop. Convention facilities. Sundries. Gift shop. Many rooms in circular tower. Cr cds: A, C, D, DS, ER, JCB, MC, V.

⊡ ⊡ ⊡ ⊡ ⊡ ⊡

★ **MARVIN'S GARDEN INN.** *27650 Northwestern Hwy (48034). Phone 248/353-6777; toll-free 888/200-5200; fax 248/353-2944.* 110 rooms, 2 story. D $40-$45; family rates. Complimentary continental breakfast. Check-out noon. TV; cable (premium). Cr cds: A, C, D, DS, MC, V.

⊡ ⊡ ⊡

Hotels

★ ★ **HILTON INN SOUTHFIELD.** *26000 American Dr (48034). Phone 248/357-1100; fax 248/799-7030. www.hilton.com.* Designed for the busy traveler, this hotel has convenient amenities to suit any guest. In spacious rooms, there are multi-line telephones and high speed Internet access. 195 rooms, 7 story. S, D $89; each additional $10; suites $175; under 12 free; weekend rates. Pet accepted, some restrictions. Check-out 1 pm. TV; cable (premium). In-room modem link. Restaurant 6-10 am, 11 am-2 pm, 5-10 pm; weekend hours vary. Bar 5 pm-midnight. Exercise equipment, sauna. Indoor pool, whirlpool. Business center. Cr cds: A, C, D, DS, ER, JCB, MC, V.

⊡ ⊡ ⊡ ⊡ ⊡ ⊡

★ ★ **MARRIOTT SOUTHFIELD DETROIT.** *27033 Northwestern Hwy (MI 10) (48034). Phone 248/356-7400; fax 248/356-5501. www.marriott.com.* In the heart of the Detroit's business district, visitors will find this hotel near many major corporate companies. With comfortable guestrooms and amenities including a pool and restaurant, guests can find good service at an affordable price. 226 rooms, 6 story. S, D $109-$129; suites $250; under 16 free; weekend rates. Crib free. Check-out noon. TV; cable, VCR available. In-room modem link. Refrigerator. Restaurant 6:30 am-11 pm. Bar 11-1 am. Health club privileges. Exercise equipment, sauna. Indoor pool, whirlpool. Meeting rooms. Concierge. Gift shop. Luxury level. Cr cds: A, C, D, DS, ER, JCB, MC, V.

⊡ ⊡ ⊡ ⊡

★ ★ ★ **THE WESTIN SOUTHFIELD DETROIT.** *1500 Town Center (48075). Phone 248/827-4000; fax 248/827-1364. www.westin.com.* 385 rooms, 12 story. S $169-$199; D $179-$209; each additional $15; suites $180-$425; under 17 free. Crib free. Valet parking $6. TV; cable (premium), VCR available. Indoor pool; whirlpool, poolside service. Restaurant 6:30 am-10:30 pm. Room service 24 hours. Bar 11-2 am; Sun noon-midnight; entertainment Tues-Sat. Check-out noon. Convention facilities. Business services available. In-room modem link. Concierge. Downhill/cross-country ski 20 miles. Exercise equipment; sauna. Refrigerators available. Luxury level. Cr cds: A, C, D, DS, JCB, MC, V.

⊡ ⊡ ⊡ ⊡ ⊡ ⊡ SC ⊡

Restaurants

★ ★ ★ **MORTON'S OF CHICAGO.** *1 Towne Sq (48076). Phone 248/354-6006; fax 248/354-6012. www.mortons.com.* The Southfield location of this Chicago based chain offers the signature tableside presentation of menu favorites, such as steaks and main lobster, along with fresh vegetables, which are presented on a cart by the animated staff. Hours: 5:30-11 pm; Sun 5-10 pm. Closed major holidays. Reservations accepted. Bar. A la carte entrees: dinner $16.95-$59.90. Specializes in fresh seafood, beef. Valet parking (dinner). Menu recited. Semi-formal steak house atmosphere. Cr cds: A, D, MC, V.

⊡

★ ★ **SWEET LORRAINE'S CAFE.** *29101 Greenfield Dr (48076). Phone 248/559-5985. www.sweetlorraines.com.* Hours: 11 am-10 pm; Fri, Sat to 11 pm; Sun to 9:30 pm; Sun brunch 11 am-4 pm. Closed some holidays. Bar. A la carte entrees: lunch $4.95-$9.95, dinner $9.45-$16.95. Sun brunch $5.95-$8.95. Specialties: pecan chicken, Jamaican jerk chicken, shrimp Creole, vegetarian entrees. Modern-style bistro. Cr cds: A, DS, MC, V.

⊡

★ ★ ★ **TOM'S OYSTER BAR.** *29106 Franklin Rd (48034). Phone 248/356-8881; fax 248/356-6500. www.tomsoysterbar.com.* One of three Detroit locations, the New England chowder house atmosphere complements the fresh seafood here. A variety of fresh raw oysters are offered, which you can order by name. Fish preparation ranges from simple to encrusted, sauced or stuffed. Specializes in seafood. Hours: Mon-Thurs. 11 am-11 pm, Fri. 11 am-midnight, Sat. 5-9 pm and Sun. 3-9 pm; closed Jan 1, Dec 25. Lunch $5-$12, dinner $10-$18. Bar. Child's meals. Reservations accepted. Outdoor dining. Cr cds: A, D, DS, MC, V.

D

South Haven (H-2)

See also Saugatuck

Pop 5,563 **Elev** 618 ft **Area code** 616 **Zip** 49090

Information South Haven/Van Buren County Lakeshore Convention & Visitors Bureau, 415 Phoenix St; 616/637-5252 or 800/SO-HAVEN

Web www.bythebigbluewater.com

A 5-mile beach on Lake Michigan and surrounding lakes make sport fishing a popular summer pastime in South Haven; numerous marinas and charter boat services are available in the area.

What to See and Do

Liberty Hyde Bailey Birthsite Museum. *903 S Bailey Ave. Phone 616/637-3251.* The 19th-century house of the famous botanist and horticulturist; family memorabilia, period furnishings, Native American artifacts. (Tues and Fri afternoons; closed holidays) **DONATION**

Michigan Maritime Museum. *260 Dyckman Ave. Phone 616/637-8078.* Exhibits of Great Lakes maps, photographs, maritime artifacts, historic boats; public boardwalk and park. (All yr) **$$**

Van Buren State Park. *23960 Ruggles Rd. 4 miles S off I-196. Phone 616/637-2788.* 326 acres include scenic wooded sand dunes. Swimming, bathhouse; hunting, picnicking, playground, concession, camping. **$$**

Special Events

Blueberry Festival. *300 Broadway St. Phone 616/637-0800.* Arts and crafts, entertainment, children's parade, 5K run. Second weekend Aug.

Harborfest. *Phone 616/637-5252.* Dragon boat races, arts and crafts, musical entertainment, children's activities. Third weekend June.

Motels/Motor Lodges

★ **ECONO LODGE AND SUITES.** *09817 M-140 Hwy (49090). Phone 616/637-5141; toll-free 800/955-1831; fax 616/637-1109. www.econolodge.com.* 60 rooms. May-Sept: S $70-$82; D $80-$90; each additional $5; suites $100-$120; under 18 free; higher rates: Tulip

Festival, some holidays; lower rates rest of year. Crib $5. Pet accepted. TV; cable (premium), VCR available (movies). Playground. Indoor pool. Complimentary coffee in rooms. Restaurant adjacent 6:30 am-8 pm; Fri, Sat to 10 pm. Bar. Check-out 11 am. Coin laundry. Valet service. Downhill ski 20 miles; cross-country ski 5 miles. Exercise room; sauna. Cr cds: A, MC, V.

🐾 🐕 🏊 ✈️ 🔧 SC

★ **LAKE BLUFF.** *76648 11th Ave (49090). Phone 616/637-8531; toll-free 800/686-1305; fax 616/637-8532. www.lakebluffmotel.com.* 49 rooms, 17 kitchens May-Sept: S $48-$74; D $65-$94; kitchen units $69-$135; weekly rates; lower rates rest of year. Crib free. TV. Heated pool; wading pool, whirlpool. Coffee in rooms. Restaurant nearby. Check-out 11 am. Business services available. Free bus depot transportation. Cross-country ski 2 miles. Sauna. Lawn games. Recreation room. Picnic tables, grills. On Lake Michigan. Cr cds: A, C, D, DS, MC, V.

D 🐕 🎿 🏊 ✈️ 🔧

B&B/Small Inns

★ ★ **YELTON MANOR BED & BREAKFAST.** *140 N Shore Dr (49090). Phone 616/637-5220; fax 616/637-4957. www.yeltonmanor.com.* 17 rooms, 3 story. No room phones. July-Labor Day: S $90-$205; D $90-$270; lower rates rest of year. TV; cable, VCR available (movies). Complimentary full breakfast. Restaurant nearby. Check-out 11 am, check-in 3 pm. Luggage handling. Concierge service. Business services available. 18-hole golf privileges. Cross-country ski 1 mile. Health club privileges. Built in 1890; antiques. Totally nonsmoking. Cr cds: A, MC, V.

🛥️ 🎿 🎿 🎣 🔧 🚶

Restaurant

★ **MAGNOLIA GRILLE/IDLER RIVERBOAT.** *515 Williams St, #10 (49090). Phone 616/637-8435.* Hours: 11 am-midnight. Closed Nov-mid-Apr. Reservations accepted. Continental menu. Bar. Lunch $3.50-$6.50, dinner $12.50-$18.95. Child's meals. Specializes in prime rib, seafood, Cajun dishes. Outdoor dining. On historic riverboat (1897), overlooking Black River. Cr cds: A, D, DS, MC, V.

D

Spring Lake

Restaurant

★ **ARBOREAL INN.** *18191 174th Ave (49417). Phone 616/842-3800; fax 616/842-7429.* Hours: Mon-Sat from 5 pm-10 pm. Closed Sun; some major holidays. Reservations accepted. Bar. A la carte entrees: dinner $16.95-

$32.95. Specialties: tournedos Oscar, whitefish jardiniere. Early American décor. Cr cds: A, DS, MC, V.

D

Stevensville

Restaurant

★ ★ **SCHULER'S OF STEVENSVILLE.** *5000 Red Arrow Hwy (I-94) (49127). Phone 616/429-3273; fax 616/ 429-7666. www.schulersrest.com.* Specializes in prime rib, pork chop, fresh seafood. Hours: 11 am-10 pm; Fri, Sat to 11 pm; Sun 11 am-9 pm; Holidays Noon-8 pm. Closed Dec 25. Lunch $5.95-$9.50, dinner $6.95-$24.95. Child's meals. Reservations accepted. Cr cds: A, D, DS, MC, V.

D

Tawas City (E-5)

Pop 2,009 **Elev** 587 ft **Area code** 989 **Zip** 48763

Information Tawas Area Chamber of Commerce, 402 Lake St, PO Box 608, 48764; 989/362-8643 or 800/55-TAWAS

Web www.tawas.com

A Ranger District office of the Huron-Manitee National Forest (see MANITEE and OSCODA) is located in East Tawas.

Special Events

Perchville USA. *Phone 989/362-8643.* Perch fishing festival featuring parade, fishing contests, softball. First weekend Feb.

Tawas Bay Waterfront Art Show. *443 W Lake St. Phone 989/362-8643.* Tawas City Park. More than 200 professional and amateur artists display art and craftwork; juried show. First weekend Aug.

Motels/Motor Lodges

★ **DALE MOTEL.** *1086 S US-23 (48763). Phone 989/ 362-6153; fax 989/362-6154.* 16 rooms. June-Nov: S $40-$60; D $50-$65; each additional $4; lower rates rest of year. TV; cable (premium). Complimentary coffee in rooms. Restaurant nearby. Check-out 11 am. Bus depot transportation. Cross-country ski 7 miles. Refrigerators. Cr cds: A, MC, V.

⬛ ⬛ ⬛ SC

★ ★ **TAWAS BAY HOLIDAY INN.** *300 E Bay St (48730). Phone 989/362-8601; toll-free 800/336-8601; fax 989/362-5111. www.tawasholidayinn.com.* 103 rooms, 2 story. July-Aug: S, D $59-$169; each additional $8; suites $184; under 18 free; ski, golf plans; higher rates: major holidays, Perchville

USA; lower rates rest of year. Crib free. Pet accepted. Check-out 11 am. TV; cable (premium). In-room modem link. Valet services, coin laundry. Restaurant 6:30 am-10 pm. Bar 11 am-midnight; Fri, Sat 10-2 am; entertainment Mon-Sat. Room service. Free supervised children's activities (July-Aug). Playground. Health club privileges. Sauna. Game room. Indoor pool, whirlpool, poolside service. Golf privileges. Cross-country ski 15 miles. Lawn games. Beach; paddleboats, rafts. Meeting rooms, business center. Sundries. Gift shop. Cr cds: A, C, D, DS, JCB, MC, V.

D ⬛ ⬛ ⬛ ⬛ ⬛ ⬛ ⬛ ⬛ ⬛ SC ⬛

★ **TAWAS MOTEL - RESORT.** *1124 US 23 (48763). Phone 989/362-3822; toll-free 888/263-3260; fax 989/ 362-3822. www.tawasmotel.com.* 21 rooms. June-Aug: S $40-$60; D $45-$65; each additional $5; lower rates rest of year. Crib $5. TV; cable (premium). Pool; whirlpool. Playground. Complimentary coffee. Check-out 11 am. Cross-country ski 15 miles. Sauna. Game room. Lawn games. Refrigerators; some in-room whirlpools. Cr cds: A, C, DS, MC, V.

D ⬛ ⬛ ⬛ ⬛ ⬛ ⬛

Three Rivers (I-2)

See also Kalamazoo

Pop 7,413 **Elev** 810 ft **Area code** 616 **Zip** 49093

Information Three Rivers Area Chamber of Commerce, 103 Portage Ave; 616/278-8193

Web www.trchamber.com

What to See and Do

Swiss Valley Ski Area. *10 miles W on MI 60, then N on Patterson Hill Rd, in Jones. Phone 616/244-5635 or 616/ 244-8016 (snow conditions).* Rentals, ski shop, snowmaking; NASTAR; restaurant, cafeteria, bar. Vertical drop 225 feet. Night skiing. (Dec-Mar, daily) $$$$

B&B/Small Inns

★ ★ **MENDON COUNTRY INN.** *440 W Main St (49072). Phone 616/496-8132; toll-free 800/304-3366; fax 616/496-8132. www.rivercountry.com/mci.* 18 rooms, 2 story. No room phones. S, D $69-$159; each additional $10. Children over 12 years only. TV in sitting room. Complimentary continental breakfast. Restaurant nearby. Check-out 11 am, check-in 3 pm. Luggage handling. Concierge service. Business services available. 18-hole golf privileges. Cross-country ski 15 miles. Some refrigerators. Built in 1843; antiques. Totally nonsmoking. Cr cds: A, MC, V.

D ⬛ ⬛ ⬛ ⬛ ⬛ ⬛

★ ★ **SANCTUARY AT WILDWOOD.** *58138 N M 40, Jones (49061). Phone 269/244-5910; toll-free 800/ 249-5910. www.sanctuaryatwildwood.com.* 11 rooms, 2 story. No room phones. Mid-May-Oct: S,D $159-$219; each additional $10; lower rates rest of year. Complimentary continental breakfast. Check-out 11 am, check-in 3 pm. TV. Restaurant nearby. Pool. Cross-country ski on site. Totally nonsmoking. Cr cds: A, DS, MC, V.

D 🔧 🏂 ⛷️ 🏋️ 🐾 ♨️ 🛩️ 🚶

Traverse City (E-2)

Settled 1847 **Pop** 15,155 **Elev** 600 ft **Area code** 231

Information Traverse City Convention and Visitors Bureau, 101 W Grandview Pkwy, 49684; 231/947-1120 or 800/TRAVERS

Web www.mytraversecity.com

A 1-acre cherry orchard, planted here in the 1880s, has multiplied to such an extent that today the entire region produces more than 75 million pounds of cherries a year. Traverse City is now one of the largest cherry-marketing cities in the country, as well as a year-round resort. There are six ski areas within 35 miles of town. More than 30 public and private golf courses are also found in the area.

What to See and Do

Clinch Park. *181 E Grandview Pkwy. Phone 231/922-4904 (zoo) or 231/922-4905 (museum).* Some fees. Zoo and aquarium featuring animals native to Michigan (mid-Apr-Nov, daily). Con Foster Museum has exhibits on local history, Native American and pioneer life, and folklore (Memorial Day-Labor Day, daily). Steam train rides; marina (May-Oct). Docked in marina is

> **Schooner *Madeline.*** *Phone 231/946-2647.* Full-scale replica of 1850s Great Lakes sailing ship. Original Madeline served as first school in Grand Traverse region. Tours (early May-late Sept, Wed-Sun afternoons).

Dennos Art Center. *1701 E Front St. On campus of Northwestern Michigan College. Phone 231/922-1055.* Three galleries; incl one of the largest collections of Inuit art in the Midwest. (Daily)

Hickory Hills. *2000 Randolph St. 2 miles W of Division St . Phone 231/947-8566.* Five rope tows; snowmaking, patrol; snack bar. Vertical drop 250 feet. (Mid-Dec-mid-Mar, daily; closed Jan 1, Dec 25) Lighted cross-country trails (fee). **$$$**

Interlochen Center for the Arts. *4000 MI 137 (49643). 13 miles SW via US 31, then 2 miles S on MI 137, in Interlochen. Phone 231/276-6230.* The Interlochen Arts Academy, a fine arts boarding high school, is located here

(Sept-May). Concerts by students, faculty, and internationally known guests; art exhibits, drama and dance productions (all year). Approximately 2,500 students assemble here every summer to study music, art, drama, and dance (see SPECIAL EVENTS).

Interlochen State Park. *15 miles SW via US 31, then S on MI 137, in Interlochen, adjacent to National Music Camp. Phone 231/276-9511.* A 187-acre park with sand beach on Green and Duck lakes. Swimming, bathhouse, fishing, boating (rentals, launch); picnicking, playground, concession, camping, pavilion. Standard fees. **$$**

L. Mawby Vineyards/Winery. *7 miles N via MI 22 toward Suttons Bay, then 1 mile W on Hilltop Rd, 1/4 mile N on Elm Valley Rd. Phone 231/271-3522.* Wine tasting. Guided tours (May-Oct, Thurs-Sat; by appointment only). **FREE**

Scenic drive. *N on MI 37.* Extends length of Old Mission Peninsula. At tip is the midway point between the North Pole and the Equator (the 45th parallel). On it stands the Old Mission Lighthouse, one of the first built on the Great Lakes.

Sugar Loaf Resort. *4500 Sugar Loaf Mountain Rd. 7 miles W on MI 72, then 11 miles NW on County 651, follow signs. Phone 231/228-5461 or 800/952-6390.* Triple, five double chairlifts, three surface lifts; rentals, school, snowmaking; 20 slopes; snowboarding; 17 miles of groomed and tracked cross-country trails. Night skiing. (Dec-Mar, daily) Three restaurants, two bars, entertainment. Vertical drop 500 feet. Kids Klub for children, nursery. 18-hole golf; mountain biking (rentals). **$$$$**

Tall Ship *Malabar.* *13390 S West-Bay Shore Dr. Phone 231/941-2000.* Tours of the classic topsail schooner (Late May-early Oct, four times daily). Bed-and-breakfast lodging. **$$$$**

Special Events

Downtown Traverse City Art Fair. *100 E Front St. Phone 231/264-8202.* Late Aug.

Interlochen Arts Camp. *Interlochen Center for the Arts. Phone 231/276-6230.* A variety of performing arts events by students and visiting professionals. Mid-June-early Sept.

Mesick Mushroom Festival. *10798 Maple Rd. Phone 231/885-2679.* Carnival, rodeo, baseball tournament, flea market, music, parade, mushroom contest, food wagons. Second weekend May.

National Cherry Festival. *108 W Grandview Pkwy (49684). Phone 231/947-1120.* More than 150 activities, including pageants, parades, concerts, fireworks, air show, Native American pow-wow and crafts, children's contests. Early July.

Motels/Motor Lodges

★ **BAYSHORE RESORT.** *833 E Front St (49686). Phone 231/935-4400; toll-free 800/634-4401; fax 231/935-0262. www.bayshore-resort.com.* 120 rooms, 4 story. D $110-$200; each additional $10; under 12 free. Complimentary continental breakfast. Check-out 11 am. TV; cable (premium). Laundry services. Exercise equipment. Game room. Indoor pool, whirlpool. Downhill/cross-country ski 5 miles. Free airport transportation. Cr cds: A, C, D, DS, MC, V.

⬛ ⊠ ≈ ⼊ ✈ ⊠

★ **BEACH CONDOMINIUMS.** *1995 US 31 N (49686). Phone 231/938-2228; fax 231/938-9774.* 30 kitchen units, 3 story. D $119-$239; package plans. Check-out 11 am. TV; cable (premium). On bay; sand beach, lake swimming. Pool, whirlpool. Downhill ski 1 1/2 miles, cross-country ski 4 1/2 miles. Cr cds: A, D, DS, MC, V.

⬛ ⊠ ⼤ ⊠ ≈ ⊠

★ **BEST WESTERN FOUR SEASONS MOTEL.** *305 Munson Ave (49686). Phone 231/946-8424; toll-free 800/528-1234; fax 231/946-1971. www.bestwestern.com.* 111 rooms. D $101-$139; each additional $7; under 18 free. Check-out 11 am. TV; cable (premium), VCR available. Game room. 2 pools, 1 indoor; whirlpool. Downhill ski 3 miles, cross-country ski 6 miles. Cr cds: A, C, D, DS, MC, V.

⬛ ⊠ ≈ ⊠ SC

★ **DAYS INN.** *420 Munson Ave (49686). Phone 231/941-0208; toll-free 800/329-7466; fax 231/941-7521. www.daysinn.com.* 182 rooms, 2 story. Mid-June-Labor Day S, D $119-$135; each additional $2-$5; suites $139-$150; under 12 free; lower rates rest of year. Crib free. TV; cable (premium), VCR available. Indoor pool; whirlpool. Playground. Complimentary continental breakfast. Coffee in rooms. Restaurant adjacent 7 am-10 pm. Check-out 11 am. Coin laundry. Meeting rooms. Business services available. Free airport transportation. Downhill ski 3 miles; cross-country ski 6 miles. Some in-room whirlpools. Cr cds: A, C, D, DS, ER, JCB, MC, V.

⬛ ⊠ ≈ ✈ ⊠ SC

★ **ELK RAPIDS BEACH RESORT.** *8975 N Bayshore Dr (49629). Phone 231/264-6400; toll-free 800/784-0049. www.elkrapidsbeachresort.com.* 25 kitchen units, 3 story. No elevator. D $89-$195; each additional $10. Check-out 10:30 am. TV; cable. Laundry services. Opposite lake, beach. Pool. Downhill, cross-country ski 17 miles. Cr cds: A, DS, MC, V.

⬛ ⊠ ≈ ⊠

★ **GRAND BEACH RESORT HOTEL.** *1683 N US Hwy 31 N (49686). Phone 231/938-4455; toll-free 800/968-1992; fax 231/938-4435. www.grandbeach.com.* 95 rooms, 3 story. D $130-$158; each additional $10; ski, golf plans. Complimentary continental breakfast. Check-out 11 am. TV; cable (premium), VCR (movies $3). Laundry services. Exercise equipment. Game room. On lake; swimming beach. Indoor pool, whirlpool. Downhill, cross-country ski 2 miles. Cr cds: A, C, D, DS, MC, V.

⬛ ⊠ ≈ ⼊ ⊠

★ **HAMPTON INN.** *247 N Division St (49686). Phone 231/946-8900; toll-free 800/426-7866; fax 231/946-2817. www.hampton-inn.com.* 127 rooms, 4 story. June-Sept: S $49-$129; D $69-$159; under 18 free; lower rates rest of year. Crib free. TV; cable (premium). Indoor pool; whirlpool. Complimentary continental breakfast. Check-out noon. Meeting room. Business services available. In-room modem link. Valet service Mon-Fri. Golf privileges. Downhill/cross-country ski 5 miles. Exercise equipment. Some refrigerators. Opposite beach. Cr cds: A, D, DS, MC, V.

⬛ ⊠ ⼤ ≈ ⼊ ⼤ ✈ ⊠

★ **HERITAGE INN.** *417 Munson Ave (49686). Phone 231/947-9520; toll-free 800/968-0105; fax 231/947-9523.* 39 rooms, 2 story. D $90-$140; each additional $4-$6. Check-out 11 am. TV; cable (premium), VCR (movies $2). Continental breakfast. Exercise equipment. Game room. Pool. Downhill ski 3 miles, cross-country ski 6 miles. Cr cds: A, C, D, DS, MC, V.

⬛ ⼤ ⼤ ⊠ ≈ ⼊ ✈ ⊠

★★ **HOLIDAY INN.** *615 E Front St (49686). Phone 231/947-3700; toll-free 800/888-8020; fax 231/947-0361. www.holiday-inn.com.* 179 rooms, 4 story. June-Labor Day: S, D $149-$199; each additional $8; under 19 free; lower rates rest of year. Crib free. Pet accepted. TV; cable (premium). Indoor pool; whirlpool. Restaurant 7-1 am. Room service. Check-out 11 am. Meeting room. Business services available. Bellhops. Sundries. Gift shop. Valet service. Free airport, bus depot transportation. Downhill ski 5 miles; cross-country ski 8 miles. Exercise equipment; sauna. Game room. Lawn games. Some refrigerators. Cr cds: A, C, D, DS, JCB, MC, V.

⬛ ⼧ ≈ ⼊ ⊠

★ **MAIN STREET INN.** *618 E Front St (49686). Phone 231/929-0410; toll-free 800/255-7180; fax 231/929-0489. www.mainstreetinnsusa.com.* 93 rooms, 20 kitchen units. June-Aug: S, D $59.95-$199.95; each additional $5; kitchen units $99.95; under 18 free; lower rates rest of year. Crib free. Pet accepted. TV; cable (premium), VCR available (movies). Heated pool. Check-out 11 am. Coin laundry. Meeting room. Business services available. Downhill ski 5 miles; cross-country ski 8 miles. Opposite beach. Cr cds: A, C, D, DS, ER, MC, V.

⬛ ⼧ ⊠ ≈ ⊠ SC

★ **NORTH SHORE INN.** *2305 US 31 N (49686). Phone 231/938-2365; toll-free 800/968-2365; fax 231/938-2368. www.northshoreinn.com.* 26 rooms, 3 story. D $69-$195; under 18 free. Check-out 11 am. TV; cable (premium), VCR available. Laundry services. Pool. Downhill/cross-country ski 1 mile. Totally nonsmoking. Cr cds: A, DS, MC, V.

★ **PINECREST.** *360 Munson Ave (49686). Phone 231/947-8900; toll-free 800/223-4433; fax 231/947-8900.* 35 rooms, 2 story. D $95-$110. Complimentary continental breakfast. Check-out 11 am. TV; cable (premium), VCR (movies). Pool, whirlpool. Cross-country ski 6 miles. Cr cds: A, C, D, DS, MC, V.

★ **POINTES NORTH INN.** *2211 US 31 N (49686). Phone 231/938-9191; toll-free 800/968-3422; fax 231/938-0070.* 52 rooms, 3 story. D $135-$145; under 12 free. Complimentary continental breakfast. Check-out 11 am. TV; cable; VCR available (movies $3). Private beach. Pool. Downhill/cross-country ski 1 1/2 miles. Cr cds: A, MC, V.

★ **SUGAR BEACH RESORT HOTEL.** *1773 US 31 N (49686). Phone 231/938-0100; toll-free 800/509-1995; fax 231/938-0200.* 95 rooms, 3 story. D $64-$198; each additional $5-$10. Complimentary continental breakfast. Check-out 11 am. TV; cable (premium), VCR (movies). Laundry services. Exercise equipment. Game room. Indoor pool, whirlpool. Downhill ski 3 miles, cross-country ski 5 miles. Cr cds: A, C, D, DS, MC, V.

★ **TRAVERSE BAY INN.** *2300 US 31 N (49686). Phone 231/938-2646; toll-free 800/968-2646; fax 231/938-5845. www.traversebayinn.com.* 24 rooms, 2 story. D: $69-$199; under 12 free. Pet accepted. Check-out 11 am. TV; cable (premium), VCR available (movies). Laundry services. Game room. Beach opposite. Pool, whirlpool. Downhill/cross-country ski 1 mile. Cr cds: A, DS, MC, V.

Hotel

★ ★ **PARK PLACE HOTEL.** *300 E State St (49684). Phone 231/946-5000; toll-free 800/748-0133; fax 231/946-2772. www.park-place-hotel.com.* Located near Grand Traverse Bay and the airport. 140 rooms, 10 story. June-Sept: S, D $109-$189; each additional $15; suites $289-$398; ski, golf plans; lower rates rest of year. Crib $10. TV; cable (premium); VCR, DVD available. Indoor pool; whirlpool. Restaurant 6:30 am-10 pm. Room service. Bar 11 am-midnight; Fri, Sat to 2 am. Coffee in rooms. Check-out 11 am. Meeting rooms. Business services available. In-room modem link. Gift shop. Free airport, bus depot

transportation. Valet service. Downhill ski 5 miles; cross-country ski 1 mile. Exercise equipment; sauna. Bathroom phones, refrigerators. Some balconies. Restored to 1930s appearance; Victorian décor. Cr cds: A, D, DS, MC, V.

Resorts

★ ★ ★ **CRYSTAL MOUNTAIN RESORT.** *12500 Crystal Mtn Dr (49683). Phone 231/378-2000; toll-free 800/968-9686; fax 231/378-2998. www.crystalmountain.com.* A great vacation spot, this premier resort has plenty to offer in all seasons. Guests can come for great snowskiing in the winter or mountain biking and water recreations in the summer and choose from many luxurious lodging options. 230 rooms, 2-3 story, 29 suites, 17 condos. A/C in motel, most condos/houses. Jan-Feb, mid-June-Aug S, D $80-$300; each additional $15; condos, houses $250-$600; weekends (2-day min); family, weekly rates; ski, golf plans; MAP available; higher rates holidays; lower rates rest of year. Crib $5. TV; cable, VCR; some DVDs. 2 pools, 1 indoor; whirlpool, poolside service. Playground. Supervised children's activities (seasonal; ages 6 and under). Dining room 7 am-9 pm. Snack bar. Bar; hours vary. Coffee in rooms. Check-out noon, check-in 5 pm (6 pm in winter). Coin laundry. Grocery, package store 2 miles. Meeting rooms. Business center. Bellhops. Concierge. Gift shop. Airport transportation. Sports director. Tennis $7/hour, pro. 36-hole golf, greens fee $33-$82 (with cart), 10-acre golf practice center, driving range, putting greens, pro shop. Downhill/cross-country ski on site; rentals. Sleighing. Hiking. Bicycles (rentals). Lawn games. Chairlift rides (summer). Social director. Game room. Exercise room. Many refrigerators, wet bars. Balconies. Some fireplaces. Picnic tables, grills. Cr cds: A, D, DS, MC, V.

★ ★ ★ **GRAND TRAVERSE RESORT AND SPA.** *100 Grand Traverse Village Blvd (49610). Phone 231/938-2100; toll-free 800/748-0303; fax 231/938-5494. www.grandtraverseresort.com.* The majestic beauty of the area will leave guests relaxed and invigorated, so will the spa. 660 rooms, 200 kitchen condos (1-3 bedroom), 50 studio condos, 17 story. May-Oct S, D $150-$210; each additional $15; condos $130-$275; suites $420-$590; under 18 free; family rates; weekly, ski, golf plans; lower rates rest of year. Crib free. Check-out noon, check-in 11 am. TV; cable (premium), VCRs/DVDs. In-room modem link. Private patios, balconies. Some refrigerators; fireplaces. Valet service. Coin laundry, package store 1 mile. Dining room 6:30 am-11 pm. Bar noon-2 am; entertainment. Room service 7 am-11 pm. Deli. Supervised children's activities; to age 15. Exercise room, sauna. Massage. Sports director. Game room. Swimming beach, snack bar. 4 pools, 2 indoor; 2 whirlpools, poolside serv, lifeguard. 54-hole golf Apr-Nov, greens fee $35-$55 for 9 holes, $40-$140 for

18 holes, pro, putting green, driving range. Indoor tennis $20, pro. Downhill ski 3 miles, cross-country ski on site. Ski rentals; ice rink, rentals. Picnics. Paddleboats, jet skis. Horse-drawn carriage rides (summer), horse-drawn sleigh rides (winter). Airport transportation on property shuttle. Business center, convention facilities. Concierge. Gift shop. Fish store. Cr cds: A, C, D, DS, ER, JCB, MC, V.

D ⚿ ⩯ SC ⚲

★ ★ **SUGAR LOAF RESORT.** *4500 Sugar Loaf Mtn Rd, Cedar (49621). Phone 231/228-5461; toll-free 800/952-6390; fax 231/228-6545.* 150 rooms in 2-4 story lodge, 53 townhouses (2-4 bedrm), 2 story, 16 condo units. July-Aug S, D $69-$109; each additional $10; studio rooms $120-$130; kitchen units $145-$320; under 18 free; MAP available; ski, golf plans; higher rates Christmas holidays; lower rates rest of year. Crib free. TV; cable. 3 pools, 1 indoor; whirlpool. Supervised children's activities (Dec-Mar, July-Aug). Dining room 7-11 am, 5-10 pm; hours vary off-season. Bar 4 pm-midnight. Check-out 11 am, check-in 5 pm. Meeting rooms. Business services available. Gift shop. Tennis. 36-hole championship golf, greens fee $25-$80, pro, putting green, driving range. Lawn games. Downhill/cross-country ski on site; instructor, rentals, ski shop. Entertainment. Game room. Exercise equipment. Bike rentals. Some refrigerators. 3,500-foot paved airstrip. Cr cds: A, C, D, DS, MC, V.

D ⩯ ⚿ ⩯ ⚲ ⩯ SC

Restaurants

★ **AUNTIE PASTA'S.** *2030 S Airport Rd (49684). Phone 231/941-8147; fax 231/941-8301.* American, Italian menu. Hours: 11 am-10 pm; Sun from noon. Closed Thanksgiving, Dec 24-25. Dinner $8.50-$17.50. Bar to 11 pm. Child's menu. Casual attire. Outdoor dining. Cr cds: A, DS, MC, V.

D

★ ★ ★ **BOWERS HARBOR INN.** *13512 Peninsula Dr (49686). Phone 231/223-4333; fax 231/223-4228. www.michiganmenu.com.* This historic converted family mansion overlooks Grand Traverse Bay, and serves such favorites as fish in a bag, rack of lamb, lobster tails, steaks and seafood in a fine dining atmosphere, accompanied by an extensive wine list. American menu. Hours: 5-10 pm; Fri, Sat to 11 pm; Nov-Apr hours vary. Closed Thanksgiving, Dec 24-25. Dinner $16-$32. Bar. Entertainment. Child's menu. Casual attire. Valet parking. Outdoor dining. Totally nonsmoking. Cr cds: A, DS, MC, V.

D ⩯

★ **LA SENORITA.** *1245 S Garfield St (49686). Phone 231/947-8820; fax 231/947-1149.* Mexican menu. Hours: 11 am-10 pm; Fri, Sat to 11 pm; Sun noon-10 pm; summer to 11 pm, Fri, Sat to midnight. Closed Easter, Thanks-

giving, Dec 25. Dinner $6.95-41.99. Bar 4 pm-midnight. Child's menu. Casual attire. Cr cds: A, D, DS, MC, V.

D

★ ★ **REFLECTIONS.** *2061 US 31N (49686). Phone 231/938-2321; fax 231/938-9711. www.waterfrontinntc.com.* American menu. Hours: 7 am-2:30 pm, 5-9 pm; Sun brunch 11 am-2 pm. Closed Thanksgiving, Dec 24, 25. Dinner $18-$24. Bar to 11 pm. Children's meals. Casual attire. Cr cds: A, C, D, DS, MC, V.

D

★ **SCHELDE'S.** *714 Munson Ave (49686). Phone 231/946-0981; fax 231/946-2807. www.michiganmenu.com.* American menu. Hours: 11 am-10 pm; Fri, Sat to 11 pm; Sun brunch. Closed Thanksgiving, Dec 24, 25. Dinner $9.95-$16. Bar 11 am-midnight. Salad bar. Child's menu. Casual attire. Cr cds: A, DS, MC, V.

D

★ ★ ★ **WINDOWS.** *7677 S West Bay Shore Dr (49684). Phone 231/941-0100; fax 231/941-4963. www.windowstc.com.* Just a few miles north of Traverse City, this restaurant, set on Grand Traverse Bay, offers seafood, lamb and duck, as well as an extensive wine list. Save room for their rich homemade desserts such as truffles and ice cream. American, French menu. Hours: 5-10 pm. Closed Dec 25; also Mon Sept-May and Sun Nov-May. Dinner $29-$38. Child's menu. Casual attire. Outdoor dining. Totally nonsmoking. Cr cds: A, D, DS, MC, V.

D ⩯ SC

Troy (H-5)

See also Detroit, Pontiac, Warren

Settled 1820 **Pop** 72,884 **Elev** 670 ft **Area code** 248

Information Chamber of Commerce, 4555 Investment Dr, Suite 300, 48098; 248/641-8151

Web www.troychamber.com

The year 1819 saw the first land grants in the area that was eventually to become Troy. By 1837 the city was becoming a center for trade between Detroit and Pontiac; today Troy is the home of many large corporations.

What to See and Do

Stony Creek Metropark. *1460 Mead Rd. Approximately 6 miles N on MI 150 (Rochester Rd) to 26 Mile Rd. Phone 810/781-4242.* More than 4,000 acres. Swimming beaches with bathhouse, lifeguard (Memorial Day-Labor Day, daily), fishing, boating (ramp, rentals); bicycling (rentals, trails), winter sports, picnicking, playground, golf (fee). Nature center with trails, exhibits. Pets on leash only. **$**

Troy Museum and Historical Village. *60 W Wattles Rd, 1 mile NE of I-75, Big Beaver Rd exit. Phone 248/524-3570.* Village museum incl 1820 log cabin, 1832 Caswell House, 1877 Poppleton School, 1880 general store, 1890 blacksmith shop, and 1900 print shop; exhibits, displays. (Tues-Sun; closed holidays) **FREE**

Motels/Motor Lodges

★ ★ **COURTYARD BY MARRIOTT.** *1525 E Maple Rd (48083). Phone 248/528-2800; fax 248/528-0963. www.marriott.com.* 147 rooms, 3 story, 14 suites. S $89; D $99; suites $109; under 16 free; weekly, weekend rates; higher rates special events. Crib free. TV; cable (premium), VCR available. Indoor pool; whirlpool. Complimentary coffee in rooms. Breakfast available. Restaurant adjacent 11-1 am. Check-out noon. Coin laundry. Meeting rooms. Business center. In-room modem link. Valet service. Downhill ski 15 miles. Exercise equipment. Refrigerator in suites. Balconies. Cr cds: A, C, D, DS, JCB, MC, V.

⊡ ⛱ 🏃 ⛷ 🚶

★ **DRURY INN.** *575 W Big Beaver Rd (48084). Phone 248/528-3330; toll-free 800/325-8300; fax 248/528-3330. www.druryinn.com.* 153 rooms, 4 story. D $66-$76; each additional $6; under 18 free. Pet accepted, some restrictions. Complimentary continental breakfast. Check-out noon. TV; cable (premium), VCR available. In-room modem link. Health club privileges. Pool. Cross-country ski 4 miles. Cr cds: A, C, D, DS, MC, V.

⊡ 🐾 🏊 ⛱ ⛷ SC

★ **FAIRFIELD INN.** *32800 Stephenson Hwy (48071). Phone 248/588-3388; fax 248/588-3388. www.fairfieldinn.com.* 134 rooms, 3 story. S, D $55-$69; each additional $7; under 18 free; weekend rates. Crib free. TV; cable (premium). Pool. Complimentary continental breakfast. Restaurant adjacent 11-2 am. Check-out noon. Valet service. Health club privileges. Cr cds: A, C, D, DS, MC, V.

⊡ 🏊 ⛷ SC

★ **HAMPTON INN.** *32420 Stephenson Hwy (48071). Phone 248/585-8881; fax 248/585-9446. www.hamptoninn.com.* 124 rooms, 4 story. S $53-$65; D $57-$70; under 18 free. Crib free. Pet accepted, some restrictions. TV; cable (premium). Complimentary continental breakfast. Restaurant nearby. Check-out noon. Meeting room. In-room modem link. Valet service. Exercise equipment; sauna. Cr cds: A, C, D, DS, MC, V.

🐾 ⛷ 🚶

★ ★ **HOLIDAY INN.** *2537 Rochester Ct (48083). Phone 248/689-7500; toll-free 800/465-4329; fax 248/689-9015. www.holiday-inn.com.* 150 rooms, 4 story. S, D $99-$144; suites $119; under 18 free; weekend rates. Crib free. Pet accepted. TV; cable. Pool. Restaurant 6:30 am-noon, 5:30-10 pm; Sat, Sun from 7 am.

Room service. Bar. Check-out noon. Coin laundry. Meeting rooms. In-room modem link. Valet service. Cross-country ski 5 miles. Exercise equipment; sauna. Cr cds: A, C, D, DS, JCB, MC, V.

⊡ 🐾 🏊 🏃 ⛷ 🚶

★ **RED ROOF INN TROY.** *2350 Rochester Ct (48083). Phone 248/689-4391; toll-free 800/redroof; fax 248/689-4397. www.redroof.com.* 109 rooms, 2 story. S $53-$69; D $64-$76; 3 or more $58.99; under 18 free. Crib free. Pet accepted. TV; cable (premium). Restaurant nearby. Check-out noon. In-room modem link. Cross-country ski 10 miles. Cr cds: A, C, D, DS, MC, V.

🐾 ⛷ SC

★ ★ **SOMERSET INN.** *2601 W Big Beaver Rd (48084). Phone 248/643-7800; toll-free 800/228-8769; fax 248/643-2296. www.somersetinn.com.* 250 rooms, 13 story. S $159; D $179; each additional $15; suites $290-$325; family, weekend rates. Crib free. TV; cable. Heated pool. Restaurant 6 am-11 pm; Sat, Sun from 7 am. Room service. Bar 11-1 am. Check-out noon. Meeting rooms. Business center. In-room modem link. Bellhops. Valet service. Shopping arcade. Exercise equipment. Cr cds: A, C, D, DS, MC, V.

⊡ 🐕 🍴 ⛱ 🏃 🚶 ⛷ 🏃

Hotels

★ ★ ★ **HILTON NORTHFIELD.** *5500 Crooks Rd (48098). Phone 248/879-2100; fax 248/879-6054. www.hilton.com.* 191 rooms, 3 story. S, D $159; each additional $10; suites $250-$350; under 18 free; family, weekend rates; package plans. Crib free. Pet accepted, some restrictions. TV; cable (premium). Indoor pool. Coffee in rooms. Restaurant 6:30 am-11 pm; Sat, Sun from 7 am. Room service. Bar 10:30-2 am; entertainment. Check-out noon. Meeting rooms. Business center. In-room modem link. Bellhops. Valet service. Sundries. Cross-country ski 3 miles. Exercise equipment; sauna. Health club privileges. Game room. Some refrigerators. Private patios, balconies. Cr cds: A, C, D, DS, ER, MC, V.

⊡ 🐾 🏊 🍴 ⛱ 🏃 ⛷ SC 🏃

★ ★ ★ **MARRIOTT TROY.** *200 W Big Beaver Rd.(48084). Phone 248/680-9797; f ax 248/680-9774. www.marriott.com.* Business travelers should stay in the "Room That Works" suite, with workdesks and data ports. Leisure guests can enjoy nearby skiing and golfing. 350 rooms, 17 story. S $164-$169; D $194-$199; each additional $30; suites $600; under 18 free; weekend rates. Crib free. Pet accepted. Valet parking $4/day, $8/overnight; free garage. TV; cable (premium), VCR available. Indoor pool; whirlpool, poolside service. Restaurant 7 am-11 pm. Bar 4 pm-1 am; entertainment Tues-Sat. Check-out noon. Convention facilities. Business services available. In-room modem link. Concierge. Gift shop. Cross-country ski 5 miles. Exercise equipment; sauna. Refrigerators available. Luxury level. Cr cds: A, C, D, DS, ER, JCB, MC, V.

D ⊕ ⇲ ⇱ ⋈ ⊠ SC

All Suites

★ ★ ★ **EMBASSY SUITES.** *850 Tower Dr (48098). Phone 248/879-7500; toll-free 800/embassy; fax 248/879-9139. www.embassysuites.com.* 251 suites, 8 story. S, D $85-$175; each additional $20; under 18 free; weekend rates. Crib free. TV; cable. Indoor pool; whirlpool, poolside service. Coffee in rooms. Restaurant 6:30 am-10 pm. Bar 11:30 am-midnight. Check-out noon. Convention facilities. In-room modem link. Gift shop. Cross-country ski 4 miles. Exercise equipment; sauna. Bathroom phones, refrigerators, minibars. Cr cds: A, C, D, DS, JCB, MC, V.

D ⇲ ⇱ ⋈ ⊠ SC

Extended Stay

★ ★ **RESIDENCE INN BY MARRIOTT.** *2600 Livernois Rd (48083). Phone 248/689-6856; fax 248/689-3788. www.residenceinn.com.* 152 kitchen suites, 2 story. May-Sept S $109-$129; D $119-$179; family, weekly, weekend, holiday rates; holidays (2-day minimum); lower rates rest of year. Crib free. Pet accepted, some restrictions; $6/day. Complimentary continental bkfst, coffee in rooms. Check-out noon. TV; cable (premium), VCR available. In-room modem link. Balconies. Valet services, coin laundry. Restaurant opposite 7 am-8 pm. Health club privileges. Heated pool, whirlpool. Downhill/cross-country ski 20 miles. Picnic tables. Cr cds: A, C, D, DS, ER, JCB, MC, V.

D ⊕ ⇲ ⇱ ⋈ ⊠

Restaurants

★ ★ **MON JIN LAU.** *1515 E Maple Rd (48083). Phone 248/689-2332; fax 248/689-6407. www.monjinlau.com.* Asian, American menu. Specialties: Mongolian rack of lamb, chili pepper squid, Chinese angel hair pasta. Hours: 11-1 am; Fri to 2 am; Sat 4 pm-2 am; Sun 3 pm-midnight; holidays 4 pm-2 am. Closed Thanksgiving, Dec 25. Lunch $7.50-$11.95, dinner $11.95-$22.95. Bar. Reservations accepted. Cr cds: A, MC, V.

D

★ ★ **PICANO'S.** *3775 Rochester Rd (48083). Phone 248/689-8050; fax 248/689-4360.* Closed some major holidays. Italian menu. Bar. Lunch $7-$10, dinner $8-$16. Specializes in veal, chicken, pasta. Own pasta. Valet parking. Modern Italian décor; mural. Cr cds: A, D, DS, MC, V.

D

Wakefield (B-5)

See also Ironwood

Pop 2,318 **Elev** 1,550 ft **Area code** 906 **Zip** 49968

What to See and Do

Indianhead Mountain-Bear Creek Ski Resort. *500 Indianhead Rd, 1 mile W on US 2, then 1 mile N. Phone 906/229-5181 or 800/346-3426.* Quad, triple, three double chairlifts; Pomalift, two T-bars; beginner's lift; patrol, school, rentals; NASTAR (daily), snowmaking; lodge (see RESORT), restaurants, cafeterias, bars, nursery. Longest run 1 mile; vertical drop 638 feet. (Nov-mid-Apr, daily) **$$$$**

Motel/Motor Lodge

★ **REGAL COUNTRY INN.** *1602 US 2 E (49968). Phone 906/229-5122; fax 906/229-5755. www.westernup.com/regalinn.* 18 rooms, 2 story. July-Aug, mid-Nov-Easter: S $43-$80; D $55-$90; each additional $10; higher rates Christmas holidays; lower rates rest of year. Crib free. TV; cable. Complimentary continental breakfast. Restaurant nearby. Check-out 11 am. Downhill ski 2 miles; cross-country ski 6 miles. Sauna. 1950s ice cream parlor on premises. Cr cds: A, DS, MC, V.

⇲ ⍩ ⋈ ⊠ ⍬

Resort

★ ★ **INDIANHEAD MOUNTAIN RESORT.** *500 Indianhead Mountain Rd (49968). Phone 906/229-5181; toll-free 800/346-3426; fax 906/229-5920. www.indianheadmtn.com.* 62 rooms, 2-3 story, 51 chalets, 32 condo units. S, D $58-$160; under 12 free; mid-week rates; ski plan. Closed mid-Apr-June, Oct-mid-Nov. Crib available. Pet accepted. Complimentary continental breakfast. Check-out 11 am, check-in 4 pm. TV; cable, VCR available (movies). Dining room 7:30 am-9 pm. Bar 8-2 am; Sun from noon; summer from 4 pm. Supervised children's activities (Nov-mid-Apr). Playground. Exercise room, sauna. Game room. Indoor pool, whirlpool. 9-hole, par 3 golf, greens fee $6-$10. Tennis. Downhill ski on site. Hiking, nature trails, mountain biking. Meeting rooms, business services. Cr cds: A, DS, MC, V.

D ⊕ ⇲ ⍩ ⍬ ⋈ ⊠ SC

Warren (H-6)

See also Detroit, Saint Claire, Troy

Pop 144,864 **Elev** 615 ft **Area code** 810

Information Chamber of Commerce, 30500 Van Dyke Ave, Suite 118, 48093; 810/751-3939

Web www.wcschamber.com

Warren, a northern suburb of Detroit, is the third largest city in Michigan. It is home of the General Motors Technical Center, designed by Eero Saarinen, as well as other offices of many large automotive manufacturers. A small farmland community until the 1930s, Warren erupted almost overnight when General Electric's Carboloy Division established a factory in the area. Soon other major manufacturers set up plants in Warren and the city boomed.

Motels/Motor Lodges

★ ★ **BEST WESTERN GEORGIAN INN.** *31327 Gratiot Ave (48066). Phone 810/294-0400; toll-free 800/446-1866; fax 810/294-1020.* 111 rooms, 2 story. Mid-May-mid-Sept: S, D $60-$73; each additional $5; suites $135; kitchen units $81; under 12 free; lower rates rest of year. Crib free. Pet accepted, some restrictions. TV; cable. Heated pool; poolside service. Restaurant 6 am-11 pm. Room service. Bar. Check-out noon. Coin laundry. Meeting rooms. Business services available. In-room modem link. Valet service. Exercise equipment. Game room. Cr cds: A, C, D, DS, MC, V.

★ ★ **BEST WESTERN STERLING INN.** *34911 Van Dyke Ave (48312). Phone 810/979-1400; toll-free 800/953-1400; fax 810/979-7962. www.sterlinginn.com.* 160 rooms, 2-3 story. S, D $161-$171; each additional $6; suites $135-$275; under 18 free; weekend rates. Crib free. TV; cable. Indoor pool; whirlpool. Restaurant 6-11 pm; Fri to midnight; Sat 7 am-midnight; Sun 7 am-10 pm. Room service. Bar from 11 am; Sat to midnight; Sun noon-10 pm. Check-out noon. Meeting rooms. Business center. In-room modem link. Valet service. Exercise equipment; sauna. Refrigerators; some in-room whirlpools, bathroom phones. Cr cds: A, C, D, DS, MC, V.

★ ★ **COURTYARD BY MARRIOTT.** *30190 Van Dyke Ave (48093). Phone 810/751-5777; fax 810/751-4463. www.marriott.com.* 147 rooms, 3 story, 14 suites, 113 kitchen units. S $85; D $95; each additional $10; suites $95-$105; under 5 free; weekend rates. Crib free. TV; cable (premium), VCR available. Indoor pool; whirlpool. Complimentary coffee in rooms. Breakfast available.

Restaurant adjacent open 24 hours. Check-out 1 pm. Coin laundry. Meeting rooms. In-room modem link. Valet service. Exercise equipment. Refrigerator in suites. Balconies. Cr cds: A, C, D, DS, MC, V.

★ **FAIRFIELD INN.** *7454 Convention Blvd (48092). Phone 810/939-1700; fax 810/939-1700. www.fairfieldinn.com.* 132 rooms, 3 story. S, D $45-$59; each additional $7; under 18 free. Crib free. Complimentary continental breakfast. Check-out noon. TV; cable (premium). In-room modem link. Valet service. Restaurant nearby. Heated pool. Cr cds: A, C, D, DS, MC, V.

★ **HAMPTON INN.** *7447 Convention Blvd (48092). Phone 810/977-7270; toll-free 800/426-7866; fax 810/977-3889. www.hamptoninn.com.* 124 rooms, 3 story. S $52-$57; D $58-$63; suites $75-$81; under 18 free; weekend rates. Crib $6. TV; cable (premium). Complimentary continental breakfast. Restaurant nearby. Check-out noon. Meeting rooms. In-room modem link. Valet service. Cross-country ski 20 miles. Refrigerator, wet bar in suites. Cr cds: A, C, D, DS, MC, V.

★ **HOLIDAY INN EXPRESS.** *11500 E 11 Mile Rd (48089). Phone 810/754-9700; toll-free 800/465-4329; fax 810/754-0376. www.holiday-inn.com.* 125 rooms, 2 story. S, D $62; under 17 free; weekend rates. Crib free. TV; cable (premium). Pool. Complimentary continental breakfast. Restaurant adjacent 11 am-midnight. Check-out noon. Meeting rooms. In-room modem link. Valet service. Cr cds: A, C, D, DS, ER, JCB, MC, V.

★ **HOMEWOOD SUITES.** *30180 N Civic Center Blvd (48093). Phone 810/558-7870; toll-free 800/225-5466; fax 810/558-8072. www.homewoodsuites.com.* 76 kitchen suites, 3 story. D $114. Pet accepted, some restrictions; refundable fee. Complimentary continental breakfast. Check-out noon. TV; cable (premium), VCR. In-room modem link. Health club privileges. Exercise equipment. Pool, whirlpool. Downhill, cross-country ski 20 miles. Business center. Cr cds: A, C, D, DS, MC, V.

★ **RED ROOF INN.** *26300 Dequindre Rd (48091). Phone 810/573-4300; fax 810/573-6157. www.redroof.com.* 136 rooms, 2 story. S $32.99-$42.99; D $46.99-$53.99; 3 or more $44.99-$60.99; under 18 free; higher rates special events. Crib free. Pet accepted, some restrictions. TV; cable (premium). Complimentary coffee. Restaurant nearby. Check-out noon. Business services available. In-room modem link. Cr cds: A, C, D, DS, MC, V.

Extended Stay

★ ★ RESIDENCE INN BY MARRIOTT. *30120 Civic Center Blvd (48093). Phone 810/558-8050; fax 810/558-8214. www.marriott.com.* 133 kitchen suites, 3 story. Mid-May-mid-Sept: S, D $109; under 18 free; weekly, weekend rates; lower rates rest of year. Crib free. Pet accepted; $50 deposit and $8/day. TV; cable (premium), VCR. Pool; whirlpool. Complimentary continental breakfast. Complimentary coffee in rooms. Restaurant nearby. Check-out noon. Coin laundry. In-room modem link. Valet service. Exercise equipment. Health club privileges. Some balconies. Picnic tables. Cr cds: A, C, D, DS, ER, JCB, MC, V.

D ⟲ ⤢ ✕ ⤢ SC

Restaurant

★ ★ ANDIAMO ITALIA. *7096 E 14 Mile Rd (48092). Phone 586/268-3200; fax 586/268-3224. www.andiamoitalia.com.* Hours: 11 am-11 pm; Fri to midnight; Sat 4 pm-midnight; Sun 4-9 pm. Closed some major holidays. Italian menu. Bar. Lunch $8-$14, dinner $9-$22. Specialties: gnocchi, bocconcini di vitello. Valet parking. Cr cds: A, MC, V.

D

Whitehall (G-2)

See also Muskegon

Pop 3,027 **Elev** 593 ft **Area code** 231 **Zip** 49461

Information White Lake Area Chamber of Commerce, 124 W Hanson St; 231/893-4585 or 800/879-9702

Web www.whitelake.org

What to See and Do

Montague City Museum. *N on US 31 Business, at Church and Meade sts in Montague. Phone 231/894-6813.* History of lumbering era, artifacts; displays on Montague resident Nancy Ann Fleming, who was Miss America 1961. (June-Aug, Sat and Sun) **DONATION**

White River Light Station Museum. *6199 Murray Rd, S of the channel on White Lake. Phone 231/894-8265.* In 1875 lighthouse made of Michigan limestone and brick; ship relics and artifacts include binnacle, ship's helm, chronograph, compasses, sextant, charts, models, photographs, paintings. View of Lake Michigan's sand dunes along coastline. (Memorial Day-Labor Day, Tues-Sun; Sept, wkends) **$$**

World's Largest Weather Vane. *Just S of town on US 31 Business, at edge of White Lake in Montague.* This 48-foot-tall structure weighs 4,300 pounds and is topped with a model of the lumber schooner Ella Ellenwood that once traveled the Great Lakes. Trademark of Whitehall Products Ltd, the company that created it, the vane is mentioned in the Guinness Book of Records.

Special Events

Summer concerts. *124 W Hanson St. Phone 231/893-4585. White Lake Music Shell, Launch Ramp Rd, in Montague. Phone 231/893-4585.* Every Tues mid-June-late Aug.

White Lake Arts & Crafts Festival. *Funnel Field. Phone 231/893-4585.* 150 exhibitors. Father's Day weekend.

Wyoming (G-2)

Restaurant

★ ★ WYOMING CATTLE CO. *1820 44th St SW (49509). Phone 616/534-0704; fax 616/534-1361. www.michiganmenu.com.* American menu. Hours: 11 am-10 pm; Fri, Sat to 11 pm. Closed Thanksgiving, Dec 24, 25. Dinner $8.95-$21.95. Bar to 11 pm. Children's meals. Casual attire. Reservations required 8 or more persons. Outdoor dining. Cr cds: A, DS, MC, V.

D

Ypsilanti (H-5)

See also Ann Arbor

Settled 1823 **Pop** 24,846 **Elev** 720 ft **Area code** 734 **Zip** 48197

Information Ypsilanti Area Visitors and Convention Bureau, 301 W Michigan Ave, Suite 101; 734/482-4920

Web www.ypsichamber.org

Established as a Native American trading post, this city was later named for a young Greek patriot, Demetrius Ypsilanti. The city had stations on the Underground Railroad before the Civil War. There are many fine examples of Greek Revival architecture. A two-block area, known as Depot Town, has renovated houses and storefronts, most of which are at least 150 years old, as well as antique shops and restaurants.

What to See and Do

Eastern Michigan University. *202 Pierce Hall. Phone 734/487-1849 or (734) 487-4636.* (1849) 25,000 students. The university is home to Quirk/Sponberg Dramatic Arts Theaters, Pease Auditorium, Bowen Field House, Rynearson Stadium, Olds Student Recreation Center; Ford Art Gallery with changing exhibits (Mon-Fri; phone 313/487-1268; free); Intermedia Art Gallery (free). Tours (by appt) depart from historic Starkweather Hall. (Daily)

Ford Lake Park. *9075 S Huron River Dr. Phone 734/485-6880 or 734/544-3800.* This park offers fishing, boating (launch; fee); volleyball, tennis, and handball courts; horseshoes, softball field, four picnic shelters. (Daily; some fees May-Sept) **$$**

Ypsilanti Historical Museum. *220 N Huron St. Phone 734/482-4990.* Victorian house with 11 rooms, including a special children's room and craft room; exhibits. (Thurs, Sat, Sun) Ypsilanti Historical Archives are located here and are open for research pertaining to local history and genealogy (Mon-Fri mornings). **DONATION**

Ypsilanti Monument and Water Tower. *Cross and Washtenaw sts.* Marble column with a bust of Demetrius Ypsilanti, Greek patriot. Century-old water tower.

Special Event

Ypsilanti Heritage Festival. *106 W Michigan Ave. Phone 734/483-4444.* Riverside Park. Classic cars, arts and crafts, 18th-century encampment, jazz competition, and continuous entertainment. Third full weekend Aug.

Hotel

★ ★ ★ **MARRIOT AT EAGLE CREST.** *1275 S Huron St (48197). Phone 734/487-2000; toll-free 800/228-9290; fax 734/481-0773. www.marriott.com.* In the town of Ypsilanti, visitors will find a rich and unique heritage here that natives call their own. 236 rooms, 8 story. May-Oct S, D $95-$135; under 12 free; golf plan; weekend rates; lower rates rest of year. Crib free. TV; cable (premium), VCR available. Indoor pool; whirlpool. Restaurant 6:30 am-10 pm. Bar 11-2 am; Sun noon-midnight. Check-out noon. Convention facilities. Business services available. In-room modem link. Concierge. Gift shop. 18-hole golf, pro, putting green, driving range. Exercise equipment; sauna. Health club privileges. Game room. Bathroom phones. Luxury level. Cr cds: A, C, D, DS, ER, MC, V.

[D] [≈] [⅄] [⨍] [≋] [SC]

Restaurant

★ ★ **HAAB'S.** *18 W Michigan Ave (48197). Phone 734/483-8200; fax 734/483-9676. wwwhaabs.com.* Hours: 11 am-9 pm; Fri, Sat to 10 pm. Closed Dec 25. Reservations accepted. Bar. Lunch $4-$8, dinner $8-$19. Child's meals. Specializes in steak. Early American décor. Building dates from 19th-century. Family-owned. Cr cds: A, C, D, DS, MC, V.

[SC]

From Michigan, it's easy to cross the border to see the possibilities Canada has to offer. Take a few days to explore the cosmopolitan city of Toronto, or spend a few hours taking in the many gardens and casinos in Windsor. Or maybe a dinner cruise in Sault Ste. Marie is more your speed. Whichever activities you enjoy, chances are you can find them in Canada.

Sault Ste. Marie, ON (B-4)

1 1/2 hours, 88 miles from Mackinaw City, MI

Pop 83,300 **Elev** 580 ft (177 m) **Area code** 705

Information Chamber of Commerce, 334 Bay St, P6A 1X1; 705/949-7152

Web www.ssmcoc.com

Founded and built on steel, Sault Ste. Marie is separated from its sister city in Michigan by the St. Mary's River. Lake and ocean freighters traverse the river, which links Lake Huron and Lake Superior—locally known as "the Soo."

What to See and Do

Agawa Canyon Train Excursion. *Phone 705/946-7300; 800/242-9287.* A scenic day trip by Algoma Central Railway through a wilderness of hills and fjordlike ravines. 2-hour stopover at the canyon. Dining car on train. (June-mid-Oct, daily; Jan-Mar, weekends only) Advance ticket orders available by phone. **$$$$**

Boat cruises. *65 Foster Dr. Phone 705/253-9850.* 2-hour boat cruises from Norgoma dock, next to Holiday Inn on MV Chief Shingwauk and MV Bon Soo through American locks; also 3-hour dinner cruises. (June-mid-Oct) Contact Lock Tours Canada, PO Box 424, P6A 5M1. **$$$$**

Sault Ste. Marie Museum. *690 Queen St E. Phone 705/759-7278.* Local and national exhibits in a structure originally built as a post office. Skylight Gallery traces history of the region dating back 9,000 years; includes prehistoric artifacts, displays of early industries, re-creation of 1912 Queen St house interiors. Durham Gallery displays traveling exhibits from the Royal Ontario Museum and locally curated displays. Discovery Gallery for children features hands-on exhibits. (Daily; closed holidays)

Special Events

Algoma Fall Festival. *1007 Trunk Rd. Phone 705/949-0822.* Visual and performing arts presentations by Canadian and international artists. Late Sept-late Oct.

Ontario Winter Carnival Bon Soo. *269 Queen St E. Phone 705/759-3000.* Features more than 100 events: fireworks, fiddle contest, winter sports, polar bear swim, winter playground sculptured from snow. Last weekend Jan-1st weekend Feb.

Motels/Motor Lodges

★ ★ ★ **ALGOMAS WATER TOWER INN.** *360 Great Northern Rd (P6A 5N3). Phone 705/949-8111; toll-free 800/461-0800; fax 705/949-1912. www.watertowerinn.com.* Take a stroll through the waterfall garden and enjoy the beautiful outdoors. 180 rooms, 5 story. S, D $79-$99; each additional $7; suites $130-$290; under 18 free; ski plans. Crib free. Pet accepted. TV; cable (premium), VCR available. Heated pool; whirlpool. Restaurant 7 am-11 pm. Room service 7-11 am, 5-10 pm. Bar noon-1 am. Check-out noon. Meeting rooms. Valet service. Airport transportation. Sundries. Cross-country ski 5 miles. Exercise equipment. Some refrigerators, microwaves; whirlpool in suites. Cr cds: A, C, D, DS, ER, JCB, MC, V.

D 🐾 🏊 🖼 🏃 🔄 SC

★**BEST WESTERN GREAT NORTHERN.** *229 Great Northern Rd; Hwy 17N (P6B 4Z2). Phone 705/942-2500; fax 705/942-2570. www.bestwestern.com.* 211 units, 2-7 story. S $86-$109; D $96-$122; each additional $10; suites $150-$275; under 18 free; package plans. Crib free. Pet accepted. TV; cable, VCR available. 2 pools, 1 indoor; whirlpool. Restaurant 7 am-11 pm. Room service. Bar to midnight. Check-out noon. Meeting rooms. Business services available. Bellhops. Valet service (Mon-Fri). Sundries. Downhill ski 20 miles; cross-country ski 3 miles. Exercise equipment. Miniature golf; water slide. Bowling. Game rooms. Some refrigerators. Cr cds: A, C, D, DS, ER, JCB, MC, V.

D 🐾 🏊 🖼 🏃 🔄 SC

★ ★ **HOLIDAY INN..** *208 St Mary's River Dr (P6A 5V4). Phone 705/949-0611; fax 705/945-6972. www.holiday-inn.com.* 195 rooms, 9 story. June-mid-Oct: S, D $92-$139; each additional $10; suites $175-$275; under 12 free; lower rates rest of year. Crib free. Pet accepted. TV; cable (premium). Indoor pool; whirlpool. Restaurant 6:30 am-10 pm. Room service. Bar 11-1 am. Check-out 4 pm.

Meeting rooms. In-room modem link. Bellhops. Valet service. Sundries. Gift shop. Airport transportation. Exercise equipment; sauna. Game room. Refrigerator in some suites. Cr cds: A, C, D, DS, ER, JCB, MC, V.

D 🐾 🏊 🖼 🏃 🔄 SC ✈

★ ★ **QUALITY INN BAY FRONT.** *180 Bay St (P6A 6S2). Phone 705/945-9264; fax 705/945-9766. www.qualityinn. com.* 109 rooms, 7 story. Sept-mid-Oct: S $102-$165; D $112-$165; each additional $10; family rates; ski, package plans; lower rates rest of year. Crib free. TV; cable (premium), VCR available. Indoor pool; whirlpool. Coffee in rooms. Restaurant 7 am-midnight. Room service. Bar from 11:30 am. Check-out 1 pm. Meeting rooms. Bellhops. Valet service. Downhill/cross-country ski 8 miles. Exercise equipment; sauna. Some refrigerators. Cr cds: A, C, D, DS, ER, JCB, MC, V.

D 🏊 🖼 🏃 🔄 SC

Restaurants

★ **GIOVANNI'S.** *516 Great Northern Rd (P6B 4Z9). Phone 705/942-3050; fax 705/942-3980.* Italian menu. Specialties: family-style dinners. Hours: 11:30 am-midnight; Sun to 11 pm. Closed Jan 1, Labour Day, Dec 25. Lunch $5-$8, dinner $7-$15. Bar. Children's meals. Reservations accepted. Cr cds: A, MC, V. a ss**New Marconi.** *480 Albert St W (P6A 1C3). Phone 705/759-8250; fax 705/759-0850.* Italian, Amer menu. Specialties: barbecued ribs, steak, seafood. Own pasta. Hours: noon-11 pm. Closed Sun; Jan 1, Dec 25. Reservations accepted. Service bar. Lunch $4.25-$8.50, dinner $8-$50. Complete meals: dinner $16.95. Family-owned. Cr cds: A, D, ER, MC, V.

D

Toronto, ON

4 hours, 381 miles form Detroit, MI

Settled 1793 **Pop** 3,400,000 **Elev** 569 ft (173 m) **Area code** 416

Information Convention & Visitors Association, Queens Quay Terminal at Harbourfront, 207 Queens Quay W, M5J 1A7; 416/203-2500 or 800/363-1990

Web www.torontotourism.com

Toronto is one of Canada's leading industrial, commercial, and cultural centers. From its location on the shores of Lake Ontario, it has performed essential communications and transportation services throughout Canadian history. Its name derives from the native word for meeting place, as the area was called by the Hurons who led the first European, Etienne Brule, to the spot. In the mid-1800s the Grand Trunk and Great Western Railroad and the Northern Railway connected Toronto with the upper St. Lawrence, Portland, Maine and Chicago, Illinois.

After French fur traders from Québec established Fort Rouille in 1749, Toronto became a base for further Canadian settlement. Its population of Scottish, English, and United States emigrants was subject to frequent armed attacks, especially during the War of 1812 and immediately thereafter. From within the United States, the attackers aimed at annexation; from within Canada, they aimed at emancipation from England. One result of these unsuccessful threats was the protective confederation of Lower Canada, which later separated again as the province of Québec, and Upper Canada, which still later became the province of Ontario with Toronto as its capital.

Toronto today is a cosmopolitan city with many intriguing features. Once predominantly British, the population is now exceedingly multicultural—the United Nations deemed Toronto the world's most ethnically diverse city in 1989. A major theater center with many professional playhouses, including the Royal Alexandra Theatre, Toronto is also a major banking center, with several architecturally significant banks. Good shopping can be found throughout the city, but Torontonians are most proud of their "Underground City," a series of subterranean malls linking more than 300 shops and restaurants in the downtown area. For professional sports fans, Toronto offers the Maple Leafs (hockey), the Blue Jays (baseball), the Raptors (basketball), and the Argonauts (football). A visit to the Harbourfront, a boat tour to the islands or enjoying an evening on the town should round out your stay in Toronto.

What to See and Do

Art Gallery of Ontario. *317 Dundas St W. Phone 416/977-0414.* Changing exhibits of paintings, drawings, sculpture, and graphics from the 14th-20th centuries including Henry Moore Collection; permanent Canadian Collection and Contemporary Galleries; films, lectures, concerts. (Tues-Sun; winter Wed-Sun; closed Jan 1, Dec 25) **FREE** admission Wed evenings. **$$$** Behind gallery is

> **The Grange.** *317 Budas St W.* A Georgian house (Circa 1817) restored and furnished in early Victorian style (1835-1840). (Same hours as Art Gallery) Free with admission to Art Gallery.

Bata Shoe Museum. *327 Bloor St W. Phone 416/979-7799.* Sonja, Imelda, Imelda, Sonja. When Mrs. Sonja Bata's passion for collecting historical shoes began to surpass her personal storage space, the Bata family established The Bata Shoe Museum Foundation. Architect Raymond Moriyama's award-winning five-story, 3,900-square-foot building now holds more than 10,000 shoes, artfully arranged in four galleries to celebrate the style and function of footwear throughout 4,500 years of history. One permanent exhibition, 'All About Shoes,' showcases a collection of 20th-century celebrity shoes; artifacts on exhibit range from Chinese bound foot shoes and ancient Egyptian sandals to chestnut crushing clogs and Elton John's platforms. Talk about standing toe-to-toe with history.

Black Creek Pioneer Village. *1000 Murray Ross Pkwy. 2 miles (3 km) N on Hwy 400, E on Steeles, then 1/2 mile (1 km) to Jane St. Phone 416/736-1733.* Step back in time to a village in 1860s Ontario, when life was much simpler—if you were hearty enough to handle it. In the village of Black Creek, workers wearing period costumes welcome you into 35 authentically restored homes, workshops, public buildings and farms, and demonstrate skills such as open-hearth cooking, bread-making, looming, milling, blacksmithing, sewing, and printing. (Hours vary by month; call for schedule; closed Dec 25) **$$$**

Bloor/Yorkville area. *Bounded by Bloor St W, Avenue Rd, Davenport Rd, and Yonge St.* If the last time you visited Toronto was 30 years ago, and still have images of flower children handing out flowers on Bloor Street, you're in for a surprise. The barefoot girl who gave you a daisy is now a 45-year-old who shops at the very spot where she used to stand. The Bloor/Yorkville area is one of Toronto's most elegant shopping and dining sections, with art galleries, nightclubs, music, designer couture boutiques, and first-rate art galleries. The area itself is fun to walk around, with a cluster of courtyards and alleyways. There's also a contemporary park in the heart of the neighborhood with a huge piece of granite called "The Rock." It was brought here from the Canadian Shield, a U-shaped region of ancient rock covering about half of Canada, causing the first part of North America to be permanently elevated above sea level.

Bruce Trail/Toronto Bruce Trail Club. *Phone 416/763-9061.* Canada's first and longest footpath, the Bruce Trail runs 437 miles along the Niagara Escarpment from Niagara to the Bruce Peninsula. It provides the only public access to the Escarpment, a UNESCO World Biosphere Reserve. While the Toronto Bruce Trail Club is the largest and, some say, the best organized of the many biking and hiking clubs in the area, you can contact the Toronto Convention and Visitors Bureau (416/203-2600) for Toronto access, and names of organizations that offer activities on the trail. Note: Although the Toronto Bruce Trail Club has members, most of its activities can be attended by the general public. (Call for info on meeting places for hikes)

Canada's Sports Hall of Fame. *Lakeshore Blvd at Strachan Ave. Phone 416/260-6789.* Erected to honor the country's greatest athletes in all major sports, Canada's Sports Hall of Fame features exhibit galleries, a theater, a library, archives, and kiosks that show videos of Canada's greatest moments in sports. Don't miss the Heritage Gallery (lower level), which contains artifacts showcasing the development of 125 years of sport. Also, stop in at the 50-seat "Red" Foster Theatre, which projects highlights from films that highlight Canadian sports, such as "The Terry Fox Story." **FREE**

Casa Loma. *One Austin Terrace. 1 1/2 miles (2 km) NW of downtown. Phone 416/923-1171.* Grab an audio cassette and a floor plan and take a self-guided tour of this domestic castle, built in 1911 over three years at a cost of $3.5 million. As romantic as he was a shrewd businessman, Sir Henry Pellatt—who immediately realized the profitability potential when Thomas Edison developed steam-generated electricity, and founded the Toronto Electric Light company—had an architect create this medieval castle. Soaring battlements, secret passageways, flowerbeds warmed by steam pipes, secret doors, servant's rooms, and an 800-foot tunnel are just some of the treats you'll discover. (Daily; closed Jan 1, Dec 25) **$$$** Adjacent is

Spadina. *285 Spadina Rd. Phone 416/392-6910.* (Circa 1865) Home of financier James Austin and his descendants; Victorian and Edwardian furnishings and fine art; restored gardens. (Tues-Sun, afternoons; closed holidays) **$$**

City parks. *Phone 416/392-1111.* Listed below are some of Toronto's many parks. Contact the Department of Parks and Recreation.

Allan Gardens. *19 Horticultural Ave. W side of Sherbourne St to Jarvis St between Carlton St and Gerrard St E. Phone 416/392-7288.* Indoor/outdoor botanical displays, wading pool, picnicking, concerts. (Daily) **FREE**

Edwards Gardens. *777 Lawrence Ave E. NE of Downtown, at Leslie Ave E and Lawrence St. Phone 416/392-8186.* Civic garden center; rock gardens, pools, pond, rustic bridges. (Daily) **FREE**

Grange Park. *Dundas and Beverley sts, located behind the Art Gallery of Ontario.* Wading pool, playground. Natural ice rink (winter, weather permitting). (Daily) **FREE**

High Park. *Between Bloor St W and The Queensway at Parkside Dr, near lakeshore. Phone 416/392-1111.* If you're after a low-key adventure after a few days of sight-seeing, High Park is your respite. Financier John T. Colborne, who built the mansion next door, also purchased 160 acres of land intending to develop a 'satellite village' for Toronto. But he couldn't sell his before-his-time concept of a subdivision, so he donated the land to the city. Today, High Park is an urban oasis, with expanses of grasses for sports, picnicking, and cycling; a large lake that freezes in the winter; a small zoo, a swimming pool, tennis courts, and bowling greens. **FREE**

Queen's Park. *Queen's Park Crescent. Phone 416/325-7500.* Ontario Parliament Buildings are located in this park. (Daily) **FREE**

Riverdale Park. *W side of Broadview Ave, between Danforth Ave & Gerrard St E. Phone 416/392-1111.* Summer: swimming, wading pools; tennis, playgrounds, picnicking, band concerts. Winter: skating; 19th-century farm. (Daily)

Toronto Island Park. *9 Queens Quay. S across Inner Harbour. Phone 416/392-8186; 416/392-8193.* Just seven minutes by ferry from Toronto lie 14 beautiful islands ripe for exploration. The land was originally a peninsula, but a series of storms in the mid-1800s caused a part of the land to break off into islands. The three major ones are Centre, Ward's, and Algonquin, with Centre being the busiest. This is partly because it's home to Centreville, an old-fashioned amusement park, with an authentic 1890s carousel, flume ride, turn-of-the-century village complete with a Main Street, tiny shops, a firehouse, and even a small working farm. But the best thing to do on Centre Island or any of the 14, is to rent a bike and explore the 612 acres of park and shaded paths. Try to get lost; that's half the fun. **FREE**

⭐ **CN Tower.** *301 Front St W. Phone 416/868-6937; 416/360-8500 (information).* Is it the Sears Tower in Chicago? The Petronas Towers in Kuala Lumpur? The Ostankino Tower in Moscow? No. The tallest freestanding structure in the world is Toronto's CN Tower. At 1,815 feet from the ground to the tip of its communications aerial, it towers over the rest of the city. If you'd like to see Toronto from the eye view of a blue jay, take the elevator to the top, where on a clear day it's said you can see the spray coming off Niagara Falls 62 miles away. But any level provides spectacular views. Don't miss the ground floor's "Tour of the Universe," a multi-media voyage set in 2019 with human guides and robots. **$$$$** Here is

Virtual World. *Phone 416/360-8500.* Two virtual reality-based adventures, Battletech and Red Planet, allow users to navigate in a world of fantasy. (Daily)

Colborne Lodge. *Colborne Lodge Dr & The Queensway. Phone 416/392-6916.* The successful 19th-century architect John Howard was just 34 when he completed this magnificent manor, named for the architect's first patron, Upper Canada Lieutenant Governor Sir John Colborne. It stands today as an excellent example of Regency-style architecture, with its stately verandas and lovely placement in a beautiful setting. Howard, far ahead of his time, also purchased 160 acres adjacent to the manor, intending to develop a "satellite village." But given the distance from 1837 Toronto, no one seemed ready for the concept of subdivisions. Fortunately, Howard held no grudge: After his death, he donated the land to form the present-day heart of High Park, a peaceful urban oasis in the heart of the bustling city. (Tues-Sun; closed Mon, Jan 1, Good Friday, Dec 25-26) **$$**

Dragon City Shopping Mall. *280 Spadina Ave. Phone 416/596-8885.* Located in the heart of Chinatown, the Dragon City Shopping Mall consists of more than 30 stores and services that allow you to immerse yourself in Chinese culture. Buy Chinese herbs, look at quality Asian jewelry, browse chic Chinese housewares and gifts, or admire

Oriental arts and crafts. After your admiration has grown and your wallet has, perhaps, contracted, treat yourself to a meal at the Sky Dragon Cuisine in the Dragon City tower, an upscale Chinese restaurant with a beautiful view of the Toronto skyline.

Easy and The Fifth. *225 Richmond W. Phone 416/979-3000.* A dance club for the over-25 crowd, the music is tango to Top 40, the dress code is upscale casual, and the atmosphere is loft-apartment-open, with two bars and several specialty bars (such as The Green Room, where you can shoot pool, play craps, and smoke a cigar to the accompaniment of live jazz). On Thursdays from 6pm-10pm, enjoy cocktail hour with a complimentary buffet. **$$$**

Eaton Centre. *220 Yonge St. Phone 416/598-2322.* Yes, a shopping mall is Toronto's top tourist attraction. And, with due respect to The Sony Store, The Canadian Naturalist, Groucho's Cigars, Sushi-Q, Baskits, London Style Fish & Chips, and the other 285 shops in the mall, it has to do with more than just goods and services. This 3 million-square-foot building is a masterpiece of architecture and environment. Its glass roof rises 127 feet above the mall's lowest level. The large, open space contains glass-enclosed elevators, dozens of long, graceful escalators, and porthole windows. A flock of fiberglass Canadian geese floats through the air. Even if it usually makes you break out in hives, this is one window shopping experience worth making. (Daily)

Elgin & Winter Garden Theatre Centre. *189 Yonge St. Phone 416/872-5555; 416/314-2841 (tour info).* The 80-year history of the two theatres speaks more volumes than one of its excellent productions. Built in 1913, it was designed as a "double-decker" theater complex with the Winter Garden Theatre built seven stories above the Elgin Theatre. Each theater was a masterpiece in its own right: The Elgin was ornate, with gold leaf, plaster cherubs and elegant opera boxes; the walls of the Winter Garden were hand-painted to resemble a garden, and its ceiling was a mass of beech bows and twinkling lanterns. Through the years the stages saw the likes of George Burns and Gracie Allen, Edger Bergen and Charlie McCarthy, Milton Berle, and Sophie Tucker before the complex fell into disrepair. A 2 1/2-year $30 million restoration began in 1987, and included such things as cleaning the walls of the Winter Garden with hundreds of pounds of raw bread dough to avoid damaging the original hand-painted water color art work. The Ontario Heritage Foundation offers year-round guided tours on Thursdays at 5 pm and Saturdays at 11 am.

Exhibition Place. *S off Gardener Expy, on Lakeshore Blvd. Phone 416/393-6000.* Designed to accommodate the Canadian National Exhibition this 350-acre (141-hectare) park has events year-round, as well as the Marine Museum of Upper Canada. (Aug-Sept, daily)

First Canadian Place. *1 First Canadian Pl, 100 King St W. Phone 416/862-8138.* If only you worked here. You'd have access to a personal shopper to buy your groceries or pick up that asymmetrical slit skirt (very hot right now); and a concierge to plan your business meetings or take care of entertaining out-of-town CEOs. As it is, you can only take advantage of 120 unique shops and boutiques, unusual restaurants, massage or spa services and ever-interesting on-going art exhibits. Between 10 am-2 pm there are special promotions, sidewalk sales, and performances as diverse as Opera Atelier's staging of The Marriage of Figaro highlights to the dancing monks of the Tibetan Dikung Monastery. (Mon-Fri; some shops and restaurants open Sat-Sun)

George R. Gardiner Museum of Ceramic Art. *111 Queen's Park, opposite Royal Ontario Museum. Phone 416/586-8080.* One of the world's finest collections of Italian majolica, English Delftware, and 18th-century continental porcelain. (Daily; closed Jan 1, Dec 25) **DONATION**

Gibson House. *5172 Yonge St (ON 11), in North York. Phone 416/395-7432.* Home of land surveyor and local politician David Gibson; restored and furnished to 1850s style. Costumed interpreters conduct demonstrations. Tours. (Tues-Sun; closed holidays) **$$**

Gray Line bus tours. *184 Front St E. Phone 416/594-3310.* Contact 184 Front St E, Suite 601, M5A 4N3.

Harbourfront Centre. *235 Queens Quay W at foot of York St. Phone 416/973-3000; fax 416/973-6055.* This 10-acre waterfront community is alive with theater, dance, films, art shows, music, crafts, and children's programs. Most events free. (Daily)

Hazelton Lanes. *55 Avenue Rd. Phone 416/960-3910.* Stores that look like movie sets. Stores that sell stunning, $850 gold vermeil, sterling silver, and swarovski crystal hair clips. Stores that have entire floors devoted to pens. This is Hazelton Lanes, one of Toronto's most exclusive shopping centers, with shops, boutiques, and services designed to turn blood blue. Even if you aren't in the mood (yawn) to buy, take a stroll anyway, and see if you can spot a celeb or two; Whoopie Goldberg, Kate Hudson, Alanis Morrisette, Samuel L. Jackson, and Harrison Ford have all been known to walk by and buy. (Daily)

Historic Fort York. *100 Garrison Rd. Garrison Rd, SE near junction Bathurst and Fleet sts by Strachan Ave. Phone 416/392-6907.* It may not have seen a lot of action—just one battle during the War of 1812—but Fort York's place in Toronto's history is secure. It is the birthplace of modern Toronto, having played a major role in saving York—now Toronto—from being invaded by 1,700 hundred American troops. Today's Fort York has Canada's largest collection of original War of 1812 buildings and is a designated National Historic Site. (Daily; closed Jan 1, last 2 wks Dec) **$$**

Hummingbird Centre for the Performing Arts. *1 Front St E at Yonge St. Phone 416/393-7469 or 716/812-2262 (tickets); 416/872-2262 (tickets); fax 416/393-7454.* Stage presentations of Broadway musicals, dramas, and concerts by international artists. Home of the Canadian Opera Company and National Ballet of Canada. Pre-performance dining; gift shop.

Huronia Historical Parks. *63 miles (101 kilometers) N via Hwy 400, then 34 miles (55 kilometers) N to Midland on Hwy 93. Phone 705/526-7838.* Two living history sites animated by costumed interpreters. (Daily) **$$$** Consists of

Discovery Harbour. *196 Jury St. Church St, Penetanguishene.* Marine heritage center and reconstructed 19th-century British Naval dockyard. Established in 1817, site includes 19th-century military base. Now rebuilt, the site features eight furnished buildings and orientation center. Replica of 49-foot (15-meter) British naval schooner HMS *Bee;* also HMS *Tecumseth* and *Perseverance.* Costumed interpreters bring base to life, circa 1830. Sail training and excursions (daily). Audiovisual display; free parking, docking, picnic facilities. Theater; gift shop, restaurant. (Victoria Day-Labour Day, Mon-Fri; after Labour Day-Sept, daily) **$$$**

Ste.-Marie among the Hurons. *(1639-1649)* Reconstruction of 17th-century Jesuit mission that was Ontario's first European community. Twenty-two furnished buildings including native dwellings, workshops, barn, church, cookhouse, hospital. Candlelight tours, canoe excursions. Cafe features period-inspired meals and snacks. Orientation center, interpretive museum. Free parking and picnic facilities. (Victoria Day wkend-Oct, daily) E of Midland on Hwy 12. World-famous Martyrs' Shrine (site of papal visit) is located across the highway. Other area highlights incl pioneer museum, replica indigenous village, Wye Marsh Wildlife Centre. **$$$**

Kortright Centre for Conservation. *9550 Pine Valley Dr, Woodbridge; 12 miles (19.3 kilometers) NW via Hwy 400, Major MacKenzie Dr exit, then 2 miles (3 km) W, then S on Pine Valley Dr. Phone 905/832-2289.* Environmental center with trails, beehouse, maple syrup shack, wildlife pond, and plantings. Naturalist-guided hikes (daily). Cross-country skiing (no rentals); picnic area, cafe; indoor exhibits and theater. (Daily; closed Dec 24 and 25) **$$**

Little Italy. *W of Bathurst St between Euclid Ave and Shaw St.* After the British, Italians make up the largest cultural group in Toronto. They settled around College St, just west of Bathurst between Euclid and Shaw, in what became Toronto's first "Little Italy." Although the Italian community moved north as it grew, the atmosphere of Little Italy remains. During the day the coffee shops, billiard halls, and food markets are filled with animated discussions about politics, family, and soccer; when

night falls, the area becomes one of the hippest places in Toronto. Restaurants and bars open onto the sidewalks, fashionable cafes are everywhere, color splashes the area, music fills the air'and there's not a bad meal to be had. Two items of note: Café Diplomatico (594 College St), called "The Dip" by locals, is often used as a set by filmmakers. And anyone looking for a little political humor need go just one block south of The Dip, where you'll find the intersection of 'Clinton' and 'Gore' streets.

Mackenzie House. *82 Bond St. Phone 416/392-6915.* Restored 19th-century home of William Lyon Mackenzie, first mayor of Toronto; furnishings and artifacts of the 1850s; 1840s print shop. Group tours (by appt). (Tues-Sun, afternoons; closed holidays) **$$**

Marine Museum of Upper Canada. *Exhibition Place. Phone 416/392-1765.* Contains exhibits depicting waterways of central Canada, the Great Lakes-St. Lawrence System; shipping memorabilia; marine artifacts; wireless room; fur trade exhibit. Adjacent is an 80-foot (24-meter) steam tugboat preserved in dry berth; 12-foot (4-meter) tall operating marine triple-expansion steam engine is also on display. (Tues-Sun; closed Jan 1, Good Fri, Dec 25, 26)

The Market Gallery. *95 Front St E. Phone 416/392-7604.* Exhibition center for Toronto Archives; displays on city's historical, social, and cultural heritage; art, photographs, maps, documents, and artifacts. (Wed-Sat, also Sun afternoons; closed holidays) **FREE**

Martin Goodman Trail. *You can pick up the trail almost anyhwhere along the waterfront, but best to contact Toronto Parks and Recreation fot succinct directions. Phone 416/392-8186.* Leave it to fitness-conscious Toronto not just to have a beautifully maintained waterfront, but to build a trail that takes you from one end to the other. The Martin Goodman Trail is a public jogging/biking/hiking/rollerblading path that connects all the elements of the waterfront, traversing 13 miles. It also runs past several spots for bike and blade rentals, so if you start out walking and change your mind, no worries.

McMichael Canadian Art Collection. *N via ON 400 or 427, 10365 Islington Ave in Kleinburg. Phone 905/893-1121.* Works by Canada's most famous artists—the Group of Seven, Tom Thomson, Emily Carr, David Milne, Clarence Gagnon, and others. Also Inuit (Eskimo) and contemporary indigenous art and sculpture. Restaurant; book, gift shop. Constructed from hand-hewn timbers and native stone, the gallery stands in 100 acres (40 hectares) on the crest of Humber Valley; nature trail. (June-early Nov, daily; rest of year, Tues-Sun; closed Dec 25) **$$$**

Medieval Times. *Exhibition Place, Dufferin Gate. Phone 416/260-1234.* If you or anyone in your family would like to play the part of an honored guest of the King of Spain—which means eating a hearty meal with your fingers while watching knights of old joust on hard-charging stallions—you've come to the right place. This 11th century castle was created to replicate an 11th century experience, complete with knightly competitions and equestrian displays. As for the eating with your hands part, not to worry—there's not a spaghetti strand in sight. **$$$$**

Mt. Pleasant Cemetery. *375 Mount Pleasant Rd. Phone 416/485-9129.* One of the oldest cemeteries in North America, the Mt. Pleasant Cemetery is the final resting place of many well-known Canadians, including Sir Frederic Banting and Charles Best, the discoverers of insulin; renowned classical pianist Glenn Gould; and Prime Minister William Lyon Mackenzie King, who led Canada through WWII. The grounds hold rare plants and shrubs as well as a Memorial Peony Garden, and its many paths are used frequently by walkers and cyclists and those who just want a few quiet moments. (Daily)

Old City Hall. *100 Queen St W. Phone 416/392-7341.* The story of Toronto's Old City Hall begins as a story of how an important building begins life as a plan (small p) and suddenly becomes a Plan (large P). It took three years to design, ten years to build, and came in at $2 million over budget when it opened in 1889. But everyone agreed it was gorgeous. Over the years it fell into disrepair, and was saved from the wrecking ball and declared a National Historic Site by the Historic Sites and Monuments Board of Canada in 1989. It now stands as a majestic, living tribute to 100 years of history and architecture. (Mon-Fri) **FREE**

Ontario Parliament Buildings. *111 Wellesley St W. Queen's Park. Phone 416/325-7500.* Guided tours of the Legislature Building and walking tour of grounds. Gardens; art collection; historic displays. (Victoria Day-Labour Day, daily; rest of year, Mon-Fri; closed holidays) **FREE**

Ontario Place. *955 Lakeshore Blvd W. Phone 416/314-9811; 416/314-9900 (recording); fax 416/314-9993. www.ontarioplace.com.* A 96-acre (39-hectare) cultural, recreational, and entertainment complex on three artificial islands in Lake Ontario. Including outdoor amphitheater for concerts, two pavilions with multimedia presentations, Cinesphere theater with IMAX films (year-round; fee); children's village. Three villages of snack bars, restaurants, and pubs; miniature golf; lagoons, canals, two marinas; 370-foot (113-meter) water slide, showboat, pedal and bumper boats; Wilderness Adventure Ride. (Mid-May-early Sept; daily) Parking fee. **$$$$**

Ontario Science Centre. *770 Don Mills Rd, at Eglinton Ave E, 6 miles (10 km) NE via Don Valley Pkwy, in Don Mills. Phone 416/429-4100 (recording).* Hundreds of hands-on exhibits in the fields of space, technology, communications, food, chemistry, and earth science. Demonstrations on electricity, papermaking, metal casting, lasers, cryogenics.

OmniMax theater (fee). Special exhibitions. This is a high tech playground in Learning Command Central—and it's really for kids. Ten huge exhibition halls in three linked pavilions are filled with exhibits on space and technology. You can stand at the edge of a black hole, watch bees making honey, test your reflexes, your heart rate or your grip strength, use pedal power to light lights or raise a balloon, hold hands with a robot, or land a spaceship on the moon. Throughout the museum there are slide shows and films that demonstrate various aspects of science, and two Omnimax theaters show larger-than-life films. Plan to spend the whole day. (Daily; closed Dec 25) **$$**

Parachute School of Toronto. *Phone 800/361-5867.* There is growing evidence that learning vacations are gaining in popularity. If this is the sort of learning that makes you feel smarter—jump on it. First you'll have morning instruction, in the afternoon you'll jump. See how easy? Be sure to call ahead to make sure the school's plane is flying that day. Sometimes they know things about the weather you don't. **$$$$**

Paramount Canada's Wonderland. *9580 Jane St, 18 miles (29 kilometers) N on Hwy 400. Phone 905/832-7000; fax 905/832-7419.* More than 125 attractions in eight themed areas offer 11 live stage shows and 50 rides, including Vortex and Top Gun (suspended roller coasters). Splash Works, a 10-acre area offers 15 water-related rides and attractions (mid-June-Labour Day, weather permitting; free with Pay-One-Price admission). Special events, fireworks displays, top-name entertainment. (May and Sept, weekends; June-Aug, daily)

The Pier: Toronto's Waterfront Museum. *Central Harbourfront at 245 Queen's Quay W. Phone 416/597-0965.* Original 1930s pier building on Toronto's celebrated waterfront includes two floors of hands-on interactive displays, rare historical artifacts, re-creations of marine history stories, art gallery, boat-building center, narrated walking excursions, children's programs. (Mar-Oct, daily) **$$$$**

Royal Ontario Museum. *100 Queen's Park. Phone 416/586-5549; 416/586-8000 (recording).* to 1000-800 BCE. The discovery has been officially recognized by UNESCO as "Canada's contribution to the United Nations Decade for Cultural Development." (Daily; closed Jan 1, Dec 25) **$$$$**

Scarborough Civic Centre. *150 Borough Dr in Scarborough. Phone 416/396-7216.* Houses offices of municipal government. Guided tours (daily; closed Dec 25). Concert Sun afternoons.

Second City. *56 Blue Jays Way. Phone 416/343-0011.* The Toronto branch of the famous Improv Club has turned out its own respectable list of veterans. Among those who have trained here are Gilda Radner, Mike Meyers, Martin

Short, Ryan Stiles, and dozens of others who have set the standards for improvisational comedy. The nightly shows are topical and frequently hilarious, but don't leave just yet; the post-show improve sessions are the ones that will have you trying to keep your sides from splitting.

Shopping on Queen Street West. *A downtown stretch from University Ave to Bathurst St.* If your style is cool and happening, welcome to Mecca. Here's where you'll find vintage clothing stores, trendy home furnishings, hip styles and stylish funk that used to be original grunge and street vendor bohemia. You'll also find the handiwork of many up-and-coming fashion designers. In between the boutiques are antique stores, used bookstores, and terrific bistros and cafes. But beware of the heaps of pasta served with heaps of attitude.

SkyDome. *1 Blue Jays Way. Phone 416/341-2770; fax 416/341-3110.* Many people go to see the Toronto Blue Jays play a great game of baseball, others go to see Canada's Argonauts take to the gridiron. But others go to see the place where the two hometown teams play: the Skydome, the first stadium in the world with a retractable roof. It takes 20 minutes and costs $500 every time every time somebody wants the sun in. But who wants to watch a baseball game under a roof? (Tours given daily) **$$$**

Spadina Historic House and Garden. *285 Spadina Rd. Phone 416/392-6910.* Built for financier James Austin and his family, this 50-room house has been restored to its 1866 Victorian glory and is open to those who want to see how the upper most of the city's upper crust spent quiet evenings at home. It's filled with the family's art, artifacts and furniture, and until 1982 it was filled with the family itself; that's when the last generation of Austins left, and the house was turned over to public ownership. Docents tend to the glorious gardens and orchard, which are open to the public in the summer. Tours are given every 15 minutes. (Jan-Mar, weekends only; Apr-Dec, daily)

St. Lawrence Centre for the Arts. *27 Front St E. Phone 416/366-7723 (box office).* Performing arts complex features theater, music, dance, films, and other public events.

The St. Lawrence Market. *92 Front St E. Phone 416/392-7219.* In 1803 Governor Peter Hunt designated an area of land to be 'market block.' Today, the St. Lawrence Market provides a good snippet of the way Toronto used to be, with enough of the character of the original architecture to make you feel as though the old city were alive and well. Some of the wide avenues, too, are reminiscent of European cities. The market itself, Toronto's largest indoor market, sells 14 different categories of foods: incredibly fresh seafood, poultry, meat, organic produce, baked goods, gourmet teas and coffees, plus fruit and flowers. And you'll be hard-pressed to find a better selection of cheese in all of Toronto.

Todmorden Mills Heritage Museum & Arts Centre. *67 Pottery Rd, 2 1/4 miles (4 kilometers) N, off Don Valley Pkwy in East York on Pottery Rd between Broadview and Bayview Aves. Phone 416/396-2819.* Restored historic houses; Parshall Terry House (1797) and William Helliwell House (1820). Also museum; restored 1899 train station. Picnicking. (May-Sept, Tues-Sun; Oct-Dec, Mon-Fri) **$$**

Toronto Blue Jays (MLB). *1 Blue Jays Way. Phone 416/341-1000; fax 416/341-1177.* SkyDome.

Toronto Maple Leafs (NHL). *40 Bay St. Phone 416/815-5700. ; fax 416/359-9213.* Air Canada Centre.

Toronto Raptors (NBA). *40 Bay St. Phone 416/366-DUNK.* Air Canada Centre,

Toronto Stock Exchange. *The Exchange Tower, 2 First Canadian Pl (King and York Sts). Phone 416/947-4676.* Stock Market Place visitor center has multimedia displays, interactive games, and archival exhibits to aid visitors in understanding the market. **FREE**

Toronto Symphony. *Roy Thomson Hall, 60 Simcoe St. Phone 416/593-4828; fax 416/598-3375.* Classical, pops and children's programs; Great Performers series. Wheelchair seating, audio enhancement for hearing-impaired.

Toronto Tours Ltd. *60 Harbour St 5th Floor. Phone 416/869-1372.* Four different boat tours of Toronto Harbour. **$$$$**

University of Toronto. *25 King's College Circle. Downtown, W of Queen's Park. Phone 416/978-5000 (tours).* (1827) 55,000 students. Largest university in Canada. Guided walking tours of magnificent Gothic buildings begin at Hart House and incl account of campus ghost (June-Aug, Mon-Fri; free).

Woodbine Racetrack. *15 miles (24 kilometers) N via Hwy 427 in Etobicoke. Phone 416/675-RACE; fax 416/213-2123.* The only track in North America that can offer both standardbred and thoroughbred racing on the same day, Woodbine is home to Canada's most important race course events. It hosts the $1 million Queen's Plate, North America's oldest continuously run stakes race; the $1 million ATTO; the $1.5 million Canadian International, and the $1 million North America Cup for Standardbreds. It also has an outstanding grass course; it was here, in 1973, that Secretariat bid farewell to racing with his win of the grass championship. Woodbine has 1,700 slot machines, and many different dining options for those times when you might need intake instead of outgo. **FREE**

Young People's Theatre. *165 Front St E. Phone 416/862-2222; fax 416/363-5136.* Professional productions for the entire family. (Sept-May, daily; Aug, weekends only)

Special Events

Beaches International Jazz Festival. *1976A Queen St E (M4L 1H8). Phone 416/698-2152.* For four days every summer since 1989, the Beaches community of Toronto has resonated with the sound of world-class jazz at the Beaches International Jazz Festival, a musical wonder that attracts nearly a million people to the water's edge. More than 40 bands play nightly, with over 700 musicians casting their spell over a crowd that includes children waving glow sticks, toe-tapping seniors and just about everyone in-between. In addition to international artists (with a focus on Canadians), the Festival also serves as a springboard for talented amateurs. Late July. **FREE**

The Bloor Yorkville Wine Festival. *55 Bloor St W, Suite 220.* In the late 1990s three separate organizations, among them the Wine Council of Ontario, began a festival that has grown to include more than 70 wineries from 11 countries. Activities include five days of international wine tastings, dinners, parties, and discussions that are held at various restaurants, bars, and hotels all over town. There is also a strong educational element to the festival, with seminars held throughout the week. If you're truly a wine aficionado you'll definitely want to wait until Saturday, the last day of the festival, which will include eight specially designed wine- and food-related seminars. And if you're a novice, sign up for the 'Pre-Tasting Seminar' to learn how swish, sip, and savor like the pros.

Canadian International. *555 Rexdale Blvd. Phone 416/675-7223.* Woodbine Racetrack. World-class thoroughbreds compete in one of Canada's most important races. Mid-late Oct.

Canadian National Exhibition. *Lake Shore Blvd & Strachan Ave. Phone 416/393-6000.* Exhibition Place on the lakefront. This gala celebration originated in 1879 as the Toronto Industrial Exhibition for the encouragement of agriculture, industry, and the arts, although agricultural events dominated the show. Today sports, industry, labor, and the arts are of equal importance to CNE. The "Ex," as it is locally known, is so inclusive of the nation's activities that it is a condensed Canada. A special 350-acre (141-hectare) park has been built to accommodate the exhibition. Hundreds of events incl animal shows, parades, exhibits, a midway, water and air shows. Virtually every kind of sporting event is represented, from frisbee-throwing to the National Horse Show. Mid-Aug-Labour Day.

Caribana. *Exhibition Place Lake Shore Blvd & Strachan Ave. Phone 416/465-4884.* Caribbean music, grand parade, floating nightclubs, dancing, costumes, food at various locations throughout city. Late July-early Aug.

Celebrate Toronto Street Festival. *City Hall, 100 Queen St W. Phone 416/395-0490.* Each July, on the first weekend after Canada Day, Toronto's Yonge Street—the longest street in the world—is transformed into more than 500,000 square feet of free entertainment, with something for people of all ages and all tastes. Each of five intersections along Yonge Street runs its own distinctive

programming mix; one has nothing but family entertainment, another has world music, a third has classic rock, and so forth. Jugglers, stilt-walkers, and buskers enliven street corners; spectacular thrill shows captivate pedestrians. Opening ceremonies, on Friday night of this weekend event, are usually at the intersection of Yonge and Eglinton; call for schedule. Early July. **FREE**

Chin International Picnic. *Lake Shore Blvd & Strachan Ave. Phone 416/531-9991.* At Paramount Canada's Wonderland. Contests, sports, picnicking. First weekend July.

Designs on Ice. *100 Queen St W. Phone 416/395-0490.* Not only do you have to be handy with a pick, you have to be awfully quick. This ice sculpture competition gives contestants exactly 48 hours to chisel a block of ice into a winter work of art. Each year brings a different theme. A recent one, for example, was J.R.R. Tolkien's epic *The Lord of the Rings,* which brought forth a wonderland of hobbits, dwarves, trolls, orcs, wizards, and elves. The public chooses the winners, and the Awards Ceremony is part of a family skating party with live music. The sculptures stay up as long as the weather cooperates. Which, in Toronto, might be a very long time indeed. Last weekend Dec. **FREE**

International Caravan. *Phone 416/977-0466.* Fifty pavilions scattered throughout the city present ethnic food, dancing, crafts. Third week June.

Outdoor Art Show. *Queen & Bay Sts. Nathan Phillips Sq. Phone 416/408-2754.* Mid-July.

Royal Agricultural Winter Fair. *Lake Shore Blvd & Strachan Ave. Phone 416/263-3400.* Coliseum Building, Exhibition Place. World's largest indoor agricultural fair exhibits the finest livestock. Food shows; Royal Horse Show features international competitions in several categories. Early Nov.

Sunday Serenades. *5100 Yonge St. Phone 416/338-0338.* See if moonlight becomes you, and play Fred and Ginger under the stars at Mel Lastman Square. Each Sunday evening in June and July you can Lindy Hop, Big Apple, and Swing to live big band and swing music from the '30s, '40's and '50s. It's free and easy'and lots of fun. **FREE**

Toronto International Film Festival. *Eaton Centre. Phone 416/968-3456.* Celebration of world cinema in downtown theaters; Canadian and foreign films, international movie makers, and stars. Phone 416/967-7371. Early Sept.

Toronto Kids Tuesday. *100 Queen St W.* For four consecutive Tuesdays in July and August, Nathan Philips Square is turned into a kids' fantasyland where everyone and everything is devoted to them. There's entertainment, face painting, coloring, chalk art, make-and-tale crafts, make your own t-shirts, build-a-kite; it depends on who is entertaining, and what the theme of the day is. The Stylamanders brought zany choreography and championship yo-yo tricks for their popular song 'Hop, Skip and Jump,' which was followed by a high-energy day of play, including interactive games with the Toronto Maple Leafs. No matter who entertains or what the theme, you'll be sure to find a crowd of happy kids. **FREE**

Toronto Wine and Cheese Show. *6900 Airport Rd (L4V 1E8). Phone 416/229-2060.* Here's your chance to try award-winning wines without the award-winning price tags. A mainstay since 1983, the Toronto Wine and Cheese Festival brings a world of top-tier wines, beers, lagers, ales, single malt whiskies, cheeses and specialty food to town. There are also famous chefs sharing their recipes, an exquisite collection of cigars to sample, tips on buying the perfect bottle of wine, and free seminars by well-known food and wine experts presented for both education and enjoyment. It's a great family event, as long as your family is all post-teen; no one under the age of 19 is admitted. Mid-Apr. **$$$$**

Motels/Motor Lodges

★ ★ **BEST WESTERN CARLTON PLACE.** *33 Carlson Ct (M9W 6H5). Phone 416/675-1234; fax 416/675-3436. www.bestwestern.com.* 524 rooms, 12 story. S $160-175; D $175-$190; each additional $15; suites $250-$350; under 18 free; weekend, mid-week rates. Crib free. Parking in/out $5/day. TV; cable (premium). Indoor pool; whirlpool. Complimentary coffee in rooms. Restaurant 6:30-1 am. Room service 24 hours. Bar 11-1 am. Check-out 1 pm. Meeting rooms. Business center. Gift shop. Airport transportation. Exercise equipment; sauna. Health club privileges. Minibars. Cr cds: A, C, D, DS, ER, JCB, MC, V.

D ⚏ 🏋 ✈ 🖥 SC 🏃

★ ★ **BEST WESTERN PRIMROSE.** *111 Carlton St (M5B 2G3). Phone 416/977-8000; fax 416/977-6323. www.bestwestern.com.* 338 rooms, 23 story. S, D $149; each additional $10; suites $275; under 16 free. Crib free. Garage $12.50. TV; cable. Pool. Complimentary coffee in rooms. Restaurant 6:30 am-10 pm. Bar 11-1 am. Check-out 11 am. Meeting rooms. Business center. Exercise equipment; sauna. Cr cds: A, C, D, DS, ER, JCB, MC, V.

D ⚏ 🏋 🖥 SC 🏃

★ **COMFORT HOTEL DOWNTOWN.** *15 Charles St E (M4Y 1S1). Phone 416/924-1222; fax 416/927-1369. www.comfortinn.com.* 108 rooms, 10 story. S $109; D $119; each additional $10; suites $129-$139; under 18 free; weekend rates. Crib $10. Parking $9. TV; cable (premium), VCR available. Restaurant noon-10 pm. Piano bar. Check-out 11 am. Meeting rooms. Business services available. Health club privileges. Refrigerators; microwaves available. Cr cds: A, C, D, DS, ER, JCB, MC, V.

🖥 SC 🏃 🏋

★ **DAYS INN DOWNTOWN.** *30 Carlton St (M5B 2E9). Phone 416/977-6655; toll-free 800/329-7466; fax 416/977-0502. www.daysinn.com/daysinn.html.* 536 rooms, 23 story. S, D $119-$135; each additional $15; under 16 free. Crib free. Pet accepted, some restrictions. Covered parking $15/day. TV; cable. Indoor pool. Restaurant 7 am-10 pm. Bar 11:30-2 am. Check-out 11 am. Coin laundry. Meeting rooms. Business services available. Sundries. Barber, beauty shop. Sauna. Some refrigerators. Sun deck. Cr cds: A, D, DS, ER, JCB, MC, V.

🐾 ⚏ 🖥 SC

★ ★ **HOLIDAY INN - DON VALLEY.** *1100 Eglinton Ave E (M3C 1H8). Phone 416/446-3700; fax 416/446-3701. www.holiday-inn.com.* 298 rooms, 14 story. S, D $115-$155; each additional $10; suites $175-$325; family, weekend, weekly rates. Crib free. Pet accepted, some restrictions. TV; cable (premium), VCR available (movies). Complimentary coffee in lobby. Restaurant 6:30 am-11 pm. Room service. Bar 6 pm-2 am; entertainment Thurs-Sat. Check-out noon. Convention facilities. Business center. In-room modem link. Concierge. Shopping arcade. Barber, beauty shop. Free valet parking. Airport, train station transportation. Indoor tennis, pro. Cross-country ski 1/4 mile. Exercise equipment; sauna. Indoor/outdoor pool; whirlpool, poolside serv, lifeguard. Playground. Supervised children's activities (June-Sept); ages 5-12. Game room. Lawn games. Bathroom phones, refrigerators. Many balconies. Cr cds: A, C, D, DS, ER, JCB, MC, V.

D 🐾 ⚏ 🏌 ⚏ 🏋 🖥 SC 🏃 ✈

★ **HOLIDAY INN EXPRESS TORONTO.** *50 Estates Dr (M1H 2Z1). Phone 416/439-9666; toll-free 800/465-4329; fax 416/439-4295. www.holiday-inn.com.* 138 rooms, 2-3 story. No elevators. S $59; D $79; each additional $10; under 19 free; weekend rates. Crib free. TV; cable (premium). Complimentary continental breakfast. Restaurant adjacent 11:30-1 am, Sat, Sun from 4:30 pm. Check-out 11 am. Meeting rooms. Business services available. Health club privileges. Cr cds: A, C, D, DS, ER, JCB, MC, V.

D 🖥 SC

★ ★ **HOLIDAY INN YORKDALE.** *3450 Dufferin St (M6A 2V1). Phone 416/789-5161; toll-free 800/465-4329; fax 416/785-6845. www.holiday-inn.com.* 365 rooms, 12 story. S $149.95; D $164.95; each additional $15; suites $350; under 12 free; weekend rates. Crib free. TV; cable (premium). Heated pool; whirlpool. Supervised children's activities. Complimentary coffee in rooms. Restaurant 6 am-11 pm. Bar 11-1 am. Check-out noon. Meeting rooms. Business center. Exercise equipment; sauna. Recreation room. Minibars. Some balconies. Cr cds: A, C, D, DS, ER, JCB, MC, V.

D ⚏ 🏋 🖥 SC 🏃

★ **HOWARD JOHNSON EAST.** 940 Progress Ave (M1G 3T5). Phone 416/439-6200; fax 416/439-5689. www.hojo.com. 186 rooms, 6 story. S $109; D $119; each additional $10; under 18 free; weekend rates; package plan. Crib free. Pet accepted. TV; cable (premium). Heated pool; whirlpool. Restaurant 6:30 am-2 pm, 5-10 pm. Room service. Bar 4:30 pm-1 am. Check-out noon. Coin laundry. Meeting rooms. Business services available. Valet service. Sundries. Gift shop. Exercise equipment; sauna. Health club privileges. Microwaves available. Cr cds: A, C, D, DS, ER, JCB, MC, V.

D 🏃 🏊 👤 🐾 **SC**

★ **HOWARD JOHNSON INN.** 89 Avenue Rd (M5R 2G3). Phone 416/964-1220; toll-free 800/446-4656; fax 416/964-8692. www.hojo.com. 71 rooms, 8 story. S $124; D $134; each additional $10; under 19 free; weekend rates off-season. Crib free. Pet accepted, some restrictions. Parking $6.50/day. TV; cable (premium), VCR available. Complimentary continental breakfast. Check-out 1 pm. Meeting rooms. Business services available. Health club privileges. Cr cds: A, D, DS, ER, MC, V.

🏃 🐾 **SC**

★★**QUALITY HOTEL.** 2180 Islington Ave (N9P 3P1). Phone 416/240-9090; fax 416/240-9944. www.qualityinn.com. 198 rooms, 12 story. S, D $89-$139; each additional $10; under 18 free; package plans; higher rates special events. Crib free. Pet accepted. TV; cable (premium). Restaurant 6 am-midnight. Bar from 11 am. Check-out 11 am. Meeting rooms. In-room modem link. Microwaves available. Near airport. Cr cds: A, D, DS, ER, JCB, MC, V.

D 🏃 ✈ 🐾 **SC**

★★ **QUALITY HOTEL.** 111 Lombard St (M5C 2T9). Phone 416/367-5555; fax 416/367-3470. www.qualityinn. com. 196 rooms, 16 story. S $139; D $149; each additional $10; under 18 free. Crib free. Pet accepted. Garage $11.75/day. TV; cable. Check-out 11 am. Business services available. Exercise equipment. Health club privileges. Cr cds: A, D, DS, ER, JCB, MC, V.

D 🏃 👤 🐾 **SC**

★★ **QUALITY SUITES.** 262 Carlingview Dr (M9W 5G1). Phone 416/674-8442; toll-free 800/228-5151; fax 416/674-3088. www.qualityinn.com. 254 suites, 12 story. S, D $120-$145; each additional $5; under 18 free; weekend, holiday rates. Crib free. Pet accepted. TV; cable (premium). Complimentary coffee in rooms. Restaurant 6:30-1 am. Bar. Check-out 11 am. Meeting rooms. Business services available. No bellhops. Gift shop. Downhill/cross-country ski 15 miles. Exercise equipment. Health club privileges. Minibars; microwaves available. Cr cds: A, D, DS, ER, JCB, MC, V.

D 🏃 🏊 👤 🐾 **SC**

★★ **RADISSON HOTEL TORONTO.** 55 Hallcrown Pl (M2J 4R1). Phone 416/493-7000; fax 416/493-0681. www.radisson.com. 228 rooms, 9 story. S, D $98-$103; each additional $10; suites $225; under 17 free; weekend rates. Crib free. TV; cable (premium). Indoor pool; whirlpool. Complimentary coffee in rooms. Restaurant 7 am-10 pm. Bar. Check-out noon. Meeting rooms. Business services available. Sauna. Cr cds: A, C, D, DS, ER, JCB, MC, V.

D 🏊 🐾 **SC**

★**RAMADA HOTEL & SUITES.** 300 Jarvis St (M5B 2C5). Phone 416/977-4823; fax 416/977-4830. www.ramada.com. 102 rooms, 10 story, 44 suites. S $155; D $170; each additional $15; suites $185-$265; under 18 free. Crib free. Garage parking $15. TV; cable (premium). Indoor pool; whirlpool. Complimentary coffee in rooms. Restaurant 7 am-2 pm, 5-9 pm. Bar from 11 am. Check-out 11 am. Meeting rooms. Business services available. Concierge. Downhill/cross-country ski 10 miles. Exercise equipment; sauna. Recreation room. Refrigerators. Cr cds: A, C, D, DS, ER, JCB, MC, V.

🏊 🏊 👤 🐾 **SC**

★**RAMADA HOTEL TORONTO AIRPORT.** 2 Holiday Dr (M9C 2Z7). Phone 416/621-2121; fax 416/621-9840. www.ramada.com. 60; each additional $10; suites $250-$350; under 18 free; weekly, weekend rates; lower rates rest of year. Crib free. Pet accepted. TV; cable (premium). Indoor/outdoor pool; whirlpool. Complimentary coffee in rooms. Restaurant 6 am-11 pm. Room service. Bar 11:30-1 am. Check-out noon. Business services available. In-room modem link. Bellhops. Valet service. Free airport transportation. Exercise equipment; sauna. Some minibars; microwaves available. Cr cds: A, C, D, DS, ER, JCB, MC, V.

D 🏃 🏊 👤 ✈ 🐾 **SC**

★**RAMADA PLAZA.** 185 Yorkland Blvd (M2J 4R2). Phone 416/493-9000; fax 416/493-5729. www.ramada.com. 285 rooms, 10 story. S, D $105-$165; each additional $15; suites $175-$300; under 18 free; weekend rates. Crib free. TV; cable (premium). Indoor pool. Coffee in rooms. Restaurant 6:30 am -10:30 pm; Sat from 7 am. Bar 11-2 am; Sun to 11 pm. Check-out noon. Meeting rooms. Business center. In-room modem link. Exercise equipment; sauna. Health club privileges. Game room. Recreation room. Some in-room whirlpools. Luxury level. Cr cds: A, C, D, DS, ER, JCB, MC, V.

D 🏊 👤 🐾 **SC** 🏃

★**SEA HORSE INN.** 2095 Lakeshore Blvd W (On 2) (M8V 1A1). Phone 416/255-4433; fax 416/251-5121. 74 rooms, 1-3 story. S $57-$72; D $57-$89; each additional $5; suites $85-$170; under 18 free. TV; cable (premium). Pool; whirlpool. Playground. Complimentary continental breakfast. Check-out 11 am. Meeting rooms. Sauna. Refrigerators. Picnic tables, grills. On Lake Ontario. Cr cds: A, C, D, DS, ER, MC, V.

🏊 🐾 **SC**

★**TRAVELODGE AIRPORT.** *925 Dixon Rd (M9W 1J8). Phone 416/674-2222; toll-free 888/483-6887; fax 416/674-5757. www.travelodge.com.* 283 rooms, 17 story. S $120; D $140; each additional $10; suites $140-$275; under 18 free; weekend rates. Crib free. Pet accepted. TV, cable (premium). Indoor pool; whirlpool. Complimentary continental breakfast. Restaurant 11-2 am. Bar. Check-out 1 pm. Convention facilities. Business services available. In-room modem link. Airport transportation. Sauna. Health club privileges. Gift shop. Cr cds: A, D, DS, ER, MC, V.

D 🐾 ⌘ ✈ ≋ SC

★**TRAVELODGE EAST.** *20 Milner Business Ct (M1B 3C6). Phone 416/299-9500; fax 416/299-6172. www.travelodge.com.* 156 rooms, 6 story. S, D $71-$81; each additional $6; suites $85-$105; under 17 free. Pet accepted. TV; cable (premium). Indoor pool; whirlpool. Complimentary coffee in rooms. Restaurant 11-2 am. Room service noon-11 pm. Check-out 11 am. Meeting rooms. Business services available. Sundries. Health club privileges. Microwaves available. Cr cds: A, C, D, DS, ER, JCB, MC, V.

D 🐾 ⌘ ≋ SC

★**TRAVELODGE NORTH.** *50 Norfinch Dr (M3N 1X1). Phone 416/663-9500; fax 416/663-8480. www.travelodge.com.* 184 rooms, 6 story. S $89; D $97; each additional $8; under 17 free. Crib free. Pet accepted, some restrictions. TV; cable (premium). Indoor pool; whirlpool. Coffee in rooms. Restaurant 7-1 am. Room service. Bar. Check-out 11 am. Meeting rooms. Business services available. Sundries. Cr cds: A, C, D, DS, ER, MC, V.

D 🐾 ⌘ ≋ SC

★ **TRAVELODGE YORKDALE.** *2737 Keele St (M3M 2E9). Phone 416/636-4656; fax 416/633-5637. www.hojo.com.* 367 rooms, most A/C, 10 story, 27 suites. S, D $129-$179; each additional $10; suites $175-$375; family rates; package plans. Crib free. Pet accepted. TV; cable (premium), VCR available. Indoor pool. Supervised children's activities (June-Sept); ages 4-12. Complimentary coffee in rooms. Restaurant 6:30 am-11 pm; Sun to 10 pm. Bar 11-1 am. Check-out noon. Meeting rooms. Business services available. Free garage parking. Downhill/cross-country ski 10 miles. Exercise equipment; sauna. Game room. Recreation room. Some minibars; microwaves available. Cr cds: A, C, D, DS, ER, JCB, MC, V.

D 🐾 ⌘ 🏋 ≋ SC

★★★**VALHALLA INN.** *1 Valhalla Inn Rd (M9B 1S9). Phone 416/239-2391; fax 416/239-8764. www.valhalla-inn.com.* 240 rooms, 2-12 story. S $160; D $170; each additional $10; suites $150-$275; under 18 free; weekend rates. Crib free. Pet accepted. TV; cable (premium). Heated pool. Coffee in rooms. Restaurant 6 am-11 pm; dining room noon-2:30 pm, 6-10 pm. Room service. Bars 11-2 am; entertainment. Check-out 1 pm.

Meeting rooms. Business center. In-room modem link. Bellhops. Valet service. Sundries. Free airport transportation. Health club privileges. Some bathroom phones. Private patios, balconies. Grills. Cr cds: A, C, D, DS, ER, MC, V.

🐾 ⌘ ✈ SC 🏃 ✈

Hotels

★ **BOND PLACE.** *65 Dundas St E (N5B 2G8). Phone 416/362-6061; fax 416/360-6406. www.bondplacehoteltoronto.com.* 286 rooms, 18 story, 51 suites. May-Oct: S, D $89-$109; each additional $15; suites $104-$134; under 15 free; lower rates rest of year. Crib free. Parking, in/out $11. TV; cable (premium), VCR available. Restaurant 7 am-11 pm. Room service 11 am-10 pm. Bar 5 pm-1 am. Check-out 11 am. Meeting rooms. Business services available. Cr cds: A, C, D, DS, ER, MC, V.

D ≋ SC

★★★ **CROWNE PLAZA TORONTO CENTRE.** *225 Front St W (M5V 2X3). Phone 416/597-1400; toll-free 800/422-7969; fax 416/597-8128. www.crowneplaza.com.* The property is located in the heart of Toronto's entertainment, financial, theater, and fashion districts. 587 rooms, 25 story. S, D $239-$279; each additional $20; suites $375-$600; under 12 free; weekend rates. Crib free. Check-out noon. Check-in 3 pm. TV; cable (premium), VCR available. In-room modem link. Minibars; microwaves available. Coffee in rooms. Restaurant (see also ACCOLADE). Bar 11:30-2 am; nightly entertainment. Exercise room, massage, sauna. Indoor pool, wading pool, whirlpool, Indoor pool; wading pool, whirlpool, poolside service. Valet parking. Meeting rooms, business center. Concierge. Upscale and luxurious decor. Cr cds: A, C, D, DS, ER, JCB, MC, V.

D ⌘ 🏋 ≋ SC 🏃

★★★**DELTA CHELSEA INN.** *33 Gerrard St W (M5G 1Z4). Phone 416/595-1975; toll-free 800/268-1133; fax 416/585-4375. www.deltahotels.com.* 1,590 rooms, 26 story. S $245-$275; D $265-$295, each additional $15; suites $255-$375, under 18 free; weekend rates. Pet accepted. Check-out 11 am, check-in 3 pm. TV; cable, VCR available. Room service Room service 24 hours. Restaurant, bar, entertainment. Supervised children's activities; ages 2-13. Children's activity center, babysitting services available. In-house fitness room, health club privileges, sauna. Game room. Indoor pool, whirlpool. Valet parking. Business center. Cr cds: A, C, D, DS, ER, JCB, MC, V.

D 🐾 ⌘ 🏋 ≋ SC 🏃

★★ **DELTA TORONTO AIRPORT.** *801 Dixon Rd (N9W 1J5). Phone 416/675-6100; fax 416/675-4022. www.deltahotels.com.* 251 rooms, 8 story. S, D $115-$165; each additional $15; suites $170-$220; under 18 free;

package plans. Crib free. Pet accepted, some restrictions. TV; cable (premium). Indoor pool. Supervised children's activities (June-Aug). Restaurant 6 am-11 pm. Room service 24 hours. Bar 11:30-2 am. Check-out 1 pm. Convention facilities. Business center. Bellhops. Valet service. Gift shops. Exercise equipment; sauna. Health club privileges. Minibars; microwaves available. Cr cds: A, C, D, DS, ER, JCB, MC, V.

[D] [icons] SC [icon]

★ ★ **DELTA TORONTO EAST.** 2035 Kennedy Rd (M1T 3G2). Phone 416/299-1500; fax 416/299-8959. www.deltahotels.ca. This property allows its guests to explore the Toronto area from outside the downtown core. 368 rooms, 14 story. S, D $219; each additional $15; suites $365-$620; under 18 free; weekend rates. Crib free. Pet accepted. TV; cable. Indoor pool; wading pool; whirlpool. Free supervised children's activities (weekends, school holidays); ages 3-15. Restaurants 6:30-2 am. Room service 24 hours. Bar 11-2 am. Check-out noon. Convention facilities. Business services available. In-room modem link. Concierge. Gift shop. Barber, beauty shop. Covered valet parking. Putting green. Exercise room; sauna. Game room. Luxury level. Cr cds: A, D, DS, ER, JCB, MC, V.

[D] [icons] SC

★ ★ ★ **FAIRMONT ROYAL YORK.** 100 Front St W (M5J 1E3). Phone 416/368-2511; fax 416/368-2884. www.fairmont.com. 1,365 rooms, 22 story. S, D $189-$289; each additional $20; suites $295-$1,750; under 18 free; package plans. Crib free. Pet accepted. Check-out noon. TV; cable. Minibars; refrigerators, microwaves available. Restaurant 6:30 am-10:30 pm. Bar noon-2 am; entertainment. Room service 24 hours. Health club privileges. Exercise room, massage, sauna. Pool, wading pool, whirlpool. Barber, beauty shop. Garage (fee). Business center, convention center/facilities. Concierge. Luxury level. Cr cds: A, D, DS, ER, JCB, MC, V.

[D] [icons] SC [icon]

★ ★ ★ ★ **FOUR SEASONS HOTEL TORONTO.** 21 Avenue Rd (M5R 2G1). Phone 416/964-0411; toll-free 800/819-5053; fax 416/964-2301. www.fourseasons.com. The standard-setting Four Seasons Hotel has a stylish home in Toronto. The 32-story headquarters is located in the Yorkville District, a fashionable and dynamic neighborhood filled with specialty shops and galleries. The guest rooms are sublimely comfortable and feature fine furnishings and impressive artwork. Guests stay on track with fitness regimes while staying here, with both a fitness center and an indoor-outdoor pool. The spa offers a variety of massages, all of which are also available in the privacy of a guestroom. Toronto's dining scene is well represented at the Four Seasons, with four sensational restaurants. The eclectic décor and the striking glass art make the Studio Café a favorite place for casual dining, while the contemporary, sleek style of Avenue attracts

the chic. No visit is complete without dining at Truffles (see also TRUFFLES), where a mouthwatering menu transports diners to the French countryside. 380 rooms, 32 story. S $325-$485; D $365-$525; each additional $30; suites $755; under 18 free; weekend rates. Pet accepted. Valet parking. Complimentary continental breakfast. Check-out noon, check-in 3 pm. TV; cable (premium), VCR available (movies). In-room modem link. Room service 24 hours. Restaurant, bar, entertainment. Baby-sitting services available. In-house fitness room, sauna. Massage. Indoor/outdoor pool; whirlpool. Business center. Concierge. Cr cds: A, D, DS, JCB, MC, V.

[D] [icons] SC [icon]

★ ★ ★ **HILTON.** 145 Richmond St W (M5H 2L2). Phone 416/869-3456; fax 416/869-3187. www.hilton.com. 601 rooms, 32 story. Apr-Nov: S, D $239-$259; each additional $20; suites $249-$1,600; family rates; package plans; lower rates rest of year. Crib free. Garage $17.50. TV; cable (premium). Indoor/outdoor pool; whirlpool, poolside service in summer. Restaurant 6:30 am-11 pm. Room service 24 hours. Bar 11:30-2 am. Check-out noon. Convention facilities. Business center. Exercise equipment; sauna. Massage. Minibars. Luxury level. Cr cds: A, C, D, DS, ER, JCB, MC, V.

[D] [icons] [icon]

★ ★ **HOLIDAY INN.** 970 Dixon Rd (M9W 1J9). Phone 416/675-7611; toll-free 800/465-4329; fax 416/675-9162. www.holiday-inn.com. 445 rooms, 12 story. S, D $160-$175; suites $230-$430; weekend rates. Crib free. Pet accepted. TV; cable (premium). 2 heated pools, 1 indoor; whirlpool. Playground. Coffee in rooms. Restaurant 6 am-11 pm. Room service to 1 am. Bar 11-2 am; Sun noon-11 pm. Check-out 1 pm. Meeting rooms. Business center. Concierge. Barber, beauty shop. Free airport transportation. Exercise equipment; sauna. Recreation room. Minibars. Cr cds: A, C, D, DS, ER, JCB, MC, V.

[D] [icons] SC [icon]

★ ★ **HOLIDAY INN.** 600 Dixon Rd (M9W 1J1). Phone 416/240-7511; toll-free 800/491-4656; fax 416/240-7519. www.holiday-inn.com. 186 rooms, 2-5 story. S, D $89-$150; each additional $10; suites $129-$155; under 18 free. Crib free. Pet accepted, some restrictions. TV; cable. Heated pool; wading pool, poolside service. Coffee in rooms. Restaurant open 24 hours. Check-out 1 pm. Meeting rooms. Business services available. Airport transportation. Exercise equipment. Cr cds: A, C, D, DS, ER, JCB, MC, V.

[D] [icons] SC

★ ★ **HOLIDAY INN.** 370 King St W (M5V 1J9). Phone 416/599-4000; toll-free 800/263-6364; fax 416/599-7394. www.holiday-inn.com. 425 rooms, 20 story. S, D $189; each additional $15; suites $269; family rates; package plans. Crib free. Garage $16. TV; cable, VCR available. Heated rooftop pool; poolside serv, lifeguard.

Complimentary coffee in rooms. Restaurant 6:30-2 am. Bar from 11 am. Check-out noon. Convention facilities. Business center. Concierge. Gift shop. Exercise equipment; sauna. Massage. Wet bars. Cr cds: A, C, D, DS, ER, JCB, MC, V.

D ⊠ 🏊 🏋 ⛷ SC 🚶

★★★**HOTEL INTER-CONTINENTAL TORONTO.** *220 Bloor St W (M5S 1T8). Phone 416/960-5200; fax 416/960-8269. www.interconti.com.* The wood paneling, brass accents, fresh flowers, and Art Deco style of the lobby create a refreshing décor that flows into the brightly colored rooms. 210 rooms, 8 story. S, D $365-$405; suites $450-$2,000. Pet accepted. Check-out 1 pm. Check-in 3 pm. TV; cable (premium), VCR available (movies). In-room modem link. Room service Room service 24 hours. Restaurant, bar. In-house fitness room, massage. Sauna. Indoor pool. Valet parking. Business center. Concierge. Cr cds: A, C, D, ER, JCB, MC, V.

D ⊠ 🏊 🏋 ⛷ SC 🚶

★ **INN ON THE PARK.** *1100 Eglinton Ave E (M3C 1H8). Phone 416/444-2561; fax 416/446-3308. www.innonthepark.com.* 270 rooms, 23 story. S, D $175-$235; each additional $20; suites $250-$800; under 18 free; weekend rates. Crib free. Check-out noon. TV; cable (premium), VCR available (movies). In-room modem link. Some private patios, balconies. Bathroom phones; some minibars. Restaurant 6:30 am-midnight. Bar 11:30-1 am; vocalist Fri-Sat. Free supervised children's activities (June-Sept); ages 5-12. Courtyard/playground games. Exercise equipment, sauna. Recreation room. 2 heated pools, 1 indoor; whirlpool. Cross-country ski opposite hotel. Barber, beauty shop. Complimentary parking. Meeting rooms, business center. Concierge. Cr cds: A, C, D, DS, ER, JCB, MC, V.

D ⊠ 🏊 🏋 ⛷ SC 🚶

★★★ **INTERNATIONAL PLAZA.** *655 Dixon Rd (M9W 1J4). Phone 416/244-1711; fax 416/244-8031. www.internationalplaza.com.* 415 rooms, 12 story. S, D $170; each additional $10; suites $350-$500; under 18 free; weekend rates. Crib free. Pet accepted. Valet parking $6. TV; cable (premium). Indoor pool; wading pool, poolside serv, lifeguard. Supervised children's activities; ages 3-12. Restaurant 6:30 am-11 pm. Room service 24 hours. Bar 11-2 am. Check-out noon. Convention facilities. Business center. Concierge. Gift shop. Beauty, barber shop. Exercise equipment; sauna. Massages. Game room. Refrigerators. Minibars in suites. Cr cds: A, D, DS, ER, MC, V.

D 🐾 🏊 🏋 ⛷ 🚶

★★★ **LE ROYAL MERIDIEN KING EDWARD.** *37 King St E (M5C 1E9). Phone 416/863-9700; fax 416/367-5515. www.lemeridien-kingedward.com.* Built in 1903 during the time of Edward VII, this stately hotel has a luxurious lobby of rich fabrics, marble pillars,

and soaring ceilings. Both business and leisure guests will find the business-district location convenient with theaters, restaurants, and shops nearby. From martinis in the plush lounge to bedtime mints on pillows, this is classy service the old-fashioned way. 294 rooms, 9 and 16 story. S $205-$360; D $230-$385; suites $435-$510; under 12 free; weekend rates. Crib free. Covered parking, valet $24. TV; cable (premium), VCR available. Restaurants 6:30 am-2:30 pm, 5-11 pm (see also CHIARO'S). Room service 24 hours. Bars 11:30-1 am. Check-out noon. Convention facilities. Business center. In-room modem link. Concierge. Shopping arcade. Beauty shop. Exercise equipment; sauna. Whirlpools. Massage. Health club privileges. Bathroom phones, minibars; microwaves available. Cr cds: A, C, D, ER, JCB, MC, V.

D 🏋 ⛷ SC 🚶

★★★ **MARRIOTT TORONTO AIRPORT.** *901 Dixon Rd (M9W 1J5). Phone 416/674-9400; toll-free 800/905-2811; fax 416/674-8292. www.marriott.com.* 424 rooms, 9 story. S, D $240; suites $300-$1,200; under 18 free; weekend rates. Crib free. TV; cable (premium). Indoor pool; whirlpool. Restaurants 6 am-11 pm. Bar noon-2 am. Check-out noon. Convention facilities. Business center. Gift shop. Covered parking. Free airport transportation. Exercise equipment; sauna. Luxury level. Cr cds: A, C, D, DS, ER, JCB, MC, V.

D ⊠ 🏋 ✈ ⛷ SC 🚶

★★★ **MARRIOTT.** *90 Bloor St E (M4W 1A7). Phone 416/961-8000. www.marriott.com.* 258 rooms, 6 story. S, D $195-$325; under 18 free. Crib available. Check-out noon, check-in 4 pm. TV; cable (premium). In-room modem link. Minibars; many refrigerators in suites. Restaurant 6:30 am-10 pm. Bar to midnight. Exercise equipment. Meeting rooms, business center. Concierge. Cr cds: A, C, D, DS, ER, JCB, MC, V.

D 🏋 ⛷ 🚶

★★★ **MARRIOTT TORONTO EATON CENTRE.** *525 Bay St (N5G 2L2). Phone 416/597-9200; toll-free 800/905-0667; fax 416/597-9211. www.marriotteatoncentre.com.* In the financial district and near the theatre district, this property attracts all types of visitors with its extensive offerings. There is a top-floor pool overlooking the city. 459 rooms, 18 story. Check-out noon, check-in 3 pm. TV; cable (premium), VCR available. Room service 24 hours. Restaurant, bar. In-house fitness room, spa, sauna. Indoor pool, whirlpool, poolside service. Valet parking. Business center. Concierge. Cr cds: A, C, D, DS, ER, JCB, MC, V.

D ⊠ 🏋 ⛷ SC 🚶

★★★★**METROPOLITAN HOTEL TORONTO.** *108 Chestnut St (M5G 1R3). Phone 416/977-5000; fax 416/599-3317. www.metropolitan.com.* All of Toronto is within easy reach from the Metropolitan Hotel, making it an obvious choice for discerning travelers. Not far from the financial district, the hotel also enjoys close proximity to world-renowned shopping, art galleries, and museums. The 26-story hotel has the services of a large property and the intimacy of a private residence. Blonde woods, earth tones, and simple furnishings deliver a calming sense to guests in the guest rooms. The accommodations are a dream, featuring the latest technology, from faxes, laser printers, modems, and multi-line telephones to stereo equipment. Fully staffed fitness and business centers are also on hand to assist all guests with their goals. Hemispheres (see also HEMISPHERES) scours the globe for culinary inspiration, and the beige and black dining room of Lai Wah Heen (see also LAI WAH HEEN) is a serene setting for its luscious Cantonese cuisine. Considered an excellent example of authentic dim sum, this restaurant is a local sensation. 425 rooms, 26 story. S, D $240-$380; each additional $30; suites $490-$1,800; weekend rates. Pet accepted, some restrictions. Parking, in/out $19/$24. Check-out noon. TV; cable (premium), VCR available (free movies). In-room modem link. Restaurant 6:30 am-11:30 pm. Bar 11-1 am. Exercise equipment, sauna. Indoor pool; whirlpool. Business center. Concierge. Eaton Centre 2 blocks. Cr cds: A, D, DS, ER, JCB, MC, V.

D ⬛ ⬛ ⬛ ⬛ SC ⬛

★★NOVOTEL TORONTO CENTRE. 45 The Esplanade (M5E 1W2). Phone 416/367-8900; fax 416/360-8285. www.novotel.com. This property has a great location near the CN Tower, the Eaton Center, and other attractions. 262 rooms, 9 story. S, D $205; each additional $20; suites $215; under 16 free; weekend rates. Crib free. Pet accepted. Garage, in/out $13.50. TV; cable (premium). Indoor pool; whirlpool. Restaurant 6 am-midnight. Bar 11-2 am. Check-out 1 pm. Meeting rooms. Business services available. Exercise equipment; sauna. Minibars. Cr cds: A, D, DS, ER, JCB, MC, V.

D ⬛ ⬛ ⬛ ⬛ SC

★★★★PARK HYATT TORONTO. 4 Avenue Rd (M5R 2E8). Phone 416/925-1234; toll-free 800/977-1497; fax 416/924-6693. www.parkhyatt.com. The Park Hyatt Toronto calls the stylish Yorkville area home. Located at the intersection of Avenue Rd and Bloor St, this hotel has some of the world's leading stores just outside its doors. The hotel echoes its fashionable neighborhood in its interiors. The Art-Deco lobby is at once soothing and vibrant with its soft, yellow light and gleaming marble floors. The public and private spaces have a rich feeling completed with handsome furnishings, and a clean, modern look dominates the rooms and suites. The demands of the world dissipate at the Stillwater Spa, where blissful and innovative therapies are offered. Step inside this spa and your cares will be lifted away almost immediately. Overlooking the lobby and the streets of Yorkville, the Mezzanine is a popular gathering place for locals and hotel guests alike. International dishes are the specialty at

Annona, while the grilled steaks and seafood of Morton's of Chicago are always a tasty treat. 346 rooms, 18 story. S, D $499, suites $559; each additional $40, under 17 free. Pet accepted. Valet parking. Check-out noon, check-in 3 pm. TV; VCR available. Room service 24 hours. Restaurant, bar. Babysitting services available. Spa, sauna, steam room. Whirlpool. Free airport transportation. Business center. Concierge. Cr cds: A, D, DS, JCB, MC, V.

D ⬛ ⬛ ⬛ ⬛ SC ⬛

★★QUALITY HOTEL MIDTOWN. 280 Bloor St W (M5S 1V8). Phone 416/968-0010; toll-free 800/424-6423; fax 416/968-7765. www.choicehotels.ca/cn312. 209 rooms, 14 story. Pet accepted. Check-out 11 am, check-in 1 pm. TV; cable. Restaurant, bar. Health club privileges. Cr cds: A, C, D, DS, JCB, MC, V.

D ⬛ ⬛ SC

★★RADISSON HOTEL TORONTO-MARKHAM. 50 E Valhalla Dr (L3R 0A3). Phone 905/477-2010; fax 905/477-2026. www.radisson.com. Located in the heart of Markham's corporate community, "Silicon Valley North", this property is convenient to the downtown core and is 20 minutes from the Pearson International Airport. A great choice for corporate travelers and small conventions. 204 rooms, 15 story, 26 suites. S, D $220; each additional $15; suites $250; under 19 free; weekly, weekend rates; golf plans; higher rates Dec 31. Crib free. Complimentary continental breakfast. Complimentary coffee in rooms. Check-out noon. Minibars; microwaves available. Restaurant 6:30 am-11 pm. Bar 11-2 am. Exercise equipment, sauna. Recreation room. Indoor pool, whirlpool. 18-hole golf privileges. Tennis privileges. Downhill/cross-country ski 12 miles. Picnic tables. Meeting rooms, business services. Gift shop. Cr cds: A, C, D, DS, ER, JCB, MC, V.

D ⬛ ⬛ ⬛ ⬛ ⬛ ⬛ SC

★★RADISSON PLAZA HOTEL ADMIRAL. 249 Queens Quay W (M5J 2N5). Phone 416/203-3333; fax 416/203-3100. www.radisson.com. Visitors can relax on the promenade deck where they can enjoy the view of Toronto's waterfront. 157 air-cooled rooms, 8 story, 17 suites. Early-May-mid-Nov: S, D $265-$295; each additional $20; suites from $495; family, weekend rates. Crib free. Parking $15/day. TV; cable (premium). Heated pool; whirlpool, poolside service. Complimentary coffee in rooms. Restaurant 7 am-11 pm. Room service 24 hours. Bar 11:30-1 am. Check-out noon. Meeting rooms. Business services available. Concierge. Gift shop. Health club privileges. Bathroom phones, minibars. On waterfront; nautical theme throughout. View of Harbour. Cr cds: A, C, D, DS, ER, JCB, MC, V.

D ⬛ ⬛ SC

★★**RADISSON SUITE TORONTO AIRPORT.** *640 Dixon Rd (M9W 1J1). Phone 416/242-7400; fax 416/242-9888. www.radisson.com.* 215 suites, 14 story. S, D $204-$216; under 18 free. Crib free. Pet accepted, some restrictions. TV; cable, VCR available. Complimentary continental breakfast. Restaurant 6:30 am-11 pm. Bar 11-1 am. Check-out noon. Meeting rooms. Business center. In-room modem link. Concierge. Gift shop. Free valet parking. Exercise equipment. Minibars, microwaves available. Cr cds: A, C, D, DS, ER, JCB, MC, V.

D 🐾 ⚓ 🏋 🏊 SC 🚶

★★★**REGAL CONSTELLATION.** *900 Dixon Rd (M9W 1J7). Phone 416/675-1500; fax 416/675-1737. www.regal-hotels.com.* Located minutes from the L. B. Pearson International Airport and downtown Toronto, this hotel is also the largest conference center in Canada. 710 rooms, 8-16 story. S, D $95-$165; each additional $15; suites from $275; under 18 free; weekend package plan. Crib free. Pet accepted, some restrictions. Valet parking $9.25/day. TV; cable (premium), VCR available. 2 heated pools, 1 indoor/outdoor; whirlpool, poolside service in season. Restaurant 6:30 am-11 pm; dining room 11 am-2 pm, 5:30-10 pm. Room service 24 hours. Bar 11-1 am; entertainment Thurs-Sat. Check-out noon. Concierge. Convention facilities. Business center. Gift shop. Beauty shop. Airport transportation. Exercise equipment; sauna. Some balconies. Cr cds: A, C, D, DS, ER, JCB, MC, V.

D 🐾 ⚓ 🏋 ✈ 🏊 SC 🚶

★★★**RENAISSANCE AT SKYDOME.** *1 Blue Jays Way (M5V 1J4). Phone 416/341-7100; toll-free 800/237-1512; fax 416/341-5091. www.renaissancehotels.com.* 348 rooms, 11 story, 26 suites. May-Oct: S, D $169-$179; each additional $30; suites from $299-$559; under 18 free; weekend rates; package plans; lower rates rest of year. Crib available. Pet accepted. Garage parking $16; valet $22. TV; cable, VCR available. Indoor pool. Complimentary coffee in rooms. Supervised children's activities (June-Sept). Restaurant 7-1 am. Room service 24 hours. Bar. Check-out 9:30 am-noon. Convention facilities. Business center. Concierge. Gift shop. Health club privileges. Massage. Minibars. Modern facility within SkyDome complex; lobby and some rooms overlook playing field. Cr cds: A, C, D, DS, ER, JCB, MC, V.

D 🐾 ⚓ 🏊 SC 🚶

★★★**SHERATON CENTRE.** *123 Queen St W (M5H 2M9). Phone 416/361-1000; fax 416/947-4854. www.sheraton.com.* An underground connection joins this property to the Eaton Center Mall. 1,382 rooms, 43 story. Late June-Dec: S $275; D $285; each additional $20; suites $450-$850; under 18 free; weekend rates; lower rates rest of year. Covered parking, valet $22/day. TV; cable (premium), VCR available. Indoor/outdoor pool; whirlpool, poolside service (summer), lifeguard. Supervised children's activities (daily July-mid-Sept; weekends rest of year). Complimentary coffee in rooms. Restaurant 6 am-11 pm. Room service 24 hours. Bars. Check-out noon. Convention facilities. Business center. Concierge. Shopping arcade. Barber, beauty shop. Exercise equipment; sauna. Massage. Recreation room. Minibars; microwaves available. Private patios, balconies. Waterfall in lobby; pond with live ducks. Cr cds: A, C, D, ER, JCB, MC, V.

D ⚓ 🏋 🏊 SC 🚶

★★★**SHERATON GATEWAY.** *Toronto International Airport, Terminal 3 (L5P 1C4). Phone 905/672-7000; fax 905/672-7100. www.sheraton.com.* This hotel is conveniently located at the Toronto airport. 474 rooms, 8 story. S, D $190-$240; each additional $15; suites $420-$800; under 18 free; weekly, weekend rates. Crib free. Pet accepted. Garage parking $9.50; valet $18. TV; cable (premium), VCR available. Indoor pool; whirlpool. Restaurant 6 am-11 pm. Room service 24 hours. Bar 11-1 am. Check-out noon. Convention facilities. Business center. Concierge. Shopping arcade. Barber, beauty shop. Free airport transportation. Exercise equipment; sauna. Massage. Minibars. Modern facility connected by climate-controlled walkway to Terminal 3. Cr cds: A, C, D, DS, ER, JCB, MC, V.

D 🐾 ⚓ 🏋 ✈ 🏊 SC 🚶

★★★**SHERATON PARKWAY HOTEL TORONTO NORTH.** *600 Hwy 7 E (L4B 1B2). Phone 905/881-2121. www.sheraton.com.* 312 rooms, 10 story. S, D $195-$325; under 18 free. Crib available. Check-out noon, check-in 4 pm. TV; cable (premium). In-room modem link. Minibars; many refrigerators in suites. Restaurant 6:30 am-10 pm. Bar to midnight. Exercise equipment. Indoor pool, whirlpool. Meeting rooms, business center. Concierge. Cr cds: A, C, D, DS, ER, JCB, MC, V.

D ⚓ 🏋 🏊 🚶

★★★**SUTTON PLACE.** *955 Bay St (M5S 2A2). Phone 416/924-9221; fax 416/324-5617. www.suttonplace.com.* A landmark for more than 30 years, this hotel has a central location adjacent to Queen's Park and minutes from fashionable Yorkville. 292 rooms, 33 story. S, D $320; each additional $20; suites $390-$1,500. Pet accepted. Check-out noon. Check-in. TV; cable (premium), VCR available (movies). Room service 24 hours. Restaurant, bar, entertainment. Babysitting services available. In-house fitness room, health club privileges, spa, spa, massage, sauna. Indoor pool, poolside service. Valet parking. Business center. Concierge. Cr cds: A, C, D, ER, JCB, MC, V.

D 🐾 ⚓ 🏋 🏊 SC 🚶

★★**TOWN INN.** *620 Church St (M4Y 2G2). Phone 416/964-3311; fax 416/924-9466. www.towninn.com.* 200 kitchen units (1-2 bedrm), 26 story. June-Dec: S $95-$125; D $110-$135; each additional $15; under 12 free; monthly rates; lower rates rest of year. Crib free. Pet accepted. Garage $14. TV; cable (premium). Heated pool. Complimentary continental breakfast. Restaurant

7-10 am. Check-out 11 am. Meeting rooms. Business services available. Tennis. Exercise equipment. Health club privileges; saunas. Refrigerators, microwaves. Balconies. Cr cds: A, C, D, ER, MC; V.

[D] [🏇] [🏊] [🏄] [🏃] [⊠] [SC]

★ ★ ★ **WESTIN HARBOUR CASTLE.** *1 Harbour Sq (M5J 1A6). Phone 416/869-1600. www.westin.com.* 980 rooms, 20 story. S, D $250-$375; under 18 free. Crib available. Check-out noon, check-in 4 pm. TV; cable (premium). In-room modem link. Minibars; many refrigerators in suites. Restaurant 6:30 am-10 pm. Bar to midnight. Exercise equipment. Indoor pool, whirlpool. Meeting rooms, business center. Concierge. Cr cds: A, C, D, DS, ER, JCB, MC, V.

[D] [🏊] [🏃] [⊠] [🏃]

★ ★ ★ **WESTIN PRINCE.** *900 York Mills Rd (M3B 3H2). Phone 416/444-2511; fax 416/444-9597. www.westin.com.* Located in the center of downtown Toronto, this hotel is just minutes from both the Ontario Science Centre and the Ford Centre for the Performing Arts. 381 rooms, 22 story. S $210-$245; D $230-$265; each additional $20; suites $340-$1,800; under 18 free; weekend rates. Crib free. Check-out 1 pm. TV; cable (premium), VCR available (movies). In-room modem link. Balconies. Refrigerators. Restaurant 6:30 am-10 pm. Bar 11:30-2 am; entertainment Mon-Sat. Room service 24 hours. Playground. Health club privileges. Exercise equipment, sauna. Game room. Pool, whirlpool, poolside service. 18-hole golf privileges. Tennis. Barber, beauty shop. Business center, convention center/facilities. Concierge. Cr cds: A, C, D, DS, ER, JCB, MC, V.

[D] [🏂] [🏄] [🏊] [🏃] [⊠] [🏃]

★ ★ ★ ★ **WINDSOR ARMS HOTEL.** *18 St. Thomas St (M5S 3E7). Phone 416/971-9666; fax 416/921-9121. www.windsorarmshotel.com.* Behind the castlelike façade of the Windsor Arms Hotel is one of Toronto's chicest lodgings. Edgy, yet classic, it is a well-heeled hipster's dream. The accommodations in this intimate and stylish hotel are sleek, modern, and sublime, with mahogany or birch furnishings, frosted glass screens, and Frette linens. Guilty pleasures include the extraordinary 24-hour butler service. This hotel is truly a slice of the good life. The Tea Room serves a traditional tea by day, and at night is transformed into Toronto's only Champagne and caviar bar. The stunning décor of the Courtyard Café attracts the fashionable set; Club 22 entertains with piano entertainment and live bands; and the Cigar Lounge offers decadent treats. Guests feeling a bit overindulged head for the fitness center and spa to work off their gastronomical sins and escape the worries of the world. 28 suites. TV. Restaurant. Spa. Exercise room. Pool. Business center. Cr cds: A, DS, MC, V.

[🏊] [🏃] [🏃]

★ ★ ★ **WYNDHAM BRISTOL PLACE HOTEL.** *950 Dixon Rd (M9W 5N4). Phone 416/675-9444; fax 416/675-4426. www.wyndham.com.* 287 rooms, 15 story. S, D $214-$350; each additional $10; suites from $625; under 18 free; weekend rates; package plans. Crib free. Check-out 1 pm. TV; cable (premium). In-room modem link. Some private patios. Minibars; bathroom phone, whirlpool in some suites. Coffee in rooms. Restaurant 6:30 am-10 pm (see also ZACHARY'S). Bar 11-2 am; entertainment Mon-Fri. Room service 24 hours. Exercise equipment, sauna. Indoor/outdoor pool; poolside service. Valet parking. Free airport transportation. Business center, convention center/facilities. Concierge. Cr cds: A, C, D, DS, ER, JCB, MC, V.

[D] [🏊] [🏃] [🏄] [⊠] [SC] [🏃]

Resort

★ ★ ★ **INN AT MANITOU.** *Center Rd (P0G 1C0). Phone 705/389-2171. www.manitou-online.com.* 22 rooms, 3 story. S, D $250-$400. Check-out noon. Check-in 4 pm. TV; cable (premium). In-room modem link. Restaurant 6:30 am-10 pm. Bar to midnight. Exercise equipment, spa. Golf. Tennis. Meeting rooms, business services. Concierge. Cr cds: A, ER, MC, V.

[🏂] [🏃] [🏃]

All Suites

★ ★ ★ **EMBASSY SUITES.** *8500 Warden Ave (L6G 1A5). Phone 905/470-8500; fax 905/477-8611. www.embassysuites.com.* This hotel is just 20 minutes from downtown Toronto and across the street from the Markham Theatre for the Performing Arts. 332 suites, 10 story. S, D $160-$180; each additional $20; weekend rates; under 18 free. Crib free. Valet parking $3. TV; cable (premium). Indoor pool; whirlpool. Complimentary full breakfast. Coffee in rooms. Restaurant 6:30 am-midnight. Bar 11-2 am. Check-out noon. Convention facilities. Business center. Shopping arcade. Barber, beauty shop. Exercise room; sauna, steam room. Game room. Minibars; microwaves available. Extensive grounds; elaborate landscaping. Elegant atmosphere. Cr cds: A, C, D, DS, ER, JCB, MC, V.

[D] [🏊] [🏃] [⊠] [SC] [🏃]

B&B/Small Inns

★ ★ ★ **MILLCROFT.** *Phone 519/941-8111; fax 519/941-9192. www.millcroft.com.* This property is only a 40-minute drive outside of Toronto. 52 rooms, 2 story. D $235-$325. Complimentary continental breakfast. Check-out noon, check-in 4 pm. Guest laundry. Restaurant (see also MILLCROFT INN). Bar. Exercise equipment, sauna. Game room. Whirlpool, poolside service. Golf privileges. Tennis. Cross-country ski on site.

100 acres on Credit River. Former knitting mill (1881). Cr cds: A, D, ER, MC, V.

⬜ 🏊 🎿 ⛷ 🎣 🚶 ⛷

Restaurants

★★★**360.** *301 Front St W (M5V 2T6). Phone 416/ 362-5411. www.cntower.ca.* As the name suggests, this restaurant completes a 360 degree rotation offering a breathtaking view from the CN Tower. The scenery inside is attractive as well, with its colorful decor and fresh, seasonal menu. Continental menu. Specializes in fresh rack of lamb, prime rib, corn-fed free-range chicken. Own baking. Hours: 11 am-2:30 pm, 5-10:30 pm; Sun from 10:30 am. Reservations accepted. Bar. Wine cellar. A la carte entrees: lunch, dinner $19-$38. Sun brunch from $35. Revolving restaurant; view of harbor and city. Cr cds: A, C, D, DS, ER, MC, V.

Ⓓ

★★★ **ACCENTS.** *955 Bay St (M5S 2A2). Phone 416/ 324-5633; fax 416/924-1778. www.tasteoflife.com.* Located in the Sutton Place Hotel, the eclectic menu at this restaurant has something to offer for everyone in the dinner party. Continental menu. Specializes in market-fresh cuisine. Hours: 6:30 am-11:30 pm. Reservations accepted. Bar. Wine cellar. A la carte entrees: breakfast $2.95-$10.50, lunch $11.50-$14.50, dinner $22-$36. Pianist Thurs-Sat. Parking. Continental atmosphere. Cr cds: A, D, ER, MC, V.

Ⓓ

★★ **ARKADIA HOUSE.** *2007 Eglinton Ave E (M1L 2M9). Phone 416/752-5685.* Greek menu. Hours: 11:30 am-3 pm, 4 pm-midnight. Closed Dec 24. Dinner $11.95-$15.95. Bar. Children's menu. Cr cds: A, C, D, ER, MC, V.

ⓈⒸ

★★ **ARLEQUIN.** *134 Avenue Rd (M5R 2H6). Phone 416/928-9521; fax 416/928-5060. www.tasteoflife.com.* French, Mediterranean menu. Hours: 8:30 am-10 pm; Fri, Sat to 11 pm. Closed Mon, most major holidays. Dinner $10.95-$36. Bar. Cr cds: A, C, D, DS, ER, MC, V.

Ⓓ

★★★ **AUBERGE DU POMMIER.** *4150 Yonge St (M2P 2C6). Phone 416/222-2220; fax 416/222-2580. www.oliverbonacini.com.* Located north of the city, this restaurant in an industrial park manages to feel like it is actually in rural France. The attentive service and comfortable decor are pleasing. French, American cuisine with North American twist. Hours: 11:30 am-2:30 pm, 5-10:30 pm; Sat from 5 pm. Closed Sun; some holidays. Bar. Children's meals. Reservations required. Cr cds: A, D, MC, V.

★★★ **AVALON.** *270 Adelaide St W (M5H 1X6). Phone 416/979-9918; fax 416/599-2006. www.torontolife.com.* Chef/owner Chris McDonald and executive chef Erik Nowak create a new menu almost daily due to their commitment to providing only what is fresh and seasonal. Guests return again and again to experience the variety and quality of food presented. Hours: noon-2:30 pm, 5:30-10 pm; Mon, Tues from 5:30 pm; Fri to 11 pm; Sat 5:30-11 pm. Closed Sun; most major holidays. Dinner $30-$40. Bar. Cr cds: A, D, ER, MC, V.

★★ **BANGKOK GARDEN.** *18 Elm St (M5G 1G7). Phone 416/977-6748; toll-free 877/279-3766; fax 416/977-8280. www.bangkokgarden.ca/restaurant.htm.* Imagine the soothing sound of water running through a quiet brook, rays of light shining through a skylight garden. This relaxing atmosphere paried with exotic Thai cuisine is the perfect match for a pleasant dining experience. Thai menu. Hours: 11:30 am-2:30 pm, 5-10 pm; Sat, Sun from 5 pm. Buffet (Mon, Fri): lunch $9.95. Dinner $19.95-$25. Bar. Children's menu. Cr cds: A, D, ER, MC, V.

Ⓓ

★★ **BAROOTES.** *220 King St W (M5H 1K4). Phone 416/979-7717; fax 416/979-0292.* International menu. Specialties: fresh stir-fry, Thai satay combination, grilled marinated lamb tenderloin. Hours: 11:30 am-2:30 pm, 5-10:30 pm. Closed Sun; Jan 1, Dec 25. Reservations accepted. Bar. A la carte entrees: lunch $8.95-$12.95, dinner $11.50-$24.95. Traditional dining room. Cr cds: A, D, MC, V.

Ⓓ

★★★ **BIAGIO.** *155 King St E (M5C 1G9). Phone 416/ 366-4040; fax 416/366-4765. www.torontolife.com.* Located in the historic St. Lawrence Hall, near the theater district, this modern Italian restaurant serves specialties from the north. An ornate ceiling and a lovely patio with a fountain add to the ambiance. Northern Italian cuisine. Hours: noon-2:30 pm, 6-10 pm; Sat from 6 pm; closed Sun, Jan 1 & Dec 25. Dinner $15-$33. Reservations accepted. Cr cds: D, MC, V.

Ⓓ

★★ **BISTRO 990.** *990 Bay St (M5S 2A5). Phone 416/ 921-9990; fax 416/921-9497. www.bistro990.com.* Hours: noon-10:30 pm; Sat from 5:30 pm. Closed Sun. Dinner $24.90. Bar. Outdoor seating. Cr cds: A, C, D, DS, MC, V.

Ⓓ

★ **BUMPKINS.** *21 Gloucester St (M4Y 1L8). Phone 416/922-8655; fax 416/922-0242.* French, Amer menu. Specialty: shrimp Bumpkins. Hours: noon-2:30 pm, 5-11 pm; Sat from 5 pm. Closed Sun. A la carte entrees: lunch $3.95-$8.50, dinner $8.75-$20.95. Child's meals. Outdoor dining. Cr cds: A, D, ER, MC, V.

Ⓓ

★★★★**CANOE.** *66 Wellington St W (M5K 1H6). Phone 416/364-0054; fax 416/364-4273. www.oliverbonacini.com.* Canoe is a tranquil place to dine. During the day, warm light streams in through the tall windows, filling the elegantly minimalist restaurant with golden tones. At night, a warm glow comes from the room's perfect amber-hued lighting, and the dining room swells with a chic crowd; the sexy cocktail list makes the bar quite popular. Whether you're having lunch or dinner, Canoe, one of restaurateur Oliver Bonacini's many stylish Toronto eateries (others include Jump and Auberge du Pommier), is a stunning venue in which to experience creative, satisfying regional Canadian cuisine. While dazzling ingredients tend to be sourced from wonderful local producers, many organic, the kitchen borrows flavors and techniques from the world at large, including Asia, France, and the American South. The end product is inventive food and an equally original room that take your breath away. Hours: 11:30 am-2:30 pm, 5-10:30 pm. Closed Sat, Sun; holidays. Dinner $25-$34. Bar to 11:30 pm. Reservations accepted. Totally nonsmoking. Cr cds: A, C, D, ER, MC, V.

D

★ ★ **CARMAN'S CLUB.** *26 Alexander St (M8V 2K8). Phone 416/924-8558; fax 416/924-7638. www.toronto.com/ carmans.* The restaurant opened in 1963. The intimacy of the setting enhances the richness of the menu. Specialties: rack of lamb, Dover sole. Own pastries. Hours: 5:30 pm-midnight. Closed Good Friday, Dec 25. Reservations accepted. Service bar. Wine cellar. Complete meals: dinner $31.95-$35.95. Child's meals. In pre-1900 house; fireplaces. Family-owned. Cr cds: A, MC, V.

D

★★★**CENTRO GRILL & WINE BAR.** *2472 Yonge St (M4P 2H5). Phone 416/483-2211; fax 416/483-2641. www.c entrorestaurant.com.* A lot of tastes are rolled into one destination at this contemporary European restaurant with a downstairs sushi and oyster bar. The wood floors; red, high-backed chairs; white tablecloths; and silver-accented decor create a colorful, New Age-style dining room, and the worldly menu is never a bore with novelties like caribou chop with juniper berry oil, Alsatian spatzle, and Arctic cloudberry sauce. European, Continental menu. Hours: 5-11:30 pm. Closed Sun.; most major holidays. Dinner $34-$42. Bar with pianist (Mon-Wed), 4-piece band (Thurs-Sat). Valet parking. Cr cds: A, D, ER, MC, V.

D

★ ★ ★ ★ **CHIADO.** *864 College St (M6H 1A3). Phone 416/538-1910; fax 416/538-8383. www.torontolife.com.* Albino Silva is the chef-owner and loving force behind Chiado, a charming, authentic Portuguese bistro named after the oldest neighborhood in his native Lisbon. Enter the cozy dining room and you are instantly hungry: the air is heavy with the scent of seafood, garlic, and herbs, and a cutting board overflowing with Silva's fresh-baked bread stares you down as you enter the front room. Paying homage to the old seaside town but updating dishes for a more modern sensibility, Chiado features what might best

be described as nouvelle Portuguese cuisine. No matter what title you give it, the food is first-rate and fabulous. You'll find an ocean's worth of fresh fish, simply prepared with olive oil and herbs, as well as innovative takes on pheasant, game, and poultry. To add to the authenticity of the experience, Chiado has the largest collection of fine Portuguese wines in North America and a superb selection of vintage ports. Portuguese classical cuisine. Hours: noon-3 pm, 5-11 pm; Sun from 5 pm. Closed Dec 24-26. Dinner $17.75-$30. Children's menu. Reservations accepted. Cr cds: A, C, D, DS, ER, MC, V.

★ ★ ★ **CHIARO'S.** *37 King St E (M5C 1E9). Phone 416/863-4126; fax 416/863-4127. www.toprestaurants.com/ toronto/chiaros.htm.* The dining room is plush and comfortable and the service is attentive. Continental menu. Specialties: rack of lamb, Dover sole. Hours: 5-10 pm. Closed Sun. Reservations accepted. Bar to 1 am. Wine cellar. Dinner $24-$43. Child's meals. Valet parking. Cr cds: A, D, ER, MC, V.

D

★ ★ **DAVID DUNCAN HOUSE.** *125 Moatfield Dr (M3B 3L6). Phone 416/391-1424; fax 416/391-5302. www.davidduncanhouse.com.* Dark oak, dim lighting, and stained-glass windows help create the luxurious setting of this acclaimed restaurant. But what is most noteworthy is the richness of its cuisine. Hours: 11:30 am-3 pm, 5-11 pm; Sat, Sun from 5 pm. Dinner $22-$42. Bar. In restored, Gothic Revival house (1865) with elaborate gingerbread and millwork, antiques, stained-glass skylight. Jacket. Valet parking. Cr cds: A, D, MC, V.

D

★ ★ ★ **THE DOCTOR'S HOUSE.** *21 Nashville Rd (LOJ 1CO) hone 905/893-1615; fax 905/893-0660. www.toronto.com/thedoctorshouse.* This large restaurant is just minutes away from the art gallery in this picturesque town. Continental menu. Hours: 11-1 am; Sun brunch 10:30 am-3 pm. Dinner $50-$60. Sun brunch. Bar. Children's menu. Outdoor seating. Cr cds: A, MC, V.

D

★ ★ **DYNASTY CHINESE.** *131 Bloor St W (M5S 1R1). Phone 416/923-3323; fax 416/923-1826. www.toronto.com/dynasty.* Hours: 11 am-11 pm; Sat, Sun from 10 am. Dinner $15. Entertainment. Cantonese menu. Cr cds: A, MC, V. **$$**

D 🖼

★★**ELLAS.** *702 Pape Ave (M4K 3S7). Phone 416/463-0334; fax 416/694-1286. www.ellas.com.* Why travel far when one can immerse oneself in all the flavors of Greece at Toronto's oldest Greek restaurant? Repeatedly visited by world-famous celebrities, this is one dining experience not to be missed. Greek menu. Specializes in lamb, shish kebab, seafood. Own pastries. Hours: 11-1 am; Sun to

11 pm. Closed Dec 25. Reservations accepted. Bar. Lunch $7.95-$9.95, dinner $9.95-$24.95. Ancient Athenian décor; sculptures. Family-owned. Cr cds: A, C, D, DS, MC, V.

D **SC**

★ ★ ★ ★ **THE FIFTH.** *225 Richmond St W (M5V 1W2). Phone 416/979-3000. www.easyandthefifth.com.* It takes work to make it to The Fifth. First, an alley entrance to leads you to The Easy, an upscale nightclub and former speakeasy. Once inside The Easy, you are directed onto a Persian rug-lined vintage freight elevator. There, an old-school attendant takes you to floor number five. Exit and you have finally arrived at The Fifth, a treasured contemporary French restaurant and supper club. Truly special in every sense, The Fifth is a stunning, intimate, living room-like space with a stone fireplace, blond hardwood floors, picture windows, white linen-draped tables and chairs, and soft candle lighting. The food is of the delicious updated French variety, and the dishes are perfectly prepared, beautifully presented, and easily devoured. In warm weather, retire to the outside deck and enjoy the smooth sounds of live jazz under the stars. Hours: 6-10 pm. Closed Sun-Wed. Dinner prix fixe: $75. Entertainment: pianist, trio. Reservations required. Cr cds: A, D, ER, MC, V.

★ **GRANO.** *2035 Yonge St (M4S 2A2). Phone 416/440-1986; fax 416/440-1996. www.grano.ca.* Italian menu. Specializes in pasta. Hours: 10 am-11 pm. Closed Sun; major holidays. Reservations accepted. Bar. Lunch $7.95-$13.95, dinner $8.95-$15.95. Outdoor dining. Italian street café ambience. Cr cds: A, D, MC, V.

D

★ ★ **GRAZIE.** *2373 Yonge St (M4P 2C8). Phone 416/488-0822; fax 416/488-0565. www.grazie.ca.* Italian menu. Specializes in pizza, pasta. Hours: noon-11 pm; Fri, Sat to midnight. Closed some major holidays. Reservations accepted. Bar. A la carte entrees: lunch, dinner $7.50-$14. Child's meals. Bistro atmosphere. Cr cds: A, MC, V.

D

★ **GUILD INN.** *201 Guildwood Pkwy (M1E 1P6). Phone 416/261-3331; fax 416/261-5675.* Continental menu. Specialties: rack of lamb, prime rib. Salad bar. Own baking. Hours: 7 am-10 pm; Sun brunch 10:30 am-2:30 pm. Reservations accepted. Bar. Wine list. Breakfast $2.75-$8.50, lunch $6.50-$15.95, dinner $15.90-$29.50. Sun brunch $17.95. Child's meals. Garden setting in former artist's colony. Cr cds: A, MC, V.

D

★ **HAPPY SEVEN.** *358 Spadina Ave (M5T 2G4). Phone 416/971-9820.* Chinese menu. Hours: 11:30-5 am. Dinner $7.95-$12.95. Bar to 2 am. Fish, crab, lobster tanks. Cr cds: MC, V.

D

★ ★ ★ **HARVEST CAFE.** *1100 Eglinton Ave E (M3C 1H8). Phone 416/444-2561; fax 416/446-3308. www.innonthepark.ca.* Continental menu. Hours: 6:30 am-11 pm. Breakfast $5-$13, dinner $23.50. Children's menu. Reservations accepted. Valet parking. Cr cds: A, D, DS, ER, MC, V.

D

★ ★ ★ **HEMISPHERES.** *110 Chestnut St (M5G 1R3). Phone 416/599-8000; fax 416/977-9513. www.metropolitan.com.* Located in the chic Metropolitan Hotel in the heart of Toronto (see also THE METROPOLITAN HOTEL), Hemispheres takes on the distinct challenge of offering a menu that blends, as its name suggests, the cultures and cuisines of the Earth's pair of hemispheres. The task is a tough one, as fusion can often turn into failure, but the kitchen at Hemispheres manages to pull it off. Most dishes incorporate an Asian slant but stay true to classic European technique. With intimate lighting and an impressive collection of modern art adorning the buttercup-yellow walls, the contemporary space has a lively energy to it, which may explain why it is perpetually crowded with a stylish, just-shy-of-trendy crowd. In addition to glamorous diners and eclectic fare, Hemispheres boasts one of Toronto's most extensive wine cellars. For a special treat, reserve the private Chef's Table Room and take a peek at the behind-the-scenes magic as the night unfolds. Continental menu. Hours: 6:30 am-10:30 pm. Closed Sun. Reservations accepted. Dinner $12-$48. Children's menu. Cr cds: A, DS, ER, JCB, MC, V.

D

★ ★ **IL POSTO NUOVO.** *148 Yorkville Ave (M5R 1C2). Phone 416/968-0469; fax 416/968-2329. www.ilposto.ca.* Italian menu. Hours: noon-2:30 pm, 6-10:30 pm. Closed Sun; holidays. Dinner $11-$35. Outdoor seating. Cr cds: A, D, DS, MC, V.

D

★ ★ **JACQUES BISTRO DUPARC.** *126-A Cumberland St (M5R 1A6). Phone 416/961-1893; fax 416/486-6445.* Specializes in sweet bread, rack of lamb. Hours: 11:30 am-3 pm, 5-10:30 pm. Closed Sun. Reservations required. Wine, beer. Lunch $10.95-$18.50; dinner $10.95-$26.95. Entertainment. Cr cds: A, C, D, DS, ER, MC, V.

★ ★ ★ **JOSO'S.** *202 Davenport Rd (M5R 1J2). Phone 416/925-1903; fax 416/925-6567.* The walls are covered with the chef's racy art and celebrity pictures at this popular restaurant, which offers a unique but excellent Mediterranean cuisine. Specializes in Italian dishes, seafood. Hours: 11:30 am-2:30 pm, 5:30-11 pm; Sat from 5:30 pm. Closed Sun; some major holidays. Reservations accepted. A la carte entrees: lunch $7-$19, dinner $14-$27. Child's meals. Outdoor dining. Wine cellar. Cr cds: A, D, MC, V.

★ **KALLY'S.** 430 Nugget Ave (M1S 4A4). Phone 416/293-9292; fax 416/293-6854. Specializes in steak, ribs. Salad bar. Hours: 11:30 am-10 pm; Sun 4-9 pm. Closed holidays; also 1st Mon in Aug. Service bar. A la carte entrees: lunch $4.45-$14.95, dinner $8.45-$14.95. Child's meals. Parking. Pyramid-shaped skylights. Cr cds: A, D, DS, ER, MC, V.

D SC

★★★**LA FENICE.** 319 King St W (M5V 1J5). Phone 416/585-2377; fax 416/585-2709. The stark, modern dining room of this downtown Italian restaurant recalls the chic design aesthetic of Milan. Italian menu. Specializes in fresh seafood, pasta. Hours: 11:30 am-2:30 pm, 5:30-10:30 pm; Sat from 5:30 pm. Closed Sun; major holidays. Reservations accepted. Bar to 1 am. Wine list. A la carte entrees: lunch $10.50-$24, dinner $16.50-$26. Sleek Milanese-style trattoria. Near theater district. Cr cds: A, D, DS, MC, V.

★ ★ ★ **LAI WAH HEEN.** 108 Chestnut St (M5G 1R3). Phone 416/977-9899; fax 416/977-8027. www.metropolitan.com/lwh. Lai Wah Heen, meaning "luxurious meeting place", is truly luxurious with its two level dining room featuring black granite, 12-foot ceilings and solarium-style glass wall. Exotic herbs and spices, skillful use of tropical fruits, and seafood dishes of exquisite refinement make for a sumptuous Cantonese menu rich with Pacific Rim flare. For an intimate dinner, dim sum or banquet, Lai Wah Heen delivers a true Hong Kong experience in the heart of Toronto. Hours: 11:30 am-3 pm, 5:30-10:30 pm. Dinner $40-$60. Cantonese menu. Cr cds: A, D, DS, ER, JCB, MC, V.

D

★ **LE PAPILLION.** 16 Church St (M5E 1M1). Phone 416/363-0838. French menu. Specialties: crápes Bretonne, French onion soup. Hours: noon-2:30 pm, 5-10 pm; Fri, Sat to midnight; Sun brunch to 3 pm. Closed Mon. Reservations accepted. Bar. Lunch, dinner $7.75-$18.95. Sun brunch $18. Child's meals. French country kitchen décor. Braille menu. Cr cds: A, D, DS, ER, MC, V.

D

★ **LE PARADIS.** 166 Bedford Rd (M5R 2K9). Phone 416/921-0995; fax 416/921-1585. www.leparadis.com. Dinner menu changes daily. Hours: noon-11 pm; Sat 5:30-11 pm; Mon, Sun 5:30-10 pm. Closed Jan 1, Dec 24, 25. Dinner $11.95-$14.95. Bar. Reservations required Fri, Sat (dinner). Outdoor seating. Cr cds: A, D, MC, V.

★ **MARCHE BCE PLACE.** 42 Yonge St (M5E 1T1). Phone 416/366-8986; fax 416/366-9437. Specialties: Caesar salad, crepes, waffles. Hours: 7:30-2 am; Fri, Sat to 4 am. Lunch $10-$15, dinner $15-$20. Wine list. Entertainment: Latin band, clowns; Tues, Wed, Sun. Children's meals. Reservations accepted. Cr cds: A, C, D, DS, ER, MC, V.

D

★ **MATIGNON.** 51 Ste Nicholas St (M4Y 1W6). Phone 416/921-9226; fax 416/921-2119. Specialties: rack of lamb, duck breast, la darne de saumon aux câpres. Hours: 11:30 am-2:30 pm, 5-10 pm. Reservations accepted. Bar. A la carte entrees: lunch $8.25-$15.95, dinner $13.50-$17.95. French atmosphere. Cr cds: A, MC, V.

★ ★ **MERCER STREET GRILL.** 36 Mercer St (M5V 1H3). Phone 416/599-3399. www.mercerstreetgrill.com. Specializes in lentil-crusted sea bass with jasmine rice papaya mint sambal and light green curry sauce, hand-rolled Belgian chocolate sushi. Hours: 5-10 pm; Fri, Sat to 11 pm. Reservations accepted. Wine list. Dinner $24-$30. Entertainment. Exotic Japanese Garden. Cr cds: A, D, MC, V.

D

★ ★ **MILLCROFT INN.** Phone 519/941-8111; fax 519/941-9192. www.millcroft.com. A restaurant with a substantial reputation for fine dining make any occasion a time to celebrate. Located in Millcroft Inn, this restaurant offers special menus for holidays. Be sure to sample their vintage wines. Continental menu. Hours: 7:30-10 am, noon-2 pm, 6-9 pm; Sat, Sun 8-10:30 am; Sun brunch noon-2:30 pm. Dinner $25-$40. Sun brunch. Bar from 11 am. Restored knitting mill (1881) on the Credit River. Valet parking. Cr cds: A, D, DS, ER, MC, V.

D

★ **MILLER'S COUNTRY FARE.** 5140 Dundas St W (M9A 1C2). Phone 416/234-5050; fax 416/233-6747. Hours: 11 am-10 pm; Fri to 11 pm; Sat 10 am-11 pm; Sat, Sun brunch to 2:30 pm. Closed Dec 25. Dinner Lunch, dinner $6.25-$13.95. Sat, Sun brunch. Bar from 11 am. Children's menu. Cr cds: A, D, ER, MC, V.

D

★ ★ ★ **MISTURA.** 265 Davenport Rd (M5R 1J9). Phone 416/515-0009; fax 416/515-7931. Hours: 5-11 pm. Closed Sun; major holidays; also Victoria Day. Reservations accepted. Italian menu. A la carte entrees: dinner $18.50-$21.75. Specialties: beet risotto, veal chops, turkey breast. Parking. Cr cds: A, C, D, ER, MC, V.

D

★ ★ ★ **NORTH 44 DEGREES.** 2537 Yonge St (M4P 2H9). Phone 416/487-4897www.north44restaurant.com; fax 416/487-2179. Style, serenity, and elegance infuse every aspect of North 44 Degrees. From the recently renovated loftlike dining room awash in muted, sandy tones to the world-class New Continental cuisine created nightly by chef-owner Mark McEwan, North 44 Degrees is a sublime and sexy dining experience. A sophisticated crowd fills the restaurant, named for the city's latitude, on most nights, happily gathering in this airy space to dine on inventive and beautiful culinary creations. From behind the stoves, McEwan enlists the finest local produce, fish, poultry, and meats to support his cross-cultural menu, expertly blending the bright flavors of Asia with those of Italy, France, and Canada. The service is smooth, refined, and in perfect harmony with the cool space and stellar cuisine. Continental menu. Hours: 5-11 pm. Closed Sun; holidays. Reservations accepted. Bar. Dinner $14.95-$39.95. Entertainment Wed-Sat. Valet parking available. Cr cds: A, D, MC, V.

D

★ ★ **OLD MILL.** *21 Old Mill Rd (M8X 1G5). Phone 416/236-2641; toll-free 866/653-6455; fax 416/236-2749. www.oldmilltoronto.com.* Continental menu. Hours: noon-2:30 pm, 3-5 pm, 5:30-10 pm; Sat 5:30-11 pm; Sun 5:30-9 pm; Sun brunch 10:30 am-2:30 pm. Closed Dec 24. Dinner $29-$43. Sun brunch. Bar. Entertainment except Sun. Children's menu. Jacket (dinner). Cover charge (Fri, Sat from 8 pm) $3.50. Cr cds: A, C, DS, ER, JCB, MC, V.

D

★ **OLD SPAGHETTI FACTORY.** *54 The Esplanade (M5E 1A6). Phone 416/864-9761; fax 416/864-0956. www.oldspaghettifactory.net.* Italian menu. Hours: 11:30 am-11 pm; Fri, Sat to midnight. Closed Dec 24. Dinner $8.99-$14.99. Bar. Children's menu. Outdoor seating. Cr cds: A, C, D, DS, ER, MC, V.

D

★ ★ ★ **OPUS.** *37 Prince Arthur Ave (M5R 1B2). Phone 416/921-3105; fax 416/921-9353. www.opusrestaurant.com.* This plush Yorkville restaurant is at the same time elegant, romantic, and filled with the energy of Toronto's powerful and moneyed elite. Continental menu. Hours: 5:30-11:30 pm. Closed Jan 1, Dec 25-27. Dinner $24-$32. Bar to 2 am. Outdoor seating. Cr cds: A, D, ER, MC, V.

★ ★ ★ **ORO.** *45 Elm St (M5G 1H1). Phone 416/597-0155. www.ororestaurant.com.* This restaurant has changed hands and names many times since it opened in 1922 and is famous for its patrons who include Ernest Hemingway and Prime Minister Jean Chretien. The decor is contemporary and elegant as is the food. Hours: noon-2 pm, 5-10 pm; Sat 5:30-10 pm. Closed Sun, holidays. Dinner $20-$42. Entertainment. Cr cds: A, D, ER, MC, V.

D ▨

★ ★ ★ **PANGAEA.** *1221 Bay St (M5R 3P5). Phone 416/920-2323; fax 416/920-0002. www.pangaearestaurant. com.* This modern eatery's industrial façade doesn't do its interior space justice. Once guests enter, they'll relish the softer, calming effects of the dining room's vaulted ceiling and exotic floral arrangements. Chef Martin Kouprie creates sophisticated continental cuisine using the wealth of each season's harvest. Tired Bloor St shoppers will find this a great place to break for lunch or tea. Continental menu. Hours: 11:30 am-11:30 pm. Closed Sun; holidays.

Dinner $18-$39. Bar. Skylight ceiling. Cr cds: A, D, DS, ER, MC, V.

D

★ ★ **PASTIS.** *1158 Yonge St (M4W 2L9). Phone 416/928-2212; fax 416/928-1632.* Skilled preparation and artful presentation of the menu is served in a sophisticated bistro environment. This midtown restauant is popular with business professionals and a local favorite among the well-heeled. French cuisine. Hours: 5:30-11 pm. Closed Sun, Mon. Dinner $13-$22. Cr cds: A, D, MC, V. **$$**

D

★ ★ **PIER 4 STOREHOUSE.** *245 Queen's Quay W (M5J 2K9). Phone 416/203-1440; fax 416/203-6292.* Hours: noon-2:30 pm; 4:30 pm-midnight; Sun 11:30-12:30 am. Closed Jan 1, Dec 25. Dinner $16.50-$35.95. Bar. Children's menu. Located at water end of a quay on Toronto Bay. Outdoor seating. Cr cds: A, D, DS, MC, V.

D

★ ★ **PREGO.** *15474 Yonge St (L4G 1P2). Phone 905/727-5100; fax 905/727-5103.* Italian menu. Specializes in baked rack of lamb, pasta. Hours: 11:30 am-2:30 pm, 5:30-10:30 pm; Sat from 5:30 pm; Sun 5-9:30 pm. Closed Mon; Jan 1, Good Friday, Dec 25, 26. Reservations accepted. Bar. A la carte entrees: lunch $7.50-$11.95, dinner $9.50-$23.50. Parking. Casual atmosphere. Cr cds: A, ER, MC, V.

D

★ ★ ★ **PROVENCE.** *12 Amelia St (M4X 1A1). Phone 416/924-9901; fax 416/924-9680. www.provencerestaurant.com.* Dining here is like a trip to southern France, enhanced by a full menu of the cuisine of the region. French menu. Hours: noon-1 am; Sat, Sun brunch noon-2 pm. Closed Dec 25. Lunch $9.95-$32, dinner $9.95-$32. Sun brunch. Bar. Cr cds: A, ER, MC, V.

D

★ **QUARTIER.** *2112 Yonge St (M4S 2A5). Phone 416/545-0505; fax 416/545-0506.* French menu. Hours: 11 am-2:30 pm, 5-10:30 pm; early-bird dinner 5-6 pm. Closed most major holidays. Dinner $20-$35. Bar. Reservations required Sat (dinner). Outdoor seating. Cr cds: A, C, D, DS, ER, MC, V.

D

★ **RIVOLI CAFE.** *332 Queen St W (M5V 2A2). Phone 416/596-1908; fax 416/596-7351. www.rivoli.ca.* Asian, Caribbean menu. Hours: 11:30-2 am. Dinner $12-$20. Bar. Outdoor seating. Totally nonsmoking. Adjacent club offers comedy/variety shows evenings. Cr cds: A, MC, V.

D

★ ★ **RODNEY'S OYSTER HOUSE.** *469 kingstreet w toronto (M5V 1V4). Phone 416/363-8105; fax 416/363-6638. www.rodneysoysterhouse.com.* Specializes in oysters, mollusks. Hours: 11:30-1 am. Closed Sun. Reservations required. Wine, beer. Lunch, dinner $6.50-$30. Entertainment. Cr cds: A, C, D, DS, ER, MC, V.

🖼

★ **THE ROSEDALE DINER.** *1164 Yonge St (M4W 2L9). Phone 416/923-3122. www.zeygezunt.com.* Hours: 11:30 am-midnight; Sat 11-1 am; Sun 11 am-11 pm; Sat, Sun brunch 11 am-3:30 pm. Closed Easter, Dec 25. Reservations accepted. Eclectic menu. Bar. A la carte entrees: lunch $9.50-$15, dinner $10-$28. Sat, Sun brunch $6.95-$15. Child's meals. Specialties: herb-crusted rack of lamb, fresh saffron spaghettini, slow-roasted chicken Dijonaise. Street parking. Outdoor dining. 1940s décor and music. Cr cds: A, D, DS, MC, V.

★ ★ **ROSEWATER SUPPER CLUB.** *19 Toronto St (M5C 2R1). Phone 416/214-5888; fax 416/214-2412. www.libertygroup.com.* This decadent restaurant-cum-nightclub is a 3-level extravaganza, complete with a three-story mosaic waterfall, cigar lounge, pool table, Persian carpets. The food and wine compete with the setting and the beautiful crowd for attention. Continental menu. Own baking. Hours: noon-2:30 pm, 5:30-11 pm; Sat from 5:30 pm. Closed Sun; major holidays; also July 1, Dec 26. Reservations accepted. Bar 11:30-2 am. Wine cellar. A la carte entrees: lunch $9.95-$15.95, dinner $19-$32. Pianist. Early 20th-century atmosphere; elaborate Victorian crown moldings and cathedral-style windows. Totally nonsmoking. Cr cds: A, DS, MC, V.

Ⓓ

★ ★ **SARKIS.** *67 Richmond St E (M5C 1N9). Phone 416/214-1337.* Hours: 5:30-10:30 pm; Fri, Sat to 11:30 pm. Closed Sun, holidays. Reservations accepted. Wine list. Dinner $15-$25. Entertainment. Cr cds: A, D, ER, MC, V.

Ⓓ 🖼

★ ★ **SASSAFRAZ.** *100 Cumberland St (M5R 1A6). Phone 416/964-2222; fax 416/964-2402. www.cafesassafraz.com.* French menu. Specialties: Angus strip steak. Hours: 11:30-2 am. Lunch $11-$20, dinner $25-$35. Beer, wine. Reservations accepted. Cr cds: A, ER, MC, V.

Ⓓ

★ ★ ★ ★ **SCARAMOUCHE.** *1 Benvenuto Pl (M4V 2L1). Phone 416/961-8011; fax 416/961-1922. www.toronto.com.* Up on a hillside overlooking the dazzling downtown lights, Scaramouche is the perfect hideaway for falling in love with food (or your dining companion). This modern, bi-level space is known for its fantastic contemporary French fare and is often jammed with dressed-up, savvy locals. The restaurant is divided between a formal dining room upstairs and a modestly priced pasta bar downstairs. The latter is a casual bistro offering a selection of stunning handmade pastas as well as non-noodle standards like steak frites. The more elegant dining room is where you'll be treated to the restaurant's famed contemporary French fare. While the menu changes seasonally, specialties of the house may include squab, lobster, and filet, plus a coconut cream pie that is as memorable and fantastic as the view. Continental, French menu. Hours: 5:30-10 pm; Sat to 11 pm. Closed Sun; holidays. Dinner $22.75-$36.75. Bar to midnight. Reservations accepted. Free valet parking. Cr cds: A, D, DS, MC, V.

Ⓓ

★ ★ **SENATOR.** *249 Victoria St (M5B 1T8). Phone 416/364-7517; fax 416/364-3784. www.toronto.com/senator.* Specializes in steak, seafood. Hours: 11:30 am-2:30 pm, 5 pm-midnight. Closed Mon; some major holidays. Reservations accepted. Bar. A la carte entrees: lunch $13.95-$19.95, dinner $20.95-$36.95. Parking. 1920s decor; in heart of theatre district. Cr cds: A, D, MC, V.

Ⓓ

★ ★ ★ **SPLENDIDO.** *88 Harbord St (M5S 1G5). Phone 416/929-7788; fax 416/929-3501. www.spendidoonline.com.* Located in the middle of the University of Toronto, this restaurant is a popular pick for parents' weekends when kids get a chance to go out for "real food." Continental menu. Hours: 5-11 pm. Closed Sun, Mon & major holidays. Dinner $20-$40. Bar. Valet parking. Cr cds: A, ER, MC, V.

Ⓓ

★ **SPRING ROLL ON YONGE.** *693 Yonge St (M4Y 2B3). Phone 416/972-7655; fax 416/972-6677. www.springrollsonline.com.* Specialties: seafood. Hours: 11 am-11 pm; Fri, Sat to midnight; Sun noon-11 pm. Lunch $6.95-$8.95, dinner $6.95-$13.95. Beer, wine. Entertainment. Reservations accepted. Cr cds: MC, V.

Ⓓ

★ **SUSHI BISTRO.** *204 Queen St W (M5V 1Z2). Phone 416/971-5315; fax 416/971-9145. www.toronto.com.* Japanese menu. Specialties: shrimp and mushrooms, sushi rolls, sashimi. Hours: noon-2:45 pm, 5-10 pm; Fri, Sat noon-midnight. Closed Sun; major holidays. Reservations accepted. Bar. A la carte entrees: lunch $7.25-$11, dinner $8.50-$18. Child's meals. Traditional Japanese food in modern setting. Cr cds: A, D, DS, MC, V.

Ⓓ

★ ★ **TAKE SUSHI.** *22 Front St W (M5J 1N7). Phone 416/862-1891; fax 416/862-2356.* Japanese menu. Hours: 11:45 am-2:30 pm, 5:30-10:30 pm; Sat 5:30-10:30 pm. Closed Sun; also major holidays. Dinner $20-$30. Cr cds: A, D, JCB, MC, V.

Ⓓ SC

★ **THAI FLAVOUR.** *1554 Avenue Rd (M5M 3X5).* *Phone 416/782-3288.* Thai menu. Specialties: cashew nut chicken, pad Thai, basil shrimp. Hours: 11 am-3 pm, 5-11 pm; Sun 5-10 pm. Closed Jan 1, Dec 25. Reservations accepted. Service bar. A la carte entrees: lunch, dinner $7.45-$9.50. Cr cds: A, D, MC, V.

★ **TIGER LILY'S NOODLE HOUSE.** *257 Queen St W (M5V 1Z4). Phone 416/977-5499; fax 416/535-7839.* Pan-Asian menu. Specializes in home-style egg roll. Hours: 11: 30 am-9 pm; Wed to 10 pm; Thurs-Sat to 11 pm. Closed most major holidays. A la carte entrees: lunch, dinner $7.95-$12.95. Totally nonsmoking. Cr cds: A, MC, V.

D

★ **TOMMY COOKS.** *1911 Eglinton Ave E (M1L 2L6). Phone 416/759-4448; fax 416/759-6760.* Hours: 11 am-midnight; Sat from 4 pm; Sun 4-10 pm; Sun brunch 11 am-2:30 pm. Dinner $7.95-$29.95. Bar to 1 am. Children's menu. Cr cds: A, D, ER, MC, V.

D

★ **TRAPPER'S.** *3479 Yonge St (M4N 2N3). Phone 416/ 482-6211; fax 416/482-6253.* Continental menu. Specializes in fresh fish, steak, pasta. Hours: 11:30 am-2:30 pm, 5-10:30 pm; Sat from 5 pm; Sun 5-9:30 pm. Closed Dec 25. Reservations accepted. Bar. A la carte entrees: lunch $8.50-$11.50, dinner $13.95-$25.95. Child's meals. Casual dining. Cr cds: A, D, DS, MC, V.

D

★ ★ ★ **TRUFFLES.** *21 Avenue Rd (M5R 2G1). Phone 416/964-0411; fax 416/964-8699. www.fourseasons.com.* Filled with light and luxury, Truffles' dining room feels like the parlor room of a fabulous art collector with impeccable taste. Soaring ceilings, rich wood moldings, large bay windows, and deep-chocolate velvet seating set an airy, sophisticated, but minimalist stage for the works of a talented group of local artisans, sculptors, and artists that are on display. Located in the Four Seasons (see also FOUR SEASONS HOTEL TORONTO), Truffles is known for its distinct, stylized brand of modern Provençal-style cuisine. As the name suggests, the coveted mushrooms do indeed show up on the menu; the restaurant's signature dish is spaghettini with Perigord Black Gold and a light truffle froth. Truffles is often the chosen locale for power dinners but is also ideal for intimate conversation. Smooth service and an extensive wine list make Truffles a truly inspired dining event. French cuisine. Hours: 6-11 pm. Dinner a la carte entrees: $28-$40: prix fixe: 5-course $62, 3-course $49. Bar. Reservations required. Cr cds: A, D, DS, MC, V.

D

★ ★ **VANIPHA LANNA.** *471 Eglinton Ave W (M5N 1A7). Phone 416/484-0895; fax 416/484-7415.* Thai menu. Specializes in Northern Thai dishes. Hours: noon-11 pm; Sat to midnight. Closed Sun; most major holidays.

Reservations accepted Fri, Sat. A la carte entrees: lunch $6.25-$9.95; dinner $8.25-$12.50. Thai décor. Totally nonsmoking. Cr cds: A, MC, V.

D

★ ★ **VILLA BORGHESE.** *2995 Bloor St W (M8X 1C1). Phone 416/239-1286; fax 416/245-4870.* Italian menu. Specializes in fresh fish, veal, pepper steak. Own pasta. Hours: noon-midnight; Sat, Sun from 4 pm. Closed Mon; Easter, Dec 25. Reservations accepted. Bar. Lunch $8-$15, dinner $11.95-$23.95. Entertainment. Italian villa décor. Cr cds: A, D, DS, ER, MC, V.

D

★ **XANGO.** *106 John St (M5V 2E1). Phone 416/593-4407; fax 416/593-7184.* South American menu. Specialty: raw fish marinated in lime juice. Hours: 5 pm-2 am. Closed Mon; Dec 24-26. Reservations accepted. Bar. A la carte entrees: dinner $19-$28. Outdoor dining. Converted house with veranda. Cr cds: A, MC, V.

★ ★ **ZACHARY'S.** *950 Dixon Rd (M9W 5N4). Phone 416/675-9444; fax 416/675-4426. www.toronto.com.* If you're looking for superior dining in refined surroundings, look no further. A stunning room with low ceilings and rich colors, this restaurant provides an original, continually changing menu. Chinese menu, Continental menu. Hours: noon-2:30 pm, 6-10 pm; Sat from 6 pm; Sun brunch 11 am-2:30 pm. Dinner $25-$39, Sunday brunch $23.95. Bar 11-1 am. Reservations accepted. Valet parking. Cr cds: A, D, DS, MC, V.

D SC

Windsor, ON (H-5)

5 minutes, 4 miles from Detroit, MI

Pop 192,083 **Elev** 622 ft (190 m) **Area code** 519

Information Convention & Visitors Bureau of Windsor, Essex County and Pelee Island, 333 Riverside Dr W, City Centre Mall, Suite 103, N9A 5K4; 519/255-6530 or 800/265-3633

Web www.city.windsor.on.ca/cvb

Windsor is located at the tip of a peninsula and is linked to Detroit, Michigan by the Ambassador Bridge and the Detroit-Windsor Tunnel. Because of its proximity to the United States, it is often referred to as the Ambassador City. Windsor is also known as the City of Roses for its many beautiful parks. The Sunken Gardens and Rose Gardens in Jackson Park boast more than 500 varieties of roses. Coventry Garden & Peace Fountain has the only fountain floating in international waters. Whatever the nickname, for many people traveling from the United States, Canada begins here. Windsor is a cosmopolitan city, designated a bilingual-bicultural area because of the French influence so much in evidence. Windsor also has a symphony orchestra, theaters, a light opera company, art galleries, nightlife, and all the amenities of a large city. Within its boundaries are 900 acres (364 hectares) of parks giving the city the charm of a rural environment. With easy access to lakes Erie and St. Clair and such pleasure troves as Pelee Island, it is also the major city in Canada's "Sun Parlor," Essex County. Mild climate and beautiful beaches make Windsor an excellent place to visit all year.

What to See and Do

Art Gallery of Windsor. *3100 Howard Ave. Phone 519/969-4494.* Collections consist of Canadian art, including Inuit prints and carvings, with emphasis on Canadian artists from the late 18th-century to the present. Children's gallery; gift shop. (Tues-Sun; closed holidays) **FREE**

Casino Windsor. *377 Riverside Dr E. Phone 519/258-7878; 800/991-7777; fax 519/985-5834.* The casino overlooks the Detroit skyline and is easily accessible from a number of hotels. (Daily)

Colasanti Farms, Ltd. *28 miles (45 kilometers) SE, on Hwy 3 near Ruthven. Phone 519/322-2301.* Over 25 greenhouses with acres of exotic plants; large collection of cacti; farm animals, parrots, and tropical birds; crafts; mini-putt; restaurant. (Daily; closed Jan 1, Dec 25) **FREE**

★ **Coventry Gardens and Peace Fountain.** *Riverside Dr E and Pillette Rd. Phone 519/253-2300.* Riverfront park and floral gardens with 75-ft-high (23-m) floating fountain; a myriad of 3-D water displays with spectacular night illumination (May-Sept, daily). Concessions. (Daily) **FREE**

Fort Malden National Historic Park. *18 miles (29 kilometers) S via City Rd 20, in Amherstburg. Phone 519/736-5416.* Ten-acre (four-hectare) park with remains of fortification, original 1838 barracks, and 1851 pensioner's cottage; visitor and interpretation centers with exhibits. (Daily) Contact PO Box 38, 100 Laird Ave, N9V 2Z2. **$$**

Heritage Village. *20 miles (32 kilometers) SE via ON 3, then 5 miles (8 kilometers) S of Essex on County Rd 23. Phone 519/776-6909.* Historical artifacts and structures on 54 acres (22 hectares). Log cabins (1826 and 1835), railway station (1854), house (1869), church (1885), schoolhouse (1907), barber shop (Circa 1920), general store (1847); transportation museum. Special events. Picnic facilities. **$$**

Jack Miner Bird Sanctuary. *332 Road 3 W. 27 miles (44 kilometers) SE via ON 3 and 29S, 2 miles (3 kilometers) N of Kingsville. Phone 519/733-4034.* Canada geese and other migratory waterfowl; ponds; picnicking; museum. Canada geese "air shows" during peak season (Mar and late Oct-Nov; daily). (Mon-Sat) **FREE**

John Freeman Walls Historic Site & Underground Railroad Museum. *At Puce in Maidstone Township; Hwy 401 E from Windsor to Puce Rd exit N. Phone 519/258-6253.* John Freeman Walls, a fugitive slave from North Carolina, built this log cabin in 1846. It subsequently served as a terminal of the Underground Railroad and the first meeting place of the Puce Baptist Church. It has remained in the possession of Walls's descendants. (May-Oct, by appointment only)

North American Black Historical Museum. *18 miles (29 kilometers) S on City Rd 20, exit Richmond St E, at 227 King St in Amherstburg. Phone 519/736-5433.* Chronicles achievements of black North Americans, many of whom fled the US for freedom in Canada. Permanent exhibits on Underground Railroad; artifacts, archives, genealogical library. (Apr-Nov, Wed-Fri, also Sat and Sun afternoons) **$$**

Park House Museum. *219 Dalhousie St, 18 miles (29 kilometers) S via City Rd 20, on the King's Naval Yard, near Fort Malden in Amherstburg. Phone 519/736-2511.* Solid log, clapboard-sided house (Circa 1795), considered to be oldest house in area. Built in Detroit, moved here in 1799. Restored and furnished as in the 1850s. Demonstrations of tinsmithing; pieces for sale. (June-Aug, daily; rest of year, Tues-Fri and Sun) **$**

Point Pelee National Park. *30 miles (48 kilometers) SE via ON 3, near Leamington. Contact Chief of Visitor Services, Rural Route 1, Leamington, N8H 3V4. Phone 519/322-2365; 519/322-2371 (migration line).* The park is a six-square-miles (16-square-kilometers) tip of the Point Pelee peninsula. Combination dry land and marshland, the park also has a deciduous forest and is situated on two major bird migration flyways. More than 350 species have been sighted in the park. A boardwalk winds through the 2,500 acres (1,011 hectares) of marshland. Fishing, swimming, canoeing; picnicking, trails, and interpretive center, biking (rentals), transit ride (free). (Daily) **$$$**

University of Windsor. *401 Sunset Ave. Phone 519/253-4232.* 16,000 students. On campus is Essex Hall Theatre, featuring seven productions/season (Sept-Mar, fee; box office phone 519/253-4565).

Willistead Manor. *1899 Niagara St, at Kildare Rd. Phone 519/253-2365.* (1906) Restored English Tudor mansion built for Edward Chandler Walker, son of famous distiller Hiram Walker, on 15 acres (6 hectares) of wooded parkland; elegant interiors with hand-carved woodwork; furnished in turn-of-the-century style. (July-Aug, Sun and Wed; Sept-June, first and third Sun of each month) **$$**

Windsor's Community Museum. *254 Pitt St W. Phone 519/253-1812.* Exhibits and collections interpret the history of Windsor and southwestern Ontario. Located in the historic Francois Baby House. (Tues-Sat, also Sun afternoons; closed holidays) **FREE**

Wreck Exploration Tours. *303 Concession 5, Leamington, ON N8H 3V5. Phone 519/326-1566; 888/229-7325.* Exploration of a 130-year-old wreck site. Shoreline cruise; artifact orientation. (May-Oct, reservations required)

Special Events

International Freedom Festival. *Riverside Dr & Ouelette Ave. Phone 519/252-7264.* Two-week joint celebration by Detroit and Windsor with many events, culminating in fireworks display over the river. Phone 519/252-7264. Late June-1st week July.

Leamington Tomato Festival. *Sea Cliff Dr & Erie. Phone 519/326-2878. Leamington. Phone 519/326-2878.* Mid-Aug.

Motels/Motor Lodges

★★ **BEST WESTERN CONTINENTAL INN.** *3345 Huron Church Rd (N9E 4H5). Phone 519/966-5541; fax 519/972-3384. www.bestwestern.com.* 71 rooms, 2 story. S $66-$76; D $70-$80; each additional $6-$10; under 12 free. TV; cable (premium), VCR available. Heated pool. Restaurant 7 am-10 pm. Room service. Check-out 11 am. Meeting rooms. Cr cds: A, C, D, DS, ER, MC, V.

⌁ ⌁ SC

★ **COMFORT INN.** *1100 Richmond St (N7M 5J5). Phone 519/352-5500; fax 519/352-2520. www.comfortinn.com.* 81 rooms, 2 story. May-Sept: S $57-$95; D $65-$105; each additional $4; under 19 free; weekend rates; lower rates rest of year. Crib free. Pet accepted. TV; cable. Complimentary coffee in lobby. Restaurant adjacent 9 am-10 pm. Check-out 11 am. Cr cds: A, C, D, DS, ER, JCB, MC, V.

D ⌁ ⌁ SC

★★ **MARQUIS PLAZA.** *2530 Ouellette Ave (N8X 1L7). Phone 519/966-1860; fax 519/966-6619. www.royalmarquis.com.* 97 rooms, 2 story. S $48-$150; D $60; each additional $5; suites $90-$150. Crib $5. Pet accepted, some restrictions; $10. TV; cable (premium), VCR available. Check-out noon. Meeting rooms. Cr cds: A, D, ER, MC, V.

D ⌁ ⌁ SC

★★ **ROYAL MARQUIS.** *590 Grand Marais E (N8X 3H4). Phone 519/966-1900; toll-free 800/265-5032; fax 519/966-4689. www.royalmarquis.com.* 99 rooms, 5 story, 14 suites. S $70; D $80; each additional $5; suites $90-$175; under 12 free; weekend rates; higher rates prom. Crib $5. Pet accepted, some restrictions; $10. TV; cable (premium), VCR available. Indoor pool; whirlpool. Supervised children's activities; ages 5-10. Restaurant 6:30 am-10 pm. Room service. Bar; entertainment Thurs-Sun. Check-out noon. Meeting rooms. Valet service. Concierge. Barber, beauty shop. Cross-country ski 5 miles. Exercise equipment; sauna. Luxurious furnishings, atmosphere. Cr cds: A, D, ER, MC, V.

D ⌁ ⌁ ⌁ ⌁ ⌁

★★ **WHEELS INN.** *615 Richmond St (N7M 1R2). Phone 519/351-1100; fax 519/436-5541. www.wheelsinn.com.* 350 rooms, 2-10 story. S, D $102.88-$154.88; each additional $5; suites $188.88-$208.88; under 18 free; lower rates mid-week. Crib free. TV; cable. 2 pools, 1 indoor/outdoor; whirlpools, water slides. Restaurant 7-1 am. Room service 7-11 am, 5 pm-midnight. Bar noon-1 am; entertainment except Sun. Check-out 11:30 am. Convention facilities. Business center. Gift shop. Miniature golf. Exercise room; sauna, steam room. Bowling. Game room. Recreation room. Some balconies. Resort atmosphere; more than 7 acres of indoor facilities. Atrium. Cr cds: A, C, D, DS, ER, JCB, MC, V.

D ⌁ ⌁ ⌁ SC ⌁

Hotels

★★★ **HILTON WINDSOR.** *277 Riverside Dr W (N9A 5K4). Phone 519/973-5555. www.hilton.com.* 305 rooms, 25 story. S, D $275-$350; under 18 free. Crib available. Check-out noon, check-in 4 pm. TV; cable (premium). In-room modem link. Minibars; many refrigerators in suites. Restaurant 6:30 am-10 pm. Bar to midnight. Exercise equipment. Indoor pool, whirlpool. Meeting rooms, business center. Concierge. Cr cds: A, D, DS, ER, MC, V.

D ⌁ ⌁ ⌁ ⌁

★★ **RADISSON.** *333 Riverside Dr W (N9A 5K4). Phone 519/977-9777; toll-free 800/267-9777; fax 519/977-1411. www.radisson.com.* Located on the waterfront, this hotel offers a spectacular view of the Detroit skyline. The location is near many attractions. 207 rooms, 19 story. S, D $95; under 12 free. Crib free. Pet accepted, some restrictions. Garage available. TV; cable (premium). Indoor pool; whirlpool. Complimentary full breakfast. Restaurant nearby. Check-out noon. Meeting rooms. In-room modem link. Exercise equipment; saunas. Minibars. Cr cds: A, C, D, DS, ER, JCB, MC, V.

D ⌁ ⌁ ⌁ ⌁ SC

Restaurants

★★ **CHATHAM STREET GRILL.** *149 Chatham St W (N9A 5M7). Phone 519/256-2555; fax 519/256-0346.* Specializes in fresh seafood, certified Angus beef. Hours: 11:30 am-midnight; Sat from noon; Sun 5-11 pm. Closed major holidays; Good Friday. Lunch $5.95-$13.95, dinner $14.95-$24.95. Bar. Reservations accepted. Cr cds: A, C, D, ER, MC, V.

★★ **COOK SHOP.** *683 Ouellette Ave (N9A 4J4). Phone 519/254-3377.* Italian, continental menu. Specializes in pasta, steak, rack of lamb. Hours: 5-10 pm; Fri, Sat to midnight. Closed Mon; Dec 24, 25; also Aug. Reservations required. Service bar. Dinner $7.65-$16.85. Parking. Cr cds: A, MC, V.

★ ★ **PASTA SHOP.** *683 Ouellette Ave (N9A 4J4).* *Phone 519/254-1300.* Italian, continental menu. Specialties: steak Diane, veal scalloppini. Hours: 5-10 pm; Fri, Sat to midnight. Closed Mon; Dec 24, 25; also Aug. Reservations required. Service bar. Dinner $11.50-$16.85. Parking. Open kitchen; intimate dining. Cr cds: A, MC, V.

★ ★ **TOP HAT SUPPER CLUB.** *73 University Ave E (N9A 2Y6). Phone 519/253-4644; fax 519/253-4646.* Specializes in steak, seafood, baby-back ribs. Hours: 11 am-midnight; Fri, Sat to 2 am. Reservations accepted. Bar. Lunch $4-$10, dinner $6.50-$25. Child's meals. Entertainment Fri, Sat. Parking. Fireplace. Family-owned. Cr cds: A, D, MC, V.

D

★ ★ **TUNNEL BAR-B-Q.** *58 Park St E (N9A 3A7). Phone 519/258-3663; fax 519/258-2923. www.tunnel-bar-b-q.com.* Specializes in barbecued ribs, chicken, steak. Hours: 8-2 am; Fri, Sat to 4 am. Closed Dec 25. Wine, beer. Breakfast $3.25-$5.95, lunch $4.25-$7.95, dinner $7.45-$18.95. Child's meals. Old English décor. Family-owned. Cr cds: D, MC, V.

D

★★**YE OLDE STEAK HOUSE.** *46 Chatham St W (N9A 5M6). Phone 519/256-0222; fax 519/256-1311.* Hours: 11:30 am-10 pm; Fri to 11 pm; Sat 4-11 pm: Sun from 4 pm. Closed Jan 1, Good Friday, Dec 25. Dinner $11-$36. Bar to 1 am. Children's menu. Cr cds: A, D, MC, V.

D

Minnesota

Mother of the Mississippi and dotted by more than 4,000 square miles of water surface, Minnesota is not the "land of 10,000 lakes" as it so widely advertises—a recount indicates that the figure is closer to 12,000. Natives of the state may tell you that the lakes were stamped out by the hooves of Paul Bunyan's giant blue ox, "Babe"; geologists say they were created by retreating glaciers during the Ice Age. They are certainly the Minnesota vacationland's prize attraction.

Although Minnesota borders on Canada and is 1,000 miles from either ocean, it is nevertheless a seaboard state thanks to the St. Lawrence Seaway, which makes Duluth, on Lake Superior, an international port and the world's largest inland freshwater port.

Dense forests, vast grain fields, rich pastures, a large open pit iron mine, wilderness parks, outstanding hospitals and universities, high-technology corporations, and a thriving arts community—these are facets of this richly endowed state.

This is the get-away-from-it-all state: you can fish in a lake, canoe along the Canadian border, or search out the Northwest Angle, which is so isolated that until recently it could be reached only by boat or plane. In winter you can ice fish, snowmobile, or ski the hundreds of miles of downhill and cross-country areas. If you are not the outdoor type, there are spectator sports, nightlife, shopping, music, theater, and sightseeing in the Twin Cities (Minneapolis/St Paul).

Explored by Native Americans, fur traders, and missionaries since the dawn of its known history, Minnesota surged ahead on the economic tides of lumber, grain, and ore. The state has 92,000 farms covering 30 million acres; its agricultural production ranks high in sugar beets, butter, turkeys, sweet corn, soybeans, sunflowers, spring wheat, hogs, and peas. Manufacturing is important to Minnesota's economy. It also is a wholesale transportation hub and financial and retailing center of the Upper Midwest.

Population: 4,375,099
Area: 79,548 square miles
Elevation: 602-2,301 feet
Peak: Eagle Mountain (Cook County)
Entered Union: May 11, 1858 (32nd state)
Capital: St. Paul
Motto: Star of the North
Nickname: Gopher State, North Star State
Flower: Pink and White Ladyslipper
Bird: Common Loon
Tree: Norway Pine
Fair: August in St. Paul
Time Zone: Central
Website: www.exploreminnesota.com
Fun Fact: Minnesota has one recreational boat per every six people, more than any other state.

The flags of four nations have flown over Minnesota as it passed through Spanish, French, and British rule, finally becoming part of the United States in segments in 1784, 1803, and 1818. A territory in 1849, Minnesota was admitted as a state less than a decade later. The Dakota (Sioux) War was a turning point in the state's history, claiming the lives of 400 settlers and an unknown number of Native Americans in 1862. It marked the end of Sioux control in the domain they called "the land of the sky-tinted waters." The vast forests poured out seemingly unending streams of lumber and the people spun legends of Paul Bunyan, an enduring part of American folklore. With the first shipment of iron ore in 1884, Minnesota was on its way to a mine-farm-factory future.

When to Go/Climate

This state of lakes and prairieland offers warm summers, cool falls, wet springs, and cold winters.

Calendar Highlights

FEBRUARY

John Beargrease Sled Dog Marathon (*Duluth*). *Phone 218/722-7631.* Approximately 500-miles, 5-day marathon from Duluth to Grand Portage and back. About 20 to 25 mushers compete.

Winter Carnival (*St. Paul*). *Phone 651/223-4700.* Citywide happening, with ice and snow carving; parades, sports events, parties, pageants.

JUNE

Judy Garland Festival (*Grand Rapids*). *Phone 218/ 327-9276 or 800/664-JUDY.* Museum. Discussions and presentations on Judy Garland's life and accomplishments. Viewing of *The Wizard of Oz*, children's activities, gala dinner.

Vikingland Drum Corps Classic (*Alexandria*). *Phone Chamber of Commerce, 320/763-3161 or 800/ 235-9441.* National drum and bugle corps perform in the state's only field show competition.

JULY

Heritagefest (*New Ulm*). *Phone 507/354-8850.* Old World-style celebration highlighting German traditions and culture; music, food, arts and crafts.

Features entertainers from around the area and from Europe.

Laura Ingalls Wilder Pageant (*Tracy*). *Phone 507/ 859-2174.* Celebration of the life of Laura Ingalls Wilder, author of the *Little House* books.

Minneapolis Aquatennial (*Minneapolis*). Parades, aquatic events, sports events, entertainment.

Paul Bunyan Water Carnival (*Bemidji*). *Phone Chamber of Commerce, 218/751-3541 or 800/458-2223.* Water show, parade, fireworks.

AUGUST

Bayfront Blues Festival (*Duluth*). *Phone 218/722-4011.* Three days of nonstop blues performances.

Minnesota State Fair (*St. Paul*). Fairgrounds. *Phone 651/642-2200.* Horse show, kids' days, all-star revue; agricultural exhibitions and contests; more than 1 million visitors each year; 300 acres of attractions.

WE Country Music Fest (*Detroit Lakes*). *Soo Pass Ranch. Phone 218/847-1340 or 800/493-3378.* Three-day event featuring many top country musicians and groups.

AVERAGE HIGH/LOW TEMPERATURES (°F)

International Falls

Jan 12/-10	May 65/40	Sept 64/43
Feb 19/-4	June 73/55	Oct 52/33
Mar 33/11	July 79/55	Nov 33/17
Apr 50/28	Aug 76/52	Dec 17/-2

Minneapolis/St. Paul

Jan 21/3	May 69/48	Sept 71/50
Feb 27/9	June 79/63	Oct 59/39
Mar 39/23	July 84/63	Nov 41/25
Apr 57/36	Aug 81/60	Dec 26/10

Parks and Recreation

Water-related activities, hiking, riding, various other sports, picnicking and visitor centers, as well as camping, are available in many of these areas. A $20 annual permit is required for vehicles entering a state park: good for a calendar year. A $4 daily permit is also available. Permits may be purchased at parks. Camping: $8-$12/night, electric hookup $3 additional; limited to 2 weeks in any one park, and reservations are accepted in all parks. In state forests, camping, backpack, or canoe-in sites are $7/night. There are small fees for other services. Fees subject to change. Parks are open year-round; however, summer facilities vary in their opening and closing dates. All state parks are game refuges; hunting is prohibited. Pets are allowed on leash only. For further info contact Information Center, Minnesota Dept of Natural Resources, 500 Lafayette Rd, St Paul 55155; 651/296-6157 or 888/MINNDNR.

FISHING AND HUNTING

There's every kind of freshwater fishing here. Many of the lakes have more than 50 pounds of game fish per acre; the total catch in the state is as high as 20 million pounds a year. Dip a line for walleye, large or smallmouth bass, crappie, northern pike, muskellunge, brook, brown, rainbow or lake trout, or panfish.

Nonresident fishing license, $34; nonresident family license, $47; nonresident 24-hr license, $8.50; nonresident 3-day license, $21; nonresident 7-day license, $24; trout stamp, $8.50. Nonresident small game license, $61. Fees subject to change. For a more complete summary of hunting, fishing, and trapping regulations contact Dept of Natural Resources, 500 Lafayette Rd, St. Paul 55155-4040. Phone 651/296-6157.

Driving Information

Safety belts are mandatory for all persons in front seat of a vehicle. Children under 12 years must be restrained anywhere in vehicle: ages 4-11 must use a regulation safety belt; under age 4 must be in a federally approved safety seat. Phone 651/282-6558.

INTERSTATE HIGHWAY SYSTEM

The following alphabetical listing of Minnesota towns in this book show that these cities are within 10 miles of the indicated interstate highways. Check a highway map for the nearest exit.

Highway Number	Cities/Towns within ten miles
Interstate 35	Albert Lea, Bloomington, Cloquet, Duluth, Faribault, Hinckley, Lakeville, Minneapolis, Northfield, Owatonna, St. Paul.
Interstate 90	Albert Lea, Austin, Blue Earth, Fairmont, Jackson, Luverne, Rochester, Winona.
Interstate 94	Alexandria, Anoka, Bloomington, Elk River, Fergus Falls, Minneapolis, Moorhead, St. Cloud, St. Paul, Sauk Centre.

Additional Visitor Information

Minnesota travel info is available free from the Minnesota Travel Information Center, 500 Metro Square, 121 7th Pl East, St. Paul 55101. Phone 651/296-5029 or 800/657-3700, for info on special events, recreational activities, and places of interest. Also available are: *Minnesota Guide; Minnesota Explorer,* a free seasonal newspaper with events and attraction info, incl a calendar of events for each season; canoeing, hiking, backpacking, biking, and fishing brochures; a state map and directories to restaurants, accommodations, and campgrounds, as well as regional and community tourism publications.

There are twelve travel info centers at entry points and along several traffic corridors of Minnesota; visitors will find the info provided at these stops very helpful in planning their trip through the area. Their locations are as follows: northbound I-35 at Iowa border; US 53, 10 miles south of Eveleth; I-90 at South Dakota border near Beaver Creek; I-90 at Wisconsin border near La Crescent; US 2, 10 miles east of North Dakota border near Fisher; US 61, 5 miles S of Canadian border near Grand Portage (May-Oct); US 53 in International Falls; I-94 at North Dakota border in Moorhead; I-94 at Wisconsin border near Lakeland; I-35 and US 2W in Duluth; US 59 and MN 60, 5 miles N of Iowa border near Worthington; US 10 S of St Cloud.

MINNESOTA'S RIVER TOWNS

Though the Mississippi River starts far to the northwest of Minneapolis and St. Paul, its most scenic and oft-visited section is found along Highway 61. Drive southeast out of the Twin Cities, tracing the Mississippi River along Minnesota's border with Wisconsin to the southern end of Highway 16. The sights begin in earnest in Hastings, a town started in 1819 and home to some very well-preserved Hudson River Gothic Revival-style residences. The road passes the Cannon River, where travelers can make a pit stop for some fine biking along a multiuse path. Red Wing is a still-thriving old wheat town with excellent bed-and-breakfast inns, hotels, and a theater. Water lovers enjoy little Frontenac State Park, which rests along the shoreline of lake Pepin, the widest spot on the Mississippi River. Wabasha is one of the state's oldest towns; many of its ornate Victorian buildings have been renovated. South of Wabasha, numerous antebellum structures have been lovingly restored and are open for tours. **(Approximately 125 miles)**

EXPLORING THE LAKES AND FORESTS OF THE GREAT NORTH WOODS

Departing from Grand Rapids, this loop route winds through the Chippewa National Forest, along the shores of innumerable lakes (there are over 1,000 in the national forest alone) and through massive stands of sugar maple, pine, oak, and birch. Historically, the vast forests of northern Minnesota have been home to logging camps and lumbermen; more mythically, these are the woods where the legends of Paul Bunyan took root.

From Grand Rapids, drive west on Highway 2 toward Deer River, a logging and agricultural center. Immediately west of town, take Highway 46 northward. The route, designated the Avenue of Pines Scenic Byway, enters the Chippewa National Forest. Wildlife is plentiful throughout the Chippewa National Forest; the highest concentration of breeding eagles in the lower 48 states can be found here. Also watch for black bears, beavers, timber wolves, and white-tailed deer. The lakes are filled with walleye.

Turn at signs for Lake Winnibigoshish and Winnie Dam. The lake—affectionately called Big Winnie—pools the waters of the Mississippi River, and canoeing and rafting the fast-flowing stream are popular activities below Winnie Dam. Campgrounds, swimming beaches and picnic areas line the lake.

North of Winnie Dam, the route enters the corridor of red pines for which the byway is named. Many of the pines along the highway were planted in the 1930s by the Civilian Conservation Corps (the CCC). Cut Foot Sioux Lake is named for a warrior slain in a 1748 battle between the Chippewa and the Sioux. On the shores of the lake are a fish hatchery and a national forest visitor center, with evening naturalist events and exhibits about the flora and fauna of the forest. Adjacent to the center is a historic log ranger station, built in 1908.

Just east of Highway 46, on the shores of Little Cut Foot Sioux Lake, is Turtle Mound, a sacred ritual site for the Native Americans of the area. This turtle-effigy is actually an intaglio, a rare form of "mound" building where the image is sunk in the ground rather than raised above it. The Dakota Sioux constructed the effigy in the 18th century, before the arrival of Europeans to the area. After the Ojibwe people drove the Sioux westward, they adopted the site into their religious observances. A short 1/2-mile trail leads to this curious site, which continues to be used as a place of worship for practitioners of traditional native religion.

North of Squaw Lake, pastures and farms break up the dense forest; at Northome, the byway terminates at Highway 71. Turn west and drive 16 miles to Blackduck, and turn south on Highway 39. In fall this route, locally called the Scenic Highway, is especially beautiful as it cuts through forests of oak, maple, aspen, and birch turned a brilliant mosaic of color by the first frost. Creeks and rivers provide openings in the forest, and you can glimpse black spruce bogs and expansive wetlands occupied by waterfowl, beavers, and songbirds.

Across from Rabideau Lake is Camp Rabideau, a restored CCC camp open to visitors in summer. The camp was built in 1935, and until 1940 it housed hundreds of workers who spent summers planting trees and building roads, ranger stations, fire towers, and other infrastructure projects in Chippewa National Forest. A 1-mile interpretive trail winds through the camp.

The largest lake along this route is Cass Lake. On the lake's south shore is Norway Beach, with a long white-sand swimming beach, four campgrounds, and hiking trails. The interpretive center here offers ranger-led activities in summer and also rents boats. A popular boat excursion is Star Island, unusual because the island has another lake at its center. At Highway 2, turn east and return to Grand Rapids. **(Approximately 150 miles)**

Aitkin (D-3)

See also Brainerd, Deerwood, Onamia

Pop 1,698 **Elev** 1,2901 ft **Area code** 218 **Zip** 56431

Information Aitkin Area Chamber of Commerce, PO Box 127; 218/927-2316

Web www.aitkin.com

Once the bed of Lake Aitkin and since drained by the deep channel of the Mississippi, the city now produces wild rice and other crops. Fishing enthusiasts, bound for one of the hundreds of lakes in Aitkin County, often stop here.

What to See and Do

Mille Lacs Lake. *41334 Shakopee Lake Rd. 14 miles S on US 169. (See ONAMIA)*

Rice Lake National Wildlife Refuge. *State Highway 65. 23 miles E on MN 210, then 5 miles S, off MN 65 near McGregor. Phone 218/768-2402.* An 18,127-acre refuge that includes 4,500-acre Rice Lake; migration and nesting area for ducks and Canada geese along Mississippi Flyway. Walking and auto trails; fishing. Headquarters (Mon-Fri; closed hols). Area (Daily). **FREE**

Savanna Portage State Park. *County Rd 14 & McGregor. 8 miles NE on US 169, then 14 miles E on US 210 to McGregor, then 7 miles N on MN 65, 10 miles NE on County 14. Phone 218/426-3271.* A 15,818-acre wilderness area built around historic portage linking Mississippi River and Lake Superior. Swimming; fishing; boating (electric motors only; rentals), canoeing; hiking; cross-country skiing, snowmobiling; picnicking; camping. Standard fees.

Special Events

Fish House Parade. *Phone 218/927-2316.* Fri after Thanksgiving.

Riverboat Heritage Days. *Phone 218/927-2316.* Third weekend July.

Albert Lea (H-4)

See also Austin, Blue Earth

Settled 1855 **Pop** 18,310 **Elev** 1,299 ft **Area code** 507 **Zip** 56007

Information Albert Lea/Freeborn County Convention & Visitors Bureau, 143 W Clark; 507/373-3938 or 800/345-8414

Web www.freeborncounty.com/alcvb

An important agriculture, manufacturing, and distribution center, Albert Lea bears the name of the officer who surveyed the area. Albert Lea is the seat of Freeborn County.

What to See and Do

Fountain Lake. *Fountain St & Ridge Ave. Phone 507/377-4370.* Numerous parks offer picnicking, hiking, fishing, swimming, and boating.

Freeborn County Historical Museum, Library, and Village. *1031 N Bridge Ave. Phone 507/373-8003.* Restored buildings include schoolhouse, general store, sheriff's office and jail, blacksmith and wagon shops, post office, train depot, church and log cabin. Museum has displays of tools, household items, firefighting equipment, toys, musical instruments. Library specializes in Freeborn County history and genealogy. (May-Sept, Tues-Sat)

Myre-Big Island State Park. *Rt. 3 BOX 33. 3 miles E at junction I-35 & I-90. Phone 507/379-3403.* 1,600 acres. Prairie pothole landscape includes rare white pelicans; hundreds of wildflowers; hiking, cross-country skiing; camping. Standard fees. **$**

Story Lady Doll and Toy Museum. *131 N Broadway Ave. Phone 507/377-1820.* Collection of 400 storybook dolls on display. Every other month museum exhibits uinque dolls from area collectors. Gift shop has collector, designer, and ethnic dolls; puppets; and charms. (Daily; closed hols).

Special Events

Big Island Rendezvous and Festival. *202 N Broadway Ave. Bancroft Bay Park. Phone 507/373-3938 or 800/658-2526.* Reenactment of the fur trade period; bluegrass music; ethnic food. First full weekend Oct.

Freeborn County Fair. *Bridge Ave and Richway Dr. Fairgrounds. Phone 507/373-6965.* Just N of city limits on Bridge St. Entertainment; livestock exhibits; midway. Five days late July or early Aug.

Motels/Motor Lodges

★ **BUDGET HOST.** *2301 E Main St (56007). Phone 507/373-8291; toll-free 800/218-2989; fax 507/373-4043. www.budgethost.com.* 124 rooms, 3 story. S $46-$56; D $59-$69; each additional $5; under 18 free. Crib free. Pet accepted. TV. Indoor pool; wading pool, whirlpool. Restaurant 6:30 am-9:30 pm. Bar 5 pm-midnight, closed Sun; entertainment weekends. Check-out 11 am. Coin laundry. Meeting rooms. Business services available. Sundries. Cross-country ski 1 mile. Exercise equipment; sauna. Game room. Cr cds: A, C, D, DS, MC, V.

⊞ 🐾 🎣 ➳ 🏋 ⊠ **SC**

★ **SUPER 8 MOTEL.** *2019 E Main St (56007). Phone 507/377-0591. www.super8.com.* 60 rooms, 3 story. No elevator. S $38; D $52; each additional $4. Crib $2. Pet accepted. Complimentary coffee in lobby Mon-Fri. Check-out 11 am. TV; cable, VCR available (movies $5). Restaurant adjacent. Cross-country ski 1 mile. Snowmobile trail adjacent. Business services available. Sundries. Cr cds: A, C, D, DS, MC, V.

Alexandria (E-2)

See also Glenwood, Sauk Centre

Settled 1866 **Pop** 7,838 **Elev** 1,400 ft **Area code** 320 **Zip** 56308

Information Chamber of Commerce, 206 Broadway; 320/763-3161 or 800/245-ALEX

Web www.alexandriamn.org

Easy access to hundreds of fish-filled lakes attracts a steady stream of tourists. The city has a manufacturing and trade industry base. Red River fur traders first explored this area, followed by settlers, one of whom gave the city his name.

What to See and Do

Lake Carlos State Park. *2601 County Rd 38 NE. 8 miles N on MN 29, then 2 miles W on County 38. Phone 320/852-7200.* A 1,236-acre park. Swimming, fishing, boat ramp; hiking, bridle trails; ski trails, snowmobiling; picnicking; camping. Sandy shoreline. Standard fees.

Runestone Museum. *206 Broadway. Phone 320/763-3160.* Runic inscriptions on graywacke stone carry a 1362 date, supporting belief of exploration of North America long before Columbus discovered the New World. Found at the roots of a tree in 1898, authenticity of the stone has been the subject of great controversy. Also restored log cabins, farm artifacts, horse-drawn machinery, schoolhouse. (Mon-Sat, also Sun afternoons) Children with adult only. **$$**

Special Events

Ole Oppe Fest. *206 Broadway St. Phone 800/235-9441.* Dunk tanks, face painting, museum tours, street dance. Memorial weekend.

Vikingland Band Festival. *206 Broadway St.* Twenty select high school marching bands compete in state's largest summer marching band competition. Last Sun June.

Vikingland Drum and Bugle Corps Classic. *206 Broadway St. Phone 800/235-9441.* National drum and bugle corps perform in state's only field show competition. June.

Motels/Motor Lodges

★ **AMERICINN MOTEL.** *4520 S Hwy 29 (56308). Phone 320/763-6808; toll-free 800/634-3444; fax 320/763-6808. www.americinn.com.* 53 rooms, 2 story. Memorial Day-Labor Day: S $64.90-$120.90; D $64.90-$140.90; each additional $6; under 12 free; lower rates rest of year. Pet accepted. Complimentary continental breakfast. Check-out 11 am. TV; cable (premium). Restaurant adjacent 6 am-11 pm. Health club privileges. Indoor pool, whirlpool. Cr cds: A, C, D, DS, MC, V.

★ **BEST INN.** *507 W 50th Ave (56308). Phone 320/762-5161; fax 320/762-5337. www.bestinn.com.* 46 rooms, 2 story. May-Aug: S $45.90-$66.90; D $56.90-$66.90; each additional $5; under 18 free; lower rates rest of year. Complimentary continental breakfast. Check-out 11 am. TV; cable (premium). In-room modem link. Restaurant nearby. Indoor pool, whirlpool. Downhill ski 10 miles, cross-country ski 1 mile. Cr cds: A, C, D, DS, ER, MC, V.

★ ★ **HOLIDAY INN.** *5637 MN 29 S (56308). Phone 320/763-6577; toll-free 800/465-4329; fax 320/762-2092. www.holiday-inn.com.* 149 rooms, 2 story. S, D $59-$109; under 18 free. Crib free. Pet accepted. Check-out noon. TV; cable (premium), VCR (movies). In-room modem link. Valet services, free laundry. Restaurant 6 am-10 pm; from 7 am Sat-Mon. Bar 4 pm-1 am, entertainment except Sun. Room service. Exercise equipment, sauna. Recreation room. Indoor pool, wading pool, whirlpool. Meeting rooms, business services. Sundries. Cr cds: A, C, D, DS, JCB, MC, V.

Resort

★ ★ **ARROWWOOD RESORT AND CONFERENCE CENTER.** *2100 Arrowwood Ln (56308). Phone 320/762-1124; fax 320/762-0133. www.radisson.com.* Beautiful sunsets and sparkling waters set the stage for this modern 450-acre resort on Lake Darling. Guests can enjoy horseback riding, swimming, tennis, golf, and much more. 200 rooms, 5 suites, 18 story. June-Sept: S, D $119-$179; each additional $15; suites $209-$269; family, weekly rates; golf plans; lower rates rest of year. Pet accepted, some restrictions; $50 deposit. Check-out noon, check-in after 4 pm. TV; cable (premium), VCR available (movies). In-room modem link. Dining room 6:30 am-10 pm. Bar 11-1 am. Room service. Supervised children's activities (June-Sept). Exercise equipment, sauna. Game room. 2 pools, 1 indoor, whirlpool, poolside service.

Greens fee $25. Indoor/outdoor tennis. Downhill ski 20 miles, cross-country ski adjacent. Boats, launching ramp, dockage, motors, rowboats, canoes, pontoon boats, paddleboats. Jet skis. Waterskiing. Sailboats, nature trails, ice-skating, tobogganing, sleighrides, snowmobiles. Bicycles. Free airport transportation. Cr cds: A, D, DS, MC, V.

Anoka (F-4)

See also Minneapolis, Saint Paul

Settled 1844 **Pop** 17,192 **Elev** 870 ft **Area code** 763

Information Anoka Area Chamber of Commerce, 12 Bridge Square, 55303; 763/421-7130

Web www.anokaareachamber.com

Once rivaling Minneapolis as the metropolitan center of the state, Anoka continues as a thriving industrial city at the confluence of the Mississippi and Rum rivers. A city of parks and playgrounds, Anoka is minutes away from ten well-stocked lakes.

What to See and Do

Anoka County History Center. *2136 3rd Ave N. Phone 763/421-0600.* Built in 1904 as a home and medical office for two doctors. Now it preserves the history of the county. Photographs, artifacts. Tours (fee). (Tues-Fri, afternoons; first Sat of each month, mornings) **$$**

Father Hennepin Stone. *Near mouth of Rum River.* Inscription reads "Father Louis Hennepin—1680"; possibly carved by the Franciscan explorer.

Jonathan Emerson Monument. *City Cemetery.* Old settler inscribed 2,500 words from the Bible and personal philosophy on monument, erected it, and died a year later.

Special Event

Anoka County Suburban Fair. *3203 St Francis Blvd. Phone 763/427-4070.* NTPA Tractor/truck pull, PRCA rodeo, demolition derbies, free entertainment, beer garden. Exhibits and an "old farm place." Last week July.

Restaurant

★ ★ **THE VINEYARD.** *1125 W Main St. Phone 763/427-0959.* American menu. Closed Thanksgiving, Dec 25. Lunch, dinner. Bar. Children's menu. Casual attire. Nonsmoking seating. Cr cds: A, DS, MC, V. **$**

Austin (H-4)

See also Albert Lea, Owatonna

Founded 1856 **Pop** 21,907 **Elev** 1,198 ft **Area code** 507 **Zip** 55912

Information Convention & Visitors Bureau, 104 11th Ave NW; 507/437-4563 or 800/444-5713

Web www.austincvb.com

Named for a pioneer settler, Austin became the county seat after two citizens stole the county records from another contender. The act aroused the voters, who cast their ballots for Austin. The Hormel Institute here, a unit of the Graduate School of the University of Minnesota, does research on fats and oils and their effect on heart disease. Austin's meat and food processing plants are an important industry; livestock, grain, and vegetables from a 100-mile radius are delivered here.

What to See and Do

Austin Fine Arts Center. *1301 18th Ave NW. Phone 507/433-8451.* Features local artists. (Fri-Sun) Oak Park Mall. **FREE**

J.C. Hormel Nature Center. *1304 21st St NE. N off I-90, at 1304 NE 21st St. Phone 507/437-7519.* Located on the former estate of Jay Hormel, the center includes interpretive building (Mon-Sat, also Sun afternoons; closed major holidays); footpaths; woods, pond, streams, meadows; also cross-country skiing in winter, canoeing in summer. (Daily) **FREE**

Mower County Historical Center. *Mower County Fairgrounds. 12th St and 6th Ave SW. Phone 507/437-6082.* Restored buildings include original Hormel building, log cabin, church, depot, country school; also steam locomotive, firefighting equipment and horse-drawn carriages; Native American artifacts; telephone museum; guide service (summer only). (June-Aug, daily; rest of year, by appt) **$$**

Special Events

Mower County Fair. *700 12th Ave SW. Phone 507/437-4561. Fairgrounds, 12th St and 4th Ave SW.* Mid-Aug.

National Barrow Show. *1 Hormel Place. Fairgrounds. Phone 507/437-5306.* Second week Sept.

SpamTown USA Festival/Spam Jam. *329 N Main St. Phone 507/437-4561.* First weekend July.

Motel/Motor Lodge

★ ★ **HOLIDAY INN.** *1701 4th St NW (55912). Phone 507/433-1000; toll-free 800/985-8850; fax 507/433-8749. www.holiday-inn.com.* 121 rooms, 12 suites, 2 story. S $59-$79; D $69-$89; each additional $10; suites $88-$150; under 19 free. Crib available. Pet accepted. TV; cable (premium). Indoor pool; wading pool, whirlpool, poolside service. Complimentary coffee in lobby. Restaurant 6 am-10 pm. Room service. Bar 11-1 am; entertainment Mon-Sat. Check-out 11 am. Coin laundry. Meeting rooms. Business services available. In-room modem link. Airport, train station transportation. Exercise equipment; sauna. Game room. Refrigerator in suites. Cr cds: A, D, DS, JCB, MC, V.

D ⛵ ⛱ ✕ ⊠ SC

Baudette (B-3)

Pop 1,146 **Elev** 1,086 ft **Area code** 218 **Zip** 56623

Information Lake of the Woods Area Tourism Bureau, PO Box 518; 218/634-1174 or 800/382-3474

Web www.lakeofthewoodsmn.com

On the Rainy River, Baudette is the gateway to the waters and thousands of islands of the Lake of the Woods area. Across the border from Ontario, it is an important trade and commerce center for a farm area producing seed potatoes, flax, alfalfa, clover, and small grain crops. It is also a 24-hour port of entry, with a toll-free bridge to Canada. (For Border Crossing Regulations, see MAKING THE MOST OF YOUR TRIP.)

What to See and Do

Lake of the Woods. *12 miles N on MN 172.* This lake is partly in the US, partly in Canada. Noted for fishing, sandy beaches and scenic beauty; more than 2,000 square miles in area, with 14,000 charted islands and 65,000 miles of shoreline. Famous for walleyed pike. Maps of driving tours through lush forests and wildlife areas are available from the Tourism Bureau. Also here is

Zippel Bay State Park. *3684 54th Ave NW. 1 mile W on MN 11 to MN 172, 12 miles N to County 8, then 9 miles W. Phone 218/783-6252.* A 2,946-acre park. Swimming; fishing; boating (ramps). Hiking, snowmobiling. Picnicking. Camping. Beach area. Standard fees.

Lake of the Woods County Museum. *8th Ave SE. Phone 218/634-1200.* Museum of local history. (Late May-Sept, Tues-Sat) **FREE**

Northwest Angle/Islands. A Minnesota peninsula connected to Canada and separated by Lake of the Woods. Fishing. Lodging.

Rainy River. *70 miles from Rainy Lake, flows NW into Lake of the Woods.* Fishing, boating.

Red Lake Wildlife Management Area and Norris Camp. *Phone 218/783-6861.* 285,000 acres. Songbirds, bald eagles, moose, wolves, bears, grouse, deer and waterfowl; hunting permitted in season; blueberry picking; camping (permit required). Norris Camp is a historic CCC camp from the 1930s. **FREE**

Motel/Motor Lodge

★ **WALLEYE INN MOTEL.** *Hwy 11W (56623). Phone 218/634-1550; toll-free 888/634-5944; fax 218/634-1596.* 39 rooms, 2 story. S $35; D $45.50-$52.90; each additional $5; suites $59-$90; under 12 free. Crib $4. TV; cable (premium). Complimentary continental breakfast. Restaurant nearby. Check-out 11 am. Business services available. Health club privileges. Microwaves available. Cr cds: A, DS, MC, V.

D ⊠

Bemidji (C-2)

Settled 1894 **Pop** 11,245 **Elev** 1,350 ft **Area code** 218

Information Convention & Visitors Bureau, PO Box 66, 56619; 218/759-0164 or 800/458-2223

Web www.visitbemidji.com

Northland vacations support this city in a lake and forest area at the foot of Lake Bemidji (beh-MID-jee). Logging and Native American trails, wooded shorelines, and scenic rivers are just a few minutes away. Bemidji started as a trading post, became a lumber boomtown, a dairy and farming center, and is now enjoying the bounty of a new cycle of forest harvests. Once strictly a summer vacation area, Bemidji is host to winter sports enthusiasts, spring anglers, fall hunters, and nature lovers.

What to See and Do

Bemidji State University. *1500 Birchmont Dr NE. Overlooking Diamond Point and Lake Bemidji. Phone 218/755-2040 for appointment and calendar of campus events.* (1919). (5,400 students) Renowned for peat research, music programs, environmental studies, accounting, industrial technology. Guided tours.

Bemidji Tourist Information Center. *MN 197 (Paul Bunyan Dr).* Houses collection of Paul Bunyan tools and artifacts with amusing descriptions. Fireplace of the States has stones from every state (except Alaska and Hawaii) and most Canadian provinces. (Memorial Day-Labor Day, daily; rest of year, Mon-Fri) **FREE** Adjacent is

Paul Bunyan and "Babe". Giant replicas of Paul Bunyan and "Babe," the Blue Ox; one of the most photographed statues in America.

Lake Bemidji State Park. *3401 State Park Rd NE. 6 miles NE off US 71. Phone 218/755-3843.* A 1,688-acre park. Swimming, picnicking, fishing, hiking in a virgin pine forest. Boating (ramp, rentals); cross-country skiing; camping; biking. Naturalist programs. Visitor center. Standard fees.

Special Events

Annual 4th of July Water Carnival. *Phone 218/444-4401.* Water show, parade, fireworks. July 4 weekend.

Beltrami County Fair. *Phone 218/759-1425.* Agricultural exhibits, carnival rides, nightly entertainment. Early Aug.

Paul Bunyan Playhouse. *314 Beltrami Ave NW. Downtown. Phone 218/751-7270.* Plays and musicals; professional casts. Wed-Sun. Reservations advised. Mid-June-mid-Aug.

Motels/Motor Lodges

★ **AMERICINN.** *1200 Paul Bunyan Dr NW (56601). Phone 218/751-3000; toll-free 800/634-3444. www.americinn.com.* 59 rooms, 2 story. June-Sept: S $65-$111, D $71-$125; each additional $6; under 12 free; ski plan; lower rates rest of year. Complimentary continental breakfast. Check-out 11 am. TV; cable (premium). In-room modem link. Restaurant adjacent open 24 hours. Sauna. Indoor pool, whirlpool. Downhill/cross-country ski 18 miles. Cr cds: A, D, DS, MC, V.

D ⬚ ⬚ ⬚ ⬚

★ **BEST WESTERN.** *2420 Paul Bunyan Dr NW (56601). Phone 218/751-0390; fax 218/751-2887. www.bestwestern.com.* 60 rooms, 2 story. July-Labor Day: S $39-$55; D $40-$75; each additional $6; under 18 free; lower rates rest of year. Complimentary continental breakfast. Check-out 11 am. TV; VCR available (movies). Restaurant adjacent open 24 hours. Health club privileges. Indoor pool, whirlpool. Downhill ski 12 miles, cross-country ski 4 miles. Cr cds: A, C, D, DS, JCB, MC, V.

D ⬚ ⬚ ⬚

★ **COMFORT INN.** *3500 Comfort Dr (56619). Phone 218/751-7700; fax 218/751-8742. www.comfortinn.com.* 61 rooms, 18 suites, 2 story. Mid-June-early Sept: S $49; D $59; each additional $5; suites $59-$89; under 19 free; lower rates rest of year. Crib free. Complimentary continental breakfast. Check-out noon. TV; cable, VCR available (movies). In-room modem link. Refrigerator in suites, in-room whirlpool in some suites. Valet services. Restaurant adjacent 6 am-10 pm. Sauna. Indoor pool, whirlpool. Airport transportation. Business services. Sundries. Cr cds: A, C, D, DS, MC, V.

D ⬚ ⬚

★ ★ **NORTHERN INN.** *3600 Moberg Dr NW (56601). Phone 218/751-9500; toll-free 800/667-8485; fax 218/751-8122.* The only full service hotel in Bemidji. Try Gangelhoff's for dinner and every Saturday, the hotel has stand up comedy at The InnProv. 123 rooms, 2 story. Mid-May-Oct: S $59-$69; D $69-$79; each additional $10; suites $130; family rates; lower rates rest of year. Pet accepted. Check-out noon. TV; VCR available (movies). In-room modem link. Restaurant 6 am-10 pm; Fri, Sat to 11 pm. Bar 3 pm-1 am; Sat, Sun from noon. Room service. Exercise equipment, sauna. Game room. Indoor pool, whirlpool, poolside service. Downhill ski 10 miles, cross-country ski 4 miles. Free airport transportation. Cr cds: A, C, D, DS, JCB, MC, V.

D ⬚ ⬚ ⬚ ⬚ ⬚ ⬚

★ **SUPER 8 MOTEL.** *1815 Paul Bunyan Dr NW (56601). Phone 218/751-8481; toll-free 800/800-8000; fax 218/751-8870. www.super8.com.* 101 rooms, 2 story. S $38-$65; D $40-$59; suites $45-$70; each additional $5; under 12 free. Crib free. TV; cable (premium). Complimentary continental breakfast. Restaurant nearby. Check-out 11 am. Business services available. Downhill ski 15 miles; cross-country ski 3 blocks. Whirlpool. Sauna. Cr cds: A, C, D, DS, MC, V.

D ⬚ ⬚ SC

Resort

★ ★ ★ **RUTTGER'S BIRCHMONT LODGE.** *530 Birchmont Beach Rd NE (56601). Phone 218/751-1630; toll-free 888/788-8437; fax 218/751-9519. www.ruttger.com.* This spectacular resort is a perfect vacation spot for all seasons. With sandy beaches, sailing, tennis, snowmobile trails and more, this family-owned paradise has played host to some very high-profile guests including Woodrow Wilson and Malcolm Forbes. In 3-story lodge 28 rooms, 11 kitchen units, 29 (1-4 bedroom) cottages. Fewer units late Sept-early May. Some A/C. No elevator. Late June-mid-Aug: S $66-$69; D $78-$148; MAP available; family rates; package plans; lower rates rest of year. Crib $4. Check-out 11:30 am, check-in after 4:30 pm. TV; cable. In-room modem link. Fireplace in most cabins, some refrigerators. Coin laundry. Dining room (seasonal) 7:30-10:30 am, 11:30 am-2 pm, 5:30-8:30 pm. Bar (seasonal) noon-1 am. Free supervised children's activities (June-Labor Day). Exercise room, sauna. Sports director, social director. 2 pools, 1 indoor, whirlpool, poolside service. 18-hole golf privileges, greens fee $28. Tennis. Downhill ski 15 miles, cross-country ski on site. Boats, motors, boat launch, dockage, sailboats, waterskiing instruction. Airport, bus depot transportation. Meeting rooms, business services. Grocery, package store 4 miles. Screened porches. Indoor, outdoor games. Movies. Cr cds: A, DS, MC, V.

D ⬚ ⬚ ⬚ ⬚ ⬚ ⬚ ⬚

Bloomington (F-4)

See also Minneapolis

Pop 86,335 **Elev** 830 ft **Area code** 952

Information Convention and Visitors Bureau, 7900 International Dr, Suite 990, 55425; 952/858-8500 or 800/346-4289

Web www.bloomingtonmn.org

Bloomington, located south of Minneapolis, is one of the state's largest cities.

City Fun Fact–Bloomington

The Mall of America in Bloomington is the size of 78 football fields–9.5 million square feet.

What to See and Do

★ **Mall of America.** *I-494 exit 24th Ave S, bounded by 81st St, Killebrew Dr, MN 77 and 24th Ave S.* Phone 952/883-8800. A retail/family entertainment complex with more than 500 stores and restaurants. Features Knott's Camp Snoopy, a 7-acre indoor theme park with rides and entertainment; LEGO Imagination Center with giant LEGO models and play areas; Golf Mountain miniature golf course; 14-screen movie complex; Underwater World, a walk-through aquarium. (Daily) Separate fees for activities.

Minnesota Valley National Wildlife Refuge. *3815 E 80th St.* Phone 952/854-5900. One of the only urban wildlife refuges in the nation. A 34-mile corridor of marsh and forest that is home to coyotes, badgers and bald eagles; the refuge offers miles of trails for hiking, biking, horseback riding, and skiing. (Daily)

Minnesota Zoo. *13000 Zoo Blvd. E on I-494, then S on MN 77 in Apple Valley.* Phone 952/432-9000. Simulated natural habitats house 450 species of animals and 2,000 varieties of plants. Includes Discovery Bay, IMAX theater, Minnesota tropics, Ocean and Discovery Trails sections; 1 1/4 miles monorail. (Daily; closed Dec 25) **$$$**

Valleyfair. *1 Valleyfair Dr. 7 miles S on I-35W, then 9 miles W on MN 101 in Shakopee.* Phone 952/445-6500. A 68-acre family amusement park bordering the Minnesota River. More than 75 rides and attractions, including four roller coasters, three water rides, antique carousel and special rides for children. Entertainment: IMAX Theater plus musical shows. (Memorial Day-Labor Day, daily; May and Sept, some weekends) **$$$$**

Special Event

Renaissance Festival. *Hwy 169 S & Hwy 41.* Re-creation of 16th-century Renaissance village celebrating a harvest holiday. Entertainment, ethnic foods, 250 arts and crafts shops, games, equestrian events. Phone 952/445-7361. 7 weekends beginning mid-Aug.

Motels/Motor Lodges

★ **BAYMONT.** *7815 Nicollet Ave (55420).* Phone 952/881-7311; fax 952/881-0604. www.baymontinn.com. 190 rooms, 2 story. No elevator. Complimentary continental breakfast. Check-out noon, check-in 3 pm. TV; cable (premium). In-room modem link. Downhill ski 10 miles, cross-country ski 1/2 mile. Cr cds: A, C, D, DS, MC, V.
🄳 🖾 🖳

★ **HAMPTON INN.** *7740 Flying Cloud Dr (55344).* Phone 952/942-9000; fax 952/942-0725. www.hamptoninn.com. 122 rooms, 3 story. S $69-$79; D $75-$79; under 18 free. Crib free. Complimentary continental breakfast. Check-out noon. TV; cable (premium). In-room modem link. Coffee in rooms. Restaurant nearby. Downhill ski 6 miles, cross-country ski 1 mile. Meeting rooms, business services. Cr cds: A, C, D, DS, MC, V.
🄳 🖾 🖳

★★ **RAMADA INN THUNDERBIRD CONFERENCE CENTER.** *2201 E 78th St (55425).* Phone 952/854-3411; toll-free 800/328-1931; fax 952/854-1183. www.thunderbirdhotel.com. 263 rooms, 2 story. Pet accepted. Check-out 11 am, check-in 3 pm. TV. Restaurant, bar, entertainment, room service. In-house fitness room, sauna. Game room. Indoor pool, outdoor pool, children's pool, whirlpool. Downhill ski 10 miles, cross-country ski 1 mile. Free airport transportation. Business center. Cr cds: A, C, D, DS, ER, JCB, MC, V.
🄳 🖦 🏊 🖾 🍽 🖳 🆂🅲 🏃

★ **RAMADA LIMITED.** *250 N River Ridge Cir (55337).* Phone 952/890-9550; fax 952/890-5161. www.ramada.com. 94 rooms, 30 suites, 2 story. May-Oct: S $69; D $79; each additional $8; suites $99-$280; under 18 free; lower rates rest of year. Check-out noon. TV; cable (premium), VCR available (movies). Bar. Indoor/outdoor pool, whirlpool. Suites decorated in different themes. Cr cds: A, C, D, DS, MC, V.
🄳 🏊 🖳

Hotels

★ **CLARION HOTEL.** *8151 Bridge Rd (55437).* Phone 952/830-1300; toll-free 800/328-7947; fax 952/830-1535. www.thebloomingtonhotel.com. 252 rooms, 18 story. Pet accepted. Check-out 11 am, check-in 3 pm. TV. In-room modem link. Restaurant, bar. Health club privileges, sauna. Game room. Indoor pool, whirlpool. Downhill ski

5 miles, cross-country ski 1 miles. Free airport transportation. Cr cds: A, C, D, DS, JCB, MC, V.

D ● ● ● ✕ ● SC

★ **COMFORT INN.** *1321 E 78th St (55425). Phone 952/854-3400; fax 952/854-2234. www.comfortinnmsp.com.* 273 rooms, 5 story. S, D $79-$129; each additional $7; suites $145; under 17 free. Check-out 11 am, check-in 3 pm. TV; cable (premium). Restaurant, bar. In-house fitness room, health club privileges. Indoor pool. Downhill ski 10 miles, cross-country ski 1 mile. Free airport transportation. Cr cds: A, C, D, DS, ER, JCB, MC, V.

D ● ● ● ✕ ✕ ● SC

★★ **COUNTRY INN & SUITES.** *2221 Killebrew Dr (55425). Phone 952/854-5555; fax 952/854-5564. www.countryinns.com.* 234 rooms, 6 story. Complimentary continental breakfast. Check-out noon, check-in 3 pm. TV; cable (premium). Restaurant, bar. In-house fitness room. Indoor pool, whirlpool. Downhill ski 14 miles, cross-country 1 mile. Free airport transportation. Cr cds: A, C, D, DS, MC, V.

D ● ● ✕ ●

★★ **EMBASSY SUITES.** *7901 34th Ave S (55425). Phone 952/854-1000; fax 952/854-6557. www.embassysuites.com.* Visitors here will appreciate the beauty of the garden atrium with bubbling brooks and waterfalls. Located at the airport, this hotel is a nice retreat for the business traveler. It offers 2-room suites and a host of convenient amenities. 219 rooms, 10 story. S, D $149-$159; each additional $10; under 18 free. Check-out noon, check-in 3 pm. TV; cable (premium). In-room modem link. Restaurant, bar. In-house fitness room, sauna. Indoor pool, whirlpool. Downhill ski 15 miles, cross-country ski 2 miles. Free airport transportation. Business center. Cr cds: A, C, D, DS, JCB, MC, V.

D ● ● ✕ ✕ ● ●

★ **FAIRFIELD INN.** *2401 E 80th St S (55425). Phone 952/858-8475. www.fairfieldinn.com.* 134 rooms, 4 story. Complimentary continental breakfast. Check-out noon, check-in 3 pm. TV; cable (premium). Indoor pool, whirlpool. Downhill ski 15 miles, cross-country ski 1 miles. Cr cds: A, C, D, DS, MC, V.

D ● ● ✕

★ **HAMPTON INN.** *4201 W 80th St. (55437). Phone 952/835-6643; fax 952/835-7217. www.hampton-inn.com.* 135 rooms, 4 story. Complimentary continental breakfast. Check-out noon, check-in 3 pm. TV; cable (premium). In-room modem link. In-house fitness room. Downhill, cross-country ski 2 miles. Free airport transportation. Cr cds: A, C, D, DS, ER, JCB, MC, V.

D ● ✕ ✕ ● SC

★★ **HILTON.** *3800 E 80th St (55425). Phone 952/854-2100; toll-free 800/637-7453; fax 952/854-1039. www.hilton.com.* 300 rooms, 15 story. S, D $150-$225; each additional $20; under 17 free. Pet accepted. Check-out noon, check-in 3 pm. TV; cable (premium), VCR available. Restaurant, bar. In-house fitness room. Indoor pool, whirlpool. Business center. Cr cds: A, C, D, DS, ER, JCB, MC, V.

D ● ● ✕ ✕ ● ●

★★ **HOLIDAY INN.** *1201 W 94th St (55431). Phone 952/884-8211; fax 952/881-5574. www.holiday-inn.com.* 171 rooms, 4 story. S, D $89-$109 under 19 free. Check-out 11 am, check-in 3 pm. TV. In-room modem link. Restaurant, bar, room service. In-house fitness room, sauna. Game room. Indoor pool, whirlpool. Downhill ski 6 miles. Free airport transportation. Business center. Cr cds: A, D, DS, JCB, MC, V.

D ● ● ✕ ● ●

★★★ **MARRIOTT.** *2020 E 79th St (55425). Phone 952/854-7441; fax 952/854-7671. www.marriott.com.* Located just five minutes from the airport, guests will also appreciate that this hotel is adjacent to the famous Mall of America, the largest shopping mall in the country. 473 rooms, 2-5 story. S $69-$175; D $69-$195; under 18 free; weekend rates. Check-out noon, check-in 4 pm. TV; cable (premium). In-room modem link. Restaurant, bar, room service. In-house fitness room. Indoor pool. Free airport transportation. Business center. Luxury level. Cr cds: A, C, D, DS, ER, JCB, MC, V.

D ● ✕ ● ●

★★ **RADISSON HOTEL SOUTH & PLAZA TOWER.** *7800 Normandale Blvd (55439). Phone 952/835-7800; toll-free 800/333-3333; fax 952/893-8419. www.radisson.com/minneapolismn_south.* 565 rooms, 22 story. S $149; D $159; each additional $15; suites $250-$450; under 18 free. Pet accepted. Check-out noon, check-in 3 pm. TV; VCR available. In-room modem link. Restaurant, bar. In-house fitness room, sauna. Indoor pool, whirlpool. Downhil/cross-country ski 2 miles. Airport transportation. Cr cds: A, C, D, DS, ER, JCB, MC, V.

D ● ● ● ✕ ● SC

★★★ **SOFITEL MINNEAPOLIS.** *5601 W 78th St (55439). Phone 952/835-1900; fax 952/835-2696. www.sofitel.com.* 282 rooms, 6 story. S $132-$209; D $132-$229; each additional $15; weekend rates. Pet accepted. Check-out noon, check-in 3 pm. TV; cable (premium), VCR available. In-room modem link. Restaurant, bar. In-house fitness room, massage. Downhill/cross-country ski 1 mile. Valet parking. Airport transportation. Business center. Concierge. Cr cds: A, C, D, JCB, MC, V.

D ● ● ● ✕ ✕ ● ●

★ ★ **WYNDHAM GARDEN HOTEL.** *4460 W 78th St Cir (55435). Phone 952/831-3131; fax 952/831-6372. www.wyndham.com.* 209 rooms, 8 story. S $119-$129; D $129-$139; each additional $10. Check-out noon, check-in 3 pm. TV; cable (premium). In-room modem link. Room service, restaurant, bar. Indoor pool, whirlpool. Downhill/cross-country ski 2 miles. Free airport transportation. Cr cds: A, C, D, DS, ER, JCB, MC, V.

D ⛷ ≋ 🏋 ✈ ⊠ SC

Restaurants

★ ★ **CIAO BELLA.** *3501 Minnesota Dr (55435). Phone 952/841-1000; fax 952/841-9141.* The service, the food (portions are serious) and the bustling bar scene are all draws at this Italian-influenced American restaurant. It's hard to resist the glamorous interior, especially when owner Rick Webb makes certain the philosophy is good, solid fun. Italian menu. Menu changes seasonally. Closed Sun; holidays. Lunch, dinner. Bar. Casual attire. Outdoor seating. Cr cds: A, DS, MC, V. **$$$**

D

★ **DA AFGHAN.** *929 W 80th St (55420). Phone 952/888-5824. www/daafghan.com.* Middle Eastern, Greek menu. Hours: 5-10 pm; Fri, Sat to 11 pm; Sun to 9 pm, closed Mon; Dec 24, 25. Lunch $4.95-$9.95, dinner $8.95-$16. Children's menu. Reservations accepted. Cr cds: A, MC, V.

D

★ **DAVID FONG'S.** *9329 Lyndale Ave S (55420). Phone 952/888-9294. www.davidfongs.com.* Chinese menu. Closed Sun; most major holidays. Lunch, dinner. Bar. Children's menu. Casual attire. Cr cds: A, D, MC, V. **$$**

D

★ ★ ★ **KINCAID'S.** *8400 Normandale Lake Blvd (55437). Phone 952/921-2255; fax 952/921-2252. www. r-u-i.com.* Touted as a fish, chop and steakhouse, this establishment delivers with a menu of well-portioned dishes, such as rock-salt-roasted prime rib. The decor is reminiscent of a turn-of-the-century saloon and service carries on this relaxed, social-center style. Steak menu. Closed Thanksgiving, Dec 25. Lunch, dinner. Bar. Children's menu. Casual attire. Patio dining. Cr cds: A, D, DS, MC, V.

D

★ ★ **LA FOUGASSE.** *5601 W 78th St (55439). Phone 952/835-1900. www.sofitel.com.* French/Mediterranean menu. Lunch, dinner, Sun brunch. Bar. Casual attire. Valet parking available. Outdoor dining. Cr cds: A, C, D, DS, MC, V. **$$**

D

★ **TEJAS.** *3910 W 50th St (55424). Phone 952/926-0800; fax 952/926-8444. www.tejasrestaurant.com.* Southwestern menu. Hours: 11:30 am-10 pm; Fri, Sat to 10:30 pm, closed Sundays. Lunch $5.25-$8.50, dinner $7-$17. Reservations accepted. Patio dining in summer. Totally nonsmoking. Cr cds: A, D, MC, V.

D

Blue Earth (H-3)

See also Albert Lea, Fairmont

Pop 3,745 **Elev** 1,093 ft **Area code** 507 **Zip** 56013

Information Chamber of Commerce, 118 E Sixth St; 507/526-2916

Web www.chamber.blue-earth.mn.us

The city gets its name from the Blue Earth River, which circles the town. The river was given the Native American name "Mahkota" (meaning blue earth) for a blue-black clay found in the high river banks. The town is the birthplace of the ice cream sandwich, and a 55 1/2-foot statue of the Jolly Green Giant stands in Green Giant Park.

What to See and Do

Faribault County Historical Society. *405 E 6th St. (Wakefield House) Phone 507/526-5421.* Maintained as a pioneer home with furnishings depicting life between 1875-1900 (Tues-Sat afternoons; also by appointment). Also 1870 rural school, an original log house, an Episcopal Church (1872), the Etta C. Ross Museum (limited hours), and an antique museum. **FREE**

The Woodland School and Krosch Log House. *N Main St. at jct I-90. Located at Faribault County Fairgrounds. Phone 507/526-5421.* The Woodland School (Circa 1870) is furnished as were 1-room schools in the early 20th century. The Krosch Log House (Circa 1860) was once home to a family of 11 children. Inquire for tours.

Special Events

Citywide Garage Sales. *118 E 6th St. Phone 507/526-2916.* Late Apr.

Faribault County Fair. *Giant Dr and Blue Earth. Fairgrounds. Phone 507/854-3374.* Carnival, 4-H exhibits, entertainment. Fourth week July.

Upper Midwest Woodcarvers and Quilters Expo. *405 E 6th St. Phone 507/526-2916.* Mid-Aug.

Motel/Motor Lodge

★ **SUPER 8 MOTEL.** *1420 Giant Dr (56013). Phone 507/526-7376; toll-free 800/800-8000; fax 507/526-2246. www.super8.com.* 42 rooms. S $59.98; D $60.98; each additional $6; under 12 free. Crib. TV; cable (premium), VCR available. Restaurant adjacent 6 am-10 pm. Check-out 11 am. Meeting rooms. Continental breakfast. Business services available. Gift shop. Whirlpool. Cr cds: A, C, D, DS, MC, V.

D ◹ SC

Brainerd (E-3)

See also Aitkin, Deerwood, Little Falls, Onamia

Founded 1870 **Pop** 12,353 **Elev** 1,231 ft **Area code** 218 **Zip** 56401

Information Brainerd Lakes Area Chamber of Commerce, 124 N 6th St, PO Box 356; 218/829-2838 or 800/450-2838

Web www.explorebrainerdlakes.com

Brainerd calls itself the "hometown of Paul Bunyan" and is the center of lore and legend about the giant lumberjack and his blue ox, Babe. On the Mississippi River at the geographical center of the state, the city was once part of a dense forest used by the Chippewa as a hunting ground and blueberry field. Created by the Northern Pacific Railroad, Brainerd was named for the wife of a railroad official. There are 465 pine-studded, sandy-bottomed lakes within a 25-mile radius and over 180 lodging choices. Golfing, fishing, canoeing, swimming, and water sports are available in the summer; skiing and snowmobiling in the winter.

What to See and Do

Crow Wing County Historical Society Museum. *320 Laurel St, adjacent to Courthouse. Phone 218/829-3268.* Restored sheriff's residence and remodeled jail features exhibits on domestic life, logging, mining and the railroad. Research library. (Mon-Sat; closed holidays) **$$**

Paul Bunyan Amusement Center. *1900 Fairview Rd N. W at junction MN 210, 371. Phone 218/829-6342* (summer only). A 26-foot animated Paul Bunyan, 15-foot Babe, the blue ox; 27 rides in amusement park, lumbering exhibits, trained animals, picnic grounds. 21-hole miniature golf. (Memorial Day-Labor Day, daily) **$$$**

Paul Bunyan State Trail. *State Hwy 371 and Excelsior Rd.* 100-mile recreational trail for joggers, walkers, bikers, hikers, and snowmobilers (rentals avail). Trail passes by six communities, nine rivers, and 21 lakes.

Recreational Areas. *Phone Chamber of Commerce.* Swimming at hundreds of lakes in the area. Also boating, canoe routes, fishing, waterskiing, playground, golf courses, picnicking, hiking, biking, camping; snowmobile and ski trails.

Special Events

Brainerd International Raceway. *4343 Hwy 371 N. 7 miles N on MN 371. Phone 810/249-5530.* Motor racing events. Early May-mid-Aug.

Crow Wing County Fair. *2000 13th St. Phone 218/824-1065.* Amusement rides; livestock; entertainment. Five days early Aug.

Icefest. *Phone 218/829-2838.* Ice sculptures, carving. Bands, races, dance, golf. Second weekend Jan.

Motels/Motor Lodges

★ **COUNTRY INN & SUITES - BAXTER.** *1220 Dellwood Dr N (56401). Phone 218/828-2161; fax 218/825-8419. www.countryinns.com.* 68 rooms, 2 story. Mid-May-Sept: S, D $73-$83; suites $99-$119; under 18 free; higher rates auto races; lower rates rest of year. Pet accepted. Complimentary continental breakfast. Check-out noon. TV; cable (premium), VCR available (movies). In-room modem link. Health club privileges, sauna. Indoor pool, whirlpool. Cross-country ski 1 1/2 miles. Cr cds: A, C, D, DS, MC, V.

D ◹ ⋈ ⋈ ◹

★ **DAYS INN.** *45 N Smiley Rd (56468). Phone 218/963-3500; toll-free 800/329-7466; fax 218/963-4936. www.daysinn.com.* 43 rooms, 2 story. Mid-May-Sept: S $51-$65; D $54-$73; each additional $5; suites $84-$95; under 12 free; higher rates special events; lower rates rest of year. Crib free. Pet accepted; $25 deposit. TV; cable, VCR available (movies). Indoor pool; whirlpool. Complimentary continental breakfast. Restaurant nearby. Check-out 11 am. Coin laundry. Downhill ski 15 miles; cross-country ski 3 blocks. Cr cds: A, C, D, DS, MC, V.

D ◹ ⋈ ⋈ ◹ SC

★ **DAYS INN.** *1630 Fairview Rd (56425). Phone 218/829-0391; fax 218/828-0749. www.daysinn.com.* 60 rooms, 2 story. May-Sept: S $48-$57; D $54-$66; each additional $6; higher rates special events; lower rates rest of year. Crib free. Pet accepted, some restrictions. TV; cable (premium). Complimentary continental breakfast. Restaurant adjacent open 24 hours. Check-out 11 am. Business services available. Downhill ski 15 miles; cross-country ski 1 mile. Cr cds: A, MC, V.

D ◹ ⋈ ⋈ SC

★ **PAUL BUNYAN INN.** *1800 Fairview Rd N (56425). Phone 218/829-3571; toll-free 877/728-6926; fax 218/829-0506. www.paulbunyancenter.com.* 34 rooms, 8 suites. Memorial Day weekend-Labor Day: S $38-$60; D $60-$70; suites $85-$110; lower rates rest of year. Complimentary continental breakfast. Check-out noon. TV; cable (premium). Restaurant adjacent open 24 hours. Sauna. Indoor pool, whirlpool. Downhill ski 15 miles, cross-country ski 1 mile. Paul Bunyan Amusement Center adjacent. Cr cds: A, D, DS, MC, V.

★★ **RAMADA INN.** *2115 S 6th St (56401). Phone 218/ 829-1441; fax 218/829-1444. www.holiday-inn.com.* 150 rooms, 2 story. Mid-May-early Sept: S, D $65-$89; under 18 free; lower rates rest of year. Crib free. Pet accepted. Check-out noon. TV; cable. In-room modem link. Valet services, coin laundry. Restaurant 6 am-2 pm, 5-10 pm, bar 3 pm-1 am. Room service. Sauna. Recreation room. Indoor pool, whirlpool, poolside service. Tennis. Downhill ski 7 miles, cross-country ski 3 miles. Free airport, bus depot transportation. Meeting rooms, business services. Bellhops. Cr cds: A, C, D, DS, JCB, MC, V.

★**SUPER 8 MOTEL.** *501 Edgewood Dr; Hwy 371 N (56425). Phone 218/828-4288; toll-free 800/800-8000. www.super8.com.* 63 rooms, 2 story. S $48; D $56. Crib available. TV; cable (premium). Continental breakfast. Restaurant nearby. Check-out 11 am. Guest laundry. Business services available. Sundries. Downhill ski 13 miles; cross-country ski 1 mile. Game room. Cr cds: A, C, D, DS, MC, V.

Resorts

★★ **CRAGUN'S PINE BEACH LODGE AND CONFERENCE CENTER.** *11000 Cragun's Rd (56401). Phone 218/829-3591; toll-free 800/272-4867; fax 218/ 829-9188.* 285 rooms, 1-2 story, 50 kitchen units. July-Aug and wkends: S, D $139-$187; family, weekly rates; package plans; MAP available; lower rates rest of year. Service charge 15%. Check-out noon, check-in 5 pm. TV. Fireplaces. Restaurant 5:30-9 pm (summer), dining room 6:30-8 pm. Bar 5 pm-1 am, entertainment. Barbecues. Free supervised children's activities (mid-June-mid-Sept); ages 4-12. Exercise equipment, saunas. 2 pools, 1 indoor, whirlpools. Golf privileges. 8 tennis courts, 2 indoor, 6 lighted. Downhill ski 9 miles, cross-country ski on site. Private beaches. Lake excursions. Boats, motors, canoes, sailboats, pontoon boats, snowmobile trails. Airport transportation. Cr cds: A, DS, MC, V.

★★ **GRAND VIEW LODGE.** *23521 Nokomis Ave (56468). Phone 218/963-2234; toll-free 800/432-3788; fax 218/963-0261. www.grandviewlodge.com.* 12 rooms, 65 cottages, 2 story. Mid-June-mid-Aug, MAP: S, D $205-$290; AP, EP available; family, weekly rates; lower rates rest of year. Service charge 15%, no tipping. Check-out 12:30 pm, check-in 4:30 pm. TV; VCR available. Some fireplaces. Dining room 7-10 am, noon-1 pm, 6-9 pm, bar

11:30-1 am. Free supervised children's activities (Memorial Day-Labor Day, daily except Sun); ages 3-12. Game room. Whirlpool, poolside service. 54-hole golf. Outdoor tennis. Cross-country ski on site. Lawn games, bicycles. Boats, motors, canoes, paddle boats, kayaks, pontoon boat. Waterskiing. Water sports. Private beach. Overlooks Gull lake. Airport transportation. Cr cds: A, DS, MC, V.

★★**MADDEN'S ON GULL LAKE.** *11266 Pine Beach Peninsula (56401). Phone 218/829-2811; toll-free 800/642-5363; fax 218/829-6583. www.maddens.com.* As Minnesota's largest resort, it encompasses over 1,000 acres of land. 41 rooms, 3 story. July-late Aug, MAP: $102-$155/person; EP: S, D $81-$284; each additional $30; family, weekly rates; weekly and package plans off-season; lower rates mid-Apr-June, late Aug-mid-Oct. Closed rest of year. Check-out 1 pm, check-in 4:30 pm. TV; VCR available. In-room modem link. Many fireplaces. Dining room (July-Aug) 8 am-6 pm, bar 11-1 am, entertainment. Pizzeria 5:30 pm-1 am. Supervised children's activities (July-mid-Aug); ages 4-12. Exercise equipment, saunas. Game room. 5 pools, 3 indoor; whirlpools, poolside service. 63-hole golf, greens fee $23. Tennis. Lawn games, bicycles. Boats; motors, sailboats, kayaks, water bikes, pontoon boats, rowboats, speedboats. Airport transportation. Movies. Private beaches. On Gull Lake. 2,600-foot airstrip 1/2 mile. Cr cds: A, MC, V.

Restaurants

★**BAR HARBOR SUPPER CLUB.** *8164 Interlaken Rd (56468). Phone 218/963-2568; fax 218/963-2841.* Closed Dec 24, 25. Lunch, dinner. Bar. Entertainment Wed-Sun. Children's menu. Outdoor dining. Cr cds: A, C, D, DS, MC, V. **$$**

★**IVEN'S ON THE BAY.** *5195 N Hwy 371 (56401). Phone 218/829-9872; fax 218/829-6666.* Specialties: fresh seafood, pasta. Hours: 5-9 pm; Fri, Sat to 10 pm; Sun brunch 9:30 am-1:30 pm; early-bird dinner to 5:30 pm, closed some major holidays. Dinner $10.95-$19.75. Sun brunch $6.95-$10.95. Bar. Children's meals. Reservations accepted. Contemporary nautical décor; lakeside dining. Cr cds: A, MC, V.

Burnsville

Restaurant

★**LEEANN CHIN.** *14023 Aladrich Ave S (55337). Phone 952/898-3303. www.leeannchin.com.* Hours: 11:30 am-10 pm; Fri, Sat to 11 pm; Sun, Mon to 9 pm. Closed Memorial Day, Thanksgiving, Dec 25. Reservations accepted. Chinese menu. Bar. Lunch $5-$7, dinner $7-$12. Specialties: Asian tacos, soy-garlic rotisserie chicken. Own noodles. Outdoor dining. Casual, Asian décor. Cr cds: A, D, DS, MC, V.

D

Cloquet (D-4)

See also Duluth

Pop 10,885 **Elev** 1,204 ft **Area code** 218 **Zip** 55720

Information Cloquet Area Chamber of Commerce, 225 Sunnyside Dr, PO Box 426; 218/879-1551 or 800/554-4350

Motel/Motor Lodge

★ **AMERICINN.** *111 Big Lake Rd (55720). Phone 218/879-1231; toll-free 800/634-3444; fax 218/879-2237. www.americinn.com.* 51 rooms, 2 story. S $55; D $64; each additional $4. Pet accepted. Complimentary continental breakfast. Check-out 11 am. TV; cable (premium). Restaurant adjacent open 24 hours. Sauna. Indoor pool, whirlpool. Cr cds: A, C, D, DS, MC, V.

D

Cook (C-4)

Pop 680 **Elev** 1,306 ft **Area code** 218 **Zip** 55723

Information Cook Area Chamber of Commerce, PO Box 296; 800/648-5897

Web www.cookminnesota.com

Almost at the center of the "arrowhead country," Cook provides access to outdoor vacations, serves the logging industry, and is the western gateway to Superior National Forest. A Ranger District office of the forest is located here.

What to See and Do

Lakes. Fishing in this area is excellent for northern pike, panfish, crappie and walleye.

> **Elbow Lake.** *26 Central Ave S. 10 miles N on County 24.* 2,000 acres, 12 islands.

> **Lake Vermilion.** *3068 Vermilion Dr. 5 1/2 miles NE via County 24 or County 78. Phone 218666-2627.*

> **Pelican Lake.** *21 miles N on US 53.* 54 miles of shoreline, 50 islands, sandy beaches; fishing for northern pike and panfish.

Motel/Motor Lodge

★ **NORTH COUNTRY INN.** *4483 US 53 (55771). Phone 218/757-3778; fax 218/757-3116. www.northcountryinn.com.* 12 rooms. May-Sept: S $44.90, D $52.90; each additional $6; under 12 free; lower rates rest of year. Crib free. Pet

accepted. Complimentary coffee in lobby. Check-out 11 am. TV; cable (premium), VCR available. Restaurant nearby. Picnic tables. Cr cds: A, DS, MC, V.

D

Coon Rapids

Restaurant

★★ **SEASONS.** *MN 242 and Foley Blvd (55448). Phone 763/755-4444.* Continental menu. Hours: 11:30 am-2 pm, 5-9 pm; Sun brunch 10 am-1 pm. Lunch $4.25-$7.25, dinner $9.25-$20, Sun brunch $12.95. Bar. Children's menu. Reservations accepted. Totally non-smoking. Cr cds: A, DS, MC, V.

D

Crookston (C-1)

See also Thief River Falls, Grand Forks

Settled 1872 **Pop** 8,119 **Elev** 890 ft **Area code** 218 **Zip** 56716

Information Convention & Visitors Bureau, 118 Fletcher St, PO Box 115; 218/281-4320 or 800/809-5997

Web www.visitcrookston.com

Crookston is the major city of the broad and level Red River valley, carved by glacial Lake Agassiz. A branch of the University of Minnesota is located here.

What to See and Do

Central Park. *N Ash St, on Red Lake River. Phone 218/281-1232.* Playground, picnicking, boat ramp, fishing, canoeing; tent, trailer and RV camping (Mid-May-Oct 1, fee), showers. Indoor swimming pool adjacent. Civic arena, roller skating (May-Oct), ice-skating (Nov-Mar), indoor tennis (Apr-Oct). **$$$**

Polk County Historical Museum. *719 E Robert St. US 2E. Phone 218/281-1038.* Houses several rooms depicting early days of America including an original log cabin, one-room schoolhouse and a building with antique machinery. Also on the premises are a chapel and miniature train exhibit. (Mid-May-mid-Sept, daily; rest of year, by appt) **DONATION**

Special Event

Ox Cart Days. *Phone 800/809-5997.* Third weekend Aug.

Motel/Motor Lodge

★★ **NORTHLAND INN.** *2200 University Ave (56716). Phone 218/281-5210; toll-free 800/423-4541; fax 218/*

281-1019. 74 rooms, 2 story. S $49-$56; D $55-$62; each additional $6. Crib free. Check-out noon. TV; cable (premium). In-room modem link. Restaurant 6:30 am-2 pm, 5-9:30 pm; Fri, Sat to 10 pm, bar 4 pm-1 am. Game room. Indoor pool, whirlpool. Meeting rooms, business services. Sundries. Cr cds: A, D, DS, MC, V.

⬜ 🏊 ⛵ SC

Deer River (C-3)

See also Grand Rapids, Hibbing

Pop 838 **Elev** 1,291 ft **Area Code** 218 **Zip** 56636

Information Chamber of Commerce, PO Box 505; 218/246-8055 or 888/701-2226

Web www.deerriver.org

A harvesting point for lumber products of Chippewa National Forest, Deer River also serves nearby farms as well as hunting and fishing camps. A Ranger District office of the Chippewa National Forest is located here.

What to See and Do

Chippewa National Forest. *200 Ash Ave NW (56633). At W edge of city, access on MN 46. Phone 218/335-8600.* (See Grand Rapids)

Cut Foot Sioux Lakes. *15 miles NW on both sides of MN 46.* Fishing, hunting, camping. Turtle and snake Indian mounds along shore.

Deerwood (D-3)

See also Crosslake

Pop 524 **Elev** 1,079 ft **Area code** 218 **Zip** 56444

Motel/Motor Lodge

★ **COUNTRY INN.** *23884 Front St (56444). Phone 218/534-3101; fax 218/534-3685. www.countryinns.com.* 38 rooms, 2 story. Late May-Aug: S, D $65-$85; each additional $6; under 18 free; lower rates rest of year. Pet accepted, some restrictions. Complimentary continental breakfast. Check-out 11 am. TV; cable (premium), VCR available (movies). Restaurant nearby. Sauna. Game room. Indoor pool, whirlpool. Cross-country ski 1 mile. Cr cds: A, D, DS, ER, JCB, MC, V.

⬜ 🎿 🏊 ⛵

Resort

★ ★ **RUTTGER'S BAY LAKE LODGE.** *25039 Tame Fish Lake Rd (56444). Phone 218/678-2885; toll-free 800/450-4545; fax 218/678-2864. www.ruttgers.com.* Founded in 1898, this rustic lodge is rich with family pride and history. 30 rooms, 2 story. MAP, July-Aug: for 2-6, $122-$155/person; EP $125-$335/day; family rates, package plans; lower rates rest of year. Check-out noon, check-in 5 pm. TV; VCR available (movies). Some fireplaces in kitchen units. Dining room (public by res) 7-10 am, noon-2 pm, 6-8 pm. Bar noon-midnight. Free supervised children's activities (MAP guests mid-June-Labor Day); ages 4-12. Exercise equipment, saunas. Game room. 3 pools, 1 indoor, whirlpools. 27-hole golf, pro. Lawn games. Private beach. Boats, launching ramp, motors; canoes, sailboat, kayaks, paddleboat. Waterskiing instruction. Lodge overlooks lake. Cr cds: A, DS, MC, V.

⬜ 🎿 🏊 🎿 ⛵

Detroit Lakes (D-2)

See also Moorhead, Park Rapids

Pop 6,635 **Elev** 1,365 ft **Area code** 218 **Zip** 56501

Information Detroit Lakes Regional Chamber of Commerce, PO Box 348, 56502; 218/847-9202 or 800/542-3992

Web www.visitdetroitlakes.com

A French missionary visiting this spot more than 200 years ago commented on the beautiful *détroit* (strait), and this came to be the name of the town. "Lakes" was added to promote the 412 lakes found within 25 miles. Tourism and agriculture are major sources of income.

What to See and Do

Becker County Historical Society Museum. *714 Summit Ave. Corner of Summit and W Front, two blocks off US 10. Phone 218/847-2938.* Exhibits pertaining to history of county. (Memorial Day-Labor Day, Tues-Sat; rest of year, Sat-Sun; closed holidays) **FREE**

Detroit Lakes City Park. *Washington Ave & W Lake Dr.* Picnic tables, grills, shelters; tennis courts, lifeguard (Mid-June-Aug), shuffleboard, ball diamonds; playground, boat rentals, fishing. One mi-long beach, bathhouse. Motorboat sightseeing services nearby. Shops. (June-Labor Day, daily) **FREE**

Detroit Mountain Ski Area. *2 miles E, off MN 34. Phone 218/847-1661.* Double and triple chairlifts, two T-bars, four rope tows; patrol, school, rentals, snowmaking; cafeteria. Vertical drop 235 feet. (Mid-Nov-Mar, Fri-Sun) **$$$$**

Tamarac National Wildlife Refuge. *8 miles E on MN 34, then 9 miles N on County 29. Phone 218/847-2641.* On 43,000 acres. Twenty-one lakes, abundant wild rice; trumpeter swans, grouse, beaver, deer; flyway sanctuary for thousands of songbirds, ducks, geese; picnicking, fishing. (Daily) Visitor center (Memorial Day-Labor Day, daily; rest of year, Mon-Fri; closed hols). **FREE**

Special Events

Becker County Fair. *Phone 218/847-9202.* Late Aug.

Festival of Birds. *Phone 218/847-9202.* Three-day migration celebration. Workshop, speakers, displays and guided field trips. Mid-May.

Northwest Water Carnival. *Detroit Lake, throughout city. Phone 218/847-3081.* Includes water show, races, fishing derby, parade, flea markets. Mid-July.

Polar Fest. *Phone 218/817-9202.* Weekend filled with sports, entertainment, polar plunge. Mid-Feb.

WE Country Music Fest. *Soo Pass Ranch, 3 miles S on MN 59.* 3-day event featuring many top country musicians and groups. Phone 218/847-1681. First weekend Aug.

White Earth Powwow. *Phone 218/935-0417.* Celebrates the treaty between the Sioux and Chippewa. Phone 800/542-3992. Mid-June.

Motels/Motor Lodges

★ ★ **HOLIDAY INN.** *1155 US 10 E (56501). Phone 218/847-2121; fax 218/847-2121. www.holiday-inn.com.* 98 rooms, 4 suites, 4 story. Late May-Labor Day: S, D $89-$119; under 18 free; family rates; lower rates rest of year. Crib free. Pet accepted. Check-out noon. TV; cable. In-room modem link. Lakeside rooms with private balconies. Some minibars. Valet service. Coin laundry. Restaurant 6:30 am-10 pm. Bar 11-1 am, entertainment. Room service. Sauna. Recreation room. Indoor pool, whirlpool. Downhill ski 2 miles, cross-country ski on site. Paddleboat rentals. Meeting rooms, business services. Sundries. On lake; 500-foot private beach, dockage. Cr cds: A, C, D, DS, JCB, MC, V.

D 🐾 ⌘ 🏊 🏌 SC

★ **SUPER 8 MOTEL.** *400 Morrow Ave (56501). Phone 218/847-1651; toll-free 800/800-8000; fax 218/847-1651. www.super8.com.* 39 rooms, 2 story. S $37.88-$43.88; D $42.88-$52.88; each additional $4; under 13 free. Crib free. TV; cable. Complimentary coffee in lobby. Restaurant adjacent open 24 hours. Check-out 11 am. Business services available. Downhill/cross-country ski 5 miles. Cr cds: A, C, D, DS, MC, V.

D ⌘ 🏊 SC

Resort

★ ★ **FAIR HILLS.** *24270 County Hwy 20 (56501). Phone 218/532-2222; toll-free 800/323-2849; fax 218/532-2068. www.fairhillsresort.com.* With endless fun-filled activities, it's no wonder this is a very popular resort for family vacations. From talent shows, the famous Hootenanny, an old-fashioned soda fountain, water sports, golf, and more, the memories will be a treasure for all. 100 rooms. Late June-mid-Aug, AP: weekly, S, D $634 each; kitchen cabins; EP: weekly $542-$1,554; family rates; varied lower rates mid-May-late June, mid-Aug-late Sept. Closed rest of year. Service charge 15%. Check-out noon, check-in 4. Some fireplaces. Dining room (public by res) 8-9 am, noon-1 pm, 5:30-7 pm. Free supervised children's activities (mid-June-mid Aug); ages 4-14. Children's pool, whirlpool. 27-hole golf. Tennis. Recreation dirs. Indoor, outdoor games. Waterskiing, instruction; boats, motors, canoes, sailboats, water bikes, windsurfing; launching ramp, dockage. Airport transportation. Private beach. On Pelican Lake. Cr cds: A, D, DS, MC, V.

D 🍴 🏌 ⌘ ✈ 🏊

Restaurants

★ ★ **FIRESIDE.** *1462 E Shore Dr (56501). Phone 218/847-8192.* Specialties: charcoal-grilled steak, barbecued ribs, seafood. Hours: 5:30-10:30 pm; days vary off-season. Closed late Nov-Mar. Dinner $7.95-$16.75. Family-owned. Children's meals. Open charcoal grill. Fireplace. Overlooks Big Detroit Lake. Cr cds: A, D, DS, MC, V.

D

★ **LAKESIDE.** *200 W Lake Dr (56501). Phone 218/847-7887; fax 215/847-7887.* Closed most major holidays. Dinner, Sun brunch. Bar. Children's menu. Former hotel built in 1891. Outdoor dining. Cr cds: DS, MC, V.

D

Duluth (D-5)

Founded 1856 **Pop** 85,493 **Elev** 620 ft **Area code** 218

Information Convention & Visitors Bureau, 100 Lake Place Dr, 55802; 218/722-4011 or 800/4-DULUTH

Web www.visitduluth.com

At the western tip of Lake Superior, Duluth is a world port thanks to the St Lawrence Seaway. Ships of many countries fly their flags at its 49 miles of docks. This gives the products of Minnesota and the Northwestern states better access to markets of the world and stimulates development of new industries converting raw materials to finished goods. One of the foremost grain exporting ports in the nation, Duluth-Superior Harbor also handles iron ore, coal, limestone, petroleum products, cement, molasses, salt, grain, soybean oil, soybeans, wood pulp, paper, and chemicals. The twin ports are the westernmost water terminus for goods consigned to the Northwest.

High bluffs rise from the lakeshore, protecting the harbor from the elements. Minnesota Point, a sandbar extending 7 miles from Minnesota to the Wisconsin shore, protects the inner harbor.

There are two ways for ships to enter the Duluth-Superior Harbor: one by way of the Superior side, called the Superior Entry; and the other, the Duluth Ship Canal, with an aerial lift bridge located a few blocks south of downtown Duluth. The distance between the two is about 8 miles.

As the state's gateway to the sea, Duluth is a business, industrial, cultural, recreational, and vacation center. The great Minnesota northwoods begin almost at the city's boundaries. From here the North Shore Drive (see GRAND MARAIS) follows Lake Superior into Canada; other highways fan out to the lake country, the great forests, and south to the Twin Cities. The headquarters of the Superior National Forest is located here.

Long a fur trading post, Duluth is the city of early voyageurs, Chippewa, and French and British explorers. The first major shipment from the twin ports of Duluth and Superior was 60 canoe loads of furs in 1660. Modern commerce started in 1855 following construction of the lock at Sault Ste. Marie, Michigan, the eastern entrance to Lake Superior. The French explorer Daniel Greysolon, Sieur du Lhut, landed here in 1679. The city takes its name from him.

What to See and Do

Aerial Lift Bridge. *525 Lake Ave S. Foot of Lake Ave. Phone 218/722-3119.* (138-feet high, 336-feet long, 900 tons in weight). Connects mainland with Minnesota Point, lifting 138 ft in less than a minute to let ships through.

⭐ **The Depot, St. Louis County Heritage and Arts Center.** *506 W Michigan St. Phone 218/727-8025.* Building was originally Union Depot (1890); houses three museums, a visual arts institute, and four performing arts organizations. (Daily, closed holidays) **$$$** Admission includes

> **Duluth Children's Museum.** *Phone 218/733-7543.* Natural, world, and cultural history; featuring giant walk-through tree in habitat exhibit.

> **Depot Square.** *(Lower level)* Reproduction of 1910 Duluth street scene with ice cream parlor, storefronts, gift shops, trolley rides.

> **Lake Superior Railroad Museum.** Extensive displays of historic railroad equipment and memorabilia. Trolley car rides and periodical excursions, some using steam locomotives.

> **St. Louis County Historical Society.** *Phone 218/733-7580.* Settlement of northern Minnesota; logging, mining, railroading, and pioneer life exhibits.

Duluth-Superior Excursions. *323 Harbor Dr (55802). Foot of 5th Ave W and waterfront. Phone 218/722-6218.* Two-hr tour of Duluth-Superior Harbor and Lake Superior on the Vista King and Star. (Mid-May-mid-Oct, daily) Also dinner and dance cruises. **$$$**

Enger Tower. *On Skyline Dr at 18th Ave W.* Tower providing best view of Duluth-Superior; dedicated in 1939 by Norway's King Olav V, then Crown Prince; dwarf conifer and Japanese gardens, picnic tables on grounds. **FREE**

Fitger's Brewery Complex. *600 E Superior St. Phone 218/722-8826.* Historic renovated brewery transformed into more than 25 specialty shops and restaurants on the shore of Lake Superior. Summer courtyard activities. (Daily; closed Jan 1, Easter, Thanksgiving, Dec 25) From here take

> **Duluth Lakewalk.** *Phone 800/4-DULUTH.* Walk along Lake Superior to the Aerial Lift Bridge; statues, kiosks; horse and buggy rides. **FREE**

Glensheen. *3300 London Rd. Phone 218/726-8910 (recording) or 218/724-8864.* (Circa 1905-1908). Historic 22-acre Great Lake estate on W shore of Lake Superior; owned by University of Minnesota. Tours. Grounds (Daily). Mansion (May-Oct, daily; rest of year, wkends; closed hols). **$$$**

Jay Cooke State Park. *500 MN 210 E. SW via MN 23, 210, adjoining gorge of St. Louis River. Phone 218/384-4610.* Located on 8,813 acres of rugged country; fishing; cross-country skiing, snowmobiling; picnicking; camping (electric hookups, dump station); visitor center. Standard fees.

Karpeles Manuscript Library Museum. *902 E 1st St. Phone 218/727-3967.* Holds original drafts of US Bill of Rights, Emancipation Proclamation, Handel's Messiah, and others. (June-Aug, daily; rest of year, Tues-Sun) **FREE**

Lake Superior Maritime Visitors Center. *600 Lake Ave S. Canal Park Dr next to Aerial Bridge. Phone 218/727-2497.* Ship models, relics of shipwrecks, reconstructed ship cabins; exhibits related to maritime history of Lake Superior and Duluth Harbor and the Corps of Engineers. Vessel schedules and close-up views of passing ship traffic. (Apr-mid-Dec, daily; rest of year, Fri-Sun; closed Jan 1, Thanksgiving, Dec 25) **FREE**

Lake Superior Zoological Gardens. *7210 Fremont St. Phone 218/723-3748.* 12-acre zoo with more than 80 exhibits; picnicking. (Daily) **$$$**

Leif Erikson Park. *11th Ave E and London Rd. Phone 218/723-3377.* Statue of Norwegian explorer and half-size replica of boat he sailed to America in A.D. 997. Rose Garden. (May-mid-Sept, daily) **FREE**

North Shore Scenic Railroad. *Departs from the Depot, 506 W Michigan St. Phone 218/722-1273 or 800/423-1273.* Narrated sightseeing trips along 28 miles of Lake Superior's scenic North Shore, from Duluth to Two Harbors. Other excursions avail: Duluth to Lester River, Pizza Train. Trips range from 1 1/2-6 hours. (Apr-Oct, daily) **$$$**

Park Point Recreation Center. *At tip of Minnesota Point.* 200-acre playground; picnicking; boat ramp; swimming facilities, lifeguard. (June-Labor Day, daily) **FREE**

Scenic North Shore Drive. *MN 61 from Duluth to Canada along Lake Superior.*

Site of Fond du Lac. *On St. Louis River.* Originally a Native American village, later a trading post; school, mission established here in 1834.

Skyline Parkway Drive. A 27-mile scenic road along bluffs of city constructed during 1930s; view from 600 feet overlooks harbor, lake, bay and river.

Spirit Mountain Ski Area. *9500 Spirit Mountain Pl. 10 miles S on I-35, exit 249. Phone 218/628-2891; 800/642-6377.* Two quad, two triple, double chairlifts; patrol, school, rentals, snowmaking; bar, cafeteria; children's center. Twenty-four runs, longest run 5,400 feet; vertical drop 700 feet. (Nov-Mar, daily) Half-day rates. Snowboarding; tubing. Cross-country trails (Dec-Apr, daily) **$$$$**

S/S *William A. Irvin*. *350 Harbor Dr; on the waterfront, adjacent to Duluth Convention Center. Phone 218/722-5573.* Guided tours of former flagship of United States Steel's Great Lakes fleet that journeyed inland waters from 1938-1978. Explore decks and compartments of restored 610-foot ore carrier, including the engine room, elaborate guest staterooms, galley, pilothouse, observation lounge, elegant dining room. Free parking. **$$$**

University of Minnesota, Duluth. *10 University Dr. 10 University Dr. Phone 218/726-8000.* (1902). (7,800 students) On campus are

Marshall W. Alworth Planetarium. *10 University Dr. Phone 218/726-7129.* Shows (Wed; closed holidays). **FREE**

Tweed Museum of Art. *Phone 218/726-8222.* Exhibits of 19th- and 20th-century paintings; contemporary works. (Tues-Sun; closed holidays) **DONATION**

Special Events

Bayfront Blues Festival. *Commerce St & Canal Park Dr. Phone 715/722-4011.* Early Aug.

International Folk Festival. *11th Ave & London Rd. Leif Erikson Park. Phone 218/722-7425.* Folk music, dancing, crafts, foods. First Sat Aug.

John Beargrease Sled Dog Marathon. *218 W Superior St. Phone 218/722-7631.* Mid-Jan.

Motels/Motor Lodges

★ **ALLYNDALE MOTEL.** *510 N 66th Ave W (55807). Phone 218/628-1061; toll-free 800/341-8000.* 21 rooms.

Mid-Apr-mid-Oct: S $38; D $43-$48; each additional $5; lower rates rest of year. Crib $5. Pet accepted, some restrictions; $5. TV; cable. Playground. Complimentary coffee. Restaurant nearby. Check-out 11 am. Downhill/cross-country ski 1 1/2 miles. Refrigerators, microwaves. Picnic tables. Cr cds: A, C, D, DS, MC, V.

★ **BEST WESTERN EDGEWATER.** *2400 London Rd (55812). Phone 218/728-3601; toll-free 800/777-7925; fax 218/728-3727. www.bestwestern.com.* 282 rooms, 5 story. June-mid-Oct: S $59-$99, D $69-$139; each additional $6; suites $98-$169; under 18 free; ski plans; lower rates rest of year. Pet accepted, some restrictions. Complimentary continental breakfast. Check-out noon. TV; cable (premium). Restaurant adj. Exercise equipment, sauna. Game room. Indoor pool, whirlpool. Downhill ski 7 miles, cross-country ski 1 mile. Miniature golf. Lawn games. Business center. Cr cds: A, C, D, DS, ER, JCB, MC, V.

★ **COMFORT INN.** *3900 W Superior St (55807). Phone 218/628-1464; toll-free 800/228-5151; fax 218/624-7263. www.comfortinn.com.* 81 rooms, 2 story, 10 kitchen units. May-Oct: S $61; D $72; each additional $5; suites $108; kitchen units (no equipment) $82; under 18 free; lower rates rest of year (except weekends). Crib free. TV; cable (premium). Indoor pool; whirlpool. Complimentary continental breakfast. Restaurant adjacent open 24 hours. Check-out 11 am. Coin laundry. Meeting room. Business services available. Sauna. Microwaves available. Cr cds: A, C, D, DS, JCB, MC, V.

★ **COMFORT SUITES.** *408 Canal Park Dr (55802). Phone 218/727-1378; toll-free 800/228-5151; fax 218/727-1947. www.comfortinn.com.* 82 rooms, 3 story. Early June-Sept: S, D $105-$115; suites $155; under 18 free; higher rates special events; lower rates rest of year. Complimentary continental breakfast. Check-out 11 am. TV; cable (premium). In-room modem link. Laundry services. Restaurant adjacent 8 am-11 pm. Indoor pool; whirlpools. Downhill/cross-country ski 5 miles. Cr cds: A, C, D, DS, JCB, MC, V.

★ **DAYS INN.** *909 Cottonwood Ave (55811). Phone 218/727-3110; fax 218/727-3110. www.daysinn.com.* 86 rooms, 2-3 story. No elevator. June-mid-Oct: S $59-$82; D $68-$82; each additional $6; higher rates special events; lower rates rest of year. Crib free. Pet accepted. Complimentary continental breakfast. Check-out noon. TV; cable (premium), VCR available. Restaurant opposite open 24 hours. Business services available. Cr cds: A, C, D, DS, ER, JCB, MC, V.

★ **SUPER 8 MOTEL.** *4100 W Superior St (55807). Phone 218/628-2241; fax 218/628-2241. www.duluth.com/ super8.* 59 rooms, 2 story. Late May-early Sept: S $56-$69; D $66-$69; each additional $3; under 12 free; higher rates special events; lower rates rest of year. Crib free. Complimentary continental breakfast. Check-out 11 am. TV; cable (premium). Coin laundry. Restaurant opposite open 24 hours. Sauna. Whirlpool. Downhill/cross-country ski 5 miles. Business services. Cr cds: A, C, D, DS, MC, V.

[D] [⚐] [⇔]

Hotels

★ ★ **FITGERS INN.** *600 E Superior St (55802). Phone 218/722-8826; toll-free 888/348-4377; fax 218/722-8826. www.fitgers.com.* Housed in what was once a thriving brewery, this historic hotel has a European style with modern facilities. 62 rooms, 5 suites, 20 story. May-Oct: S $80-$95, D $80-$135; suites $150-$250; under 17 free; lower rates rest of year. Pet accepted, some restrictions. Check-out noon. TV; cable (premium), VCR available. In-room modem link. Some fireplaces. Bar 11 am-11 pm, entertainment weekends. Health club privileges, exercise equipment. Part of renovated 1858 brewery; shops, theater adjacent. Most rooms overlook Lake Superior. Cr cds: A, C, D, DS, MC, V.

[D] [⚐] [𝕏] [⇔]

★ ★ **HOLIDAY INN HOTEL & SUITES DOWN-TOWN WATERFRONT.** *200 W First St (55802). Phone 218/722-1202; toll-free 800/477-7089; fax 218/722-0233. www.holidayinnduluth.com.* 353 rooms, 16 story. S, D $89-$119; each additional $10; suites $89-$235; ski, package plans. Crib free. Check-out noon. TV; cable. In-room modem link. Refrigerators. Microwave, wet bar in suites. Coffee in rooms. Restaurant 6:30 am-11 pm. Bar 11-1 am. Health club privileges, exercise equipment, saunas. Indoor pools, whirlpool. Downhill/cross-country ski 7 miles. Free garage parking. Meeting rooms. Adjacent large shopping complex. Cr cds: A, C, D, DS, ER, JCB, MC, V.

[D] [⇔] [𝕏] [⇔] [SC]

★ ★ **RADISSON HOTEL DULUTH, HARBOR-VIEW.** *505 W Superior St (55802). Phone 218/727-8981; fax 218/727-0162. www.radisson.com.* Located downtown and connected to the indoor skyway system. 268 rooms, 16 story. June-mid-Oct: S, D $80-$110; each additional $10; suites $135-$250; under 18 free; package plans; lower rates rest of year. Bar 11:30-1 am; closed Sun. Crib free. Pet accepted. Check-out noon. TV; cable, VCR available. Restaurant (See also TOP OF THE HARBOR). Bar 11:30-1 am; closed Sun. Health club privileges, sauna. Indoor pool, whirlpool, poolside service. Downhill/cross-country ski 10 miles. Meeting rooms, business services. Cr cds: A, C, D, DS, ER, JCB, MC, V.

[D] [⚐] [⇔] [⇔] [⇔]

Restaurants

★ ★ ★ **BELLISIO'S.** *405 Lake Ave S (55802). Phone 218/727-4921; fax 215/720-3804. www.grandmas restaurants.com.* The restaurant features wine racks from floor to ceiling and white tablecloths with full table settings to help guests enjoy a true Italian experience. Italian menu. Lunch, dinner. Bar. Cr cds: A, C, D, DS, MC, V. **$$**

[D]

★ **GRANDMA'S CANAL PARK.** *522 Lake Ave S (55802). Phone 218/727-4192; fax 218/723-1986.* Closed some major holidays. Lunch, dinner. Bar. Children's menu. Under Aerial Lift Bridge at entrance to harbor. Cr cds: A, D, DS, MC, V. **$**

[D] [SC]

★ ★ **PICKWICK.** *508 E Superior St (55802). Phone 218/727-8901; fax 218/786-0228.* The wood-paneled dining area and antique-filled rooms of this historic bar and restaurant offer incredible views of Lake Superior. The continental menu is an eclectic mix of regional and internationally influenced dishes from smoked white fish to Grecian lamb chops. Closed Sun; major holidays. Lunch, dinner. Bar. Children's menu. Cr cds: A, C, D, DS, MC, V. **$$**

[D]

★ **TOP OF THE HARBOR.** *505 W Superior St (55802). Phone 218/727-8981. www.radisson.com.* Specializes in steak, salmon, trout. Hours: 6:30 am-2 pm, 4:30-10 pm; Fri, Sat 5-10 pm; early-bird dinner Thurs-Sun 11 am-8 pm. Breakfast $4.25-$9.95, lunch $9.95-$19.95. Dinner $16-$26. Service bar. Child's meals. Reservations accepted. Cr cds: A, D, DS, ER, MC, V.

[SC]

Elk River (F-3)

See also Anoka, Minneapolis, Saint Cloud, Saint Paul

Pop 11,143 **Elev** 924 ft **Area code** 763 **Zip** 55330

Information Elk River Area Chamber of Commerce, 509 Hwy 10; 763/441-3110

Web www.elkriverchamber.org

What to See and Do

Oliver H. Kelley Farm. *15788 Kelley Farm Rd. 2 miles SE on US 10, 52. Phone 763/441-6896.* Birthplace of National Grange and organized agriculture. Now a living history farm of the mid-19th century (May, Sept-Oct, Sat-Sun, holidays; June-Aug, Thurs-Mon). Visitor center. **$$$**

Sherburne National Wildlife Refuge. *17076 293rd Ave. 13 miles N on MN 169, then 5 miles W on County 9. Phone 763/389-3323.* Wildlife observation; interpretive hiking and cross-country skiing trails in season; hunting, fishing; canoeing. Includes a self-guided auto tour route (weekends and holidays). **FREE**

Motel/Motor Lodge

★ **AMERICINN.** *17432 US Hwy 10 (55330). Phone 763/441-8554; toll-free 800/634-3444. www.americinn.com.* 40 rooms, 2 story. Pet accepted. Complimentary continental breakfast. Check-out 11 am, check-in 3 pm. TV; VCR (movies). Sauna. Indoor pool, whirlpool. Cross-country ski 3 blocks. Mississippi River 1 block. Cr cds: A, D, DS, MC, V.

Ely (C-5)

See also Tower

Settled 1883 **Pop** 3,968 **Elev** 1,473 ft **Area code** 218 **Zip** 55731

Information Chamber of Commerce, 1600 E Sheridan St; 218/365-6123 or 800/777-7281

Web www.ely.org

A vacation and resort community, Ely is also gateway to one of the finest canoeing areas, Boundary Waters Canoe Area Wilderness, and is in the heart of the Superior National Forest. A Ranger District office of this forest is located here. From the Laurentian Divide, south of here, all waters flow north to the Arctic.

What to See and Do

Canoe trips. *Phone Chamber of Commerce for info.* Canoes, equipment, supplies. Guides available.

Canoe Country Outfitters. *629 E Sheridan St. Phone 218/365-4046.* Offers complete and partial ultra-light outfitting for trips to BWCAW and Quetico Park. Boat fishing trips and fly-in canoe trips; also camping, cabins on Moose Lake. (May-Oct, daily)

Tom and Woods' Moose Lake Wilderness Canoe Trips. *5855 Moose Lake Rd. 20 miles NE on Moose Lake. Phone Toll 800 322-5837.* Family, weekly rates. Specializes in ultra-lightweight canoe trips. (May-Sept)

Dorothy Molter Museum. *2002 E Sheridan. Phone 218/365-4451.* Last living resident of the Boundary Waters Canoe Area Wilderness who passed away Dec, 1986. Museum has two of her furnished cabins as they were in the wilderness. (Memorial Day-Sept, daily) **$$**

Greenstone outcropping. *13th Ave E and Main St.* Only surface ellipsoidal greenstone in US, judged to be more than two billion years old.

International Wolf Center. *E on MN 169. Phone 800/ELY-WOLF.* Houses wolf pack; exhibits. (May-mid-Oct, daily; rest of year, Sat-Sun)

Native American Pictographs. *7 miles N via MN 88 and 116 (Echo Trail).* Cliff paintings can be seen on Hegman Lake. These are simple exhibits of art painted by tribes who inhabited the region long ago.

Superior-Quetico Wilderness. *Superior in the US, Quetico in Canada.*

Vermilion Interpretive Center. *1900 E Camp St. Phone 218/365-3226.* Presentation of local history through photos, tapes, film, artifacts and displays; focuses on heritage of local people and land. (Apr-Oct, daily) **$**

Special Events

Blueberry Arts Festival. *Phone 218/365-6123.* Last full weekend July.

Harvest Moon Festival. *Phone 218/365-6123.* Weekend after Labor Day.

Voyageur Winter Festival. *1600 E. Sheridan. Phone 218/365-6123.* Ten days beginning first Sat Feb.

Motels/Motor Lodges

★**SUPER 8 MOTEL.** *1605 E Sheridan St (55731). Phone 218/365-2873; fax 218/365-5632. www.super8.com.* 30 rooms, 2 story. S $55; D $65; each additional $5; under 12 free. Crib free. Complimentary coffee in lobby. Check-out 11 am. TV; cable. Whirlpool. Sauna. Cross-country ski 1 mile. Business services. Cr cds: A, C, D, DS, MC, V.

★**WESTGATE MOTEL.** *110 N 2nd Ave W (55731). Phone 218/365-4513; toll-free 800/806-4979; fax 218/365-5364.* 17 units, 2 story. S $40-$50; D $55-$65; each additional $5; under 5 free. Crib free. Pet accepted, some restrictions; $5/day. TV; cable. Complimentary continental breakfast. Restaurant nearby. Check-out 10:30 am. Business services available. Free airport transportation. Downhill ski 20 miles; cross-country ski 1 mile. Cr cds: A, MC, V.

Eveleth (C-4)

See also Cook, Hibbing, Tower, Virginia

Founded 1893 **Pop** 4,064 **Elev** 1,610 ft **Area code** 218 **Zip** 55734

Information Eveleth Area Chamber of Commerce, 122 Grant Ave; 218/744-1940

Web www.evelethchamber.org

Site of a large taconite operation, mines within a 50-mile radius produce a large amount of the nation's requirements of iron ore. Located about one mile west of town on County Highway 101, Leonidas Overlook provides a panoramic view of the taconite operations and Minntac Mine.

What to See and Do

US Hockey Hall of Fame. *801 Hat Trick Ave (US 53). Phone 218/744-5167 or 800/443-7825.* Museum honoring American players and the sport; theater. (Daily; closed some major holidays) **$$**

Motels/Motor Lodges

★★EVELETH INN. *US 53 (55734). Phone 218/744-2703; fax 218/744-5865.* Hockey fans unite in Eveleth where the largest hockey stick in the world is located! This inn offers guests a kid-friendly environment with an Olympic-sized pool, mini golf course, volleyball court and on-site restaurant. 145 rooms, 2 story. S, D $59-$92; under 19 free. Pet accepted. Check-out noon. TV; cable (premium). Restaurant 6 am-10 pm. Bar 4 pm-1 am. Room service. Sauna. Indoor pool. Cr cds: A, C, D, DS, JCB, MC, V.

D ⊀ ☒ ☒

★SLOVENE MOTEL. *303 Hat Trick Ave (55734). Phone 218/744-3427; toll-free 800/628-2526.* 21 rooms. S $31; D $45; each additional $3. Crib free. TV; cable. Complimentary coffee in lobby. Restaurant nearby. Downhill/cross-country ski 10 miles. Sauna. Whirlpool. Cr cds: A, DS, MC, V.

☒ ☒ SC

★ SUPER 8 MOTEL. *I-90 & Hwy 15 (55734). Phone 218/744-1661; fax 218/744-4343. www.super8.com.* 54 rooms, 2 story. Mid-May-late Oct: S $55.88; D $59.88-$64.88; each additional $5; under 12 free; ski, golf plans; lower rates rest of year. Crib $1. Complimentary continental bkfst, coffee in rooms. Check-out 11 am. TV; cable (premium). Coin laundry. Restaurant opposite 6 am-10 pm. Sauna. Game room. Indoor pool, whirlpool. Downhill ski 20 miles, cross-country ski 10 miles. Meeting rooms, business services. Cr cds: A, MC, V.

D ☒ ⫟ ☒ ☒ SC

Fairmont (H-3)

See also Blue Earth, Jackson

Pop 11,265 **Elev** 1,185 ft **Area code** 507 **Zip** 56031

Information Convention & Visitors Bureau, 1201 Torgerson Dr; 507/235-5547

Web www.fairmontcvb.com

Fairmont, the seat of Martin County, is 10 miles north of the Iowa line at the junction of I-90 and MN 15. Situated on a north-south chain of lakes, fishing and water sports are popular pastimes. A group of English farmers who arrived in the 1870s and were known as the "Fairmont sportsmen" introduced fox hunting into southern Minnesota.

What to See and Do

Fairmont Opera House. *45 Downtown Plaza. Phone 507/238-4900 or 800/657-3280.* Built in 1901, historic theater has been completely restored. Guided tours. Fees for productions vary. (Mon-Fri, also by appointment; closed holidays) **FREE**

Martin County Historical Society and Pioneer Museum. *304 E Blue Earth Ave. Phone 507/235-5178.* Operated by Martin County Historical Society; pioneer memorabilia, Native American artifacts. (Mon-Sat) Under 12 years with adult only. **FREE**

Motels/Motor Lodges

★ BUDGET INN. *1122 N State St (56031). Phone 507/235-3373; fax 507/235-3286.* 43 rooms. S $26-$42; D $35-$49. Crib free. TV; cable. Indoor pool; whirlpool. Sauna. Complimentary coffee in lobby. Restaurant nearby. Check-out 11 am. Meeting room. Cross-country ski 2 miles. Cr cds: A, C, D, DS, MC, V.

☒ ☒ ☒ SC

★ HOLIDAY INN. *I-90 & Hwy 15 (56031). Phone 507/238-4771; fax 507/238-9371. www.holidayinnfairmont.com.* 105 rooms, 2 story. S $62-$79; D $72-$89; under 18 free. Check-out noon. TV; cable. In-room modem link. Balconies. Coin laundry. Restaurant 6 am-10 pm. Bar 11-1 am. Room service. Sauna. Indoor pool, wading pool, whirlpool, poolside service. Cross-country ski 2 miles. Free airport transportation. Meeting rooms, business services. Sundries. Cr cds: A, C, D, DS, JCB, MC, V.

D ☒ ☒ ☒

★ SUPER 8 MOTEL. *1200 Torgerson Dr (56031). Phone 507/238-9444; toll-free 800/800-8000; fax 507/238-9371. www.super8.com.* 47 rooms, 2 story. S, D $47-$57; each additional $5; under 12 free. Crib $5. Pet accepted. TV; cable. Continental breakfast. Restaurant opposite 6 am-10 pm. Check-out noon. Business services available. Free airport transportation. Cr cds: A, C, D, DS, MC, V.

D ⫟ ☒ SC

Restaurant

★ THE RANCH FAMILY RESTAURANT. *1330 N State St (56031). Phone 507/235-3044.* Closed Dec 25. Breakfast, lunch, dinner. Bar. Children's menu. Casual, family-style dining. Cr cds: DS, MC, V. **$**

D SC

Faribault (G-4)

See also Lakeville, Le Sueur, Mankato, Northfield, Owatonna, Saint Peter

Settled 1826 **Pop** 17,085 **Elev** 971 ft **Area code** 507 **Zip** 55021

Information Faribault Area Chamber of Commerce, 530 Wilson Ave, PO Box 434; 507/334-4381 or 800/658-2354

Web www.faribaultmn.org

In 1826, Alexander Faribault, a French-Canadian fur trader, built the largest of his six trading posts here. Faribault now is known for Faribo wool blankets and Tilt-A-Whirl amusement rides. The town, seat of Rice County, is surrounded by 20 area lakes and 3,000 acres of parkland. Faribault is also home to several historic landmarks, including the Cathedral of Our Merciful Saviour, built in 1869, and the limestone buildings of Shattuck-St. Mary's Schools, founded in 1858.

What to See and Do

Alexander Faribault House. *12 NE 1st Ave. Phone 507/334-7913.* (1853). House of the fur trader for whom the town was named. Period furnishings; museum of Native American artifacts and historical items. (May-Sept, Mon-Fri (daily); rest of year, by appt) **$**

Fairbault Woolen Mill Company. *1500 NW 2nd Ave. Phone 507/334-1644.* Wool blankets, items made in century-old mill on the Cannon River. Factory store, mill seconds. Check in at store for 45-minute guided tour (Mon-Fri; closed first 2 weeks July). **FREE**

Rice County Historical Society Museum. *1814 NW 2nd Ave. adjacent to county fairgrounds. Phone 507/332-2121.* Slide show; video presentation; Native American and pioneer artifacts; turn-of-the-century Main St; works of local artists. Nearby are log cabin, church, one-room schoolhouse and two steel annexes. (June-Aug, wkends; rest of year, Mon-Fri) **$$**

River Bend Nature Center. *1000 Rustad Rd. SE via MN 60, on Rustad Rd. Phone 507/332-7151.* More than 700 acres of mixed habitat including woodlands, prairie, ponds and rivers. Ten miles of trails (cross-country in winter) meander through the area. (Daily) **FREE**

Special Event

Tree Frog Music Festival. *122 1st Ave NE. Phone 507/334-4381.* Two-day event featuring headliner concert each day. Arts and crafts. Mid-Sept.

Motel/Motor Lodge

★ **SELECT INN.** *4040 Hwy 60 W (55021). Phone 507/334-2051; toll-free 800/641-1000; fax 507/334-2051. www.selectinn.com.* 67 rooms, 2 story. S $37; D $43-$58; each additional $5; under 13 free. Pet accepted. Complimentary continental breakfast. Check-out 11 am. TV; cable (premium). Restaurant adjacent open 24 hours. Game room. Indoor pool. Cr cds: A, C, D, DS, MC, V.

D 🐾 ⛱ 🏊 SC

Fergus Falls (E-1)

Settled 1857 **Pop** 12,362 **Elev** 1,196 ft **Area code** 218 **Zip** 56537

Information Chamber of Commerce, 202 S Court St; 218/736-6951

Web www.fergusfalls.com

Fergus Falls was named in honor of James Fergus, who financed Joseph Whitford, a frontiersman who led an expedition here in 1857. The town is the seat of Otter Tail County, which has 1,029 lakes. The city has a remarkable park and recreation system.

What to See and Do

Otter Tail County Historical Society Museum. *1110 W Lincoln Ave. Phone 218/736-6038.* Modern facility featuring dioramas and changing exhibits interpreting regional history; also library, archives and genealogical materials. (Daily; closed some major holidays) **$$**

Pebble Lake City Park. *205 S Peck St. SE on US 59. Phone 218/739-3205.* Picnicking, swimming, beach. 18-hole golf (Apr-Sept, daily; fee). Park open early June-late Aug, daily.

Motels/Motor Lodges

★ **DAYS INN.** *610 Western Ave (56537). Phone 218/739-3311; toll-free 800/329-7466; fax 218/736-6576. www.daysinn.com.* 57 rooms, 2 story. S $38-$42.90; D $48.90-$52.90; each additional $3; under 12 free. Crib free. Pet accepted; $5. TV; cable. Indoor pool; whirlpool. Complimentary continental breakfast. Restaurant adjacent 6 am-midnight. Check-out 11 am. Business services available. Sundries. Health club privileges. Downhill/cross-country ski 2 miles. Cr cds: A, C, D, DS, JCB, MC, V.

D 🐾 ✈ ⛱ 🏊 SC

★ **SUPER 8 MOTEL.** *2454 College Way (56537). Phone 218/739-3261. www.super8.com.* 32 rooms, 2 story. S, D $35-$55; each additional $5. Crib $2. Complimentary coffee. Check-out 11 am. TV; cable (premium). Restaurant adjacent open 6 am-midnight. Business services. Cr cds: A, MC, V.

D 🏊 SC

Restaurant

★ ★ **MABEL MURPHY'S EATING LTD.** *MN 210 W (56537). Phone 218/739-4406. www.mabelmurphysmn.com.* Lunch, dinner. Bar. Children's menu. Cr cds: A, D, DS, MC, V. **$$**

D

Glenwood (E-2)

See also Morris, Sauk Centre

Pop 2,573 **Elev** 1,350 ft **Area code** 320 **Zip** 56334

Information Chamber of Commerce, 202 N Franklin St; 320/634-3636 or 800/304-5666

What to See and Do

Chalet Campsite. *956 S Hwy M104. 1/2 mile S on MN 104. Phone 320/634-5433.* Boating (launch), swimming beach, bicycling, picnicking, playground, tennis court, camping (fee), rest rooms, showers. (Mid-May-Sept, daily)

Department of Natural Resources, Area Fisheries Headquarters. *1 1/2 miles W on N Lakeshore Dr, MN 28, 29. Phone 320/634-4573.* Trout in display ponds (Mon-Fri; closed hols). Grounds (Daily). **FREE**

Pope County Historical Museum. *809 S Hwy 104. 1/2 mile S on MN 104. Phone 320/634-3293.* Helbing Gallery of Native American arts and crafts; country store, school and church; exhibits of local history, farm machinery and artifacts; furnished log cabin (1880). (Memorial Day-Labor Day, Tues-Sun; rest of year, Tues-Sat) **$$**

Special Events

Pope County Fair. *Phone 320/634-3636.* First week Aug.

Scout Fishing Derby. *Phone 320/634-3636.* First weekend Feb.

Terrace Mill Heritage Festival. *Phone 320/278-3278.* Last weekend June.

Terrence Mill Fiddlers' Contest. *Phone 320/278-3278.* Late Sept.

Waterama. *Phone 320/634-3636.* Water carnival; contests, parade. Last full weekend July.

Motel/Motor Lodge

★ **SCOTWOOD MOTEL.** *MN 55 and MN 28 (56334). Phone 320/634-5105.* 46 rooms, 2 story. S $35-$42; D $42-$45; each additional $5. Crib $5. TV; cable (premium). Indoor pool; whirlpool. Complimentary continental breakfast. Restaurant nearby. Check-out 11 am. Game room. Cr cds: A, D, DS, MC, V.

Resort

★ ★ **PETERS' SUNSET BEACH RESORT.** *20000 S Lakeshore Dr (56334). Phone 320/634-4501; toll-free 800/356-8654. www.petersresort.com.* Located on beautiful Lake Minnewaska, this golf resort has breathtaking views and lush landscaping. With golf, a swimming beach, boating, fishing, and much more, the whole family will enjoy the fun-filled adventures here. 24 lodge rooms, 27 kitchen units. Mid-June-mid-Aug: cottages for 1-9, $114-$267; MAP, family rates; golf plans; 2-4 day min stay: holidays, some wkends; lower rates May-mid-June, mid-Aug-Oct. Closed rest of year. Check-out 12:30 pm, check-in 4:30 pm. TV; VCR available (movies). Dining room (public by res) 7:30-9:30 am, 7-8:30 pm. Saunas. 18-hole golf, greens fee $28. Tennis. Bicycles. Boats, motors, rowboats; launching ramp. Some room phones. Cr cds: A, MC, V.

Restaurant

★ ★ **MINNEWASKA HOUSE SUPPER CLUB.** *24895 MN 28 (56334). Phone 320/634-4566; toll-free 800/828-0882.* Closed most holidays. Lunch, dinner. Bar. Entertainment. Cr cds: A, MC, V.

D SC

Grand Marais (C-6)

See also Grand Portage, Lutsen

Pop 1,171 **Elev** 688 ft **Area code** 218 **Zip** 55604

Information Grand Marais Information Center, 13 N Broadway, PO Box 1048; 218/387-2524 or 888/922-5000

Web www.grandmarais.com

This municipality on the rocky north shore of Lake Superior is the major community in the northeast point of Minnesota. The area resembles the tip of an arrow and is known as the "arrowhead country." The cool climate and pollen-free air, as well as lake and stream fishing, abundant wildlife, water sports, camping, and stretches of wilderness, make this a leading resort area. A Ranger District office of the Superior National Forest is located here.

What to See and Do

Canoe trips. Canoes, equipment, guides. For map, folder, names of outfitters contact Grand Marais Information Center.

⭐ **Grand Portage National Monument.** *38 miles NE on MN 61.*

Gunflint Trail. *Starting at NW edge of town, the road goes N and W 58 miles to Saganaga Lake on the Canadian border.*

Penetrates into area of hundreds of lakes where camping, picnicking, fishing, canoeing are available.

⭐ **North Shore Drive.** *MN 61 along Lake Superior from Duluth to Pigeon River (150 miles).* Considered one of the most scenic shore drives in the US.

Special Events

Cook County Fair. *Five blocks N on MN 61. Phone 218/ 387-2524.* Late Aug.

Fisherman's Picnic. *Phone 218/387-2524.* Parade, rides, dancing, queen's coronation; food. First week Aug.

Motels/Motor Lodges

⭐ **ASPEN LODGE.** *E US Hwy 61 (55604). Phone 218/387-2500; fax 218/387-2647.* 52 rooms. Mid-June-mid-Oct, mid-Dec-mid-Mar: S $39-$88; D $42-$129; suites $65-$145; package plans; lower rates rest of year. Pet accepted, some restrictions. Complimentary continental breakfast. Check-out 11 am. TV; cable (premium). In-room modem link. Guest laundry. Restaurant nearby. Sauna. Indoor pool, whirlpool. Downhill ski 18 miles, cross-country ski 1 mile. Snowmobiling. Cr cds: A, D, DS, MC, V.

D 🐾 ⛱ ⇶ ⛷

⭐ **BEST WESTERN.** *Hwy 61 E (55604). Phone 218/ 387-2240; fax 218/387-2244. www.bestwestern.com.* 66 rooms, 2-3 story. June-Oct: D $79-$129; suites $109-$179; lower rates rest of year. Pet accepted. Complimentary continental breakfast. Check-out 11 am. TV; cable (premium), VCR available (movies). Fireplaces. Restaurant nearby. Private beach on lake. Whirlpool. Downhill ski 18 miles, cross-country ski 1/2 mile. Snowmobiling. Views of Lake Superior. Cr cds: A, C, D, DS, ER, JCB, MC, V.

D 🐾 ⛱ ⇶ SC

⭐⭐ **EAST BAY HOTEL AND DINING ROOM.** *Wisconsin St (55604). Phone 218/387-2800; toll-free 800/ 414-2807; fax 218/387-2801. www.eastbayhotel.com.* 36 rooms, 4 suites, 2-3 story. No A/C. Mid-May-Oct: S, D $51-$124.50; suites $125-$150; under 12 free; lower rates rest of year. Crib free. Pet accepted. Check-out 11 am. TV; cable. Some in-room whirlpools, refrigerators. Microwave, fireplace, wet bar in suites. Restaurant 7 am-2 pm, 5-9 pm. Bar 11 am-9 pm, entertainment. Room service. Massage. Whirlpool. Downhill ski 18 miles, cross-country ski 5 miles. On lake. Cr cds: A, DS, MC, V.

D 🐾 ⛱ ⛷

⭐⭐ **NANIBOUJOU LODGE.** *20 Naniboujou Trl (55604). Phone 218/387-2688. www.naniboujou.com.* 24 rooms, 2 story. No A/C. No room phones. Mid-May-late Oct: S $65; D $80; each additional $10; under 3 free; lower rates rest of year. Winter hours weekends only. Crib $10. Check-out 10:30 am. Some fireplaces. Restaurant 8 am-10:30 am, 11:30 am-2:30 pm, 5:30-8:30 pm. On lake/river. Cross-country ski on site. Business services. Totally non-smoking. Cr cds: DS, MC, V.

D 🐾 ⛷

⭐ **SHORELINE.** *20 S Broadway (55604). Phone 218/387-2633; toll-free 800/247-6020; fax 218/387-2499. www.grandmaraismn.com.* 30 rooms, 2 story. No A/C. Mid-June-mid-Oct, mid-Dec-mid-Mar: S, D $49-$99; each additional $8; package plans; lower rates rest of year. Crib free. Complimentary continental breakfast. Check-out 11 am. TV; cable (premium). In-room modem link. Refrigerators. Restaurant nearby. Downhill ski 18 miles, cross-country ski 1 mile. Snowmobiling. Beach on Lake Superior. Business services. Gift shop. Cr cds: A, C, D, DS, MC, V.

🐾 ⛷ SC

⭐ **SUPER 8 MOTEL.** *1711 W US 61 (55604). Phone 218/387-2448; toll-free 800/247-6020; fax 218/387-9859. www.super8.com.* 35 rooms. Mid-June-mid-Oct and mid-Dec-mid-Mar: S, D $40-$108; each additional $8; package plans; lower rates rest of year. Crib free. Pet accepted, some restrictions. Complimentary continental breakfast. Check-out 11 am. TV; cable (premium). In-room modem link. Refrigerators. Guest laundry. Restaurant nearby. Whirlpool. Sauna. Downhill ski 18 miles, cross-country ski 2 miles. Snowmobiling. Business services. Cr cds: A, C, D, DS, MC, V.

D 🐾 ⛱ ⛷

Resort

⭐⭐ **BEARSKIN LODGE.** *124 E Bearskin Rd (55604). Phone 218/388-2292; toll-free 800/338-4170; fax 218/388-4410. www.bearskin.com.* 4 kitchen units (1-3 bedroom) in 2-story lodge, 11 kitchen cottages (2-3 bedroom). No A/C. Lodge: S, D $125-$208; each additional $46; kitchen cottages: D $90-$306; each additional $46; package plans. Crib available. Check-out 10 am, check-in 4 pm. Some balconies, screened porches. Fireplaces, microwaves. Coin laundry. Dining room (reservations required) 6 pm. Box lunches. Free supervised children's activities (June-Aug); ages 3-13 years. Playground. Whirlpool. Sauna. Private swimming beach. Cross-country ski on site. Boats, motors, canoes. Fishing guides. Private docks. Grills, picnic tables. Hiking trails, mountain bikes. Business services. Grocery, package store 5 miles. Wine, beer. Nature program. Cr cds: A, DS, MC, V.

D 🐾 ⛱

Restaurant

★ **BIRCH TERRACE.** *W 6th Ave (55604). Phone 218/387-2215; fax 218/387-2215.* Dinner. Bar. Children's menu. Northwoods mansion built 1898; fireplaces. Cr cds: DS, MC, V. **$$**

D

Grand Portage (C-6)

What to See and Do

Ferry Service to Isle Royale National Park. *Phone 715/392-2100.* From Grand Portage there is passenger ferry service to Isle Royale National Park within Michigan state waters (Mid-May-late Oct).

Grand Portage National Monument Once this area was a rendezvous point and central supply depot for fur traders operating between Montreal and Lake Athabasca. Partially reconstructed summer headquarters of the North West Company include stockade, great hall, kitchen and warehouse. The Grand Portage begins at the stockade and runs 8 1/2 miles NW from Lake Superior to Pigeon River. Primitive camping at Fort Charlotte (accessible only by hiking the Grand Portage or by canoe). Buildings and grounds (mid-May-mid-Oct, daily). Trail (all-year).

Grand Rapids (C-3)

See also Hibbing

Settled 1877 **Pop** 7,976 **Elev** 1,290 ft **Area code** 218 **Zip** 55744

Information Grand Rapids Area Chamber of Commerce, The Depot, 1 NW 3rd St; 218/326-6619 or 800/472-6366

Web www.grandmn.com

At the head of navigation on the Mississippi River, Grand Rapids was named for nearby waters. For years it served as a center for logging. Paper production and tourism are the principal industries today. Seat of Itasca County, Grand Rapids serves as a diverse regional center at the western end of the Mesabi Iron Range. A number of open pit mines nearby have observation stands for the public. The forested area surrounding the town includes more than a thousand lakes. Four of them—Crystal, Hale, Forest, and McKinney—are within the city limits.

What to See and Do

Canoeing. On Mississippi River, N on Bigfork waters to Rainy Lake, Lake of the Woods; also to Lake Itasca and on many nearby rivers.

Central School. *10 NW 5th St. Phone 218/326-6431.* Heritage center housing historical museum, Judy Garland display, antiques, shops and a restaurant. (Daily)

Chippewa National Forest. *200 Ash Ave NW. Between Grand Rapids and Bemidji on US 2. Phone 218/335-8600.* Has 661,400 acres of timbered land; 1,321 lakes, with 699 larger than 10 acres; swimming, boating, canoeing, hiking, hunting, fishing, picnicking, camping (fee); winter sports. Bald eagle viewing; several historic sites.

Forest History Center. *2609 County Rd 76. 3 miles SW via S US 169. Phone 218/327-4482.* Center includes a museum building, re-created 1900 logging camp and log drive wanigan maintained by Minnesota Historical Society as part of an interpretive program. Early Forest Service cabin and fire tower, modern pine plantation, living history exhibits; nature trails. (June 1-Labor Day, daily). **$$$**

Judy Garland Birthplace and Children's Museum. *2727 US 169 S. Phone 218/327-9276 or 800/664-JUDY.* Childhood home of actress. (Daily) **$$**

Pokegama Dam. *34385 S US Hwy 2. Phone 218/326-6128.* Camping on 21 trailer sites (hookups, dump station; 14-day maximum); picnicking, fishing. **$$$$**

Quadna Mountain Resort Area Convention Center. *100 Quadna Rd. 18 miles S on US 169, 1 mile S of Hill City. Phone 218/697-8444.* Quad chairlift, 2 T-bars, rope tow; patrol, school, rentals, snowmaking; motel, lodge and restaurant. Cross-country trails. 16 runs, longest run 26,430 feet, vertical drop 350 feet. (Thanksgiving-mid-Mar, Fri-Tues) Also golf, outdoor tennis, horseback riding, lake activities in summer. **$$$$**

Scenic State Park. *56956 Scenic Hwy # 7. 12 miles N on US 169, then 32 miles N on County 7. Phone 218/743-3362.* Primitive area of 3,000 acres with seven lakes. Swimming; fishing; boating (ramp, rentals), hiking; cross-country skiing, snowmobiling; picnicking; camping (electrical hookups); lodging; interpretive programs. Standard fees.

Special Events

Itasca County Fair. *1336 NE 3rd Ave. Fairgrounds, on Crystal Lake. Phone 218/326-6619.* Mid-Aug.

Judy Garland Festival. *2727 Pokegama Ave S. Phone 218/327-9276.* Museum. Late June.

***Mississippi Melodie* Showboat.** *16th Ave W, on Mississippi River. Phone 218/259-0814.* Amateur musical variety show. Three weekends July.

Northern Minnesota Vintage Car Show and Swap Meet. *Itasca County Fairgrounds. Phone 218/743-3893.* Late July. Phone 218/743-3893.

North Star Stampede. *Phone 218/743-3893.* Three-day rodeo. Late July.

Tall Timber Days and US Chainsaw Carving Championships. *Downtown. Phone 800/472-6366.* Early Aug.

Motels/Motor Lodges

★ **AMERICINN OF GRAND RAPIDS.** *1812 S Pokegama Ave (55744). Phone 218/326-8999; toll-free 800/634-3444; fax 218/326-9190. www.americinn.com.* 43 rooms, 2 story. Mid-June-Labor Day: S $52-$66, D $71-$86; each additional $6; under 17 free; lower rates rest of year. Complimentary continental breakfast. Check-out 11 am. TV; cable (premium). Restaurant nearby. Sauna. Indoor pool, whirlpool. Downhill/cross-country ski 18 miles. Cr cds: A, D, DS, MC, V.

⊡ ⊠ ⊠ ✈ ✕ ⊠

★**COUNTRY INN.** *2601 S US 169 (55744). Phone 218/327-4960; fax 218/327-4964.* 59 rooms, 2 story. June-Aug: S, D $74; each additional $5; under 18 free; lower rates rest of year. Pet accepted, some restrictions. Complimentary continental breakfast. Check-out noon. TV; cable (premium). Restaurant adjacent 6:30 am-10 pm. Indoor pool, whirlpool. Downhill ski 10 miles, cross-country 2 miles. Cr cds: A, D, DS, MC, V.

⊡ ⊠ ⊠ ⊠ ⊠

★ ★ **SAWMILL INN.** *2301 S Pokegama Ave (55744). Phone 218/326-8501; toll-free 800/235-6455; fax 218/326-1039. www.sawmillinn.com.* 124 rooms, 2 story. S $57-$85; D $67-$85; each additional $4; suites $88-$110; under 12 free. Pet accepted. Check-out noon. TV. Restaurant 6:30 am-10 pm; Sun to 9 pm. Bar 11-1 am. Room service. Sauna. Game room. Indoor pool, whirlpool, poolside service. Downhill/cross-country ski 18 miles. Free airport transportation. Cr cds: A, C, D, DS, MC, V.

⊡ ⊠ ⊠ ⊠ ✈ ✕ ⊠

★ **SUPER 8 MOTEL.** *1702 S Pokegama Ave (55744). Phone 218/327-1108. www.super8.com.* 58 rooms, 2 story. S, D $59-$62. Crib $2. Complimentary continental breakfast. Check-out 11 am. TV; cable (premium). In-room modem link. Guest laundry. Restaurant nearby. Downhill ski 18 miles, cross-country ski 1 mile. Business services. Shopping nearby. Cr cds: A, C, D, DS, MC, V.

⊠

Granite Falls (F-2)

See also Marshall, Redwood Falls

Pop 3,083 **Elev** 920 ft **Area code** 320 **Zip** 56241

Information Chamber of Commerce, 155 7th Ave, PO Box 220; 320/564-4039

Web www.granitefalls.com

What to See and Do

Lac qui Parle State Park. *County Rd 33 & Hwy 7. 14 miles NW on US 212, 8 miles NW on US 59, then 4 1/2 miles W on County 13. Phone 320/752-4736.* Approximately 529 acres. On Lac qui Parle and Minnesota rivers. Dense timber. Swimming, fishing; boating (ramps); hiking, riding; cross-country skiing; picnicking; camping. Standard fees. (Daily)

Olof Swensson Farm Museum. *151 Pioneer Dr. 4 miles N on County 5, then 2 1/2 miles W on County 15. Phone 320/269-7636.* A 22-room brick family-built farmhouse, barn and family burial plot on a 17-acre plot. Olof Swensson ran unsuccessfully for governor of Minnesota, but the title was given to him by the community out of respect and admiration. (Memorial Day-Labor Day, Sun) **$$**

Upper Sioux Agency State Park. *9805 Hwy 67. 8 miles SE on MN 67. Phone 320/564-4777.* 1,280 acres. Boating (ramps, canoe campsites). Bridle trails. Snowmobiling. Picnicking. Semi-modern campsite; rustic horserider campground. Visitor center. Standard fees.

Yellow Medicine County Museum. *726 Prentice St. 1/2 mile from center of town via MN 67. Phone 320/564-4479.* Depicts life in the county and state dating from the 1800s. Two authentic log cabins and bandstand on site. Also here is an exposed rock outcropping estimated to be 3.8 billion years old. (Mid-May-mid-Oct, daily except Mon; mid-Apr-mid-May, Tues-Fri) **FREE**

Special Event

Western Fest Stampede Rodeo. *155 7th Ave. Phone 320/564-4039.* Rodeo, street dances, parade. Weekend after Father's Day.

Motel/Motor Lodge

★ **VIKING JR MOTEL.** *1250 W Hwy 212 (56241). Phone 320/564-2411.* 20 rooms. S $28; D $31-$42; each additional $3. Crib $3. Pet accepted. TV; cable, VCR available (movies). Check-out 11 am. Cr cds: A, DS, MC, V.

⊠ ⊠ SC

Hastings (F-4)

See also Minneapolis, Northfield, Red Wing, Saint Paul

Settled 1850 **Pop** 15,445 **Elev** 726 ft **Area code** 651 **Zip** 55033

Information Hastings Area Chamber of Commerce & Tourism Bureau, 111 E 3rd St; 651/437-6775 or 888/612-6122

Web www.hastingsmn.org

Diversified farming and industry are the mainstays of this community, founded by a trader who felt the area was a good town site.

What to See and Do

Afton Alps. *6600 Peller Ave S. 10 miles N via US 61, MN 95. Phone 651/436-5245; 800/328-1328.* Three triple, 15 double chairlifts, two rope tows; patrol, school, rentals; snowmaking; store, cafeteria, snack bar; bar. Longest run 3,000 feet; vertical drop 330 feet. (Nov-Mar, daily) **$$$$**

Alexis Bailly Vineyard. *18200 Kirby Ave. Phone 651/437-1413.* First vineyard to make wine with 100 percent Minnesota-grown grapes. Wine tastings (June-Oct, Fri-Sun). Group tours (by appt).

Carpenter St. Croix Valley Nature Center. *12805 St. Croix Trail, 2 miles N via US 61, then 3 miles E via US 10. Phone 651/437-4359.* Environmental education center with more than 15 miles of hiking trails and one miles of shoreline on the St. Croix River. Various seasonal programs and activities (some fees). (Daily; closed major holidays)

Historic Walking Tour. A self-guided tour featuring the historic buildings of Hastings, including the exterior of the LeDuc-Simmons Mansion and Norrish "Octagon House." Tour booklets with background detail and map are available at the Chamber of Commerce. Guided tours by appointment.

Ramsey Mill. *E 18th St & McNamara. On MN 291 on the Vermillion River. Phone Toll 800 222-7077.* Remains of first flour mill in state, built by Governor Alexander Ramsey in 1857.

Treasure Island Resort and Casino. *5734 Sturgeon Lake Rd. S on US 61, 316 to Welch, follow signs. Phone 800/222-7077.* This 24-hour casino offers blackjack, slots, bingo and pull-tabs. Buffet, sports bar. Marina. National local entertainment. (Daily)

Special Event

Rivertown Days. *Phone 651/437-6775.* Gala community-wide festival. Riverfront activities; exhibits and tours; sporting events; fireworks. Mid-July.

Motels/Motor Lodges

★ **AMERICINN.** *2400 Vermillion St (55033). Phone 651/437-8877; toll-free 800/634-3444; fax 651/437-8184. www.americinn.com.* 43 rooms, 2 story. S $52.90-$95.90; D $58.90-$95.90; each additional $6; under 12 free. Complimentary continental breakfast. Check-out 11 am. Check-in 3 pm. TV; cable (premium), VCR available. Downhill ski 11 miles, cross-country ski 1 mile. Cr cds: A, C, D, DS, MC, V.
D ⊠ ⬚ SC

★ **SUPER 8 MOTEL.** *2250 Vermillion St (55033). Phone 651/438-8888. www.super8.com.* 50 rooms, 2 story. Apr-Sept: S $43-$46; D $49-$56; each additional $6; lower rates rest of year. Crib $3. Complimentary continental breakfast. Check-out 11 am. Check-in 3 pm. TV; cable. Exercise room. Restaurant nearby. Cr cds: A, MC, V.
D ⬚ SC

B&B/Small Inns

★ ★ ★ **ROSEWOOD HISTORIC INN.** *620 Ramsey St (55033). Phone 651/437-3297; toll-free 888/746-7966; fax 651/437-4129. www.thorwoodinn.com.* This property offers two inns built in the 1880s, both offering large suites with a private bath, a whirlpool tub or a fireplace, complimentary fruits and pastries, breakfast in the dining room or in guests suites, all near the historic downtown area. 6 rooms, 2 suites, 3 story. S, D $137-$177; suites $247; each additional $15; under 12 free. Complimentary full breakfast. Check-out noon, check-in 4 pm. TV available; VCR available. Dinner available with notice. In-room modem link. Fireplaces in each room. Downhill ski 6 miles, cross-country ski 3 miles. Historic houses built 1880; antiques, marble fireplaces. Cr cds: A, DS, MC, V.
⊠ ⬚

Restaurant

★ **MISSISSIPPI BELLE.** *101 E 2nd St (55033). Phone 651/437-4814; fax 651/437-2403.* Specializes in fresh seafood, steak. Steak menu. Hours: 11 am-2 pm, 4:30-9 pm; Fri to 10 pm; Sat 4:30-10 pm; Sun noon-7 pm. Closed Mon. Lunch $6.95-$9, dinner $10.95-$41. Children's menu. Reservations accepted . Dining in the tradition of the riverboat era (1855-1875); riverboat steel engravings. Cr cds: A, DS, MC, V.
D

Hibbing (C-4)

See also Cook, Deer River, Eveleth, Grand Rapids, Virginia

Settled 1893 **Pop** 18,046 **Elev** 1,489 ft **Area code** 218 **Zip** 55746

Information Chamber of Commerce, 211 E Howard St, PO Box 727; 218/262-3895 or 800/4-HIBBING

Web www.hibbing.org

Here is the world's largest open-pit iron mine, which produced one-quarter of the ore mined in the country during WWII. Hibbing calls itself the "iron ore capital of the world." On the Mesabi (Native American for "sleeping giant") Iron Range, Hibbing mines and processes taconite, yielding a rich iron concentrate. Frank Hibbing, the town's founder, built the first hotel, sawmill, and bank building.

In 1918, when the Hull-Rust pit encroached on the heart of town, the community was moved on wheels two miles south. The move was not completed until 1957. A local bus line, begun here in 1914 with an open touring car, is now the nationwide Greyhound Bus system. Hibbing was the boyhood home of singer-guitarist Bob Dylan.

What to See and Do

Bus Tour. *211 E Howard St. Phone 218/262-3895.* 3-hour bus tour of town and nearby taconite plant. Includes stops at Paulucci Space Theatre, high school. (Mid-June-mid-Aug, Mon-Fri) For information **$$**

Hull-Rust Mahoning Mine. *1200 E Howard St. N of town. Phone 218/262-3895.* Observation building provides view of "Grand Canyon of Minnesota," mining area extending three miles. Individual mines have merged through the years into single pit producing hundreds of millions of tons. Deepest part of pit, on E side, dips 535 feet into earth. Observation building; self-guided walking tours. (Mid-May-Sept, daily) Contact the Chamber of Commerce for further info. **FREE**

★ **Ironworld Discovery Center.** *Highway 169 W. 5 miles NE on US 169 in Chisholm. Phone 800/372-6437.* Displays and audiovisual presentations interpret culture and history of the iron mining industry and its people. Ethnic craft demonstrations and food specialties; entertainment; scenic train rides; outdoor amphitheater. (May-Sept, daily) (See ANNUAL EVENTS) **$$$**

McCarthy Beach State Park. *7622 McCarthy Beach Rd. 20 miles NW on County 5.* Approximately 2,566 acres. Virgin pine, two lakes. Swimming, fishing, boating (ramp, rentals); cross-country skiing; hiking; snowmobiling; camping; naturalist (summer). Standard fees. **$$**

Minnesota Museum of Mining. *Memorial Park Complex. 6 miles NE via MN 73, on W Lake St in Chisholm. Phone 218/254-5543.* Records the past 70 years of iron mining; equipment, exhibits, models; jet and rotary drills, steam engine, ore cars and railroad caboose, 120-ton Euclid and fire trucks; first Greyhound bus, and steam railroad diorama. (Mid-May-mid-Sept, daily) Self-guided tours. Picnicking. **$$**

Paulucci Space Theatre. *1502 E 23rd St. Phone 218/262-6720.* General interest programs from astronomy to dinosaurs, using stars, slides, special effects and hemispheric film projection; multimedia theater with tilted-dome screen; display area; gift shop. Shows (June-Aug, daily; Sept-May, Sat-Sun). **$$**

Special Events

Last Chance Curling Bonspiel. *Memorial Building. Phone 218/263-4379.* International curling competition on 14 sheets of ice. Early Apr.

Minnesota Ethnic Days. *Ironworld USA. Phone 218/254-7959.* A series of celebrations of ethnic heritage. Entertainment, history, crafts and food. Each day devoted to different nationality. July.

St. Louis County Fair. *Fairgrounds, 12th Ave. Phone 218/254-7959.* Cattle and rock exhibits, auto races, carnival midway. Early Aug.

Motel/Motor Lodge

★ **SUPER 8 MOTEL.** *1411 E 40th St (55746). Phone 218/263-8982. www.super8.com.* 49 rooms, 2 story. Apr-Sept: S, D $37-$50; suites $42-$64; each additional $3; under 13 free; weekly rates; higher rates special events; lower rates rest of year. Crib free. Pet accepted, some restrictions; $25 deposit. Complimentary coffee in lobby. Check-out 11 am. TV; cable (premium), VCR available. Restaurant opposite 6 am-11 pm. Cross-country ski 2 miles. Meeting rooms, business services. Cr cds: A, C, D, DS, MC, V.

Hinckley (E-4)

See also Mora

Pop 946 **Elev** 1,030 ft **Area code** 320 **Zip** 55037

What to See and Do

Hinckley Fire Museum. *106 US 61. Phone 320/384-7338.* Old Northern Pacific Railroad Depot houses museum that depicts the disastrous forest fire that swept across Hinckley in 1894. Mural, video tape, diorama, reconstructed living quarters. (May-Oct, Tues-Sun) **$$**

North West Company Fur Post. *County Rd 7. Phone 320/629-6356.* A reconstruction of an 1800 fur trade outpost, based on archaeological findings and other research; picnic area. (May-Labor Day, Tues-Sat and Sun afternoons) **FREE**

St. Croix State Park. *15 miles E on MN 48, then S. Phone 320/384-6591.* A 34,037-acre park. Swimming (lake), fishing, canoeing (Memorial Day-Labor Day, rentals); hiking, riding trails, cross-country skiing, snowmobiling; picnicking, sicross-mi blacktop wooded bike trail, camping (electric, dump station). Standard fees.

Motels/Motor Lodges

★ **DAYS INN.** *104 Grindstone Ct (55037). Phone 320/384-7751; toll-free 800/559-8951; fax 320/384-6403. www.daysinn.com.* 69 rooms, 2 story. S $55-$85; D $60-$90; each additional $5; suites $90-$135; under 18 free. Crib free. Pet accepted; $5. Complimentary continental breakfast, coffee in rooms. Check-out 11 am. TV; cable, VCR available. Some refrigerators, microwaves available. Coin laundry. Restaurant adjacent open 24 hours. Sauna. Indoor pool, whirlpool. Cross-country ski 10 miles. Business services. Cr cds: A, C, D, DS, JCB, MC, V.

★ **GRAND NORTHERN INN.** 604 Weber Ave (55037). Phone 320/384-7171; toll-free 800/558-0612; fax 320/745-4659. 101 rooms, 2 story. May-Sept: D $69-$89; each additional $10; whirlpool rooms $85-$129; under 19 free; lower rates rest of year. Pet accepted. Complimentary continental breakfast. Check-out noon. TV; cable. Sauna. Indoor pool, whirlpool. Cross-country ski 10 miles. Cr cds: A, MC, V.

★ **SUPER 8.** 2811 Hwy 23 (55735). Phone 320/245-5284; fax 320/245-2233. www.super8.com. 31 rooms, 2 story. S $45-$98; D $61-$148; each additional $4; under 12 free. Crib free. Pet accepted. Complimentary continental breakfast. Check-out 11 am. TV; cable (premium). Coin laundry. Restaurant opposite 6 am-10 pm. Game room. Whirlpool. Cross-country ski opposite. Business services. Cr cds: A, C, D, DS, MC, V.

Restaurants

★ ★ **CASSSIDY'S.** I-35 and Hwy 48 (55037). Phone 320/384-6129. American menu. Breakfast, lunch, dinner. Children's menu. Cr cds: DS, MC, V. **$**

★ **TOBIE'S.** 504 Fire Monument Rd (55037). Phone 320/384-6174. www.tobies.com. Closed Dec 25. Breakfast, lunch, dinner. Bar. Entertainment Thurs-Sun. Cr cds: A, D, DS, MC, V. **$**

International Falls (B-4)

Pop 8,325 **Elev** 1,124 ft **Area code** 218 **Zip** 56649

Information International Falls Area Chamber of Commerce, 301 2nd Ave; 218/283-9400 or 800/325-5766

Web www.intlfalls.org

In addition to tourism, converting trees and wood chips into paper is big business here. The town takes its name from a 35-foot drop of the Rainy River, now concealed by a reservoir above a dam that harnesses the water power. International Falls is a port of entry to Canada by way of Fort Frances, ON. (For border crossing regulations, see MAKING THE MOST OF YOUR TRIP.)

What to See and Do

Boise Cascade Paper Mill. 2nd St & 4th Ave. Phone 218/285-5511. No cameras allowed. No children under ten years. Proper footwear required. Tours (June-Aug, Mon-Fri; closed hols). Reservations advised. **FREE**

Fishing. Rainy Lake. E along international boundary. Walleye, sand pike, muskie, crappie, perch, bass. **Rainy River.** W along international boundary. Walleye, sand pike, sturgeon, northern pike.

Grand Mound History Center. 6749 Highway 11. 17 miles W via MN 11. Phone 218/285-3332. Several ancient Native American burial mounds exist in this area, the largest being the Grand Mound, which has never been excavated. Interpretive center offers audiovisual program, sound system exhibit and 1/4-mile trail to mound site. (May-Aug, daily; rest of year, weekends; also by appointment) **FREE**

International Falls City Beach. 3 1/2 miles E on MN 11. Sandy beach for swimming; picnic grounds, play equipment.

Smokey the Bear Statue. Municipal Park. NW edge of business district. Giant symbol of the campaign against forest fires. In park is a giant thermometer, standing 22 feet tall; it electronically records the temperature. Also in the park is

Bronko Nagurski Museum. Highlighting the life and career of football hero Bronko Nagurski; features exhibits, diorama, audiovisual program, photographs and archives.

Koochiching Museums. 214 6th Ave. Phone 218/283-4316. Exhibits, manuscripts, pictures, articles used by early settlers in area. (Mon-Fri) **$$**

⭐ **Voyageurs National Park** Voyageurs National Park is on Minnesota's northern border and lies in the southern part of the Canadian Shield, representing some of the oldest rock formations in the world. Over 1/3 water, the park is water-based and rugged, but varied, with most trails and campsites accessible by boat. Rolling hills, bogs, beaver ponds, swamps, islands, and large and small lakes make up the vast scenery. Voyageurs has a cool climate with short, warm summers and long winters. Common summer activities include boating, swimming, fishing (with some of the best bass and walleye water in the US), hiking, and camping, while outdoor enthusiasts enjoy skiing, snowmobiling, and snowshoeing during the colder months. A rich location for wildlife viewing, Voyagers is located in black bear country, and designated campsites are equipped with bear lockers for food storage. If a locker is not available, be prepared to hang your food, as bear-proofing food storage is required. In the summer, park-sponsored programs include interpretive walks, children's activities, and canoe trips. In the winter, activities include candlelight skiing and snowshoe hikes. Lodging is available in the park during the summer months at Kettle Falls Hotel, and house boats are available for rent. (Closed Jan 1, Thanksgiving, Dec 25)

Motels/Motor Lodges

★ **DAYS INN.** *2331 Hwy 53 S (56649). Phone 218/283-9441; toll-free 800/329-7466. www.daysinn.com.* 60 rooms, 2 story. S $46-$58; D $60-$70; under 18 free. Crib free. Pet accepted, some restrictions. TV; cable (premium). Complimentary continental breakfast. Restaurant adjacent open 24 hours. Check-out noon. Business services available. Exercise equipment; sauna. Whirlpool. Cr cds: A, C, D, DS, JCB, MC, V.

⬛⬛⬛ SC

★ ★ **HOLIDAY INN.** *1500 Hwy 71 (56649). Phone 218/283-8000; toll-free 800/331-4443; fax 218/283-3774. www.holidayinnifalls.com.* 127 rooms, 2 story. S, D $79.95-$89; suites $85-$149; family rates. Crib free. Pet accepted. Check-out noon. TV; cable (premium). In-room modem link. Some refrigerators, microwaves available. Coin laundry. Restaurant 6:30 am-10 pm. Bar, room service. Health club privileges, Sauna. Indoor pool, wading pool, whirlpool. Free airport transportation. Meeting rooms, business services. Bellhops. Sundries. View of Rainy River. Cr cds: A, D, DS, JCB, MC, V.

⬛⬛⬛⬛⬛ SC

★ **SUPER 8 MOTEL.** *2326 Hwy 53 Frontage Rd (56649). Phone 218/283-8811; fax 218/283-8880. www.super8.com.* 53 rooms, 2 story. Mid-May-Sept: S $33-$37; D $45-$62, suites $62-$76; each additional $6; under 12 free; lower rates rest of year. Crib free. Complimentary coffee in lobby. Check-out 11 am. TV; cable (premium). In-room modem link. Refrigerator, in-room whirlpool, minibar in suites. Some microwaves. Coin laundry. Restaurant nearby. Business services. Cr cds: A, C, D, DS, MC, V.

⬛⬛ SC

Itasca State Park (C-2)

28 miles N on US 71. Phone 218/266-2100.

In the deep forests that cover most of the 32,000 acres of this park, there is a small stream just 15 steps across; this is the headwaters of the Mississippi River at its source, Lake Itasca. The name of the park and the lake itself is a contraction of the Latin *veritas caput,* meaning "true head." The lake is the largest of more than 100 that sparkle amid the virgin woodlands. The park offers swimming, fishing, boating (ramp, rentals); snowmobiling, cross-country skiing, biking (rentals), and hiking. There are cabins, camping and picnic grounds, and a lodge that offers food service (see RESORT). In the summer there are daily boat

cruises aboard the Chester Charles, from Douglas Lodge Pier to the headwaters of the Mississippi River (fee). A lookout tower, Aiton Heights, in the southeastern part of the park just off the ten-mile wilderness drive, provides a bird's eye view of the park. American Indian burial mounds and a pioneer cabin are some of the many historical sites preserved at Itasca. The University of Minnesota's forestry school and biological station operate here during the summer.

The Naturalist program provides self-guided and guided hikes, auto tours, boat launch tours, campfire programs, and evening movies on history and features of the area. Exhibits show many animals and plants native to the state, as well as park history. Inquire at the entrance gates for details. Standard entrance fees. (For further information contact Itasca State Park, HC05, Box 4, Lake Itasca, 56470-9702; phone 218/266-2114)

Rapid River Logging Camp. *3 miles N via US 71, 2 1/2 miles E on County 18 and follow signs. Phone 218/732-3444.* Authentic logging camp with nature trail; antiques; serves lumberjack meals; logging demonstrations (Tues and Fri). See sluiceway in the river. (Memorial Day weekend-Labor Day weekend, daily) **FREE**

Jackson (H-2)

See also Fairmont

Founded 1856 **Pop** 3,559 **Elev** 1,312 ft **Area code** 507
Zip 56143

Information Chamber of Commerce, 82 W Ashley St; 507/847-3867

Web www.jacksonmn.com

A peaceful community on the banks of the Des Moines River, Jackson processes the farm produce of the fertile river valley and also manufactures industrial farm equipment. Thirteen blocks of Jackson's business district are on the National Register of Historic Places.

What to See and Do

Fort Belmont. *Phone 507/847-3867.* Blacksmith shop, 19th-century farmhouse, historic church, sodhouse and other buildings; Native American artifacts. (Memorial Day-Labor Day, daily). **$$**

Kilen Woods State Park. *4 miles N on US 71, then 5 miles W. Phone 507/662-6258.* 219 acres of forested hills in Des Moines Valley. Fishing, hiking, snowmobiling, picnicking, camping (hookups, dump station); visitor center. Standard fees.

Monument to Slain Settlers. *State St & Riverside Dr. Ashley Park.* Marks scene of attack by the Sioux in 1857.

Special Events

County Fair. *Phone 507/847-3867.* Late July-early Aug.

Town and Country Day Celebration. *Main St. Phone 507/847-3867.* Third Sat July.

Motels/Motor Lodges

★ ★ **BEST WESTERN COUNTRY MANOR INN.** *2007 Hwy 71 N (56143). Phone 507/847-3110; toll-free 800/528-1234. www.bestwestern.com.* 41 rooms. S $40-$48; D $50-$62; each additional $4. Crib free. Check-out noon. TV; cable. In-room modem link. Restaurant 6 am-10 pm. Bar 11-12:30 am. Sauna. Indoor pool, wading pool, whirlpool. Meeting rooms, business services. Sundries. Cr cds: A, C, D, DS, MC, V.

D ⚊ 🏊 SC

★**BUDGET HOST.** *950 Hwy 71 N (56143). Phone 507/847-2020; toll-free 800/283-4678; fax 507/847-2022. www.budgethost.com.* 24 rooms. S, D $36-$55; each additional $4. Crib $4. TV; cable. Coffee in rooms. Restaurant nearby. Check-out 10 am. In-room modem link. Sundries. Cross-country ski 2 miles. Golf opposite. Cr cds: A, C, D, DS, MC, V.

🏊 ⚊

Lake Elmo

Restaurant

★ ★ ★ **LAKE ELMO INN.** *3442 Lake Elmo Ave (55042). Phone 651/777-8495.* Guests enjoy the hearty portions of rich, creative cuisine, charming outdoor seating and a stellar Sunday brunch. Continental menu. Hours: Hrs: 11 am-2 pm, 5-10 pm; Sun 10 am-2 pm, 4:30-8:30 pm. Closed Closed some major holidays. Lunch $6-$11.95, dinner $14-$30, Sun brunch $16.95. Bar to midnight. Child's meals. Casual elegance in restored inn (1881). Reservations accepted. Outdoor dining. Cr cds: A, C, D, DS, MC, V.

D

Lake Kabetogama (B-4)

See also International Falls

Pop 60 **Elev** 1,155 ft **Area Code** 218 **Zip** 56669

Information Kabetogama Lake Association, Inc, 9903 Gamma Rd; 218/875-2621 or 800/524-9085

Web www.kabetogama.com

Kabetogama Lake is the central entrance to Voyageurs National Park.

What to See and Do

Kabetogama Lake. *7 miles NE off US 53.* 22 miles long, 6 miles wide, with hundreds of miles of rugged shoreline, numerous islands, secluded bays for fishing, sand beaches, woodland trails, snowmobiling, cross-country skiing, hunting for partridge, deer, bear; many resorts.

Voyageurs National Park. *Off US 53 on County Roads 122 and 123. (See INTERNATIONAL FALLS) Phone 218/283-9821.*

Lakeville (A-10)

See also Hastings, Minneapolis, Northfield, Red Wing, Saint Paul

Pop 24,854 **Elev** 974 ft **Area code** 952 **Zip** 55044

Information Lakeville Area Chamber of Commerce & Visitors Bureau, PO Box 12; 952/469-2020 or 888/525-3845

Web www.lakevillechambercvb.org

Motel/Motor Lodge

★ **MOTEL 6.** *11274 210th St (55044). Phone 952/469-1900; toll-free 800/466-8356; fax 952/469-5359. www.motel6.com.* 85 rooms, 2 story. S $30-$34; D $36-$42; under 17 free. Crib free. Pet accepted. Complimentary coffee in lobby. Restaurant opposite 7 am-11 pm. Check-out noon. Downhill ski 5 miles; cross-country ski 2 miles. Cr cds: A, C, D, DS, MC, V.

D 🐾 🏊 ⚊ SC

B&B/Small Inns

★ ★ ★ **SCHUMACHER'S HOTEL.** *212 W Main St (56071). Phone 952/758-2133; toll-free 800/283-2049; fax 952/758-2400. www.schumachershotel.com.* 16 rooms, 2 story. S, D $140-$250. Check-out 11:30 am, check-in 3 pm. Restaurant (See also SCHUMACHER'S). Bar to 11 pm; Fri, Sat to midnight. Cross-country ski 1 mile. Built in 1898. Decor resembles country inns, hotels in Bavaria, southern Bohemia and Austria. Cr cds: A, C, D, DS, MC, V.

D 🏊 ⚊

Restaurant

★ ★ **SCHUMACHER'S.** *212 W Main St (56071). Phone 952/758-2133; toll-free 800/283-2049. www.schumachershotel.com.* Fifty miles outside the Twin Cities, the German-style cuisine is worth the trip, especially if you can arrange a stay at the inn. Sample sauerbraten with stuffing and Czech dumplings, elk steaks with cranberry relish, and banana cream pie. Continental menu. Specialties: veal, game dishes. Own baking. Hours: 7 am-9 pm; Fri, Sat to 10 pm. Breakfast $3-$10, lunch $5-$19, dinner $28-$37. Bar. Wine list. Reservations accepted. Decor resembles country inns in Bavaria, Austria and southern Bohemia. Cr cds: A, C, D, DS, MC, V.

D

Le Sueur (G-3)

See also Fairbault, Mankato, Saint Peter

Pop 3,714 **Elev** 800 ft **Area Code** 507 **Zip** 56058

Information Chamber of Commerce, 500 N Main St, Suite 106; 507/665-2501

Web www.lesueurchamber.org

This town on the Minnesota River was named for Pierre Charles le Sueur, who explored the river valley at the end of the 17th century. The Green Giant Company, one of the world's largest packers of peas and corn, was founded here and merged with Pillsbury in 1980. Home office of Le Sueur Inc and plant sites for ADC Telcommunications, UNIMIN, and Le Sueur Cheese are located here.

What to See and Do

W.W. Mayo House. *118 N Main St. Phone 507/665-3250.* (1859). Home of Mayo Clinic founder; restored to 1859-1864 period when Dr. Mayo carried on a typical frontier medical practice from his office on the 2nd floor. Adjacent park is location of Paul Granland's bronze sculpture The Mothers Louise. (June-Aug, Tues-Sat; May and Sept-Oct, Sat only) **$**

Litchfield (F-3)

See also Minneapolis, Willmar

Pop 6,041 **Elev** 1,132 ft **Area code** 320 **Zip** 55355

Information Chamber of Commerce, 219 N Sibley Ave; 320/693-8184

Web www.litch.com

What to See and Do

Meeker County Historical Society Museum. *308 N Marshall Ave. Phone 320/693-8911.* The museum stands behind the Grand Army of the Republic Hall. Includes a log cabin, old barn display, blacksmith shop, general store and Native American display. Original newspapers, furniture and uniforms are also exhibited. (Tues-Sun afternoons, also by appointment; closed major holidays except Memorial Day)

Grand Army of the Republic Hall. Built in 1885, the hall has two rooms in original condition. Commemorates the members of the GAR (Grand Army of the Republic). **DONATION**

Motel/Motor Lodge

★ **SCOTWOOD.** *1017 E Hwy 12 (55355). Phone 320/693-2496; toll-free 800/225-5489; fax 320/693-2496.* 35 rooms, 2 story. S $44.95-$59.50; D $58.95-$99.75; each additional $5. Crib free. Pet accepted, some restrictions. Complimentary continental breakfast. Check-out 11 am. TV; cable (premium). Restaurant nearby. Sundries. Cr cds: A, DS, MC, V.

D

Little Falls (E-3)

See also Onamia, Saint Cloud

Pop 7,232 **Elev** 1,120 ft **Area code** 320 **Zip** 56345

Information Convention & Visitors Bureau, 606 First St SE; 320/616-4959 or 800/325-5916.

Web www.littlefallsmn.com

This town gets its name from the rapids of the Mississippi River. The seat of Morrison County, it is a paper milling town and a center of the small boat industry.

What to See and Do

Charles A. Lindbergh House and History Center. *1200 Lindbergh Dr S, S edge of town, on W bank of Mississippi River. Phone 320/632-3154.* Home of C.A. Lindbergh, former US congressman, and Charles A. Lindbergh, famous aviator. Homestead restored to its 1906-1920 appearance with much original furniture; visitor center has exhibits, audiovisual program, gift shop. (May-Labor Day, daily; Sept-Oct, weekends) Adjacent is

Charles A. Lindbergh State Park. *1201 Lindbergh Dr S. Phone 320/616-2525.* 436 acres. Hiking; cross-country skiing; picnicking; camping (hookups, dump station). Standard fees. **$$**

Charles A. Weyerhaeuser Memorial Museum. *2151 Lindbergh Dr S. Phone 320/632-4007.* Museum and resource center for Morrison County and regional history. (Tues-Sat; summer Tues-Sun; closed holidays) **FREE**

Minnesota Military Museum. *15000 Hwy 115. Camp Ripley, 7 miles N on MN 371, W on MN 115. Phone 320/632-7374.* Located in a former regimental headquarters, the museum documents US military history as experienced by Minnesotans, from frontier garrisons to the Persian Gulf. Exhibits; military decorations; tanks and aircraft. (Sept-May, Thurs-Fri; late May-late Aug, Wed-Sun) **FREE**

Primeval Pine Grove Municipal Park. *Broadway Ave & NW 10 St. Phone 320/616-5500.* Picnicking, playground, zoo with native animals (all year); stand of virgin pine. (May-Sept, daily) **FREE**

Motel/Motor Lodge

★ **SUPER 8 MOTEL.** *300 12th St NE (56345). Phone 320/632-2351; toll-free 800/800-8000; fax 320/632-2351. www.super8.com.* 51 rooms, 2 story. S $48; D $55-$60. Crib free. TV; cable. Coffee in rooms. Restaurant nearby. Check-out 11 am. Sundries. Cr cds: A, C, D, DS, MC, V.

D ⊠ SC

Lutsen (C-6)

See also Grand Marais

Pop 290 **Elev** 671 ft **Area code** 218 **Zip** 55612

Information Lutsen-Tofte Tourism Association, PO Box 2248, Tofte, 55615; 888/616-6784

Web www.61north.com

What to See and Do

Lutsen Mountains Ski Area. *467 Ski Hole Rd. 1 1/2 miles SW on MN 61, then 1 1/2 miles N. Phone 218/663-7281.* Seven double chairlifts, surface lift; school, rentals; snowmaking; lodge (see RESORTS), cafeteria, bar. Longest run 2 miles; vertical drop 1,088 feet. Gondola. (Mid-Nov-mid-Apr, daily) Cross-country trails. **$$$$** Also here are

Alpine Slide. *467 Ski Hole Rd. Phone 218/663-7281.* Chairlift takes riders up mountain to slide; riders control sled on 1/2 mile track down mountain. (May-mid-Oct) Concession & picnic area. **$$$$**

Mountain Tram. *467 Ski Hole Rd. Phone 218/663-7281.* 2-miles round trip sightseeing ride to the highest point on the North Shore. Particularly scenic view in fall. (May-mid-Oct). Horseback riding. (Mid-May-mid-Oct, fee) **$$$**

Motels/Motor Lodges

★ **BEST WESTERN CLIFF DWELLER.** *6452 US 61 (55604). Phone 218/663-7273.* 22 rooms, 2 story. April-Oct, Dec-May: S, D $69-$99; each additional $8; package plans; lower rates rest of year. Pet accepted, some restrictions. Check-out 11 am. TV; cable (premium). In-room modem link. Restaurant (late June-Sept) 7 am-9 pm. Downhill ski 3 miles, cross-country ski adjacent. Cr cds: A, C, D, DS, ER, JCB, MC, V.

D ⬤ ⤢ ⛷ ⊠

★★★**BLUEFIN BAY ON LAKE SUPERIOR.** *US 61 (55615). Phone 218/663-7296; toll-free 800/258-3346; fax 218/663-8025. www.bluefinbay.com.* Found on Lake Superior in a wilderness area, visitors can relax in front of their fireplace or in their private Jacuzzi. 72 units, 56 kitchen units, 2 story. No A/C. Late Dec-Mar, June-Oct: S, D, kitchen units $69-$345; each additional $10; under 12 free; ski plans; higher rates; ski weekends, holidays;

lower rates rest of year. Crib free. Pet accepted. Check-out noon. TV; VCR available (movies). Balconies, fireplaces, in-room whirlpools, microwaves, Complimentary coffee in rooms. Coin laundry. Restaurant 7:30 am-10 pm. Bar 3 pm-1 am. Supervised children's activities. Playgrounds. Exercise equipment, massage, sauna. Game room. 2 pools, 1 indoor, whirlpool. 18-hole golf privileges. Downhill ski 9 miles, cross-country ski opposite. Lawn games, grills. Meeting rooms, business services. Gift shop. Cr cds: DS, MC, V.

D ⬤ ⤢ ⛷ ⤢ ⛷ ⊠

★ **MOUNTAIN INN.** *County Rd 5 (55612). Phone 218/663-7244; toll-free 800/686-4669; fax 218/663-7248. www.mtn-inn.com.* 30 rooms, 2 story. Jan-Mar, July-mid-Oct: S, D $55-$99; each additional $8; under 18 free; weekend rates; ski, golf plans; holidays (2-day minimum); lower rates rest of year. Crib free. Pet accepted, some restrictions. Complimentary continental breakfast. Check-out noon. TV; cable (premium). Microwaves, refrigerators, wet bars. Restaurant opposite 7 am-11 pm. Sauna. 18-hole golf privileges, greens fee $41, pro, putting green, driving range. Downhill ski 1 block, cross-country ski on site. Jan-Mar, July-mid-Oct: S, D $55-$99; each additional $8; under 18 free; weekend rates; ski, golf plans; holidays (2-day minimum); lower rates rest of year. Picnics/tables. Business services. Cr cds: DS, MC, V.

D ⬤ ⤢ ⛷ ⊠ SC

Resorts

★★ **CARIBOU HIGHLANDS LODGE.** *371 Ski Hill Rd (55612). Phone 218/663-7241; toll-free 800/642-6036; fax 218/663-7920. www.caribouhighlands.com.* This lodge is located in the Lutsen Mountains on the north shore of Lake Superior. 110 units, 1-3 story. Feb-Mar: S, D $100-$600; kitchen units $180-$600; weekly, weekend, holiday rates; ski, golf plans; weekends Feb-Mar (3-day minimum), also weekends mid-July-Labor Day (2-day minimum); lower rates rest of year. Check-out 11 am, check-in 4:30 pm. TV; cable; VCR available (movies). Fireplaces. Coin laundry 18 miles. Restaurant 7-1 am. Bar 11-1 am. Room service. Supervised children's activities; ages 4-12. Exercise equipment, sauna. Game room. 2 pools, 1 indoor. 18-hole golf privileges, greens fee $39. Tennis. Downhill/cross-country ski on site. Bicycle rentals. Fishing/hunting guides. Hiking. Horse stables. Sleighing. Rental equipment available. Cr cds: MC, V.

D ⬤ ⚒ ⤢ ⛷ ⤢ ⛷ ⊠

★★**CASCADE LODGE.** *3719 W US 61 (55612). Phone 218/387-1112; toll-free 800/322-9543. www.cascadelodgemn.com.* 12 rooms in 2-story lodge, 11 cabins, 4 motel units (1-2 bedroom), 8 kitchens. No A/C. Late June-mid-Oct and late Dec-late Mar: Lodge D $66-$110; each additional $11-$13; cabins, kitchen units $106-$185; motel units D $66-$106; family rates; package plans. Crib

$5. Check-out 11 am, check-in after 1 pm. TV; VCR available (movies). Fireplaces, some in-room whirlpools, refrigerators. Coin laundry. Dining room 7:30 am-8 pm. Box lunches. Playgrounds. Sauna. Recreation room. Downhill ski 11 miles, cross-country ski adjacent. Bicycles, canoes, grills, Hiking trails. Picnics/tables. Meeting rooms, business services. Grocery. Lodge rooms totally nonsmoking. Indoor, outdoor games. Cr cds: A, DS, MC, V.

⊠ ⊠ **SC**

Luverne (H-1)

See also Pipestone, Sioux Falls

Pop 4,382 **Elev** 1,450 ft **Area code** 507 **Zip** 56156

Information Luverne Area Chamber of Commerce, 102 E Main St; 507/283-4061 or 888/283-4061

Web www.luvernemn.com

What to See and Do

Blue Mounds State Park. *5 miles N of I-90 on US 75, 1 mile E on County 20. Phone 507/283-1307.* A 2,028-acre park. Main feature is Blue Mound, 1 1/2 miles long quartzite bluff. Buffalo can be observed in park. Swimming, fishing, boating; snowmobiling; picnicking; camping; visitor center. Standard fees. **$$**

Motel/Motor Lodge

★ **SUPER 8 MOTEL.** *I-90 and US 75 (56156). Phone 507/283-9541. www.super8.com.* 36 rooms, 2 story. S, D $42-$65; suites $56-$67; each additional $5. Crib free. Pet accepted. Check-out 11 am. TV; cable (premium). Cr cds: A, D, DS, MC, V.

D 🐾 ⊠

Mankato (G-3)

See also Faribault, Le Sueur, New Ulm, Saint Peter

Founded 1852 **Pop** 31,477 **Elev** 785 ft **Area code** 507

Information Chamber & Convention Bureau, 112 Riverfront Dr, PO Box 999, 56002; 507/345-4519 or 800/657-4733

Web www.mankato.com

In a wooded valley where the Minnesota and Blue Earth rivers join, Mankato (Native American for "blue earth") takes its name from the blue clay that lines the riverbanks. Settled by Eastern professional men, farmers, and Scandinavian and German immigrants, Mankato today enjoys an economy based on farming, retailing, manufacturing, and distributing.

What to See and Do

Hubbard House. *606 S Broad St. Phone 507/345-4154 or 507/345-5566.* (1871) Historic Victorian home with cherry woodwork, three marble fireplaces, silk wall coverings, signed Tiffany lampshade; carriage house; Victorian gardens. **$$**

Land of Memories. *S via US 169, then E at municipal campground sign. Camping Phone 507/387-8649.* Picnicking, camping (hookups, dump station, rest rooms), fishing, boating (launch), nature trails. **$$$**

Minneopa State Park. *54497 Gadwall Rd. 3 miles W off US 60. Phone 507/389-5464.* A 1,145-acre park. Scenic falls and gorge; historic mill site; fishing, hiking, picnicking, camping. Standard fees. Adjacent is

Minneopa-Williams Outdoor Learning Center. *Phone 507/625-3281.* Wide variety of native animals and vegetation; information stations; outdoor classrm. (Daily) **FREE**

Mount Kato Ski Area. *20461 Hwy 66. 1 mile S on MN 66. Phone 507/625-3363.* Five quad, three double chairlifts; patrol, school, rental; snowmaking; cafeteria; bar. (Nov-Apr, daily) **$$$$**

Sibley Park. *End of Park Lane.* Fishing, picnicking; river walk, playground, zoo (daily); rest rooms; beautiful gardens, scenic view of rivers. **FREE**

Tourtelotte Park. *N end of Broad St, on Mabel St. Phone 507/387-8649.* Picnicking, playground. Swimming pool (early June-Labor Day, daily; fee), wading pool. **$**

Motels/Motor Lodges

★★ **BEST WESTERN HOTEL & RESTAURANT.** *1111 Range St (56003). Phone 507/625-9333; fax 507/386-4592. www.bestwestern.com.* 147 rooms, 2 story. S $53-$84; D $69-$99; each additional $6; under 18 free. Crib free. Check-out noon. TV; cable, VCR available (movies). Coffee in rooms. Coin laundry. Restaurant 6 am-9 pm. Bar, room service. Sauna. Recreation room. Indoor pool, whirlpool. Downhill ski 6 miles, cross-country ski 1 mile. Free airport transportation. Meeting rooms, business services. Sundries. Cr cds: A, C, D, DS, JCB, MC, V.

D ⊠ ⊠ ✈ ⊠ **SC**

★ **DAYS INN.** *1285 Range St (56001). Phone 507/387-3332. www.daysinn.com.* 50 rooms, 2 story. S $39-$64; D $49-$69; suites $65-$135; under 18 free. Crib free. Pet accepted. Complimentary continental breakfast. Check-out 11 am. TV; cable. In-room modem link. Restaurant nearby. Indoor pool, whirlpool. Downhill skiing, cross-country ski 5 miles. Business services. Cr cds: A, C, D, DS, JCB, MC, V.

D 🐾 ✈ ⊠ ⊠

★ ★ **HOLIDAY INN MANKATO, MN.** *101 E Main St (56001). Phone 507/345-1234; fax 507/345-1248. www.holiday-inn.com.* 151 rooms, 4 suites, 4 story. S $59-$69; D $69-$79; each additional $6; suites $89; under 19 free. Crib free. Check-out noon. TV; cable. In-room modem link. Valet services, coin laundry. Restaurant 7 am-10 pm. Bar 3 pm-1 am. Room service. Exercise equipment. Recreation room. Indoor pool, whirlpool, poolside service. Putting green. Downhill ski 4 miles, cross-country ski 1 mile. Meeting rooms, business services. Sundries. Civic Center nearby. Cr cds: A, C, D, DS, JCB, MC, V.

D ⊠ ⌦ 🧍 ⊠

★ **SUPER 8 MOTEL.** *Hwy 169 N & 14 (56001). Phone 507/387-4041; toll-free 800/800-8000; fax 507/387-4107. www.super8.com.* 61 rooms, 3 story. S, D $45-$85; Crib $1. TV; cable. Complimentary coffee in lobby. Restaurant adjacent open 24 hours. Check-out 11 am. Business services available. In-room modem link. Downhill ski 5 miles; cross-country ski 2 miles. Whirlpool. Cr cds: A, C, D, DS, MC, V.

D ⊠ ⌦ SC

Mantorville

Restaurant

★ ★ **HUBBELL HOUSE.** *MN 57 (55955). Phone 507/635-2331; fax 507/635-5280. www.hubbell-house.com.* Seafood menu, Steak menu. Specialties: in steak, barbecued ribs, seafood. Hours: 11:30 am-2 pm, 5-10 pm; Sun 11:30 am -9:30 pm; early-bird dinner Tues-Fri 5-6 pm. Closed Mon; Jan 1, Thanksgiving, Dec 24-25. Lunch $5-$9.95, dinner $9.95-$22. Bar to 1 am. Family-owned. Child's menu. Reservations accepted; required weekends. Country inn built in 1854; antiques. Cr cds: A, D, DS, MC, V.

D

Marshall (G-2)

See also Granite Falls, Redwood Falls, Tracy

Pop 12,023 **Elev** 1,170 ft **Area code** 507 **Zip** 56258

Information Marshall Area Chamber of Commerce, 1210 E College Dr, PO Box 352B; 507/532-4484

Web www.marshall-mn.org

Crossroads of five highways, Marshall is a major industrial and retail center for the southwest part of Minnesota.

What to See and Do

Camden State Park. *1897 County Rd 68.* 10 miles S, off MN 23. Phone 507/865-4530. More than 2,200 acres in forested Redwood River Valley. Swimming, fishing; hiking, riding, cross-country skiing, snowmobiling; picnicking, camping. Standard fees.

Southwest State University. *1501 State St. Phone 507/537-6255.* (1963) 5,000 students. Liberal arts and technical programs. Planetarium (fee), museum, and greenhouse (daily; closed holidays; free). **FREE**

Special Events

International Rolle Bolle Tournament. *Phone 507/532-4484.* 150 teams compete for prize money. Mid-Aug.

Shades of the Past 50's Revival Weekend. *Phone 507/532-4484.* Over 500 classic and collector cars. Flea market, swap meet, street dance. First weekend June.

Motels/Motor Lodges

★ ★ **BEST WESTERN.** *1500 E College Dr (56258). Phone 507/532-3221; fax 507/5324089. www.bestwestern.com.* 100 rooms, 2 story. S $43-$60; D $53-$60; suites $79-$84; under 17 free. Crib free. Pet accepted. Check-out noon. TV; cable. In-room modem link. Restaurant 6:30 am-2 pm, 5-9:30 pm; weekend hours vary. Bar noon-11:30 pm. Room service. Sauna. Indoor pool, whirlpool, poolside service. Cross-country ski 1 mile. Free airport, bus depot transportation. Meeting rooms, business services. Sundries. Cr cds: A, C, D, DS, MC, V.

D 🐾 ⊠ ⌦ ⊠

★ **SUPER 8 MOTEL.** *1106 E Main St (56258). Phone 507/537-1461. www.super8.com.* 50 rooms, 2 story. S $42-$52; D $42-$75; suites $78-$130; each additional $5. Crib free. Pet accepted. Check-out 11 am. TV; cable (premium). Coin laundry. Restaurant adjacent 6 am-10 pm. Cross-country ski 1 mile. Meeting rooms, business services. Cr cds: A, C, D, DS, MC, V.

D 🐾 ⊠ 🧍 ⊠

★ ★ **TRAVELER'S LODGE.** *1425 E College Dr (56258). Phone 507/532-5721; toll-free 800/532-5721; fax 507/532-4911.* 90 rooms, 1-2 story. S $36; D $44; each additional $4; under 12 free. Crib free. Pet accepted. Complimentary continental breakfast. Check-out noon. TV; cable (premium), VCR available (movies $3.50). Restaurant adjacent open 24 hours. Cross-country ski 1 mile. Free airport transportation. Meeting rooms, business services. Sundries. Cr cds: A, C, D, DS, MC, V.

🐾 ⊠ 🧍 ⊠ 🧍

Minneapolis (F-4)

See also Bloomington, Saint Paul

Settled 1847 **Pop** 368,383 **Elev** 687-980 ft **Area code** 612

Information Greater Minneapolis Convention & Visitors Assn, 4000 Multifoods Tower, 33 S 6th St, 55402; 612/661-4700 or 888/676-6757

Web www.minneapolis.org

Across the Mississippi from Minnesota's capital, St. Paul, is this handsome city with skyscrapers, lovely parks, and teeming industries. Minneapolis still has a frontier vigor; it is growing and brimming with confidence in itself and its future. Clean and modern, a north country fountainhead of culture, Minneapolis is also a university town, a river town, and a lake town.

A surprising array of nightlife, a revitalized downtown with many fine stores, a rich, year-round sports program, a symphony orchestra, and theaters provide an excellent opportunity to enjoy the niceties of city life. Minneapolis has one of the largest one-campus universities in the country and more than 400 churches and synagogues. Hunting and fishing, which are among the state's major tourist attractions, are easily accessible. The Minneapolis park system, with over a hundred parks, has been judged one of the best in the country. The city has also been a consistent winner of traffic safety awards.

Capital of Upper Midwest agriculture, with one of the largest cash grain markets in the world, Minneapolis is the processing and distribution center for a large sector of America's cattle lands and grainfields. Several of the largest milling companies in the world have their headquarters here. Graphic arts, electronics, medical technology, machinery, lumber, paper, and chemicals are also major industries.

Minneapolis was born when two mills were built to cut lumber and grind flour for the men of a nearby fort. Despite the fact that these were reservation lands and that cabins were torn down by army troops almost as soon as settlers raised them, the community of St. Anthony developed at St. Anthony Falls around the twin mills. In 1885, the boundaries of the reservation were changed, and the squatters' claims became valid. The swiftly growing community took the new name of Minneapolis (Minne, a Sioux word for water, and polis, Greek for city).

What to See and Do

American Swedish Institute. *2600 Park Ave. Phone 612/871-4907.* This museum is housed in a turn-of-the-century, 33-room mansion and features hand-carved woodwork, porcelainized tile stoves, and sculpted ceilings, plus Swedish fine art and artifacts. (Tues, Thurs-Sat noon-4 pm; Wed noon-8 pm; Sun 1-5 pm; closed Mon, holidays) **$**

Basilica of St. Mary. *88 N 17th St. Hennepin Ave between 16th and 17th sts. Phone 612/333-1381.* Renaissance architecture patterned after Basilica of St. John Lateran in Rome. (Daily)

Buck Hill. *15400 Buck Hill Rd. 14 miles S on I-35W or I-35E, in Burnsville. Phone 952/435-7174.* Quad, three double chairlifts, J-bar, three rope tows; snowmaking; patrol, school, rentals; restaurant, bar, cafeteria. (Thanksgiving-Mar, daily) **$$$$**

Eloise Butler Wildflower Garden and Bird Sanctuary. *Theodore Wirth Pkwy and Glenwood Ave. Phone 612/370-4903.* Horseshoe-shaped glen contains natural bog, swamp; habitat for prairie and woodland flowers and birds. Guided tours. (April 1-Oct 15, daily 7:30 am-30 minutes before sunset) **FREE**

Guthrie Theater. *725 Vineland Pl. 1 block S of junction I-94 and I-394. Phone 612/377-2224.* Produces classic plays in repertory, as well as new works. (Nightly Tues-Sun; matinees Wed, Sat, Sun)

Hennepin History Museum. *2303 Third Ave S. Phone 612/870-1329.* Permanent and temporary exhibits on the history of Minneapolis and Hennepin County. Includes collection of textiles, costumes, toys, and material unique to central Minnesota. Research library and archive. (Sun, Wed, Fri-Sat 10 am-5 pm; Tues 10 am-2 pm; Thurs 1-8 pm; closed Mon, holidays) **$**

Hubert H. Humphrey Metrodome. *900 S Fifth St. Phone 612/332-0386.* Sports stadium. Home of Minnesota Twins (baseball), Minnesota Vikings (football), and University of Minnesota football. Seats up to 63,000. (Mon-Fri and special events) **$$**

Lyndale Park Gardens. *3900 Bryant Ave S. Off E Lake Harriet Pkwy and Roseway Rd, on the NE shore of Lake Harriet. Phone 612/661-4800.* Four distinctive gardens: one for roses, two for perennials, and the Peace (rock) Garden. Displays of roses, bulbs, other annuals and perennials; exotic and native trees; rock garden; two decorative fountains; adjacent to bird sanctuary. Apr-Sept is the best time to visit. (Daily 7:30 am-10 pm) **FREE**

MetroConnections. *1219 Marquette Ave. Phone 612/333-8687; toll-free 800/747-8687.* Motorcoach tours include Twin Cities Highlights (Jan-Nov); Stillwater, a historic river town (June-Oct); and Lake Minnetonka (June-Aug). **$$$$**

Minneapolis City Hall. *350 S 5th St. Phone 612/673-2491.* (1891). Father of Waters statue in rotunda, carved of largest single block of marble produced from quarries of Carrara, Italy. Self-guided tours. Guided tours 1st Wed of month. (Mon-Fri; closed holidays) **FREE**

Minneapolis College of Art and Design. *2501 Stevens Ave S. Phone 612/874-MCAD.* Founded in 1886. 560 students. Four-year college of fine arts, media arts, and design. MCAD Gallery (daily; closed holidays). **FREE**

Minneapolis Grain Exchange. *400 S 4th St. Phone 612/321-7101.* Visit cash grain market and futures market. Tours (Tues-Thurs). Visitors' balcony; reservations required (mornings; closed hols). **FREE**

Minneapolis Institute of Arts. *2400 Third Ave S. Phone 612/870-3131.* Masterpieces from every age and culture. Collection of more than 80,000 objects covers American and European painting, sculpture, decorative arts; period rooms, prints and drawings, textiles, photography; American, African, Oceanic, Asian, and ancient Asian objects. Lectures, classes, films (fee), special events (fee); restaurants. (Tues, Wed, Fri-Sat 10 am-5 pm; Thurs 10 am-9 pm; Sun 11 am-5 pm; closed July 4, Thanksgiving, Dec 25) **FREE**

Minnehaha Park. *Minnehaha Pkwy and Hiawatha Ave S, along the Mississippi. Phone 612/370-4939.* Minnehaha Falls, immortalized as the "laughing water" of Longfellow's epic poem Song of Hiawatha; statue of Hiawatha and Minnehaha; picnicking; Stevens House, first frame house built west of the Mississippi. Park (May-mid-Oct, daily). **FREE**

Minnesota Lynx (WNBA). *600 First Ave N. Phone 612/673-8400.* Team plays at the Target Center.

Minnesota Timberwolves (NBA). *600 First Ave N. Phone 612/337-DUNK.* Team plays at the Target Center.

Minnesota Twins (MLB). *34 Kirby Puckett Pl. Phone 612/375-1366.* Team plays at the Metrodome.

Minnesota Vikings (NFL). *900 S Fifth Ave. Phone 612/338-4537.* Team plays at the Metrodome.

⭐ **Nicollet Mall.** *700 Nicollet Mall. Downtown. Phone 612/332-3101.* A world-famous shopping promenade with a variety of shops, restaurants, museums, and art galleries, as well as entertainment ranging from an art show to symphony orchestra performances (see SPECIAL EVENTS). No traffic is allowed on this avenue except for buses and cabs. Beautifully designed with spacious walkways, fountains, shade trees, flowers, and a skyway system, it is certainly worth a visit. Also here is

> **IDS Tower.** *80 S 8th St.* 775 feet, 57 stories; one of the tallest buildings between Chicago and the West Coast.

River City Trolley. *1301 2nd Ave S. Phone 612/204-0000.* A 40-minute loop traverses the core of downtown, passing through the Mississippi Mile, St Anthony Falls, and the Warehouse District. A Chain of Lakes tour is also available. On-board narration; tours run approximately every 20 minutes. (May-Oct, daily, also Fri and Sat evenings) **$**

St. Anthony Falls. *Main St SE and Central Ave.* Head of the navigable Mississippi, site of village of St. Anthony. A public vantage point at the upper locks and dam provides a view

of the falls and of the operation of the locks. Also includes a renovated warehouse with shops and restaurants.

University of Minnesota, Twin Cities. *On E and W banks of Mississippi, University Ave SE. Phone 612/624-6888.* (1851) (39,315 students) One of the largest single campuses in United States. Several art galleries and museums on campus. Tours. On Campus are

> **Bell Museum of Natural History.** *17th and University Ave SE. For information phone 612/624-7083.* Dioramas show Minnesota birds and mammals in natural settings; special traveling exhibits; exhibits on art, photography and natural history research change frequently. Touch and See Room encourages hands-on exploration and comparison of natural objects. (Tues-Sun; closed Thanksgiving, Dec 25) **$$**

> **Frederick R. Weisman Art Museum.** *333 E River Rd. Phone 612/625-9494.* Striking exterior is oddly shaped stainless steel designed by Frank Gehry. Inside are collections of early 20th-century and contemporary American art, Asian ceramics, and Native American Mimbres pottery. **FREE**

Walker Art Center. *725 Vineland Place. Phone 612/375-7622.* Permanent collection of 20th-century painting, sculpture, prints and photographs; also changing exhibits, performances, concerts, films, lectures. (Gallery open Tues, Wed, Fri-Sat 10 am-5 pm; Thurs 10 am-9 pm; Sun 11 am-5 pm; closed Mon; free admission on the first Thurs and Sat of each month) **$$** Opposite is

> **Minneapolis Sculpture Garden.** *Vineland Place & Lyndale Ave S. Phone 612/375-7577.* Ten-acre urban garden features more than 40 sculptures by leading American and international artists; glass conservatory. (Daily 6 am-midnight) **FREE**

Special Events

Minneapolis Aquatennial. *43 Main St SE. Phone 612/661-4700; 612/331-8371.* Parades, aquatic events, sports events, entertainment. Mid-July.

Minnesota Orchestra. *1111 Nicollet Ave. Orchestra Hall. Box office phone 612/371-5656.* Mid-Sept-June.

Showboat. *On University of Minnesota campus, on Mississippi River. Phone 612/625-4001 for schedule and ticket info.* During the 1800s, melodramas, comedies and light opera were presented on riverboats; University Theater productions preserve this tradition aboard an authentic, air-conditioned sternwheeler moored on the river. Tues-Sun. July-Aug.

Sommerfest. *Orchestra Hall, 1111 Nicollet Mall. Phone 612/371-5656.* Summer concert series of Minnesota Orchestra with Viennese flavor; food booths. July-Aug.

University Theatre. *120 Rarig Center, 330 21st Ave S, on University of Minnesota campus. Phone 612/625-4001.*

Student-professional productions of musicals, comedies and dramas in four-theatre complex. Early Oct-late May.

Motels/Motor Lodges

★ **AMERICINN.** *21800 Industrial Blvd (55374). Phone 763/428-4346; toll-free 800/634-3444; fax 763/428-2117. www.americinn.com.* 61 rooms, 2 story. Pet accepted. Complimentary continental breakfast. Check-out 11 am, check-in 3 pm. TV; cable (premium), VCR available. Indoor pool, whirlpool. Cr cds: A, C, D, DS, MC, V. **$**

D ◄≋ ⩫

★ **BAYMONT INN & SUITES.** *6415 James Cir N (55430). Phone 763/561-8400; fax 763/560-3189. www.baymontinn.com.* 99 rooms, 3 story. S $43-$66; D $51-$74. Complimentary continental breakfast. Check-out noon. TV; cable (premium). In-room modem link. Restaurant nearby. Cross-country ski 1/2 mile. Cr cds: A, C, D, DS, MC, V.

D ⩻ ⩫

★ **BEST WESTERN KELLY INN.** *5201 NE Central Ave (55441). Phone 763/571-9440; toll-free 800/780-7234; fax 763/571-1720. www.bestwestern.com.* 95 rooms, 2 story. Rates. Pet accepted. Complimentary continental breakfast. Check-out 11 am, check-in 3 pm. TV; cable (premium). Room service. Sauna. Game room. Indoor pool, whirlpool. Cr cds: A, C, D, DS, MC, V. **$**

D ◄≋⩫ ⩬

★ **CHANHASSEN INN.** *531 W 79th St (55317). Phone 952/934-7373; fax 952/934-7373.* 7 rooms, 2 story. S $56-$61; D $61-$66; each additional $5; under 16 free. Complimentary continental breakfast. Check-out 2 pm. TV. In-room modem link. Guest laundry. Cr cds: A, C, D, DS, MC, V.

D ⩫

★ **COMFORT INN.** *1600 James Cir N (55430). Phone 612/560-7464; toll-free 800/228-5150; fax 612/560-7464. www.comfortinn.com.* 60 rooms, 3 story. June-Sept: S $74.95-$79.95; D $79.95-$84.95; each additional $5; under 19 free; lower rates rest of year. TV; cable (premium). Complimentary continental breakfast. Restaurant adjacent 6 am-11 pm. Check-out 11 am. Meeting rooms. Business services available. Game room. Some refrigerators, microwaves. Cr cds: A, C, D, DS, MC, V.

⩫ SC

★ **DAYS INN.** *2149 Program Ave (55112). Phone 763/786-9151; fax 612/786-2845. www.daysinn.com.* 70 rooms, 2 story. S $37-$51; D $46-$71; each additional $5; under 15 free; higher rates special events. Complimentary continental breakfast. Check-out 11 am. TV; cable (premium). Restaurant adjacent open 24 hours. Bar. Cross-country ski 3 miles. Cr cds: A, C, D, DS, MC, V.

D ⩻ ⩫

★ **DAYS INN.** *2407 University Ave SE (55414). Phone 612/623-3999; fax 612/331-2152. www.daysinn.com.* 131 rooms, 6 story. Complimentary continental breakfast. Check-out 11 am, check-in 3 pm. TV. In-room modem link. Downhill ski 10 miles, cross-country ski 1 mile. Cr cds: A, C, D, DS, JCB, MC, V. **$**

D ⩻ ⩫

★ **HAMPTON INN.** *10420 Wayzata Blvd (55305). Phone 952/541-1094; toll-free 800/426-7866; fax 612/541-1905. www.hamptoninn.com.* 127 rooms, 4 story. S $74-$89; D $89-$94; under 18 free. Complimentary continental breakfast. Check-out noon. TV; cable (premium). In-room modem link. Restaurant nearby. Downhill ski 25 miles, cross-country ski 1 mile. Cr cds: A, C, D, DS, MC, V.

D ⩻ ⩫

★ ★ **RADISSON HOTEL ROSEVILLE.** *2540 N Cleveland Ave (55113). Phone 651/636-4567; fax 651/636-7110. www.radisson.com.* 256 rooms, 4 story. June-Labor Day: S, D $69-$119; each additional $10; under 19 free; lower rates rest of year. Crib free. TV; cable. Indoor pool; wading pool, whirlpool. Complimentary coffee in rooms. Restaurant 6:30 am-10 pm. Room service. Bar 3 pm-1 am. Check-out noon. Meeting rooms. Business services available. Valet service. Coin laundry. Exercise equipment; sauna. Game room. Some refrigerators. Cr cds: A, C, D, DS, ER, JCB, MC, V.

D ⩺ 🕴 ⩫ SC

★ **SUPER 8.** *6445 James Cir N (55430). Phone 763/566-9810; fax 763/566-8680. www.super8.com.* 102 rooms, 2 story. S, D $63-$73; suites $89-$119; each additional $5; under 12 free. Crib free. Complimentary continental breakfast. Check-out 11 am. TV; cable (premium). Restaurant adjacent. Business services. Cr cds: A, C, D, DS, MC, V.

D ⩫

Hotels

★ **BEST WESTERN.** *405 S 8th St (55404). Phone 612/370-1400; toll-free 800/372-3131; fax 612/370-0351. www.bestwestern.com.* 159 rooms, 4 story. Complimentary continental breakfast. Check-out noon, check-in 3 pm. TV; cable (premium). In-room modem link. In-house fitness room, sauna. Indoor pool, whirlpool, poolside service. Cr cds: A, C, D, DS, ER, MC, V. **$$**

D ⩺ 🕴

★ ★ **CROWNE PLAZA.** *618 Second Ave S (55402). Phone 612/338-2288; toll-free 800/556-7827; fax 612/338-6194. www.crowneplaza.com.* Located in downtown Minneapolis, this hotel is connected to the city's Skywalk system making for easy access to shopping, dining, sports and entertainment. A fitness and business center is offered along with the Rosewood Room Restaurant. 223 rooms, 11 story. Check-out 1 pm, check-in 3 pm. TV; VCR available (movies). In-room modem link. Restaurant, bar. In-house fitness room. Cross-country ski 1 mile. Luxury level. Cr cds: A, C, D, DS, ER, JCB, MC, V. $$

★ ★ **DOUBLETREE GUEST SUITES.** *1101 LaSalle Ave (55403). Phone 612/332-6800; toll-free 800/662-3232; fax 612/332-8246. www.doubletree.com.* Located only one block from the Nicollet Mall in downtown Minneapolis' shopping and theater district. It offers 230 suites with either two double or one king size bed, a wet bar and more. 230 suites, 12 story. Check-out noon, check-in 3 pm. TV; cable (premium). In-room modem link. Restaurant, bar. In-house fitness room, sauna. Cross-country ski 1 mile. Cr cds: A, C, D, DS, ER, JCB, MC, V.

★ ★ **DOUBLETREE PARK PLACE.** *1500 Park Pl Blvd (55416). Phone 612/542-8600; fax 612/542-8063. www.doubletree.com.* This hotel offers a quiet suburban location along with the convenience of being near downtown Minneapolis. Visitors can enjoy a Vikings, Twins, or Timberwolves game at the nearby Hubert H. Humphery Metrodome. 297 rooms, 15 story. Check-out noon, check-in 3 pm. TV; cable (premium). In-room modem link. Room service 24 hours. Restaurant, bar. In-house fitness room, sauna. Game room. Indoor pool, whirlpool. Cross-country ski 2 miles. Cr cds: A, C, D, DS, ER, JCB, MC, V. $

★ ★ **EMBASSY SUITES.** *425 S 7th St (55415). Phone 612/333-3111; fax 612/333-7984. www.embassysuites.com.* A 6-story atrium filled with tropical plants will greet visitors as they enter the hotel. Located in the business and financial district, the property is near the Target Center, Orpheum Theatre, fine shops, and entertainment. 216 suites, 6 story. Check-out noon, check-in 3 pm. TV; cable (premium). In-room modem link. Restaurant, bar. In-house fitness room, sauna, steam room. Indoor pool, whirlpool. Cross-country ski 1 mile. Cr cds: A, C, D, DS, JCB, MC, V. $

★★**FOUR POINTS BY SHERATON MINNEAPOLIS.** *1330 Industrial Blvd (55413). Phone 612/331-1900; toll-free 800/777-3277; fax 612/331-6827. www.fourpoints.com.* 252 rooms, 8 story. Pet accepted. Check-out noon, check-in 3 pm. TV; cable (premium). In-room modem link. Restaurant, bar, entertainment. In-house fitness room, sauna. Indoor pool, whirlpool, poolside service. Cross-country ski 1 mile. Airport transportation. Luxury level. Cr cds: A, C, D, DS, ER, MC, V. $$

★ ★ ★ **THE GRAND HOTEL MINNEAPOLIS.** *615 Second Ave S (55402). Phone 612/288-8888. www.grandhotelminneapolis.com.* 140 rooms, 12 story. Check-out noon, check-in 3 pm. TV; cable (premium), VCR available. Restaurant, bar. Babysitting services available. In-house fitness room, spa. Indoor pool. Business center. Cr cds: A, C, D, DS, ER, JCB, MC, V. $$

★ ★ **HILTON.** *1001 Marquette Ave S (55403). Phone 612/376-1000; fax 612/397-4875. www.hilton.com.* Found in the heart of downtown, this hotel is connected by skyway to the Minneapolis Convention Center and is near Orchestra Hall, Guthrie Theater, great shopping, dining, and more. The hotel offers all the expected services and facilities. 821 rooms, 25 story. Check-out noon, check-in 3 pm. TV; cable (premium), VCR available. In-room modem link. Restaurant, bar. In-house fitness room, sauna. Pool, whirlpool, poolside service. Cross-country ski 1 mile. Concierge. Cr cds: A, C, D, DS, MC, V. $$

★ ★ **HILTON MINNEAPOLIS NORTH.** *2200 Freeway Blvd (55430). Phone 763/566-8000. www.hilton.com.* 176 rooms, 10 story. Pet accepted. Check-out noon, check-in 3 pm. TV; cable (premium), VCR available. Restaurant, bar. In-house fitness room. Business center. Cr cds: A, C, D, DS, JCB, MC, V. $$

★ ★ **HOLIDAY INN.** *1500 Washington Ave S (55454). Phone 612/333-4646; toll-free 800/448-3663; fax 612/333-7910. www.metrodome.com.* 265 rooms, 14 story. S, D $119-$159; each additional $10; suites $149.50; under 18 free. Crib free. Pet accepted. Check-out noon. TV; cable (premium). In-room modem link. Coffee in rooms. Restaurant 6:30 am-11 pm, bar 4 pm-1 am. Exercise equipment. Indoor pool. Garage $8. Airport transportation. Meeting rooms, business services. Gift shop. Cr cds: A, C, D, DS, ER, JCB, MC, V.

★ ★ ★ **HYATT REGENCY.** *1300 Nicollet Mall (55403). Phone 612/370-1234; fax 612/370-1463. www.hyatt.com.* Located in the heart of the downtown business and financial district, this hotel offers access to the Minneapolis Convention Center via the city's skywalk. It is near the Guthrie Theatre, Walker Art Center, and much more. 533 rooms, 24 story. Check-out noon, check-in 3 pm. TV; VCR available (movies). In-room modem link. Restaurant, bar. In-house fitness room, health club privileges. Indoor pool, whirlpool. Cross-country ski 1 mile. Parking. Airport transportation. Concierge, luxury level. Cr cds: A, C, D, DS, ER, MC, V. $$

★ ★ ★ **THE MARQUETTE.** *710 Marquette Ave (55402). Phone 612/333-4545; toll-free 800/328-4782; fax 612/288-2188. www.marquettehotel.com.* Located in the downtown area, this hotel is connected to shops, restaurants, and entertainment by the city's skywalk system. Each guestroom ad suite features a mini bar, a large seating area and a room safe. 277 rooms, 19 story. Pet accepted. Check-out noon, check-in 3 pm. TV; cable (premium), VCR available. In-room modem link. Restaurant, bar. In-house fitness room. Cross-country ski 1 mile. Business center. Luxury level. Cr cds: A, C, D, DS, JCB, MC, V. **$$$**

★ ★ ★ **MARRIOTT CITY CENTER MINNEAPOLIS.** *30 S 7th St (55402). Phone 612/349-4000; toll-free 800/228-9290; fax 612/332-7165. www.marriott.com.* Linked by the enclosed skywalk to many of the city's offices and shopping complexes in the downtown area, this hotel is very convenient. It offers 583 guestrooms, 83 suites, a health club and more. Golf courses and tennis facilities are nearby. 583 rooms, 31 story. Pet accepted. Check-out noon, check-in 3 pm. TV; cable (premium), VCR available (movies). In-room modem link. Restaurant, bar. In-house fitness room, health club privileges, massage, sauna. Cross-country ski 1 mile. Valet parking. Business center. Luxury level. Cr cds: A, C, D, DS, ER, JCB, MC, V. **$$**

★ ★ ★ **MARRIOTT SOUTHWEST MINNEAPOLIS.** *5801 Opus Pkwy (55343). Phone 952/935-5500; fax 952/935-0753. www.marriott.com.* 321 rooms, 17 story. Pet accepted. Complimentary continental breakfast. Check-out noon, check-in 4 pm. TV; cable (premium), VCR available. Restaurant, bar. In-house fitness room. Indoor pool, whirlpool. Business center. Cr cds: A, C, D, DS, ER, JCB, MC, V. **$$**

★ ★ ★ **MILLENNIUM HOTEL MINNEAPOLIS.** *1313 Nicollet Mall (55403). Phone 612/332-6000; fax 612/359-2160. www.millennium-hotels.com.* With 325 guestrooms located on downtown's Nicollett Mall and near theaters, museums, and other attractions, this hotel is a great place for all travelers. It offers a restaurant, lounge, indoor pool, health club and more. 322 rooms, 14 story. Pet accepted. Check-out noon, check-in 3 pm. TV; cable (premium). In-room modem link. Restaurant, bar. In-house fitness room, health club privileges, sauna. Indoor pool. Cross-country ski 1 mile. Airport transportation available. Cr cds: A, C, D, DS, JCB, MC, V. **$$**

★ ★ ★ **NORTHLAND INN AND EXECUTIVE CONFERENCE CENTER.** *7025 Northland Dr (55428). Phone 763/536-8300; toll-free 800/441-6422; fax 763/536-8790. www.northlandinn.com.* Quality and customer satisfaction is what makes this well-designed hotel so popular for corporate travelers. 231 rooms, 8 story. S, D $125-$195; under 12 free. Crib free. Check-out noon. TV; cable (premium), VCR available. In-room modem link. Refrigerators. Valet services. Restaurant 6:30 am-10 pm. Bar to 1 am. Exercise equipment. Game room. Indoor pool, whirlpool, poolside service. Downhill ski 20 miles, cross-country 1 mile. Meeting rooms, business services. Concierge. Sundries, gift shop. Cr cds: A, C, D, DS, JCB, MC, V.

★ ★ **RADISSON.** *3131 Campus Dr (55441). Phone 763/559-6600; fax 763/559-1053. www.radisson.com.* Set in picturesque marshlands, this hotel is near many attractions including French Regional Park, the Ridgedale Shopping Mall, and more. The hotel offers fine dining, great meeting space and exceptional exercise facilities. 243 rooms, 6 story. Pet accepted. Check-out noon, check-in 3 pm. TV; cable (premium), VCR available. In-room modem link. Restaurant, bar. In-house fitness room, sauna. Indoor pool, whirlpool, poolside service. Lighted outdoor tennis courts. Downhill ski 20 miles, cross-country ski 2 miles. Racquetball. On wooded site. Cr cds: A, C, D, DS, ER, JCB, MC, V. **$**

★ ★ **RADISSON HOTEL METRODOME.** *615 Washington Ave SE (55414). Phone 612/379-8888; toll-free 800/822-6757; fax 612/379-8436. www.radisson.com.* Conveniently located between downtown Minneapolis and St. Paul, this hotel offers well-furnished guestrooms and suites. It is near the University of Minnesota's campus, museums, sporting events, family attractions, and a busy night life. 304 rooms, 8 story. Check-out noon, check-in 3 pm. TV; VCR available. In-room modem link. Restaurant, bar. In-house fitness room, health club privileges. Downhill ski 20 miles, cross-country ski 1 mile. Cr cds: A, C, D, DS, ER, JCB, MC, V. **$$**

★ ★ **RADISSON PLAZA.** *35 S 7th St (55402). Phone 612/339-4900; toll-free 800/333-3333; fax 612/337-9766. www.radisson.com.* 357 rooms, 17 story. S, D $178-$258; each additional $10; suites $310-$410; under 18 free. Crib free. Check-out noon. TV; cable (premium), VCR available. In-room modem link. Restaurant 6 am-11 pm. Bar 11-1 am, entertainment, room service 24 hours. Exercise room, sauna. Cross-country ski 1 mile. Meeting rooms, business services. Concierge. Shopping arcade. Luxury level, Atrium lobby; fountain, marble columns. Cr cds: A, C, D, DS, ER, JCB, MC, V.

★ ★ ★ **THE WHITNEY HOTEL.** *150 Portland Ave (55401). Phone 612/375-1234; fax 612/376-7512. www.thewhitneyhotel. com.* Located on the historic Riverfront, this hotel offers European style along with a view of the Mississippi River and the St. Anthony Falls. It is near many golf courses, attractions and a local health club with fitness facilities. 96 rooms, 8 story. Check-out noon, check-in 3 pm. TV; cable (premium), VCR available. In-room modem link. Room service 24 hours. Restaurant, bar. Parking, valet parking. Airport transportation. Concierge. Cr cds: A, C, D, DS, MC, V. **$$**

D ◻

B&B/Small Inns

★ ★ **NICOLLET ISLAND INN.** *95 Merriam St (55401). Phone 612/331-1800; toll-free 800/331-6528; fax 612/331-6528. www.nicolletislandinn.com.* 24 rooms, 2 story. Pet accepted. Check-out noon, check-in 3 pm. TV; cable (premium). In-room modem link. Restaurant, bar, room service. Cr cds: A, C, D, DS, ER, JCB, MC, V. **$**

D ◻ ◻

Restaurants

★ ★ **510 RESTAURANT.** *510 Groveland Ave (55403). Phone 612/874-6440. www.510restaurant.com.* Originally a glittery 1920s-era hotel, this restaurant's grand opulence is a step back in time. The food is wonderfully inventive and artistic. American, French menu. Hours: 5-9 pm, closed Sun. Dinner $15-$26. Cr cds: A, C, D, DS, MC, V.

D

★ **BLACK FOREST INN.** *1 E 26th St (55404). Phone 612/872-0812; fax 612/872-0423. www.blackforestinnmpls. com.* Hours: 11-1 am; Sun noon-midnight. German menu. Lunch $3.50-$8, dinner $5.50-$15. Specialties: sauerbraten, Wiener schnitzel, bratwurst. Outdoor dining. German décor. Family-owned. Cr cds: A, C, D, DS, MC, V.

D

★ ★ **CAFE BRENDA.** *300 1st Ave N (55401). Phone 612/342-9230. www.cafebrenda.com.* Vegetarian, seafood menu. Specialties: in fresh broiled rainbow trout, organic chicken enchiladas. Hours: 11:30 am-2 pm, 5:30-9 pm; Fri to 10 pm, Sat 5:30-10 pm. Closed Sun; most major holidays. Lunch $6-$10, dinner $9-$16. Dinner Parking (dinner). Bar. Totally nonsmoking. Reservations accepted. Cr cds: A, DS, MC, V.

D

★ ★ ★ **CAFE UN DEUX TROIS.** *114 S 9th St (55402). Phone 612/673-0686; fax 612/673-0349.* Delicious classic bistro fare offering creative and exquisite dishes. The dining room is beautiful but not stuffy. Staff is professional yet friendly. It's France without the French.

Eclectic, bistro atmosphere with murals, mirrors on walls. French bistro menu. Hours: 11:30 am-10 pm; Fri, Sat to 11 pm. Closed Sun; most major holidays. Lunch $7.95-$17.50, dinner $45-$55, dinner Free valet parking (dinner). Bar. Reservations accepted. Cr cds: A, C, D, MC, V.

D

★ ★ **CAMPIELLO.** *1320 W Lake St (55408). Phone 612/825-2222; fax 612/825-2162. www.damico.com.* Italian menu. Hours: 5-10 pm; Fri, Sat to 11 pm; Sun 10:30 am-2:30 pm (brunch), 5-10 pm. Closed Dec 25. Dinner $10.75-$25.95. Sun brunch . Bar to midnight. Valet parking available. Outdoor seating. Cr cds: A, D, DS, MC, V.

D

★ **CARAVELLE.** *2529 Nicollet Ave S (55404). Phone 612/871-3226.* Chinese menu. Hours: 11 am-9 pm; Sat from noon; Sun noon-7 pm. Closed July 4, Thanksgiving, Dec 25. Dinner $5.95-$15. Cr cds: MC, V.

★ ★ **CHRISTOS.** *2632 Nicollet Ave S (55408). Phone 612/871-2111. www.christos.com.* Greek menu. Hours: 11 am-10 pm; Fri to 10:30 pm; Sat noon-10:30 pm; Sun noon-9 pm. Closed most major holidays. Dinner $9.95-$13.95. Cr cds: A, C, D, DS, MC, V.

D

★ ★ ★ **D'AMICO CUCINA.** *100 N 6th St (55403). Phone 612/338-2401; fax 612/337-5130. www.damico.com.* Dinner only is served at this elegant Italian fine dining restaurant, offering pasta dishes, and an exceptional Italian wine list, including many fine reserve selections. Try the gnocchi. Italian menu. Specializes in modern Italian cuisine. Hours: 5:30-10 pm; Fri, Sat to 11 pm; Sun 5-9 pm. Closed Sun; major holidays. Dinner $21-$29.50. Bar. Piano Fri, Sat. Restored warehouse. Reservations accepted. Cr cds: A, D, DS, MC, V.

D

★ ★ **FIGLIO.** *3001 Hennepin Ave S (55408). Phone 612/822-1688; fax 612/822-0433.* American menu. Hours: 11:30-1 am; Fri, Sat to 2 am. Dinner $7.50-$18.95. Bar. Outdoor seating. Cr cds: A, D, DS, MC, V.

D

★ **GARDENS - SALONICA.** *19 5th St NE (55413). Phone 612/378-0611; fax 612/378-2300.* Hours: 11 am-9 pm; Fri, Sat to 10 pm. Closed Sun; Thanksgiving, Dec 25. Greek menu. Bar. Lunch, dinner $5-$10. Specializes in lamb dishes. Own pasta. Casual dining; Greek décor. Cr cds: A, C, D, DS, MC, V.

D

★ ★ **GIORGIO.** *2451 Hennepin Ave (55405). Phone 612/374-5131.* Hours: 11:30 am-2:30 pm, 5-11 pm; Sun 5-11 pm. Closed Thanksgiving, Dec 24, 25. Reservations accepted weekdays. Italian menu. Wine, beer. Lunch $2.95-$10.95, dinner $2.95-$16.50. Specialties: marinated leg of lamb, calamari steak. Outdoor dining. Italian décor. Cr cds: D, MC, V.

D

★ ★ ★ **GOODFELLOW'S.** *40 S 7th St (55402). Phone 612/332-4800. www.goodfellowsrestaurant.com.* This former Forum-Cafeteria space feels like a trip back to the 1930s, albeit a luxurious trip, with a décor of polished wood, Art Deco fixtures, and jade accents. Executive chef Kevin Cullen's regional American offerings highlight local, seasonal ingredients and may include a lamb trio of grilled chop, sweet-onion strudel and seared leg with marjoram sauce. The Forum space offers four private dining/meeting rooms. Hours: 11:30 am-2 pm, 5:30-9 pm; Fri to 10 pm; Sat 5:30-10 pm. Closed Sun; holidays. Lunch $7-$16, dinner $30-$38. Bar. Reservations accepted. Cr cds: A, C, D, DS, MC, V.

D

★ **ICHIBAN JAPANESE STEAK HOUSE.** *1333 Nicollet Mall Ave (55403). Phone 612/339-0540.* Japanese menu. Closed Easter, Thanksgiving, Dec 24. Dinner. Bar. Children's menu. Cr cds: A, C, D, DS, MC, V. **$$**

D SC

★ **IT'S GREEK TO ME.** *626 W Lake St (55408). Phone 612/825-9922.* Greek menu. Hours: 4 pm-midnight; Sat, Sun from 11 am. Closed Mon; major holidays. Dinner $7.75-$16.95. Bar. Outdoor seating. Cr cds: A, D, MC, V.

D

★ **J.D. HOYT'S.** *301 Washington Ave N (55401). Phone 612/338-3499; fax 612/338-1560. www.jdhoyts.com.* Cajun/Creole menu. Closed some major holidays. Breakfast, lunch, dinner, Sun brunch. Bar. Casual attire. Valet parking available. Outdoor seating, non-smoking seating. Cr cds: A, D, DS, MC, V. **$**

D

★ ★ ★ **JAX CAFE.** *1928 University Ave NE (55418). Phone 612/789-7297. www.jaxcafe.com.* The bar is adorned with stained glass windows of the seven dwarfs at this restaurant specializing in steaks. There is a fireplace in the dining room for cozy winter dining and a patio for the summer. Hours: 11 am-10:30 pm; Sun to 9 pm; Sun brunch 10 am-1:30 pm. Closed major holidays. Dinner $15-$35. 11 am-10:30 pm; Sun to 9 pm; Sun brunch 10 am-1:30 pm. Sun brunch $14.50. Reservations accepted. Cr cds: A, D, DS, MC, V.

D

★ **JERUSALEM'S.** *1518 Nicollet Ave S (55403). Phone 612/871-8883.* Hours: 11 am-10 pm; Fri to 11 pm; Sat, Sun noon-10 pm. Closed Thanksgiving, Dec 25. Reservations accepted. Middle Eastern menu. Bar. Lunch $4.25-$8.25, dinner $9.95-$15.95. Specializes in vegetarian

combinations. Middle Eastern tapestries on walls. Cr cds: C, D, DS, MC, V.

D

★ **KIKUGAWA.** *43 SE Main St (55414). Phone 612/378-3006; fax 612/378-0819. www.kikugawa-sushi.com.* Hours: 11:30 am-2 pm, 5-10 pm; Sat noon-2 pm, 5-11 pm; Sun noon-2:30 pm, 4:30-9:30 pm. Closed Jan 1, Thanksgiving, Dec 25. Reservations accepted. Japanese menu. Bar. Lunch $4.95-$10, dinner $9.50-$26.50. Specialties: sukiyaki, sushi bar. Parking. Modern Japanese décor. Overlooks Mississippi River. Cr cds: A, D, DS, MC, V.

D

★ **THE KING AND I.** *1346 LaSalle Ave (55403). Phone 612/332-6928; fax 612/338-4293. www.kingandithai.com.* Thai menu. Hours: 11-1 am; Sat from 5 pm. Closed Sun. Dinner $12-$30. Informal dining. Cr cds: A, D, DS, MC, V.

D

★ ★ ★ **LUCIA'S.** *1432 W 31st St (55408). Phone 612/825-1572; fax 612/824-4553. www.lucias.com.* This lively bistro offers a weekly changing menu that focuses on seasonal dishes, and a complimenting wine list. The adjacent wine bar allows diners the option to choose from an ever-evolving wine list, with many options by the glass. Contemporary American menu. Menu changes weekly. Hours: 11:30 am-2:30 pm, 5:30-9:30 pm; Fri, Sat to 10 pm; Sun 10 am-2 pm, 5:30-9 pm; Sat, Sun brunch 10 am-2 pm. Closed Mon; most major holidays. Lunch $9-$11, dinner $12.95-$22.95, Sat, Sun brunch $5.95-$11.95. Bar. Reservations accepted. Outdoor dining. Cr cds: MC, V.

D

★ ★ ★ **MANNY'S.** *1300 Nicollet Mall (55403). Phone 612/339-9900.* This Manhattan-style steakhouse offers traditional meat entrees with a la carte sides served family-style. Hardwood floors and a bustling atmosphere make this an active dining space. Hours: 5:30-10 pm; Sun to 9 pm. Closed major holidays. Reservations accepted. Bar. A la carte entrees: $28-$50. Specializes in steak, lobster. Contemporary décor. Cr cds: A, D, DS, MC, V.

D

★ ★ ★ **MORTON'S OF CHICAGO.** *555 Nicollet Mall (55402). Phone 612/673-9700. www.mortons.com.* Consistent with expectations, this outlet serves famed steaks and seafood. A knowledgeable staff explains the menu in a fun tableside presentation. A warm, club-like atmosphere welcomes a martini-sipping, steak-eating crowd. Steak menu. Closed Dec 25, Jan 1. Lunch, dinner. Bar. Casual attire. Cr cds: A, D, MC, V. **$$**

D

★ ★ **NEW FRENCH CAFE.** *128 N 4th St (55401). Phone 612/338-3790.* Hours: 7 am-2 pm, 5:30-10 pm; Fri to 11 pm; Sat 5:30-11 pm; Sun 5-9 pm; Sat, Sun brunch

8 am-2 pm. Reservations accepted. Country and contemporary French menu. Bar 11-1 am, Sun from 6 pm. Breakfast $3.95-$7.95, lunch $6.95-$11, dinner $16.95-$23. Prix fixe dinner: $18. Sat, Sun brunch $3.50-$10.75. Specializes in duck, seafood. Outdoor dining (bar). Remodeled building (1900); French bistro theme. Cr cds: A, D, MC, V.

D

★ **NYE'S POLONAISE.** *112 E Hennepin Ave (55414). Phone 612/379-2021. www.nyespolonaise.com.* Polish, American menu. Hours: 11 am-11 pm; Sun 5-10 pm. Closed Dec 25. Dinner $17-$30. Bar to 1 am. Casual attire. Polka Thurs-Sat. Cr cds: A, D, DS, MC, V.

D

★★★**OCEANAIRE SEAFOOD INN.** *1300 Nicollet Mall (55403). Phone 612/333-2277; fax 612/305-1923.* A stunning oyster bar displaying eight varieties glistens with shaved ice at the entrance of this retro-style, seafood room. Reminiscent of a 1930s ocean liner, the Hyatt Regency restaurant serves both simple preparations and more-involved specialties. The all-American, childhood dessert favorites, including root beer floats and Dixie cups, are a fun touch. Fresh seafood menu changes daily. Hours: 5-10 pm, Fri, Sat to 11 pm. Dinner $27.95. Cr cds: A, C, D, DS, MC, V.

D

★★**ORIGAMI.** *30 N 1st St (55401). Phone 612/333-8430. www.origamirestaurant.com.* Japanese menu. Hours: 11 am-2 pm, 5-9:30 pm; Fri to 10:30 pm;Sat 5-10:30 pm; Sun 5-9 pm. Closed Jan1, Dec 25. Dinner $7-$25. Outdoor seating. Cr cds: A, D, DS, MC, V.

D

★★★**PALOMINO.** *825 Hennepin Ave (55402). Phone 612/339-3800; fax 612/339-1628. www.r-u-i.com.* One of the trendiest concepts in the country, this European bistro-style restaurant offers an unusual combination of rustic, hardwood-fired Mediterranean cooking and a chic, bustling ambiance. The oft-changing menu offers the season's best, prepared in distinctive style. Mediterranean menu. Hours: 11:15 am-2:30 pm, 5-10 pm; Fri, Sat to 11 pm; Sun 5-10 pm. Closed Thanksgiving Day, Dec 25. Lunch $4.50-$16.95, dinner $6.95-$50. Bar to 1 am. Reservations accepted. Cr cds: A, D, DS, MC, V.

D

★ **PICKLED PARROT.** *13000 Technology Dr (55344). Phone 952/975-1800.* Hours: 11-1 am; Sun 10 am-10 pm; Sun brunch 10 am-2 pm. Closed Jan 1, Dec 24, 25. Dinner $8-$25. Sun brunch. Bar. Cr cds: A, C, D, DS, MC, V.

D

★★**PING'S SZECHUAN BAR AND GRILL.** *1401 Nicollet Ave S (55403). Phone 612/874-9404; fax 612/874-0647.* Chinese menu. Hours: 11 am-10 pm; Fri to midnight; Sat noon-midnight; Sun noon-9 pm. Closed Thanksgiving. Dinner $9-$14. Bar. Valet parking. Cr cds: A, C, D, DS, MC, V.

D

★ **PRACNA ON MAIN.** *117 Main St (55414). Phone 612/379-3200.* American menu. Lunch, dinner, late night. Bar. Casual attire. Outdoor seating, non-smoking seating. Cr cds: A, D, DS, MC, V. **$**

D

★★★**RUTH'S CHRIS STEAK HOUSE.** *920 2nd Ave S (55402). Phone 612/672-9000; fax 612/672-9102. www.ruthschris.com.* This classic steakhouse serves the fast-paced business crowd at its central downtown location. Specialties: in steak. Hours: 5-10:30 pm. Closed Thanksgiving, Dec 25. Dinner $35-$45. Bar. Reservations accepted. Elegant décor. Complimentary valet parking. Cr cds: A, D, MC, V.

D

★ **SAWATDEE.** *607 Washington Ave S (55415). Phone 612/338-6451; fax 612/338-6498. www.sawatdee.com.* Seafood, Thai menu. Specialties: in pad Thai, Bangkok seafood special. Hours: 11 am-9:30 pm; Fri, Sat to 10:30 pm. A la carte entrees: lunch, dinner $8.25-$24, lunch Buffet: 8.95. Bar. Reservations accepted. Cr cds: A, C, D, DS, MC, V.

D

★ **SHUANG CHENG.** *1320 SE 4th St (55414). Phone 612/378-0208.* Hours: 10 am-10 pm; Fri, Sat 11 am-11 pm; Sun 4-10 pm. Chinese menu. Lunch $3.55-$4.75, dinner $4.50-$10.95. Specializes in seafood, pork, chicken. Casual décor. Cr cds: A, DS, MC, V.

D

★ **SIDNEY'S PIZZA CAFE.** *2120 Hennepin Ave (55405). Phone 612/870-7000.* Italian, Amer menu. Specialties: in pizza, pasta. Hours: 7 am-11 pm; Fri to midnight; Sat 10 am-midnight; Sun 10 am-11 pm. Closed Dec 24, 25. Breakfast, lunch /dinner $4.95-$9.95. Beer, wine. Outdoor dining. Casual décor. Cr cds: D, DS, V.

D

★★ **SOPHIA.** *65 SE Main St (55414). Phone 612/379-1111; fax 612/379-2507. www.sophia-mpls.com.* French, Continental menu. Hours: 11 am-3 pm, 5-9:45 pm; Fri, Sat to 11:45 pm; Sun 11 am-3 pm. Closed Jan 1, Dec 25. Lunch $5.95-$13, dinner $14-$27. Bar. Outdoor dining. Cr cds: A, D, DS, MC, V.

D

Minnetonka

Restaurant

★ **MARSH.** *15000 Minnetonka Blvd (55345). Phone 952/935-2202; fax 952/935-9685. www.themarsh.com.* Menu changes daily. Hours: 7 am-8 pm; Sat 8 am-8:30 pm; Sun 8 am-5 pm; Sun brunch 11 am-2 pm. Closed Dec 25. Dinner $6-$14. Sun brunch. Bar. Children's menu. Outdoor seating. Cr cds: A, MC, V.

D

Moorhead (D-1)

See also Detroit Lakes

Founded 1871 **Pop** 32,295 **Elev** 903 ft **Area code** 218

Information Chamber of Commerce of Fargo Moorhead, 321 N 4th St, PO Box 2443, Fargo, ND, 58108-2443; 701/237-5678

Web www.moreheadrowan.com

Along with the neighboring city to the west, Fargo, ND, Moorhead is considered an agricultural capital. A shipping and processing center for agricultural products, the town is also a retailing and distribution point. The biggest industries are sugar refining and grain malting. Millions of pounds of sugar are produced annually from beets raised in and near Clay County. Moorhead is the home of Moorhead State University, Concordia College, and Northwest Technical College-Moorhead.

What to See and Do

Comstock Historic House. *506 8th St S. Phone 218/233-0848.* (1882) 11-room home of Solomon Comstock, the founder of Moorhead State University, and his daughter Ada Louise Comstock, who was the first full-time president of Radcliffe College (1923-1943). House has period furniture, historical artifacts. Guided tours. (June-Sept, Sat and Sun) **$**

Heritage-Hjemkomst Interpretive Center. *202 1st Ave N. Phone 218/299-5511.* Home of the Hjemkomst, a Viking ship that sailed to Norway in 1982, the Stave Church and the Red River Valley Heritage exhibit. Also major traveling exhibits. (Mon-Sat, also Sun afternoons; closed Jan 1, Easter, Dec 25) **$$**

Regional Science Center-Planetarium. *1104 7th Ave S. Phone 218/236-3982.* Offers variety of astronomy programs. (Sept-May, Sun-Mon; summer, Thurs) Minnesota State University Moorhead campus, **$$**

Special Event

Scandinavian Hjemkomst Festival. *Phone 218/299-5511.* Late June.

Motel/Motor Lodge

★ **SUPER 8 MOTEL.** *3621 S 8th St (56560). Phone 218/233-8880; toll-free 800/800-8000. www.super8.com.* 61 rooms, 2 story. S $35; D $40-$49; each additional $4; under 12 free. Crib $2. TV; cable. Complimentary continental breakfast. Restaurant nearby. Check-out 11 am. Coin laundry. Business services available. Game room. Cr cds: A, MC, V.

D ⊠ SC

Mora (E-4)

See also Hinckley

What to See and Do

Fishing. Snake River. *Runs along N, S and W perimeters of city.* Canoeing. **Fish Lake.** *5 miles S off MN 65.* **Ann Lake.** *8 miles NW, off MN 47.* **Knife Lake.** *8 miles N on MN 65.*

Kanabec History Center. *805 Forest Ave W. W Forest Ave. Phone 320/679-1665.* Exhibits, gift shop, picnic area, hiking and ski trails; research information. (Daily; closed Jan 1, Thanksgiving, Dec 24-25) **$$**

Special Events

Bike Tour. *Phone 320/679-1677.* Third Sat Sept.

Canoe Race. *Phone 320/679-1081.* First Sat May.

Half-Marathon. *Phone 320/679-1838.* Third Sat Aug.

Vasaloppet Cross-Country Ski Race. *Phone 800/368-6672.* Second Sun Feb.

Morris (E-1)

Pop 5,613 **Area code** 320 **Zip** 56267

Information Morris Area Chamber of Commerce & Agriculture, 507 Atlantic Ave; 320/589-1242

Web www.morrischamber.org

Morris is the county seat of Stevens County and provides a regional shopping center for west central Minnesota. The surrounding area offers good fishing and hunting and is known for wildfowl, especially pheasants. The Wetland Management office is located here and manages seven counties along with 43,000 acres of waterfowl protection areas.

What to See and Do

Pomme de Terre City Park. *2 3/4 miles E on County 10.* A 363-acre public recreational area along Pomme de Terre River; picnicking, canoeing, fishing; camping (hookups; fee), nature and bicycle trail; swimming beach; sand volleyball court; concession. (Apr-Oct, daily) **FREE**

University of Minnesota, Morris. *600 E 4th St. 4th and College sts. For information Phone 320/589-6050.* (1960). (2,000 students) Humanities Fine Arts Center Gallery presents changing contemporary exhibits (Oct-mid-June, Mon-Fri) and performing arts series (Oct-Apr). Tours.

Special Event

Prairie Pioneer Days. *Phone 320/589-1242.* Arts and crafts, parade, games and activities. Second weekend July.

Motel/Motor Lodge

★ ★ **BEST WESTERN PRAIRIE INN.** *200 Hwy 28 E (56267). Phone 320/589-3030; toll-free 800/565-3035. www.bestwestern.com.* 78 rooms, 2 story. S, D $34-$84; under 17 free. Crib free. Pet accepted, some restrictions. Complimentary continental breakfast. Check-out 11 am. TV; cable (premium). Restaurant 6:30 am-10 pm. Bar 4 pm-1 am. Sauna. Game room. Indoor pool, wading pool, whirlpool, poolside service. Meeting rooms, business services. Cr cds: A, C, D, DS, MC, V.

D ⛵ 🚶

New Ulm (G-3)

See also Redwood Falls, Saint Peter

Founded 1854 **Pop** 13,132 **Elev** 896 ft **Area code** 507 **Zip** 56073

Information New Ulm Convention & Visitors Bureau, 1 N Minnesota, Box 862; 507/233-4300 or 888/4-NEWULM

Web www.ic.new-ulm.mn.us

Settled by German immigrants who borrowed the name of their home city, New Ulm is one of the few planned communities in the state. After more than a century, it still retains the order and cleanliness of the original settlement. The city today is in the center of a prosperous agricultural and dairy area and has developed a substantial business community. There is a visitor center at 1 North Minnesota Street (May-Oct, daily; Nov-Apr, Mon-Sat).

What to See and Do

Brown County Historical Museum. *2 N Broadway St. Center St and Broadway. Phone 507/354-2016.* Former post office. Historical exhibits on Native Americans and pioneers; artwork; research library with 5,000 family files. (Mon-Fri, also Sat and Sun afternoons; closed holidays) **$**

Flandrau. *1300 Summit Ave. Located at the city limits, on S Summit Ave; 1 mile S on MN 15, then W. Phone 507/233-9800.* Comprised of 801 acres on Cottonwood River. Swimming; cross-country skiing (rentals); camping; hiking. Standard fees.

Fort Ridgely. *14 miles W on US 14, then 12 miles N on MN 4. Phone 507/426-7840.* A 584-acre park. Fort partly restored; interpretive center (May-Labor Day, daily). Nine-hole golf course (fee); cross-country skiing; camping; hiking; annual historical festival. Standard fees.

The Glockenspiel. *4th N and Minnesota sts. Phone 507/354-4217.* A 45-foot-high musical clock tower with performing animated figures; carillon with 37 bells. Performances (three times daily; noon, 3 pm and 5 pm).

Harkin Store. *2 N Broadway St. 8 miles NW of town via County 21. Phone 507/354-8666.* General store built by Alexander Harkin in 1870 in the small town of West Newton. The town died when it was bypassed by the railroad, but the store stayed open as a convenience until 1901, when rural free delivery closed the post office. The store has been restored to its original appearance and still has many original items on the shelves. Special programs in summer months. (Summer, Tues-Sun; May-Sept, weekends) **$**

Hermann's Monument. *Center & Monument sts. On the bluff W of city in Hermann Heights Park. Phone 507/354-4217.* Erected by a fraternal order, monument recalls Hermann the Cheruscan, a German hero of A.D. 9. Towering 102 feet, monument has winding stairway to platform with view of city and Minnesota Valley. (June-Labor Day, daily) Picnic area. **$**

Schell Garden and Deer Park. *Schells Park. S on MN 15, then W on 18th St; on Schell Brewery grounds. Phone 507/354-5528.* Garden with deer and peacocks (all year). Brewery tours, museum, gift shop. (Memorial Day-Labor Day, daily; rest of year, Sat) **$**

Special Events

Brown County Fair. *1200 N State St. Fairgrounds Phone 507/354-2223.* Aug.

Fasching. *118 N Minnesota St. Phone 507/354-8850.* Traditional German winter festival. Includes German food, music; costume ball. Phone 507/354-8850. Late Feb.

Heritagefest. *118 N Minnesota St. Phone 507/354-8850.* Old World-style celebration highlighting German traditions and culture through music, food, arts and crafts. Features entertainers from around the area and from Europe. Phone 507/354-8850. Two weekends Mid-July.

Motels/Motor Lodges

★ **COLONIAL INN.** *1315 N Broadway St (97060).*
Phone 507/354-3128; toll-free 888/215-2143. 24 rooms, 10
with shower only. S $26-$50; D $34-$65. Crib free. Complimentary coffee in lobby. Check-out 11 am. TV; cable
(premium). Restaurant nearby. Cross-country ski 1 mile.
Cr cds: A, DS, MC, V.

★ ★ **HOLIDAY INN.** *2101 S Broadway St (56073).*
*Phone 507/359-2941; toll-free 877/359-2941; fax 507/354-
7147. www.holiday-inn.com.* 120 rooms, 6 suites, 2 story.
S, D $69-$89; each additional $10; suites $89-$129; under
19 free. Crib free. Check-out noon. TV; cable (premium).
In-room modem link. Valet services. Restaurant 6:30 am-
2 pm, 5-10 pm. Bar 11-1 am, entertainment, room service.
Sauna. Game room. Indoor pool, whirlpool. Cross-coun-
try ski 2 miles. Meeting rooms, business center. Cr cds: A,
D, DS, JCB, MC, V.

Restaurants

★ **D.J.'S.** *1200 N Broadway (56073). Phone 507/354-
3843.* German, Amer menu. Hours: 6 am-9 pm; Sat, Sun
from 7 am. Closed Dec 24, 25. Breakfast $1.59-$6.99,
lunch $3.15-$6, dinner $5.25-$11.95.

★ **VEIGEL'S KAISERHOF.** *221 N Minnesota St
(56073). Phone 507/359-2071; fax 507/354-2006.* German
cuisine. Hours: Mon.-Sun. 11 am-9 pm, closed Dec .25.
Lunch $4-$8, dinner $9-$18. Bar to 1 am. Child's menu.
Reservations accepted. Cr cds: A, C, D, DS, MC, V.

Northfield (G-4)

See also Minneapolis, Owatonna, Red Wing, Saint Paul

Founded 1855 **Pop** 14,684 **Elev** 919 ft **Area code** 507
Zip 55057

Information Northfield Area Chamber of Commerce, 500
Water St S, PO Box 198; 507/645-5604 or 800/658-2548

Web www.northfieldchamber.com

This bustling, historic river town, located 30 miles south
of the Twin Cities, offers a captivating blend of the old
and new. Its history is one of the most dramatic of any
Midwestern community. Each year on the weekend after
Labor Day, thousands flock here to share in the retelling of
the defeat of Jesse James and his gang who, on September
7, 1876, were foiled in their attempt to raid the Northfield

Bank in what proved to be one of the last chapters in the
brutal saga of the Old West.

This history has been preserved in the Northfield Bank
Museum at 408 Division St, keystone of the city's unique
historical downtown district. The well-preserved storefronts house boutiques, antique stores, and other interesting shops.

What to See and Do

Carleton College. *1 N College St. NE edge of town on MN
19. Phone 507/646-4000.* (1866). (1,800 students) Liberal
arts. Arboretum (455 acres) has hiking and jogging trails
along Cannon River. Also here is a 35-acre prairie maintained by college. Tours of arboretum and prairie with
advance notice. Summer theater programs.

Nerstrand Woods State Park. *9700 170th St E. 12 miles SE,
off MN 246. Phone 507/334-8848.* More than 1,280 acres,
heavily wooded; hiking, cross-country skiing, snowmobiling; picnicking, camping (dump station). Standard fees.

Northfield Arts Guild. *304 Division St S. Downtown. Phone
507/645-8877.* Exhibits of local and regional fine arts
housed in historic YMCA Building (1885); juried handcrafted items. (Mon-Sat; closed holidays) **FREE**

St. Olaf College. *1520 St Olaf Ave. 1 mile W of business
district. Phone 507/646-2222.* (1874). (3,000 students)
Famous for its choir, band, and orchestra, which tour
nationally and abroad. Steensland Art Gallery (Daily).
Home of national offices and archives of Norwegian-
American Historical Association.

Special Event

Defeat of Jesse James Days. *Phone 507/645-5604.* Raid
reenactment, parade, outdoor arts fair, rodeo. Four days
beginning weekend after Labor Day.

Motels/Motor Lodges

★ ★ **COUNTRY INN BY CARLSON, NORTH-
FIELD.** *300 S Hwy 3 (55057). Phone 507/645-2286;
toll-free 800/456-4000; fax 507/645-2958.* 54 rooms, 2
story. S $47-$82; D $53-$88; each additional $6; suites
$82-$88; under 18 free. Crib free. Complimentary continental breakfast. Check-out noon. TV; cable (premium).
Refrigerators. Coin laundry. Restaurant nearby. Indoor
pool, whirlpool. Downhill ski 20 miles, cross-country ski
1 mile. Cr cds: A, C, D, DS, MC, V.

★ **SUPER 8 MOTEL.** *1420 Riverview Dr (55057). Phone
507/663-0371; toll-free 800/800-8000. www.super8.com.* 40
rooms, 2 story. S $40-$49; D $51-67; suite $76-$81. Crib free.
Check-out 11 am. TV. Restaurant adjacent. Cross-country
ski 1 mile. Business services. Cr cds: A, C, D, DS, MC, V.

B&B/Small Inns

★★ARCHER HOUSE HOTEL. *212 Division St (55057). Phone 507/645-5661; toll-free 800/247-2235; fax 507/645-4295. www.archerhouse.com.* 34 rooms, 3 story. D $40. Check-out 11 am, check-in 3 pm. TV; cable (premium), VCR available. Dining room 6:30 am-10 pm. Room service. Downhill ski 20 miles, cross-country ski 1 mile. Built 1877; antiques, country décor. On river. Cr cds: A, MC, V.

D ⊠

Onamia (E-3)

Pop 676 **Elev** 1,264 ft **Area code** 320 **Zip** 56359

What to See and Do

Mille Lacs Kathio State Park. *15066 Kathio Park Rd. 8 miles NW on US 169, then 1 mile S on County Rd 26. Phone 320/532-3523.* Comprises 10,577 acres surrounding main outlet of Mille Lacs Lake. Evidence of Native American habitation and culture dating back over 4,000 years. Here in 1679, Daniel Greysolon, Sieur du Lhut, claimed the upper Mississippi region for France. Swimming, fishing, boating (rentals); hiking, riding trails; cross-country skiing (rentals), snowmobiling; picnicking; camping (dump station). Interpretive center. Standard fees. **$$**

Resort

★★IZATY'S GOLF AND YACHT CLUB. *40005 85th Ave. Phone 320/532-3101; toll-free 800/533-1728; fax 320/532-3208. www.izatys.com.* Offering both hotel rooms and two, three, and four bedroom town homes, this resort has something for every vacationer. Two golf courses are found at the resort along with a full marina, an indoor and outdoor pool. 28 in lodge rooms, 2 story. D $65-$125; townhouses $115-$389 (2-day min wkends); family rates; golf plan. Check-out noon, check-in 4 pm. TV; VCR available (movies). Fireplaces. Dining room 7 am-10 pm. Bar 11-1 am. Free supervised children's activities (Memorial Day-Labor Day); ages 4-10 years. Sauna. Game room. 1 outdoor pool, 1 indoor, whirlpool. Cross-country ski on site. Lawn games. Motors, pontoons, launch serv, boat marina. Fishing guides. Snowmobiles. Cr cds: A, D, DS, MC, V.

D ⊠ ⊠

Owatonna (G-4)

See also Faribault, Northfield, Rochester

Settled 1854 **Pop** 19,386 **Elev** 1,154 ft **Area code** 507 **Zip** 55060

Information Chamber of Commerce and Tourism, 320 Hoffman Dr; 507/451-7970 or 800/423-6466

Web www.owatonna.org

Legend has it that the city was named after a beautiful but frail Native American princess named Owatonna. It is said that her father, Chief Wabena, had heard about the healing water called "minnewaucan." When the waters' curing powers restored his daughter's health, he moved his entire village to the site now known as Mineral Springs Park. A statue of Princess Owatonna stands in the park and watches over the springs that are still providing cold, fresh mineral water.

What to See and Do

Minnesota State Public School Orphanage Museum. *540 W Hills Cir. Phone 507/451-2149. Phone 507/451-2149.* This museum is on the site of a former orphanage that housed nearly 13,000 children from 1866–1945. The main building is on the National Registry of Historic Places. (Daily) **FREE**

Norwest Bank Owatonna, NA Building. *101 N Cedar Ave, at Broadway. Phone 507/451-7970.* Completed in 1908 as the National Farmers Bank, this nationally acclaimed architectural treasure was designed by one of America's outstanding architects, Louis H. Sullivan. The cube like exterior with huge arched stained-glass windows by Louis Millet quickly earned the building widespread recognition as, according to one historian, "a jewel box set down in a prairie town."

Owatonna Arts Center. *435 Garden View Ln, West Hills Complex. Phone 507/451-0533.* Housed in a historic Romanesque structure. Permanent collection includes 100-piece collection of garments from around the world, and 14-foot stained-glass panels featured in the Performing Arts Hall. Outdoor sculpture garden has works by Minnesota artists John Rood, Richard and Donald Hammel, Paul Grandlund, and Charles Gagnon. Changing gallery shows every month. **DONATION**

Village of Yesteryear. *1448 Austin Rd. Phone 507/451-1420.* Eleven restored pioneer buildings from mid-1800s include church, two log cabins, schoolhouse, large family home, old fire department and country store; depot, farm machinery bldg, blacksmith shop; museum; period furnishings, memorabilia and a C-52 locomotive caboose (1905). (May-Sept, afternoons except Mon) **$$**

Motels/Motor Lodges

★ BUDGET HOST INN. *745 State Ave (55060). Phone 507/451-8712; fax 507/451-4456.* 27 rooms, 2 story. S $29-$38; D $32-$48; each additional $5. Crib $5. Check-out 11 am. TV; cable. Restaurant adjacent. Cross-country ski 1 mile. Meeting rooms. Coffee in lobby. Cr cds: A, MC, V.

⊠ ✕

★ **RAMADA INN.** *1212 N I-35 (55060). Phone 507/ 455-0606; fax 507/455-3731. www.ramada.com.* 117 rooms, 2 story. S $47-$57; D $54-$64; each additional $5. Crib free. Check-out noon. TV; cable. Coin laundry. Restaurant 6 am-2 pm, 5-9 pm. Bar 4 pm-1 am. Room service. Sauna. Indoor pool, whirlpool. Cross-country ski 1 mile. Free airport transportation. Business services. Sundries. Cr cds: A, C, D, DS, JCB, MC, V.

D ⊠

★ **SUPER 8 MOTEL.** *1818 Hwy 14 W; I-35 & Hwy 14 W (55060). Phone 507/451-0380; fax 507/451-0380.* 60 rooms, 2 story. S $44-$48; D $53-$60; each additional $3-$5. Crib $3. TV; VCR (movies). Complimentary continental breakfast. Restaurant adjacent open 24 hours. Check-out 11 am. Business services available. Sundries. Cross-country ski 1 mile. Cr cds: A, C, D, DS, MC, V.

D ⊠ ⊠ SC

Park Rapids (D-2)

See also Detroit Lakes, Walker

Founded 1880 **Pop** 2,863 **Elev** 1,440 ft **Area code** 218 **Zip** 56470

Information Chamber of Commerce, PO Box 249; 218/ 732-4111 or 800/247-0054

Web www.parkrapids.com

This resort center is surrounded by 400 lakes, nearly as many streams, and beautiful woods. There are more than 200 resorts within 20 miles. Fishing is excellent for bass, walleye, northern pike, muskie, and trout.

What to See and Do

Hubbard County Historical Museum/North Country Museum of Arts. *Court Ave at Third St. Phone 218/732-5237.* Historical museum has displays on pioneer life, including pioneer farm implements, one-room schoolhouse, and foreign wars. Museum of arts has five galleries of contemporary art and also features a section on 15th- to 18th-century European art. (May-Sept, Tues-Sat; Feb-Apr, Tues-Sun)

Motel/Motor Lodge

★ **SUPER 8 MOTEL.** *1020 E 1st St (56470). Phone 218/732-9704; toll-free 800/800-8000. www.super8.com.* 62 rooms, 2 story. S $45-$75; D $60-$80; suites $95-$125; each additional $5; under 13 free. Crib $2. TV; cable. Complimentary breakfast. Restaurant nearby. Check-out 11 am. Guest laundry. Business services available. In-room modem link. Whirlpool. Sauna. Recreation room. Cr cds: A, C, D, DS, JCB, MC, V.

D ⊠ SC

Pine River (D-3)

See also Brainerd, Walker

Pop 871 **Elev** 1,290 ft **Area code** 218 **Zip** 56474

Resorts

★ ★ ★ **DRIFTWOOD RESORT AND GOLF COURSE.** *RR 1 Box 404 (56474). Phone 218/568-4221; fax 218/568-4222. www.driftwoodresort.com.* This is a full service country resort that offers 24 individual cabins along with tons to keep guests busy and relaxed. A great golf courses is available as well as tennis facilities, row boats, kayaks, a great dining room and much more. 8 kitchen units, 27 cottages (1-4 bedrooms). July-mid-Aug, weekly: $546 each; map available; family rates mid-Aug-late Sept. Closed rest of year. Crib available. Check-out noon, check-in 4 pm. Refrigerators. Coin laundry. Dining room 8-9:30 am, noon-1 pm, 6-7:30 pm. Entertainment; movies, dancing. Box lunches, snacks. Free supervised children's activities (mid-May-Sept); ages 2-13. Heated pool, wading pool. 9-hole golf, putting greens. Tennis, pro. Canoes, rowboats, sailboats, motors; launching facilities. Sternwheel paddleboat cruises available. Nature walk/trail. Business services. Grocery, package store 4 1/2 miles. Barbecues, outdoor buffet Mon. Recreation director. Minnesota resort museum. Pony rides. Indoor, outdoor games. Recreation hall. 55 acres. Cr cds: A, MC, V.

D ⚂

★ ★ **PINEY RIDGE LODGE.** *6023 Wildamere Dr (56474). Phone 218/587-2296; toll-free 800/450-3333; fax 218/587-4323. www.pineyridge.com.* 12 cottages (1-4 bedrm), 8 with kitchen 14 deluxe condo kitchen units. Mid-June-late Aug, weekly: $700-$1,575 (2-6 persons); weekend rates; lower rates May-mid-June, late Aug-late-Sept. Closed rest of year. Crib available. Check-out 10 am, check-in 4 pm. Fireplaces, refrigerators. Coin laundry. Dining room 8-10 am, 11:30 am-3 pm, 5-10 pm. Box lunches, snack bar. Free supervised children's activities (mid-June-Labor Day). Sauna. Soc director. Recreation room. 18-hole, pro shop. Lawn games, Dockage, boats, motors, canoes. Grills, picnics/tables. Airport, bus depot transportation. Business services. Grocery, package store 6 1/2 miles. Private club 8-11 pm. Movies. Cr cds: MC, V.

D ⊠

Pipestone (G-1)

See also Sioux Falls

Settled 1874 **Pop** 4,554 **Elev** 1,738 ft **Area code** 507 **Zip** 56164

Information Chamber of Commerce, 117 8th Ave SE, PO Box 8; 507/825-3316 or 800/336-6125

Web www.pipestoneminnesota.com

County seat and center of a fertile farming area, Pipestone is host to visitors en route to Pipestone National Monument. Some of the red Sioux quartzite from the quarries shows up in Pipestone's public buildings. George Catlin, famous painter of Native Americans, was the first white man to report on the area.

What to See and Do

Pipestone County Museum. *113 S Hiawatha Ave. Phone 507/825-2563.* Prehistory, early settlement, Native American, pioneer exhibits; research library, gift shop. Tours. (Daily, closed holidays) **$$**

Split Rock Creek State Park. *6 miles SW on MN 23, then 1 mile S on County 20. Phone 507/348-7908 or 800/766-6000.* On 1,300 acres. Swimming; fishing (accessible to the disabled); boating (rentals). Hiking; cross-country skiing; picnicking; camping (dump station). Standard fees.

Special Events

Hiawatha Pageant. *117 8th Ave SE. Phone 507/825-3316. Just S of Pipestone National Monument entrance.* Outdoor performance. All seats reserved; ticket office opens 1 pm on show dates, phone 507/825-3316 or contact the Chamber of Commerce. Last two weekends July and first weekend Aug.

Watertower Festival. *Courthouse lawn. Phone 507/825-3316.* Large arts and crafts show; parade. Last Fri and Sat June.

Motels/Motor Lodges

★ **ARROW MOTEL.** *600 8th Ave NE (56164). Phone 507/825-3331; fax 507/825-5638.* 17 rooms. S $27; D $39; each additional $4. Crib. Pet accepted. Complimentary continental breakfast. Check-out 11 am. TV; cable (premium). Restaurant opposite 6 am-9 pm. Pool. Gift shop. Shaded lawn. Cr cds: A, DS, MC, V.

D ⊠

★ **SUPER 8 MOTEL.** *605 8th Ave SE (56164). Phone 507/825-4217; fax 507/825-4219. www.super8.com.* 39 rooms, 2 story. S $38-$50; D $72-$80; each additional $4; under 12 free. Crib $1. Check-out 11 am. TV; cable (pre-

mium). Some in-room whirlpools. Restaurant adjacent 6 am-10 pm. Business services. Cr cds: A, C, D, DS, MC, V.

D ⊠

Hotel

★★ **HISTORIC CALUMET INN.** *104 W Main St (56164). Phone 507/825-5871; fax 507/825-4578.* This historic inn, which features rooms full of antiques, was built from Sioux Quartzite in 1888. Guests will be awed by the two-story lobby with its tin ceiling and will enjoy a nightcap at the large antique oak bar in Cally's Lounge, which was once the bank! 40 rooms, 4 story. S, D $50-$65; each additional $4; under 12 free. Complimentary continental breakfast. Check-out 11 am. TV; cable (premium), VCR available (movies). In-room modem link. Restaurant 9 am-9 pm. Bar 4 pm-1 am. Cr cds: A, MC, V.

D ⊠ SC

Restaurant

★ **LANGE'S CAFE.** *110 8th Ave SE (56164). Phone 507/825-4488.* Hours: Open 24 hours. Breakfast $1.29-$6.95, lunch $3.25-$6.95 , dinner $4.25-$13.95. Casual, family-style dining. Reservations accepted. Cr cds: MC, V.

D ⊠

Pipestone National Monument (G-1)

See also Pipestone

(On US 75, MN 23, 30, adjacent to north boundary of Pipestone)

The ancient pipestone in the quarries of this 283-acre area is found in few other places. The Native Americans quarried this reddish stone and carved it into ceremonial pipes. Pipestone deposits, named catlinite for George Catlin, who first described the stone, run about a foot thick, though most usable sections are about two inches thick. Principal features of the monument are **Winnewissa Falls,** flowing over quartzite outcroppings; **Three Maidens,** group of glacial boulders near quarries; **Leaping Rock,** used by Native Americans as a test of strength of young men who attemped to leap from the top of quartzite ridge to its crest, 11 feet away; **Nicollet Marker,** inscription on boulder recalls visit here in 1838 of Joseph Nicollet's exploring party. He carved his name and initials of members of his party, including Lieutenant John C. Frémont.

Established as a national monument in 1937, Pipestone protects the remaining red stone and preserves it for use by Native Americans of all tribes. The visitor center has exhibits, slides, pipe-making demonstrations, and a self-guided tour booklet for the circle trail and other information; also here is Upper Midwest Indian Cultural Center with craft displays. (Daily; visitor center closed Jan 1, Dec 25) Phone 507/825-5464.

Red Wing (G-4)

See also Hastings, Lakeville, Northfield, Saint Paul

Founded 1836 **Pop** 15,134 **Elev** 720 ft **Area code** 651 **Zip** 55066

Information Visitors and Convention Bureau, 418 Levee St; 651/385-5934 or 800/498-3444

Web www.redwing.org

Established as a missionary society outpost, this community bears the name of one of the great Dakota chiefs, Koo-Poo-Hoo-Sha (wing of the wild swan dyed scarlet). Red Wing industries produce leather, shoes, precision instruments, malt, flour, linseed oil, diplomas, rubber, and wood products.

What to See and Do

Biking. *306 Mills St W. Phone 507/263-0508.* Wheel passes needed for biking. For further information, contact the Cannon Valley Trail office. (18 years and over only)

Cannon Valley Trail. *500 LaFayette Rd N. Phone 651/263-0508; 651/258-4141 (snow conditions).* Twenty-mi cross-country skiing trail connects Cannon Falls, Welch, and Red Wing. **$$**

Goodhue County Historical Museum. *1166 Oak St. Phone 651/388-6024.* One of state's most comprehensive museums. Permanent exhibits relate local and regional history from glacial age to present. Extensive collection of Red Wing pottery; artifacts from Prairie Island Native American community. (Tues-Sun; closed holidays) **FREE**

Hiking. A 1 1/2 miles hiking trail to top of Mt. LaGrange (Barn Bluff) with scenic overlook of Mississippi River. Cannon Valley Trail provides 25 miles of improved trail following Cannon Bottom River to Cannon Falls. **FREE**

Mount Frontenac. *9 miles S on US 61. Phone 651/388-5826; 800/488-5826.* Three double chairlifts, three rope tows; patrol, school, rentals; snowmaking; cafeteria. Vertical drop 420 feet. (Nov-mid-Mar, Wed-Sun; closed Dec 25) Also 18-hole golf course (Mid-Apr-Oct; fee). **$$$$**

Red Wing Stoneware. *4909 Moundview Dr. Phone 651/388-4610.* Popular stoneware facility; visitors can watch artisans create various types of pottery. Call for hours.

Sheldon Theatre. *443 W Third St. Phone 651/385-3667.* The US's first municipal theater, opened 1904. Perfor-

mances available regularly. Group tours available. (June-Oct, Fri-Sat; Nov-May, Sat).

Soldiers' Memorial Park/East End Recreation Area. *Skyline Dr.* On plateau overlooking city and river; 476 acres; 5 miles of hiking trails. **Colvill Park.** On Mississippi. Also waterpark (June-Aug, fee), playground; boat launching, marina. **Bay Point Park.** On Mississippi. Showers, boat launching, marina, picnicking, playground, walking trail. (May-Oct, daily)

Welch Village. *26685 County 7 Blvd. 12 miles NW on US 61, then 3 miles S on County 7 to Welch. Phone 651/258-4567.* Three quad, five double, triple chairlifts, Mitey-mite; patrol, rentals; snowmaking; cafeteria. Longest run 4,000 feet; vertical drop 350 feet. (Nov-Mar, daily; closed Dec 25) **$$$$**

Special Events

Fall Festival of the Arts. *Phone 651/385-5934.* First weekend Oct.

River City Days. *Phone 651/385-5934.* First weekend Aug.

Motels/Motor Lodges

★**BEST WESTERN.** *752 Withers Harbor Dr (55066). Phone 651/388-1577; fax 612/388-1150. www.quiethouse.com.* 51 rooms, 2 story. S $74-$157; D $84-$167; under 12 free. Pet accepted. Check-out 11 am. TV. In-room modem link. Exercise equipment. Indoor pool, outdoor pool, whirlpool. Cr cds: A, C, D, DS, MC, V.

D ⬛ ⬛ ⬛ ⬛

★ **DAYS INN.** *955 E 7th St (55066). Phone 651/388-3568; toll-free 800/329-7466; fax 651/385-1901. www.daysinn.com.* 48 rooms. S, D $40.50-$80.50; each additional $5; under 13 free. Pet accepted. Complimentary continental breakfast. Check-out 11 am. TV; cable. Complimentary coffee in rooms. Restaurant nearby. Indoor pool, whirlpool. Downhill ski 7 miles, cross-country ski 1 mile. Business services. Municipal park, marinas opposite. Cr cds: A, C, D, DS, JCB, MC, V.

D ⬛ ⬛ ⬛ ⬛ SC

★ **RODEWAY INN.** *235 Withers Harbor Dr (55066). Phone 651/388-1502; toll-free 800/228-2000; fax 651/388-1501.* 39 rooms, 2 story. S $39-$57; D $49-$67; each additional $5; suites $59-$130. Crib $5. TV; cable (premium), VCR available (movies). Indoor pool; whirlpool. Restaurant adjacent 6 am-midnight. Check-out 11 am. Business services available. Downhill ski 12 miles; cross-country ski 1 mile. Cr cds: A, C, D, DS, JCB, MC, V.

D ⬛ ⬛ ⬛ SC

★ **SUPER 8 MOTEL.** *232 Withers Harbor Dr (55066). Phone 651/388-0491; fax 651/388-1066. www.super8.com.* 60 rooms, 2 story. June-Dec: S $48-$57; D $57-$67; suites $70-$100; higher rates Sat; lower rates rest of year. Crib $3. Complimentary continental breakfast in lobby. Check-out 11 am. TV; cable (premium), VCR avail, (movies). Restaurant adjacent 6 am-11 pm. Indoor pool. Downhill ski 12 miles. Business services. Cr cds: A, C, D, DS, MC, V.

🄳 ⌕ ⌕ ⌕

Hotel

★ ★ **ST. JAMES.** *406 Main St (55066). Phone 651/388-2846; toll-free 800/252-1875; fax 651/388-5226. www.st-james-hotel.com.* Built in 1875, this hotel offers 19th-century Victorian style along with modern amenities. It is located on the bank of the Mississippi River in the heart of Red Wing, near many local attractions, restaurants, and shops. 60 rooms, 2-5 story. S, D $96-$225; under 18 free. TV; cable (premium), VCR available. In-room modem link. Restaurant 6:30 am-9:30 pm. Bar 11-12:30 am, entertainment Fri, Sat. Health club privileges. Downhill/cross-country ski 10 miles. Free covered parking. Airport transportation. Overlooks Mississippi. Cr cds: A, C, D, DS, MC, V.

🄳 ⌕ ⌕ ✕

B&B/Small Inns

★ ★ **GOLDEN LANTERN INN.** *721 East Ave (55066). Phone 651/388-3315; toll-free 888/288-3315; fax 651/385-9178. www.goldenlantern.com.* 5 rooms, 2 story. No room phones. D $99-$215. Accepts children by arrangement. Complimentary full breakfast. Check-out 11 am, check-in 4-5 pm. Restaurant nearby. Downhill ski 8 miles, cross-country ski 1 mile. Tudor brick house built 1932. Totally nonsmoking. Cr cds: A, DS, MC, V.

⌕

Restaurant

★ **LIBERTY'S.** *303 W 3rd (55066). Phone 651/388-8877. www.libertyonline.com.* Continental menu. Specialties: in ribs, burgers. Hours: 8 am-11 pm; Fri, Sat to 1 am. Closed most major holidays. Breakfast $2.50-$7.95, lunch $3-$7, dinner $3-$17.95. Sun brunch 9:30 am-2 pm; $8.25. Bar to 1 am. Casual décor. Reservations accepted. Cr cds: A, D, DS, MC, V.

🄳 🆂🅲

Redwood Falls (G-2)

Pop 4,859 **Elev** 1,044 ft **Area Code** 507 **Zip** 56283

Information Redwood Area Chamber and Tourism, 200 S Mill St, PO Box 21; 507/637-2828 or 800/657-7070

Web www.redwoodfalls.org

What to See and Do

Lower Sioux Agency and Historic Site. *32469 Redwood County Hwy 2. 7mi E of Redwood Falls. Phone 507/697-6321.* Exhibits, trail system, and restored 1861 warehouse trace history of the Dakota in Minnesota from the mid-17th century through the present. (May-Sept, daily; rest of year, by appt)

Ramsey Park. *W edge of town, off MN 19.* A 200-acre park of rugged woodland carved by Redwood River and Ramsey Creek. Includes picnicking, trail riding, cross-country ski trail, hiking; golf; camping. Small zoo, playground shelters, 30-foot waterfall.

Special Event

Minnesota Inventors Congress. *805 E Bridge St. Phone 507/637-2344.* Redwood Valley School. Exhibit of inventions by adult and student inventors; seminars. Food; arts and crafts; parade; also resource center. Three days second full weekend June.

Rochester (G-4)

See also Spring Valley

Settled 1854 **Pop** 70,745 **Elev** 1,297 ft **Area code** 507

Information Convention & Visitors Bureau, 150 S Broadway, Suite A, 55904; 507/288-4331 or 800/634-8277

Web www.rochestercvb.org

The world-famous Mayo Clinic has made what was once a crossroads campground for immigrant wagon trains a city of doctors, hospitals, and lodging places. Each year thousands of people come here in search of medical aid. One of the first dairy farms in the state began here, and Rochester still remains a central point for this industry. Canned goods, fabricated metals, and electronic data processing equipment are among its industrial products.

What to See and Do

Mayo Clinic. *200 1st St SW. Phone 507/284-9258.* Over 30 buildings now accommodate the famous group practice of medicine that grew from the work of Dr. William Worrall Mayo and his sons, Dr. William James Mayo and Dr. Charles Horace Mayo. There are now 1,041 doctors at the clinic as well as 935 residents in training in virtually every medical and surgical specialty. The 14-story Plummer Building (1928) includes medical library and historical exhibit. The Conrad N. Hilton and Guggenheim buildings (1974) house clinical and research laboratories. The 19-story Mayo Building (1955, 1967) covers an entire block. It houses facilities for diagnosis and treatment. Clinic tours (Mon-Fri; closed holidays). **FREE** Also here is

> **The Rochester Carillon.** *In the tower of the Plummer Building.* Concerts (schedule varies). **FREE**

Mayowood. *1195 W Circle Dr SW. Phone 507/282-9447 or 507/287-8691 (recording).* Home of Drs C. H. and C. W. Mayo, historic 38-room country mansion on 15 acres; period antiques, works of art. **$$$**

Olmsted County History Center and Museum. *1195 W Circle Dr SW. Corner of County Rds 22 and 25. Phone 507/282-9447.* Changing historical exhibits (Daily; closed hols); research library (Mon-Fri; closed hols). **$**

Plummer House of the Arts. *1091 Plummer Ln SW. Entrance is at corner of 12th Ave and 9th St. Phone 507/281-6160.* Former estate of Dr. Henry S. Plummer, a 35-year member of the Mayo Clinic. 11 acres remain, with formal gardens, quarry, water tower. 5-story house is English Tudor mansion (Circa 1920) with original furnishings and slate roof. Tours (June-Aug, Wed afternoons, also first and third Sun afternoons). **$$**

Whitewater State Park. *20 miles E on US 14, then 7 miles N on MN 74. Phone 507/932-3007.* An 1,822-acre park. Limestone formations in a hardwood forest. Swimming, fishing; hiking, cross-country skiing; picnicking; primitive camping. Interpretive center. Standard fees.

Motels/Motor Lodges

★ **AMERICINN STEWARTVILLE.** *1700 Second Ave NW (55976). Phone 507/533-4747; toll-free 800/634-3444; fax 507/533-4747.* 29 rooms. S $40-$45; D $45-$50; each additional $6; under 12 free. Crib free. Complimentary continental breakfast. Check-out 11 am. TV; cable. Restaurant nearby. Business services. Cr cds: A, DS, MC, V.

D ⬜ SC

★★ **BEST WESTERN APACHE.** *1517 16th St SW (55902). Phone 507/289-8866; fax 507/292-0000. www.bestwestern.com.* 151 rooms, 3 story. S $60-$199; D $64-$219; each additional $5; suites $85-$159; under 18 free; weekend rates. Pet accepted. Complimentary breakfast. Check-out noon. TV; cable (premium), VCR available.

In-room modem link. Valet services. Restaurant 6:30 am-10 pm. Bar 5 pm-1 am. Room service. Game room. Indoor pool, whirlpool. Cross-country ski 2 miles. Free airport transportation. Meeting rooms, business services. Sundries. Tropical atrium. Cr cds: A, C, D, DS, JCB, MC, V.

D ⬜ ⬜ ⬜ ⬜ SC

★ **BEST WESTERN FIFTH AVENUE.** *20 NW 5th Ave (55901). Phone 507/289-3987. www.bestwestern.com.* 63 rooms, 3 story. S, D $56; each additional $5; under 18 free. Pet accepted. Check-out noon. TV; cable (premium). Restaurant nearby. Indoor pool. Cross-country ski 1 mile. Cr cds: A, C, D, DS, ER, JCB, MC, V.

D ⬜ ⬜ ⬜ ⬜

★★ **BEST WESTERN SOLDIERS' FIELD.** *401 6th St SW (55902). Phone 507/288-2677; fax 507/282-2042. www.bestwestern.com.* 21 rooms, 90 kitchen units, 8 story. S, D, kitchen suites $69-$84; each additional $5; under 12 free. Crib free. Complimentary breakfast Mon-Fri. Check-out noon. TV; cable. Coin laundry. Restaurant 6 am-10 pm. Bar 4 pm-closing, entertainment. Exercise equipment. Game room, recreation room. Indoor pool, wading pool, whirlpool. Cross-country ski 1 block. Free airport, bus depot transportation. Meeting rooms, business services. Gift shop. Cr cds: A, C, D, DS, JCB, MC, V.

D ⬜ ⬜ ⬜ ⬜ ⬜ SC

★ **COMFORT INN.** *1625 S Broadway (55904). Phone 507/281-2211; toll-free 800/305-8470; fax 507/288-8979. www.comfortinn.com.* 162 rooms, 5 story. S, D $79; each additional $10; under 17 free. Crib free. Pet accepted, some restrictions. Complimentary continental breakfast. Check-out noon. TV; cable (premium). In-room modem link. Some private patios. Microwaves, refrigerators, Coffee in rooms. Valet services, coin laundry. Restaurant 11 am-2 pm, 5-10 pm. Bar 4 pm-midnight. Room service. Sauna. Indoor pool, whirlpool. Meeting rooms, business services. Cr cds: A, C, D, DS, JCB, MC, V.

D ⬜ ⬜ ⬜ SC

★ **DAYS INN.** *111 28th SE St (55904). Phone 507/286-1001; toll-free 800/329-7466. www.daysinn.com.* 128 rooms. S $46-$62; D $52-$62; each additional $5; under 18 free. Crib free. Pet accepted. TV; cable (premium). Complimentary continental breakfast. Restaurant nearby. Check-out noon. Business services available. Free airport transportation. Cross-country ski 2 miles. Cr cds: A, C, D, DS, ER, JCB, MC, V.

D ⬜ ⬜ ⬜ SC

★ **ECONO LODGE.** *519 3rd Ave SW (55902). Phone 507/288-1855; toll-free 800/553-2666. www.econolodge.com.* 62 rooms, 2 story, 6 kitchens S, D $43-$46; each additional $5; kitchen units $45; under 18 free. Crib free. TV; cable. Restaurant nearby. Check-out noon. Coin laundry. Cross-country ski 1 mile. City park opposite. Cr cds: A, C, D, DS, MC, V.

★**EXECUTIVE INN.** *116 5th St SW (55902). Phone 507/289-1628; toll-free 888/233-9470.* 59 rooms, 2 story. S, D $29-$39; under 18 free. Crib free. Complimentary continental breakfast. Check-out noon. TV; cable. Some refrigerators. Coin laundry. Sauna. Pool, indoor pool. Cross-country ski 2 miles. Sundries. Cr cds: A, DS, MC, V.

★ ★ **EXECUTIVE INN.** *9 3rd Ave NW (55901). Phone 507/289-8646; toll-free 800/533-1655; fax 507/282-4478. www.kahler.com.* 266 rooms, 9 story. S $71-$102; D $81-$112; each additional $10; under 18 free. Crib free. Pet accepted. TV; cable (premium). Indoor pool; whirlpool. Complimentary continental breakfast. Restaurant 6 am-9 pm. Bar 3-9 pm. Check-out 2 pm. Meeting room. Business services available. In-room modem link. Sundries. Grocery store. Valet service. Coin laundry. Cross-country ski 1 mile. Exercise equipment; sauna. Recreation room. Some refrigerators. Cr cds: A, MC, V.

★ **HAMPTON INN.** *1755 S Broadway (55904). Phone 507/287-9050; toll-free 800/426-7866; fax 507/287-9139. www.hamptoninn.com.* 105 rooms, 3 story. S $74-$79; D $84-$89; under 18 free. Crib free. Complimentary continental breakfast. Check-out noon. TV; cable (premium). Refrigerators. Valet services, coin laundry. Restaurant nearby. Exercise equipment. Indoor pool, whirlpool. Cross-country ski 1 mile. Meeting rooms, business services. Cr cds: A, C, D, DS, MC, V.

★ ★ **HOLIDAY INN SOUTH.** *1630 S Broadway (55904). Phone 507/288-1844. www.holiday-inn.com.* 195 rooms, 5 suites, 2 story, 7 kitchens S, D $59-$69; each additional $7; kitchen units $79-$119. Crib free. Pet accepted. TV; cable. Indoor pool. Restaurant 6 am-10 pm; Fri, Sat to 11 pm. Room service. Bar 11:30-1 am. Check-out 2 pm, Sat noon. Coin laundry. Meeting rooms. Business services available. Valet service. Sundries. Free airport, bus depot transportation. Recreation room. Cr cds: A, D, DS, JCB, MC, V.

★ ★ **QUALITY INN & SUITES.** *1620 1st Ave SE (55904). Phone 507/282-8091; toll-free 800/228-5151. www.qualityinn.com.* 41 suites, 2 story. S, D $69-$165; each additional $7; under 18 free. Crib free. Pet accepted. Complimentary continental breakfast. Check-out noon. TV; cable (premium). In-room modem link. Complimentary coffee in rooms. Coin laundry. Restaurant nearby. Airport transportation. Cr cds: A, C, D, DS, JCB, MC, V.

★ **RAMADA LIMITED.** *435 16th Ave NW (55901). Phone 507/288-9090; fax 507/292-9442. www.ramada.com.* 120 rooms, 3 story, 20 kitchen units. S $52-$72; D $57-$77; each additional $10; under 18 free. Crib free. Pet accepted. TV; cable (premium). Indoor pool. Coffee in rooms. Restaurant 11 am-10 pm. Check-out noon. Coin laundry. Valet service. Sundries. Refrigerators, microwaves. Cr cds: A, C, DS, JCB, MC, V.

★ **RED CARPET INN.** *2214 S Broadway (55904). Phone 507/282-7448; toll-free 800/658-7048.* 47 rooms, 6 kitchen units, 2 story. S $36; D $40-$42; each additional $5; kitchen units $28.95-$31.95; under 12 free; weekend rates. Crib free. Pet accepted. Complimentary coffee in lobby. Check-out noon. TV; cable. Coin laundry. Restaurant nearby. Indoor pool. Cross-country ski 1 mile. Meeting rooms, business services. Sundries. Cr cds: A, DS, MC, V.

★ **ROCHESTER KNIGHTS INN.** *106 21st St SE (55904). Phone 507/282-1756. www.super8.com.* 80 rooms, 2 story. S, D $45-$60; under 18 free. Crib free. Complimentary continental breakfast. Check-out noon. TV; cable (premium). Some refrigerators, wet bars. Restaurant nearby. Cross-country ski 2 miles. Business services. Cr cds: A, C, D, DS, MC, V.

★ **ROCHESTER SOUTH THRIFTLODGE.** *1837 S Broadway (55904). Phone 507/288-2031; toll-free 800/890-3871.* 27 rooms. S, D $33-$50; each additional $5. Crib free. Pet accepted. TV; cable. Complimentary coffee in lobby. Restaurant nearby. Check-out noon. Cross-country ski 1 mile. Cr cds: A, C, D, DS, MC, V.

★ **SUPER 8.** *1230 S Broadway (55904). Phone 507/288-8288. www.super8.com.* 88 rooms. S $52-$60; D $57-$65; each additional $5; under 18 free. Crib free. Pet accepted. Check-out noon. TV; cable. In-room modem link. Restaurant adjacent open 24 hours. Cross-country ski adjacent. Cr cds: A, D, DS, MC, V.

Hotels

★ ★ **HOLIDAY INN CITY CENTER.** *220 S Broadway (55904). Phone 507/252-8200; toll-free 800/241-1597; fax 507/288-6602. www.kahler.com.* 170 rooms, 8 story. S, D $89-$99; each additional $10; suites $89-$252; under 18 free. Crib free. TV; cable (premium). In-room modem link. Restaurant 6:30 am-2 pm, 5:30-10 pm; Sat, Sun from 7 am. Bar 5 pm-midnight. Cross-country ski 2 miles. Meeting rooms, business services. Cr cds: A, C, D, DS, JCB, MC, V.

★★★ **KAHLER HOTEL.** *20 2nd Ave SW (55902). Phone 507/282-2581; toll-free 800/533-1655; fax 507/285-2775. www.kahler.com.* Located across from the Mayo Clininc in the downtown area. 700 rooms, 11 story. S $59-$140; D $69-$150; each additional $10; suites $350-$1,500; under 18 free. Crib free. Pet accepted. Check-out 2 pm. TV; cable. In-room modem link. Refrigerators. Restaurant 6:30 am-11 pm, 5:30-9 pm. Bar 11-12:45 am, entertainment except Sun. Health club privileges, exercise equipment, sauna. Game room. Indoor pool, whirlpool, poolside service. Cross-country ski 2 miles. Barber, beauty shop. Airport transportation. Meeting rooms, business services. Drug store. Original section English Tudor; vaulted ceilings, paneling. Walkway to Mayo Clinic. Cr cds: A, C, D, JCB, MC.

★★★ **MARRIOTT AT MAYO CLINIC ROCHESTER.** *101 1st Ave SW (55902). Phone 507/280-6000; fax 507/280-8531. www.kahler.com.* Near the Galleria Mall, Miracle Mile Shopping Complex, tennis facilities, and many golf courses. 194 rooms, 9 story. S, D $179-$219; suites $295-$1,800; under 18 free. Crib free. Pet accepted, some restrictions. Check-out 2 pm. TV; cable. In-room modem link. Refrigerators, some bathroom phones, minibars. Restaurant 6:30 am-10 pm. Bar 11 am-11 pm, entertainment. Exercise equipment, sauna. Game room. Indoor pool, whirlpool. Barber, beauty shop. Meeting rooms, business services. Concierge. Gift shop, drug store. Luxury level. Mayo Medical Complex adjacent. Cr cds: A, MC, V.

★★ **RADISSON PLAZA.** *150 S Broadway (55904). Phone 507/281-8000; toll-free 800/333-3333; fax 507/281-4280. www.radisson.com.* 207 guestrooms and five suites with whirlpool tubs are offered by this downtown hotel with skyway access to the Mayo Clinic, Government Center, shopping, dining and entertainment. The property is only eight miles from the Rochester Airport. 212 rooms, 11 story. S, D $89-$119; suites $139-$295. Crib free. Check-out noon. TV; cable (premium). In-room modem link. Refrigerator in suites. Coin laundry. Restaurant 6:30 am-midnight. Bar 11-1 am. Exercise equipment, sauna. Indoor pool, whirlpool. Cross-country ski 1 mile. Meeting rooms, business services. Concierge. Gift shop. Cr cds: A, C, D, DS, ER, JCB, MC, V.

Restaurants

★ **AVIARY.** *4320 US 52 N (55901). Phone 507/281-5141.* Steak menu. Closed most major holidays. Lunch, dinner. Bar. Many trees, plants. Cr cds: A, D, DS, MC, V. **$**

★★ **BROADSTREET CAFE AND BAR.** *300 1st Ave NW (55901). Phone 507/281-2451; fax 509/278-9804. www.broadstreet-cafe.com.* Mediterranean menu. Specialties: in boursin chicken breast, Canadian walleye. Hours: 11 am-9:30 pm; Sat, Sun 5-9:30 pm. Closed Easter, Thanksgiving, Dec 25. Lunch $9.95-$11.95, dinner $22.75-$33.50. Bar. Former warehouse. Casual décor. Reservations accepted. Cr cds: A, MC, V.

★★ **CHARDONNAY.** *723 2nd St SW (55902). Phone 507/252-1310.* French, American menu. Closed Sun; major holidays. Lunch, dinner. 4 dining rooms in remodeled house. Cr cds: A, C, D, DS, MC, V. **$**

★ **HENRY WELLINGTON.** *216 1st Ave SW (55902). Phone 507/289-1949; fax 507/289-0450. www.henrywellington.com.* Hours: Mon.-Fri 11 am-11 pm, Sat. 4 pm-11 pm and Sun 4 pm-10 pm, closed July 4, Thanksgiving, Dec 24, 25. Lunch $6-$8.45, dinner $9-$19. Bar. Outdoor seating. Cr cds: A, D, MC, V.

★ **JOHN BARLEYCORN.** *2780 S Broadway (55904). Phone 507/285-0178.* Hours: 11 am-2 pm, 5-10 pm; Sat, Sun from 5 pm. Open all year round. Lunch $4.25-$7.25, dinner $5.95-$23.95. Bar. Salad bar. Reservations accepted. Cr cds: A, C, D, DS, MC, V.

★ **MICHAEL'S FINE DINING.** *15 S Broadway (55904). Phone 507/288-2020. www.michaelsfinedining.com.* Greek, Amer menu. Hours: 11 am-11 pm; early-bird dinner Mon-Thurs 3-5 pm, Fri, Sat to 5:30 pm. Closed Sun; most holidays. Lunch $6-$8, dinner $8-$22.95. Bar to midnight. Child's menu. Reservations accepted. Cr cds: A, D, DS, MC, V.

★ **SANDY POINT.** *18 Sandy Point Ct NE (55906). Phone 507/367-4983.* Closed Dec 25. Lunch, dinner. Bar. Children's menu. Cr cds: A, C, D, DS, MC, V. **$**

Roseau (B-2)

Pop 2,396 **Elev** 1,048 ft **Area Code** 218 **Zip** 56751

What to See and Do

Hayes Lake State Park. *48990 County Rd 4. 15 miles S on MN 89, then 9 miles E on County 4. Phone 218/425-7504.* A 2,950-acre park. Swimming, fishing, hiking, cross-country skiing, snowmobiling, picnicking, camping (dump station). Standard hours, fees.

Pioneer Farm and Village. *2 1/2 miles W via MN 11. Phone 218/463-2187 or 218/463-2690.* Restored buldings include log barn, museum, church, parish hall, equipped printery, log house, school, store, blacksmith shop and post office. Picnicking. (Mid-May-mid-Sept; schedule varies) **FREE**

Roseau City Park. *11th Ave SE.* 40-acre park with canoeing, hiking and picnicking. Camping (electric and water hook-ups, dump station).

Roseau County Historical Museum and Interpretive Center. *110 2nd Ave NE. Phone 218/463-1918.* Natural history, collection of mounted birds and eggs; Native American artifacts and pioneer history. (Tues-Sat; closed holidays) **$**

Roseau River Wildlife Management Area. *27952 400th St. 20 miles W and N via MN 11, 89 and County Rd 3. Phone 218/463-1557.* More than 2,000 ducks raised here annually on 65,000 acres. Bird watching area, canoeing on river, hunting during season, with license. **FREE**

Saint Cloud (F-3)

Founded 1856 **Pop** 48,812 **Elev** 1,041 ft **Area code** 320

Information St Cloud Area Covention & Visitors Bureau, 30 S 6th Ave, PO Box 487, 56302; 320/251-2940 or 800/264-2940

Web www.stcloudcvb.com

Its central location makes St. Cloud a convention hub and retail center for the area. The granite quarried here is prized throughout the United States. This Mississippi River community's architecture reflects the German and New England roots of its early settlers.

What to See and Do

City Recreation Areas. Riverside Park. *1529 Northway Dr. Phone 320/255-7256.* Monument to Zebulon Pike who discovered and named the nearby Beaver Islands in 1805 during exploration of the Mississippi. Shelter; flower gardens; wading pool, tennis, picnicking, lighted cross-country skiing. 1725 Kilian Blvd. **Wilson Park,** picnicking; boat landing, tennis, disc golf course. 625 Riverside Dr NE. Lake **George Eastman Park,** swimming (Early June-mid-Aug, daily; fee); skating (Late Dec-early Feb, daily; free); paddleboats (fee), fishing, picnicking. 9th Ave and Division. **Municipal Athletic Complex,** indoor ice-skating (Mid-June-mid-May, phone 320/255-7223 for fee and schedule information). 5001 8th St N. **Whitney Memorial Park,** walking trails, playground, picnicking, softball and soccer. **Northway Dr. Heritage Park,** nature trails, skating, cross-country skiing, earth-covered shelter; nearby is an interpretive heritage museum (Memorial Day-Labor Day, daily; rest of year, Tues-Sun; closed

holidays; fee) with replica of working granite quarry and historical scenes of central Minnesota. 33rd Ave S.

Clemens Gardens & Munsinger Gardens. *13th St and Kilian Blvd. Phone 800/264-2940.* Clemens Gardens features, among other gardens, the White Garden, based upon Kent, England's White Garden at Sissinghurst Garden. Munsinger Gardens is surrounded by pine and hemlock trees. (Memorial Day-Labor Day) **FREE**

College of St. Benedict. *7 miles W on I-94 in St Joseph. Phone 320/363-5777 or -5308 for schedules.* (1887). (1,742 women) On campus is the $6 million Ardolf Science Center. Guided tours. Art exhibits, concerts, plays, lectures and films in Benedicta Arts Center. Also here is

St. Benedict's Convent. *NW via I-94, in St Joseph at 104 Chapel Lane. For further info Phone 320/363-7100.* (1857). Community of more than 400 Benedictine women. Tours of historic Sacred Heart Chapel (1913), and archives. Gift and crafts shop; Monastic Gardens.

Minnesota Baseball Hall of Fame. *10 4th Ave S. St Cloud Civic Center. Second floor. Phone 320/255-7272.* Features great moments from amateur and professional baseball. (Mon-Fri) **FREE**

Powder Ridge Ski Area. *16 miles S on MN 15. Phone 320/398-7200; 800/348-7734.* Quad, two double chairlifts, J-bar, rope tow; patrol, school, rentals; snowmaking; bar, cafeteria. (Mid-Nov-Mar, daily) Fifteen runs. **$$$$**

St. Cloud State University. *4th Ave S, overlooking Mississippi River. Phone 320/255-3151.* (1869). (15,600 students) Marked historical sites; anthropology museum, planetarium, art gallery (Mon-Fri; closed holidays and school breaks).

St. John's University and Abbey, Preparatory School. *13 miles W on I-94 in Collegeville. Phone 320/363-2573.* (1857) (1,900 university students) Impressive modern abbey, university, church and Hill Monastic manuscript library, other buildings designed by the late Marcel Breuer; 2,450 acres of woodlands and lakes.

Stearns History Museum. *235 S 33rd Ave. Phone 320/253-8424.* Located in a 100-acre park, the center showcases cultural and historical aspects of past and present life in central Minnesota; contains replica of working granite quarry; agricultural and automobile displays; research center and archives. (Daily; closed holidays) **$$**

Special Events

Mississippi Music Fest. *Riverside Park. Phone 320/255-2205.* Late April.

Wheels, Wings & Water Festival. *Phone 320/251-0083.* June.

Motels/Motor Lodges

★★ **BEST WESTERN AMERICANNA INN AND CONFERENCE CENTER.** *520 S US 10 (56304). Phone 320/252-8700; toll-free 800/950-8701. www.bestwestern.com.* 63 rooms, 2 story. S $57-$73; D $67-$80; each additional $5; suites for 2-6, $74.95-$99.95; under 19 free. Crib $2. Pet accepted, some restrictions. Check-out 11 am. TV; cable (premium). In-room modem link. Complimentary coffee in rooms. Valet services. Restaurant 11 am-10 pm; Sun to 9 pm. Bar 10:30-1 am, entertainment, room service. Sauna. Game room. Indoor pool, whirlpool. Meeting rooms, business services. Sundries. Cr cds: A, C, D, DS, MC, V.

★**COMFORT INN.** *4040 2nd St S (56301). Phone 320/251-1500; toll-free 800/228-5150; fax 320/251-1111. www.comfortinn.com.* 63 rooms, 2 story. S, D $45.95-$66.95; each additional $6; under 18 free. Crib $7. TV; cable (premium). Complimentary continental breakfast. Restaurant nearby. Check-out 11 am. Coin laundry. Meeting rooms. Business services available. Sundries. Exercise equipment; sauna. Cr cds: A, C, D, DS, ER, JCB, MC, V.

★ **DAYS INN.** *420 Hwy 10 SE (56304). Phone 320/253-0500; toll-free 800/329-7466. www.daysinn.com.* 78 rooms, 2 story. S $38.95-$56.95; D $45.95-$59.95; each additional $7; under 18 free. Crib free. Pet accepted. TV; cable (premium). Indoor pool; whirlpool. Complimentary continental breakfast. Check-out 11 am. Business services available. Sundries. Downhill ski 10 miles; cross-country ski 1 mile. Cr cds: A, C, D, DS, MC, V.

★**FAIRFIELD INN.** *4120 2nd St S (56301). Phone 320/654-1881. www.fairfieldinn.com.* 57 rooms, 10 suites, 3 story. S $46.95-$64.95; D $49.95-$69.95; each additional $6; under 19 free. Crib free. TV; cable (premium). Indoor pool; whirlpool. Complimentary continental breakfast. Restaurant adjacent open 24 hours. Check-out 11 am. Meeting rooms. Business services available. In-room modem link. Downhill ski 18 miles; cross-country ski 1 mile. Game room. Some refrigerators. Cr cds: A, C, D, DS, MC, V.

★★ **HOLIDAY INN ST. CLOUD.** *75 37th Ave S (56301). Phone 320/253-9000; toll-free 800/465-4329; fax 320/253-5998. www.holiday-inn.com.* 257 rooms, 43 suites, 3 story. S, D $74-$99; suites $89-$179; under 19 free. Crib free. Check-out 11 am. TV; cable (premium). Coffee in rooms. Restaurant 6 am-2 pm, 5-10 pm; Sun from 7 am. Bar 11-1 am. Exercise equipment, sauna. 5 indoor pools, wading pool, whirlpool, poolside service. Meeting rooms, business services. Cr cds: A, C, D, DS, MC, V.

★ **MOTEL 6.** *815 S 1St St (56387). Phone 320/253-7070; toll-free 800/466-8356; fax 320/253-0436. www.motel6.com.* 93 rooms, 2 story. S $29-$39; D $35-$45; under 18 free. Crib free. TV; cable (premium). Restaurant nearby. Check-out noon. Business services available. In-room modem link. Downhill ski 10 miles. Cr cds: A, C, D, DS, MC, V.

★★ **QUALITY INN.** *70 S 37th Ave (56301). Phone 320/253-4444; fax 320/259-7809. www.qualityinn.com.* 89 units, 2 story. Mid-June-early Sept: S $39-$42; D $44-$49; each additional $7; under 18 free; lower rates rest of year. Crib free. Pet accepted, some restrictions. TV; cable (premium). Restaurant nearby. Check-out noon. Sauna. Whirlpool. Cr cds: A, C, D, DS, JCB, MC, V.

★ **SUPER 8.** *50 Park Ave S (56302). Phone 320/253-5530; toll-free 800/843-1991; fax 320/253-5292. www.super8.com.* 68 rooms, 2 story. S $36-$43; D $42.88-$58.88; each additional $5; under 13 free. Crib free. Pet accepted. TV; cable (premium). Complimentary continental breakfast. Restaurant adjacent open 24 hours. Check-out 11 am. Meeting rooms. Business services available. Downhill ski 8 miles; cross-country ski 1 miles. Cr cds: A, C, D, DS, MC, V.

Restaurant

★ **D. B. SEARLE'S.** *18 5th Ave S (56301). Phone 320/253-0655.* Specialties: French onion soup, stuffed popovers. Hours: Mon.-Thurs. 11 am-9 pm, Fri.-Sat. 9:30 pm, and Sun. 5 pm-8 pm; closed some holidays. Lunch $6.49-$7.39, dinner $5.95-$19.75. Built 1886. Reservations accepted. Cr cds: A, DS, MC, V.

Saint Paul (F-4)

See also Hastings, Minneapolis, Stillwater

Settled 1840 **Pop** 272,235 **Elev** 874 ft **Area code** 651

Information Convention and Visitors Bureau, 175 W Kellogg Blvd, Suite 502, 55102; 651/265-4900 or 800/627-6101

Web www.stpaulcvb.org

Distribution center for the great Northwest and dignified capital of Minnesota, stately St. Paul had its humble beginnings in a settlement known as "Pig's Eye." At the great bend of the Mississippi and tangent to the point where the waters of the Mississippi and Minnesota rivers meet, St. Paul and its twin city, Minneapolis, form a mighty northern metropolis. Together they are a center for computers, electronics, medical technology, printing, and publishing. In many ways they complement each other, yet they are also friendly rivals. Fiercely proud of their professional athletes (the baseball Minnesota Twins, the football Minnesota Vikings, and the basketball Minnesota Timberwolves), the partisans of both cities troop to the Hubert H. Humphrey Metrodome Stadium in Minneapolis (see), as well as other arenas in the area, to watch their heroes in action.

A terraced city of diversified industry and lovely homes, St. Paul boasts 30 lakes within a 30-minute drive, as well as more than 90 parks. St. Paul is home to 3M Companies and other major corporations.

The junction of the Mississippi and Minnesota rivers was chosen in 1807 as the site for a fort that later became known as Fort Snelling. Squatters soon settled on the reservation lands nearby, only to be expelled in 1840 with one group moving a few miles east and a French-Canadian trader, Pierre Parrant, settling at the landing near Fort Snelling. Parrant was nicknamed "Pig's Eye," and the settlement that developed at the landing took this name.

When Father Lucien Galtier built a log cabin chapel there in 1841, he prevailed on the settlers to rename their community for Saint Paul. A Mississippi steamboat terminus since 1823, St. Paul prospered on river trade, furs, pioneer traffic, and agricultural commerce. Incorporated as a town in 1849, it was host to the first legislature of the Minnesota Territory and has been the capital ever since.

A number of institutions of higher education are located in St. Paul, including University of Minnesota—Twin Cities Campus, University of St. Thomas, College of St. Catherine, Macalester College, Hamline University, Concordia University, Bethel College, and William Mitchell College of Law.

What to See and Do

6th Street Center Skyway. *56 E 6th St, located in the center of downtown.* Created out of the second level of 6th Street Center's 5-story parking garage. The center includes shops and restaurants. (Daily; closed major holidays)

Alexander Ramsey House. *St. 265 S Exchange St. Phone 651/296-0100.* (1872). Home of Minnesota's first territorial governor; original furnishings. Guided tours; reservations suggested. (Fri-Sat; closed Dec 25) **$$$**

Cathedral of St. Paul. *239 Selby Ave. Phone 651/228-1766. (Roman Catholic)* (1915). Dome 175 feet high; central rose window. (Daily)

City Hall and Court House. *15 W Kellogg Blvd. Phone 651/266-8023.* (1932). Prominent example of Art Deco, with Carl Milles' 60-ton, 36-feet-tall onyx Vision of Peace statue in the lobby.

Como Park. Midway & Lexington Pkwys. *Midway and Lexington Pkwys. Phone 651/266-6400 651/487-8200 (Zoo & Conservatory).* A 448-acre park with 70-acre lake. Conservatory features authentic Japanese garden and tea house; "Gates Ajar" floral display, zoo. (Daily) Amusement area (Memorial Day-Labor Day, daily) with children's rides (fee). 18-hole golf course (fee).

Gray Line Bus Tours. Greyhound Bus Depot. (See MINNEAPOLIS)

Gray Line Twin Cities Tour. *Phone 952/469-5020.* Bus tour of the Twin Cities area departs from the Mall of America and includes Minnehaha Falls, Fort Snelling, and the Saint Paul Cathedral (daily 10:15 am; weekends only in late May-late Aug; no tours on July 4). **$$$$**

Gray Line Twin Cities Tour. *Phone 952/469-5020.* Bus tour of the Twin Cities area departs from the Mall of America and includes Minnehaha Falls, Fort Snelling, and the Saint Paul Cathedral (daily 10:15 am; weekends only in late May-late Aug; no tours on July 4). **$$$$**

James J. Hill House. *240 Summit Ave. Phone 651/297-2555.* (1891). Showplace of city when built for famous railroad magnate. Reservations suggested. (Wed-Sat; closed holidays) **$$**

Landmark Center. *75 W 5th St. Phone 651/292-3228 or -3230 (tours).* Restored Federal Courts Building constructed in 1902; currently center for cultural programs and gangster history tours. Houses four courtrooms and four-story indoor courtyard (the Cortile). Includes restaurant, archive gallery, auditorium, Schubert Club Keyboard Instrument Collection (Mon-Fri), and the Minnesota Museum of American Art. (Daily; closed holidays 45-minute tours (Thurs and Sun; also by appointment); self-guided tours (Daily). **FREE**

Luther Seminary. *2481 Como Ave. Phone 651/641-3456.* (1869). (780 students) On campus is the Old Muskego Church (1844), first church built by Norse immigrants in America; moved to present site in 1904. Tours.

Minnesota Children's Museum. *10 W 7th St. Phone 651/225-6000.* Hands-on learning exhibits for children up to 10 years old; museum store stocked with unique puzzles, maps, toys, games, books. Self-guiding. (Memorial Day-Labor Day, daily; rest of year, Tues-Sun) **$$$**

Minnesota History Center. *345 Kellogg Blvd W. Phone 651/296-6126 or 800/657-3773 (exc Twin Cities).* Home to the Historical Society, the center houses a museum with interactive exhibits, extensive genealogical collection; special events, gift shop, restaurant. (Daily; hours may vary. **FREE**

Minnesota Museum of American Art—Landmark Center. *75 5th St W. Phone 651/292-4355.* Changing exhibits and gallery of contemporary Midwest artists and new art

Historic St. Paul

The center of St. Paul contains a number of historic structure and cultural institutions, as well as the Minnesota state capitol. A morning or afternoon stroll easily links all of the following sites.

Begin at Rice Park, located at 5th and Market streets, Established 150 years ago, this park—with its vast old trees, manicured lawns, flowers, and fountains, is an oasis of nature in the midst of urban St. Paul. Surrounding the park are some of the city's most noted landmarks. Facing the park to the east is the St. Paul Hotel (350 Market St), built in 1910 as the city's finest. After a loving refurbishment, it is once again one of the city's premier luxury hotels. Step inside to wander the lobby, which is filled with chandeliers, oriented carpets, and fine furniture.

Facing Rice Park from south is the handsome turn-of-the-20th-century St. Paul Public Library. To the west, the Ordway Music Theatre (345 Washington St) is an elegant concert hall where the St. Paul Chamber Orchestra and the Minnesota Orchestra frequently perform. The Landmark Center, facing Rice Park to the north (75 West 5th St), is a castlelike federal courthouse built in 1902. A number of galleries and arts organizations are now housed in the structure, including the Minnesota Museum of American Art.

Cross St. Peter St and continue east on East 6th St. At Cedar St is Town Center Park, the world's largest indoor park, complete with trees, fountains, flowers, and a carousel. From the north side of the park there good views of the state capitol. Exit the north end of the park onto 7th St, walk one block east to Wabasha Street, and turn north. At the corner of Wabasha and Exchange streets is the World Theater (10 Exchange St), from where Garrison Keillor frequently broadcasts *The Prairie Home Companion*, the acclaimed public radio show.

One block north is the Science Museum of Minnesota (30 East 10th St) with exhibits on geology, paleontology, and the sciences, and the William L. McKnight-3M Omnitheater, with a 76-foot-wide domed screen. From the main entrance of the Science Museum, walk up Cedar St toward the capitol building, passing through the parklike Capitol Mall. The magnificent Minnesota Capitol sits on a hill overlooking the city and is crowned by the world's largest unsupported dome. Wander the marble-clad hallways, or join a free tour of the legislative chambers.

From the capitol, follow John Ireland Blvd south to the Cathedral of St. Paul. Modeled after St. Peter's Basilica in Rome, this 3,000-seat church occupies the highest point in St. Paul. Just south of the cathedral is the James J. Hill House at 240 Summit Ave. This late 19th-century, 5-story mansion was built by James Hill, founder of the Great Northern Railroad. When built, this mansion was the largest and most expensive private home in the upper Midwest. Tours are offered. Return to downtown St. Paul along Kellogg Blvd.

forms. Also Museum School and store. (Tues-Sun; closed holidays) **DONATION**

Minnesota Wild (NHL). *317 Washington St. Phone 651/222-WILD*. Team plays at Xcel Energy Center.

Mounds Park. *Mounds Blvd and Burns Ave, in Dayton's Bluff section. Phone 651/266-6400*. More than 25 acres of park containing prehistoric Native American burial mounds. 18 mounds existed on this site in 1856, six remain. Picnic facilities, ball field, view of Mississippi River.

Science Museum of Minnesota. *120 W Kellogg Phone 651/221-9444*. Technology, anthropology, paleontology, geography and biology exhibits; 3-D laser show; William L. McKnight 3M Omnitheater. (Daily) Also here is

Great American History Theatre. *30 10th St E (55101). Phone 651/292-4323*. Original works with American and Midwestern themes. (Sept-May, Thurs-Sun) **$$$**

Sibley Historic Site. *1357 Sibley Memorial Hwy (State Hwy 13). Phone 651/452-1596*. (1835). Home of General Henry Sibley, first governor, now preserved as museum. On same grounds is Faribault House Museum (1837), home of pioneer fur trader Jean Baptiste Faribault, a museum of the Native American and fur trade era. (May-Oct, Tues-Sun) **$$**

⭐ **Sightseeing Cruises.** *Harriet Island Park, W of Wabasha bridge and Boom Island in Minneapolis. Phone 651/227-1100*. Authentic Mississippi River sternwheelers Harriet Bishop, Betsy Northrop and Jonathan Padelford make 1 3/4-hour narrated trips to Historic Fort Snelling. Sidewheeler Anson Northrup makes trip through lock at St Anthony Falls. Dinner, brunch cruises also available. Showboat tours available.(Memorial Day-Labor Day, daily; May and Sept, weekends)

State Capitol. *75 Constitution Ave. Phone 651/296-2881*. (1896-1905). Designed in the Italian Renaissance style by Cass Gilbert and decorated with murals, sculpture, stencils and marble, the Capitol opened in 1905. 45-minute guided tours leave on the hr; last tour leaves one hour before closing (group reservations required). (Daily; closed some major holidays) **FREE**

University of Minnesota, Twin Cities Campus. *Phone 612/ 625-5000.* (1851). 39,315 students. Campus tours; animal barn tours (for small children). Near campus is

> **Gibbs Museum of Pioneer & Dakotah Life.** *2097 W Larpenteur Ave, Falcon Heights. Phone 651/646-8629.* (1854). Restored furnished farmhouse depicting life of Pioneers and Dakotahs at the turn of the century. Includes two barns and a one-room schoolhouse. Interpretations, demonstrations, summer schoolhouse program. (May-Oct, Tues-Fri, also Sun afternoons) **$$**

Special Events

Minnesota State Fair. *Fairgrounds, N 1265 Snelling Ave. Phone 651/642-2200.* Midway, thrill show, horse show, kids' days, all-star revue; more than one million visitors each year; 300 acres of attractions. Phone 651/642-2200. Late Aug-early Sept.

Winter Carnival. *75 5th St W. Phone 651/223-4700.* Throughout city. One of the leading winter festivals in America; ice and snow carving; parades, sports events, parties, pageants. Last weekend Jan-first weekend Feb.

Motels/Motor Lodges

★ ★ **BEST WESTERN.** *1780 E County Rd D (55109). Phone 651/770-2811; toll-free 800/780-7234. www.bestwesternmaplewood.com.* 118 rooms, 2 story. S, D $89-$129; each additional $4; under 18 free. Crib free. Pet accepted; $5 deposit. Check-out noon. TV; cable (premium). In-room modem link. Microwaves, Coffee in rooms. Valet services, coin laundry. Restaurant 6:30 am-2 pm, 5-10 pm. Bar 4 pm-1 am, entertainment Fri, Sat. Room service. Health club privileges, sauna. Game room. Indoor pool, whirlpool. Meeting rooms, business services. Sundries. Cr cds: A, C, D, DS, MC, V.

⌨ ⌨ ⌨ SC

★ **EXEL INN OF ST. PAUL.** *1739 Old Hudson Rd (55106). Phone 651/771-5566; fax 651/771-1262. www.exelinns.com.* 100 rooms, 3 story. Pet accepted. Complimentary continental breakfast. Check-out noon, check-in 3 pm. TV; cable (premium). In-room modem link. Laundry services. Game room. Downhill ski 15 miles; cross-country ski 2 miles. Cr cds: A, D, DS, MC, V. **$**

⌨ ⌨ ⌨ ⌨ SC

★ ★ **HOLIDAY INN.** *1010 W Bandana Blvd (55108). Phone 651/647-1637; toll-free 800/465-4329; fax 651/647-0244. www.holiday-inn.com.* 109 rooms, 6 suites, 2 story. S, D $79-$129; suites $101-$131. Crib free. TV; cable (premium). Indoor pool; wading pool, whirlpool. Complimentary continental breakfast. Check-out noon. Meeting rooms. Business services available. In-room modem

link. Valet service. Downhill ski 15 miles; cross-country ski 1 mile. Sauna. Some refrigerators. Motel built within exterior structure of old railroad repair building; old track runs through lobby. Shopping center adj; connected by skywalk. Cr cds: A, C, D, DS, ER, JCB, MC, V.

⌨ ⌨ ⌨ ⌨ SC

★ ★ **HOLIDAY INN ST. PAUL EAST.** *2201 Burns Ave (55119). Phone 651/731-2220; toll-free 800/465-4329; fax 651/731-0243. www.holiday-inn.com.* 195 rooms, 8 story. S, D $125; under 19 free; weekend rates. Crib free. Check-out noon. TV; cable (premium). In-room modem link. Some bathroom phones. Valet services, coin laundry. Restaurant 6 am-2 pm, 5-10 pm; Sat, Sun from 7 am. Bar 4 pm-1 am. Room service. Exercise equipment, sauna. Game room. Indoor pool, whirlpool. Downhill ski 10 miles, cross-country ski 1/2 mile. Meeting rooms, business services. Bellhops. Sundries, gift shop. Luxury level. Cr cds: A, C, D, DS, JCB, MC, V.

⌨ ⌨ ⌨ ⌨ ⌨

★ **SUPER 8 MOTEL.** *285 Century Ave N (55119). Phone 651/738-1600; toll-free 800/800-8000; fax 651/738-9405. www.super8.com.* 110 rooms, 4 story. Late May-early Sept: S $48.88-$61.88; D $55.88-$66.88; each additional $5; under 12 free; lower rates rest of year. Crib free. Pet accepted; $50 refundable. Complimentary breakfast buffet. Check-out 11 am. TV; cable (premium). In-room modem link. Microwaves, refrigerators. Coin laundry. Restaurant adjacent. Game room. Downhill ski 15 miles, cross-country ski 2 miles. Picnics/tables. Airport transportation. Business services. Sundries. Cr cds: A, D, DS, MC, V.

⌨ ⌨ ⌨ SC

Hotels

★ ★ **COUNTRY INN.** *6003 Hudson Rd (55125). Phone 651/739-7300; toll-free 800/456-4000; fax 651/731-4007. www.countryinns.com.* 158 rooms, 2 story. Complimentary continental breakfast. Check-out noon, check-in 3 pm. TV; cable (premium). In-room modem link. Restaurant, bar, room service. In-house fitness room, sauna. Game room. Indoor pool, whirlpool. Downhill ski 12 miles, cross-country ski 11 miles. Concierge. Cr cds: A, C, D, DS, MC, V. **$**

⌨ ⌨ ⌨ ⌨ ⌨ SC

★ ★ **CROWNE PLAZA.** *2700 Pilot Knob Rd (55121). Phone 651/454-3434; toll-free 800/465-4329; fax 651/454-4904. www.crowneplaza.com.* Located just 5 miles from the airport and Mall of America, this full service hotel offers transportation to and from both locations and free parking. 187 rooms, 6 story. S, D $119-$129; suites $129-$149; under 20 free. Check-out noon. TV; cable (premium). In-room modem link. Restaurant 7 am-11 pm. Bar. Health club privileges. Free airport transportation. Cr cds: A, C, D, DS, JCB, MC, V.

[D] [≈] [⚓] [✈] [⊠] [SC]

★ ★ **EMBASSY SUITES.** *175 E 10th St (55101). Phone 651/224-5400; toll-free 800/362-2779; fax 651/224-0957. www.embassystpaul.com.* It is located near the Science Museum of Minneapolis, Galtier Plaza, the Mall of America, and much more. 210 suites, 8 story. S $159-$179; D $169-$189; each additional $10; under 12 free; wkend, holiday rates. Crib free. Complimentary full breakfast. Check-out noon. TV; cable (premium). In-room modem link. Microwaves, refrigerators, wet bars, Coffee in rooms. Coin laundry. Restaurant 11 am-10 pm. Bar to 1 am. Exercise equipment, sauna, steam room. Indoor pool, whirlpool. Free airport transportation. Meeting rooms, business services. Gift shop. Atrium with pond, waterfalls, fountains, ducks; many plants and trees. Cr cds: A, C, D, DS, ER, JCB, MC, V.

[D] [✈] [≈] [⚓] [✈] [⊠] [SC]

★ ★ **FOUR POINTS BY SHERATON.** *400 Hamline Ave N (55104). Phone 651/642-1234; toll-free 800/535-2339; fax 651/642-1126. www.sheraton.com.* 197 rooms, 4 story. Check-out noon, check-in 3 pm. TV; cable (premium). In-room modem link. Restaurant, bar, room service. In-house fitness room, health club privileges. Beach. Indoor pool, whirlpool. Downhill ski 15 miles, cross-country ski 7 miles. Cr cds: A, C, D, DS, MC, V. **$**

[D] [✈] [≈] [⚓] [⊠]

★★**HAMPTON INN.** *1000 Gramsie Rd (55126). Phone 651/482-0402; toll-free 800/HAMPTON; fax 651/482-8917. www.hamptoninn.com.* 120 rooms, 2 story. Complimentary continental breakfast. Check-out 11 am, check-in 3 pm. TV; cable (premium). In-room modem link. Coin laundry. Restaurant, bar, room service. In-house fitness room. Indoor pool, whirlpool. Cr cds: A, C, D, DS, MC, V. **$**

[≈] [⚓] [⊠] [SC]

★ ★ **RADISSON RIVERFRONT.** *11 E Kellogg Blvd (55101). Phone 651/292-1900; fax 651/224-8999. www.radisson.com.* This hotel is located in downtown near many attractions, shopping and dining. It offers 479 spacious guestrooms, a pool and Jacuzzi, workout facilities open 24 hours a day and a restaurant found on the 22nd floor with a great view of the river. 475 rooms, 22 story. S $150; D $180; each additional $10; under 18 free; package plans. Crib free. Garage parking $12.50. TV; cable (premium), VCR available. Indoor pool. Restaurant 6:30 am-10:30 pm; Fri, Sat to 11:30 pm. Bars 11:30-1 am. Check-out noon. Convention facilities. Business services available. In-room modem link. Concierge. Downhill ski 15 miles; cross-country ski 4 miles. Exercise equipment. Health club privileges. Some refrigerators. Indoor skyway

to major stores, businesses. Luxury level. Cr cds: A, C, D, DS, ER, JCB, MC, V.

[D] [✈] [≈] [⚓] [⊠] [SC]

★ ★ ★ **THE SAINT PAUL HOTEL.** *350 Market St (55102). Phone 651/292-9292; toll-free 800/292-9292; fax 651/228-9506.* A Historic Hotel of America, this beautifully restored property was founded in 1910 by wealthy businessman Lucius Ordway and still maintains an old-style, European charm. The 254-room hotel has hosted many famous individuals while still maintaining a commitment to business and leisure visitors to this capital city. Most rooms have splendid downtown, Rice Park, or St. Paul Cathedral views. 254 rooms, 12 story. Check-out noon, check-in 3 pm. TV. In-room modem link. Restaurant, bar. In-house fitness room, health club privileges. Business center. Concierge. Connected to downtown skyway system. Cr cds: A, MC, V. **$$**

[⚓] [⚓]

Restaurants

★ **CECIL'S.** *651 S Cleveland (55116). Phone 651/698-0334; fax 651/699-2303. www.cecilsdeli.com.* Hours: 9 am-8 pm. Breakfast $1.75-$4.50, lunch, dinner $3-$7.50. Cr cds: MC, V.

★ **CIATTI'S.** *850 Grand Ave (55105). Phone 651/292-9942; fax 651/292-0195.* Italian menu. Closed Dec 24, 25. Lunch, dinner, Sun brunch. Bar. Children's menu. Casual attire. Cr cds: A, DS, MC, V. **$**

[D]

★ ★ **DAKOTA BAR AND GRILL.** *1021 E Bandana Blvd (55108). Phone 651/642-1442. www.dakotacooks.com.* Jazz fans will enjoy this modern restaurant in Bandana Square. Regional ingredients are used in such eclectic dishes as pheasant fritters. Along with the extensive wine list, guests can enjoy dining on the outdoor patio in the summer. Hours: 5-10 pm; Sun brunch 11 am-2:30 pm. Closed Sun. Dinner $16-$27. Bar 4 pm-midnight; Fri, Sat to 1 am. Live music. Located in restored railroad building in historic Bandana Square. Outdoor seating. Cr cds: A, D, DS, MC, V.

[D]

★ **DIXIE'S.** *695 Grand Ave (55105). Phone 651/222-7345; fax 651/225-8248. www.dixiesrestaurants.com.* Southern, Cajun menu. Closed Thanksgiving Dec 25. Lunch, dinner, Sun brunch. Bar. Children's menu. Casual attire. Outdoor seating. Informal dining. Cr cds: A, C, D, DS, MC, V. **$**

[D]

★ ★ ★ **FOREPAUGH'S.** *276 S Exchange St (55102). Phone 651/224-5606; fax 651/224-5607. www.forepaughs.com.* Some say the ghost of the former owner haunts this romantic 3-story home St. Paul, with its 9 dining rooms complete with lace curtains. The French menu has English "subtitles", and they offer shuttle service to nearby theaters. French menu. Hours: 11:30 am-2 pm, 5:30-9:30 pm; Sat from 5:30 pm; Sun 5-8:30 pm; Sun brunch 10:30 am-1:30 pm. Closed some holidays. Dinner $15.75-$21. Sun brunch . Bar to 1 am; Sun to midnight. Children's menu. Restored mansion (1870); 9 dining rooms. Valet parking available. Outdoor seating. Cr cds: A, D, MC, V.

[D]

★ **GALLIVAN'S.** *354 Wabasha St (55102). Phone 651/ 227-6688; fax 651/292-9700. www.minnesotamenus.com.* American menu. Closed Sun; major holidays. Lunch, dinner. Bar. Entertainment Fri, Sat. Casual attire. Cr cds: A, C, D, DS, MC, V. **$**

[D]

★ **GREEN MILL RESTAURANT & BAR.** *57 S Hamline Ave (55105). Phone 651/698-0353; fax 651/ 698-8439. www.greenmill.com.* Italian, American menu. Hours: 11 am-2 pm, 4-10 pm; Fri to 11 pm; Sat 4-11 pm; Sun 4-10 pm; Closed Dec 24 eve-Dec 25. Dinner $7-$14. Cr cds: A, D, DS, MC, V.

[D]

★ ★ ★ **KOZLAKS ROYAL OAK.** *4785 Hodgson Rd (55126). Phone 651/484-8484; fax 651/484-7753.* Guests really receive the royal treatment here, beginning with personalized note pads or matchbooks left on the table. Mood enhancing colored lights reflect beauty from the dozens of flowers and etched-glass windows to the scenic garden seating. Hours: 11 am-2:30 pm, 4-9:30 pm; Fri to 10:30 pm; Sat 4-10:30 pm; Sun 10 am-1:30 pm (brunch), 4-8:30 pm; early-bird dinner Sun-Fri to 5:45 pm. Lunch $5.50-$12. Dinner $15.50-$27. Sun brunch $9.95-$16.95. Bar to midnight; Fri, Sat to 1 am. Child's menu. Reservations accepted. Outdoor seating. Cr cds: A, DS, MC, V.

[D]

★ **LEEANN CHIN.** *214 E 4th St (55101). Phone 651/224-8814; fax 651/224-8746. www.leeannchin.com.* Chinese menu. Specialties: in Cantonese, mandarin and Szechwan dishes. Hours: 11 am-2:30 pm, 5-9 pm; Fri, Sat to 10 pm. Closed major holidays. Lunch, dinner $4.59-$13.95. Service bar. Totally nonsmoking, Child's menu. Reservations accepted. Contemporary decor. Cr cds: A, D, DS, MC, V.

[D]

★ ★ **LEXINGTON.** *1096 Grand Ave (55105). Phone 651/222-5878; fax 651/222-8230.* The comfortable, clubby dining room is chandelier-lit and boasts a curving mahogany bar. Since 1935, the restaurant has prepared such traditional favorites as chateaubriand and prime rib in a simple and straightforward manner. French Provincial décor. Hours: 11 am-10 pm; Fri, Sat to 11 pm; Sun

4-9 pm; Sun brunch 10 am-3 pm. Closed Dec 25. Lunch $6.95-$11.95, dinner $9.95-$27. Sun brunch $4.95-$11.95. Bar. Children's menu. Reservations accepted. Cr cds: A, D, DS, MC, V.

[D]

★ **LINDEY'S PRIME STEAKHOUSE.** *3600 Snelling Ave N (55112). Phone 651/633-9813. www.lindsey.com.* Steak menu. Closed Sun; major holidays. Dinner. Bar. Children's menu. Casual attire. Non-smoking seating. Cr cds: A, DS, MC, V. **$$**

[D]

★ **MANCINI'S CHAR HOUSE.** *531 W 7th St (55102). Phone 651/224-7345.* Hours: 5-11 pm; Fri, Sat to 12:30 am. Closed major holidays. Bar to 1 am. Dinner $10-$29. Specializes in steak, lobster. Entertainment Wed-Sat. Parking. Open charcoal hearths; 2 fireplaces. Family-owned. Cr cds: DS, MC, V.

[D]

★ ★ **MUFFULETTA IN THE PARK.** *2260 Como Ave (55108). Phone 651/644-9116; fax 651/644-5329.* Continental menu. Hours: 11:30 am-2:30 pm, 5-9:30 pm; Fri, Sat to 10 pm; Sun 10 am-2 pm, 5-8 pm; winter hours vary. Closed some major holidays. Dinner $7.95-$22.95, Sun brunch $7.95-$11.95. Reservations accepted. Outdoor dining. Totally nonsmoking. Cr cds: A, D, DS, MC, V.

[D]

★ ★ **RISTORANTE LUCI.** *470 Cleveland Ave S (55105). Phone 651/699-8258. www.ristoranteluci.com.* No surprises, just the kind of food everyone wants to eat all the time; simple and satisfying. Italian menu, Seafood menu. Hours: 5-9:30 pm; Fri, Sat to 10:30 pm; Sun 4:30-9 pm. Closed Sun, Mon; most major holidays. Dinner $7.75-$26. Child's menu. Reservations accepted. Totally nonsmoking. Cr cds: A, MC, V.

★ ★ **THE ST. PAUL GRILL.** *350 Market St (55102). Phone 651/224-7455. www.stpaulhotel.com.* The masculine decor of wood floors, oriental rugs and dim lighting overlooks beautiful Rice Park. American menu. Lunch, dinner, Sun brunch. Bar. Casual attire. Valet parking available. Cr cds: A, DS, MC, V. **$**

[D]

★ ★ **SAKURA.** *350 St. Peter St #338 (55102). Phone 651/224-0185; toll-free www.sakurastpaul.com; fax 651/ 225-9350.* Japanese menu. Hours: 11:30 am-2:30 pm, 5-10:30 pm; Fri, Sat to 11 pm; Sun to 9:30 pm. Closed Jan 1, Thanksgiving, Dec 25. Lunch $6-$18.50, dinner $15-$25. Bar. Reservations accepted. Cr cds: A, D, DS, MC, V.

[D]

★ **SAWATDEE.** *289 E 5th St (55101). Phone 651/222-5859; fax 651/222-7524. www.sawatdee.com.* Thai menu. Closed Sun; most major holidays. Lunch, dinner. Bar. Casual attire. Cr cds: A, DS, MC, V. **$**

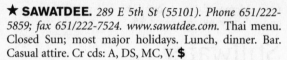

★★ **TOBY'S ON THE LAKE.** *249 Geneva Ave N (55128). Phone 651/739-1600. www.tobysonthelake.com.* Specialties: in prime rib, steak, fresh seafood. Hours: 11 am-2:30 pm, 5-10 pm; Sat 11 am-11 pm; Sun 11 am-9 pm; Sun brunch to 2 pm. Closed Dec 25. Lunch $5.95-$13.50, dinner $11.95-$23.95. Sun brunch $5.95-$9.95. Bar. Child's menu. Reservations accepted. Outdoor dining, Olde English atmosphere. Overlooks Tanners Lake. Cr cds: A, D, DS, MC, V.

★★★ **W. A. FROST AND COMPANY.** *374 Selby Ave (55102). Phone 651/224-5715; fax 651/224-7945. www.wafrost.com.* Located in the historic Dakotah Building, the four dining rooms are decorated with Victorian-style wallpaper, furnishings and oil paintings. Hours: 11:15 am-1:30 pm, 5:30-10 pm; Fri, Sat to 11 pm; Sun from 10:30 am, closed some major holidays. Dinner $6.95-$30. Sun brunch. Bar 11:15 am-midnight; Fri, Sat to 1 am; Sun from 10:30 am. Children's menu. Three dining rms; Victorian-style décor. Renovated pharmacy (1887). Valet parking Fri, Sat. Outdoor seating. Totally nonsmoking. Cr cds: A, C, D, DS, MC, V.

Saint Peter (G-3)

Founded 1853 **Pop** 9,421 **Elev** 770 ft **Area Code** 507 **Zip** 56082

Information Saint Peter Area Chamber of Commerce, 101 S Front St; 507/934-3400 or 800/473-3404

Web www.tourism.st-peter.mn.us

What to See and Do

Eugene Saint Julien Cox House. *500 N Washington Ave. Phone 507/931-2160.* (1871). Fully restored home is best example of Gothic Italianate architecture in the state. Built by town's first mayor; late Victorian furnishings. Guided tours. (June-Aug, Wed-Sun; May and Sept, Sat and Sun afternoons) **$$**

Gustavus Adolphus College. *800 W College Ave. Phone 507/933-8000.* (1862). (2,300 students) On campus are Old Main (dedicated 1876); Alfred Nobel Hall of Science and Gallery; Lund Center for Physical Education; Folke Bernadotte Memorial Library; Linnaeus Arboretum; Schaefer Fine Arts Gallery; Christ Chapel, featuring door and narthex art by noted sculptor Paul Granlund.

At various other locations on campus are sculptures by Granlund, sculptor-in-residence, including one depicting Joseph Nicollét, mid-19th-century French explorer & cartographer of the Minnesota River Valley. Campus tours. In Oct, the college hosts the nationally known Nobel Conference, which has been held annually since 1965.

Treaty Site History Center. *1851 N Minnesota Ave. Phone 507/931-2160.* County historical items relating to Dakota people, explorers, settlers, traders and cartographers and their impact on the 1851 Treaty of Traverse des Sioux. Archives. Museum shop. (Daily; closed major holidays) **$$**

Sauk Centre (E-2)

Pop 3,581 **Elev** 1,246 ft **Area code** 320 **Zip** 56378

Information Sauk Centre Area Chamber of Commerce, PO Box 222; 320/352-5201

Web www.saukcentrechamber.com

This is "Gopher Prairie," the boyhood home of Sinclair Lewis and the setting for Main Street, as well as many of his other novels. The town is at the southern tip of Big Sauk Lake.

What to See and Do

Sinclair Lewis Boyhood Home. *812 Sinclair Lewis Ave. Phone 320/352-5201.* Restored home of America's first Nobel Prize-winning novelist. Original furnishings; family memorabilia. (Memorial Day-Labor Day, Tues-Sun; rest of year, by appt) **$$**

Sinclair Lewis Interpretive Center. *1220 Main St S. At junction I-94, US 71. Phone 320/352-5201.* Exhibits include original manuscripts, photographs, letters; 15-minute video on the author's life; research library. (Labor Day-Memorial Day, Mon-Fri; Memorial Day-Labor Day, daily) **FREE**

Special Event

Sinclair Lewis Days. *Phone 320/352-5201.* Third weekend July.

Motel/Motor Lodge

★ **SUPER 8 MOTEL.** *322 12th St S (56378). Phone 320/352-6581; fax 320/352-6584. www.super8.com.* 38 rooms, 2 story. S, D $43-$62; each additional $5; under 12 free. Crib $2.50. Pet accepted, some restrictions. Check-out 11 am. TV; cable (premium). Indoor pool. Business services. Cr cds: A, DS, MC, V.

Spring Park

Restaurant

★ ★ ★ **LORD FLETCHER'S OF THE LAKE.** *3746 Sunset Dr (55384). Phone 952/471-8513; fax 952/471-8937. www.lordfletchers.com.* The atmosphere at this popular nautical respite resembles the peacefulness of a country English inn, with cozy fireplaces for cooler days. Local ingredients and unusual flavors make up the inventive dishes. Hours: 11:30 am-2:30 pm, 5-10 pm; Sun 4:30-9:30 pm; Sun brunch 11 am-2 pm. Closed Jan 1, Dec 24-Dec 25. Reservations accepted. English, Amer menu. Bar. Wine list. Lunch $6.25-$11.50, dinner $12.95-$22.95. Sun brunch $10.95. Specializes in beef, fish, prime rib. Outdoor dining. Mesquite charcoal grill. Old English décor; fireplaces, wine kegs, antiques. Boat dockage. Cr cds: A, D, DS, MC, V.

D

Spring Valley (H-4)

Pop 2,461 **Elev** 1,279 ft **Area Code** 507 **Zip** 55975

Information Spring Valley Chamber of Commerce, PO Box 13; 507/346-7367

As the name suggests, there are many large springs in this area. Geologists find the underground rivers, caves, and limestone outcroppings here of particular interest.

What to See and Do

Forestville/Mystery Cave State Park. *6 miles E on MN 16, 4 miles S on County 5, then 2 miles E on County 12. Phone 507/352-5111.* A 3,075-acre park in the Root River valley with a historic townsite. Fishing; hiking; bridle trails. Cross-country skiing, snowmobiling; picnicking; camping. Standard fees.

Mystery Cave. *Route 2 Preston MN. Phone 507/352-5111.* 60-minute guided tours; 48°F in cave. (Memorial Day-Labor Day, daily; mid-Apr-Memorial Day, weekends) Picnicking. Vehicle permit required (additional fee). **$$$**

Methodist Church. *221 W Courtland St. Phone 507/346-7659.* (1876). Victorian Gothic architecture; 23 stained-glass windows. Laura Ingalls Wilder site. Lower-level displays include country store, history room; military and business displays. (June-Aug, daily; Sept-Oct, wkends; also by appt) **$$**

Washburn-Zittleman House. *220 W Courtland St. Phone 507/346-7659.* (1866). Two-story frame house with period furnishings, quilts; farm equipment, one-room school, toys. (Memorial Day-Labor Day, daily; Sept-Oct, weekends; also by appointment) **$$**

Stillwater (F-4)

See also Taylors Falls

Settled 1839 **Pop** 13,882 **Elev** 700 ft **Area code** 651 **Zip** 55082

Information Chamber of Commerce, 423 S Main St, Brick Alley Bldg; 651/439-4001

Web www.ilovestillwater.com

Center of the logging industry in pioneer days, Stillwater became a busy river town, host to the men who rode the logs downriver and the lumbermen who cleared the forests.

What to See and Do

★ **St. Croix Scenic Highway.** MN 95 runs 50 miles from Afton to Taylors Falls along the "Rhine of America," the St. Croix River.

Washington County Historical Museum. *602 N Main St. Phone 651/439-5956.* Former warden's house at old prison site; mementos of lumbering days (1846-1910); pioneer kitchen, furniture. (May-Oct, Thurs-Sun; also by appointment) **$$**

William O'Brien State Park. *16 miles N on MN 95. Phone 651/433-0500.* A 1,273-acre park. Swimming, fishing, boating (ramp); hiking, cross-country skiing, picnicking, camping (hookups, dump station). Standard fees.

Special Events

Lumberjack Days. *423 Main St S. Phone 651/439-7700.* Last weekend July.

Rivertown Art Fair. *Lowell Park. Phone 651/430-2306.* Third weekend May.

Motels/Motor Lodges

★ **BEST WESTERN.** *1750 W Frontage Rd (55082). Phone 651/430-1300; toll-free 800/647-4039; fax 651/430-0596. www.bestwestern.com/stillwaterinn.* 59 rooms, 2 story. Pet accepted. Complimentary continental breakfast. Check-out 11 am, check-in 3 pm. TV; cable (premium). In-room modem link. Indoor pool, whirlpool. Downhill ski 20 miles, cross-country ski 2 miles. Cr cds: A, C, D, DS, ER, JCB, MC, V. **$**

D

★ **COUNTRY INN & SUITES BY CARLSON.** *2200 W Frontage Rd (55082). Phone 651/430-2699; toll-free 800/456-4000; fax 651/430-1233.* 66 rooms, 2 story.

Complimentary continental breakfast. Check-out 11 am, check-in 3 pm. TV; cable (premium). In-room modem link. Game room. Indoor pool, whirlpool. Downhill ski 15 miles, cross-country ski 2 miles. Cr cds: A, D, DS, MC, V. **$**

D ⊠ ⊠ ⊠ SC

★ **SUPER 8 MOTEL.** *2190 W Frontage Rd (55082). Phone 651/430-3990; toll-free 800/800-8000. www.super8.com.* 49 rooms, 2 story. Complimentary continental breakfast. Check-out 11 am, check-in 1 pm. TV; cable (premium). Laundry services. Downhill ski 15 miles; cross-country ski 2 miles. Near St. Croix River. Cr cds: A, C, D, DS, MC, V. **$**

D ⊠ ⊠ SC

Hotels

★ ★ **LUMBER BARON'S HOTEL.** *101 S Water St (55082). Phone 651/439-6000; fax 651/430-9393. www.lumberbarons.com.* This intimate Victorian-style hotel offers 36 guestrooms that overlook the scenic St. Croix River. The property is located in the historic downtown of Stillwater. 41 rooms, 3 story. Complimentary full breakfast. Check-out 11 am, check-in 4 pm. TV. Fireplaces. Restaurant, bar. Cr cds: A, D, DS, MC, V. **$**

D ⊠

B&B/Small Inns

★ ★ ★ **AFTON HOUSE INN.** *3291 S St. Croix Trl (55001). Phone 651/436-8883; toll-free 877/436-8883; fax 651/436-6859. www.aftonhouseinn.com.* For a great escape, this romantic country inn is the perfect answer. Whether curling up with a book in the pine loft or taking a cruise on the St. Croix River, guests will find uninterrupted peace and relaxation here. 25 rooms, 2 story. S, D $49-$275; AP available; mid-week rates. Check-out 11 am, check-in 2 pm. TV; VCR available. Fireplaces. Restaurant, room service. Downhill skiing, cross-country ski 2 miles. Airport transportation. River cruises available. Cr cds: A, DS, MC, V.

D ⊠ ⊠

★ ★ **COVER PARK MANOR BED AND BREAKFAST.** *15330 58th St N (55082). Phone 651/430-9292; toll-free 877/430-9292; fax 651/430-0034. www.coverpark.com.* 42 rooms, 2 suites, 2 story. No elevator, no room phones. S $99-$195, D $109-$195; holidays (2-day minimum). Complimentary full bkfst, Complimentary afternoon refreshments. Check-out 11:30 am, check-in 4 pm. Some fireplaces, in-room whirlpools. Restaurant nearby. Victorian house built in 1882; antiques. Totally nonsmoking. Cr cds: A, DS, MC, V.

D ⊠ ⊠

★ ★ ★ **LOWELL INN.** *102 2nd St N (55082). Phone 651/439-1100; toll-free 888/569-3554; fax 651/439-4686. www.lowellinn.com.* Located in the historic area of Stillwater, on the banks of the beautifull St. Croix River, this hotel is a convenient getaway spot from the Twin Cities. Each of the hotel's rooms are individually decorated with fine furnishings. 23 rooms, 3 story. S $89; D $129; higher rates Fri, Sat (MAP). Check-out noon. TV. Restaurant, bar 11:30 am-2:30 pm, 5:30 pm-1 am; Sun, holidays noon-11 pm. Downhill ski 15 miles, cross-country ski 9 miles. Cr cds: A, C, D, DS, MC, V.

⊠

Restaurants

★ ★ **AFTON HOUSE.** *3291 S St. Croix Trl (55001). Phone 651/436-8883. www.aftonhouseinn.com.* Tableside presentations complete with the traditional flame effects, are featured at this historic inn, with such dishes as caesar salad, steak Diane, and dessert items like cherries jubilee, banana's foster and strawberries Victoria. Hours: 11:30 am-10 pm; Sat to 11 pm; Sun 10 am-9 pm; Sun brunch to 2 pm. Closed Dec 25; also Mon, Jan-Apr. Breakfast $3.50-$6.95, lunch $7.95-$14.99, dinner $14.95-$28.75. Sun brunch $12.95. Bar to 1 am. Entertainment Fri-Sat. Child's menu, Renovated inn (1867); nautical décor. Reservations accepted. Cr cds: A, DS, MC, V.

D

★ ★ ★ **BAYPORT COOKERY.** *328 5th Ave N (55003). Phone 651/430-1066. www.bayportcookery.com.* With only one nightly seating, diners can plan on an adventure of innovative cuisine at this St. Croix River Valley destination. Even city dwellers travel to experience the daily changing dinners featuring artistic presentations of local ingredients. Contemporary Amer menu. Closed Sun; major holidays. Dinner 5-course dinner $46, with wine option $75. Reservations required. Totally nonsmoking. Sitting: Wed-Sun 7 pm. Cr cds: A, DS, MC, V.

D

★ **GASTHAUS BAVARIAN HUNTER.** *8390 Lofton Ave N (55082). Phone 651/439-7128; fax 651/439-0562. www.gasthausbavarianhunter.com.* German menu. Closed some major holidays. Lunch, dinner, brunch. Bar. Children's menu. Casual attire. Reservations accepted. Outdoor seating, totally nonsmoking. Accordianist Fri eve, Sun afternoon. Cr cds: A, MC, V. **$**

D

★ ★ **LOWELL INN RESTAURANT.** *102 N 2nd St (55082). Phone 651/439-1100. www.lowellinn.com.* Journey back to colonial times at this "Mount Vernon of the

West". Traditional preparations are showcased, complete palate cleansing sorbets and finger bowls, lending the air of the past, or try the fondue room for something a bit different. Swiss, Amer menu. Hours: 8 am-10 pm. Closed Thanksgiving, Dec 24, 25. Breakfast $4.35-$8.95, lunch $7.95-$14.95, dinner $15-$24, dinner Prix fixe: dinner $60 (Swiss fondue Bourguigonne). Bar to 1 am; Sun, holidays to 11 pm. Child's menu. Reservations accepted. Cr cds: A, DS, MC, V.

[D] [SC]

Superior National Forest (B-4)

See also Crane Lake, Ely, Grand Marais, Tower, Virginia

On N side of Lake Superior, W to Virginia, N to Canadian border, E to Grand Marais

With more than 2,000 beautiful clear lakes, rugged shorelines, picturesque islands, and deep woods, this is a magnificent portion of Minnesota's famous northern area.

The Boundary Waters Canoe Area Wilderness, part of the forest, is perhaps the finest canoe country in the United States (travel permits required for each party, $9 for advance reservations, phone 800/745-3399). Scenic water routes through wilderness near the international border offer opportunities for adventure. Adjacent Quetico Provincial Park is similar, but guns are prohibited. Entry through Canadian Customs (see Border Crossing Regulations in MAKING THE MOST OF YOUR TRIP) and Park Rangers' Ports of Entry.

Boating, swimming, water sports; fishing and hunting under Minnesota game and fish regulations; winter sports; camping (fee), picnicking, and scenic drives along Honeymoon, Gunflint, Echo, and Sawbill trails.

For further info contact Forest Supervisor, 8901 Grand Avenue Pl, Duluth 55808; 218/626-4300.

Taylors Falls (F-4)

See also Saint Paul, Stillwater

Settled 1838 **Pop** 694 **Elev** 900 ft **Area Code** 612 **Zip** 55084

Information Taylors Falls Chamber of Commerce, PO Box 235; 612/465-6315, 612/257-3550 (Twin Cities) or 800/447-4958 (outside 612 area)

Web www.wildmountain.com

What to See and Do

Boat Excursions. *37350 Wild Mountain Rd. Phone 612/465-6315, 612/257-3550 or 800/447-4958. Also, Taylors Falls Adventurers, 612/465-6501 or 800/996.* Taylors Falls Scenic Boat Tour. Base of bridge, downtown. (Early May-mid-Oct, daily); 30-minutes, 3-mile trip through St. Croix Dalles; also 1 1/3-hour, 7-mile trip on Taylors Falls Queen or Princess. Scenic, brunch, luncheon and dinner cruises; fall color cruises. Also Taylors Falls one-way canoe rentals to Osceola or Williams O'Brien State Park, trips (with shuttle) (May-mid-Oct, daily).

Interstate. *1 mile S on MN 8. Phone 612/465-5711.* A 295-acre park. Geologic formations. Boating (ramp), canoe rentals, fishing, hiking, picnicking, camping (electric hookups, dump station). Excursion boat (fee). Standard fees.

★ St. Croix and Lower St. Croix National Scenic Riverway. *Phone 715/483-3284.* From its origins in northern Wisconsin the St Croix flows southward to form part of the Minnesota-Wisconsin border before joining the Mississippi near Point Douglas. Two segments of the river totaling more than 250 miles have been designated National Scenic Riverways and are administered by the National Park Service. Information headquarters (mid-May-Oct, daily; rest of year, Mon-Fri); two information stations (Memorial Day-Labor Day, daily).

W.H.C. Folsom House. *120 Government Rd. Phone 612/465-3125.* (1855). Federal/Greek Revival mansion reflects New England heritage of early settlers; many original furnishings. (Memorial Day weekend-mid-Oct, daily) **$$**

Wild Mountain Ski Area. *37350 Wild Mountain Rd. 7 miles N on County 16. Phone 651/257-3550; 800/447-4958.* Four quad chairlifts, two rope tows; patrol, school, rentals; snowmaking; cafeteria. Twenty-three runs, longest run 5,000 feet; vertical drop 300 feet. (Nov-Mar, daily) **$$$$** Also here is

Water Park. *37200 Wild Mountain Rd. Phone 651/257-3550.* Alpine slides and go-karts. (Memorial Day-Labor Day, daily).

Wild River. *10 miles NW via MN 95, then 3 miles N on County 12. Phone 612/583-2125.* On 6,706 acres in the St Croix River Valley. Fishing, canoeing (rentals); 35 miles of trails for hiking, cross-country skiing and 20 miles of horseback riding trails; picnicking; primitive and modern camping (electric hookups, dump station). Interpretive center and Trail Center (Daily). Standard hours, fees.

Thief River Falls (B-1)

Pop 8,010 **Elev** 1,133 ft **Area code** 218 **Zip** 56701

Information Chamber of Commerce, 2017 Hwy 59 SE; 218/681-3720 or 800/827-1629

Web www.ci.thief-river-falls.mn.us

What to See and Do

Agassiz National Wildlife Refuge. *23 miles NE via MN 32 to County 7E. Phone 218/449-4115.* Approximately 61,500 acres of forest, water and marshland. A haven for 280 species of migratory and upland game birds; 41 species of resident mammals. Refuge headquarters (Mon-Fri; closed holidays); auto tour route (daily, except winter). No camping. **FREE**

Motels/Motor Lodges

★ ★ **BEST WESTERN INN.** *1060 Hwy 32 S (56701). Phone 218/681-7555; toll-free 800/780-7234; fax 218/681-7721. www.bestwestern.com.* 78 rooms. S, studio rooms $49-$57; D $59-$67; each additional $4; under 18 free. Crib free. TV; cable (premium). Indoor pool; whirlpool. Complimentary coffee in rooms. Restaurant 6 am-10 pm. Room service. Bar 3 pm-1 am; entertainment. Check-out noon. Meeting rooms. Business services available. In-room modem link. Sundries. Free airport transportation. Cross-country ski 3 miles. Exercise equipment. Game room. Refrigerators. Cr cds: A, C, D, DS, MC, V.

⬚ ⬚ ⬚ ⬚ ⬚ SC

★ **C'MON INN.** *1586 Hwy 59 S (56701). Phone 218/681-3000; toll-free 800/950-8111; fax 218/681-3060.* 44 rooms, 2 story. S $44-$57; D $51-$65; each additional $7; suites $74-$94; under 12 free. Crib free. Pet accepted, some restrictions. TV; cable (premium). Indoor pool; whirlpool. Complimentary continental breakfast. Restaurant nearby. Check-out noon. Meeting room. Business services available. In-room modem link. Game room. Balconies. Cr cds: A, DS, MC, V.

⬚ ⬚ ⬚ ⬚ SC

★ **SUPER 8 MOTEL.** *1915 Hwy 59 S (56701). Phone 218/681-6205; toll-free 888/890-9568; fax 218/681-7519. www.super8.com.* 46 rooms. S, D $40-$60; each additional $4; under 16 free. Crib free. TV; cable (premium). Complimentary continental breakfast. Restaurant adjacent 6:30 am-11 pm. Check-out 11 am. Business services available. Cr cds: A, C, D, DS, MC, V.

⬚ ⬚ SC

Tower (C-4)

Founded 1882 **Pop** 502 **Elev** 1,400 ft **Area Code** 218 **Zip** 55790

What to See and Do

Lake Vermilion. *515 Main St. Phone 218/753-2301.* 40 miles long, 1,250 miles of wooded shoreline, 365 islands varying in size from specklike rocks to Pine Island, which is 9 miles long and has its own lake in its interior. Fishing for walleye, northern pike, bass, and panfish. Swimming, boating, water sports; hunting for duck, deer, and small game in fall; snowmobiling and cross-country skiing; camping and lodging. Primarily located in Superior National Forest.

Soudan Underground Mine State Park. *2 miles E on MN 169, in Soudan. Phone 218/753-2245.* Has 1,300 acres including site of the Soudan Mine, the state's first underground iron mine (52°F; 2,400 feet) in operation 1882-1962. Self-guided tour of open pits, engine house, crusher building, drill shop, interpretive center; one-hr guided underground mine tour includes train ride (fees). Hiking trails. Picnic area. (Memorial Day-Labor Day, daily) Standard fees. **$$$**

Steam Locomotive and Coach. *51 end Main St, near junction MN 135, 169. Phone 218/753-2301.* Locomotive (1910) served Duluth & Iron Range Railroad. Coach is now a museum housing early logging, mining and Native American displays. (Memorial Day-Labor Day, daily; early spring and late fall, by appointment) On grounds is a tourist info center and gift shop. **DONATION**

Tracy (G-2)

Pop 2,059 **Elev** 1,395 ft **Area Code** 507 **Zip** 56175

Information Chamber of Commerce, Prairie Pavilion, 372 Morgan St; 507/629-4021

Web www.tracymn.com/chamber

What to See and Do

Lake Shetek State Park. *163 State Park Rd. 14 miles S on County 11 and 38. Phone 507/763-3256.* Comprises 1,011 acres on one of largest lakes in SW Minnesota. Monument to settlers who were victims of the Dakota Conflict in 1862; restored pioneer cabin. Swimming, fishing, boating (ramp, rentals); hiking, snowmobiling, picnicking, camping. Standard fees. Naturalist (Late May-early Sept).

⭐ **Laura Ingalls Wilder Museum and Tourist Center.** *7 miles E on US 14, in Walnut Grove at 330 8th St. Phone*

507/859-2358. This tribute to Laura Ingalls Wilder is five buildings of museums. The depression in the ground where the dugout used to be, and the rock and spring mentioned in On the Banks of Plum Creek are all 1 1/2 miles N of Walnut Grove; fee per vehicle at farm site. (May-Oct, daily; rest of year, by appt) **$$**

Special Event

Laura Ingalls Wilder Pageant. *313 Main St. Phone 507/859-2174. 7 miles E on US 14, 1 mile W of Walnut Grove.* Story of the Ingalls family of Walnut Grove in the 1870s. Daughter was Laura Ingalls Wilder, author of the Little House books. July.

Two Harbors (D-5)

See also Duluth

Founded 1884 **Pop** 3,651 **Elev** 699 ft **Area code** 218 **Zip** 55616

Information Two Harbors Area Chamber of Commerce, 1026 7th Ave; 218/834-2600 or 800/777-7384

Web www.twoharbors.com/chamber

Two Harbors was given its start when the Duluth & Iron Range Railroad reached Lake Superior at Agate Bay. Ore docks were constructed immediately and the city became an important ore shipping terminal. Today it is a bustling harbor community nestled between the twin harbors of Agate Bay and Burlington Bay.

What to See and Do

Depot Museum. *520 South Ave. In depot of Duluth & Iron Range Railroad, foot of Waterfront Dr. Phone 218/834-4898.* Historic depot (1907) highlights the geological history and the discovery and mining of iron ore. Mallet locomotive (1941), world's most powerful steam engine, on display. (May, wkends; Memorial Day-Oct, daily) **$**

Gooseberry Falls State Park. *3206 Hwy 61. 14 miles NE on MN 61. Phone 218/834-3855.* A 1,662-acre park. Fishing, hiking, cross-country skiing, snowmobiling, picnicking, camping (dump station). State park vehicle permit required. Standard fees.

Lighthouse Point and Harbor Museum. *520 South Ave. Off MN 61, on Waterfront Dr at Lighthouse Point. Phone 218/834-4898.* Displays tell the story of iron ore shipping and the development of the first iron ore port in the state. A renovated pilot house from an ore boat is located on the site. Shipwreck display. Tours of operating lighthouse. (May-Nov 1, daily) **$$**

Split Rock Lighthouse State Park. *3755 Split Rock Lighthouse. 20 miles NE on MN 61. Phone 218/226-6377 (park) or -6372 (historic site).* 1,987 acres. Lighthouse served as guiding sentinel for north shore of Lake Superior from 1910-1969. Also in the park is a historic complex (fee) which includes fog-signal bldg, keeper's dwellings, several outbldgs and the ruins of a tramway (mid-May-mid-Oct, daily). Waterfalls. Picnicking. Cart-in camping (fee) on Lake Superior, access to Superior Hiking Trail. State park vehicle permit required. Standard hours, fees. **$$**

Motel/Motor Lodge

★★**COUNTRY INN BY CARLSON.** *1204 7th Ave (55616). Phone 218/834-5557; toll-free 800/456-4000; fax 218/834-3777.* 46 rooms, 2 story. Mid-May-mid-Oct: S, D $59-$109; each additional $5; under 18 free; higher rates special events; lower rates rest of year. Crib free. Pet accepted, some restrictions; $5/day. Complimentary continental breakfast. Check-out 11 am. TV; cable (premium), VCR available (movies). Microwaves, Some refrigerators, wet bars, coffee in rooms. Coin laundry. Restaurant adjacent 6 am-11 pm. Sauna. Indoor pool, whirlpool. Cross-country ski 1 mile. Business services. Cr cds: A, C, D, DS, MC, V.

D ⊠ ⊠ ⊠ ⊠ SC

Resort

★★★**SUPERIOR SHORES RESORT.** *1521 Superior Shores Dr (55616). Phone 218/834-5671; toll-free 800/242-1988; fax 218/834-5677. www.superiorshores.com.* 104 rooms in 3-story lodge, 42 kitchen units in 3-story townhouses. Mid-June-mid Oct: S, D $49-$69; under 18 free; weekly rates; weekends (2-day min), holidays (3-day min); lower rates rest of year. Pet accepted. Check-out 11 am, check-in by arrangement. TV; cable, VCR (movies). Balconies, microwaves, Many refrigerators, Restaurant 7 am-9 pm. Bar 11-1 am. Sauna. Game room. 3 pools, 1 indoor, whirlpool. Cross-country ski opposite. Grills, Hiking trails. Picnics/tables, snow mobiles. Meeting rooms, business services. Gift shop. Cr cds: A, DS, MC, V.

D ⊠ ⊠ ⊠ ⊠ ⊠

Virginia (C-4)

See also Cook, Eveleth, Hibbing, Tower

Founded 1892 **Pop** 9,410 **Elev** 1,437 ft **Area code** 218 **Zip** 55792

Information Virginia Area Chamber of Commerce, 403 1st St N, PO Box 1072; 218/741-2717

Web www.virginiachamber.com

Born of lumbering, Virginia is nurtured by mining and vacationing. Great open iron ore pits mark the surrounding green countryside—man-made canyons are right at the city limits. Vacationers come to Virginia en route to the Boundary Waters Canoe Area Wilderness, Superior National Forest, and Voyagers National Park. A Ranger District office of the Superior National Forest is located nearby.

What to See and Do

Mine View in the Sky. *403 1st St N. S edge of town on US 53. Phone 218/741-2717.* Observation building (and visitor's info center) gives view of a Mesabi Range open-pit mine 650 feet below. (May-Sept daily) **FREE**

World's Largest Floating Loon. *1409 N Broadway. Phone 218/741-2717.* Listed in the Guinness Book of World Records, this 20-feet long, 10-feet high, 7 1/2-feet wide, fiberglass loon swims on Silver Lake (located in the heart of the city) during the summer months.

Motels/Motor Lodges

★ **LAKESHORE MOTOR INN.** *404 N 6th Ave (55792). Phone 218/741-3360; toll-free 800/569-8131; fax 218/741-3363.* 11 rooms, 3 suites, 2 story. Mid-May-Aug: S $36; D $44-$48; each additional $4; family rates; lower rates rest of year. Crib available. Pet accepted. TV; cable. Complimentary coffee in rooms. Whirlpool. Restaurant nearby. Check-out 11 am. Gift shop. Downhill ski 18 miles; cross-country ski 4 miles. Cr cds: A, MC, V.

⬛ ⬛ ⬛ ⬛ **SC**

★ **SKI VIEW.** *903 17th St N (55792). Phone 218/741-8918; toll-free 800/255-7106; fax 218/749-3279.* 59 rooms, 2 story. S $32; D $44; each additional $4. Crib $5. Pet accepted. Complimentary continental breakfast. Check-out 11 am. TV; cable (premium). Microwaves available. Coffee in rooms. Restaurant nearby. Sauna. Downhill skiing, cross-country ski 20 miles. Snowmobile trails adjacent. Cr cds: A, C, D, DS, MC, V.

⬛ ⬛ ⬛

Walker (D-3)

See also Bemidji, Park Rapids, Pine River

Pop 950 **Elev** 1,336 ft **Area code** 218 **Zip** 56484

Information Chamber of Commerce, PO Box 1089; 218/547-1313 or 800/833-1118

Web www.leech-lake.com

At the foot of Chippewa National Forest and Leech Lake, Walker serves tourists heading for adventures among woods and waters. Snowmobiling and cross-country skiing are popular sports here. The town is named for a pioneer lumberman and landowner. A Ranger District office of the Chippewa National Forest (see GRAND RAPIDS) is located here.

What to See and Do

Leech Lake. *MN 200/371.* Third largest lake in the state; fishing and swimming.

Motel/Motor Lodge

★ **AMERICINN.** *Hwy 371 & 34 (56484). Phone 218/547-2200; toll-free 800/757-9135. www.americinn.com.* 37 rooms, 2 story. S $43.90-$56.90; D $59.90-$65.90; each additional $6; suites $64.90-$96.90; under 12 free. Complimentary continental breakfast. Check-out 11 am. TV; VCR available (movies). Restaurant adjacent 7 am-9 pm. Sauna. Indoor pool, whirlpool. Cross-country ski 10 miles. Cr cds: A, D, DS, MC, V.

⬛ ⬛ ⬛ ⬛

Willmar (F-2)

See also Granite Falls, Litchfield

Founded 1869 **Pop** 17,531 **Elev** 1,130 ft **Area code** 320 **Zip** 56201

Information Willmar Area Chamber of Commerce, 2104 E Hwy 12; 320/235-0300 or 800/845-8747

Web www.willmarareachamber.com

What to See and Do

Kandiyohi County Historical Society Museum. *610 Hwy 71 NE. 1 mile N on US 71 Business. Phone 320/235-1881.* Steam locomotive, country schoolhouse, restored house (1893); historical exhibits, agriculture building, research library. (Memorial Day-Labor Day, daily; rest of year, Mon-Fri; also by appointment; closed major holidays) **DONATION**

Sibley State Park. *800 Sibley Park Rd. 15 miles N on US 71. Phone 320/354-2055.* A 2,600-acre park; was a favorite hunting ground of first governor of state, for whom park is named. Swimming, fishing, boating (ramps, rentals); horseback riding, hiking; cross-country skiing, snowmobiling; camping (dump station); nature center. Standard fees.

Motels/Motor Lodges

★ ★ **AMERICINN MOTEL AND SUITES.** *2404 E Hwy 12 (56201). Phone 320/231-1962; toll-free 800/634-3444. www.americinn.com.* 30 rooms, 2 story. S $59.99;

D $69.99; each additional $6; under 13 free. Crib free. Complimentary continental breakfast. Check-out 11 am. TV; cable (premium). Restaurant adjacent open 24 hours. Indoor pool, whirlpool. Cross-country ski 1 mile. Meeting rooms, business services. Cr cds: A, DS, MC, V.

⬜ ⬜ ⬜ ⬜

★ **DAYS INN.** 225 28th St SE (56201). Phone 320/231-1275; toll-free 877/241-5235; fax 320/231-1275. www.torgersonproperties.com. 59 rooms, 2 story. S, D $59; each additional $6; under 18 free. Crib free. Pet accepted. Complimentary continental breakfast. Check-out 11 am. TV; cable (premium). Restaurant nearby. Exercise equipment, sauna. Cr cds: A, C, D, DS, JCB, MC, V.

⬜ ⬜ ⬜ ⬜

★ ★ **HOLIDAY INN.** 2100 E Hwy 12 (56201). Phone 320/235-6060; toll-free 877/405-4466; fax 320/235-4231. www.holiday-inn.com. 98 rooms, 2 story. S $63-$69; D $73-$79; each additional $10; under 18 free. Crib free. Pet accepted. Complimentary coffee in lobby. Check-out noon. TV; cable (premium). In-room modem link. Some balconies. Restaurant 6 am-10 pm. Bar 4 pm-1 am. Room service. Indoor pool, wading pool, whirlpool, poolside service. Business services. Cr cds: A, D, DS, MC, V.

⬜ ⬜ ⬜ ⬜

★ **SUPER 8 MOTEL.** 2655 S 1st St (56201). Phone 320/235-7260; toll-free 800/800-8000; fax 320/235-5580. www.super8.com. 60 rooms, 3 story. No elevator. S, D $37-$55; each additional $5; under 12 free. Crib free. Pet accepted. TV; cable (premium). Complimentary coffee in lobby. Restaurant nearby. Check-out 11 am. Business services available. Cr cds: A, DS, MC, V.

⬜ ⬜ ⬜ SC

Winona (G-5)

See also Rochester

Settled 1851 **Pop** 25,399 **Elev** 666 ft **Area code** 507 **Zip** 55987

Information Convention & Visitors Bureau, 67 Main St, PO Box 870; 507/452-2272

Web www.visitwinona.com

New Englanders and Germans came to this site on the west bank of the Mississippi and built an industrial city graced with three colleges. An early lumbering town, Winona today is one of the state's leading business and industrial centers and home of Winona State University.

What to See and Do

Fishing. Whitman Dam and Locks #5. *12 miles N on US 61.* **Dresbach Dam and Locks #7.** *15 miles S on US 61.* **Lake Winona.** *S side of town.* Float and boat fishing.

Garvin Heights. *Huff St and Garvin Heights Rd.* Accessible via Huff St. Park with 575-feet bluff, offering majestic views of the Mississippi River Valley. Picnic area. (Dawn-dusk)

Julius C. Wilkie Steamboat Center. *Phone 507/454-1254.* Replica and exhibits. (June-Oct, Tues-Sun) Levee Park. **$**

Prairie Island Park. *Prairie Island Rd, 3 miles N off US 61.* Camping (Apr-Oct), picnicking, water, rest rooms, fireplaces. Fishing (all-year). Some fees.

Upper Mississippi River National Wildlife and Fish Refuge. *51 E 4th St. 51 E 4th St. Phone 507/452-4232* (Mon-Fri). From Wabasha, MN, extending 261 miles to Rock Island, IL, the refuge encompasses 200,000 acres of wooded islands, marshes, sloughs and backwaters. Abounds in fish, wildlife & plants. (Daily) Twenty percent of the refuge is closed for hunting and trapping until after duck hunting season. Boat required for access to most parts of refuge.

Winona County Historical Society Museum. *160 Johnson St. Phone 507/454-2723.* Country store; blacksmith, barber shops; Native American artifacts; logging and lumbering exhibits; early vehicles and fire fighting equipment, award-winning children's exhibit, gift shop, library. (Daily; closed some major holidays) **$$** The society also maintains

> **Bunnell House.** *710 Johnson St. 5 miles S on US 14, 61 in Homer. Phone 507/452-7575.* (Circa 1850). Unusual mid-19th-century Steamboat Gothic architecture; period furnishings. (Memorial Day-Labor Day, Wed-Sun; Labor Day-second weekend Oct, weekends only; rest of year, by appointment) Also here is Carriage House Museum Shop (same schedule). **$$**

Special Events

Victorian Fair. *160 Johnson St. Phone 507/452-2272.* Living history; costumed guides; boat rides. Late Sept.

Winona Steamboat Days. *Phone 507/452-2272.* Late June.

Motels/Motor Lodges

★ ★ **BEST WESTERN RIVERPORT INN.** *900 Bruski Dr (55987). Phone 507/452-0606; toll-free 800/595-0606; fax 507/452-6489. www.bestwestern.com.* 106 rooms, 3 story. May-Oct: S $59-$89; D $69-$99; each additional

$10; suites $69-$89; under 13 free; lower rates rest of year. Crib free. Pet accepted; $10. Complimentary continental breakfast. Check-out 11 am. TV; cable (premium), VCR available. Some refrigerators. Restaurant 11 am-10 pm. Bar Bar 11-1 am. Room service. Game room. Indoor pool, whirlpool. Downhill ski 8 miles, cross-country ski 1 mile. Meeting rooms. Gift shop. Cr cds: A, C, D, DS, MC, V.

D ⊶ ⊠ ⊠ ⊠ SC

★ **DAYS INN.** *420 Cottonwood Dr (55987). Phone 507/454-6930; toll-free 800/329-7466; fax 507/454-7917. www.daysinn.com.* 58 rooms, 2 story. S $42-$56; D $43-$62; each additional $6; under 18 free. Crib free. TV; cable. Complimentary continental breakfast. Restaurant nearby. Check-out 11 am. Cross-country ski 1 miles. Cr cds: A, C, D, DS, MC, V.

D ⊠ ⊠ SC

★ ★ **QUALITY INN WINONA.** *956 Mankato Ave (55987). Phone 507/454-4390; toll-free 800/228-5151; fax 507/452-2187. www.qualityinn.com.* 112 rooms, 2 story. S $50-$75; D $55-$85; each additional $10; family rates. Crib free. Complimentary coffee in rooms. Check-out 11 am. TV; cable. Complimentary coffee in rooms. Valet services. Restaurant 24 hours. Bar 4 pm-1 am, Sun from 11 am. Room service. Indoor pool, whirlpool. Cross-country ski 1 mile. Meeting rooms. Sundries. Cr cds: A, C, D, DS, JCB, MC, V.

D ⊠ ⊠ ⊠ SC

★ **STERLING MOTEL.** *1450 Gilmore Ave (55987). Phone 507/454-1120; toll-free 800/452-1235.* 32 rooms. S $29-$38; D $45-$59; each additional $4; family rates. Crib free. Check-out 11 am. TV; cable (premium). Restaurant adjacent open 24 hours. Cross-country ski 1 mile. Cr cds: A, D, DS, MC, V.

⊠ ⊠

★ **SUPER 8 MOTEL.** *1025 Sugar Loaf Rd (55987). Phone 507/454-6066; toll-free 800/800-8000. www.super8.com.* 61 rooms, 3 story. No elevator. S, D $41-$59; each additional $5; family rates. Crib $2. TV; cable. Complimentary continental breakfast. Restaurant nearby. Check-out 11 am. Cross-country ski 1 mile. Cr cds: A, C, D, DS, MC, V.

D ⊠ ⊠ SC

Winnipeg, the provincial capital of Manitoba, is roughly 100 miles north of the Minnesota border. While visiting Minnesota, take advantage of the proximity and take a few days to visit our neighbor to the north. Whether you're a sports fan, a ballet aficionado, a shopaholic, or a foodie, Winnipeg has activities to suit all interests.

Winnipeg, MB

2 hours 45 minutes, 70 miles from St. Vincent, MN

Pop 650,000 **Elev** 915 ft (279 m) **Area code** 204

Information Tourism Winnipeg, 279 Portage Rd, R3B 2B4; 204/943-1970 or 800/665-0204

Web www.tourism.winnipeg.mb.ca

Winnipeg, the provincial capital, is situated in the heart of the continent and combines the sophistication and friendliness of east and west. The city offers much for any visitor, including relaxing cruises on the Assiniboine and Red rivers, Rainbow Stage summer theater in Kildonan Park, the Manitoba Theatre Centre, the Winnipeg Symphony, the Manitoba Opera, and the renowned Royal Winnipeg Ballet. Sports fans will enjoy the Blue Bombers in football and the Manitoba Moose hockey team. Shopping, nightlife, gourmet restaurants—Winnipeg has it all.

What to See and Do

Assiniboine Park. *2355 Corydon Ave. Phone 204/986-3989.* A 376-acre (152-hectare) park features colorful English and formal gardens; the Leo Mol Sculpture Garden; conservatory with floral displays; duck pond; playgrounds; picnic sites; cricket and field hockey area; refreshment pavilion; miniature train; bicycle paths; fitness trail. Assiniboine Park Zoo has collection of rare and endangered species, tropical mammals, birds, and reptiles; children's discovery area featuring variety of young animals (daily). Park (daily). **FREE**

Birds Hill Provincial Park. *8 miles N on Hwy 59. Phone 204/222-9151.* A 8,275-acre (3,350-hectare) park situated on a glacial formation called an eskar. Large population of whitetail deer; many orchid species. Interpretive, hiking, bridle, and bicycle trails; rollerblading path; snowshoe, snowmobile, and cross-country skiing trails (winter). Interpretive programs. Swimming; camping and picnicking at 81 1/2-acre (33-hectare) lake (seasonal). Riding stables (phone 204/222-1137). Per vechicle (May-Sept) **$$**

⭐ **Centennial Centre.** *555 Main St.* Complex includes concert hall, planetarium, Museum of Man and Nature, Manitoba Theatre Centre Building. Here are

> **Manitoba Museum of Man and Nature.** *190 Rupert Ave.* Eight galleries interpret Manitoba's human and natural history: Orientation; Earth History (geological background); Arctic-Subarctic; Boreal Forest; Nonsuch (full-size replica of 17th-century ship); and Urban. (Victoria Day-Labour Day, daily; rest of year, Tues-Sun) **$$**

> **Planetarium.** Circular, multipurpose audiovisual theater. Wide variety of shows; subjects include cosmic catastrophes and the edge of the universe. In the Science Gallery, visitors can learn about science through hands-on exhibits (separate admission fee). (Same days as museum) **$$**

"Dalnavert". *61 Carlton St. Phone 204/943-2835.* Restored Victorian residence (1895) of Sir Hugh John Macdonald, premier of Manitoba, depicting lifestyle and furnishings of the period. Gift shop. Guided tours (Mar-Dec, Tues-Thurs, Sat and Sun; rest of year, Sat and Sun only) **$$**

The Forks National Historic Site. *Pioneer Blvd, opposite Water and Pioneer Aves at Provencher Bridge. Phone 204/983-2007; 204/983-5988.* Situated on 10 acres at the confluence of the Red and Assiniboine rivers. Riverside promenade; walkways throughout. Historical exhibits, playground; evening performances. Special events. (May-Sept) Grounds (all year). Adjacent area open in winter for skating, cross-country skiing. **FREE**

Legislative Building. *Broadway and Osborne. Phone 204/945-5813.* Example of neoclassical architecture. Grounds contain statues of Queen Victoria, Lord Selkirk, George Cartier. Tours (June-Aug, Mon-Fri; Sept-June, by appointment) **FREE**

Lower Fort Garry National Historic Site of Canada. *20 miles (32 kilometers) N on Hwy 9. Phone 204/785-6050.* Hudson's Bay Co fur trade post restored to the 1850s. Original buildings; blacksmith shop, farmhouse, Ross cottage, furloft, Governor's house, sales shop; indigenous encampment. Visitor center with exhibits and artifacts of the fur trade society; costumed tour guides. Restaurant, gift shop. (Mid-May-Labour Day, daily) **$$**

Oak Hammock Marsh Wildlife Management Area. *14 miles (23 kilometers) N via Hwy 7 or 8, then 5 miles (8 kilometers) to Hwy 67. Phone 204/467-3300.* More than 8,000 acres (3,238 hectares) of marshland and grassland wildlife habitat. Attracts up to 300,000 ducks and geese during spring (Apr-mid-May) and fall migration (Sept-Oct). Nature trails; picnic sites, marsh boardwalk, viewing mounds, drinking water. Conservation center with displays, interpretive programs (daily; fee). **FREE**

Paddlewheel/River Rouge boat and bus tours. *Phone 204/942-4500.* Floating restaurant, moonlight dance, and sightseeing cruises (May-Sept); also guided tours on double-decker buses. Bus/cruise combinations available. Contact PO Box 3930, Postal Station B, R2W 5H9. **$$$$**

Ross House. *140 Meade St N, between Euclid and Sutherland aves. Phone 204/943-3958; 204/947-0559.* (1854) Oldest building in the original city of Winnipeg; first post office in western Canada. Displays and period-furnished rooms depict daily life in the Red River Settlement. (June-Aug, Wed-Sun) **FREE**

Royal Canadian Mint. *520 Lagimodière Blvd. Phone 204/257-3359.* (1976) One of the world's most modern mints; striking glass tower, landscaped interior courtyard. Tour allows viewing of coining process; coin museum. (Early May-late Aug, Mon-Fri; closed holidays) **$**

Seven Oaks House Museum. *Rupertsland Ave, in West Kildonan area. Phone 204/339-7429; 204/986-3031.* Oldest habitable house in Manitoba (1851). Log construction, original furnishings, housewares. Adjoining buildings incl general store, post office. (Mid-June-Sept, daily; mid-May-mid-June, Sat and Sun) **$**

St.-Boniface Museum. *494 ave Taché. Phone 204/237-4500.* (1846) Housed in oldest structure in the city, dating to the days of the Red River Colony; largest oak log construction in North America.

Winnipeg Art Gallery. *300 Memorial Blvd. Phone 204/786-6641.* Canada's first civic gallery (1912). Eight galleries present changing exhibitions of contemporary, historical, and decorative art, plus North America's largest collection of Inuit art. (Summer, daily; rest of year, Tues-Sun; closed holidays) Programming incl tours, lectures, films, concerts. Restaurant. **$$**

Special Events

Canada's Royal Winnipeg Ballet. *Centennial Concert Hall. Phone 204/956-2792.* Performs mix of classical and contemporary ballets. Oct-May.

Festival du Voyageur. *In St.-Boniface, Winnipeg's "French Quarter."Phone 204/237-7692.* Winter festival celebrating the French-Canadian voyageur and the fur trade era. Ten days mid-Feb.

Folklorama. *Pavilions throughout city. Phone 204/982-6210.* Multicultural festival featuring up to 40 pavilions. Singing, dancing, food, cultural displays. Aug.

Manitoba Opera Association. *Portage Place. Phone 204/942-7479.* Nov-May.

Red River Exhibition. *Phone 204/888-6990.* Large event encompassing grandstand shows, band competitions, displays, agricultural exhibits, parade, entertainment, midway, petting zoo, shows, food. Late June-early July.

Winnipeg Folk Festival. *Birds Hill Provincial Park, 8 miles N on Hwy 59. Phone 204/231-0096.* More than 100 regional, national, and international artists perform; nine stages; children's village; evening concerts. Juried crafts exhibit and sale; international food village. Early July.

Winnipeg Symphony Orchestra. *Centennial Concert Hall. Phone 204/949-3999 (box office).* Classical, pops, and children's concerts. Sept-May.

Motels/Motor Lodges

★ ★ **BEST WESTERN VICTORIA INN.** *1808 Wellington Ave (R3H 0G3). Phone 204/786-4801; toll-free 800/928-4067; fax 204/786-1329. www.bestwestern.com.* 288 rooms, 5 story. S $79; D $84; suites $175; under 16 free. Crib free. Pet accepted. TV; cable. 1 indoor; whirlpool, poolside service. Restaurant 7 am-11 pm. Room service. Bar 11:30-1 am. Check-out noon. Meeting rooms. Business services available. In-room modem link. Bellhops. Gift shop. Free airport transportation. Some refrigerators. Cr cds: A, C, D, DS, ER, MC, V.

★ **COMFORT INN.** *1770 Sargent Ave (R3H0C8). Phone 204/783-5627; fax 204/783-5661. www.hotelchoice.com.* 81 rooms, 2 story. Mid-June-mid-Sept: S, D $85-$95; each additional $10; under 18 free; weekend rates; lower rates rest of year. Crib free. Pet accepted. TV; cable. Complimentary coffee in lobby. Continental breakfast available. Restaurant nearby. Check-out 11 am. Business services available. In-room modem link. Valet service. Cr cds: A, C, D, DS, JCB, MC, V.

★ ★ **COUNTRY INN & SUITES.** *730 King Edward St (R3H 1B4). Phone 204/783-6900; fax 204/775-7197. www.countryinns.com.* 77 units, 3 story, 36 suites. S $65-$95; D $75-$105; each additional $10; under 18 free; weekend rates. Crib free. Pet accepted, some restrictions. TV; cable (premium), VCR (free movies). Complimentary coffee in rooms. Complimentary

continental breakfast. Restaurant adjacent 7 am-11 pm. Check-out noon. Coin laundry. Business services available. Sundries. Valet service. Refrigerators. Cr cds: A, C, D, DS, MC, V.

★ ★ **HOLIDAY INN.** *1330 Pembina Hwy (R3T 2B4). Phone 204/452-4747; toll-free 800/423-1337; fax 204/284-2751. www.hi-winnipeg.mb.ca.* 170 rooms, 11 story. S $159; D $179; each additional $10; suites $250; under 19 free; weekend rates. Crib free. Pet accepted. Check-out noon. TV; cable, VCR available. In-room modem link. Coffee in rooms. Valet services, coin laundry. Restaurant 6:30 am-11 pm; weekend hours vary. Bar, room service. Exercise equipment. Indoor pool, wading pool, whirlpool, poolside service. Free airport transportation. Meeting rooms, business services. Bellhops. Sundries. Cr cds: A, C, D, DS, ER, JCB, MC, V.

★ **HOWARD JOHNSON HOTEL.** *1740 Ellice Ave (R2K 0R2). Phone 204/775-7131; toll-free 800/665-8813; fax 204/788-4685. hojo.com.* 155 rooms, 5 story. S, D $54-$72; each additional $10; under 16 free; package plans. Crib $10. Check-out noon. TV; cable. Coin laundry. Restaurant 7 am-9 pm. Bar 11-2 am, entertainment, room service. Sauna. Indoor pool, whirlpool, poolside service. Free airport transportation. Meeting rooms, Business services available. Bellhops. Gift shop. Cr cds: A, D, MC, V.

Hotels

★ ★ **CHARTER HOUSE.** *330 York Ave (R3C 0N9). Phone 204/942-0101; toll-free 800/782-0175; fax 204/956-0665.* 90 rooms, 5 story. S, D $65-$125; under 18 free; weekly, weekend rates. Crib $10. Pet accepted. TV; cable, VCR available (movies). Restaurant 7 am-11 pm. Bar 11-2 am. Check-out 11 am. Meeting rooms. Business services available. In-room modem link. Balconies. Cr cds: A, C, D, DS, MC, V.

★ ★ **DELTA WINNIPEG.** *350 St. Mary Ave (R3C 3J2). Phone 204/942-0551; fax 204/943-8702. www.deltahotels.com.* 392 rooms, 18 story. S $155; D $165; each additional $15; suites $195-$485; under 18 free. Crib available. Check-out noon. TV; cable (premium). In-room modem link. Balconies, refrigerators, Complimentary coffee in room. Coin laundry. Restaurant 6:30-1 am. Room service 24 hours. Exercise room, Exercise room; sauna. 2 pools, 1 indoor, wading pool, whirlpool. Airport transportation. Meeting rooms, business services. Luxury level. Cr cds: A, D, DS, ER, JCB, MC, V.

★★★**THE FAIRMONT WINNIPEG.** *Phone 204/957-1300. www.fairmont.com.* 340 rooms, 20 story. S, D $175-$275; each additional $20; under 17 free. Crib available. Check-out noon. TV; cable (premium), VCR available. Some refrigerators, minibars, Complimentary coffee, newspaper in rooms. Restaurant 6 am-10 pm. Exercise room. Meeting rooms, business center. Gift shop. Cr cds: A, C, D, DS, JCB, MC, V.

★★**HOLIDAY INN AIRPORT WEST.** *2520 Portage Ave (R3J 3T6). Phone 204/885-4478; fax 204/831-5734. www.holiday-inn.com/winnipeg-arpt.* 226 rooms, 8 kitchen units, 15 story. S $139; D $149; each additional $10; suites $145-$186; under 19 free; weekend rates. Crib free. Check-out 1 pm. TV; cable. In-room modem link. Balconies, refrigerators, Some minibars, Coffee in rooms. Coin laundry. Restaurant 6:30 am-11 pm. Bar 11:30-2 am, entertainment. Supervised children's activities, ages 3-11. Exercise equipment, sauna. Game room. Free airport transportation. Meeting rooms, business center. Cr cds: A, D, DS, ER, JCB, MC, V.

★★**RADISSON DOWNTOWN.** *288 Portage Ave (R3C 0B8). Phone 204/956-0410; fax 204/947-1129. www.radisson.com.* 272 rooms, 29 story. S, D $129-$199; each additional $15; suites $229; under 18 free; weekend rates. Crib free. Pet accepted. Check-out 1 pm. TV; cable (premium), VCR available (movies). In-room modem link. Minibars, Coffee in rooms. Restaurant 6:30 am-10 pm; Sat, Sun from 7 am. Bar 11:30-1 am. Room service 24 hours. Exercise equipment, sauna. Indoor pool, poolside service. Garage parking $10. Meeting rooms, business center. Concierge. Gift shop. Cr cds: A, C, D, DS, ER, JCB, MC, V.

★★**RADISSON SUITE HOTEL WINNIPEG AIRPORT.** *Phone 204/783-1700; fax 204/786-6588. www.radisson.com/winnipegca_airport.* Providing a quiet, comfortable home to the business and leisure traveler alike, the 1-bedroom suites are ideal for any extended traveling. 149 suites, 6 story. S $139; D $189; each additional $15; under 17 free; weekend and holiday rates. Crib free. Complimentary continental breakfast. Check-out noon. TV; cable. Refrigerators, wet bars, Complimentary coffee in rooms. Restaurant 7 am-10 pm. Bar 11:30 am-midnight. Room service 24 hours. Exercise equipment, sauna. 2 pools, 1 indoor, whirlpool, poolside service. Free airport transportation. Meeting rooms. Business services available. Gift shop. Cr cds: A, C, D, DS, ER, JCB, MC, V.

★★★**SHERATON WINNIPEG HOTEL.** *161 Donald St. (R3C 1M3). Phone 204/942-5300; toll-free 800/463-6400; fax 204/943-7975. www.sheraton.com.* This hotel is conveniently located three blocks from the convention center. 271 rooms, 21 story. S $130-$145; D $140-$155; under 18 free; weekend rates. Crib free. Pet accepted. Underground parking, valet $9/day. TV; cable (premium). Indoor pool; whirlpool. Coffee in rooms. Restaurant 6:30 am-11 pm. Room service 24 hours. Bar 11-1 am. Check-out noon. Convention facilities. Business services available. In-room modem link. Concierge. Gift shop. Sauna. Health club privileges. Many refrigerators. Many balconies. Cr cds: A, D, ER, MC, V.

Restaurants

★★ **AMICI.** *326 Broadway (R3C 0S5). Phone 204/943-4997. www.amiciwpg.com.* Italian menu. Hours: 11:30 am-2 pm, 5-10 pm; Sat from 5 pm. Closed Sun; most major holidays. Dinner $15-$40. Bar to 11 pm. Children's menu. Reservations accepted. Cr cds: A, D, MC, V.

★★ **HY'S STEAK LOFT.** *216 Kennedy (R3C 1T1). Phone 204/942-1000. www.hyssteakhouse.com.* Seafood menu, Steak menu. Hours: 5-11 pm; Fri, Sat to midnight; Sun to 9 pm. Closed major holidays. Dinner $22.95-$45. Bar 4 pm-midnight; Sat from 5 pm. Reservations accepted. Cr cds: A, D, ER, MC, V.

★★ **ICHIBAN JAPANESE STEAKHOUSE AND SUSHI BAR.** *189 Carlton St (R3C 3H7). Phone 204/925-7400.* Hours: 4:30-10 pm. Fri, Sat to 10:30 pm. Closed major holidays. Reservations accepted. Japanese menu. Bar 4:30-10 pm, Fri, Sat to 10:30. Dinner $17.95-$35. Specialties: Imperial dinner, Empress dinner, sushi. Teppanyaki cooking. Japanese garden atmosphere. Cr cds: A, D, MC, V.

Wisconsin

Virgin forests blotted out the sky over Wisconsin when the first French voyageurs arrived more than three centuries ago. Rich in natural resources, modern conservation concepts took strong root here; Wisconsin's 15,000 lakes and 2,200 streams are teeming with fish, and millions of acres of its publicly owned forest are abundant with game.

People of many heritages have contributed to the state's colorful past, busy industries, and productive farms. Wisconsin is famous for the breweries of Milwaukee, great universities, forests, paper mills, dairy products, and diverse vacation attractions.

Wisconsin is the birthplace of the statewide primary election law, worker's compensation law, unemployment compensation, and many other reforms that have since been widely adopted. It produced Senator Robert M. La Follette, one of the 20th century's foremost progressives, and many other honored citizens.

The Badger State acquired its nickname during the lead rush of 1827, when miners built their homes by digging into the hillsides like badgers. It is "America's dairyland," producing much of the nation's milk and over 30 percent of all cheese consumed in the United States. It is a leader in the production of hay, cranberries, and ginseng, and harvests huge crops of peas, beans, carrots, corn, and oats. It is the leading canner of fresh vegetables and an important source of cherries, apples, maple syrup, and wood pulp. A great part of the nation's paper products, agricultural implements, and nonferrous metal products and alloys are manufactured here.

The Wisconsin summer is balmy, and the winter offers an abundance of activities, making the state a year-round vacationland that lures millions of visitors annually. They find a land of many contrasts: rounded hills and narrow valleys to the southwest, a huge central plain, rolling prairie in the southeast, and the north, majestic with forests, marshes, and lakes.

Native Americans called this land *Ouisconsin* ("where the waters gather"). French explorer Jean Nicolet, seek-

Population: 4,891,769
Area: 54,424 square miles
Elevation: 581-1,951 feet
Peak: Timms Hill (Price County)
Entered Union: May 29, 1848 (30th state)
Capital: Madison
Motto: Forward
Nickname: Badger State
Flower: Wood Violet
Bird: Robin
Tree: Sugar Maple
Fair: August, in Milwaukee
Time Zone: Central
Website: www.travelwisconsin.com
Fun Facts: Wisconsin produces more milk than any state.

ing the Northwest Passage to the Orient, landed near Green Bay in 1634 and greeted what he thought were Asians. These Winnebago made a treaty of alliance with the French, and for the next 125 years a brisk trade in furs developed. The British won Wisconsin from the French in 1760 and lost it to the United States after the American Revolution.

Shortly before Wisconsin became a state it was a battleground in the Black Hawk War. After the campaign, word spread of the state's beauty and fertile land in the East, and opened the doors to a flood of settlers.

The rich lead mines brought another wave of settlers, and the forests attracted lumbermen—both groups remained to till the soil or work in the factories.

Diversified industry, enhanced recreational facilities, the trade opportunities opened by the St. Lawrence Seaway, and enlightened agricultural techniques promise continuing prosperity for Wisconsin.

When to Go/Climate

Cool forests and lake breezes make northern Wisconsin summers pleasant and comfortable, while the southern farmland is often hot. Temperatures from northern to southern Wisconsin can vary as much as 20°F. Winters are often snowy and harsh statewide. Fall

Calendar Highlights

JANUARY

World Championship Snowmobile Derby (*Eagle River*). *Phone 800/359-6315.* More than 300 professional racers fight for the championship.

FEBRUARY

American Birkebeiner (*Cable*). *Phone 800/872-2753.* Cross-country ski race. More than 6,000 participants from 40 states and 15 countries.

Winter Festival (*Cedarburg*). *Phone 262/377-9620 or 800/827-8020.* Ice carving and snow sculpture contests, bed and barrel races across ice, winter softball and volleyball, Alaskan malamute weight pull, snow goose egg hunt; torchlight parade, horse-drawn sleigh rides.

MAY

Festival of Blossoms (*Door County*). *Phone 920/743-4456 or 800/527-3529.* Month-long celebration of spring, with a million daffodils and blooming cherry and apple trees.

Great Wisconsin Dells Balloon Rally (*Wisconsin Dells*). *Phone 800/223-3557.* More than 90 hot-air balloons participate in contests and mass liftoffs.

JUNE

Summerfest (*Milwaukee*). *Phone 800/273-3378.* Eleven different music stages; food.

Walleye Weekend Festival and Mercury Marine National Walleye Tournament (*Fond du Lac*). *Phone 800/937-9123.* Lakeside Park. Fish fry, food, entertainment, sports competitions.

JULY

Art Fair on the Square (*Madison*). *Phone 608/257-0158.* Capitol Concourse. Exhibits by 500 artists and craftspersons; food, entertainment.

AUGUST

EAA (Experimental Aircraft Association) International Fly-In Convention (*Oshkosh*). *Phone 920/235-3007 (air show lodging info) or 920/426-4800 (general information).* Wittman Regional Airport. One of the nation's largest aviation events. More than 500 educational forums, workshops, and seminars; daily air shows; exhibits; more than 12,000 aircraft.

Wisconsin State Fair (*Milwaukee*). *Phone 414/266-7000.* State Fair Park in West Allis. Entertainment, 12 stages, auto races, exhibits, contests, demonstrations, fireworks.

---

is the best time to visit, with brilliant foliage, harvests, and festivals.

AVERAGE HIGH/LOW TEMPERATURES (°F)

Green Bay

Jan 23/6	May 67/44	Sept 69/49
Feb 27/10	June 76/54	Oct 57/39
Mar 39/21	July 81/59	Nov 42/27
Apr 54/34	Aug 78/57	Dec 28/13

Milwaukee

Jan 26/12	May 64/45	Sept 71/53
Feb 30/16	June 75/55	Oct 59/42
Mar 40/26	July 80/62	Nov 45/31
Apr 53/36	Aug 78/61	Dec 31/18

Parks and Recreation

Water-related activities, hiking, bicycling, riding, various other sports, picnicking and visitor centers, as well as camping, are available in many of these areas. From May-Oct, camping is limited to 3 weeks; fee is $9-$12/unit/night; electricity $3. Camps can be taken down or set up between 6 am and 11 pm. Motor vehicle sticker for nonresidents: daily $10; annual $30; residents: daily $5; annual $20. For additional info contact Wisconsin Department of Natural Resources, Bureau of Parks & Recreation, PO Box 7921, Madison 53707. Phone 608/266-2181.

FISHING AND HUNTING

Wisconsin, eager to have visitors share the abundance of fish in the lakes and streams, posts few barriers. The state is very conservation-minded; regulations have been developed to ensure equally good fishing in the future. Fishing licenses: nonresident over 16, 4-day $15; 15-day $20; annual $34; family 15-day, $30; annual family $52; licenses expire Mar 31. Two-day Great Lakes, $10. A trout stamp must be purchased by all licensed anglers in order to fish for trout in inland waters, $7.25. A salmon and trout stamp is required, except those having a 2-day license, to fish the Great Lakes, $7.25. For further info contact the Wisconsin Department of Natural Resources, Customer Service and Licensing, PO Box 7921, Madison 53707. Phone 608/266-2621.

The Department of Natural Resources issues separate pamphlets on trapping big game, pheasant, and waterfowl hunting regulations. Hunting licenses: nonresident, furbearer $150; small game $75; archery $135; deer $135; 5-day small game $43. Hunting migratory birds requires a special federal stamp ($15), obtainable at any post office, as well as a state stamp ($7). A pheasant stamp ($7.25) is also required. Special hunting regulations apply to minors; contact Dept of Natural Resources for further info. **Note:** License fees subject to change.

Wisconsin waters boast trout, muskellunge, northern pike, walleye, large and smallmouth bass, and panfish throughout the state; salmon is primarily found in the Lake Superior/Michigan area; lake sturgeon in Winnebago Waters/St. Croix/Wisconsin, Chippewa, Flambeau, and Menominee rivers; and catfish in Wolf, Mississippi, and Wisconsin rivers. Inquire for seasons and bag limits.

Driving Information

Safety belts are mandatory for all persons in designated seating spaces within the vehicle. Children under 4 years of age must be in an approved safety seat anywhere in vehicle. Children ages 4-8 years may use a regulation safety belt. Phone 608/266-3212.

Interstate Highway System

The following alphabetical listing of Wisconsin towns in this book shows that these cities are within 10 miles of the indicated interstate highways. Check a highway map for the nearest exit.

Highway Number	Cities/Towns within ten miles
Interstate 43	Cedarburg, Green Bay, Manitowoc, Milwaukee, Port Washington, Sheboygan.
Interstate 90	Baraboo, Beloit, Janseville, La Crosse, Madison, Mauston, Portage, Sparta, Tomah, Wisconsin Dells.
Interstate 94	Baraboo, Black River Falls, Eau Claire, Hudson, Kenosha, Madison, Milwaukee, Oconomowoc, Portage, Racine, Tomah, Watertown, Waukesha, Wauwatosa, Wisconsin Dells.

Additional Visitor Information

The Wisconsin Department Tourism, PO Box 7976, Madison 53707. Phone 608/266-2161, 800/372-2737 (northern IL, IA, MI, MN, WI only) or 800/432-TRIP (anywhere in US), produces and distributes a variety of publications covering sports, attractions, events, and recreation. When requesting info, ask for *Adventure Guide, Events/Recreation Guide, Heritage Guide, Where to Stay in Wisconsin, Guide to State Golf Courses, Campground Directory,* and/or state highway map.

There are several tourist information centers in Wisconsin. Visitors who stop will find helpful information and brochures. They are located in Beloit (I-90); Genoa City (US 12), (seasonal); Grant County (US 151/61), (seasonal); Hudson (I-94); Hurley (US 51); Kenosha (I-94); La Crosse (I-90); Madison (201 W Washington Ave); Prairie du Chien (211 Main St), (seasonal); Superior (305 E 2nd St), (seasonal). There is also an info center in Chicago, IL (140 S Dearborn St, Room 104).

Wisconsin offers a fabulous system of bicycle routes. To order a free guide to bicycling in Wisconsin contact the Department of Tourism, PO Box 7976, Madison 53707. Phone 608/266-2161, 800/432-8747, or 800/372-2737.

CRANBERRY HIGHWAY

Cranberries are the big money crop around Wisconsin Rapids. In fall, mechanical harvesters sweep across 13,000 acres of cranberry marshes, dislodging the bright red berries that then float to the surface creating a crimson sea of fruit. Although fall is an ideal time to visit, travel "The Cranberry Highway" year-round, stopping perhaps for a cranberry shake or cranberry muffin or to visit a cheese factory for "Cran-jack" cheese, studded with dried fruit. The full route runs approximately 40 miles and includes visits to numerous marsh areas, historic sites, museums, markets, shops, and restaurants. A south loop covers about 70 miles and is described below.

Begin in downtown Wisconsin Rapids at Paul Gross Jewelers (241 Oak St), where you can pick up a gold cranberry rake necklace complete with ruby cranberry. Then stop at South Wood County Historical Museum (3rd St between East Grand Ave and Riverview Expy) for a look at local history and changing displays, including a cranberry exhibit.

Continue on 3rd St to WI 54, which traces the Wisconsin River through Port Edwards. Stop at Alexander House Art & History Center (1131 Wisconsin River Dr), a combination art gallery and historical museum is located in a stately, colonial home along the banks of the river. Continue on WI 54 and take County D south. Along the way, visit Glacial Lake Cranberries for a thorough introduction to Wisconsin's cranberry industry, which produces about 150 million pounds of fruit annually. Operated by third-generation cranberry farmers, it offers Marsh Tours year-round. A gift shop carries fresh fruit in season and the Stone Cottage accommodates up to four guests. From here, continue south on County D, then east on WI 173 to County Z south. At the intersection of County Z and Wakely Rd in Nekoosa find Historic Point Basse, an 1837 living history site that stages events throughout the year. It protects an endangered historic site placed on the National Register of Historic Places in 2001.

Golfers tired of shelling out outrageous green fees enjoy the lower costs at the region's championship courses. Lake Arrowhead at Nekoosa (one mile off WI 13), with two challenging 18-hole courses, is ranked by *Golf Digest* as one of the nation's best golf values. It charges only $62 per round (with cart). Another golfing bargain awaits at The Ridges (east on County Z), where greens fees are only $55 (with cart) for 18 holes with challenging elevations and plenty of water and woods—white birch, green willows, and towering pines. From the clubhouse restaurant watch golfers tee-off for the back nine with a shot from an 80-foot-high ridge into a valley flanked by tall pines and a twisting creek.

A shopping find is Studio of Good Earth, located on 52nd St, just a 1/2 mile north of Hwy 53. Operated by William and Annette Gudim, the studio offers the work of more than 45 artists and crafters, ranging from paintings, calligraphy, and baskets to weavings, handmade paper, and stained glass. Included are Annette's pottery and William's woodwork. Find lots of bird feeders and bird baths among quality traditional and contemporary arts and crafts at prices based on the local economy—remarkably lower than those at well-traveled resorts. Take time to enjoy the Gudims' beautiful flower gardens.

For an aerial view of cranberry marshes, head for Wings Air Charter (at Alexander Field). Short flights cost $10 per person ($55 for a 30-minute flight for three persons). From Airport Avenue, head north on Lincoln St to Grand Ave to find luxury lodgings at the Hotel Mead and Conference Center (451 East Grand Ave), where a $9-million expansion added an 89-room, 4-story tower, bringing the total number of rooms and suites to 157. All new guestrooms have refrigerators, coffeemakers, hair dryers, and desks with work space and data ports. The Mead has an indoor swimming pool and sauna, a fitness center, two restaurants, and a lively bar with entertainment. Breakfast in the Grand Avenue Grill features cranberry French toast.

Local eateries in Wisconsin Rapids include Harriet's Kitchen Nook (9041 US 13 S) which, contrary to its blue-painted tables and cutesy motif, has true diner lineage. It's a good spot to find breakfast pancakes, eggs, and superb hash browns (this is also a potato-growing country). It is derigueur to include a glass of cranberry juice with breakfast. Another local time-warp eatery is Herschleb's (640 16th St N), where carhops serve burgers, homemade soups (try chicken with dumplings), and their own brand of ice cream (which in cranberry harvest season includes cranberry swirl flavor). This is an excellent spot for shakes, malts, and floats. Prices are retro, too.

(Approximately 40 miles)

Algoma (E-6)

See also Green Bay, Sturgeon Bay

Settled 1818 **Pop** 3,353 **Elev** 600 ft **Area code** 920 **Zip** 54201

Information Algoma Area Chamber of Commerce, 1226 Lake St; 920/487-2041 or 800/498-4888

Web www.algoma.org

What to See and Do

Ahnapee State Trail. *Hwy S and Hwy M. Phone 920/487-2041 or 800/498-4888.* More than 15 miles of hiking and biking along the Ahnapee River; snowmobiling. (Daily) **FREE**

Kewaunee County Historical Museum. *10 miles S via WI 42. Court House Sq, 613 Dodge St in Kewaunee. Phone 920/388-4410.* Century-old building; displays incl a letter written by George Washington, wood carvings, child's playroom with toys of 1890-1910 period, sheriff's office, ship models, old farm tools, and artifacts. (Memorial Day-Labor Day, daily; rest of year, by appt) **DONATION**

Von Stiehl Winery. *115 Navarino St. Phone 920/487-5208 or 800/955-5208.* Housed in 140-year-old brewery. Wine, cheese, and jelly tasting at end of tour. Under 21 only with adult (wine tasting); no smoking. Gift shop; candy shop features homemade fudge. (May-Oct, daily; rest of year, Fri-Sun) **$**

Motel/Motor Lodge

★**RIVER HILLS MOTEL.** *820 N Water St (54201). Phone 920/487-3451; toll-free 800/236-3451; fax 920/487-2031.* 30 rooms. D $40-$60. Crib $3. Pet accepted, some restrictions; $3. TV; cable (premium). Coffee in lobby. Check-out 11 am. Business services available. Refrigerators available. Boat dock, public ramps nearby. Cr cds: MC, V.

D ⊠ ⌂

Restaurant

★ **CAPTAIN'S TABLE.** *133 N Water St (WI 42 N) (54201). Phone 920/487-5304.* Hours: 5 am-9 pm; Nov-May hours vary. Closed Thanksgiving, Dec 25. Breakfast $1.85-$5.95, lunch $1.55-$4.50, dinner $4.95-$9.95. Children's menu. Cr cds: MC, V.

D SC

Antigo (D-4)

See also Wausau

Settled 1876 **Pop** 8,276 **Elev** 1,498 ft **Area code** 715 **Zip** 54409

Information Chamber of Commerce, 329 Superior St, PO Box 339; 715/623-4134 or 888/526-4523

Web www.newnorth.net/antigo.chamber

What to See and Do

F. A. Deleglise Cabin. *404 Superior St. 7th and Superior sts, on grounds of public library. Phone 715/627-4464 or 715/623-3038.* (1878) First home of city's founder. (May-Sept, Wed-Mon) **DONATION**

Restaurant

★ **BLACKJACK STEAK HOUSE.** *800 S Superior St (54409). Phone 715/623-2514.* Specializes in seafood, prime rib. Hours: 4;30pm- 10pm, Sun buffet 11 am-3 pm. Closed Tues, Dec 24-25. Buffet Sun buffet $8.50. Dinner $5.50-$20. Bar. Salad bar. Child's meals. Reservations accepted. Friday fish fry $6.75-$8.75. Cr cds: A, DS, MC, V.

D

Appleton (E-5)

See also Green Bay, Neenah-Menasha, Oshkosh

Settled 1848 **Pop** 65,695 **Elev** 780 ft **Area code** 920

Information Fox Cities Convention & Visitors Bureau, 3433 W College Ave, 54914; 920/734-3358 or 800/236-6673

Web www.foxcities.org

Located astride the Fox River, Appleton's economy centers around the manufacture of paper and paper products and insurance and service industries.

What to See and Do

✪ **Charles A. Grignon Mansion.** *1313 Augustine St, 8 miles E off US 41 in Kaukauna. Phone 920/766-3122.* (1837) First deeded property in Wisconsin (1793); restored Greek Revival house of one of the area's early French-Canadian settlers; period furnishings, displays; summer events. Picnic area. Tours. (June-Aug, daily; rest of year, by appt) **$$**

Fox Cities Children's Museum. *100 College Ave, in Avenue Mall. Phone 920/734-3226.* Hands-on exhibits; climb through a human heart, play in the New Happy Baby Garden, or visit Grandma's Attic. (Tues-Thurs 9 am-5 pm; Fri 9 am-8 pm; Sat 10 am-5 pm; Sun noon-5 pm; closed Mon)

Lawrence University. *706 E College Ave at Lawe St. For campus tours contact Admissions Office. Phone 920/832-6500.* (1847) 1,400 students. Merged in 1964 with Milwaukee-Downer College. On campus are.

Music-Drama Center. *420 E College Ave. Phone 920/832-6611.* Summer theater (mid-June-Aug), phone 920/734-8797. (1959) Quarters for Conservatory of Music, concert hall, practice rooms, classrms; Cloak Theater, an experimental arena playhouse; Stansbury Theater. Concerts and plays (academic year).

Wriston Art Center. *613 E College Ave. 1/2 block S of College Ave on Lawe St. Phone 920/832-6621.* Traveling exhibits, lectures, and art shows. (Sept-May, Tues-Sun; schedule may vary; closed holidays) **FREE**

Outagamie Museum. *330 E College Ave. Phone 920/735-9370 or 920/733-8445.* Features local technology and industrial accomplishments. Major exhibit themes incl electricity, papermaking, agriculture, transportation, communications. Also an extensive exhibit devoted to Appleton native Harry Houdini. (Sept-May, Tues-Sun; rest of year, daily; closed holidays) **$$**

Motels/Motor Lodges

★ ★ **BEST WESTERN MIDWAY HOTEL.** *3033 W College Ave (54914). Phone 920/731-4141; toll-free 800/528-1234; fax 920/731-6343. www.bestwestern.com.* 105 rooms, 2 story. S $72-$112; D $82-$122; each additional $10; under 18 free; weekend rates. Crib free. Pet accepted, some restrictions; $10. Complimentary full breakfast (Mon-Fri). Check-out 11 am. TV; cable. In-room modem link. Coffee in rooms. Restaurant 6:30 am-11 pm. Bar 11-1 am. Room service. Health club privileges. Exercise equipment, sauna. Recreation room. Indoor pool; whirlpool. Free airport transportation. Meeting rooms, business services. Sundries. Cr cds: A, C, D, DS, MC, V.

D 🐾 🏊 🏋 🛒 SC ✈

★ ★ **DAYS INN.** *200 N Perkins St (54914). Phone 920/735-2733; fax 920/735-5588. www.ramada.com.* 91 units, 2 story. S $60-$80; D $70-$100; each additional $5; suites $80-$110; under 18 free. Crib free. Pet accepted, some restrictions. TV; cable (premium), VCR available (movies). Indoor pool; whirlpool. Complimentary breakfast buffet. Restaurant adjacent. Bar 11-1 am. Check-out noon. Coin laundry. Meeting rooms. Business services available. Valet service. Sundries. Free airport, bus depot

transportation. Exercise equipment. Some refrigerators. Cr cds: A, C, D, DS, MC, V.

D 🐾 🏊 🛒 ✈

★ **EXEL INN.** *210 N Westhill Blvd (54914). Phone 920/733-5551; toll-free 800/367-3935; fax 920/733-7199. www.exelinns.com.* 104 rooms, 2 story. S $38.99; D $46.99-$105; each additional $4; under 18 free. Crib free. Pet accepted, some restrictions. TV; cable (premium). Complimentary continental breakfast. Restaurant adjacent 6 am-11 pm. Check-out noon. Business services available. In-room modem link. Exercise equipment. Health club privileges. Some in-room whirlpools; refrigerators; microwaves available. Cr cds: A, C, D, DS, MC, V.

D 🐾 🏋 🛒 SC

★ ★ **HOLIDAY INN.** *150 S Nicolet Rd (54914). Phone 920/735-9955; toll-free 800/465-4329; fax 920/735-0309. www.holiday-inn.com.* 228 units, 8 story. S $69-$99; D $69-$109; each additional $10; suites $139-$199.95; under 19 free; weekend rates; higher rates: Packer games, EAA Fly-In. Crib free. TV; cable (premium), VCR available. Indoor pool; whirlpool, poolside service. Complimentary coffee in rooms. Restaurant 6 am-2 pm, 5-10 pm. Bar 3 pm-1 am; weekends 11-2 am. Check-out noon. Coin laundry. Meeting rooms. Business center. In-room modem link. Gift shop. Free airport transportation. Cross-country ski 4 miles. Exercise room; sauna. Massage. Refrigerator, microwave in suites. Cr cds: A, C, D, DS, JCB, MC, V.

D 🏊 🏋 ✈ 🛒 🚶

★ **ROADSTAR INN.** *3623 W College Ave (54914). Phone 920/731-5271; toll-free 800/445-4667; fax 920/731-0227.* 102 rooms, 2 story. S $35; D $41; each additional $5; suites $42.95-$47; under 15 free; higher rates special events. Pet accepted. TV; cable (premium). Complimentary continental breakfast. Restaurant adjacent 7 am-9 pm. Check-out noon. Guest laundry. Sundries. Cr cds: A, C, D, DS, MC, V.

D 🐾 🏋 🚶 🛒

★ ★ **WOODFIELD SUITES.** *3730 W College Ave (54914). Phone 920/734-7777; fax 920/734-0049. www.woodfieldsuites.com.* 98 rooms, 2 story. S $100; D $110; each additional $10; under 19 free. Crib free. TV; cable (premium), VCR available. 2 pools, 1 indoor; whirlpool. Complimentary continental breakfast. Coffee in rooms. Restaurant adjacent 6 am-11 pm. Bar from 11 am. Check-out noon. Meeting room. Business services available. In-room modem link. Valet service. Sundries. Free airport transportation. Tennis. Sauna. Bowling. Game room. Recreation room. Lawn games. Refrigerators. Cr cds: A, C, D, DS, JCB, MC, V.

D 🐾 🏊 🚶 🛒 🏋 ✈ 🏊

Hotel

★ ★ ★ **RADISSON.** *333 W College Ave (54913). Phone 920/733-8000; toll-free 800/242-3499; fax 920/733-9220. www.parkplazapapervalley.com.* 394 rooms, 7 story. S $99-$119; D $109-$129; each additional $10; suites $129; under 18 free; weekend packages. Crib free. TV; cable (premium), VCR available. Indoor pool; whirlpool, poolside service. Complimentary coffee. Restaurant 6:30 am-11 pm. Bar 11-1 am. Check-out noon. Convention facilities. Business center. In-room modem link. Shopping arcade. Barber, beauty shop. Free airport, bus depot transportation. Miniature golf. Exercise equipment; sauna. Game room. Recreation room. Some refrigerators, microwaves. Cr cds: A, C, D, DS, ER, JCB, MC, V.

⊡ ⊠ 🛇 🛅 🗲 ⊠ 🛉 🏌 ✕ 🛇 SC 🏃

Restaurant

★★**GEORGE'S STEAK HOUSE.** *2208 S Memorial Dr (54915). Phone 920/733-4939; fax 920/733-3731. www.foodspot.com/georges.* Closed Sun; holidays. Lunch, dinner. Bar. Piano bar. Children's menu. Cr cds: A, D, DS, MC, V. **$**

⊡

Ashland (B-3)

See also Bayfield

Founded 1854 **Pop** 8,695 **Elev** 671 ft **Area code** 715 **Zip** 54806

Information Ashland Area Chamber of Commerce, 320 4th Ave W, PO Box 746; 715/682-2500 or 800/284-9484

Web www.visitashland.com

Located on Chequamegon Bay, which legend says is the "shining big sea water" of Longfellow's Hiawatha, Ashland is a port for Great Lakes ships delivering coal for the Midwest. It is also a gateway to the Apostle Islands. Papermaking machinery, fabricated steel, and other industrial products provide a diversified economy.

What to See and Do

Copper Falls State Park. *WI 169 and Copper Falls Rd. S off WI 13, 169 in Mellen. Phone 715/274-5123.* This 2,500-acre park has more than 8 miles of river; nature and hiking trails provide spectacular views of the river gorge and the falls. Swimming, fishing, canoeing; backpacking, cross-country skiing, picnicking, playground, concession, primitive and improved camping (hookups, dump station). Standard fees. (Daily) **$$$**

Fishing. In Chequamegon Bay and in 65 trout streams and inland lakes (license and stamp required). Ice fishing is a popular winter sport. Also spring smelting and deep sea trolling in Lake Superior. Public boat landing at Sunset Park; RV park adjacent to Sunset Park (hookups, dump station).

Northland College. *1411 Ellis Ave. Phone 715/682-1699.* (1892) 750 students. Founded to bring higher education to the people of the isolated logging camps and farm communities of northern Wisconsin. On campus are Sigurd Olson Environmental Institute, in an earth-sheltered, solar-heated building; and historic Wheeler Hall (1892), constructed of brownstone from the nearby Apostle Islands.

Special Event

Bay Days Festival. *101 Lake Shore Dr W. Phone 800/284-9484.* Sailboat regatta, art fair, bicycle and foot races, ethnic food booths, entertainment, dancing. Third weekend July.

Motels/Motor Lodges

★ ★ **BEST WESTERN HOLIDAY HOUSE.** *Lake Shore Dr (US 2/63/WI 13) (54806). Phone 715/682-5235; toll-free 800/452-7749; fax 715/682-4730. www.bestwestern.com.* 65 rooms, 2 story. Mid-May-early Oct: S $46-$103; D $51-$118; each additional $5; winter weekend packages; lower rates rest of year. Crib free. Pet accepted; $20 and $100 deposit. Check-out 11 am. TV; cable (premium). Many balconies. Coffee in rooms. Restaurant 7 am-1 pm, 4:30-10 pm. Bar. Sauna. Indoor pool, whirlpool. Downhill ski 15 miles; cross-country ski opposite. Cr cds: A, D, DS, MC, V.

🛋 🛇

★ **SUPER 8.** *1610 W Lake Shore Dr (54806). Phone 715/682-9377; fax 715/682-9377. www.super8.com.* 70 rooms, 2 story. Mid-June-Sept: S $58.88-$65.88; D $59.88-$74.88; each additional $5; under 12 free; lower rates rest of year. Crib free. Pet accepted, some restrictions. TV; cable (premium), VCR available. Indoor pool; whirlpool. Complimentary coffee in lobby. Check-out 11 am. Coin laundry. Business services available. In-room modem link. Cross-country ski 10 miles. Microwaves available. Opposite Lake Superior. Cr cds: A, C, D, DS, ER, MC, V.

⊡ 🐾 🛇 🗲 ✕ 🛋 🏃 🛇 🛇

Hotel

★ ★ **CHEQUAMEGON.** *101 W Lakeshore Dr (54806). Phone 715/682-9095; toll-free 800/946-5555; fax 715/682-9410.* On the shores of Lake Superior guests will find a gracious home with refined air, a classic setting, and elegant dining. 65 rooms, 3 story. D $85-$95; each additional $10; under 12 free. Check-out 11 am. TV; cable (premium). Restaurant, dining room, bar. Sauna. Indoor pool, whirlpool. Large veranda overlooks marina. On Lake Superior. Cr cds: A, DS, MC, V.

[D] [symbols]

Baileys Harbor (D-6)

(Door County)

Settled 1851 **Pop** 780 **Elev** 595 ft **Area code** 920 **Zip** 54202

Information Door County Chamber of Commerce, 1015 Green Bay Rd, PO Box 406, Sturgeon Bay 54235; 920/743-4456 or 800/527-3529

Web www.doorcountyvacations.com

Bailey's Harbor is the oldest village in Door County, with one of the best harbors on the east shore. Range lights, built in 1870 to guide ships into the harbor, still operate. Its waters feature charter fishing for trout and salmon.

What to See and Do

Bjorklunden. *WI 57, 1 mile S of Baileys Harbor Phone 920/839-2216.* A 425-acre estate, owned by Lawrence University (Appleton), with a replica of a Norwegian wooden chapel (stavkirke). The chapel was handcrafted by the original owners, the Boynton family, during the summers of 1939-1947. Seminars in the humanities are held on the estate each summer. Tours of chapel. (Mid-June-Aug, Mon and Wed) **$$**

Kangaroo Lake. *S on WI 57.* Swimming, fishing, boating; picnicking.

Special Event

Baileys Harbor Brown Trout Tournament. *Phone 920/743-4456.* Late Apr.

Resort

★ ★ **GORDON LODGE.** *1420 Pine Dr (54202). Phone 920/839-2331; toll-free 800/830-6235; fax 920/839-2450. www.gordonlodge.com.* This hotel is a nature enthusiasts' home away from home. 20 rooms. D $100-$212; each additional $29. Closed mid-Oct-mid-May. Complimentary full breakfast (in season). Check-out noon, check-in 4 pm. TV; cable (premium). Some fireplaces. Dining room, bar, entertainment. Exercise equipment. Private sand beach. Pool, whirlpool. Tennis, lighted courts. Bicycles. Row boats. Cr cds: A, DS, MC, V.

[symbols]

Restaurants

★ ★ **COMMON HOUSE.** *8041 WI 57 (54202). Phone 920/839-2708; fax 920/839-2708.* Hours: 5:30-10 pm.

Reservations accepted. No A/C. Bar. Dinner $10-$26.95. Child's meals. Own desserts. Old-fashioned wood stove in dining room. Cr cds: DS, MC, V.

[D]

★ ★ **FLORIAN II.** *Hwy 57 (54202). Phone 920/839-2361.* Hours: 5-9 pm; Sat, Sun 8 am-2:30 pm, 5-9 pm. Closed Nov-Mar. Reservations accepted. Bar. Buffet: breakfast $5.95. Dinner $9.95-$19.95. Child's meals. Specializes in prime rib, roast duck, barbecued ribs. Salad bar. Entertainment Fri, Sat. Solarium dining; overlooks Lake Michigan. Dock. Family-owned. Cr cds: MC, V.

[D] [SC]

★ **SANDPIPER.** *8166 WI 57 (54202). Phone 920/839-2528.* Specialties: chicken, fish. Own soups. Hours: 7 am-9 pm; hours vary off-season. Closed Nov-Mar. Breakfast $3.95-$5.95, lunch $1.75-$6.95, dinner $6.95-$12.95. Beer, wine. Children's menu. Outdoor dining. Fish boil mid-May-Oct Mon-Sat: $10.50. Cr cds: MC, V.

[D]

Baraboo (F-4)

See also Portage, Prairie du Sac, Reedsburg, Wisconsin Dells

Founded 1830 **Pop** 9,203 **Elev** 894 ft **Area code** 608 **Zip** 53913

Information Chamber of Commerce, PO Box 442; 608/356-8333 or 800/BARABOO

Web www.baraboo.com/chamber

A center for the distribution of dairy products, Baraboo is a neatly ordered town of lawns, gardens, parks, homes, and factories. The city is the original home of the Ringling Brothers and Gollmar circuses and still holds memories of its circus-town days. It was founded by Jean Baribeau as a trading post for the Hudson's Bay Company. Beautiful spring-fed Devil's Lake is three miles south of town.

What to See and Do

★ **Circus World Museum.** *550 Water St. Phone 608/356-8341.* Has 50 acres and eight buildings of circus lore; original winter quarters of Ringling Brothers Circus. Live circus acts under "Big Top," daily circus parade, display of circus parade wagons, steam calliope concerts, P. T. Barnum sideshow, wild animal menagerie; carousel, band organ. Unloading circus train with Percheron horses; picnic facilities. (Early May-mid-Sept, daily) Exhibit Hall open year-round. **$$$$**

Devil's Head Resort. *S-6330 Bluff Rd. 12 miles SE via WI 113, 78 at S-6330 Bluff Rd, in Merrimac. Phone 608/493-2251.* Area has triple, six double, three quad chairlifts;

four rope tows; patrol, school, rentals, snowmaking; lodge, restaurants, cafeteria, bars. Longest run 1 3/4 miles; vertical drop 500 feet. (Dec-Mar, daily) Night skiing; cross-country trails. Golf, 18 holes. Swimming pool, whirlpool. Tennis courts. Mountain Biking. **$$$$**

Devil's Lake State Park. *S5975 Park Rd. 3 miles S of Baraboo on WI 123. Phone 608/356-6618. Phone 608/356-8301.* Per vehicle $5-$10. **Ice Age National Scientific Reserve.** Naturalists explain evidence of Wisconsin glaciation; exhibits of local Ice Age features; trails; under development. Also included in the reserve are Northern Unit Kettle Moraine State Forest (see FOND DU LAC) and two state parks, Mill Bluff (see TOMAH) and Interstate (see ST. CROIX FALLS). Per vehicle $5-$10. **$$$**

Ho-Chunk Casino & Bingo. *S3214A US 12. Phone Toll 800/ 746-2486.* Gaming casino featuring 48 blackjack tables, 1,200 slot machines, video poker, and keno. (Daily, 24 hours)

International Crane Foundation. *E11376 Shady Lane Rd. Phone 608/356-9462.* A nonprofit organization promoting the study and preservation of cranes. Features cranes and their chicks from all over the world. Movies, displays, nature trails. (May-Oct, daily) Guided tours (Memorial Day-Labor Day, daily; Sept-Oct, weekends) **$$$**

Mid-Continent Railway Museum. *E8948 Diamond Hill Rd. 5 miles W via WI 136, then 2 miles S to North Freedom. Phone 608/522-4261.* Restored 1894 depot, complete 1900 rail environment; steam locomotives, coaches, steam wrecker, snowplows; artifacts and historical exhibits. Picnic area, gift shop. (Mid-May-Labor Day, daily; after Labor Day-mid-Oct, weekends only) 1-hour steam train round-trip on a branch of C & NW Railroad line, which once served early iron mines and rock quarries. Leaves North Freedom (same dates as museum; four departures daily). **$$$**

Mirror Lake State Park. *E10320 Fern Dell Rd. 2 miles W off US 12. Phone 608/254-2333.* A 2,050-acre park with swimming, fishing, boating, canoeing; hiking, cross-country skiing, picnicking, playground, camping (fee; electric hookups, dump station). Standard fees. (Daily) **OTHER**

Sauk County Historical Museum. *531 4th Ave. Phone 608/356-1001.* Houses 19th-century household goods, textiles, toys, china, military items, pioneer collection, Native American artifacts, circus memorabilia, natural history display, photos; research library. (May-Oct, Tues-Sun) **$**

Motels/Motor Lodges

★ ★ **QUALITY INN.** *626 W Pine St (53913). Phone 608/356-6422; toll-free 800/355-6422; fax 608/356-6422. www.qualityinn.com.* 84 rooms, 5 story, 12 suites.

Memorial Day-Labor Day: S $70-$80; D $70-$85; each additional $5; suites $125-$150; under 17 free; ski, golf plans; lower rates rest of year. Crib $4. TV; cable. Indoor pool; whirlpool. Complimentary coffee in rooms. Restaurant 7 am-10 pm. Room service. Bar 10-1 am. Check-out 11 am. Coin laundry. Meeting rooms. Business services available. Valet service. Sundries. Downhill ski 12 miles. Exercise equipment; sauna. Health club privileges. Game room. Refrigerator, wet bar, whirlpool in suites. Cr cds: A, C, D, DS, JCB, MC, V.

⊡ 🐾 ⛴ 🏌 ➰ 🏂 ⤬ SC 🚶

★ **SPINNING WHEEL MOTEL.** *809 8th St (53913). Phone 608/356-3933.* 25 rooms. S $33-$53; D $35-$63; each additional $6; under 12 free. Crib $6. Pet accepted. TV; cable (premium). Restaurant nearby. Downhill ski 10 miles; cross-country ski 5 miles. Cr cds: A, DS, MC, V.

⊡ 🐾 ⛴ ⤬ SC

Bayfield (A-3)

See also Ashland

Pop 686 **Elev** 700 ft **Area code** 715 **Zip** 54814

Information Chamber of Commerce, 42 S Broad St, PO Box 138; 715/779-3335 or 800/447-4094

Web www.bayfield.org

What to See and Do

Apostle Islands National Lakeshore. *415 Washington Ave. N and E off Bayfield Peninsula. Phone 715/779-3397.* Eleven miles of mainland shoreline and 21 islands of varying size. The lakeshore area features hiking, boating, fishing; primitive campsites on 18 islands. Two visitor centers, in Bayfield (all year) and at Little Sand Bay (Memorial Day-Sept), 13 miles NW of Bayfield. National Lakeshore Headquarters/Visitor Center (daily; free). Boat trips provided by

Apostle Islands Cruise Service. *Rittenhouse Ave. City Dock. Reservations advised, inquire for schedule. Phone 715/779-3925.* Lake Superior cruises to Apostle Islands on the Island Princess (May-early Oct, departures daily); also Stockton Island shuttle with Raspberry Island Lighthouse Adventure: 2-hour layover and naturalist hike. **$$$$**

Lake Superior Big Top Chautauqua. *3 miles S on WI 13, then W on Ski Hill Rd. Phone 715/373-5552; 888/244-8368.* Outdoor theater; features folk and bluegrass performances; musicals and theater pieces. (June-Labor Day, Wed-Sat eves; some Tues, Sun, and matinee performances)

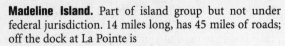

Madeline Island. Part of island group but not under federal jurisdiction. 14 miles long, has 45 miles of roads; off the dock at La Pointe is

Madeline Island Ferry Line. *1 Washington Ave. Phone 715/747-2051.* The *Island Queen, Nichevo II,* and the *Madeline Bayfield* make frequent trips. (Apr-Jan, daily) **$$**

Madeline Island Historical Museum. *Col. Wood Ave and Main St. Phone 715/747-2415.* Located near the site of an American Fur Company post and housed in a single building combining four pioneer log structures. (Late May-early Oct, daily; fee) There are motels, housekeeping cottages, and restaurants on the island. Guided bus tours. Marina; camping in two parks, cross-country skiing.

Mount Ashwabay Ski Area. *3 miles S on WI 13. Phone 715/779-3227.* T-bar, four rope tows; patrol, school, rentals; snow-making machine; restaurant, cafeteria, concession, bar. Longest run 1,500 feet; vertical drop 317 feet. (Dec-Mar, Wed, Sat-Sun; Christmas week, daily) Half-day rates; night skiing (Wed and Sat); cross-country skiing (Tues-Sun), 24 miles of trails.

Special Events

Apple Festival. *42 S Broad St. Phone 800/447-4094.* First full weekend Oct.

Bayfield Festival of Arts. *2 E Front St Memorial Park. Phone 800/447-4094.* Last full weekend July.

Great Schooner Race. *2 E Front St. Phone 800/447-4094.* Last weekend Sept.

Run on Water. *2 E Front St Bayfield Lakeside Pavillion. Phone 800/447-4094.* First Sat Feb.

Sailboat Race Week. *2 E Front St Bayfield Lakeside Pavillion. Phone 800/447-4094.* First week July.

Motels/Motor Lodges

★ **BAYFIELD INN.** *20 Rittenhouse Ave (54814). Phone 715/779-3363; fax 715/779-9810. www.bayfieldinn.com.* 21 rooms, 2 story. No A/C. June-Sept: S $50; D $75-$95; each additional $10; weekends 2-day min (July-Aug); higher rates Apple Festival; lower rates rest of year. TV; cable, VCR available (movies). Complimentary continental breakfast. Restaurant 11:30 am-9 pm. Room service. Check-out 11 am. Business services available. Downhill ski 5 miles; cross-country ski on-site. Sauna. Health club privileges. Game room. On lake. Cr cds: DS, MC, V.

★ **SUPER 8.** *Harbor View Dr (54891). Phone 715/373-5671; fax 715/373-5674. www.super8.com.* 35 rooms, 2 story. July-Sept: S $69.98-$75.98; D $79.98-$84.98; each additional $5; suite $89.98-$99.98; under 12 free; weekly and holiday rates; higher rates Apple Fest; lower rates rest of year. Crib free. Pet accepted, some restrictions; $25. TV; cable. Complimentary continental breakfast. Restaurant adjacent 4-10 pm. Check-out 11 am. Business services available. Downhill/cross-country ski 8 miles. Sauna. Whirlpool. Game room. On lake. Cr cds: A, C, D, DS, MC, V.

★ **WINDFIELD INN.** *225 E Lynde Ave (54814). Phone 715/779-3252; fax 715/779-5180.* 31 rooms, 26 A/C, 1-2 story, 6 kitchen apartments (1-2 bedrm). June-Oct: S, D $69; kitchen apartments $98-$135; lower rates rest of year. Crib free. Pet accepted. TV; cable. Complimentary coffee in rooms. Restaurant nearby. Check-out 11 am. Downhill/cross-country ski 8 miles. Some balconies. Sun deck. 4 wooded acres on shore of Lake Superior. Cr cds: A, MC, V.

B&B/Small Inns

★ ★ ★ **OLD RITTENHOUSE INN.** *301 Rittenhouse Ave (54814). Phone 715/779-5111; toll-free 800/779-2129; fax 715/779-5887. www.rittenhouseinn.com.* Travelers looking for something a little different can find it in the whimsical romance of this charming inn. Considered by many as the preferred lodging for romance and weekend getaways, this inn consists of two extraordinary Victorian homes and one charming cottage, all located just blocks from the historic district of downtown Bayfield. Guests will delight in the comfortably appointed guestrooms, with lovely antiques. 19 units in 3 guest houses, 2-3 story. No room phones. Complimentary continental breakfast in main house. Check-out noon, check-in 3:30 pm. Downhill ski 3 miles, cross-country ski 1 mile. Fireplaces. Restaurant. Individually decorated rooms in 3 restored Victorian houses; antique furnishings. Cr cds: MC, V. **$**

Restaurant

★ ★ ★ **OLD RITTENHOUSE.** *301 Rittenhouse Ave (54814). Phone 715/779-5111. www.rittenhouseinn.com.* Romantic and elegant dining at its finest. Hours: 5-9 pm. Reservations accepted. Cr cds: MC, V. **$$**

Beaver Dam (F-5)

See also Watertown, Waupun

Settled 1841 **Pop** 14,196 **Elev** 879 ft **Area code** 920 **Zip** 53916

Information Chamber of Commerce, 127 S Spring St; 920/887-8879

Web www.beaverdamchamber.com

What to See and Do

Beaver Dam Lake. *WI 33 and County B. Phone 920/885-6766.* 14 miles long. Fishing for bullhead, perch, crappie, walleye, and northern pike; ice fishing, boating (docks, ramps), waterskiing; waterfowl hunting. (Daily) **FREE**

Dodge County Historical Museum. *105 Park Ave. Phone 920/887-1266.* In 1890 Romanesque building; Chinese and Native American artifacts, spinning wheels, dolls. (Tues-Sat, afternoons; closed holidays) **FREE**

Special Events

Dodge County Fair. *W7435 WI 33 E. Phone 920/885-3586.* Fairgrounds, 3 miles E on WI 33. Five days mid-late Aug.

Swan City Car Show. *S University & Mill St. Swan City Park. Phone 920/887-7000.* Father's Day.

Motels/Motor Lodges

★★ **BEST WESTERN CAMPUS INN.** *815 Park Ave (53916). Phone 920/887-7171; toll-free 800/572-4891; fax 920/887-7171. www.bestwestern.com.* 94 rooms, 4 story. S, D $68-$82; each additional $5; suites $85-$110; under 12 free. Crib $4. TV; cable (premium), VCR available. Indoor pool; whirlpool. Restaurant 6 am-11 pm. Room service. Bar 4 pm-2 am. Check-out 11 am. Coin laundry. Meeting rooms. In-room modem link. Valet service. Sundries. Putting green. Game room. Some in-room whirlpools. Cr cds: A, C, D, DS, MC, V.

⬚ ⬚ ⬚

★ **GRAND VIEW.** *1510 N Center St (53916). Phone 920/885-9208; fax 920/887-8706.* 22 rooms. S $30.94; D $40.89-$46.41; each additional $4. Crib $3. Pet accepted, some restrictions. TV; cable (premium). Check-out 11 am. Cr cds: A, C, DS, MC, V.

⬚

★ **MAYVILLE INN.** *Hwy 28 W (53050). Phone 920/387-1234; fax 920/387-1234. www.mayvilleinn.com.* 29 rooms, 2 story. S, D $52; each additional $6; under 12 free. Crib free. TV; cable. Complimentary continental breakfast. Restaurant nearby. Bar. Check-out 11 am. Meeting room. Business services available. In-room modem link. Gift shop. Cross-country ski 5 miles. Whirlpool. Some refrigerators, wet bars. Cr cds: A, DS, MC, V.

⬚ ⬚ ⬚ ⬚ ⬚ ⬚ ⬚

Beloit (H-4)

See also Delavan, Janesville

Settled 1836 **Pop** 35,573 **Elev** 750 ft **Area code** 608 **Zip** 53511

Information Convention and Visitors Bureau, 1003 Pleasant St; 608/365-4838 or 800/4-BELOIT

Web www.visitbeloit.com

In 1837, the town of Colebrook, New Hampshire, moved almost en masse to this point at the confluence of Turtle Creek and Rock River. The community, successively known as Turtle, Blodgett's Settlement, and New Albany, was finally named Beloit in 1857. The New Englanders, determined to sustain standards of Eastern culture and education, founded Beloit Seminary soon after settling; this small coeducational school became Beloit College. Today the city's economy centers around the college, food processing, and the production of heavy machinery.

What to See and Do

Angel Museum. *656 Pleasant St. Phone 608/362-9099.* Collection of 11,000 angels made from everything from leather to china. Oprah Winfrey has donated over 500 angels from her private collection. (Mon-Sat 10 am-5 pm; Sun afternoons; closed holidays)

Beloit College. *700 College St. On US 51. Phone 608/363-2000.* (1846) 1,100 students. Noted for Theodore Lyman Wright Museum of Art (academic year, daily). Logan Museum of Anthropology has changing displays of Native American and Stone Age artifacts. Campus contains prehistoric mounds. Campus tours (by appointment).

Hanchett-Bartlett Homestead. *2149 St. Lawrence Ave. Phone 608/365-7835.* (1857) Restored historic limestone homestead on 15 acres is built in the transitional Greek Revival style, with Italianate details; restored in period colors. House contains furnishings of the mid-19th century; limestone barn houses collection of farm implements. On the grounds is a 1-room schoolhouse (1880); picnic area. (June-Sept, Wed-Sun afternoons; also by appointment) **$**

Special Event

Riverfest. *Riverside Park at Hwys 81 & 51. Phone 608/365-4838.* Music festival with top-name performers; more than 50 bands feature variety of music. Food, carnival rides, children's entertainment. Mid-July.

Motels/Motor Lodges

★ **COMFORT INN.** *2786 Milwaukee Rd (53511). Phone 608/362-2666; fax 608/362-2666. www.comfortinn.com.* 56 rooms, 2 story, 16 suites. June-Sept: S $45-$65; D $50-$70; each additional $5; suites $55-$75; under 18 free; weekly rates; higher rates special events; lower rates rest of year. Crib free. Pet accepted. TV; cable (premium), VCR available (movies). Indoor pool; whirlpool. Complimentary continental breakfast. Restaurant nearby. Check-out 11 am. Business services available. Game room. Refrigerator in suites. Cr cds: A, C, D, DS, JCB, MC, V.

⬛ 🐾 🏊 🖼

★ **HOLIDAY INN EXPRESS.** *2790 Milwaukee Rd (53511). Phone 608/365-6000; fax 608/365-1974. www.holiday-inn.com.* 73 rooms, 2 story. S $49-$65; D $60-$70; each additional $6; under 18 free. Crib free. TV; cable (premium). Complimentary breakfast. Coffee in rooms. Check-out noon. Meeting room. Business services available. Valet service. Cr cds: A, C, D, DS, JCB, MC, V.

⬛ 🏊 🚶 🖼

★ ★ **RAMADA INN.** *200 Dearborn Ave (61080). Phone 815/389-3481; toll-free 800/465-4329; fax 815/389-3481. www.holiday-inn.com.* 166 rooms, 2 story. S $59-$85; D $67-$97; each additional $8; under 18 free. Crib free. TV; cable. Heated pool; whirlpool. Restaurant 6 am-10 pm. Room service. Bar 11 am-midnight. Check-out noon. Meeting rooms. Business center. Valet service (Mon-Fri). Cross-country ski 5 miles. Exercise equipment. Sun deck. Cr cds: A, C, D, DS, JCB, MC, V.

⬛ 🏊 🏊 🚶 🖼 SC 🚶

Restaurant

★ ★ **BUTTERFLY CLUB.** *5246 E County Rd X (53511). Phone 608/362-8577; fax 608/362-8277.* Closed Mon; Jan 1, Dec 24-25. Dinner. Bar. Entertainment Fri, Sat. Children's menu. Outdoor dining. Cr cds: A, D, DS, MC, V. **$**

⬛

Black River Falls (E-3)

See also Sparta, Tomah

Pop 3,490 **Elev** 796 ft **Area code** 715 **Zip** 54615

Information Black River Area Chamber of Commerce, 120 N Water St; 715/284-4658 or 800/404-4008

Web www.blackrivercountry.com

In 1819, when the Black River countryside was a wilderness of pine, one of the first sawmills in Wisconsin was built here. Among the early settlers were a group of Mormons

from Nauvoo, Illinois (see). Conflict developed with local landowners, and the Mormons soon returned to Nauvoo. The seat of Jackson County, Black River Falls is situated on the Black River, which offers boating and canoeing. The area is also noted for deer hunting and winter sports.

What to See and Do

Black River Falls State Forest. *910 WI 54 E. 6 miles E on WI 54. Phone 715/284-1400.* A 66,000-acre forest. Swimming, fishing, boating, canoeing; hiking, cross-country skiing, snowmobiling, bridle trail, picnicking, playground, camping (fee). Lookout tower; abundant wildlife. Self-guided auto trail. All motor vehicles must have parking sticker. (Daily) Standard fees. **$$**

Thunderbird Museum. *In Hatfield, 10 miles NE via US 12, County K exit at Merrillan. Phone 715/333-5841.* Exhibits include Native American artifacts dating back to paleolithic man, weapons, minerals, dolls, coins, stamps, art. (May-Sept, weekends or by appointment) **$$**

Special Event

Winnebago Pow-Wow. *3 miles NE via WI 54, at Red Cloud Memorial Pow-Wow Grounds. Phone 715/284-4658.* Dancing. Held twice annually: Sun and Mon, Memorial Day and Labor Day weekends.

Motels/Motor Lodges

★ ★ **BEST WESTERN ARROWHEAD LODGE.** *600 Oasis Rd (54615). Phone 715/284-9471; toll-free 800/284-9471; fax 715/284-9664. www.bestwestern.com.* 144 rooms, 3 story, 30 suites. S $59-$75; D $65-$85; each additional $5; suites $66.95-$179.95; under 12 free. Crib $3. Pet accepted. Complimentary full breakfast. Check-out noon. TV; cable. In-room modem link. Restaurant 6:30 am-2 pm, 5-10 pm. Bar, entertainment Sat. Playground. Sauna. On lake; docks, swimming beach. Indoor pool, whirlpool. Nature/fitness trail. Snowmobile trails. Meeting rooms, business services. Sundries. Cr cds: A, C, D, DS, ER, JCB, MC, V.

⬛ 🐾 🛁 🏊 🖼 🖼

★ **DAYS INN.** *Phone 715/284-4333; toll-free 800/356-8018; fax 715/284-9068. www.daysinn.com.* 86 rooms, 2 story. S $44.99-$61.99; D $51.99-$69.99; suites $75-$110; under 12 free. Crib free. Pet accepted. TV; cable, VCR available. Sauna. Indoor pool; whirlpool. Complimentary continental breakfast. Restaurant adjacent 6 am-11 pm. Check-out noon. Coin laundry. Meeting room. Business services available. In-room modem link. Downhill ski 15 miles; cross-country ski 1 mile. Health club privileges. Game room. Cr cds: A, C, D, DS, MC, V.

⬛ 🐾 🏊 🏊 🚶 🖼 SC

Boulder Junction (B-4)

See also Eagle River, Land O Lakes, Manitowish Waters, Minocqua, Sayner, Woodruff

Pop 1,000 **Elev** 1,640 ft **Area code** 715 **Zip** 54512

Information Chamber of Commerce, PO Box 286; 715/385-2400 or 800/466-8759

Web www.boulderjct.org

This secluded little village within the Northern Highland-American Legion State Forest is the gateway to a vast recreational area with woodlands, scenic drives, streams, and several hundred lakes where fishing for muskellunge is excellent. Indeed, "Musky Capital of the World" is its registered trademark. Boulder Junction also offers various winter activities, including snowmobiling, cross-country skiing, and ice fishing. In nearby state nurseries, millions of young pine trees are raised and shipped all over the state for forest planting.

What to See and Do

Northern Highland-American Legion State Forest. *4125 CTH M. Phone 715/385-3521.* A 225,000-acre forest with swimming beaches, waterskiing, fishing, boating, canoeing; hiking, cross-country skiing, snowmobiling, picnicking, improved and primitive camping (896 sites on lakes; dump station; fee), sites also along water trails. Standard fees. (Daily) **$$**

Special Event

Musky Jamboree/Arts and Crafts Fair. *W7435 Hwy 33 E. Phone 715/385-2400.* Second Sun.

Restaurant

★ ★ **GUIDE'S INN.** *County M (54512). Phone 715/385-2233.* Continental menu. Hours: 4-10 pm. Closed Sun, Thanksgiving Day, Easter, Dec 25. Dinner $6.50-$19.95. Bar. Child's meals. Cr cds: MC, V.

D

Brown Deer

Restaurant

★ ★ **RIVER LANE INN.** *4313 W River Ln (53223). Phone 414/354-1995.* Hours: 11:30 am-2:30 pm, 5-10 pm. Closed Sun; Dec. 25th, Thanksgiving Day . Lunch $8-$15, dinner $17-$25. Bar. Cr cds: A, DS, MC, V.

D

Burlington (G-5)

See also Delavan, Elkhorn, Fontana, Lake Geneva

Settled 1835 **Pop** 8,855 **Elev** 766 ft **Area code** 262 **Zip** 53105

Information Chamber of Commerce, 112 E Chesnut St, PO Box 156; 262/763-6044

Web www.burlingtonareachamber.com

Originally called Foxville, Burlington was renamed for the city in Vermont by a group of settlers arriving in 1835. It is the home of the Liar's Club, an organization dedicated to the preservation of the art of telling tall tales. A prize is awarded each year to the contributor who submits the most incredible "stretcher."

What to See and Do

Green Meadows Farm. *33603 High Dr, 5 miles N via WI 36, 3 miles W of Waterford on WI 20. Phone 262/534-2891.* Operating farm offers daily guided tours; pony rides, tractor-drawn hayrides; more than 20 "hands-on" animal areas; picnic areas. (May-June, Tues-Sat; July-Labor Day, Oct, daily; closed Sept) Pumpkin picking in Oct. **$$$**

Historic Burlington. Visit 22 historic spots in the city, including the Lincoln Monument and the Meinhardt Homestead.

Spinning Top Exploratory Museum. *533 Milwaukee Ave. Phone 262/763-3946 or 262/728-5623.* Exhibits and displays dealing with tops, yo-yos, gyroscopes; top games, demonstrations; 35 tops for hands-on experiments. Video presentations.

Tall Tales Trail. 17-stop walking tour featuring tall tales preserved on plaques and mounted on public buildings and storefronts.

Special Events

Aquaducks Water Ski Show. *Fischer Park on Browns Lake. Phone 262/763-6044.* Performance each Sat evening; rain date Sun. June-Labor Day.

Chocolate City Festival. *Parade: 112 E Chestnut. Phone 262/763-3300.* Two-day, city-wide celebration including arts and crafts fair (fee), parade, entertainment. Weekend after Mother's Day.

Motel/Motor Lodge

★ **AMERICINN - MOTEL.** *205 S Browns Lake Dr (53813). Phone 414/534-2125; toll-free 800/634-3444; fax 414/534-2125. www.americinn.com.* 37 rooms, 2 story. D $62-$75; each additional $6; under

12 free. Complimentary continental breakfast. Check-out 11 am. TV; cable (premium). Sauna. Indoor pool, whirlpool. Cr cds: A, D, DS, MC, V.

D ⌖ ⌖ SC

Cable (B-2)

See also Hayward

Pop 817 **Elev** 1,370 ft **Area code** 715 **Zip** 54821

Information Cable Area Chamber of Commerce, PO Box 217; 715/798-3833 or 800/533-7454

Web www.cable4fun.com

What to See and Do

Mount Telemark Ski Area. *3 miles E on County M. Phone 715/798-3999.* Area has two chairlifts, two T-bars, rope tow; alpine and nordic ski schools, rentals, patrol, snowmaking; nursery, restaurants, cafeteria, bar, lodge. Longest run 1/2 mile; vertical drop 370 feet. (Thanksgiving-Mar, daily) Cross-country trails (Dec-Mar, daily; rentals), more than 40 miles of trails. Hiking, bridle, and bicycle trails rest of year; also 18-hole golf, eight tennis courts (four indoor).

Special Event

American Birkebeiner. *11 Main St. Phone 715/634-5025.* Cross-country ski race. More than 6,000 participants from 40 states and 15 countries. 55 kilometers. Late Feb.

Cedarburg (F-5)

See also Milwaukee, Port Washington

Pop 9,895 **Elev** 780 ft **Area code** 262 **Zip** 53012

Information Chamber of Commerce, PO Box 104; 262/377-9620 or 800/CDR-BURG

Web www.cedarburg.org

Cedarburg, surrounded by rich farmlands and protected forests and wetlands, has many beautiful old homes built in the 1800s. Many buildings in the historic downtown area have been restored.

What to See and Do

Cedar Creek Settlement and Winery. *W6340 Bridge Rd, at N Washington. Phone 262/377-8020.* Stone woolen mill (1864) converted into a winery; houses shops, art studios, and restaurants. Winery makes strawberry, cranberry, and grape wines; museum of antique winemaking tools. (Daily; closed holidays) **$**

Special Events

House Tour. *Cedarburg Cultural Center W62 N546 Washington. Phone 262/375-3676.* Tour of historic homes in the area. First full weekend June.

Ozaukee County Fair. *W65 N796 Washington Ave. (Firemen's Park and County Grounds). Phone 262/377-9620.* Educational and commercial exhibits, carnival, entertainment. Late July-early Aug.

Strawberry Festival. *W63N641 Washington Ave. Phone 262/377-9620.* Strawberry foods, contests, craft fair, entertainment. Fourth full weekend June.

Wine and Harvest Festival. *N70W6340 Bridge Rd #21. Cedar Creek Winery. Phone 262/377-9620.* Grape-stomping contests, farmers market, arts and crafts fair, scarecrow contest; entertainment, food. Third weekend Sept.

Winter Festival. *W63N641 Washington Ave. Phone 262/377-9620.* Ice carving and snow sculpture contests, bed and barrel races across ice, winter softball and volleyball, Alaskan malamute weight pull, snow goose egg hunt; torchlight parade, horse-drawn sleigh rides. First full weekend Feb.

Motels/Motor Lodges

★ **BEST WESTERN QUIET HOUSE SUITES.** *10330 N Port Washington Rd (53092). Phone 262/241-3677; fax 414/241-3707. www.bestwestern.com.* 54 rooms, 2 story. D $111-$200; each additional $10. Pet accepted; fee. Complimentary continental breakfast. Check-out 11 am. TV; cable (premium). In-room modem link. Exercise equipment. Indoor, outdoor pool, whirlpool. Cr cds: A, C, D, DS, MC, V.

D ⌖ ⌖ ⌖ ⌖

★ **BREEZE INN TO THE CHALET.** *10401 N Port Washington Rd (53092). Phone 262/241-4510; toll-free 800/343-4510; fax 414/241-5542.* 41 rooms, 2 story. May-Oct: S $41-$68; D $48-$68; each additional $7; suites $85-$150; under 12 free; weekly rates; higher rates special events, holidays; lower rates rest of year. Crib free. Pet accepted, some restrictions. TV; cable (premium). Restaurant 6 am-9 pm; Fri to 9:30 pm; Sat, Sun from 7 am. Bar. Check-out 11 am. Meeting room. Business services available. Many refrigerators. Cr cds: A, C, D, DS, MC, V.

D ⌖ ⌖ ⌖

B&B/Small Inns

★ **STAGECOACH INN BED AND BREAKFAST.** *W61 N 520 Washington Ave (53012). Phone 262/375-0208; toll-free 888/375-0208; fax 414/375-6170. www.stagecoach-inn-wi.com.* 12 rooms, 3 story, 6 suites. Phone available. S $65-$75; D $75-$95; each additional $10; suites $115. TV; cable. Complimentary continental breakfast. Coffee in rooms. Restaurant nearby. Bar. Check-out

11 am, check-in 4 pm. Business services available. Cross-country ski 3 miles. Restored stagecoach inn (1853); antiques. Some in-room whirlpools, fireplaces. Totally nonsmoking. Cr cds: A, D, DS, MC, V.

★★★**WASHINGTON HOUSE INN.** *W62 N573 Washington Ave (53012). Phone 262/375-3550; toll-free 800/ 554-4717; fax 414/375-9422. www.washingtonhouseinn.com.* Experience all the personal touches added to make this inn feel like home. Each of the rooms is furnished with antique appointments and down comforters. 34 rooms, 3 story. S, D $69-$189; each additional $10. TV; cable (premium), VCR available. Complimentary continental breakfast buffet. Restaurant opposite. Check-out noon, check-in 3 pm. Meeting room. Business center. Cross-country ski 5 miles. Sauna. Many in-room whirlpools; some fireplaces. In a Victorian Cream City brick building (1886); antiques, historic memorabilia. Rms named after city's pioneers. Cr cds: A, D, DS, MC, V.

Restaurant

★ **KOWLOON.** *W63 N145 Washington Ave. Phone 262/375-3030; fax 262/375-3051.* Chinese menu. Hours: 11:30 am-9 pm; Fri to 10 pm; Sat 4:30-10 pm; Sun 4-9 pm. Closed Mon. Dinner $5.25-$10.25. Bar. Cr cds: A, D, DS, MC, V.

Chippewa Falls (D-2)

See also Eau Claire, Menomonie

Settled 1836 **Pop** 12,727 **Elev** 902 ft **Area code** 715 **Zip** 54729

Information Chamber of Commerce, 10 S Bridge St; 715/723-0331

Web www.chippewachamber.org

Water has replaced lumber as the prime natural resource of this city on the Chippewa River. Jean Brunet, a pioneer settler, built a sawmill and then a dam here. Soon the area was populated by lumberjacks. Today, hydroelectric power is channeled to the industries of Chippewa Falls, which has water noted for its purity.

What to See and Do

Brunet Island State Park. *23125 255th St. N via US 53, then E on WI 64 in Cornell. Phone 715/239-6888.* A 1,032-acre river island park. Swimming, fishing (pier), boating, canoeing; nature and hiking trails, cross-country skiing, picnicking, playground, camping (electric hookups, dump station). Standard fees. (Daily) **$$$**

Chippewa Falls Zoo. *109 E Spruce St. Irvine Park, N on WI 124. Phone 715/723-3890.* Concentrates on native animals. Also picnic tables, playground, tennis courts, pool. Fee for some activities. (May-Oct, daily) **FREE**

Cook-Rutledge Mansion. *505 W Grand Ave. Phone 715/ 723-7181.* (1870s) Restored Victorian mansion. Guided tours (June-Aug, Thurs-Sun; rest of year, by appointment). **$$$**

Lake Wissota State Park. *18127 CTH O. 8 miles E on WI 29. Phone 715/382-4574.* A 1,062-acre park with swimming, waterskiing, fishing, boating, canoeing; hiking, cross-country skiing, picnicking, playground, concession, camping (dump station, electro-hookups; reservations accepted). Observation points. Standard fees. (Daily) **$$$**

Special Events

Northern Wisconsin State Fair. *Fairgrounds. 330 Jefferson Ave. Phone 715/723-2861.* Early or mid-July.

Pure Water Days. *Downtown. 10 S Bridge St. Phone 715/ 723-0331.* Canoe paddling, sport competitions, contests, parade, dances, beer garden, food. Second weekend Aug.

Motels/Motor Lodges

★★ **AMERICINN.** *11 W South Ave (54729). Phone 715/723-5711; toll-free 800/634-3444; fax 715/723-5254. www.americinn.com.* 62 rooms, 2 story. D $65-$91. Pet accepted; fee. Check-out 11 am. TV; cable (premium). In-room modem link. Indoor pool, whirlpool. Cr cds: A, C, D, DS, MC, V.

★ **COUNTRY INN.** *1021 W Park Ave (54729). Phone 715/720-1414; fax 715/720-1414.* 62 rooms, 2 story. May-Sept: S $54.90-$98.90; D $62.90-$106.90; each additional $8; under 18 free; lower rates rest of year. Crib available. TV; cable (premium). Complimentary continental breakfast. Coffee in rooms. Restaurant nearby. Check-out 11 am. Business services available. In-room modem link. Indoor pool; whirlpool. Some refrigerators. Cr cds: A, D, DS, MC, V.

★ **GLEN LOCH MOTEL.** *1225 Jefferson Ave (54729). Phone 715/723-9121; toll-free 800/470-2755; fax 715/ 723-7020.* 19 rooms. S $26; D $36-$44; each additional $4. TV; cable (premium). Complimentary coffee in lobby. Check-out 11 am. Picnic tables. Cr cds: MC, V.

★ **IMA INDIANHEAD.** *501 Summit Ave (54729). Phone 715/723-9171; fax 715/723-6142.* 27 rooms. S, D $40-$46; each additional $5. Crib available. Pet accepted. TV; cable (premium), VCR available. Complimentary coffee in lobby. Restaurant adjacent. Check-out

11 am. Valet service. Some refrigerators. On bluff overlooking city. Cr cds: A, DS, MC, V.

D 🐾 🖼

★ ★ **PARK INN.** *1009 W Park Ave (54729). Phone 715/723-2281; toll-free 800/446-9320; fax 715/723-2281. www.parkinn.com.* 67 rooms. S $50-$57; D $57-$64; each additional $7. Crib available. Pet accepted, some restrictions. TV; cable. Indoor pool; whirlpool. Restaurants 6:30 am-1:30 pm, 5-9:30 pm. Room service. Bar. Checkout noon. Meeting rooms. Business services available. Valet service. Sundries. Some wet bars. Cr cds: A, C, D, DS, ER, JCB, MC, V.

D 🐾 🖼 🖼 SC

Restaurants

★ ★ **EDELWEISS STEAK HOUSE AND MOTEL.** *8988 WI 124 (54729). Phone 715/723-7881.* German, American menu. Hours: 4:30-9:30 pm; Sun 10:30 am-2 pm, 4:30-9:30 pm. Closed Mon (winter); Dec 24, 25. Dinner $6.75-$16.95. Bar to 1 am. Reservations accepted. Bavarian décor; beamed ceiling; loft dining area. Cr cds: DS, MC, V.

D

★ **LINDSAY'S ON GRAND.** *24 W Grand Ave (54729). Phone 715/723-4025.* Hours: 6 am-9 pm. Closed Jan 1, Thanksgiving, Dec 25. Breakfast $2.75-$4.85, lunch, dinner $4.55-$7.95. Child's meals. Specialties: cod fillet, glazed ham steak. Own pasta. Casual family restaurant. Cr cds: MC, V.

D

Crandon (C-4)

See also Rhinelander, Three Lakes

Pop 1,958 **Elev** 1,629 ft **Area code** 715 **Zip** 54520

Information Chamber of Commerce, 201 S Lake Ave, PO Box 88; 715/478-3450 or 800/334-3387

Web www.crandonwi.com

What to See and Do

Camp Five Museum and "Lumberjack Special" Steam Train Tour. *11 miles E on US 8 and WI 32 in Laona. Phone 715/674-3414.* Old steam train ride to Camp Five Museum complex; harness and an active blacksmith shop, 1900 country store, logging museum with audiovisual presentation, nature center with diorama featuring area wildlife, 30-minute guided forest tour, hayrack/pontoon boat trip (fee); children's playground, concession. (Mid-June-late Aug, four departures daily; closed Sun) **$$$$**

Motel/Motor Lodge

★ **FOUR SEASONS MOTEL.** *304 W Glen St (54520). Phone 715/478-3377; toll-free 888/81MOTEL; fax 715/478-3785.* 20 rooms. S $38; D $45; under 6 free. Crib free. TV; cable (premium). Coffee in rooms. Checkout 11 am. Business services available. Refrigerators. Cr cds: DS, MC, V.

D 🐾 🖼 🖼 🖼

Delavan (G-5)

See also Elkhorn, Fontana, Lake Geneva

Settled 1836 **Pop** 6,073 **Elev** 940 ft **Area code** 262 **Zip** 53115

Information Delavan Chamber of Commerce, 52 E Walworth Ave; 262/728-5095 or 800/624-0052

Web www.delavanwi.org

Between 1847 and 1894, Delavan was the headquarters of 28 different circuses. The original P. T. Barnum circus was organized here during the winter of 1870-1871 by William C. Coup. Spring Grove and St. Andrew's cemeteries are "last lot" resting places for more than 100 members of the 19th-century circus colony. Today many flowering crabapple trees grace the town, blooming usually in mid-May.

Restaurant

★ ★ **MILLIE'S.** *N 2484 County O (53115). Phone 262/728-2434.* Closed Mon (exc July-Aug); Thanksgiving, Dec 25; also Tues-Fri Jan-Feb. Breakfast, lunch, dinner. Bar. On 80-acre farm; English gardens, gazebo. **$**

D

Devil's Lake State Park (F-4)

3 miles S of Baraboo on WI 123.

These 11,050 acres, with spring-fed Devil's Lake as the greatest single attraction, form Wisconsin's most beautiful state park. Remnants of an ancient mountain range surround the lake, providing unique scenery. The lake, 1 1/4 miles long, is in the midst of sheer cliffs of quartzite that rise as high as 500 feet above the water. Unusual rock formations may be found at the top of the bluffs. The park has a naturalist in residence who may be contacted for information concerning year-round nature hikes and programs. Sandy swimming beaches with bathhouses, concessions, and boat landings are at either end. No motorboats are permitted. The park provides hiking and cross-country skiing trails, picnic grounds, improved tent and trailer facilities (electric hookups, dump station), and a nature center. The lake is restocked yearly. Native American mounds include the Eagle, Bear, and Lynx mounds. General tourist supplies are available at the north and south shores. Standard fees. (Daily) Contact the Park Superintendent, S5975 Park Rd, Baraboo 53913. Phone 608/356-8301. Per vehicle **$$$**

Ice Age National Scientific Reserve. Naturalists explain evidence of Wisconsin glaciation; exhibits of local Ice Age features; trails; under development. Also included in the reserve are Northern Unit Kettle Moraine State Forest and two state parks, Mill Bluff and Interstate Per vehicle **$$$**

Dodgeville (G-3)

See also Mount Horeb, New Glarus, Platteville

Founded 1827 **Pop** 3,882 **Elev** 1,222 ft **Area code** 608 **Zip** 53533

Information Dodgeville Chamber of Commerce, 178 1/2 N Iowa St, Suite 201; 608/935-5993

Web www.dodgeville.com

What to See and Do

Governor Dodge State Park. *4175 WI 23. 3 miles N via US 151, WI 23. Phone 608/935-2315.* A 5,029-acre park with 95-acre and 150-acre lakes. Rock formations, white pine. Swimming, bathhouse, fishing, boating (electric motors only; ramps), canoeing (rentals); bicycle, hiking, and bridle trails; cross-country skiing, snowmobiling, picnicking, playgrounds, concession, camping (electric hookups, dump station), backpack campsites, horse campground. Nature programs (June-Aug). Standard fees. (Daily)

Motels/Motor Lodges

★ ★ **DON Q INN.** *3656 WI 23 (53533). Phone 608/935-2321; toll-free 800/666-7848; fax 608/935-2416.* 61 rooms, 3 story. Mid-May-Oct: S, D $69-$89; each additional $8; specialty rooms $79-$255; under 18 free; lower rates rest of year. Crib $8. TV. Indoor/outdoor pool; whirlpool. Complimentary continental breakfast. Restaurant 5-8:30 pm. Check-out noon. Meeting rooms. Cross-country ski 1 1/2 miles. Some in-room whirlpools. Game room. Imaginatively furnished; rustic décor. Cr cds: A, D, DS, MC, V.

⏚ ✦ ⛵ ⊠

★ **NEW CONCORD INN.** *3637 State Rd 23 (53533). Phone 608/935-3770; toll-free 800/348-9310; fax 608/935-9605. www.concordinn.com.* 63 rooms, 3 story. D $74; each additional $6; under 12 free. Complimentary continental breakfast. Check-out 11 am. TV; cable

(premium). Game room. Indoor pool, whirlpool. Cross-country ski 2 miles. Cr cds: A, DS, MC, V.

⒟ ⏚ ✦ ✦ ⛵ ⊠

Door County

Famous for its fish boils, foliage, and 250 miles of shoreline, Door County is a peninsula with Green Bay on the west and Lake Michigan on the east. Its picturesque villages, rolling woodlands, limestone bluffs, and beautiful vistas are the reason the area is often referred to as the Cape Cod of the Midwest.

Door County offers year-round recreational opportunities. Spring and summer bring fishing, sailing, beachcombing, camping, hiking, biking, and horseback riding. Thousands of acres of apple and cherry blossoms color the landscape in late May. There is excellent scuba diving in the Portes des Mortes (Death's Door) Straits at the tip of the peninsula, where hundreds of shipwrecks lie in the shifting freshwater sands. Fall colors can be viewed from the endless miles of trails and country roads, which become cross-country ski routes in winter.

Many artists reside here, as is evidenced by the towns' shops, galleries, and boutiques. Summertime theater and concerts also attract tourists.

The taste of the peninsula is unquestionably the legendary fish boil. Trout or whitefish and potatoes and onions are cooked in a cauldron over an open fire. When the fish has almost finished cooking, kerosene is thrown onto the fire, creating a huge flame and causing the unwanted oils to boil out and over the pot.

Door County Chamber of Commerce, 1015 Green Bay Rd, PO Box 406, Sturgeon Bay, 54235, 920/743-4456 or 800/527-3529, has winter and summer schedules of events, maps and details on recreational facilities. For a free vacation guide, phone 800/52-RELAX.

The following towns in Door County are included in this travel planner (For full information on any one of them, see the individual alphabetical listing): Bailey's Harbor, Egg Harbor, Ellison Bay, Ephraim, Fish Creek, Sister Bay, Sturgeon Bay, and Washington Island.

Eagle River (C-4)

See also Land O Lakes, Rhinelander, Saint Germain, Three Lakes

Pop 1,374 **Elev** 1,647 ft **Area code** 715 **Zip** 54521

Information Eagle River Area Chamber of Commerce, PO Box 1917; 715/479-6400 or 800/359-6315

Web www.eagle-river.com

The bald eagles that gave this town its name are still occasionally seen, and the Eagle chain of 28 lakes, the largest inland chain of freshwater lakes in the world, is an outstanding tourist attraction. Eagle River has developed as a center of winter sports. The result is lake vacationers in summer and ski fans, both cross-country and downhill, and snowmobilers in winter. There are more than 11 miles of cross-country ski trails on Anvil Lake trail, and 600 miles of snowmobile trails and several hiking areas are in the Nicolet National Forest. A Ranger District office of the Nicolet National Forest (see THREE LAKES) is located here.

What to See and Do

Trees For Tomorrow Natural Resources Education Center. *519 Sheridan St. Phone 715/479-6456.* Demonstration forests, nature trail; "talking tree." (Daily) Outdoor skills and natural resource programs with emphasis on forest ecology and conservation. Cross-country skiing. Orienteering. Natural resources workshops (fee). Guided tours (Tues and Thurs, summer). **FREE**

Special Events

Cranberry Fest. *164 Forest Vilas County Fairgrounds. Phone 800/359-6315.* Cranberry bog tours, events. First weekend Oct.

Klondike Days. *1311 Hwy 45 N. Phone 715/479-4456.* Oval sled dog races, winter events. Mid- Feb.

National Championship Musky Open. *164 Forest Vilas County Fairgrounds. Phone 715/479-6400.* Third weekend Aug.

World Championship Snowmobile Derby. *1311 US 45 N. 1 1/2 miles N on US 45. Phone 715/479-4424.* Third weekend Jan.

Motels/Motor Lodges

★ **DAYS INN.** *844 WI 45 N, 844 Railroad St N (54521). Phone 715/479-5151; toll-free 800/356-8018; fax 715/479-8259. www.daysinn.com.* 93 rooms, 2 story. D $59-$99; each additional $5; under 18 free. Pet accepted. Complimentary continental breakfast. Check-out 11 am. TV; cable. Laundry services. Sauna. Game room. Indoor pool, whirlpool. Cross-country ski 1/2 mile. Cr cds: A, MC, V.

★★ **EAGLE RIVER INN AND RESORT.** *5260 WI 70 W (54521). Phone 715/479-2000; toll-free 877/479-2051; fax 715/479-9198. www.eriver-inn.com.* 36 units, 2 story, 7 suites, 8 kitchens Late June-Aug, Christmas week, weekends Jan-Feb: S $59-69; D $79-$99; each additional $10; suites $149-$169; kitchen units $79-$109; under 12 free; weekly rates; ski, golf plans; lower rates rest of year. Crib $10. TV; cable. Indoor pool; whirlpool. Restaurant 4-9 pm in season. Room service. Bar. Check-out 11 am. Meeting rooms. Business services available. Gift shop. Cross-country ski 2 miles. Exercise equipment; sauna. Miniature golf. Boats. In-room whirlpool in some suites. Balconies. Picnic tables. On lake; dock. Cr cds: A, DS, MC, V.

★ **WHITE EAGLE.** *4948 WI 70 W (54521). Phone 715/479-4426; toll-free 800/782-6488; fax 715/479-3570. www.whiteeaglemotel.com.* 22 rooms. No A/C. Mid-June-mid-Oct: S, D $52-$75; lower rates rest of year. Crib free. Pet accepted; $10. TV; cable (premium). Heated pool; whirlpool. Sauna. Complimentary coffee. Restaurant nearby. Check-out 10:30 am. Cross-country ski 3 miles. Snowmobile trails. Paddleboat, pontoon boat. Refrigerators available. Picnic tables. On Eagle River; private piers. Driving range, miniature golf opposite. Cr cds: DS, MC, V.

Resorts

★★ **CHANTICLEER INN.** *1458 E Dollar Lake Rd (54521). Phone 715/479-4486; toll-free 800/752-9193; fax 715/479-0004. www.chanticleerinn.com.* 13 motel rooms, 2 story, 8 kitchen villas, 50 units (1-3 bedrm) in 20 town houses, 20 with kit., most A/C. S, D $69-$89; each additional $10; under 16 free; golf, package plans; higher rates: winter holidays, snowmobile derby. Crib $10. TV. Playground. Complimentary coffee in motel rooms. Dining room 8-10 am, 5:30-9:30 pm. Box lunches, snacks. Bar. Check-out 10:30 am, check-in 3 pm. Grocery, package store 2-1/2 miles. Coin laundry. Meeting rooms. Business services available. Gift shop. Free airport transportation. 2 tennis courts, 1 lighted. 9-hole golf adj, daily greens fee. 2 sand beaches; boats, motors, canoes, pontoon boats. Cross-country ski on site. Recreation room. Fishing guides, clean and store area. Fireplace in villas/condos. Private patios or balconies in townhouses and suites. Cr cds: A, DS, MC, V.

★ **GYPSY VILLA RESORT.** *950 Circle Dr (54521). Phone 715/479-8644; toll-free 800/232-9714; fax 715/479-8780. www.gypsyvilla.com.* 21 kitchen cottages (1-4-bedroom), 6 A/C. Kitchen. cottages $345-$1,818/week (2-6 persons); daily rates; MAP available. Crib free. Garage parking (fee). Pet accepted. TV; VCR available. Wading pool; whirlpool. Playground. Free supervised children's activities (June-Aug). Check-out noon, check-in 3 pm. Coin laundry. Meeting rooms. Phone available. Business services available. Grocery, package store 2 miles. Tennis. Private swimming beach. Boats, waterskiing. Bicycles. Lawn games. Soc director. Game room. Exercise equipment; sauna. Fish/hunt guides. Fireplaces; some in-room whirlpools. Private patios. Picnic tables, grills. Most cottages on Cranberry Island. Cr cds: A, MC, V.

Restaurant

★ **BAERTSCHY'S PINE GABLES SUPPER CLUB.** *5009 WI 70 W (54521). Phone 715/479-7689.* German menu. Hours: from 5 pm, closed Tues. Dinner $15-$27. Bar. Cr cds: A, D, DS, MC, V. **$**

D

Eau Claire (D-2)

See also Chippewa Falls, Menomonie

Settled 1844 **Pop** 56,856 **Elev** 796 ft **Area code** 715

Information Eau Claire Convention Bureau, 3625 Gateway Dr, Suite F, 54701; 715/831-2345 or 800/344-3866

Web www.eauclaire-info.com

Once a wild and robust lumber camp and sawmill on the shores of the Eau Claire and Chippewa rivers, the city has turned to diversified industry. The name is French for "clear water."

What to See and Do

Chippewa Valley Museum. *1204 Carson Park Dr. Carson Park. Phone 715/834-7871.* "Paths of the People" Ojibwe exhibit, "Settlement and Survival" 1850-1925 history of Chippewa Valley. Street scene, 21-room doll house, agricultural wing, old-fashioned ice cream parlor, research library. Log house (1860); Sunnyview School (1880). Gift shop. (Tues-Sun) **$$**

Dells Mills Museum. *E 18855 County V. 20 miles SE via WI 12, 3 miles N of Augusta via WI 27 on County V. Phone 715/286-2714.* (1864) Historic 5-story water-powered flour and grist mill built of hand-hewn timbers; wooden pegged. One-room schoolhouse museum. Gun shop, antique shop. (May-Oct, daily) **$$$**

⭐ **Paul Bunyan Logging Camp.** *1110 Carson Park Dr. Carson Park, Clairemont Ave to Menomonie St, E to Carson Park Dr. Phone 715/835-6200.* Restored 1890s logging camp with bunkhouse, cook shack, blacksmith shop, dingle, filers shack, barn; heavy equipment display. Artifacts, film at interpretive center. (First Mon in Apr-first Mon in Oct) **$$**

University of Wisconsin-Eau Claire. *105 Garfield Ave. Park and Garfield aves. Phone 715/836-2637.* (1916) 10,500 students. Planetarium, bird museum, greenhouses; dramatic productions, musical events, art gallery (free). Putnam Park arboretum, a 230-acre tract of forest land kept in its natural state, has self-guided nature trails.

Motels/Motor Lodges

★ **ANTLERS MOTEL.** *2245 S Hastings Way (54701). Phone 715/834-5313; toll-free 800/423-4526; fax 715/*

839-7582. 33 rooms, 1-2 story. S $38-$45; D $46-$52; each additional $5. Crib free. TV; cable (premium). Playground. Restaurant adjacent open 24 hours. Check-out 11 am. Cr cds: A, MC, V.

✈

★ ★ **BEST WESTERN ATRIUM INN.** *2851 Hendrickson Dr (54701). Phone 715/835-2242; toll-free 800/528-1234; fax 715/835-1027. www.midwayhotels.com.* 109 rooms, 2 story. S $59-$68; D $71-$79; each additional $12; under 18 free. Crib free. TV; cable (premium), VCR available. Indoor pool; whirlpool. Complimentary full breakfast Mon-Fri. Coffee in rooms. Restaurant 6:30 am-2 pm, 5-9 pm; Sat, Sun 7 am-2 pm, 5-9 pm. Room service. Bar 4 pm-1 am, Sun noon-9 pm; entertainment. Check-out 11 am. Meeting rooms. Business services available. In-room modem link. Valet service. Sundries. Free airport, bus depot transportation. Sauna. Domed recreation area. Game room. Cr cds: A, C, D, DS, MC, V.

D ✈ 🍴 🏋 ≈ 🏊 🏃 ✈

★ ★ **BEST WESTERN WHITE HOUSE INN.** *1828 S Hastings Way (54701). Phone 715/832-8356; toll-free 877/213-1600; fax 715/836-9686. bestwestern.com.* 66 rooms, 1-2 story. S, D $64-67; each additional $5. Crib $5. TV; cable (premium). Indoor pool; whirlpool. Complimentary afternoon refreshments. Restaurant 4:30-11 pm. Check-out 11 am. Business services available. In-room modem link. Valet service. Sauna. Health club privileges. Game room. Refrigerators; some in-room whirlpools. Sun deck. Cr cds: A, C, D, DS, MC, V.

D 🍴 🏋 ≈ ⛷ SC 🏃

★ **COMFORT INN.** *3117 Craig Rd (54701). Phone 715/833-9798; fax 715/833-9798. www.comfortinn.com.* 56 rooms, 2 story. June-Aug: S $62.95-$70.95; D $67.95-$75.95; each additional $5; under 18 free; lower rates rest of year. Crib available. Pet accepted. TV; cable (premium). Indoor pool. Complimentary continental breakfast. Restaurant nearby. Check-out 11 am. Business services available. In-room modem link. Cross-country ski 2 miles. Cr cds: A, C, D, DS, JCB, MC, V.

D 🍴 ≈ ⛷

★ **EXEL INN.** *2305 Craig Rd (54701). Phone 715/834-3193; toll-free 800/367-3935; fax 715/839-9905.* 100 rooms, 2 story. S $33.99-$45; D $44.99-$60; each additional $5. Crib free. Pet accepted. TV; cable (premium). Complimentary continental breakfast. Coffee in rooms. Restaurant adjacent open 24 hours. Check-out noon. Business services available. Exercise equipment. Cr cds: A, C, D, DS, ER, JCB, MC, V.

D 🍴 🏃 ≈ SC

★ **HAMPTON INN.** *2622 Craig Rd (54701). Phone 715/833-0003; toll-free 800/426-7866; fax 715/833-0915. www.hamptoninn.com.* 106 rooms, 3 story. S $59-$74;

D $64-$79; under 18 free; higher rates weekends. TV; cable (premium). Indoor pool; whirlpool. Complimentary continental breakfast. Restaurant opposite 6 am-11 pm. Check-out noon. Meeting rooms. Business services available. In-room modem link. Cross-country ski 2 miles. Exercise equipment. Cr cds: A, C, D, DS, MC, V.

⊡ 🖾 🖾 🕱 🖾 SC

★ **HEARTLAND INN.** *4075 Commonwealth Ave (54701). Phone 715/839-7100; toll-free 800/334-3277; fax 715/839-7050. www.heartlandinn.com.* 88 rooms, 2 story. S $65-$75; D $70-$80; each additional $5; under 17 free. Crib available. Pet accepted. Complimentary continental breakfast. Check-out noon. TV; cable (premium), VCR available. In-room modem link. Restaurant nearby. Sauna. Indoor pool, whirlpool. Cross-country ski 5 miles. Meeting rooms, business services. Sundries. Cr cds: A, C, D, DS, MC, V.

⊡ 🖾 🖾 🖾 🖾 SC

★ **MAPLE MANOR MOTEL.** *2507 S Hastings Way (54701). Phone 715/834-2618; toll-free 800/624-3763; fax 715/834-1148. www.themaplemanor.com.* 36 rooms. S $29-$35; D $35-$45; each additional $5; weekly rates. Crib $3. Pet accepted. TV; cable (premium). Complimentary full breakfast. Restaurant 6:30 am-1:30 pm. Bar to 11 pm. Check-out 11:30 am. Sundries. Many refrigerators. Picnic tables. Cr cds: A, D, DS, MC, V.

🖾 🖾 SC

★★ **QUALITY INN.** *809 W Clairmont Ave (54701). Phone 715/834-6611; toll-free 800/638-7949; fax 715/834-6611. www.qualityinn.com.* 120 rooms, 2 story. S $52-$75; D $60-$75; each additional $10; suites $69-$139; under 18 free; Sun rates. Crib free. Pet accepted. TV; cable (premium), VCR available. 2 pools, 1 indoor; whirlpool. Complimentary full breakfast Mon-Fri. Restaurant 6 am-10 pm; Fri, Sat to 10:30 pm. Room service. Bar 11-2 am; entertainment Tues-Sat. Check-out noon. Meeting rooms. Business services available. In-room modem link. Valet service. Sundries. Sauna. Recreation room. Private patios, balconies. Cr cds: A, C, D, DS, ER, JCB, MC, V.

⊡ 🖾 🖾 🖾 SC

★★ **RAMADA INN CONFERENCE CENTER.** *1202 W Clairemont Ave (54701). Phone 715/834-3181; toll-free 800/482-7829; fax 715/834-1630. www.ramada-eauclaire.com.* 233 rooms, 2-5 story. S $59-99; D $69-$109; each additional $10. Crib free. TV; cable (premium). 2 indoor pools. Restaurant. Bar; Sun from noon. Check-out 11 am. Meeting rooms. Business services available. In-room modem link. Valet service. Free airport transportation. Cr cds: A, C, D, DS, JCB, MC, V.

⊡ 🖾 🖾 🕱 🖾 🖾 🖾 🕱 🖾 🖾

★ **ROADSTAR INN.** *1151 W MacArthur Ave (54701). Phone 715/832-9731; toll-free 800/445-4667; fax 715/832-0690.* 62 rooms, 2 story. S $28-$38; D $37-$44; each additional $3; under 16 free. Crib available. TV; cable (premium). Complimentary continental breakfast. Restaurant nearby. Check-out 11 am. Some refrigerators. Cr cds: A, C, D, DS, MC, V.

⊡ 🖾 🖾

B&B/Small Inns

★★★ **FANNY HILL VICTORIAN INN.** *3919 Crescent Ave (54703). Phone 715/836-8184; toll-free 800/292-8026; fax 715/836-8180. www.fannyhill.com.* A beautiful river view is the claim to fame in this elegant inn with a classic air. Each room is appointed with Victorian touches to cap off the true romantic sense in the air. 11 rooms. Complimentary full breakfast. Check-out 11 am, check-in 2:30 pm. TV; cable (premium). Restaurant. Victorian garden overlooking Chippewa River. Dinner theater on premises. Totally nonsmoking. Cr cds: A, D, DS, MC, V. **$**

⊡ 🖾

Restaurant

★★ **FANNY HILL INN AND DINNER THEATRE.** *3919 Crescent Ave (54703). Phone 715/836-8184. www.fannyhill.com.* Continental menu. Seafood menu, Steak menu. Hours: 5-9 pm; Sun brunch 10 am-2 pm. Closed Mon, Tues (summer only); Dec 24-25. Dinner $18-$45, dinner theater Thurs-Sun. Sun brunch $14.95. Bar. Reservations accepted required for dinner theatre. Cr cds: A, D, DS, MC, V.

⊡

Edgerton

Restaurant

★★ **COACHMAN'S GOLF RESORT.** *984 County Trunk A (53534). Phone 608/884-8484. www.coachman.com.* Hours: 11 am-9 pm; Fri, Sat to 10 pm; Sun brunch 9 am-2 pm. Closed Dec 24 evening, Dec 25. Reservations accepted. Bar. Lunch $4-$7, dinner $7.75-$16.95. Sun brunch $10.50. Specializes in roast duck, charcoal-grilled steak. Salad bar. Parking. English country inn atmosphere. Guest rooms available. Cr cds: A, DS, MC, V.

⊡

Egg Harbor (D-6)

(Door County)

Pop 183 **Elev** 600 ft **Area code** 920 **Zip** 54209

Information Door County Chamber of Commerce, 1015 Green Bay Rd, PO Box 406, Sturgeon Bay 54235; 920/743-4456 or 800/527-3529

Web www.doorcountyvacations.com

This town in Door County is on the shores of Green Bay.

Special Event

Birch Creek Music Center. *3 miles E via County E.* Phone *920/868-3763.* Concert series in unique barn concert hall. Early-mid-July: percussion series; mid-July-mid-Aug: big band series. Other concerts and events through Labor Day.

Motels/Motor Lodges

★ ★ **ALPINE INN.** *7715 Alpine Rd (54209). Phone 920/868-3000.* 52 motel rooms, 3 story, 5 suites; 30 kitchen cottages. No elevator. No room phones. Mid-June-Labor Day: S $60.50-$82; D $71-$96; each additional $10; suites $96; kitchen cottages $104-$271 or $640-$1,146/wk; MAP available; family, weekly rates; golf plan; lower rates Memorial Day-mid-June, Labor Day-mid-Oct. Closed rest of year. Crib $5. Pet accepted, some restrictions. TV. Heated pool. Playground. Supervised children's activities (July-Aug); ages 3-8. Restaurant 7:30-11 am, 5:45-8:30 pm. Bar to midnight. Check-out 10 am. Meeting rooms. Business services available. Bellhops. Gift shop. Tennis. 27-hole golf, greens fee, putting green. Game room. Recreation room. Some refrigerators; microwaves available; wet bar in cottages. Picnic tables, grills. Swimming beach. Cr cds: A, DS, MC, V.

★ ★ **ASHBROOKE SUITES.** *7942 Egg Harbor Rd (54209). Phone 920/868-3113; toll-free 877/868-3113; fax 920/868-2837.* 36 rooms, 2 story. D $99-$169. Closed Dec; also weekdays Nov-Apr. Children over 13 years only. Complimentary continental breakfast. Check-out 11 am. TV; cable (premium). Some fireplaces. Exercise equipment, sauna. Indoor pool, whirlpool. Cross-country ski 5 miles. Totally nonsmoking. Cr cds: A, MC, V.

★ ★ **BAY POINT INN.** *7933 WI 42 (54209). Phone 920/868-3297; toll-free 800/707-6660; fax 920/868-2876. www.baypointinn.com.* This all-suite property overlooks Door County's beautiful, wooded shoreline. Accommodations are filled with country-home furnishings. 10 rooms, 2 story. $140-$200; each additional $12. Complimentary continental breakfast. Check-out 11 am. TV; VCR (free movies). Some fireplaces. Pool, whirlpool. Cross-country ski 6 miles. Business center. Cr cds: A, D, DS, MC, V.

★ ★ **EGG HARBOR LODGE.** *7965 WI 42 (54209). Phone 920/868-3115. www.eggharborlodge.com.* Set high above Green Bay, this hotel offers a spectacular and romantic view of the area. The lodge offers a variety of amusement and leisure options for guests to enjoy in this tranquil setting. 25 rooms, 3 story. D $111-$250; additional $25. Closed Nov-Apr. Children over 17 years only. Check-out 11 am. TV; cable (premium). Pool, whirlpool. Tennis. Cr cds: A, MC, V.

★★ **LANDING RESORT.** *7741 Egg Harbor Rd (54209). Phone 920/868-3282; toll-free 800/851-8917; fax 920/868-2689.* 60 kitchen units, 2 story. June-Aug: S $111-$125; D $134-$205; each additional $10; under 7 free; weekly rates; lower rates rest of year. Crib $5. TV; cable (premium), VCR (movies $3). 2 pools, 1 indoor; whirlpool. Playground. Restaurant nearby. Check-out 11 am. Business services available. Tennis. Game room. Microwaves. Private patios. Picnic tables, grills. On 5 wooded acres. Cr cds: DS, MC, V.

★ **LULL-ABI MOTEL.** *7928 Egg Harbor Rd (54209). Phone 920/868-3135; fax 920/868-1695. www.lullabimotel.com.* 23 rooms, 2 story, 5 suites. July-Oct: D $69-$95; each additional $15; suites $84-$95; lower rates rest of year. TV; cable (premium). Complimentary coffee in lobby. Restaurant nearby. Check-out 11 am. Whirlpool. Refrigerator, microwave, minibar in suites. Cr cds: A, DS, MC, V.

Restaurants

★ **GRANT'S OLDE STAGE STATION TAVERN.** *7778 Egg Harbor Rd (54209). Phone 920/868-3247. Oldestagesstation.com.* American menu, Italian menu. Hours: 11 am-2 am, Sun 8 am-2 am, closed Dec 25. Buffet breakfast $7.95. Dinner $4.50-$15.50. Bar. Child's meals. Former stagecoach stop (1889). Outdoor dining. Cr cds: MC, V.

★ **VILLAGE CAFE.** *7918 Egg Harbor Rd (54209). Phone 920/868-3342.* Hours: 7 am-2 pm. Breakfast $2.55-$7.50 Specializes in breakfast entrees. Lunch $4.95-$9.50. Outdoor dining on screened-in deck. Cr cds: DS, MC, V.

Elkhart Lake (F-5)

See also Fond du Lac, Sheboygan

Pop 1,019 **Elev** 945 ft **Area code** 920 **Zip** 53020

Information Chamber of Commerce, 41 E Rhine St, PO Box 425; 920/876-2922

Web www.elkhartlake.com

This lake resort, famous for its good beaches, is one of the state's oldest vacation spots.

What to See and Do

Broughton-Sheboygan County Marsh. *W7039 County SR. 1 mile NE on County J. Phone 920/876-2535.* A 14,000-acre wildlife area. Fishing, boating, canoeing; duck hunting, camping (53 sites; hookups), lodge, restaurant. Standard fees. **FREE**

Little Elkhart Lake. A 131-acre lake with heavy concentrations of pike, walleye, bass, and panfish.

Old Wade House Historic Site. *2 miles N on County P, then SW via County P and A in Greenbush. Phone 920/ 526-3271.* Restored Old Wade House (1850), early stagecoach inn. Nearby are smokehouse, blacksmith shop, mill dam site; and Jung Carriage Museum housing more than 100 restored horse and hand-drawn vehicles. Picnicking, concession. Horse-drawn carriage rides. (May-Oct, call for schedule) **$$$**

Timm House. *1600 Wisconsin Ave. Approximately 15 miles N via WI 32, NW via WI 57 in New Holstein at 1600 Wisconsin Ave. Phone 920/898-9006 or 920/898-5205.* (1892) 10-room, Victorian-style house contains period furniture; guided tours. (June-Sept, Sun; rest of year, by appointment) **$** Admission includes

> **Pioneer Corner Museum.** *Main St. Phone 920/ 898-9006.* Exhibits of early German immigrant furniture; extensive button collection; general store and post office; Panama Canal memorabilia. (June-Sept, Sun; rest of year, by appointment)

Special Event

Road America. *N7390 Highway 67. 1 1/2 miles S on WI 67. Phone 800/365-7223.* Located on 525 rolling, wooded acres; a closed-circuit 4-mi sports car racecourse with 14 turns. One of the most popular events of the season is the CART Indy race, which draws top-name race teams. Mon-Fri, June-Sept.

Resorts

★★**OSTHOFF RESORT.** *101 Osthoff Ave (53020). Phone 920/876-3366; toll-free 800/876-3399; fax 920/876-3228. www.osthoff.com.* Located on the shores of the scenic Elkhart Lake and inside the premier Oshtoff Resort, awaits a culinary delight successfully designed to please the senses while enhancing the tastebuds. Serving exquisite cuisine set amidst the beautiful scenery makes for a truly delectable meal. 145 kitchen units, 4 story. May-mid-Oct: suites $169-$369; under 18 free; family rates; package plans; weekends, holidays 2-3 day minimum (in season); higher rates special events; lower rates rest of year. Crib $5. Complimentary coffee in rooms. Check-out noon, check-in 3 pm. TV; cable (premium), VCR available (movies). cable (premium), VCR available (movies). Balconies. Fireplaces; many in-room whirlpools. Valet services, coin laundry. Restaurant 7 am-10 pm. Bar 8 am-11 pm. Supervised children's activities; ages 4-12. Playground. Snack bar. Exercise equipment, spa, massage, sauna. Sports director. Social director. Game room; recreation room. On lake. 3 pools, 1 indoor; whirlpool, poolside service. 36-hole golf privileges, pro. Lighted tennis. Cross-country ski on-site. Picnics. Lawn games. Bicycle rentals. Boats. Fishing/hunting guides; clean and store. Hiking. Snowmobiles. Waterskiing. Beauty shop. Business services. Totally nonsmoking. Cr cds: A, D, DS, MC, V.

D ⚒ ✈ 🎿 🍴 ➰ ⛷ 🐟 🏃 🏊 ⊠

★ **VICTORIAN VILLAGE ON ELKHART LAKE.** *279 Lake St (53020). Phone 920/876-3323; toll-free 877/ 860-9988; fax 920/876-3484. www.vicvill.com.* 120 units, 17 in main building. MAP, June-Sept: S, D $70-$195; children $17.95-$19.95; weekly rates; EP available; weekend packages; lower rates rest of year. Crib free. TV; VCR available. 2 pools, 1 indoor. Free supervised children's activities (June-Sept); ages 3-12. Dining room 8-10 am, 6:30-8 pm. Box lunches, snack bar, picnics. Bar 8-1 am. Check-out 11:30 am, check-in 4 pm. Convention facilities. Business services available. In-room modem link. Sports director. Miniature golf. Private beach; swimming, waterskiing; boats, motors, rowboats, canoes, sailboats, paddleboats, pontoons, jet skis. Hiking trails. Lawn games. Social director; entertainment. Game room. Recreation room. Balconies. Picnic tables. Dock. Cr cds: A, DS, MC, V.

D ⚒ 🐟 🍴 🏊 ✈ ⊠

B&B/Small Inns

★★★**52 STAFFORD.** *52 S Stafford St (53073). Phone 920/893-0552; fax 920/893-1800. www.classic innsofwisconsin.com.* Remodeled to be reminiscent of a fine Irish manor home, the luxurious furnishings and atmosphere make guests feel more like their on the Emerald Isle than in Wisconsin. 19 rooms, 4 suites, 3 story. No elevator. S, D $99.50-$149.50; suites $149.50. Complimentary continental breakfast. Check-out 10:30 am, check-in 3 pm. TV; cable. Dining room 5-9 pm; opens 9:30pm Fri, Sat. Built 1892; restored and furnished as an Irish guest house. Four-poster beds. Cr cds: A, D, DS, MC, V.

★ ★ **YANKEE HILL INN BED AND BREAKFAST.** *405 Collins St (53073). Phone 920/892-2222; fax 920/ 892-6228. www.yankeehillinn.com.* 12 rooms, 2 story. S, D $80-$113 each additional $15. Complimentary full breakfast. Check-out 11 am, check-in 3 pm. TV in common room; cable, VCR available. Restaurant nearby. Downhill/cross-country ski 1 mile. Huson house built in 1870; Gothic Italianate home. Huson house built in 1891; Queen Anne home. 2 separate houses: Henry H. Gilbert L. Totally nonsmoking. Cr cds: A, DS, MC, V.

Elkhorn (G-5)

See also Burlington, Fort Atkinson, Janesville, Waukesha

Settled 1837 **Pop** 5,337 **Elev** 1,033 ft **Area code** 262 **Zip** 53121

Information Chamber of Commerce, 114 W Court St; 262/723-5788

Web www.elkhorn-wi.org

What to See and Do

Alpine Valley Ski Resort. *W2501 County Rd D. 1 1/2 miles S off I-43 on County D and Townline Rd near East Troy. Phone 262/642-7374.* Resort has quad, five triple, three double chairlifts; four rope tows; patrol, school, rentals; snowmaking; restaurant, cafeteria, bar. Longest run 3,000 feet; vertical drop 388 feet. (Dec-mid-Mar, daily; closed Dec 24 afternoon) Night skiing. Also motel; indoor/outdoor pools, whirlpool; golf, tennis. **$$$$**

Watson's Wild West Museum. *W 4865 Potter Rd. Phone 262/723-7505.* Re-creation of general store, storytelling, western-style barbecues. (May-Oct, Tues-Sun) **$$**

Webster House. *9 E Rockwell St. Phone 262/723-4248.* Restored 19th-century home of Joseph Philbrick Webster, composer of "Sweet Bye and Bye" and "Lorena." Mounted game bird collection. (Memorial Day-mid-Oct, Wed-Sat afternoons; Apr, by appointment) **$$**

Special Events

Festival of Summer. *100 W Walworth St. Phone 262/723-5788.* Town Square Arts and crafts fair; custom car show. First weekend Aug.

Walworth County Fair. *411 E Court St. NE via WI 11 E to city limits. Phone 262/723-3228.* Agricultural fair, grandstand entertainment, and harness racing. Six days ending Labor Day.

Ellison Bay (D-6)

(Door County)

Pop 250 **Elev** 610 ft **Area code** 920 **Zip** 54210

Information Door County Chamber of Commerce, 1015 Green Bay Rd, PO Box 406, Sturgeon Bay 54235; 920/743-4456 or 800/527-3529

Web www.doorcountyvacations.com

This resort area is near the northern end of Door County. Fishing and boating are popular here; public launching ramps and charter boats are available. This is also considered a good area for scuba diving.

What to See and Do

Death's Door Bluff. Near top of peninsula between the mainland and Washington Island. According to legend, 300 Native Americans, attempting a surprise attack, were betrayed and dashed to death against the rocks. Also named because of the large number of ships lost here.

Ferry to Washington Island. *8 miles E and N on WI 42 to Northport Pier, in Gills Rock. Contact Washington Island Ferry Line. Phone 920/847-2546.* Enclosed cabin plus open deck seating. 30-minute trip. (Year-round) Also accommodates cars and bicycles (fees vary). (Daily) **$$$**

Newport State Park. *NE of town on County Rd NP. Phone 920/854-2500.* A 2,370-acre wilderness park with 11 miles of Lake Michigan shoreline. Beach. Hiking, cross-country ski trails; picnicking, backpack and winter camping. Standard fees.

Special Event

Old Ellison Bay Days. *Phone 920/743-4456.* Parade, fishing contests, fish boil, bazaars, fireworks. Late June.

Motels/Motor Lodges

★ **GRAND VIEW MOTEL.** *11885 WI 42 (54210). Phone 920/854-5450; toll-free 800/258-8208; fax 920/854-7538. www.thegrandview.com.* 28 rooms, 2 story. D $82; each additional $7; under 14, $3. Closed late Oct-early Apr. Complimentary continental breakfast. Check-out 11 am. TV; VCR available. Some fireplaces. Bicycles. Totally nonsmoking. Cr cds: A, MC, V.

★ **SHORELINE RESORT.** *12747 WI 42 (54210). Phone 920/854-2606; fax 414/854-5971. www.shorelineresort.com.* 16 rooms, 2 story. July-Aug: S, D $89-$94; kitchen unit $99; lower rates May-June, Sept-Oct. Closed rest of year. Crib free. TV. Restaurant adjacent 7 am-9 pm. Wine, beer. Check-out 11 am. Business services available. Gift shop. Refrigerators, microwaves. Balconies. Picnic tables, grills. Overlooks Green Bay. Totally nonsmoking. Cr cds: DS, MC, V.

⬚ ⬚ ⬚ ⬚

Resort

★ ★ **WAGON TRAIL.** *1041 County Rd ZZ (54210). Phone 920/854-2385; fax 920/854-5278. www.wagontrail.com.* 72 rooms in 2-story lodge, 8 suites, 16 kits; 30 houses, 8 kitchen cottages. July-Aug: S, D $109-$169; each additional $10; suites $159-$239; kitchen cottages $175-$250; houses $175-$260; under 18 free in lodge; lower rates rest of year. Crib free. TV; cable. Indoor pool; whirlpool. Playground. Restaurant (see also GRANDMA'S SWEDISH). Box lunches. Check-out 10 am, check-in 3 pm. Coin laundry. Meeting rooms. Business services available. Package store 1 mile. Gift shop. Bakery shop. Tennis. Private beach, marina. Boats; motors. Cross-country ski on site; rentals. Exercise room; sauna. Bicycle rentals. Lawn games. Game room. Some refrigerators, in-room whirlpools; microwaves available. Some patios, fireplaces in cottages. Picnic tables, grills. On shores of Rowley's Bay; extensive wooded grounds. Cr cds: DS, MC, V.

⬚ ⬚ ⬚ ⬚ ⬚ ⬚ ⬚ ⬚

B&B/Small Inns

★ ★ **HARBOR HOUSE INN.** *12666 WI 42 (54210). Phone 920/854-5196; fax 920/854-9917. www.door-country-inn.com.* 15 units, shower only, 2 story. No room phones. Closed Nov-Apr. Pet accepted, some restrictions. Complimentary continental breakfast. Check-out 10 am, check-in 3 pm. TV. Sauna. Victorian-style house built 1904; many antiques. Totally nonsmoking. Cr cds: A, MC, V. $

⬚ ⬚ ⬚

Restaurant

★ **VIKING.** *12029 WI 42 (54210). Phone 920/854-2998; fax 920/854-9281. www.doorcountyfishboil.com.* Hours: 6 am-9 pm; to 7 pm in winter. Closed Easter, Thanksgiving, Dec 25. Wine, beer. Breakfast $1.99-$8.95, lunch $2.60-$7.95, dinner $7.25-$14.95. Fish boil $11.25. Child's meals. Specializes in fresh fish, whitefish chowder. Outdoor dining. Cr cds: A, DS, MC, V.

⬚

Elm Grove

Restaurants

★ **THE CHOCOLATE SWAN.** *13320 Watertown Plank Rd (53122). Phone 262/784-7926; fax 262/*

784-7161. Hours: 11 am-6 pm; Fri to 8:30 pm; Sat from 10 am. Closed Sun; holidays. Totally nonsmoking. Dessert menu only. Desserts $1.75-$5.75. Tea room ambiance. Cr cds: C, MC, V.

★ ★ **ELM GROVE INN.** *13275 Watertone Plank Rd (53122). Phone 262/782-7090. www.elmgroveinn.com.* Continental menu. Hours: 11:30 am-2 pm, 5-9:30 pm; Sat from 5 pm. Closed Sun; Jan. 1, Thanksgiving, Dec. 25. Lunch $9-$14, dinner $22-$35. Bar to midnight. Reservations accepted. Cr cds: A, D, DS, MC, V.

⬚

Ephraim (D-6)

(Door County)

Founded 1853 **Pop** 261 **Elev** 600 ft **Area code** 920 **Zip** 54211

Information Door County Chamber of Commerce, 1015 Green Bay Rd, PO Box 406, Sturgeon Bay 54235; 920/743-4456 or 800/527-3529

Web www.doorcountyvacations.com

Moravian colonists founded the second Ephraim here after leaving the first town of that name, now a part of Green Bay; a monument at the harbor commemorates the landing of Moravians in 1853. The village is now a quaint resort community and a center for exploration of the north and west shores of Door County.

Special Event

Fyr-Bal Fest. Phone 920/854-4989. Scandinavian welcome to summer. Fish boil, Blessing of the Fleet, art fair, lighting of the bonfires on the beach at dusk, coronation of Viking Chieftain. Three days mid-June.

Motels/Motor Lodges

★ ★ **EDGEWATER RESORT MOTEL.** *10040 Hwy 42 (54211). Phone 920/854-2734; fax 920/854-4127.* 38 units, 2 story. July-Aug, Sept-Oct (weekends): S, D $90-$146; lower rates May-June. Closed Nov-Apr. Crib free. TV; cable (premium). Heated pool. Restaurant. Check-out 11 am. Refrigerators. On Green Bay. Cr cds: DS, MC, V.

⬚ ⬚

★ **EPHRAIM GUEST HOUSE.** *3042 Cedar St (54211). Phone 920/854-2319; toll-free 800/589-8423. www.ephraim guesthouse.com.* 14 rooms, 2 story. D $90-$150; each additional $10. Check-out 11 am. TV; cable (premium), VCR. Some fireplaces. Laundry services. Whirlpool. Cross-country ski 3 miles. Bay 1 block. Cr cds: A, DS, MC, V.

⬚ ⬚ ⬚ ⬚ ⬚ SC

★ **EPHRAIM MOTEL.** *10407 Water St (54211). Phone 920/854-5959. www.ephraimmotel.com.* 28 rooms, 2 story. July-mid-Aug, Oct: S, D $80-$85 each additional $10; under 6 free; lower rates May-June, Sept. Closed rest of year. Crib free. TV; cable. Heated pool. Complimentary continental breakfast. Restaurants nearby. Check-out 11 am. Meeting room. Refrigerators, microwaves. Balconies. Cr cds: MC, V.

⬛ ⬛

★★ **EPHRAIM SHORES MOTEL.** *10018 Water St (54211). Phone 920/854-2371; fax 920/854-4926. www.ephraimshores.com.* 46 rooms, 2 story. D $85-$100; each additional $10; suites $180; under 12, $4; 12-18, $8; under 4 free. Crib $3. TV; cable. Indoor pool; whirlpool. Playground. Coffee in rooms. Restaurant 8 am-8 pm. Check-out 10:30 am. Business services available. Sundries. Game room. Exercise equipment. Recreation room. Bicycles. Refrigerators; some in-room whirlpools. Sun deck. On Green Bay, overlooking Eagle Harbor. Totally nonsmoking. Cr cds: MC, V.

⬛ ⬛ ⬛ ⬛

★ **EVERGREEN BEACH.** *9944 Water St (54211). Phone 920/854-2831; toll-free 800/420-8130; fax 920/854-9222. www.evergreenbeach.com.* 30 rooms, 1-2 story. D $99-$112; each additional $6-$10. Closed late Oct-late May. Complimentary continental breakfast. Check-out 10:30 am. TV; cable (premium). On Eagle Harbor; private beach. Pool. Lawn games. Totally nonsmoking. Cr cds: A, DS, MC, V.

⬛ ⬛ ⬛

★ **PINE GROVE MOTEL.** *10080 WI 42 (54211). Phone 920/854-2321; toll-free 800/292-9494; fax 920/854-2511.* 44 rooms, 2 story. D $88-$103; each additional $12. Closed Nov-Apr. Check-out 11 am. TV; cable (premium). Laundry services. Exercise equipment. Game room. On bay; private sand beach. Indoor pool, whirlpool. Cr cds: DS, MC, V.

⬛ ⬛ ⬛

★ **SOMERSET INN AND SUITES.** *10401 N Water St (54211). Phone 920/854-1819; toll-free 800/809-1819; fax 920/854-9087. www.somersetinndc.com.* 20 rooms, 2 story. D $79-$99; each additional $10. Check-out 11 am. TV; cable (premium). 2 pools, 1 indoor, whirlpool. Cross-country ski 1 mile. Totally nonsmoking. Cr cds: DS, MC, V.

⬛ ⬛ ⬛ ⬛

★ **TROLLHAUGEN LODGE.** *10176 WI 42 (54211). Phone 920/854-2713; toll-free 800/854-4118. trollhaugenlodge.com.* 13 rooms, showers only. July-Aug, 3 weekends in Oct: S, D $49-$99; kitchen cottage $125; under 2 free; weekly rates; weekends (2-day minimum); higher rates special events; lower rates Sept-Oct, mid-Apr-

June. Closed rest of year. TV; cable, VCR available. Complimentary continental breakfast. Restaurant nearby. Check-out 10 am. Refrigerators; many microwaves; some fireplaces. Some balconies. Picnic tables, grills. Cr cds: DS, MC, V.

⬛ ⬛ ⬛ ⬛

B&B/Small Inns

★★★ **EAGLE HARBOR INN.** *9914 Water St (54211). Phone 920/854-2121; toll-free 800/324-5427; fax 920/854-2121. www.eagleharbor.com.* Guests get a warm feeling when approaching this inn with classical styling. Enjoy the serenity of the wooded areas surrounding the hotel, or take a stroll down to the beach nearby. 9 inn rooms, 1-2 story, 32 suites. S, D $64-149; suites, July-Aug: $165-$189; lower rates rest of year. TV; cable (premium), VCR. Indoor pool. Playground. Full breakfast for inn guests. Restaurant nearby. Check-out 10 am, check-in 3 pm. Meeting room. Business services available. In-room modem link. Cross-country ski 1 mile. Exercise equipment; sauna. Massage. Microwaves available. In-room whirlpool, fireplace in suites. Picnic tables, grills. Opposite beach. Decorated with turn-of-the-century antiques. Cr cds: DS, MC, V.

⬛ ⬛ ⬛ ⬛ ⬛ ⬛ ⬛ ⬛ ⬛ ⬛

★★ **EPHRAIM INN.** *9994 Pioneer Ln (54211). Phone 920/854-4515; fax 920/854-1859. www.theephraiminn.com.* 16 rooms, 2 story. S, D $135. Closed Nov-Apr (Mon-Thurs). Children over 12 years only. TV. Complimentary full breakfast. Check-out 11 am, check-in 3 pm. Opposite beach. Overlooks Green Bay. Each room has different theme. Cr cds: A, DS, MC, V.

⬛ ⬛ ⬛ ⬛ ⬛ ⬛

★ **FRENCH COUNTRY INN BED AND BREAKFAST.** *3052 Spruce Ln (54211). Phone 920/854-4001; fax 920/854-4001.* 7 rooms in main building, 5 share bath rooms, 1 cottage. kitchen units, 2 story. No A/C. May-Oct: S, D $67-$94; kitchen cottage $89-$99; weekly rates; lower rates rest of year. Children over 12 years only in main building. Complimentary continental breakfast. Check-out 11 am, check-in 3 pm. TV in cottage. Restaurant nearby. Cross-country ski 1 mile. Built 1912. Near bay. Totally nonsmoking. Cr cds: A, MC, V.

⬛ ⬛

Restaurant

★ **OLD POST OFFICE RESTAURANT.** *10040 Water St (54211). Phone 920/854-4034.* Hours: 7:30-11 am, 5:30-8 pm. Closed Nov-Apr. Breakfast $2.50-$7.50. Child's meals. Reservations accepted. Fish boil $15.50. Cr cds: MC, V.

⬛

Fish Creek (D-6)

(Door County)

Pop 200 **Elev** 583 ft **Area code** 920 **Zip** 54212

Information Door County Chamber of Commerce, 1015 Green Bay Rd, PO Box 406, Sturgeon Bay 54235; 920/743-4456 or 800/52-RELAX

Web www.doorcountyvacations.com

This picturesque Green Bay resort village, with its many interesting shops, is in Door County.

What to See and Do

Peninsula State Park. N off WI 42. Phone 920/868-3258. A 3,763-acre park with nine miles of waterfront includes sandy and cobblestone beaches; caves, cliffs; observation tower. Swimming, fishing, boating, waterskiing; hiking, bicycle trails; cross-country skiing, snowmobiling, picnic grounds, playground, concession, camping (471 sites, hookups, dump station). Naturalist programs. Eighteen-hole golf course (mid-May-mid-Oct). Standard fees. $$$

Special Event

American Folklore Theatre. *Peninsula State Park Amphitheater. Phone 920/868-1100.* Original folk musical productions based on American lore and literature. Limited fall season. Mon-Sat, July-Aug.

Motels/Motor Lodges

★ **BEOWULF LODGE.** *3775 WI 42 (54212). Phone 920/868-2046; toll-free 800/433-7592; fax 920/868-2381. www.beowulflodge.com.* 60 rooms, 2 story, 9 suites, 26 kitchens May-Oct: S, D $60-$90; suites $120-$140; kitchen units $95; lower rates rest of year. Crib $10. TV; cable, VCR available. Indoor pool; whirlpool. Complimentary coffee in lobby. Restaurant nearby. Check-out 10 am. Coin laundry. Business services available. Tennis. Downhill ski 20 miles; cross-country ski on site. Game room. Some refrigerators; microwaves available. Picnic tables, grills. Cr cds: DS, MC, V.

★ **BY THE BAY MOTEL.** *Hwy 42 (54212). Phone 920/868-3456.* 15 rooms, 2 story. Mid-June-Labor Day and Oct: S, D $84-$120; each additional $8; some lower rates off-season. Closed Nov-Apr. Crib $5. TV; cable (premium). Restaurant adjacent 7 am-9 pm. Check-out 10:30 am. Business services available. Public beach opposite. Totally nonsmoking. Cr cds: DS, MC, V.

★ **CEDAR COURT.** *9429 Cedar St (54212). Phone 920/868-3361; fax 920/868-2541. www.cedarcourt.com.* 11 rooms, 2 story, 9 kitchen cottages. Late June-Aug: S $62-$85; D $78-$120; suites $115; cottages $115-$235; each additional $5-$10; under 12 free; weekly, 3-day weekend rates; ski plan; honeymoon package; lower rates rest of year. Crib free. Complimentary coffee in rooms. Check-out 11 am. TV; cable, VCR available. Balconies. Refrigerators; microwaves available; some in-room whirlpools. Restaurant nearby. Heated pool. Downhill ski 20 miles; cross-country ski 1 mile. Picnic tables. Business services. Totally nonsmoking. Cr cds: DS, MC, V.

★ **HOMESTEAD.** *4006 WI 42 (54212). Phone 920/868-3748; toll-free 800/686-6621; fax 920/868-2874. www.homesteadsuites.com.* 33 rooms, 2 story. D $79-$129; each additional $10; under 12 free; package plans. Complimentary continental breakfast. Check-out 11 am. TV; cable (premium), VCR available (movies $4). In-room modem link. Exercise equipment, sauna. Indoor pool, whirlpool. Cross-country ski adjacent. Bike trail adjacent. Adjacent to Peninsula State Park. Cr cds: DS, MC, V.

★ **JULIE'S PARK CAFE AND MOTEL.** *4020 WI 42 (54212). Phone 920/868-2999; fax 920/868-9837. www.juliesmotel.com.* 12 units. Late-June-late Aug: S, D $75-$92; lower rates rest of year. Crib free. Pet accepted, some restrictions. TV; cable (premium). Restaurant 7 am-10 pm. Check-out 10 am. Cross-country ski adjacent. Gazebo. Totally nonsmoking. Cr cds: A, MC, V.

B&B/Small Inns

★ ★ **BEACH HOUSE.** *4117 Main St (54212). Phone 920/868-2444; fax 920/868-9833. www.thorphoseinn.com.* 4 inn rooms, 9 kitchen units. Air Condition Rooms. July-Aug:D $95-$195; kitchen cottages $85-$185. Complimentary continental breakfast (inn guests). Check-out 11 am, check-in 3 pm. TV; cable (premium), VCR available. Some in-room whirlpools, fireplaces; microwaves available. Restaurant nearby. Downhill ski 20 miles; cross-country ski 5 blocks. Bikes. Built 1902; many antiques, library. Totally nonsmoking (inn). Cr cds: A, MC, V.

★ ★ **HARBOR GUEST HOUSE.** *9484 Spruce St (54212). Phone 920/868-2284; fax 920/868-1535. www.doorcounty.org/lodging/hgh.html.* 7 kitchen suites (1-2-bedrm), 2 story. July-mid-Oct: kitchen suites $165-$225; family rates; lower rates rest of year. Crib $5. TV; cable (premium). Complimentary coffee in rooms. Restaurant nearby. Check-out 10 am, check-in 3 pm.

Cross-country ski on site. Boat slips available. Microwaves, fireplaces. Some balconies. Grills. View of Green Bay. Cr cds: MC, V.

D ⬆ 🏊 ⊠

★ ★ **SETTLEMENT COURTYARD INN.** *9126 WI 42 (54212). Phone 920/868-3524; fax 920/868-3048. www.settlemeninn.com.* 32 kitchen units, 2 story. July-Oct: S $64-$116; D $119-$224; each additional $5-$10; suites $129-$174; under 4 free; weekly rates; lower rates rest of year. Check-out 11 am, check-in 3 pm. TV; VCR available. Fireplaces; microwaves available. Restaurant nearby. Cross-country ski on site. Hiking trails. Continental breakfast in season. Cr cds: A, DS, ER, MC, V.

D ⬆ 🏊 🍴 🎿 🚶 ⊠

★ ★ ★ **THE WHISTLING SWAN INN.** *4192 Main St (54212). Phone 920/868-3442; toll-free 888/277-4289; fax 920/868-1703.* This quaint country-style inn has a lot to offer in addition to a comfortable stay. The boutiques in the lobby level draw many people looking for fine clothing and more for the whole family. 7 rooms, 2 suites, 2 story. D, suites $119-$162. Complimentary full breakfast. Check-out 11 am, check-in 3 pm. TV available; cable (premium). Renovated country inn (1887); antique furnishings. Totally nonsmoking. Cr cds: A, DS, MC, V.

⬆ 🎿 🏊 🚶 ⊠

★ ★ **WHITE GULL INN.** *4225 Main St (54212). Phone 920/868-3517; fax 920/868-2367. www.whitegullinn.com.* 13 rooms, 1-2 story. D $132-$256 Cottages $194-$325: Check-out 11 am, check-in 3 pm. TV; in cottages; cable (premium), VCR (free movies). Fireplaces. Restaurant. Airport transportation. Cross-country ski 1 mile. Built 1896; library, antiques. Totally nonsmoking. Cr cds: A, C, D, DS, MC, V.

D 🏊 🍴 ⊠ 🚶 ✈

Restaurants

★ ★ **C AND C SUPPER CLUB.** *WI 42 (54212). Phone 920/868-3412.* Seafood menu, Steak menu. Hours: 4:45-10 pm; Nov-Apr hours vary. Dinner $9.75-$21.99. Bar 11-2 am. Entertainment Fri, Sat Summertime only. Child's meals. Reservations accepted. Cr cds: D, DS, MC, V.

D

★ **COOKERY.** *WI 42 (54212). Phone 920/868-3634; fax 920/868-2831. www.cookeryfishcreek.com.* Hours: 7 am-9 pm; Nov-Apr, weekends only. Breakfast $3.95-$7.95, lunch $5.99-$7.95, dinner $9.95-$13.95. Children's menu, Totally nonsmoking. Cr cds: MC, V.

D

★ **PELLETIER'S.** *4199 Main St (54212). Phone 920/868-3313.* Hours: 7:30 am-8 pm. Closed Nov-mid-May. Reservations accepted; required fish boil. Wine, beer.

Breakfast $2.25-$6.25, lunch $3.25-$9.95. Fish boil dinner: $11.25. Specializes in crêpes, fish boil. Own soups. Parking. Patio dining. Nautical décor. Family-owned.

D

★ ★ **SUMMERTIME.** *1 N Spruce St (54212). Phone 920/868-3738. www.thesummertime.com.* Specializes in South African-style barbecue ribs , Greek menu, Italian menu. Hours: 7:30 am-10 pm; Fri, Sat to 11 pm. Breakfast $1.95-$6.95, lunch $2.95-$7.95, dinner $6.95-$39. Reservations accepted. Outdoor dining. Cr cds: A, MC, V.

D SC

★ ★ **WHITE GULL INN.** *4225 Main St (54212). Phone 920/868-3517. www.whitegullinn.com.* Hours: 7:30 am-2:30 pm, 5-8 pm. Closed Thanksgiving, Dec 25. Reservations accepted. Wine, beer. Breakfast $4-$8, lunch $4-$8, dinner $14.95-$19. Fish boil Wed, Fri-Sun evenings: $14.95. Child's meals. Parking. Turn-of-the-century décor. Family-owned. Cr cds: A, D, DS, MC, V.

D

Fond du Lac (F-5)

See also Green Lake, Oshkosh, Waupun

Settled 1835 **Pop** 42,000 **Elev** 760 ft **Area code** 920

Information Convention & Visitors Bureau, 171 S Pioneer Rd St; 920/923-3010 or 800/937-9123, ext 71

Web www.fdl.com

Located at the foot of Lake Winnebago and named by French explorers in the 1600s, Fond du Lac, "foot of the lake," was an early outpost for fur trading, later achieving prominence as a lumbering center and railroad city.

What to See and Do

Galloway House and Village. *336 Old Pioneer Rd. Phone 920/922-6390.* Restored 30-room Victorian mansion with four fireplaces, carved woodwork, and stenciled ceilings; village of late 1800s; 24 buildings including 1-room schoolhouse, print shop, general store, operating gristmill, museum with collection of Native American artifacts; war displays; other area artifacts. (Memorial Day-Labor Day, daily; rest of Sept, Sat and Sun) **$$$**

Kettle Moraine State Forest, Northern Unit. *17 miles SE on US 45 to Waucousta, then E on County F. Phone 262/626-2116.* The forest is being developed as part of Ice Age National Scientific Reserve (see DEVI. The forest's 30,000 acres include Long and Mauthe Lake Recreation Areas, scenic Kettle Moraine Dr. Swimming, waterskiing, fishing, boating, canoeing. There are 58 miles of hiking and bridle trails. Snowmobiling, cross-country skiing, picnicking, camping available

(338 sites, hookups, dump station), incl primitive and winter camping. Observation tower. Forest Supervisor is in Campbellsport. Standard fees. (Daily) **$$$$** Also here is

> **Ice Age Visitors Center.** *N2875 Hwy 67. Phone 920/533-8322.* Films, slides, and panoramas show visitors how glaciers molded Wisconsin's terrain; naturalists answer questions. (Daily; closed Jan 1, Dec 25) **FREE**

Lakeside Park. *650 N Main St. N end of Main St. Phone 920/989-6846.* A 400-acre park on Lake Winnebago. Boating (ramps, canoe rentals); petting zoo, playground, rides, picnic area; lighthouse. (June-Aug, daily) (See SPECIAL EVENT) **FREE**

Lake Winnebago. *US 41 and N Main. Phone 800/937-9123 x35.* Boating, sailing, windsurfing, waterskiing, fishing, ice-fishing, sturgeon spearing (last two weeks in Feb), ice-boating, snowmobiling.

⭐ **Octagon House.** *276 Linden St. Phone 920/922-1608.* A 12-room octagonal house built in 1856 by Isaac Brown and designed by Orson Fowler has hidden rm, secret passageways, and an underground tunnel. Period antiques, dolls, clothing; native American display, ship collection, spinning wheel demonstrations. Carriage house has pony carriages. 90-minute guided tours Mon, Wed, Fri, afternoons. **$$$**

Silver Wheel Manor. *N 6221 County K; E on WI 23, S on County K. Phone 920/922-1608.* A 30-room mansion that was once part of 400-acre farm established 1860; antique furnishings; collection of more than 1,200 dolls and accessories; model trains; circus room, photography room. (Mon, Wed, Fri, Sat, mornings) **$$$**

St. Paul's Cathedral. *Phone 920/921-3363.* Episcopal. English Gothic limestone structure with wood carvings from Oberammergau, Germany, rare ecclesiastical artifacts, and a variety of stained-glass windows; cloister garden. Self-guided tours (by appointment).

Special Event

Walleye Weekend Festival and Mercury Marine National Walleye Tournament. *Lakeside Park. 555 N Park Ave. Phone 920/923-6555.* Fish fry, food, entertainment, sports competions. Second weekend June.

Motels/Motor Lodges

⭐ **DAYS INN.** *107 N Pioneer Rd (54935). Phone 920/923-6790; toll-free 800/329-7466; fax 920/923-6790. www.daysinn.com.* 59 rooms, 2 story. S $39.95-$45.95; D $55.95-$60.95; each additional $6; under 17 free. Crib free. Pet accepted; $3. TV; cable (premium). Complimentary continental breakfast. Check-out 11 am. Business services available. In-room modem link. Cr cds: A, C, D, DS, JCB, MC, V.

D ⮝ ⮠ SC

⭐ **ECONO LODGE.** *649 W Johnson St (54935). Phone 920/923-2020; fax 920/929-9352. www.econolodge.com.* 48 rooms, 2 story. S $44-$64; D $44-$65; each additional $5; higher rates special events. Crib $3. TV; cable (premium). Indoor pool; whirlpool. Complimentary continental breakfast. Restaurant nearby. Check-out 11 am. Business services available. Refrigerators. Cr cds: A, C, D, DS, JCB, MC, V.

D ⮝ ⮠ SC

⭐⭐ **HOLIDAY INN.** *625 W Rolling Meadows Dr (54937). Phone 920/923-1440; fax 920/923-1366. www.holiday-inn.com.* 141 rooms, 2 story. S $72-$115; D $82-$125; under 19 free. Crib free. Pet accepted. TV; cable (premium), VCR available. Indoor pool; whirlpool. Coffee in rooms. Restaurant 7 am-10 pm. Room service. Bar 11-1 am. Check-out 11 am. Coin laundry. Meeting rooms. In-room modem link. Bellhops. Valet service. Sundries. Free airport transportation. Exercise equipment; sauna. Recreation room. Golf course opposite. Microwaves available. Cr cds: A, D, DS, JCB, MC, V.

D ⮝ ⮠ ⮠ ⮠ ⮠ SC

⭐ **NORTHWAY MOTEL.** *301 S Pioneer Rd (54935). Phone 920/921-7975; toll-free 800/850-7339; fax 920/921-7983. www.visitwisconsin.com/fondulac.* 19 rooms. June-Oct: S $30-$35; D $49-$55; each additional $5; under 12 free; weekly rates; higher rates special events; lower rates rest of year. Crib $4. Pet accepted; $7. TV; cable. Complimentary continental breakfast. Coffee in rooms. Check-out 11 am. Cross-country ski 10 miles. Refrigerators, microwaves available. Picnic tables, grills. Cr cds: A, DS, MC, V.

D ⮝ ⮠ ⮠ SC

⭐⭐ **RAMADA PLAZA.** *1 N Main St (54935). Phone 920/923-3000; toll-free 800/272-6232; fax 920/923-2561. www.ramada.com.* 132 rooms, 8 story. Mid-June-late Aug: S $59-$79; D $59-$89; each additional $10; suites $95-$200; under 18 free; higher rates special events; lower rates rest of year. Crib free. TV; cable (premium). Complimentary coffee in rooms. Restaurant 6:30 am-2:30 pm, 5-9 pm. Bar; entertainment weekends. Check-out 11 am. Meeting rooms. Business services available. In-room modem link. Cross-country ski 2 miles. Exercise equipment; sauna. Massage. Indoor pool; whirlpool. Refrigerator, wet bar in suites; microwaves available. Luxury level. Cr cds: A, C, D, DS, JCB, MC, V.

D ⮠ ⮠ ⮠ SC ⮠

Restaurants

⭐ **SALTY'S SEAFOOD AND SPIRITS.** *503 N Park Ave (54935). Phone 920/922-9940.* Specialties: seafood, prime rib, steak. Salad bar. Hours: 11 am-10 pm; weekends to 11 pm. Closed holidays. Lunch, dinner $3.95-$12.95. Bar. Nautical decor. Cr cds: A, DS, MC, V.

D

★ ★ **SCHREINER'S.** *168 N Pioneer Rd (54935). Phone 920/922-0590; fax 920/922-1992. www.fdlchowder.com.* Hours: 6:30 am-8:30 pm; mid-July-mid-Aug to 10 pm. Closed Thanksgiving; Dec 24 eve, 25; Easter. Breakfast $2.50-$4, lunch, dinner $5.50-$10. Children's menu. Cr cds: A, DS, MC, V.

D

Fontana (H-5)

See also Beloit, Elkhorn, Lake Geneva

Pop 1,635 **Elev** 900 ft **Area code** 262 **Zip** 53125

Located on the western shore of Geneva Lake in territory once occupied by the Potawatomi, this town was named for its many springs.

Resort

★ ★ ★ **ABBEY RESORT & FONTANA SPA.** *269 Fontana Blvd (53125). Phone 262/275-6811; toll-free 800/558-2405; fax 414/275-3264. www.theabbeyresort.com.* Situated on 90 lush acres and set on the water's edge, this elegant resort and spa delights guests with its restaurants, exquisitely prepared dishes, crisp linens and wonderful selection of wines to complement any meal. 334 rooms, 2 story, 20 condos. S, D $99-$195; each additional $12; under 12 free; suites $175-$280; kitchen units $280; package plans. Crib free. Check-out noon, check-in 4 pm. TV; cable, VCR. In-room modem link. Private patios and balconies (condos). Valet services. Dining rooms 7 am-10 pm. Bar 11-2 am. Room service. Snack bar. Supervised children's activities; ages 5-12. Exercise equipment, sauna. Full-service spa. Massage. Game room, recreation room. On Geneva Lake. 5 pools, 2 indoor; whirlpool, poolside service. Recreation director. Tennis. Downhill ski 10 miles; cross-country ski 2 miles. Lawn games. Bicycles. Waterskiing, marina, boats. Barber, beauty shop. Airport transportation. Business center. Convention facilities. Concierge. Gift shop. Cr cds: A, C, D, DS, MC, V.

D 🏊 🚣 ⛵ 🎿 ⛷ 🚶 🎾 ✈

Fort Atkinson (G-5)

See also Janesville, Madison, Watertown

Settled 1836 **Pop** 10,227 **Elev** 790 ft **Area code** 920 **Zip** 53538

Information Chamber of Commerce, 244 N Main St; 920/563-3210 or 888/733-3678

Web www.fortchamber.com

In 1872, William Dempster Hoard, later governor of Wisconsin, organized the Wisconsin State Dairyman's Association here. He toured the area, drumming up support by preaching the virtues of the cow, "the foster mother of the human race." More than any other man, Hoard was responsible for Wisconsin's development as a leading dairy state. Nearby are Lake Koshkonong, a popular recreation area, and Lake Ripley, where Ole Evinrude invented the outboard motor in 1908.

What to See and Do

Hoard Historical Museum. *407 Merchants Ave. Phone 920/563-7769.* Housed in historic home (1864), museum features pioneer history and archaeology of the area; period rooms, antique quilt, bird room, old costumes and clothing, antique firearms; reference library; permanent and changing displays. (June-Aug, Tues-Sun; rest of year, Tues-Sat; closed Thanksgiving, Dec 25) **FREE** Also here is

Dwight Foster House. *407 Merchants Ave. Phone 920/563-7769.* (1841) Historic home of city's founder; five-room, two-story Greek Revival frame house is furnished in the period, with many original pieces. (June-Aug, Tues-Sun; rest of year, Tues-Sat; closed Thanksgiving, Dec 25) **FREE**

National Dairy Shrine Museum. *407 Merchant's Ave. Phone 920/563-7769.* Traces development of the dairy industry for past 100 years. Collection of memorabilia; exhibits incl old creamery, replica of early dairy farm kitchen, old barn, and milk-hauling equipment. Multimedia presentation. (June-Aug, Tues-Sun; rest of year, Tues-Sat; closed Thanksgiving, Dec 25) **FREE**

Panther Intaglio. *1236 Riverside Dr.* Panther-shaped prehistoric earthwork; dates to A.D. 1000. Discovered by Increase Lapham in 1850.

Motel/Motor Lodge

★ **SUPER 8 FORT ATKINSON.** *225 S Water St E (53538). Phone 920/563-8444; toll-free 800/800-8000; fax 920/563-8444. www.super8.com.* 40 rooms, 3 story. S $47-$49; D $50-$55; each additional $10; suites $75; under 12 free; higher rates wkends, holidays, special events. Crib $5. Pet accepted, some restrictions. TV; cable. Complimentary continental breakfast. Restaurant nearby. Bar 4 pm-midnight; Fri, Sat to 1 am; entertainment. Check-out 11 am. Meeting rooms. Sundries. Downhill/cross-country ski 5 miles. Overlooks Rock River. Patio and deck chairs on riverbank. Cr cds: A, C, D, DS, MC, V.

D 🐾 🛏 ⛷ 🏊 SC

Fox Point

Restaurants

★ ★ ★ **MANIACI'S CAFE SICILIANO.** *6904 N Santa Monica Blvd (53217). Phone 414/352-5757.* After nearly 25 years under the watchful eyes of Arthur and Rose Maniaci, chef Anthony Mandella is now at the helm of this intimate Italian-Sicilian restaurant known for caring service. Continental menu. Specialties: veal, fish, pasta. Own pasta. Hours: 4-10 pm. Closed Sun; holidays; also week of July 4. Dinner $17.50-$32.95. Wine cellar. Service bar. Family-owned. Children's menu. Reservations accepted. Sicilian decor with brick columns, tile floors. Cr cds: A, MC, V.

★ ★ **NORTH SHORE BISTRO.** *8649 N Port Washington Rd (53217). Phone 414/351-6100; fax 414/351-1443.* Hours: 11 am-10 pm; Sat to 11 pm; Sun from 4 pm. Closed Thanksgiving Day, Dec. 25. Lunch $6-$9.25, dinner $6-$24.95. Bar. Casual bistro atmosphere. Reservations accepted . Outdoor dining. Cr cds: A, MC, V.

Ⓓ

Galesville (E-2)

See also La Crosse

Pop 1,278 **Elev** 712 ft **Area code** 608 **Zip** 54630

What to See and Do

State parks. Fishing, boating, canoeing; hiking, picnicking, playgrounds, camping (electric hookups, dump stations). Standard fees.

Merrick State Park. *S2965 WI 35. 22 miles NW on WI 35. Phone 608/687-4936.* A 324-acre park along Mississippi River. Canoeing; camping. (Daily)

Perrot State Park. *W26247 Sullivan Rd. 2 miles W on Trempealeau. Phone 608/534-6409.* Trempealeau Mtn, a beacon for voyageurs for more than 300 years, is in this 1,425-acre park. Nicolas Perrot set up winter quarters here in 1686; a French fort was built on the site in 1731. Cross-country skiing. Vistas, bluffs. Standard fees. (Daily)

Motel/Motor Lodge

★**SONIC MOTEL.** *21278 W State St (54630). Phone 608/582-2281.* 24 rooms, 2 kitchens S $36.95; D $40.95-$48.95. Crib free. TV; cable (premium). Complimentary coffee in rooms. Check-out 11 am. Gift shop. Cross-country ski 5 miles. Cr cds: MC, V.

Germantown

Restaurants

★ ★ **JERY'S OLD TOWN INN.** *N 116 W 15841 Main St (53022). Phone 262/251-4455; fax 262/250-2282.* Hours: 4-10 pm; Fri, Sat to 10:30 pm; Sun to 9 pm. Reservations accepted. Bar. Dinner $12.95-$24.95. Child's meals. Specialty: barbecue baby-back pork ribs. Own baking. Casual dining; pig theme throughout. Cr cds: A, MC, V.

Ⓓ

★ ★ **LOHMANN'S STEAK HOUSE.** *W183 N9609 Appleton Ave (53051). Phone 262/251-8430; fax 262/251-8432. www.foodspot.com/lohmanns.* Hours: 11:30 am-2 pm, 5-10 pm. Closed Sun; holidays. Lunch $4.50-$10.25, dinner $10.50-$42. Bar. Children's menu. Reservations accepted Reservations accepted. Cr cds: A, D, DS, MC, V.

Ⓓ

Green Bay (E-5)

Pop 96,466 **Elev** 594 ft **Area code** 920

Information Visitor & Convention Bureau, 1901 S Oneida St, 54307-0596; 920/494-9507 or 888/867-3342

Web www.greenbay.org

The strategic location that made Green Bay a trading center as far back as 1669 today enables this port city to handle nearly 1.8 million tons of cargo a year. The region was claimed for the King of France in 1634, and was named La Baye in 1669 when it became the site of the mission of St. Francis. It then saw the rise of fur trading, a series of Native American wars, and French, British, and US conflicts. Although it became part of the United States in 1783, Green Bay did not yield to American influence until after the War of 1812, when agents of John Jacob Astor gained control of the fur trade. Oldest settlement in the state, Green Bay is a paper and cheese producing center as well as a hub for health care and insurance. It is also famous for its professional football team, the Green Bay Packers.

What to See and Do

Children's Museum of Green Bay. *320 N Adams St. Upper Level Washington Commons Mall. Phone 920/432-4397.* Hands-on exhibits and interactive programs. Areas incl the Hospital, Submarine, Fire Truck, Police Station, Bank, and Grocery Store. (Daily; closed holidays) **$$**

Green Bay Botanical Gardens. *2600 Larsen Rd. Phone 920/490-9457.* Educational and recreational facility. Formal rose garden; children's garden; four season garden; gift shop. (Tues-Sun, daily) **$**

Green Bay Packer Hall of Fame. *855 Lombardi Ave. Brown County Expo Centre, across from Lambeau Field. Phone 920/499-4281 or 888/442-7225.* History of team from 1919 to present; a unique collection of multimedia presentations, memorabilia, hands-on activites, NFL films. (Daily; closed holidays) **$$$**

Green Bay Packers (NFL). *1265 Lombardi Ave. Phone 920/496-5700.* Lambeau Field,

Hazelwood Historic Home Museum. *1008 S Monroe Ave. Phone 920/437-1840.* (1837-1838) Greek Revival house where state constitution was drafted. (Memorial Day-Labor Day, Mon-Fri; rest of year, by appointment) **$$**

Heritage Hill State Park. *2640 S Webster. Phone 920/448-5150.* 40-acre living history museum; complex of 26 historical buildings illustrate the development of northeast Wisconsin. (Memorial Day-Labor Day, Tues-Sun; Dec, Sat-Sun) Christmas festival (Fri-Sun in Dec). **$$$**

National Railroad Museum. *2285 S Broadway. Phone 920/437-7623.* Seventy-five steam locomotives, diesels, and cars; train rides; exhibit building; theater; gift shop. (May-mid-Oct, daily; weekdays rest of year)

Neville Public Museum. *210 Museum Pl. Phone 920/448-4460.* Science, history, and art collections and exhibits. (Daily; closed Mon, holidays) **DONATION**

Northeastern Wisconsin Zoo. *4378 Reforestation Rd. Phone 920/434-7841.* Over 43 acres of animals in natural settings. Children's zoo. Exhibits include Wisconsin Trail, International and Northern trail. (Daily) **$**

Oneida Nation Museum. *W892 EE Rd, 7 miles SW on US 41 to County Rd EE. Phone 920/869-2768.* Permanent and "hands-on" exhibits tell story of Oneida Nation. (Tues-Fri; closed holidays) **$**

University of Wisconsin-Green Bay. *2420 Nicolet Dr. Phone 920/465-2000.* (1965) 5,000 students. Campus built on 700 acres. Weidner Center for the Performing Arts. Also here is Cofrin Memorial Arboretum; 9-hole golf course (fee); Bayshore picnic area. Tours of campus (by appointment).

Special Event

Waterboard Warriors. *County Rd ZZ S Wrightstown County Park. Brown County Fairgrounds. Phone 920/468-1967.* Waterski shows performed by skiers from the area. Tues and Thurs (evenings). June-Aug.

Motels/Motor Lodges

★ **BAYMONT INN.** *2840 S Oneida St (54304). Phone 920/494-7887; toll-free 877/229-6668; fax 920/494-4370. www.baymontinn.com.* 80 rooms, 2 story. D $72; under

18 free. Pet accepted, some restrictions. Complimentary continental breakfast. Check-out noon. TV; cable (premium), VCR available (movies). Health club privileges. Cross-country ski 10 miles. Business center. Cr cds: A, C, D, DS, MC, V.

★ ★ **BEST WESTERN MIDWAY HOTEL.** *780 Packer Dr (54304). Phone 920/499-3161; toll-free 800/528-1234; fax 920/499-9401. www.bestwestern.com.* 145 rooms, 2 story. S $70-$76; D $81-$87; each additional $7; under 12 free. Crib free. TV. Indoor pool; whirlpool. Restaurant 7 am-10 pm. Room service. Bar 11-1 am. Check-out 11 am. Meeting rooms. Business services available. In-room modem link. Bellhops. Valet service. Sundries. Free airport transportation. Downhill ski 10 miles; cross-country ski 5 miles. Exercise equipment; sauna. Health club privileges. Game room. Lambeau Field adjacent. Cr cds: A, C, D, DS, MC, V.

★ **COMFORT INN.** *2841 Ramada Way (54304). Phone 920/498-2060; toll-free 800/288-5150; fax 920/498-2060. www.comfortinn.com.* 60 rooms, 2 story. S $54-$79; D $64-$89; each additional $5; under 17 free; higher rates: Packers football games, EAA Fly-in, Dec 31; lower rates weekdays. Crib free. Pet accepted, some restrictions. Complimentary continental breakfast. Check-out 11 am. TV; cable (premium). In-room modem link. Valet services. Restaurant nearby. Health club privileges. Indoor pool, whirlpool. Cross-country ski 5 miles. Business services. Cr cds: A, C, D, DS, ER, JCB, MC, V.

★ **DAYS INN.** *406 N Washington St (54301). Phone 920/435-1478; fax 920/435-3120. www.daysinn.com.* 98 rooms, 5 story. S $55-$85; D $65-$95; suites $70-$100; each additional $5; under 18 free. Crib free. Pet accepted. TV. Indoor pool. Restaurant 6:30 am-2 pm, 5-9 pm. Room service. Bar 3 pm-midnight. Check-out noon. Meeting rooms. Business services available. In-room modem link. Valet service. Sundries. Health club privileges. Microwaves available. Overlooks Fox River. Cr cds: A, C, D, DS, JCB, MC, V.

★ **EXEL INN.** *2870 Ramada Way (54304). Phone 920/499-3599; fax 920/498-4055. www.exelinns.com.* 105 rooms, 2 story. S $44.99-$54.99; D $51.99-$56.99; each additional $5; under 18 free. Crib free. Pet accepted, some restrictions. Complimentary continental breakfast. Check-out noon. TV; cable. In-room modem link. Restaurant adjacent open 24 hours. Health club privileges. Business services. Cr cds: A, C, D, DS, MC, V.

★ **FAIRFIELD INN.** 2850 S Oneida St (54304). Phone 920/497-1010; toll-free 800/228-2800; fax 920/497-3098. www.fairfieldinn.com. 63 rooms, 3 story. May-Sept: S $63; D $69; each additional $6; under 18 free; higher rates special events; lower rates rest of year. Complimentary continental breakfast. Check-out noon. TV; cable (premium). Restaurant adjacent open 24 hours. Health club privileges. Indoor pool, whirlpool. Cross-country ski 3 miles. Business services. Cr cds: A, C, D, DS, MC, V.

⊡ ⊠ ⊠

★★ **HOLIDAY INN.** 2580 S Ashland Ave (54304). Phone 920/499-5121; fax 920/499-6777. www.holiday-inn.com. 147 rooms, 2 story. June-Aug: S $80-$90; D $90-$100; each additional $10; suites $110; under 18 free; lower rates rest of year. Crib free. Complimentary coffee in rooms. Check-out noon. TV; cable (premium). Some refrigerators. Restaurant 6:30 am-1:30 pm, 5:30-10 pm. Room service. Health club privileges. Game room. Indoor pool, whirlpool. Free airport transportation. Meeting rooms, Business center. Cr cds: A, C, D, DS, JCB, MC, V.

⊡ ⊠ ⊠ SC ⊼

★★ **HOLIDAY INN.** 200 Main St (54301). Phone 920/437-5900; toll-free 800/457-2929; fax 920/437-1192. www.holiday-inn.com. 149 rooms, 7 story. S, D $92; family rates. Crib free. Pet accepted, some restrictions. Check-out noon. TV; cable (premium). Coffee in rooms. Valet services, coin laundry. Restaurant 6 am-10 pm. Bar 10-1 am; entertainment, room service. Health club privileges. Sauna. Indoor pool, whirlpool. On Fox River; marina. Meeting rooms, business services. Sundries. Luxury level. Cr cds: A, C, D, DS, ER, JCB, MC, V.

⊡ ⊠ ⊠ ⊠

★ **MARINER MOTEL.** 2222 Riverside Dr (54301). Phone 920/437-7107; fax 920/437-2877. 23 rooms, 2 story. S $39.95-$50; D $44.95-$58.95; each additional $5; under 18 free; higher rates special events. Crib $5. Complimentary continental breakfast. Check-out 11 am. TV; cable. Patios. Refrigerators; microwaves available. Restaurant 11:30 am-2 pm, 5-9 pm; Fri, Sat to 10 pm. Room service. Health club privileges. Cross-country ski 10 miles. Lawn games. Beauty shop. Meeting rooms. On Fox River; dock. Cr cds: A, C, D, DS, MC, V.

⊡ ⊠ ⊠ SC

★ **ROAD STAR INN.** 1941 True Ln (54304). Phone 920/497-2666; toll-free 800/445-4667; fax 920/497-4754. 63 rooms, 2 story. July-Oct: S $34; D $40; each additional $3; under 15 free; higher rates: special events, wkends; lower rates rest of year. Pet accepted. TV; cable. Complimentary continental breakfast. Restaurant nearby. Check-out 11 am. Some refrigerators, wet bars. Cr cds: A, C, D, DS, MC, V.

⊡ ⊠

★ **SKY LITE.** 2120 S Ashland Ave (54304). Phone 920/494-5641; fax 920/494-4032. 23 rooms, some kitchens S $29.50-$35; D $39.50-$56; under 12 free. Crib $5. Pet accepted, some restrictions. TV; cable (premium). Restaurant nearby. Check-out 11 am. Coin laundry. Sundries. Microwaves available. Picnic tables. Cr cds: A, DS, MC, V.

⊡ ⊠ ⊠ ⊠

★ **SUPER 8.** 2868 S Oneida St (54304). Phone 920/494-2042; fax 920/494-6959. www.super8.com. 84 rooms, 2 story. Mid-June-Oct: S $55-$60; D $65-$70; lower rates rest of year. Crib free. Pet accepted. TV; cable, VCR available. Complimentary continental breakfast. Restaurant nearby. Check-out 11 am. Coin laundry. Meeting room. Business services available. Sauna. Health club privileges. Whirlpool. Microwaves available. Cr cds: A, C, D, DS, MC, V.

⊡ ⊠ ⊠ ⊠ ⊠ ⊠ ⊠ ⊠

Hotel

★★ **RADISSON INN.** 2040 Airport Dr (54313). Phone 920/494-7300; fax 920/494-9599. www.radisson.com. This hotel caters to making the guest's stay as relaxing as possible. 299 rooms, 3, 6 story. D $119; each additional $10; under 18 free, TV; cable. In-room modem link. Some fireplaces. Laundry services. Restaurant, bar, entertainment, room service. Health club privileges. Exercise equipment, sauna. Indoor pool, whirlpool. Free airport transportation. Cr cds: A, C, D, DS, ER, JCB, MC, V.

⊡ ⊠ ⊠ ⊠ ⊠

B&B/Small Inns

★★★ **ASTOR HOUSE.** 637 S Monroe Ave (54301). Phone 920/432-3585; toll-free 888/303-6370; fax 920/436-3145. www.astorhouse.com. The only bed and breakfast in Green Bay, this charming 1880s Victorian house serves up intimate home-style hospitality, featuring five distinct rooms. 5 rooms, shower only, 3 story. Complimentary continental breakfast. Check-out 11 am, check-in 4-6 pm. TV; cable; VCR (movies). In-room modem link. Built in 1888; antiques. Totally nonsmoking. Cr cds: A, DS, MC, V.

⊠

★★★ **JAMES STREET INN.** 201 James St (54115). Phone 920/337-0111; toll-free 800/89SUITE; fax 920/337-6135. Upon entering this enchanting inn, guests are lured to relaxation by the simple elegance and romantic lobby with all of its charming furnishings, including the magnificent antique mahogany and cherry fireplace. Guests will appreciate the elegant accommodations, personal and attentive service, and classically appointed guestrooms, some featuring private waterfront decks and panoramic views of the Fox River. 36 rooms, 4 story. S $69-$129; D $89-$219; each additional $5; suites $89-

$139; under 12 free. Complimentary continental breakfast; afternoon refreshments. Check-out Noon, check-in 3 pm. TV; cable (premium), VCR available (movies). Restaurant nearby. Cross-country ski 2 miles. Old flour mill built 1858. Cr cds: A, D, DS, MC, V.

Restaurants

★ ★ **EVE'S SUPPER CLUB.** *2020 Riverside Dr (54301). Phone 920/435-1571; fax 920/435-2899.* Specializes in steak, seafood. Hours: 11 am-2 pm, 5-10 pm; Sat from 5 pm. Closed Sun; Thanksgiving, Dec 24, 25. Lunch $2.50-$13.95, dinner $6.75-$26.95. Bar. Reservations accepted Mon-Thurs. Cr cds: A, D, DS, MC, V.

D

★ ★ **WELLINGTON.** 1060 Hansen Rd (54304). Phone 920/499-2000; fax 920/499-7894. Closed Sun; holidays. Lunch, dinner. Children's menu. Outdoor dining. Cr cds: A, D, MC, V. **$$**

D

Green Lake (F-4)

See also Fond du Lac, Waupun

Pop 1,064 **Elev** 828 ft **Area code** 920 **Zip** 54941

Information Chamber of Commerce, 550 Mill St, PO Box 386; 920/294-3231 or 800/253-7354

This county seat, known as the oldest resort community west of Niagara Falls, is a popular four-season recreational area. Green Lake, 7,325 acres, is the deepest natural lake in the state and affords good fishing, including lake trout, swimming, sailing, powerboating, and iceboating.

What to See and Do

Green Lake Conference Center/American Baptist Assembly. *W2511 WI 23. Phone 920/294-3323.* A 1,000-acre all-yr vacation-conference center. Activities incl indoor swimming; fishing; cross-country skiing (rentals), tobogganing, ice-skating, camping (fee), hiking, biking, tennis, 36-hole golf. (Daily) **$**

Lake Cruises. *643 Illinois Ave. At Heidel House, Illinois Ave. Phone 920/294-3344 or 800/444-2812.* A 1 1/4 hour narrated cruise. (June-Aug, daily; May, Sept-Oct, Sat-Sun) Also dinner, brunch cruises; private charters. **$$$**

Motels/Motor Lodges

★ **AMERICINN.** *1219 W Fond du Lac St (54971). Phone 920/748-7578; fax 920/748-7897. www.americinn.com.* 42 rooms, 2 story. D $70-$80; each additional $6; under 12 free. Complimentary continental breakfast. TV; cable

(premium). Sauna. Indoor pool, whirlpool. Cross-country ski 6 miles. Cr cds: A, D, DS, MC, V.

★ **BAYVIEW MOTEL & RESORT.** *439 Lake St (54941). Phone 920/294-6504; fax 920/294-0888. www.vbe.com/~bayview.* 17 rooms, 2 story, 7 kitchens May-Oct: S $84; D $94; each additional $6; suites $190; golf plans; lower rates rest of year. Crib $6. TV; cable. Coffee in rooms. Restaurant nearby. Check-out 10 am. Cross-country ski 5 miles. Pontoon, fishing boats; motors, launching ramp, dockage, boat trailer parking. Fish clean/ store. Picnic tables, grills. On lake. Cr cds: MC, V.

Resort

★ ★ ★ **HEIDEL HOUSE.** *643 Illinois Ave (54941). Phone 920/294-3344.* 205 rooms, 4 story. S, D $155-$275; each additional $25; under 17 free. Crib available. 2 heated pools. TV; cable (premium), VCR available. Complimentary coffee, newspaper in rooms. Restaurant 6 am-10 pm. Check-out noon. Meeting rooms. Business center. Gift shop. Exercise room. Some refrigerators, minibars. Cr cds: A, C, D, DS, MC, V.

B&B/Small Inns

★ ★ **CARVER'S ON THE LAKE.** *N5529 Co Rd A (54941). Phone 920/294-6931. www.carversonthelake.com.* 9 rooms, 2 with shower only, 2 story. Complimentary continental breakfast. Check-out 11 am, check-in 3 pm. TV; cable. Restaurant. Built 1925; antiques. Some room phones. Totally nonsmoking. Cr cds: MC, V. **$**

★ **OAKWOOD LODGE.** *365 Lake St (54941). Phone 920/294-6580. www.wisvactions.com/oakwoodlodge/.* 12 rooms, 2 story. No A/C. No room phones. May-Sept: S, D $95-$135; each additional $20; golf plans; lower rates rest of year. Closed Nov-Apr. Complimentary full breakfast. Check-out 11 am, check-in 3 pm. TV in sitting room; cable (premium), VCR available. Golf on premise. Cross-country ski 5 miles. Built 1866; antique furnishings. Totally nonsmoking. Cr cds: MC, V.

Restaurants

★ ★ **ALFRED'S SUPPER CLUB.** *506 Hill St (54941). Phone 920/294-3631; fax 920/294-0631. www.foodspot.com.* American menu. Hours: 5-11 pm. Closed Mon in winter. Dinner $14-$28. Bar. Children's menu. Reservations accepted. Cr cds: A, DS, MC, V.

D

★★★**CARVER'S ON THE LAKE.** *N5529 County Rd A (54941). Phone 920/294-6931. www.carversonthelake.com.* The English country decor and cozy atmosphere of this inn and restaurant draw visitors for new-American cuisine along the lake's eastern shore. Linger over a drink fireside at the Great Room bar. Hours: 5 pm to closing. Closed Mon. Reservations accepted. Bar. Wine list. Dinner $16-$26. Child's meals. Specializes in fresh seafood, regional dishes, pasta. Own baking. Dining in old English country house; antiques. Cr cds: MC, V.

★★**NORTON'S MARINE DINING ROOM.** *380 S Lawson Dr (54941). Phone 920/294-6577; fax 920/294-6922.* Hours: 11 am-3 pm, 5-10 pm. Closed Dec 24, 25. Bar to 2 am. Lunch $3.25-$11.95, dinner $8.50-$39.95. Specializes in steak, seafood. Outdoor dining. Overlooks Green Lake. Cr cds: A, MC, V.

Ⓓ

Hartland

Restaurant

★★**SEVEN SEAS.** *1807 Nagawicka Rd (53029). Phone 262/367-3903. www.weissgerbers.com.* Hours: 5-10 pm; Sat from 5 pm; Sun brunch from 11 am; Sun 4-9 pm. Closed Tues (Oct-Apr). Reservations accepted. German, Amer menu. Bar. Dinner $14.95-$42. Sun brunch $14.95. Child's meals. Specializes in Wiener schnitzel, roast duck, seafood. Outdoor dining. Overlooks Lake Nagawicka; nautical décor. Cr cds: A, D, DS, MC, V.

Ⓓ

Hayward (C-2)

See also Spooner

Settled 1881 **Pop** 1,897 **Elev** 1,198 ft **Area code** 715 **Zip** 54843

Information Hayward Area Chamber of Commerce, 101 W 1st St; 715/634-8662

Web www.haywardlakes.com

A Ranger District office of the Chequamegon National Forest is located here.

What to See and Do

National Freshwater Fishing Hall of Fame. *10360 Hall of Fame Dr, Jct Hwy B & WI 27. Phone 715/634-4440.* A 143-foot long and 4 1/2-story high walk-thru "muskie"; the mouth serves as an observation deck. Museum and educational complex contains more than 400 mounts representing many world species; world records and record photo gallery and library; thousands of angling artifacts; 350 outboard motor relics. Project covers six acres and incl five other museum display buildings. (Mid-Apr-Nov, daily) Snack shop, gift shop, playground with fish theme. **$$**

Special Event

Lumberjack World Championship. *County B. Phone 715/634-2484.* On County B. Logrolling, tree chopping, climbing, and sawing. Late July.

Motels/Motor Lodges

★**AMERICINN.** *15601 US 63 N (54843). Phone 715/634-2700; toll-free 800/634-3444; fax 715/634-3958. www.americinn.com.* 42 rooms, 2 story. D $55-$101; each additional $6; under 18 free. Pet accepted, some restrictions; fee. Complimentary continental breakfast. Check-out 11 am. TV; cable (premium), VCR available. Sauna. Game room. Indoor pool, whirlpool. Downhill ski 20 miles; cross-country ski adjacent. Cr cds: A, D, DS, MC, V.

Ⓓ 🐾 ➤ ≈

★**BEST WESTERN NORTHERN PINE INN.** *9966 N WI 27 (54843). Phone 715/634-4959; toll-free 800/777-7996; fax 715/634-8999. www.bestwestern.com.* 39 rooms. D $54-$79; each additional $5; under 12 free. Complimentary continental breakfast. Check-out 11 am. TV; cable. Sauna. Game room. Pool, whirlpool. Downhill ski 20 miles, cross-country ski 1 mile. Cr cds: A, C, D, DS, MC, V.

Ⓓ ➤ ≈ ⊠

★**CEDAR INN.** *15659 WI 27 (54843). Phone 715/634-5332; toll-free 800/776-2478; fax 715/634-1343.* 23 rooms. Memorial Day-early Oct: S $46-$56; D $51-$71; each additional $5; suites $100-$130; under 5 free; higher rates Birkebeiner Ski Race; lower rates rest of year. Crib $5. Pet accepted; some restrictions. TV; cable (premium). Complimentary continental breakfast. Restaurant nearby. Check-out 10:30 am. Business services available. In-room modem link. Cross-country ski 3 miles. Sauna. Whirlpool. Refrigerators; microwaves available. Cr cds: A, DS, MC, V.

Ⓓ 🐾 ⚡ ➤ 🧍 ✈ ⊠

★**COUNTRY INN AND SUITES.** *WI 27 S (54843). Phone 715/634-4100; toll-free 800/456-4000; fax 715/634-2403.* 66 rooms, 2 story. D $68-$78; each additional $6; under 18 free. Pet accepted, some restrictions. Complimentary continental breakfast. Check-out noon. TV; cable (premium). In-room modem link. Restaurant, bar, room service. Game room. Indoor pool, whirlpool. Cross-country ski 4 miles. Cr cds: A, D, DS, MC, V.

Ⓓ 🐾 ⚡ ➤ ≈ ⊠

★ **NORTHWOODS MOTEL.** *9854 WI 27 N (54843). Phone 715/634-8088; toll-free 800/232-9202; fax 715/634-0714.* 9 rooms. S $35-$55; D $45-$60; each additional $5; kitchen suite $65; family rates; higher rates special events (3-day min). Crib free. Pet accepted. TV; cable. Complimentary coffee in lobby. Check-out 10 am. Downhill ski 19 miles; cross-country ski 3 miles. Cr cds: DS, MC, V.

★ **SUPER 8.** *10444 N WI 27 (54843). Phone 715/634-2646; fax 715/634-6482. www.super8.com.* 46 rooms, 1-2 story. Apr-Sept: S $46.69; D $54.79-$63.79; each additional $5; under 12 free; higher rates special events; lower rates rest of year. Crib $5. Pet accepted. TV; cable (premium). Indoor pool; whirlpool. Complimentary coffee in lobby. Restaurant adjacent 5:30 am-9 pm. Check-out 11 am. Cross-country ski 2 miles. Game room. Cr cds: A, D, DS, MC, V.

Restaurant

★ **KARIBALIS.** *10590 Main St (54843). Phone 715/634-2462.* Seafood menu, Steak menu. Hours: Memorial Day-Labor Day: Mon-Sat 11am-9pm, Sun 11am-8pm, closed Easter, Thanksgiving, Dec 25. Dinner $5.95-$15.95. Bar open 11am-10pm, Salad bar. Children's menu. Reservations accepted. Outdoor dining in summer, nonsmoking seating. Cr cds: A, DS, MC, V.

Howard

Restaurant

★★ **RIVER'S BEND.** *792 Riverview Dr (54303). Phone 920/434-1383.* Specialties: prime rib, steak, seafood. Salad bar. Hours: 11:30 am-2 pm, 5-10 pm; Fri to 10:30 pm; Sat 5-10:30 pm; Sun 4:30-9 pm. Closed holidays. Lunch $3.95-$8, dinner $7-$29. Bar to 1 am. Children's menu. Reservations accepted. Local artwork on display. Overlooks Duck Creek. Cr cds: A, D, DS, MC, V.

Hudson (D-1)

Pop 6,378 **Elev** 780 ft **Area code** 715 **Zip** 54016

Information Hudson Area Chamber of Commerce, 502 2nd St; 715/386-8411 or 800/657-6775

Web www.hudsonwi.org

What to See and Do

Octagon House. *1004 3rd St. Phone 715/386-2654.* (1855) Octagonal home furnished in the style of gracious living of the 1800s; garden house museum with country store and lumbering and farming implements; carriage house museum with special display areas. (May-Oct, Tues-Sun; first three weeks Dec; closed holidays) **$$**

Willow River State Park. *1034 County Trunk A. 5 miles N on County A. Phone 715/386-5931.* A 2,800-acre park with swimming, fishing, boating, canoeing; cross-country skiing, picnicking, camping (hookups, dump station). Naturalist programs (summer only). River scenery with two dams. Standard fees. (Daily) **$$**

Motels/Motor Lodges

★★ **BEST WESTERN HUDSON HOUSE INN.** *1616 Crest View Dr (54016). Phone 715/386-2394; toll-free 800/528-1234; fax 715/386-3167. www.bestwestern.com.* 102 rooms, 1-2 story. S $60-$82; D $69-$90; each additional $6; studio room $81-$160; under 13 free. Crib free. TV; cable (premium). Indoor pool. Restaurant 5-9 pm. Room service from 9 am. Bar 11:30-1 am; entertainment Fri, Sat. Check-out 11 am. Meeting rooms. Business services available. In-room modem link. Sundries. Beauty shop. Downhill ski 8 miles. Cr cds: A, C, D, DS, MC, V.

★ **COMFORT INN.** *811 Dominion Dr (54016). Phone 715/386-6355; toll-free 800/725-8987; fax 715/386-9778. www.comfortinn.com.* 60 rooms, 2 story. S $44.95-$62.95; D $47.95-$72.95; each additional $5; under 18 free. Crib free. Pet accepted, some restrictions; $50. TV; cable (premium), VCR available. Indoor pool; whirlpool. Complimentary continental breakfast. Restaurant nearby. Check-out 11 am. Guest laundry. Business services available. Cr cds: A, C, D, DS, JCB, MC, V.

B&B/Small Inns

★★★ **PHIPPS INN.** *1005 3rd St (54016). Phone 715/386-0800; toll-free 888/865-9388. www.phippsinn.com.* Nestled in scenic St. Croix Valley, this Queen Anne-style inn offers a quiet retreat in a lavish setting. 6 rooms, 3 suites, 3 story. No room phones. Complimentary full breakfast. Check-out 11 am, check-in 4:30-6 pm. Restored Queen Anne-style Victorian mansion (1884); formal music room with baby grand piano, two parlors, 3 porches. Totally nonsmoking. Cr cds: A, MC, V.

Hurley (B-3)

See also Manitowish Waters

Founded 1885 **Pop** 1,782 **Elev** 1,493 ft **Area code** 715 **Zip** 54534

Information Chamber of Commerce, 316 Silver St; 715/561-4334

Web www.hurleywi.com

Originally a lumber and mining town, Hurley is now a winter sports center.

What to See and Do

Iron County Historical Museum. *303 Iron St. Iron St at 3rd Ave S. Phone 715/561-2244.* Exhibits of county's iron mining past; local artifacts, photo gallery. (Daily; closed Dec 25) **FREE**

Whitecap Mountain Ski Area. *County Rd E. 8 miles W on WI 77 to Iron Belt, then 3 miles W on County E. Phone 715/561-2776 or 800/933-SNOW.* Area has six chairlifts, rope tow; patrol, school, rentals; nursery; restaurant, cafeteria, concession area. Longest run 1 1/2 miles; vertical drop 450 ft. (Nov-Mar, daily) Half-day rates. **$$$$**

Special Events

Iron County Heritage Festival. *316 Silver St. Phone 715/561-4334.* 316 Silver St. Various heritage themes and costumed cast of characters. Last Sat July.

Paavo Nurmi Marathon. *316 Silver (54534). Phone 715/561-3290.* Begins in Upson, SW via WI 77. Oldest marathon in state. Related activities Fri-Sat. Second weekend Aug.

Red Light Snowmobile Rally. *316 Silver St. Phone 715/561-4334.* Second weekend Dec.

Motel/Motor Lodge

★ ★ **RAMADA INN.** *1000 10th Ave N (54534). Phone 715/561-3030; fax 715/561-4280.* 100 rooms, 2 story. S $48-$65; D $62-$77; each additional $6; under 19 free; higher rates some winter holiday weeks and winter weekends. Crib free. Pet accepted. TV; cable. Indoor pool; whirlpool. Restaurant 7 am-2 pm, 5:30-10 pm. Room service. Bar 11-1 am. Check-out noon. Coin laundry. Meeting rooms. Business services available. Valet service. Downhill/cross-country ski 15 miles. Snowmobile trails. Game room. Cr cds: A, D, DS, MC, V.

D ⬛ 🐾 🏊 ⛷ 🌊

Janesville (G-4)

See also Beloit, Fort Atkinson, Madison

Founded 1836 **Pop** 52,133 **Elev** 858 ft **Area code** 608

Information Janesville Area Convention & Visitors Bureau, 51 S Jackson St, 53545; 608/757-3171 or 800/487-2757

Web www.janesville.com

In 1836, pioneer Henry F. Janes carved his initials into a tree on the bank of the Rock River. The site is now the intersection of the two main streets of industrial Janesville. Janes went on to found other Janesvilles in Iowa and Minnesota. Wisconsin's Janesville has a truck and bus assembly plant that offers tours. Because of its 1,900 acres of parkland, Janesville has been called "Wisconsin's Park Place."

What to See and Do

General Motors Corporation. *1000 Industrial Ave. Phone 608/756-7681.* Guided tours (Mon-Thurs; closed holidays). No cameras. Reservations required. **FREE**

Lincoln-Tallman Restorations. *440 N Jackson St, 4 blocks N on US 14 Business. Phone 608/752-4519.* Tallman House (1855-1857), 26-room antebellum mansion of Italianate design considered among the top 10 mid-19th-century structures for the study of American culture at the time of the Civil War. Restored Greek Revival Stone House (1842). Horse Barn (1855-1857) serves as visitor center and museum shop. Tours (daily). **$$$**

Milton House Museum. *18 S Janesville St in Milton, 8 miles NE at junction WI 26, 59. Phone 608/868-7772.* (1844) Hexagonal building constructed of grout; underground railroad tunnel connects it with original log cabin; country store; guided tours. (Memorial Day-Labor Day, daily; May, Sept-mid-Oct, weekends, also Mon-Fri by appointment) **$$**

Municipal parks. Riverside. *2200 Parkside Dr (53547). N Washington St, N on US 14 Business.* **Palmer.** *E Racine St, E on US 14 Business, exit WI 11.* Wading pool, swimming beach; picnicking, tennis courts, exercise course, 9-hole golf, concession. **Traxler.** *N Parker Dr, 1/2 mile N on US 51.* Boat launching ramps for Rock River, fishing, children's fishing pond; picnicking, ice-skating; water ski shows, rose gardens. (Daily, May-Sept) **Rockport.** *2800 Rockport Rd. Phone 608/755-3025.* Swimming pool, bathhouse; cross-country skiing; hiking. Wading pool, fishing, boat launch; picnicking, hiking, cross-country skiing, tennis courts, 18-hole golf, concession. **FREE**

Rotary Gardens. *1455 Palmer Dr. Phone 608/752-3885.* 15-acre botanical garden (Daily). Gift shop.

Special Event

Rock County 4-H Fair. *100 Craig Ave. Rock County 4-H Fairgrounds. Phone 608/754-1470.* One of the largest 4-H fairs in country. Exhibits, competitions, carnival, grandstand shows, concerts. Last week July.

Motels/Motor Lodges

★ ★ **BEST WESTERN.** *3900 Milton Ave (53545). Phone 608/756-4511; fax 608/756-0025. www.bestwestern. com.* 106 rooms, 3 story. May-Sept: S, D $65-$80; each additional $5; suites $95-$140; under 12 free; lower rates rest of year. Crib free. Pet accepted. TV; cable. Indoor pool; whirlpool. Complimentary coffee in rooms. Restaurant 6-9 pm; weekends 7 am-10 pm. Room service. Bar 4 pm-1 am. Check-out noon. Meeting rooms. Business services available. Airport transportation. Exercise equipment. Game room. Cr cds: A, C, D, DS, MC, V.

D ⬛ 🏊 ✕ SC

★ ★ **RAMADA INN.** *3431 Milton Ave (53545). Phone 608/756-2341; toll-free 800/433-7787; fax 608/756-4183. www.ramada.com.* 189 rooms, 2 story. S $56-$62; D $62-$70; suites $125-$150; each additional $10; under 18 free. Crib free. TV; cable (premium). Complimentary continental breakfast (Mon-Fri). Indoor pool; whirlpool. Restaurant 6 am-1:30 pm, 5-10 pm. Room service. Bar 11-1 am. Check-out noon. Meeting rooms. Business services available. Sundries. Gift shop. Putting green. Exercise equipment; sauna. Game room. Cr cds: A, C, D, DS, ER, JCB, MC, V.

D 🐾 ✈ 🏊 ✕ ✈ 🏃

Kenosha (G-6)

See also Lake Geneva, Milwaukee, Racine

Settled 1835 **Pop** 80,352 **Elev** 610 ft **Area code** 262

Information Kenosha Area Convention & Visitors Bureau, 812 56th St, 53140; 262/654-7307 or 800/654-7309

Web www.kenoshacvb.com

A major industrial city, port, and transportation center, Kenosha was settled by New Englanders. The city owns 84 percent of its Lake Michigan frontage, most of it developed as parks.

What to See and Do

Bong State Recreation Area. *17 miles W via WI 142; 9 miles W of I-94. Phone 262/878-5600 or 262/652-0377.* A 4,515-acre area. Swimming, fishing, boating; hiking, bridle, and off-road motorcycle trails; cross-country skiing, snowmobiling, picnicking, guided nature hikes, nature center, special events area; family, group camping (fee). **$$$**

Carthage College. *2001 Alford Park Dr, WI 32, northern edge of city on lakeside. Phone 262/551-8500.* (1847) 2,100 students. Civil War Museum in Johnson Art Center (Mon-Fri; closed holidays). **FREE**

Factory outlet stores. *Phone 262/857-7961 (Original Outlet Mall); 262/857-2101 (Prime Outlets at Pleasant Prairie).* More than 170 outlet stores can be found at **Original Outlet Mall,** 7700 120th Ave; and Prime **Outlets at Pleasant Prairie,** 11211 120th Ave. (Daily)

Kemper Center. *6501 3rd Ave. Phone 262/657-6005.* Approximately 11 acres. Several buildings incl Italianate Victorian mansion (1860); complex has more than 100 different trees, rose collection; mosiac mural; outdoor tennis courts, picnic area; also Anderson Art Gallery (Thurs-Sun afternoons). Guided tours by appointment. (Office, Mon-Fri; grounds, daily) **FREE**

Kenosha County Historical Society and Museum. *220 51st Pl. Phone 262/654-5770.* Items and settings of local and Wisconsin history, Native American material, folk and decorative art. Research library. (Tues-Sun afternoons; closed holidays) **FREE**

Rambler Legacy Gallery. *5500 1st Ave. Civic Center. Phone 262/653-4140.* Lorado Taft dioramas of famous art studios; Native American, Oceanic, and African arts; Asian ivory and porcelain, Wisconsin folk pottery; mammals exhibit, dinosaur exhibit. Changing art, natural history exhibits. (Daily; closed holidays) **DONATION**

Southport Marina. *97 57th St. From 97th to 57th Sts. Phone 262/657-5565.* 2-mile walkway on Lake Michigan; playground. (Daily) **FREE**

University of Wisconsin-Parkside. *900 Wood Rd. Phone 262/595-2355.* (1968) 5,100 students. A 700-acre campus. Buildings are connected by glass-walled interior corridors that radiate from $8-million trilevel Wyllie Library Learning Center. Nature, cross-country ski trails. Tours.

Special Event

Bristol Renaissance Fair. *12550 120th Ave. 6 miles SW via I-94, Russell Rd exit, just N of the IL/WI state line. Phone 847/395-7773; 800/52-FAIRE.* Re-creation of a 16th-century European marketplace featuring royal knights and swordsmen, master jousters, musicians, mimes, dancers, and hundreds of crafters and food peddlers. Richly gowned ladies, tattered beggars, barbarians, and soldiers stroll the grounds. Procession is heralded by trumpets and the royal drum corps. Nine weekends beginning last weekend June.

Motels/Motor Lodges

★ **BAYMONT INN.** *7540 118th Ave (53158). Phone 262/857-7911; fax 414/857-2370. www.baymontinn.com.* 95 rooms, 2 story. D $69-$79; each additional $7; under 18 free. Pet accepted. Complimentary continental breakfast.

Check-out noon. TV; cable (premium). In-room modem link. Downhill ski 15 miles. Cr cds: A, C, D, DS, MC, V.

[D] [icons] SC

★ **HOLIDAY INN EXPRESS.** *5125 6th Ave (53140). Phone 262/658-3281. www.holiday-inn.com.* 111 rooms, 5 story. S $64-$125; D $79-$135; under 19 free. Crib free. Check-out 11 am. TV; cable (premium). Sauna. On Lake Michigan. Indoor pool, whirlpool. Meeting rooms, business services. Cr cds: A, D, DS, JCB, MC, V.

[D] [icons]

★ **KNIGHTS INN.** *7221 122nd Ave (53142). Phone 414/857-2622; fax 414/857-2375. www.knightsinn.com.* 113 rooms, 14 kitchens June-Oct: S, D $47.95-$69.95; each additional $5; kitchen units $62.95-$68.95; under 18 free; higher rates weekends; lower rates rest of year. Crib free. Pet accepted. TV. Complimentary coffee in lobby. Restaurant nearby. Check-out noon. Business services available. Cr cds: A, C, D, DS, MC, V.

[D] [icons] SC

Restaurants

★ ★ **HOUSE OF GERHARD.** *3927 75th St (53142). Phone 262/694-5212. www.foodspot.com.* German, American menu. Hours: 11:30 am-10 pm. Closed Sun; Dec 24-25; also 1 week early July. Dinner $8.95-$16. Bar. Children's menu. Cr cds: A, D, DS, MC, V.

[D]

★ ★ **MANGIA TRATTORIA.** *5717 Sheridan Rd (53140). Phone 262/652-4285; fax 262/652-9313.* Italian menu. Hours: 11:30 am-2 pm, 5-9 pm; Fri to 10 pm; Sat 5-10 pm; Sun 3-8 pm. Closed holidays. Dinner $3.95-$29.95. Bar. Outdoor seating. Cr cds: A, D, DS, MC, V.

[D]

Kohler (F-6)

See also Sheboygan

Pop 1,989 **Area code** 920 **Zip** 53044

Information Sheboygan County Chamber of Commerce, 712 Riverfront Dr, Suite 101, Sheboygan 53081; 920/457-9495 or 800/457-9497

Web www.destinationkohler.com

Kohler, a small town near Sheboygan, has gained a reputation as one of the region's top resort destinations. One of the nation's first planned communities, designed with the help of the Olmstead Brothers firm of Boston, MA, Kohler began as a "garden at the factory gate and headquarters for the country's largest plumbing manufacturer. Running through Kohler is seven miles of the Sheboygan River and a 500-acre wildlife sanctuary.

What to See and Do

Great Gingerbread Holiday Festival: Gingerbread house creations designed and executed by area school children at the Waelderhaus. Dec

Industry in Action Tour: Three-hour walking tour inside the massive Kohler Company pottery, brass works, and cast iron foundry. View the work of craftsman during the manafacturing of the plumbing products.

John Michael Kohler Arts Center. *608 New York Ave. Phone 920/458-6144.* Changing contemporary art exhibitions, galleries, shop, historic house; theater, dance, and concert series. Center's exhibitions emphasize craft-related forooms, installation works, photography, new genres, ongoing cultural traditions and the work of self-taught artists. (Daily; closed holidays) **FREE**

Kohler Andrae State Park. *1520 Old Park Rd. S on I-43 exit 120, on Lake Michigan. Phone 920/451-4080.* Includes 1,000 acres of woods and sand dunes. Swimming, bathhouse; nature and cross-country ski trails, picnicking, playgrounds, concession, camping (105 sites, electric hookups), winter camping. Nature center (closed winter). Standard fees. (Daily)

Kohler Design Center: 36,000 square feet, three story exhibition center of kitchen and bath design ideas, and the newest Kohler plumbing products. Museum of Kohler Company, village history and Kohler Company Art Collection gallery. (Daily)

Traditional Holiday Illumination: More than 200,000 lights on trees surrounding Kohler hospitality facilities create a winter fantasyland in the Kohler Village. Thanksgiving-February

Waelderhaus. *1100 W Riverside Dr. 1 mile S off County PP, on W Riverside Dr in Kohler. Phone 920/452-4079.* Reproduction of chalet and furnishings of Kohler family home in Austrian Alps. Guided tours (afternoons, three departures daily; closed holidays). **FREE**

Hotel

★ ★ **INN ON WOODLAKE.** *705 Woodlake Rd (53044). Phone 920/452-7800; toll-free 800/919-3600; fax 920/452-6288. www.innonwoodlake.com.* Situated between the meadows and the Southern shore of Wood Lake, this property gives guests the choice of a prairie view or a lake view from their room. 121 rooms, 3 story. D $164-$315; each additional $10; under 16 free. Complimentary continental breakfast. Check-out noon. TV; cable (premium), VCR available (movies). Health club privileges, exercise equipment, sauna. Indoor pool, whirlpool. Cross-country ski. Cr cds: A, C, D, DS, MC, V.

[D] [icons]

Resort

★ ★ ★ **THE AMERICAN CLUB.** *444 Highland Dr (53044). Phone 920/457-8000; toll-free 800/344-2838; fax 920/457-0299. www.americanclub.com.* Located in the charming village of Kohler, The American Club offers a country getaway only one hour north of Milwaukee. Travelers stay and play here, and with the wide variety of available activities, visitors are never at a loss for something to do. Avid golfers wax poetic about the resort's four 18-hole courses sculpted out of the rugged terrain by renowned course architect Pete Dye. Whistling Straits calls to mind the natural beauty of Scotland and Ireland in its design, while Blackwolf Run is often considered the top public course in America. After a competitive round of golf, a tennis match, or a workout at the fitness center, guests succumb to the relaxing wonders of the Kohler Waters Spa. Everyone finds a favorite among ten distinctive dining establishments, and after a delicious meal, guests find the comfort of their tastefully appointed accommodations just right for a restful end to a wonderful day. 237 rooms, 3 story. May-Oct: S $235-$900; D $265-$900; each additional $15; under 17 free; lower rates rest of year. Check-out noon. TV; cable (premium), VCR available (movies). In-room modem link. Restaurant (see THE IMMIGRANT). Bar 11:30-1 am; entertainment, dancing. Room service 24 hours. Exercise room. Spa. 72-hole golf. Indoor/outdoor tennis. Cross-country ski on site. Carriage rides; bicycles. Hunting, trap shooting and fishing. Business center. Concierge. Cr cds: A, C, D, DS, JCB, MC, V.

D ⬛ ⬛ ⬛ ⬛ ⬛ ⬛ ⬛ SC

Restaurant

★ ★ ★ **THE IMMIGRANT.** *Highland Dr (53044). Phone 920/457-8000. www.americanclub.com.* Exquisite food and exceptional service radiates through the six rooms decorated to salute the European ethnic mix of early Wisconsin settlers. Regional American menu. Specialties: fresh fish, game, beef. Own baking. Hours: 6-10 pm; Sat to 11 pm. Closed Sun, Mon. A la carte entrees: dinner $24-$35. Bar, wine cellar. Entertainment Fri, Sat. Jacket. Reservations required. Cr cds: A, C, D, DS, MC, V.

D

Lac du Flambeau (C-4)

See also Manitowish Waters, Minocqua, Woodruff

Pop 1,423 **Elev** 1,635 ft **Area code** 715 **Zip** 54538

Information Chamber of Commerce, PO Box 158; 715/588-3346 or 877/588-3346

Web www.lacduflambeauchamber.com

The French gave this village the name "Lake of the Torch" because of the Chippewa practice of fishing and canoeing at night by the light of birch bark torches. Located in the center of the Lac du Flambeau Reservation, the village is tribal headquarters for more than 1,200 Chippewa still living in the area. It is also the center for a popular, lake-filled north woods recreation area. The reservation boasts 126 spring-fed lakes and its own fish hatchery.

What to See and Do

Lac du Flambeau Chippewa Museum and Cultural Center. *603 Peace Pipe Rd. Downtown. Phone 715/588-3333.* Displays of Native American artifacts, fur trading, and historical items. Chippewa craft workshops (May-Oct). (Mon-Sat; also by appointment) $$

Waswagoning Ojibwe Village. *2750 County Rd H. 1 miles N on County H. Phone 715/588-3560.* Twenty acres of Ojibwe culture with guided tours. (Memorial Day-Labor Day). $$$

Special Events

Colorama. *622 Peace Pipe Ln. Downtown. Phone 715/588-3346.* Last Sat Sept.

Powwows. *603 Peace Pipe. At Indian Bowl, fronting on Lake Interlaken. Phone 715/588-3333.* Dancing by Wa-swa-gon Dancers. Tues evenings. July-mid-Aug.

Resort

★ ★ **DILLMAN'S BAY PROPERTIES.** *3285 Sandlake Lodge Ln (54538). Phone 715/588-3143; fax 715/588-3110. www.dillmans.com.* 16 units, 18 cottages. No A/C. EP, mid-May-mid-Oct: daily, from $51/person; weekly, from $343/person; family rates. Closed rest of year. Crib free. Pet accepted. TV in lobby, some rooms. Playground. Dining by reservations. Check-out 10 am, check-in noon. Package store. Meeting rooms. Sports dir in summer. Tennis. Practice fairway. Sand beaches; waterskiing; windsurfing; scuba diving; boats, motors, kayaks, sailboats, canoes, pontoon boats; private launch, covered boathouse. Bicycles. Lawn games. Hiking trails. Social director; wine and cheese party Sun. Nature study, photography, painting workshops. Recreation room. Fishing clean and store area. Some fireplaces; refrigerator, microwave in suites and cottages. On 250 acres. Cr cds: MC, V.

D ⬛ ⬛ ⬛ ⬛ ⬛ ⬛ ⬛ ⬛ ⬛ SC ⬛

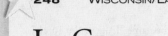

La Crosse (F-2)

See also Galesville, Sparta

Settled 1842 **Pop** 51,003 **Elev** 669 ft **Area code** 608

Information La Crosse Area Convention and Visitor Bureau, 410 E Veterans Memorial Dr, 54601; 608/782-2366 or 800/658-9424

Web www.explorelacrosse.com

An agricultural, commercial, and industrial city, La Crosse is washed by the waters of the Mississippi, the Black, and La Crosse rivers. Once a trading post, it was named by the French for the native game the French called lacrosse. More than 200 businesses and industries operate here today.

What to See and Do

Goose Island County Park. *W6488 County Rd GI. 3 miles S on WI 35, then 2 miles W on County GI. Phone 608/788-7018.* Beach, fishing, boat ramps; hiking trails, picnicking, camping (electric hookups). (Mid-Apr-mid-Oct, daily) **$$$**

Granddad Bluff. *400 La Crosse St. Phone 608/789-7533.* Tallest (1,172 ft) of the crags that overlook the city; it provides a panoramic view of the winding Mississippi, the tree-shaded city, and the Minnesota and Iowa bluffs. Picnic area. (May-late Oct, daily) Surfaced path to shelter house and top of bluff for the disabled. **FREE**

Hixon House. *429 N 7th St. Phone 608/782-1980.* (Circa 1860) 15-room home; Victorian and Asian furnishings. Visitor information center and gift shop in building that once served as wash house. (Memorial Day-Labor Day, daily) **$$**

Industrial tour. City Brewery. *1111 S 3rd St. Phone 608/785-4200 or 800/433-BEER.* 1-hour guided tours. Gift shop. (Mon-Sat; closed holidays) **FREE**

***La Crosse Queen* Cruises.** *Boat Dock, Riverside Park, W end of State St. Phone phone 608/784-2893 or 608/784-8523.* Sightseeing cruise on the Mississippi River aboard 150-passenger, double-deck paddlewheeler (early May-mid-Oct, daily). Also dinner cruise (Fri night, Sat and Sun). Charters (approximately Apr-Oct).

Mount La Crosse Ski Area. *2 miles S on WI 35. Phone 608/788-0044 or 800/426-3665.* Area has three chairlifts, rope tow; patrol, rentals, school; snowmaking; night skiing; cafeteria, bar. Longest run 1 mile; vertical drop 516 feet. (Thanksgiving-mid-Mar, daily; closed Dec 25) Half-day rates on weekends, holidays. Cross-country trails (Dec-mid-Mar, daily).

Swarthout Museum. *112 S 9th St. Phone 608/782-1980.* Changing historical exhibits ranging from prehistoric times to the 20th century. (Memorial Day-Labor Day, Tues-Sat; rest of year, Tues-Sun; closed holidays) **FREE**

Special Events

La Crosse Interstate Fair. *W4985 County Hwy M. La Crosse Fairgrounds Speedway. 11 miles E on I-90 in West Salem. Phone 800/658-9424.* Stock car racing, farm exhibits; carnival, entertainment. Mid-July.

Oktoberfest. *1 Oktoberfest Dr. S side of town. Phone 800/658-9424.* Six days beginning last weekend Sept or first weekend Oct.

Riverfest. *410 Veterns Memorial Dr. Riverside Park. Phone 608/782-6000.* 5-day festival with river events, music, food, entertainment, fireworks, children's events. Early July.

Motels/Motor Lodges

★ ★ **BEST WESTERN.** *1835 Rose St (54603). Phone 608/781-7000; fax 608/781-3195. www.bestwestern.com.* 121 rooms, 2 story. S $54-$76; D $68-$95; each additional $10; under 18 free. Crib free. TV; cable (premium), VCR. Indoor pool; whirlpool. Complimentary coffee in rooms. Restaurant 6:30 am-10 pm. Room service to 9 pm. Bar 11:30-1 am; entertainment Tues-Sat. Check-out noon. Meeting rooms. Business services available. In-room modem link. Valet service. Sundries. Downhill/cross-country ski 10 miles. Exercise equipment; sauna. Recreation room. On river; dockage. Private beach. Cr cds: A, C, D, DS, MC, V.

⊡ 🐾 🏊 🛥 🏃 🎿 🏊 🚶

★ **DAYS INN CONFERENCE CENTER.** *101 Sky Harbour Dr (54603). Phone 608/783-1000; fax 608/783-2948. www.daysinn.com.* 148 rooms, 2 story. S $59-$84; D $59-$89; each additional $5; under 18 free. Crib free. TV; cable. Sauna. Indoor pool; whirlpool. Complimentary coffee in rooms. Restaurant 6:30 am- 2 pm, 5-9 pm. Room service. Bar 4:30 pm-1 am. Check-out 11 am. Meeting rooms. Business services available. Valet service. Sundries. Downhill/cross-country ski 10 miles. Game room. Cr cds: A, C, D, DS, ER, JCB, MC, V.

⊡ 🐾 🏊 🎿 🛥 🏃 ✈ 🚶

★ **EXEL INN.** *2150 Rose St (54603). Phone 608/781-0400; toll-free 800/367-3935; fax 608/781-1216. www.exelinns.com.* 102 rooms, 2 story. S $31.99-$47.99; D $38.99-$54.99; each additional $4; suite $80-$100; under 19 free. Crib free. Complimentary continental breakfast. Check-out noon. TV. Coin laundry. Restaurant nearby. Game room. Cr cds: A, C, D, DS, ER, MC, V.

⊡ 🐾 🏊 🚶

★ **HAMPTON INN LA CROSSE.** *2110 Rose St (54603). Phone 608/781-5100; toll-free 800/426-7866; fax 608/781-3574. www.hamptoninn.com.* 101 rooms, 2 story.

S, D $69-$109; under 19 free. Crib free. TV; cable. Complimentary continental breakfast. Restaurant adjacent open 24 hours. Check-out noon. Meeting rooms. Whirlpool. Cr cds: A, C, D, DS, JCB, MC, V.

★ **NIGHT SAVER INN.** *1906 Rose St (54603). Phone 608/781-0200; toll-free 800/658-9497; fax 608/781-0200. www.visitor-guide.com/nights.* 73 rooms, 2 story. Mid-May-Oct: S $$44; D $54; under 12 free; lower rates rest of year. Crib available. TV; cable (premium), VCR available. Complimentary continental breakfast. Restaurant opposite 6 am-11 pm. Check-out 11 am. Business services available. In-room modem link. Downhill ski 8 miles; cross-country ski 1 mile. Exercise equipment. Whirlpool. Cr cds: A, C, D, DS, MC, V.

★ **ROADSTAR INN.** *2622 Rose St (54603). Phone 608/781-3070; toll-free 800/445-4667; fax 608/781-5114.* 110 rooms, 2 story. S $36-$46; D $42-$52; each additional $5; under 15 free; higher rates special events. TV; cable (premium). Complimentary continental breakfast. Restaurant adjacent open 24 hours. Check-out noon. Downhill/cross-country ski 8 miles. Some refrigerators, wet bars. Cr cds: A, D, DS, MC, V.

★ **SUPER 8.** *1625 Rose St (54603). Phone 608/781-8880; toll-free 800/800-8000; fax 608/781-4366. www.super8.com.* 82 rooms, 2 story. S $72-$82; D $82-$92; each additional $5; under 18 free. Crib free. Pet accepted, some restrictions; $5/day. Complimentary continental breakfast. Check-out 11 am. TV. Some in-room whirlpools. Coin laundry. Restaurant nearby. Indoor pool, whirlpool. Meeting rooms. Sundries. Cr cds: A, C, D, DS, MC, V.

Hotel

★★**RADISSON HOTEL LA CROSSE.** *200 Harborview Plz (54601). Phone 608/784-6680; fax 608/784-6694. www.radisson.com.* Providing a lovely view of the river, the spacious accommodations at this hotel are designed to make guests feel at home. 169 rooms, 8 story. D $99-$139; each additional $10; under 18 free. Pet accepted. Check-out noon. TV; cable. Restaurant, bar, entertainment. Exercise equipment. Indoor pool. Downhill/cross-country ski 8 miles. Free airport transportation. Overlooks Mississippi River. Cr cds: A, C, D, DS, ER, JCB, MC, V.

Restaurants

★★**FREIGHTHOUSE.** *107 Vine St (54601). Phone 608/784-6211; fax 608/784-6280. www.freighthouserestaurant. com.* Hours: 4pm-10 pm daily; Fri, Sat 5-10:30 pm. Closed Easter, Thanksgiving, Dec 24-25. Dinner $11.95-$35.95. Bar to 1 am. Former freight house of the Chicago, Milwaukee, and St. Paul Railroad (1880). Outdoor dining overlooking river. Cr cds: A, D, DS, MC, V.

★★**PIGGY'S.** *328 S Front St (54601). Phone 608/784-4877; fax 608/784-7576. www.piggys.com.* Specializes in ribs, pork chops, prime steaks. Hours: 11 am-10 pm; Fri, Sat to 11 pm; Sun from 4-10 pm. Closed Memorial Day, Labor Day, Dec 24-25. Lunch $3.45-$9.95, dinner $15.95-$24.95. Bar. Children's menu. Reservations accepted. Cr cds: A, D, DS, MC, V.

Ladysmith (C-2)

Pop 3,938 **Elev** 1,144 ft **Area code** 715 **Zip** 54848

Information Rusk County Visitor Center, 205 W 9th St; 715/532-2642 or 800/535-7875

Web www.ruskcounty.org

Ladysmith, county seat of Rusk County, is located along the Flambeau River. The economy is based on processing lumber and marketing dairy and farm produce. There are fishing and canoeing facilities in the area.

What to See and Do

Flambeau River State Forest. *E on US 8 to Hawkins, then N on County M to County W, near Winter. Phone 715/332-5271.* A 91,000-acre forest. Canoeing river, swimming, fishing, boating; backpacking, nature and hiking trails, mountain biking, cross-country skiing, snowmobiling, picnicking, camping (dump station). Standard fees. (Daily)

Special Events

Leaf it to Rusk Fall Festival. *Phone 715/532-2642.* County-wide events. Last weekend Sept.

Northland Mardi Gras. *Parade Starts at Middle School 115 E 6th St. S Events at Memorial Park. Phone 715/532-2642.* Third weekend July.

Rusk County Fair. *E 3rd St Fairgrounds. Phone 715/532-2639.* Four days mid-Aug.

Motels/Motor Lodges

★★ **BEST WESTERN EL RANCHO.** *8500 W Flambeau Ave (54848). Phone 715/532-6666; fax 715/532-7551. www.bestwestern.com.* 27 rooms. S $46-$50; D $54-$62; each additional $4; under 12 free. Crib $9. Pet accepted. TV; cable (premium). Restaurant 11 am-2 pm, 4:30-

9:30 pm. Bar to 1 am. Check-out 11 am. Business services available. Downhill ski 15 miles; cross-country ski on site. Cr cds: A, C, D, DS, MC, V.

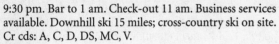

★ **EVERGREEN MOTEL.** *1201 Lake Ave W (54848). Phone 715/532-3168; toll-free 800/828-3168; fax 715/532-3168.* 20 rooms. S $30; D $40; each additional $4. Crib $4. Pet accepted, some restrictions. TV; cable (premium). Complimentary coffee in rooms. Restaurant nearby. Check-out 11 am. Downhill/cross-country ski 7 miles. Picnic tables. Cr cds: A, DS, MC, V.

Lake Delton

Restaurants

★ ★ **DEL-BAR.** *800 Wisconsin Dells Pkwy (53940). Phone 608/253-1861; fax 608/258-1871. www.dells.com/delbar.html.* Specializes in custom-cut steak, pasta, fresh seafood. Hours: 4:30-10 pm; June-Aug to 10:30 pm. Closed Thanksgiving, Dec 25. Dinner $17-$35. Bar. Friday fish fry $9.95. Cr cds: A, D, DS, MC, V.

★ ★ **WALLY'S HOUSE OF EMBERS.** *935 Wisconsin Dells Pkwy (53940). Phone 608/253-6411; fax 608/253-2433. www.dells.com/embers.html.* Hours: 4:30 pm-midnight. Reservations accepted. Bar. Dinner $9.90-$22.90. Child's meals. Specializes in hickory-smoked ribs, steak, fresh seafood. Entertainment weekends. Outdoor gazebo; garden. Family-owned. Cr cds: A, MC, V.

★ **WINTERGREEN GRILLE.** *60 Gasser Rd #A (53940). Phone 608/254-7686; fax 608/253-6235. www.dells.com/wintergrn.html.* Hours: 7 am-9 pm. Sun breakfast buffet 8-11:30 am Memorial Day-Labor Day. Amer, Italian menu. Wine, beer. Breakfast $3.50-$7.95, lunch $4.75-$7.95, dinner $9.95-$17.95. Sun buffet $5.95. Child's meals. Specializes in ribs, pizza. Parking. Cr cds: A, D, DS, MC, V.

Lake Geneva (G-5)

See also Burlington, Elkhorn, Fontana, Kenosha

Settled 1840 **Pop** 5,979 **Elev** 880 ft **Area code** 262 **Zip** 53147

Information Geneva Lake Area Chamber of Commerce, 201 Wrigley Dr; 262/248-4416 or 800/345-1020

Web www.lakegenevawi.com

This is a popular and attractive four-season resort area. Recreational activities include boating, fishing, swimming, horseback riding, camping, hiking, biking, golf, tennis, skiing, cross-country skiing, ice fishing, snowmobiling, and ice boating.

What to See and Do

Big Foot Beach State Park. *1452 Hwy H. 1 mile S on WI 120. Phone 262/248-2528.* A 272-acre beach park on Geneva Lake. Swimming (lifeguard on duty mid-June-Labor Day, weekends only), fishing; picnicking, playground, winter sports, camping. Standard fees. (Daily) **$$$**

Excursion boats. *812 Wrigley Dr. Riviera Docks. Phone 262248-6206 or 800/558-5911.* 2-hour round-trip and one-hour rides; also lunch, Sun brunch, dinner cruises. (May-Oct, daily) Reservations required. Mail boat (mid-June-mid-Sept, once daily). **$$$$**

Geneva Lake. This 5,230-acre lake provides a variety of game fish in clear waters. The surrounding hills are heavily wooded with elm, maple, and oak trees.

Grand Geneva Resort. *7036 Grand Geneva Way. 2 miles E at junction US 12 and WI 50. Phone 800/558-3417.* Area has three chairlifts, two rope tows; patrol, school, rentals; snowmaking; lodging (see RESORT); restaurant, cafeteria, concession, bar. Longest run 1/4 mile; vertical drop 211 feet (Dec-Mar, daily) Cross-country trails, night skiing. **$$$$**

Wilmot Mountain. *3 miles N of Antioch, IL on IL 83, then W on WI County C; 1 mile S of Wilmot, WI on IL state line. Phone 262/862-2301.* Quad, three triple, four double chairlifts, six rope tows; patrol, school, rentals, snowmaking; restaurant, cafeteria, bar. Longest run 2,500 feet; vertical drop 230 feet. Night skiing. (Mid Nov-Mar, daily; closed Dec 24 evening)

Special Events

Venetian Festival. *Flatiron Park, 201 Wrigley Dr. Phone 262/248-4416.* Rides, games, food; lighted boat parade and fireworks. Third weekend Aug.

Winterfest. *201 Wrigley Dr. Riviera Park at the lakefront. Phone 262/248-4416.* Host of US Snow Sculpting Championships. Early Feb.

Motels/Motor Lodges

★ ★ **AMBASSADOR.** *415 S Wells St (53147). Phone 262/248-3452; fax 414/248-0605.* 18 rooms. Late May-mid-Sept: S $65-$135; lower rates rest of year. TV. Indoor pool; whirlpool, sauna. Complimentary continental breakfast. Restaurant nearby. Check-out 11 am. Meeting rooms. Business services available. Tennis. Downhill/cross-country ski 2 miles. Miniature golf adjacent. Some refrigerators, whirlpools. Totally nonsmoking. Cr cds: A, DS, MC, V.

⬜🏊🏌🏖🚶🏃🚫

★ **BUDGET HOST DIPLOMAT.** *1060 S Wells St (53147). Phone 262/248-1809; toll-free 800/264-5678; fax 414/248-1809. www.budgethost.com.* 23 rooms, 2 story. Apr-Oct: S $41-$71; D $51-$101; under 12 free; ski plan; higher rates some holidays; lower rates rest of year. Crib free. TV; cable (premium), VCR available. Pool. Complimentary coffee in lobby. Check-out 11 am. Business services available. Downhill/cross-country ski 2 miles. Balconies. Picnic tables. Cr cds: A, DS, MC, V.

⬜🏊🚫

★★ **INTERLAKEN RESORT AND COUNTRY SPA.** *W 4240 WI 50 (53147). Phone 262/248-9121; toll-free 800/225-5558; fax 414/245-5016. www.interlakenresort.com.* This serene resort promotes an air of pure relaxation and hosts several wonderful views. 144 rooms in 3-story lodge, 100 kitchen villas. Lodge: S, D $49-$169; each additional $10; villas for 1-6, $140 $260; under 12 free; package plans available. Crib free. Check-out noon. TV; VCR (movies). Valet services. Restaurant 7 am-10 pm. Bar 11-1 am; weekend entertainment. Room service. Free supervised children's activites (June-Labor Day; also holidays). Exercise equipment, sauna, steam room. Game room. 3 pools, 1 indoor; wading pool, whirlpool, poolside service. Tennis. Downhill ski 5 miles; cross-country ski on site. Snowmobiles; ice skates. Boats, waterskiing, windsurfing. Barber, beauty shop. Meeting rooms, business services. Concierge (seasonal). Sundries. Gift shop. Cr cds: A, C, D, DS, MC, V.

⬜🏊🏌🏖🚶🏃🚫

Resort

★★★**GRAND GENEVA RESORT & SPA.** *7036 Grand Geneva Way (53147). Phone 262/248-8811; toll-free 800/558-3417; fax 414/249-4763. www.grandgeneva.com.* Guests can let the friendly staff introudce them to their home. Plenty of recreational choices. 355 rooms, 3 story. S, D $179-$279; each additional $10; under 18 free. Crib free. TV; cable (premium), VCR (movies). 3 pools, 2 indoor; whirlpool. Playground. Supervised children's activities; ages 4-12. Complimentary coffee in rooms. Restaurants 6:30 am-10 pm; Bar 11:30-2 am; entertainment. Check-out noon, check-in 4 pm. Convention facilities. Business center. In-room modem link. Valet service. Gift shop. Airport transportation. Indoor, outdoor tennis, pro. 36-hole golf, pro, driving range, putting green. Paddleboats, hydrobikes. Downhill/cross-country ski on site. Bicycle rentals. Exercise room; sauna, steam room. Spa center. Private patios, balconies. 1,300 acres of wooded, meadowland with private lake. Cr cds: A, C, D, DS, JCB, MC, V.

⬜🏊🏌🏖🚶🏃✈🚫

B&B/Small Inns

★★ **FRENCH COUNTRY INN.** *W 4190 West End Rd (53147). Phone 262/245-5220; fax 414/245-9060. www.frenchcountryinn.com.* 24 rooms, 2 story. May-Oct: S, D $105-$155; suites $115-$155; lower rates rest of year. Crib free. Complimentary full breakfast. Check-out noon, check-in 3 pm. TV; cable (premium). Dining room 5-10 pm; Fri, Sat to 10:30 pm. On lake; beach. Pool. Golf-privileges. Downhill ski 12 miles; cross-country ski 1 mile. Business services. Portions of guest house built in Denmark and shipped to US for Danish exhibit at the 1893 Columbian Exposition in Chicago. Cr cds: MC, V.

⬜🏊🏌🏖🚶🚫

Restaurants

★ **POPEYE'S GALLEY AND GROG.** *811 Wrigley Dr (53147). Phone 262/248-4381.* Hours: 11 am-10 pm; Fri, Sat to 11 pm; winter 11:30 am-9 pm; Fri, Sat to 10 pm. Closed Dec 25. Bar. Lunch, dinner $5.95-$15.95. Child's meals. Parking. Nautical décor. Glass-enclosed deck with view of Geneva Lake. Cr cds: A, DS, MC, V.

⬜

★★ **RISTORANTE BRISSAGO.** *7036 Grand Geneva Way (53147). Phone 262/248-8811. www.grandgeneva.com.* Named after a town on Lake Maggiore in the Italian-Swiss countryside, this restaurant enjoys a Midwestern, countryside home all its own. The dining room is just one of the options at the Grand Geneva Resort and Spa. Hours: 5:30-10 pm; Fri, Sat to 11 pm. Closed Mon. Reservations accepted. Italian menu. Bar. Wine list. A la carte entrees: dinner $9.75-$27. Specialties: osso buco Milanese, gamberi Mediterraneo, antipasto. Valet parking. Views of lake and wooded hills. Cr cds: A, D, DS, MC, V.

⬜

Land O Lakes (B-4)

Pop 700 **Elev** 1,700 ft **Area code** 715 **Zip** 54540

Information Chamber of Commerce, US 45, PO Box 599; 715/547-3432 or 800/236-3432

Web www.ci.land-o-lakes.wi.us

This lovely village, on the Michigan border amid more than 100 lakes, serves as a center for tourist traffic. Fishing and boating in the area are exceptional. East of town is Lac Vieux Desert, source of the Wisconsin River.

Motel/Motor Lodge

★ **PINEAIRE RESORT MOTEL.** *2091 WI 45 (95449). Phone 906/544-2313.* 9 cottages, 7 with shower only. No A/C, room phones. Cottages $35-$45; each additional

$5; under 8 free. Crib free. Pet accepted. TV. Restaurant nearby. Check-out 10 am. Cross-country ski on site. Snowmobiling. Picnic tables, grills. Cr cds: A, MC, V.

Resort

★★SUNRISE LODGE. *5894 W Shore Rd (54540). Phone 715/547-3684; toll-free 800/221-9689; fax 715/547-6110. www.sunriselodge.com.* 22 units in 21 cottages, 18 kitchens No A/C in cottages. May-Oct, AP: S $80; D $150; EP: S $49; D $59; weekly, family rates; fall plan; Nov-Apr, EP only: D $55-$125. Crib available. Pet accepted. Playground. Dining room 7:30-10 am, 11:30 am-2 pm, 5-7:30 pm; Sun 7:30-11 am, noon-3 pm; weekends only in winter. Box lunches. Meeting room. Business services available. Airport, bus depot transportation. Tennis. Miniature golf. Private beach; boats, motors, canoes. Cross-country ski on site. Lawn games. Exercise trail. Nature trail. Bicycles. Recreation room. Fish/hunt guides; clean and store area. Refrigerators. Picnic tables, grills. Spacious grounds. On Lac Vieux Desert. Cr cds: DS, MC, V.

Madison (G-4)

See also Mount Horeb, New Glarus, Prairie du Sac

Settled 1837 **Pop** 191,262 **Elev** 863 ft **Area code** 608

Information Greater Madison Convention & Visitors Bureau, 615 E Washington Ave, 53703; 608/255-2537 or 800/373-6376

Web www.visitmadison.com

Madison was a virgin wilderness in 1836 when the territorial legislature selected the spot for the capital and the state university. Today this "City of Four Lakes," located on an isthmus between Lake Mendota and Lake Monona, is a recreational, cultural, and manufacturing center. Both the university and state government play important roles in the community.

Madison has a rich architectural heritage left by Frank Lloyd Wright and the Prairie School movement. There are a number of Wright buildings here; many are private homes and not open to the public but may be viewed from the outside.

What to See and Do

Dane County Farmers' Market. *200 Martin Luther King, Jr. Blvd. (Two locations) Capitol Sq and 200 Martin Luther King, Jr. Blvd. Phone 608/424-6714.* Festive open-air market selling Wisconsin produce and agricultural products. Capitol Sq (May-Oct, Sat); Martin Luther King, Jr Blvd (May-Oct, Wed).

Edgewood College. *855 Woodrow St. Phone 608/257-4861.* (1927) 1,725 students. A 55-acre campus on Lake Wingra; Native American burial mounds.

First Unitarian Society. *900 University Bay Dr. Phone 608/233-9774.* A classic example of Wright's Prairie School work. (May-Sept, Mon-Fri afternoons, also Sat mornings; closed holidays and two weeks Aug) **$$**

Henry Vilas Park Zoo. *702 S Randall Ave on Lake Wingra. Phone 608/258-9490.* World-famous for successful orangutan, Siberian tiger, spectacle bear, penguin, and camel breeding programs. Zoo exhibits incl 600 specimens consisting of 140 species. Petting zoo, picnic area on an island in Lake Wingra's lagoon, bathing beach, tennis courts. (Daily) **FREE**

Lake Kegonsa State Park. *2405 Door Creek Rd. 13 miles SE via I-90, then S on County N. Phone 608/873-9695.* A 343-acre park. Swimming, waterskiing, fishing, boating; hiking and nature trails, picnicking, playground, camping (May-mid-Oct, dump station). Standard fees. (Daily)

Madison Art Center. *211 State St in Civic Center. Phone 608/257-0158.* Features modern and contemporary art by international, national, regional, and local artists; permanent collection. Tours (by appointment, fee). (Tues-Sun; closed holidays) **FREE**

Madison Children's Museum. *100 State St. Phone 608/256-6445.* Hands-on museum. Special craft and activity programs every weekend. (Tues-Sun, daily; closed holidays) **$$**

Olbrich Botanical Gardens. *3330 Atwood Ave. Phone 608/246-4551.* Contains 14 acres of horticultural displays incl annuals, perennials, shrubs, hybrid roses, lilies, dahlias, spring bulbs, rock and herb gardens. All-American Rose Selection Demonstration Garden. Garden building has a tropical conservatory housed inside a 50-foot high glass pyramid; tropical ferns, palms, flowering plants; waterfall, stream. (Daily; closed Dec 25) **$**

Self-driving tour. These are private homes and not open to the public. However, they may be viewed from the outside. **Airplane House** (1908), *120 Ely Place;* **Dr. Arnold Jackson House** (1957), *3515 W Beltline Hwy;* **Lamp House** *(1899), 22 N Butler St;* **J. C. Pew House** (1939), *3650 Lake Mendota Dr;* **Louis Sullivan's Bradley House,** *106 N Prospect;* "**Jacobs I**" **House** (1937), *441 Toepfer Ave.*

State Capitol. *2 E Main St. Capitol Sq. Phone 608/266-0382.* Dominates the center of the city. The white granite building has a classic dome topped by Daniel Chester French's gilded bronze statue Wisconsin. Tours (daily; closed most major holidays). **FREE**

State Historical Museum. *30 N Carroll St, located on Capitol Sq, junction State, Mifflin, and Carroll sts. Phone 608/264-6555.* Permanent exhibits explore the history of

Native American life in Wisconsin; gallery with changing Wisconsin, US history exhibits. Theater. (Tues-Sat) **FREE**

University of Wisconsin-Madison. *716 Langdon St. 7 blocks W of Capitol. Maps and general information at Visitor and Information Place, N Park and Langdon Sts; or at Campus Assistance Center, 420 N Lake St. Phone 608/263-2400.* (1849) 41,948 students. The 929-acre campus extends for more than 2 miles along S shore of Lake Mendota. On campus are

> **Carillon Tower.** *1160 Observatory Dr. Phone 608/263-1900.* 56 bells; afternoon concerts (Sun).

> **Elvehjem Museum of Art.** *800 University Ave. Phone 608/263-2246.* Paintings, sculpture, decorative arts, prints, Japanese woodcuts, other artworks from 2300 B.C. to present day; changing exhibits; 80,000-volume Kohler Art Library. (Tues-Sun; closed Jan 1, Thanksgiving, Dec 25) **FREE**

> **Geology Museum.** *1215 W Dayton St, corner of W Dayton and Charter sts. Phone 608/262-2399.* 6-foot rotating globe, rocks, minerals, a black light display, a walk-through cave, meteorites, and fossils incl the skeletons of a giant mastodon and dinosaurs. (Mon-Fri, daily, also Sat mornings; closed holidays) **FREE**

> **Memorial Library.** *728 State St. Langdon and Lake sts. Phone 608/262-3193.* More than five million volumes; collection of rare books.

> **Observatory and Willow drives.** Scenic drives along shore of Lake Mendota.

> **Washburn Observatory.** *1401 Observatory Dr. Phone 608/262-9274.* Public viewing first and third Wed evenings of each month (weather permitting). **FREE**

Wisconsin Veterans Museum. *30 W Mifflin St. Phone 608/267-1799.* Dioramas, exhibits of events from Civil War to Persian Gulf War. (June-Sept, daily; rest of year, Mon-Sat; closed holidays) **FREE**

Special Events

Art Fair on the Square. *2 E Main. Phone 608/257-0158.* Exhibits by 500 artists and craftspersons; food, entertainment. Contact Madison Art Center. Mid-July.

Concerts on the Square. *2 E Main. Phone 608/257-0638.* 6-week series; Wed evenings. Late June-early Aug.

Dane County Fair. *Alliant Energy Center. Phone 608/224-0500.* Mid-July.

Paddle & Portage Canoe Race. *Gorham & Blair sts. Phone 608/255-1008.* July.

Motels/Motor Lodges

★ ★ **BEST WESTERN.** *22 S Carroll St (53703). Phone 608/257-8811; toll-free 800/279-8811; fax 608/257-5995. www.bestwestern.com.* 213 rooms, 9 story. S $94-$99; D $104-$114; each additional $10; suites $149-$159; under 12 free; higher rates special events. Crib free. Pet accepted. TV; cable (premium). Heated pool; whirlpool. Restaurants 6 am-11 pm. Bar 2 pm-closing. Check-out noon. Meeting rooms. Business services available. In-room modem link. Gift shop. Free covered parking; valet. Free airport transportation. Exercise equipment. Some in-room whirlpools. Cr cds: A, C, D, DS, MC, V.

[D] [symbols]

★ **BEST WESTERN.** *650 Grand Canyon Dr (53719). Phone 608/833-2400; toll-free 800/847-7919; fax 608/833-5614. www.bestwestern.com.* 101 suites, 2 story. D $49-$109; each additional $5; under 17 free. Pet accepted. Complimentary full breakfast. Check-out noon. TV; cable. In-room modem link. Laundry services. Health club privileges. Exercise equipment. Cr cds: A, C, D, DS, ER, JCB, MC, V.

[D] [symbols] SC

★ **ECONO LODGE.** *4726 E Washington Ave (53704). Phone 608/241-4171; fax 608/241-1715. www.econolodge.com.* 98 rooms, 2 story. S $39-$41.95; D $45.95-$57.95; each additional $4; theme rooms $50.95-$62.95; under 18 free. Crib $3. TV; cable. Complimentary continental breakfast. Restaurant nearby. Check-out noon. Laundry facilities. Meeting room. Business services available. Sundries. Some microwaves. Cr cds: A, C, D, DS, JCB, MC, V.

[D] [symbols] SC

★ ★ ★ **EDGEWATER HOTEL.** *666 Wisconsin Ave (53703). Phone 608/256-9071; toll-free 800/922-5512; fax 608/256-0910. www.theedgewater.com.* Lake view rooms loaded with the latest in modern features await guests at this getaway on Lake Mendota. 116 rooms, 8 story. S, D $79-$160; suites $189-$389. Crib free. Pet accepted, some restrictions. Check-out noon. TV; cable (premium). Some microwaves. Valet services. Restaurant (see also ADMIRALTY). Bar 11-12:30 am. Room service 6:30 am-10:30 pm. Health club privileges. Massage. On Lake Mendota; swimming beach. Free garage. Free airport transportation. Meeting rooms, business services. Cr cds: A, C, D, MC, V.

[D] [symbols]

★ **EXEL INN.** *4202 E Towne Blvd (53704). Phone 608/241-3861; toll-free 800/356-8013; fax 608/241-9752. www.exelinn.com.* 101 rooms, 2 story. May-Sept: S $39.99-$54; D $48.99-$63; each additional $4; under 18 free; weekly rates; higher rates special events; lower rates rest of year. Crib free. Pet accepted, some restrictions. TV; cable (premium). Complimentary continental breakfast. Coffee in rooms. Restaurant nearby. Check-out noon. Business services available. In-room modem link. Sundries. Coin laundry. Cross-country ski

3 miles. Exercise equipment. Health club privileges. Game room. Some refrigerators; microwaves available. Cr cds: A, C, D, DS, MC, V.

[D] [icons] SC

★**FAIRFIELD INN.** *4765 Hayes Rd (53704). Phone 608/249-5300; fax 608/240-9335. www.fairfieldinn.com.* 135 rooms, 3 story. S, D $44-$62; under 18 free. Crib free. TV; cable (premium). Heated pool. Complimentary continental breakfast. Restaurants nearby. Check-out noon. Business services available. Cr cds: A, C, D, DS, ER, JCB, MC, V.

[D] [icons] SC

★ **HAMPTON INN.** *4820 Hayes Rd (53704). Phone 608/244-9400; toll-free 800/426-7866; fax 608/244-7177. www.hampton-inn.com.* 116 rooms, 4 story. S $69-$89; D $79-$99; under 19 free; higher rates special events. Crib free. TV; cable. Indoor pool; whirlpool. Complimentary continental breakfast. Coffee in rooms. Restaurant nearby. Check-out noon. Meeting rooms. Business services available. Cross-country ski 10 miles. Exercise equipment. Microwaves available. Cr cds: A, C, D, DS, MC, V.

[D] [icons]

★ ★ **HOWARD JOHNSON PLAZA HOTEL.** *525 W Johnson St (53705). Phone 608/251-5511; toll-free 800/446-4656; fax 608/251-4824. www.hojo.com.* 163 rooms, 7 story. S $82-$135; D $92-$145; each additional $10; studio rooms $92-$145; suite $125-$150; under 18 free. Crib free. TV; cable. Indoor pool; whirlpool. Coffee in rooms. Restaurant 6 am-10 pm. Room service. Bar 4:30 pm-12:45 am. Check-out noon. Meeting rooms. Business services available. Valet service. Sundries. Free airport transportation. Cross-country ski 1 mile. Exercise equipment. Health club privileges. Refrigerators, microwaves available. Cr cds: A, C, D, DS, ER, JCB, MC, V.

[D] [icons] SC

★★**IVY INN HOTEL.** *2355 University Ave (53705). Phone 608/233-9717; toll-free 877/IVYINN1; fax 608/233-2660. www.ivyinnhotel.com.* 57 rooms, 2 story. S $64-$74; D $74-$79; each additional $10; under 13 free. Crib free. Pet accepted. TV; cable. Restaurant 7 am-2 pm, 5-8 pm. Bar 4 pm-midnight. Check-out noon. Business services available. Valet service. Sundries. Cr cds: A, D, DS, MC, V.

[D] [icons]

★ **SELECT INN.** *4845 Hayes Rd (53704). Phone 608/249-1815; toll-free 800/641-1000; fax 608/249-1815. www.selectinn.com.* 96 rooms, 3 story. June-mid-Sept: S $33.90-$53.90; D $41.90-$53.90; each additional $4; under 18 free. Pet accepted; $25 deposit. TV; cable. Complimentary continental breakfast. Restaurant nearby. Check-out 11 am. Meeting room. Business services available. Sundries. Whirlpool. Some refrigerators, microwaves, minibars. Cr cds: A, C, D, DS, MC, V.

[D] [icons] SC [icon]

Hotels

★ ★ ★ **MADISON CONCOURSE HOTEL & GOVERNOR'S CLUB.** *1 W Dayton St (53703). Phone 608/257-6000; toll-free 800/356-8293; fax 608/257-5280. www.concoursehotel.com.* Stylish and warm are often used to describe this inn. 356 rooms, 13 story. S $109-$159; D $119-$169; each additional $10; suites $200-$350; under 18 free. Crib free. TV; cable. Pool; whirlpool. Coffee in rooms. Restaurant 6:30 am-10 pm. Bar 11-1 am; entertainment. Check-out noon. Convention facilities. Business center. Barber. Gift shop. Free garage. Airport transportation. Cross-country ski 3 miles. Exercise equipment; sauna, steam room. Health club privileges. Some in-room whirlpools. Luxury level. Cr cds: A, C, D, DS, MC, V.

[D] [icons] SC [icon]

★★★**MARRIOTT MADISON WEST.** *1313 John Q. Hammons Dr (53582). Phone 608/831-2000. www.marriott.com.* 295 rooms, 10 story. S, D $115-$199; each additional $15; under 17 free. Crib available. Pet accepted. Indoor pool. TV; cable (premium), VCR available. Complimentary coffee, newspaper in rooms. Restaurant 6 am-10 pm. Check-out noon. Meeting rooms. Business center. Gift shop. Some refrigerators, minibars.refrigerators, minibars. Cr cds: A, C, D, DS, MC, V.

[icons]

★ ★ ★ **SHERATON.** *706 John Nolen Dr (53713). Phone 608/251-2300; toll-free 800/325-3535; fax 608/251-1189. www.sheraton.com.* 237 rooms, 7 story. S $99; D $119; each additional $10; under 18 free; weekend rates. Crib free. TV; cable. Indoor pool; whirlpool. Restaurant 11:30 am-2 pm, 5-10 pm. Bar 5 pm-1 am. Room service 6:30-11 am. Check-out noon. Meeting rooms. Gift shop. Exercise equipment; sauna. Game room. Luxury level. Cr cds: A, C, D, DS, ER, JCB, MC, V.

[D] [icons]

B&B/Small Inns

★ ★ ★ **ANNIE'S BED AND BREAKFAST.** *2117 Sheridan Dr (53704). Phone 608/244-2224; fax 608/244-2224. www.bbinternet.com/annies.* One block from the shores of Lake Mendota, many of the rooms here offer beautiful valley views. Enjoy a peaceful stay after you see all that Madison has to offer just minutes away. 2, 2-bedroom suites, 2 story. Suites $129; each additional $40; 2-day minimum. Adults only. Complimentary full breakfast. Complimentary coffee in library. Check-out noon, check-in 4-6 pm. TV; free VCR movies. In-room modem link. Refrigerators. Health club privileges. Near Lake Mendota. Whirlpool. Cross-country ski adjacent. Picnic tables. Business services. Overlooks park. Cr cds: A, MC, V.

[icons]

★ ★ **COLLINS HOUSE B&B.** *704 E Gorham St (53703). Phone 608/255-4230. www.collinshouse.com.* 5 rooms, 3 story. S $75-$130; D $85-$140. Crib free. TV in sitting room; VCR available (free movies). Complimentary full breakfast. Restaurant nearby. Check-out noon, check-in 4 pm. Cross-country ski 3 miles. Some in-room whirlpools, fireplaces; microwaves available. Balconies. Former residence of lumber industry executive (1911); example of Prairie School style of architecture. View of Lake Mendota. Totallly nonsmoking. Cr cds: A, MC, V.

🏊

Extended Stay

★ ★ **RESIDENCE INN BY MARRIOTT.** *501 D'Onofrio Dr (53719). Phone 608/833-8333; fax 608/833-2693. www.residenceinn.com.* 80 kitchen suites, 2 story. Kitchen. suites $120-$175; higher rates special events. Crib free. Pet accepted, some restrictions. TV; cable. Heated pool; whirlpool. Complimentary continental breakfast. Restaurant nearby. Check-out noon. Coin laundry. Meeting rooms. Valet service. Exercise equipment. Health club privileges. Microwaves. Private patios, balconies. Picnic tables, grills. Cr cds: A, C, D, DS, ER, JCB, MC, V.

🄳 🔧 🏊 🏃 🐾

Restaurants

★ ★ ★ **ADMIRALTY.** *666 Wisconsin (53703). Phone 608/256-9071. www.theedgewater.com.* This dining room boasts spectacular sunset views over Lake Mendota and a classic, continental menu. The space carries Old World charm with its leather chairs, framed photographs, and tableside preparations of dishes. Continental menu. Hours: 6:30-10 am, 11 am-2 pm, 5-10 pm; Sun brunch 11 am-2 pm. Dinner $22-$35. Sun brunch . Bar. Entertainment Fri, Sat (summer, fall). Outdoor seating. Cr cds: A, D, MC, V.

🄳

★ ★ **CHINA HOUSE.** *1256 S Park St (53715). Phone 608/257-1079. www.madisonchinahouse.com.* Hours: 11:30 am-10 pm; Fri, Sat to 11 pm. Reservations accepted. Chinese menu. Bar. A la carte entrees: lunch $3.75-$4.75, dinner $5.95-$9.25. Specializes in Szechwan and Hunan cuisine. Parking. Chinese décor. Cr cds: A, C, MC, V.

🄳

★ **ELLA'S DELI.** *2902 E Washington Ave (53704). Phone 608/241-5291.* Kosher-style deli menu. Hours: 10 am-11 pm; Fri, Sat to midnight. Closed Thanksgiving, Dec 24-25. Dinner $3.50-$9.95. Outdoor carousel. Cr cds: MC, V.

🄳

★ **ESSEN HAUS.** *514 E Wilson St (53703). Phone 608/255-4674; fax 608/258-8632. www.essenhaus.com.* German, American menu. Specialties: authentic German cuisine, prime rib, fresh fish. Hours: 5-10 pm; Fri to 11 pm; Sat 4-11 pm; Sun 3-9 pm. Closed Mon; Jan 1, Dec 24-25. Dinner $12.95-$18.95. Bar from 3 pm. Entertainment. Children's menu. Reservations accepted. Parking. Old World atmosphere; extensive stein collection. Cr cds: MC, V.

🄳

★ ★ ★ **L'ETOILE.** *25 N Pinckney (53703). Phone 608/251-0500; fax 608/251-7577. www.letoile-restaurant.com.* This second-floor dining room may be hard to find, but it's worth the search for some of this university town's best dining. Chef/owner Odessa Piper changes her menu weekly to highlight the wares of local markets and organic farooms. French, American menu. Specialties: seasonal and regional dishes. Menu changes daily. Hours: from 5:30 pm; Fri, Sat from 5 pm. Closed Sun; holidays. Dinner $20-$30. Bar. Reservations accepted. Contemporary decor; original artwork. View of capitol. Cr cds: D, DS, MC, V.

★ ★ **MARINER'S INN.** *5339 Lighthouse Bay Dr (53704). Phone 608/246-3120. www.marinersinn.com.* Hours: from 5 pm; Fri-Sun from 4:30 pm. Closed some holidays. Bar. Dinner $14.99-$19.99. Specializes in steak, seafood, legendary hash browns. Own cheesecake. Parking. Nautical décor. View of lake; dockage. Family-owned. Cr cds: MC, V.

🄳

★ **NAU-TI-GAL.** *5360 Westport Rd (53704). Phone 608/246-3130. www.nautigal.com.* Hours: 11:30 am-10 pm; Fri, Sat to 10:30 pm (summer); Sun 10 am-9 pm; Sun brunch to 2 pm. Closed Jan 1, Thanksgiving, Dec 25; also Super Bowl Sun, Mon Nov-Feb. Dinner $7.99-$18. Sun brunch. Bar. Outdoor seating. Cr cds: MC, V.

🄳

★ ★ **QUIVEY'S GROVE.** *6261 Nesbitt Rd (53719). Phone 608/273-4900. www.quiveysgrove.com.* Specialties: regional Wisconsin dishes, turtle pie. Hours: 11 am-10 pm. Closed holidays. Lunch $5.75-$7.50, dinner $7.75-$22.50. Bar. Children's menu. Converted historic mansion and stables (1855); many antiques. Reservations accepted. Parking. Cr cds: A, DS, MC, V.

🄳

★ **SA-BAI THONG.** *2840 University Ave (53705). Phone 608/238-3100.* Hours: 11 am-10 pm; Sun from 5 pm. Closed Jan 1, Thanksgiving, Dec 25. Reservations accepted. Thai menu. Wine, beer. A la carte entrees: lunch $4.95-$6.25, dinner $6.95-$11.95. Specializes in seafood, curry dishes. Contemporary Thai décor. Totally nonsmoking. Cr cds: A, DS, MC, V.

🄳

Manitowish Waters (B-3)

See also Minocqua, Woodruff

Pop 686 **Elev** 1,611 ft **Area code** 715 **Zip** 54545

Information Chamber of Commerce, PO Box 251, 54545; 715/543-8488 or 888/626-9877

Web www.manitowishwaters.org

Manitowish Waters is in Northern Highland-American Legion State Forest, which abounds in small and medium-size lakes linked by streams. Ten of the fourteen lakes are navigable without portaging, making them ideal for canoeing. There are 16 campgrounds on lakes in the forest (standard fees) and 135 overnight campsites on water trails. Canoe trips, fishing, swimming, boating, waterskiing, and snowmobiling are popular here.

What to See and Do

Cranberry bog tours. *Hwy 51 Airport Rd. Community Center. Phone 715/543-8488.* Tours begin with a video and samples, then follow guides in own vehicle. (Late July-early Oct, Fri)

Motel/Motor Lodge

★ **GREAT NORTHERN.** *Phone 715/476-2440; fax 715/476-2205.* 80 rooms, 2 story. No A/C. S, D $59-$69; each additional $10; under 10 free. Pet accepted. TV; cable (premium). Sauna. Indoor pool; whirlpools. Complimentary continental breakfast. Restaurant. Bar 5 pm-2 am. Check-out 11 am. Meeting rooms. Business services available. Gift shop. Cross-country ski 1 mile. Game room. On lake; swimming beach, boats. Cr cds: DS, MC, V.

D ⚓ 🛥 💪 🏊 ⛷ 🏖 ⛵

Restaurants

★ ★ **LITTLE BOHEMIA.** *County W (54545). Phone 715/543-8433. www.littlebohemia.net.* Hours: 4-11 pm; June-Aug expanded hours. Closed Wed; Feb and Mar. Reservations accepted. No A/C. Bar. Dinner $10.95-$22.95. Child's meals. Specializes in ribs, steak, roast duck. Rustic décor. Site of a 1930s shoot-out between John Dillinger and the FBI; musuem. Cr cds: DS, MC, V.

★ ★ **SWANBERG'S BAVARIAN INN.** *140 CONTY HWY W (54545). Phone 715/543-2122; fax 715/543-2047.* Continental menu. Hours: 11:30 am-9 pm. Closed Sun. Lunch $4.95-$7.50, dinner $10.95-$25. Bar. Children's menu. Reservations accepted. Cr cds: DS, MC, V.

D

Manitowoc (E-6)

See also Green Bay, Sheboygan, Two Rivers

Settled 1836 **Pop** 32,520 **Elev** 606 ft **Area code** 920 **Zip** 54220

Information Manitowoc-Two Rivers Area Chamber of Commerce, 1515 Memorial Dr, PO Box 903, 54221-0903; 920/684-5575 or 800/262-7892

Web www.mtvcchamber.com

A shipping, shopping, and industrial center, Manitowoc has an excellent harbor and a geographical position improved by the completion of the St. Lawrence Seaway. Shipbuilding has been an important industry since the earliest days. During World War II Manitowoc shipyards produced nearly 100 vessels for the United States Navy including landing craft, wooden minesweepers, sub chasers, and 28 submarines. Manitowoc is the home of one of the largest manufacturers of aluminum ware and is a leader in the state's canning industry. Nearby lakes and streams provide excellent fishing.

What to See and Do

Hidden Valley Ski Area. *1815 Maple St. Phone 920/682-5475, or 920/863-2713 (snow report).* Area has double chairlift, two surface lifts; patrol, school, rentals; snowmaking; snack bar, bar. Longest run is 2,600 feet; vertical drop 200 feet. (Dec-Mar, Fri-Sun; night skiing Tues-Fri) **$$$$**

Lake Michigan car ferry. *900 S Lakeview Dr. Trips to Ludington, MI. Phone 920/684-0888 or 800/841-4243.* Departs from dock at S Lakeview Dr. (Early May-Oct, daily; advance reservations strongly recommended)

Lincoln Park Zoo. *1215 N 8th St. Phone 920/683-4537.* Array of animals in attractive settings; picnic, recreational facilities. (Daily) **FREE**

Pine Crest Historical Village. *924 Pine Crest Ln. I-43 exit 152, then 3 miles W on County JJ, then left on Pine Crest Lane. Phone 920/684-5110.* Site of 22 historic buildings depicting a typical turn-of-the-century Manitowoc county village. (May-Labor Day, daily; Sept-mid-Oct, Fri-Sun; also two weekends late Nov-early Dec) **$$$**

Rahr-West Art Museum. *610 N 8th St at Park St. Phone 920/683-4501.* Victorian house with period rooms; American art; collection of Chinese ivory carvings. Modern art wing featuring changing exhibits. (Daily; closed holidays) **DONATION**

Wisconsin Maritime Museum. *75 Maritime Dr. Phone 920/684-0218.* Exhibits depict 150 years of maritime history including model ship gallery; narrated tours through the *USS COBIA,* a 312-foot WWII submarine. (Daily; closed holidays) **$$$**

Marinette (D-6)

See also Oconto, Peshtigo

Settled 1795 **Pop** 11,843 **Elev** 598 ft **Area code** 715 **Zip** 54143

Information Chamber of Commerce, 601 Marinette Ave, PO Box 512; 715/735-6681 or 800/236-6681

Web www.cybrzn.com/chamber

Located along the south bank of the Menominee River, Marinette is named for Queen Marinette, daughter of a Menominee chief. An industrial and port city, it is also the retail trade center for the surrounding recreational area.

What to See and Do

City Park. *2000 Alice Ln. Carney Ave. Phone 715/732-0558.* Picnicking, camping (electric hookups, dump station; May-Sept). **$$$**

Fishing, whitewater rafting, canoeing. Trout streams, lakes, and the Peshtigo River nearby. Inquire at Chamber of Commerce.

Marinette County Historical Museum. *On Stephenson Island, US 41 at state border. Phone 715/732-0831.* Features logging history of area; miniature wood carvings of logging camp; Native American artifacts. Tours by appointment. (Memorial Day-Sept, daily) **DONATION**

Special Event

Theatre on the Bay. *750 W Bay Shore St, University of Wisconsin Center/Marinette County. Phone 715/735-4300.* Comedies, dramas, musicals. June-Aug.

Motels/Motor Lodges

★★ **BEST WESTERN.** *1821 Riverside Ave (54143). Phone 715/732-1000; toll-free 800/338-3305; fax 715/732-0800. www.bestwestern.com.* 120 rooms, 6 story. S $65-$69; D $69-$75; each additional $6; under 18 free. Crib free. TV; cable; VCR available (movies). Indoor pool. Coffee in rooms. Restaurant 6 am-10 pm. Room service. Bar 11-1 am. Check-out noon. Meeting room. Business services available. Valet service. Sundries. Cross-country ski 1 mile. Game room. Cr cds: A, C, D, DS, ER, JCB, MC, V.

⬜ 🐾 🏊 🎿 📠 🛥 ✕ 🛄 SC

★ **SUPER 8.** *1508 Marinette Ave (54143). Phone 715/735-7887; fax 715/735-7455. www.super8.com.* 68 rooms, 2 story. Mid-May-Sept: S $46; D $52; under 12 free; lower rates rest of year. Crib free. Pet accepted, some restrictions. TV; cable (premium). Complimentary continental breakfast. Check-out 11 am. Meeting rooms. Business services available. Cross-country ski 5 miles. Sauna. Whirlpool. Cr cds: A, D, DS, MC, V.

⬜ 🐾 🏊 🛥 SC

B&B/Small Inns

★★ **LAUERMAN GUEST HOUSE INN.** *1975 Riverside Ave (54143). Phone 715/732-7800. www.explore wisconsin.com\lauermanguesthouseinn.* 7 rooms, 3 story. S $53; D $85; each additional $10. Complimentary full breakfast. Check-out 11 am, check-in 2 pm. Cross-country ski 1 mile. Free airport, bus depot transportation. Cr cds: A, DS, MC, V.

🛥 SC

Marshfield (E-3)

See also Stevens Point, Wisconsin Rapids

Settled 1872 **Pop** 19,291 **Elev** 1,262 ft **Area code** 715 **Zip** 54449

Information Visitors & Promotion Bureau, 700 S Central St, PO Box 868; 715/384-3454 or 800/422-4541

Web www.mtecnserv.com/macci

Marshfield, a city that once boasted one sawmill and 19 taverns, was almost destroyed by fire in 1887. It was rebuilt on a more substantial structural and industrial basis. This is a busy northern dairy center, noted for its large medical clinic, manufactured housing wood products, and steel fabrication industries.

What to See and Do

Upham Mansion. *212 W Third St. Phone 715/387-3322 or 800/422-4541.* (1880) Italianate, mid-Victorian house built entirely of wood. Some original furniture, custommade in the factory of the owner. (Wed and Sun afternoons) **FREE**

Wildwood Park and Zoo. *630 S Central Ave. off WI 13 (Roddis Ave), S of business district or off 17th St from Central Ave S. Phone 715/384-4642 or 800/422-4541.* Zoo houses a variety of animals and birds, mostly native to Wisconsin. (Mid-May-late Sept, daily; rest of year, Mon-Fri) **FREE**

Special Events

Central Wisconsin State Fair. *Fair Park. Vine Ave and 14th St. Phone 715/387-1261.* Six days ending Labor Day.

Dairyfest. *Vetrans Park, 7th and Central. Phone 800/ 422-4541.* Salute to the dairy industry. First weekend June.

Fall Festival. *Wildwood Park 17th & Central. Phone 800/ 422-4541.* Mid-Sept.

Mauston (F-3)

See also Wisconsin Dells

Settled 1840 **Pop** 3,439 **Elev** 883 ft **Area code** 608 **Zip** 53948

Information Greater Mauston Area Chamber of Commerce, 503 WI 82, PO Box 171; 608/847-4142

What to See and Do

Buckhorn State Park. *W8450 Buckhorn Park Ave. 11 miles N via County rds 58 and G, near Necedah. Phone 608/565-2789.* A 2,504-acre park with facilities for swimming, waterskiing, fishing, boating, canoeing; hunting, hiking, nature trails, picnicking, playground, backpack and canoe camping. (Daily) Standard fees. **$$**

Motels/Motor Lodges

★ **K AND K MOTEL.** *219 US 12/16 (54618). Phone 608/ 427-3100; fax 608/427-3824. rkelsingamwt.net.* 14 rooms. S $30-$35; D $37.95-$50; each additional $5; higher rates special events. Crib free. Pet accepted; fee. TV; cable, VCR available (movies $5). Coffee in lobby. Restaurant opposite 11 am-10 pm. Check-out 10 am. Coin laundry. Business services available. Refrigerators, microwaves. Cr cds: A, MC, V.

D 🐾 🛄 🖂 SC

★ **TRAVELODGE.** *1700 E Bridge St (53950). Phone 608/562-5141; toll-free 888/895-6200; fax 608/562-6205. www.travelodge.com.* 72 rooms. S $30-$49; D $42-$59; each additional $5; studio rooms $49-$59. Crib free. TV; cable. Playground. Restaurant 6:30 am-9 pm. Bar 11:30-1 am. Check-out 11 am. Meeting room. Recreation room. Cr cds: A, D, DS, JCB, MC, V.

D 🖂 SC

Guest Ranch

★★ **WOODSIDE RANCH TRADING POST.** *W 4015 WI 82 (53948). Phone 608/847-4275; toll-free 800/ 646-4275. www.woodsideranch.com.* 14 rooms in 2-story lodge, 23 cottages (1-, 2- and 3-bedroom). No room phones. AP, late June-late Sept, late Dec-late Feb: S $210/ week; D $370/week; each additional $175-$420/week; lower rates rest of year. Crib free. Pet accepted. Complimentary coffee in lobby. Check-out 10 am, check-in 1: 30 pm. TV in lobby. Fireplace in cottages. Coin laundry. Dining room; sittings at 8 am, 12:30 and 5:30 pm. Bar

Snack bar, picnics. Bar 8-2 am; entertainment Tues, Sat. Free supervised children's activities. Playground. Sauna. Sports director. Social director. Game room. Recreation room. Pool; wading pool, poolside service. Tennis. Downhill/cross-country ski on site. Snack bar, picnics, picnics. Boats. Hiking. Sleighing, sledding. Gift shop. Swimming. On 1,400 acres. Cr cds: DS, MC, V.

D 🐾 🛶 🎿 🎿 🏊 🛥

Menomonee Falls (G-5)

See also Milwaukee, Wauwatosa

Settled 1843 **Pop** 26,840 **Elev** 840 ft **Area code** 262 **Zip** 53051

Information Menomonee Falls Chamber of Commerce, N 88 W 16621 Appleton Ave, PO Box 73, 53052; 262/ 251-6565 or 800/801-6565

What to See and Do

Bugline Recreation Trail. *Appleton Ave.* A 12-mile trail located on the former Chicago, Milwaukee, St. Paul, and Pacific Railroad right-of-way. Bicycling, hiking, jogging, horseback riding (some areas), cross-country skiing, snowmobiling. Dogs allowed (on leash).

Old Falls Village. *N96W15791 County Line Rd. 1/2 mile N on County Line Rd. Phone 262/255-8346.* Miller-Davidson farmhouse (1858) of Greek Revival style, decorative arts museum, 1851 schoolhouse, carriage house, barn museum, 1890 railroad depot, two restored log cabins,1873 Victorian cottage; extensive grounds, picnic area. (May-Sept, Sun; also by appointment) **$**

Sub-Continental Divide. *Main St, 1 block W of Town Line Rd. Phone 262/251-6565 or 800/801-6565.* Water falling west of this crest of land goes into the Fox River Watershed and eventually into the Gulf of Mexico via the Mississippi River. Water falling on the east side goes into the Menomonee River watershed and enters the St. Lawrence Seaway by flowing through the Great Lakes.

Motel/Motor Lodge

★ **SUPER 8.** *N96 W17490 County Line Rd (53022). Phone 414/255-0880; toll-free 800/800-8000; fax 414/255-7741. www.super8.com.* 81 rooms, 2 story. June-Sept: S $55; D $62-$72; each additional $5; suites $60-$65; under 12 free; lower rates rest of year. Crib free. Pet accepted; $50 refundable. TV; cable (premium). Complimentary continental breakfast. Restaurant adjacent open 24 hours. Check-out 11 am. Coin laundry. Business services available. Cr cds: A, C, D, DS, MC, V.

D 🐾 🖂 SC

Restaurant

★ ★ ★ **FOX AND HOUNDS.** *Phone 262/628-1111. www.ratzsch.com.* This renowned spot, located a few miles west of Milwaukee, is set in an authentic-feeling, 1845 log cabin. It's worth thinking ahead for a reservation at the Friday fish fry. American menu. Hours: 5-10 pm. Closed Mon; Jan 1, Dec 24 & 25. Dinner A la carte entrees: $15-$27. Bar. Child's meals. Reservations accepted. Cr cds: A, D, DS, MC, V.

Ⓓ

Menomonie (D-2)

See also Chippewa, Falls, Eau Claire

Settled 1859 **Pop** 13,547 **Elev** 877 ft **Area code** 715 **Zip** 54751

Information Chamber of Commerce, 700 Wolske Bay Rd, Suite 200; 715/235-9087 or 800/283-1862

Located on the banks of the Red Cedar River, Menomonie is home of the University of Wisconsin-Stout and was once headquarters for one of the largest lumber corporations in the country. The decline of the lumber industry diverted the economy to dairy products. Recently several new industries have located here, giving the city a more diversified economic base.

What to See and Do

Caddie Woodlawn Park. *W25 & C. 10 miles S on WI 25. Phone 715/235-2070.* Two century-old houses and log smokehouse in 5-acre park; memorial to pioneer girl Caddie Woodlawn. Picnicking. (Daily) **FREE**

Empire in Pine Lumber Museum. *E4541 County Rd C. 7 miles S on WI 25 in Downsville. Phone 715/664-8690.* Lumbering artifacts, slides of life in lumber camps; primitive furniture, displays incl original pay office. (Early May-Oct, daily; mid-Apr-early May, by appointment) **FREE**

Mabel Tainter Memorial Building. *205 Main St. Phone 715/235-9726 or 800/236-7675.* Hand-stenciled and ornately carved cultural center constructed in 1889 by lumber baron Andrew Tainter in memory of his daughter Mabel. Theater with performing arts season; reading room, pipe organ. Gift shop. Guided tours (daily). **$$**

Wilson Place Museum. *101 Wilson Ct. Wilson Cir. Phone 715/235-2283.* Victorian mansion (1846); former residence of Senator James H. Stout, founder of University of Wisconsin. Almost all original furnishings. Guided tours (Memorial Day-Labor Day, daily; closed Jan 1, Thanksgiving, Dec 25) **$$**

Special Events

Victorian Christmas. *101 Wilson Ct. Wilson Place Museum. Phone 715/235-2283.* Daily, mid-Nov-Dec.

Winter Carnival. *Pine Ave and Broadway, Wakanda Park. Phone 715/235-9087.* Second weekend Feb.

Motels/Motor Lodges

★ **BEST WESTERN INN.** *1815 N Broadway (54751). Phone 715/235-9651; toll-free 800/622-0504; fax 715/235-6568. www.bestwestern.com.* 135 rooms. D $59-$119; each additional $4; under 12 free. Pet accepted, some restrictions; fee. Check-out 11 am. TV; cable (premium). Bar. Cross-country ski 2 miles. Cr cds: A, C, D, DS, MC, V.

Ⓓ 🔁 🔀 🔀 SC

★ **BOLO COUNTRY.** *207 Pine Ave (54751). Phone 715/235-5596; toll-free 800/553bolo; fax 715/235-5596. www.thebolocountryinn.com.* 25 rooms. S, D $49-$79. Pet accepted. TV; cable (premium). Complimentary continental breakfast. Restaurant 11 am-10 pm. Bar 11-1 am. Check-out noon. Meeting rooms. Picnic tables. Cr cds: A, MC, V.

Ⓓ 🔁 🔀

Mequon

Restaurant

★ ★ **RIVERSITE.** *11120 N Cedarburg Rd (53092). Phone 262/242-6050.* Specializes in seafood, steak. Hours: 5-10 pm. Closed Sun; major holidays. Dinner $22.95-$32.95. Bar. Reservations accepted. Cr cds: A, MC, V.

Ⓓ

Milwaukee (G-6)

See also Major Cities, Major Cities

Settled 1822 **Pop** 628,088 **Elev** 634 ft **Area code** 414

Information Greater Milwaukee Convention & Visitors Bureau, 101 W Wisconsin Ave, 53203; 414/273-3950 or 800/231-0903

Web www.officialmilwaukee.com

Suburbs Menomonee Falls, Port Washington, Waukesha, Wauwatosa.

Thriving and progressive, Milwaukee has retained its *Gemütlichkeit*—though today's lively conviviality is as likely to be expressed at a soccer game or at a symphony concert as at the beer garden. This is not to say that raising beer steins has noticeably declined as a popular local form of exercise. While Milwaukee is still the beer capital of the nation, its leading single industry is not brewing but the manufacture of X-ray apparatus and tubes.

Long a French trading post and an early campsite between Chicago and Green Bay, the city was founded by Solomon Juneau, who settled on the east side of the Milwaukee River. English settlement began in significant numbers in 1833, and was followed by an influx of Germans, Scandinavians, Dutch, Bohemians, Irish, Austrians, and large numbers of Poles. By 1846, Milwaukee was big and prosperous enough to be incorporated as a city. In its recent history perhaps the most colorful period was from 1916-40 when Daniel Webster Hoan, its Socialist mayor, held the reins of government.

The city's Teutonic personality has dimmed, becoming only a part of the local color of a city long famous for good government, a low crime rate, and high standards of civic performance.

With a history going back to the days when the Native Americans called this area Millioki, "gathering place by the waters," Milwaukee has undergone tremendous development since World War II. The skyline changed with new building, an expressway system was constructed, the St. Lawrence Seaway opened new markets, new cultural activities were introduced, and 44 square miles were tacked onto the city's girth.

Today a city of 96.5 square miles on the west shore of Lake Michigan, where the Milwaukee, Menomonee, and Kinnickinnic rivers meet, Milwaukee is the metropolitan center of five counties. "The machine shop of America" ranks among the nation's top industrial cities and is a leader in the output of diesel and gasoline engines, outboard motors, motorcycles, tractors, wheelbarrows, padlocks, and, of course, beer.

As a result of the St. Lawrence Seaway, Milwaukee has become a major seaport on America's new fourth seacoast. Docks and piers handle traffic of ten lines of oceangoing ships.

The city provides abundant tourist attractions including professional and college basketball, hockey, and football, major league baseball, top-rated polo, soccer, and auto racing. There is also golf, tennis, swimming, sailing, fishing, hiking, skiing, tobogganing, and skating. For the less athletic, Milwaukee has art exhibits, museums, music programs, ballet, and theater including the Marcus Center for Performing Arts. Its many beautiful churches include St. Josaphat's Basilica, St. John Cathedral, and the Gesu Church.

What to See and Do

Annunciation Greek Orthodox Church. *9400 W Congress St. Phone 414/461-9400.* Domed structure designed by Frank Lloyd Wright.

Betty Brinn Children's Museum. *929 E Wisconsin Ave, near the lakefront. Phone 414/291-0888.* Hands-on exhibits; workshops; performances. (June-Labor Day, daily) **$$**

Bradford Beach. The city's finest bathing beach, with bathhouse, concessions. **FREE**

Captain Frederick Pabst Mansion. *2000 W Wisconsin Ave, downtown. Phone 414/931-0808.* (1893) Magnificent house of the beer baron; exquisite woodwork, wrought iron, and stained glass; restored interior. Guided tours. (Daily; closed holidays) **$$$**

Charles Allis Art Museum. *1801 N Prospect Ave, near the lakefront. Phone 414/278-8295.* Art treasures from the United States, Near East, Far East, and Europe dating from 600 B.C. to the 1900s; personal collection of Charles Allis in his preserved Tudor-style mansion. (Wed-Sun afternoons) **$$**

City Hall. *200 E Wells St, downtown. Phone 414/286-3285.* (1895) Milwaukee landmark of Flemish Renaissance design. Common Council Chamber and Anteroom retain their turn-of-the-century character; ornately carved woodwork, leaded glass, stenciled ceilings, and two large stained glass windows; ironwork balconies surround eight-story atrium. (Mon-Fri; closed holidays) **FREE**

Court of Honor. 3-block area serving as a monument to the city's Civil War dead. Bounded by Marquette University on the west and the downtown business district on the east, it contains an 18-story YMCA building, the Public Library, many towering churches, and statues of historic figures.

Iroquois Boat Line Tours. *1823 S Kinnickinnick Ave. Board at Clybourn St Bridge on W bank of Milwaukee River. Phone 414/294-9450.* View lakefront, harbor, lighthouse, breakwater, and foreign ships in port. (Late June-Aug, daily) **$$$$**

Kilbourntown House. *4400 W Estabrook Dr, in Estabrook Park, 5 miles N on I-43, Capitol Dr E exit. Phone 414/273-8288.* (1844) Excellent example of Greek Revival architecture; restored and furnished in the 1844-1864 period. (Late June-Labor Day, Tues, Thurs, Sat-Sun) **FREE**

Marcus Center for the Performing Arts. *929 N Water St, downtown. Phone 414/273-7206.* Strikingly beautiful structure, overlooking the Milwaukee River, with four theaters, reception areas, and parking facility connected by a skywalk. Outdoor riverfront Peck Pavilion. Also here is

Milwaukee Ballet. *929 N Water St. Phone 414/643-7677 or 414/273-7206 (box office).* Classical and contemporary ballet presentations. (Sept-May)

Marquette University. *1217 W Wisconsin Ave. Phone 414/288-3178.* (1881) 11,000 students. On campus are

Haggerty Museum of Art. *530 N 13th St. Phone 414/288-7290.* Paintings, prints, drawings, sculpture, and decorative arts; changing exhibits. (Daily) **FREE**

Marquette Hall's 48-bell carillon. *1217 W Wisconsin Ave.* One of the largest in the country. Occasional concerts. **FREE**

St. Joan of Arc Chapel. *14th St and Wisconsin Ave. Phone 414/288-6873.* (15th-century) Brought from France and reconstructed on Long Island, NY in 1927 and here in 1964. Tours (daily).

Miller Brewing Company. *4251 W State St. Phone 414/931-BEER.* 1-hour guided tour, includes outdoor walking. (May-Sept, Mon-Sat; rest of year, Tues-Sat; closed holidays)

Milwaukee Brewers (MLB). *1 Brewers Way. Phone 414/902-4400.* Miller Park,

Milwaukee Bucks (NBA). *1001 N 4th St. Phone 414/227-0500.* Bradley Center,

Milwaukee County Historical Center. *910 N Old World, 3rd St at Pere Marquette Park, downtown. Phone 414/273-8288.* Milwaukee history and children's exhibits; archive library housed in bank building (1913). (Daily; closed holidays) **FREE**

Milwaukee County Zoo. *10001 W Blue Mound Rd, 6 miles W. Phone 414/771-3040.* On 194 wooded acres. Mammals, birds, reptiles, and fish exhibited in continental groupings with native backdrops. World-renowned predator/prey outdoor exhibits. Miniature train travels on a 1 1/4-mile track (fee); guided tours on Zoomobile (fee). Park (daily). **$$$**

Milwaukee Public Museum. *800 W Wells St, downtown. Phone 414/278-2700.* Natural and human history museum; unique "walk-through" dioramas and exhibits; life-size replicas of dinosaurs. Rain forest, Native American, and special exhibits. IMAX Dome Theater. Shops; restaurant. (Daily) **$$$**

Discovery World Museum of Science, Economics and Technology. *815 N James Lovell St, downtown. Phone 414/765-9960.* Museum with more than 140 participatory exhibits. Entrepreneurial village, stock wall, and Into Einstein's Brain show. (Daily; closed holidays)

Humphrey IMAX Dome Theater. *710 W Wells St. Phone 414/319-4629.* A 275-seat theater; giant wrap-around domed screen. **$$$**

Mitchell Park Horticultural Conservatory. *524 S Layton Blvd at W Pierce St. Phone 414/649-9800.* Superb modern design, three self-supporting domes (tropical, arid, and show dome) feature outstanding seasonal shows and beautiful exhibits all year. Each dome is almost half the length of a football field in diameter and nearly as tall as a 7-story building. Also gift shop, picnic area; parking (free). (Daily) **$$**

Old World Third Street. *Between W Wells St and W Highland Blvd.* Downtown walking tour for gourmets, historians, and lovers of antiques and atmosphere. Incl the Milwaukee Journal Company's history of the newspaper. Most shops (Mon-Sat).

Pabst Theater. *144 E Wells St, downtown. Phone 414/286-3663 or 414/286-3665.* (1895) Center of Milwaukee's earlier cultural life; restored to its original elegance. Lavish decor and excellent acoustics enhance the charm of the theater. Musical and dramatic events. Tours (Sat; free).

Park system. *9480 W Watertown Plank Rd. Phone 414/257-6100.* One of the largest in the nation, with 14,681 acres; 137 parks and parkways, community centers, five beaches, 19 pools, 16 golf courses, 134 tennis courts, and winter activities include cross-country skiing, skating, sledding. Fees vary. Of special interest is

Whitnall Park. *S 92nd St and Whitnall Park Dr. Phone 414/425-1130.* A 640-acre park with Boerner Botanical Gardens (parking fee) featuring the Rose Garden, one of the All American Selection Gardens; also nature trails, woodlands, formal gardens, wildflowers, shrubs, test gardens, fruit trees, rock, and herb gardens; Wehr Nature Center. 18-hole golf (fee). (Early Apr-mid-Oct, daily) **FREE**

Port of Milwaukee. *2323 S Lincoln Memorial Dr. Phone 414/286-3511.* Incl Inner Harbor, formed by Milwaukee, Menomonee, and Kinnickinnic rivers, and the commercial municipal port development in the Outer Harbor on the lakefront. Ships flying foreign flags may be seen at Jones Island on Milwaukee's south side.

Schlitz Audubon Center. *1111 E Brown Deer Rd. Phone 414/352-2880.* Center has 225 acres of shoreline, grassland, bluff, ravine, and woodland habitats with a variety of plants and wildlife including fox, deer, skunk, and opossum; self-guided trails; some guided programs. (Tues-Sun). **$$**

University of Wisconsin-Milwaukee. *2200 E Kenwood Blvd. Phone 414/229-4961.* Also an art museum and three art galleries are open to the public. *3203 N Downer Ave, .* (1956) 25,400 students. The Manfred Olson Planetarium (fee) offers programs Fri and Sat evenings during academic year.

Villa Terrace Decorative Arts Museum. *2220 N Terrace Ave, near the lakefront. Phone 414/271-3656.* (1923) this Italian Renaissance-style house serves as a museum for decorative arts. Guided tours (reservations required). (Wed-Sun afternoons; closed Jan 1, Dec 25) **$$**

★ **War Memorial Center.** *750 N Lincoln Memorial Dr. Phone 414/273-5533.* An imposing modern monument to honor the dead by serving the living; designed by Eero Saarinen. Provides facilities for civic groups and houses the

Milwaukee Art Museum. *700 N Lincoln Memorial Dr, near the lakefront. Phone 414/224-3200.* Permanent collection of American and European masters; folk, decorative and contemporary art. Special exhibits;

films and tours. (Tues-Sun; closed Jan 1, Thanksgiving, Dec 25) **$$$**

Special Events

Ethnic Festivals. *Henry Maier Festival Grounds, 200 N Harbor Dr. Phone 414/273-3950.* Incl African, Arabian, German, Italian, Irish, Asian, Mexican, and Polish, take place throughout the summer. Convention and Visitors Bureau has information. May-Sept.

Great Circus Parade. *Lincoln Memorial Dr and Mason. Phone 608/356-8341.* Downtown. This re-creation of an old-time circus parade incl bands, costumed units, animals, and unusual collection of horsedrawn wagons from the Circus World Museum. Mid-July.

Holiday Folk Fair. *State Fair Park. 81st & Greenfield. Phone 414/225-6225.* The Wisconsin Center. Continuous ethnic entertainment, 300 types of food from around the world, cultural exhibits, workshops. Phone 414/225-6225. Weekend before Thanksgiving.

Summerfest. *Henry Maier Festival Grounds, 200 N Harbor Dr. Lakefront, E of downtown. Phone 800/273-3378.* Eleven different music stages; food. Late June-early July.

Wisconsin State Fair. *8100 W Greenfield Ave. State Fair Park in West Allis, bounded by I-94, GreenfieldAve, 76th and 84th Sts. Phone 414/266-7000 or 800/884-FAIR.* Entertainment, 12 stages, auto races, exhibits, contests, demonstrations, fireworks. Aug.

Motels/Motor Lodges

★**BAYMONT INN & SUITES.** *5442 N Lovers Ln (53225). Phone 414/535-1300; toll-free 800/428-3438; fax 414/535-1724. www.baymontinns.com.* 140 rooms, 3 story. D $84-$94; each additional $7; under 18 free. Pet accepted, some restrictions. Complimentary continental breakfast. Check-out noon. TV; cable (premium), VCR available. In-room modem link. Cr cds: A, C, D, DS, MC, V.

★ ★ **BEST WESTERN MIDWAY HOTEL.** *251 N Mayfair Rd (53226). Phone 414/774-3600; toll-free 800/528-1234; fax 414/774-5015. www.bestwestern.com.* 116 rooms, 3 story. S $94-$129; D $104-$139; each additional $10. Crib free. TV; cable (premium). Indoor pool; whirlpool. Complimentary coffee in rooms. Restaurant 6 am-10 pm. Room service. Bar 11-1:30 am. Check-out noon. Coin laundry. Meeting rooms. Business services available. In-room modem link. Bellhops. Sundries. Valet service. Free airport, train station, bus depot transportation. Exercise equipment, sauna. Some refrigerators. Cr cds: A, C, D, DS, MC, V.

★★**CLARION HOTEL.** *5311 S Howell Ave (53207). Phone 414/481-2400; fax 414/481-4471. www.clarionhotel.com.* 180 rooms, 3 story. S, D $70-$99; suites $89-$150; each additional $5; under 18 free. Crib $7. TV; cable (premium). Indoor pool. Complimentary continental breakfast. Restaurant 7 am-10 pm; Sun 9 am-9 pm. Room service. Bar 11 am-11 pm. Check-out 11 am. Coin laundry. Meeting rooms. Business services available. Bellhops. Free airport transportation. Exercise equipment. Cr cds: A, C, D, DS, JCB, MC, V.

★ **EXEL INN.** *5485 N Port Washington Rd (53217). Phone 414/961-7272; toll-free 800/367-3935; fax 414/961-1721. www.exelinn.com.* 125 rooms, 3 story. S $39.99-$63.99; D $49.99-$76.99; each additional $7; under 17 free; weekend rates; higher rates special events. Crib free. Pet accepted, some restrictions. TV; cable (premium). Complimentary continental breakfast. Restaurant adjacent open 24 hours. Check-out noon. Coin laundry. Business services available. In-room modem link. Sundries. Game room. Some in-room whirlpools; microwaves available. Cr cds: A, C, D, DS, MC, V.

★ **EXEL INN.** *1201 W College Ave (53154). Phone 414/764-1776; fax 414/762-8009. www.exelinn.com.* 110 rooms, 2 story. S $33.99-$79.99; D $34.99-$89.99; each additional $4; under 18 free. Crib free. Pet accepted. TV; cable (premium). Complimentary continental breakfast. Restaurant opposite 6 am-noon. Check-out noon. Coin laundry. Business services available. In-room modem link. Free airport transportation. Microwaves available. Cr cds: A, C, D, DS, MC, V.

★ ★ **FOUR POINTS BY SHERATON AIRPORT.** *4747 S Howell Ave (53207). Phone 414/481-8000; toll-free 800/558-3862; fax 414/481-8065. www.fourpoints.com.* 510 rooms, 6 story. S, D $89-$119; each additional $10; suites $225-$295; under 17 free; package plans. Crib free. TV; cable (premium). 2 heated pools, 1 indoor; whirlpool. Restaurants 6 am-10 pm. Bar 11-2 am. Check-out noon. Meeting rooms. Business center. In-room modem link. Gift shop. Barber, beauty shop. Free airport transportation. Indoor tennis. Exercise equipment; sauna. Game room. Some refrigerators. Cr cds: A, C, D, DS, MC, V.

★★**FOUR POINTS BY SHERATON.** *8900 N Kildeer Ct (53209). Phone 414/355-8585; fax 414/355-3566. www.sheraton.com.* 149 rooms, 6 story. S $124-$137; D $134-$147; each additional $10; suites $141-$225; under 18 free; weekend rates. Crib free. Check-out noon. TV; cable (premium), VCR available. In-room modem link. Some refrigerators; microwaves available. Coffee in rooms. Valet services. Restaurant 6:30 am-10:30 pm. Bar 10-2 am. Room service. Health club privileges. Sauna. Indoor/outdoor pool; whirlpool, poolside service. Cross-country ski 3 miles. Barber. Airport transportation. Meeting rooms, business services. Cr cds: A, C, D, DS, JCB, MC, V.

[D] [≈] [≈] [✈] [≈] [SC]

★**HAMPTON INN.** *5601 N Lovers Ln Rd (53225). Phone 414/466-8881; toll-free 800/426-7866; fax 414/466-3840. www.hamptoninn.com.* 107 rooms, 4 story. S, D $69-$99; under 18 free; higher rates: special events, summer weekends. Crib free. TV; cable. Indoor pool; whirlpool. Complimentary continental breakfast. Restaurant adjacent. Check-out noon. Meeting room. Business services available. In-room modem link. Valet service. Exercise equipment. Microwaves available. Cr cds: A, C, D, DS, MC, V.

[D] [≈] [✈] [≈] [SC]

★ ★ **HOLIDAY INN.** *611 W Wisconsin Ave (53203). Phone 414/273-2950; toll-free 800/465-4329; fax 414/ 273-7662. www.holiday-inn.com.* 245 rooms, 10 story. S $99-$129; D $109-$139; each additional $10; suites $119-$199; under 18 free; higher rates special events. TV; cable (premium). Pool. Coffee in rooms. Restaurant 6 am-10 pm. Room service. Bar from 4 pm. Check-out noon. Meeting rooms. Business center. In-room modem link. Valet service. Free valet parking. Exercise equipment. Cr cds: A, C, D, DS, ER, JCB, MC, V.

[D] [乔] [≈] [✈] [乔] [≈] [SC] [乔]

★ **HOSPITALITY INN.** *4400 S 27th St (53220). Phone 414/282-8800; toll-free 800/825-8466; fax 414/282-7713. www.hospitalityinn.com.* 167 rooms. D $60-$200. Complimentary continental breakfast. Check-out noon. TV; cable (premium). Exercise equipment. 2 indoor pools, whirlpool. Free airport transportation. Cr cds: A, MC, V.

[D] [≈] [✈] [✈] [≈] [SC]

★ **MANCHESTER SUITES AIRPORT.** *200 W Grange Ave (53207). Phone 414/744-3600; toll-free 800/ 723-8280; fax 414/744-4188. www.manchestersuites.com.* 123 suites, 4 story. D $85-$109; each additional $8; under 14 free. Complimentary full breakfast. Check-out noon. TV; cable (premium). In-room modem link. Health club privileges. Free airport transportation. Cr cds: A, C, D, DS, MC, V.

[✈] [乔]

★ **MANCHESTER SUITES NORTHWEST.** *11777 W Silver Spring Dr (53225). Phone 414/ 462-3500; toll-free 800/723-8280; fax 414/462-8166. www. manchestersuites.com.* 123 suites, 4 story. Suites $79-$129; under 14 free. Complimentary full breakfast. Check-out noon. TV; cable. In-room modem link. Exercise equipment. Cr cds: A, C, D, DS, MC, V.

[D] [乔] [≈] [SC]

★ ★ **RAMADA INN.** *633 W Michigan St (53203). Phone 414/272-8410; toll-free 800/228-2828; fax 414/272-*

4651. *www.ramada.com.* 155 rooms, 7 story. S $70-$90; D $78-$101; each additional $10; suites $105-$145; under 18 free; weekend rates. Crib free. TV; cable (premium), VCR available (movies). Heated pool. Restaurant 6 am-10 pm. Room service. Bar 11-2 am. Check-out noon. Meeting rooms. Business services available. In-room modem link. Valet service. Downhill ski 15 miles; cross-country ski 7 miles. Exercise equipment. Cr cds: A, C, D, DS, JCB, MC, V.

[D] [≈] [≈] [乔] [≈] [SC]

★ **RED ROOF INN.** *6360 S 13th St (53154). Phone 414/764-3500; toll-free 800/843-7663; fax 414/764-5138. www.redroof.com.* 108 rooms, 2 story. S $36.99-$58.99; D $41.99-$69.99; under 18 free. Crib free. Pet accepted. TV; cable (premium). Complimentary coffee in lobby. Check-out noon. Business services available. Cr cds: A, C, D, DS, MC, V.

[D] [🐾] [≈]

★ ★ **WESTWOOD INN HOTEL & SUITES.** *201 N Mayfair Rd (53226). Phone 414/771-4400; toll-free 800/ 531-3966; fax 414/771-4517. www.westwoodhotel.com.* 230 rooms, 3 story. May-Sept: S $84; D $99; under 18 free; lower rates rest of year. Crib free. Pet accepted, some restrictions. TV; cable (premium). Indoor pool; whirlpool. Playground. Restaurant 6 am-1 pm, 5-9 pm. Room service. Bar 3 pm-1 am; Fri, Sat to 2 am. Check-out noon. Coin laundry. Meeting rooms. Business services available. Valet service. Exercise equipment; sauna. Picnic tables. Cr cds: A, D, DS, MC, V.

[D] [≈] [≈] [乔] [乔] [≈]

Hotels

★ ★ **COURTYARD BY MARRIOTT.** *300 W Michigan St (53203). Phone 414/291-4122; toll-free 800/321-2211; fax 414/291-4188.* 169 rooms, 6 story. Check-out noon, check-in 3 pm. TV; cable (premium). In-room modem link. Laundry services. In-house fitness room. Indoor pool. Cr cds: A, C, D, DS, MC, V.

[≈]

★ ★ ★ **HILTON.** *509 W Wisconsin Ave (53203). Phone 414/271-7250; fax 414/271-1039. www.hilton.com.* Those looking to stay in the downtown area will enjoy all this hotel has to offer, with its location very near to local theaters, museums and major businesses. 500 rooms, 25 story. S, D $89-$199; each additional $20; suites $225-$1,000; under 18 free; weekend plan. Crib free. TV; cable (premium). Indoor pool. Restaurant 6:30 am-10 pm. Bar 11-1 am. Check-out noon. Convention facilities. Business services available. In-room modem link. Concierge. Gift shop. Barber, beauty shop. Exercise equipment; sauna. Cr cds: A, C, D, DS, ER, JCB, MC, V.

[D] [🏊] [≈] [乔] [≈] [乔]

★ ★ ★ **HILTON.** *4700 N Port Washington Rd (53212). Phone 414/962-6040; toll-free 800/445-8667; fax 414/962-6166. www.hilton.com.* On the banks of the Milwaukee River, this hotel provides a modern and convenient environment for guests. Minutes away from many attractions including sports arenas, museums, the zoo and a brewery. 163 rooms, 5 story. S $99-$127; D $114-$142; each additional $15; suites $180-$370; studio rooms $120-$135; family rates. TV; cable (premium). Indoor pool. Coffee in rooms. Restaurant 6:30 am-10 pm. Bar 11 am-midnight. Check-out noon. Meeting rooms. Business services available. In-room modem link. Exercise equipment. Some refrigerators. Overlooks river. Cr cds: A, C, D, DS, ER, JCB, MC, V.

⊡ 🛏 🏋 ⛷ SC

★ ★ **HOTEL WISCONSIN.** *720 N Old World 3rd St (53203). Phone 414/271-4900; fax 414/271-9998.* 234 rooms, 11 story. Mid-June-Sept: S, D $69-$76; each additional $8; suites $85; kitchen units $69-$82; under 17 free; lower rates rest of year. Crib free. Pet accepted. TV; cable (premium), VCR available. Restaurant 6 am-10 pm. Check-out 11 am. Meeting room. Business services available. Concierge. Sundries. Valet service. Coin laundry. Game room. Health club privileges. Some refrigerators; microwaves available. Cr cds: A, D, DS, MC, V.

🏋 🏂 ⛷

★ ★ ★ **HYATT REGENCY.** *333 W Kilbourn Ave (53203). Phone 414/276-1234; toll-free 800/233-1234; fax 414/276-6338. www.milwaukeehyatt.com.* This hotel delights guests with spacious and elegantly appointed guestrooms, as well as offering Milwaukee's only revolving-rooftop restaurant which affords guests panoramic views of the city's skyline. 484 rooms, 22 story. S $99-$179; D $124-$204; each additional $25; parlor rooms $95-$150; suites $295-$750; under 18 free; weekend rates; package plans. TV; cable (premium), VCR available (movies). Restaurants 6:30 am-midnight (see also POLARIS). Bar from 11 am, Fri, Sat to 2 am. Check-out noon. Convention facilities. Business center. Concierge. Gift shop. Exercise equipment. Cr cds: A, C, D, DS, ER, MC, V.

⊡ 🏋 🏂 🛏 ⛷ 🚶

★ ★ **PARK EAST.** *916 E State St (53202). Phone 414/276-8800; toll-free 800/328-7275; fax 414/765-1919. www.parkeasthotel.com.* 159 rooms, 5 story. S $88-$112; D $98-$122; each additional $10; suites $120-$200; under 18 free. Crib $5. TV; cable (premium), VCR (movies). Complimentary continental breakfast. Restaurant 11 am-11 pm. Check-out noon. Meeting rooms. Business services available. Exercise equipment. Health club privileges. Some in-room whirlpools, refrigerators, wet bars; microwaves available. Cr cds: A, C, D, DS, MC, V.

⊡ 🏊 🏋 🛏 ⛷ 🚶

★ ★ ★ **THE PFISTER HOTEL.** *424 E Wisconsin Ave (53202). Phone 414/273-5025; toll-free 800/558-8222; fax 414/273-5027. www.thepfister.com.* The attentive staff is ready to serve at this refined hotel with the classic atmosphere in the heart of the financial district. 378 rooms, 23 story. D $139-$264; each additional $20; under 18 free. Check-out noon, check-in 3 pm. TV; cable (premium), VCR available (movies). In-room modem link. Laundry. Restaurant 6:30 am-11 pm. Bar 11-2 am, entertainment. Room service 24 hours. Exercise room. Heated indoor pool. Parking; valet available. Airport transportation. Business center. Concierge. Cr cds: A, C, D, DS, ER, JCB, MC, V.

⊡ 🛏 🏋 ⛷ SC 🚶

★ ★ ★ **RADISSON HOTEL MILWAUKEE AIRPORT.** *6331 S 13th St (53221). Phone 414/764-1500; toll-free 800/303-8002; fax 414/764-6531. www.radisson.com.* This property is a convenient few minutes from downtown. 159 rooms, 3 story. S $69-$90; D $79-$110; each additional $10; under 18 free. Crib free. Pet accepted. TV. Indoor pool. Playground. Restaurant 6 am-1 pm, 5-10 pm; Sat, Sun from 7 am. Room service. Bar. Check-out 11 am. Coin laundry. Meeting rooms. Business services available. Bellhops. Sundries. Free airport transportation. Exercise equipment; saunas. Game room. Balconies. Cr cds: A, C, D, DS, ER, JCB, MC, V.

✈

★ ★ ★ **RADISSON HOTEL MILWAUKEE WEST.** *2303 N Mayfair Rd (53226). Phone 414/257-3400; fax 414/257-0900. www.radisson.com.* 150 rooms, 8 story. S $89-$159; D $99-$169; each additional $10; under 18 free; lower rates weekends. Crib free. TV; cable (premium). Sauna. Indoor pool. Coffee in rooms. Restaurant 6 am-2 pm, 5-10 pm. Room service. Bar 11-2 am. Check-out noon. Meeting rooms. Business services available. In-room modem link. Bellhops. Sundries. Free airport transportation. Cross-country ski 2 miles. Cr cds: A, C, D, DS, ER, JCB, MC, V.

⊡ 🏋 🏊 🛏 ✈ ⛷ SC 🚶

★ ★ ★ **SHERATON BROOKFIELD.** *375 S Moorland Rd (53005). Phone 262/786-1100.* 389 rooms, 12 story. S, D $150-$225; each additional $20; under 17 free. Crib available. Pet accepted. 2 heated pools. TV; cable (premium), VCR available. Complimentary coffee, newspaper in rooms. Restaurant 6 am-10 pm. Check-out noon. Meeting rooms. Business center. Gift shop. Exercise room. Some refrigerators, minibars. Cr cds: A, C, D, DS, JCB, MC, V.

🐾 🚶

★ ★ **WYNDHAM HOTEL.** *139 E Kilbourn Ave (53202). Phone 414/276-8686; toll-free 800/822-4200; fax 414/276-8007. www.wyndham.com.* 221 rooms, 10 story, 77 suites. S, D $142-$192; each additional $10; under 18 free; weekend rates. Crib free. Garage $10. TV; cable, VCR available. Complimentary coffee in rooms. Restaurant 6: 30 am-2 pm, 5-10 pm. Bar 11-2 am; entertainment Fri-Sat. Check-out noon. Meeting rooms. Business services available. Gift shop. Exercise equipment; sauna, steam room. Whirlpool. Cr cds: A, C, D, DS, ER, JCB, MC, V.

⧈ ⊀ ⊠

All Suites

★★★EMBASSY SUITES MILWAUKEE WEST.
1200 S Moorland Rd (53005). Phone 262/782-2900; toll-free 800/444-6404; fax 414/796-9159. www.embassysuites.com. Minutes from downtown. 203 suites, 5 story. S, D, suites $99-$500; each additional $20; under 12 free; weekend rates; package plans. Crib free. Pet accepted, some restrictions. TV; cable (premium). Indoor pool; whirlpool. Complimentary full breakfast. Complimentary coffee in rooms. Restaurant 11 am-11 pm. Bar to 1 am. Check-out noon. Meeting rooms. Business center. In-room modem link. Concierge. Free airport transportation. Tennis privileges. Golf privileges. Exercise equipment; sauna, steam room. Game room. Refrigerators, microwaves, wet bars. Cr cds: A, C, D, DS, JCB, MC, V.

⧈ ⊰ ⊠ ⊀ ⊠ ⊠

Restaurants

★ AU BON APPETIT.
1016 E Brady St (53202). Phone 414/278-1233. www.aubonappetit.com. Mediterranean menu. Hours: 5-9 pm; Fri, Sat to 10 pm. Closed Sun, Mon; holidays. Dinner $10.95-$14.95. Cr cds: MC, V.

⧈

★BALISTRERI'S BLUE MOUND INN.
6501 W Blue Mound Rd (53213). Phone 414/258-9881. www.balistreris. com. Italian, American menu. Hours: 11-1 am; Fri to 2 am; Sat 4 pm-2 am; Sun 4 pm-1 am. Closed Thanksgiving, Dec 24, 25. Dinner $14-$28. Bar. Cr cds: A, D, DS, MC, V.

★ ★ ★ BARTOLOTTA'S LAKE PARK BISTRO.
3133 E Newberry Blvd (53211). Phone 414/962-6300; fax 414/962-4248. www.bartolottas.com. Restaurateur Joe Bartolotta, who also owns Bartolotta Ristorante in Wauwatosa, serves authentic, Italian dishes and many wood-fired-oven specialties in this lovely, Paris-like dining room. The second-story location in the Lake Park Pavilion affords beautiful Lake Michigan views. French menu. Hours: 11:30 am-2 pm, 5:30-9 pm; Fri to 10 pm; Sat 5-10 pm; Sun 10:30 am-2 pm (brunch), 5-8 pm. Closed holidays. Dinner $12-$22. Sun brunch. Bar. Children's menu. Cr cds: A, D, DS, MC, V.

⧈

★ ★ BAVARIAN INN.
700 W Lexington Blvd (53217). Phone 414/964-0300; fax 414/964-0302. www. bavarianinnmil.com. German, American menu. Hours: 11:30 am-2:30 pm, 5-9 pm; Fri to 10 pm; Sat 5-9 pm; Sun brunch 10:30 am-2 pm. Closed Mon; Jan 1, July 4, Dec 24, 25. Dinner $7.95-$14.95. Sun brunch. Bar. Children's menu. Cr cds: A, DS, MC, V.

⧈

★ ★ ★ BOULEVARD INN.
925 E Wells St (53202). Phone 414/765-1166. www.boulevardinn.com. Located in the Cudahy Tower in downtown Milwaukee with a spectacular view of Lake Michigan, this fine-dining restaurant has been a tradition for 50 years. Enjoy the classical pianist and attentive service, in addition to the diverse menu and the elegant flourishes. Specialties: fresh fish, veal, German dishes. Own baking. Hours: 11:30 am-9 pm; Fri, Sat to 10 pm; Sun from 10:30 am; Sun brunch to 2 pm. Closed holidays. Lunch $7.50-$11.50, dinner $16.95-$35.95. Sun brunch $10.45. Some tableside preparation. Bar. Wine list. Pianist. Family-owned. Children's menu. Reservations accepted. Valet parking. Overlooks Lake Michigan. Cr cds: A, C, D, MC, V.

⧈

★ ★ BUCA DI BEPPO.
1233 N Van Buren st (53202). Phone 414/224-8672. Italian menu. Hours: 5-10 pm; Fri to 11 pm; Sat, Sun from 4 pm. Closed Thanksgiving, Dec 24, 25. Dinner $10-$16. Bar. Cr cds: A, D, DS, MC, V.

★ COUNTY CLARE.
1234 N Astor St (53202). Phone 888/942-5273. www.countyclare-inn.com. Irish menu. Specialties: Irish smoked salmon, corned beef and cabbage, Irish root soup. Hours: 11:30 am-10 pm; Sun to 9 pm. Closed holidays. Lunch $3.50-$9.50, dinner $3.50-$10.95. Bar to 1 am. Traditional Irish music Sun. Irish pub décor with cut glass and dark woods. Cr cds: A, D, DS, MC, V.

⧈

★ DOS BANDIDOS.
5932 N Green Bay Ave (53209). Phone 414/228-1911. Mexican, American menu. Specialties: steak and chicken fajitas, spinach enchiladas, vegetarian dishes. Hours: 11 am-10:30 pm; Fri to 11:30 pm; Sat noon-11:30 pm; Sun 4-9 pm. Closed holidays. Lunch $3.95-$6.50, dinner $7.25-$11.95. Bar. Parking. Patio dining. Mexican cantina decor. Cr cds: A, MC, V.

⧈

★ ★ EAGAN'S.
1030 N Water St (53202). Phone 414/271-6900; fax 414/266-3225. Hours: 11 am-11 pm; Fri, Sat to 1 am; Sun brunch 11 am-2 pm. Closed holidays. Dinner $6.95-$29.95. Sun brunch. Bar. Outdoor seating. Totally nonsmoking. Cr cds: A, D, DS, MC, V.

⧈

★ ★ ★ ELSA'S ON THE PARK.
833 N Jefferson St (53202). Phone 414/765-0615. www.elsas.com. The grand, Victorian brownstone location in Cathedral Square seems an unlikely place to find such comforting dishes, but this casual spot pulls it off with a loyal lunchtime and late-night-dining crowd. Hours: 11 am-2 pm; Fri to 2:30 pm;

Sat 5 pm-2:30 am; Sun 5 pm-2 am. Dinner $5-$10. Entertainment. Cr cds: A, DS, MC, V.

D

★ ★ ★ **GRENADIER'S.** *747 N Broadway Ave (53202). Phone 414/276-0747. www.grenadiers.com.* For more than 20 years, this French continental restaurant has attracted locals and visitors alike to its elegant, romantic dining room. Specializes in Dover sole, lamb curry Calcutta, fresh seared tuna on ocean salad. Own pastries. Hours: 11:30 am-10 pm; Sat from 5:30 pm. Closed Sun; holidays. Reservations accepted. Bar. Wine cellar. Lunch a la carte entrees: $9.95-$15.95, dinner a la carte entrees: $19-$39. Degustation menu: dinner $34.95. Entertainment: pianist. Valet parking (dinner). Jacket recommended. Cr cds: A, D, DS, MC, V.

D

★ **IZUMI'S.** *2178 N Prospect Ave (53209). Phone 414/271-5278.* Hours: 11:30 am-2 pm, 5-10 pm; Fri, Sat 5-10:30 pm; Sun 4-9 pm. Closed major holidays. Reservations accepted. Japanese menu. Wine, beer. Lunch $4.95-$12.95, dinner $9-$23. Specializes in sushi, sukiyaki, teriyaki dishes. Parking. Contemporary Japanese décor. Cr cds: A, MC, V.

D

★ ★ **KARL RATZSCH'S.** *320 E Mason St (53202). Phone 414/276-2720. www.ratzsch.com.* American, German menu. Hours: 4-9:30 pm; Sat to 10:30 pm; Sun to 9 pm. Closed Sun, Holidays. Dinner $12.95-$30. Bar. Children's menu. Valet parking. Collection of rare steins, glassware. Cr cds: A, D, DS, MC, V.

★ ★ **KING AND I.** *823 N 2nd St (53203). Phone 414/276-4181; fax 414/276-4387.* Thai menu. Specialties: volcano chicken, fresh red snapper, crispy duck. Hours: 11:30 am-10 pm; Sat 5-11 pm; Sun 4-9 pm. Closed holidays. Lunch $5-$8, dinner $9-$18. Bar. Reservations accepted. Southeast Asian decor; enameled wood chairs, hand-carved teakwood, native artwork. Cr cds: A, D, DS, MC, V.

D

★ **THE KNICK.** *1030 E Juneau Ave (53202). Phone 414/272-0011; fax 414/272-0702.* Seafood menu. Hours: 6:30 am-10 pm; Fri, Sat to 11 pm; Sun 9 am-10 pm. Closed Thanksgiving, Dec 25. Breakfast $3.95-$7.95, lunch $3.95-$7.95, dinner $10.95-$19.95. Brunch. Bar. Outdoor seating. Cr cds: A, MC, V.

D

★ ★ **MADER'S.** *1037 N Old World 3rd St (53203). Phone 414/271-3377. www.maders.com.* German, Continental menu. Hours: 11:30 am-10 pm; Fri, Sat to 11:30 pm; Mon to 9 pm; Sun 10:30 am-9 pm; Sun brunch to 2 pm. Dinner $18.50-$31. Sun Brunch. Bar. Children's menu. Valet parking. Cr cds: A, D, DS, MC, V.

D

★ ★ ★ **MANIACI'S CAFÉ SICILIANO.** *6904 N Santa Monica Blvd, Fox Point (53217). 414/352-5757.* Continental menu. Specialties: veal, fish, pasta. Own pasta. Hours: 4-10 pm. Closed Sun; holidays; also week of July 4. Dinner $17.50-$32.95. Wine cellar. Service bar. Family-owned. Children's menu. Reservations accepted. Sicilian decor with brick columns, tile floors.

★ ★ ★ **MIMMA'S CAFE.** *1307 E Brady St (53202). Phone 414/271-7337. www.mimmas.com.* This family-run establishment has grown from an eight-seat eatery to a 150-seat, fine Italian restaurant with impressive faux-marble walls, paintings, chandeliers and polished-tile flooring. Italian menu. Specialties: pasta, seafood, veal. Hours: 11:30 am-2:30 pm, 5-10 pm; Fri, Sat to midnight; Sun from 5 pm. Closed holidays. A la carte entrees: lunch $6-$12, dinner $8-$30. Bar. Reservations accepted. Contemporary decor. Cr cds: A, D, DS, MC, V.

D

★ **OLD TOWN SERBIAN GOURMET HOUSE.** *522 W Lincoln Ave (53207). Phone 414/672-0206; fax 414/672-0209. www.wwbci.com/oldtown.* Serbian, American menu. Hours: 11:30 am-2:30 pm, 5-11 pm; Sat, Sun from 5 pm. Closed Mon; holidays. Lunch $5-$9, dinner $12-$20. Bar. Entertainment (weekends). Family-owned. Children's menu. Reservations accepted. Parking. Cr cds: A, DS, MC, V.

★ ★ ★ **OSTERIA DEL MONDO.** *1028 E Juneau Ave (53202). Phone 414/291-3770. www.osteria.com.* Chef and owner Marc Bianchini enhances the German landscape of Wisconsin with this authentic Italian cafe. The wine, food and desserts all transport each guest into an Italian province for an hour. The wine bar is an additional experience and adds a exquisite touch to this casual, yet intimate restaurant. Italian menu. Hours: 5-10:30 pm; Fri, Sat 5-11 pm, Sun 5-9 pm; Sun brunch 10 am-3 pm; hours vary seasonally. Closed holidays. Dinner $15-$27. Sun brunch. Bar. Outdoor seating. Totally nonsmoking. Cr cds: A, D, MC, V.

D

★ ★ ★ **PANDL'S BAYSIDE.** *8825 N Lake Dr (53217). Phone 414/352-7300. www.pandls.com.* This restaurant serves up a wonderfully cozy atmosphere in an attractive park-like setting with an elaborate salad bar, family-friendly brunches and good value. Enjoy fresh fish, steaks and the ever-popular duckling with raspberry sauce. Private rooms are available. Hours: 11:30 am-10 pm; Fri-Sat to 11:30 pm; Sun 10 am-9 pm; Sun brunch to 2 pm. Closed Labor Day, Dec 25. Dinner $12.95-$26.95. Sun brunch. Bar. Children's menu. Cr cds: A, C, D, DS, MC, V.

D

★ **PLEASANT VALLEY INN.** *9801 W Dakota St (53227). Phone 414/321-4321. www.foodspot.com/ pleasantvalleyinn.* Specialties: steak, seafood. Hours: 5-9 pm; Fri, Sat to 10 pm; Sun 4-8 pm. Closed Mon; holidays. Dinner $14-$22. Bar. Children's menu. Reservations accepted. Casual decor. Cr cds: A, D, DS, MC, V.

★ ★ **POLARIS.** *333 W Kilbourn Ave (53203). Phone 414/276-1234; fax 414/276-6338.* Hours: 11:30 am-2 pm, 5-11 pm; Sat, Sun from 5 pm. Closed Jan 1, Thanksgiving, Dec 25. Reservations accepted. Bar. A la carte entrees: lunch $5.95-$8.95, dinner $13.95-$25. Specializes in prime rib au jus, grilled veal chops, chicken tortellini. Parking. Revolving restaurant on 22nd floor. Cr cds: A, D, DS, MC, V.

D

★ ★ **PORTERHOUSE.** *800 W Layton Ave (53221). Phone 414/744-1750; fax 414/744-7804. www.foodspot.com/ porterhouse.* Hours: 11 am-2:30 pm, 5-10 pm; Fri, Sat to 11 pm; Sun 4-9 pm. Closed Mon. Dinner $11.95-$32.95. Bar. Children's menu. Cr cds: A, D, DS, MC, V.

D

★ **RED ROCK CAFE.** *4022 N Oakland Ave (53211). Phone 414/962-4545; fax 414/962-6671. www. theredrockcafe.com.* Hours: 11 am-2 pm, 5-9 pm; Fri, Sat to 10 pm; Sun from 5 pm. Closed Mon; holidays. Dinner $6.95-$27. Sun Brunch. Bar. Children's menu. Totally nonsmoking. Cr cds: A, D, MC, V.

D

★ **ROYAL INDIA.** *3400 S 27th St (53215). Phone 414/ 647-9600.* Hours: 11 am-3 pm, 5-10 pm; Fri, Sat to 10:30 pm. Reservations accepted. Indian menu. Wine, beer. Buffet: lunch $6.95. Dinner $5.95-$11.95. Specializes in tandoori dishes, seafood, lamb. Own baking. Casual Indian décor. Totally nonsmoking. Cr cds: A, MC, V.

D

★ **SAFE HOUSE.** *779 N Front St (53202). Phone 414/ 271-2007; fax 414/271-2676. www.safe-house.com.* Hours: 11:30-2 am; Fri, Sat to 2:30 am; Sun 4 pm-midnight. Dinner $5.95-$16.95. Bar. DJ Fri, Sat, magician Sun-Thurs. Cr cds: A, MC, V.

★ ★ ★ **SANFORD.** *1547 N Jackson St (53202). Phone 414/276-9608; fax 414/278-8509. www. sandfordrestaurant.com.* The site, once a grocery store owned by Sanford's family, houses a modern, sophisticated dining room offering internationally flavored, New American cuisine from an a la carte menu. An additional, five-course ethnic tasting menu is also offered on weeknights. Hours: 5:30-8:45 pm; Fri to 9 pm; Sat 5-9 pm. Closed Sun; holidays. Dinner $45-$79. Free valet parking. Cr cds: A, D, DS, MC, V.

D

★ **SAZ'S STATE HOUSE.** *5539 W State St (53208). Phone 414/453-2410. www.sazs.com.* Hours: 11 am-midnight; Sun to 10 pm; Sun brunch 10:30 am-2:30 pm. Closed Dec 24, 25. Bar. Lunch $4.25-$7.95, dinner $7.50-$19.95. Specializes in barbecued ribs, fresh fish, chicken. Parking. Outdoor dining. 1905 roadhouse. Cr cds: A, DS, MC, V.

D

★ **THREE BROTHERS.** *2414 S St. Clair St (53207). Phone 414/481-7530; fax 414/481-8652.* Serbian Menu. Hours: 5-10 pm; Fri, Sat 4-11 pm; Sun 4-10 pm. Closed Mon; holidays. Dinner $12.50-$16.50.

D

★ **TRES HERMANOS.** *1332 W Lincoln Ave (53215). Phone 414/384-9050; fax 414/384-1022. www. club3hermanos.com.* Hours: 11 am-midnight. Closed Thanksgiving, Dec 25. Reservations accepted. Mexican menu. Bar. Lunch $1.75-$5.99, dinner $1.75-$15. Child's meals. Specializes in seafood, burritos, tacos. Salad bar. Entertainment Fri, Sat. Mexican décor. Totally nonsmoking. Cr cds: A, D, DS, MC, V.

D

★ ★ **WEISSGERBER'S 3RD STREET PIER.** *1110 N Old World 3rd St (53203). Phone 414/272-0330. www.weissgerbers.com.* Hours: 11:30 am-2 pm, 5-10 pm; Sat from 5 pm; Sun 4-9 pm. Reservations accepted. Bar 11-1 am. Lunch $6-$10, dinner $15.95-$34.95. Child's meals. Specializes in seafood, steak. Own desserts. Pianist Thurs-Sat. Valet parking. Outdoor dining. Lunch, dinner cruises on Lake Michigan available. In restored landmark building on Milwaukee River. Cr cds: A, D, DS, MC, V.

D

★ ★ **WEST BANK CAFE.** *732 E Burleigh St (53212). Phone 414/562-5555.* Chinese, Vietnamese menu. Specialties: Vietnamese dishes. Own baking. Hours: 5:30-9:30 pm; Fri, Sat to 10 pm. Closed holidays. Dinner $7-$16. Service bar. Street parking. Contemporary Oriental decor. Totally nonsmoking. Cr cds: A, MC, V.

D

★ **YEN CHING.** *7630 W Good Hope Rd (53223). Phone 414/353-6677.* Hours: 11:30 am-2 pm, 4:30-9:30 pm; Fri, Sat 4:30-10 pm; Sun 11:30 am-2:30 pm, 4:30-9 pm. Mandarin menu. Service bar. Lunch $4.25-$5.50, dinner $6.50-$12. Specializes in beef, chicken, seafood. Parking. Oriental décor. Cr cds: A, D, DS, MC, V.

D

Mineral Point (G-3)

See also Dodgeville, New Glarus, Platteville

Settled 1827 **Pop** 2,428 **Elev** 1,135 ft **Area code** 608 **Zip** 53565

Information Chamber/Main St, 225 High St; 608/987-3201 or 888/764-6894

Web www.mineralpoint.com

The first settlers were New Englanders and Southerners attracted by the lead (galena) deposits. In the 1830s miners from Cornwall, England settled here. These "Cousin Jacks," as they were called, introduced superior mining methods and also built the first permanent homes, duplicating the rock houses they had left in Cornwall. Since the mines were in sight of their homes their wives called them to meals by stepping to the door and shaking a rag—so the town was first called "Shake Rag."

Visitors to Mineral Point can experience the way small towns used to be. The city offers a wide variety of shopping opportunities, including artisan galleries and working studios, antique shops, and specialty shops.

What to See and Do

Mineral Point Toy Museum. *215 Commerce. Phone 608/987-3160.* Antique and collectible doll houses, toys, and trains. (May-Oct, Fri-Sun, daily) **$$**

Pendarvis, Cornish Restoration. *114 Shake Rag St. Phone 608/987-2122.* Guided tour of six restored log and limestone homes of Cornish miners (Circa 1845). Also 40-acre nature walk in old mining area (free), which has mine shafts, wildflowers, and abandoned "badger holes." (May-Oct, daily) **$$$**

Motel/Motor Lodge

★ **REDWOOD MOTEL.** *625 Dodge St (53565). Phone 608/987-2317; toll-free 800/321-1958; fax 608/987-2317.* 28 rooms, 2 story. May-Oct: S $35-$55; D $43-$55; each additional $5; lower rates rest of year. TV; cable. Restaurant adjacent 6 am-8 pm. Check-out 11 am. Business services available. Miniature golf. Cr cds: DS, MC, V.

D ➤ 🏌 ✈ ⊠ SC

Minocqua (C-4)

See also Eagle River, Rhinelander, Saint Germain, Woodruff

Pop 3,522 **Elev** 1,603 ft **Area code** 715 **Zip** 54548

Information Minocqua-Arbor Vitae-Woodruff Area Chamber of Commerce, 8216 US 51, PO Box 1006; 715/356-5266 or 800/446-6784

Web www.minocqua.org

Minocqua is a four-season resort area known for its thousands of acres of lakes. The area contains one of the largest concentrations of fresh water bodies in America. Minocqua, the "Island City," was once completely surrounded by Lake Minocqua. Now youth camps and resorts are along the lakeshore.

What to See and Do

Area has 3,200 lakes, streams, and ponds. Contain every major type of freshwater fish found in Wisconsin. Also clear water for diving. The Min-Aqua-Bat waterski shows are held mid-June-mid-Aug on Wed, Fri, and Sun evenings. For winter sports enthusiasts there are thousands of miles of groomed snowmobile and hundreds of miles of cross-country ski trails. Inquire at Chamber of Commerce.

Circle M Corral Family Fun Park. *10295 WI 70. 2 1/2 miles W of US 51 on WI 70 W. Phone 715/356-4441.* Horseback riding, bumper boats, go-carts; train ride with robbery aboard replica C. P. Huntington; water slide; miniature golf; children's rides. Picnic area, snack bar. (Mid-May-mid-Oct, daily) **$$$**

Jim Peck's Wildwood. *10094 State Hwy 70. US 51 to WI 70, then 2 miles W. Phone 715/356-5588.* A wildlife park featuring hundreds of tame animals and birds native to the area; many can be pet at baby animal nursery; walk among tame deer; trout and musky ponds. Picnic area; nature walk; adventure boat rides; gift shop, snack wagon. (May-mid-Oct, daily) **$$$**

Minocqua Museum. *416 Chicago Ave. US 51 to 416 Chicago Ave, downtown. Phone 715/356-7666.* Ongoing display of Island City's unique history. Main gallery exhibits change annually; some permanent exhibits. (June-Sept, daily; or by appointment) **DONATION**

Minocqua Winter Park Nordic Center. *12375 Scotchman Lake Rd. 6 miles W on WI 70 to Squirrel Lake Rd, then approximately 6 miles S, follow the signs. Phone 715/356-3309.* Center has over 35 miles of groomed and tracked cross-country trails; two groomed telemarking slopes;

more than one miles of lighted trails for night skiing (Thurs-Fri only). School, shop, rentals. Heated chalet, concessions. (Dec-Mar, Thurs-Tues) **$$$$**

Northwoods Wildlife Center. *8683 Blumstein Rd. US 51 to WI 70, then 1 mile W.* Phone 715/356-7400. Wildlife hospital, wildlife educational center with tours and scheduled programs. (Mon-Sat, daily) **DONATION**

Wilderness Cruise. *7 miles S on US 51, then 7 miles on County Y to Willow Dam Rd in Hazelhurst.* Phone 715/453-3310 or 800/472-1516. 2-hour cruise on the Willow Flowage aboard the Wilderness Queen. Also brunch, dinner, and sightseeing cruises. (Mid-May-Oct, call for hours; reservations required) **$$$$**

Special Event

Northern Lights Playhouse. *10 miles S of Minocqua on US 51 in Hazelhurst.* Phone 715/356-7173. Professional repertory theater presents Broadway plays, musicals, and comedies; also Children's Theatre. Memorial Day-early Oct. **$$$$**

Motels/Motor Lodges

★ **AQUA AIRE MOTEL.** *806 WI 51N (54548).* Phone 715/356-3433; fax 715/358-9701. www.north-wis.com/aquaaire. 10 rooms, shower only. June-Aug: S $70; D $80; each additional $5; under 3 free; weekly rates; higher rates special events; lower rates rest of year. Crib free. Pet accepted, some restrictions. TV; cable (premium). Restaurant opposite 7 am-2:30 pm. Check-out 11 am. Business services available. Cross-country ski 7 miles. Refrigerators; microwaves available. Picnic tables. Cr cds: A, DS, MC, V.

★ ★ **BEST WESTERN.** *311 E Park Ave (54548).* Phone 715/356-5208; toll-free 800/852-1021; fax 715/356-1412. www.bestwestern.com. 41 rooms, 2 story. July-early Sept, holidays: S $81-$111; D $91-$111; each additional $6; 2-story chalet units available; lower rates rest of year. Pet accepted; $6. TV; cable (premium). Whirlpool; sauna. Complimentary continental breakfast. Restaurant nearby. Check-out 11 am. Business services available. Cross-country ski 10 miles. Snowmobiling. Some balconies. Picnic tables. On Lake Minocqua; dock. Cr cds: A, MC, V.

★ **NEW CONCORD INN.** *320 Front St (54548).* Phone 715/356-1800; toll-free 800/356-8888; fax 715/356-6955. www.newconcordinn.com. 53 rooms, 3 story. D $88-$115; each additional $7; under 12 free. Complimentary continental breakfast. Check-out 11 am. TV; cable (premium), VCR available. Game room. Opposite beach. Indoor pool, whirlpool. Cr cds: A, MC, V.

Restaurants

★ ★ **NORWOOD PINES.** *10171 HWY 70 W (54548).* Phone 715/356-3666. Specializes in veal, steak, seafood. Hours: 5-10 pm. Closed Sun, Dec 24-25. Dinner $8.95-$27. Friday fish fry $6.95. Cr cds: D, DS, MC, V.

★ **PAUL BUNYAN'S.** *8653 HWY 51 N (54548).* Phone 715/356-6270; fax 715/356-2780. www.paulbunyans.com. Hours: 7 am-9 pm. Closed Oct-Apr. Breakfast $7.95, lunch $5.95-$7.95, dinner $9.95-$12.95. Bar. Children's menu, 2 entrees daily; family-style service. Fri fish fry $8.95, Replica of typical 1890 logging camp. Cr cds: DS, MC, V.

★ **RED STEER.** *8230 WI 51 S (54548).* Phone 715/356-6332. www.theredsteer.com. Hours: 5 pm-closing. Closed Thanksgiving, Dec 24-25. Reservations accepted. Bar. Dinner $10.95-$19.95. Child's meals. Specializes in charcoal-broiled steak, seafood, ribs. Rustic décor. Cr cds: A, D, DS, MC, V.

★ **SPANG'S.** *318 Milwaukee St (54548).* Phone 715/356-4401. Hours: 5-10 pm. Closed Easter, Thanksgiving, Dec 24-25. Italian menu. Bar. Dinner $6.25-$13.95. Child's meals. Specializes in pasta, pizza. Cr cds: A, DS, MC, V.

Monroe (H-4)

See also Janesville, New Glarus

Pop 10,241 **Elev** 1,099 ft **Area code** 608 **Zip** 53566

Information Chamber of Commerce, 1505 9th St; 608/325-7648

Web www.monroechamber.org

A well-known community of Swiss heritage in an area of abundant dairy production, Monroe is the site of a unique courthouse with a 120-foot tall clock tower.

What to See and Do

Alp and Dell Cheesery, Deli, and Country Café. *657 2nd St.* Phone 608/328-3355. Watch cheesemaking process (Mon-Fri). Self-guided tours. Retail store (daily).

Yellowstone Lake State Park. *8495 Lake Rd (53516).* 16 miles NW on WI 81 to Argyle, then N on County N, then W on Lake Rd. Phone 608/523-4427. A 968-acre park on Yellowstone Lake. Swimming, waterskiing, fishing, boating (rentals); hiking, cross-country skiing, snowmobiling, picnicking, playground, concession, camping (electric, dump station; reservations accepted through reserve America), winter camping. Standard fees. (Daily) **$$**

Special Event

Balloon Rally. *2600 10th St. Phone 608/325-7648.* Mid-June.

Motel/Motor Lodge

★ **KNIGHTS INN MONROE, WI.** *250 N 18th Ave (53566). Phone 608/325-4138; toll-free 800/325-1178; fax 608/325-1282. www.knightsinn.com.* 65 rooms, 2 story. S $30-$40; D $59-$69; each additional $4; under 13 free. Crib free. TV; cable (premium). Complimentary coffee in lobby. Restaurant nearby. Check-out 11 am. Business services available. In-room modem link. Cr cds: A, DS, MC, V.

D 🐾 🏊 🎿

Mount Horeb (G-4)

See also Dodgeville, Madison, New Glarus

Pop 4,182 **Elev** 1,230 ft **Area code** 608 **Zip** 53572

Information Chamber of Commerce, PO Box 84; 608/437-5914 or 888/765-5929

What to See and Do

Blue Mound State Park. *4350 Mounds Park Rd. W on US 18, 1 mile NW of Blue Mounds. Phone 608/437-5711.* A 1,150-acre park with scenic views and lookout towers. Swimming pool; nature, mountain bike trails, hiking, and cross-country ski trails; picnicking, playgrounds, camping (dump station). Standard fees. (Daily) **$$$**

Cave of the Mounds. *2975 Cave of the Mounds Rd. 4 miles W on US 18/151, then follow signs to Cave of the Mounds. Phone 608/437-3038.* Colorful onyx formations in limestone cavern, rooms on two levels. Registered National Natural Landmark. One-hr guided tours. (Year-round, call for hours) Also picnic grounds, gardens, snack bar, and gift shops. **$$$**

⭐ **Little Norway.** *W via US 18/151 to Cave of the Mounds Rd, then follow signs to County JG. Phone 608/437-8211.* Norwegian pioneer faroomstead built in 1856; museum of Norse antiques. Guided tours (45 minutes). (May-late Oct, daily) **$$$**

Mount Horeb Mustard Museum. *100 W Main St. Phone 608/437-3986; toll-free 800/438-6878.* Large collection of mustards, mustard memorabilia, and samplings. (Daily)

Motel/Motor Lodge

★★ **KARAKAHL COUNTRY INN.** *1405 US 18 Business and 151 E (53572). Phone 608/437-5545; fax 608/437-5908. www.karakahl.com.* 76 rooms, 1-2 story. Mid-May-mid-Oct: S $59-$64; D $69-$174; each additional $5; suites $119; under 18 free; lower rates rest of yr; crib $4. Pet accepted, some restrictions; $5. TV; cable. Saunas. Indoor pool. Complimentary continental breakfast. Restaurant 7 am-2 pm, 5-8 pm; Fri, Sat to 10 pm; closed Sun evening. Bar 5 pm-1 am. Check-out noon. Business services available. Cross-country ski 2 blocks. Cr cds: A, DS, MC, V.

D 🐾 🏊 🎿 🎿

Nashotah

Restaurant

★ **RED CIRCLE INN.** *33013 Watertown Plank Rd (53058). Phone 262/367-4883. www/foodspot/redcircleinn.com.* Hours: 5-9:30 pm. Closed Sun and Mon; holidays. Dinner $18.95-$27.95. Bar from 4 pm. Former stagecoach stop; one of oldest restaurants in state (established 1848). Reservations accepted. Cr cds: A, DS, MC, V.

D

Neenah-Menasha (E-5)

See also Appleton, Green Bay, Oshkosh

Settled 1843 **Pop** 23,219 **Elev** 750 ft **Area code** 920 **Zip** Neenah, 54956; Menasha, 54952

Information Fox Cities Convention & Visitor Bureau, 3433 W College Ave, Appleton, 54914; 920/734-3358 or 800/236-6673

Web www.foxcities.org

Wisconsin's great paper industry started in Neenah and its twin city, Menasha. The two cities, located on Lake Winnebago, are still among the nation's leaders in dollar volume of paper products. Many paper product factories are located here in addition to large wood product plants, printing and publishing houses, foundries, and machine shops.

What to See and Do

Barlow Planetarium. *1478 Midway Rd. Phone 920/832-2848.* 3-D projections explain the stars. (Thurs, Fri evenings; Sat, Sun afternoons-evenings) **$$**

Bergstrom-Mahler Museum. *165 N Park Ave, Neenah. Phone 920/751-4658.* More than 1,800 glass paperweights; antique German glass; American regional paintings; changing exhibits. (Tues-Sun; closed holidays) Museum shop, specializing in glass. **DONATION**

Doty Cabin. *701 Lincoln St. Doty Park, Webster and Lincoln sts, Neenah. Phone 920/751-4614.* Home of Wisconsin's second territorial governor, James Duane Doty. Boating (ramp); tennis courts, picnic facilities, playgrounds; park (daily), cabin (June-mid-Aug, daily, afternoons). **DONATION**

High Cliff State Park. *N7630 State Park Rd. 9 miles E, off WI 114, on opposite shore of Lake Winnebago. Phone 920/989-1106.* A 1,139-acre park with beautiful wooded bluffs. Swimming, bathhouse, waterskiing, fishing, boating (marina); nature, hiking, snowmobile, and cross-country ski trails; picnicking, playgrounds, concession, camping (dump station). Naturalist program. Standard fees. (Daily) **$$** In the park is

High Cliff General Store Museum. *N 7630 State Park Rd. Phone 920/989-1106.* Museum depicts life in the area from 1850 to the early 1900s. Store was once the center of activity of the lime kiln community and housed the post and telegraph offices. Relic of old lime kiln oven nearby. (Mid-May-Sept, Sat-Sun and holidays) **FREE**

Smith Park. *140 Main St, Menasha. Phone 920/967-5106.* Monument to Jean Nicolet, who came in 1634 to arrange peace between Native American tribes. Tennis courts, cross-country skiing, picnic areas, pavilion, playground. Native American effigy mounds; formal gardens; historic railroad caboose representing birthplace of Central Wisconsin Railroad. (Daily) **FREE**

New Glarus (G-4)

Settled 1845 **Pop** 1,899 **Elev** 900 ft **Area code** 608 **Zip** 53574

Information New Glarus Tourism, PO Box 713; 608/527-2095 or 800/527-6838

When bad times struck the Swiss canton of Glarus in 1844, a group of 193 set out for the New World and settled New Glarus. Their knowledge of dairying brought prosperity. The town is still predominantly Swiss in character and ancestry.

What to See and Do

Chalet of the Golden Fleece. *618 2nd St. Phone 608/527-2614.* Replica of Swiss chalet, with more than 3,000 Swiss items. Guided tours. (May-Oct, daily) **$$**

New Glarus Woods State Park. *W5446 County Rd NN. 1 mile S on WI 69. Phone 608/527-2335.* Park has 38 campsites in 425 acres of wooded valleys. Picnicking, playgrounds. Standard fees. (Daily) **$$**

Sugar River State Trail. *418 Railroad St. Phone 608/527-2334.* A 24-mile trail follows abandoned railroad bed between New Glarus and Brodhead to the southeast. Hiking, biking, snowmobiling, and cross-country skiing. (Daily) **$$**

⭐ **Swiss Historical Village.** *612 7th Ave. Phone 608/527-2317.* Replicas of first buildings erected by settlers, includes blacksmith shops, cheese factory, school-house, and print shop; original furnishings and tools; guided tours. (May-Oct, daily) **$$$**

Special Events

Heidi Festival. *1701 2nd St, New Glarus High School. Phone 608/527-2095.* Mid-June.

Swiss Volksfest. *Wilhelm Tell Shooting Park, 1/2 mile N on County O. Phone 608/527-2095.* Singing, yodeling, dancing. Honors birth of Swiss confederation in 1291. First Sun Aug.

Wilhelm Tell Festival. *1 mile on County W. Tell Amphitheater, Wilhelm Tell Grounds. Phone 608/527-2095.* Alpine Festival, Swiss entertainment, Sat. Schiller's drama, Wilhelm Tell, in German, Sun; in English, Sat, Mon. Also fine arts show, Village Park, Sun. Labor Day weekend.

Motels/Motor Lodges

★ ★ **CHALET LANDHAUS INN.** *801 WI 69 (53574). Phone 608/527-5234; toll-free 800/944-1716; fax 608/527-2365. www.chaletlandhaus.com.* 67 rooms, 3-4 story. May-Oct: S $59-$69; D $86-$59; each additional $15; suites $140; family rooms $100; under 8 free; lower rates rest of year. Crib $12. TV; cable. Restaurant 7-11 am, 5:30-9 pm; Sun, Mon to 11 am. Check-out 11 am. Meeting rooms. Business services available. Cross-country ski 2 miles. Whirlpool in suites. Some balconies. Cr cds: A, DS, MC, V.

D ⊠ 🕴 🐾 ⇌ 🏋 🏃 🐾 SC 🏃

★ **SWISS-AIRE MOTEL.** *1200 WI 69 (53574). Phone 608/527-2138; toll-free 800/798-4391; fax 608/527-5818.* 26 rooms. May-Oct: S $45-$49; D $45-$65; each additional $6; under 5 free; lower rates rest of year. Crib free. Pet accepted. TV; cable. Heated pool. Complimentary continental breakfast. Check-out 11 am. Meeting rooms. Picnic tables. Cr cds: DS, MC, V.

🐾 👋 ⇌ ⊠

B&B/Small Inns

★ ★ **COUNTRY HOUSE.** *180 WI 69 (53574). Phone 608/527-5399.* 4 rooms, 2 story. S, D $65-$110. Complimentary full breakfast. Check-out 11 am, check-in 4-7 pm. Built in 1892; antiques. Totally nonsmoking. Cr cds: MC, V.

⊠

Restaurant

★ ★ **NEW GLARUS HOTEL.** *100 6th Ave (53574). Phone 608/527-5244; fax 608/527-5055. www.newglarushotel.com.* Swiss, Amer menu. Hours: 11 am-9 pm; Fri, Sat to 10 pm; Sun brunch 10:30 am-3 pm. Closed Thanksgiving, Dec 24-25; also Tues in Nov-Apr. Lunch $3.50-$9 , dinner $5-$15. Sun brunch $15.95.

A Stroll Through a Swiss Mountain Village (In Wisconsin!)

Gather brochures at the New Glarus Information Center at Railroad St and Sixth Ave, then walk one block east to First St, the town's main business thoroughfare. On the corner is the New Glarus Hotel, built in 1853 by Swiss settlers. Its main dining room occupies an old opera house (where talking movies were introduced in 1930). On an enclosed upper balcony, picture windows look out onto picturesque shops and over rooftops to surrounding green hills. Veal dishes include geschetzlets (thin slices lightly browned and served with a white wine sauce). Don't miss the baked-on-the-premises rhubarb-custard torte. The hotel has lodging in six guest rooms. Across the street are three good "foodie" stops. Chalet-style Scholo-Laden is a retail outlet for imported chocolates, homemade fudge, ice cream, and locally made cheeses. Ruef's Meat Market offers a variety of wurst, including fresh and smoked brats and landjaeger sausages favored by Swiss hunters (dried sausage that makes a great munchie). New Glarus Bakery and Tea Room is the spot for an afternoon respite or to buy tempting baked goods that include rich, dense stolen (German sweet bread).

Snuggled in the Little Sugar River valley, tiny New Glarus resembles a Swiss mountain village. And with good reason. The town was founded in 1845 by 108 immigrants from the Swiss canton of Glarus who traveled to America to escape poverty and unemployment. Today, it not unusual to see dairy herds grazing among the pretty hills, nor is it startling to hear a yodel echo across the valley. In fact, every year on the first Sunday in August, yodelers, alphornists, and folk dancers gather here to celebrate Swiss Independence Day.

Wandering downtown's few short blocks, visitors quickly realize just how much the village resembles a Swiss mountain town. Chalet-style buildings feature carved balconies decorated by colorful coats of arooms, Swiss flags and banners, and window boxes spilling with bright red geraniums. Many businesses bear Swiss-German inscriptions proclaiming the nature of the commerce conducted within. The clank of cowbells welcomes you to shops selling lace, embroidery, and raclette grills. Just east of First St. on Seventh Ave, the Chalet of the Golden Fleece Museum replicates a Swiss Bernese mountain chalet. Rocks and logs on the roof reflect a Swiss practice designed to protect slate shingles from strong mountain winds. The museum houses a collection of more than 3,000 Swiss items, from dolls to kitchenware, as well as artifacts collected from around the world (such as jeweled watch once owned by King Louis XVI, 2,000-year-old Etruscan earrings, and Gregorian chants on parchment dating from 1485). Continue east on Seventh Ave to the Swiss Historical Village Museum, a replica pioneer village with log cabins, log church, and 1-room schoolhouse. Operated by the local historical society, the museum preserves the history and records of New Glarus and tells the story of Swiss immigration and colonization. Its 14 buildings include a traditional Swiss bee house, a replica cheese factory, blacksmith's shop, general store, and a print shop that display equipment used to print the *New Glarus Post* from 1897 to 1967.

Bar. Children's menu. Reservations accepted. Polka Fri, Sat; yodeling (summer). Cr cds: A, DS, MC, V.

D

Oconomowoc (G-5)

See also Milwaukee, Watertown

Pop 10,993 **Elev** 873 ft **Area code** 262 **Zip** 53066

Information Greater Oconomowoc Area Chamber of Commerce, 152 E Wisconsin Ave; 262/567-2666

Web www.oconomowoc.com

Native Americans called this place "the gathering of waters," because of its location between Fowler Lake and Lac La Belle.

What to See and Do

Highlands Ski Hill. *965 Cannon Gate Rd. WI 67 and I-94. Phone 262/567-2577.* Area has two chairlifts, rope tow; patrol, school, rentals; snowmaking; bar. Longest run is 2,200 feet; vertical drop 196 feet. (Nov-Mar, daily) **$$$$**

Honey of a Museum. *Honey Acres, 10 miles N, on WI 67 just N of Ashippun. Phone 920/474-4411.* Bee Tree provides a close-up view of bee activities; pollination and beeswax exhibits; multimedia show about beekeeping yesterday, today, and around the world; nature walk, honey tasting. (Mid-May-Oct, daily; rest of year, Mon-Fri; closed holidays) **FREE**

Motel/Motor Lodge

★ **COUNTRY PRIDE INN.** *2412 Milwaukee St (53018). Phone 262/646-3300; fax 262/646-3491.* 56 rooms, 2 story. D $62; each additional $5. Check-out 11 am. TV; cable (premium). Sauna. Indoor pool, whirlpool. Downhill ski 6 miles, cross-country ski 1/4 mile. Cr cds: A, DS, MC, V.

D ⬛ ⬛ ⬛ ⬛ ⬛

Resort

★ ★ ★ **OLYMPIA RESORT.** *1350 Royale Mile Rd (53066). Phone 414/567-0311; toll-free 800/558-9573; fax 414/567-5934. www.olympiaresort.com.* The goal of this resort is to recreate a European-style spa in your own backyard. 256 units, 3-4 story. S, D $89-$129; each additional $20; suites $189-$249; family, ski and golf plans. TV. 2 pools, 1 indoor; whirlpool, poolside service. Coffee in rooms. Dining room 6:30 am-10 pm. Room service. Bars 11-2 am. Check-out noon, check-in 4 pm. Meeting rooms. Business services available. Grocery 1 block. Deli. Valet service. Beauty shop. Indoor, outdoor tennis. 18-hole golf, greens fee, pro, driving range. Downhill ski. Entertainment Fri, Sat; movies. Game room. Exercise room; sauna, steam room. Some refrigerators. Fireplace in suites. Cr cds: A, C, D, DS, MC, V.

D ⬛ ⬛ ⬛ ⬛ ⬛ ⬛ ⬛ SC

B&B/Small Inns

★ ★ **INN AT PINE TERRACE.** *351 E Lisbon Rd (53066) Phone 262/ 567-7463; toll-free 800/421-4667; fax 262/567-7532. www.innatpineterrace.com.* 13 rooms, 3 story. Pet accepted, some restrictions. Complimentary continental breakfast. Check-out 10:30 am, check-in 3 pm. TV; cable (premium). Heated pool. Restored mansion (1879); antique furnishings. Cr cds: A, D, DS, MC, V.

D ⬛ ⬛ ⬛ ⬛

Restaurant

★ ★ ★ **GOLDEN MAST INN.** *1270 Lacy Ln. Phone 262/ 567-7047. www.weissgerberrestaurants.com.* This favorite local restaurant offers a wide array of entrees with a German flair. German, American menu. Specializes in Wiener schnitzel, Kasseler rippchen, seafood. Hours: 5-11 pm; Sun 11 am-9; Sun brunch 11 am-2 pm. Closed Closed Mon in Oct-Apr. Dinner $17-$39, Sun brunch $9.50-$13.95. Bar. Child's meals. Reservations accepted. Outdoor dining in beer garden. Cr cds: A, DS, MC, V.

D

Oconto (D-5)

See also Green Bay, Peshtigo

Pop 4,474 **Elev** 591 ft **Area code** 920 **Zip** 54153

On Green Bay at the mouth of the Oconto River, Oconto was the home of Copper Culture people 4,500 years ago.

What to See and Do

Beyer Home. *917 Park Ave. Phone 920/834-6206.* (Circa 1868) Victorian house with furnishings of 1880-1890s. Adjacent museum annex has exhibits of Copper Culture people and antique vehicles. (June-Labor Day, Mon-Sat, also Sun afternoons) **$$**

North Bay Shore County Park. *500 Bay Rd. 9 miles N on County Y. Phone 920/834-6825.* Swimming, fishing, boating; tent and trailer sites, camping (late May-late Sept; fee). Fall Salmon Run. (Daily) **FREE**

Oshkosh (E-5)

Settled 1836 **Pop** 55,006 **Elev** 767 ft **Area code** 920

Information Oshkosh Convention & Visitors Bureau, 2 N Main St, 54901; 920/236-5250 or 800/876-5250

Web www.oshkoshcvb.org

Named for the Chief of the Menominee, Oshkosh is located on the west shore of Lake Winnebago, the largest freshwater lake within the state. The city is known for the many recreational activities offered by its lakes and rivers. This is the original home of the company that produces the famous overalls that help make Oshkosh a household word. The economy of the town, once called "Sawdust City," is centered on transportation equipment manufacturing, tourism, and candle making.

What to See and Do

⭐ **EAA Air Adventure Museum.** *3000 Poberezny Rd. Phone 920/426-4818.* More than 90 aircraft on display including home-built aircraft, antiques, classics, ultralights, aerobatic and rotary-winged planes. Special World War II collection. Extensive collections of aviation art and photography; special displays of engines, propellers, and scale models. Five theaters. Antique airplanes fly on weekends (May-Oct). (Daily; closed holidays) **$$$**

Grand Opera House. *100 High Ave, PO Box 1004. Phone 920/424-2350 (box office).* A restored 1883 Victorian Theater, offers a variety of performing arts.

Menominee Park. *1200 E Irving. On Lake Winnebago, enter off Hazel or Merritt sts. Phone 920/236-5080.* Swimming beach (lifeguard), fishing, sailing, paddleboats; tennis courts, picnic shelters, concession. Train rides, children's zoo (late May-early Sept, daily). Fee for some activities. (Daily)

Oshkosh Public Museum. *1331 Algoma Blvd. Phone 920/424-4731.* Housed in turn-of-the-century, Tudor-style mansion with Tiffany stained-glass windows and interior; also occupies adjacent addition. Apostles Clock, china and glassware collection; life-sized dioramas depicting French exploration, British occupation, pioneer settlement, and native wildlife; antique fire and train equipment; meteorites; Native American exhibits; fine and decorative art; 1913 Harley-Davidson; miniature lumber company. (Tues-Sun; closed holidays) **FREE**

Paine Art Center and Arboretum. *1410 Algoma Blvd, at jct WI 21, 110. Phone 920/235-6903.* Tudor-revival house; period rooms, European and American paintings and sculpture, Asian rugs, furniture and decorative arts; Arboretum and display gardens. (Tues-Sun afternoons; closed holidays) **$$**

Rebel Alliance Theater. *445 N Main St. Phone 920/426-8580 (box office).* Non-profit organization dedicated to bringing the live theater experience to Fox Valley.

University of Wisconsin-Oshkosh. *800 Algoma Blvd. Phone 920/424-0202 or 800/624-1466.* (1871) 11,000 students. Priebe Art Gallery, Reeve Memorial Union, Kolf Sports and Recreation Center. Campus tours (Mon-Fri; Sat by appointment).

Special Events

EAA Air Venture. *3000 Poberezny Rd. Phone 920/426-4800.* (Experimental Aircraft Association). Held at Wittman Regional Airport. One of the nation's largest aviation events. More than 500 educational forums, workshops, and seminars; daily air shows; exhibits; more than 12,000 aircraft. Late July-early Aug.

Oshkosh Public Museum Art Fair. *1331 Algoma Blvd. On Oshkosh Public Museum grounds. Phone 920/424-4731.* Featuring original fine art by over 200 quality artists from around the country. Music, entertainment, concessions. Early July.

Sawdust Days. *Menominee Park Hazel St & E Irving Ave. Phone 920/235-5584.* Commemorates lumbering era. Early July.

Motels/Motor Lodges

★ **BAYMONT INN.** *1950 Omro Rd (54901). Phone 920/233-4190; fax 920/233-8197. www.baymontinn.com.* 100 rooms, 2 story. D $57.95-$73.95; each additional $7; under 18 free. Pet accepted, some restrictions. Complimentary continental breakfast. Check-out noon. TV; cable. In-room modem link. Cross-country ski 2 miles. Cr cds: A, C, D, DS, MC, V.

D ⬛ ⬛ ⬛ ⬛

★ **FAIRFIELD INN.** *1800 S Koeller St (54901). Phone 920/233-8504; fax 920/233-8504. www.fairfieldinn.com.* 57 rooms, 3 story, 10 suites. June-Sept: S $51.95-$61.95; D $57.95-$77.95; each additional $6; suites $67.95-$74.95; under 18 free; lower rates rest of year. Crib $5. TV; cable (premium). Indoor pool; whirlpool. Complimentary continental breakfast. Restaurant nearby. Check-out noon. Meeting rooms. Business services available. In-room modem link. Game room. Some refrigerators, microwaves. Cr cds: A, C, D, DS, ER, JCB, MC, V.

D ⬛ ⬛ ⬛

★ **HOLIDAY INN EXPRESS HOTEL & SUITES.** *2251 Westowne Ave (54904). Phone 920/303-1300; toll-free 888/522-9472; fax 920/303-9330. www.hiexpress.com.* 68 rooms, 3 story, 28 suites. June-Aug: S $75-$89; D $85-$99; suites $79-$175; under 19 free; higher rates special events; lower rates rest of year. Crib available. Pet accepted. TV; cable. Complimentary continental breakfast. Complimentary coffee in rooms. Restaurant nearby. Check-out 11 am. Meeting rooms. Business services available. In-room modem link. Coin laundry. Free airport transportation. Downhill ski/cross-country ski 2 miles. Exercise equipment. Indoor pool; whirlpool. Many refrigerators, microwaves, minibars; some in-room whirlpools. Cr cds: A, C, D, DS, ER, JCB, MC, V.

D ⬛ ⬛ ⬛ ⬛ ⬛ ⬛ ⬛ ⬛ SC ⬛

★ **HOWARD JOHNSON INN.** *1919 Omro Rd (54902). Phone 920/233-1200; fax 920/233-1135. www.hojo.com.* 100 rooms, 2 story. May-Aug: S $55-$70; D $60-$75; each additional $5; under 18 free; lower rates rest of year. Crib free. Pet accepted, some restrictions. TV; cable. Indoor pool; whirlpool. Coffee in rooms. Restaurant adjacent 6 am-10 pm. Bar 4 pm-1 am. Check-out noon. Meeting room. Business services available. Private patios, balconies. Cr cds: A, C, D, DS, MC, V.

D ⬛ ⬛ ⬛ ⬛ ⬛ ⬛ SC ⬛

★ ★ **RAMADA INN.** *500 S Koeller St (54902). Phone 920/233-1511; fax 920/233-1909. www.ramada.com.* 129 rooms, 2 story. S $40-$50; D $50-$60; each additional $10; under 18 free; weekend rates. Pet accepted. TV; cable (premium). Indoor pool; whirlpool, poolside service. Restaurant 7 am-10 pm. Room service. Check-out noon. Coin laundry. Meeting rooms. Business center. Bellhops. Valet service. Sundries. Free airport transportation. Exercise equipment; sauna. Microwaves available. Cr cds: A, C, D, DS, MC, V.

D ⬛ ⬛ ⬛ ⬛ ⬛ ⬛ SC

Hotel

★ ★ ★ **PARK PLAZA INTERNATIONAL.** *1 N Main St (54901). Phone 920/231-5000; toll-free 800/365-4458; fax 920/231-8383. www.parkplazaoshkosh.com.* Convenient to the convention center. 179 rooms, 8 story. S, D $95-$105; suites $125; under 18 free. Pet accepted, some restrictions. TV; cable (premium), VCR available. Indoor pool; whirlpool, poolside service. Restaurant 6:30 am-10 pm. Bar 11-1 am. Check-out noon. Meeting rooms. Business center. In-room modem link. Concierge. Free covered parking. Free airport transportation. Exercise equipment. Health club privileges. Some refrigerators; microwaves available. View of river. Luxury level. Cr cds: A, D, DS, MC, V.

Resort

★ ★ ★ **PIONEER RESORT & MARINA.** *1000 Pioneer Dr (54902). Phone 920/233-1980; toll-free 800/683-1980; fax 920/426-2115. www.pioneerresort.com.* Enjoy the height of relaxation at the only island resort in Wisconsin. 192 rooms, 2-3 story. Memorial Day-Labor Day: S, D $89-$129; each additional $10; suites $299; under 18 free; package plans. Crib free. TV; cable (premium), VCR available. 2 pools, 1 indoor; wading pool, whirlpool. Supervised children's activities; ages 5-12. Restaurants 7 am-10 pm. Bar 10:30-1 am. Check-out noon. Business services available. In-room modem link. Free airport transportation. Tennis. Exercise equipment. Massage. Social director. Lawn games. Guest bicycles. Some in-room whirlpools, microwaves. On lake; boat rentals, marina, sailing. Cr cds: A, D, DS, MC, V.

Restaurants

★ ★ **ROBBINS.** *1810 Omro Rd (54902). Phone 920/235-2840; fax 920/235-2906.* Specializes in steak, seafood, pasta. Hours: 11 am-10 pm; Fri, Sat to 11 pm; Sun to 9 pm. Closed Dec 25. Lunch $4.45-$9.95, dinner $6.45-$18.95. Bar to 2 am. Children's menu. Reservations accepted. Non-smoking seating. Cr cds: A, DS, MC, V.

★ **WISCONSIN FARMS.** *2450 Washburn (54904). Phone 920/233-7555; fax 920/233-7520. www.foodspot.com/wifarmsrest/index.html.* Hours: 5 am-8 pm; Fri, Sat to 9 pm. Closed Thanksgiving, Dec 25. Breakfast $1.35-$7.95, lunch $3.50-$15.99, dinner $2.95-$15.99. Children's menu. Reservations accepted. Cr cds: DS, MC, V.

Park Falls (C-3)

See also Lac du Flambeau, Manitowish Waters

Pop 3,104 **Elev** 1,490 ft **Area code** 715 **Zip** 54552

Information Park Falls Area Chamber of Commerce, 400 S 4th Ave S, Suite 8; 715/762-2703 or 800/762-2709

Web www.parkfalls.com

Park Falls has been proclaimed "ruffed grouse capital of the world," since more than 5,000 acres within this area have been used to create a natural habitat for the bird.

What to See and Do

Chequamegon National Forest. *1170 Fourth Ave S. E on WI 29, 70, or US 8 and 2; also NW on WI 13 and 63. A District Ranger office is located here. Phone 715/762-2461.* Aspen, maple, pine, spruce, balsam, and birch on 855,000 acres. Rainbow Lake and Porcupine Lake Wildernes areas; Great Divide National Scenic Byway. Canoeing on south fork of Flambeau River, the north and south forks of the Chippewa River and Namekagon River; muskellunge, northern pike, walleye, and bass fishing; hunting for deer, bear, and small game; archery. Blueberry and raspberry picking. Swimming, boat launching; Ice Age and North Country national scenic trails; hiking, motorcycle, cross-country skiing, and snowmobile trails; camping (May-Sept; some sites to Dec) on a first-come basis (fee). Pets must be leashed. Resorts and cabins are located in and near the forest. (Daily) **FREE**

Concrete Park. *82 36th St. 22 miles S via WI 13 in Phillips. Phone 800/762-2709.* Fred Smith's concrete and glass statues include northwoods people, folklore, fantasies, historic personages, Native Americans, angels, and animals. (Daily) **FREE**

Old Town Hall Museum. *W 7213 Pine St. Phone 715/762-4571.* Artifacts of logging era (1876-1930); replica of turn-of-the-century living room and kitchen; county historic display; old opera house. (June-Labor Day, Fri and Sun afternoons) **FREE**

Post Office Lumberjack Mural. *109 N 1st St. Phone 715/762-4575.* In 1938 the US Government provided artists the opportunity to submit artwork to be displayed in local post offices throughout the country. The Park Falls Post Office features one of the 2,200 that were finally selected. The restored mural, covering one entire wall, depicts the history of logging. (Mon-Sat)

Special Event

Flambeau Rama. *400 4th Ave S. Downtown. Phone 715/762-2703.* 4-day event includes parades, arts and crafts show, Evergreen Road Run, games. Early Aug.

Peshtigo (D-6)

See also Menominee, Oconto

Pop 3,154 **Elev** 600 ft **Area code** 715 **Zip** 54157

Information City Clerk, City Hall, 331 French St, PO Box 100; 715/582-3041

On October 8, 1871, the same day that the Chicago fire claimed 250 lives, 800 people died in Peshtigo, virtually unpublicized, when the entire town burned to the ground in a disastrous forest fire. A monument to those who died in the fire is located in the Peshtigo Fire Cemetery on Oconto Ave. The city is now a manufacturing center.

What to See and Do

Badger Park. *N Emery Ave on Peshtigo River. Phone 715/582-4321 or 715/582-3041.* Swimming, fishing (northern, bass, coho salmon); tent and trailer sites (electric hookups), playground. (May-Oct, daily) **$$$$**

Peshtigo Fire Museum. *400 Oconto Ave. Phone 715/582-3244.* Local historical items. (Memorial Day-early Oct, daily) **FREE**

Platteville (G-3)

Pop 9,708 **Elev** 994 ft **Area code** 608 **Zip** 53818

Information Chamber of Commerce, 275 US 151 W, PO Box 16; 608/348-8888

Web www.platteville.com

Sport fishing is very popular in the many streams in the area as are ice fishing on the Mississippi River and hunting for upland game, waterfowl, and deer. The world's largest letter "M" was built on Platteville Mound in 1936 by mining engineering students; it is lit twice each year for the University of Wisconsin-Platteville's homecoming and Miner's Ball.

What to See and Do

Mining Museum. *385 E Main St. Phone 608/348-3301.* Traces the development of lead and zinc mining in the area. Guided tour includes a walk down into Bevans Lead Mine and a mine train ride (May-Oct, daily). Changing exhibits (Nov-Apr, Mon-Fri). **$$$** Admission includes

Rollo Jamison Museum. *405 Main St. Phone 608/348-3301.* Museum contains a large collection of everyday items collected by Jamison during his lifetime, including horse-drawn vehicles, tools, and musical instruments.

Stone Cottage. *W Madison and Lancaster (53818). Corner of West, Madison, and US 81. Phone 608/348-8888.* (1837)

Much of the interior is the original furnishing of the home; 2-feet thick walls of dolomite Galena limestone. Was private residence until 1960s. **$**

Special Events

Dairy Days Celebration. *Pitt and Water sts Legion Field. Phone 608/348-8888.* Carnival, parade, food, live music, tractor and truck pulls, car show, 4-H exhibits. First weekend after Labor Day.

Wisconsin Shakespeare Festival. *198 Ullsvik Center. In Center for the Arts on campus of University of Wisconsin-Platteville. Phone 608/342-1398.* Nightly Tues-Sun; matinees Wed, Sat, and Sun. Phone 608/342-1298. Early July-early Aug.

Motels/Motor Lodges

★ ★ **BEST WESTERN.** *300 W US 151 (53818). Phone 608/348-2301; toll-free 800/528-1234; fax 608/348-8579. www.bestwestern.com.* 74 rooms, 2 story. S $45-$67; D $72-$77; each additional $5-$7; suites $110-$150; under 18 free. Crib $3. Pet accepted, some restrictions. TV; cable. Indoor pool; whirlpool. Complimentary coffee in lobby. Restaurants 6 am-11 pm. Check-out noon. Business services available. Exercise equipment; saunas. Game room. State university 5 blocks. Cr cds: A, C, D, DS, MC, V.

⬛ ⬛ ⬛ ⬛

★ **BEST WESTERN WELCOME INN-LANCASTER.** *420 W Maple St (53813). Phone 608/723-4162; fax 608/723-4843. www.bestwestern.com.* 22 rooms, 2 story. D $46; under 12 free. Complimentary continental breakfast. Check-out 11 am. TV; cable (premium). Laundry services. Cr cds: A, C, D, DS, MC, V.

⬛ ⬛ ⬛ ⬛

Motel/Motor Lodge

★ **SUPER 8 - PLATTEVILLE.** *100 WI 80/81 S (53818). Phone 608/348-8800; fax 608/348-7233. www.super8.com.* 73 rooms, 2 story. S $41-$47; D $48-$64; each additional $5; suites $125. Crib $4. Pet accepted; $10. TV; cable (premium). Complimentary continental breakfast. Restaurant adjacent open 24 hours. Check-out 11 am. Coin laundry. Meeting rooms. Sauna. Whirlpool. Some bathroom phones, refrigerators. Balconies. Overlooks stream. Gazebo. Cr cds: A, MC, V.

⬛

B&B/Small Inns

★ **WISCONSIN HOUSE.** *2105 Main St (53811). Phone 608/854-2233; fax 608/854-2041. wisconsinhouse.com.* 8 rooms, 2 share bath, 2 suites, 3 story. No room phones. Complimentary full breakfast. Check-out 10 am, check-in 3 pm. TV in sitting room; cable; VCR available.

Built 1846; former stagecoach stop. Dinner available Sat. Totally nonsmoking. Cr cds: A, DS, MC, V.

Restaurant

★ ★ **TIMBERS.** *670 Ellen St (53818). Phone 608/ 348-2406; fax 608/348-4995.* Tradional Menu. Hours: 11 am-1:30 pm, 5-10 pm; Sun brunch 10:30 am-1:30 pm. Closed Mon & Sun nights. Lunch $4.95-$8.95, dinner $9.50-$19.95. Sun brunch $12.95. Bar from 11 am. Organist on Sat & Sun Nights only. Child's meals. Large custom-built electronic theater pipe organ. Reservations accepted. Cr cds: A, D, DS, MC, V.

Pleasant Prairie

Restaurant

★ ★ ★ **RAY RADIGAN'S.** *11712 S Sheridan Rd (53158). Phone 262/694-0455; fax 262/694-0798.* Just three miles from town, this popular stop has been a local standby since 1933. Hours: 11 am-10 pm; Fri, Sat to 11 pm; Sun from noon. Closed Mon; Dec 24-25. Reservations accepted. Bar. Lunch $5-$10, dinner $11.95-$30. Specializes in fresh seafood, steak. Own baking. Family-owned. Cr cds: A, D, MC, V.

Portage (F-4)

See also Baraboo, Prairie du Sac, Wisconsin Dells

Settled 1835 **Pop** 8,640 **Elev** 800 ft **Area code** 608 **Zip** 53901

Information Chamber of Commerce, 301 W Wisconsin St; 608/742-6242 or 800/474-2525

Portage is built on a narrow strip of land separating the Fox and Wisconsin rivers. In the early flow of traffic, goods were hauled from one river to another, providing the name for the city. Before permanent settlement, Fort Winnebago occupied this site; several historic buildings remain. Modern Portage is the business center of Columbia County.

What to See and Do

Cascade Mountain Ski Area. *NW on I-90/94, then 1/4 mile W on WI 33 to Cascade Mtn Rd. Phone 608/ 742-5588 or 800/992-2754.* Two double, three quad, three triple chairlifts, rope tow; patrol, school, snowmaking; snack bar, cafeteria, dining room, bar. 27 runs; longest run 1 mile; vertical drop 460 feet. Night skiing. (Mid-Nov-Mar, daily)

Fort Winnebago Surgeons' Quarters. *W8687 State Rd 33. 1 mile E on WI 33. Phone 608/742-2949.* Original log house (1828), surviving from Old Fort Winnebago, used by medical officers stationed at the fort. Restored; many original furnishings. Garrison school (1850-1960). (Mid-May-mid-Oct, daily) **$$**

Home of Zona Gale. *506 W Edgewater St. Phone 608/ 742-7744.* Greek Revival house built in 1906 for the Pulitzer Prize-winning novelist; some original furnishings. (Mon-Fri, by appointment) **$**

Old Indian Agency House. *Rural Rte 1. 1 mile E on WI 33 to Agency House Rd. Phone 608/742-6362 or 608/742-2739.* (1832) Restored house of John Kinzie, US Indian Agent to the Winnebago and an important pioneer; his wife Juliette wrote Wau-bun, an early history of their voyages to Fort Winnebago. Period furnishings. (May-Oct, daily; rest of year, by appointment) **$$**

Silver Lake. *N side of town. Phone 608/742-2176.* Swimming, beach, lifeguards, waterskiing, fishing (rainbow trout, largemouth bass, northern pike, panfish, muskie, walleye), boating (public landing); picnic area (shelter), playground. Parking. (Early June-Labor Day, daily) **FREE**

Motel/Motor Lodge

★ ★ **RIDGE MOTOR INN.** *2900 New Pinery Rd (53901). Phone 608/742-5306; toll-free 877/742-5306; fax 608/742-5306.* 113 rooms, 3 story, 9 kitchen suites. June-Aug: S $49-$69; D $59-$79; each additional $5; kitchen suites $100-$135; under 12 free; weekend rates; lower rates rest of year. Crib $4. TV; cable (premium), VCR available (movies). Indoor pool; whirlpool. Complimentary coffee in rooms. Restaurant 6 am-10 pm. Bar. Check-out 11 am. Coin laundry. Meeting rooms. Business services available. Downhill ski 4 miles; cross-country ski 16 miles. Exercise room; sauna, steam room. Massage. Game room. Cr cds: A, C, D, DS, MC, V.

Port Washington (F-6)

See also Cedarburg, Milwaukee, Sheboygan

Settled 1830 **Pop** 9,338 **Elev** 612 ft **Area code** 262 **Zip** 53074

Information Tourist Center located in the Pebble House, 126 E Grand Ave, PO Box 153; 262/284-0900 or 800/719-4881

Web www.discoverusa.com/wi/ptwash

Located along the shore of Lake Michigan, Port Washington has many pre-Civil War homes. The Port Washington

Marina, one of the finest on Lake Michigan, provides exceptional facilities for boating and fishing.

What to See and Do

Eghart House. *316 Grand Ave. Phone 262/284-2875.* Built in 1872; Victorian furnishings from 1850-1900 in hall, parlor, dining-living room, bedroom, kitchen, and pantry. Tours. (Late May-Labor Day, Sun afternoons; weekdays by appointment) **$**

Motels/Motor Lodges

★ ★ **BEST WESTERN HARBORSIDE.** *135 E Grand Ave (53074). Phone 262/284-9461; fax 414/284-3169. www.bestwestern.com.* 96 rooms, 5 story. S $59-$199; D $68-$199; each additional $10; under 12 free. Crib free. Pet accepted; some restrictions. Sauna. Indoor pool; whirlpool. Restaurant 6:30-10 am. Bar 4 pm-1 am. Check-out 11 am. Exercise equipment. Meeting rooms. Business services available. Valet service. Game room. On Lake Michigan; dock. Some whirlpools. Cr cds: A, C, D, DS, MC, V.

⬛ 🐾 🏊 🧍 🛝

★ ★ **WEST BEND FANTASUITES.** *2520 W Washington St (53095). Phone 262/338-0636; toll-free 800/727-9727; fax 414/338-4290.* 86 rooms, 2 story, 25 theme suites. S $59-$67; D $69-$77; each additional $8; suites $99-$179; under 18 free. Crib free. TV; cable (premium), VCR available (movies). Sauna. Indoor/outdoor pool; whirlpool. Complimentary continental breakfast. Bar. Check-out noon. Meeting rooms. Business services available. Valet service. Game room. Uniquely decorated suites with varying themes. Cr cds: A, C, D, DS, MC, V.

⬛ 🛎 🏊 🧍 🛝 🏃

Restaurants

★ ★ **BUCHEL'S COLONIAL HOUSE.** *1000 S Spring St (53074). Phone 262/284-2212.* Continental menu. Hours: 5-10 pm. Closed Sun-Mon; holidays. Dinner $11.50-$25. Bar. Children's menu. Reservations accepted. Cr cds: MC, V.

⬛

★ ★ **SMITH BROTHERS' FISH SHANTY.** *100 N Franklin St (53074). Phone 262/284-5592; fax 262/377-7923. www.foodspot.com.* Specialties: seafood, lemon meringue pie. Hours: Sun-Thurs 11 am-9 pm; Fri, Sat 11 am-10 pm, closed Thanksgiving, Dec 25. Lunch $4.95-$10.95, dinner $7.50-$15.50. Bar. Children's menu. Reservations accepted. Outdoor deck dining. Non-smoking seating. Cr cds: DS, MC, V.

⬛

Prairie du Chien (G-2)

Settled 1736 **Pop** 5,659 **Elev** 642 ft **Area code** 608 **Zip** 53821

Information Chamber of Commerce, 211 S Main St, PO Box 326; 608/326-2032 or 800/732-1673

Web www.prairieduchien.org

This is the second oldest European settlement in Wisconsin, and dates to June 1673. Marquette and Jolliet discovered the Mississippi River just south of the prairie that the French adventurers then named Prairie du Chien ("prairie of the dog") for Chief Alim, whose name meant "dog." The site became a popular gathering place and trading post. The War of 1812 led to the construction of Fort Shelby and Fort Crawford on an ancient Native American burial ground in the village. Stationed here were Jefferson Davis, later president of the Confederacy, and Zachary Taylor, later president of the United States. In 1826, Hercules Dousman, an agent for John Jacob Astor's American Fur Company, came and built a personal fortune, becoming Wisconsin's first millionaire. When Fort Crawford was moved, Dousman bought the site and erected Villa Louis, the "House of the Mound," a palatial mansion.

What to See and Do

Fort Crawford Museum. *717 S Beaumont Rd. Phone 608/326-6960.* Relics of 19th-century medicine, Native American herbal remedies, drugstore, dentist and physicians' offices. Educational health exhibits; Dessloch Theater displays "transparent twins." Dedicated to Dr. William Beaumont, who did some of his famous digestive system studies at Fort Crawford. (May-Oct, daily) **$$**

⭐ **Kickapoo Indian Caverns and Native American Museum.** *W 200 Rhein Hollow, 6 miles S on US 18, then 9 miles E on WI 60 in Wauzeka. Phone 608/875-7723.* Largest caverns in Wisconsin, used by Native Americans for centuries as a shelter. Sights incl subterranean lake, Cathedral Room, Turquoise Room, Stalactite Chamber, and Chamber of the Lost Waters. Guided tours. (Mid-May-Oct, daily) **$$$**

Nelson Dewey State Park. *12190 County Rd VV. 35 miles S via US 18, WI 35 ,and 133 near Cassville. Phone 608/725-5374.* This 756-acre park offers nature, hiking trails; camping (hookups). Standard fees. (Daily) Also here is

Stonefield. *12195 County Rd VV. Phone 608/725-5210.* Named for a rock-studded, 2,000-acre farm that Dewey (first elected governor of Wisconsin established on the bluffs of the Mississippi River.

State Agricultural Museum contains display of farm machinery. Site also features re-creation of an 1890 Stonefield Village including blacksmithy, general store, print shop, school, church, and 26 other buildings. Horse-drawn wagon rides (limited hours; fee). (Memorial Day-early Oct, Wed-Sun) **$$$**

✪ **Villa Louis.** *521 Villa Louis Rd, off US 18. Phone 608/ 326-2721.* (1870) Built on site of Fort Crawford. Restored to its 19th-century splendor. Contains original furnishings, collection of Victorian decorative arts. Surrounded by extensive grounds, bounded by the Mississippi River. Tours includes Fur Trade Museum. (May-Oct, Tues-Sun) **$$$**

Wyalusing State Park. *13081 State Park Ln. 7 miles SE on US 18, then W on County C, X. Phone 608/996-2261.* A 2,654-acre park at the confluence of the Mississippi and Wisconsin rivers. Sentinel Ridge (500 feet) provides a commanding view of the area; valleys, caves, waterfalls, springs; Native American effigy mounds. Swimming beach nearby, fishing, boating (landing), canoeing; 18 miles of nature, hiking, and cross-country ski trails; picnicking, playground, concession, camping (electric hookups, dump station). Nature center; naturalist programs (summer). Standard fees. (Daily) **$$**

Motels/Motor Lodges

★ **BEST WESTERN QUIET HOUSE & SUITES.** *Hwys 18 & 35 S (53821). Phone 608/326-4777; fax 608/ 326-4787. www.bestwestern.com.* 42 suites, 2 story. S $91; D $111; each additional $10. Pet accepted. Check-out 11 am. TV; cable (premium). In-room modem link. Exercise equipment. Indoor pool, whirlpool. Cr cds: A, C, D, DS, MC, V.

D 🐾 ⚓ 🏋 🏊 🧍 🖼

★ **BRISBOIS MOTOR INN.** *533 N Marquette Rd (53821). Phone 608/326-8404; toll-free 800/356-5850; fax 608/326-8404. www.brisboismotorinn.com.* 46 rooms. S $49-$59; D $67-$84; each additional $5; under 17 free. Crib free. TV; cable (premium). Heated pool. Playground. Complimentary coffee in rooms. Restaurant adjacent 6 am-11 pm. Check-out 11 am. Meeting room. Free airport transportation. Cross-country ski 2 miles. Cr cds: A, D, DS, MC, V.

D 🐾 🍴 🏊 🖼

★ **HOLIDAY MOTEL.** *1010 S Marquette Rd (53821). Phone 608/326-2448; toll-free 800/962-3883; fax 608/ 326-2413.* 18 rooms, 1-2 story. May-Oct: S $35-$55; D $50-$75; suite $98; each additional $5; under 16 free; lower rates rest of year. Crib free. TV; cable (premium). Complimentary coffee. Restaurant nearby. Check-out 11 am. Business services available. Cr cds: A, DS, MC, V.

D 🐾 🏊 🧍 🖼

★ **PRAIRIE MOTEL.** *1616 S Marquette Rd (53821). Phone 608/326-6461; toll-free 800/526-3776.* 32 rooms. May-Oct: S $49-$55; D $55-$65; family rates; lower rates rest of year. Pet accepted. TV; cable (premium). Heated pool. Playground. Complimentary coffee in rooms. Check-out 11 am. Cross-country ski 2 miles. Miniature golf. Lawn games. Some refrigerators. Picnic tables, grills. Cr cds: DS, MC, V.

🐾 🧍 🏊 🖼 🖼

Prairie du Sac (F-4)

See also Spring Green

Pop 2,380 **Elev** 780 ft **Area code** 608 **Zip** 53578

Information Sauk Prairie Area Chamber of Commerce, 207 Water St, Sauk City 53583; 608/643-4168

A favorite launching area for canoeists on the Wisconsin River. It is possible to see bald eagles south of the village at Ferry Bluff, where many of them winter. Watching them feed on fish in the open water is a favorite winter pastime.

What to See and Do

Wollersheim Winery. *7876 WI 188. Phone 608/643-6515 or 800/847-WINE.* (1857) Guided tours, wine tasting, cheese, gift shop. (Daily; closed holidays) **$$**

Special Event

Harvest Festival. *Wollersheim Winery. 7876 WI 188. Phone 608/643-6515.* Grape stompers competition; music; cork toss; grape spitting contest; foods. First full weekend Oct.

Racine (G-6)

See also Burlington, Kenosha, Milwaukee

Founded 1834 **Pop** 84,298 **Elev** 626 ft **Area code** 262

Information Racine County Convention and Visitors Bureau, 345 Main St, 53403; 262/634-3293 or 800/ C-RACINE

Web www.racine.org

Racine is situated on a thumb of land jutting into Lake Michigan. The largest concentration of people of Danish descent in the United States can be found here; in fact, West Racine is known as "Kringleville" because of its Danish pastry. There are more than 300 manufacturing firms located here.

What to See and Do

Architectural tour. *1525 Howe St. Reservations required. Phone 262/260-2154.* A 45-minute tour of SC Johnson Wax world headquarters designed by Frank Lloyd Wright (Fri; closed holidays). **FREE**

Charles A. Wustum Museum of Fine Arts. *2519 Northwestern Ave. Phone 262/636-9177.* Painting, photography, graphics, crafts, and sculpture displays; works of local, regional, and nationally known artists are featured. Permanent and changing exhibits. Also park and formal gardens. (Daily; closed holidays) **FREE**

Racine Heritage Museum. *701 S Main St. Phone 262/636-3926.* Cultural history of Racine includes permanent and temporary exhibits, archive, and photographic collection. (Tues-Sat; closed holidays) **FREE**

Racine Zoological Gardens. *2131 N Main St. Phone 262/636-9189.* Extensive animal collection, picnic area, swimming (beach). (Daily; closed Dec 25) **FREE**

Special Event

Salmon-A-Rama. *5 Fifth St. Lakefront. Phone 262/636-9229.* Fishing contest. Two weekends. Mid-July.

Motels/Motor Lodges

★ **KNIGHTS INN.** *1149 Oakes Rd (53406). Phone 262/886-6667; toll-free 800/843-5644; fax 414/886-6667. www.knightsinn.com.* 107 rooms, 1 story. June-Labor Day: S $40-$49; D $49-$59; each additional $7; suites $47.95-$58.95; kitchen units $58.95-$62.95; under 18 free; lower rates rest of year. Crib free. Pet accepted. TV; cable (premium), VCR available (movies). Complimentary continental breakfast. Restaurant nearby. Check-out noon. Cr cds: A, C, D, DS, MC, V.

D ⚫ 🛎 💺 🏌 ☒ 🏊 SC 🏃

★ **RIVERSIDE DAYS INN.** *3700 Northwestern Ave (53405). Phone 262/637-9311; toll-free 888/242-6494; fax 414/637-4575. www.daysinn.com.* 112 rooms, 2 story. S $49-$89; D $59-$99; each additional $6; under 18 free. Crib free. Pet accepted. TV; cable (premium). Heated pool. Complimentary coffee in rooms. Restaurant 6 am-2 pm, 5:30-9 pm. Room service. Bar 4 pm-2 am. Check-out noon. Coin laundry. Meeting rooms. Business services available. In-room modem link. Bellhops. Valet service. Sundries. Cross-country ski 3 miles. Game room. Lawn games. Picnic tables. On Root River. Cr cds: A, C, D, DS, MC, V.

D ⚫ 💺 🏌 💺 ☒ 🏊 🏊 SC 🏃

Hotel

★ ★ **MARRIOTT RACINE.** *7111 Washington Ave (53406). Phone 262/886-6100. www.marriott.com.* 222 rooms, 5 story. S, D $135-$175; each additional $20; under 17 free. Crib available. Indoor pool. TV; cable (premium), VCR available. Complimentary coffee, newspaper in rooms. Restaurant 6 am-10 pm. Check-out noon. Meeting rooms. Business center. Gift shop. Exercise room. Some refrigerators, minibars. Cr cds: A, C, D, DS, ER, JCB, MC, V.

🏊 🏃

Restaurants

★ **GREAT WALL.** *6214 Washington Ave (53406). Phone 262/886-9700.* Chinese menu, Pan-Asian menu. Hours: 11 am-8:30 pm; Fri to 9:30 pm; Sat 4-9:30 pm; Sun 11 am-2 pm. Closed Mon; holidays. Buffet Sun buffet $6.95, lunch $4.95-$5.95, dinner $6.75-$15.50. Bar. Reservations accepted. Cr cds: A, DS, MC, V.

D

★ ★ **HOB NOB.** *277 S Sheridan Rd (53403). Phone 262/552-8008; fax 262/552-8009.* Specializes in seafood, steak, duck. Hours: 5-10 pm; Sun from 4 pm. Closed Dec 24, 25; also Super Bowl Sun. Dinner $9.95-$19.95. Bar. Reservations accepted. Cr cds: A, D, DS, MC, V.

D

Reedsburg (F-3)

See also Portage, Prairie du Sac, Wisconsin Dells

Pop 5,834 **Elev** 926 ft **Area code** 608 **Zip** 53959

Information Chamber of Commerce, 240 Railroad St, PO Box 142; 608/524-2850 or 800/844-3507

Self-proclaimed "butter capital of America," Reedsburg is the home of one of the largest butter producing plants in the world. The Wisconsin Dairies plant produces more than 50,000,000 pounds of butter here each year.

What to See and Do

Carr Valley Cheese Factory. *S3797 County Rd G. 9 miles W on County K, G in La Valle. Phone 608/986-2781.* Observation area for viewing production of cheddar cheese. (Mon-Sat; closed Jan 1, Dec 25) **FREE**

Foremost Farms. *501 S Pine. Phone 608/524-2351.* Viewing window for butter making process. (Mon-Fri) **FREE**

Historical Society Log Village and Museum. *3 miles E via WI 33. Phone 608/524-2807.* Log cabin with loft, Oetzman log house (1876), log church and library, one-room schoolhouse, blacksmith shop; completely furnished kitchen, living rm, and bedrm; apothecary shop; Native American and army memorabilia. Located on 52 acres of pine forest and farm fields. (June-Sept, Sat-Sun) **DONATION**

Museum of Norman Rockwell Art. *227 S Park. Phone 608/524-2123.* One of the largest collections of Norman

Rockwell memorabilia spans the artist's 65-year career. Video. Gift shop. (Mid-May-Oct, daily; rest of year, Tues-Sun; closed holidays) **$$$**

Park Lane Model Railroad Museum. *S2083 Herwig Rd. 8 miles E on WI 23 at Herwig Rd.* Phone 608/254-8050. Features working model railroad layouts; hundreds of individual cars on display. (Mid-May-mid-Sept, daily) **$$**

Special Event

Butter Festival. *Nishan Park. County H and 8th St.* Phone 608/524-2850. 4-day festival with parade, tractor and horse pulls, carnival rides, events, arts and crafts, food. 6 days mid-June.

Rhinelander (C-4)

See also Three Lakes

Settled 1880 **Pop** 7,427 **Elev** 1,560 ft **Area code** 715 **Zip** 54501

Information Rhinelander Area Chamber of Commerce, 450 W Kemp St, PO Box 795; 715/365-7464 or 800/236-4386

Web www.ci.rhinelander.wi.us

Rhinelander is the gateway to the "world's most concentrated lake region." It lies at the junction of the Wisconsin and Pelican rivers. 232 lakes, 11 trout streams, and two rivers within a 12-mile radius make the city a thriving resort center. Fishing is good in lakes and streams, and there is hunting for upland game and deer. The logging industry, which built this area, still thrives and the many miles of old logging roads are excellent for hiking and mountain biking. Paved bicycle trails, cross-country skiing, and snowmobiling are also popular in this northwoods area.

Rhinelander is headquarters for the Nicolet National Forest; phone 715/362-3415.

What to See and Do

⭐ **Rhinelander Logging Museum.** *810 Keenan St. In Pioneer Park, on US 8, WI 47.* Phone 715/369-5004. Most complete displays of old-time lumbering in Midwest. On grounds are "Five Spot," last narrow-gauge railroad locomotive to work Wisconsin's northwoods, and a restored depot dating from late 1800s. Also on premises is one-room schoolhouse. Museum houses the "hodag," called "the strangest animal known to man." Created as a hoax, it has become the symbol of the city. (Memorial Day-Labor Day, daily) **DONATION** Also on grounds is

Civilian Conservation Corps Museum. *Kemp and Oneida Ave.* Phone 800/236-4386. Houses photographs, memorabilia, artifacts, tools, and papers that record much of the history of the CCC. The manner of clothing worn, how the enrolee was housed and fed, and the tools used in project work are on the display. (Last week May-first week Sept, daily) **FREE**

Special Events

Art Fair. *1 Courthouse Sq, Courthouse lawn.* Phone 715/365-7464. Second Sat June.

Hodag Country Festival. *5476 River Rd.* Phone 715/369-1300. 3-day country music festival featuring top-name entertainment. Phone 800/762-3803. Mid-July.

Oktoberfest. *Downtown. 156 Courtney on the Green.* Phone 715/365-7464. German music, food. Phone 800/236-4386. Mid-Oct.

Motels/Motor Lodges

⭐ **AMERICINN.** *648 W Kemp St (54501).* Phone 715/369-9600; toll-free 800/634-3444; fax 715/369-9613. www.americinn.com. 52 rooms, 2 story. D $67-$77; each additional $6; under 12 free. Pet accepted, some restrictions. Complimentary continental breakfast. Check-out 11 am. TV; cable (premium), VCR available. Laundry services. Sauna. Indoor pool, whirlpool. Cross-country ski 1 mile. Cr cds: A, D, DS, MC, V.

⭐⭐ **BEST WESTERN CLARIDGE MOTOR INN.** *70 N Stevens St (54501).* Phone 715/362-7100; toll-free 800/427-1377; fax 715/362-3883. www.bestwestern.com. 81 rooms, 2-4 story. July-Oct: S $55-$61; D $57-$66; each additional $8; suites $84-$115; under 18 free. Pet accepted. TV; cable. Indoor pool; whirlpool. Coffee in rooms. Restaurant 6:30 am-2 pm, 5-10 pm; Sun, holidays to 9 pm. Room service 5-9 pm. Bar 11 am-2 pm, 4 pm-midnight. Check-out 11 am. Laundry facilities. Meeting rooms. Business services available. Valet service. Sundries. Free airport transportation. Cross-country ski 5 miles. Exercise equipment. Cr cds: A, C, D, DS, MC, V.

⭐ **HOLIDAY INN.** *668 W Kemp St (54501).* Phone 715/369-3600; toll-free 800/465-4329; fax 715/369-3600. www.holiday-inn.com. 101 rooms, 2 story. S $55-$64; D $64-$79; each additional $8. Crib free. TV; cable, VCR available (movies). Indoor pool; whirlpool. Restaurant 6:30 am-2 pm, 5-10 pm; Sun from 7 am. Room service. Bar 11:30 am-midnight; entertainment. Check-out noon. Coin laundry. Meeting rooms. Business services available. Sundries. Free airport transportation. Downhill ski 20 miles; cross-country ski 5 miles. Exercise equipment; sauna. Game room. Cr cds: A, C, D, DS, JCB, MC, V.

Resorts

★ **HOLIDAY ACRES RESORT.** *4060 S Shore Dr (54501). Phone 715/369-1500; toll-free 800/261-1500; fax 715/369-3665.* 28 rooms in 2-story lodge, 28 kitchen cottages (1-4 bedroom; boat included; maid service available). Lodge, mid-June-late Aug, also Fri, Sat Dec 24-mid-Mar: S, D $94-$124; each additional $11.50; cottages for 2-8, $89-$264; winter weekend packages; lower rates rest of year. Pet accepted; $6. TV; cable, VCR available (movies). Indoor pool, whirlpools, sauna. Playground. Coffee in rooms. Dining room 5 am-10 pm. Box lunches, coffee shop. Room service. Bar 4 pm-1 am. Check-out 11 am (cottages in summer, 10 am). Meeting rooms. Business services available. Grocery, package store 3 miles. Gift shop in season. Airport transportation. Tennis. Sand beach; boats, motors, rafts, canoes, sailboat, windsurfing. Downhill ski 20 miles; cross-country ski on site. Snowmobile trails. Bicycles. Lawn games. Fireplace in 24 cottages, 2 lodge rooms; some screened porches. 1000 acres on Lake Thompson. Cr cds: A, C, D, DS, MC, V.

⬛🌊🏊‍♂️🏌️🏂🛶🏃🛷🚶

★ **KAFKA'S RESORT.** *4281 W Lake George Rd (54501). Phone 715/369-2929; toll-free 800/426-6674. www.kafkas-resort.com.* 10 kitchen cottages (2-3 bedroom; boat included). No A/C. Mid-June-Aug: cottages for 2-6, $500-$750/week; lower rates rest of year. No maid service. Check-out 9 am, check-in 2 pm. TV; cable. Bar 1 pm-midnight. Playground. Recreation room. Private beach, swimming; Boats, motors, canoes. Downhill ski 20 miles; cross-country ski 5 miles. Picnic tables. Lawn games. Fishing guides, clean and store area. Snowmobiling. Free airport transportation. Cr cds: A, MC, V.

⬛🌊🏌️🛶🏂✈️

Restaurants

★ ★ **RHINELANDER CAFE AND PUB.** *Phone 715/362-2424; fax 715/362-6062.* Hours: 7 am-11 pm. Closed Thanksgiving, Dec 25. Bar 10:30-1 am. Breakfast $1.50-$5.75, lunch $1.50-$10, dinner $5-$25. Child's meals. Specializes in prime rib, roast duck. Nautical décor. Family-owned. Cr cds: A, D, DS, MC, V.

⬛

★ **TULA'S FAMILY RESTAURANT.** *232 S Courtney (54501). Phone 715/369-5248; fax 715/369-5802.* Hours: 6 am-9 pm. Closed Dec 25. Breakfast $2.29-$6.95, lunch $2.79-$6.99, dinner 2.79-$14.95. Bar 11 am-midnight. Child's meals. Reservations accepted. Outdoor dining. Cr cds: DS, MC, V.

Rice Lake (C-2)

See also Spooner

Pop 7,998 **Elev** 1,140 ft **Area code** 715 **Zip** 54868

Information Rice Lake Area Chamber of Commerce, 37 S Main St; 715/234-2126 or 800/523-6318

Web www.chamber.rice-lake.wi.us

Formerly headquarters for the world's largest hardwood mills, Rice Lake has an economy based on industry and retail trade. The city and lake were named for nearby wild rice sloughs, which were an important Sioux and Chippewa food source. Surrounded by 84 lakes, the city is in a major recreation area.

Special Events

Aquafest. *37 S Main. Phone 800/523-6318.* June.

County Fair. *101 Short St. Barron County Fairgrounds. Phone 800/523-6318.* July.

Motels/Motor Lodges

★ **AMERICINN.** *2906 Pioneer Ave (54868). Phone 715/234-9060; toll-free 800/634-3444; fax 715/234-9060. www.americinn.com.* 43 rooms, 2 story. D $58-$79; each additional $6; under 13 free. Complimentary continental breakfast. Check-out 11 am. TV; cable (premium). In-room modem link. Indoor pool, whirlpool. Downhill ski 10 miles, cross-country ski 1 mile. Cr cds: A, C, D, DS, MC, V.

⬛🌊🏊‍♂️🛷 SC

★ **CURRIER'S LAKEVIEW MOTEL.** *2010 E Sawyer St (54868). Phone 715/234-7474; toll-free 800/433-5253; fax 715/736-1501. www.currierslakeview.com.* 19 rooms, 2 story. S $37-65; D $52-$85. Pet accepted. Check-out 11 am. TV; cable (premium). Continental breakfast. Private beach. Downhill/cross-country ski 18 miles. Boats, motors, dockage; paddle boats, canoes, pontoons. Snowmobile trails. Free airport transportation. Cr cds: A, DS, MC, V.

🌊🏌️🛷🛷

★ **SUPER 8.** *115 2nd St (54728). Phone 715/924-4888; fax 715/924-2538. www.super8.com.* 40 rooms, 2 story. June-Sept: S $56-$68; D $66-$84; each additional $6; under 12 free; lower rates rest of year. Crib free. TV; cable (premium). Complimentary continental breakfast. Restaurant nearby. Check-out 11 am. Business services available. In-room modem link. Indoor pool; whirlpool. Cr cds: A, C, D, DS, MC, V.

⬛🏌️🛷🛷

B&B/Small Inns

★ ★ ★ **CANOE BAY.** *Phone 715/924-4594; fax 715/924-4594. www.canoebay.com.* Canoe Bay is rather like a luxurious camp for adults, with gourmet dining, an award-winning wine cellar, and extensive amenities. Situated on 280 acres in northwestern Wisconsin, the resort's three private, spring-fed lakes are perfect for a multitude of recreational opportunities. The wilderness trails are ideal for hiking in summer months, while snowshoeing and cross-country skiing are popular during the winter. Embodying the definition of a getaway, this resort has no telephones or televisions to distract from the peaceful setting. Guests enjoy plucking books off the shelves at the Great Room's library or working out in the fitness center. The guest rooms and cottages are characterized by regional décor and offer great privacy. Couples linger over romantic evenings at the candlelit Dining Room, where an extensive wine list and a nightly tasting menu make for terrific memories. 19 units, 5 rooms in inn, 4 rooms in lodge, 10 cottages. rooms. S, D $270-$725. Adults only. Complimentary bkfst, coffee in rooms. Check-out Check-out 11 am, check-in 3 pm. Check-in Check-out 11 am, check-in 3 pm. TV; cable (premium), VCR (movies). TV; cable (premium), VCR (movies). TV; cable (premium), VCR (movies). Restaurant Restaurant sitting 6-8 pm. Room service Room service noon-8 pm. Exercise equipment. 9-hole golf privileges. Cross-country ski on site. Ice skating. Concierge service. On 2 lakes. Totally nonsmoking. Cr cds: A, DS, MC, V.

🅳 ⛷ ✈ 🕴 🏊

Restaurant

★ **NORSKE NOOK.** *2900 Pioneer Ave. Phone 715/234-1733; fax 715/234-1733. www.norskenook.com.* Hours: 5:30 am-10 pm; Sun 8 am-8 pm. Closed Thanksgiving, Dec 25, Jan 1, Easter. Breakfast $3.25-$12, Daily, lunch $3.25-$12. Dinner $3.25-$12. Child's meals. Reservations accepted. Specialzies in hot sandwiches, pies. Old-style family restaurant. Cr cds: DS, MC, V.

🅳

Richland Center (F-3)

See also Reedsburg, Spring Green

Settled 1849 **Pop** 5,018 **Elev** 731 ft **Area code** 608 **Zip** 53581

Information Richland Chamber of Commerce, 174 S Central, PO Box 128; 608/647-6205 or 800/422-1318

Web www.richlandcounty.com

This is the birthplace of famed architect Frank Lloyd Wright (1867).

What to See and Do

Eagle Cave. *16320 Cavern Ln. 12 miles SW via WI 80 and 60. Phone 608/537-2988.* Large onyx cavern contains stalactites, stalagmites, fossils. Camping (hookups; fee); marked trails, picnicking, deer farm; fishing, swimming, horseback riding; hay rides; game room. 220 acres. Guided cave tours (Memorial Day-Labor Day, daily) **$$**

Special Events

Richland County Fair. *Fairgrounds, 1/2 mile S Hwy AA & Industrial Park Dr. Phone 608/647-6859.* Early-Sept.

Wisconsin High School State Rodeo Finals. *Fairgrounds, 1/2 mile S Hwy AA & Industrial Park Dr. Phone 608/647-6859.* Late June.

Saint Croix Falls (C-1)

Settled 1837 **Pop** 1,640 **Elev** 900 ft **Area code** 715 **Zip** 54024

Headquarters for the Interstate State Park, St. Croix Falls has become a summer and winter resort area. The oldest community in Polk County, it depends on farming, industry, dairying, and the tourist trade. Lions Park north of town has picnicking and boat launching, and there are many miles of groomed snowmobile trails in Polk County. Fishing for catfish, walleye, sturgeon, and panfish is excellent in the St. Croix River and the many area lakes.

What to See and Do

Crex Meadows Wildlife Area. *325 WI 70. N via WI 87, 1 mile N of Grantsburg. Phone 715/463-2896.* This 30,000-acre state-owned wildlife area is a prairie-wetlands habitat; breeding wildlife species incl giant Canada geese, 11 species of ducks, sharp-tailed grouse, sandhill cranes, bald eagles, ospreys, trumpeter swans, and loons. Wildlife observation and photography; guided (by appointment) and self-guided tours. Canoeing; hunting, trapping (fall); hiking, picnicking, camping (Sept-Dec). (Daily) **FREE**

Governor Knowles State Forest. *325 WI 70. Headquarters 27 miles N via WI 87, just N of Grantsburg on WI 70. Phone 715/463-2898.* A 33,000-acre forest extending north and south along the St. Croix River. Fishing, boating, canoeing; hiking, bridle, snowmobile (fee), and cross-country ski trails; picnicking, group camping. (Daily)

⭐**Interstate State Park.** *2 blocks S of US 8 on WI 35. Phone 715/483-3747.* A 1,325-acre park; Wisconsin's oldest state park. Swimming, fishing, boating, canoeing; nature, hiking, and cross-country ski trails; picnicking, camping (dump station). Permanent naturalist; naturalist programs. Part of the Ice Age National Scientific Reserve.

The Reserve operates a visitor center here. (Daily) Standard fees. **$$$** In the park is

The Gorge of the St. Croix River. Forms the Dalles of the St. Croix, with volcanic rock formation, sheer rock walls, some over 200 feet tall; series of potholes, wooded hills and valley; state trout hatchery is located just N of Interstate Park (daily).

St. Croix National Scenic Riverway. *Phone 715/483-3284.* Northern unit, 200 miles of scenic riverway in mixed pine and hardwood forest. Southern unit, 52 miles of scenic riverway in mixed pine and hardwood forests, high rocky bluffs. National Park Visitor centers (daily).

Trollhaugen Ski Resort. *2232 100th Ave. 3 miles S on WI 35 to Dresser, then 3/4 mile E on County F. Phone 715/755-2955 or 800/826-7166 (WI).* Resort has three chairlifts, seven rope tows; patrol, school, rentals; snowmaking; bars, cafeterias, restaurant. 22 runs. (Early Nov-Mar, daily) **$$$$**

Motel/Motor Lodge

★ ★ **DALLES HOUSE MOTEL.** *WI 35 S (54024). Phone 715/483-3206; fax 715/483-3207.* 50 rooms, 2 story. S, D $43-$85; each additional $6. Crib $7. Pet accepted. TV; cable (premium). Sauna. Indoor pool; whirlpools. Restaurant 8 am-11 pm. Check-out 11 am. Coin laundry. Meeting room. Business services available. In-room modem link. Downhill ski 3 miles; cross-country ski 1/4 mile. Interstate State Park adjacent. Cr cds: A, C, DS, MC, V.

Saint Germain (C-4)

See also Eagle River, Minocqua, Three Lakes, Woodruff

Pop 1,100 **Elev** 1,627 ft **Area code** 715 **Zip** 54558

Restaurants

★ **ELIASON'S SOME PLACE ELSE.** *438 WI 70 (54558). Phone 715/542-3779.* Hours: 5-9 pm. Closed Mon; Dec 24-25; also Nov. Bar. Dinner $4.95-$19.95. Fri fish fry $7.50. Specializes in prime rib, lobster. Entertainment Fri, Sat. Country décor. Gift shop. Family-owned. Cr cds: MC, V.

★ **SPANG'S.** *Phone 715/479-9400; fax 715/477-2173.* Hours: 5-10 pm. Closed Easter, Thanksgiving, Dec 24-25. Italian, Amer menu. Bar. Dinner $7.25-$15.25. Child's meals. Specializes in pasta, pizza. Garden lounge. Old World atmosphere. Family-owned. Cr cds: A, DS, MC, V.

Sayner (C-4)

See also Boulder Junction, Eagle River, Minocqua, Woodruff

Pop 450 **Elev** 1,675 ft **Area code** 715 **Zip** 54560

Centrally located in the Northern Highland-American Legion State Forest and boasting 42 sparkling lakes, the Sayner-Star Lake area offers camping, waterskiing, and excellent all-year fishing. Considered the birthplace of the snowmobile, Sayner is near miles of scenic well-groomed trails.

Resort

★ ★ **FROELICH'S SAYNER LODGE.** *3221 Plum Lake Dr (54560). Phone 715/542-3261.* 11 lodge rooms, 2 story, 25 cottages (1-3 bedroom). No A/C except public rooms. Late May-Oct: S, D $40-$60; cabana: $70; cottage $70-$180. Closed rest of year. Pet accepted, some restrictions. TV; VCR available. Heated pool. Playground. Complimentary continental breakfast. Bar 4 pm-12:30 am; closed Mon, Tues. Check-out 10 am, check-in 2 pm. Grocery, coin lndry, package store 3/4 miles. Airport transportation. Tennis. Boats, motors, canoe, pontoon boat; waterskiing. Lawn games. Hiking trails. Recreation room. Fishing guides. Library. Screened porch in most cottages; some fireplaces. On Plum Lake. Cr cds: MC, V.

Shawano (D-5)

Settled 1843 **Pop** 7,598 **Elev** 821 ft **Area code** 715 **Zip** 54166

Information Chamber of Commerce, 1404 E Green Bay St, PO Box 38; 715/524-2139 or 800/235-8528

Web www.shawano.com

A city born of the lumber boom, Shawano is now a retail trade center for the small surrounding farms and produces dairy and wood products.

What to See and Do

Shawano Lake. *WI 22 and Lake Dr. 2 miles E on WI 22. Phone 800/235-8528.* Lake is 4 miles wide and 7 miles long. Fishing, boating (ramps); ice fishing, hunting. 300 miles of snowmobile trails, 8 miles of cross-country ski trails. Camping (fee).

Special Event

Flea Market. *Shawano County Fairgrounds. 211 W Green Bay St. Phone 715/526-9769.* Sun, Apr-Oct.

Motels/Motor Lodges

★ **AMERICINN.** *1330 E Green Bay St (54166). Phone 715/524-5111; fax 715/526-3626. www.americinn.com.* 47 rooms, 2 story. D $54.90-$64.90; each additional $6-$10; under 12 free. Complimentary continental breakfast. Check-out 11 am. TV; cable (premium), VCR available. In-room modem link. Sauna. Indoor pool, whirlpool. Cr cds: A, D, DS, MC, V.

⊡ 🐾 🏊 🛏 🏊

★ ★ **BEST WESTERN VILLAGE HAUS.** *201 N Airport Dr (54166). Phone 715/526-9595; toll-free 800/553-4479; fax 715/526-9826. www.bestwestern.com.* 89 rooms, 2 story. June-Aug: S $65-$95; D $65-$89; each additional $6; under 13 free; lower rates rest of year. Crib free. TV; cable. Indoor pool; whirlpool. Restaurant 6 am-9 pm; Sat 7 am-10 pm; Sun from 7 am. Bar 3 pm-2 am. Meeting rooms. Business services available. Sundries. Cross-country ski 5 miles. Game room. Near lake, river; beach swimming. Cr cds: A, C, D, DS, JCB, MC, V.

⊡ 🐾 🏊 🎿 🛏 🏃 🛏 SC 🏃

Restaurant

★ **ANELLO'S TORCHLIGHT.** *1276 E Green Bay St (54166). Phone 715/526-5680; fax 715/524-5368.* Italian, American menu. Hours: 4-10pm Daily, Fri, Sat 4pm-11pm, closed Thanksgiving Dec 24. Dinner $8.95-$29.95. Bar. Salad bar. Reservations accepted. Cr cds: A, DS, MC, V.

Sheboygan (F-6)

See also Manitowoc, Port Washington

Settled 1818 **Pop** 49,676 **Elev** 633 ft **Area code** 262 and 920

Information Sheboygan County Convention & Visitors Bureau, 712 Riverfront Dr, 53081; 920/457-9495, ext 900 or 800/457-9497, ext 900

Web www.sheboygan.org

A harbor city on the west shore of Lake Michigan, Sheboygan is a major industrial city and a popular fishing port.

What to See and Do

John Michael Kohler Arts Center. *608 New York Ave. Phone 262/458-6144.* Changing contemporary art exhibitions, galleries, shop, historic house; theater, dance, and concert series. (Daily; closed holidays) **FREE**

Kohler-Andrae State Park. *S on I-43 exit 120, on Lake Michigan. Phone 920/451-4080.* Includes 1,000 acres of woods and sand dunes. Swimming, bathhouse; nature and cross-country ski trails, picnicking, playgrounds, concession, camping (105 sites, electric hookups, dump station), winter camping. Nature center (closed winter). Standard fees. (Daily) **$$**

Lakeland College. *10 miles NW on County M off County A (access to County A from WI 42 and 57). Phone 262/565-2111.* (1862) 2,500 students. On campus are Lakeland College Museum (Wed-Thurs, also by appointment; free) and Bradley Fine Arts Gallery (Mon-Fri afternoon during school year; free).

Scenic drives. Along lakeshore on Broughton Dr, Riverfront Dr, Lakeshore Dr.

Sheboygan County Historical Museum. *3110 Erie Ave. Phone 920/458-1103.* Exhibit center plus Judge David Taylor home (1850); 2-story loghouse (1864) furnished with pioneer items; restored barn; 1867 cheese factory. (Apr-Oct, Tues-Sat; closed Good Friday, Easter, July 4) **$$**

Special Events

Bratwurst Day. *Kiwanis Park. 17th & New Jersey sts. Phone 920/457-9491.* Early Aug.

Great Cardboard Boat Regatta. *Rotary Riverview Park. Pennsylvania and 6th sts. Phone 920/458-6144.* Human-powered cardboard craft compete in various classes for fun and prizes. Part of city-wide Independence Day festivities. July 4.

Holland Fest. *118 Main St. 1 mile W off I-43 via exit 113 in Cedar Grove. Phone 920/457-9491.* Dutch traditions: wooden-shoe dancing, street scrubbing, folk fair, food, music, art fair, parade. Phone 920/668-6118. Last Fri and Sat July.

Outdoor Arts Festival. *On the grounds of John Michael Kohler Arts Center. 608 New York Ave. Phone 920/458-6144.* Multi-arts event features works by 125 juried artists; demonstrations, entertainment, refreshments. Third full weekend July.

Polar Bear Swim. *Deland Park. Niagra St & Broughton Dr. Phone 920/457-9491.* More than 350 swimmers brave Lake Michigan's icy winter waters. Jan 1.

Motels/Motor Lodges

★ **BAYMONT INN.** *2932 Kohler Memorial Dr (53081). Phone 920/457-2321; toll-free 800/301-0200; fax 920/457-0827. www.baymontinn.com.* 98 rooms, 2 story. S $46-$52; D $52-$60; under 18 free. Crib free. Pet accepted, some restrictions. Complimentary continental breakfast. Check-out noon. TV; cable (premium). Cr cds: A, C, D, DS, MC, V.

⊡ 🐾 🛏 SC

★ **BEST VALUE INN PARKWAY · SHEBOYGAN.** *3900 Motel Rd (53081). Phone 920/458-8338; fax 920/459-7470. www.bestvalueinn.com.* 32 rooms. June-Sept: S, D $59.90-$81.90; each additional $3; higher rates special events; lower rates rest of year. Crib $6. Pet accepted. TV, cable (premium). Complimentary coffee in rooms. Restaurant nearby. Check-out 11 am. Business services available. Sundries. Cross-country ski 2 miles. Refrigerators; microwaves available. Picnic tables, grills. Cr cds: A, D, DS, MC, V.

Restaurant

★★ **CITY STREETS RIVERSIDE.** *712 Riverfront Dr (53081). Phone 920/457-9050; fax 920/457-9541.* Hours: 11 am-2 pm, 5-9 pm; Fri to 10 pm; Sat 5-10 pm. Closed Sun. Lunch $4.50-$8.50, dinner $5.95-$24.95. Bar to 2 am. Reservations accepted. Beamed ceiling. Cr cds: MC, V.

D

Sheboygan Falls

Restaurant

★★ **RICHARD'S.** *501 Monroe St (53085). Phone 920/467-6401.* Hours: 4-10 pm, Sat-Mon from 5 pm. Dinner $10-$35. Bar 5 pm-midnight. Former stagecoach inn (Circa 1840s). Cr cds: DS, MC, V.

D

Sister Bay (D-6)

(Door County)

Pop 675 **Elev** 587 ft **Area code** 920 **Zip** 54234

Information Door County Chamber of Commerce, 1015 Green Bay Rd, PO Box 406, Sturgeon Bay 54235; 920/743-4456 or 800/527-3529

Web www.doorcountyvacations.com

This town is near the northern tip of Door County (see). Sister Bay was settled in 1857 by Norwegian immigrants. Today it's known for its shopping, dining, and boating opportunities, but still retains a distinct Scandinavian flavor.

Special Event

Sister Bay Fall Festival. *Phone 920/743-4456.* Fish boil, fireworks, parade, street auction. Mid-Oct.

Motels/Motor Lodges

★ **BLUFFSIDE MOTEL.** *403 Bluffside Ln (54234). Phone 920/854-2530. www.bluffside.com.* 16 units, 1-2 story, 1 suite. July-Labor Day, late Sept-Oct: S, D $55-$65; each additional $6; suite $125; lower rates May-June, weekdays after Labor Day-late Sept. Closed rest of year. Crib free. TV; cable. Complimentary coffee in rooms. Restaurant nearby. Check-out 10 am. Free airport transportation. Refrigerators; microwaves available. Picnic tables, grills. Cr cds: MC, V.

★★★ **THE CHURCH HILL INN.** *425 Gateway Dr (54234). Phone 920/854-4885; toll-free 800/422-4906; fax 920/854-4634. www.churchhillinn.com.* This inn features beautiful English country decor. The private parlors are ideal for relaxing. 34 rooms, 2 story. S $65-$105; D $65-$154; each additional $19; higher rates weekends. Children over 10 years only. TV; cable. Heated pool; whirlpool. Complimentary full breakfast; afternoon refreshments. Check-out 10:30 am. Meeting rooms. Business services available. Cross-country ski 4 miles. Exercise equipment; sauna. Some refrigerators, in-room whirlpools. Balconies. Common rooms with fireplaces. Totally non-smoking. Cr cds: MC, V.

★ **COACHLITE INN.** *830 S Bay Shore Dr (54234). Phone 920/854-5503; toll-free 800/745-5031; fax 920/854-9011.* 21 rooms, 2 story, 2 suites. Late July-late Aug: D $79; each additional $7; suites $119; lower rates rest of year. Crib $3. TV; cable. Complimentary coffee in lobby. Restaurant nearby (open in season). Check-out 10 am. Cross-country ski 3 miles. Some in-room whirlpools, microwaves. Balconies. Picnic tables. Gazebo. Cr cds: MC, V.

★★★ **COUNTRY HOUSE RESORT.** *715 Highland Rd (54234). Phone 920/854-4551; toll-free 800/424-0041; fax 920/854-9809. www.country-house.com.* This resort is an ideal romantic retreat. Enjoy beautiful rooms at night and a variety of recreational options during the days. 46 rooms, 2 story. May-Oct: S, D $84-$142; each additional $22; suites $163-$260; lower rates rest of year. Children over 13 years only. TV; cable (premium). Pool; whirlpool. Complimentary continental breakfast. Coffee in rooms. Check-out 11 am. Meeting room. Business services available. Tennis. Rowboats, dock facilities. Bicycles. Lawn games. Refrigerators; some in-room whirlpools, microwaves. Private balconies overlook water. Picnic tables, grills. Along Green Bay shoreline, on 16 wooded acres. Cr cds: A, DS, MC, V.

★ **EDGE OF TOWN MOTEL.** *11092 WI 42 (54234). Phone 920/854-2012.* 10 rooms. No room phones. Mid-June-Oct: S $39-$62; $59-$72; each additional $7; family rates; lower rates rest of year. Crib free. Pet accepted, some restrictions; $7. TV; cable (premium). Complimentary coffee in lobby. Restaurant nearby. Check-out 11 am. Refrigerators, microwaves. Cr cds: DS, MC, V.

⌨ 🏊 🛝 🍴 🏝

★ ★ **HELMS FOUR SEASONS RESORT.** *414 Mill Rd (54234). Phone 920/854-2356; fax 920/854-1836. www.helmsfourseasons.com.* 41 rooms, 2 story, 9 kitchen apartments. Mid-June-late Oct:S $65-$91; D $75-$99; each additional $8-$10; kitchen apartments $115-$200; lower rates rest of year. Crib free. TV; cable. Indoor pool; whirlpool. Complimentary continental breakfast (Labor Day-Memorial Day). Restaurant nearby. Check-out 10 am. Coin laundry. Meeting room. Gift shop. Sundries. Free airport transportation. Cross-country ski 5 miles. Snowmobiling. Sun deck. Refrigerators; some fireplaces. Many private patios, balconies. On Sister Bay, dock. Cr cds: MC, V.

⌨ 🎿 🏊 🛝 🍴 🏝 SC 🎿 🛫

★ ★ **HOTEL DU NORD.** *11000 Bayshore Dr (54234). Phone 920/854-4221; toll-free 800/582-6667; fax 920/854-2710. www.hoteldunord.com.* 56 rooms, 2 story. S, D $85-$165. Crib free. TV; VCR available (movies). Heated pool; whirlpool. Continental breakfast. Restaurant. Check-out 11 am. Coin laundry. Business services available. Sundries. Some in-room whirlpools. On Green Bay. Cr cds: A, MC, V.

⌨ 🎿 🏝

★ ★ **THE INN AT LITTLE SISTER HILL.** *2715 Little Sister Hill Rd (54234). Phone 920/854-2328; toll-free 800/768-6317; fax 920/854-2696. www.doorcountyinn.com.* 26 kitchen suites, 2 story. D $69-$119. June-Oct: kitchen suites $109-$139; each additional $10; lower rates rest of year. Crib $10. TV; cable, VCR (movies). Heated pool. Playground. Complimentary coffee in lobby. Check-out 11 am. Coin laundry. Meeting room. Refrigerators, microwaves. Some balconies. Picnic tables, grills. Cr cds: DS, MC, V.

⌨ 🏊 🍴 🏝 SC 🎿

★ ★ **NORDIC LODGE.** *2721 Nordic Dr (54234). Phone 920/854-5432; fax 920/854-5974. www.themordiclodge.com.* 33 rooms, 2 story. July-Oct: D $64-$92; each additional $5-$10; under 2 free; higher rates: Fall Festival, some holidays; lower rates rest of year. Crib free. TV; cable (premium). Indoor pool; whirlpool. Complimentary contintental breakfast. Check-out 11 am. Refrigerators; microwaves available. Balconies. Picnic tables, grills. Golf course opposite. Near Pebble Beach. Totally nonsmoking. Cr cds: MC, V.

⌨ 🎿 🍴 🏝 🏊 🛫 🏝

★ ★ **OPEN HEARTH LODGE.** *1109 S Bayshore Dr (54234). Phone 920/854-4890; fax 920/854-7486. www.pcwif.com/openhearth.* 32 rooms, 2 story. July-Oct: D $79-$94; each additional $3-$10; lower rates rest of year.

Crib free. TV; cable. Indoor pool; whirlpool. Playground. Complimentary continental breakfast. Complimentary coffee. Restaurant nearby. Check-out 11 am. Refrigerators; microwaves available. Cr cds: A, DS, MC, V.

⌨ 🏊 🏝 🏝

★ **SCANDIA COTTAGES.** *11062 Beach Rd (54234). Phone 920/854-2447. www.scandiacottages.com.* 6 kitchen cottages, 1 motel room. No room phones. June-Oct, Dec-Feb: kitchen cottages $65-$150; each additional $5-$10; family, weekly rates; ski plan; lower rates rest of year. Crib free. TV; cable. Restaurant nearby. Check-out 10 am. Cross-country ski 4 miles. Picnic tables, grills. Bay nearby. Totally nonsmoking. Cr cds: A, MC, V.

⌨ 🏊 🍴 🏝 🎿 🏝

★ **VOYAGER INN AT DOOR COUNTY.** *232 WI 57 (54234). Phone 920/854-4242; fax 920/854-2670. dcwis.com/voyagerinn.* 29 rooms. July-Aug, weekends Sept-mid-Oct: S, D $46-$84; each additional $7; lower rates May-June. Closed rest of year. Crib $5. Heated pool; whirlpool. Restaurant nearby. Check-out 11 am. Business services available. Sauna. Refrigerators; microwaves available. Some balconies, patios. Cr cds: DS, MC, V.

🍴 🏝 🏝 🛫 🏝

Resort

★ **LITTLE SISTER RESORT AT PEBBLE.** *360 Little Sister Rd (54234). Phone 920/854-4013; fax 920/854-5076. www.littlesisterresort.com.* 6 chalets, 13 cottages (1-2-bedrm). MAP only, July-Aug: weekly, chalets, cottages $360-$460/person; family rates; lower rates rest of year. Closed Nov-Apr. Crib $7. TV; cable (premium). Playground. Check-out 10 am. Grocery store 2 miles. Coin laundry. Tennis. Hiking. Bicycles. Lawn games. Boat rentals. Balconies. Picnic tables. On swimming beach. Cr cds: MC, V.

⌨ 🎿 🍴 🏝

Restaurants

★ **AL JOHNSON'S SWEDISH RESTAURANT.** *702 Bay Shore Dr (54234). Phone 920/854-2626; fax 920/854-9650.* American menu. Hours: 6 am-9 pm; Nov-Apr to 8 pm. Closed Thanksgiving, Dec 25. Dinner $9.75-$14.95. Children's menu. Goats graze on grass-covered roof. Cr cds: A, DS, MC, V.

★ ★ **HOTEL DU NORD.** *11000 Bay Shore Dr (54234). Phone 920/854-7972.* Hours: 7:30 am-2 pm, 5:30-10 pm; Sun brunch 9:30 am-12:30 pm. Reservations accepted. Bar 4:30 pm-midnight. Breakfast $4-$8, lunch $6-$10, dinner $16.25-$22. Sun brunch $11.95. Child's meals. Overlooks Green Bay. Cr cds: A, D, MC, V.

⌨

★ **NORTHERN GRILL AND PIZZA.** *321 Country Walk Dr (54234). Phone 920/854-9590.* Hours: 11 am-11 pm. Bar. Lunch $2.50-$5.25, dinner $9.95-$14.95. Child's meals. Specializes in homemade pizza, smoked barbeque ribs, local fish. Outdoor dining. Cr cds: DS, MC, V.

D

Sparta (F-3)

See also Black River Falls, La Crosse, Tomah

Settled 1849 **Pop** 7,788 **Elev** 793 ft **Area code** 608 **Zip** 54656

Information Chamber of Commerce, 111 Milwaukee St; 608/269-4123 or 608/269-2453

Sparta is the home of several small industries manufacturing, among other items, dairy products, brushes, and automobile parts. The area is also well-known for its biking trails. Fort McCoy, a US Army base, is five miles northeast on WI 21.

What to See and Do

Elroy-Sparta State Trail. *113 White St. Phone 608/337-4775 or 608/463-7109.* Built on an old railroad bed, this 32-mi hard-surfaced (limestone screenings) trail passes through three tunnels and over 23 trestles. Biking (fee). (Apr-Oct, daily) **$$**

Motels/Motor Lodges

★ **BEST NIGHTS INN.** *303 W Wisconsin St (54656). Phone 608/269-3066; toll-free 800/201-0234; fax 608/269-3175. www.bestnightsinn.bizonthe.net.* 28 rooms. Mid-May-Oct: S $38-$72; D $48-$89; each additional $7; under 16 free; lower rates rest of year. Crib available. Pet accepted. TV; cable. Restaurant opposite open 24 hours. Check-out 11 am. Refrigerators. Cr cds: A, DS, MC, V.

D

★ **BUDGET HOST HERITAGE MOTEL.** *704 W Wisconsin St (54656). Phone 608/269-6991; toll-free 800/658-9484.* 22 rooms, 2 story. S $35; D $38; each additional $3. Crib $5. Pet accepted. TV; cable (premium). Pool; whirlpool. Restaurant adjacent open 24 hours. Check-out 11 am. Cr cds: A, C, D, DS, MC, V.

★ **COUNTRY INN BY CARLSON.** *737 Avon Rd (54656). Phone 608/269-3110; fax 608/269-6726.* 61 rooms, 2 story. S $60-$68; D $56-$70; under 18 free. Pet accepted. Complimentary continental breakfast. Check-out noon. TV; cable (premium), VCR available (movies). Laundry services. Bar. Indoor pool, whirlpool. Downhill

ski 7 miles, cross-country ski 1 mile. Cr cds: A, D, DS, MC, V.

★ **DOWNTOWN MOTEL.** *509 S Water St (54656). Phone 608/269-3138.* 17 rooms. S $32-$39.95; D $36-$45; each additional $3; under 12 free. Crib free. TV; cable (premium). Restaurant 6 am-1 pm. Check-out 11 am. Cr cds: DS, MC, V.

B&B/Small Inns

★ ★ **JUSTIN TRAILS COUNTRY INN.** *7452 Kathryn Ave (54656). Phone 608/269-4522; toll-free 800/488-4521; fax 608/269-3280. www.justintrails.com.* 4 rooms, 1-2 story. D $85-$225; family rates. Complimentary full breakfast. Check-out noon, check-in 3 pm. Cross-country ski on site. Restored 1920s farmhouse; log cabins. Cr cds: A, D, DS, MC, V.

Spooner (C-2)

See also Hayward, Rice Lake

Settled 1883 **Pop** 2,464 **Elev** 1,065 ft **Area code** 715 **Zip** 54801

Information Spooner Area Chamber of Commerce, 122 N River St; 715/635-2168 or 800/367-3306

Web www.spoonerwisconsin.com

Once a busy railroad town, Spooner is now a popular destination for fishermen and nature lovers.

What to See and Do

Railroad Memories Museum. *424 Front St. Phone 715/635-3325.* Memorabilia, model railroad in old Chicago & Northwestern depot. (Mid May-mid-Oct, daily) **$$**

St. Croix National Scenic Riverway. *Phone 715/635-8346.* One of two in the US; excellent canoeing (Class #1 rapids) and tubing. Contact Chamber of Commerce or National Park Service Information Station in Trego.

Trego Lake Park. *W5665 Trego Park Rd. 1/4 mile N, junction US 53, 63 in Trego. Phone 715/635-9931 or 715/635-2091.* Heavily wooded area on the Namekagon River (Wild River). Fishing, boating, canoeing, inner tubing; hiking, picnicking, camping (electric hookups). (May-Sept) **$$$**

Special Events

Spooner Car Show. *W Beaver Brook Ave & Hwy 63 Washburn County Fairgrounds. Phone 715/635-3740.* Early June.

Spooner Rodeo. *W Beaver Brook Ave & Hwy 63 Washburn County Fairgrounds. Phone 800/367-3306.* PRCA approved. Country music. Mid-July.

Motels/Motor Lodges

★ **COUNTRY HOUSE.** *717 S River St (54801). Phone 715/635-8721.* 22 rooms. June-Oct: S $39-$75; D $54-$85; each additional $5; under 12 free; lower rates rest of year. Crib $4. Pet accepted, some restrictions; fee. TV; cable, VCR available. Complimentary coffee in rooms. Restaurant adjacent 6:30 am-9 pm. Check-out 11 am. Business services available. Cr cds: A, C, D, DS, MC, V.

[icons]

★ **GREEN ACRES MOTEL.** *N 4809 US 63 S (54801). Phone 715/635-2177.* 21 rooms. Late May-Aug: S, D $59-$76; each additional $5; higher rates rodeo; lower rates rest of year. Crib $5. Pet accepted, some restrictions; $5. TV; cable (premium). Complimentary coffee in lobby. Check-out 10 am. Business services available. Cross-country ski 2 miles. Playground. Lawn games. Microwaves available. Picnic tables, grills. Cr cds: A, DS, MC, V.

[icons]

Spring Green (G-3)

See also Dodgeville, Mineral Point, Prairie du Sac

Pop 1,283 **Elev** 729 ft **Area code** 608 **Zip** 53588

Information Chamber of Commerce, PO Box 3; 608/588-2042 or 800/588-2042

Web www.springgreen.com

This is where Frank Lloyd Wright grew up, built his home (Taliesin East), and established the Taliesin Fellowship for the training of apprentice architects.

What to See and Do

⭐ **House on the Rock.** *5754 WI 23. 9 miles S on WI 23. Phone 608/935-3639.* Designed and built by Alexander J. Jordan atop a chimney-like rock, 450 feet above a valley. Waterfalls, trees throughout house; collections of antiques, Asian objets d'art, and automated music machines (many of the musical exhibits require additional money to activate the automation mechanism). Restaurant. (Mid-March-late Oct, daily) **$$$$**

⭐ **Taliesin.** *5607 County Hwy C. 3 miles S on WI 23. Phone 608/588-7948.* Features Frank Lloyd Wright's home, studio, farm, and school. (May-Oct, daily) **$$$$**

Tower Hill State Park. *5808 County Hwy C. 3 miles E on US 14, then S on County Hwy C. Phone 608/588-2116.* Park has 77 acres of wooded hills and bluffs overlooking the Wisconsin River. Site of Pre-Civil War shot tower and early lead-mining village of Helena. Fishing, canoeing;

picnicking (shelter), playgrounds, camping. Standard fees. (Daily) **OTHER**

Special Event

American Players Theatre. *E2930 Golf Course Rd. Phone 608/588-2361.* Theater arts center for the classics. Summer performances in outdoor amphitheater (Tues-Sun; also matinees Tues-Fri in Sept and Oct) Mid-June-early Oct.

Motels/Motor Lodges

★ **PRAIRIE HOUSE MOTEL.** *E4884 US 14 (53588). Phone 608/588-2088; toll-free 800/588-2088; fax 608/588-7965. www.execpc.com/shift~phouse.* 51 rooms, 1 story. July-Aug: S $47-$80; D $57-$80; each additional $5; under 18 free; lower rates rest of year. Crib $5. TV. Complimentary coffee in lobby. Restaurant nearby. Check-out 11 am. Meeting room. Cross-country ski 5 miles. Exercise equipment; sauna. Whirlpool. Some refrigerators. Cr cds: A, DS, MC, V.

[icons]

★ ★ **ROUND BARN LODGE.** *US 14 (53588). Phone 608/588-2568; fax 608/588-2100. www.roundbarn.com.* 44 rooms, 2 story. June-Aug: S, D $79.50; each additional $5; suites $109.50; under 6 free; lower rates rest of year. Crib free. TV; cable (premium). Indoor pool; whirlpool. Complimentary coffee in lobby. Restaurant 7 am-9 pm. Check-out 11 am. Meeting room. Cross-country ski 5 miles. Cr cds: A, D, DS, MC, V.

[icons]

Restaurant

★ ★ **POST HOUSE.** *127 E Jefferson (53588). Phone 608/588-2595. www.posthousespringgreen.com.* Specialties: prime rib, roast duck. Hours: 11 am-2 pm, 5-9 pm; Fri, Sat to 10 pm; Sun 11 am-8 pm. Closed Mon, Tues (Nov-Apr); holidays. Lunch $5.75-$7, dinner $8.50-$14.50. Bar. Children's menu. Reservations accepted. Outdoor dining. Contemporary American decor. Cr cds: MC, V.

[icon]

Stevens Point (E-4)

See also Marshfield, Wisconsin Rapids

Settled 1838 **Pop** 23,006 **Elev** 1,093 ft **Area code** 715 **Zip** 54481

Information Stevens Point Area Convention and Visitors Bureau, 23 Park Ridge Dr; 715/344-2556 or 800/236-4636

Web www.easy-axcess.com/spacvb

A diversified community on the Wisconsin River near the middle of the state, Stevens Point was established as a trading post by George Stevens, who bartered with the Potawatomi. Incorporated as a city in 1858, today it has a number of industries and markets the dairy produce and vegetable crops of Portage County.

What to See and Do

George W. Mead Wildlife Area. *2148 County Rd S. 15 miles NW on US 10 to Milladore, then 5 miles N on County S. Phone 715/457-6771.* Preserved and managed for waterfowl, fur bearers, deer, prairie chickens, ruffed grouse, and other game and nongame species. Limited fishing; hunting, bird-watching, hiking. (Mon-Fri) **FREE**

Stevens Point Brewery. *2617 Water St, corner of Beer and Water sts. Phone 715/344-9310.* (1857) The brewery tour has been described as one of the most interesting in the country. (Mon-Sat, reservations suggested). **$**

University of Wisconsin-Stevens Point. *2100 Main St. Phone 715/346-4242.* (1894) 8,500 students. Across the entire front of the 4-story Natural Resources Building is the world's largest computer-assisted mosaic mural. Museum of Natural History has one of the most complete collections of preserved birds and bird eggs in the country (academic year, daily). Planetarium show in Science Hall (academic year, Sun). Fine Arts Center houses 1,300 American Pattern glass goblets.

Motels/Motor Lodges

★ **BAYMONT INN & SUITES.** *4917 Main St (54481). Phone 715/344-1900; fax 715/344-1254. www.baymontinn.com.* 80 rooms, 3 story. S $39.95-$49.95 D $47.95-$51.95; under 19 free. Pet accepted. Complimentary continental breakfast. Check-out noon. TV; cable (premium). In-room modem link. Laundry services. Cross-country ski 1 mile. Cr cds: A, C, D, DS, MC, V.

★ **COMFORT SUITES.** *300 N Division St (54481). Phone 715/341-6000; toll-free 800/221-2222; fax 715/341-8908. www.comfortsuites.com.* 105 suites, 3 story. S, D $74-$129; each additional $10; under 18 free. Crib free. TV; VCR (movies). Indoor pool; whirlpool. Complimentary continental breakfast. Complimentary coffee in rooms. Restaurant adjacent open 24 hours. Check-out noon. Coin laundry. Meeting rooms. Business services available. In-room modem link. Valet service. Sundries. Cross-country ski 2 miles. Exercise equipment. Refrigerators; some in-room whirlpools, wet bars. Cr cds: A, C, D, DS, JCB, MC, V.

★★ **HOLIDAY INN.** *800 Victor's Way (54481). Phone 715/341-1340; toll-free 800/922-7880; fax 715/341-9446. www.holiday-inn.com.* 295 rooms, 2-6 story. S $79-$99;

D $89-$109; each additional $10; suites $99-$168; under 18 free. Crib free. Pet accepted. Check-out 11 am. TV; cable, VCR (movies). In-room modem link. Valet services, coin laundry. Restaurant 6:30 am-10 pm; Fri, Sat to 11 pm. Bar 11-1 am; entertainment. Room service. Exercise equipment, sauna. Indoor pool, whirlpool, poolside service. Downhill ski 20 miles; cross-country ski 1 mile. Free airport transportation. Business services, Convention facilities. Sundries. Gift shop. Cr cds: A, D, DS, MC, V.

★ **POINT MOTEL.** *209 Division St (54481). Phone 715/344-8312; fax 715/344-8312.* 44 rooms, 2 story. S $33; D $37-$42; each additional $4. Crib $4. Pet accepted. TV; cable, VCR available. Complimentary continental breakfast. Check-out 11 am. Meeting room. Cr cds: A, D, DS, MC, V.

Restaurant

★★★ **THE RESTAURANT AND PAGLIACCI'S.** *1800 N Point Dr (54481). Phone 715/346-6010; fax 715/346-6608.* There are actually two restaurants in one at this small town destination. Specialties: pasta, veal, seafood. Own baking. Hours: 5-9 pm; Fri, Sat to 10 pm. Closed Sun; holidays. A la carte entrees: dinner $5-$17. Bar. Wine list. Reservations accepted. Outdoor dining. Cr cds: A, MC, V.

Sturgeon Bay (D-6)

See also Green Bay (Door County)

Settled 1870 **Pop** 9,176 **Elev** 588 ft **Area code** 920 **Zip** 54235

Information Door County Chamber of Commerce, 1015 Green Bay Rd, PO Box 406; 920/743-4456 or 800/527-3529

Web www.doorcountyvacations.com

Sturgeon Bay, in Door County, sits at the farthest inland point of a bay where swarms of sturgeon were once caught and piled like cordwood along the shore. The historic portage from the bay to Lake Michigan, used for centuries by Native Americans and early explorers, began here. The Sturgeon Bay ship canal now makes the route a waterway used by lake freighters and pleasure craft. The city is the county seat and trading center. Two shipyards and a number of other industries are located here. Ten million pounds of cherries are processed every year in Door County.

What to See and Do

Cave Point County Park. *10 miles NE via WI 57, County Hwy D. Phone 920/823-2400.* Wave-worn grottoes and caves in limestone bluffs. Sand dunes, beautiful landscapes nearby.

★ Door County Museum. *4th Ave and Michigan St. Phone 920/743-5809.* Old-time stores; fire dept with antique trucks; county memorabilia and photographs. Video presentation. Gift shop. (May-Oct, daily) **DONATION**

The Farm. *4 miles N on WI 57. Phone 920/743-6666.* ndings; pioneer farmstead; wildlife display. (Memorial Day-Mid Oct, daily) **$$$**

Potawatomi State Park. *2 miles NW. Phone 920/746-2890.* 1,200-acre woodland along the shores of Sturgeon Bay. Limestone bluffs. Waterskiing, fishing, boating, canoeing; nature, hiking, snowmobile, cross-country ski, and bicycle trails; downhill skiing. Picnicking, playgrounds, camping (125 sites, 23 hookups), winter camping. Standard fees.

Robert La Salle County Park. *County J & County U. SE on Lake Michigan. Phone 800/527-3529.* Site where La Salle and his band of explorers were rescued from starvation by friendly Native Americans. Monument marks location of La Salle's fortified camp. Picnicking.

US Coast Guard Canal Station. *2501 Canal Rd. Phone 920/743-3367.* At entrance to ship canal on Lake Michigan. Coast Guard provides maritime law enforcement patrols, search and rescue duties, weather reports; lighthouse. Tours (by appointment). **FREE**

Special Events

Annual Sturgeon Bay Harvest Fest. *Along Third Ave. Phone 800/301-6695.* Art show, huge craft show, farmers market, food booths, music and entertainment. Late Sept.

Shipyards Tour. *Phone 920/746-2286.* Early May.

Motels/Motor Lodges

★ BAY SHORE INN. *4205 N Bay Shore Dr (54235). Phone 920/743-4551; toll-free 800/556-4551; fax 920/743-3299. www.bayshoreinn.net.* 30 rooms, 3 story. S, D $79-$179. Check-out 11 am. TV; cable (premium), VCR. Laundry services. Game room. On swimming beach. 2 pools, 1 indoor; whirlpool. Tennis. Cross-country ski 6 miles. Bicycles, paddle boats. Cr cds: A, DS, MC, V.

★ BEST WESTERN MARITIME INN. *1001 N 14th Ave (54235). Phone 920/743-7231; fax 920/743-9341. www.bestwestern.com.* 91 rooms, 2 story. D $88-$99; each additional $7; under 12 free; package plans. Complimentary continental breakfast. Check-out 11 am. TV; cable (premium). Game room. Indoor pool, whirlpool.

Downhill/cross-country ski 5 miles. Cr cds: A, C, D, DS, MC, V.

★ CHAL-A MOTEL. *3910 WI 42 and 57 (54235). Phone 920/743-6788.* 20 rooms. S $29-$49; D $34-$54; each additional $4. Crib $5. Complimentary coffee in lobby. Check-out 10:30 am. TV. Downhill ski 7 miles. Museum on premises; features collections of cars, toys, and dolls. Cr cds: MC, V.

★★ CHERRY HILLS LODGE. *5905 Dunn Rd (54235). Phone 920/743-4222; toll-free 800/545-2307; fax 920/743-4222. www.golfdoorcounty.com.* 31 rooms, 2 story. July-Aug, weekends in Sept: S, D $109-$139; each additional $15; golf plan; lower rates rest of year. TV. Heated pool; whirlpool. Dining room 7-10:30 am, 11 am-2 pm, 6-9 pm. Bar; entertainment. Check-out 11 am. Meeting rooms. Business services available. Gift shop. 18-hole golf, greens fee $19-$28. Downhill/cross-country ski 7 miles. Refrigerators, minibars. Patios, balconies. Picnic tables. Totally nonsmoking. Cr cds: A, C, D, DS, MC, V.

★ CLIFF DWELLERS RESORT. *3540 N Duluth Ave (54235). Phone 920/743-4260.* 16 rooms, 1-2 story, 12 cabins. S, D $95-$105; each additional $10-$15; package plans. Closed Nov-Apr. Check-out 11 am. TV; cable. Sauna. Pool, whirlpool. Tennis. Lawn games. Bicycles. Rowboats. Breakfast tray in rooms. Overlooks Sturgeon Bay. Cr cds: A, DS, MC, V.

★ HOLIDAY MOTEL. *29 N 2nd Ave (54235). Phone 920/743-5571; fax 920/743-5395.* 18 rooms, 2 story. July-Aug: S $26-$50; D $39-$69; each additional $5; under 18 free; weekly rates; higher rates: weekends Sept, Oct; weekends (2-day minimum); lower rates rest of year. Crib free. Pet accepted, some restrictions; $5. TV; cable, VCR available (free movies). Complimentary continental breakfast. Restaurant nearby. Check-out 11 am. Business services available. Cross-country ski 4 miles. Refrigerators; microwaves available. Cr cds: A, D, DS, MC, V.

★★ LEATHEM SMITH LODGE AND MARINA. *1640 Memorial Dr (54235). Phone 920/743-5555; toll-free 800/336-7947; fax 920/743-5355. www. teathemsmithlodge.com.* 63 rooms, 2 story, 16 suites. Late June-Aug and late Dec: S, D $80-$96; each additional $15; suites $120-$186; under 12 free; 2-day min holidays (some higher rates); lower rates rest of year. Crib $10. TV; cable, VCR available (movies $3.75). Heated pool; poolside service. Playground. Check-out 11 am. Meeting rooms. Business services available. Gift shop. Tennis. 9-hole par 3 golf; greens fee $6, putting green. Downhill/cross-country ski 6 miles. Lawn games. Some refrigerators, microwaves. 48-slip marina with boat ramp. Cr cds: A, MC, V.

★ ★ **WHITE BIRCH INN.** *1009 S Oxford (54235). Phone 920/743-3295; fax 920/743-6587.* 14 units, 2 story, 3 suites. May-mid-Oct: S, D $75-$150; each additional $10; lower rates rest of year. Crib free. TV. Complimentary continental breakfast. Restaurant 11:30 am-1:30 pm, 5:30-9:30 pm; Sat from 5 pm. Room service. Check-out 11:30 am. Gift shop. Free airport transportation. Cross-country ski 6 miles. Picnic tables. Southwestern décor; Native American artifacts. Cr cds: MC, V.

Resort

★ ★ ★ **STONE HARBOR RESORT.** *107 N 1st Ave (54235). Phone 920/746-0700.* 126 rooms, 5 story. S, D $175-$275; each additional $25; under 17 free. Crib available. Indoor pool. TV; cable (premium), VCR available. Complimentary coffee, newspaper in rooms. Restaurant 6 am-10 pm. Check-out noon. Meeting rooms. Business center. Gift shop. Exercise room. Some refrigerators, minibars. Cr cds: A, C, D, DS, MC, V.

B&B/Small Inns

★ ★ ★ **BARBICAN INN.** *132 N 2nd Ave (54235). Phone 920/743-4854; toll-free 877/427-8491.* This beautiful inn close to historic Sturgeon Bay features comfortable suites each appointed with unique themes. 18 suites, 2 story. No room phones. D $120-$190; package rates. Complimentary continental breakfast. Check-out 11 am, check-in 2 pm. TV; cable (premium), VCR. In-room whirlpools, refrigerators, fireplaces. Restaurant nearby. Room service. Downhill/cross-country ski 10 miles. Restored Victorian houses (1873); antiques. Former residence of local lumber baron. Cr cds: MC, V.

★ ★ **CHADWICK INN.** *25 N 8th Ave (54235). Phone 920/743-2771; fax 920/743-4386. www.thechadwickinn.com.* 3 suites, 3 story. Complimentary continental breakfast in rooms. Check-out noon, check-in 2 pm. TV; cable (premium), VCR available. Fireplaces. Built 1895; original woodwork, antique glassware, Chickering piano (1823). Cr cds: A, MC, V. **$**

★ ★ ★ **CHANTICLEER GUEST HOUSE.** *4072 Cherry Rd (County HH) (54235). Phone 920/746-0334; fax 920/746-1368. www.chanticleerguesthouse.com.* Romance, serenity, peace, and relaxation are just a few words that can describe the guest experience here. Nestled among the orchards or Door County, this bed and breakfast is truly one of the finest and most unique. 8 rooms, 3 story. Adults only. Complimentary continental breakfast. Check-out 11 am, check-in 2 pm. TV; VCR. Sauna. Heated pool. Cross-country ski on site. Hiking trail. Country house built 1916 on 30 acres; gazebo and sheep. Cr cds: A, DS, MC, V. **$$**

★ **GRAY GOOSE BED AND BREAKFAST.** *4258 Bay Shore Dr (54235). Phone 920/743-9100; fax 920/743-9165.* 5 rooms, 2 story. No room phones. D $90-$100; each additional $15; under 12 free; holidays 2-day minimum. Complimentary full breakfast. Check-out 11 am, check-in 3 pm. Premium cable TV in common rm; VCR available (movies). Some fireplaces. Downhill ski 10 miles. Built in 1862. Totally nonsmoking. Cr cds: MC, V.

★ ★ ★ **SCOFIELD HOUSE BED AND BREAKFAST.** *908 Michigan St (54235). Phone 920/743-7727; toll-free 888/463-0204; fax 920/743-7727. www.scofieldhouse.com.* Built in 1901, this elegant inn welcomes guests to enjoy a very delightful stay in appointed guestrooms filled with lovely antiques. This desirable inn is able to charmingly combine the comforts of modern amenities while maintaining all the charm and ambiance of a turn-of-the-century mansion. 6 rooms, 3 story. No room phones. S, D $112-$220. Complimentary full breakfast; afternoon refreshments. Check-out 11 am, check-in 3 pm. TV; cable (premium), VCR (free movies). Restaurant nearby. Downhill/cross-country ski 6 miles. Totally nonsmoking. Cr cds: MC, V.

★ ★ ★ **WHITE LACE INN.** *16 N 5th Ave (54235). Phone 920/743-1105; toll-free 877/948-5223; fax 920/743-8180. www.whitelaceinn.com.* 18 rooms, 2 story. D $69-$235; ski rates; lower rates Sun-Thurs Nov-Apr. Adults only. Complimentary breakfast. Check-out 11 am, check-in 3 pm. TV in most rms; VCR available. Some fireplaces. Downhill/cross-country ski 5 miles. Four buildings built 1880, 1900. White-columned front porch. Totally nonsmoking. Cr cds: A, C, DS, MC, V.

Restaurants

★ ★ **INN AT CEDAR CROSSING.** *336 Louisiana St (54235). Phone 920/743-4249. www.innatcedarcrossing.com.* Hours: 7 am-9 pm; Fri, Sat to 9:30 pm. Closed Dec 25. Dinner $8.95-$32. Bar. Victorian storefront (1884); antique furnishings, fireplaces. Reservations accepted. Totally nonsmoking. Cr cds: A, DS, MC, V.

★ ★ **MILL SUPPER CLUB.** *4128 HWY 42/57 (54235). Phone 920/743-5044.* Seafood menu. Hours:

4:30 pm-1 am. Closed Mon; Easter, Thanksgiving, Dec 24, 25. Dinner $7.95-$36.95. Bar. Children's menu, non-smoking seating. Cr cds: MC, V.

D

Superior (B-2)

Founded 1852 **Pop** 27,134 **Elev** 642 ft **Area code** 715 **Zip** 54880

Information Tourist Information Center, 305 Harborview Parkway; 800/942-5313.

Web www.visitsuperior.com

At the head of Lake Superior, with the finest natural harbor on the Great Lakes, Superior-Duluth has been one of the leading ports in the country in volume of tonnage for many years. The Burlington Northern Docks and taconite pellet handling complex are the largest in the United States. More than 200 million bushels of grain are shipped in and out of the area's elevators each year. Here is the largest coal-loading terminal in the United States with 12 coal docks in the Superior-Duluth area, also a briquet plant, a shipyard, a refinery, and a flour mill. Production of dairy products is also a major industry. Long before its founding date, the city was the site of a series of trading posts. The University of Wisconsin-Superior is located here.

What to See and Do

Amnicon Falls State Park. *10 miles E on US 2. Phone 715/398-3000 or 715/399-3111.* An 825-acre park with many small waterfalls and interesting rock formations. Hiking, picnicking, camping. Standard fees. (Daily) $$

Barker's Island. *Marina Dr and US 2 (53) Phone 800/942-5313.* Boating (launching ramps, marina); picnic facilities, lodging, dining. Also here are

Duluth-Superior Excursions. *250 Marina Dr (54880). Phone 218/722-6218.* A 1 3/4-hour narrated tour of Superior-Duluth Harbor and Lake Superior on excursion boats(Mid-May-mid-Oct, daily) Also lunch and dinner cruises. $$$$

The *S.S. Meteor*. *Phone 715/392-5712.* (1896) Last remaining whaleback freighter, the *Meteor* is moored here and is open to visitors as a maritime museum. (May-Sept, daily) $$

Brule River State Forest. *30 miles SE via US 2. Phone 715/372-4866.* On 40,218 acres. Fishing, boating, canoeing; nature, hiking, snowmobile, and cross-country ski trails; picnicking, camping. Standard fees. (Daily) $$$$

Fairlawn Mansion and Museum. *906 E 2nd St. Phone 715/394-5712.* Restored 42-room Victorian mansion overlooking Lake Superior. First floor and exterior fully restored and furnished. (Daily; closed most major holidays) $$$

Old Fire House and Police Museum. *23rd Ave E and 4th St. Phone 715/398-7558.* Firehouse (1898) serving as a museum devoted to the history of police and fire fighting. Historical vehicles, artifacts. (June-Aug; daily) $$

Pattison State Park. *6294 WI 35 S. 15 miles S on WI 35. Phone 715/399-3111.* Has 1,476 acres of sand beach and woodlands. Swimming, fishing, canoeing; nature, hiking, and cross-country ski trails; picnic grove, playgrounds, primitive and improved camping (electric hookups, dump station). Nature center. Outstanding park attraction is Big Manitou Falls (165-foot drop), the highest waterfall in the state. Little Manitou Falls (31-foot drop) is located upstream of the main falls. Standard fees. (Daily)

Superior Municipal Forest. *N 28th St and Billings Dr.* Has 4,500 acres of scenic woods bordering the shores of the St. Louis River. Fishing, boating; hiking, jogging, cross-country skiing, archery. **FREE**

Wisconsin Point. *Moccasin Mike Rd and Wisconsin Point Rd. On shores of Lake Superior. Phone 800/942-5313.* Popular for picnicking by light of driftwood fires. Swimming, fishing; bird-watching. **FREE**

Special Events

Head-of-the-Lakes Fair. *4700 Tower Ave. Fairgrounds. Phone 715/394-7848.* July.

Miller Lite Northern Nationals Stock Car Races. *Superior Speedway. 4700 Tower Ave. Phone 715/394-7848.* Sept.

Motels/Motor Lodges

★ ★ **BARKER'S ISLAND INN.** *300 Marina Dr (54880). Phone 715/392-7152; toll-free 800/344-7515; fax 715/392-1180. www.visitduluth.com/barkers.* 114 rooms, 2 story. Mid-June-mid-Oct: S, D $65-$109; suites $135; weekday rates; higher rates: Grandma's Marathon, Dec 31; lower rates rest of year. Crib free. TV; cable. Sauna. Indoor pool; whirlpool. Restaurant 7 am-9 pm. Room service. Bar noon-1 am (summer), 4 pm-1 am (winter). Check-out 11 am. Coin laundry. Meeting rooms. Business services available. Sundries. Lighted tennis. Downhill ski 10 miles; cross-country ski 5 miles. Game room. Cr cds: A, C, D, DS, MC, V.

D

★ **BEST WESTERN BAY WALK INN.** *1405 Susquehanna Ave (54880). Phone 715/392-7600; fax 715/392-7680. www.bestwestern.com.* 50 rooms, 2 story. S $60-$100; D $55-$81; each additional $6; under 16 free. Pet accepted, some restrictions. Complimentary continental breakfast. Check-out 11 am. TV; cable (premium), VCR available (movies). Laundry services. Sauna. Game room. Indoor pool, whirlpool. Downhill ski 7 miles, cross-country ski 1 mile. Cr cds: A, C, D, DS, ER, JCB, MC, V.

★ **BEST WESTERN BRIDGEVIEW.** *415 Hammond Ave (54880). Phone 715/392-8174; toll-free 800/777-5572; fax 715/392-8487. www.bestwestern.com.* 96 rooms, 2 story. S $60-$100; D $10-$100; each additional $5; under 18 free. Pet accepted. Complimentary continental breakfast. Check-out noon. TV; cable (premium). Laundry services. Bar. Sauna. Indoor pool, whirlpool. Downhill/cross-country ski 8 miles. Cr cds: A, C, D, DS, ER, JCB, MC, V.

★ **SUPER 8.** *4901 E 2nd St (54880). Phone 715/398-7686; fax 715/398-7339. www.super8.com.* 40 rooms, 2 story. May-Sept: S $49-$65; D $59-$75; under 12 free; lower rates rest of year. Crib free. TV; cable (premium). Complimentary continental breakfast. Restaurant adjacent 7 am-11 pm. Check-out 11 am. Business services available. Downhill ski 20 miles; cross-country ski adjacent. Cr cds: A, C, D, DS, MC, V.

Restaurant

★ ★ **SHACK SMOKEHOUSE AND GRILLE.** *3301 Belknap St (54880). Phone 715/392-9836; fax 715/392-4831. www.shackonline.com.* 9-$6.99, dinner $9.99-$17.99. Specializes in authentic hickory-smoked barbeque, local seafood, prime rib. Own soups. Family-owned. Cr cds: D, DS, MC, V.

Three Lakes (C-4)

See also Cramden, Eagle River, Rhinelander, Saint Germain

Pop 1,900 **Elev** 1,637 ft **Area code** 715 **Zip** 54562

Information Three Lakes **Information** Bureau, 1704 Superior St, PO Box 268; 715/546-3344 or 800/972-6103

Web www.threelakes.com

Between Thunder Lake and the interlocking series of 28 lakes on the west boundary of Nicolet National Forest, Three Lakes is a provisioning point for parties exploring the forest and lake country.

What to See and Do

Three Lakes Winery. *6971 Gogebic St. Corner of WI 45 and County A. Phone 715/546-3080.* Produces fruit wines.

Winery tours (late May-mid-Oct, daily); wine tasting (all year; must be 21 or over to taste wine). **FREE**

Tomah (F-3)

See also Sparta

Pop 7,570 **Elev** 960 ft **Area code** 608 **Zip** 54660

Information Greater Tomah Area Chamber of Commerce, 306 Arthur St, PO Box 625; 608/372-2166 or 800/94-TOMAH

Web www.tomahwisconsin.com

Tomah is Wisconsin's "Gateway to Cranberry Country." This was also the home of Frank King, the creator of the comic strip "Gasoline Alley"; the main street was named after him. Lake Tomah, on the west edge of town, has boating, waterskiing, fishing, ice-fishing, and snowmobiling.

What to See and Do

Little Red Schoolhouse Museum. *Superior Ave. In Gillett Park. Phone 608/372-2166.* Built in 1864, in use until 1965; many original furnishings, books. (Memorial Day-Labor Day, afternoons) **FREE**

Mill Bluff State Park. *15819 Funnel Rd. 7 miles E, off US 12, 16. Phone 608/427-6692 or 608/337-4775.* Has 1,258 acres with rock bluffs. Swimming; picnicking, camping. Being developed as part of Ice Age National Scientific Reserve. Standard fees. (Daily) **$$**

Necedah National Wildlife Refuge. *W7996 20th St W. 6 miles E via WI 21 near Necedah. Phone 608/565-2551.* Water birds may be seen during seasonal migrations; lesser numbers present during the summer. Resident wildlife incl deer, wild turkey, ruffed grouse, wolf, and bear. Viewing via 11-mile self-guided auto tour or one-mi self-guided foot trail. (All year, daily; office, Mon-Fri; foot trail, mid-Mar-mid-Nov only; auto tour is along township roads, which may close due to inclement weather) **FREE**

Wildcat Mountain State Park. *WI 33 E. 25 miles S via WI 131, 33, near Ontario. Phone 608/337-4775.* Has 3,470 acres of hills and valleys. Trout fishing in Kickapoo River, Billings and Cheyenne creeks. Canoeing; nature, hiking, bridle, and cross-country ski trails; picnicking, playgrounds, camping. Observation points provide panoramic view of countryside. Standard fees. (Daily)

Special Event

Cranberry Festival. *402 Pine St. Main St in Warrens. Phone 608/378-4200.* Late Sept.

Motels/Motor Lodges

★ **COMFORT INN.** *305 Wittig Rd (54660). Phone 608/372-6600; toll-free 800/288-5150; fax 608/372-6600. www.comfortinn.com.* 52 rooms, 2 story. May-Aug: S, D $52.95-$79.95; each additional $5; under 18 free; lower rates rest of year. Crib available. Pet accepted. TV; cable (premium). Indoor pool; whirlpool. Complimentary continental breakfast. Restaurant adjacent. Check-out 11 am. Business services available. Downhill ski 15 miles; cross-country 1/2 mile. Some refrigerators. Cr cds: A, C, D, DS, JCB, MC, V.

D ⌖ ⚡ ⇌ ⊠ SC

★ ★ **HOLIDAY INN.** *WI 21 (54660). Phone 608/372-3211; fax 608/372-3243. www.holiday-inn.com.* 100 rooms, 2 story. Mid-May-Labor Day: S $72; D $78; each additional $6; family rates; lower rates rest of year. Crib free. TV. Sauna. Heated pool; whirlpool, poolside service. Restaurant 6 am-2 pm, 5-10 pm. Room service. Bar. Check-out noon. Coin laundry. Meeting rooms. Business services available. In-room modem link. Valet service. Sundries. Cross-country ski 1/2 mile. Game room. Recreation room. Some refrigerators. Cr cds: A, C, D, DS, MC, V.

D ⌖ ⚡ ⛏ ⇌ ⊠ ⇥ ⊠

★ **LARK INN.** *229 N Superior Ave (54660). Phone 608/372-5981; toll-free 800/447-5275; fax 608/372-3009. www.larkinn.com.* 25 rooms, 1-2 story, 3 kitchens S $49-$58; D $59-$68; each additional $5; kitchens $60-$70; under 16 free. Crib $3. Pet accepted. TV; cable (premium), VCR available (movies $2.50). Restaurant 6 am-11 pm. Room service. Check-out 11 am. Coin laundry. Sundries. Downhill ski 10 miles; cross-country ski 1 mile. Some refrigerators. Picnic tables. Cr cds: A, C, D, DS, MC, V.

D ⌖ ⚡ ⛏ ⇌ ⇥ ⊠ ⊠

★ **REST WELL MOTEL.** *25491 US 12 (54660). Phone 608/372-2471.* 12 rooms, 10 with shower only. No room phones. S $35-$40; D $25-$55. Pet accepted. TV. Check-out 10 am. Downhill ski 10 miles; cross-country 1 mile. Cr cds: MC, V.

⇌ ⛏ ⇥ ⊠

★ **SUPER 8.** *1008 E McCoy Blvd (54660). Phone 608/372-3901; fax 608/372-5792. www.super8.com.* 64 rooms, 2 story. Mid-June-late Sept: S, D $42.98-$104.98; each additional $5; under 19 free; lower rates rest of year. Crib free. Pet accepted. TV; cable. Complimentary continental breakfast. Restaurant adjacent open 24 hours. Check-out 11 am. Coin laundry. Business services available. Downhill ski 12 miles; cross-country ski 1 mile. Some refrigerators. Cr cds: A, C, D, DS, MC, V.

D ⌖ ⚡ ⛏ ⇥ ⊠

Restaurant

★★ **BURNSTAD'S.** *WI 12 & 16E (54660). Phone 608/372-3277. www.burnstads.com.* Continental menu. Hours: 8 am-9 pm; Sun 8 am-8 pm. Closed Jan 1, Dec 25. Dinner $7.95-$14.95. Totally nonsmoking. Cr cds: A, D, DS, MC, V.

D

Two Rivers (E-6)

See also Green Bay, Manitowac, Sheboygan

Pop 13,030 **Elev** 595 ft **Area code** 920 **Zip** 54241

Information Manitowoc-Two Rivers Area Chamber of Commerce, 1515 Memorial Dr, PO Box 903, Manitowoc 54221-0903; 920/684-5575 or 800/262-7892

Web www.manitowoc.com

A fishing fleet in Lake Michigan and light industry support Two Rivers.

What to See and Do

Point Beach State Forest. *9400 County Trunk O.* Phone 920/794-7480. A 2,900-acre park with heavily wooded areas, sand dunes, and beach along Lake Michigan. Nature, hiking, snowmobile, and cross-country ski trails; ice skating. Picnicking, playgrounds, concession, improved camping, winter camping. Nature center. Standard fees. (Daily) **$$**

Rogers Street Fishing Village Museum. *2102 Jackson St.* Phone 920/793-5905. Artifacts of commercial fishing industry; 60-year-old diesel engine; artifacts from sunken vessels; 1886 lighthouse; life-size woodcarvings. Art and craft galleries feature local area artists. (June-Aug, daily) **$**

Washington Island (C-6)

(Door County)

Settled 1869 **Pop** 623 **Elev** 600 ft **Area code** 920 **Zip** 54246

Information Door County Chamber of Commerce, 1015 Green Bay Rd, PO Box 406, Sturgeon Bay 54235; 920/743-4456 or 800/527-3529

Web www.doorcountyvacations.com

Washington Island, six miles off the coast of Door County is one of the oldest Icelandic settlements in the United States. Many Scandinavian festivals are still celebrated.

Surrounding waters offer excellent fishing. The island may be reached by ferry.

What to See and Do

Rock Island State Park. *Little Lake Rd, NW corner of island. Phone 920/847-2235 (mid-Apr-mid-Nov); 920/847-2500 (rest of year).* Reached by privately-operated ferry (June-Oct, daily; fee) from Jackson Harbor located at the NE corner of island. This 912-acre park was the summer home of electric tycoon, C. H. Thordarson. Buildings in Icelandic architectural style. Potawatomi Lighthouse (1836) on northern point. Swimming, fishing, boating; nature trail, more than 9 miles of hiking and snowmobile trails, picnicking, primitive camping (no supplies available). No vehicles permitted. Standard fees. (Daily)

Washington Island Museum. *Little Lake Rd, NW corner of island. Phone 920/847-2522.* Native American artifacts; antiques; rocks and fossils. (May-mid-Oct, daily)

Special Event

Scandinavian Dance Festival. *Phone 920/847-2179.* Dance festival and Viking Games. Early Aug.

Motels/Motor Lodges

★ ★ **FINDLAY'S HOLIDAY INN AND VIKING VILLAGE.** *Main Rd (54246). Phone 920/847-2526; toll-free 800/522-5469; fax 920/847-2752. www.holidayinn.net.* 16 rooms. Some A/C. S $76-$85; D $85-$110; under 6 free; weekly rates. Crib free. Check-out 10 am. TV. Restaurant (See also FINDLAY'S HOLIDAY INN). Health club privileges. On Lake Michigan; beach. Lawn games. Business services. Gift shop. Cr cds: MC, V.

[D] [🐾]

★ **VIKING VILLAGE MOTEL.** *Main Rd (54246). Phone 920/847-2551; toll-free 800/522-5469; fax 920/847-2752. www.holidayinn.net.* 12 kit units. No A/C. S $65-$85; D $75-$110; each additional $5; suites $95-$120; under 6 free; weekly rates. Crib free. Pet accepted. TV. Coffee in rooms. Restaurant 7 am-1:30 pm, 5:30-7:30 pm. Check-out 10 am. Health club privileges. Refrigerators; some microwaves, fireplaces. Cr cds: MC, V.

[D] [🐾] [🐾]

Restaurant

★ ★ **FINDLAY'S HOLIDAY INN.** *Main Rd (54246). Phone 920/847-2526. www.holidayinn.net.* Hours: 7-10:30 am, 11:30 am-2 pm, 5:30-7:30 pm. Closed Nov-Apr. Reservations accepted. Wine, beer. Breakfast $2-$7, lunch $3.50-$10, dinner $5-$12. Specializes in seafood. Salad bar. Entertainment. Norwegian décor. Totally nonsmoking. Cr cds: A, MC, V.

[D]

Watertown (G-5)

See also Beaver Dam, Fort Atkinson, Oconomowoc

Settled 1836 **Pop** 19,142 **Elev** 823 ft **Area code** 262 **Zip** 53094

Information Chamber of Commerce, 519 E Main St; 262/261-6320

Waterpower, created where the Rock River falls 20 feet in two miles, attracted the first New England settlers. A vast number of German immigrants followed, including Carl Schurz, who became Lincoln's minister to Spain and Secretary of the Interior under President Hayes. His wife, Margarethe Meyer Schurz, established the first kindergarten in the United States. Watertown, with diversified industries, is in the center of an important farming and dairy community.

What to See and Do

★ **Octagon House and First Kindergarten in USA.** *919 Charles St. Phone 262/261-2796.* Completed in 1854 by John Richards, the 57-room mansion has 40-foot spiral cantilever hanging staircase; Victorian-style furnishings throughout, many original pieces. On grounds are restored kindergarten founded by Margarethe Meyer Schurz in 1856 and 100-year-old barn with early farm implements. (May-Oct, daily) **$$**

Special Event

Riverfest. *Labaree and Division, Riverside Park. Phone 920/261-6320.* Four-day event; craft show, carnival, raft race, entertainment. Early Aug.

Waukesha (G-5)

See also Milwaukee

Settled 1834 **Pop** 56,958 **Elev** 821 ft **Area code** 262

Information Waukesha Area Convention & Visitors Bureau, 223 Wisconsin Ave, 53186; 262/542-0330 or 800/366-8474

Web www.wauknet.com/visit

Mineral springs found here by pioneer settlers made Waukesha famous as a health resort; in the latter half of the 19th century, it was one of the nation's most fashionable. Before that it was an important point on the Underground Railroad. *The American Freeman* (1844-1848) was published here. Today the city is enjoying important industrial growth. Carroll College lends the city a gracious academic atmosphere. The name Waukesha (by the little fox) comes from the river that runs through it. The river, along with the city's many parks and wooded areas, adds to a beautiful atomosphere for leisure activities.

What to See and Do

Kettle Moraine State Forest, Southern Unit. *S91 W39091 WI 59. 17 miles SW on WI 59. Phone 262/594-2135.* Contains 20,000 acres of rough, wooded country as well as Ottawa and Whitewater lakes. Swimming, waterskiing, fishing, boating, canoeing. Trails: hiking, 74 miles; bridle, 50 miles; snowmobile, 52 miles; cross-country ski, 40 miles; nature, 3 miles. Picnicking, playground, primitive and improved camping (electric hookups, dump station), winter camping. Standard fees. (Daily) **$$**

⭐ **Old World Wisconsin.** *S103W37890 WI 67. 14 miles SW on WI 67; 1 1/2 miles S of Eagle. Phone 262/594-6300.* A 576-acre outdoor museum with more than 65 historic structures (1840-1915) reflecting various ethnic backgrounds of Wisconsin history. Restored buildings include church, town hall, schoolhouse, stagecoach inn, blacksmith shop, and ten complete 19th-century farmsteads. All buildings furnished in period artifacts; staffed by costumed interpreters. Tram system; restaurant. (May-Oct, daily) **$$$$**

Waukesha County Museum. *101 W Main St at East Ave. Phone 262/548-7186.* Historical exhibits (Tues-Sat, also Sun afternoons; closed holidays). Research library (Tues-Sat; closed holidays; fee). **FREE**

Special Events

Fiesta Waukesha. *Frame Park, 1120 Baxter St. On Fox River banks. Phone 262/547-0887.* Music, folklore, dance, diverse food, and cultural activities. Mid-June.

Holiday Fair, Christmas Walk, and Annual Parade. *Downtown. Phone 262/549-6154.* Merchants offer special bargains, festive treats. Mid-Nov.

Waukesha County Fair. *2417 Silvernail Rd. Phone 262/544-5922.* Incl performances by top-name Country and Western and rock artists. Mid-July.

Waukesha JanBoree. *Frame Park, 1120 Baxter St. Phone 262/524-3737.* Three days of winter activities. Late Jan.

Motels/Motor Lodges

⭐**FAIRFIELD INN.** *20150 W Blue Mound Rd. Phone 262/785-0500; fax 414/785-1966. www.fairfieldinn.com.* 135 rooms, 3 story. S $54.95-$95.95; D $64.95-$95.95; each additional $10; under 18 free. Crib free. TV; cable (premium). Pool. Complimentary continental breakfast. Restaurant adjacent 6-1 am. Check-out noon. Business

services available. In-room modem link. Cr cds: A, C, D, DS, MC, V.

🄳 ⌷ 🚶 ⌷ ⌷

⭐ **HAMPTON INN.** *575 N Barker Rd (53045). Phone 414/796-1500; toll-free 800/426-7866; fax 414/796-0977. www.hamptoninn.com.* 120 rooms, 4 story. S, D $99; under 18 free; higher rates special events. Crib free. TV; cable (premium). Indoor pool; whirlpool. Complimentary continental breakfast. Restaurant adjacent 6 am-3 am. Check-out noon. Meeting room. Business services available. Sundries. Cr cds: A, C, D, DS, MC, V.

🄳 ⌷ ⌷ **SC**

⭐ **RAMADA LIMITED WAUKESHA.** *2111 E Moreland Blvd (53186). Phone 262/547-7770; toll-free 888/298-2054; fax 262/547-0688. www.ramada.com.* 92 rooms, 2 story. July-Aug: S, D $65-$89; each additional $6; under 19 free; higher rates special events; lower rates rest of year. Crib available. TV; cable (premium); VCR available. Sauna. Whirlpool. Complimentary continental breakfast. Restaurant adjacent. Check-out 11 am. Business services available. Some refrigerators. Cr cds: A, C, D, DS, MC, V.

🄳 ⌷ 🚶 ⌷

⭐ **SELECT INN.** *2510 Plaza Ct (53186). Phone 414/786-6015; toll-free 800/641-1000; fax 414/786-5784. www.selectinn.com.* 101 rooms, 2-3 story. No elevator. S, D $39-$51; under 12 free. Pet accepted; $25 refundable. TV; cable. Complimentary continental breakfast. Check-out 11 am. Meeting room. Business services available. Cross-country ski 5 miles. Some refrigerators. Cr cds: A, C, D, DS, MC, V.

🄳 ⌷ ⌷ ⌷ **SC**

⭐ ⭐ **WYNDHAM GARDEN HOTEL.** *18155 Bluemound Rd (53045). Phone 414/792-1212; toll-free 800/822-4200; fax 414/792-1201. www.wyndham.com.* 178 rooms, 3 story. S, D $59-$169; weekend rates; higher rates special events. Crib available. TV; cable, VCR available. Indoor pool; whirlpool. Complimentary coffee in rooms. Restaurant 7 am-9 pm. Bar 4 pm-midnight. Check-out noon. Meeting rooms. Business services available. In-room modem link. Sundries. Valet service. Free Milwaukee airport transportation. Exercise equipment. Game room. Balconies. Picnic tables. Cr cds: A, C, D, DS, JCB, MC, V.

🄳 ⌷ 🚶 ⌷ ⌷ **SC**

Hotel

⭐ ⭐ ⭐ **MARRIOTT WAUKESHA.** *W 231 N 1600 (53186). Phone 262/574-0888.* 283 rooms, 6 story. S, D $150-$199; each additional $20; under 17 free. Crib available. Indoor pool. TV; cable (premium), VCR available. Complimentary coffee, newspaper in rooms. Restaurant

6 am-10 pm. Check-out 11 am. Meeting rooms. Business center. Gift shop. Exercise room. Some refrigerators, minibars. Cr cds: A, C, D, DS, MC, V.

Restaurant

★ ★ ★ WEISSGERBER'S GASTHAUS INN.
2720 N Grandview Blvd (53188). Phone 262/544-4460. www.weissgerbers.com. Milwaukee's traditional German restaurant and beer garden. Original German entrees provide a gourmet tour through the Old World. The warm woodwork, fieldstone fireplaces and colorful stained glass windows provide a comfortable and intimate atmosphere in all our rooms and lounge. American, German menu. Hours: 11:30 am-2 pm, 5-10 pm; Sat from 5 pm; Sun 4-9 pm. Dinner $16-$22. Bar. Outdoor beer garden. Cr cds: A, DS, MC, V.

Waupaca (E-4)

See also Stevens Point, Wautoma

Pop 4,957 **Elev** 870 ft **Area code** 715 **Zip** 54981

Information Waupaca Area Chamber of Commerce, 221 S Main; 715/258-7343 or 888/417-4040

Web www.waupacaareachamber.com

This community, near a chain of 22 lakes to the southwest, is a boating, fishing, and tourist recreation area.

What to See and Do

Canoeing and tubing. *N 2498 W Columbia Lake Dr. On the Crystal and Little Wolf rivers.* 2- to 3-hour trips. (May-Labor Day) Contact Chamber of Commerce.

Covered Bridge. *Fulton (54W) & Joann Ln. 3 miles S on Hwy K near the Red Mill Colonial Shop. Phone 715/258-7343.* A 40-foot lattice design with 400 handmade oak pegs used in its construction.

Hartman Creek State Park. *N2480 Hartman Creek Rd. 6 miles W via WI 54, then 1 1/2 miles S on Hartman Creek Rd. Phone 715/258-2372.* A 1,400-acre park with 300-foot sand beach on Hartman Lake. Swimming, fishing, boating (no gasoline motors), canoeing; nature, hiking, snowmobile, and cross-country ski trails; picnicking, camping (dump station), winter camping. Standard fees. (Daily) $$$

Scenic cruises. *N2757 County Rd QQ. 4 miles SW via WI 54 and County QQ at Clear Water Harbor. Phone 715/258-2866.* Sternwheeler Chief Waupaca offers 1 1/2-hour cruises on eight lakes of the Chain O' Lakes. Also cruises

aboard motor yacht Lady of the Lakes. (Memorial Day-Sept, daily) Private evening charters arranged. $$$

South Park. *Main and Junction sts. Mirror and Shadow lakes, S end of Main St. Phone 715/258-7343.* Offers swimming beach, bathhouse, fishing dock, boat landing; picnicking. Also in park is

> **Hutchinson House Museum.** *Main St and Shadow Lake Rd. End of Main St in South Park. Phone 715/258-7343.* Restored 12-room Victorian pioneer home (1854); furnishings, artifacts; herb garden; Heritage House.Contact the Chamber of Commerce. $

Special Events

Fall-O-Rama. *S Main and Hwy K, South Park. Phone 715/258-7343.* Arts and crafts fair, entertainment, food. Third Sat Sept.

Strawberry Fest. *111 S Main, Downtown Square. Phone 715/258-7343.* Arts and crafts, entertainment, fresh strawberries. Third Sat June.

Motel/Motor Lodge

★★BAYMONT INN & SUITES. *110 Grand Seasons Dr (54981). Phone 715/258-9212; toll-free 877/880-1054; fax 715/258-4294. www.baymontinns.com.* 90 rooms, 3 story. Late May-early Sept: S $69-$79; D $79-$109; each additional $10; suites $89-$140; under 18 free; family rates; package plans; higher rates special events; lower rates rest of year. Crib free. Pet accepted. Complimentary continental breakfast (Mon-Sat). Check-out 11 am. TV; cable (premium). In-room whirlpools, refrigerators, microwaves in suites. Coin laundry. Restaurant 10 am-10 pm. Bar to 2 am. Exercise equipment, sauna, Massage. Game room. Indoor pool, whirlpool. Downhill ski 10 miles; cross-country ski 2 miles. Picnic tables. Meeting rooms, business services. Sundries. Cr cds: A, C, D, DS, MC, V.

Waupun (F-5)

See also Beaver Dam, Fond du Lac, Green Lake

Founded 1839 **Pop** 8,207 **Elev** 904 ft **Area code** 920 **Zip** 53963

Information Chamber of Commerce, 434 E Main; 920/324-3491

The city's Native American name means "Early Dawn of Day." Diversified crops, light industry, and three state institutions contribute to this small city's economy.

What to See and Do

City of Sculpture. *Madison St at Shaler Park.* First bronze casting of famous sculpture by James Earl Frazer, designer of Indian head nickel. Also six other historical bronze statues.

Fond du Lac County Park. *N2825 County Rd MMM. W on WI 49 to County Trunk MMM. Phone 920/324-2769.* Park has 100 acres of virgin timber on Rock River. Swimming pool (mid-June-Aug, daily; fee); picnic area (tables, fireplaces), playgrounds, camping (mid-May-Nov, daily). Park (all year). **$$$$**

Horicon National Wildlife Refuge. *W4279 Headquarters Rd. Visitor Center, 6 1/2 miles E on WI 49, then 4 miles S on Dodge County Z. Phone 920/387-2658.* Large flocks of Canada geese and various species of ducks can be seen Oct, Nov, Mar, Apr. Many visitors stop during migratory seasons to watch the birds resting and feeding on the Horicon Marsh (daylight hours). Limited hunting and fishing (inquire for dates); canoeing. Hiking trails. (Daily) **FREE**

Motel/Motor Lodge

★ **INN TOWN.** *27 S State St (53963). Phone 920/324-4211; toll-free 800/433-6231; fax 920/324-6921.* 16 rooms. S $33-$40; D $46-$53; each additional $3. Crib $3. Pet accepted. TV; cable (premium). Coffee in rooms. Restaurant nearby. Check-out 10 am. Refrigerators; microwaves available. Cr cds: A, DS, MC, V.

✈

Wausau (D-4)

See also Stevens Point

Settled 1839 **Pop** 37,060 **Elev** 1,195 ft **Area code** 715 **Zip** 54401

Information Wausau Area Convention and Visitors Bureau, 300 3rd St, Suite 200, PO Box 6190, 54402-6190; 715/845-6231, ext 324 or 800/236-9728

Web www.wausauchamber.com

Known as Big Bull Falls when it was settled as a lumber camp, the town was renamed Wausau, Native American for "Faraway Place." When the big timber was gone, the lumber barons started paper mills; paper products are still one of the city's many industries.

What to See and Do

Leigh Yawkey Woodson Art Museum. *700 N 12th St. Phone 715/845-7010.* Collection of wildlife art, porcelain, and glass; changing exhibits. (Tues-Sun; closed holidays) **FREE**

Marathon County Historical Museum. *403 McIndoe St. Phone 715/848-6143.* Former home of early lumberman Cyrus C. Yawkey. Victorian period rms; model railroad

display; changing theme exhibits. (Tues-Thurs, Sat and Sun; closed holidays) **FREE**

Special Events

Big Bull Falls Blues Festival. *Stewart Ave & River Dr, Fern Island Park. Phone 715/355-8788.* Mid-Aug.

Wisconsin Valley Fair. *17th and Stewart, Marathon Park. Phone 715/355-8788.* Early Aug.

Motels/Motor Lodges

★ **BAYMONT INN.** *1910 Stewart Ave (54401). Phone 715/842-0421; fax 715/845-5096. www.baymontinns.com.* 96 rooms, 2 story. D $64-$69; under 18 free. Pet accepted. Check-out noon. TV; cable. Continental breakfast. In-room modem link. Indoor pool. Downhill/cross-country ski 2 miles. Cr cds: A, C, D, DS, MC, V.

🐾 🌊 ➡ ⛷

★ ★ **BEST WESTERN MIDWAY HOTEL.** *2901 Martin Ave (54401). Phone 715/842-1616; toll-free 800/528-1234; fax 715/845-3726. www.bestwestern.com.* 98 rooms, 2 story. S, D $70; each additional $12; under 18 free. Crib free. Pet accepted. TV; cable. Indoor pool; whirlpool. Playground. Coffee in rooms. Restaurant 6 am-10 pm. Room service. Bar; entertainment. Check-out noon. Meeting rooms. Business services available. In-room modem link. Valet service. Free airport transportation. Downhill ski 1 mile; cross-country ski 3 miles. Recreation room. Exercise equipment; sauna. Lawn games. Some refrigerators, microwaves. Picnic tables. Cr cds: A, C, D, DS, ER, JCB, MC, V.

🗅 🐾 🍴 ⛷ 🌊 🕴 🏃 ✈ ➡

★ **EXEL INN.** *116 S 17th Ave (54401). Phone 715/842-0641; toll-free 800/367-3935; fax 715/848-1356. www.exelinns.com.* 122 rooms, 2 story. S $36.99-$46.99; D $43.99-$52.99; each additional $4; under 18 free. Crib free. Pet accepted. TV. Complimentary continental breakfast. Complimentary coffee in rooms. Restaurant nearby. Check-out noon. Business services available. Laundry facilities. Downhill ski 3 miles; cross-country ski 3 miles. Game room. View of Rib Mtn. Cr cds: A, C, D, DS, MC, V.

🗅 🐾 ➡ ⛷ **SC**

★ ★ **RAMADA INN.** *201 N 17th Ave (54401). Phone 715/845-4341; toll-free 800/754-9725; fax 715/845-4990. www.ramada.com.* 233 rooms, 6 story. S $59; D $69-$99; each additional $10. suites $119-$179; under 18 free; higher rates special events. Crib free. TV; cable (premium), VCR available. Complimentary continental breakfast. Complimentary coffee in rooms. Restaurant 6:30 am-10 pm. Room service. Bar from 3 pm. Check-out noon. Meeting rooms. Business services available. In-room modem link. Valet service. Coin laundry. Free airport transportation. Downhill/cross-country ski 2 miles. Exercise equipment; sauna. Indoor pools; wading pool, whirlpool. Game rooms.

Refrigerators, microwaves; some in-room whirlpools. Many balconies. Cr cds: A, C, D, DS, JCB, MC, V.

★ **RIB MOUNTAIN INN.** *2900 Rib Mtn Way (54401). Phone 715/848-2802; toll-free 877/960-8900; fax 715/848-1908.* 16 rooms rooms, 2 story, 4 villas, 4 townhouses. S $48-$71; D $55-$78; villas $95-$155; townhouses $125-$155; weekly, monthly rates; ski plan; higher rates: ski season, weekends. Pet accepted. Complimentary continental breakfast. Check-out 11 am. TV; cable (premium), VCR (movies). Balconies, patios. Refrigerators, fireplaces. Sauna. Driving range. Downhill ski 1/4 mile; cross-country ski 7 miles. Picnic tables. Lawn games. Business services. On Rib Mtn. Adjacent to state park. Cr cds: A, C, D, DS, MC, V.

★ **SUPER 8.** *2006 Stewart Ave (54401). Phone 715/848-2888; fax 715/842-9578. www.super8.com.* 88 rooms, 2 story. S $47-$54; D $54-$60; each additional $10; under 18 free. Crib free. Pet accepted. TV; cable. Indoor pool; whirlpool. Complimentary continental breakfast. Check-out noon. Business services available. Valet service. Sundries. Cr cds: A, D, DS, MC, V.

B&B/Small Inns

★★ **ROSENBERRY INN.** *511 Franklin St (54403). Phone 715/842-5733; fax 715/843-5659. www.rosenberryinn.com.* 8 rooms, 3 story. A/C in 4 rooms. No room phones. S $70; D $70-$100; each additional $15. Complimentary full breakfast. Check-out 11 am, check-in 3 pm. TV in sitting room; cable. Downhill/cross-country ski 5 miles. Two historic homes built 1908; Prairie School-style architecture. Cr cds: MC, V.

Restaurants

★ **CARMELO'S.** *3607 N Mountain Rd (54401). Phone 715/845-5570.* Italian menu. Hours: 5-10 pm; Sun, Mon to 9 pm. Closed holidays. Dinner $9.95-$18.95. Bar. Reservations accepted Sat-Thurs. Cr cds: A, DS, MC, V.

★★ **GULLIVER'S LANDING.** *1701 Mallard Ln (54401). Phone 715/849-8409; fax 715/843-0915. www.gulliverslanding.com.* Hours: Mon-Sun 10 am-10 pm. Closed holidays. Dinner $7.95-$29.95. Bar. Children's menu, Outdoor dining. Non-smoking seating. Dockage. Cr cds: A, DS, MC, V.

★★ **MICHAEL'S.** *2901 Rib Mountain Dr (54401). Phone 715/842-9856. www.michaelsuperclub.com.* Continental menu. Hours: 5-10 pm. Closed Sun; holidays.

Dinner $8.25-$36. Bar from 4 pm. Children's menu. Wildlife pictures on walls. Cr cds: A, DS, MC, V.

★★ **WAGON WHEEL SUPPER CLUB.** *3901 N 6th St (54403). Phone 715/675-2263. www.islpage.com/i/wagonwheel.* Seafood, Steak menu. Hours: 5-10 pm. Closed Sun. Dinner $11.75-$49.50. Bar. Reservations accepted Mon-Thurs. Non-smoking seating. Cr cds: A, DS, MC, V.

★ **WAUSAU MINE CO.** *3904 W Stewart Ave (54401). Phone 715/845-7304; fax 715/842-1575.* Hours: 11 am-midnight. Closed Easter, Thanksgiving, Dec 24-25. Dinner $3.95-$16.75. Bar. Children's menu. Reservations accepted Sun-Thurs. Non-smoking seating. Cr cds: DS, MC, V.

Wautoma (E-4)

See also Green Lake, Waupaca

Pop 1,784 **Elev** 867 ft **Area code** 920 **Zip** 54982

What to See and Do

Nordic Mountain Ski Area. *W5806 County Rd W. 8 miles N via WI 152. Phone 920/787-3324 or 800/253-7266.* Triple, double chairlifts, T-bar, pomalift, two rope tows; patrol, school, rentals; snowmaking; restaurant, cafeteria, concession, bar. Longest run 1 mile; vertical drop 265 feet. Night skiing. (Dec-mid-Mar, Thurs-Tues; closed Dec 25); 13 miles of cross-country trails (weekends only; free). **$$$$**

Wild Rose Pioneer Museum. *8 miles N on WI 22, Main St, in Wild Rose. Phone 920/622-3364.* Historical complex of buildings incl Elisha Stewart House, containing furniture of the late 19th century; pioneer hall; outbuildings; carriage house; blacksmith shop, cobbler shop, replica of general store, one-room schoolhouse, apothecary; weaving room; gift shop. Tours. (Mid-June-Labor Day, Wed and Sat afternoons; also by appointment during summer) **$**

Wauwatosa (G-5)

See also Menomonee Falls, Milwaukee

Settled 1835 **Pop** 49,366 **Elev** 634 ft **Area code** 414

Information Chamber of Commerce, 7707 W State St, 53213; 414/453-2330

What to See and Do

Lowell Damon House. *2107 Wauwatosa Ave. Phone 414/273-8288.* (1844) Community's oldest home is a classic example of colonial architecture; period furnishings. Tours (Sun, Wed; closed holidays). **FREE**

Motels/Motor Lodges

★ **EXEL INN.** *115 N Mayfair Rd (53226). Phone 414/257-0140; toll-free 800/367-3935; fax 414/475-7875. www.exelinns.com.* 123 rooms, 2 story. S $44.99-$66.99; D $55.99-$79.99; suites $105-$132; each additional (up to 4) $4; under 17 free. Crib free. Pet accepted, some restrictions. TV; cable (premium). Complimentary continental breakfast. Check-out noon. Business services available. Cr cds: A, C, D, DS, MC, V.

D ◢ ⊠ SC

★ **FORTY WINKS INN.** *11017 W Bluemound Rd (53226). Phone 414/774-2800; toll-free 800/946-5746; fax 414/774-9134.* 31 rooms (12 with shower only), 2 story. June-Aug: S, D $60-$75; each additional $6; kitchen units $65-$85; lower rates rest of year. Crib $5. TV; cable (premium). Complimentary coffee in lobby. Restaurant nearby. Check-out 11 am. Sundries. Cross-country ski 1 mile. Some refrigerators. Cr cds: A, DS, MC, V.

D ⊠

★ **HOLIDAY INN EXPRESS.** *11111 W North Ave (53226). Phone 414/778-0333; fax 414/778-0331. www. holiday-inn.com.* 122 rooms, 3 story. S, D $84-$109; suites $89-$109; under 18 free. Crib free. Complimentary continental breakfast. Check-out noon. TV; cable (premium), VCR available. Some balconies, refrigerators. Valet services. Restaurant adjacent open 24 hours. Health club privileges. Meeting rooms, business services. Cr cds: A, C, D, DS, JCB, MC, V.

D ⊱ 🎿 ⊠ SC 🚶

Restaurants

★ ★ **BARTOLOTTA'S.** *7616 W State St (53213). Phone 414/771-7910; fax 414/771-1589. www.bartolottas.com.* A classic representation of trattoria-style dining. The menu highlights fresh and authentic ingredients. This is a family-owned restaurant that has a wonderful following and promises a casual, yet rewarding dining experience. Italian menu. Hours: 5:30-9:30 pm; Fri, Sat to 5-10 pm; Sun 5-8 pm. Closed Sun; holidays. Dinner $12.95-$21.95. Bar. Entertainment. Children's menu. Outdoor dining. Totally nonsmoking. Cr cds: A, D, DS, MC, V.

D

★ ★ **JAKE'S.** *21445 W Capitol Dr (53072). Phone 414/771-0550; fax 414/771-6667. www.foodspot.com.* Hours: 5-10 pm; Sun to 9 pm. Closed holidays; also Super Bowl Sun. Dinner $15.95-$27.95. Bar. Children's menu. Totally nonsmoking. Cr cds: A, D, MC, V.

D

West Allis

Restaurant

★ ★ **SINGHA THAI.** *2237 S 108th St (53227). Phone 414/541-1234; fax 414/541-0683. www.singha-thai.com.* Thai menu. Hours: 11 am-9 pm; Fri, Sat to 10 pm. Closed holidays. Lunch $5-$10, dinner $6-$15. Reservations accepted. Cr cds: MC, V.

D

Whitefish Bay

Restaurant

★ ★ **JACK PANDL'S WHITEFISH BAY INN.** *1319 E Henry Clay St (53217). Phone 414/964-3800.* Specialties: whitefish, German pancakes, Schaum torte. Hours: 11: 30 am-2:30 pm, 5-9 pm; Fri, Sat to 10:30 pm; Sun 10:30 am-2:30 pm, 4-8 pm. Lunch $5.95-$12.95, dinner $7.95-$21.95. Bar. Children's menu, Established in 1915; antique beer stein collection. Reservations accepted. Cr cds: A, D, DS, MC, V.

Winneconne

Restaurant

★ **FIN 'N FEATHER SHOWBOATS.** *22 W Main St (54986). Phone 920/582-4305. www.in-n-feathershowboats. com.* Hours: 8 am-11 pm; winter months to 10 pm; Sun brunch 9 am-3 pm. Closed Dec 25. Reservations accepted. Bar to 2:30 am. Breakfast $1.95-$6.95, lunch, dinner $2.65-$24.95. Sun brunch buffet $9.95. Specializes in fish, Angus steak, pasta. Salad bar. Replica of riverboat; excursions available on *Showboat II*. Family-owned. Cr cds: A, MC, V.

D SC

Wisconsin Dells (F-4)

See also Baraboo, Mauston, Portage, Prairie du Sac

Settled 1856 **Pop** 2,393 **Elev** 912 ft **Area code** 608 **Zip** 53965

Information Wisconsin Dells Visitor & Convention Bureau, 701 Superior St, PO Box 390; 608/254-4636 or 800/22-DELLS

Web www.wisdells.com

Until 1931 this city was called Kilbourn, but it changed its name in the hope of attracting tourists to the nearby Dells. It seems to have worked—Wisconsin Dells has become the state's prime tourist attraction.

What to See and Do

Beaver Springs Fishing Park and Riding Stables. *600 Trout Rd, 1/2 mile S on WI 13.* Phone 608/254-2735 (*fishing*) or 608/254-2707 (*stable*). Guided one-hr rides. Spring-fed ponds stocked with trout, catfish, bass, and other fish. Pay for fish caught. Pole rental. (Apr-Oct, daily) **$$**

Christmas Mountain Village. *S944 Christmas Mountain Rd. 4 miles W on County H.* Phone 608/254-3971. Area has two double chairlifts, rope tow; patrol, school, rentals; snowmaking; restaurant, bar, snack bar. Lodge. Seven power-tilled runs; longest run 1/2 mile; vertical drop 250 feet. (Mid-Dec-mid-Mar, daily; closed Dec 24 evening) Cross-country trails; night skiing. **$$$$**

Dells Boat Tours. *11 Broadway.* Phone 608/254-8555. Guided sightseeing tours through the Dells Scenic Riverway. View of towering sandstone cliffs, narrow fern-filled canyons, and unique rock formations. Upper Dells tour is two hours with scenic shore landings at Stand Rock and Witches Gulch; Lower Dells tour is one hour and features the Rocky Island region, caverns and cliffs; complete tour is Upper and Lower Dells combined. (Mid-Apr-Oct, daily, departures every 30 minutes in July and Aug) **$$$$**

⭐ **Dells Ducks.** *1550 Wisconsin Dells Pkwy (53965). 1-1/2 miles S on US 12.* Phone 608/254-6080. One-hr land/water tour of scenic rock formations along Wisconsin River. (Late May-late Oct, daily) **$$$$**

H. H. Bennett Studio and History Center. *215 Broadway.* Phone 608/253-3523. (1865) Oldest photographic studio in the United States. The landscape and nature photography of H. H. Bennett helped make the Dells area famous. The studio is still in operation and it is possible to purchase enlargements made from Bennett's original glass negatives. (Memorial Day-Labor Day, daily; rest of year, by appointment)

Original Wisconsin Ducks. *1890 Wisconsin Dells Pkwy. 1 mile S on US 12.* Phone 608/254-8751. 1-hou r, 8 1/2-mile land and water tours on the Original Wisconsin Ducks. (Apr-Oct, daily) **$$$$**

Riverview Park & Waterworld. *US 12. 1/4 mile S on US 12.* Phone 608/254-2608. Wave pool, speed slides, tube rides, and kids pools. Grand Prix, go-carts, dune cat track. Park (late May-early Sept); admission free; fee for activities. Waterworld (late May-early Sept, daily). **$$$$**

Tommy Bartlett's Thrill Show. *560 Wisconsin Dells Pkwy. 3 miles S on US 12, in Lake Delton.* Phone 608/254-2525. Water ski theme, "Hooray for Hollywood," features juggling jokester, the Nerveless Knocks, "Mr. Sound Effects"

Wes Harrison, and colorful entrancing waters; also laser light show (evening performances only). (Late May-early Sept, daily) **$$$$** Also here is

    Tommy Bartlett's Robot World & Exploratory. *560 Wisconsin Dells Pkwy. 3 miles S on US 12.* Phone 608/254-2525. More than 150 hands-on exhibits, incl the world's only Russian Mir Space Station core module. Principles of light, sound, and motion are explored. Features robot-guided tour. (Daily) **$$$**

Wisconsin Deer Park. *583 Wisconsin Dells Pkwy. 1/2 mile S on US 12.* Phone 608/253-2041. A 28-acre wildlife exhibit. (May-mid-Oct, daily) **$$$**

Motels/Motor Lodges

⭐ **AMERICAN WORLD RESORT AND SUITES.** *400 Wiconsin Dells Pkwy (53965).* Phone 608/253-4451; toll-free 800/433-3557; fax 608/254-4770. www.americanworld. 94 rooms, 1-3 story. S, D $69-$119; each additional $7. Check-out 10 am. TV; cable. Laundry services. 6 pools, 3 indoor. Tennis. Downhill ski 7 miles, cross-country ski 3 miles. Lawn games. RV park. Cr cds: A, D, DS, MC, V.
[D] 🐾 🎿 🏊 🛟 SC

⭐ **BAKERS SUNSET BAY RESORT.** *921 Canyon Rd (53965).* Phone 608/254-8406; toll-free 800/435-6515; fax 608/253-2062. 74 rooms, 1-2 story. S, D $95-$195. Complimentary continental breakfast (off-season). Check-out 10 am. TV; cable (premium). Some fireplaces. Exercise equipment. Game room. Swimming beach. Pontoon boats. 4 pools, 2 indoor; children's pool. Lawn games. Cr cds: A, MC, V.
[D] 🛟 🏊 🏋 🛟 SC

⭐ **BEST WESTERN AMBASSADOR INN SUITES.** *610 Frontage Rd S (53965).* Phone 608/254-4477; toll-free 800/828-6888; fax 608/253-6662. www.bestwestern.com. 181 rooms, 3 story. S, D $68-$98; each additional $6; under 17 free. Check-out 11 am. TV; cable (premium), VCR available (movies). Laundry services. Sauna. Game room. 2 pools, 1 indoor, children's pool, whirlpool. Downhill/cross-country ski 4 miles. Cr cds: A, C, D, DS, MC, V.
[D] 🐾 🏊 🛟 SC

⭐ **BLACKHAWK MOTEL.** *720 Race St (53965).* Phone 608/254-7770; fax 608/253-7333. www.blackhawkmotel.com. 75 rooms, 1-2 story, 9 cabins. S, D $55-$110; each additional $5; suites $100-$160. Closed Nov-Mar. Check-out 11 am; off-season, noon. TV; cable (premium), VCR available (movies). Laundry services. Saunas. Game room. Indoor, outdoor pool, children's pool, whirlpools. Water slides. Cr cds: A, C, D, DS, MC, V.
[D] 🏊 🛟

⭐ **CAROUSEL INN AND SUITES.** *1031 Wisconsin Dells Pkwy (53965).* Phone 608/254-6554; fax 608/254-6554. 102 rooms, 2 story. S, D $130; under 18 free, higher rates weekends, holidays. Closed Oct-Apr. Check-out 11 am. TV; cable (premium), VCR available (movies $5). Game room. Indoor pool, whirlpool. Indoor water slide, outdoor waterpark. Cr cds: A, DS, MC, V.

[D] [icons]

★ **CHIPPEWA MOTEL.** *1114 Broadway (53965). Phone 608/253-3982; toll-free 800/756-2447; fax 608/254-2577. www.chippewamotel.com.* 50 rooms, 2 story. Mid-June-Labor Day: S $38-$115; D $48-$150; suites $85-$150; family rates; lower rates rest of year. Crib $4. TV; cable (premium). Indoor pool; whirlpool. Playground. Restaurant opposite 7 am-10 pm. Check-out 10 am. Coin laundry. Business services available. Sauna. Game room. Some in-room whirlpools; microwaves available. Picnic tables. Cr cds: A, DS, MC, V.

[D] [icons]

★ **COMFORT INN.** *703 Frontage Rd N (53965). Phone 608/253-3711; fax 608/254-2164. www.comfortinn.com.* 75 rooms, 3 story. Memorial Day-Labor Day: S $65-$104; D $73-$104; each additional $6; higher rates spring and fall weekends; lower rates rest of year. Crib free. TV; cable (premium). Indoor pool; whirlpool. Complimentary continental breakfast. Restaurant adjacent 6:30 am-1 pm, 5-9 pm. Check-out 11 am. Business services available. Game room. Refrigerators, microwaves. Cr cds: A, C, D, DS, JCB, MC, V.

[D] [icons]

★ **DAYS INN.** *944 WI 12/16 (53965). Phone 608/254-6444; fax 608/254-6444. www.daysinn.com.* 100 rooms, 2 story. Late June-Aug: S $85-$99; D $105-$135; each additional $5; suites $119-$152; under 12 free; lower rates rest of year. Crib free. TV; cable (premium). Indoor/outdoor pool; whirlpool. Restaurant adjacent open 24 hours. Check-out 11 am. Business services available. Downhill/cross-country ski 7 miles. Sauna. Microwaves available. Cr cds: A, D, DS, ER, MC, V.

[D] [icons]

★ ★ **HOLIDAY INN AQUA DOME.** *655 Frontage Rd (53965). Phone 608/254-8306; toll-free 800/544-3557; fax 608/254-8306. www.holiday-inn.com.* 228 rooms, 2 story. July-Labor Day: S, D $144; family rates: winter, spring; lower rates rest of year. Crib free. TV; cable (premium). 4 pools, 2 indoor; whirlpools, slides. Supervised children's activities (June-Aug); ages 2-12. Coffee in rooms. Restaurant 6:30 am-1 pm, 5-9 pm. Room service. Bar; entertainment. Check-out 10:30 am. Coin laundry. Meeting rooms. Business services available. Gift shop. Downhill/cross-country ski 8 miles. Sauna. Game room. Microwaves available. Cr cds: A, D, DS, MC, V.

[D] [icons]

★ **INDIAN TRAIL MOTEL.** *1013 Broadway (53965). Phone 608/253-2641. www.indiantrailmotel.com.* 45 rooms. D $60-$100. Closed Nov-Mar. Check-out 10 am. TV; cable (premium). 2 pools, 1 indoor; whirlpool. Lawn games. On 11 acres.s. On 11 acres. Cr cds: A, DS, MC, V.

[icons]

★ **INTERNATIONAL MOTEL.** *1311 E Broadway (53965). Phone 608/254-2431.* 45 rooms. July-Labor Day: S $35-$65; D $45-$90; lower rates May-June, after Labor Day-mid-Oct. Closed rest of year. Crib $5. Pet accepted, some restrictions. TV; cable (premium). Heated pool; wading pool. Playground. Complimentary coffee in lobby. Restaurant adjacent 7 am-midnight. Check-out 11 am. Game room. Refrigerators available. Balconies. Picnic tables on patio. Cr cds: A, C, D, DS, MC, V.

[D] [icons]

★ **LUNA INN AND SUITES.** *Phone 608/253-2661; toll-free 800/999-5862. www.dells.com/luna.* 70 rooms, 1-2 story. Mid-June-mid-Sept: S $45-$80; D $48-$99; each additional $8; suites $59-$178; lower rates mid-Sept-mid-Nov, mid-Apr-mid-June. Closed rest of year. Crib $5. TV; cable (premium), VCR. 2 pools, 1 indoor; whirlpool. Coffee in lobby. Restaurant adjacent 7 am-10 pm. Check-out 10:30 am. Some refrigerators, microwaves. Cr cds: DS, MC, V.

[D] [icons]

★ **MAYFLOWER.** *910 Wisconsin Dells Pkwy (53965). Phone 608/253-6471; toll-free 800/345-7407; fax 608/253-7617.* 72 rooms, 1-2 story. D $98-$118; each additional $6. Check-out 11 am. TV; cable (premium). Laundry services. Sauna. Game room. 2 pools, 1 indoor, children's pool, whirlpool. Downhill ski 7 miles, cross-country ski 3 miles. Cr cds: A, MC, V.

[icons]

★ **PARADISE MOTEL.** *1700 Wisconsin Dells Pkwy (53965). Phone 608/254-7333; fax 608/253-2350.* 45 rooms. Mid-June-Labor Day: S, D $60-$95; suites $85-$155; family of 6-8, $85-$175; lower rates rest of year. Crib $5. TV; cable (premium). Heated pool; wading pool, whirlpool. Playground. Restaurant nearby. Check-out 11 am. Refrigerators; some in-room whirlpools. Cr cds: A, DS, MC, V.

[D] [icons] [SC]

★ ★ **RIVER INN.** *1015 River Rd (53965). Phone 608/253-1231; toll-free 800/659-5395; fax 608/253-6145.* 54 rooms, 5 story. June-Sept: S, D $84-$159; suites $114-$159; lower rates rest of year. TV; cable (premium). 2 pools, 1 indoor; whirlpool. Playground. Coffee in rooms. Restaurant 8 am-10 pm (in season). Room service. Bar 4 pm-1 am. Check-out 11 am. Business services available. Downhill/cross-country ski 7 miles. Exercise equipment;

sauna. Refrigerators; some microwaves. Some balconies, patios. Cr cds: A, D, DS, MC, V.

⬛ 🏊 🎿 🏌 ⛷

★ **RIVIERA MOTEL AND SUITES.** *811 Wisconsin Dells Pkwy (53965). Phone 608/253-1051; toll-free 800/800-7109; fax 608/253-9038.* 58 rooms. D $89-$225. Check-out 10:30 am. TV; cable (premium). Some fireplaces. Sauna. 2 pools, 1 indoor; whirlpool, water slide. Cr cds: DS, MC, V.

⬛ 🏊 ⛷

★ **SUPER 8.** *800 Cty Hwy H (53965). Phone 608/254-6464; fax 608/254-2692. www.super8.com.* 124 rooms, 3 story. June-Sept: S $59.99; D $87.99; each additional $6; suites $150; golf plans; lower rates rest of year. Crib $4. Pet accepted, some restrictions. Complimentary continental breakfast. Coffee in rooms. Check-out 11 am. TV; cable. Restaurant adjacent 6-1 am. Sauna. Indoor pool, whirlpool. Downhill ski 5 miles; cross-country ski 3 miles. Picnic tables. Business services. Cr cds: A, C, D, DS, MC, V.

⬛ 🐾 🏊 ⛷

★★ **WINTERGREEN RESORT AND CONFERENCE CENTER.** *60 Gassek Rd (53940). Phone 608/254-2285; toll-free 800/648-4765; fax 608/253-6235. www.wintergreen-resort.com.* 111 rooms, 3 story. July-Aug: S $69-$139; D $95-$179; each additional $8; suites $109-$339; under 18 free; weekly rates; package plans; higher rates weekends (2-day min); lower rates rest of year. Crib $10. TV; cable (premium). 2 pools, 1 indoor; wading pool, whirlpool. Playground. Restaurant 7 am-9 pm. Room service. Check-out 11 am. Coin laundry. Meeting rooms. Business services available. Sundries. Gift shop. Downhill ski 12 miles; cross-country ski 2 miles. Exercise equipment; sauna. Game room. Refrigerators, microwaves, minibars; some in-room whirlpools. Balconies. Picnic tables. Indoor/outdoor water park. Cr cds: A, DS, MC, V.

⬛ 🎿 🏌 🏊 ⛷ 🚶

Resorts

★★★ **CHULA VISTA RESORT AND CONFERENCE CENTER.** *4031 N River Rd (53965). Phone 608/254-8366; toll-free 800/388-4782; fax 608/254-7653. www.chulavistaresort.com.* This Southwestern themed resort offers fun and relaxation for children of all ages. 260 rooms. Memorial Day-Labor Day: S $69-$139; D $79-$149; each additional $5; suites $165-$279; lower rates rest of year. Crib $10. Check-out 10:30 am, check-in 3 pm. TV; cable (premium). Balconies. Microwaves; some in-room whirlpools. Dining room 7:30 am-11 pm. Bar. Room service. Exercise equipment, sauna, steam room. 5 pools, 1 indoor; wading pool, whirlpool, poolside service. Golf. Miniature golf. Tennis. Downhill ski 5 miles. Hiking trails. Snowmobiling. Airport transportation.

Business services, convention facilities. Gift shop. Cr cds: A, C, D, DS, MC, V.

⬛ 🐾 🎿 🏌 🏊 ⛷ ✈ 🚶

★★★ **KALAHARI RESORT.** *1305 Kalahari Dr (53965). Phone 608/254-5466.* 272 rooms, 4 story. S, D $199-$299; each additional $15; under 17 free. Crib available. Heated pool. TV; cable (premium), VCR available. Complimentary coffee, newspaper in rooms. Restaurant 6 am-10 pm. Check-out 11 am. Meeting rooms. Business center. Gift shop. Exercise room. Some refrigerators, minibars. Extensive water park. Cr cds: A, C, D, DS, MC, V.

⛷

Wisconsin Rapids (E-4)

See also Marshfield, Stevens Point

Pop 18,245 **Elev** 1,028 ft **Area code** 715 **Zip** 54494

Information Wisconsin Rapids Area Convention & Visitors Bureau, 1120 Lincoln St; 715/422-4856 or 800/554-4484

Web www.wctc.net/chamber

A paper manufacturing and cranberry center, Wisconsin Rapids was formed in 1900 by consolidating the two towns of Grand Rapids and Centralia after the Wisconsin River had devastated large sections of both communities. At first the combined town was called Grand Rapids, but the name was changed when confusion with the Michigan city developed. Cranberry marshes here produce the largest inland cranberry crop in the world.

What to See and Do

Forest tour. *5 miles NE on County U, on banks of Wisconsin River. Phone 715/422-3789.* Self-guided walking or cross-country skiing tour of site of Consolidated Papers' first tree nursery, now planted with various types of hard and soft woods; 27 marked points of special interest on 60 acres. (Daily) **FREE**

Grotto Gardens. *6975 Grotto Ave. 7 miles N via WI 34, County C in Rudolph. Phone 715/435-3120.* A 6-acre garden park with series of religious tableaux, statues, and grottoes (daily). Picnic grounds. Gift shop/Information center (Memorial Day-Labor Day, daily). **$**

South Wood County Historical Corporation Museum. *540 3rd St S. Phone 715/423-1580.* Historical museum in town mansion. (June-Aug, Sun-Thrus, afternoons) **FREE**

Special Event

River Cities Fun Fest. *W Grand Ave and 2nd St N. Phone 715/423-1830.* Tours, car show, arts and crafts fair, water ski shows. First weekend Aug.

Motels/Motor Lodges

★ **BEST WESTERN RAPIDS MOTOR INN.** *911 Huntington Ave (54494). Phone 715/423-3211; toll-free 800/528-1234; fax 715/423-2875. www.bestwestern.com.* 43 rooms, 2 story. S $46-$54; D $49-$60; each additional $6; under 12 free; package plans. Pet accepted. Check-out 11 am. TV; cable (premium). In-room modem link. Cross-country ski 2 miles. Cr cds: A, C, D, DS, MC, V.

🅳 ⛵ 🏊 ⛷ SC

★ **CAMELOT.** *9210 WI 13 S (54494). Phone 715/325-5111.* 14 rooms, 6 with shower only. S $35-$40; D $45-$50; each additional $2; higher rates special events. Crib $5. Pet accepted. TV; cable (premium), VCR (movies). Complimentary coffee in rooms. Restaurant opposite 5:30 am-8 pm. Check-out 11 am. Downhill ski 20 miles; cross-country ski 2 miles. Pool. Refrigerators; microwaves available. Picnic tables. Cr cds: A, MC, V.

⛵ 🏂 ⛷ 🎿 ⛱ ⛷

★ **ECONO LODGE.** *3300 8th St S (54494). Phone 715/423-7000; toll-free 800/755-1488. www.econolodge.com.* 55 rooms, 2 story. S $39.95-$44; D $49.95-$54; each additional $5; under 18 free; weekends 2-day minimum Crib free. Pet accepted, some restrictions; $10. TV; cable. Complimentary coffee in rooms. Restaurant 6:30 am-10 pm. Bar 3 pm-2 am. Check-out 11 am. Meeting rooms. Business services available. In-room modem link. Many refrigerators, microwaves. Cr cds: A, C, D, DS, JCB, MC, V.

🅳 ⛵ 🏂 ⛷

★ ★ ★ **HOTEL MEAD.** *451 E Grand Ave (54494). Phone 715/423-1500; toll-free 800/843-6323; fax 715/422-7064. www.hotelmead.com.* Centrally located and considered by many as the hospitality center of central Wisconsin, this hotel caters to business travelers, leisure travelers and adventure travelers. 157 rooms, 5 story, 24 suites. S $89; D $99; each additional $10; suites $109-$115; under 18 free; package plans. Crib available. Pet accepted, some restrictions; $15. TV; cable (premium). Complimentary coffee in rooms. Restaurant 6:30 am-10 pm. Room service. Bar 11-1 am. Check-out noon. Meeting rooms. Business services available. In-room modem link. Valet service. Sundries. 18-hole golf privileges. Cross-country ski 2 miles. Exercise equipment. Indoor pool; whirlpool, poolside service. Refrigerators; some bathroom phones, microwaves, wet bars. Cr cds: A, C, D, DS, MC, V.

🅳 ⛵ 🏂 🏋 🏂 🏌 ⛷ ⛱ 🎿 🏂 🚶

★ **MAPLES MOTELS.** *4750 8th St S (54494). Phone 715/423-2590; fax 715/423-2592.* 27 rooms, 2 with shower only, 16 kitchen units. S $35-$40; D $45-$55; each additional $5; kitchen units $50-$70. Crib $5. Pet accepted. TV; cable, VCR. Complimentary coffee in suites. Restaurant opposite 5-2 am. Check-out 11 am. Business services available. In-room modem link. Cross-country ski 2 miles. Pool. Game room. Refrigerators; microwave in suites. Picnic tables, grills. Cr cds: A, MC, V.

✈

★ **QUALITY INN.** *3120 8th St (54494). Phone 715/423-5506; toll-free 800/755-1336; fax 715/423-7150. www.qualityinn.com.* 36 rooms, 2 story. No room phones. S $60-$66; D $66-$72; each additional $6; under 18 free. Complimentary continental breakfast. Check-out 11 am. TV; cable (premium). Health club privileges. Cr cds: A, C, D, DS, JCB, MC, V.

🅳 ⛷ SC

Woodruff (C-4)

See also Eagle River, Rhinelander, Saint Germain

Pop 2,000 **Elev** 1,610 ft **Area code** 715 **Zip** 54568

Information Minocqua-Arbor Vitae-Woodruff Area Chamber of Commerce, 8216 US 51 S, Minocqua, 54548; 715/356-5266 or 800/446-6784

Web www.minocqua.org

Woodruff is a four-seasons playground for families and outdoor recreationalists alike. The area has one of the largest concentrations of fresh water bodies in America, providing unlimited fishing and water activities.

What to See and Do

Kastle Rock. *9438 County Hwy J. US 51 to County Trunk J, 2 blocks E. Phone 715/356-6865.* 18-hole miniature golf with 500-foot train track. (May-Aug, daily) **$$$**

Woodruff State Fish Hatchery. *8770 Country Rd J. 2 1/2 miles SE on County Trunk J. Phone 715/356-5211.* Hatchery (mid-Apr-mid-June). Tours (Memorial Day-Labor Day, Mon-Fri) **FREE**

Special Event

Scheer's Lumberjack Show. *15648 County Rd B. US 51, 2 miles N of Minocqua to WI 47. Phone 715/634-6923.* World champion lumberjacks provide entertainment, live music. Phone 715/356-4050. June-Aug.

Side Trips

While visiting Milwaukee, plan to take a day or two and drive south an hour and a half to Chicago—you won't be disappointed. Gaze at the breathtaking skyline, stroll along the awe-inspiring lakefront, indulge in the world-famous deep-dish pizza, soak up authentic blues music, and then plan for day two of your excursion.

Chicago, IL (H-6)

1 1/2 hours, 95 miles from Milwaukee, WI

Settled 1803 **Pop** 2,896,016 **Elev** 596 ft **Area code** 312, 773

Information Chicago Office of Tourism, Chicago Cultural Center, 78 E Washington St, 60602; 312/744-2400 or 800/226-6632

Web www.ci.chi.il.us/tourism

Suburbs *North:* Evanston, Glenview, Gurnee, Highland Park, Highwood, Northbrook, Skokie, Wilmette; *Northwest:* Arlington Heights, Itasca, Schaumburg, Wheeling; *West:* Brookfield, Cicero, Downers Grove, Elmhurst, Geneva, Glen Ellyn, Hillside, Hinsdale, La Grange, Naperville, Oak Brook, Oak Park, St Charles, Wheaton; *South:* Homewood, Oak Lawn.

"I have struck a city—a real city—and they call it Chicago," wrote Rudyard Kipling. For poet Carl Sandburg, it was the "City of the Big Shoulders"; for writer A.J. Liebling, a New Yorker, it was the "Second City." Songwriters have dubbed it a "toddlin' town," and "my kind of town." Boosters say it's "the city that works"; and to most people it is "the windy city." But over and above all the words and slogans is the city itself and the people who helped make it what it is today.

The people of Chicago represent a varied ethnic and racial mix. From the Native Americans who gave the city its name—*Checagou*—to the restless Easterners who traveled west in search of land and opportunity to the hundreds of thousands of venturesome immigrants from Europe, Asia, and Latin America who brought with them the foods and customs of the Old World to the Southern blacks and Appalachians who came in hope of finding better jobs and housing, all have contributed to the strength, vitality, and cosmopolitan ambience that makes Chicago a distinctive and unique experience for the visitor.

Chicago's past is equally distinctive, built on adversity and contradiction. The first permanent settler was a black man, Jean Baptiste Point du Sable. The city's worst tragedy, the Great Fire of 1871, was the basis for its physical and cultural renaissance. In the heart of one of the poorest ethnic neighborhoods, two young women of means, Jane Addams and Ellen Gates Starr, created Hull House, a social service institution that has been copied throughout the world. A city of neat frame cottages and bulky stone mansions, it produced the geniuses of the Chicago School of Architecture (Louis Sullivan, Daniel Burnham, Dankmar Adler, William LeBaron Jenney, John Willborn Root), whose innovative tradition was carried on by Frank Lloyd Wright and Ludwig Mies van der Rohe. Even its most famous crooks provide a study in contrasts: Al Capone, the Prohibition gangster, and Samuel Insull, the financial finagler whose stock manipulations left thousands of small investors penniless in the late twenties.

Chicago's early merchants resisted the intrusion of the railroad, yet the city became the rail center of the nation. Although Chicago no longer boasts a stockyard, its widely diversified economy makes it one of the most stable cities in the country. Metropolitan Chicago has more than 12,000 factories with a $20-billion annual payroll and ranks first in the United States in the production of canned and frozen foods, metal products, machinery, railroad equipment, letterpress printing, office equipment, musical instruments, telephones, housewares, candy, and lampshades. It has one of the world's busiest airports, largest grain exchange, and biggest mail-order business. It is a great educational center (58 institutions of higher learning); one of the world's largest convention and trade show cities; a showplace, marketplace, shopping, and financial center; and a city of skyscrapers, museums, parks, and churches, with more than 2,700 places of worship.

Chicago turns its best face toward Lake Michigan, where a green fringe of parks forms an arc from Evanston to the Indiana border. The Loop is a city within a city, with many corporate headquarters, banks, stores, and other enterprises. To the far south are the docks along the Calumet River, used by ocean vessels since the opening of the St. Lawrence Seaway and servicing a belt of factories, steel mills, and warehouses. Behind these lies a maze of industrial and shopping areas, schools, and houses.

Although Louis Jolliet mapped the area as early as 1673 and du Sable and a compatriot, Antoine Ouilmette, had established a trading post by 1796, the real growth of the city did not begin until the 19th-century and the advent of the Industrial Revolution.

City Fun Facts–Chicago

1. The world's first Skyscraper was built in Chicago, 1885

2. The Chicago Public Library is the world's largest public library with a collection of more than 2 million books.

3. The abbreviation 'ORD' for Chicago's O'Hare airport comes from the old name 'Orchard Field.'

4. Chicago is home to the world's longest street: Western Ave.

5. Chicago produced the Oscar Mayer "Wienermobile," in 1936.

6. The Hostess Twinkie was first produced in Chicago in 1930.

7. Chicago is home to the world's largest food festival every summer in Grant Park–the Taste of Chicago.

In 1803, the fledging US government took possession of the area and sent a small military contingent from Detroit to select the site for a fort. Fort Dearborn was built at a strategic spot on the mouth of the Chicago River; on the opposite bank, a settlement slowly grew. Fort and settlement were abandoned when the British threatened them during the War of 1812. On their way to Fort Wayne, soldiers and settlers were attacked and killed or held captive by Native Americans who had been armed by the British. The fort was rebuilt in 1816; a few survivors returned, new settlers arrived, but there was little activity until Chicago was selected as the terminal site of the proposed Illinois and Michigan Canal. This started a land boom.

Twenty thousand Easterners swept through on their way to the riches of the West. Merchants opened stores; land speculation was rampant. Although 1837—the year Chicago was incorporated as a city—was marked by financial panic, the pace of expansion and building did not falter. In 1841, grain destined for world ports began to pour into the city; almost immediately, Chicago became the largest grain market in the world. In the wake of the grain came herds of hogs and cattle for the Chicago slaughterhouses. Tanneries, packing plants, mills, and factories soon sprang up.

The Illinois and Michigan Canal, completed in 1848, quadrupled imports and exports. Railroads fanned out from the city, transporting merchandise throughout the nation and bringing new produce to Chicago. During the slump that followed the panic of 1857, Chicago built a huge wooden shed (the Wigwam) at the southeast corner of Wacker and Lake to house the Republican National Convention. Abraham Lincoln was nominated Republican candidate for president here in 1860. The Civil War doubled grain shipments from Chicago. In 1865, the mile-square Union Stock Yards were established. Chicago was riotously prosperous; its population skyrocketed. Then, on October 8, 1871, fire erupted in a cow barn and roared through the city, destroying 15,768 buildings, killing almost 300 people, and leaving a third of the population homeless. But temporary and permanent rebuilding started at once, and Chicago emerged from the ashes to take advantage of the rise of industrialization. The labor unrest of the period produced the Haymarket bombing and the Pullman and other strikes. The 1890s were noteworthy for cultural achievements: orchestras, libraries, universities, and the new urban architectural form for which the term "skyscraper" was coined. The Columbian Exposition of 1893, a magnificent success, was followed by depression and municipal corruption.

Chicago's fantastic rate of growth continued into the 20th century. Industries boomed during World War I, and in the 1920s the city prospered as never before—unruffled by dizzying financial speculation and notorious gang warfare, an outgrowth of Prohibition. The stock market crash of 1929 brought down the shakier financial pyramids; the repeal of Prohibition virtually ended the rackets; and a more sober Chicago produced the Century of Progress Exposition in 1933. Chicago's granaries and steel mills helped carry the country through WWII. The past several decades have seen a reduction of manufacturing jobs in the area and an increase of jobs in service industries and in the fields of finance, law, advertising, and insurance. The 1996 relocation of Lake Shore Drive made it possible to create the Museum Campus, a 57-acre extension of Burnham Park. The Museum Campus provides an easier and more scenic route to the Adler Planetarium, Field Museum, and Shedd Aquarium, and surrounds these three institutions with one continuous park featuring terraced gardens and broad walkways.

Although in the eyes of some Chicago evokes the image of an industrial giant, it is also a city in which the arts flourish. Chicagoans are proud of their world-famous symphony orchestra, their Lyric Opera, and their numerous and diverse dance companies. Since 1912, Chicago has been the home of *Poetry* magazine. Chicago's theater community is vibrant, with more than 100 off-Loop theaters presenting quality drama. The collections at the Art Institute, Museum of Contemporary Art, Terra Museum of American Art, and many galleries along Michigan Ave and in the River North area are among the best in the country.

Other museums are equally renowned: the Museum of Science and Industry, the Field Museum of Natural History, the Chicago Children's Museum at Navy Pier, and the various specialty museums that reflect the ethnic and civic interests of the city.

The zoos, planetarium, and aquarium, as well as many parks and beaches along the lakefront, afford pleasure for visitors

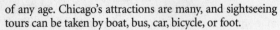
of any age. Chicago's attractions are many, and sightseeing tours can be taken by boat, bus, car, bicycle, or foot.

Buses and rapid transit lines are integrated into one system—the most extensive in the nation—with interchangeable transfers. Elevated lines run through the Loop. Subway trains run under State and Dearborn streets and run on elevated structures to both the north and south. Rapid transit lines also serve the West Side as well as O'Hare and Midway airports. Commuter trains stretch out to the far western and southern suburbs and near the Wisconsin and Indiana borders.

Driving and parking in Chicago are no more difficult than in any other major city. There are indoor and outdoor parking areas near and in the Loop; some provide shuttle bus service to the Loop or to the Merchandise Mart.

The attractions decribed under CHICAGO are arranged topically, and most contain neighborhood designations following their addresses. The Loop is considered the center of the city, with State Street running north and south and Madison Street east and west as the baselines. Attractions contain the following designations: The Loop, Near North, North, Near South, South, and West. The eastern border of the city is Lake Michigan. In addition, some attractions in outlying areas are listed.

Additional Visitor Information

For additional attractions and accommodations, see CHICAGO O'HARE AIRPORT AREA, which follows CHICAGO. When available, half-price, day-of-performance tickets are offered, with a slight service charge, at HOT TIX booths, Chicago Place at 700 N Michigan Ave, 108 N State St, 1616 Sherman Ave in Evanston, and Oak Park Visitor Center at 158 Forest Ave in Oak Park. (Tue-Sat; Sun tickets sold on Sat) For available tickets phone 312/977-1755.

Chicago magazine is helpful for anyone visiting Chicago; available at most newsstands. Key-This Week in Chicago and Where, at major hotels, provide up-to-date information. For additional information see any of the daily newspapers; special sections to look at are: Friday in the Friday Chicago Tribune; the Arts & Entertainment section in the Sunday Chicago Tribune; and the Weekend Plus section of the Friday Chicago Sun-Times. A free weekly newspaper, The Reader, provides information on local events, art, and entertainment.

There are five Illinois Travel Information centers, located at 310 S Michigan Ave, at the Sears Tower, at the James R. Thompson Center (100 W Randolph St), and at Midway and O'Hare Airports. (Mon-Fri). The Pumping Station, at the corner of Chicago and Michigan aves, houses a visitor information center that provides brochures and information on points of interest and transportation. (Daily).

Contact the Chicago Office of Tourism, Chicago Cultural Center, 78 E Washington St, 60602; 312/744-2400 or 800/226-6632. The Office of Tourism distributes an event calendar, maps and museum guides, and hotel and restaurant guides, plus other info concerning the Chicago area. (Mon-Sat, also Sun afternoons).

Transportation

Airport. O'Hare International Airport,Mannheim Rd & Kennedy Expy, 19 miles NW of Loop (see CHICAGO O'HARE AIRPORT AREA), phone 773/686-2200; Chicago Midway Airport, 5700 S Cicero Ave (approximately 8 miles S of Loop), phone 773/838-0600.

Car Rental Agencies. See IMPORTANT TOLL-FREE NUMBERS.Public Transportation. Chicago Transit Authority/Regional Transit Authority, phone 312/836-7000. Rail Passenger Service. Amtrak 800/872-7245.

What to See and Do

Adler Planetarium & Astronomy Museum. *1300 S Lake Shore Dr, on a peninsula in Lake Michigan, Near S Side. Phone 312/322-0300; 312/922-STAR (recorded schedule).* (1930) Bronze sundial by sculptor Henry Moore in entry plaza. Two-part Sky Show in Universe and Sky theaters, Zeiss VI projector, and horizon projection system; Sat and Sun morning children's shows. Exhibits on modern astronomy and astronomical techniques; Race to the Moon exhibit features videotape of first manned landing on the moon; 2.6-oz moon rock; early scientific instruments; displays on the *Voyager* probes, satellites; navigation and the use of telescopes (includes the telescope William Herschel used to discover Uranus); computerized observing station linked with Apache Point observatory in New Mexico; solar telescope. Museum (daily; closed Thanksgiving, Dec 25). **$$**

American Sightseeing Tours. *Depart from Palmer House Hotel, 17 E Monroe St. Phone 312/251-3100.*

Apollo Theater. *2540 N Lincoln Ave. Phone 773/935-6100; fax 773/935-6214.*

⭐ **Architectural tours.** *Contact Chicago Architecture Foundation, 224 S Michigan Ave, 60604. Phone 312/922-TOUR (recording).* View the city's architecture by bus, boat, bike, or on foot. Sponsored by the Chicago Architecture Foundation; approximately 50 different architectural tours of the city's neighborhoods and suburbs. (Days vary; no tours on holidays) Among tours offered are

> **Chicago Highlights Bus Tour.** *224 S Michigan Ave. Phone 312/922-3432.* This 4-hour bus tour covers the Loop, the Gold Coast, Hyde Park, three historic districts, and three university campuses; includes interior of Frank Lloyd Wright's Robie House. (Sat and Sun) Reservations required. **$$$$**

Art Deco the Chicago Way

Chicago is a textbook of Art Deco design. Look up at the facades of historic high rises, peek into the lobbies of landmark office buildings, ride an elevator or two. Begin at the Chicago Board of Trade (141 W Jackson Blvd), home to the world's oldest and largest futures exchange, formed in 1848. Ceres, the Roman goddess of grain and harvest, receives due homage with a 31-foot-tall statue atop the original 1930 building and a monumental mural in the atrium, added in the 1980s. A massive clock is ornamented with a distinctive agrarian motif. The 3-story lobby, a dazzling Art Deco masterpiece, gleams with contrasting black and buff-colored marble trimmed with silver; elevator doors are silver and black. Light fixtures behind translucent panels throw out a diffused glow, and stylized figures are abundant. Take a free guided tour and watch the frenetic trading in the "pits."

Walk a couple of blocks west for breakfast at Lou Mitchell's (563 W Jackson Blvd), known for egg dishes served in sizzling skillets. The restaurant presents boxes of Milk Duds to waiting female patrons. Then head north to the American National Bank Building (1 N LaSalle St). This 49-story limestone building, with typical Art Deco setbacks and dominant vertical lines, occupies an entire block of Chicago's financial district. A stunning Art Deco lobby features dark marble contrasted by gleaming metalwork and exquisite carved wood sconces. Outside, at the fifth-floor level, relief panels chronicle the 17th-century explorations of Rene Robert de La Salle (Vitzhum & Burns, 1930).

Turn east to the former Chicago Daily News Building (400 W Madison St). Horace Greeley, Joseph Pulitzer, and other famous journalists, as well as events from Chicago's rich newspaper history, are chronicled with stylized bas-relief figures carved by Alvin Meyer. Originally, the limestone building with dramatic setbacks and an open riverfront plaza was designed to house the newspaper's offices and plant. Inside are ornate metal elevator doors, grillwork, and terrazzo floors in a geometric pattern. Travel north to the Carbide and Carbon Building (230 N Michigan Ave). Now being renovated, this Art Deco skyscraper is as dramatically dark as its eponymous minerals. Offsetting piles of black polished granite are dark green masonry and gold terra-cotta trim. The stunning 2-story lobby features marble walls, elegant bronze grillwork, gold-and-white plaster, and recessed lights of frosted glass. Just a block or two southwest, Heaven on Seven is tucked away on the seventh floor of the Garland Building (111 N Washington St). Notable Cajun and Creole cooking includes gumbo, po' boy sandwiches, spicy jambalaya, sweet potato pie, and bread pudding.

Divert your attention from the chocolate goodies at Fanny May's street-level outlet and focus on the fifth-floor of this limestone building at 333 N Michigan Ave. 7-foot-high carved panels depicting settlers and Native Americans commemorate the site of Fort Dearborn, which overlooked the Chicago River at this spot. The lobby has terrazzo floors of black, russet, and green and brass elevator doors decorated with stylized figures. Farther north on the Magnificent Mile, look up above chic storefronts at the former Palmolive/Playboy Building (919 N Michigan Ave). Notice the dark bas-relief designs between windows of this massive, stepped building. Turn the corner onto Walton and check out the lobby. It features Art Deco lights and handsome walnut elevator doors sculpted with bas-relief figures. Ride an elevator and note that the ornate carvings continue inside. The Saloon (200 E Chestnut) is a warm, cheery steakhouse with high-quality, flavorful meat, suitably marbled and dry-aged. Be sure to try a side of bacon-scallion mashed potatoes. Décor features stenciled earth-tone walls, parchment sconces, and Native American murals.

Chicago River Boat Tour. *455 E Illinois (60611). Phone 312/942-3432.* This 1 1/2-hour tour covers north and south branches of the Chicago River with views of the city's celebrated riverfront architecture; historic 19th-century railroad bridges and warehouses, 20th-century bridgehouses, and magnificent Loop skyscrapers. (May-Sept, daily; Oct, Tue, Thur, Sat, and Sun; no tours Labor Day) Reservations required. **$$$$**

Graceland Cemetery Tour. *4001 N Clark St. Phone 773/525-1105; 312/922-TOUR.* Walking through Graceland Cemetery on the city's north side is like taking a step back into Chicago's early history. Not only will you recognize the names of the movers and shakers who put Chicago on the map—Philip Armour, Mayor Joseph Medill, Cyrus McCormick, George Pullman, Potter Palmer, and Marshall Field, to name a few—but you'll also find memorials to the people who helped build it: architects Louis Sullivan, Daniel Burnham, John Root, and Mies van der Rohe. Established in 1860, Graceland, with its winding pathways and gorgeous old trees, is perfect for solo exploration any time of the year. Throughout the cemetery you'll discover varied and artistic memorials, from Greek temples and Egyptian pyramids to Celtic crosses and ethereal angels. Highlights include Louis Sullivan's tomb for Carrie Eliza Getty, a landmark described as the beginning of modern architecture in America; Daniel Burnham's island resting place in the middle of the lake; and Mies van der Rohe's elegantly understated grave marker. (Daily) **FREE**

Loop Walking Tours. *Depart from Tour Center, 224 S Michigan Ave. Phone 312/922-3432.* Each tour is two hours long. *Early Skyscrapers* traces the origins of the Chicago School of Architecture and the skyscrapers built from 1880-1940. The tour includes the Monadnock and the Rookery. *Modern & Beyond* reviews important newer buildings, including the Federal Center, the IBM Building, and the James R. Thompson Center; also public murals and sculptures by Calder, Chagall, Miro, Picasso, Henry Moore, and Dubuffet. (Daily) **$$$**

Arie Crown Theater. *2301 S Lake Shore Dr. McCormick Place, E 23rd St and S Lake Shore Dr. Phone 312/791-6000.*

⭐ **The Art Institute of Chicago.** *122 S Michigan Ave. Michigan Ave and Adams St, in Grant Park. Phone 312/443-3600.* No visit to Chicago is complete without a stop at the Art Institute of Chicago, a local treasure with an international reputation. Adjacent to Millennium Park on South Michigan Avenue, this 1879 Beaux Arts building, originally part of the Columbian Exposition, houses more than 300,000 works of art within its ten curatorial departments. The museum has what's considered the finest and most comprehensive modern and contemporary art collection in the world, one of the largest arms collections in America, and one of the two finest collections of Japanese woodblock prints. Highlights include Georges Seurat's *A Sunday on La Grande Jatte,* 1884, Grant Wood's *American Gothic,* Edward Hopper's *Nighthawks,* 33 Monet paintings, Marc Chagall stained glass windows, a reconstructed Adler and Sullivan Chicago Stock Exchange trading room, and significant photo and architectural drawing collections. You can also attend free daily lectures, visit the well-stocked gift shop, dine at one of three restaurants, including a summertime garden, and take a special tour for the visually impaired. (Daily) Free admission Tue. **$$**

Auditorium Theater. *50 E Congress Pkwy. Phone 312/922-2110; fax 312/431-2360.*

Auditorium Building. *430 S Michigan Ave, in the Loop.* (1889) Landmark structure designed by Louis Sullivan and Dankmar Adler. Interior is noted for its intricate system of iron framing, breathtaking ornamentation, and near-perfect acoustics. Now houses Roosevelt University.

Balmoral Park Race Track. *26435 S Dixie Hwy. 25 miles S on 1-94 to IL 394, continue S to Elmscourt Ln in Crete. Phone 708/672-1414; fax 708/672-5932.* Harness racing. (All year, days vary)

Balzekas Museum of Lithuanian Culture. *6500 S Pulaski Rd, S Side. Phone 773/582-6500.* Antiques, art, children's museum, memorabilia, and literature spanning 1,000 years of Lithuanian history. Exhibits include amber, armor and antique weapons, rare maps, textiles, dolls, stamps, coins; research library. (Daily; closed Jan 1, Thanksgiving, Dec 25) Free admission Mon. **$$**

Blue Man Group. *3133 N Halsted. In the Briar Street Theater. Phone 773/348-4000.* Blue Man Group is a percussion (drums) band and performance group that's literally blue—all three members cover themselves in blue body paint. The group performs by thumping on drums, banging on barrels, and pounding on pipes. The heart-pounding, entertaining, dramatic performance includes audience members (although no one is forced to participate against his will); if you so choose, you may even get painted, too! Performances last just over two hours. **$$$$**

Briar Street Theater. *3133 N Halsted St. Phone 773/348-4000; fax 773/348-7365.*

Brookfield Zoo.

Carson Pirie Scott. *1 S State St. State and Madison sts, in the Loop. Phone 312/641-7000.* (1899) Landmark department store building is considered architect Louis Sullivan's masterpiece. Extraordinary cast-iron ornamentation on the first and second floors frames display windows like paintings. (Mon-Sat and selected Sun; closed holidays)

Chicago Botanical Garden.

Chicago Cultural Center. *78 E Washington St, in the Loop. Phone 312/744-6630; fax 312/744-2089.* If you have a free couple of hours, you may want to wander into the Chicago Cultural Center on Michigan Ave between Randolph and Washington, a gem of a building that offers a wealth of free daily programming and ongoing exhibits. The landmark building, formerly a library, features Tiffany glass domes, mosaics, and marble walls and stairs. **FREE** (Daily; closed holidays) Also here is

> **Museum of Broadcast Communications.** *78 E Washington St. Phone 312/629-6014.* This museum is one of only two broadcast communications museums in the country. The archives contain 10,000 television shows, 50,000 hours of radio, 9,000 television commercials, and 2,500 newscasts. Media buffs will have a field day, but everyone can enjoy this bounty thanks to user-friendly computers set up in viewing suites, where you can revisit classic TV shows, news broadcasts from key world events, or whatever suits your fancy. Besides the exhibits—one, of course, devoted to the Nixon-Kennedy debate that took place in Chicago—there are

interactive programs, including one in which you can "call" the play-by-play of a baseball game. You'll also find a collection of antique radios and televisions and a Radio Hall of Fame. (Daily; closed holidays) **FREE**

Chicago Fire (MLS). *425 E McFetridge. Phone 888/MLS-FIRE.* Team normally plays at Soldier Field, but will play at Cardinal Field on the campus of North Central College in Naperville until renovation of Soldier Field is completed. Games are played between April and October. **$$$$**

Chicago Fire Academy. *558 W DeKoven St, W Side. Phone 312/747-8151.* Built on site where the Great Fire of 1871 is believed to have started. **FREE**

Chicago Historical Society. *1601 N Clark St, near N Side. Phone 312/642-4600.* Changing exhibits focus on history and development of Chicago. Selected aspects of Illinois and US history including galleries devoted to costumes, decorative arts, and architecture. Pioneer craft demonstrations; hands-on gallery. (Daily; closed Jan 1, Thanksgiving, Dec 25) Free admission Mon. Additional charges for special exhibits. **$$**

Chicago Lakefront. *Phone 312/742-7529.* Chicago's lakefront reflects the vision of architect Daniel Burnham, whose 1909 Plan for Chicago specified that the shoreline remain publicly owned and enjoyed by all. It is also one of the things that make this city sparkle. After all, how many major cities have bathing beaches—31 in total—within the city limits? In addition to beaches, the lakefront sports 18 miles of bicycle, jogging, and inline skating paths,several golf courses and driving ranges, skating rinks, tennis courts, field houses, theaters, and more, all easily accessible and open to the public. Chicagoans rich and poor flock to the lakefront year-round to exercise, sunbathe, picnic, and simply enjoy the view. If you have the opportunity and the weather cooperates, rent a bicycle at Navy Pier and spend a few hours following the well-marked path north. Look for the chess players at North Avenue Beach and the skyline views from Montrose Harbor.

Chicago Loop Synagogue. *16 S Clark St, in the Loop. Phone 312/346-7370.* (1957) The eastern wall of this building is a unique example of contemporary stained glass, depicting ancient Hebraic symbols whirling through the cosmos.

Chicago Motor Coach Company. *3903 S Halsted St. Phone 312/922-8919.* Double-decker tours depart from Sears Tower at Jackson and Wacker, Field Museum, Michigan and Pearson, and Michigan and Wacker.

Chicago Neighborhood Tours. *78 E Washington St. Phone 312/742-1190.* Departs from the Chicago Cultural Center. Narrated tours visit ten different neighborhoods via motor coach bus. Tours on Sat only. Reservations strongly recommended.

Chicago Stock Exchange. *440 S LaSalle St. One Financial Pl. Phone 312/663-2980.* For a birds-eye view of high-stakes trading, there is no better place than the Visitor's Gallery on the fifth floor of the Chicago Stock Exchange. On weekdays only, visitors can watch the reality of life in the pits as aggressive young traders jockey for position, yell out their orders, and scramble to keep ahead of volatile markets. A 10-minute video runs continuously, but most of the action is where you'd expect it: on the trading floor. (Mon-Fri; closed major holidays) **FREE**

Chicago Symphony Orchestra. *220 S Michigan Ave. Phone 312/294-3333.* Long considered one of the great orchestras of the world, the CSO has been a fixture on the Chicago cultural scene for more than 100 years. It may have reached its highest acclaim under the late, great Sir Georg Solti, when so many of its recordings were virtual shoe-ins for Grammy awards, but today, with three conductors and an award-winning composer in residence, the orchestra continues to produce innovative and inspiring music in a classically beautiful setting at the newly renovated Symphony Center across from the Art Institute. While the big-name shows may sell out in advance, it is often possible to get day-of-show or single-seat tickets at the box office—especially for weeknight and Friday afternoon performances—at a reasonable price. The Symphony Center also sponsors specialty series, such as jazz and world music, which keeps its programming rich and diverse.

Chicago Temple. *77 W Washington St, in the Loop. Phone 312/236-4548.* (First Methodist Episcopal Church, 1923) At 568 feet from street level to the tip of its Gothic tower, this is the highest church spire in the world. Tours (Mon-Sat at 2 pm; tours Sun after 8:30 am and 11 am services; no tours holidays).

Chicago Theater. *175 N State St. Phone 312/443-1130; fax 312/263-9505.*

Chicago Tribune **Tower.** *435 N Michigan Ave, Near N Side. Phone 312/222-3994.* (1925) Essentially, this is a *moderne* building (36 story) with a Gothic-detailed base and crown; it does exactly what publisher Joseph Medill intended: it "thames" the Chicago River. The tower's once strong foundation has been loosening in recent years, and structural engineers have noted that the edifice has been slowly sinking at the rate of almost a foot a year due to seepage from a sublevel bog just west along the riverbank. Bits and pieces of historic structures from around the world are embedded in the exterior walls of the lower floors.

Chicago Trolley Company. *615 W 41st St. Phone 312/663-0260.* One-fee, all-day ride, with ability to hop on and off at major sites. **$$$$**

Chicago White Sox (MLB). *333 W 35th St. Phone 312/674-1000. www.whitesox.com; fax 312/674-5500.* Team Plays at U.S. Cellular Field.

Chicago Wolves (IHL). *6920 Mannheim Rd (60018). Phone 800/THE-WOLVES.* Team plays at Allstate Arena.

Chinatown. *Starts at the intersection of Cermak Rd and Wentworth Ave. Phone 312/326-5320 (Chinatown Chamber of Commerce).* Though not as large as New York's or San Francisco's Chinatowns, Chicago's Chinatown is a vibrant and lively cultural center that makes for a fascinating visit. Located south of the Loop at Cermak and Wentworth, Chinatown's boundary is marked by a tiled gateway and traditional architecture that is reflected in the smallest details, such as the rooftops, lampposts, and phone booths. Within a 10-block radius are 10,000 community members, more than 40 restaurants, 20 gifts shops, herbal and tea stores, and bakeries. Locals tend to visit on Sunday mornings for dim sum, but it's also fun to be in the neighborhood during any of the traditional festivals, including Chinese New Year, the Dragon Boat Festival, and the mid-autumn Moon Festival. Chinatown is a 10- to 15-minute cab ride from the Loop, and during summer weekends it is also accessible via a free trolley that departs from the Field Museum and from the intersection of State Street and Roosevelt Road. **FREE**

Civic Opera Building. *20 N Wacker Dr, in the Loop. Phone 312/332-2244.* (1929) On the lower levels, under 45 floors of commercial office space, is the richly Art Deco, 3,600-seat Civic Opera House, home of the Lyric Opera of Chicago.

Civic Opera House. *20 N Wacker Dr. Owned and operated by the Lyric Opera of Chicago, 20 N Wacker Dr. Phone 312/419-0033.*

Crate & Barrel. *646 N Michigan Ave (60611). Phone 312/787-5900.* This housewares and home furnishings chain got its start in Chicago in 1962 and has since grown to more than 100 stores nationwide. Its large flagship store on Michigan Ave brings in hordes of visitors drawn in by its clean designs, eye-catching colors, and reasonable prices. (Mon-Sat 10 am-7 pm, Sun 11 am-6 pm)

DePaul University. *Loop campus, 1 E Jackson Blvd. Lincoln Park campus, Fullerton and Sheffield St, Near N Side; Phone 312/362-8300.* 20,500 students. The north campus, with its blend of modern and Gothic architecture, is an integral part of Chicago's historic Lincoln Park neighborhood. The Blue Demons, DePaul's basketball team, play home games at the Allstate Arena in Rosemont (see). Tours (by appointment).

DuSable Museum of African-American History. *740 E 56th Pl, S Side. Phone 773/947-0600.* African and African-American art objects; displays of black history in Africa and the US. Extensive collection includes paintings, sculpture, artifacts, textiles, books, and photographs. (Daily; closed Jan 1, Thanksgiving, Dec 25) Free admission Sun. **$$**

⭐ **Field Museum.** *1400 S Lake Shore Dr, Near S Side. Phone 312/922-9410.* (1920) One of the largest natural history museums in the world. Includes world culture, history, animal, and gem exhibits. Egyptian tomb complex with burial shaft, chamber, and mummies. Touchable displays in the Place for Wonder; Traveling the Pacific features exhibits on Pacific natural history and cultures. Special exhibits, films, lectures, demonstrations, and performances; restaurants and gift shop. (Daily; closed Jan 1, Dec 25) List of touchables for visually impaired available. Free admission (Sept-Feb, Mon-Tue). **$$$**

Fourth Presbyterian Church. *126 E Chestnut, Near N Side. Phone 312/787-4570.* Completed in 1914, this beautiful church is a fine example of Gothic design. One of its architects, Ralph A. Cram, was a leader of the Gothic Revival in the US. Tours available by appointment or after Sun services.(Daily)

Garfield Park and Conservatory. *300 N Central Park Ave, W Side. Phone 312/746-5100.* Outdoor formal gardens. Conservatory has eight houses and propagating houses on more than five acres. Permanent exhibits. Four major shows annually at Horticultural Hall and Show House. (Daily) **FREE**

Goodman Theater. *170 N Dearborn. Phone 312/443-3800; fax 312/443-3821.*

Grant Park. *331 E Randolph St. Stretching from Randolph St to McFetridge Dr, in the Loop.* Chicago's downtown park. Contains the James C. Petrillo Music Shell. (See SPECIAL EVENTS) Also in Grant Park is

> **Buckingham Fountain.** *331 E Randolph St. Grant at Lake Shore Dr between Balboa and Jackson. Phone 312/742-7529.* When the World Cup was held in Chicago in 1994, foreign visitors identified the Buckingham Fountain as the "Bundy fountain" because of its prominent place in the opening credits of the TV show *Married with Children*. That notoriety aside, Buckingham Fountain is an integral part of Chicago and one of the largest fountains in the world. Located in Grant Park at Columbus Dr and Congress Pkwy, the fountain was given to the city by Kate Buckingham in 1927 in honor of her brother. Every minute, 133 jets spray approximately 14,000 gallons of water as high as 150 feet into the air. Every hour on the hour, there's a 20-minute water display (accompanied, at dusk, by lights and music). For locals, the fountain marks the changing seasons; when it's turned on, to much fanfare, it heralds the beginning of summer, and when it's turned off, it signals that the dreaded Chicago winter will soon follow. (May-Oct 1, daily) **FREE**

> **Petrillo Music Shell.** *Columbus Dr and Jackson Blvd (60604). Phone 312/742-7530.*

Gray Line Tours. *Phone 312/251-3107.* Tours depart from 17 E Monroe St.

Green Mill. *4802 N Broadway. Phone 773/878-5552.* The oldest jazz club in America, the Green Mill is located in the still-dicey Uptown neighborhood. It's more than a great place to hear jazz; it's also a chance to step back in time. With a vintage sign out front and a gorgeous carved bar inside, this former speakeasy of the Capone gang reeks of atmosphere (and cigarettes) of a bygone era. The jazz, however, is strictly contemporary, showcasing some of the most acclaimed musicians working today, from international performers to local luminaries such as Patricia Barber, Kurt Elling, and Von Freeman. On weeknights, you might find swing or a big band; on weekend nights, several acts pack in aficionados until the wee hours; and on Sundays, you can experience the Poetry Slam (the nation's first, hosted by Marc Smith, the "godfather" of poetry slams), where area poets test their mettle against audience reaction. (Daily) **$$$**

Hawthorne Race Course. *3501 S Laramie Ave. Phone 708/780-3700.*

Haymarket Riot Monument. *1300 W Jackson St.* Commemorates the riot that killed seven policemen when a bomb exploded during a labor strike on May 4, 1886. Statue still stirs passions over labor issues.

Holy Name Cathedral. *735 N State St, Near N Side. Phone 312/787-8040.* (Roman Catholic) Neo-Gothic architecture. (Daily) Guided tours, reservations required.

Illinois Institute of Technology. *3300 S Federal St, S Side. Phone 312/567-3000.* (1892) 6,000 students. Campus designed by Mies van der Rohe.

International Museum of Surgical Science. *1524 N Lake Shore Dr. Phone 312/642-6502.* Housed in an old mansion, museum features exhibits on the history of surgery. Main exhibit on surgical implements circa 1900. (Tue-Sat 10 am-4 pm) **$$**

Jane Addams' Hull House. *800 S Halsted St, on campus of University of Illinois at Chicago, W Side. Phone 312/413-5353.* Two original Hull House buildings, restored Hull Mansion (1856) and dining hall (1905), which formed the nucleus of the 13-building settlement complex founded in 1889 by Jane Addams and Ellen Gates Starr, social welfare pioneers. Exhibits and presentations on the history of Hull House, the surrounding neighborhood, ethnic groups, and women's history. (Mon-Fri, also Sun afternoons; closed holidays) **FREE**

John G. Shedd Aquarium. *1200 S Lake Shore Dr, at Roosevelt Rd, Near S Side. Phone 312/939-2438.* (1930) The world's largest indoor aquarium features more than 8,000 freshwater and marine animals displayed in 200 naturalistic habitats; divers hand-feed fish, sharks, eels, and turtles several times daily in the 90,000-gallon Caribbean Reef exhibit. The Oceanarium re-creates a Pacific Northwest ecosystem with whales, dolphins, sea otters, and seals. A colony of penguins inhabit a Falkland Islands exhibit; Seahorse Symphony exhibit. Food service and gift shops. (Daily; closed Jan 1, Dec 25) Free admission Mon, Tue(Sept-Feb only). **$$$$**

The John Hancock Center. *875 N Michigan Ave. Near N Side. Phone 312/751-3681; toll-free 888/875-8439 (observatory).* Anchoring North Michigan Avenue is yet another undeniable Chicago landmark, the John Hancock Center, which at 1,127 feet and 100 floors is the world's 13th tallest building. Since completion in 1969, this innovative office/residential building with its distinctive exterior X bracing, which eliminated need for inner support beams, thus increasing usable space, has won numerous architectural awards. It also claims many notables, including the world's highest residence and the world's highest indoor swimming pool. The 94th floor observatory features an open-air skywalk, a history wall chronicling Chicago's growth, multilingual sky tours, and a 360-degree view that spans 80 miles and four states (Michigan, Indiana, Wisconsin, and Illinois). The best viewing is from sunset onward, when the sun shimmers on the skyline and lake. Visitors who want to extend the experience can dine at the Signature Room, an upscale restaurant located on the building's 95th floor. (Daily) **$$**

Lincoln Park. *Stockton Dr near Fullerton to North Ave, Near N side. Phone 312/742-7529.* Largest in Chicago, stretches almost the entire length of the north end of the city along the lake. Contains statues of Lincoln, Hans Christian Andersen, Shakespeare, and others; 9-hole golf course, driving range, miniture golf, bike and jogging paths, obstacle course, protected beaches. In the Park are

Lincoln Park Conservatory. *2400 N Stockton Dr (60614). Stockton Dr near Fullerton. Phone 312/742-7736.* Has four glass buildings, 18 propagating houses, and three acres of cold frames; formal and rock gardens; extensive collection of orchids. Four major flower shows annually at Show House. (Daily) **FREE**

Lincoln Park Zoo. *2200 Cannon Dr. W entrance, Webster Ave and Stockton Dr; E entrance, Cannon Dr off Fullerton Ave. Phone 312/742-2000; toll-free www.lpzoo.com.* The Lincoln Park Zoo may be small (just 35 acres), but it has so much going for it—it's free, it's open 365 days a year, and it's a leader in education and conservation—that this gem of a zoo is a big part of the Chicago experience. Not only can visitors enjoy seeing animals from around the world, including gorillas, big cats, polar bears, exotic birds, and reptiles, but they can do so in style among architecturally significant structures, beautiful gardens, and modern visitor facilities, all in a prime location in the heart of Chicago's famed Lincoln Park. Families can double their fun at the newly renovated "Farm in the Zoo," where children can milk cows, churn butter, groom goats, and experience a working farmhouse kitchen. Also available are paddle boat rentals on the adjacent lagoon, a restaurant, and special events like family sleepovers, trick-or-treating on Halloween, and caroling to the animals at Christmas. (Daily) **FREE**

Loyola University. *Lake Shore campus, 6525 N Sheridan Rd. Downtown campus, 820 N Michigan Ave, N Side. Phone 773/274-3000 (Lake Shore campus;) 312/915-7100 (Downtown campus).* (1870) 14,300 students. Martin d'Arcy Museum of Art (Tue-Sat; closed holidays, semester breaks). Fine Arts Gallery of the Edward Crown Center; exhibits (Mon-Fri; closed holidays).

Lyric Opera of Chicago. *20 N Wacker Dr. Phone 312/419-0033.* Civic Opera House.

⭐ **The Magnificent Mile.** *Michigan Ave between Oak St and the Chicago River.* Although often compared to Rodeo Drive in Beverly Hills and Fifth Avenue in New York because of the quality and quantity of its stores, Chicago's Michigan Avenue has a vibe all its own. Known as the Magnificent Mile, this 1-mile flower-lined stretch between Oak Street and the Chicago River boasts 3.1 million square feet of retail space, 460 stores, 275 restaurants, 51 hotels, numerous art galleries, and two museums, all set among some of Chicago's most architecturally significant buildings. In addition, there are four vertical malls, including the granddaddy of them all, a newly renovated Water Tower Place; high-end department stores like Neiman Marcus, Saks Fifth Avenue, and Marshall Field's; and international retailers like Hermes, Cartier, Armani, Tiffany, and Burberry. Some of the most popular specialty stores on the "Boul Mich'" are the giant Niketown and Sony stores; American Girl Place, just off the avenue; and the new Bloomingdale's Home Store in the renovated Medinah Temple. (Daily; closed major holidays) Also on the magnificient Mile are

900 North Michigan Shops. *900 N Michigan Ave. Phone 312/915-3916.* More than 70 shops and restaurants, including Bloomingdale's and Gucci, surround a marble atrium in this mall that's adjacent to the Four Seasons. (Mon-Sat 10 am-7 pm, Sun noon-6 pm; closed holidays)

Chicago Place. *700 N Michigan Ave. Phone 312/642-4811.* This 8-story vertical mall has more than 45 stores and several restaurants. (Mon-Fri 10 am-7 pm, Sat 10 am-6 pm, Sun noon-5 pm; closed Jan 1, Easter, Dec 25)

Niketown. *669 N Michigan Ave. Phone 312/642-6363.* Since opening in 1993, this five-story sports store has become a major tourist attraction. It includes Nike Museum, a video theater, display of athletic gear worn by Michael Jordan, and a basketball court with a 28-foot likeness of His Airness. (Daily; closed holidays)

Water Tower Place. *835 N Michigan Ave. Phone 312/440-3165.* This atrium mall connected to the Ritz-Carlton has more than 100 shops, including Chicago favorite Marshall Field's, plus restaurants and a movie theater complex. (Mon-Sat 10 am-7 pm, Sun noon-6 pm; closed holidays)

Marina City. *300 N State St, N side of Chicago River, Near N Side.* (1959-1967). Condominium and commercial building complex with marina and boat storage. Includes two 550-foot-tall cylindrical buildings; home of House of Blues club and hotel. Designed by Bertrand Goldberg Associates; one of the most unusual downtown living-working complexes in the US.

Marriott Lincolnshire Resort Theater. *10 Marriott Dr. Lincolnshire. Phone 847/634-0200; fax 847/634-7022.*

Marshall Field's. *111 N State St. In the Loop. Phone 312/781-4483.* A Chicago landmark for more than a century and one of the most famous stores in the country. A traditional Chicago meeting place is under its clock, which projects over the sidewalk. On one side is an inner court rising 13 stories; on the other is a 6-story rotunda topped by a Tiffany dome made of 1.6 million pieces of glass. (Daily; closed Thanksgiving, Dec 25)

Maywood Park Race Track. *8600 W North Ave, in Maywood, I-290, exit 1st Ave N. Phone 708/343-4800; fax 708/348-2564.* Pari-mutuel harness racing. Nightly Mon, Wed, Fri. Also TV simulcast thoroughbred racing (daily).

McCormick Place Convention Complex. *2301 S Martin Luther King Dr. E 23rd St and S Lake Shore Dr, S Side. Phone 312/791-7000; fax 312/791-6543.* Nation's largest exposition and meeting complex. Exhibits, special shows, Arie Crown Theatre (see also ARIE CROWN THEATER), and restaurant facilities.

Merchandise Mart. *222 Merchandise Mart Plaza. On Wells St at the Chicago River, Near N side. Phone 312/527-7600.* The world's largest commercial building, built in 1930; restaurants, shopping, and special events; Apparel Center adjacent.

Mercury, the Skyline Cruiseline. *Wacker Dr & Michigan Ave (S side of Michigan Ave Bridge). Phone 312/332-1353.* Offers 1-hour, 1 1/2-hour, and 2-hour lake and river cruises; also Sun brunch, dinner, and luncheon cruises. (May-Oct) **$$$$**

Mexican Fine Arts Center Museum. *1852 W 19th St. Phone 312/738-1503.* Showcase of Mexican art and heritage; museum features revolving exhibits of contemporary and classical works by renowned Mexican artists. (Tue-Sun 10 am-5 pm; closed Mon, holidays) **FREE**

Monadnock Building. *53 W Jackson Blvd, in the Loop.* (1889-1891) Highest wall-bearing building in Chicago was, at the time of its construction, the tallest and largest office building in the world. It is now considered one of the masterworks of the Chicago school of architecture. Designed by Burnham & Root; south addition by Holabird & Roche (1893).

Museum of Contemporary Art. *220 E Chicago Ave. Near N Side. Phone 312/280-2660.* Just a half a block east of Michigan Avenue in the tiny Streeterville neighborhood lies Chicago's Museum of Contemporary Art, one of the nation's largest facilities dedicated to post-1945 works. With a large, rotating permanent collection and a reputation for cutting-edge exhibits, the museum showcases some of the finest artists working today, whether in painting, sculpture, video and film, photography, or performance. The museum, in a new building since 1995, also positions itself as a cultural center, and its 300-seat theater hosts a variety of programming, from lectures and films to experimental theater and music festivals. An annual highlight is the 24-hour summer solstice celebration, which attracts art lovers and partygoers in droves. The museum also has a stellar gift shop and bookstore, a restaurant run by Wolfgang Puck, and a terraced sculpture garden with views of Lake Michigan that serves as a peaceful urban sanctuary just steps from the heart of Chicago. (Tue-Sun; closed Jan 1, Thanksgiving, Dec 25) Free admission Tue. **$$**

Museum of Contemporary Photography. *600 S Michigan Ave. Phone 312/663-5554.* Museum affiliated with Columbia College Chicago focuses on photography from 1950 to the present. (Mon-Sat) **FREE**

Museum of Holography/Chicago. *1134 W Washington Blvd, West Side. Phone 312/226-1007.* Permanent collection of holograms (3-dimensional images made with lasers) featuring pieces from the US and many European and Asian countries. (Wed-Sun, afternoons; closed holidays) **$$**

⭐ **Museum of Science and Industry.** *5700 S Lake Shore Dr. 57th St and Lake Shore Dr, S Side. Phone 773/684-1414.* More than 2,000 exhibit units use visitor interaction to illustrate scientific principles and industrial concepts. Among the many displays are the "Idea Factory,"; Apollo 8 spacecraft; miniature circus with 22,000 hand-carved pieces; chick incubator; coal mine; captured German U-boat, and 16-foot-tall, walk-through human heart model. (Daily; closed Dec 25) Free admission Thur. **$$$** Also here is

> **Crown Space Center.** *5700 S Lake Shore Dr.* This 35,000-square-foot space center houses the latest in space exhibitions; 334-seat Omnimax Theater in a 76-foot diameter projection dome. **$$$**

Music Box Theatre. *3733 N Southport Ave (60613). Phone 773/871-6604.* Those raised on multiplex cinemas are in for a treat at the Music Box Theatre, a neighborhood art house that attracts a loyal following, and not just because it's one of the few places in town devoted to independent, foreign, cult, documentary, and classic films. The Music Box is one of the last surviving old-time movie palaces. Built in 1929 and restored in 1983, its style is what one architectural critic called "an eclectic mélange of Italian, Spanish, and Pardon-My-Fantasy put together with passion," including a ceiling replete with "twinkling stars and moving cloud formations, plus a genuine organ, still played on Saturday nights and at special events. The theater is also home to periodic productions of *The Rocky Horror Picture Show,* sing-a-longs to classics (for example, *The Sound of Music*), and screenings for the Chicago International Film Festival, usually held in October. The theater is located in trendy Lakeview, a neighborhood of small shops and diverse restaurants. (Daily) **$$**

National Vietnam Veterans Art Museum. *1801 S Indiana. 1801 S Indiana, S Side. Phone 312/326-0270.* Houses more than 500 pieces of fine art created by artists who served in the Vietnam War. Interactive dioramas, artifacts; museum store, cafe. (Tue-Sun; closed holidays). **$$**

Navy Pier. *600 E Grand Ave, near N Side. Phone 312/595-7437.* Known as one of the city's top venues for families, Navy Pier, an old naval station renovated during the 1990s and converted into an urban playground, seems to offer something for everyone. Its most visible attraction, the 150-foot-high Ferris wheel, offers spectacular views of the lake and skyline and is modeled after the world's first, built in Chicago in 1893. During the summer, families flock to the pier for boat cruises, free outdoor concerts, and fireworks; during the winter they can ice skate (free). Year-round, visitors can enjoy an IMAX theater, a Shakespeare theater, a stained-glass museum, a children's museum, shops and kiosks, a food court, and six restaurants catering to tastes from casual "street food" to "formal and pricey" fare (see also RIVA). Many of the pier's attractions are free, but parking can be expensive; instead, take advantage of the city's free trolley service from downtown hotels and other locations. (Daily) **FREE** Also here is

> **The Children's Museum at Navy Pier.** *700 E Grand Ave. Phone 312/527-1000.* Chock full of interesting and interactive activities, the Children's Museum at Navy Pier strikes a near-perfect balance between fun and learning. Plus, with an ever-changing slate of exhibits and activities, it's the kind of place that children can return to again and again. Overall, the exhibits encourage imagination, exploration, curiosity, and learning through experience; there's a play maze, an inventing lab where kids can perform experiments, and Treehouse Trails for children under 5 to explore the great outdoors. A recent exhibit called "Face to Face" dealt with prejudice and discrimination, and an Afghan children's art exhibit made the realities of life during wartime real for American kids. The programming is stellar, and in any given week the museum may have programs such as trilingual storytelling (English,

Spanish, and American Sign Language), sing-a-longs, art shows, ethnic festivals and celebrations, theater shows, art classes, and even a clown college for kids. (Daily; closed Mon Labor Day-Memorial Day) **$$**

The Newberry Library. *60 W Walton St, near N Side. Phone 312/943-9090.* (1887) Houses more than 1.4 million volumes and several million manuscripts. Internationally famous collections on the Renaissance, Native Americans, the Chicago Renaissance, the American West, local and family history, music history, history of printing, calligraphy, cartography, others. Exhibits open to the public. Admission to reading rooms by registration. (Tue-Sat; closed holidays) Tours (Thur, Sat). **FREE**

North Shore Center for the Performing Arts. *9501 Skokie Blvd. Phone 847/673-6300; fax 847/679-1879.*

Northwestern University Chicago Campus. *357 E Chicago Ave. Lake Shore Dr and Chicago Ave, Near N Side. Phone 312/503-8649.* (1920) 5,400 students. Schools of Medicine, Law, Dentistry, and University College

Oak Street. *Michigan Ave & Oak St, near North side.* The block between Michigan Ave and N Rush St is lined with small shops that specialize in high fashion and the avant-garde from around the world.

The Oprah Winfrey Show. *1058 W Washington St. Phone 312/591-9222 (reservations).* One of the most coveted tickets in town is for *The Oprah Winfrey Show,* taped at Harpo Studios in the West Loop area. It may be tough to plan a visit to Chicago around the show, because it generally tapes only on Tuesdays, Wednesdays, and Thursdays from September through early December and from January to June. The only way to get tickets is to call the studio's Audience Department in advance at 312/591-9222. Note that security for the show is tight and that you must be over 18 to attend (although teens ages 16 and 17 can attend with a parent or legal guardian if they bring a copy of their birth certificate for check-in). If you do get to a taping, allow yourself extra time to explore the surrounding neighborhood. Amid loft condos and meatpacking plants, you'll find some of the hottest restaurants and bars in the city. **FREE**

Oriental Institute Museum. *1155 E 58th St, on University of Chicago campus, S Side. Phone 773/702-9514.* Outstanding collection of archaeological material illustrating the art, architecture, religion, and literature from the ancient Near East. Lectures, workshops, free films (Sun; limited hours). Museum (Tue-Sun; closed Jan 1, Thanksgiving, Dec 25). **FREE**

Our Lady of Sorrows Basilica. *3121 W Jackson Blvd, W side. Phone 773/638-0159.* (1890-1902) Worth seeing are the Shrine Altar of the Seven Holy Founders of the Servites (main altar of Carrara marble) and the beautiful English Baroque steeple, chapels, paintings, and other architectural ornamentations (daily). Tours (by reservation).

Outdoor Art.

Batcolumn. *600 W Madison St. Outside the Harold Washington Social Security Administration Building plaza, in the Loop.* (1977) Designed by artist Claes Oldenburg. This 100-foot-tall, 20-ton welded steel sculpture resembles a baseball bat, set in a concrete base.

Flamingo. *Federal Center Plaza, Adams and Dearborn sts, in the Loop.* (1974) Sculptor Alexander Calder's stabile is 53 feet high and weighs 50 tons.

The Four Seasons. *First National Plaza, Monroe and Dearborn sts, in the Loop.* (1974) This 3,000-square-foot mosaic designed by Marc Chagall contains more than 320 different shades and hues of marble, stone, granite, and glass.

Miro's Chicago. *The Brunswick Building, 69 W Washington, in the Loop.* (1981) The structure, made of steel, wire mesh, concrete, broze, and ceramic tile, is 39 feet tall.

Picasso Sculpture. *50 W Washington St. At Daley Center* No one's really sure what it is, perhaps a horse, a bird, or a woman, but people around the world know what the Picasso sculpture outside Daley Plaza (50 W Washington) represents: Chicago. Since its unveiling in 1967, this 50-foot-tall, 162-ton steel work of art has become an unofficial logo and an unlikely icon for the city. Some consider it a miracle that the city's famously conservative mayor, Richard J. Daley (aka "the Boss"), would commission a work of cubist abstract expressionism from the bad boy of modern art, but with one of Chicago's leading architecture firms as liaison, the project came to fruition. It led the way for other major public art projects, including the **Miro statue** (69 W Washington), **the Chagall mosaic** (First National Plaza), **Calder's Flamingo** (Federal Center), and the **Dubuffet outside the Thompson Center** (100 W Randolph), that give the Loop its distinctive and accessible feel.

Untitled Sounding Sculpture. *200 E Randolph. Amoco Building, 200 E Randolph, in the Loop.* (1975) Unique "sounding sculpture" set in reflecting pool. Designed by Harry Bertoia.

Peace Museum. *100 N Central Park Ave. Garfield Park Dome, 1 block E and 4 blocks N of Independence St exit of Eisenhower Expressway. Phone 773/638-6450.* Exhibits focusing on the role of the arts, the sciences, labor, women, minorities, and religious institutions on issues of war and peace and on the contributions of individual peacemakers. (Tue-Fri; schedule varies)

Peggy Notebaert Nature Museum. *2430 N Cannon Dr. At Lake Shore Dr and Fullerton Pkwy. Phone 773/755-5100.*

Hands-on exploration of nature is the mission of the Peggy Notebaert Nature Museum. This newest of Chicago museums, built in 1999 as an offshoot of the Chicago Academy of Sciences, Chicago's first museum, takes its mission seriously. Here, visitors and city dwellers alike can connect with the natural world via indoor exhibits and outdoor adventures. Children can dress up like animals, adults can explore the Midwestern landscape, and urbanites can forget their cares while surrounded by wildflowers. Permanent exhibits include a 28-foot-high butterfly haven, a city science interactive display, a family water lab, a wilderness walk, and a children's gallery designed for kids ages 3 to 8. Special exhibits are real kiddie pleasers, judging by two recent ones: Grossology: The Impolite Science of the Human Body and Monster Creepy Crawlies. The museum is beautifully situated in Lincoln Park and is within walking distance of the Lincoln Park Zoo, the lagoon, and Fullerton Ave beach. (Daily) Free admission Thur. **$$**

Pheasant Run Dinner Theatre. *4051 E Main St. W on IL 64 in St. Charles. Phone 630/584-6300.*

Polish Museum of America. *984 N Milwaukee Ave, near N Side. Phone 773/384-3352.* Polish culture, folklore, immigration; art gallery, archives, and library; Paderewski and Kosciuszko rooms. (Closed Thur; Jan 1, Good Friday, Dec 25) **DONATION**

Prairie Avenue Historic District. *1800 S Prairie Ave, between 18th and Cullerton sts, S Side. Phone 312/326-1480.* Area where millionaires lived during the 1800s. **The Clarke House** (circa 1835), the oldest house still standing in the city, has been restored and now stand at a site near its original location. **The Glessner House** (1886), 1800 S Prairie Ave, is owned and maintained by the Chicago Architecture Foundation. Designed by architect Henry Hobson Richardson, the house has 35 rooms, many of which are restored with original furnishings; interior courtyard. 2-hour guided tour of both houses (Wed-Sun). Other houses on the cobblestone street are **Kimball House** (1890), 1801 S Prairie Ave, replica of a French chateau; **Coleman House** (circa 1885), 1811 S Prairie Ave, and **Keith House** (circa 1870), 1900 S Prairie Ave. Architectural tours. Free admission on Wed. **$$$**

Ravinia Festival. *Phone 847/266-5000.*

Richard J. Daley Center and Plaza. *50 W Washington St (60602). Randolph and Clark sts, in the Loop. Phone 312/603-7980.* This 31-story, 648-foot building houses county and city courts and administrative offices. In the plaza is the Chicago Picasso sculpture; across Washington St is the Chicago Miro sculpture.

River North Gallery District. With the highest concentration of art galleries outside Manhattan, Chicago's River North Gallery District, just a short walk from Michigan Ave and the Loop, offers world-class art in a stylish setting of renovated warehouses and upscale restaurants. Although the district is loosely bordered by the Chicago River, Orleans St, Chicago Ave, and State St, you'll find the majority of galleries on Superior and Franklin streets. If you happen to be in town on the second Friday of the month, wander over to the opening-night receptions (5 pm to 7 pm) for a glass of wine and a glimpse of Chicago's black-clad art scenesters. Serious collectors may want to visit Carl Hammer and Judy Saslow for Outsider Art, Ann Nathan for contemporary art, Douglas Dawson and Primitive Artworks for tribal art, Manifesto for high-end furniture, Aldo Castillo for global art, and Douglas Rosin for 20th-century modern art. (Tue-Sat) **FREE**

Robie House. *5757 S Woodlawn Ave, near University of Chicago campus, S Side. Phone 773/834-1847.* (1909) Designed by Frank Lloyd Wright, this may be the ultimate example of the Prairie house. Tours (Daily; closed holidays). **$$**

Rockefeller Memorial Chapel. *5850 S Woodlawn Ave, on University of Chicago campus. Phone 773/702-2100.* Designed by Bertram Grosvenor Goohue Associates; noted for its Gothic construction, vaulted ceiling, 8,600-pipe organ and 72-bell carillon. Guided tours by appointment.

The Rookery. *209 S La Salle St, in the Loop.* (1886) Oldest remaining steel-skeleton skyscraper in the world. Designed by Burnham & Root, the remarkable glass-encased lobby was remodeled in 1905 by Frank Lloyd Wright.

Roosevelt University. *Entrance at 430 S Michigan Ave, in the Loop. Phone 312/341-3500.* (1945) 6,400 students. Auditorium Building designed by Louis Sullivan and engineered by Dankmar Adler in 1889.

Royal George Theater. *1641 N Halsted St. Phone 312/988-9000.*

⭐ **Sears Tower.** *233 S Wacker Dr. In the Loop. Phone 312/875-9696 (skydeck).* It seems fitting that the town that gave birth to the skyscraper should lay claim to North America's tallest building (and the world's tallest until 1996). Built in 1974 by Skidmore, Owings & Merrill, the 110-story Sears Tower soars 1/4 mile (1,450 feet) above the city, making it the most prominent building in the skyline. The building, which houses 10,000 office workers and hosts 25,000 visitors daily, was constructed of black anodized aluminum in nine bundled square tubes, an innovation that provides both wind protection and the necessary support for its extraordinary height. The elevators that whisk visitors to the 103rd floor observatory are among the world's fastest, and well worth the ride. The observatory offers panoramic views of the city; on a clear day you can easily see 35 miles away. During the height of tourist season, the summer, expect long waits. (Daily) **$$**

Second City. *1616 and 1608 N Wells St. Phone 312/337-3992 (1616 N Wells St); 312/642-8189 (1608 N Wells St).*

Shoreline Marine Company. *474 N Lake Shore Dr. Departures from Shedd Aquarium, afternoons, and Buckingham Fountain, evenings. Phone 312/222-9328.* 30-minute tour of lakefront. (May-Sept, daily) **$$$**

Shubert Theater. *22 W Monroe St. Phone 312/977-1710; fax 312/977-1740.*

Six Flags Great America. (see).

Spertus Museum. *618 S Michigan Ave. in the Loop. Phone 312/322-1747.* Permanent collection of ceremonial objects from many parts of the world; sculpture, graphic arts, and paintings; ethnic materials spanning centuries; changing exhibits in fine arts; documentary films and photographs. Rosenbaum Artifact Center has hands-on exhibits on ancient Near East archaeology. (Mon-Fri, Sun; closed Sat, holidays, and Jewish holidays) Free admission Fri. **$$**

Spirit of Chicago. *455 E Illinois St. Navy Pier. Phone 312/836-7899.* Lunch, brunch, dinner, and moonlight cruises; entertainment. (Year-round) **$$$$**

Sportsman's Park Race Track. *3301 S Laramie Ave. Approximately 7 miles W. Phone 773/242-1121.*

State Street Shopping District. *In the Loop between Lake St and Jackson Blvd.* Yes, State Street is "that great street" alluded to in song. Once dubbed the busiest intersection in the world, State Street today is a Loop shopping mecca anchored by Chicago's two most famous department retailers, Marshall Field's and Carson Pirie Scott. These flagship stores have been joined by national chains, discount stores, and specialty shops. More interesting than the merchandise available for purchase, however, may be the street's architecture. Check out the graceful Louis Sullivan grillwork at Carson's main entrance, the Tiffany Dome inside Field's, and the exterior of the Hotel Burnham, a masterful renovation and restoration of the former Reliance Building, once termed "the crown jewel of Chicago architecture." For lunch, try Marshall Field's venerable Walnut Room or the Atwood Cafe (see also ATWOOD CAFE) in the Hotel Burnham. And if you need to meet up with someone, do so under the Marshall Field's clock at Washington and State as Chicagoans have done for generations. (Daily)

Steppenwolf Theater Company. *1650 N Halsted St (60614). At North Ave and Halsted; accessible by red line trains. Phone 312/335-1650.* One of the most acclaimed

theater groups in the country, Steppenwolf not only helped put Chicago theater on the map, but also gave many famous actors, including John Malkovich, Joan Allen, Gary Sinise, Laurie Metcalf, and John Mahoney, their start. The dozens of awards its shows and performers have won, including Tonys, Emmys, and Obies, belie its humble founding in a suburban church basement in 1974 by Sinise, Kinney, and Jeff Perry. Steppenwolf quickly become known for its risky choices and edgy performances, an approach critics aptly termed "rock-and-roll theater." Today, the company has its own state-of-the-art building in the Lincoln Park neighborhood (just a short cab or El train ride from downtown), which includes a studio space and a school and hosts several specialty series. Steppenwolf performances are almost uniformly excellent, with stunning sets, strong acting, and plenty of original material; theater lovers should try to reserve tickets as far in advance of their Chicago visit as possible.

Sur La Table. *50-54 E Walton St. Phone 312/337-0600.* In the 1970s, Seattle spawned this clearinghouse for hard-to-find kitchen gear, and it soon became known as a source for cookware, small appliances, cutlery, kitchen tools, linens, tableware, gadgets, and specialty foods. Sur La Table has since expanded to include cooking classes (**$$$$**), chef demonstrations, and cookbook author signings, as well as a catalog and online presence. Cooking connoisseurs discover such finds as cool oven mitts, zest graters, copper whisks, onion soup bowls, and inspired TV dinner trays. (Daily)

Swedish-American Museum Center. *5211 N Clark St. Phone 773/728-8111.* Pays tribute to Swedish heritage and history. Exhibits on Swedish memorabilia. (Tue-Sun)

Symphony Center. *220 S Michigan Ave, in the Loop. Phone 312/294-3000 (ticket information).* (1904) Historic Symphony Center is home of the Chicago Symphony Orchestra and stage for the Civic Orchestra of Chicago, chamber music groups, diverse musical attractions, and children's programs. Includes Buntrock Hall, a ballroom, rehearsal space, and restaurant.

Terra Museum of American Art. *664 N Michigan Ave. Between Huron and Erie sts. Phone 312/664-3939.* Located in the heart of the Magnificent Mile on North Michigan Ave, the Terra Museum of Art is a small, accessible museum with a big mission: to promote a greater understanding of America's artistic and cultural heritage by acquiring, exhibiting, and interpreting original works of American art. The museum is the brainchild of the late Daniel J. Terra, a former US ambassador-at-large for cultural affairs, a successful businessman, and an avid art collector who originally started the museum in the northern suburb of Evanston and moved it downtown in 1987. In addition to special exhibits, the museum has a permanent collection that includes works by Georgia O'Keefe,

Winslow Homer, Mary Cassat, and James McNeill Whistler. Free public tours are offered at noon on weekdays, and on the first Sunday of every month children ages 5 to 12 and their parents can participate in a free family fair, which includes an interactive guided tour and a hands-on studio workshop. (Tue-Sun) **DONATION**

Theatre Building. *1225 W Belmont Ave. Phone 773/327-5252.*

United Center. *1901 W Madison St. Phone 312/455-4500; fax 312/455-4511.* Affectionately known as "the house that Michael built," the United Center replaced the cavernous Chicago Stadium in the mid-1990s as the home of Chicago Bulls professional basketball team. Even though the Blackhawks professional hockey team skates here and numerous concerts and special events are held here, the giant statue of Michael Jordan in front of the building's north entrance attests to the building's true provenance. Inside is shrine to the glory years of Chicago sports: hanging from the rafters are banners from the Bulls, six straight championship seasons; the Blackhawks, Stanley Cup wins; and a variety of retired jerseys, including Jordan's number 23. Although the Bulls aren't packing in the crowds the way they did when "his airness," as the local sportswriters called him, ruled the courts, a visit to the United Center enables you to see where history took place. Tours of the arena are available through the Guest Relations office. The United Center is accessible via public transportation, but because the neighborhood is in transition, it's probably safer to take a cab or to drive (there is ample parking close by).

Chicago Blackhawks. *1901 W Madison St. At the United Center. Phone 312/455-7000.* The other powerhouse team to make its home at the United Center is the Chicago Blackhawks, one of the oldest NHL teams in the league. Although their last Stanley Cup victory was in 1961, the Hawks have a loyal (and raucous) fan base that can contest the game as hotly in their seats as the players do on the ice. And although, like all professional sports contests, Blackhawks games are marketed as family events, you still get a sense that within the plush confines of new United Center lies the same rough-and-tumble crowd that rocked the old Chicago Stadium.

Chicago Bulls. *1901 W Madison S. At the United Center. Phone 312/455-4500.*

United States Post Office. *433 W Harrison. In the Loop. Phone 312/983-7550; 312/983-7527.* (1933) Largest in the world under one roof. Individuals may join 1 1/2-hour guided group tours (Mon-Fri, three tours daily; no tours holidays and Dec). No cameras, packages, or purses. Reservations required. **FREE**

University of Chicago. *5801 S Ellis Ave, S Side. Phone 773/702-8374.* (1892) 12,750 students. It was on this campus that Enrico Fermi produced the first sustained nuclear reaction. The University of Chicago also has had one of the highest number of Nobel Prize winners of any institution. The campus includes the Oriental Institute, Robie House, Rockefeller Memorial Chapel, and David and Alfred Smart Museum of Art, on Greenwood Ave (Tue-Sun; free; phone 773/702-0200). Guided 1-hour campus tours leave from 1212 E 59th St.

University of Illinois at Chicago. *1200 W Harrison. Near I-94 and I-290, W Side. Phone 312/996-4350.* (1965) 25,000 students. Comprehensive urban university. On campus is Jane Addams' Hull House.

Untouchable Tours. *610 N Clark St. Phone 773/881-1195.* Guided tour of gangster hot spots of 1920s and 1930s. Departs from 610 N Clark St. Tour with dinner and revue also available. (Daily; reservations strongly recommended) **$$$$**

Victory Gardens Theater. *2257 N Lincoln Ave. Phone 773/549-5788; fax 773/549-2779.*

Wabash Avenue. *Wabash Ave & Congress Pkwy. S of the river to Congress Ave, in the Loop.* This unique street, always in the shadow of elevated train tracks, is known for its many specialty stores—books, music, musical instruments, records, men's clothing, tobacco, etc.—as well as being the center of the wholesale and retail jewelry trade.

★ **Walking tours of Pullman Historic District.** *614 E 113th St. Phone 773/785-3828.* Built in 1880-1884 to house the workers at George M. Pullman's Palace Car Company, the original town was a complete model community with many civic and recreational facilities. Unlike most historic districts, 9/10 of the original buildings still stand. The 1 1/2-hour tours start at the Historic Pullman Center, 614 E 113th St. Tours (May-Oct, first Sun of month; two departures). **$$**

The Old Chicago Water Tower and Pumping Station. *806 N Michigan Ave (60611). Near N Side.* One of the few buildings to survive the Great Chicago Fire of 1871 that ravaged the city, the old Water Tower and the Chicago Avenue Pumping Station are rare monuments to Chicago's early history. Built in 1869 by W. W. Boyington and granted city landmark status in 1972, these gingerbready, castlelike gothic revival buildings house a visitor's center and a city gallery and recently have become the new home to the acclaimed Lookingglass Theater company. For first-time visitors to Chicago, the old Water Tower, located at North Michigan and Chicago aves in the heart of the Magnificent Mile, makes a good starting point for getting oriented. The visitor center is stocked with information about city attractions and tours and is just steps away from shopping, restaurants, hotels, museums, entertainment, and Lake Michigan beaches. (Daily; closed Thanksgiving, Dec 25) **FREE**

Wendella. *400 N Michigan Ave, at the Wrigley Building (NW side of Michigan Ave Bridge). Phone 312/337-1446.* 1-, 1 1/2, and 2-hour lake and river cruises. (Apr-mid-Oct, daily) **$$$$**

Wicker Park/Bucktown Neighborhood. *1608 N Milwaukee. Neighborhoods start at the intersection of North, Milwaukee, and Damen aves. Blue line; stop Damen. Phone 773/384-8672.* Just a short cab or El ride northwest of downtown Chicago is one of the city's liveliest and most diverse areas, the Wicker Park/Bucktown neighborhood. You may recognize it from the film *High Fidelity*, shot on location here. The area is home to artists and musicians, urban pioneers and hipsters, plus a wealth of trendy stores and restaurants. Start at the neighborhood's epicenter, the intersection of North, Milwaukee, and Damen aves. Within a several block radius, you'll find antique stores and thrift shops, art galleries, boutiques, design studios, day spas, nightclubs, coffeehouses, bars, and nationally recognized restaurants (including MOD and SOUL KITCHEN). Be sure to walk down Pierce and Hoyne st, where the beer barons lived, as well as around the park itself for a glimpse of the grand homes from this historic neighborhood's past, a combination of German, Polish, Ukrainian, and, more recently, Latino roots.

Wrigley Building. *410 N Michigan Ave. Near N Side. Phone 312/923-8080.* Perched on the north bank of the Chicago River on Michigan Ave, the sparkling white Wrigley Building has been one of Chicago's most recognized skyscrapers since its completion in 1924 by prominent architects Graham, Anderson, Probst, and White. The building's triangular shape is patterned after the Seville Cathedral's Giralda Tower in Spain, and its ornamental design is an adaptation of French Renaissance style. Note that the building is actually two towers linked by an open walkway at street level and two enclosed walkways on the third and 14th floors. Today, the building remains the headquarters of the Wrigley family of chewing gum fame, although other firms also rent office space. At night, the exterior, clad with more than 250,000 glazed terra-cotta tiles, is floodlit, making it one of the nation's major commercial lighting displays and one of the most highly visible symbols of the city. Unfortunately, no tours of the building's interior are available.

Wrigley Field. *1060 W Addison St. Phone 312/404-CUBS.* America's second-oldest National League ballpark is also one of its most unique, located within a vibrant city neighborhood where residents often watch games from their roof decks. While the Cubs' perpetual losing streak is a running joke in Chicago, it never keeps people away from the ballpark; during the summer, it's one of the hottest tickets in town, mostly because "the Friendly Confines," as it is known, offers the ultimate old-time baseball experience. The best place to sit is in the box seats just past first and third base, where the players in their bullpens will talk to the fans. If you want to catch a homerun, try the left field bleachers, especially during batting practice.

Be sure to walk to the upper deck at sunset for spectacular views of the city. After the game, you can continue the party at one of the dozens of bars and restaurants within walking distance of the park.

Chicago Cubs (MLB). *1060 W Addison St. Phone 773/404-CUBS. Wrigley Field.*

Special Events

Air and Water Show. *1600 N Lake Shore Dr. Phone 312/744-2400 (Chicago Office of Tourism).* The nation's largest 2-day air show, attracting more than 2 million people every August, is a free event and a favorite of kids and adults alike. There are daredevil pilots, parachute teams, and jets flying in formation, as well as a water-skiing and boat-jumping component for additional thrills. The great thing about this festival is that it's visible from almost everywhere along the Chicago lakefront. Grandstand seats for the water show are located at North Avenue Beach, but some of the best viewing points are farther north, at Montrose Harbor and at the point between Belmont and Addison. Mid-Aug. **FREE**

Around the Coyote Arts Festival. *1579 N Milwaukee Ave. At the intersection of Milwaukee, North, and Damen aves. (Blue line train-Damen stop) Phone 773/342-6777.* With one of the highest concentrations of artists in the country residing in the Wicker Park/Bucktown neighborhood, it made sense to find a way to showcase their work. That's exactly what Paris art dealer Jim Happy-Delpesh did when he came back to Chicago in 1989. Although the festival revolves around the visual artists, it also encompasses cutting-edge dance, theater, poetry, film and video, fashion, and furniture design. Typically, the timing of the festival, held the second weekend in September, results in glorious early fall weather, and tens of thousands of people walk through the neighborhood visiting galleries, group shows, the Flat Iron Arts building, and artists' homes and studios. And because the neighborhood is spilling over with hip boutiques and dozens of trendy restaurants and outdoor cafés, many people make a day of it. A smaller winter version of the festival is held in February. Second weekend in Sept. **FREE**

Art Chicago. *600 E Grand Ave. Phone 312/587-3300. Navy Pier.* Worldwide artists' exhibition. Mid-May.

Chicago Auto Show. *2301 S Lake Shore Dr. Phone 312/744-3370. McCormick Place.* Hundreds of foreign and domestic cars are displayed. Second weekend in Feb.

Chicago Blues Fest. *331 E Randolph St. Phone 312/774-6630 (Chicago Office of Tourism). Grant Park.* In a city virtually synonymous with the blues, Chicago's annual Blues Fest, held in late May/early June, is the crème de la crème of blues festivals, attracting local stars such as Buddy Guy, Koko Taylor, Otis Rush, Sugar Blue, and Son Seals as well as national names like Bo Diddley, Ruth Brown, Howlin' Wolf, Muddy Waters, Honeyboy

Edwards, and the North Mississippi Allstars. With such a wealth of local talent, even the small stages and daytime shows rival the best blues clubs in the United States. Low-key and racially diverse, this free outdoor festival attracts more than 600,000 visitors over its four-day run. It's a great place to experience a true cross-section of the city while enjoying barbecue, the start of summer, and the best in traditional and contemporary blues music. Late May/early June. **FREE**

The Chicago Humanities Festival. *500 N Dearborn St, Suite 1028. Phone 312/661-1028.* For years, this festival was one of the best-kept secrets in Chicago: world-renowned authors, scholars, poets, policymakers, artists, and performers would gather for a weekend in November to celebrate the power of ideas in human culture and the role of the humanities in our daily lives. Dozens of lectures, performances, panels, and seminars, featuring names like Gore Vidal, Mira Nair, V. S. Naipul, Arthur Miller, Germaine Greer, Stephen Sondheim, and Robert Pinsky, were available to the public for just $5. Now, in its 13th year, the festival lasts for two weeks, features hundreds of events, and takes on a particular theme. For example, 2003 is Saving + Spending; past themes have included Brains + Beauty, Crime & Punishment, Work & Play, Love & Marriage, and He/She. Tickets are still only $5 per event, yet now it's better to purchase them in advance since the secret is out. Two weeks in fall. **$**

Chicago International Film Festival. *32 W Randolph St. Phone 312/425-9400 (24-hour hotline).* New films shown throughout city. Three weeks in Oct.

Chicago Jazz Fest. *331 E Randolph St. In Grant Park. Phone 312/774-6630 (Chicago Office of Tourism).* Held each Labor Day weekend for the past 25 years, this event is worth planning a trip to Chicago around. During the four days of this most prestigious of US jazz festivals, Grant Park becomes a giant outdoor jazz café with more than 300,000 people in attendance. Lesser-known and local artists perform during the day on the small stages near the food concession area, but the main headliners, world-class jazz musicians such as Herbie Hancock, Cassandra Wilson, Betty Carter, Wayne Shorter, and Roy Hargrove, take the main stage at the Petrillo Music Shell after 5 pm. You need to arrive early to get a seat near the stage, but most folks prefer to picnic on the lawn, enjoying the perfect skyline views and listening to the strategically placed speakers. Labor Day weekend. **FREE**

Chicago to Mackinac Races. *400 E Monroe St. Phone 312/744-3370.* On Lake Michigan. Third weekend in July.

Grant Park July 3 Concert. *235 S Columbus. Phone 312/744-3370. At Petrillo Music Shell.* Lakefront blazes with cannon flashes as the Grant Park Symphony welcomes Independence Day with Tchaikovsky's 1812 Overture; fireworks. July 3.

Grant Park Music Festival. *235 S Columbus. Phone 312/742-4763. At Petrillo Music Shell.* Concerts Wed, Fri, Sat, late June-Sept. **FREE**

The Magnificent Mile Lights Festival. *N Michigan Ave. Phone 312/409-5560.* As a kickoff to the holiday season, for the last 13 years the North Michigan Avenue Association has sponsored the Magnificent Lights Festival, during which the avenue's trademark tiny white lights get turned on to much fanfare. Generally held the weekend before Thanksgiving, the festival has grown to become a family day, starting with carolers, gingerbread decorating, ice-carving displays, Disney character stage shows, and a lively procession down Michigan Avenue, culminating in the lighting and fireworks spectacular. Attendance is usually high; of course, all depends on Chicago's unpredictable winter weather. Late Nov. **FREE**

Marshall Field's Holiday Window Displays. *111 N State St. Phone 312/781-1000.* Every holiday season, children and adults alike flock to Marshall Field's State St store to gaze in wonder at the elaborate and magical window displays. It's a Chicago ritual to line up outside the windows, three, four, and five deep, the day after Thanksgiving for the unveiling of the new season's displays. Although Field's has been delighting Chicagoans for more than a century with its innovative decorations, not until 1946 did its stores feature "stories" from a reenactment of "Twas the Night Before Christmas" to recent tales of Harry Potter, that progress from window to window. To avoid the crowds, visit right after Christmas. When you've stood out in the cold long enough, treat yourself to lunch in the store's elegant Walnut Room, another Chicago holiday tradition, where every table offers a view of its famous 40-plus-foot Christmas tree. Mid-Nov-mid-Jan.

Navy Pier Art Fair. *331 E Randolph St. Phone 312/744-3370. At Navy Pier.* Month-long exhibit of local artists' work. Jan. **FREE**

Spring Flower Show. *300 N Central Ave. Phone 312/746-5100.* Citywide, most notably at the Lincoln Park Conservatory. Apr.

St. Patrick's Day Parade. *Downtown Chicago. Phone 312/744-3370.* Chicago's St. Patrick's Day parade is famous around the world, not because of its size (although it is one of the largest) or its spirit (it is one of the rowdiest), but for the fact that on the day of the parade, the city dyes the Chicago River green, a tradition started during the early 1960s. If nothing else, this tells you how seriously Chicago takes the holiday. Held annually on the Saturday closest to St. Patrick's Day, the parade features dozens of bands, thousands of Irish step dancers, a multitude of floats, representatives of unions and local organizations, politicians, dignitaries, and many a surprise guest—often famous people with Chicago roots, all "wearin' the green." Mostly, however, the parade is one big party for hundreds of thousands of Chicagoans and visitors alike, where everyone gets to be Irish, at least for an afternoon. Weekend closest to St. Patrick's Day. **FREE**

Taste of Chicago. *331 E Randolph St. Phone 312/774-6630 (Chicago Office of Tourism).* What started out more than 20 years ago as way to sample cuisines from some of the city's best-known restaurants has become an all-out food fest and Fourth of July celebration that attracts more than 3.5 million visitors a year and features booths from more than 50 area vendors. At this 10-day event, you can stick to Taste favorites, Lou Malnati's pizza, Eli's cheesecake, Robinson's ribs, giant turkey drumsticks, and sautéed goat meat and plantains from Vee-Vee's African restaurant, or indulge in more refined specialties, like coconut lime sorbet, duck with lingonberries, grilled lobster tail, and alligator on a stick. In addition to food, you'll find free live music by big-name headliners, amusement park rides, and even a parent helper tent with free diapers. The crowds can get oppressive, so the earlier in the day you go, the better; don't forget to bring water, sunscreen, patience, and, perhaps, some wetnaps. Also try to buy food tickets in advance to avoid long lines. Late June-early July. **FREE**

Venetian Night. *Monroe St Harbor. Phone 312/747-2474.* Monroe St Harbor. Venetian aquatic parade, fireworks. Late July. **FREE**

Winter Delights. *Citywide. Mayor's Office of Special Events. Phone 312/744-3315.* tests. First 2 weeks in Feb.

Motel/Motor Lodge

★★**COURTYARD BY MARRIOTT.** *6610 S Cicero Ave, Bedford Park (60638). Phone 708/563-0200; toll-free fax 708/728-2841. www.courtyard.com/chicm.* 174 rooms, 5 story. Pet accepted. Check-out noon, check-in 3 pm. TV; cable (premium). In-room modem link. Restaurant, bar. Indoor pool, whirlpool. Airport transportation. Business center. Cr cds: A, C, D, DS, JCB, MC, V. **$**

⊡ ▨ ≈ ✕ 🛉 ▨ 🛉

★ **FAIRFIELD INN BY MARRIOTT MIDWAY.** *6630 S Cicero Ave (60638). Phone 708/594-0090; fax 708/728-2842. www.fairfieldinn.com.* 113 rooms, 5 story. Complimentary continental breakfast. Check-out noon, check-in 3 pm. TV; cable (premium). In-room modem link. In-house fitness room. Indoor pool; whirlpool. Free airport transportation. Cr cds: A, C, D, DS, ER, JCB, MC, V.

⊡ ≈ 🛉 ✕ SC

Hotels

★ ★ **ALLERTON CROWNE PLAZA.** *701 N Michigan Ave (60611). Phone 312/440-1500; toll-free 800/621-8311; fax 312/440-1819. www.allertoncrowneplaza.com.* 443 rooms, 25 story. Check-out noon, check-in 3 pm. TV; cable (premium), VCR available. Restaurant, bar. Babysit-

ting services available. In-house fitness room. Business center. Cr cds: A, C, D, DS, JCB, MC, V.

🛉 ▨ 🛉

★ ★ **BEST WESTERN INN OF CHICAGO.** *162 E Ohio St (60610). Phone 312/787-3100; toll-free 800/557-BEST; fax 312/573-3140. www.bestwestern.com.* 350 rooms, 22 story. Check-out noon, check-in 3 pm. TV. Restaurant, bar. In-house fitness room, health club privileges. Valet parking. Airport transportation. Cr cds: A, C, D, DS, JCB, MC, V. **$**

⊡ 🛉 ▨

★ ★ ★ **BURNHAM HOTEL.** *1 W Washington (60602). Phone 312/782-1111; toll-free 877/294-9712; fax 312/782-0899. www.burnhamhotel.com.* Reviving the historic Reliance building (predecessor of the modern skyscraper and early 1900s home of department store Carson Pirie Scott), the Burnham retains the integrity of the landmark architecture, integrating it with a whimsically elegant, clubby ambience. In the Loop near the downtown theater district, major museums, and parks, the hotel is appropriate for business or leisure travel. Rooms and suites offer dramatic views of the Chicago cityscape. The in-house Atwood Café serves upscale American comfort food (including breakfast, lunch, dinner, Sunday brunch, and pre-theater options). The hotel offers complimentary morning coffee, an evening wine reception, and 24-hour room service, as well as pampering pet treatments. 122 rooms, 15 story. Pet accepted. Check-out noon, check-in 3 pm. TV; cable (premium), VCR available. Room service 24 hours. Restaurant, bar. Babysitting services available. In-house fitness room. Cr cds: A, C, D, DS, JCB, MC, V. **$$$**

⊡ 🐾 🛉 ▨

★ ★ **COURTYARD BY MARRIOTT.** *30 E Hubbard St (60611). Phone 312/329-2500; toll-free 800/321-2211; fax 312/329-0293. www.courtyard.com.* 337 rooms, 15 story. Check-out noon, check-in 4 pm. TV; cable (premium). In-room modem link. Restaurant, bar, room service. In-house fitness room, health club privileges, spa, sauna. Indoor pool; whirlpool. Cr cds: A, C, D, DS, ER, JCB, MC, V. **$**

⊡ ≈ 🛉 ▨ SC

★ ★ ★ **CROWNE PLAZA-THE SILVERSMITH.** *10 S Wabash Ave (60603). Phone 312/372-7696; fax 312/372-7320. www.crowneplaza.com.* 143 rooms, 10 story. S, D $159-$300; each additional $20; under 17 free. Crib available. Complimentary coffee in rooms. Check-out 11 am. TV; cable (premium), VCR available. Refrigerators. Restaurant 6 am-midnight. Exercise room. Meeting rooms. Business center. Cr cds: A, C, D, DS, JCB, MC, V.

🛉 🛉

★ ★ ★ **THE DRAKE HOTEL.** *140 E Walton Pl (60611). Phone 312/787-2200; toll-free 800/553-7253; fax 312/787-0256. www.thedrakehotel.com.* A favorite landmark in the Michigan Avenue skyline, the Drake is a luxury lakefront hotel offering both spectacular views and a prime Gold Coast location. Built in 1920 as a summer resort, extensive renovations have preserved the ornate, elegant charm of this venerable classic. Amenities include executive floors, luxurious bathrooms, an exercise facility, a shopping arcade, and multiple dining options. The clubby Cape Cod Room is famous for its oyster bar and seafood, the Oak Terrace for its lakefront views, and the Coq d'Or for its piano bar. Afternoon tea in the lobby Palm Court and 24-hour room service are also offered. 537 rooms, 10 story. Check-out noon, check-in 3 pm. TV; cable (premium), VCR available. In-room modem link. Room service 24 hours. Restaurant, bar. In-house fitness room, health club privileges. Valet parking. Business center. Concierge, luxury level. Cr cds: A, C, D, DS, JCB, MC, V. **$$$**

ⓓ 🏌 🖼 🏃

★ ★ ★ **THE FAIRMONT CHICAGO.** *200 N Columbus Dr (60601). Phone 312/565-8000; fax 312/856-1032. www.fairmont.com.* Since opening in 1987, this Grant Park property has been host to a number of celebrities and political dignitaries. All 626 rooms and 66 suites have a rich yet simplified décor, spacious configuration, and individual design, including access to the on-site business center and nearby Lakeshore Athletic Club. The well-known Entre Nous restaurant serves splendid regional American cuisine with French accents. 626 rooms, 66 suites, 41 story. S, D $229-$359; each additional $35; suites $329-$3,600. Crib free. Pet accepted, some restrictions. Check-out 1 pm. TV; cable (premium), VCR available. In-room modem link. Bathroom phones, refrigerators, minibars. Valet service. Restaurant, bar 11-2 am; entertainment Tue-Sat. Room service 24 hours. Health club privileges $20/day. Golf, tennis nearby. Valet parking, in/out $33. Business center. Convention facilities. Concierge. Gift shop. Cr cds: A, C, D, DS, ER, JCB, MC, V.

ⓓ 🏊 🏌 🖼 🏃

★★★★★ **FOUR SEASONS HOTEL CHICAGO.** *120 E Delaware Pl (60611). Phone 312/280-8800; toll-free 800/332-3442; fax 312/280-9184. www.fourseasons.com/chicagofs.* Located in a 66-story building atop the world-renowned shops of 900 Michigan Avenue, the Four Seasons Hotel Chicago is a well-heeled shopper's paradise. More than 100 world-class stores, including Gucci and Bloomingdale's, await only steps from your door. This palatial skytop hotel exudes glamour, from its gleaming marble lobby with grand staircase to its regal accommodations. Even exercise is refined here, with a marvelous Roman-columned indoor pool. Occupying the 30th through 46th floors of the tower, the guest rooms afford jaw-dropping views of the magnificent skyline and Lake Michigan. From this vantage point, guests truly feel on top of the world. The accommodations have an opulent character enhanced by jewel tones, rich fabrics, and timeless furnishings. Body and mind are calmed at the spa, where a whimsical element inspires the decadent Champagne cocktail and caviar facials. 343 rooms, 66 story. Pet accepted. Check-out noon, check-in 3 pm. TV; cable (premium), VCR available. In-room modem link. Room service 24 hours. Restaurant, bar, entertainment. Babysitting services available. In-house fitness room, spa, sauna, steam room. Indoor pool, whirlpool. Valet parking. Business center. Concierge. Cr cds: A, C, D, DS, ER, JCB, MC, V. **$$$$**

ⓓ 🏊 🖼 🏌 🖼 🖼 🏃

★ ★ **HOLIDAY INN.** *300 E Ohio St (60611). Phone 312/787-6100; toll-free 800/465-4329; fax 312/787-6259. www.holiday-inn.com.* 500 rooms, 26 story. Check-out noon, check-in 3 pm. TV; cable (premium), VCR available. In-room modem link. Restaurant, bar. Babysitting services available. In-house fitness room, sauna, spa, massage. Indoor pool, outdoor pool, whirlpool. Indoor tennis. Business center. Cr cds: A, C, D, DS, ER, JCB, MC, V. **$$**

ⓓ 🏌 🖼 🖼 SC 🏃

★ ★ ★ **HOTEL ALLEGRO CHICAGO.** *171 W Randolph St (60601). Phone 312/236-0123; toll-free 800/643-1500; fax 312/236-0917. www.allegrochicago.com.* The stylishly eclectic Hotel Allegro is the result of a 1998 renovation of the Loop's historic Bismarck Hotel. This erstwhile grande dame's classic-contemporary new incarnation is exuberantly colorful, with musical and theatrical icons integrated throughout the décor. The dramatic lobby, with fireplace and baby grand piano, harkens back to the days of the grand hotel (guests can enjoy a complimentary evening wine hour). The Allegro offers multiple dining and cocktail environments, including the adjacent restaurant 312 Chicago; the Encore lounge for lunch, cocktails, or late-night dining; and room service. Special amenities are offered for canine and feline guests. 483 rooms, 19 story. Pet accepted. Check-out noon, check-in 3 pm. TV; cable (premium), VCR available. In-room modem link. Restaurant, bar. Babysitting services available. In-house fitness room. Valet parking. Business center. Concierge. Cr cds: A, C, D, DS, ER, JCB, MC, V. **$$$**

ⓓ 🏊 🏌 🖼 🏃

★ ★ ★ **HOTEL MONACO CHICAGO.** *225 N Wabash (60601). Phone 312/960-8500; fax 312/960-8538. www.monaco-chicago.com.* In the heart of downtown, between the Loop and the Magnificent Mile, the Monaco's stylishly eclectic, Euro aesthetic is equally suited to business or pleasure travel. The front desk recalls a vintage steamer trunk; the lobby has the feel of a posh living room, with a grand limestone fireplace. Colorful rooms are retreats of creature comfort, with plush furnishings, distinctive bath products (and Fuji tubs in the suites), and even a companion goldfish on request. Enjoy round-the-clock room service or visit the South Water Kitchen, the hotel's restaurant, for breakfast, lunch, or dinner. Complimentary morning coffee and evening wine service are offered, and pets are accommodated with aplomb. 192 rooms, 14 story. D $195-$250. Pet accepted. Check-out noon. TV; cable (premium), VCR available. Restaurant 6 am-10 pm. Exercise room. Business center. Cr cds: A, C, D, DS, JCB, MC, V.

★ ★ ★ **HOUSE OF BLUES.** *333 N Dearborn (60610). Phone 312/245-0333; toll-free 800/22-LOEWS; fax 312/923-2466. www.loewshotels.com.* With its exotic Gothic-Moroccan-East Indian décor, eye-popping art collection, and adjacent live concert venue, the hip House of Blues Hotel appeals to a new generation of travelers. Guest rooms are spacious and well appointed; vast meeting space and related services cater to business travelers. The namesake restaurant serves Southern American fare and hosts a popular Sunday gospel brunch. In the same complex are the chic, wine-themed bistro Bin 36 and Smith & Wollensky Steak House. The location puts guests in the heart of the River North gallery, dining, and entertainment district and close to the Loop and Michigan Avenue. 367 rooms, 15 story. Pet accepted. Check-out noon, check-in 3 pm. TV; cable (premium), VCR available. Restaurant, bar. Babysitting services available. In-house fitness room, spa. Business center. Cr cds: A, C, D, DS, MC, V. **$$**

★ ★ ★ **HYATT AT UNIVERSITY VILLAGE.** *625 S Ashland Ave (60607). Phone 312/491-1234; fax 312/529-6095. www.hyatt.com.* This hotel is conveniently located to downtown Chicago and 20 minutes from O'Hare International Airport. Amenities include a fitness center and the access to Chicago Health Club which is just 5 blocks from the hotel. Enjoy a fireside dinner at Jaxx Restaurant and then a night cap at Jaxx Lounge, both located on-site. 114 rooms, 4 story. S $145-$295; D $170-$320; each additional $25; suites $395-$795; under 18 free; package plans. Crib free. Check-out noon. TV; cable (premium), VCR available. Some refrigerators. Microwaves available. Valet services. Restaurant 6 am-10 pm. Bar 11 am-midnight. Room service. Health club privileges. Exercise equipment. Pool privileges. Tennis privileges. Valet parking. Meeting rooms. Business center. Near University of Illinois Chicago campus. Cr cds: A, C, D, DS, ER, JCB, MC, V.

★ ★ ★ **HYATT ON PRINTERS ROW.** *500 S Dearborn St (60605). Phone 312/986-1234; toll-free 800/233-1234; fax 312/939-2468. www.hyatt.com.* Located in the heart of Chicago's South Loop within walking distance of many attractions like the Art Institute and Soldier Field, this historical property offers amenities for business and leisure travelers alike. Guest rooms feature hairdryers, data ports, and cable television with movie channels. 161 rooms, 7-12 story. S $225-$325; D $250-$350; each additional $25; suites $650; weekend rates. Crib free. Check-out noon. TV; cable (premium), VCR available. Bathroom phones, minibars. Restaurant 6:30 am-10 pm (see also PRAIRIE). Bar 6:30 am-10 pm. Health club privileges. Exercise equipment. Valet parking $31; self-park $18. Airport transportation. Meeting rooms. Business services. Financial district nearby. Cr cds: A, C, D, DS, ER, JCB, MC, V.

★ ★ ★ **HYATT REGENCY CHICAGO.** *151 E Wacker Dr (60601). Phone 312/565-1234; toll-free 800/233-1234; fax 312/565-2966. www.hyatt.com.* Located on the "Magnificent Mile" in the heart of Chicago's cultural and shopping district, this hotel is within walking distance of many restaurants, boutiques, and entertainment. The property offers a business center and gift shop and guest rooms feature hairdryers, irons, data ports, and voice mail. 2,019 rooms, 34 story (East Tower), 36 story (West Tower). S $139-$295; D $139-$320; each additional $25; suites $565-$3,600; under 18 free; package plans. Crib free. Garage, in/out $33. TV; cable (premium), VCR available (movies). Restaurant (see also STETSON'S CHOP-HOUSE). Room service 24 hours. Bar 11-2 am. Check-out noon. Convention facilities. Business center. In-room modem link. Concierge. Shopping arcade. Barber, beauty shop. Health club privileges. Minibars; some in-room steam baths, whirlpools. Bathroom phone, refrigerator in suites. Luxury level. Cr cds: A, C, D, DS, ER, JCB, MC, V.

★ ★ ★ **HYATT REGENCY MCCORMICK PLACE.** *2233 S Martin Luther King Dr (60616). Phone 312/567-1234; fax 312/528-4000. www.mccormickplace.hyatt. com.* Conveniently connected by the enclosed Grand Concourse walkway to three exposition buildings, this hotel offers a splendid stay for the busy executive or the guest who just needs to unwind. Providing guests with spacious and well-furnished accommodations and just steps from downtown Chicago, State Street shopping, and Michigan Avenue, this hotel has something for everyone and guarantees return visitors by even the most discriminating traveler. 800 rooms, 33 story. Pet accepted. Check-out noon, check-in 3 pm. TV; cable (premium), VCR available. In-room modem link. Room service 24 hours. Restaurant, bar. In-house fitness room, sauna. Indoor pool. Valet parking. Business center. Concierge. Cr cds: A, C, D, DS, ER, JCB, MC, V. **$$**

★ ★ ★ **INTERCONTINENTAL CHICAGO.** *505 N Michigan Ave (60611). Phone 312/944-4100; fax 312/ 944-1320. www.intercontinental.com.* Built in 1929 as a luxury men's club (the original swimming pool remains in the fitness center), the InterContinental has undergone extensive renovations in recent years. Uniting the modern main tower and the historic north tower, the dramatic lobby is open and airy, with mosaic tile flooring, a four-story rotunda, and a grand staircase. The Magnificent Mile location, luxuriously appointed rooms with Michigan Avenue or Lake Michigan views, numerous ballrooms, and unique meeting spaces are among the draws. Room service is available 24 hours, and the hotel's restaurant, Zest, serves contemporary Mediterranean fare. High tea is also offered in the Salon. 808 rooms, 2 buildings, 26 and 42 story. Check-out noon, check-in 3 pm. TV; VCR available. In-room modem link. Room service 24 hours. Restaurant, bar, entertainment Thur-Sun. Baby sitting services available. In-house fitness room, sauna, massage. Indoor pool, poolside service. Business center. Concierge. Cr cds: A, C, D, DS, ER, JCB, MC, V. **$$$**

★ ★ ★ **LE MERIDIEN CHICAGO.** *521 N Rush St (60611). Phone 312/645-1500; toll-free 800/543-4300; fax 312/327-0598. www.lemeridien.com.* 311 rooms, 12 story. Pet accepted, some restrictions. Check-out noon, check-in 3 pm. TV; cable (premium), VCR available. Room service 24 hours. Restaurant, bar. Babysitting services available. In-house fitness room. Business center. Cr cds: A, C, D, DS, ER, JCB, MC, V. **$$$$**

★ ★ ★ **MARRIOTT CHICAGO DOWNTOWN.** *540 N Michigan Ave (60611). Phone 312/836-0100; fax 312/836-6139. www.marriott.com.* Located along the Magnificent Mile and near many Loop corporate offices, this 1,192-room property boasts 55,500 square feet of meeting space. This combined with 300 rooms specifically designed for the working traveler, with data ports, voice mail and work areas, attract business clientele. 1,192 rooms, 46 story. Pet accepted, some restrictions. Check-out noon, check-in 4 pm. TV; cable (premium), VCR available. In-room modem link. Restaurant, bar. In-house fitness room, spa, massage, sauna. Game room. Indoor pool, whirlpool. Valet parking. Business center. Concierge. Cr cds: A, C, D, DS, ER, JCB, MC, V. **$$$**

★ ★ ★ **MILLENNIUM KNICKERBOCKER.** *163 E Walton Pl (60611). Phone 312/751-8100; toll-free 866/866-8086; fax 312/751-9205. www.millennium-hotels.com.* Built in 1927 and extensively renovated in the past few years, the Millennium Knickerbocker has an updated vintage elegance layered with character. Its history includes a 1970s turn as the Playboy Towers and rumors of dodgy Capone-era connections for added flavor. The prime Magnificent Mile location puts it amidst the city's finest shopping and many great restaurants. The stately décor is light and airy, with uplifting color accents. NiX American bistro serves breakfast, lunch, and dinner; the Martini Bar offers live entertainment and 44 varieties of its namesake. Club-level rooms, 24-hour room service, meeting rooms and a business center, and the ornate, Georgian-style Crystal Ballroom are additional draws. 305 rooms, 14 story. Pet accepted, some restrictions. Check-out noon, check-in 3 pm. TV; cable (premium), VCR available. In-room modem link. Room service 24 hours. Restaurant, bar. In-house fitness room, health club privileges. Valet parking. Concierge, luxury level. Cr cds: A, C, D, DS, ER, JCB, MC, V. **$$**

★ ★ ★ **OMNI AMBASSADOR EAST.** *1301 N State Pkwy (60610). Phone 312/787-7200; toll-free 800/843-6664; fax 312/787-4760. www.omnihotels.com.* A Historic Hotel of America located in the Gold Coast neighborhood, this property is the mirror image of the Ambassador West across the street and home to the famed Pump Room restaurant. An incredible number of stars have stayed here over the years. 285 rooms, 17 story. S $149-$229; D $159-$239; each additional $20; suites $375-$1,000; under 17 free; weekend rates. Crib free. Check-out noon. TV; cable (premium). Minibars; microwaves available. Restaurant (see also PUMP ROOM). Bar 11-1 am. Room service 24 hours. Health club privileges. Exercise equipment. Valet parking $34. Airport transportation. Meeting rooms. Business services. Concierge. Cr cds: A, C, D, DS, ER, JCB, MC, V.

★ ★ ★ **OMNI CHICAGO HOTEL.** *676 N Michigan Ave (60611). Phone 312/944-6664; toll-free 800/788-6664; fax 312/266-3015. www.omnihotels.com.* In the center of Michigan Avenue within a mixed-use building sits this 347-suite property, host to many famous guests of the *Oprah Winfrey Show.* All accommodations offer spacious sitting rooms with bedrooms hidden behind French doors, great for corporate clientele needing their room to double as an office. The fourth floor Cielo restaurant provides fantastic views of the street excitement below. 347 rooms, 25 story. Pet accepted. Check-out noon, check-in 3 pm.

TV; cable (premium), VCR available. In-room modem link. Room service 24 hours. Restaurant, bar. Children's activity center, babysitting services available. In-house fitness room, health club privileges, sauna. Indoor pool, whirlpool. Valet parking. Business center. Concierge. Cr cds: A, C, D, DS, ER, JCB, MC, V. **$$**

★★★**PALMER HOUSE HILTON.** *17 E Monroe St (60603). Phone 312/726-7500; toll-free 800/445-8667; fax 312/917-1707. www.hilton.com.* Grand and gilded, the Palmer House Hilton has harbored visitors to the Windy City for 130 years, making it America's longest-operating hotel. This Loop landmark has undergone a full renovation to restore designer-builder Potter Palmer's original French Empire opulence, including the breathtaking Beaux Arts ceiling in the palatial lobby. Amenities include an 11-room penthouse suite, executive levels with private elevator, an entire floor of "deluxe-tech" conference and meeting facilities, a fitness club, and a shopping arcade. Four restaurants and bars include the 1940s-themed Big Downtown restaurant and bar and the retro Polynesian favorite, Trader Vic's. 1,639 rooms, 25 story. D $184-$354. Pet accepted. Check-out 11 am. TV; cable (premium), VCR available. In-room modem link. Restaurant 6:30-2 am. Bar 11-2 am, entertainment. Exercise room, massage, sauna, steam room. Indoor pool, whirlpool. Airport transportation. Business center. Concierge. Cr cds: A, C, D, DS, ER, JCB, MC, V.

★★★★**PARK HYATT CHICAGO.** *800 N Michigan Ave (60611). Phone 312/335-1234; toll-free 800/778-7477; fax 312/239-4000. www.parkhyattchicago.com.* From its stylish interiors to its historic Water Tower Square location, the Park Hyatt is intrinsically tied to the history of Chicago. Occupying a landmark building in the heart of the Magnificent Mile shopping area, the hotel has a sleek, modern attitude. The public and private spaces celebrate the city's long-lasting love affair with architecture and its artists. Mies van der Rohe, Eames, and Noguchi furnishings are showcased throughout the guest rooms, while photography commissioned by the Art Institute of Chicago graces the walls. A health club, spa, and salon are the perfect antidotes to stress, and the flawless service always ensures a carefree visit. The nouvelle cuisine at NoMI is a standout, although the dramatic seventh-floor views from the floor-to-ceiling windows are not for the faint of heart. To escape the urban pace, visitors head to the NoMI Garden for American barbecue favorites. 202 rooms, 18 story. Pet accepted. Check-out noon, check-in 3 pm. TV; cable (premium), VCR available. Room service 24 hours. Restaurant, bar. Babysitting services available. In-house fitness room, spa. Indoor pool, whirlpool. Business center. Cr cds: A, C, D, DS, MC, V. **$$$$**

★★★★**PENINSULA CHICAGO.** *108 E Superior St (60611). Phone 312/337-2888; fax 312/751-2888. www.peninsula.com.* Reigning over Chicago's famed Magnificent Mile, the Peninsula Chicago hotel basks in a golden aura. From the sun-filled lobby to the gleaming, gilded details, this hotel simply sparkles. With Tiffany and Ralph Lauren downstairs and Saks and Neiman Marcus across the street, the gracious bellmen outfitted in crisp white uniforms are a shopper's savior. Asian sensibilities are expertly blended with details highlighting the city's Art Deco heritage in the public spaces. Soft lighting, polished woods, and golden hues create glorious shelters in the guest rooms. Proving the point that modern amenities are a hallmark of this property, all rooms are fitted with bedside electronic control panels and flat-screen televisions. Guests escape the pressures of the everyday at the state-of-the-art exercise facility and spa, complete with an outdoor sundeck. Whether taking tea, nibbling flammekuchen, sampling Asian specialties, or savoring seafood, guests traverse the world at five distinctive dining venues. 339 rooms, 20 story. Pet accepted. Check-out noon, check-in 3 pm. TV; cable (premium), VCR available. Room service 24 hours. Restaurant, bar. Babysitting services available. In-house fitness room, spa. Indoor pool, children's pool, whirlpool. Valet parking. Business center. Cr cds: A, C, D, DS, JCB, MC, V. **$$$$**

★★★**RENAISSANCE CHICAGO HOTEL.** *1 W Wacker Dr (60601). Phone 312/372-7200; fax 312/372-0093. www.renaissancehotels.com.* This Marriott-owned Loop high-rise features stone and glass exterior towers that rise above the intersection of State and Wacker. The Renaissance is a welcome haven to its audience of business travelers and vacationers looking for a central location accessible to theaters and museums. The handsome lobby sets a posh, executive tone; comfortable rooms boast spectacular views (especially on the higher floors). The Great Street Restaurant in the hotel's atrium serves American breakfast, lunch, and dinner (and a bargain theater menu) with a view of the river. Additional amenities include 24-hour room service, expanded club level rooms, a fitness club and pool, a lobby bar, and a 24-hour Kinko's business center. 553 rooms, 27 story. Pet accepted, some restrictions. Check-out 1 pm, check-in 3 pm. TV; cable (premium), VCR available. In-room modem link. Room service 24 hours. Restaurant, bar. In-house fitness room, sauna, massage. Indoor pool, whirlpool, poolside service. Valet parking. Business center. Concierge. Luxury level. Cr cds: A, C, D, DS, ER, JCB, MC, V. **$$$**

★ ★ ★ ★ ★ **THE RITZ-CARLTON, A FOUR SEASONS HOTEL.** *160 E Pearson St (60611). Phone 312/266-1000; toll-free 800/621-6906; fax 312/266-1194. www.fourseasons.com.* Guests of the esteemed Ritz-Carlton Chicago often wonder if heaven could get any better than this. The unparalleled levels of service, commitment to excellence, and meticulous attention to detail make this one of the country's finest hotels. Gracing the upper levels of prestigious Water Tower Place on the Magnificent Mile, the hotel's guest rooms afford picture-perfect views through large windows. Rich tones and dignified furnishings define the accommodations. Managed by the Four Seasons, The Ritz-Carlton offers guests a taste of the luxe life, from the resplendent décor and seamless service to the superlative cuisine at the four restaurants and lounges. The sublime contemporary French menu and sensational ambience at the Dining Room makes it one of the most coveted tables in town. Human guests, however, are not the only ones to be spoiled-furry visitors feast in-room on filet mignon and salmon! 435 rooms, 31 story. Pet accepted. Check-out noon, check-in 3 pm. TV; cable (premium), VCR available. In-room modem link. Room service 24 hours. Restaurant, bar. Babysitting services available. In-house fitness room, spa, sauna, steam room. Indoor pool, whirlpool. Parking. Business center. Concierge. Cr cds: A, MC, V. **$$$**

D 🐾 ➳ 🏋 🏊 🚶

★★★**SHERATON CHICAGO HOTEL & TOWERS.** *301 E North Water St (60611). Phone 312/464-1000; toll-free 800/233-4100; fax 312/464-9140. www.sheratonchicago.com.* Contemporary yet comfortable, every room of the handsomely appointed Sheraton Chicago Hotel & Towers promises a sweeping view of the cityscape, the Chicago River, or Lake Michigan. The central location is just minutes from the Magnificent Mile, the Loop, Navy Pier, and McCormick Place. The spacious lobby is appointed in imported marble and rich woods, and luxurious fitness facilities feature a pool and sauna. Close to numerous fine restaurants, the Sheraton's five in-house dining options include Shula's Steak House and an indoor-outdoor café overlooking the river. Extensive and elegant meeting facilities, a full-service business center, and club-level rooms cater to business travelers. 1,200rooms, 34 suites, 34 story. S $199-$269; D $219-$289; each additional $25; suites $450-$3,500; under 17 free. Pet accepted, some restrictions. Check-out noon. TV; cable (premium), VCR available. In-room modem link. Restaurant 6-1 am. Bar 11-1:30 am; pianist, room service 24 hours. Exercise equipment, massage, sauna. Indoor pool. Business center. Concierge, luxury level. On Chicago River, near Navy Pier. Cr cds: A, C, D, DS, JCB, MC, V.

D 🐾 ➳ 🏋 🏊 🚶

★ ★ ★ **THE SUTTON PLACE HOTEL – CHICAGO.** *21 E Bellevue Pl (60611). Phone 312/266-2100; toll-free 800/810-6888; fax 312/266-2141. www.suttonplace.com.* Stylish understatement is the mantra of this luxurious 23-story hotel, an Art Deco-inspired building housing a handsome, modern interior. The prime Gold Coast location offers immediate access to such attractions as Magnificent Mile shopping, Rush Street nightlife, and some of the city's finest restaurants. Recently renovated, soundproof rooms feature deep-soaking tubs, separate glass-enclosed showers, plush robes, and lavish bath accessories. Room service is 24/7, and destination dining and people-watching are available at the Whiskey Bar & Grill. Popular with corporate travelers, Sutton Place is equally suited to private getaways—even with your pet (with some restrictions). 246 rooms, 23 story. Pet accepted. Check-out noon, check-in 3 pm. TV; cable (premium), VCR available. In-room modem link. Room service 24 hours. Restaurant, bar. In-house fitness room, health club privileges. Valet parking. Airport transportation. Business center. Concierge. Cr cds: A, C, D, DS, JCB, MC, V. **$$**

D 🐾 🏋 🏊 SC 🚶

★ ★ ★ **SWISSOTEL CHICAGO.** *323 E Wacker Dr (60601). Phone 312/565-0565; toll-free 800/73-SWISS; fax 312/565-0540. www.swissotelchicago.com.* High ceilings, dark wood and a well lit lobby provide the first glimpse into the tastefully decorated and operated Swissotel Chicago. With oversized rooms and personalized service, there's no going wrong for even the most discerning traveler. 632 rooms, 43 story. Check-out noon. TV; cable (premium), VCR available. In-room modem link. Bathroom phones, minibars. Coffee in rooms. Restaurant 6 am-10:30 pm. Bar 11-2 am. Room service 24 hours. Health club privileges. Exercise room; sauna. Massage. Indoor pool; whirlpool. Covered parking, in/out $33. Business center, convention facilities. Concierge. Gift shop. Panoramic views of city and Lake Michigan. Cr cds: A, C, D, DS, ER, JCB, MC, V. **$$**

D 🏊 🏋 🏊 🚶

★ ★ ★ **THE TALBOTT HOTEL.** *20 E Delaware Pl (60611). Phone 312/944-4970; fax 312/944-7241. www.talbotthotel.com.* Landed-gentry chic sets the tone at this smaller, traditional hotel, an elegant escape from the bustle of the upscale Gold Coast. Built in 1927 and completely renovated in recent years, the Talbott is known for European service, intimacy, and old-world comfort. The lobby is reminiscent of a Victorian living room, with two welcoming fireplaces, antiques, classic artwork, and fresh flowers. The lobby bar, Basil's, offers café fare and outdoor seating in warm weather. Talbott guests also enjoy complimentary access to the 72,000-square-foot Gold

Coast Multiplex health club. 149 rooms, 15 story. Check-out noon, check-in 3 pm. TV; cable (premium), VCR available. Restaurant, bar. Babysitting services available. Cr cds: A, C, D, DS, JCB, MC, V. **$$**

⊡ 🏃 ⊠

★ ★ **TREMONT.** *100 E Chestnut St (60611). Phone 312/751-1900; toll-free 800/621-8133; fax 312/751-8691. www.tremontchicago.com.* This 16-floor European-style hotel features 5,000 square feet of meeting space as well as 118 guest rooms. Guests have access to an on-site fitness facility but a health club is located just 1/2 block from the hotel. 118 rooms, 16 story. Pet accepted. Check-out noon. Check-in 3 pm. TV; cable (premium), VCR available. In-room modem link. Room service 24 hours. Restaurant. In-house fitness room. Parking. Concierge. Cr cds: A, C, D, DS, MC, V. **$$**

🐾 🏃 ⊠

★ ★ ★ **W CHICAGO CITY CENTER.** *172 W Adams St (60603). Phone 312/332-1200. www.whotels.com.* 390 rooms, 20 story. S, D $250-$475; each additional $35; under 17 free. Crib available. Complimentary coffee in rooms. Check-out noon. TV; cable (premium), VCR. Minibars. Restaurant 6 am-10 pm. Bar 4:30 pm-2 am; entertainment Tue-Sat. Exercise room. Meeting rooms. Business services. Cr cds: A, C, D, DS, JCB, MC, V.

⊡ 🏃 ⊠

★ ★ ★ **W CHICAGO LAKESHORE.** *644 N Lakeshore Dr (60611). Phone 312/943-9200. fax 312/255-4411. www.whotels.com.* 578 rooms, 33 story. S, D $150-$350; each additional $25; under 17 free. Crib available. Pet accepted. Complimentary coffee in rooms. Check-out noon. TV; cable (premium), VCR available. Pool; whirlpool. Some refrigerators, minibars. Restaurant 6 am-10 pm. Exercise room. Meeting rooms. Business center. Cr cds: A, C, D, DS, MC, V.

🐾 🏃 ⊠ 🏃 ⊠

★ ★ ★ ★ **WESTIN CHICAGO RIVER NORTH.** *320 Dearborn (60610). Phone 312/744-1900; toll-free 800/WESTIN-1; fax 312/527-2664. www.westinrivernorth .com.* The Westin Chicago River North enjoys a wonderful location overlooking the Chicago River in the heart of the city's financial and theater districts. This luxury hotel is an impressive sight and offers a welcoming home for business or leisure travelers visiting the Windy City. Attractive and comfortable, the rooms use a blend of brass, black, and caramel tones to create a soothing atmosphere, the furnishings a contemporary interpretation of classic design. Westin's signature Heavenly beds make for luxurious slumber, and the Heavenly baths ensure aquatic therapy. Athletic-minded guests reap the rewards of the full-service fitness center. The Kamehachi Sushi Bar delights fish lovers; the Celebrity Café features all-day dining with a focus on American dishes; and the

Hana Lounge entertains nightly with hors d'oeuvres and live music. 424 rooms, 20 story. Pet accepted. Check-out noon, check-in 3 pm. TV; cable (premium), VCR available. In-room modem link. Room service 24 hours. Restaurant, bar. Babysitting services available. In-house fitness room, sauna, spa, massage. Valet parking. Business center. Concierge. Cr cds: A, C, D, DS, JCB, MC, V. **$$**

⊡ 🐾 🏃 ⊠ 🏃

★ ★ ★ **WESTIN MICHIGAN AVENUE CHICAGO.** *909 N Michigan Ave (60611). Phone 312/943-7200; toll-free 800/WESTIN-1; fax 312/397-5580. www.westinmichigana ve.com.* Situated in the heart of downtown Chicago, this hotel is conveniently located for both the corporate traveler and the leisure traveler. Just minutes from the Loop, business travelers will find it easy to get to their meetings on time. For the leisure traveler this hotel is close to Grant Park, Navy Pier and many Art Galleries. Dining facilities are available on-site. 751 rooms, 27 story. Pet accepted, some restrictions. Check-out noon, check-in 3 pm. TV; cable (premium). In-room modem link. Room service 24 hours. Restaurant, bar. Babysitting services available. In-house fitness room, sauna, massage. Valet parking. Business center. Concierge, luxury level. Cr cds: A, C, D, DS, ER, JCB, MC, V. **$$**

⊡ 🐾 🏃 ⊠ SC 🏃

★ ★ ★ **THE WHITEHALL HOTEL.** *105 E Delaware Pl (60611). Phone 312/944-6300; toll-free 800/948-4255; fax 312/944-8552. www.thewhitehallhotel.com.* A historic Gold Coast landmark, this venerable hotel is just off the Magnificent Mile and steps from Water Tower Place. Built in 1927 and extensively renovated in recent years, the independent Whitehall retains its stature as a small sanctuary with personal service and sedate, old-world charm. Rooms combine traditional décor (including some four-poster beds) and modern technology. The California-Mediterranean restaurant, Molive, offers an excellent wine program, a bar, and outdoor dining. Additional highlights include club floors, an evening cocktail hour, and complimentary sedan service (within 2 miles). 221 rooms, 21 story. Pet accepted, some restrictions. Check-out noon, check-in 3 pm. In-room modem link. Room service 24 hours. Restaurant, bar. Babysitting services available. In-house fitness room, health club privileges. Valet parking. Concierge, luxury level. Cr cds: A, D, DS, MC, V. **$$$**

⊡ 🐾 🏃 ⊠

★ ★ ★ **WYNDHAM CHICAGO.** *633 N St. Clair St (60611). Phone 312/573-0300; toll-free 800/WYNDHAM; fax 312/274-0164. www.wyndhamchicago.com.* 417 rooms, 17 story. Check-out noon, check-in 3 pm. TV; cable (premium), VCR available. Restaurant, bar. In-house fitness room. Indoor pool, whirlpool. Business center. Cr cds: A, C, D, DS, MC, V. **$$**

⊠ 🏃 ⊠ 🏃

All Suite

★★★DOUBLETREE GUEST SUITES CHI-CAGO-DOWNTOWN. *198 E Delaware Pl (60611). Phone 312/664-1100; toll-free 800/222-TREE; fax 312/664-8627. www.doubletreehotels.com.* This all-suite hotel is located just off the "Magnificent Mile" and is easily accessible for the business traveler. This property offers guests a fitness center, pool, sauna and game room/arcade. Guests will enjoy the convenience of the on-site restaurant and bar/lounge. 345 suites, 30 story. Check-out noon, check-in 3 pm. TV; cable (premium), VCR available. In-room modem link. Room service 24 hours. Restaurant, bar. In-house fitness room, sauna. Game room. Indoor pool, whirlpool. Valet parking. Business center. Concierge. Cr cds: A, C, D, DS, ER, JCB, MC, V. **$$**

⊡ ⊠ 🏃 ⊠ SC 🏃

★★★ EMBASSY SUITES CHICAGO-DOWN-TOWN. *600 N State St (60610). Phone 312/943-3800; toll-free 800/362-2779; fax 312/943-7629. www.embassysuiteschicago.com.* Both business and family friendly, this recently renovated all-suite hotel boasts a prime River North location, just a short walk to a multitude of galleries, dining, and entertainment venues, as well as Michigan Avenue shopping. Beautifully appointed 2-room suites are modern and spacious and include kitchen appliances and sleeper sofas. Lush with greenery and fountains, the inviting lobby leads to an 11-story atrium. Immediately adjacent are both a Starbucks and the quaint Papagus Greek Taverna. Other amenities include VIP rooms; complimentary breakfast; manager's evening cocktail reception; on-site car rental; business, meeting, and conference facilities; and fitness facilities with sauna and pool. 358 suites, 11 story. S $189-$399; D $299-$439; under 12 free. Complimentary full breakfast. Check-out noon. TV; cable (premium). In-room modem link. Restaurant (see also PAPAGUS GREEK TAVERNA). Bar. Exercise equipment; sauna. Indoor pool; whirlpool. Concierge. Cr cds: A, C, D, DS, ER, JCB, MC, V.

⊡ ⊠ 🏃 ⊠ SC

B&B/Small Inns

★★ GOLD COAST GUEST HOUSE. *113 W Elm St (60610). Phone 312/337-0361; fax 312/337-0362. www.bbchicago.com.* 4 rooms, 3 story. Children over 12 years only. Complimentary continental breakfast. Check-out 11 am, check-in by arrangement. TV; VCR available. Renovated brick townhome built in 1873. Cr cds: A, DS, MC, V. **$**

⊠

★★★ OLD TOWN BED & BREAKFAST. *1442 N North Park Ave (60610). Phone 312/440-9268. www.oldtownchicago.com.* 4 rooms, 4 story. S, D $139-$199. Complimentary continental breakfast. Check-out

11 am. TV; cable (premium), VCR. Exercise room. Art Deco mansion. Cr cds: A, MC, V.

🏃

Restaurants

★★★ 312 CHICAGO. *136 N LaSalle (60602). Phone 312/696-2420. www.312chicago.citysearch.com.* Named for Chicago's urban area code, 312 Chicago is adjacent to the Hotel Allegro in the heart of the Loop's business, shopping, and theater district. The tempting menu marries fresh, contemporary Italian fare with more rustic options. The bi-level setting is clubby yet airy, with a bustling open kitchen and an aromatic rotisserie. The restaurant also serves upscale breakfast and lunch, and the chic bar is a great spot for cocktails. Menu changes seasonally. Hours: 7-10 am, 11 am-3 pm, 5-10 pm; Fri to 11 pm; Sat 7 am-noon, 5-11 pm; Sun 8 am-3 pm, 5-10 pm. Closed Jan 1, Thanksgiving, Dec 25. Dinner $13.95-$28.95. Cr cds: A, C, D, DS, MC, V.

⊡

★★ ADOBO GRILL. *1610 N Wells (60614). Phone 312/266-7999; fax 312/266-9299. www.adobogrill.com.* Fans of beyond-the-taco Mexican food will appreciate this upscale, up-tempo Old Towner known for its extensive tequila list, tableside guacamole preparation, and intriguing (and extensive) menu offerings—with some equally intriguing cocktails. The scene at night can be raucous; brunch-time is quieter. Mexican menu. Closed major holidays. Dinner, brunch. Two vintage bars. Entertainment. Children's menu. Casual attire. Outdoor seating. Cr cds: A, D, MC, V. **$$**

⊡

★ ALBERT'S CAFE & PATISSERIE. *52 W Elm St (60610). Phone 312/751-0666; fax 312/787-5576.* Contemporary American menu. Hours: 10 am-9 pm. Closed Mon; Jan 1, Dec 25 . Lunch, dinner $6.95-$12.95. Valet parking. Outdoor dining. Totally nonsmoking. Cr cds: A, D, DS, MC, V.

★★★ AMBRIA. *2300 N Lincoln Park W (60614). Phone 773/472-5959. www.lettuceentertainyou.com.* Ambria is located at the base of Lincoln Park in The Belden-Stratford, a 1922 architectural landmark turned residential hotel on Chicago's romantic lakefront. With dark mahogany walls and luxuriously appointed tabletops set with tiny shaded votive lamps, this beautiful, graceful space is filled with radiant women and striking men who glow in the room's creamy amber light. Ambria is a civilized spot, ideal for business or pleasure. The menu is as elegant as the room, with Mediterranean accents from Italy, Spain, and beyond (saffron, piquillo peppers, olives, and polenta) turning up the flavor on the kitchen's top-quality selection of fish, game, lamb, and beef. In addition to the enticing à la carte menu, the kitchen offers the Ambria Classic menu, a decadent five-course prix fixe option that should be ordered if a big enough appetite presents itself. The service is helpful, efficient, and warm, making dining here a delight on every level. French, continental menu. Menu changes seasonally; daily specialties. Closed Sun; holidays. Dinner. Bar. Children's menu. Jacket required. Reservations required. Valet parking available. Cr cds: A, C, D, DS, MC, V. **$$$**

D

★ **ANN SATHER.** *929 W Belmont Ave (60657). Phone 773/348-2378; fax 773/348-1731. www.annsather.com.* Open since 1945, this Swedish family of comfy, come-as-you-are restaurants may be best known for its sinful cinnamon rolls, but fans of all ages also appreciate the hearty Swedish and American classics (for example, Swedish pancakes with lingonberries, roast turkey dinner), the no-nonsense service, and the reasonable prices. The breakfast menu is available all day. Four additional locations can be found on the city's north side, at 5207 N Clark, 1448 N Milwaukee, 3416 N Southport, and 3411 N Broadway. Swedish, American menu. Hours: 7 am-10 pm; Fri, Sat to 11 pm. Dinner $9.95-$12.95. Bar. Cr cds: A, D, MC, V.

D SC

★ ★ **ARCO DE CUCHILLEROS.** *3445 N Halsted St (60657). Phone 773/296-6046.* Tapas menu. Closed Mon; most major holidays. Dinner, sun brunch. Bar. Casual attire. Outdoor seating. Cr cds: A, D, MC, V. **$**

D

★ ★ ★ **ARUN'S.** *4156 N Kedzie Ave (60618). Phone 773/539-1909; fax 773/539-2125. www.arunsthai.com.* Arun's version of Thai food is as similar to neighborhood take-out as caviar is to peanut butter. Regarded as the best Thai interpreter in the city, if not the country, Arun's takes a fine-dining turn with the complex cooking of Thailand, but without the attendant snobbery of many serious restaurants. A phalanx of eager, well-informed servers cheerfully work the alcove-lodged tables in the tranquil, Asian-art-filled rooms. Chef Arun Sampanthavivat prepares an original $85 prix-fixe menu nightly, proffering 12 courses, half of them small appetizers, served family style. You won't know what's on until you arrive, but the kitchen easily adapts to food and spice sensitivities. Thai menu; special chef-designed menus. Closed Mon; holidays. Dinner. Bar. Reservations required. Cr cds: A, D, DS, MC, V.

D

★ ★ ★ **ATLANTIQUE.** *5101 N Clark (60640). Phone 773/275-9191; fax 773/275-9199.* An Andersonville neighborhood joint with cooking worthy of a downtown address, Atlantique specializes in seafood. From the huge marlin over the bar to the starfish-shaped sconces, the décor plays up the menu motif. Chef and owner Jack Jones borrows from the culinary cultures of Asia, Italy, and France in dishes like panko-dusted crab cakes, warm lobster salad with truffle oil, and seared tuna au poivre. Oysters often turn up among specials, and landlubbers get interesting choices, too, such as venison and duck confit. Seafood menu. Menu changes seasonally. Closed Mon. Dinner. Bar. Entertainment. Casual attire. Reservations required weekends. Outdoor seating. Cr cds: A, D, MC, V. **$$$**

D ⊠

★ ★ ★ **ATWOOD CAFE.** *1 W Washington (60602). Phone 312/368-1900; fax 312/357-2875. www.atwoodcafe.com.* The whimsical ground-floor occupant of the Burnham Hotel, Atwood draws a cross-section of travelers, desk jockeys, theatergoers, and shoppers in for chef Heather Terhune's café menu. Modern dishes like grilled calamari and tuna carpaccio balance comfort food classics like grilled pork chops with spaetzle. Soak up the Loop scene through floor-to-ceiling windows framing the downtown bustle at lunch, and romantic, marquee-lit streetscapes at dinner. Cozy velvet banquettes and settees encourage lingering. American menu. Closed holidays. Breakfast, lunch, dinner, brunch. Bar. Entertainment. Children's menu. Casual attire. Outdoor seating. Cr cds: A, D, DS, MC, V. **$$**

D

★ ★ ★ **AUBRIOT.** *1962 N Halsted St (60614). Phone 773/281-4211; fax 773/281-4232.* Chef-owner Eric Aubriot's eponymous restaurant bridges the gap between destination French and neighborhood dining. The ambience is casually upscale; the light, contemporary cuisine is artfully presented and informed by Aubriot's pedigreed background (including apprenticeship under Alain Ducasse). When it's not on the menu, you can request his signature foie gras with chocolate sauce. The wine list evolves with the seasonal menu, and a reserve list is available. The upstairs lounge, Eau, offers ambient music and light, late-night fare. Front room tables face teeming Halsted Street (forget street parking; take a cab or use the restaurant's valet). French menu. Closed Mon; major holidays. Dinner. Bar. Casual attire. Valet parking available. Totally nonsmoking. Cr cds: A, D, MC, V. **$$**

D

★ ★ **BANDERA.** *535 N Michigan (60611). Phone 312/644-3524. www.houstons.com.* Specializes in Seattle-style BBQ salmon, wood-fire rotisserie chicken. Hours: 11:30 am-10 pm; Fri, Sat to 11 pm. Closed Sun; Thanksgiving Day, Dec 25. Lunch $6.95-$20; dinner $10-$26. Children's menu. Cr cds: A, D, MC, V.

D ⊠

★ ★ **BASTA PASTA.** *6733 Olmstead St (60631). Phone 773/763-0667; fax 773/763-1114. www.bastapastachicago.com.* Italian menu. Closed Mon. Lunch, dinner. Bar. Children's menu. Casual attire. Outdoor seating. Cr cds: A, D, MC, V. **$$**

[D]

★ **BERGHOFF.** *17 W Adams St (60603). Phone 312/427-3170. www.berghoff.com.* Hours: 11 am-9 pm; Fri to 9:30 pm; Sat to 10 pm. Closed Sun; major holidays. Reservations accepted. German, American menu. Lunch $6.50-$11, dinner $9-$17. Children's menus. In 1881 building. Family-owned since 1898. Cr cds: A, MC, V.

[D]

★ ★ **BICE.** *158 E Ontario St (62611). Phone 312/664-1474; fax 312/664-9008.* Hours: 11:30 am-10:30 pm; Fri, Sat to 11:30 pm. Closed Jan 1, Dec 25. Reservations accepted. Northern Italian menu. Bar. A la carte entrees: lunch $11-$20, dinner $14-$25. Own pastries, desserts, pasta. Valet parking (dinner). Outdoor dining. Contemporary Italian décor. Cr cds: A, D, DS, MC, V.

[SC]

★ ★ **BIG DOWNTOWN.** *124 S Wabash Ave (60603). Phone 312/917-7399. www.hilton.com.* Hours: 11-2 am. Lunch $8-$16, dinner $10-$30. Bar. Reservations accepted (dinner). Blues Wed night. Cr cds: A, D, DS, MC, V.

[D]

★ ★ **BIN 36.** *339 N Dearborn St (60610). Phone 312/755-9463; fax 312/755-9410. www.bin36.com.* Menu changes seasonally. Hours: 6:30 am-10 pm. Dinner $16-$24. Entertainment. Reservations accepted. Cr cds: A, D, DS, MC, V.

[D]

★ ★ ★ **BLACKBIRD.** *619 W Randolph St (60606). Phone 312/715-0708; fax 312/715-0774. www.blackbirdrestaurant.com.* The minimalist chic Blackbird girds style with substance. Aluminum chairs and pale mohair banquettes seat guests at tables within easy eavesdropping distance of one another. But instead of the boring details of someone's career, what you're likely to hear are raves for chef Paul Kahan's French-influenced cooking. Like the décor, his style is spare, hitting just the right contemporary notes without drowning in too many flavors. The market-driven menu changes frequently, with seasonal favorites such as homemade charcuterie, quail with foie gras, and braised veal cheeks. Noise levels are high but the elegantly attired fans who flock here consider it simply good buzz. American menu. Closed Sun; Jan 1, Thanksgiving, Dec 25. Lunch, dinner. Bar. Casual attire. Valet parking available. Outdoor seating. Cr cds: A, D, DS, MC, V. **$$$**

[D]

★ ★ **BLUE POINT OYSTER BAR.** *741 W Randolph (60661). Phone 312/207-1222; fax 312/207-1222. www.rdgchicago.com.* Seafood menu. Closed major holidays. Lunch, dinner. Bar. Entertainment. Children's menu. Casual attire. Outdoor seating. Cr cds: A, D, DS, MC, V. **$$**

[D]

★ ★ ★ **BRASSERIE JO.** *59 W Hubbard St (60610). Phone 312/595-0800; fax 312/595-0808. www.lettuceentertainyou.com.* In the brasserie tradition, Jean Joho's spacious, lively River North spot welcomes café society for a quick bite with a glass of moderately priced French wine or handcrafted beer, iced fruits de mer at the zinc bar, or a leisurely meal of robust, reasonably priced Alsatian-French fare. Menu classics include moules marinière, salade Niçoise, choucroute, coq au vin, and bouillabaisse. Light floods in from the street-level windows; vast murals, woven café chairs, and tile floors create a chic, vintage Parisian atmosphere. To finish your meal, request a visit from the "cheese chariot." French menu. Closed Thanksgiving, Dec 24 and 25. Dinner. Bar. Children's menu. Valet parking. Outdoor seating. Cr cds: A, D, DS, MC, V. **$$**

[D]

★ ★ **BRETT'S.** *2011 W Roscoe (60618). Phone 773/248-0999. www.brettsrestaurant.com.* American menu. Menu changes seasonally. Closed Mon, Tue, major holidays. Dinner, brunch. Bar. Entertainment. Casual attire. Outdoor seating. Cr cds: A, D, DS, MC, V. **$$**

[D]

★ ★ **BUCKINGHAM'S.** *720 S Michigan Ave (60605). Phone 312/922-4400. www.hilton.com.* Found in the Hilton Chicago & Towers near the lakefront, one of the cafe's claims to fame is a 300-plus scotch list. Another is the famous, $40-per-person (children get discounts) Sunday brunch. All the usual steakhouse trappings are in evidence. Hours: 5:30-10 pm. A la carte entrees: dinner $18.95-$29.95. Bar. Wine list. Child's menu. Reservations accepted. Valet parking. Elegant décor; cherrywood pillars, Italian marble; original artwork. Cr cds: A, C, D, DS, ER, JCB, MC, V.

★ ★ **CAFE BA-BA-REEBA!.** *2024 N Halsted St (60614). Phone 773/935-5000; fax 773/935-0660. www.cafebabareeba.com.* Spanish tapas menu. Lunch, dinner. Bar. Authentic Spanish tapas bar. Casual attire. Reservations required. Valet parking available. Outside patio. Cr cds: A, C, D, DS, ER, MC, V. **$**

[D]

★ ★ **CAFE BERNARD.** *2100 N Halsted (60614). Phone 773/871-2100. www.cafebernard.com.* French menu. Closed Dec 25. Dinner. Bar. Entertainment. Casual attire. Outdoor seating. Cr cds: A, D, DS, MC, V. **$$**

★ ★ **CAFE IBERICO.** *739 N LaSalle (60610). Phone 312/573-1510. www.cafe-iberico.com.* Elbow your way into this River North tapas hotspot for small plates of hot and cold Spanish fare, refreshing sangria, and casual camaraderie. The food is great for sharing, whether in a group or on a date, and the atmosphere, while boisterous during prime time, creates a festive mood. Hours: 11 am-11:30 pm; Fri to 1:30 am; Sat noon-1:30 am; Sun noon-11:30 pm. Lunch, dinner $9-$13. Entertainment. Reservations accepted. Cr cds: A, D, DS, MC, V.

★ ★ ★ **CALITERRA.** *633 N St. Clair (60611). Phone 312/274-4444; fax 312/274-0164. www.wyndham.com.* Aptly named considering its Cal-Ital culinary concept (Tuscany meets northern California), this handsome, and somewhat hidden, oasis in the Wyndham Chicago Hotel draws a well-heeled Gold Coast business and shopping crowd. Innovative seasonal fare emphasizes organic produce and non-hormone-treated meats; additional monthly specialty menus showcase a particular ingredient in various preparations. The dining room is dressed in wood and textiles, with a display kitchen and a glass mural of a grape arbor as focal points. The gracious cocktail lounge, noteworthy cheese cart, and Italian-American wine list are additional highlights. Hours: 6:30 am-10 pm. Dinner $17-$35. Children's menu. Cr cds: A, D, DS, MC, V.

D

★ **CAPE COD ROOM.** *140 E Walton (60611). Phone 312/440-8486; toll-free 800/55-DRAKE; fax 312/787-0256. www.thedrakehotel.com.* Seafood menu. Closed Dec 25. Lunch, dinner. Bar. Casual attire. Valet parking available. Outdoor seating. Cr cds: A, D, DS, MC, V. **$$**

D

★ ★ ★ **THE CAPITAL GRILLE.** *633 N St. Clair St (60611). Phone 312/337-9400; fax 312/337-1259. www.thecapitalgrille.com.* This Washington, DC-based chain deliberately cultivates the old boys' network vibe. The clubby, masculine décor features dark woods and original oil paintings of fox hunts, cattle drives, and the like. But even if cigars and cell phones aren't your thing, you'll find it hard to resist the top-notch steakhouse fare served up here. Sizable á la carte entrees like porterhouse steak, filet mignon, and broiled fresh lobster, along with traditional sides that serve three, tempt the taste buds and ensure that you'll leave feeling quite full. Beef is dry-aged on the premises for 14 days and hand-cut daily. The restaurant sits just off the Mag Mile in the same building that houses the Wyndham Chicago. Steak menu. Closed July 4, Thanksgiving, Dec 25. Lunch, dinner. Bar. Valet parking available. Cr cds: A, D, DS, MC, V. **$$$**

D

★ ★ **CARMINE'S.** *1043 N Rush St (60611). Phone 312/988-7676; fax 312/988-7957. www.rosebudrestaurants.com.* Lunch, dinner, brunch. Entertainment. Cr cds: A, D, DS, MC, V. **$$**

D ⊠

★ ★ ★ ★ **CHARLIE TROTTER'S.** *816 W Armitage Ave (60614). Phone 773/248-6228; fax 773/248-6088. www.charlietrotters.com.* Charlie Trotter's is a place for people who equate food with the highest form of art. It is also a restaurant for those who value a chef's masterful ability to transform sustenance into culinary wonder. But even those who doubt these two tenets will leave Charlie Trotter's understanding that food is not just for eating. It is for savoring, honoring, marveling at, and, most of all, thoroughly enjoying. Set inside a two-story brick townhouse, Charlie Trotter's is an intimate, peaceful temple of cuisine of the most refined and innovative variety. Trotter is the Nobel laureate of the kitchen—a mad maestro of gastronomy, if you will—and you must experience his talent for yourself to understand the hype. Charlie Trotter's offers several magnificent menus, including The Grand Tasting, The Vegetable, and The Kitchen Table Degustation. Each combines pristine seasonal products (Trotter has a network of more than 90 purveyors, many of them local small farms) with impeccable French techniques and slight Asian influences. Trotter prefers saucing with vegetable juice'Â-based vinaigrettes, light emulsified stocks, and purees as well as delicate broths and herb-infused meat and fish essences. The result is that flavors are remarkably intense, yet dishes stay light. Dining at Charlie Trotter's is an astonishing and extraordinary dining journey. Bon voyage! American menu with French and Asian influences. Closed Sun, Mon; major holidays. Dinner. Jacket required. Reservations required. Valet parking available. Totally nonsmoking. Cr cds: A, D, DS, MC, V. **$$$$**

D

★ ★ ★ **CHEZ JOEL.** *1119 W Taylor St (60607). Phone 312/226-6479; fax 312/226-6589.* Just a few minutes from the Loop, tiny Chez Joel dares to be French within the friendly confines of Little Italy. Classic bistro fare (paté, escargots, coquilles St. Jacques, coq au vin, steak frites) is seasoned with more adventurous specials and an appealing sandwich selection at lunch. The cozy room invites with a buttery glow, courtesy of soft yellow walls accented with French prints and posters; in warm weather, the outdoor garden is a charming oasis. The wine list is moderately priced, and a limited reserve list is offered. Make reservations; the secret is out. French Bistro menu. Lunch, dinner. Bar. Entertainment. Casual attire. Outdoor seating. Cr cds: A, C, D, DS, MC, V. **$$$**

D

★ ★ **CHICAGO CHOP HOUSE.** *60 W Ontario St (60610). Phone 312/787-7100; fax 312/787-3219. www.chicagochophouse.com.* Hours: 11:30 am-11 pm; Fri to 11:30 pm; Sat 4-11:30 pm; Sun 4-11 pm. Closed some major holidays. Dinner $15.95-$28.95. Bar. Entertainment. Turn-of-the-century Chicago décor. Valet parking. Cr cds: A, C, D, DS, MC, V.

★ ★ ★ **COCO PAZZO.** *300 W Hubbard St (60610). Phone 312/836-0900; fax 312/836-0257.* A renovated loft with velvet swagged curtains and rustic wood floors sets an aptly dramatic stage for the robust Italian cooking on offer at Coco Pazzo. Chef Tony Priolo mans the stoves, turning out recipes that range from the sophisticated but uncomplicated beef carpaccio with black truffle oil to the crowd-pleasing rigatoni with sausage and cream. Pastas come in appetizer portions, allowing you to save room for the traditional Italian "second plate" of Florentine steak or wood-fired salmon. A longtime River North resident, Coco Pazzo draws dealmakers among the ad and art world types working nearby. Italian menu. Hours: 11:30 am-2:30 pm, 5:30-10:30 pm; Fri to 11 pm; Sat 5:30-11 pm; Sun 5-10 pm. Closed major holidays. Dinner $15-$35. Service bar. Valet parking. Outdoor seating. Cr cds: A, DS, MC, V.

D

★ ★ ★ ★ **CROFTON ON WELLS.** *535 N Wells St (60610). Phone 312/755-1790; fax 312/755-1890. www.croftononwells.com.* Suzy Crofton's acclaimed American cuisine is served in simply stylish, neutral-chic surroundings in this River North storefront. Expect a gracious, grown-up dining experience; the quiet, understated room and absence of "scene" diminish distractions from what's on your plate. Seasonal ingredients star on classically trained Crofton's limited menu of sophisticated regional cuisine, which features bold and earthy undertones. The carefully selected, reasonably priced wine list offers perfect pairings for the menu's attractions. American menu. Hours: 11:30 am-2:30 pm, 5-10 pm; Fri to 11 pm; Sat 5-11 pm. Closed major holidays. Dinner $16-$32. Bar. Valet parking. Totally nonsmoking. Cr cds: A, D, DS, MC, V.

★ ★ ★ **CYRANO'S BISTRO AND WINE BAR.** *546 N Wells (60610). Phone 312/467-0546; fax 312/467-1850.* Cozy and unpretentious, Cyrano's is a country French getaway in Chicago's frenzied River North area. The rustic, un-Americanized menu encompasses bistro classics (including game and offal dishes), with a specialty in rotisserie meats. The décor is all sunny yellow walls, gilded mirrors, and provincial French accoutrements. The regional French wine list and bargain four-course lunch are added attractions, and an outdoor café makes diners part of the neighborhood scene in warm weather. Live cabaret and jazz entertainment is featured Fridays and Saturdays. Hours: 11:30 am-2:30 pm, 5:30-10:30 pm. Closed Sun; holidays. Dinner $14.50-$24.50. Entertainment. Cr cds: A, C, D, DS, MC, V.

D

★ ★ ★ ★ **THE DINING ROOM.** *160 E Pearson St (60611). Phone 312/266-1000; fax 312/266-1194. www.fourseasons.com.* Innovative contemporary French cuisine is served in quiet luxury at The Dining Room, the opulent restaurant of The Ritz-Carlton. The décor of this striking, clubby room is rich and luxurious, from the fabrics to the breathtaking fresh flowers updated weekly. In addition to the superb á la carte choices, a signature dish is a succulent Maine lobster served with wild mushrooms over a crisp golden lobster cake, the chef offers an adventurous, personalized eight-course tasting menu, a five-course degustation menu, and a five-course vegetarian menu. To complement the fantastic fare, the award-winning wine list emphasizes boutique wines from Bordeaux, Burgundy, and California. The service at The Dining Room is in keeping with the décor. Waiters are tuxedoed and formal, and each presentation detail matches the classic atmosphere that the dining room strives to represent. Eclectic/International menu. Menu changes daily. Closed Mon. Dinner, Sun brunch. Piano. Children's menu. Reservations required. Valet parking. Cr cds: A, C, D, DS, MC, V. **$$$**

D

★ **ED DEBEVIC'S.** *640 N Wells St (60610). Phone 312/664-1707; fax 312/664-7444. www.eddebevics.com.* Hours: 11 am-10 pm; Fri and Sat to midnight. Closed Thanksgiving, Dec 24, 25. Dinner $1-$8. Bar. Valet parking. Cr cds: A, C, D, DS, ER, MC, V.

D

★ ★ **ELI'S THE PLACE FOR STEAK.** *215 E Chicago Ave (60611). Phone 312/642-1393; fax 312/642-4089. www.eliplaceforsteak.com.* American, steak menu. Closed major holidays. Lunch, dinner. Bar. Children's menu. Casual attire. Valet parking available. Cr cds: A, D, DS, MC, V. **$$**

D

★ ★ **ERWIN.** *2925 N Halsted St (60657). Phone 773/528-7200; fax 773/528-1931. www.erwincafe.com.* Low on contrivance, high on flavor, chef-owner Erwin Dreschler's "urban heartland" cuisine is right at home in his comfy and convivial north-side restaurant. This is the thinking man's contemporary American comfort food, served amid a nature-inspired scheme of warm woods, forest green walls, and white tablecloths. The well-chosen wines, including extensive by-the-glass choices, are central to the concept of the ever-changing seasonal menu (Dreschler is a champion of local foodstuffs and leads tours of area farmers' markets). With choices like banana-cinnamon French toast, eggs Benedict, and rainbow trout, erwin is also a popular brunch destination. Closed Mon; most-major holidays. Dinner, sun brunch. Bar. Valet parking available. Cr cds: A, D, DS, MC, V. **$**

D

★ ★ ★ ★ **EVEREST.** *440 S La Salle St (60605). Phone 312/663-8920; fax 312/663-8802. www.lettuceentertainyou. com.* Perched high atop the city on the 40th floor of the Chicago Stock Exchange building, chef-owner Jean Joho's restaurant, Everest, affords spectacular views and equally fabulous contemporary French cuisine. Joho blends European influences with local, seasonal American ingredients; he is not afraid to pair noble ingredients like caviar and foie gras with humbler fruits of American soil such as potatoes and turnips. The á la carte menu offers several signature dishes, including the Fantasy of Chocolate—five different riffs on the decadent cocoa theme artfully piled onto one glorious plate. Everest's dining room is luxuriously decorated with polished gold railings, vaulted draped ceilings, mirrored walls, and, of course, floor-to-ceiling windows for fabulous unobstructed views. Creative French menu with Alsatian influence. Hours: 5:30-9 pm (last sitting); Fri, Sat to 10 pm (last sitting). Closed Sun, Mon; major holidays. Dinner $28-$38; prix fixe multicourse $79. Reservations required. Free valet parking. Cr cds: A, D, DS, MC, V.

D

★ ★ ★ **FRONTERA GRILL.** *445 N Clark St (60610). Phone 312/661-1434; fax 312/661-1830. www.fronterakitch ens.com.* Born of chef-owner Rick Bayless' genius for, and scholarly pursuit of, regional Mexican cuisine, this River North superstar's brand has become a name to reckon with. The casual, more accessible of Bayless' side-by-side duo (see also TOPOLOBAMPO), Frontera introduces a wealth of deceptively simple Mexican dishes, and a world of flavors, that you won't find at your neighborhood taco stand. An exhaustive tequila list for sipping or for shaken-to-order margaritas and a fine wine list stand up to the food. A seat here is a coveted one, as reservations are for parties of five to ten only. Try Sat brunch (the restaurant is closed Sun and Mon). Mexican menu. Hours: 11:20 am-2 pm, 5:30-9:30 pm; Fri to 10:30 pm; Sat 5-11 pm; Sat brunch 10:30 am-2:30 pm. Closed Sun, Mon. Lunch $8-$12, dinner $9-$18.95. Sat brunch $5.95-$9.50. Bar. Valet parking available. Outdoor seating. Cr cds: A, D, DS, MC, V.

D

★ ★ **GEJA'S CAFE.** *340 W Armitage Ave (60614). Phone 773/281-9101; fax 773/281-0849. www.gejascafe.com.* The fondue craze never ended at this venerable Lincoln Park classic, always at or near the top of all those "most romantic" lists. It's dark and cozy inside, and after all, there is something flirtatious about swirling your food around in a pot and occasionally crossing forks with your tablemate(s) to the stylings of live flamenco guitar music. Fondue menu. Closed major holidays. Dinner. Bar. Live music. Casual attire. Variety of wines sold by the glass. Cr cds: A, D, DS, MC, V. **$$$**

★ ★ **GENE & GEORGETTI.** *500 N Franklin St (60610). Phone 312/527-3718; fax 312/527-2039. www.gene andgeorgetti.com.* A veteran steakhouse with a masculine, insider's ambience and a past (it opened in 1941, long before River North was a hip 'hood), Gene & Georgetti is an old-school Chicago carnivore's haunt. Prime steaks, gigantic "garbage salad," and gruff service are among the draws. Steakhouse menu. Hours: 11:00 am-midnight. Closed Sun; major holidays; also first week in July. Dinner $14-$39.75. Bar. Valet parking. Cr cds: A, MC, V.

D

★ ★ ★ **GIBSON'S STEAKHOUSE.** *1028 N Rush St (60611). Phone 312/266-8999; fax 312/787-5649. www. gibsonssteakhouse.com.* The theme at Gibson's is outsized, from the massive steaks on the plate to the stogie-puffing personalities'—a blend of politicians, sports figures, celebrities, and conventioneers, who energize the room. Carnivores crave the generous porterhouses here, but the kitchen also manages to issue some of the sea's biggest lobster tails and desserts that easily feed a four-top. Do call for a reservation, but don't be surprised if you still have to wait. In that case, squeeze into the smoky, convivial bar, order a martini, and prepare to make new friends. Steak, seafood menu. Closed Easter, Thanksgiving, Dec 24 and 25. Lunch, dinner. Bar. Piano. Casual attire. Valet parking available. Outdoor seating. Cr cds: A, D, DS, MC, V. **$$**

D

★ ★ **GIOCO.** *1312 S Wabash (60605). Phone 312/939-3870; fax 312/939-3858.* A riot of earthy flavors is in store at this chic former speakeasy in the South Loop. The simply sophisticated Italian food is offered up in a comfortable setting that's simultaneously rustic and clubby'—and the seasonal outdoor patio is a rare treat in this up-and-coming neighborhood. Italian menu. Menu changes seasonally. Closed holidays. Lunch, dinner. Bar. Entertainment. Casual attire. Cr cds: A, D, MC, V. **$$**

D

★ ★ **GREEK ISLANDS.** *200 S Halsted St (60661). Phone 312/782-9855; fax 312/454-0937.* Greek menu. Closed Thanksgiving, Dec 25. Dinner. Bar. Casual attire. Valet parking available. Outdoor seating. Cr cds: A, D, DS, MC, V. **$**

D

★ ★ **HARRY CARAY'S.** *33 W Kinzie St (60610). Phone 312/828-0966; fax 312/828-0962. www.harrycarays.com.* Hours: 11:30 am-2:30 pm, 5-10:30 pm; Fri, Sat to 11 pm; Sun 4-10 pm. Closed Dec 25. Reservations accepted. Italian, American menu. Bar. A la carte entrees: lunch, dinner $8.95-$39.95. Valet parking. Baseball memorabilia. Cr cds: A, DS, MC, V.

D

★ ★ **HATSUHANA.** *160 E Ontario St (60611). Phone 312/280-8808; fax 312/280-4545. www.hatsuhana.com.* Sushi menu. Closed Sun; major holidays. Lunch, dinner. Casual attire. Outdoor seating. Cr cds: A, C, D, DS, MC, V. **$$**

★★**INDIAN GARDEN.** *2546 W Devon Ave (60659). Phone 773/338-2929; fax 773/338-3930. www.theindiangarden.com.* Indian menu. Buffet, lunch, dinner. Bar. Casual attire. Reservations required. Cr cds: A, D, MC, V. **$$**

[D] [SC]

★ ★ **IXCAPUZALCO.** *2919 N Milwaukee (60618). Phone 773/486-7340; fax 773/486-7348.* Authentic, regional Mexican fare is the draw at this unpretentious neighborhood storefront. While a few dishes are recognizable renditions, Ixcapuzalco presents an opportunity to savor more intriguing, less familiar preparations for lunch, dinner, or Sunday brunch. There's also a traditional mole of the day, paired with a variety of meats. Dozens of premium tequilas may be sipped or shaken into margaritas. Candlelight and white tablecloths, rustic hand-carved wood chairs, and brilliant-hued artwork warm the small, smoke-free main dining room (which can be noisy due to the presence of the small, open kitchen; the back room is quieter). Mexican menu. Menu changes seasonally. Closed Tue. Lunch, dinner, brunch. Bar. Entertainment. Casual attire. Cr cds: A, D, DS, MC, V. **$$$**

[D]

★ ★ **JANE'S.** *1655 W Cortland (60622). Phone 773/862-5263. www.janesresaurant.com.* Eclectic American menu. Menu changes seasonally. Closed major holidays. Dinner, brunch. Bar. Entertainment. Casual attire. Outdoor seating. Cr cds: A, MC, V. **$$**

[D]

★ **JOE'S BE-BOP CAFE.** *600 E Grand Ave (60611). Phone 312/595-5299; fax 312/832-6986. www.joesbebop.com.* Barbecue menu. Hours: 11 am-11 pm; Fri, Sat to midnight. Closed Thanksgiving, Dec 25. Dinner $7.50-$18.95. Bar. Children's menu. Valet parking. Outdoor seating. Cr cds: A, D, DS, MC, V.

[D]

★ **JOHN'S PLACE.** *1202 W Webster (60614). Phone 773/525-6670.* Hours: 11 am-10 pm; Fri to 11 pm; Sat 8 am-11 pm; Sun 8 am-9 pm. Closed Mon. Lunch $5.95-$8.95, dinner $17.95-$54.95. Brunch $6.95-$8.95. Entertainment. Children's menu. Reservations accepted. Cr cds: A, D, DS, MC, V.

[D] [⊠]

★★★**KIKI'S BISTRO.** *900 N Franklin (60610). Phone 312/335-5454; fax 312/335-0614.* Long before bistros were blossoming all over town, this little charmer on an out-of-the-way corner in River North was pleasing patrons with its traditional bistro fare and regional specials. The softly lit dining rooms are appointed in wood, rose-pink draping and upholstery, and lace curtains. A somewhat older crowd frequents cozy, casual Kiki's for its romantic, country inn ambience, reliable kitchen, and free valet parking (a real boon in this bustling neighborhood). It's also fun to dine at the bar here. French bistro menu. Closed Sun; major holidays. Lunch, dinner. Bar. Casual attire. Cr cds: A, D, DS, MC, V. **$$**

[D]

★ ★ **KLAY OVEN.** *414 N Orleans St (60610). Phone 312/527-3999.* White tablecloths, exotic textiles, and tasteful serving carts set the tone for fine Indian dining at Klay Oven. Offerings include several tandoori options, plenty of vegetarian choices, and eight varieties of fresh-baked bread. Wine and beer options exceed expectations, and the lunch buffet is a great deal for the quality. Indian menu. Hours: 11:30 am-2:30 pm, 5:30-10:30 pm. Closed major holidays. A la carte entrees: lunch buffet $7.95, dinner $6.95-$25.95. Bar. Reservations accepted. Cr cds: A, DS, MC, V.

[D]

★ ★ **LA BOCCA DELLA VERITA.** *4618 N Lincoln (60618). Phone 773/784-6222; fax 773/784-6272. www.laboccachicago.com.* Italian menu. Closed Mon; major holidays. Lunch, dinner. Entertainment. Casual attire. Outdoor seating. Cr cds: A, D, DS, MC, V. **$$**

[D]

★ ★ ★ **LA SARDINE.** *111 N Carpenter (60607). Phone 312/421-2800; fax 312/421-2318. www.lasardine.com.* Perhaps a bit large for a bistro, La Sardine nevertheless delivers the requisite aromas, creature comforts, and menu classics. Warm and bustling (and sometimes noisy) despite a fairly industrial West Loop location, La Sardine draws both hip and mature urbanites for the likes of escargots, brandade, bouillabaisse, roast chicken, and profiteroles. Servers wear butcher aprons; the walls are buttery yellow; and those scents waft from an open kitchen and rotisserie. The impressive wine list includes some hard-to-find French selections. French menu. Closed Sun; major holidays. Lunch, dinner. Bar. Entertainment. Casual attire. Cr cds: A, C, D, DS, MC, V. **$$**

[D]

★★**LA STRADA.** *155 N Michigan Ave (60601). Phone 312/565-2200; fax 312/565-2216. www.lastradaristorante.com.* Northern Italian menu. Hours: 11:30 am-10 pm; Fri to 11 pm, Sat 5-11 pm; early-bird dinner 5-6:30 pm. Closed Sun; some major holidays. A la carte entrees: lunch $12-$18, dinner $14-$32, 7 course $75. Tableside cooking. Bar. Wine cellar. Pianist from 5 pm. Reservations accepted. Valet parking. Cr cds: A, D, DS, MC, V.

[D]

★ ★ **LAWRY'S PRIME RIB.** *100 E Ontario St (60611). Phone 312/787-5000; fax 312/787-1264. www.lawrysonline.com.* Steak menu. Closed Dec 25. Lunch, dinner. Bar. In 1896 McCormick mansion. Casual attire. Valet parking (dinner). Chicago counterpart of famous California restaurant. Cr cds: A, D, DS, MC, V. **$$$**

SC

★ ★ **LE BOUCHON.** *1958 N Damen Ave (60647). Phone 773/862-6600; fax 773/524-1208. www.lebouchonofchicago.com.* French menu. Closed Sun; major holidays. Dinner. Bar. French bistro décor with lace curtains, pressed-tin ceiling. Casual attire. Cr cds: A, C, D, DS, MC, V. **$$**

D

★ ★ ★ **LES NOMADES.** *222 E Ontario St (60611). Phone 312/649-9010; fax 312/649-0608. www.lesnomades.net.* Les Nomades is a serene little spot tucked away from the bustle of Michigan Avenue in an elegant turn-of-the-century townhouse. Romantic and intimate, with a fireplace, hardwood floors, deep cozy banquettes, and gorgeous flower arrangements, Les Nomades was originally opened as a private club. It is now open to the public, and what a lucky public we are. While many of Chicago's hottest dining rooms are filled with as much noise as they are with wonderful food, Les Nomades is a peaceful, reserved restaurant that offers perfect service and a magnificent menu of French fare flecked with Asian accents. Excessive noise is not present to distract you from the task at hand. Any spontaneous exclamations of love directed toward the delicious dishes you are consuming (game, foie gras, scallops, lamb, and fish among them) should be kept to a quiet roar, as the tables are closely spaced and exclamations of wonder are often shared. Dining here is a wonderful gastronomic experience, thus this is not a place for a casual dinner. Men are required to dine in jackets and ties, and women are comparably fitted for the occasion. Even children who are rightfully pampered by the attentive staff dress in their holiday best for a memorable evening. French menu. Closed Sun, Mon; holidays. Dinner. Bar. Jacket required. Valet parking available. Totally nonsmoking. Cr cds: A, C, D, MC, V. **$$$**

D

★ **MAGGIANO'S.** *516 N Clark St (60610). Phone 312/644-7700. www.maggianos.com.* Southern Italian menu. Hours: 11:30 am-2 pm, 5-10 pm; Fri to 11 pm; Sat 11:30 am-11 pm; Sun noon-10 pm. Closed Dec 25. A la carte entrees: lunch $7.95-$14.95, dinner $9.95-$29.95. Bar. Reservations accepted. Valet parking. 1940s, family-style décor with wood columns and bistro-style seating. Outdoor dining. Cr cds: A, C, D, DS, MC, V.

D

★ ★ **MARCHE.** *833 W Randolph St (60607). Phone 312/226-8399; fax 312/226-4169. www.marche-chicago.com.* French Bistro menu. Closed major holidays. Lunch, dinner. Bar. Casual attire. Valet parking available. Outdoor seating. Cr cds: A, D, MC, V. **$$$**

D

★ ★ **MARYSOL.** *812 W Randolph St (60607). Phone 312/563-1763; fax 312/563-1773.* Cuban menu. Closed Sun; major holidays. Dinner. Bar. Casual attire. Outdoor seating. **$$**

D

★ ★ ★ **MERITAGE.** *2118 N Damen (60647). Phone 773/235-6434. www.meritagecafe.com.* For a storefront Bucktown restaurant, Meritage aims high, dishing seafood-focused fare inspired by the cuisine and wines of the Pacific Northwest. Pacific Rim influences edge into seared salmon with taro pancake and Japanese spiced roast scallops. Meat lovers and red wine drinkers are ably served with seared lamb and duck confit. Though the spacious outdoor patio is enclosed and heated in winter, only a canopy cloisters the space in summer, making Meritage one of the city's best open-air eateries. American menu. Closed major holidays. Dinner, Sun brunch. Bar. Casual attire. Outdoor seating. Cr cds: A, D, DS, MC, V. **$$$**

★ ★ ★ **MIA FRANCESCA.** *3311 N Clark St (60657). Phone 773/281-3310; fax 773/281-6671. www.miafrancesca.com.* The original of an ever-expanding family of restaurants, still-trendy (and loud) Mia Francesca packs 'em in for the earthy, ever-changing, moderately priced northern Italian fare. The casually stylish, colorful crowd is comprised of all ages and persuasions; the décor manages to be simultaneously sleek and warm. The second floor is a bit calmer; the outdoor tables are a lucky score for summer dining. Long waits at the vintage bar or in the coach house are often part of the dining experience here, as Mia takes no reservations. Italian menu. Closed Thanksgiving, Dec 25. Dinner. Bar. Children's menu. Reservations not accepted. Valet parking available. Cr cds: A, D, MC, V. **$**

D

★ ★ ★ **MIKE DITKA'S.** *100 E Chestnut (60611). Phone 312/587-8989. www.mikeditkaschicago.com.* Former Chicago Bears coach Mike Ditka's namesake restaurant is manly, naturally, yet surprisingly civilized. While a museum installation-quality sports memorabilia display decorates the clubby restaurant, the patrons exhibit more steakhouse than stadium behavior. Conveniently located near the Magnificent Mile and its many hotels and shopping destinations, Ditka's dishes up generous portions of quality meats (including a massive signature pork chop and "training table" pot roast), as well as seafood, pastas, and salads. The cigar-friendly bar is a louder, more casual destination for snacks and televised sports; upstairs, the cigar lounge features live piano music. American menu. Closed Dec 25. Lunch, dinner, brunch. Bar. Entertainment Wed-Sat. Children's menu. Casual attire. Outdoor seating. Cr cds: A, C, D, DS, MC, V. **$$$**

D

★ ★ ★ **MIRAI SUSHI.** *2020 W Division (60622). Phone 773/862-8500; fax 773/862-8510. www.miraisushi. com.* Wicker Park's funky-hip sushi hotspot is serious about sushi. Offering more than just your everyday maki and nigiri, Mirai ups the ante on sushi (fish is flown in daily, and some selections are still swimming), sake (a generous list), and Japanese culinary creativity (with an intriguing menu items and specials). The bi-level restaurant boasts a bright, smoke-free main-floor dining area and sushi bar, your best bet for experiencing the sushi specials; the upstairs sake bar is dark and seductive, with a choice of barstools, tables, or sleek lounge furniture, with deejay music on weekends. Sushi menu. Closed major holidays. Dinner. Bar. Entertainment. Casual attire. Outdoor seating. Cr cds: A, D, DS, MC, V. **$**

D

★ ★ ★ **MK.** *868 N Franklin St (60610). Phone 312/482-9179; fax 312/482-9171. www.mkchicago.com.* Style meets substance at Michael Kornick's mk, where refined yet real contemporary cuisine is offered in a perfectly compatible setting. The seasonal American food is clean and uncontrived, the multitiered architectural space linear and neutral without severity. Mergers (stylish couples) and acquisitions (salt-and-pepper-haired types in fashionable eyewear) are all a part of the mk dining experience, as are knowledgeable service, a fine wine list (including private-label selections), and excellent desserts. Degustation menus are available, and the chic lounge area is perfect for a before-or-after glass of bubbly. American menu. Closed holidays; week of July 4. Dinner. Bar. Entertainment. Cr cds: A, C, D, JCB, MC, V. **$$$**

D

★ ★ ★ **MOD.** *1520 N Damen Ave (60622). Phone 773/252-1500.* Don't let the trippy, geometric-acrylic décor fool you; the food here is serious enough, as evidenced by the commitment to seasonal ingredients and composed plate presentations. The American fare, wine list, and background music could all be described as intelligently eclectic, making MOD. a hit with both the hipster Wicker Park crowd and more seasoned, suited-up diners with a sense of adventure. A happening bar scene, Sunday brunch, and seasonal outdoor dining add to the restaurant's appeal. Contemporary American menu. Menu changes seasonally. Dinner, Sun brunch. Bar. Outdoor seating. Cr cds: A, D, MC, V.

D

★ ★ ★ **MON AMI GABI.** *2300 N Lincoln Park W (60614). Phone 773/348-8886. www.leye.com.* French Bistro menu. Closed major holidays. Dinner. Bar. Entertainment. Children's menu. Casual attire. Outdoor seating. Cr cds: A, D, DS, MC, V. **$$**

D

★ ★ ★ **MORTON'S OF CHICAGO.** *1050 N State St (60610). Phone 312/266-4820; fax 312/266-4852. www.mortons.com.* This steakhouse chain, which originated in Chicago in 1978, appeals to serious meat lovers. With a selection of belt-busting carnivorous delights (like the house specialty, a 24-ounce porterhouse), as well as fresh fish, lobster, and chicken entrées, Morton's rarely disappoints. If you just aren't sure what you're in the mood for, the tableside menu presentation may help you decide. Here, main course selections are placed on a cart that's rolled to your table, where servers describe each item in detail. Hours: 5:30-11 pm; Sun 5-10 pm. Closed major holidays. Dinner $19.95-$34.95. Bar. Valet parking. Cr cds: A, C, D, DS, JCB, MC, V.

D

★ ★ ★ **NICK'S FISHMARKET.** *51 S Clark (60603). Phone 312/621-0200; fax 312/621-1118. www. nicksfishmarketchicago.com.* Though Nick's specializes in seafood, it acts in every other way like a steakhouse. Consider the dark, subterranean room with low ceilings and attentive tuxedoed waiters. Traditional preparations like lobster bisque and lobster thermador encourage the simile. But in the kitchen, Nick is all about fish. An operation born in Hawaii in the mid-1960s, Nick's reveals its roots in Hawaiian fish specials and the "Maui Wowie" salad. Appetizers feature shellfish, sashimi, and caviar, followed by sole, salmon, and lobster entrees. The street-level bar serves casual versions. American menu. Closed Sun; major holidays. Lunch, dinner. Bar. Piano (Tue-Sun, dinner). Children's menu. Valet parking. Cr cds: A, D, DS, JCB, MC, V. **$$$**

D

★ ★ ★ **NINE.** *440 W Randolph St (60606). Phone 312/575-9900. www.n9ne.com.* American menu. Closed Sun; major holidays. Lunch, dinner. Bar. Casual attire. Cr cds: A, D, MC, V. **$$$**

D

★ ★ **NIX.** *163 E Walton Pl (60611). Phone 312/867-7575; toll-free 866/866-8086; fax 312/751-9205. www. millenium-hotels.com.* American menu. Breakfast, lunch, dinner, Sun brunch. Bar. Children's menu. Casual attire. Valet parking available. Outdoor seating. Cr cds: A, C, D, DS, MC, V. **$$$**

D SC

★ **NOLA'S.** *1856 W North Ave (60622). Phone 773/395-4300; fax 773/395-1253.* American, Cajun/Creole menu. Closed major holidays. Dinner. Bar. Children's menu. Casual attire. Outdoor seating. **$$**

D

★ ★ ★ **NOMI.** *800 N Michigan Ave (60611). Phone 312/239-4030; fax 312/239-4029. www.nomirestaurant.com.* A posh perch over Chicago's famed Magnificent Mile, NoMI (an acronym for North Michigan) is the Park Hyatt's stylish, civilized destination for critically acclaimed contemporary French cuisine. Asian influences are evident in sushi and sashimi selections on the sophisticated menu. Luxurious materials combine in the streamlined décor, highlighted by an eye-catching art collection, glittering open kitchen, and scintillating view from floor-to-ceiling windows. The wine list is both impressive and extensive, with 3,000 or so bottles. NoMI also serves breakfast and lunch and offers outdoor terrace dining in fair weather. French menu. Breakfast, lunch, dinner. Bar. Reservations required. Outdoor seating. Cr cds: A, D, DS, MC, V. **$$$**

D

★ ★ ★ **NORTH POND CAFE.** *2610 N Cannon Dr (60614). Phone 773/477-5845; fax 773/477-3234. www.northpondrestaurant.com.* North Pond delivers a dining experience like no other. Seasonal, contemporary American food emphasizing regional ingredients is paired with an all-American wine list and served in a one-of-a-kind location on the Lincoln Park lagoon. The handsome Arts and Crafts décor gives the feeling that Frank Lloyd Wright had a hand in the proceedings. No roads lead here; cab it or look for parking along Cannon Drive, and then follow the garden path to the restaurant. Sunday brunch is a refined indulgence, and outdoor dining is a special treat in seasonable weather. Menu changes seasonally. Hours: 11:30 am-2 pm, 5:30-10 pm; Sun 11 am-2 pm, 5:30-10 pm. Closed Mon; holidays. Dinner $24-$32. Sun brunch. Entertainment. Outdoor seating. Cr cds: A, D, MC, V.

D

★ **NORTHSIDE CAFE.** *1635 N Damen (60647). Phone 773/384-3555; fax 773/384-6337.* American menu. Closed Thanksgiving, Dec 24 and 25. Lunch, dinner. Bar. Entertainment. Casual attire. Outdoor seating. Cr cds: A, D, DS, MC, V. **$$**

D

★ ★ ★ **ONE SIXTYBLUE.** *160 N Loomis (60607). Phone 312/850-0303; fax 312/829-3046. www.onesixtyblue.com.* Award-winning, haute contemporary cuisine and sleek, high-styled décor by famed designer Adam Tihany define this adult, urban dining experience in the West Loop. Bold American fare with French roots is at home in the contemporary yet comfortable dining room, done in dark wood and citrus hues with discreet lighting and great sightlines. The open kitchen and dramatic wine storage are focal points. A cocoa bar offers sinful chocolate creations; the chic lounge is a hot cocktail spot. The buzz over former Chicago Bull Michael Jordan's partnership is a mere whisper now that his limelight has dimmed. American menu. Menu changes seasonally. Closed Sun; holidays. Dinner. Bar. Entertainment. Casual attire. Cr cds: A, D, MC, V. **$$$**

D

★ ★ **PALM.** *323 E Wacker Dr (60601). Phone 312/616-1000; fax 312/616-3717. www.thepalm.com.* Steak menu. Lunch, dinner. Bar. Casual, energetic atmosphere; caricatures of celebrities and regular customers line walls. Casual attire. Valet parking available. Outdoor dining. Cr cds: A, C, D, DS, MC, V. **$$$**

D

★ **PAPAGUS GREEK TAVERNA.** *620 N State St (60610). Phone 312/642-8450; fax 312/642-8132. www.leye.com.* Hours: 11:30 am-10 pm; Sat 11:30 am-midnight; Sun 2:30-10 pm. Reservations accepted. Greek menu. Bar. A la carte entrees: lunch $3.95-$14, dinner $7.75-$24.95. Valet parking. Outdoor dining. Rustic, country taverna atmosphere. Cr cds: A, C, D, DS, MC, V. **$**

D

★ **PARTHENON.** *314 S Halsted St (60661). Phone 312/726-2407; fax 312/726-3203. www.theparthenon.com.* Greek menu. Closed Thanksgiving, Dec 25. Lunch, dinner. Bar. Children's menu. Casual attire. Valet parking available. Cr cds: A, C, D, DS, MC, V. **$**

D

★ **PENNY'S NOODLE SHOP.** *3400 N Sheffield (60657). Phone 773/281-8222.* Thai menu. Closed Mon; major holidays. Lunch, dinner. Entertainment. Casual attire. Outdoor seating. Cr cds: A, D, MC, V. **$**

D

★ **PIZZERIA UNO.** *29 E Ohio St (60611). Phone 312/321-1000. www.unos.com.* Pizza. Closed Thanksgiving, Dec 25. Lunch, dinner. Bar. Children's menu. Casual attire. Outdoor seating. Cr cds: A, C, D, DS, ER, MC, V. **$**

D

★ ★ **PRINTER'S ROW.** *550 S Dearborn St (60605). Phone 312/461-0780; fax 312/461-0624. www.printers-row.com.* Local legend Michael Foley changes his contemporary American menu with the seasons, and the results are usually (but not always) quite fine. Dishes of game and seafood tend to be especially tasty. Service can be erratic on occasion. Contemporary American menu. Closed Sun; major holidays. Lunch, dinner. Bar. In old printing building (1897). Casual attire. Cr cds: A, D, DS, MC, V. **$$$**

D

★ ★ ★ **PUMP ROOM.** *1301 N State Pkwy (60610). Phone 312/266-0360; fax 312/266-1798. www.pumproom.com.* This revered Chicago classic combines the grand, gracious hotel dining of yesteryear with contemporary French-American fare. Having undergone several chef changes in recent years (and a major renovation a few years ago), the Pump Room remains popular with tourists and special-occasion celebrants. Booth One lives on, complete with vintage telephone; the bar could have been transported from a Thin Man set. The photo wall is a sentimental journey down the memory lane of film, music, and politics. Highlights include live music with a small dance floor and Sunday Champagne brunch; the "upscale casual"dress code attests to the times. American menu. Breakfast, lunch, dinner, Sun brunch. Bar. Entertainment Thur-Sat. Children's menu. Jacket required. Valet parking available. Cr cds: A, C, D, DS, MC, V. **$$$**

D

★ **REDFISH.** *400 N State St (60610). Phone 312/467-1600; fax 312/467-0325.* Hours: 11:30 am-10 pm; Fri to 11 pm; Sat noon-11 pm; Sun noon-10 pm. Closed most major holidays. Reservations accepted. Cajun/Creole menu. Bar to midnight. Lunch $10-$18, dinner $15-$18. Children's meals. Jazz and blues Thur-Sat. Valet parking. Outdoor dining. Louisiana roadhouse with Mardi Gras décor; masks, voodoo doll displays. Cr cds: A, D, DS, MC, V.

D

★ ★ **REDLIGHT.** *820 W Randolph St (60607). Phone 312/733-8880. www.redlight-chicago.com.* Chinese, Thai menu. Closed Jan 1, Thanksgiving, Dec 25. Lunch, dinner. Bar. Casual attire. Valet parking available. Outdoor seating. Cr cds: A, C, D, MC, V. **$**

D

★ ★ **RIVA.** *700 E Grand Ave (60611). Phone 312/644-7482; fax 312/206-7035. www.stefanirestaurants.com.* Seafood menu. Closed Thanksgiving, Dec 24 and 25. Lunch, dinner. Bar. Children's menu. Casual attire. Valet parking available. Outdoor seating. Cr cds: A, C, D, DS, MC, V. **$$**

D

★ ★ **ROSEBUD.** *1500 W Taylor (60607). Phone 312/942-1117. www.rosebudrestaurants.com.* Italian menu. Closed. Lunch, dinner. Bar. Entertainment. Casual attire. Outdoor seating. Cr cds: A, D, DS, MC, V. **$$**

D

★ ★ **RUSSIAN TEA TIME.** *77 E Adams St (60603). Phone 312/360-0000; fax 312/360-0575. www.russianteatime.com.* Russian, Ukrainian menu. Hours: 11 am-11 pm; Mon to 4 pm; Fri to midnight; Sat noon-midnight; Sun 1-9 pm. Closed Jan 1, Memorial Day. Dinner $18-$27. Bar. Totally nonsmoking. Traditional caviar service. Russian dolls on display. Cr cds: A, D, DS, MC, V.

D

★ ★ **SALOON.** *200 E Chestnut St (60611). Phone 312/280-5454; fax 312/280-6986. www.saloonsteakhouse.com.* Steak menu. Closed major holidays. Lunch, dinner. Bar. Casual attire. Cr cds: A, C, D, DS, MC, V. **$$$**

D

★ ★ **SALPICON.** *1252 N Wells St (60610). Phone 312/988-7811; fax 312/988-7715. www.salpicon.com.* In a town where chef Rick Bayless and his Frontera Grill rule the gourmet Mexican roost, Salpicon remains an in-the-know treasure. Chef Priscilla Satkoff grew up in Mexico City and honors her native cuisine here with rich moles, tender roasted meats, and upscale twists on both, such as ancho chile quail. The extensive wine list, managed by the chef's husband, has won numerous awards. But it's hard to get past the 50-some tequilas on offer to mix in margaritas (knowing servers ably steer agave gringos). Salpicon's boldly colored interiors generate a spirit of fiesta. Mexican menu. Closed Thanksgiving, Dec 25. Dinner, Sun brunch. Bar. Valet parking available. Outdoor dining. Cr cds: A, D, DS, MC, V.

D

★ ★ **SANTORINI.** *800 W Adams St (60607). Phone 312/829-8820; fax 312/829-6263. www.santoriniseafood.com.* Greek menu. Closed Thanksgiving, Dec 25. Lunch, dinner. Bar. Children's menu. Casual attire. Valet parking available. Simulated Greek town. Outdoor seating. Cr cds: A, D, DS, MC, V. **$$**

D

★ **SAYAT NOVA.** *157 E Ohio St (60611). Phone 312/644-9159; fax 312/644-6234.* Hours: 11:30 am-10:30 pm; Sat noon-11 pm; Sun 3-10 pm. Closed major holidays. Reservations accepted. Armenian menu. Bar. Lunch $6.95-$11.95, dinner $9.90-$16.95. Family-owned. Cr cds: A, C, D, DS, MC, V.

D

★ ★ **SCOOZI.** *410 W Huron (60610). Phone 312/943-5900; fax 312/943-8969. www.lettuceentertainyou.com.* Hours: 11:30 am-2 pm, 5-9:30 pm; Fri to 10:30 pm; Sat 5-10:30 pm; Sun 4-9 pm. Closed Thanksgiving, Dec 25. Reservations accepted. Italian menu. Bar. A la carte entrees: lunch $7-$15, dinner $7-$21. Specializes in woodburning-oven pizza, antipasti. Own pasta, desserts. Valet parking. Outdoor dining. Casual atmosphere with loft-style ceilings, woodburning oven and antipasti bar. Cr cds: A, D, DS, MC, V.

D

★ ★ ★ **SEASONS.** *120 E Delaware Pl (60611). Phone 312/649-2349; fax 312/649-2372. www.fourseasons.com.* Dining at Seasons, the upscale and elegant restaurant of the Four Seasons, is the sort of experience that may cause whiplash. Your head will whip back and forth as you watch stunning plates pass by in the

rich and refined dining room. Each dish looks better than the next. On a nightly basis, the dining room is filled with food envy. Perhaps this is because the kitchen prepares every plate with a deep respect for ingredients, making every inventive dish on the menu of New American fare a delight to admire from afar and devour from up close. The chef offers three prix fixe menus: vegetarian, five-course, and eight-course. What's more, while a restaurant of this stature could easily feel pretentious, the staff's warmth and charm makes dining here easy and comfortable, a pleasure from start to finish. American, French menu. Bar. Children's menu. Lunch, dinner, Sun brunch. Bar. Piano, jazz trio Sat. Children's menu. Valet parking available. Casual attire. Cr cds: A, C, D, DS, ER, MC, V. **$$$**
D

★★ **SHAW'S CRAB HOUSE.** *21 E Hubbard St (60611). Phone 312/527-2722; fax 312/527-4740. www.shaws-chicago.com.* Seafood menu. Closed Thanksgiving, Dec 25. Lunch, dinner. Bar. Entertainment Tue, Thur 7-10 pm. Casual attire. Valet parking available. Outdoor seating. Cr cds: A, C, D, DS, MC, V. **$$$**
D

★★ **SIGNATURE ROOM AT THE 95TH.** *875 N Michigan Ave (60611). Phone 312/787-9596; fax 630/968-7779. www.signatureroom.com.* American menu. Closed Jan 1, Dec 25. Lunch, dinner, Sun brunch. Bar. Piano. Casual attire. Cr cds: A, D, DS, MC, V. **$$**
D

★★ **SOUK.** *1552 N Milwaukee Ave (60622). Phone 773/227-1818; fax 773/278-1408. www.soukrestaurant.com.* Mediterranean menu. Dinner. Bar. Casual attire. Cr cds: A, D, DS, MC, V. **$$**
D

★★★ **SOUL KITCHEN.** *1576 N Milwaukee (60622). Phone 773/342-9742; fax 773/342-9798.* Original art, beaded lamps, and the generous use of leopard print put the funk in Soul Kitchen. An R&B soundtrack out-shouts the clamor of groups who storm the place on weekends. Helped by a star location at the Wicker Park intersection of North, Damen, and Milwaukee, this perennial favorite slings Southern food from a lively open kitchen. Entrees range from barbecued shrimp to jerk chicken, but it's the rave-worthy crab cakes and sautéed oysters on the starter list that you shouldn't miss. Menu changes seasonally. Hours: 5-10:30 pm. Sun brunch 10 am-2 pm. Closed holidays. Dinner $12-$20. Brunch $7-$16. Entertainment. Reservations accepted. Cr cds: A, C, D, DS, JCB, MC, V.
D ▨

★★★ **SPAGO.** *520 N Dearborn St (60610). Phone 312/527-3700; fax 312/527-3353. www.wolfgangpuck.com.* The famed LA import serves up Wolfgang Puck's brand of contemporary American cuisine, running the gamut from creative to comfort food (including those now-legendary wood-fired pizzas). Both the prices and the décor have been toned down since the restaurant's opening; a makeover has subdued the former go-go 1980s color extravaganza to a more soothing, neutral palette. The handsome space, now done in warm woods, curves, and geometric shapes, is more compatible with the power business and the well-heeled tourist crowd (attire is "business casual"). The signature open kitchen and the wall of original Robert Rauschenbergs remain, as does the upstairs cigar lounge. American menu. Closed Sun; holidays. Lunch, dinner. Bar. Casual attire. Valet parking. Cr cds: A, D, MC, V. **$$$**
D

★★★ **SPIAGGIA.** *980 N Michigan Ave (60611). Phone 312/280-2750; fax 312/943-8560. www.spiaggiarestaurant.com.* Next to Spiaggia, you'd have to fly to Milan to get a dose of the sort of contemporary, sophisticated Italian cuisine served here. Chef Tony Mantuano has a light, refined touch, working with artisanal and exotic ingredients like Piemontese beef and seasonal white truffles. Expect frequent menu changes, but typical dishes include wood-roasted scallops with porcini mushrooms and parmesan shavings, pumpkin risotto with seared foie gras, and lamb chops with slow-cooked lamb shoulder. Favored by both expense accounts and special occasion affairs, the opulent tri-level room completes the seduction, offering each table a view over Lake Michigan. Italian menu. Closed holidays. Dinner. Bar. Piano. Jacket required (dinner). Reservations required. Valet parking available. Cr cds: A, C, D, DS, MC, V. **$$$$**
D

★★★★ **SPRING.** *2039 W North Ave (60647). Phone 773/395-7100. www.springrestaurant.net.* You don't expect it of the bohemian Wicker Park surroundings, but Spring is one of the city's most sophisticated foodies. Chef Shawn McClain has a deft touch with seafood, the specialty here prepared with Asian touches. Artistic but unfussy dishes change seasonally but might include tuna tartare with quail egg or cod in crab and sweet pea sauce. Lodged in a former bathhouse with the white ceramic wall tiles to prove it, Spring faces east for inspiration, greeting diners in the foyer with a Zen-inspired rock garden. American menu. Closed early Jan; major holidays. Dinner. Bar. Casual attire. **$$$**
D

★★★ **STETSON'S CHOPHOUSE.** *151 E Wacker Dr (60601). Phone 312/565-1234.* Steakhouse menu. Hours: 4:30-10 pm. A la carte entrees: dinner $16-$30. Bar. Wine list. Children's menu. Reservations accepted. Valet parking. Cr cds: A, D, DS, MC, V.

★★ **STREETERVILLE GRILLE.** *301 E North Water St (60611). Phone 312/670-0788.* Hours: 11:30 am-2 pm, 5:30-10 pm; Fri to 10:30 pm; Sat 5-10:30 pm. Closed Sun;

Jan 1, Dec 25. Reservations accepted. Service bar. Lunch $8-$17. A la carte entrees: dinner $18-$30. Specializes in steak, prime rib, pasta. Valet parking. Cr cds: A, D, DS, MC, V.

D

★ **SU CASA.** *49 E Ontario St (60611). Phone 312/943-4041; fax 312/943-6480.* Hours: 11:30 am-11 pm; Fri, Sat to midnight. Closed Thanksgiving, Dec 25. Reservations accepted. Mexican menu. Bar. Lunch, dinner $4.95-$12.95. Valet parking. Outdoor dining. 16th-century Mexican décor; Mexican artifacts. Cr cds: A, D, DS, MC, V.

D

★★**SUSHI WABI.** *842 W Randolph St (60607). Phone 312/563-1224; fax 312/563-9579. www.sushiwabi.com.* Chicago's first in a wave of hipster sushi bars draws a fashionable crowd to the West Loop market district for the fresh fish, industrial-chic atmosphere, and late-night deejay music. The clubby (noisy) scene is secondary to the seafood, and savvy sushi lovers know that reservations are a must. Japanese, Sushi menu. Closed holidays. Lunch, dinner. Bar. Entertainment: Wed, Fri, Sat. Casual attire. Reservations required. Cr cds: A, D, DS, MC, V. **$$**

D ⊠

★★ **SZECHWAN EAST.** *340 E Ohio St (60611). Phone 312/255-9200; fax 312/642-3907. www.chicagobest chinesefood.com.* Chinese menu. Chinese décor with large golden Buddha, etched glass. Hours: 11:30 am-10 pm; Sun brunch to 2 pm. Closed Thanksgiving. Buffet lunch $8.95. A la carte entrees: dinner $7.95-$23.95. Sun brunch $15.95. Bar to 1 am. Reservations accepted. Valet parking. Outdoor dining. Cr cds: A, C, D, DS, MC, V.

★★ **TIZI MELLOUL.** *531 N Wells (60610). Phone 312/670-4338; fax 312/670-4254.* Menu changes seasonally. Hours: 5:30-11 pm; Thur 5-10 pm; Fri, Sat 5-11 pm; Sun 5:30-10 pm. Dinner $14-$20. Entertainment. Reservations accepted. Cr cds: A, C, D, DS, MC, V.

D ⊠

★ **TOAST.** *2046 N Damen (60647). Phone 773/772-5600.* American menu. Closed major holidays. Breakfast, lunch. Casual attire. **$**

★★ **TOPOLOBAMPO.** *445 N Clark St (60610). Phone 312/661-1434. www.fronterakitchens.com.* Pioneering chef-owner Rick Bayless is a cookbook author, television personality, and perennial culinary award winner with a devoted following. His celebration of the regional cuisines of Mexico is realized at Topolobampo, the upscale counterpart to his famed Frontera Grill—and the shrine where the faithful gather to revel in the bright, earthy flavors of his fine-dining Mexican fare. The seasonal menu is paired with a tome of premium tequilas and an excellent wine list. White tablecloths and colorful folk art help set the tone for a memorable Mexican meal. Mexican menu. Hours: 11:30 am-2 pm, 5:30-9:30 pm; Fri, Sat 5:30-10:30 pm. Closed Sun, Mon. Dinner $15-$29. Bar. Valet parking. Cr cds: A, D, DS, MC, V.

D

★★★**TRATTORIA NO. 10.** *10 N Dearborn St (60602). Phone 312/984-1718. www.trattoriaten.com.* A rustic yet elegant respite from the hectic rush of the Loop business district, Trattoria No. 10 welcomes with arched ceilings, murals, and ceramic tile floors. House-made ravioli is a specialty, as are pastas, risottos, and fresh seafood selections on the menu of updated Italian classics. A popular lunch and dinner spot for downtown denizens, Trattoria No. 10 is perhaps best known for its bountiful, bargain-priced cocktail hour buffet—a great pre-theater option or pick-me-up after museums and shopping. Italian menu. Hours: 11:30 am-2 pm, 5:30-9 pm; Fri to 10 pm; Sat 5:30-10 pm. Closed Sun; major holidays. Dinner $10.95-$22.95. Bar. Valet parking. Cr cds: A, C, D, DS, MC, V.

D

★★★★**TRU.** *676 N St. Clair (60611). Phone 312/202-0001; fax 312/202-0003. www.trurestaurant.com.* Awash in white and set in a chic lofty space, TRU's modern, airy dining room is a stunning stage for chef–co-owner Rick Tramonto's savory, progressive French creations and co-owner pastry chef Gale Gand's incredible, one-of-a-kind sweet and savory endings. Tramonto offers plates filled with flawless ingredients that are treated to his unmatched creativity and artistic flair. The result is food that is precious and, some say, overdone. Indeed, many of the plates are so beautiful and complicated that you may not want to dig and ruin the presentation, or you may be unable to decipher the appropriate way to consume the dish. Do yourself a favor and bring a camera; that way, you can admire the dishes long after you have devoured them. TRU offers three- to eight-course "Collections" (prix fixe menus) and a unique and extraordinary four-course dessert and Champagne dessert tasting from the unconventional Gale Gand of the Food Network. Like the savory side of the menu, the desserts have a distinctive sense of ingredient choice, style, and humor. Ingredient choice, style, and humor. Progressive French menu. Hours: 5:30-10 pm; Fri, Sat 5 to 11 pm. Dinner $45-$65; prix fixe $75-$125. Jacket required. Reservations required. Valet parking available. Totally nonsmoking. Cr cds: A, D, DS, MC, V.

D

★ **TUCCI BENUCCH.** *900 N Michigan Ave (60611). Phone 312/266-2500; fax 312/266-7702. www.leye.com.* Italian menu. Closed Thanksgiving, Dec 25. Lunch, dinner. Bar. Children's menu. Casual attire. Totally nonsmoking. Cr cds: A, D, DS, MC, V. **$$**

D

★ ★ **TUSCANY.** *1014 W Taylor St (60612). Phone 312/829-1990; fax 312/829-8023. www.stefanirestaurants.com.* Northern Italian menu. Closed Jan 1, Dec 25. Lunch, dinner. Bar. Valet parking available. Cr cds: A, D, DS, MC, V. **$$**

D

★ **TWIN ANCHORS RESTAURANT AND TAVERN.** *1655 N Sedgwick St (60614). Phone 312/266-1616.* Make no bones about it: Chicago is a meat-and-potatoes kind of town, and there are few things that native Chicagoans like more than a great slab of ribs. Choices abound, but a local favorite is Twin Anchors Restaurant and Tavern in the Old Town neighborhood just north of downtown (and a fairly short cab ride away). Although this former speakeasy was reincarnated as a restaurant in 1932, it maintains its hole-in-the-wall appeal, complete with diner-style booths, linoleum tabletops, a jukebox stocked with an eclectic mix of tunes, and an extensive collection of beers. The real attraction, however, is the ribs; rumor has it that they were Frank Sinatra's favorites. Order them zesty, like a local, and then let the feast begin. The menu may be limited, but the portions are generous. If ribs aren't your style, the hamburgers and filet mignon are also excellent. Be prepared for a long wait, though; this 60-seat restaurant fills up fast. Barbecue menu. Lunch, dinner. Bar. Casual attire. Outdoor seating. **$$**

D

★ ★ **VINCI.** *1732 N Halsted St (60614). Phone 312/266-1199. www.vinci-group.com.* Italian menu. Closed Mon; most major holidays. Dinner, Sun brunch. Bar. Children's menu. Casual attire. Valet parking (dinner). Cr cds: A, D, DS, MC, V. **$$**

D

★ ★ **VIVERE.** *71 W Monroe St (60603). Phone 312/332-4040; fax 312/332-2656. www.italianvillage-chicago.com.* Italian menu. Hours: 11:30 am-2:30 pm, 5-10 pm; Fri to 11 pm; Sat 5-11 pm. Closed Sun; major holidays. Dinner $16-$35. Bar. Valet parking. Cr cds: A, D, DS, MC, V.

D

★ ★ **VIVO.** *838 W Randolph (60607). Phone 312/733-3379; fax 312/733-4436. www.vivo-chicago.com.* With the distinction of having pioneered the now-booming Randolph Street restaurant row, Vivo continues to draw a hip crowd for its groovy, contemporary grotto atmosphere (exposed brick, candlelight, and piles of wine bottles) and straightforward Italian fare. The antipasti spread near the entrance is a welcoming, authentic touch. Italian menu. Closed Jan 1, Dec 25. Lunch, dinner. Bar. Casual attire. Valet parking available. Outdoor seating. Cr cds: A, D, MC, V. **$$$**

D

★ ★ ★ **WATUSI.** *1540 W North Ave (60622). Phone 773/862-1540. www.watusichicago.com.* Dinner. Entertainment: Wed. Cr cds: A, D, DS, MC, V.

D

★ **WISHBONE.** *1001 W Washington (60607). Phone 312/850-2663; fax 312/850-4332. www.wishbonechicago.com.* Hours: 7 am-3 pm, 5-10 pm; Sat, Sun from 8 am. Closed holidays. Lunch $3.50-$13, dinner $7-$15. Brunch $4-$12. Entertainment. Children's menu. Reservations accepted. Cr cds: A, C, D, DS, MC, V.

D

★ ★ ★ **ZEALOUS.** *419 W Superior (60610). Phone 312/475-9112.* Charlie Trotter protégé Michael Taus runs Zealous with a Trotter-like attention to detail and innovation. Menus change constantly, but you can expect the daring, like veal sweetbread-topped beignets, taro root and mushroom ravioli with sea-urchin sauce, and star-anise braised veal cheeks. Put yourself in the chef's hands with a five- or seven-course degustation menu. This is event dining, amplified by the thoughtful Asian-influenced décor. Bamboo planters, skylit 18-foot ceilings, and a glass-clad wine room make Zealous a fitting resident of the River North gallery district. Menu changes seasonally. Hours: 5:30-10:30 pm. Closed Sun. Dinner á la carte entrees: $18-$29. Bar. Entertainment. Reservations required. Cr cds: A, DS, MC, V.

D

Index

Establishment names are listed in alphabetical order followed by their classificiaton and then city and state. The classification symbols are: [S] for Special Events, [W] for What to See and Do, [AS] for All Suites, [BB] for B&Bs/Small Inns, [CAS] for Casinos, [CON] for Villas/Condos, [CONF] for Conference Centers, [EX] for Extended Stays, [HOT] for Hotels, [MOT] for Motels/Motor Lodges, [RAN] for Guest Ranches, [RST] for Resorts, and [RES] for Restaurants.

Notes

Notes

Notes

Notes

Notes

Notes

Notes

Notes

Notes

Notes

Notes

Notes